1 MONTH OF
FREE
READING

at
www.ForgottenBooks.com

By purchasing this book you are eligible for one month membership to ForgottenBooks.com, giving you unlimited access to our entire collection of over 1,000,000 titles via our web site and mobile apps.

To claim your free month visit:

www.forgottenbooks.com/free1087985

ISBN 978-0-331-46971-4
PIBN 11087985

LETTER

OF

THE SECRETARY OF STATE,

TRANSMITTING A REPORT ON THE

COMMERCIAL RELATIONS OF THE UNITED STATES

WITH

FOREIGN NATIONS,

FOR

THE YEAR ENDED SEPTEMBER 30, 1864.

WASHINGTON:
GOVERNMENT PRINTING OFFICE.
1865.

Be it enacted by the Senate and House of Representatives of the United States of America in Congress assembled, That it shall be the duty of the Secretary of State to lay before Congress, annually, at the commencement of its session, in a compendious form, all such changes and modifications in the commercial systems of other nations, whether by treaties, duties on imports and exports, or other regulations, as shall have come to the knowledge of the department.

Approved August 16, 1842.

Be it enacted by the Senate and House of Representatives of the United States of America in Congress assembled, That, in addition to the changes and modifications in the commercial systems of other nations, now required by said act, it shall be the duty of the Secretary of State to lay before Congress, annually, within sixty days after the commencement of each ordinary session, as a part of said report, all other commercial information communicated to the State Department by consular and diplomatic agents of this government abroad, or contained in the official publications of other governments, which he shall deem sufficiently important.

Approved August 18, 1856.

ANNUAL REPORT

ON

FOREIGN COMMERCE

FOR THE

YEAR ENDED SEPTEMBER 30, 1864.

FEBRUARY 11, 1865.—Referred to the Committee on Commerce and ordered to be printed.

DEPARTMENT OF STATE, *Washington, February 9, 1865.*

SIR: In compliance with the acts of Congress of August 16, 1842, and August 18, 1856, I have the honor to transmit herewith a Report on the Commercial Relations of the United States with foreign nations for the year ended September 30, 1864.

I have the honor to be, sir, your obedient servant,

WILLIAM H. SEWARD.

Hon. SCHUYLER COLFAX,
Speaker of the House of Representatives.

CONTENTS OF PART I.

CONTENTS.

CONTENTS.

CONTENTS OF PART II.

List of countries and the ports in each country from which consular returns of commerce and navigation may be found in the tables.

PART I.

ABSTRACTS

OF

CONSULAR RETURNS

AND

OFFICIAL PUBLICATIONS.

1864.

ABSTRACTS

CONSULAR RETURNS

AND

OFFICIAL PUBLICATIONS.

GREAT BRITAIN.

Statement of the imports from the United States to Great Britain and Ireland of the principal articles of United States produce, and their values, in the ten months ended October 31, 1864, compared with the corresponding period of the year 1863.

Articles.	Quantity.		Value.	
	1863.	1864.	1863.	1864.
Cotton—raw .... pounds.	48,168	131,853	$2,242,431	$7,817,320
Corn—wheat .... bushels.	14,013,320	11,145,040	18,539,184	17,278,068
flour .... cwt.	2,302,290	1,709,898	7,099,559	4,938,740
Tobacco—stemmed .... pounds.	6,042,957	5,435,674	1,945,983	1,572,347
unstemmed........ do...	21,721,594	27,106,227	4,828,668	5,822,401
manf'd and snuff... do...	2,363,067	5,438,162	1,787,285	3,104,035

Statement of the exports to the United States of the principal articles of British and Irish produce in the eleven months ended November 30, 1864, compared with the corresponding period of 1863.

Articles.		Quantity.		Value.	
		1863.	1864.	1863.	1864.
Alkali—soda	cwt	770,509	817,835	$354,346	$286,939
Beer and ale	barrels	7,008	9,182	144,517	195,913
Cotton manufactures—piece goods of all kinds, plain, printed, or colored	yards	63,733,256	62,284,709	6,855,569	7,902,195
Coals	tons	281,421	197,997	894,320	613,949
Earthenware and porcelain	packages	57,485	63,253	1,066,112	1,841,198
Linen manufactures—piece goods of all kinds	yards	63,950,365	71,155,003	8,612,242	11,174,819
thread	pounds	1,864,825	1,636,260	869,070	855,038
Metals—iron, pig, and puddled	tons	42,865	66,828	585,402	1,015,998
iron, wrought, all sorts	tons	10,489	12,082	896,726	1,184,894
steel, unwrought	tons	14,663	14,171	2,309,507	2,240,663
iron, bar, angle, bolt, and rod	tons	51,90	72,401	2,155,634	3,405,428
railroad,	tons	60,710	105,090	1,817,032	3,872,324
castings	tons	1,691	633	88,218	68,113
hoops, sheets, and boiler plates	tons	16,864	18,809	770,232	1,055,942
lead, pig, rolled, sheet, piping, tubing, and shot	tons	2,012	10,914	202,776	1,119,404
tin plates	tons	622,066	508,439	3,346,330	3,037,671
Oil—seed	gallons	20,386	353,373	17,588	1,227,838
Salt	tons	66,531	81,531	125,583	167,009
Silk manufactures—broad piece goods, fancy silks and satins, velvet, &c	yards	514,910	412,633	450,362	355,009
handkerchiefs, scarfs, and shawls	dozen	3,222	15,937	18,150	83,586
ribbons of silk only	pounds	20,547	23,282	114,940	136,405
Spirits, (British)	gallons	93,625	88,630	58,868	53,622
Woollen and worsted manufact's, mixed or unmixed with other materials, cloths, kerseymeres	yards	4,567,630	5,173,594	2,955,894	3,865,715
carpets and druggets	yards	1,610,011	1,557,027	1,109,260	1,348,428
carpets and rugs	number	227,786	196,356	339,478	296,735
stuffs	yards	41,767,406	45,880,606	8,312,003	9,713,734

Comparative statement showing the quantities of raw cotton imported to and exported from Great Britain and Ireland for eleven months of the years 1863 and 1864.

IMPORTED INTO.

Countries whence exported.	1863. (eleven months.)	1864. (eleven months.)
From United States ....pounds..	5,174,512	13,346,704
Brazil ....pounds..	20,493,424	32,298,560
Egypt ....pounds..	78,606,864	119,376,768
British East Indies.....................pounds..	331,999,136	423,870,944
Other countries ....pounds..	92,461,600	32,520,880
Total pounds............................	528,735,536	621,413,856

EXPORTED FROM.

Countries to which exported.	1863. (eleven months.)	1864. (eleven months.)
To Russia, northern ports ....pounds..	17,099,936	24,902,752
Prussia................................pounds..	11,052,272	5,562,256
Hanover...............................pounds..	6,096,160	51,695,792
Hanse Towns..........................pounds..	40,294,240	53,960,032
Holland ....pounds..	40,302,528	45,003,952
Other countries.......................pounds..	101,857,056	97,786,352
Total.............................	216,702,192	228,911,136
	312,033,344	392,502,720
Retained for consumption.......................... Total imported, (as above)................	528,735,536	621,413,856

Comparative statement showing the quantities of raw cotton imported into the United Kingdom, and the countries whence imported, from January 1 to December 31, during twenty years, and also during eleven months ended November 30, 1864.

Years.	United States.	Brazil.	Mediterranean.	British possessions in the East Indies.	British West Indies and British Guiana.	Other countries.	Total.
	Pounds.	*Pounds.*	*Pounds.*	*Pounds.*	*Pounds.*	*Pounds.*	*Pounds.*
1844	517,218,622	21,084,744	12,406,327	88,639,776	1,707,194	5,054,641	646,111,304
1845	626,650,412	20,167,633	14,614,699	58,437,426	1,394,447	725,336	721,979,953
1846	401,949,393	14,746,321	14,978,47	34,340,143	1,201,857	1,140,113	467,856,274
1847	364,599,291	9,966,922	4,814,268	83,934,614	793,953	598,587	474,707,615
1848	600,247,468	19,971,378	7,231,861	84,101,961	640,437	827,036	713,020,161
1849	634,504,050	20,738,13	17,369,843	70,838,515	944,307	1,074,164	755,469,012
1850	493,153,112	30,299,982	18,931,414	118,872,742	238,913	2,090,698	663,576,861
1851	596,638,962	19,339,104	16,950,525	122,026,976	446,529	1,377,653	757,379,749
1852	765,630,94	26,506,144	48,058,640	84,922,432	703,696	3,960,992	929,79948
1853	658,451,706	24,190,628	98,353,575	181,845,160	350,428	2,064,162	895,278,749
1854	722,151,346	24,577,952	23,503,003	119,536,009	409,110	1,730,081	887,353,149
1855	681,629,424	21,830,714	32,904,153	145,179,216	168,452	6,992,755	891,751,952
1856	780,040,016	29,910,832	34,616,844	190,496,624	462,784	6,439,398	1,023,886,304
1857	654,758,048	18,617,872	24,882,144	250,338,14	1,443,568	7,986,160	969,318,896
1858	833,237,776	22,478,060	38,246,112	132,722,576	367,898	11,148,032	1,034,342,176
1859	961,707,264	17,295,864	38,196,096	192,330,840	592,256	10,773,616	1,225,989,072
1860	1,115,890,608	17,200,336	44,036,696	204,141,164	1,060,784	8,532,720	1,390,938,752
1861	819,500,528	19,145,392	40,892,096	368,040,448	*	10,261,328	1,256,984,736
1862	6,778,128	20,493,424	49,242,148	315,629,216	*	28,612,192	419,506,976
1863	5,174,512	32,298,560	78,646,864	331,999,136	*	92,461,600	528,936
1864, (eleven months)	13,346,704		119,376,768	423,670,944	*	32,520,880	621,413,856

* Included in "Other countries."

Comparative statement showing the quantities of wool (sheep, lamb, and alpaca) imported into the United Kingdom from various countries during a period of twenty years ended December 31, 1863, and also during eleven months of the year 1864.

Years.	Spain.	Germany, viz: Meck-lenburg, Hanover, Hanse Towns, and Oldenburg.	Other countries of Europe.	British possessions in South Africa.	British possessions in the East Indies.	British settlements in Australia.	South America.	Other countries.	Total.
	Pounds.	Pounds.	Pounds.	Pounds.	Pounds.	Pounds.	Pounds.	Pounds.	Pounds.
1844	918,863	21,847,684	15,313,067	2,197,143	2,765,853	17,602,247	3,760,063	1,86,81	65,713,761
1845	1,074,540	18,484,736	17,606,515	3,512,924	3,975,966	24,177,317	6,468,338	1,53,69	76,813,855
1846	1,020,476	15,888,705	11,733,601	2,954,457	4,570,981	21,783,346	4,890,273	2,94,83	65,255,469
1847	424,408	12,673,814	7,935,697	3,477,392	3,063,142	36,056,815	7,255,560	1,665,780	62,592,598
1848	106,638	14,429,161	7,094,098	3,497,250	5,907,435	39,030,567	8,851,211	924,487	70,984,847
1849	127,569	12,750,011	11,432,354	5,377,495	4,182,653	35,879,171	6,914,525	1,004,679	76,766,647
1850	440,751	9,166,731	8,705,262	5,700,599	3,473,252	39,018,221	5,296,648	2,518,384	74,326,778
1851	383,150	8,919,236	14,263,156	5,816,591	4,549,280	41,810,117	6,252,680	3,420,157	83,311,975
1852	233,413	12,765,253	13,389,140	6,384,796	7,880,24	43,107,301	6,232,680	3,661,082	93,761,458
1853	154,146	11,584,800	26,861,166	7,221,448	12,400,869	47,076,010	6,134,334	4,357,978	119,126,449
1854	424,300	11,448,518	14,481,483	8,223,598	14,965,191	47,489,650	7,106,708	2,954,921	106,121,995
1855	68,760	6,125,686	8,119,408	11,075,965	14,283,535	49,142,306	8,076,317	3,375,148	99,300,446
1856	55,090	8,687,781	14,480,869	11,305,188	15,346,578	52,052,139	9,306,896	3,167,430	116,211,392
1857	397,238	6,088,002	23,802,520	14,267,828	19,370,741	49,303,655	10,046,381	7,257,028	129,749,898
1858	110,510	10,595,186	17,926,869	16,557,504	17,333,307	51,104,560	9,759,779	3,024,216	126,738,723
1859	153,874	12,036,125	27,145,518	14,269,343	14,363,403	59,166,618	1,950,029	1,656,050	133,384,634
1860	1,000,257	9,292,942	28,570,342	16,574,345	20,214,173	68813,903	‡	4,027,303	148,396,577
1861	‡	‡	24,417,987	18,676,296	1,161,004	6944,929	‡	16,421,342	146,990,522
1862	‡	‡	32,771,183	15,966,909	1807,136	6944,929	‡	15,788,943	147,839,100
1863	‡	‡	25,390,648	16,641,812	16,474,377	74,110,734	‡	19,433,096	152,050,607
1864	‡	‡	35,490,533	16,946,504	16,450,088	95,333,861	‡	19,618,642	183,769,998

* Eleven months.   † Included in "Other countries of Europe."   ‡ Included in "Other countries."

Statement showing the custom revenue of the United Kingdom for the years 1826, 1841, 1853, and 1863.

Years.	NUMBER OF ARTICLES SUBJECT TO DUTY.			Gross amount of customs revenue received.	Aggregate British and foreign tonnage entered and cleared.
	Principal articles.	Subdivisions.	Total on the list.		
1826....	432	848	1,280	£19,562,000	5,074,611 tons.
1841....	564	488	1,052	23,515,000	9,418,547 "
1853....	230	236	466	22,506,000	18,390,910 "
1863....	52	90	142	23,232,000	26,738,733 "

Years.	TOTAL VALUE OF IMPORTS.		VALUE OF EXPORTS.		
	Official.	Real.	Real value of British produce.	Official value of foreign and colonial produce.	Real value of foreign and colonial produce.
1826....	£37,686,000	Not ascertained.	£31,536,000	£10,076,000	Not ascertained.
1841....	64,377,000	Not ascertained	51,634,000	14,723,000	Not ascertained.
1854*....	124,426,000	£152,389,000	97,184,000	29,752,000	£18,636,000
1863....	171,913,000	248,980,000	146,489,000	54,914,000	49,485,000

* 1854 is here taken instead of 1853, as it was the first year for which the real value of imports and foreign exports was ascertained.

Statement showing the average daily amount of tonnage entered and cleared upon each working day for the years 1826, 1841, 1853, 1863.

1826 .... 16,360 tons.   1853 .... 59,323 tons.
1841 .... 30,381 tons.   1863 .... 86,250 tons.

Statement showing the average amount of imports for home consumption and exports of domestic produce together, for each individual, of the chief countries of Europe for the year 1862.

	£. s.		£. s.
Russian empire	0 14*	France	4 15
Sweden	2 13*	Spain	1 13*
Denmark	4 8	Austria	1 9*
Holland	12 18†	Greece	2 7
Belgium	9 2	United Kingdom	12 2

*Total imports and exports.
†Including a large amount of Dutch colonial produce re-exported.

Rates of import duty upon certain manufactured articles, per cwt., by the tariff of the principal countries in Europe.

Principal countries in Europe.	Yarns.			Cotton tissues.		Linen tissues.
	Cotton, single, unbleached.	Linen, single, unbleached.	Woollen, undyed.	Unbleached cloth.	Prints.	Unbleached cloth.
	£. s. d.	£. s. d.	£. s. d.	£. s. d.	£. s. d.	£. s. d.
Russia	1 17 11	1 12 6	2 3 4	7 11 9	14 1 9	25¼ per ct. to 27¼ per ct. ad valorem.
Sweden	0 15 11	1 13 3	0 19 11	2 13 2	5 19 8	6 12 11
Norway	0 11 5	0 11 5	1 10 6	1 2 11	5 14 5	0 7 8 to 1 2 11
Denmark	0 5 9	0 10 8	0 14 4	1 14 4	3 16 4	0 2 5 to 0 14 4
Z-Verein	0 9 2	0 6 1	0 1 6	7 12 5	7 12 5	0 12 2
Hamburg	Free.	Free.	Free.	5 p. c. ad val.	⅓ p. c. ad val.	Free.
Holland	Free.	0 2 7	Free.	5 p. c. ad val.	5 p. c. ad val.	5 p. c. ad val.
Belgium	0 6 1 to 0 16 3	0 4 1 to 0 8 2	0 8 2	1 0 4 to 6 1 11	15 p. c. ad val.	15 p. c. ad val.
France	0 6 1 to 6 1 11	0 6 1 to 2 0 8	0 10 2 to 2 0 8	6 1 11 to 6 1 11	15 p. c. ad val.	0 11 5 to 2 7
Portugal	1 10 10 and 3 p. c. additional.	2 17 2 and 3 p. c. additional.	7 14 5 and 3 p. c. additional.	1 2 10 to 1 14 14 and 3 p. c. additional.	6 5 9 and 3 p. c. additional.	5 2 11 and 3 p. c. additional.
Spain:— In Spanish vess'ls	4 8 5 to 5 0 7	0 11 2	3 13 2	6 3 6	9 5 0	2 16 11 to 10 13 5
In foreign vess'ls	5 6 2 to 6 0 5	0 13 5	4 7 11 to 6 7 1	7 8 5	11 2 7	3 8 1 to 12 16 1
Italy	0 4 8 to 0 9 4	0 4 8	0 18 8	0 16 8	2 6 9	0 9 4 to 1 3 5
Austria	0 10 8	0 5 3	0 10 7	4 5 4	10 13 4	1 12 0
Switzerland	0 1 8	0 1 8	0 1 8	0 1 8	0 6 6	0 1 8 to 0 6 6
Greece	0 5 8	0 14 2	Not stated.	0 10 2	1 2 8	2 2 6
Turkey	0 9 4	7.20 p. c. ad valorem.	7.20 p. c. ad valorem.	0 8 10	0 0 6 to 0 1 1¼ per piece.	7.20 p. c. ad valorem.

Rates of import duty upon certain manufactured articles, per cwt., by the tariff of the principal countries in Europe—Continued.

Principal countries in Europe.	Woollen tissues.		Iron.		Paper.	
	Woollen cloth.	Worsted stuffs.	Pig.	Bar.	For printing.	For writing. plain.
	£ s. d.	£ s. d.	£ s. d.	£ s. d.	£ s. d.	£ s. d.
Russia	17 6 9 to 30 6 10	26 0 2	0 0 6¼	0 3 9¼	2 19 7	2 19 7
Sweden	9 19 5	9 19 5	Free.	Free.	0 8 0	0 15 11 to 0 19 11
Norway	3 1 10 to 4 15 4	3 1 10 to 4 15 4	Free.	0 0 10½	0 7 8	0 19 1
Denmark	5 14 5	3 16 4	Free.	0 0 10½	0 5 9	0 9 6
Zollverein........	4 11 5	7 12 5	0 1 0½	0 4 6½	0 3 0½	0 15 3
Hamburg	½ p. c. ad val.	½ p. c. ad val.	Free.	Free.	½ p. c. ad val.	½ p. c. ad val.
Holland	5 p. c. ad val.	5 p. c. ad val.	Free.	Free.	5 p. c. ad val.	5 p. c. ad val.
Belgium..........	10 p. c. ad val.	10 p. c. ad val.	0 0 5	0 1 2½	0 3 3	0 3 3
France	10 p. c. ad val.	10 p. c. ad val.	0 0 9½	0 2 5½	0 3 3	0 3 3
Portugal	5 2 11 and 3 p. c. additional.	17 3 0 to 28 11 8 and 3 p. c. additional.	0 0 5½ and 3 p. c. additional.	0 0 8½ and 3 p. c. additional.	0 3 5 and 3 p. c. additional.	1 2 10 add 3 p. c. additional.
Spain—						
In Spanish ves'ls	14 4 7 to 19 1 2	8 9 9 to 14 4 7	0 0 10½	0 4 0½	10 p. c. ad val.	0 14 , 3 to 1 2 4
In foreign ves'ls.	17 1 6 to 22 17 4	10 3 9 to 17 1 6	0 1 0½	0 4 10½	12 p. c. ad val.	0 17 1 to 1 6 10
Italy	10 p. c. ad val.	10 p. c. ad val.	Free.	0 2 4	0 4 0½	0 4 0½
Austria	5 6 8	5 6 8	0 0 10½	0 4 3½	0 6 5	0 16 3
Switzerland	0 6 6	0 6 6	0 0 2½	0 0 9½	0 2 10½	0 2 10½
Greece	2 2 6	5 13 4	0 0 1½	0 0 6½	0 3 4½	0 3 4½
Turkey	7.20 p. c. ad valorem.	0 1 2½ to 0 2 2½ per piece.	0 0 4	0 0 8	7.20 p. c. ad valorem.	7.20 p. c. ad valorem.

Table of articles subject to duty on importation into the United Kingdom.

RATES OF DUTY.

	£ s. d.
Beer and ale, all kinds of, per barrel...........................	1 0 0
Cards, playing, per dozen packs................................	3 9
Chicory or other substitutes for coffee raw, per cwt..............	1 6 6
Chicory or other substitutes for coffee roasted or ground, per pound.	4
Chloroform, per pound..	3 0
Cocoa, raw, per pound..	1
Cocoa paste or chocolate, per pound............................	2
Cocoa husks and shells, per cwt...............................	2 0
Coffee, per pound...	3
Coffee, kiln-dried, roasted, or ground, per pound.................	4
Confectionery, succades, and dried cherries, per pound............	1
Corn and grain of all kinds, per cwt...........................	3
Meal and flour of all kinds, biscuit, bread, and starch, per cwt......	4½
Collodion, per gallon..	1 4 0
Currants, figs, fig-cake, prunes, and raisins, per cwt.............	7 0
Dice, per pair..	1 1 0
Essence of spruce, ten per cent. ad valorem.	
Ether, per gallon...	1 5 0

	£.	s.	d.
Malt, per quarter...	1	5	0
Pepper of all sorts, 6d. per pound and five per cent. thereon.			
Pickles preserved in vinegar, per gallon........................			1
Plate, gold, ounce troy..		17	0
Plate, silver, gilt or ungilt, ounce troy...... ✦...................		1	6
Powder, hair, and other kinds, per cwt........................			4½
Plums, dried or preserved, per cwt............................		7	0
Plums, preserved in sugar, per pound.........................			1
Ships of wood, with their tackle, foreign or colonial built, on their registration thereof as British ships, per ton of gross register....		1	0
Spirits and strong waters unsweetened, brandy and Geneva, per proof gallon...		10	5
Rum of and from any foreign country, being the country of its production, per proof gallon.....................................		10	2
Rum from any country, not the country of its production, per proof gallon...		10	5
Tafia of and from any colony of France, and rum and spirits of and from a British possession, per proof gallon....................		10	2
Unenumerated...		10	5
Other spirits, sweetened or mixed, so that the degree of strength cannot be ascertained by Sykes's hydrometer, viz: Rum shrub, liqueurs, and cordials of and from a British possession, per proof gallon...		10	2
Perfumed spirits for perfumery only, and water, Cologne, not in flasks		14	0
Perfumed spirits in flasks, not more than 30 to the gallon, per flask.			6
Unenumerated, per gallon.....................................		14	0
Sugar candy, brown or white and refined, or equal in quality thereto, per cwt..		12	10
Sugar—White, clayed, or equal in quality thereto, not being refined, per cwt..		11	8
Yellow, muscovado, and brown clayed, or equal in quality thereto, and not equal to white clayed, per cwt...........		10	8
Brown muscovado, or equal in quality thereto, and not equal to yellow muscovado or brown clayed, per cwt........		9	4
Any other sugar not equal in quality to brown muscovado, per cwt... ..		8	2
Cane juice, per cwt...................................		6	7
Molasses, per cwt...		3	6
Tea, per pound...		1	0
Tobacco manufactured, viz: stemmed, stripped, or unstemmed, containing 10 pounds or more of moisture in every 100 pounds weight thereof, (with five per cent. thereon,) per pound..............		3	0
Tobacco manufactured, containing less than 10 pounds of moisture in every 100 pounds weight thereof..........................		3	6
Tobacco manufactured, viz: Cigars...........................		5	0
Cavendish or negrohead.............................		4	6
Snuff containing more than 13 pounds of moisture to every 100 pounds weight thereof.........................		3	9
Snuff not containing more than 13 pounds of moisture to the 100 pounds weight thereof......................		4	6
Other manufactured tobacco, cavendish or negrohead, manufactured in bond in the United Kingdom from unmanufactured tobacco on the entry thereof for home consumption.......................................		4	0
Varnish, viz: Containing any quantity of alcohol or spirits, per gal.		12	0

	£.	s.	d.
Vinegar...	0	0	3
Wine and lees of wine under 26 degrees of proof spirits..........		1	0
Under 42 degrees of proof spirits in bottles, per gallon..........		2	6
And an additional duty of 3d per gallon for every degree of strength above the height above specified.			
Wood and timber, viz : Hewn, per load.........................		1	0
Sawed or split, planed or dressed, staves not exceeding 72 inches in length, nor 7 inches in breadth, nor 3¼ inches in thickness, per load...................................		2	0
Hoops and shovel hilts, per load.........................		2	0
Lathwood and firewood.................................		1	0
Wood and timber for ship-building and tree-nails, per load....		1	0
Furniture and hard woods, (except veneers,) and all other woods, (except dyewoods.).................................		1	0

ENGLAND.

MANCHESTER—HENRY W. LORD, *Consul.*

APRIL·28, 1864.

I have the honor to enclose a copy of a despatch which I have this day forwarded to the Secretary of the Treasury on the subject of sterling exchange.

It has been my desire for some time past to present to your excellency some remarks on the subject of sterling exchange. I have hitherto refrained from doing so lest I should obtrude upon a subject outside the proper sphere of my duty. It has, however, been my good fortune to offer suggestions to the government on one or two other points deemed important, which suggestions have been adopted and proved beneficial ; and, as Manchester is a city making greater sales of property to American merchants than are made by any other city, all of which merchandise to be invoiced under my own cognizance, and all paid for in sterling exchange, I trust you will pardon me if I ask a few moments attention.

The price of sterling exchange outside of certain limits, not very considerable in extent, is governed by the price of gold.

It is nevertheless true that the price of gold may be governed, and that absolutely, by the price of exchange ; or if not, yet sufficiently so for the purposes set forth in this letter.

It is important, to the end that I have in view, to note that the transactions in exchange are, as a rule, *bona fide*. Persons buy exchange because they want it. The transactions in gold, on the contrary, to a very large extent, are speculative. Persons buy gold because they wish to make a bet on its probable value next week. So that although gold is the basis of exchange, and the operations in gold very much larger than in sterling exchange, yet it is probable that the *bona fide* transactions in exchange are larger than the *bona fide* transactions in gold. I mean, simply, that the operations in exchange for necessary purposes are larger than in gold, the transactions in the latter being to such an extent fictitious ; as when a Wall street broker sells to another $50,000 to be delivered at a future day, the seller may never expect to deliver nor the buyer to receive a dollar in gold ; they "settle" by quotations, and the profit or loss is according as the one may have succeeded in "Bearing down" or the other in "Bulling" up the market.

The actual need of gold on the part of the citizen is probably nearly confined his necessities, for the payment of duties on foreign merchandise, and to make good such balances abroad as are not provided for by the sales of American productions.

The amount of exchange required is equal to the whole value of foreign merchandise purchased ; nevertheless, the nominal demand for gold is doubtless immensely greater than that for exchange.

However this may be subject to important modifications, it is clearly true that the required amount of exchange is sufficiently large, if it can be governed, to govern in its turn the price of gold.

Is the latter advisable on the part of the government ? If so, and recent measures adopted as to furnishing gold for customs leads me to suppose that it is, then I am convinced that if government will provide for the sale of gold, deliverable in London, that is to say, sterling exchange, then the price of exchange may be regulated at any given point, provided that point is not lower than exchange is, compared with currency, intrinsically worth.

There is doubtless some point at which, during the suspension of specie payments, gold has its proper value. It is also true that there is an extent to which gold may be advanced beyond its real value compared with the currency of the country, and its fluctuations may be influenced by all the appliances which are practiced in Wall street and elsewhere for the purposes of mere speculation. Every change of a cent in the price of gold is a virtual change in the value of everything possessed as property within the United States to about the same extent.

Thus it is possible for a few men operating upon eccentricities of public feeling, and compelling to their use every fitful gust of rumor from distant battle-fields, and without in fact touching or expecting to touch a dollar in gold, cause fluctuations in commercial values to the extent of millions by a single day's "transactions."

If gold may be fairly worth a premium over currency within reasonable limits—call its value 110, 120, or 140—my proposition is, to get it gradually reduced to the proper point, and then to hold it there, with slight variations, and to do this mainly through the medium of sterling exchange. For illustration, I will suppose the desired and equitable point of value for gold to be 140. It can never get much above that point if merchants can procure what sterling exchange they want for legitimate purposes at 151 to 152, that being about the relative value of exchange with gold at 140, the sovereign being counted at $4 40 in buying exchange, instead of $4 84.5, its (the sovereign's) real value.

Sixty-day sterling exchange is now, while I write, say 190, gold 176, 177. Let government instruct its bankers in London to accept sixty-day drafts, and instruct its bankers in New York (which instructions, in both cases, should, I think, be confidential) to be prepared at all, or at most, times to sell exchange to all who shall apply for it. Direct such New York agent to offer exchange to-day at 188, to-morrow at 186, the third day a little lower still, and from that time it will fall by its own gravity, and the agent will only have to follow it down to 150, where he may hold it, and which point it will reach probably within a month after the process shall have commenced. Gold will then be 138 to 140.

If government loses something by this directly, it will not need to be much, and thousands will be indirectly saved for every dollar that is directly lost; and many millions will be saved to the country, besides the advantage of keeping business steady, itself a consideration of great importance in these exceptional times.

The greatest blow that the Manchester trade with America has experienced was when the price of exchange fell at once 30 to 40 per cent. Merchants did not recover their senses for three months after it, so great is the fear of wide fluctuations. The same effect was universal throughout the States at home.

The direct loss on the sale of exchange as contemplated need not be large, because the government agent will not have to provide the whole, nor a very large part, of the exchange wanted, as other parties will have as much exchange to dispose of as they have now, and be as ready to sell it. And if it should be otherwise, the custom of selling sixty-day bills gives ample time to provide for their payment from the money received from their sale. If a banker of good credit, whom I will suppose to act under instructions, offers exchange for 150, sixty-day bills, after having gradually reduced the rates to that point, other bankers will offer to sell at that rate, and the first-named can, if desirable, buy of others in New York nearly as much as he will sell, and use for the purchase the same currency that he collects for the sale.

Thus with great diffidence I submit what I had desired to say on this subject, feeling at the same time that a proposition so obvious must doubtless have often occurred to the government, and perhaps also have been urged by scores of other correspondents than myself, and by the department rejected for good reasons. Nevertheless, looking upon the matter as a business project, and in the light of a commercial experience, I can see no valid reason why the plan should not work as indicated.

Hon. SALMON P. CHASE,
    Secretary of the Treasury.

LEEDS—J. W. MARSHALL, *Consul.*

FEBRUARY 9, 1864.

I enclose No. 1, a statement of the exports to the United States from this consular district for the year ending September 30, 1863, so far as the consular records exhibit the same. Considerable quantities of goods manufactured in and shipped from this district were invoiced and certified elsewhere, especially at Manchester and Liverpool, so that I am confident the actual exports were much in excess of the result stated, $12,900,509 64.

*   *   *   *   *   *   *

I estimate that the exports from this district to the United States from October 1, 1862, to September 30, 1653, amounted to fifteen or eighteen millions of dollars, paying into our treasury five to six millions in duties.

In reference to the state of trade I may observe that while the limited supply of cotton of greatly increased prices pressed heavily on the manufacturing industry of Lancashire, the production of the staple manufactures of Leeds, Bradford, Huddersfield, Halifax, and other towns in Yorkshire engaged in woollen or flax manufacture, was stimulated thereby, and Sheffield was compensated for any slackness in the cutlery trade by an increased demand for iron and steel. Full employment was therefore within the reach of the manufacturing population of this district, and the year may be characterized as one of great prosperity for this interest.

Statement showing the exports from Leeds to the United States for the year ended September 30, 1864.

	£	s.	d.
Steel, cutlery, iron, &c., &c., manufactures of same........	324, 722	8	9¼
Wool, flax, yarn, twine, woollens, unions, mohair, worsted, cotton, silks, &c...................................	790, 400	12	8½
Waste, shoddy, flocks, &c.............................	26, 511	9	0
Carpet and binding for same, rugs, mats................	119, 383	4	11
Skins, leather, &c., &c...............................	23, 381	16	11

	£	s.	d.
Dye goods	1,581	6	3½
Plaster	292	12	9
Hosiery	2,554	1	6
Thread	29,867	7	4
Grease	234	12	4
Pitch	13	2	1
Brandy	41	3	3
Cheese, wood-model, ale and porter	1,108	4	6
Mustard	29	10	0
Seed	119	7	0
Hair seating, cow's hair	3,342	0	5
Earthenware, glass bottles	70	10	.0
Botanical specimens, book and an album, containing photographs	5	0	0
$6,406,507 07 equal at $4 84 per £ to	1,323,658	9	9½

*Statement of the exports to the United States, from the Leeds consular district,
for the year ended September 30, 1863.*

	£	s.	d.
Wool, flax, cotton, and the manufactures thereof, embracing cloths, worsted stuff goods, tow and woollen yarns, linen thread, cotton and shoe thread, twine, carpets, carpet binding, rugs, mats, hosiery, &c.	1,809,558	17	1
Waste, shoddy, flocks	47,494	13	6
	1,857,053	10	7

	$8,988,139	08
Iron, steel, and manufactures thereof, embracing machinery, cutlery, &c., optical instruments, umbrella frames, and grindstones	3,729,432	96
Skins, leather, grease, &c., &c.	116,526	97
Paints, oils, Paris white, and dyestuffs	42,303	41
Miscellaneous: Ale, brandy, cheese, wood-model, mustard, garden seeds, hair seating, cow's hair, earthenware, glass, cliffstone and coal	24,101	41
	12,900,503	83

Of this amount, $12,900,503 83, there was certified at

Leeds	$6,406,507	09
Bradford	3,750,994	93
Sheffield	2,043,264	08
Huddersfield	665,227	97
Hull	35,510	51
Total	12,901,504	58

Classified report of invoices, Bradford, nine months preceding Sept'r 30, 1863

Articles.	Quarter ending Mar. 31, 1863.	Quarter ending June 30, 1863.	Quarter ending Sept. 30, 1863.	Total.
Worsted stuffs	£202,094 13 10	£161,587 9 8½	£362,338 16 0	£726,011 1 6½
Woollen goods	254 17 8	705 4 10	....	960 2 6
Yarn	....	523 5 6	1,777 12 3	2,300 17 9
Wool, shoddy, &c.	....	14,512 13 3	6,471 11 3	20,983 4 6
Canvas	323 3 10	....	....	323 3 10
Cotton goods	202 14 4	111 14 9	....	314 9 1
Iron and steel	3,097 9 10	5,708 18 0	5,882 2 3	16,688 10 1
Machinery	1,480 15 8	2,641 2 0	2,849 7 0	6,971 1 8
Grease	75 3 0	42 13 0	328 6 9	446 5 1
Total	309,513 18 2	185,833 3 4½	379,643 17 6	*774,998 19 0½

* Equal, at $4 84 per £, to $3,750,994 93.

FEBRUARY 12, 1864.

I have the honor to advise you that I forward herewith the returns of invoices certified at the consular offices in this district for the quarter ended December 31, 1863, as follows:

Amount certified at Leeds	$891,930 58
Do.......Bradford	2,108,369 60
Do........Sheffield	1,278,113 64
Do........Huddersfield	453,801 45
Do........Hull	12,510 92
Total	4,744,726 19

MAY 11, 1864.

I beg to inform you that I transmit herewith the returns and invoices certified at the consular offices in this district during the quarter ended March 31, 1864, as follows:

Amount certified at Leeds	$1,216,655 78
Do.......Bradford	3,325,458 65
Do........Sheffield	1,358,958 85
Do........Huddersfield	884,830 50
Do........Hull	26,960 50
Total	6,812,864 28

Summary statement of the invoices certified at the several offices of the Leeds consular district for the quarters ended June 30 and September 30, 1864.

Amount certified at Leeds, quarter ended June 30, 1864	$998,126 28
Do..........do........do....September 30, 1864	312,959 38
Do........Sheffield .....do....June 30, 1864	1,241,350 71
Do........do........do....September 30, 1864	801,333 64
Do........Bradford.....do....June 30, 1864	2,546,082 44
Do.........do........do....September 30, 1864	1,459,144 32
Do........Huddersfield..do....June 30, 1864	713,915 34
Do..........do........do....September 30, 1864	283,470 53

| Amount certified at Hull, quarter ended June 30, 1864 ..... | $18,851 72 |
| Do..........do.......do ...September 30, 1864. | 6,111 18 |

Total 8,381,345 54

CARDIFF—CHARLES D. CLEVELAND, *Consul.*

JANUARY 28, 1864.

The British government manages the whole business of shipping seamen much better than we do, and we might advantageously take a leaf out of their book. By its laws, all shipping agents are appointed by the board of trade and licensed by the government; and no one else can engage a seaman for a British vessel under a penalty of £20 for each seaman so engaged, and the captain is under a like penalty for employing any other person than those appointed by the government. The established fee is 2s. 6d., or 60 cents each man, which goes to the shipping agent, and pays him well. If he takes anything more, either from the captain or men, he is fined £5 for each case, and is deprived of his office. The regular fee which the shipping-masters here have agreed among themselves to take from our men is $2 50, but they often take $5.

In the case of British vessels, the crews are always shipped by the shipping agent before a "shipping-master," as he is called, at the custom-house, and every captain, also, must pay off his crew before this same "shipping-master." These are admirable regulations; and I wish we might adopt something like them on the other side of the Atlantic.

MARCH 1, 1864.

Annexed I give you the exports of coal and iron from this port for the last three years:

	Tons coal.	Tons iron.
1861...	1,127,232	122,493
1862...	1,323,531	172,352
1863...	1,485,385	212,892

In last year (1863) this coal and iron were taken away in 4,659 vessels. Of these there were belonging to Great Britain, 1,769; to France, 1,406; to Italy, 287; to Austria, 226; to the United States, 138; to Norway, 138; to Denmark, 106; to Hanse Towns, 95; to Pompeia, 89; to Holland, 75; to Russia, 64; to Sweden, 57; to fifteen other places, 209.

Though the United States here ranks the 5th in the *number of vessels*, we are certainly the 3d, and probably the 2d, in *tonnage*, as a greater part of the French vessels are "luggers" of 20 or 30 tons.

BRISTOL—ZEBINA EASTMAN, *Consul.*

FEBRUARY 20, 1864.

I have the honor to transmit herewith to the State Department the following tabular statement of goods shipped from this consular district to the United States, as shown by invoices verified at this consulate and the several dependencies, for the two quarters closing with the end of the year 1863.

Notwithstanding the high rate of exchange, the reports show a gradual increase in the amount of exports for the past two quarters, though there was an apparent decline for the second quarter of the year, as appears from the tabular statement from this office of August 5, 1863.

H. Ex. Doc. 60——2

Statement showing the exports to the United States from the consular district of Bristol for the quarter ended September 30, 1863.

Places	Cotton and woollen goods, carpets, &c.	Linen goods, twine, webbing, &c.	Silk goods.	Glass and crockery.	Pearl buttons, cutlery, needles.	Jewelry, watches, &c.	Guns and gun materials.	Hardware.	Miscellaneous.	Total.
	£ s. d.	£ s. d.	£ s. d.	£ s. d.	£ s. d.	£ s. d.	£ s. d.	£ s. d.	£ s. d.	£ s. d.
Bristol	16 0 4			*276 8 8				9,372 0 0	85 7 5	10,187 16 1
Birmingham	1,263 5 4	438 0 0	463 0 0		8,565 6 10	4,950 4 3	7,871 0 3	66,530 15 0	67,762 11 4	160,859 2 11
Worcester	2,391 12 6	990 8 0	1,382 9 6	2,432 11 9	961 6 10	150 5 0		178 0 0		4,385 3 10
Gloucester								3,000 0 0		3,000 0 0
Total	3,670 17 10	1,428 8 0	1,845 9 6	2,708 19 10	8,896 13 8	5,100 9 3	7,871 0 3	79,081 1 9	67,847 18 9	178,389 2 10

Statement showing the exports to the United States from the consular district of Bristol for the quarter ended December 31, 1863.

Places	Cotton and woollen goods, carpets, &c.	Linen goods, twine, webbing, &c.	Silk goods.	Glass and crockery.	Pearl buttons, cutlery, needles.	Jewelry, watches, &c.	Guns and gun materials.	Hardware.	Miscellaneous.	Total.
	£ s. d.	£ s. d.	£ s. d.	£ s. d.	£ s. d.	£ s. d.	£ s. d.	£ s. d.	£ s. d.	£ s. d.
Bristol	1,110 8 6	2,195 18 10	3,615 10 0	†483 13 0	9,111 6 0	6,577 5 0		8,195 8 0	860 11 2	11,695 11 0
Birmingham	1,888 10 6		576 19 6	3,716 19 4	1,389 9 7	222 8 6	8,505 7 0	120,425 8 4	38,381 17 3	192,411 10 5
Worcester		967 9 0						103 0 0	4,309 6 8	8,568 5 0
Gloucester								4,000 0 0		4,000 0 0
Total	2,998 19 0	3,163 7 10	4,192 0 6	4,200 12 4	10,500 15 7	6,799 13 6	8,505 7 0	132,712 16 4	43,551 15 1	216,655 7 2

* Bath or Bristol brick.   † Bristol brick.

The total amount of exports for the year 1863 is as follows:

	£.	s.	d.
First quarter, ended March 31	149, 472	19	0
Second quarter, ended June 30	101, 375	5	6
Third quarter, ended September 30	178, 382	2	10
Fourth quarter, ended December 31	216, 655	7	2
Total amount for the year	645, 885	14	6

The exports from the district of Bristol are mechanical productions from the inland towns and of a large section of what is called the midland of England, and in most cases are shipped from the port of Liverpool. Indeed, very few of the goods that are specified in the invoices verified at the consular office of Bristol are exported from this port, but fall into the great current of commerce and transportation that flows from Liverpool. The business of this consulate and the dependencies shows a large variety of goods, and reveals the sources of industry in many isolated points and in places of no public reputation, which helps to make up the grand aggregate of the mechanical productions of this nation. Thus we have at Sydney, in Gloucestershire, the locality of sheet-iron manufacture; and at another place the block tin, being all the product of the south of England. At Worcester, or vicinity, are the manufacturers of needles, and a class of china ware; also the world-wide Worcestershire sauce, and which is extensively shipped to the United States, and even to California. And at Kidderminster are carpet manufactories, which supply our countrymen so extensively; at Coventry the principal place of the silk works, and the weaving of ribbons. The only place in the world where the widely known and heavy article of export called the Bristol brick is made is in this vicinity, but neither at Bath nor at Bristol, but at Bridgewater, a place on the Bristol channel thirty or forty miles southwest.

They form the item of quite a large number of the invoices of this consulate, but do not swell large its amount in value of exports, and yet, heavy and bulky as they are as an article for transportation, not one thousand of them has been shipped to the United States from the port of Bristol, but are all forwarded past this port to Liverpool or London for shipment. The new invoice regulations, and perhaps the restriction in the cotton manufacture, have brought out a new article of export from this district, viz: a variety of the linen product made at Bridgeport, on the English channel, a place almost exclusively devoted to the manufacture of linen lines and cordage, and particularly lines and nets for fishing. About one-half of the invoices verified at Bristol for the past two quarters were for goods of this description from Bridgeport, which are all entered at the port of Boston.

Oil-cloths and dyes and dye colors are manufactured at Bristol.

Hair-cloths, for seating of chairs and sofas, come from Castle Carey, in Somerset, and from near Glastonbury; invoices of wool or felt rugs, most elegantly colored and prepared from the skins of sheep and lambs with the wool left on.

The largest amount of business by far is done at Birmingham. It embraces every variety of merchandise and manufactures, preponderating to the iron and hardware trade. Guns and gun material form rather a large item in the department of the hardware or iron-work of Birmingham for a single one, but not by any means so large as the public impression is as to its trade with the United States, as is indicated by the invoices of legitimate business, as having been shipped from Birmingham to the loyal portion of the United States.

The effect of the new law in regard to verifying invoices has been to change radically the character of the business done in the jurisdiction of this consulate.

The shipping business has very much declined, but the income from fees has been more than realized against the loss of the shipping from the entire amount of business in invoices.

MAY 6, 1864.

I have the honor to transmit below, as part of this despatch, classification of the exports from this consular district, as shown by invoices verified at this and the offices of its dependencies.

The business of the quarter indicates no change of note from the business of previous quarters, of which I have heretofore remarked in full; there is but a slight decrease in the sum total of the amount of exports of British produce. It is presumed, from a number of causes, that hereafter there will be a large decline, which is not to be regretted, in the present state of exchange, and with a great falling off of products received from the United States.

Statement of exports of goods and merchandise to the United States from the consular district of Bristol for the quarter ended March 31, 1864.

Where from.	Cotton and woolen goods, carpets, &c.	Linen goods, twines, webbing, &c.			Silk goods.	Glass and crockery.	Pearl buttons, cutlery, needles, &c.	Jewelry, watches, pens, &c.	Guns and gun materials.	Hardware.	Miscellaneous.			Total.		
	£	£	s.	d.	£	£	£	£	£	£	£	s.	d.	£	s.	d.
Bristol	3,296	2,95	7	1	10,173	3,361	5,809	11,745	8,903		1,423	18	11	3,919	6	4
Birmingham		1,86	0	0		115	500	778		195,468	20,035	17	5	190,299	17	0
Worcester	8,081									2,360	2,382	18	0	14,156	18	5
Total														208,369	1	5

JULY 26, 1864.

I have the honor to enclose herewith, and making part of this despatch, the abstract or statement of the amount of goods and merchandise shipped from this consular district to the United States for the quarter ended June 30, 1864.

The aggregate, compared with the previous quarter, shows a small falling off, but not so great as would be supposed from the increased rate of the tariff, for a part of the time, and the very high rate of exchange.

Statement showing the description and value of the exports of Bristol to the United States, also the country from whence sent, during the quarter ended June 30, 1864.

Article.	Bristol.	Birmingham.	Worcester.	Grand total.
	£ s. d.	£ s. d.	£ s. d.	£ s. d.
Cotton and woollen goods, carpets, &c..............	....	4,515 00 0	2,248 00 0	....
Linen goods, twine, webbing, &c..............	1,746 00 0	3,060 00 0	....	....
Silk goods..............	....	3,687 00 0	....	....
Glass and crockery........	135 00 0	3,763 00 0	734 00 0	....
Pearl buttons, cutlery, needles, &c..............	....	8,332 00 0	....	....
Jewelry, watches, pens, &c.	....	6,507 00 0	....	....
Guns and gun material, &c.	....	11,916 00 0	....	....
Hardware..............	1,261 00 0	106,047 00 0	3,060 00 0	....
Miscellaneous..............	2,165 14 3	28,278 12 5	6,289 10 8	....
Total value..........	5,307 14 3	176,105 12 5	12,331 10 8	193,744 17 4

Statement showing the total value of the exports to the United States from the Bristol consular district during the quarter ended September 30, 1864.

	£	s.	d.
Bristol...	1,651	4	4
Birmingham..	80,777	13	3
Worcester..	5,810	12	0
Gloucester...	2,699	9	2
	90,939	11	9

OCTOBER 5, 1864.

There has recently issued from the press in this country a document entitled the "Wreck Register and Chart for 1863," which contains much statistical information upon the subject of wrecks and the loss of life at sea, and the preservation of life by life-boats, which may be of peculiar interest to those in the United States who are investigating these subjects. The synopsis of this report I submit.

The Wreck Register and Chart for 1863.

The return of the registrar general of seamen shows that during the past year 413,972 vessels—representing a tonnage of nearly 62 millions—entered inwards and cleared outwards from British ports. The estimated value of the goods carried on board these ships was upwards of four hundred millions sterling.

*   *   *   *   *   *   *

We find that the number of wrecks and casualties, including collisions, reported as having occurred on the coasts of the United Kingdom during 1863 is 2,001. This number, which is in excess by 174 of the wrecks reported in 1862, is above the annual average of the ten years ending 1863.   The numbers for the last five years are as follows, viz : 1859, 1,416 ; 1860, 1,379 ; 1861, 1,495 ; 1862, 1,827 ; and 1863, 2,001—total, 8,117.   The fearful increase in 1863 was owing to the great number of casualties in the gales of October, November, and December of that year ; and the marked increase in 1862 is owing mainly to the 542 wrecks and casualties which happened in the gales of January, October, and December.

Out of 2,001 wrecks and casualties in 1863, 882 are reported to have been caused by stress of weather, and 214 from various and unknown causes.   Again, 61 were lost from defects in the ships, or in their gear or equipment, and 176 from inattention and negligence.   The 1,096 vessels lost by stress of weather and various other causes unknown we must charitably suppose were inevitable ; yet we cannot help thinking that if the storm warning signals on the coast had been diligently attended to a considerable proportion of those 1,096 shipwrecks might have been avoided.   But the loss of 237 ships from negligence and defects in their equipments is inexcusable, and calls loudly for investigation—if not on account of the valuable property thus lost forever to the country, surely on that of the precious lives sacrificed on these disastrous occasions—in order that every effort might be made to prevent such an annual waste of life and property.

During the same period 5,096 lives were saved by life-boats and the rocket apparatus, fishing-boats, and other means.   In the absence of these appliances the sacrifice of human life would no doubt be terrible to contemplate.   The number of collisions reported in 1863 is 331, against 338 in 1862 and 323 in 1861, or 317 being the annual average of the seven years ended 1863.   Of these 331 collisions 216 happened at night and 113 in the daytime ; 133 were caused by " bad look-outs," " neglecting to show lights," and " neglect or misapplication of the road at sea."   The remainder were more or less the result of "accident," "unsound gear,"or "negligence."   *   *   *   *   *

During the past six years 399 lives have been lost from collisions in our seas—a truly distressing fact ; and if fishing-smacks and boats were not often at hand to render prompt and efficient services to the poor people this large number would undoubtedly be enormously increased.

The total number of wrecks and casualties from all causes reported during the year 1863 is 2,001, against 1,827 reported in 1862.   It is above the number reported during any one of the eight years preceding, and is 661 above the annual average of the eight years ending 1862.   The tonnage of these wrecks is thus given :

		Vessels.
Vessels under 50 tons		404
51 and under 100 "		494
101 " 300 "		867
301 " 600 "		158
601 " 900 "		46
901 " 1,200 "		18
1,201 and upwards "		14
Total		2,001

Of the total number of ships to which casualties have happened in 1863, 1,649 were British ships, 272 foreign ships, and the country and employment of 80 were unknown.

The greatest number of casualties happened to ships laden with coals, ores, bricks, &c., or, in other words, to ships of the collier class, as will be seen from the accompanying list, viz: .

Colliers laden. 614
Colliers light. 114
Iron and copper ore, &c. 146
Stone, &c. 115
Timber 101
Fishing-smacks and other laden vessels 689
Vessels in ballast (not colliers). 174
Passengers and general cargo 48
                                                         ─────
        Total ships 2,001

Again, it appears that 614 casualties happened with the wind at and under force 7, or from a calm to a moderate gale, and that 1,050 happened with the wind above force 7, or from a fresh gale to a hurricane.

The number of persons who perished in 1863 from wrecks was 620, while in 1862 it was 690.

It is satisfactory to know that, notwithstanding the larger number of casualties in 1863, there is a great falling off in the number of lives lost, and that it is 161 below the annual average of the last twelve years.

The total number of lives lost from 1854 to 1863 is really frightful to contemplate. It was 7,786, and this, let it be remembered, is not a casual loss. It is a continual if not an ever-increasing one. The drain on our sailors and fishermen goes on year after year, notwithstanding all the benevolent and strenuous efforts made at the present day to stay the ravage. The sea is dreadfully exacting in its demands, and season after season, when the equinoctial gales blow, when the winter sets in, our shores are converted into altars, on which the ocean, as during last winter, offers his victims by hundreds. It is unlikely that we shall ever effectually obtain the mastery over the waves; but even at this moment we are able to contend successfully with them in their blind efforts to swallow up life against our endeavours to save. During the fearful gales of October, November, and December last nearly 500 lives were rescued by life-boats alone; and undoubtedly a very large proportion must have perished in the absence of these noble services.

The number of lives saved during the past year was 5,096, and the total number of lives rescued by life-boats, the rocket and mortar apparatus, smacks, and other means, during the past eight years, is 25,254—a number sufficient to man a considerable fleet.

The Board of Trade, the coast-guard, and our boatmen and fishermen continue to work cordially with the National Life-boat Institution in the great and important work of saving the lives of shipwrecked persons on our coasts; and when one remembers that by means of its life-boats and of fishing-boats—to the crews of which it has given liberal rewards for their laudable exertions—it has contributed to the saving of nearly 14,000 persons, cold must the heart of that man be which does not feel a thrill of joy coming over it at such an announcement.

There are at present 182 life-boats on the coasts of the United Kingdom belonging to the Royal National Life-boat Institution and other bodies. The mortar and rocket apparatus stations now number 239, and are under the management of the coast-guard and the Board of Trade.

During the past year 417 lives (besides 17 vessels) were saved by the life-boats of the National Institution alone, and upwards of 300 by shore boats and other means, for which it granted rewards. A sum of £1,297 was expended by the institution in rewards; and £13,819 on its various establishments round the coasts of the British Isles.

FALMOUTH—ALFRED FOX, *Consul.*

AUGUST 30, 1864.

In the hope that the information may be useful to the government, I transmit the enclosed paper containing extracts from the " Mineral Statistics of the United Kingdom for the year 1863."

Mineral Statistics.

The following are extracts from *The Mineral Statistics of the United Kingdom for the year* 1863, by Robert Hunt, F. R. S., Keeper of Mining Records.

Gold.—The quantity of gold produced from two British mines amounted to 552 ozs., of the value of £1,747; the returns for 1862 being 5,299 ozs., of the value of £20,390.

Tin.—The tin ore (black tin) smelted in 1863 amounted to 15,157 tons according to the returns of sales made each month by the tin smelters; the returns, as shown by the dues paid to the stannary court, giving 14,224 tons. This arises from the circumstance that, although the ore may have been sold in December, the dues on that ore may not be paid for a month or more after the sale. The actual increase in the quantity of tin ore raised and sold in 1863 was 830 tons, the quantity of metallic tin (white tin) produced being 10,006 tons.

Copper.—The production of copper from British mines still exhibits a falling off. During last year 210,947 tons of this mineral were produced from 222 mines, the quantity in 1862 having been 224,171 tons. This ore yielded to the smelter 14,247 tons of copper.

Lead.—The mines of the United Kingdom gave 91,283 tons of ore during the year, against 95,311 tons produced in 1862. Of lead we obtained from this ore 68,220 tons, the value of this metal being £1,418,985.

Silver.—The lead obtained gave 613,266 ozs. of silver; to this must be added 20,738 ozs., produced from ores so excessively rich in silver as to be returned as silver ores, making altogether 634,004 ozs., of the value of £174,351.

Zinc.—The production of zinc ore has somewhat increased, the quantities sold in 1863 amounting to 13,699 tons, which gave 3,835 tons of metallic zinc, of the value of £90,889.

Pyrites—Sulphur ores.—The quantities of these ores obtained from British mines still exhibit a decline of 95,376 tons, of the value of £62,035, being the produce of 1863, against 98,433 tons produced in 1862. The ores, however, fetched a higher price.

Iron.—Of iron ores of different kinds 9,088,060 tons were obtained. This was employed in making 4,510,040 tons of pig-iron, having the value of £11,275,100

Coal.—There has been a large increase in the production of this mineral, 86,292,215 tons having been sold and used. The export trade has been less active than usual, therefore the employment of this large quantity is entirely due to the demands of British manufacturers.

General Summary of which returns are given for 1863.

Minerals.	Quantity.	Value.
Gold quartz.........................tons	385	£1,500
Tin ore........................... "	15,157	963,985
Copper ore........................... "	212,947	1,100,554
Lead ore...........................	91,283	1,193,530
Silver ore...........................	88	5,703
Zinc ore...........................	12,941	29,968
Pyrites........................... "	95,376	62,035

Minerals.		Quantity.	Value.
Wolfram ....tons		13	£67
Uranium................................cwts.		3	23
Gossans ....tons		4,424	4,576
Arsenic ....do.		1,444	1,200
Iron ore.................................do.		9,101,552	3,240,890
Coal (sold and used) ....do.		86,292,215	20,572,945
Earthy minerals (estimated)..............do.		....	1,975,000
Total value of minerals produced in 1863................			29,151,976

Metals produced from British minerals and coals.

Gold..............................ounces		552	£1,747
Tin................................tons		10,006	1,170,702
Copper ....do.		14,247	1,409,608
Lead ....do.		68,220	1,418,985
Silver ....ounces		634,004	174,351
Zinc ....tons		3,835	90,889
Iron, pig ....do.		4,510,040	11,275,100
Total value of the above			15,541,382
Estimated value of other metals			250,000
Coals...			20,578,945
Total value of the metals obtained and coal produced in 1863........................			36,364,327

To produce the above results direct employment has been given to at least 500,000 men, so that our mineral industries may be considered as alone supporting a population of nearly 3,000,000, in addition to adding much to the general wealth of the kingdom, and especially to the wealth of those whose capital has been employed in mining operations.

SCOTLAND.

DUNDEE—JAMES SMITH, *Consul.*

OCTOBER 15, 1864.

In transmitting my annual report upon trade, commerce and manufactures of this consular district, allow me to state that the field of my duties is chiefly confined to the town of Dundee, situated on the river Tay, within twelve miles of the German ocean, now having a population of fully 100,000; it has long been the centre of the linen trade in Scotland. The other towns in Forfarshire, (in which Dundee is situated,) and in which this trade is carried on, are Arbroath, Forfar, and Montrose, and in addition in many villages in the district.

Formerly the raw material used in the manufacture of linens consisted of flax, tow, codilla, and hemp, imported principally from the Russian and Prussian ports in the Baltic, and from Archangel, but since about the year 1838 a new fibre from India has been introduced, viz: jute, which now constitutes by far the greater portion of the manufactures of the town. Although altogether a different fibre from flax, the product of both is generally classified under the head of "linens and the linen trade."

To show the extent of this staple trade the following is an approximation, as nearly as possible, of the imports and exports into and from Dundee. It is to be remarked that both the raw material, especially flax, (as almost the whole jute is consumed in Dundee,) to supply the neighboring towns, is imported partly into Dundee, and the linens manufactured in the surrounding district are likewise exported from this port.

Importations into Dundee from June 1, 1863, to May 31, 1864.

	Tons.
Flax, tow, and codilla	35,914
Jute	54,488
Hemp	1,023
Total	91,425

Exported from Dundee from June 1, 1863, to May 31, 1864, linens and yarns, about 70,000 tons. The value of the raw material may be estimated at about two millions and one-half, whilst the value of the linens and yarns will be about four millions sterling. During the year 1863, about 11,000 tons of flax, tow, and codilla were imported into Arbroath, Aberdeen, and Montrose.

The number of spindles in Forfarshire employed in spinning are now about 230,000, whilst the power-looms reach to about 8,000. Large quantities of manufactures are still made by hand, but hand-loom weaving is being gradually superseded by power, so much so, that unless in exceptional cases it will in the course of time have no existence.

In consequence of the great prosperity attending the linen trade of the district during the last two years, very considerable additions are now being made both to the spinning works and to the power-loom.

It is difficult to estimate the quantity of linens used in the United Kingdom and that sent abroad, but it is believed that about one-half is exported, and the other half consumed in the United Kingdom.

Dundee, in consequence of being situated on the east coast of the island, has little direct shipping for exporting the linens, but they are sent to London, Liverpool, and Glasgow, and thence exported to the various markets of the world. The linens manufactured in this district are exported very largely to the United States, and to Canada, South America, the West Indies, Australia, and to the continent of Europe, principally *via* Hamburg. Here also a large trade in yarns is carried on with Spain.

As already stated, it is believed that for the last year one-half, namely, two millions sterling, of the whole manufactures sent from this district is exported to foreign countries. I beg to append to this report details of the value of the consular certificates which have been granted from October 1, 1861, to September, 30, 1864, amounting in all to £2,241,976 4s. 9d. sterling, or $10,851,164 98. As the value of the consular certificates granted for the year ended 30th September last amounts to £1,110,063 13s. 3d. sterling, or $5,372,708 12, it will be seen that an exceedingly large proportion of the goods manufactured in this district are sent to the United States, and it has been long well known that the United States is by far the best customer for Dundee and the neighborhood, so much so, that any sudden check to the usual demand for the market there would be very serious in its results to this part of the country. This is also conspicuously shown by comparing the value of the goods exported through my consulate with the total value of all the linens exported to the United States from the United Kingdom in 1863, which is detailed in the table appended to this report. Since the rebellion, the diminution in the production of cotton goods with the greatly increased cost of these manufactures, the linen and jute trades have experienced an extraordinary impetus, and the late prosperity may be traced as almost entirely due to this event. Whilst the raw material used in the manufactures of the district has been increased in value, the demand for the manufactures has been such as to raise their price to a point scarcely ever previously experienced. To show fully what the demand has been and still is, I beg to append the prices of leading articles on 1st January, 1862, and at the date of this report.

Yarns.	1st Jan'y, 1862.		Sept., 1864.	
	s.	*d.*	*s.*	*d.*
2 lbs. flax per spindle	1	8¼	2	8½
3 " " " "	2	1	3	3
3 " tow " "	1	11½	3	1
6 " " " "	2	5¾	3	9
7 " jute " "	2	6	2	11
26 per Osnaburg		3½		5⅜
Long flax canvas No. 1		13		16½
Merchant navy " 1		10		12½
12 per 40 in. 10½ oz. jute, Hessian, sent very largely to the United States		2¾		4¼
16 per 40 in. tow, Hessian		3¾		5¼
2⅝ lbs. 3 bushel sacks, each		8¾		13
10 lbs. wool jacks, "		31		47

The following statement, taken from the Board of Trade returns for the years 1861 and 1863, exhibits very fully, as already stated, the large proportion of the linens which are sent to the United States. It also brings out well the increase in the trade which has arisen from the circumstances before mentioned.

Linens exported from the United Kingdom in 1861 and 1863.

	Yards.	Value.
1861.—To United States	21,169,077	£642,696
" all other countries	95,153,392	2,928,435
Total yards	116,322,469	3,571,131
1863.—To United States	73,088,420	2,074,774
" all other countries	107,307,547	3,846,534
Total yards	180,395,967	5,921,308

A very large quantity of coal is used in Dundee for the various public works, and as no coal is found in Forfarshire it is all imported from Fifeshire and the north of England. The other important imports are guano, timber, and grain.

There are also several companies engaged in the Greenland and Davis Straits seal and whale fishery, the oil of which is principally used in the manufacture of jute into yarns.

In the year 1863 there were brought in 615 tons of whale blubber and 18 tons whalebone. Among other works in the neighborhood is one for the manufacture of coarse paper. The paper manufacturers complain much of the export duty on rags which the various countries on the continent of Europe have imposed. Latterly, to make up for the want of rags, a fibre named "esparto" has been imported from Spain, which is gradually being more largely used; this fibre is used in connexion with other materials. During the seven months of the present year, 27,856 tons of esparto and other vegetable fibre have been imported into the United Kingdom.

The harbor of Dundee is very safe and commodious; at average spring tides there is a depth of 18 feet of water, and there are three wet docks as also a graving dock and a patent slip. The shore dues, which are not extravagant, for the year ended 31st May last, amounted to £31,588. The shipping belonging to the port numbers 207 vessels, with a registered tonnage of 46,434 tons. A number of vessels are employed bringing the flax from the Baltic and Archangel, as also (as already stated) in the whale fishery. Vessels fetch timber also from Norway, the Baltic, and the Canadas. Several ships, the largest of which is 1,500 tons register, are likewise engaged in bringing jute direct from Calcutta. From 1st January of this year to the present time fully twelve thousand tons have been imported in this manner. Occasionally a few vessels sail direct to Australia or India; but, as already stated, little direct shipping with exports exists with foreign countries.

The number of vessels that has entered the harbor for the year ended 31st May, 1864, with their tonnage, is as follows:

		Tonnage.
Foreign vessels	531	104,750
Coasting vessels	1,786	207,087
River vessels	771	24,176
Total	3,088	336,013

No United States vessels have arrived at this port during the past year. In 1863 there were three arrivals of United States vessels from Calcutta, but there is no direct trade between this port and the United States.

APPENDIX.

Statement showing the description and value of exports from Dundee to the United States from October 1, 1861, to September 30, 1864.

Ports.	Merchandise.	Value.
	Quarter ended December 31, 1861.	£ *s.* *d.*
New York.....	Jute, jute cloth, wool bagging, and canvas	20,324 9 8
Boston........	Jute, jute goods, and canvas	8,646 13 8
San Francisco .	Canvas and carpeting	4,779 9 4
Philadelphia...	Canvas and wooden rollers.........................	866 9 2
Baltimore	Canvas	271 13 5
	Total..	24,888 15 3
	At $4 84 to the pound sterling, equal to............	$168,861 61
	Quarter ended March 31, 1862.	
New York	Jute bagging, woollen bagging, and linen goods	20,433 16 5
Boston.........	Jute goods and linen canvas	15,768 4 10
San Francisco .	Jute goods and linen canvas	3,973 4 7
Philadelphia...	Linen goods.......................................	2,268 18 1
Baltimore	Linen goods.......................................	532 7 8
	Total.......................................	42,976 11 7
	At $4 84 to the pound sterling, equal to	$208,006 64
	Quarter ended June 30, 1862.	
New York.....	Hemp carpeting and linen goods.....................	30,045 14 11
Boston........	Linen goods.......................................	12,950 10 6
San Francisco .	Jute and linen goods	6,985 15 7
Philadelphia...	Linen goods.......................................	963 6 3
Baltimore	Linen goods.......................................	1,449 15 9
	Total.......................................	52,395 3 0
	At $4 84 to the pound sterling, equal to............	$253,592 52
	Quarter ended September 30, 1862.	
New York.....	Linen goods.......................................	55,459 12 9
Boston........	Linen goods.......................................	16,878 19 9
San Francisco .	Linen goods.......................................	6,763 1 2
Philadelphia...	Linen goods.......................................	2,101 0 9
Baltimore	Linen goods.......................................	308 15 10
	Total.......................................	81,511 10 3
	At $4 84 to the pound sterling, equal to............	$394,515 72
	Quarter ended December 31, 1862.	
New York.....	Linen goods and yarn..............................	215,007 10 5
Boston........	Flax-linen goods, yarn, and grinding stones	65,250 16 6
San Francisco .	Linen goods.......................................	15,955 6 3
Philadelphia ..	Linen goods.......................................	3,943 13 9
Portland......	Linen goods.......................................	1,977 3 7
Baltimore	Linen goods.......................................	238 0 11
	Total.......................................	302,372 11 5
	At $4 84 to the pound sterling, equal to............	$1,463,483 24

Statement showing the description and value of exports, &c.—Continued.

Ports.	Merchandise.	Value.
	Quarter ended March 31, 1863.	£ s. d.
New York.....	Paper, linen goods, and yarn.........................	175,083 14 9
Boston	Linen goods, flax, and tow...........................	66,268 13 1
San Francisco .	Linen goods...	15,922 17 8
Baltimore	Linen goods...	2,145 3 11
Philadelphia...	Linen goods...	1,601 9 4
	Total.......................................	261,021 18 9
	At $4 84 to the pound sterling, equal to.............	$1,263,346 34
	Quarter ended June 30, 1863.	
New York.....	Marmalade and linen goods	110,917 4 9
Boston........	Flax, tow, and linen goods	48,981 17 10
San Francisco .	Linen goods...	17,536 2 1
Baltimore	Linen goods...	1,442 16 11
Philadelphia...	Linen goods...	980 14 1
	Total.......................................	179,858 14 11
	At $4 84 to the pound sterling, equal to.............	$870,516 33
	Quarter ended September 30, 1863.	
New York.....	Linen goods, flax, and machinery	112,875 9 5
Boston........	Linen goods, pig iron, tow, and mats	32,708 16 5
San Francisco .	Linen goods...	28,324 15 4
Philadelphia ..	Linen goods...	2,978 5 2
	Total.......................................	176,887 6 4
	At $4 84 to the pound sterling, equal to	$856,134 61
	Quarter ended December 31, 1863.	
New York.....	Linen goods...	259,102 6 5
Portland	Linen goods...	25,574 17 8
San Francisco .	Linen goods...	19,827 18 2
Boston	Linen goods...	17,144 7 5
Philadelphia...	Linen goods...	3,311 18 11
Baltimore	Linen goods...	901 2 5
	Total.......................................	325,862 11 0
	At $4 84 to the pound sterling, equal to	$1,577,174 74
	Quarter ended March 31, 1864.	
New York.....	Plants, yarn, flax, granite, jute, tow, stones, linen goods, and marmalade	241,936 12 3
Boston........	Tow yarn, plants, twine, flax, and linen goods	41,799 4 4
Portland	Linen goods and yarn	31,372 7 0
San Francisco .	Linen goods and yarn	7,529 0 0
Philadelphia ..	Linen goods and yarn	6,067 3 9
Baltimore	Linen goods and yarn	2,529 9 5
	Total	331,233 16 9
	At $4 84 to the pound sterling, equal to.............	$1,603,171 77

Statement showing the description and value of exports, &c.—Continued.

Ports.	Merchandise.	Value.
	Quarter ended June 30, 1864.	£ *s.* *d.*
New York.....	Bleaching powder, stones, marmalade, twine, paper, tar, machinery, yarn, and linen goods.............	227,565 15 6
Boston	Twine, yarns, flax, tow, hemp, nets, glass, and linen goods...	33,684 5 5
San Francisco.	Twine and linen goods ....:........................	12,727 15 6
Portland	Yarn and linen goods.............................	6,042 19 1
Philadelphia...	Linen goods.......................................	4,123 10 5
Baltimore	Linen goods	1,787 7 5
	Total............................:......:	285,933 13 4
	At $4 84 to the pound sterling, equal to..............	$1,383,918 95
	Quarter ended September 30, 1864.	
New York.....	Machinery, flax, yarn, and linen goods	117,404 8 3
Boston	Machinery, flax, yarn, and linen goods...............	37,632 2 5
San Francisco.	Linen goods.......................................	10,148 17 3
Baltimore	Linen goods	1,224 18 9
Philadelphia...	Linen goods	623 5 6
	Total.............	167,033 12 2
	At $4 84 to the pound sterling, equal to..............	$808,442 66

RECAPITULATION.

	£ *s.* *d.*
Quarter ended December 31, 1861	34,888 15 3
Quarter ended March 31, 1862	42,976 11 7
Quarter ended June 30, 1862....	52,395 3 0
Quarter ended September 30, 1862.....................................	81,511 10 3
Total...................,............................	211,772 0 1
At $4 84 to the pound sterling, equal to................................	$1,024,976 50
Quarter ended December 31, 1862 ....:..	302,372 11 5
Quarter ended March 31, 1863...	261,021 18 9
Quarter ended June 30, 1863..	179,858 14 11
Quarter ended September 30, 1863.....................................	176,887 6 4
Total...	920,140 11 5
At $4 84 to the pound sterling, equal to................................	$4,453,480 36
Quarter ended December 31, 1863	325,862 11 0
Quarter ended March 31, 1864	331,233 16 9
Quarter ended June 30, 1864	285,933 13 4
Quarter ended September 30, 1864.....................................	167,033 12 2
Total..	1,110,063 13 3
At $4 84 to the pound sterling, equal to	$5,372,708 12

LEITH—NEIL McLACHLAN, *Consul.*

DECEMBER 31, 1863.

* * * The value of the goods exported from this district for the quarter ended this date amounted to £60,519 11s., showing an increase over the corresponding quarter of 1862 of £24,536.

The goods exported were principally linens, ale, paper, books, carpets, cork, sailcloth, gelatine, India-rubber, &c.

There are no ships to report this quarter. * *

Nothing transpired in this consular district during the last year worthy of report, and no ship-building of any amount.

H. Ex. Doc. 60——3

Statement showing the description and quantity of imports at Leith, and whence shipped, during the year ended December 31, 1863.

Countries	GRAIN									OTHER ARTICLES						
	Wheat.	Barley.	Oats.	Peas.	Beans.	Tares.	Rye.	Malt.	Total.	Flour.	Meal.	Wood.	Guano.	Flax.	Tow.	Hemp.
	Qrs.	*Qrs.*	*Qrs.*	*Qrs.*	*Qrs.*	*Qrs.*	*Qrs.*	*Qrs.*	*Qrs.*	*Bags.*	*Bags.*	*Loads.*	*Tons.*	*Tons.*	*Tons.*	*Tons.*
Scotland	2,238	7,781	30,350	10	684	7	52	1,350	42,518	2,457	369	2,134	14	15	48	15
England	16,998	90	113	2,189	1,100	1,457	7	80	21,957	8,697		134	4,108	41	1	1,900
Holland	976	1,695	394	661	1,897				4,453	38		8		86	169	
Hanse Towns	18,371	3,277	1,097	908	10,669	1,739			35,338	85,967				28		2
Denmark	91,966	33,797	61,145	2,557	3,975	511	674		192,481	3,679						
Prussia	930,397	193,811	15,678	46,458	4,197	2,364			432,579	2,617		3,147		46		
Norway	4,679											20,391				
Sweden	99,614	339	90,985	43		68			94,987			6,344				
Mecklenburg									30,076	16						
Russia	53,453		4,661	57	3,177				59,114	1,000		19,671		1,066	405	2,201
Hanover			969		1,043				4,322			2				
Oldenburg									1,062							
Belgium												5				
France	1,255	675	361						2,391	6,641				155	8	
Turkey	2,941	13,597	6,059						92,550	664		13,117				
British North America	10,100								10,100			14	714			
Foreign North America	3,631								3,631			344	11,071			
South America													1,313			
Africa					810				810							
Total for 1863	465,520	185,116	141,143	52,173	96,248	6,160	703	1,400	877,171	111,768	399	58,811	17,290	1,439	631	4,118
Total for 1862	475,885	169,921	92,117	32,634	31,884	3,256	40	1,479	807,156	90,110	304	53,561	11,312	1,643	718	5,903
Increase		15,195	49,096	19,539	5,638		663		70,015	21,658	95	5,250	5,908		87	
Decrease	10,995					2,904		79						204		1,785

Statement showing the description and quantity of exports from Leith, and the countries where shipped, during the year ended December 31, 1863.

Countries.	EXPORTS.		
	Coals.	Pig iron.	Malleable iron.
	Tons.	*Tons.*	*Tons.*
Scotland	2,961	154	435
England	4,692	4,962	141
Holland	507	22,533	60
Hanse Towns	8,742	27,180	1,148
Denmark	3,183	1,037	21
Prussia	759	30,459	289
Norway	1,179	110	16
Sweden	514	305	22
Mecklenburg	56		
Russia	5,188	3,480	25
Belgium	841		
France	2,336	9,268	
Spain	1,452		
Portugal	274		
Italy	5,334	244	
Malta	85		
Greece	545		
Egypt	1,414		
British North America	5,469	194	
Foreign North America	737	500	
South America	3,069		
West Indies	1,810		3
Australia	521	493	17
Africa	397		1
Total tons for 1863	52,085	100,939	2,178
Total tons for 1862	41,703	75,867	999
Increase	10,382	25,072	1,179

Statement showing the number and tonnage of vessels arrived at and departed from Leith for the year ended December 31, 1863.

Ports	British Sailing Vessels — Loaded		— Ballast		British Steam Vessels — Loaded		— Ballast		Foreign Vessels — Loaded		— Ballast		Total		Total for the year 1863	
	No.	*Tons.*	*No.*	*Tons.*	*No.*	*Tons.*	*No.*	*Tons.*	*No.*	*Tons.*	*No.*	*Tons.*	*No.*	*Tons.*	*No.*	*Tons.*
Arrived from—																
Ports in Frith of Forth	1,822	85,457	131	5,154	388	23,364	49	4,902	4	1,096	4	1,098	2,398	119,901	1,790	83,438
Other ports in Scotland	1,695	41,041	97	5,169	93	23,777	9	1,436	5	359			830	48,782	735	39,419
London	52	4,312	9	2,946	110	62,501	1	587	4	591	1	963	189	68,737	151	66,098
Other ports in England	966	17,507	6	997	158	39,359	33	2,404	5	1,394			469	61,294	639	54,963
Ireland	16	538											4	538	5	653
Holland		1,951			49	90,951	3	1,410	49	3,194	2	2,546	110	96,036	104	94,593
Hanse Towns			1	962	96	37,478			5	464			104	40,750	84	94,570
Denmark	3	329			10	3,540			343	27,568			356	31,437	256	30,373
Prussia	108	10,559			63	30,063			313	94,504			384	65,146	416	63,343
Norway	2	95							107	14,524			109	14,319	107	13,497
Sweden	5	639							41	4,165			46	6,388	41	4,693
Mecklenburg	2	520			7	5,350			36	4,390			38	4,385	3	3,686
Russia	47	8,796							87	14,396			141	98,445	136	30,798
Hanover									13	738			13	738	15	939
Oldenburg									3	143			3	143	1	71
Belgium	90	2,146	1	465	1	630			13	1,088			35	4,199	37	4,497
France	31	2,951			44	8,888	1	499	13	499			88	12,194	84	10,855
Spain	14	1,134	1	856	1	199			6	976			19	2,465	12	915
Portugal	24	4,107			1	169			5	593			30	4,688	30	4,967
Italian States	3	1,955							5	1,976			29	2,831	29	3,563
Turkey	3	464							6	1,681			17	3,145	14	3,836
Egypt	3	792											9	792	2	469
North America (British)	22	10,751							9	1,416			96	12,369	95	11,904
North America (Foreign)	9	2,949							4		4		4	1,948	6	1,924
South America	13	7,785							5	3,715			18	11,460	17	9,397
West Indies	3	688							1	313			3	1,001	3	988
Africa	4	1,068	1						1	983			5	1,361	5	692
Australia															1	390
Total, 1863	3,170	203,494	169	10,149	1,021	224,383	96	11,238	968	110,119	7	3,837	5,425	573,220	4,669	486,904
Total, 1862	2,355	156,845	184	8,066	1,001	210,769	43	4,551	900	104,509	6	1,434	4,489	486,174		
Increase	815	46,649			20	23,614	53	6,687	68	5,610	1	2,403	936	87,046		
Decrease			15	2,083												
Sailed for—																
Ports in Frith of Forth	997	13,169	2,061	138,459	396	22,559	41	4,908	9	881	705	79,251	4,301	259,920	2,950	200,498
Other ports in Scotland	34	34,394	46	2,902	96	4,094	4	97			4	995	194	41,782	648	36,724
London	66	3,750		1,053	105	60,407	1	295	3	317			176	65,859	137	61,859
Other ports in England	9	3,768	1	8,646	158	39,012	38	2,684			292	4,331	466	58,341	350	4,510
Ireland		149											9	149	6	413

Holland													
Hanse Towns													
Denmark													
Prussia													
Norway											140		
Sweden													
Mecklenberg											1,800	9	
Russia													
Belgium											42	1	
France													
Spain													
Portugal													
Italian States													
Malta													
Egypt											1,801	2	
Greece													
North America, (British)													
North America, (Foreign)													
South America													
West Indies													
East Indies													
Australia													
Africa													
Total for 1863	495,022	4,517		5,668	91,369	1,052	22,323	196	9,413	82	235,780	1,034	134,536
Total for 1862			83,394	4,517	89,154	807	17,882	115	6,316	53	210,116	992	97,250
Increase				1,151	2,915	945	4,641	11	3,097	29	25,664	42	36,996

IRELAND.

CORK—EDWIN G. EASTMAN, *Consul.*

OCTOBER 25, 1864.

* * * I have the honor herewith to present my annual report of commerce.

There are no changes to record in the custom-house or other regulations affecting American interests. The first part of the present year was one of great commercial prosperity throughout the kingdom of Great Britain and Ireland; but, owing to speculation and contracting, it has been followed by a revulsion, and, at the present time, the people are passing through a commercial crisis similar to the one in 1857. The Galway Steamship Company has been dissolved and their steamers sold for the want of sufficient business to make them profitable, shareholders losing about all they invested.

The telegraph has been completed from this to Cape Clear, off which place steamers are now intercepted, and we receive news from America some six hours earlier than formerly. I notice a gradual change taking place in this country in the construction of vessels. Instead of wood, as formerly, iron is now almost universally used; and owing to the many modern improvements in steam engines effecting a great saving of fuel, large iron "cargo steamers," as they are called, are run at an average speed of about ten knots, at a very small expense. A line of these vessels, known as the National Steam Navigation Company, has been established between London, Liverpool, and New York. They have performed their work with great regularity and punctuality. During the coming season it will be increased to a weekly line. * * * * * *

The crops throughout Ireland have, during the past year, yielded an abundant harvest, thus affording many persons the means of reaching the goal of their ambition, "emigrating to America."

Emigration has continued unabated to the present time. I enclose herewith a statement of the number of emigrants from this port for the United States during the past year, and also an account of the imports and exports to and from the United States, showing the amount and value of the direct trade with this port:

Statement showing the number of emigrants from Cork to the United States direct, during each quarter of the year ended September 30, 1864.

Quarter ended December 31, 1863 .... 6, 621
Quarter ended March 31, 1864 .... 3, 151
Quarter ended June 30, 1864 .... 10, 743
Quarter ended September 30, 1864 .... 6, 545

Total 27, 060

Statement showing the description, quantity, and value of the imports at Cork, with the name of the port whence shipped during the several quarters of the year ended September 30, 1864.

Date.	Whence shipped.	Description.	Quantity.	Value.
			Qrs.	£ s. d.
Quarter ended Dec'r 31, 1863..	New York..	Wheat.......	18,640	186,400 00 00
" " March 31, 1864..	..... do	....do	13,806	138,060 00 00
" " June 30, 1864..	..... do	....do	3,205	32,050 00 00
" " Sept'r 30, 1864..	..... do	....do	15,117	151,170 00 00
Total......			50,768	507,680 00 00

Statement showing the description and value of the exports from Cork to the United States, with the name of the port where shipped, during the several quarters of the year ended September 30, 1864.

Date.	Where shipped.	Description.	Value.
			£ s. d.
Quarter ended December 31, 1863.......	Mostly to N. York, via Liverpool.	Whiskey and magnesia.	750 18 09
" " March 31, 1864...........	New York......	Magnesia	264 04 10
" " June 30, 1864............	New York......	Magnesia, whiskey, and calicoes.	829 02 10
" " September 30, 1864......	New York......	Whiskey and magnesia..	745 02 11
Total value of exports.............			2,589 09 04

BELFAST—JOHN YOUNG, *Consul.*

FEBRUARY 10, 1864.

I have the honor to enclose a statement of the value of invoices certified at this office during the quarters ending September 30 and December 31, 1863:

	£	s.	d.
On September 30, 1863, value was....................	196,876	19	10
On December 31, 1863, value was	249,181	19	9

JUNE 30, 1864.

Statement showing the value of the invoices certified at the United States consulate, Belfast, during the quarter ended March 31 and June 30, 1864.

Quarter ended March 31, 1864................... £324,459 $1,622,295
Quarter ended June 30, 1864. 225,130   1,125,650

OCTOBER 1, 1864.

* * The value of goods shipped from this district during the last quarter to the different ports in the United States amounts to £43,622 9s. 11d., showing a decrease of £4,580 1s. 9d.

POSSESSIONS AND DEPENDENCIES.

CANADA.

MONTREAL—D. THURSTON, *Vice-Consul General.*

JULY 7, 1864.

I have the honor to inform you that the Canadian Parliament, at the session just closed, enacted the following law in amendment to the act respecting "duties and customs, and the collection thereof, and to alter the duties on certain goods:"

1. In addition to the ad valorem duties of customs payable thereon, under any act now in force, there shall be imposed, levied, and collected on gin, rum, cordials, spirits of wine, and alcohol, not being whiskey or brandy, a specific duty of customs of fifteen cents for every gallon, wine measure, thereof, of the strength of proof by Sykes's hydrometer, and so in proportion for any greater strength or any less quantity than a gallon.

2. In addition to the specific duty of customs payable thereon, under any act now in force, there shall be imposed, levied, and collected on whiskey a further specific duty of customs of fifteen cents for every gallon, wine measure, thereof, of the strength of proof by Sykes's hydrometer, and so in proportion for any greater strength or any less quantity than a gallon.

3. In addition to the ad valorem duty of customs payable thereon, under any act now in force, there shall be imposed, levied, and collected on brandy a specific duty of customs of fifteen cents for every gallon, wine measure, thereof, of the strength of proof of Sykes's hydrometer, and so in proportion for any greater strength or any less quantity than a gallon.

4. The duties imposed by the foregoing sections shall be held to have come into force on the 11th day of May in the present year, 1864, and shall be held to have been payable on all such goods as aforesaid imported into this province, or taken out of the warehouse for consumption therein, upon or after the said day.

5. In addition to the ad valorem duty of customs payable thereon, under any act now in force, there shall be imposed, levied, and collected, on the several descriptions of manufactured tobacco hereinafter mentioned, the specific duties of customs following—that is to say:

On cavendish, plug, twist, and all descriptions of manufactured tobacco, sweetened or not sweetened, except that hereinafter specially mentioned, and otherwise charged with duty, for every pound, ten cents.

On common and smoking tobacco (*tabac frini*) made from impressed tobacco, whether from the leaf and stems together, or exclusively from stems, and on shoots or other refuse, separated from fine-cut tobacco in the process of manufacture, for every pound, five cents.

On snuff and snuff flour, manufactured from tobacco, ground dry, for every pound, ten cents.

On tobacco, fine-cut, manufactured to be sold or delivered loose, in bulk or in packages, papers, wrappers, or boxes, for every pound, fifteen cents.

On Canadian twist, otherwise called *tabac blanc en torquette*, being the impressed leaf rolled and twisted, for every pound, two cents.

On every pound of snuff, damp, moist, or pickled, eight cents.

On cigars per 1,000, according to the value thereof, as hereinafter, viz:

Value not over $10 per 1,000 .... $2
Value over $20, not over $40 per 1,000 4
Value over $40 per 1,000 5

And the said duties shall be held to have come into force on the 1st day of June of the present year, 1864, and shall be held to have been payable on all such goods as aforesaid imported in this province, or taken out of warehouse for consumption therein, upon or after the said day.

6. Every package or parcel of raw or manufactured tobacco, or of cigars, or snuff imported or brought into this province after the passing of this act, whether entered at the custom-house for warehouse or for consumption, shall have attached thereto, by the proper officer of customs, such stamp as may be directed by regulation established by the minister of finance.

7. The following articles, heretofore classed as cordials, and chargeable as such with the duties of customs imposed on cordials—that is to say : Ginger wine, orange wine, lemon wine, gooseberry wine, strawberry wine, raspberry wine, elder wine, and currant wine, shall, after the passing of this act, cease to be rated and chargeable with duty as cordials, and shall be rated and chargeable with an ad valorem duty of twenty per cent. as unenumerated articles.

8. In addition to the duties of customs now payable on the following articles there shall be imposed, levied, and collected thereon the following specific duties of customs—that is to say: On vinegar, four cents per gallon ; on refined petroleum, five cents per gallon ; on naphtha, six cents per gallon.

9. The present ad valorem duties of customs upon the following articles are hereby repealed, and the following specific duties of customs shall be imposed, levied, and collected thereon—that is to say : On benzule, fifteen cents per gallon ; on crude petroleum, four cents per gallon.

Summary statement showing the total value of imports into Montreal for the quarter ended September 30, 1864, and also the names of the countries whence derived.

Recapitulation.	Total value.	Great Britain.	N. America.	West Indies.	United States.	Other foreign countries.
Goods paying specific duty	$10,570	$4,989			$6,281	
Goods paying sp ad ium duty						
Goods paying 100 per cent. ad ium duty	708,733	106,138	$9,240	$67,495	249,956	$275,904
Goods paying 40 per cent. ad valorem duty	32,685	20,358	9		9,650	2,668
Goods paying 30 per cent. ad valorem duty	29,623	13,858	11		11,701	4,053
Goods paying 25 per cent. ad valorem duty	5,922,118	4,551,366	11,091	444	339,333	319,984
Goods paying 20 per cent. ad valorem duty	75				75	
Goods paying 15 per cent. ad ium duty	521,367	468,735	336		23,596	28,710
Goods paying 10 per cent. ad valorem duty	499,624				199,624	
Free goods, coin, and ition	2,206,694	962,182	43,665		1,184,302	16,545
Other free goods						
Total	9,231,489	6,126,896	64,352	67,939	2,384,508	647,864

Summary statement showing the total value of the exports of the produce of Canada, from Montreal, during the quarter ended September 30, 1864, with the names of the countries where shipped.

Recapitulation.	Total value.	Great Britain.	N. America.	West Indies.	United States.	Other foreign countries.
Produce of the mine	$528		$595		$528	
Produce of the forest	424,849	$379,921	20,088	$1,300	42,063	$970
Animal and other products	525,186	434,337	84,712		50,478	19,383
Agricultural products	920,113	809,554	10,248		91,608	4,239
Manufactures	88,103	70,585	4,910	2,261	4,078	931
Other articles	116,000	109,900			1,190	
Total	2,074,779	1,804,297	121,453	3,561	119,945	25,523

MARCH 8, 1864.

There is also appended a comparative statement of vessels built at Quebec in each year, between the years 1852 and 1864, inclusive, exhibiting the number, tonnage, and average. From this table it will be observed that the yearly aggregate tonnage has largely increased in the twelve years, comparing 1852 with 1864; also a still greater increase in the number of vessels. It should be added that the number, and of course the tonnage, is not yet completed for 1864.

A comparative statement of vessels built at Quebec in each year between the years 1852 and 1864, inclusive, showing the number, tonnage, and average.

Year.	Number.	Tonnage.	Average tonnage.
1852	23	21,572	937,913
1853	43	48,039	1,117,186
1854	44	44,951	1,021,613
1855	31	28,827	929,903
1856	40	33,107	827,675
1857	48	36,619	762,896
1858	24	20,121	838,375
1859	17	10,169	598,176
1860	22	18,367	834,863
1861	27	22,617	837,666
1862	27	23,149	857,370
1863	63	54,287	861,700
1864	63	56,348	894,412

APRIL 20, 1864.

I have the honor to furnish your department with a recent order, passed in government council, relative to tolls upon certain commodities on the provincial canals being rescinded.

GOVERNMENT HOUSE, QUEBEC,
Saturday, April 16, 1864.

Present: His excellency the governor general in council.

His excellency was pleased to lay before the council a memorandum, dated 8th April instant, from the honorable the minister of finance, representing that, by the tariff of tolls on the provincial canals, established by order in council of 13th day of June, 1859, as well as by previous tariffs since 1853, certain exemptions were created in favor of salt, iron, wheat, flour and corn, under the conditions therein mentioned, and that it is expedient that such exemptions, which, by the tariff of the 15th April, 1863, have not been continued, should be revived and re-established.

Whereupon his excellency in council was pleased to order, and it is hereby ordered, under and by virtue of the authority given and conferred by the twenty-eighth chapter of the Consolidated Statutes of Canada, that upon, from and after this sixteenth day of April instant, the following articles, having paid full tolls through the St. Lawrence canal, be passed free through the Welland canal; and if tolls shall have been previously paid thereon through the Chambly canal, that such tolls be refunded at the canal office at Montreal, viz: iron of all kinds, salt; and that the following articles, having paid full tolls through the Welland canal, be passed free through the St. Lawrence and Chambly canals, viz: wheat, flour, corn.

WILLIAM H. LEE, *C. E. C.*

APRIL 30, 1864.

I have the honor to forward to your department a recent regulation in the fisheries branch of the crown lands department, approved by his excellency the governor general in council.

Department of crown lands—Fisheries branch.

QUEBEC, *April 25, 1864.*

The following regulations relating to claims for fishing bounties, under chapter sixty-two of the Consolidated Statutes of Canada, have been approved by the governor general in council on the 23d instant:

First. Claimants for fishing bounties shall, in addition to the several requirements specified in the fisheries act, furnish sufficient proof to the satisfaction of any collector of customs to whom application for a certificate may be made, that the vessel has been engaged exclusively in actual fishing during the space of at least three consecutive months, or for any other period of consecutive time up to four months, no intermediate voyage or occupation being reckoned therein.

Second. The time during which each vessel is so engaged in fishing may be proved by the owner and two other competent witnesses, all of whom shall be sworn by the collector of customs; and a journal or log-book, kept day by day on board each vessel, shall be produced and its entries verified on oath by the owner, master or skipper, and such journal or log-book must state the particulars of the voyage, the daily catch by the crew, the locality where so occupied, and also the time of departure from and arrival at any port or place during the time computed as such fishing voyage.

Third. Proofs shall be also required by any collector of customs that the vessel for which bounty is claimed has not been during the fishing season—which season shall in each case be reckoned as the period of constant fishing named in the act and alleged by the claimant—engaged in trading or carrying cargoes.

Fourth. Probable claimants for fishing bounties should, on the granting of licenses to fish for the bounty, be apprised of the requirements of the act and of these regulations; and that unless they be conformed to in every respect certificates will not be granted by the collector of customs.

ANDREW RUSSELL, *Assistant Commissioner.*

JUNE 2, 1864.

I have the honor to correspond under this date, and beg leave to enclose a schedule of the excise duty on manufactured tobacco *now levied and in force;* also, the corresponding increase made in duties of customs *now also levied and in force,* the same having been agreed to and by law established on the 31st of May, 1864.

Resolutions to be moved by the honorable Mr. Galt, in committee of ways and means:

1. That it is expedient to levy an excise duty on manufactured tobacco, and that a corresponding increase be made in the duties of customs now levied on the importation of that article into this province.

2. That upon, from and after the 31st day of May instant no person, firm, or association shall manufacture tobacco in any way for sale without having first obtained a license to do so, or a permit as hereinafter mentioned, for which license he or they shall pay annually $25.

3. That on the several descriptions of manufactured tobacco hereinafter mentioned there shall be levied and collected, from and after the 31st of May instant, the duties of excise following—that is to say:

Class A. On cavendish, plug, twist, and all descriptions of manufactured tobacco, sweetened or not sweetened, except those hereinafter specially mentioned and otherwise charged with excise duty, for every pound..$0 10

Class B. On common cut smoking tobacco *(tabac frisé)* made from unpressed tobacco, whether from the leaf and stems together or exclusively from stems; on shorts or other refuse separated from fine-cut tobacco in the process of manufacture, for every pound............... 0 05

Class C. On snuff and snuff flour manufactured from tobacco ground dry, per pound 0 10

Class D. On tobacco fine-cut, manufactured to be sold or delivered loose, in bulk, or in packages, papers, wrappers or boxes, for every pound... 0 15

Class E. On Canadian twist, otherwise called *tabac blanc en torquette*, being the unpressed leaf rolled and twisted, for every pound......... 0 02

Class F. On cigars per 1,000 according to the value thereof as hereunder, viz :

    Value not over $4 per 1,000 .... 1 00
    Value over $4 and not over $10 per 1,000.................... 2 00
    Value over $10 and not over $20 per 1,000.................. 3 00
    Value over $20 and not over $40 per 1,000.................. 4 00
    Value over $40 per 1,000.................................. 5 00

4. That in addition to the ad valorem duty of customs now by law imposed and levied on manufactured tobacco of every description, there be levied and collected upon, from and after the said 31st of May instant, on the several descriptions of manufactured tobacco hereinbefore mentioned, the specific duties following—that is to say :

On every pound of manufactured tobacco included in class A and not excepted therefrom..$0 10

On every pound of manufactured tobacco mentioned in class B........ 0 05

On every pound of snuff and snuff flour mentioned in class C......... 0 10

On every pound of manufactured tobacco mentioned in class D......... 0 15

On every pound of tobacco of the description mentioned in class E.... 0 02

And on every pound of snuff, damp, moist, or pickled................ 0 08

And on cigars, per 1,000, as hereunder, viz :

On every 1,000 cigars, value not over $10........................... 2 00

On every 1,000 cigars, value over $10 and not over $20.............. 3 00

On every 1,000 cigars, value over $20 and not over $40.............. 4 00

On every 1,000 cigars, value over $40.............................. 5 00

5. That it is expedient that upon, from and after the said 31st day of May instant, all stocks of manufactured tobacco of every description and color, whether the same be wholly or only partly manufactured, in the possession of the manufacturer or manufacturers of the said tobacco, shall at once become and be subject to the payment of the excise duty hereinabove mentioned, and no part of the said stocks of manufactured tobacco shall be allowed to leave the tobacco manufactory or the stores or premises thereunto belonging and appertaining in which such stocks may be deposited, to go into consumption, without permit or warrant of the proper officer of excise and the payment of the duties mentioned in the foregoing resolutions, and all such stocks may be immediately examined, secured, and stamped by the collector of inland revenue or other proper officer of excise.

6. That pending the final passing of the act to be introduced in accordance with the foregoing resolutions, the collector of inland revenue in each of the revenue districts or divisions, in which any one or more tobacco manufactories may be situated, shall grant to the person, firm, or association carrying on or

working such tobacco manufactory or manufactories, a permit in writing under his official signature, authorizing such person, firm, or association to carry on and work such tobacco manufactory until a license for the same can issue in due course of law, and such permit shall be held a sufficient authority for carrying on and working such tobacco manufactory.

JUNE 3, 1864.

I have the honor to enclose a return of the number of passengers arrived at this port from the opening of navigation to June 1, 1864, issued from the government immigration office.

Return of the number of passengers arrived at the port of Quebec from the opening of navigation to the 1st June, 1864.

	Cabin.	Steerage.	Total.
From England	113	1,168	1,281
From Ireland	8	1,035	1,043
From Scotland	12	512	524
From Germany	1	446	447
From Norway	3	891	894
Total	137	4,052	4,189
To corresponding period last year	318	3,961	4,279
Decrease this year			90
Arrived by steamers			2,472
Arrived by sailing vessels			1,717
Total			4,189

Nationalities.		Destinations.	
English	777	Lower provinces	7
Irish	1,543	Eastern townships	75
Scotch	155	Montreal	271
Germans	549	Central dis't east of Toronto.	482
Norwegians	915	Toronto and west of Toronto.	517
Swedes	32	Remained in Quebec	34
Danes	93		
Other countries	129		
Total	4,189	Remained in Canada	1,386

Went to Eastern States	1,105	
Went to Western States	1,698	
		2,803
Total		4,189

A. C. BUCHANAN, *Chief Agent.*

GOVERNMENT IMMIGRATION OFFICE, *Quebec, June* 1, 1864.

JUNE 18, 1864.

I have the honor to enclose a comparative statement of the tonnage and number of arrivals and departures of vessels by sea at and from this port during the years ended June 16, 1863 and 1864.

Comparative statement of arrivals and tonnage at this port from sea in 1863 and 1864, up to the 16th of June in each year.

1863—642 vessels .... 347,103 tons.
1864—367 vessels .... 216,649 tons.

Less this year... 275 vessels..................... 130,454 tons.

Arrival of ocean mail steamers at this port in 1863 and 1864, up to the 16th June in each year.

1863—7 steamers .... 10,285 tons.
1864—8 steamers .... 11,966 tons.

More this year... 1 steamer..................... 1,681 tons.

Comparative statement of arrivals and tonnage of vessels from the lower ports to the 16th of June in each year.

1863—17 vessels .... 1,753 tons.
1864—10 vessels..................... 971 tons.

Less this year... 7 vessels..................... 782 tons.

Comparative statement of arrivals and tonnage of vessels from sea to the 16th June in each year.

1864—385 vessels .... 229,586 tons.
1863—666 vessels..................... 359,141 tons.

Less this year... 281 vessels..................... 129,555 tons.

Comparative statement of vessels and tonnage cleared at this port to the 16th instant for sea, including steamships.

1864—231 vessels .... 155,396 tons.
1863—206 vessels .... 121,222 tons.

More this year... 25 vessels..................... 34,174 tons.

Comparative statement of vessels, &c., cleared from this port for ports without the province, including steamers, &c., to the 16th instant.

1864—39 vessels, &c..................... 2,679 tons.
1863—45 vessels, &c..................... 3,112 tons.

Less this year... 6 vessels, &c..................... 433 tons.

Comparative statement of total clearances at this port for European ports and ports without the province to the 16th instant, including steamers.

```
        1864—270 vessels, &c.................. 158, 075 tons.
        1863—251 vessels, &c.................. 124, 334 tons.

More this year...  19 vessels, &c.................. 33, 741 tons.
```

Comparative statement of arrivals and tonnage of vessels from sea to the 1st September in each year.

```
        1864—746 vessels...................... 419, 050 tons.
        1863—994 vessels...................... 503, 995 tons.

Less this year... 248 vessels...................... 84, 945 tons.
```

Comparative statement of the arrivals and tonnage of steamships from sea to the 1st September in each year.

```
        1864—26 steamships.................... 36, 048 tons.
        1863—26 steamships.................... 32, 287 tons.

        .............................. 3, 761 more this year.
```

Comparative statement of the arrivals and tonnage of vessels from the lower ports to the 1st September in each year.

```
        1863—88 vessels....................... 7, 885 tons.
        1864—68 vessels....................... 7, 388 tons.

Less this year... 20 vessels....................... 497 tons.
```

Comparative statement of vessels and tonnage cleared at this port to the 1st September for sea, &c., including steamships.

```
        1864—579 vessels...................... 440, 047 tons.
        1863—838 vessels...................... 471, 700 tons.

Less this year... 259 vessels...................... 31, 653 tons.
```

Comparative statement of vessels cleared for ports without the province to September 1 in each year.

```
        1864—105 vessels...................... 6, 878 tons.
        1863—104 vessels...................... 7, 099 tons.

More this year...  1 vessel ...................... 221 less this year.
```

Comparative statement of timber, masts, bowsprits, spars, staves, &c., measured and culled to date.

	1862.	1863.	1864.
Waney white pine.........................	546, 171	469, 733	436, 835
White pine.................................	17, 978, 108	20, 304, 197	16, 221, 495
Red pine...................................	3, 171, 278	4, 280, 901	3, 037, 721
Oak..	1, 747, 115	1, 161, 542	2, 208, 884
Elm..	1, 190, 887	2, 476, 105	1, 711, 533
Ash..	248, 639	670, 005	167, 067
Basswood..................................	13, 481	38, 008	12, 713
Butternut..................................	3, 429	7, 473	5, 998
Tamarac...................................	1, 008, 969	2, 367, 651	666, 130
Birch and maple...........................	186, 465	234, 768	231, 279
Masts and bowsprits, (pieces).............	475	1, 135	937
Spars, (pieces)............................	1, 248	2, 892	4, 300
Standard staves...........................	1, 048. 0. 2. 3	1, 000. 6. 1. 8	880. 1. 3. 12
West India staves.........................	1, 469. 6. 2. 29	2, 705. 6. 0. 26	2, 901. 2. 2. 20
Barrel staves..............................	2. 5. 1. 15	54. 5. 1. 3	20. 2. 3. 2

WM. QUINN, *Supervisor.*

SUPERVISOR OF CULLERS' OFFICE,
Quebec, September 2, 1864.

H. Ex. Doc. 60——4

Recapitulation of exports from Quebec for the quarter ending September 30, 1864.

Description.	Total value.	EXPORTED TO—				
		Great Britain.	BRITISH COLONIES.		United States.	Other foreign countries.
			North America.	West Indies.		
Products of the mine	$6,764	$2,898	$76			$3,790
Products of the fisheries	56		56			
Products of the forest	3,181,597	3,081,116	6,367			133,994
Animals and their products	43,307	9,429	33,818			60
Agricultural products	198,661	30,454	95,967	$130		
Manufactures	29,432	7,396	98,077	3,407	$552	
Coin and bullion	9,958	9,958				
Other articles	2,943	68	2,874			2,940
Total value of exports	3,394,717	3,081,319	167,235	3,527	552	149,064

Comparative return of the value of goods entered for consumption at the port of Quebec, showing the countries whence imported, for the quarter ending September 30, 1864.

Description.	Total value.	Great Britain.	British North America.	United States.	Other foreign countries.	Amount of duty.
Goods paying specific duty	$2,206	$565		$1,621		$1,085 70
Goods paying specific and ad valorem duties	128,550	30,061	$3,708	45,008	$49,753	57,367 17
Goods paying 100 per cent. ad valorem						
Goods paying 40 ...... do	119			119		47 60
Goods paying 30 ...... do	6,749	2,978		1,178	2,563	2,034 91
Goods paying 25 ...... do	3,284	3,350		.34		845 99
Goods paying 20 ...... do	810,989	746,178	408	37,438	98,965	162,197 58
Goods paying 15 ...... do	639	639			105	95 92
Goods paying 10 ...... do	174,871	171,396		3,385		17,397 46
Free goods, coin and bullion	76,811		105	76,811		
Other free goods	614,142	497,493	32,988	58,371	25,290	
Total	1,818,460	1,452,600	37,909	223,945	104,706	941,069 33

Value of foreign reprints of British copyrights, $74, and duty thereon, at 12½ per cent., $9 26.

Comparative statement showing the supply, export from, and stock of lumber at Quebec, to the 1st December, for the years 1860, 1861, 1862, 1863, and 1864, respectively, and an average of five years preceding.

Articles.	Average of five years, 1855 to 1859.	Supply.—From returns from supervisor and others, for years ending 1st December.				
		1860.	1861.	1862.	1863.	1864.
TIMBER.						
Oak............feet.	1,617,874	1,086,160	1,447,682	2,206,483	1,668,818	3,717,012
Elm............ do.	1,338,347	1,176,224	1,048,491	1,671,776	2,953,817	2,649,897
Ash .... do.	179,481	105,968	82,177	295,403	683,835	189,778
Birch . ... do.	139,064	514,348	275,304	181,890	213,869	246,841
Tamarac ....do.	394,948	199,528	351,494	1,285,563	2,661,679	935,289
W'te pine, sq., } do.	16,410,525	18,564,205	{ 15,730,547	21,627,853	21,617,465	23,737,268
Do., waney .. }			6,734,962	748,614	185,969	735,360
Red pine........ do.	2,147,555	3,631,125	3,045,573	4,039,991	5,105,029	5,348,638
STAVES.						
Standard......mille.	1,851	1,473	1,010	1,453	1,930	1,817
Puncheon.... do .	2,589	2,441	2,138	2,386	4,688	4,623
Barrel . ... do .	16	5	11	21	76	22
DEALS.						
Pine .. ...standard.	1,999,504	2,812,595	2,893,075	2,334,296	2,505,608	3,013,115
Spruce.... do .	784,877	1,172,086	1,283,921	815,158	629,657	742,120
LATHWOOD.						
Red pine and hemlock....cords.	3,260	819	3,254	5,224	1,715	2,999

Articles.	Average of five years,1855 to 1859.	Export.—From customs returns for years ending 1st December.				
		1860.	1861.	1862.	1863.	1864.
TIMBER.						
Oak............feet	1,106,791	1,485,400	1,725,160	1,463,680	2,085,280	2,463,560
Elm .... do.	1,129,752	1,021,560	1,269,320	1,099,200	2,128,840	1,957,960
Ash .... do.	111,240	88,440	96,560	99,840	306,760	121,800
Birch .... do.	172,065	462,160	255,320	165,480	430,720	358,280
Tamarac .. .. do.	84,410	58,240	50,240	57,120	243,680	190,120
W'te pine, sq., } do.	14,458,649	18,252,600	19,447,920	15,493,080	23,147,520	20,032,520
Do. waney .. }						
Red pine ....do.	2,213,349	2,502,880	2,855,240	2,491,120	4,049,600	3,999,440
STAVES.						
Standard......mille.	1,616	1,851	1,383	1,282	2,211	1,826
Puncheon.... do .	2,351	3,163	{ 2,478	2,191	3,564 {	2,679
Barrel .... do .	2	....				32
DEALS.						
Pine .. .standard. }	3,728,064	4,668,850	4,927,817	3,493,299	5,207,158 {	3,686,000
Spruce . do . }						711,237
LATHWOOD.						
Red pine and hemlock ...cords	4,380	6,013	6,965	4,296	5,616	6,168

Comparative statement showing the supply, export, &c.—Continued.

Articles.	Average of five years, 1855 to 1859.	Total stock.—Including merchantable and culls, on the 1st December.				
		1860.	1861.	1862.	1863.	1864.
TIMBER.						
Oak .... feet.	1,375,019	1,348,477	958,627	1,298,608	651,145	1,793,082
Elm .... do.	1,192,521	1,068,854	793,761	998,978	1,595,909	2,332,10¹
Ash .... do.	133,892	112,030	48,696	157,288	441,894	406,215
Birch .... do.	22,153	119,321	203,211	225,380	69,103	74,
Tamarac .. .. do.	665,918	22,201	52,409	303,639	1,098,695	1,048,
W'te pine, sq., } do.	11,217,373	11,390,354	{ 7,971,000	15,354,942	13,998,578	17,561,567
Do. waney.. }			{ 6,346,602	3,949,944	1,224,365	301,908
Red pine .... do.	2,356,910	2,649,157	2,707,199	3,407,583	4,197,305	5,382,922
STAVES.						
Standard ..... mille.	1,192	1,390	984	1,173	857	916
Puncheon .... do .	1,477	1,829	1,226	1,100	2,292	3,808
Barrel .... do .	1	....	....	....	45	18
DEALS.						
Pine . ..... standard.	1,426,507	1,246,160	1,577,469	2,029,141	1,352,016	1,584,577
Spruce ... do .	346,916	617,478	569,210	541,660	338,608	561,589
LATHWOOD.						
Red pine and hemlock ... cords.	2,047	1,396	296	3,042	2,126	1,400

Condensed statement of goods entered for consumption at Quebec, with the values thereof, showing the countries whence imported, during the quarter ended December 31, 1864.

Description.	Total value.	Great Britain.	B. N. America.	B. W. Indies.	United States.	France.	Germany.	Other foreign countries.	Am't of duty.
Goods paying specific duty	$1,710	$796			$684				$779 40
Goods paying specific and ad valorem duties	84,906	18,448	$12,642	$11,946	19,741	$2,553		$10,576	36,554 93
Goods paying 30 ....do	6,119	4,450	4		470			1,194	1,835 00
Goods paying 25 ....do	2,095	1,999			103				963 70
Goods paying 20 ....do	276,466	235,993	504		98,783	1,871	$1,034	10,994	55,294 00
Goods paying 15 ....do									
Goods paying 10 ....do	43,469	49,177	759		596		7		4,346 32
Free goods, coin and bullion	50,417				50,417				
Other free goods	270,342	204,546	37,007	47	98,023	498		503	
Total	735,518	506,381	50,909	11,993	127,047	4,910	1,041	31,397	99,333 55

Condensed statement of the exports of the produce of Canada, from Quebec, during the quarter ended December 31, 1864, and showing to what country the same were exported.

Description.	Total value.	Great Britain.	B. N. America.	B. W. Indies.	United States.	France.	Other foreign countries.
Produce of the mines	$1,984	$990	$110		$194		$40
Produce of the fisheries	889		829				
Produce of the forest	1,849,554	1,763,564	1,914	$1,805	1,339	$32,295	29,337
Animals and their products	38,106	15,982	23,771	214			
Agricultural products	66,487	6,834	59,439	9,086		50	
Manufactures	15,013	1,503	4,374				
Coin and bullion	1,025	1,025					
Other articles	1,702	251	147		304		
Thirty-five vessels, built from July 1 to December 31, register tons 33,114, at $41	1,357,674	1,357,674					
Total	3,330,654	3,167,133	88,884	11,105	1,767	32,345	29,430

Comparative statement showing the arrivals and tonnage of vessels at the port of Quebec for the years 1860 to 1864, together with the average of the five years from 1855 to 1859.

	Vessels.	Tons.
Average of the five years 1855 to 1859	906	470,811
1860	1,169	652,894
1861	1,364	809,303
1862	1,191	673,507
1863	1,401	742,431
1864	1,098	624,026

RECAPITULATION OF 1863.

British	882	504,764
American	3	3,095
Norwegian	142	80,972
Swedish	4	2,655
Prussian	26	18,538
French	2	1,054
Spanish	3	1,415
Portuguese	27	6,987
Danish	1	172
Hamburg	6	3,683
Mecklenburg	2	741
Total	1,098	624,026

Comparative return of imports, exports, and duties at Quebec, for 1863–'64.

Value of exports for the year ending December 31, 1863	$11,087,748 00
Value of exports for the year ending December 31, 1864	9,859,034 00
Decrease in 1864	1,228,714 00
Value of imports for the year ending December 31, 1863	5,024,691 00
Value of imports for the year ending December 31, 1864	5,209,319 00
Increase in 1864	184,628 00
Duties collected in the year ending December 31, 1863	587,982 17
Duties collected in the year ending December 31, 1864	721,056 33
Increase in 1864	133,074 16
Total collections of all kinds for the year ending December 31, 1863	635,023 51
Total collections of all kinds for the year ending December 31, 1864	789,457 95
Increase in 1864	154,434 44

JULY 28, 1864.

I have the honor to enclose herewith printed copies of the "*sanitary orders*" passed by the provincial government in 1854, and now in force, together with a copy of a resolution adopted by the board of health of the city of Halifax, on the 25th instant, which has just been furnished at my request by the provincial secretary, relating to vessels coming directly from the ports of New York, Boston, and Baltimore. * * * * *

OFFICE OF BOARD OF HEALTH,
Halifax, July 25, 1864.

Extract from minutes of a meeting of the board of health held this day:

"*Resolved,* That hereafter it shall only be necessary for the health officer to visit vessels coming directly from New York, Boston, and Baltimore, except such ships having surgeons attached to them, and that his excellency the lieutenant governor and the executive council be requested to establish the same table of fees for the port of Halifax as that adopted for the ports of the province."

SANITARY ORDERS.

By his Excellency Colonel Sir JOHN GASPARD LEMARCHANT, knight, lieutenant governor, commander-in-chief in and over her Majesty's province of Nova Scotia and its dependencies, &c., &c., &c.

J. GASPARD LEMARCHANT.

Whereas, on the ground of extensive observations of medical men in different portions of the globe, the opinion now generally prevails that sanitary regulations are, in every respect, preferable to quarantine restrictions for preventing the introduction and spread of infectious disease in communities:

I do therefore, by the advice of her Majesty's executive council of this province, hereby order and direct—

1st. That when a vessel shall arrive at any port of this province, the captain shall report to the pilot or revenue officer all cases of sickness of whatever kind, other than ordinary sea-sickness, that may be on board.

2d. That the revenue officer, or pilot, shall send notice thereof to the health officer of the port, or should there be no such officer, to any other duly qualified medical practitioner of the place.

3d. That the captain, if need be, shall provide a boat and men to convey such notice, and to bring back such medical officer or practitioner to examine the case or cases of sickness on board.

4th. That the health officer thus notified shall go on board, and having examined the cases of sickness on board, shall use such means as are necessary and proper for their recovery.

5th. In case the health officer shall find the vessel in a filthy condition or over-crowded, or that there is danger of disease spreading on board, he shall cause the sick to be taken on shore, and the vessel to be thoroughly cleansed, and in every such case the captain, agents, or owners of the vessel shall be held responsible for all the necessary expenses incurred in cleansing the vessel or providing suitable apartments for the sick, for their removal thereto, and their treatment therein.

6th. In case of the existence of any contagious or infectious disease on board of any vessel arriving in port, the health officer is hereby authorized to take such measures for the protection of the passengers and crew on board, as also the community on shore, as are prescribed in the several regulations in cap. 54, sections 8 and 9, of Revised Statutes of Nova Scotia.

7th. That for the services thus rendered, the health officer shall be entitled to charge a reasonable sum, to be paid by the captain or agents of the vessel on behalf of the owner.

8th. That no vessel, subject by these sanitary regulations to be examined, shall be admitted to entry until a certificate of such examination, signed by the health officer, shall be exhibited, nor shall such vessel be admitted to entry or clearance until all the fees and charges authorized by these sanitary orders have been paid, as directed in chapter 54, section 3, of the Revised Statutes of Nova Scotia.

9th. In case of dispute in respect to such charges, such dispute, where the bill of charges does not exceed twenty pounds, shall be determined summarily before any two justices of the peace, as to the amount which is reasonable according to the accustomed rate of charge within the place, for distance and for attendance on patients of the like condition and class in life.

10th. That the table of fees payable to health officers, in all ports of the province, Halifax excepted, shall be as follows:

For visiting all vessels above 100 tons burden liable to be examined. £0 15 0
Of and under 100 tons...................................... 0 7 6
Certificate of release...................................... 0 5 0

    Fees at Halifax payable by the vessel:

For visiting a vessel having emigrants, or more than ten steerage
  passengers on board, or coming from an infected place 1 10 0
For inspecting passengers...................................... 0 10 0
For each subsequent visit, made necessary either by sickness or request 0 15 0
For certificate of release...................................... 0 6 3

11th. That all pilots and revenue officers shall keep and carry with them copies of these sanitary regulations and instructions thereon.

12th. That any violation or disobedience of any sanitary order hereby made shall be deemed a misdemeanor, and shall subject the person guilty thereof to a penalty not exceeding one hundred pounds.

    Given under my hand and seal at arms, at Halifax, this 20th day of Oc-
[L. S.] tober, A. D. 1852, and in the 16th year of her Majesty's reign.
    By his excellency's command:

                         JOSEPH HOWE.
God save the Queen.

At a council held at the government house on the 2d day of August, 1854— present his excellency the lieutenant governor, &c., &c., &c.—it is ordered, That at all the ports in this province, except Halifax, each health officer shall be entitled to demand, in addition to the fees prescribed by the sanitary orders established for this province on the 20th October, 1852, sixpence currency for every mile of distance from the residence of the health officer to the vessel required to be visited, if the distance shall exceed two miles.

        PICTOU—B. HAMMETT NORTON, *Consul.*

                            MARCH 19, 1864.

  * * * From developments daily making I am satisfied that Nova Scotia will, at no distant day, prove the richest portion of the continent of North America. Her gold fields are now attracting the attention of capitalists

both in England and in the United States. From the latter an immense amount of money is being invested in her coal, copper, and gold mines.

The general assembly now in session have passed a bill for the construction of a railroad to Pictou, thus uniting Halifax by rail with the waters of the Gulf of St. Lawrence.   *   *   *   *   *

OCTOBER 4, 1864.

I have the honor of submitting my annual report of the trade and commerce of this port, Sidney and Lingan, for the year ended September 30, 1864.

The principal article of export is coal, and a larger quantity has been shipped the present year than at any former one.

New mines have been opened and are now in working order at Glace bay, Cow bay, and a number of other localities.

Below is a statement of coal shipped to the United States from the Sidney mines, Gorrie mines, at Cow bay, and Little Brasdor mines, for the year ended September 30, 1864:

Sidney mines exported coal to the value of..........	$34,761 45
Gorrie mines, at Cow bay, exported coal to the value of	23,787 00
Little Brasdor mines exported coal to the value of.....	1,412 00
	59,960 45

Statement of exports and imports at the port of Lingan for the year ended September 30, 1864:

Amount of exports	$92,166 00
Amount of imports	1,000 00

Table showing imports of the U. States into the port of Pictou for the year ended Sept. 30, 1864.

Descript'n.	IN BRITISH SHIPS.		IN FOREIGN SHIPS.	
	Quantities.	Value.	Quantities.	Value.
Ashes, vegetable potash ....pounds..	473	$41 00		
Agricultural implements ....pieces..	3,117	2,058 60		
Butter and lard....................pounds..	310	32 00		
Burning fluid....................gallons..	585	453 00		
Bread, fine.......................pounds..	1,165	83 00		
navy ....pounds..	686	29 00		
Bricks, fire.......................number..	2	135 00		
Candles..........................pounds..	120	60 00		
Cheese...........................pounds..	6,773	895 00		
Coffee ....pounds..	1,520	194 00		
Cordage ....pounds..	1,940	188 13	560	$84 60
Cotton and linen manufactures.......pieces..	42	785 18		
Carriages ....number..	24	500 53		
Clocks ....packages..	34	389 00		
Drugs and apothecary wares..... packages..	133	1,482 69		
Dyestuffs ....packages..	121	378 42		
Flour, wheat....................barrels..	10,305	48,036 00	40	250 00
corn-meal ....barrels..	273	836 00		
Fruit, green ....packages..	624	1,295 00		
dried ....packages..	20	77 85		
raisins ....pounds..	2,263	195 00		
Furniture ....packages..	1,258	4,778 77		
Glassware........................packages..	116	2,024 82		
Hides ....number..	1,065	5,496 00		
Hats and caps ....packages..	15	1,055 97		
Hardware ....packages and pieces..	25,015	8,913 84		
Hops ....packages..	1	27 94		
Iron, viz: stoves, grates, &c.......number..	167	2,259 58		
India-rubber manufactures ......packages..	4	291 30		
Leather, sole ....pounds..	2,084	503 00		
upper and harness..........packages..	4	72 04		
boots and shoes ....packages..	81	7,912 20		
Lime ....pounds..	1,200	849 00	500	200 00
Musical instruments . ...pieces..	4	560 75		
Molasses ....gallons..	62	25 00		
Marble, wrought ....packages..	6	76 50		
unwrought.............packages..	48	109 00		
Naval stores ....barrels..	193	397 15		
Nuts ....packages..	33	231 20		
Oakum ....pounds..	1,000	76 00		
Oil, coal ....gallons..	4,899	2,160 00		
lard ....gallons..	2,031	1,671 00		
Paper and paper manufactures...packages..	86	394 60		
Printed books....................packages..	34	1,307 00		
Printer's ink.....................packages..	4	23 80		
Paints and putty.................packages..	24	198 00		
Pork and hams..................packages..	15	257 00		
Rice ....pounds..	98	5 00		
Seeds ....packages..	39	194 34		
Soap ....packages..	20	128 00		
Stationery ....packages..	3	233 50		
Spirits, say strong wines...........gallons..	3¼	3 00		
Sugar, refined ....pounds..	6,057	661 34		
Tea ....pounds..	1,683	611 40		
Tobacco, leaf....................pounds..	97,112	13,265 00		
manufactured ....pounds..	346	110 00		
cigars and snuff ....pounds..	11	88 31		
Vegetables, onions...............pounds..	2,380	112 00	275	11 00
other kinds ....pounds..	12	36 00		
Woollen manufactures ....packages..	8	1,073 00		
Wood, viz: lumber ..		227 00	250	6 00
Unenumerated packages	889	4,264 56		
Total......................................		120,838 31		551 00

Statement showing the exports from Pictou in British and foreign vessels, for the year ended September 30, 1864.

Description.	IN BRITISH VESSELS.		IN FOREIGN VESSELS.	
	Quantity.	Value.	Quantity.	Value.
Coal...	134,856	$335,631	43,567	$108,783
Fish—mackerel	63	240	....	....
Grain—oats	1,000	420	....	....
Grindstones	160	3,200	....	....
Do.	224	2,150	....	....
Hay	75	600	....	....
Hides and skins.............................	350	350	....	....
Iron—scrap	96	1,486	....	....
Wool	1,876	624	....	....
Unenumerated—rags, &c.	117	2,189	....	....
Total...........................	....	346,892	....	108,783

Vessels entered from and cleared for the United States in the year ended September 30, 1864.

ENTERED.

BRITISH.		FOREIGN.	
Number.	Tonnage.	Number.	Tonnage.
228..............................	40,144	123...........................	35,329

CLEARED.

455..............................	77,535	96...........................	27,276

NEWFOUNDLAND.

Information has been received at this department from Mr. C. O. Leach, the consul of the United States at St. John's, Newfoundland, of the passage of an act by the general assembly "which," as the consul remarks, "provides that hereafter all vessels entering this port shall pay a tonnage fee of five cents per ton, in addition to the twenty-four cents now charged for light dues, which, with the pilotage, will make the port charges amount to about thirty-eight to forty cents per ton."

The following sections of the act are printed for general information:

15. It shall be lawful for the governor in council to direct the appropriation to the purposes of the said company of the proceeds of any duty that may be laid upon coal imported into St. John's.

16 The following rates shall be paid by all vessels entering and clearing at the custom-house at the port of St. John's, and the proceeds applied to the support of the company, namely:

1. By all vessels entering or clearing at the custom-house upon or from foreign voyages, a rate of five cents per ton of their register tonnage, to be paid at the time of their first entry or clearance.

2. By all vessels clearing at the custom-house for the sealing voyage, a rate of five cents per ton of their register tonnage, to be paid at the time of such clearance.

3. By all vessels engaged in coasting voyages, or voyages to the Labrador, a rate of five cents per ton of their register tonnage, to be paid at their first entry or clearance at the said custom-house, in each year.

SEC. 17. Such rates shall be paid at the times aforesaid by the masters or owners of such vessels, and shall be collected and recovered in the same manner and by the like means as light dues are now collected and recovered in the said port: *Provided,* That no vessel shall be compelled to pay water rate oftener than once in one year, nor to a greater amount, whatever her tonnage may be, than twenty dollars.

SEC. 18. In consideration of the payment of such rates the vessels paying the same shall be entitled to receive from the hose of the company, at any wharf within reach, from a hydrant at which such vessel may lie, a full supply of water, upon each occasion of such payment, without further charge; and the master shall also be at liberty upon all other occasions to take water from any of the public fountains.

ST. JOHN'S—CONVERSE O. LEACH, *Consul.*

MARCH 9, 1864.

In compliance with instructions contained in your despatch No. 22, I now have the honor to enclose a statement, showing what was the tariff of Newfoundland before and after the reciprocity treaty went into operation, by which it will be seen that the duty on articles not entitled to entry duty free was increased very materially after the effecting of the treaty. Table No. 2, also enclosed, will show more particularly the increase of duty, the articles on which the increase was made, and the date of the alteration.

****

Table No. 3 shows the total value of goods entitled to free entry under the treaty, that have been imported from different countries during the years 1850 to 1863. Table No. 4 shows the quantity and value of each article included in return No. 3. Table No. 5 shows the value of imports and exports to and from each country from 1857 to 1863, and the amount of duty collected on the imports from each country. Table No. 6 shows the quantity and value of each article, being the product of this colony, exported to the United States, for each year from 1851 to 1863; and table No. 7 shows the total imports of bread from all countries for the same years.

****

Tabular statement showing the tariff of Newfoundland before and after the reciprocity treaty went into effect.

Description.	1850.	1854.	1856.	1862.
	£ s. d.	£ s. d.	£ s. d.	£ s. d.
Ale, porter, cider, and perry, viz:				
in bottles, the dozen, containing two galls	10 per ct.	....	0 0 9	0 1 0
in casks, per gallon..................	10 per ct.	....	0 0 3	0 0 4
Apples ....per barrel..	0 1 6	....	0 1 6	....
Anchors ....per £100..	5 0 0	....	5 0 0	5 10 0
Bacon, hams, and smoked beef.....per cwt..	0 5 0	....	0 7 6	0 8 3
Beef, salted and cured.....per barrel..	0 2 0	....	0 2 0	*0 2 0
Bread or biscuit.......... ....per cwt..	0 0 3	....	0 0 3	*0 0 3
Butter ....do....	0 2 0	....	0 3 0	*0 3 0
Barley and oats...................per £100..	5 0 0	....	5 0 0	5 10 0
Cheese ....cwt..	0 5 0	....	0 5 0	0 5 6
Chocolate and cocoa..................do....	0 5 0	....	0 9 4	*0 9 4
Cigars ....per lb..	0 5 0	....	0 10 0	0 11 0
Coffee ....per cwt..	0 5 0	....	0 9 4	*0 9 4
Coals......................per ton..	0 1 0	....	0 1 0	....
Candles of all kinds.............per £100..	7 10 0	....	10 0 0	11 0 0
Clocks, watches, and furniture ....do....	10 0 0	....	10 0 0	11 0 0
Canvas ....do....	5 0 0	....	5 0 0	5 10 0
Cordage and cables...............do....	5 0 0	....	5 0 0	5 10 0
Copper and composition for shipping,				
sheathing, bars, bolts, and nails..per £100.	5 0 0	....	5 0 0	5 10 0
Cork and corkwood ....do....	5 0 0	....	5 0 0	5 10 0
Flour....................... ....per barrel..	0 1 6	....	0 1 6	*0 1 6
Feathers and feather beds............per lb..	5 per ct..	....	0 0 1	*0 0 1
Fruit, dried........................do....	5 per ct..	....	0 0 1	*0 0 1½
other descriptions ....per £100..	5 0 0	....	10 0 0	11 0 0
Fishing tackle ....do....	5 0 0	....	5 0 0	5 10 0
Horses ....each..	0 10 0	....	0 10 0	Exempt.
Iron, viz: bar, bolt, sheathing, and				
sheet........................per £100..	5 0 0	....	5 0 0	5 10 0
Indian corn........................do....	5 0 0	....	5 0 0	5 10 0
Indian and oat meal..............per barrel..	0 0 6	....	0 0 6	*0 0 6
Lumber ....per 1,000 feet..	0 2 6	....	0 2 6	....
Medicines ....per £100..	5 0 0	....	5 0 0	5 10 0
Molasses ....per gallon..	0 0 1½	....	0 0 2½	0 0 2½
Oakum ....per £100..	5 0 0	....	5 0 0	5 10 0
Pork ....per barrel..	0 3 0	....	0 3 0	*0 3 0
Peas..........................per £100..	5 0 0	....	5 0 0	5 10 0
Pitch from turpentine................do....	5 0 0	....	5 0 0	5 10 0
Poultry and fresh meat..............do....	5 0 0	....	5 0 0	5 10 0
Salt ....per ton..	0 0 6	....	0 0 6	0 0 6
Shooks and staves, manufactured .per £100..	5 0 0	....	5 0 0	11 0 0
Shingles ....per M..	0 1 0	....	0 1 0	....
Spirits, viz: brandy, gin, whiskey,				
&c.......per gallon..	0 3 0	....	0 4 0	0 5 0
rum.....................do....	0 0 9	0 1 0	0 1 6	0 2 6
Sugar, viz: loaf and refined.........per cwt..	0 7 6	....	0 12 0	*0 12 0
unrefined..................do	0 5 0	....	0 7 6	0 8 3
bastard ....do	0 5 0	....	0 7 6	0 10 0
Tea.............................per lb..	0 0 3	....	0 0 4	0 0 5
Timber, including balk and scantling .per ton..	0 1 6	....	0 1 0	....
Tobacco, viz: manufactured.........per lb..	0 0 2	....	0 0 3	*0 0 3
stems ....per cwt..	0 2 0	....	0 2 0	*0 2 0
Vinegar ....per gallon..		....	0 0 3	*0 0 3
Wines, viz: in bottles............do......	0 3 0	....	†0 5 0	0 6 0
port, Madeira, and hock,				
not bottled...........do......	0 2 0	....	†0 4 0	0 5 0
sherry ....do......	0 2 0	....	†0 2 6	*0 3 0
claret ....do......	0 2 0	....	†0 2 0	*0 2 6
Goods, wares, and merchandise not otherwise				
enumerated and described, and not other-				
wise exempt ....per £100..	5 0 0	....	10 0 0	11 0 0

* And 10 per cent. thereon.   † And 12½ per cent. thereon.

Tabular statement showing the articles on which the duty has been increased, the amount of increase, and the date when the change was made, by the tariff of Newfoundland.

Articles.	1850. Duty.	1856. Duty.	Increase.	1862. Duty.	Increase since 1850.
Bacon hams, &c..........per cwt..	$1 20	$1 80	60 cts. per cwt.	$1 98	78 cts. per cwt.
Chocolate and cocoa......per cwt..	1 20	2 24	$1 04 per cwt.	*2 24	*$1 04 per cwt.
Cigars..................per M..	1 20	2 40	1 20 per M ..	2 64	1 44 per M.
Coffee................per cwt..	1 20	2 24	1 04 per cwt.	*2 24	*1 04 per cwt.
Candles, all kinds................	7½ per ct.	10 per ct.	2½ per cent.	11 per ct.	3½ per ct.
Molasses ....per gal..	3 cents.	5 cents.	2 cents.	5 cents.	2 cents.
Rum......................per gal..	24 cents.	36 cents.	12 cents....	60 cents.	36 cents.
Refined sugar..........per cwt..	$1 80	$2 88	$1 08	$2 88	*$1 08
Unrefined sugar..........per cwt..	1 20	1 80	60 cents....	1 98	78 cents.
Bastard sugar............per cwt..	1 20	1 80	60 cents....	2 40	$1 20
Tea..................per lb..	6 cents.	8 cents.	2 cents....	10 cents.	4 cents.
Tobacco, manufactured....per lb..	4 cents.	6 cents.	2 cents....	*6 cents.	*2 cents.
Wines, in bottles ....per gal..	72 cents.	$1 20	48 cents....	$1 44	72 cents.
port, Madeira, and not bottled ....per gal..	48 cents.	96 cents.	48 cents....	1 20	72 cents.
sherry, & not bot'd per gal..	48 cents.	60 cents.	12 cents....	72 cents.	24 cents.
Manufactured goods not otherwise mentioned	5 per ct.	10 per ct.	5 per cent.	11 per ct.	6 per cent.

* And 10 per cent. thereon.

Tabular statement showing the total value of goods which are admitted free under the reciprocity treaty imported into Newfoundland during the years 1850 to 1863 inclusive, specifying the value of imports, from each country affected by the treaty.

Years.	Great Britain.	British N. American colonies.	Jersey.	Canada.	Nova Scotia.	New Brunswick.	Prince Edward's Island.	United States.	Countries not affected by the reciprocity treaty.	Total.
	£	£	£	£	£	£	£	£	£	£
1850	14,234	154,567						132,242		301,043
1851	8,687	147,294						162,293		318,304
1852	11,033	160,594						194,151	19,128	314,836
1853	12,510	151,164						146,267	22,740	332,681
1854	11,292	152,976						184,137	16,874	365,279
1855	17,586	138,533						309,705	23,179	499,003
1856	16,963	198,530						334,362	7,514	557,369
1857	24,394		908	59,904	102,422	9,609	11,970	254,810	24,967	489,004
1858	13,131		1,893	52,228	95,792	9,281	13,487	268,547	20,169	474,588
1859	15,188		1,116	49,946	105,279	8,934	15,350	289,392	22,046	507,251
1860	13,362		26	40,762	105,578	2,584	20,327	278,079	11,948	472,666
1861	12,133		241	60,075	91,949	5,038	14,376	296,557	11,621	491,990
1862	15,417		95	48,333	69,148	2,332	11,401	289,153	5,402	441,281
1863	15,254		846	37,785	85,199	3,758	9,058	289,217	7,398	448,445

Tabular statement showing the quantity and value of articles subject to free entry under the reciprocity treaty that have been imported from all countries for the years 1850 to 1863, inclusive.

Articles.	1850.		1851.		1852.		1853.		1854.		1855.		1856.	
	Quantity.	*Value.*	*Quantity.*	*Value.*	*Quantity.*	*Value.*	*Quantity.*	*Value.*	*Quantity.*	*Value.*	*Quantity.*	*Value.*	*Quantity.*	*Value.*
Animals: horses .... No.	79	$718	53	$836	70	$750	41	$605	15	$919	19	$316	28	$454
oxen and cows .. No.	3,041	22,547	2,699	21,960	3,609	29,861	2,735	13,437	2,075	12,975	2,670	15,285	3,056	22,509
sheep and swine . No.	4,011	2,164	2,998	1,770	3,834	2,398	3,911	3,009	2,858	2,735	2,745	2,674	2,911	1,920
Bacon and hams .... cwt.	502	1,300	319	764	290	754	779	2,264	558	1,587	694	2,257	729	2,508
Beef, salted .... bbls.	1,478½	4,452	3,672	6,997	2,483	4,604	2,023	3,931	2,627	5,760	1,601	4,159	4,249	11,152
Butter .... cwt.	10,225	27,690	11,692	32,909	12,228	34,496	16,518	54,137	12,000	43,555	14,860	51,838	17,798	49,395
Cheese .... cwt.	309	595	728	1,336	356	839	374	977	374	1,013	333	1,059	479	1,663
Coal .... tons.	21,707	19,169	19,235	15,668	23,563	16,670	23,892	15,786	21,861	18,603	21,525	22,402	27,099	20,739
Corn, &c.: barley and oats. bush.	23,148	1,773	35,384	2,023	27,466	1,546	26,596	2,053	23,186	2,166	24,668	2,727	50,936	4,615
bran .... bush.	816	61	1,256	84	48	96	5,148	551	4,814	963	2,488	1,455	6,746	1,303
flour .... lbs.	127,841	128,869	145,639	155,345	125,008	125,108	122,099	135,321	103,632	173,170	119,725	263,067	166,274	267,932
Indian meal ... bbls.	15,670	14,083	8,014	6,406	3,739	2,871	13,185	11,295	17,829	19,385	22,542	21,194	24,656	23,993
Indian corn ... bush.	3,400	1,255	16,648	2,274	445	179	884	144	4,950	962	6,522	1,912	5,737	955
oatmeal .... lbs.	1,239	1,181	1,212	1,208	1,238½	1,170	2,683	2,459	2,121	2,928	1,695	2,684	3,695	3,759
peas .... 1 lbs.	1,075	598	2,136	304	2,503	1,237	1,492	1,127	2,365	2,009	1,822	2,598	3,650	3,130
wheat .... bush														
Fish: dry cod .... qtls.														
haddock .... qtls.														
herring .... boxes.					1,446	85	394	27	210	21	180	88	1,076	96
mackerel										24		15		7
oysters .... bush.					557	96	579	89	300	99	880	141	489	183
salmon						75		12		36				47
Fruit: apples and plums bbls.	1,705	813	1,788	726	5,314	2,291	1,279	658	1,849	979	2,589	1,233	3,775	1,631
Lard .... cwt.					27	83	84½	188	36	130	83	261	113	363
Meat and poultry		2,304		2,214		1,566		2,061		1,535		2,283		5,377
Pitch and tar .... bbls.	4,625	2,178	3,797	1,565	3,606½	1,816	4,739	2,536	3,597	2,622	4,047	2,614	5,083	3,127
Pork .... bbls.	24,345½	53,871	18,067	43,917	17,800	64,942	21,638	63,450	19,744½	53,056	21,865	70,212	27,164	95,949
Potatoes and vegetables .. bush.	22,257	2,463	29,151	3,053	83,490	6,402	69,645	5,437	51,197	5,460	50,954	7,728	87,600	11,482
Rice .... cwt.	1,080	740	1,100	771	887	680	1,797	1,478	895	937	1,775	2,030	1,851	1,719
Stone		2,083		525		600		1,190		724		1,943		495
Tobacco: leaf .... cwt.	10	24			100	284	40	112					8	40
stems .... cwt.	74	25	121	46	28	15	59	57	38	17	66	56	82	39
Wood: billets .... M.														
board and lapk .... M.	3,769	6,494	7,152	10,814	4,840½	9,723	2,035	3,707	2,118	6,117	2,777	5,471	3,988	9,889
laths .... M.	120	185	150	240	430	82					80	19	132	49
masts and spars .... No.	463	206	1,554	617	1,750	450	252	154	645	456	410	642	1,390	1,440
palings .... M.														
shingles .... M.	4,632	1,907	5,150	1,886	4,669	1,504	3,999	1,677	4,028	1,750	3,066	2,488	5,663	2,332
staves .... M.					18	34	566½	1,689	268	1,493	816	4,716	1,804	6,167
heading .... M.														
timber & scantling . tons.	1,580	1,372	4,291	2,747	1,280½	1,599	868	1,049	1,335	1,792	1,562	2,137	811	910
Total		301,043		318,304		314,836		339,681		365,979		499,003		557,369

Tabular statement showing the quantity and value of articles subject to free entry under the reciprocity treaty that have been imported from all countries for the years 1850 to 1863, inclusive—Continued.

Articles.		1857. Quantity.	1857. Value.	1858. Quantity.	1858. Value.	1859. Quantity.	1859. Value.	1860. Quantity.	1860. Value.	1861. Quantity.	1861. Value.	1862. Quantity.	1862. Value.	1863. Quantity.	1863. Value.
Animals: horses	No.	114	$1,725	87	$1,740	111	$2,290	94	$2,940	119	$2,380	75	$1,500	91	$1,890
oxen and cows	No.	3,402	17,010	3,692	18,110	3,308	18,540	3,794	18,970	9,873	14,365	1,997	9,985	3,275	16,375
sheep and swine	No.	3,861	1,990	4,373	2,285	4,216	2,140	4,561	2,350	5,470	2,789	1,469	9,300	4,359	2,184
Bacon and hams	cwt.	619	2,088	1,000½	2,955	934	2,956	849	2,592	908	2,558	1,190	3,317	4,872	6,946
Beef, salted	bbl.	2,875	6,050	2,771	5,325	2,994	4,564	3,713	5,662	2,573	3,927	2,321	3,556	2,936	3,359
Butter	cwt.	90,460	77,711	90,677	60,987	91,303	63,164	19,895	58,615	30,879½	62,064	15,964½	44,563	19,400	58,358
Cheese	cwt.	40,743	2,935	901	2,237	854	2,928	749	2,006	864½	2,108	465	1,193	757	1,848
Coal	tons	34,319	83,461	35,937	17,689	37,631	18,816	41,594	30,789	43,028	21,514	37,494	18,747	38,080	19,010
Corn, &c.: barley and oats	bush.	664	2,665	54,609	4,108	60,481	4,608	77,851	5,881	57,405	4,423	48,407	3,794	43,329	3,370
bran	bush.		100			3,027	927	668	65		65	2,700	503	250	19
flour	bbl.	152,892	183,397	165,683	190,591	180,645	907,735	171,157	196,830	191,110	219,777	226,334	226,334	947,791	923,011
Indian meal	bbl.	8,762	5,915	8,919	2,006	2,518	2,375	1,144	2,798	2,596	4,697	10,128	6,846	7,236	4,585
Indian corn	bush.	4,969	867	8,257	1,049	2,278	348	900	135	2,170	697	14,037	6,465	4,130	689
oatmeal	bbl.	1,944	1,190	1,447	1,528	1,820	2,447	1,271	1,865	2,798	3,681	2,503	2,990	4,056	1,066
peas	bbl.	2,986	2,374	2,193	1,511	3,414	3,149	2,092	1,963	1,834	1,679	2,839	1,658	2,908	1,986
wheat	bush.	940	30									3,311	4,000		
Fish: dry cod	qtls											376	1,890		
haddock	qtls	1,811	181	9,365	836	9,794	978	9,938	984	5,769	577	383	135	14,692	11,116
herring	boxes		9		4								38		
mackerel		2,668	477	389	110	1,077	169	785	118	773	115	566	90	1,317	139
oysters	bush.													983	63
salmon															
Fruit: apples and plums	bbl.	9,857½	1,440	2,354	9,161	3,298	1,664	6,980	2,784	3,321	1,296	4,131	894	5,931	1,188
Lard	cwt.	91	397	913	846	9,169½	1,649	6,146	2,584	159	608	306	593	299	814
Meat and poultry			4,903		6,636		9,113		9,074		7,494		6,647		5,981
Pitch and tar	bbl.		3,964	4,105	2,019	5,389	4,105	4,756	3,610	4,510	7,610		5,551	4,109	6,101
Pork	bbl.	6,150	100,596	39,594	102,188	33,186	100,541	30,403	91,818	33,127	99,690	34,006	68,774	39,628	57,592
Potatoes and vegetables	bush.	27,866	6,021	66,985	4,953	116,904	6,994	187,519	1,563	97,501	5,914	111,691	6,641	101,349	5,660
Rice	cwt.	1,719	1,194	2,174	1,491	9,114½	1,305	1,391	978	1,713	1,310	1,937	1,364	1,807	1,525
Stone		102	309	414	384	394½	402	46	417		358	98	988	981	780
Tobacco: leaf	cwt.	35	49	107	145	116	119	36	176	72	176	98	364	103	1,009
stems				87	150		163		51	51	51	198	179		144
Wood: billets	M.	7,680	16,360	9,580	19,165	10,500	21,092	8,419	16,839	7,104	14,211	4,890	9,780	4,107	8,214
board and plank	M.	724	147	311	49	619	108	1,256	51	949	50	515	103	375	78
laths	M.	1,397	1,397	1,546	1,546	1,408	1,408	1,734	1,754	1,879	1,679	353	192	568	568
masts and spars	No.							51	153	18	56	64	192	13	39
palings	M.							731	2,911	11,796	3,539	6,942	1,873	6,702	2,011
shingles	M.	14,274	4,983	12,920	3,679	8,296	9,691	631	4,416	391	737	176	1,522	118	825
staves	M.	2,636	18,459	9,212	14,509	9,593	18,166	67	133						
heading	M.					392	786								
timber & scantling	tons	2,978	2,278	2,297	2,297	4,169	4,169	2,376	2,376	2,038	2,038	1,065	1,085	2,163	2,163
Total			498,004		474,588		507,251		472,666		491,990		441,281		448,845

Tabular statement showing the value (in sterling) of imports from and exports to each country, and amount of duty collected on the imports from the countries specified below, for the years 1857 to 1863, inclusive.

Countries.	1857. Value of imports.	Value of exports.	Duty collected on imports.	1858. Value of imports.	Value of exports.	Duty collected on imports.	1859. Value of imports.	Value of exports.	Duty collected on imports.	1860. Value of imports.	Value of exports.	Duty collected on imports.
Canada	63,929	94,385	980 5 2	54,524	91,609	394 8 6	53,308	9,299	549 5 7	42,453	10,380	108 11 3
Nova Scotia	131,801	70,048	4,961 10 4	196,417	56,970	4,943 7 7	132,311	43,919	4,292 17 11	140,327	39,448	7,600 15 4
New Brunswick	8,672	376	31 8 0	9,414	670	15 18 0	9,553	3,697	57 7 1	2,708	784	13 9 6
Prince Edward's Island	12,057	921	13 10 0	13,848	758	40 14 0	15,589	1,165	17 5 8	90,746	1,614	44 11 0
United States	340,527	87,328	17,013 11 3	323,896	113,107	19,081 1 2	381,748	106,989	14,145 11 2	364,733	81,800	15,842 12 7
Total	556,902	183,058	21,619 4 9	528,509	196,033	17,475 8 11	573,503	164,049	18,972 7 5	570,841	133,960	23,729 19 8
United Kingdom	577,877	551,185		450,856	621,779		530,696	375,440		489,967	353,025	
Guernsey and Jersey	10,066	4,108		13,818	8,900		13,946	11,673		15,781	15,781	
Gibraltar		4,983						1,082				
Malta		5,330			6,444			3,007			3,214	
Mauritius		9,603									6,067	
Hanseatic Towns	118,335	103,905		74,715	7,365		89,736	190,633		74,598	197,595	
Spain	8,916	149,479		16,504	83,306		10,387	85,555		11,144	155,553	
Portugal	15,433	88,143		8,815	103,186		7,545	49,407		11,181	34,529	
Italian States	2,719		78,615 3 0	123	37,981	78,615 3 0			96,455 17 7	508		88,916 7 7
Denmark	5,051											
Naples					3,667		185				4,050	
Sicily											1,388	
Ionian Islands					1,667							
Sweden	199	3,640										
France	47,177	105,190		33,961	61,394		2,481	3,157		37,107	86,367	
British West Indies	69,496	39,001		46,336	55,401		34,925	90,434		44,406	51,817	
Other West Indies					639		59,069	58,241				
Madeira					186						172	
St. Pierre	1,374			1,528			1,347			1,167		
Brazil	467	322,338		287	308,741		333	340,875		44	229,098	
Australia					1,957							
Total	1,413,439	1,651,171	122,361 7 1	1,172,862	1,318,836	96,090 11 11	1,264,136	1,357,113	115,428 5 0	1,254,128	1,271,712	106,646 7 3

H. Ex. Doc. 60——5

Tabular statement showing the value (in sterling) of imports from and exports to each country, &c.—Continued.

Countries.	1861 Value of imports.	1861 Value of exports.	1861 Duty collected on imports.	1862 Value of imports.	1862 Value of exports.	1862 Duty collected on imports.	1863 Value of imports.	1863 Value of exports.	1863 Duty collected on imports.	Total Value of imports.	Total Value of exports.	Total Duty collected on imports.
	£	£	£ s. d.	£	£	£ s. d.	£	£	£ s. d.	£	£	£ s. d.
Canada	61,971	16,016	157 0 6	50,548	19,001	155 0 11	42,923	8,449	729 8 11	368,330	109,079	2,446 0 10
Nova Scotia	123,018	41,798	5,602 7 3	90,306	37,019	6,359 10 3	107,706	34,980	6,809 8 6	853,086	307,185	40,033 16 10
New Brunswick	5,192	1,065	15 15 10	2,351		1 8 4	3,860	2,872	14 10 4	42,941	8,394	150 9 5
Prince Edward's Island	14,887	1,390	40 0 10	11,729	969	32 6 11	9,315	1,716	31 0 11	98,101	8,473	219 9 4
United States	359,080	33,472	10,007 12 11	345,797	47,729	9,920 8 9	344,044	60,043	10,031 12 3	3,439,515	530,448	88,332 10 1
Total	564,058	93,741	15,822 16 8	501,012	104,656	15,971 15 2	507,148	108,060	17,609 6 11	3,801,973	963,579	131,300 19 6
United Kingdom	401,907	378,019		353,813	397,019		442,080	399,712		3,945,976	2,806,199	
Guernsey and Jersey	9,167	1,290		10,459	11,693		8,878	5,653		79,585	58,328	
Gibraltar		1,372						2,525			9,292	
Malta	94			65	2,633		159			159	17,881	
Mauritius											12,277	
Hanseatic Towns	69,368	2,797		46,339	3,936		52,353	302,154		565,450	14,118	
Spain	11,485	171,602		7,672	206,394		9,109	133,664		75,138	1,335,493	
Portugal	10,499	116,411		9,400	204,806		9,979	30,051		69,785	950,564	
Italian States	99	34,283		77	41,501		207			5,743	308,545	575,051 17 8
Denmark			66,325 18 3			68,878 13 7			80,117 15 4	5,051		
Naples	486	1,560		128	6,722		80			925,450	3,697	
Sicily					1,675					841	12,332	
Ionian Islands											7,570	
Sweden												
France	29,886	76,223		94,954	67,526		13,988	66,705		199	3,157	
British West Indies	53,957	37,298		49,727	40,845		33,812	15,658		9,481	553,735	
Other West Indies										219,308	297,661	
Madeira										356,798	839	
St. Pierre	2,226	61		3,423			2,686	300			719	
Brazil	69	175,865			152,775			168,941		14,051	1,718,653	
Australia										1,213	1,957	
	1,152,857	1,092,551	82,148 14 11	1,007,082	1,171,723	84,850 8 9	1,077,278	1,223,353	97,727 2 3	8,401,769	9,096,439	706,259 17 2

Imports from the United States, amounting to £2,439,515 sterling, for seven years, pay £88,332 10s. 1d. duty, or about 3¼ per cent.
Imports from British North American colonies, amounting to £1,362,458 sterling, for seven years, pay £42,848 9s. 5d. duty, or about 3 1-5 per cent.
Imports from other countries, amounting to £4,599,796 sterling, for seven years, pay £575,051 17s. 8d. duty, or about 12½ per cent.

Tabular statement showing the quantity and value of Newfoundland produce exported to the United States for the years 1851 to 1863, inclusive.

Years.	Codfish.		Salmon.		Herring.		Cod oil.		Refined cod oil.		Seal oil.		Seal skins and hides.		Fish and oils not enumerated.	Total.
	Quintals.	Value.	Tierces.	Value.	Barrels.	Value.	Tuns.	Value.	Tuns.	Value.	Tuns.	Value.	Number.	Value.	Value.	Value.
1851	14,795	£4,684	2,781	£7,570	1,706	£967	14	£647	17½	£1,894	1	£30	753	£113	£253	£16,634
1852	43,630	31,988	2,950	7,068	4,475	3,195	540	16,438	40	3,596	1,728½	57,469	16,626	2,415	97	100,188
1853	91,467	12,707	1,581	5,638	4,563	3,818	396½	10,646	64	1,941	64	525	6,003	900	198	37,654
1854	83,570	15,644	666	5,656	2,545	1,089	448	1,467	14½	2,987	5	900	900	25		92,444
1855	65,779	40,731	2,910	9,948	8,904	6,943	181	7,953	59	2,334	154	540			1,215	68,997
1856	64,583	40,374	1,131	5,081	6,639	4,755	759	31,137	98	1,478	372½	14,676	5,370	806	1,417	100,570
1857	38,597	94,947	2,188	11,450	18,478	11,546	390	12,883	91	2,348	433	15,016	9,286	1,854	1,436	81,499
1858	44,498	31,508	1,556	7,077	31,947	13,279	1,194	39,298	33½	3,679	505½	16,685			983	102,978
1859	90,965	29,949	2,213	10,512	30,133	15,062	1,309½	34,041	55½	3,506	254½	7,639	97	17	1,858	108,987
1860	94,621	18,466	1,898	9,016	27,460	13,730	1,014½	36,377	36	18	199	5,763			1,769	77,687
1861	9,557	6,919	822	4,110	16,944	8,122	295½	8,909	30	2,100	68½	9,912	1,050	157	658	30,934
1862	12,708	8,258	1,778	7,119	11,601	5,801	950½	6,915	95	2,548	4	183	2,690	1,300	982	30,605
1863	13,947	14,947	2,668	8,750	27,197	19,031	181½	8,699							2,329	56,997
		271,061		94,168		106,510		197,625		26,301		121,356		7,567		838,799

Statement showing the total imports of bread from all countries into Newfoundland for the years 1851 to 1863, inclusive, the average quantity, and amount of duty received thereon.

Years.	HAMBURG. Quantity. (Cwt.)	HAMBURG. Duty. (£)	GREAT BRITAIN. Quantity. (Cwt.)	GREAT BRITAIN. Duty. (£)	UNITED STATES. Quantity. (Cwt.)	UNITED STATES. Duty. (£)	BRITISH N. AMERICAN COLONIES. Quantity. (Cwt.)	BRITISH N. AMERICAN COLONIES. Duty. (£)	CHANNEL ISLAND. Quantity. (Cwt.)	CHANNEL ISLAND. Duty. (£)	ST. PIERRE. Quantity. (Cwt.)	ST. PIERRE. Duty. (£)	Total. (Cwt.)
1851	58,260	728	14,227	178	5,840	73	4,869	61	1,735	29			84,931
1852	55,821	698	7,811	96	4,552	57	6,655	83	2,694	34			77,537
1853	63,974	1,060	11,965	150	9,354	117	13,273	166	2,813	35			121,379
1854	52,209	653	10,846	136	11,664	150	9,387	117	1,000	13			85,406
1855	57,339	1,093	14,978	187	10,187	102	3,663	46	866	10			117,025
1856	63,981	799	9,606	3	7,913	98	6,023	Free..	530	6			88,063
1857	69,555	1,119	4,165	4	6,749	84	2,049	Free..	1,040	13	16	4 0	104,174
1858	58,181	727	3,648	46	3,077	38	1,793	22	1,874	23	32	8 0	68,605
1859	70,942	887	6,613	83	718	9	1,691	21	1,459	18	10	2 6	81,403
1860	69,464	763	8,369	117	1,479	19	1,104	14	593	6			70,962
1861	51,489	644	4,339	54	1,900	94	1,100	14	1,085	13	50	12 6	59,903
1862	38,098	517	4,317	72	3,773	50	2,609	32	1,905	14	121	1 17 0	51,053
1863	41,023	594	3,193	46	1,736	25	4,011	50	1,098	14			51,661
Total	810,366	10,272	105,090	1,174	69,242	846	58,827	626	17,694	221	229	3 4 0	
Average	62,374	790	8,064	90	5,326	65	4,525	48	1,371	17	18	0 5 0	

MARCH 22, 1864.

I have the honor to enclose herewith a copy of "An act for the regulation of the currency" of this colony passed at the last session of the legislative assembly, which substitutes dollars and cents for the pounds, shillings and pence now in use.

This act having lately received the sanction of the Queen, will go into effect on the 1st day of July next.

AN ACT for the regulation of the currency.—Passed March 25, 1863.

Be it enacted by the governor, legistive council, and assembly, in legislative session convened, as follows:

I. The denomination of money in the currency of this colony shall be dollars and cents, in which currency the cent shall be the one-hundredth part of a dollar; and all public accounts shall be kept, all public moneys paid and received, all verdicts received and judgments entered, and other legal proceedings taken, in such currency.

II. The British sovereign of lawful weight shall be held to be equal to and shall be a legal tender and pass current for four dollars and eighty cents currency; and all parts of the sovereign shall pass current and be a legal tender in currency after the like rate, according to the proportion they respectively bear to the sovereign.

III. The gold eagle of the United States, coined after the first July, eighteen hundred and thirty-four, and while the standard of fineness for gold coins then fixed by the laws of the United States remains unchanged, and weighing ten pennyweights eighteen grains, troy weight, shall pass current and be a legal tender for nine dollars and eighty-five cents currency; and all multiples and parts of such eagle of like date and proportionate weight shall pass current and be a legal tender in currency after the like rate, according to the proportion they respectively bear to the eagle.

IV. The silver coins of the United Kingdom, while lawfully current therein, shall pass current and be a legal tender for sums in currency after the rate fixed as aforesaid for the gold coins of the United Kingdom, according to the proportion such silver coins bear to such gold coins: Provided, that no tender in silver coin to a greater amount than ten dollars shall be valid.

V. The foreign gold coin called the doubloon, containing three hundred and sixty-two grains of pure gold, shall pass and be a legal tender in currency for fifteen dollars and thirty-five cents.

VI. The American, Peruvian, Mexican, Columbian, and old Spanish dollars, being of the full weight of four hundred and sixteen grains, and containing not less than three hundred and seventy-three grains of pure silver, shall pass current and shall be a legal tender at the rate of one hundred cents each; and the several divisions of such coins shall pass current and be a legal tender in currency after the like rate, according to the proportion such divisions shall respectively bear to the coins of which they are parts: Provided, that no tender of such coins to a greater amount than ten dollars shall be valid.

VII. It shall be lawful for the governor in council to obtain and import such quantity of copper or bronze cents and half cents as may be necessary for the purpose of this act, which cents and half cents shall be a legal tender for any amount not exceeding twenty-five cents; and when and after this act shall have come into operation, the copper coinage then in circulation shall be called in, and one half of its circulating value paid to the holder; and no other copper or bronze coins, other than British sterling, pence, and halfpence, of bronze, shall pass current in this colony: Provided, that no person be entitled to be paid for any such copper coins then in circulation until he shall have made and signed, before a stipendiary magistrate, an affidavit setting forth that he had not been in any way concerned in the importation of such coin, or of any part thereof, but was in the possession of the same in the ordinary course of his trade or business on the day on which this act shall have come into operation.

VIII. Such gold and silver coins, representing dollars, or multiples or divisions of the dollar currency, as her Majesty shall see fit to direct to be struck for that purpose, shall, by such names, and at such rates, and for such amounts, as her Majesty, by her proclamation, shall assign, pass current and be a legal tender in this colony; the standard of fineness of such coins being the same as that now adopted for coins of the United Kingdom, and their intrinsic value bearing the same proportion to their current value as British coins, respectively, bear to their current value under this act.

IX. Her Majesty may at any time declare, by proclamation, that any other gold or silver coins of any foreign state shall, when of the weights assigned therein, pass current and be a legal tender at rates in currency to be assigned to them respectively in such proclamation, such rates being proportionate to the quantity of pure gold and silver contained in such coins, as compared with the rates of British coins current under this act.

X. Gold coins current under this act shall be a legal tender by tale so long as they shall not want more than two grains of the weight assigned to them by this act, or by her Majesty's proclamation : Provided, that in any one payment above fifty pounds, the person paying may pay, or the person receiving may insist onr eceiving the said British gold coins by weight, at the rate of eighteen dollars and sixty-nine and a half cents per ounce troy, and the said gold coins of the United States, by weight, at the rate of eighteen dollars aud thirty-two nine-sixteenths of a cent per ounce troy.

XI. All existing liabilities, whether under act of the legislature, judgment, rule or order of a court of judicature, or private contract, shall be discharged, as follows : The pound of present currency, by payment of four dollars ; the pound of local sterling, (equal to twenty-three shillings and twelve-thirteenths of a penny of present currency,) by payment of four dollars and sixty-one cents ; and the pound British sterling, (equal to twenty-four shillings of present currency,) by payment of four dollars and eighty cents ; and nothing in this act shall affect the rights of parties claiming local sterling or British sterling under any act of the legislature, or private contract, now subsisting.

XII. In all future contracts the term pound shall mean and be equivalent to four dollars currency ; and the term pound sterling shall mean and be equivalent to four dollars and eighty cents currency.

XIII. Any person who shall falsely make or counterfeit any coin resembling, or apparently intended to resemble or pass for, any gold or silver coin current under or by virtue of this act or any proclamation thereunder, or who shall import into this colony any such false or counterfeit coin, shall be guilty of felony, and, being convicted thereof. shall be liable, at the discretion of the court, to transportation beyond seas for life, or for any term not less than seven years, or to be imprisoned, with hard labor, for any term not exceeding four years ; and every such offence shall be deemed to be complete, although the coin so made or counterfeited shall not be in a fit state to be uttered, or the counterfeiting thereof shall not be finished or perfected.

XIV. Any person who shall tender, utter, or put off any such false or counterfeit coin, knowing the same to be false or counterfeit, shall be guilty of a misdemeanor, and, being convicted thereof, shall be imprisoned, with hard labor, for any term not exceeding one year.

XV. This act shall not be in force until sanctioned by her Majesty, nor until a day thereafter to be fixed by proclamation of his excellency the governor, published in the Royal Gazette.

St. John, N. B.—James Q. Howard, *Consul.*

October 10, 1864.

I have the honor herewith to transmit a brief annual report of the trade of this consular district, in obedience to instructions contained in section 648 of the Consular Manual.

There have been no modifications in the custom-house or sanitary regulations of this port since my last annual report, nor has there been any change in the tariff or duties, or in the customary port charges.

Trade seems to have followed its usual channels, except that there has been, since January 1, 1864, a diminution in the quantity of lumber and fish shipped to the American market.

This is owing to the high rate of exchange between St. John and New York during the past year. This rate reached 60 per cent. in August last, which of course was too high a rate of discount to enable St. John merchants to sell in the New York or Boston markets with profit. The bank rate of exchange is now 49 per cent., and the revival of business with the United States is in proportion to the fall in gold and exchange. * * * *

An impression seems to exist in the minds of many provincial people that our prosperity is their misfortune, and our misfortune their gain. They seem to think that there is a necessary antagonism or hostility between the interests of the provinces and the States.

They forget the simplest lesson of history that prosperity to us is prosperity to them, and that by the geographical position and conformation of the continent the interests of the different provinces and states of North America are identical.

By the following tables, which exhibit the value of imports and exports for each year since 1844, it will be seen that 1863 has been one of the most prosperous years in the way of trade and commerce that this province has yet enjoyed:

Table showing the value in dollars of the imports and exports of the province of New Brunswick from and to all countries during the last twenty years.

Year.	Imports.	Exports.	Year.	Imports.	Exports.
1844....	$3,840,475 00	$2,874,417 00	1854...	$9,930,110 00	$5,300,232 00
1845....	5,309,790 00	3,780,595 00	1855...	5,725,320 00	3,966,629 00
1846....	4,972,877 00	4,256,462 00	1856...	7,301,654 00	5,152,085 00
1847....	5,401,574 00	3,342,715 00	1857...	6,801,926 00	4,405,320 00
1848....	3,021,158 00	3,068,155 00	1858...	5,581,200 00	3,891,739 00
1849....	3,330,849 00	2,887,017 00	1859...	6,796,963 00	6,182,910 00
1850....	3,914,549 00	2,632,072 00	1860...	6,944,452 00	4,398,585 00
1851....	4,705,440 00	3,705,715 00	1861...	5,943,038 00	4,546,037 00
1852....	5,330,885 00	3,822,408 00	1862...	6,199,698 00	3,856,536 00
1853....	8,237,318 00	5,147,957 00	1863...	7,658,462 00	4,940,781 00

Table showing the value in dollars of the imports and exports of the province of New Brunswick from and to the United States during the last twenty years.

Year.	Imports.	Exports.	Year.	Imports.	Exports.
1844....	$995,923 00	$81,163 00	1854...	$3,413,923 00	$470,064 00
1845....	1,499,102 00	134,112 00	1855...	3,757,257 00	591,009 00
1846....	1,430,429 00	76,132 00	1856...	3,429,672 00	832,728 00
1847....	1,632,468 00	214,291 00	1857...	3,016,848 00	761,745 00
1848....	1,172,525 00	213,854 00	1858...	2,708,376 00	785,769 00
1849....	1,269,897 00	247,593 00	1859...	3,240,456 00	1,132,867 00
1850....	1,258,310 00	371,520 00	1860...	3,303,441 00	1,192,214 00
1851....	1,588,008 00	398,534 00	1861...	3,014,736 00	843,139 00
1852....	1,887,408 00	402,301 00	1862...	2,960,707 00	889,416 00
1853....	2,755,536 00	584,918 00	1863...	3,550,382 00	1,224,913 00

Statement showing the description and value of the principal importations of New Brunswick during the year 1863.

Haberdashery, cottons, woollens, velvets, silk, &c............	$1,617,714 00
Wheat flour....................................	1,224,311 00
Hardware and all manufactures of iron....................	742,768 00
Tea...	278,784 00
Canvas and cordage................................	249,149 00
Meats of all kinds................................	241,408 00
Spirits, wines, and cordials..........................	209,443 00
Tobacco, snuff, and cigars..........................	208,914 00
Molasses and treacle..............................	189,349 00
Sugar of all kinds................................	188,615 00
Sails and rigging................................	182,642 00
Copper and patent metal...........................	144,251 00
Coals..	110,390 00

The principal exports in 1863 may be classed as follows :

Produce of the forests, including furs...................	$3,657,096 00
Produce of the fisheries..............................	265,724 00

A considerable amount of capital has been invested by citizens of the United States in mills, situated at St. John, for the manufacture of lumber, and a much larger amount is being invested in coal and copper mines, several of which are now profitably worked. The mineral resources of the province, which I believe are great, are rapidly being developed by intelligent and energetic Americans.

TRINIDAD—EDWARD H. FITH, *Vice-Consul.*

MARCH 1, 1864.

I have the honor to transmit the annual report of the trade and commerce of Trinidad for the year ended December 31, 1863.

During the early part of the year there was great depression among the planters and merchants, caused by the low rates ruling for sugar with European markets; but latterly there has been a revival in trade in consequence of a rise in the price of sugar, which, it is expected, will be maintained during the ensuing season.

The arrivals from the States during the year have been 41 American vessels, whereas the previous year there were 66, which shows a decrease of 25 vessels, doubtless caused by so many having changed their flag.

The imports have not decreased; on the contrary, the island has been abundantly supplied with breadstuffs and provisions, which have been sold at ruinous rates to the shippers.

The exports for the year reach the sum of $216,079 44.

*   *   *   *   *   *   *   *

I am led to believe, from all accounts, that the sugar and cocoa crop will be a fair one. Some of our planters have turned their attention to the cultivation of cotton.   *   *   *   *   *   *   *

N. L. HUMPHREY, *Consul.*

OCTOBER 1, 1864.

The total value of imports into this island for the year ended June 30, 1864, may be stated in round numbers at three million three hundred and thirty thousand dollars, of which goods to the value of about $880,000 came from the United States; $360,000 from France; $140,000 from Venezuela. A very small portion comes from Spain and other countries, and the large balance from Great Britain and its dependencies. I subjoin a list of goods from the United States, with their values in round numbers:

7,000 barrels bread	$29,000
230,000 pounds candles	36,000
14,000 bushels corn	13,500
45,000 pounds fish	2,500
255,000 pounds lard	57,000
1,300,000 pounds salt meats	128,500
15,000 pounds butter	3,000
100,000 pounds cheese	14,000
7,500 barrels meal	28,500
50,000 barrels flour	275,000
60,000 feet lumber	1,500
1,700 pounds refined sugar	3,000
70,000 pounds tobacco	47,000
Matches	4,500
Oil-meal and oil-cake	43,500
Peas	9,000
Shooks and staves	46,500
Wines	5,500
Malt liquor	6,000
Medicines	4,000
Coal and lard oils	11,500
Potatoes	1,000
Vinegar	1,000
Miscellaneous	9,000
	780,000

Of the above merchandise a little more than one-third was imported in vessels sailing under the United States flag, although another third, at least, doubtless came in American bottoms, under foreign flags.

The total value of imports may be set down at about the same as the previous year. The rates of freights to and from the United States during the year may be set down at from $6 to $8 per ton. The exports for the year are as follows:

39,656 hogsheads, 673 tierces, 5,643 barrels sugar, valued at	$3,852,000
13,066 puncheons molasses	312,000
652 puncheons rum	22,000
5,045,180 pounds cocoa	505,000
86,000 pounds cotton	18,000
8,000 pounds coffee	1,500
Total amount	4,710,500

The exports to the United States, consisting principally of sugar, molasses, and cocoa, together with a few cargoes of old metals and a small quantity of hides from Venezuela, amount to about $280,000, of which only about $75,000 were shipped in American vessels.

The sugar crop of the present year exceeds that of last by over 2,000 hogsheads in quantity, and owing to the larger advance, full fifty per centum, in prices, it exceeds it in value by some $1,400,000. The rate of exchange on London is quoted pretty regularly at 90 days' sight; purchasing, $475 per £100; selling, $482 per £100. I have seen no quotations since my arrival here of exchange on the United States.

The prospect for the coming crop is flattering.

A company has been formed with an ample capital for the manufacture of petroleum from the celebrated asphaltum lake in the southeast part of the island, which, if successful, will materially increase its trade and prosperity.

TURK'S ISLAND—JOHN E. NEWPORT, *Consul.*

MAY 9, 1864.

As the best evidence that direct steam communication between the United States and these islands is now actually established, I beg leave to inform you that hereafter a steamer will leave New York regularly every month for Jamaica, calling here both on her way to and from the latter place.

After the present month, I understand that the time of departure from New York will be at a later date than the 20th.

*　　*　　*　　*　　*　　*　　*　　*　　*

It is authoritatively stated that the Saladin and other small vessels at present on the line will be withdrawn, and larger and swifter ones substituted.

*　　*　　*　　*　　*　　*　　*　　*　　*

Return of the number of vessels passed the light-house at Grand Turk between sunrise and sunset from 1st January to 1st July, 1864.

Steamers	12
Ships	1
Barks	34
Brigs	141
Schooners	97
Total	285

JOHN ADAMS, *Light-house Keeper.*

JULY 26, 1864.

Herewith please find a "schedule of the public revenue of the Turk's and Caicos islands for the quarter ended June 30, 1864, in comparison with the corresponding quarter in 1863."

I have reduced the general results stated in said schedule from British currency into dollars and cents, and they are as follows:

The imports for the quarter ended June 30, 1863, amounted to $3,813 62; for the corresponding quarter in 1864 they were $5,604 98, showing an increase of $1,791 36.

The exports for the June quarter in 1863 were $920 80; for the same period in the present year $1,394 08, being a gain of $473 28. From other sources of revenue there appears to be a falling off of $1,074 06; for during the quarter aforesaid in 1863, $3,067 72 derived therefrom, whereas only $1,993 66 was obtained in the corresponding quarter of 1864.

The number of bushels of salt exported during the above period in 1863 was 174,160, and only 139,408 bushels were exported during the June quarter of this year, being a decrease of 34,752 bushels.

On the whole, the public revenue of this colony for the quarter ended June 30, 1864, in comparison with the corresponding quarter of 1863, is greater by the sum of $1,190 58. The expenditure is $1,120 94 more.

TURK'S AND CAICOS ISLANDS.

Schedule of the public revenue for the quarter ended 30th June, 1864, in comparison with the corresponding quarter in 1863.

IMPORTS.

	1864.			1863.		
	£	s.	d.	£	s.	d.
Alcohol	4	16	0	0	0	0
Ale, porter, cider, &c.	18	6	10	2	4	0
Beans and peas	0	19	0	1	2	9
Baywater	0	12	0	0	0	0
Bread	11	4	3	7	19	3
Butter	15	10	11	10	4	3
Candles	6	5	9	7	12	9
Cattle	0	0	0	1	5	0
Cheese	8	19	4	9	12	5
Chocolate	2	0	6	0	6	0
Cigars	1	4	11	0	0	0

	1864.			1864.		
	£	s.	d.	£	s.	d.
Coffee	3	5	2	28	17	7
Cordage	2	12	1	0	4	4
Cordials	10	0	0	0	13	9
Corn	7	19	0	7	10	5
Fish, dried and pickled	7	18	0	47	10	0
Flour, wheat	140	16	4	70	1	3
Flour, meal and rye	4	5	6	5	2	9
Lard	10	19	6	8	2	5
Lumber and shingles	13	16	6	38	2	11
Meat, salted or cured	31	11	0	32	4	7
Molasses, sirup, and honey	22	15	0	21	9	2
Oils	7	15	6	5	2	4
Paint	0	5	0	0	0	0
Pitch	0	0	6	0	2	0
Raisins, currants, figs, &c	2	17	5	1	3	3
Rice	11	15	9	3	2	8
Rum, brandy, gin, &c	280	19	0	262	4	0
Sheep and goats	1	1	0	1	5	0
Shrub	4	19	0	0	0	0
Soap	12	19	0	5	5	5
Spirits of turpentine	0	0	6	0	0	0
Sugar	77	7	4	17	15	4
Tea	2	17	0	8	1	6
Tobacco	7	0	10	5	18	3
Wine	25	5	4	4	4	7
Ad valorem duties	406	13	4	180	0	2
	1,167	14	1	794	10	1

EXPORTS.

	£	s.	d.	£	s.	d.
Salt.—1864, 139,408 bushels; 1863, 174,160 bushels	290	8	8	191	16	8

RECAPITULATION.

	£	s.	d.	£	s.	d.
Imports	1,167	14	1	794	10	1
Exports	290	8	8	191	16	8
	1,458	2	9	1,986	6	9

EXPENDITURE.

	£	s.	d.
Salaries and allowances	2,041	11	4¾
Miscellaneous	206	15	8½
	2,248	7	1¼

D. T. SMITH,
Receiver General and Treasurer.

RECEIVER GENERAL'S OFFICE,
Grand Turk, July 21, 1864.

October 15, 1864.

I have the honor to transmit some valuable information relative to the Caicos islands, which constitute much the largest, and, in an agricultural point of view, the wealthiest portion of this colony. The information in question appears in the shape of a letter from some of the principal inhabitants and land owners in the Caicos, addressed to the chief executive of this presidency, and I am indebted to his honor President Moir for the same.   *   *   *

TURK'S AND UAICOS ISLANDS, *February* 20, 1863.

Sir: The undersigned, who have resided for many years on the Caicos islands, beg to submit such information as they have been able to obtain respecting the resources of these islands. In the early settlement of this part of the colony, large quantities of cotton were produced and exported to England direct, in vessels which brought out supplies of British goods. This was done during the existence of slavery, when labor was secure, and when there were fully 3,000 inhabitants. The cultivation of this valuable commodity may be carried on as advantageously as ever; it requires only labor, energy, and some capital, in which the present scattered settlers are deficient, having no disposition to give their attention to anything beyond a supply of daily or weekly wants, and this scantily. To procure such information as your honor requires respecting the agricultural produce of these islands, it will require a skilful person to give the land a fair trial. At present it is difficult to ascertain what an acre of land will produce, as the settlers cultivate the soil in detached pieces, which suits their habits. It is the opinion of those persons capable of judging, that if agriculture were properly attended to it would pay 100 per cent. better than salt-raking, in proportion to the outlay.

The cost of clearing land is from 16 shillings to 24 shillings per acre; less when there are no trees to be cut down.

The value of vegetables, fruits, corn, and other productions may be estimated as follows :

Indian corn, per bushel, from 4s. to 6s.; Guinea corn, per bushel, from 3s. to 5s. (These may be produced in abundance.)

Sweet potatoes, 4s. per bushel.

Pumpkins, from 2s. to 4s. per dozen.

Sugar-cane, 10s. to 16s. 8d. per hundred.

Cassava grows well, but is seldom sold.

Yams, 8s. to 10s. per 100 lbs.

Plantains, not in abundance, 16 for 1s.

Oranges of superior quality, 4s. to 6s. per 100.

Bananas, from 1s. to 4s. per bunch.

Avocado pears, from 2s. 6d. to 3s. per dozen.

Limes, lemons, sour oranges, and all the fruits of a tropical climate, may be produced in great abundance and of excellent quality. A superior quality of tobacco may be produced. Cocoa-nut trees may grow there, but are not generally cultivated, although the soil, in many parts of the Caicos islands, seems well adapted for their production.

Sheep, horned cattle, and horses thrive well. Sheep sell from 14s. to 20s. per head, and when well fed weigh from 16 to 20 lbs. per quarter, the mutton being considered of superior quality.

Cattle sell, according to size, from £3 to £10; sometimes at a higher rate; and if such stock were well attended to, might be raised in sufficient numbers to supply the Turk's Island market, where beef is sold from 8d. to 10d. per lb.; mutton, 10d., and pork, 8d.

Horses sell from £6 to £12. Turtle, fish, crabs, concks, lobsters, and other shell-fish abound, so do wild ducks, pigeons, and other game; in fact, the islands are capable of producing all that may be had in any of the West Indies.

The cost of a wattled and plastered cottage, with two floors, 16 by 20 feet, 10 feet high, is from £25 to £30; a small cottage, with one floor, much less.

Facilities for obtaining wood for building purposes are great, as there are valuable forests of pine, yellow-wood, mahogany, spruce, and pitch-pine.

Braziletto and ebony wood have been exported in considerable quantities during the past year. Lime of excellent quality can be burned in any quantity from stone, shells, or coral, at from 4d. to 5d. per bushel. Fuel is abundant. The cost of a common fishing-boat is from £4 to £6. A good sized sail-boat, for bringing produce to market, will cost from £30 to £50.

Agricultural wages may be quoted at from £1 to £1 10s. per month, with rations; but the laborers will seldom engage themselves, except by the day, at from 2s. to 2s. 6d. They are not fond of work, and will do as little as they can.

Heavy rains may be expected during the summer months, and the productions of these islands are generally brought to market in May and December.

The general mode of travelling is on foot. In some parts of Middle Caicos the roads which were once very good are now so completely overgrown as to be impassable by horses.

The islands are generally healthy. Some neglected and damp localities are subject to fevers in the fall of the year, which are not of a dangerous type. In fact, the Turk's and Caicos islands may be considered among the most healthy portions of the world, and we may proudly and thankfully invite the invalids of northern climates to seek for the restoration of health in this colony, which numbers have already done with great success.

The Caicos islands can boast of having the strongest and most healthy individuals in a tropical climate. Their food consists principally of fish, corn, vegetables, and shell-fish, and they frequently attain the advanced age of 70 or 90 years.

Owing to the great indolence of most of the settlers, as well as their want of agricultural skill, very little would be raised did it not grow spontaneously. If so much is, therefore, produced at the Caicos in the present state, and under such circumstances, what may not be done by industry and skilful cultivation?

Mr. TUCKER and others *to President Moir.*

KINGSTON, JAMAICA—R. J. C. HITCHINS, *Vice-Consul.*

JUNE 30, 1864.

The operations of trade between this port and the United States are at present almost altogether confined to the importation of the breadstuffs required for consumption. The increase of duties in the United States has checked shipments the.e of the island produce of which the crops are now almost harvested. Exports to the United States are thus almost confined to dyewoods, of which logwood forms a principal part. Sales of imported goods are generally made at a credit of 60 to 90 days, payable by acceptances on which two names not connected in business are required; and on these acceptances the banks, if willing to cash the same, require a discount and commission equal to 9 per cent., which is charged to the party for whose account the sales are made. Produce of the island is sold for cash, unless in particular cases, when the credit depends on agreement, but is never beyond 60 to 90 days; also for approved acceptances with two names. The discount on this is generally chargeable to the purchasers. There are no bounties on any goods exported. Rum is shipped from the bonded warehouses, in which it is placed on receipt at the shipping ports to secure the excise duty, a large amount on which was lost previous to this precaution; other produce is subject only to an export duty. Imported goods, subject to duty, are exported from the bonded warehouses, free of any charge, by the government. The customary rate of commission for purchasing and shipping goods is 5 per cent. if without funds, and 2½ per cent. if in funds. The usual brokerage on the sale of merchandise is 5 per cent. on European and 2½ per cent. on American products, if for cash; but where a *del credere* or advance is required a further 2½ per cent. is generally charged. The expenses on shipments are never included in the price of the article, but always charged separately to the party concerned. The costs of transport to a place of shipment are seldom, if ever, set down as a separate charge. Should the produce be transported coastwise, then there is usually a charge; but sometimes this is paid by the vessel on which it is shipped, or a lighter is thus provided.

Steamships belonging to the Pacific and West India Company, taking this port en route to Aspinwall, Santa Martha, and Vera Cruz, returning through this in a double line to Liverpool, have increased the trade of this port, and the greater part of all produce, excepting sugar and rum, is now shipped on steam vessels to England.

A coasting steamer has commenced running, intended originally for a feeder to these lines, but the business hitherto has been so great that the cargoes for these steamers have been but a small part, and already another steamer is required.

The restriction on foreign vessels in the coasting trade of the colonies will always prevent the introduction of American steamers or these would be much patronized, particularly by passengers. The original cargo or passengers are only now allowed to be carried coastwise, in whole or in part, and in loading the whole or a part of a cargo can be taken from one port to another, but no island produce or cargo shipped on the island, or passengers taken on board in one port, can be debarked in another.

Railroads and telegraphs have been constructed between Kingston and Spanish Town only.

JOHN W. CAMP, *Vice-Consul.*

DECEMBER 10, 1864.

I have the honor to enclose herewith "A," statement of navigation and commerce of the United States at this port; "B," exports to the United States from the port of Kingston, made up from invoices certified at this consulate; "C," imports from the United States into this island—all for the year ending 30th September, 1864. Also, "D," total imports and exports of Jamaica for the quarter and years ending 30th September, 1864, '63, '62, and '61, as made to the house of assembly by the collector and comptroller of her Majesty's customs for Jamaica.

The figures in schedule "C" may not be entirely exact in every particular, but are as nearly so as I have been able to make them, and are sufficiently so for all purposes of information.

The great falling off in the exhibits of American shipping at this port for the year ending September, 1864, and the two previous years, as compared with previous exhibits, is chiefly due to the transfer of American vessels engaged in this trade to foreign flags. A secondary cause is the establishment of a regular monthly steamer between this port and New York, by means of which large importations are made that formerly found their way hither by sailing vessels.

In addition to the regular mail steamer that makes monthly trips under subsidy from the Jamaica government, there is now in operation one steamer of the "New York and Columbian Steamship Company's" new line running between New York and Santa Martha, Savinilla, and Carthagena, touching at Kingston on both outward and return voyages. I am informed that additional vessels will soon be put on this line, which will cause further reduction in the business done by sailing vessels.

Statement showing the imports and exports for the quarter and years ended September 30, 1864, 1863, 1862, and 1861, agreeably to 9th Victoria, chap. 14.

IMPORTS.

ARTICLES.	Quarter ended September 30, 1864.	For year ended September 30, 1864.	For year ended September 30, 1863.	For year ended September 30, 1862.	For year ended September 30, 1861.
BREADSTUFFS.					
Flour..................barrels..	26,566	104,540	96,066	102,623	67,902
Cornmeal..............barrels..	4,750	18,128	16,349	26,286	7,123
Bread and biscuits......cwt. qrs. lbs..	979 3 24	3,452 3 3	3,896 2 8	4,230 0 00	2,938 2 18
Rice......................lbs..	2,777,656	6,183,713	6,751,947	5,156,486	2,979,612
Corn..................bushels..	8,442	22,311	22,846	26,488	30,415
Peas, beans, and calavances......bushels..	207	708	842	1,128	2,269
Barley, oats, and rye..........bushels..	160	570	1,785	2,426	2,356
Wheat...............bushels..		4,103	9,896	13,188	12,645
SALTED PROVISIONS.					
Beef......................barrels..	893	2,789	2,897	2,878	2,021
Pork......................barrels..	2,852	10,303	13,377	14,981	9,766
Pickled tongues ....barrels..	223	691	1,004	537	969
Dry tongues, beef, hams, and sausages.cwt..	588	2,113	2,590	2,489	1,779
Butter.................firkins—56 lbs..	4,080	9,447	9,957	11,321	10,139
Lard..................firkins—60 lbs..	2,375	7,594	6,876	7,436	4,990
FISH.					
Salmon, pickled..............barrels..	137	1,138	1,076	1,178	842
smoked..............cwt..	1	5	29	....	842
Smoked herrings..........boxes..	633	5,048	4,117	3,045	3,700
Mackerel...............barrels..	3,632	20,219	19,447	15,836	10,562
Alewives...............barrels..	1,499	3,414	3,587	5,473	4,536
Herrings...............barrels..	4,686	38,711	34,425	33,074	34,072
Codfish................quintals..	15,684	69,548	81,084	82,803	92,664
SPIRITS.					
Brandy.................gallons..	3,202	16,127	15,432	17,205	9,853
Gin...................gallons..	658	5,623	5,679	5,321	3,376
Ale and beer..........tuns, h. g..	35 19	337 387	286 327	552	745
do................gallons..	170 } 211 }	207 } 159 }	175 } 119 }	35	203
Cider and Perry..............tuns..	2	6	3	1	....
do................gallons..	42	101	198	55	196
Wine, in bulk..............tuns..	19	119	112	115	128
do................gallons..	22	146	190	230	206
Wine, in bottles.............tuns..	5	34	28	20	27
do................gallons..	201	133	75	8	139
MISCELLANEOUS.					
Refined sugar...............lbs..	9,586	54,561	54,288	35,872	46,265
....................lbs..	476	1,647	2,234	1,795	1,225
Tea.....................lbs..	5,797	15,782	15,007	11,145	11,037
Candles, sperm.............boxes..	3	9	139	88	452
composition...........boxes..	1,619	2,792	2,312	2,915	2,273
tallow ....boxes..	3,633	15,571	14,045	16,248	11,736
Soap..................boxes..	5,469	26,951	38,099	38,516	36,483
do...................gallons..	14,468	69,191	79,380	85,305	65,083
Salt....................cwt..	7,793	22,879	37,451	65,377	23,443
Tobacco, manufactured.........lbs..	41,441	110,929	132,756	169,488	200,416
leaf..............lbs..	17,478	136,552	154,922	148,998	211,091
Bricks.................number..	41,600	341,600	392,198	677,093	642,890
Coal...................tons..	6,586	33,690	90,610	28,019	16,890
LIVE STOCK.					
Horses ....number..		22	2	25	43
Mares ....number..	....	....	....	....	....
Asses ....number..	....	1	1	....	....
Cattle ....number..	....	1	5	307	348
Swine ....number..	3	10	16	26	42
Sheep and goats.........number..	5	13	5	....	7
LUMBER.					
Red oak staves..........number..	2,200	280,414	413,834	139,045	673,829
White oak staves and heading....number..	....	7,760	172,949	242,017	414,283
Standard shooks...........number..	513	12,834	11,731	15,195	10,474
Puncheon shooks..........number..	371	13,190	74,163	23,754	12,249
White pine lumber...........feet..	865,640	3,891,351	2,690,719	4,407,438	3,250,057
Pitch pine lumber...........feet..		60,119	50,724	94,437	872,356
Cypress shingles..........number..		110,000	222,000		1,307,407
Cedar shingles..........number..	1,546,001	7,540,601	4,468,050	2,720,700	3,343,165
Wood staves............number..	34,250	420,840	449,900	613,170	587,925

Statement showing the imports and exports, &c.—Continued.

EXPORTS.

ARTICLES.	Quarter ended September 30, 1864.	For year ended September 30, 1864.	For year ended September 30, 1863.	For year ended September 30, 1862.	For year ended September 30, 1861.
Sugar.............................hhds..	7,972	25,124	29,898	33,097	32,077
Do.................................tierces..	1,180	3,872	4,320	4,480	3,309
Do.................................barrels..	1,407	5,866	4,732	5,406	6,245
Rum ....puncheons .	5,015	13,502	17,258	19,831	20,625
Do................................hhds..	8	12	22	71	71
Do................................qr. casks..	85	129	21	24	45
Molasses...........................casks..			1		
Coffee.............................lbs..	1,113,163	5,424,184	8,485,731	5,601,157	6,766,954
Pimento...........................lbs..	471,267	8,929,870	4,466,855	5,536,513	8,863,249
Ginger.............................cwt..	1,276	6,071	7,210	7,512	6,337
Arrowroot.........................lbs..	3,136	37,204	12,884	22,316	32,088
Logwood...........................tons..	8,832	27,828	29,984	30,895	17,013
Fustic.............................tons..	1,642	3,951	1,261	1,190	1,668
Lancewood spars..................number..	378	1,811	1,054	2,735	2,905
Mahogany and other woods..........tons..	15	15	1		5
Do................do.................feet..		2,000	21,175	13,399	1,936
Succades.......................cwt. qrs. lbs..	26 3 9	125 2 5	269 0 19	215 3 1	162 0 18
Santa, or shrub..................gallons..	56	56	175		55
Beeswax.....................cwt. qrs. lbs..	291 3 10	878 1 24	884 3 22	852 1 20	694 1 0
Honey ....cwt. qrs. lbs..	214 3 9	661 3 4	663 0 0	745 2 16	738 0 24
Coconuts.........................number..	165,409	738,736	808,613	830,571	999,276
Cotton.............................lbs..	3,942	19,147	15,352	1,949	
Lignumvitæ and ebony ....tons..	271	377	194	405	268
Copper ore.........................tons..				16 5-20	14 2-20
Lead ore...........................tons..					
Horses.............................number..	1	3	4	27	2
Mules ....number..		50	84		32
Neat cattle........................number..		30	150		

Statement showing the imports from the United States into the island of Jamaica for the year ended 30th September, 1864.

Flour..........	104,540 barrels.	Tallow candles..	15,000 boxes.
Corn-meal......	18,128 barrels.	Composition can-	
Bread and biscuit	3,452 cwt.	dles	699 boxes.
Corn	22,311 bushels.	Manufactured to-	
Peas and beans..	600 bushels.	bacco........	69,330 pounds.
Wheat.........	4,130 bushels.	Leaf tobacco....	102,414 pounds.
Beef	2,700 barrels.	Cheese	1,135 cwt.
Pork	10,303 barrels.	R. O. staves	210,310
Dry hams and		W. O. staves....	6,000
tongues	1,585 cwt.	W. P. lumber...	2,432,094 feet.
Butter	5,904 firkins.	Cyprus shingles.	110,000
Lard	7,594 firkins.		

Statement showing the exports from the port of Kingston to the United States for the year ended September 30, 1864.

	LOGWOOD.		FUSTIC.		METALS.		RUM.	
	Quantity.	Value.	Quantity.	Value.	Quantity.	Value.	Quantity.	Value.
	tons. cwt. qrs.	£ s. d.	tons. cwt. qrs.	£ s. d.	tons. cwt. qrs. lbs.	£ s. d.	puncheons.	£ s. d.
Fourth quarter, 1863	1,908 3 2	2,504 8 7	61 18 0	167 0 8	1 8 0 8	592 7 10	45	414 11 7
First quarter, 1864	2,379 7 0	4,791 3 0	9 0 0	27 0 0	44 16 0 0	392 9 10	27	297 13 9
Second quarter, 1864	1,904 10 0	2,418 14 0	30 10 0	103 19 0	35 8 0 25	465 16 4	338	3,438 16 0
Third quarter, 1864	2,053 10 0	3,986 19 0	40 14 0	142 7 7	8 0 0 5	234 11 0	5	63 18 0
Total	6,844 0 2	13,641 4 7	142 2 0	440 10 3	89 12 1 10	2,225 5 0	415	4,214 19 4

Statement showing the exports from Kingston—Continued.

	SUGAR.		COFFEE.		PIMENTO.		GINGER.	
	Quantity.	Value.	Quantity.	Value.	Quantity.	Value.	Quantity.	Value.
	tons. cwt. qrs. lbs.	£ s. d.	cwt. qrs. lbs.	£ s. d.	cwt. qrs. lbs.	£ s. d.	cwt. qrs. lbs.	£ s. d.
Fourth quarter, 1863	128 13 2 0	2,647 12 7	6,453 1 0	17,312 3 5	6,342 0 6	4,688 19 4	3 2 20	5 10 8
First quarter, 1864	47 9 2 6	1,094 9 0	8,993 3 9	18,080 11 1	7,902 0 22	6,056 4 10	130 2 0	221 18 0
Second quarter, 1864			4,249 2 14	13,982 8 10	4,592 1 17	3,225 14 5	137 0 0	345 4 7
Third quarter, 1864			264 3 16	916 9 3	16 1 0	13 5 0	132 0 0	445 7 7
Total	176 3 0 6	3,742 1 7	19,961 2 11	50,291 13 1	18,852 3 17	13,982 6 11	403 0 24	1,098 1 6

Statement showing the exports from Kingston—Continued.

	COCOA-NUTS		TOBACCO		LIMES AND ORANGES		WOOLLEN GOODS		GUANO	
	Quantity.	Value.	Quantity.	Value.	Quantity.	Value.	Quantity.	Value.	Quantity.	Value.
		£ s. d.	cwt. qrs. lbs.	£ s. d.	barrels.	£ s. d.		£ s. d.	tons.	£ s. d.
Fourth quarter, 1863	1,500	3 15 0	94 0 20	964 12 0	49	18 0 6	4 cases.	133 6 6	125	240 0 0
First quarter, 1864					342	133 9 0	2 bags.	1 11 6		
Second quarter, 1864										
Third quarter, 1864										
Total	1,500	3 15 0	94 0 20	964 12 0	391	151 9 6	4 cases, 2 bags	134 17 6	125	240 0 0

Statement showing the exports from Kingston—Continued.

	BITTER WOOD.		LIME-JUICE.		ARROWROOT.		RAGS.		BEESWAX.	
	Quantity.	Value.	Quantity.	Value.	Quantity.	Value.	Quantity.	Value.	Quantity.	Value.
	tons.	£ s. d.	puncheons.	£ s. d.	cwt. qrs. lbs.	£ s. d.	cwt. qrs. lbs.	£ s. d.	pounds.	£ s. d.
Fourth quarter, 1863	93	37 9 0			146 2 0	398 14 10	139 0 0	38 18 2	131	8 4 9
First quarter, 1864	174	26 0 0	3	18 5 0			39 2 15	11 6 0	636	40 1 0
Second quarter, 1864	60	72 10 10	6	35 3 0						
Third quarter, 1864										
Total	100 4	136 0 2	9	53 8 0	146 2 0	398 14 10	178 2 15	50 4 2	767	48 5 9

Summary statement showing the exports from Kingston to the United States during the year ended September 30, 1863.

Articles.	Quarter ended December 31, 1862.			Quar. ended March 31, 1863.			Quarter ended June 30, 1863.			Quarter ended September 30, 1863.			Total.		
Logwood ...	£4,881	19	11	£5,415	7	10	£2,260	4	4	£2,940	16	3	£15,498	8	4
Coffee	11,114	5	10	16,647	6	7	956	8	2	493	8	11	29,211	9	6
Pimento	1,304	8	6	2,057	9	6	190	10	10	....			3,572	8	10
Rum	244	1	1	124	19	1	473	9	3	286	4	3	1,128	13	8
Sundries ...	149	12	8	667	3	1	972	4	2	349	5	8	2,138	5	7
Total.....	17,784	8	0	24,912	6	1	4,782	16	9	4,069	15	1	51,549	5	11

PRINCE EDWARD ISLAND—J. H. SHERMAN, *Consul.*

NOVEMBER —, 1864.

I have the honor to submit this my annual report:

As no important changes have occurred since my last report, this one will necessarily be brief. The only feature deserving of particular notice is the unexampled prosperity of the island in its agricultural and financial departments.

The crops were very large, and the prices obtained abroad, principally in the United States, were highly remunerative. The export of oats alone amounted the past year to one and a half million of bushels.

	£	s.	d.
The total value of goods imported was, in sterling.........	293,431	4	10
Against the previous year of...........................	211,240	18	6
Showing an increase of...............................	82,190	6	4

	£	s.	d.
The impost and excise duties on the past year's importations were..	30,704	17	8
Those of the previous year were........................	25,704	6	5
Showing an increase of...............	5,000	11	3

EXPORTS.

	£	s.	d.
The total value of exports the past year was.............	209,472	9	6
The total value the previous year......................	150,549	2	1
Showing an increase of...............................	58,923	7	5

	£	s.	d.
The new vessels built on Prince Edward Island the past year number 100, of an aggregate burden of 24,991 tons; calculating the value of this shipping at £5 per ton, sterling, the amount should be added to the general exports of	209,472	9	6

	£	s.	d.
For shipping	124,955	0	0
Total exports	334,427	9	6
Against total imports	293,431	4	10
Leaving a balance in favor of the colony, of sterling	40,996	4	8

As usual, the exports to the United States exceed the aggregate amount exported to all other parts of the world.

ARTICLES OF EXPORT.

The principal articles of export (exclusive of shipping) are agricultural products. Of these the following amounts were shipped the past year, viz:

Oats	1,459,130 bushels.
Barley	74,959 bushels.
Potatoes	408,122 bushels.
Dry fish	15,086 quintals.
Pickled fish	7,570 barrels.

Statement showing the value in sterling of the imports and exports of Prince Edward Island, from and to the United States, during the last twenty years, viz: from 1844 to 1863, both years included.

Years.	Imports.	Exports.
1844	£1,432 18 7	£1,257 3 11
1845	2,803 8 4	3,065 10 0
1846	4,064 6 8	1,325 3 6
1847	7,065 13 2	821 10 0
1848	16,381 6 8	1,283 17 6
1849	16,516 9 11	6,482 10 6
1850	8,320 15 7	11,077 6 0
1851	16,981 9 6	20,976 15 1
1852	34,271 3 7	28,371 0 5
1853	37,583 7 6	24,100 2 6
1854	39,167 13 10	16,356 11 0
1855	43,241 17 10	33,398 14 6
1856	34,915 13 0	18,013 18 5
1857	50,296 0 0	48,452 0 0
1858	42,004 0 0	63,823 0 0
1859	62,055 19 4	87,899 12 2
1860	56,429 6 4	78,405 17 8
1861	43,009 2 4	46,775 7 11
1862	46,929 19 11	43,466 16 4
1863	84,771 18 10	105,733 16 5
Total	648,249 10 11	641,086 13 10

Statement showing the value in sterling of the imports and exports of Prince Edward Island, from and to all countries, from the year 1830 to the year 1863, both inclusive.

Year.	Imports.			Exports.			Year.	Imports.			Exports.		
	£	s.	d.	£	s.	d.		£	s.	d.	£	s.	d.
1830	56,430	0	0	33,588	15	11	1847...	143,647	3	5	71,228	14	2
1831	63,826	18	5	42,535	13	.7	1848...	129,532	5	8	40,222	8	9
1832	70,068	8	11	31,739	15	0	1849...	115,208	8	4	55,657	15	11
1833	93,338	0	11	35,128	18	2	1850...	123,117	1	10	59,694	16	1
1834	111,595	14	6	41,191	16	8	1851...	133,882	2	0	68,604	12	4
1835	61,155	6	11	47,215	12	0	1852...	171,971	2	3	106,256	19	7
1836	90,759	18	7	46,973	19	7	1853...	210,678	3	1	127,346	17	9
1837	82,907	16	2	37,235	0	0	1854...	273,929	1	2	151,213	12	6
1838	94,547	11	0	62,419	1	11	1855...	268,406	8	9	147,114	14	9
1839	136,210	3	5	73,100	18	1	1856...	237,707	6	8	111,980	4	0
1840	144,440	1	11	62,120	17	9	1857...	258,728	0	0	134,465	0	0
1841	127,164	19	6	68,323	8	6	1858...	186,229	0	0	135,071	0	0
1842	101,518	2	9	58,157	14	10	1859...	234,698	3	3	178,680	6	11
1843	187,945	11	9	56,015	15	5	1860...	230,054	0	0	201,434	3	4
1844	97,110	19	0	59,158	14	8	1861...	209,995	15	11	163,114	7	10
1845	121,937	17	4	70,204	12	2	1862...	211,240	18	6	150,549	2	1
1846	127,920	4	9	74,551	10	10	1863...	293,431	4	11	209,472	9	6
	1,768,877	15	0	899,662	5	1		3,433,396	5	9	2,112,107	5	6

Statement showing the total sterling value of the imports and exports of the province of Prince Edward Island, from and to each country, in the year ended December 31, 1863.

Ports of—	Imports.			Exports.		
United Kingdom	£122,880	5	6¼	£21,949	0	9
Nova Scotia	66,890	11	5¼	38,511	12	3
New Brunswick	19,975	3	11	23,340	5	4
Newfoundland	1,865	15	3	11,241	12	4
Bermuda and West Indies	3,969	5	7	5,769	0	8
Saint Pierre	292	11	3	1,207	13	10
Canada	6,152	8	3	1,255	12	11
Cape of Good Hope				429	11	0
Magdalenes	302	3	0	34	4	0
United States	71,103	0	8	105,733	16	5
Total	293,431	4	11	209,472	9	6

FISHERIES.

The fisheries, prosecuted almost exclusively by our citizens on the coasts of this island, have richly rewarded our enterprising people, and during the past year have been large, and prices ruled high during the latter part of the season.

There have been no wrecks of American vessels on the coast of this island, and no American seamen have applied for relief.

The light and anchorage duties have not been changed during the past year.

There has been a line of screw steamers established the present summer between Boston and the city of Charlottetown, on this island, which has been very successful. Two steamers make, together, regular weekly trips. One is of eight hundred tons burden, and the other of between three and four hundred tons burden. They are both owned in Boston.   *   *   *

Laws of Prince Edward Island.

CAP. I.

AN ACT for raising a revenue. Passed April 30, 1864.

Whereas it is deemed expedient to further continue and amend the hereinafter recited act: Be it therefore enacted, by the lieutenant governor, council, and assembly, as follows:

I. The act made and passed in the nineteenth year of the reign of her present Majesty, entitled "An act for raising a revenue," and to consolidate and amend the several acts therein mentioned, save and except such clauses and parts thereof as are hereby repealed, shall be, and the same is hereby, continued, with certain amendments hereinafter mentioned, until the first day of May, which will be in the year of our Lord one thousand eight hundred and sixty-five.

II. From and after the passing of this act, and until the said first day of May, one thousand eight hundred and sixty-five, there shall be raised, levied, and paid, on the several articles hereinafter mentioned, imported or brought into this island from any place or country whatsoever, the several impost duties, rates, or impositions inserted, described, and set forth in figures in the table of duties hereinafter contained, denominated "table of impost duties," opposite to and against the said respective articles, as therein mentioned, described, and enumerated, and according to the value, number, and quantity thereof, as therein specified; the first column of duties in the said table denoting the *ad valorem* duty, or amount payable on every one hundred pounds worth of the article imported, which shall be in like proportion for any less amount than one hundred pounds worth; and the second column denoting the specific duty on each article; and the said duties shall be calculated on the actual value or amount of the invoice when reduced into the lawful current money of this island, which said several duties, rates, and impositions, shall be in lieu of all duties, rates, and impositions imposed by the hereinbefore recited act; and the amount of any invoice of dutiable goods imported from the United States of America into this island, made out in dollars and cents, shall, for all the purposes of this act, be reduced into the current money of this island, by allowing for each dollar the sum of six shillings of the said current money, or such other sum as the lieutenant governor of this island, in council, shall, from time to time, fix and determine the rate so fixed by the government, to be published in the Royal Gazette, weekly, and in like proportion for any smaller part or fraction of a dollar.

Tab'e of impost duties referred to in the preceding act.

Articles.	Percentage (ad valorem) duty on every £100 currency value per invoice.			Other duties.		
	£	s.	d.	£	s.	d.
Anchors and chain cables	1	0	0			
Blocks and deadeyes	5	0	0			
Boots and shoes of all kinds	12	10	0			
Buffalo robes	10	0	0			
Burning fluid, kerosene, paraffine, rock, combination and all other descriptions of oils, manufactured from coal, per gallon				0	0	7½
Books, being the reprints of British authors, under the imperial act 11th Vic., cap. 28	20	0	0			
Canvas, sail-cloth, and cordage	2	0	0			
Clothes, ready-made, namely, coats, overcoats, vests, jackets, and trowsers	12	10	0			
Coffee, green, per lb				0	0	2
Coffee, roasted or ground, per lb				0	0	3
Chocolate, broma, or cocoa paste, per lb				0	0	3
Cigars	20	0	0			
Cider, per gallon				0	0	5
Clocks	25	0	0			
Copper composition bars, bolts, rudder braces, clinch rings, sheets, and sheathing nails	2	0	0			
All wheel machinery, and machinery for manufacturing or to be used in the formation of clocks	20	0	0			
Carriages of all kinds	12	10	0			
Bar iron	5	0	0			
Jewelry of all kinds	10	0	0			
Leather of all kinds except sole leather	6	5	0			
Sole leather, per lb				0	0	1
Porter, ale, and beer, per gallon				0	0	5
Jordan and shelled almonds, per lb				0	0	3
Rigging	2	0	0			
Rum or other distilled spirituous liquors imported into this island, not exceeding the strength of proof by Sykes's hydrometer, and so in proportion for any greater strength than the strength of proof, and landed at the ports of Charlottetown, Georgetown, Summerside, and Souris, per gallon				0	1	6
Rum or other distilled spirituous liquors imported into this island, for every gallon thereof, of any strength under and not exceeding the strength of proof 28 by the bubble; and for every bubble below 28 in number by the bubble, an additional 1½d. per gallon				0	0	1½
Molasses, per gallon				0	0	4
Patent medicines	30	0	0			
Salt, per ton				0	0	6
Sails	2	0	0			
Spirituous liquors, on all manufactured or distilled in this island, per gallon				0	0	6
Steam engines and boilers	2	0	0			
Sugar, refined, per lb				0	0	3
Sugar, brown or muscovado, per cwt				0	7	0
Confectionery of all kinds, per lb				0	0	4
Tea, per lb				0	0	4
Fine bread and crackers of all kinds except ship bread and navy bread	10	0	0			

Table of impost duties—Continued.

Articles.	1st column. Percentage (ad valorem) duty on every £100 currency value per invoice.	2d column. Other duties.
	£ s. d.	£ s. d.
Tobacco, manufactured, per lb	....	0 0 6
Tobacco, manufactured in this island...................	....	0 0 4
Watches and all machinery to be used in the formation thereof......	10 0 0	
Sails, rigging, and ships' materials, saved from vessels wrecked on the coast of this island, not belonging to this island, duty payable on account of sales......................	10 0 0	
Ships' stores and cordage saved from wrecks or sold in vessels stranded, to pay the same duty as in cases of importation.		
Where a vessel not belonging to this island is stranded and condemned, or sold whilst stranded, a duty shall be paid on the amount of sales of her hull, rigging, and materials, whether she be again got off or there broken up......................	10 0 0	
Wines, claret and all other light wines, (except port and sherry,) the first class of which is under twenty pounds sterling, per pipe..	25 0 0	
Port and sherry, and all other wines costing over twenty pounds sterling per pipe, per gallon, in addition to five per cent. ad valorem duty.....................	5 0 0	0 4 0
Spirits, namely, brandy imported into this island at the ports of Charlottetown, Georgetown, Summerside, and Souris, not exceeding the strength of proof by Sykes's hydrometer, and so in proportion for any greater strength than the strength of proof, per gallon....	....	0 4 6
Spirits, namely, brandy, imported into this island at any other ports, for every gallon thereof of any strength under and not exceeding the strength of proof of 28 by the bubble.....................	....	0 4 6
And for every bubble below 28 in number, by the bubble, an additional 3d. per gallon......................	....	0 0 3
Spirits, namely, gin, cordials, and whiskey imported into this island at the ports of Charlottetown, Georgetown, Summerside, and Souris, not exceeding the strength of proof by Sykes's hydrometer, and so in proportion for any greater strenth than the strength of proof, per gallon......................	....	0 3 6
Spirits, namely, gin, cordials, and whiskey imported into this island at any other ports, for every gallon thereof of any strength, under and not exceeding the strength of proof of 28 by the bubble......	....	0 3 6
And for every bubble below 28 in number, by the bubble, an additional 3d. per gallon......................	....	0 0 3
Lemon sirup, shrub, santa, and gingerette, per gallon............	....	0 1 0
Tinctures, per gallon......................	....	0 2 0
Currants, raisins, prunes, figs, and all other kinds of dried fruits, per lb......................	....	0 0 1
Articles manufactured of wood, and such articles of which wood forms the principal part, not hereinbefore enumerated............	12 10 0	
Corn brooms, matches, trunks, valises, portmanteaus, and looking-glasses......................	12 10 0	
Oakum......................	2 0 0	
Iron bars and straps intended for strapping riders and knees of ships.	2 0 0	
On all goods, wares, and merchandise not above enumerated, except as hereinafter mentioned and excepted......................	10 0 0	

III. All articles in the following table, imported from any country or colony whatsoever, shall be exempt from duty, to.wit:

All articles imported by the lieutenant governor for his own use; ashes, namely, potashes and pearlashes; baggage: apparel, household effects, working tools and implements used and in use of persons or families arriving in this island, if used abroad by them, and not intended for any other person or persons, or for sale; barrels and half barrels of all kinds; books (printed) of all kinds, not prohibited to be imported into the United Kingdom; maps and charts; blocks, rigging, and sails, which may have been used to take new vessels from this island to a market for sale, if such blocks, rigging, and sails shall be returned forthwith, after the sale of the vessel, direct to this island, by the exporter thereof, and shall have previously paid, and shall have been charged with the duties by law imposed thereon, on the first importation thereof into this island; butter; broomcorn and bark; ship and pilot bread; cheese; coal; dyewoods of all kinds, (ground and unground;) engines, (fire;) flax; fish of all kinds, and products of fish, and all other creatures living in the water; furs, skins, and tails, undressed; fruits, dried and undried, grown in the United States of America; grain, flour, and breadstuffs of all kinds; gypsum, ground and unground; grindstones, hewn, wrought, or unwrought; hemp and tow, unmanufactured; hides; horns; iron, (pig;) lard; lime; manures; meats, fresh, smoked, and salted; oil, (fish;) organs and bells imported expressly for any church, chapel, or sacred edifice in this island, and intended to be placed therein; ores of metals of all kinds; ordnance or commissariat stores, or war munitions of any kind; or military baggage or clothing brought into this island for the use of her Majesty's army, navy, or militia, by any commissary or other person in her Majesty's service; military clothing and accoutrements for the use of her Majesty's volunteer corps in this island; printing paper, royal and demy, in use for newspapers; poultry, eggs; pitch, tar, and rosin; pelts; plants, shrubs, and trees; rags; rice; seeds and vegetables; slate; stone or marble, sawn or in its crude or unwrought state; burr or limestone; stock (live) of all kinds, for breeding purposes; seines; staves; tallow; teasels: timber and lumber of all kinds, round, hewn, and sawed, unmanufactured; firewoods; tobacco, unmanufactured; wool.

IV. All and every the powers and authorities, provisions, rules, regulations, directions, penalties, forfeitures, clauses, matters and things in the said recited act of the nineteenth Victoria, chapter one, shall severally and respectively be duly observed, practiced, and applied to, and put in execution in relation to the duties thereby and hereby imposed and granted, as well during the time hereby limited, as after the expiration thereof, for securing, levying, collecting, and recovering the said duties, and all arrears thereof, and all penalties and forfeitures that may have heretofore been incurred under and by virtue of the said recited act; and for suing for and recovering all such penalties as shall have been or may be incurred in relation to the said duties, as fully and effectually, to all intents and purposes, as if the same powers and authorities, rules, regulations, directions, penalties, forfeitures, clauses, matters and things, were particularly repeated and re-enacted in the body of this act, with reference to the said duties hereby or thereby granted and imposed.

V. No rum, brandy, gin, or alcohol shall be imported or brought into this island in any cask or package not capable of containing at least sixty gallons; and any person offending against the provisions of this section shall forfeit ten pounds for every cask or package, and the liquor shall be forfeited: provided, that nothing in this section contained shall apply to any such liquors imported into this island from Europe, the British West Indies, or any British possessions in North America.

VI. On the seizure of any goods, wares, and merchandise by any landwaiter or preventive officer, under the provisions of the said hereinbefore recited act, the duties on such goods, wares, and merchandise shall be first paid into the public tr asury within thirty days after the sale thereof, and the balance or residue of the proceeds arising from such sale, after the payment of the duties as aforesaid, shall be paid to or equally divided between the officer or officers making the seizure, together with three-fourth parts of all fines relating to such seizure; which shall be sued for and recovered in the name or names of such officer or officers making the seizure, or by an information filed by the attorney general.

VII. No goods, wares, or merchandise shall be liable to forfeiture by reason of the same not having been duly entered by the master of the ship or vessel in which the same shall have been imported : Provided always, that such goods, wares, or merchandise shall have been duly entered according to law by the importer or consignee thereof, or other person interested in the same.

VIII. No ship or vessel shall be liable to seizure, detention, or forfeiture, under the provisions of the said recited act, by reason of any breach or violation of the said act having been committed by the master (not being the owner) of such ship or vessel, unless the owner or owners of such ship or vessel shall, either directly or indirectly, be privy or accessory to, or in some way concerned in, the breach or violation of such act as aforesaid.

IX. All masters of ships, coasting, fishing, and of all other vessels whatsoever, whether laden or in ballast, coming into any harbor, port, river, creek, or any other part of the coasts of this island, shall, before breaking bulk, or landing passengers or baggage, and within twenty-four hours after their arrival, make report in writing, upon oath, to the collector of impost for the harbor or district wherein such vessel shall have arrived ; and the masters of all vessels having on board any wines, gin, brandy, rum, or other distilled spirituous liquors, tea, tobacco, goods, wares, or merchandise, of what nature or kind soever, shall also specify in such report the kinds of casks, packages, parcels, boxes, trunks, bales, and all other manner of things in which such wines, gin, brandy, rum, or other distilled spirituous liquors, tea, tobacco, goods, wares, and merchandise shall or may be contained, together with the marks and numbers thereof, and that they have not landed, nor suffered to be landed, sold, bartered, or exchanged, any wine, gin, brandy, rum, or other distilled spirituous liquors, tea, tobacco, goods, wares, or merchandise, at any port or place within this island, or on the coasts thereof, since their sailing from the port or place where the same were laden on board any ship or vessel for exportation, which oath the said collector is empowered to administer in the form following :

You, A B, do swear that the report which you have made, (read, or heard read, as the case may be,) and subscribed, contains a just and true account of all wines, gin, brandy, rum, or other spirituous liquors, tea, tobacco, goods, wares, or merchandise laden on board the   at the port of or any other port or ports, or elsewhere, before or since your sailing from   ; and that you have not landed, nor suffered to be landed, sold, or delivered, bartered, or exchanged, any wine, rum, brandy, gin, or other distilled spirituous liquors, tea, tobacco, goods, wares, or merchandise, at any port or place within this island, or on the coast thereof, since your sailing from   , or since your sailing from any other place. So help you God.

X. In every case, where any ship or vessel shall report or enter at any excise office or custom-house within this island, preparatory to, or with the intention of, trading or selling any goods, wares, or merchandise which she may have on board, the cargo of such vessel shall immediately thereafter be landed or checked by the collector of impost or controller of customs, or any landwaiter or revenue officer, for the port or place where the same shall be so entered ; and the duties to which the cargo on board such vessel, when so landed or checked in manner aforesaid, shall be found to be liable, shall be paid, or the payment thereof secured in manner prescribed by the said recited act of the nineteenth Victoria, chapter one, as amended by this act.

XI. When any landwaiter or preventive officer shall have made a seizure of any goods prohibited, or unlawfully imported, or attempted to be unlawfully imported, or landed in this island, it shall be the duty of such officer, and he is hereby required, to furnish to the nearest collector of impost a list or account of the goods so seized, before proceeding to the sale thereof, and which sale shall be made known by posting a notice thereof in the form prescribed in the schedule marked (A,) to this act annexed, in twelve of the most public places, at and in the vicinity of the place where such sale is to take place, at least fifteen days previous to such sale ; and the collector or collectors of impost who may receive such list of seizures, as aforesaid, are hereby required to furnish the same. annually, to the treasurer of this island, who shall lay the same before the house of assembly at the next session thereof.

XII. For the better and more effectually securing the several duties, fines, forfeitures, and penalties arising by virtue of this or any other act relating to the revenue now or hereafter to be in force, the chief justice, or, in his absence, any other judge of the supreme court, is hereby authorized and empowered, on application made by the attorney general, or other officer prosecuting on the part of the crown for that purpose, to grant a bailable writ or warrant against any person liable for the said duties, penalties, fines, and forfeitures ; and such person shall be imprisoned or detained in the county jail until he shall have given bail to answer the judgment and costs in any action to which he shall have rendered himself liable, or then commenced or pending against him for such duties, fines, forfeitures, and penalties.

XIII. There shall be allowed and paid on all wines, gin, brandy, rum, or other distilled spirituous liquors, tea, tobacco, and all goods, wares, and merchandise that have already been or that shall hereafter be imported into this island, or manufactured therein, on exportation of the same therefrom, a drawback equal in amount to the whole duty paid or secured to be paid on such on the importation thereof.

XIV. Any revenue officer having reasonable cause to suspect goods liable to forfeiture to be in any particular building, may, in company with any justice of the peace for the county where the building is situate, who is hereby required to accompany him, enter such building at any time between sunrise and sunset; but if the doors are fastened, then admission shall be first demanded, and the purpose for which entry is required, when declared, if admission shall not be given, the justice shall order the officer forcibly to enter, and when, in either case, entry shall be made. the officer shall search the building and seize all forfeited goods.

XV. Duties on goods importable before the coming into operation of an act imposing new duties, and whereon the duties have not been paid or secured, shall be collected under the new law, but forfeitures shall be recovered under the law under which they were incurred, notwithstanding such law may have expired.

XVI. During the continuance of this act it shall be lawful for the lieutenant governor, or other administrator of the government for the time being, to grant licenses to distil, extract, or manufacture spirituous liquors in this island, which licenses shall be in force from the date thereof, respectively, until the first day of May, one thousand eight hundred and sixty-five, and the rate or price of every such license shall be twenty-five pounds for each and every distillery, which sum shall be paid into the treasury of this island for the use of her Majesty's government ; and every person who shall pay the said sum of twenty-five pounds, or shall enter into, sign, seal, and execute a bond and warrant of attorney, with one good and sufficient surety, before the collector of impost for the district wherein the distillery of the person so seeking such license shall be situate, conditioned to pay such sum within six months, with interest thereon, from the date thereof, and shall produce to the treasurer of this island a certificate from such collector of the fact of such bond and warrant of attorney having been given for the amount aforesaid, (which bond and warrant of attorney the collector is hereby required to take before granting such certificate,) such person shall be entitled to receive a license to distil, extract, or manufacture spirituous liquors during the period for which such license shall be granted. The bond and warrant of attorney, to be given as last hereinbefore prescribed, shall be of like form and effect as the bond and warrant of attorney hereafter to be given by the importers of goods, wares, and merchandise to secure the payment of duties thereon, under the provisions of the said recited act, of the nineteenth Victoria, chapter one, as amended by this act.

XVII. It shall be unlawful for any person during the continuance of this act to distil, extract, or manufacture spirituous liquors in this island without having first obtained such license as aforesaid; and any person or persons who shall so distil, extract, or manufacture spirituous liquors, without first having obtained a license therefor, for every distillery as hereinbefore required, shall, for each and every offence, forfeit and pay to her Majesty a fine not exceeding one hundred pounds, to be paid into the treasury of this island, for the use of her Majesty's government.

XVIII. The owner or owners of any distilling, or other person or persons who shall manufacture any distilled spirituous liquors in this island, and in case such distillery shall be conducted or carried on by any servant or servants having the care and management of the same, such owners, masters, or servants, respectively, shall, on the first Monday in June, and on every first Monday in every alternate month hereafter, in each year during the continuance of this act, render a just and true account in writing, to the nearest collector of impost and excise, of the quantity of all spirituous liquors distilled or manufactured by him or them for the two months then last past; and shall also, in such account, state whether the spirituous liquors therein referred to have been distilled from molasses, or barley, or grain, and how much from each, respectively, and shall make and subscribe before the said collector the following oath, which oath the said collector is hereby required to administer:

"I, A B, do swear that the account which I have now rendered and subscribed contains a just and true account of all the rum, brandy, gin, or whiskey distilled by me, (or if entry be made by foreman or servant,) for any person or persons, since the   day of   last past; and, also, that the substances from which the same have been extracted or manufactured are truly mentioned and stated in the said account.   So help me God."

XIX. And the said owner, master, or servant, after making and subscribing the before-mentioned oath, shall forthwith pay or secure unto the said collector of impost and excise the amount of duty imposed and due on such liquors so manufactured, as aforesaid, during the two months then last past, the same to be paid or secured as directed by this act in the case of liquors or other goods and merchandise imported into this island.

XX. If any person shall neglect or refuse to make such return, or shall make a false return of the quantity of spirituous liquors so manufactured or distilled by him, or of the substances from which the same have been manufactured, or shall refuse to pay or secure the amount of duties on such liquors, such person shall, for each and every offence, forfeit and pay the sum of twenty pounds, and shall likewise forfeit the license to manufacture or distil, so granted to him as aforesaid, and no license shall or may be granted to any person whomsoever to manufacture or distil in the distillery of any person whose license shall be so forfeited and cancelled, for the period of six months next after the same shall have been so cancelled.

XXI. For the better detecting persons distilling, extracting, or manufacturing spirituous liquors, without license, as aforesaid, and also the better to enable the officers of the revenue collecting the duties imposed by this or any other act of the legislature on the distillation, extraction, manufacturing or importation of such spirituous liquors, or other dutiable articles, it shall be lawful for any collector of import, collector of the navigation laws, preventive officer, or other person appointed for collecting, securing, or protecting the revenue, and he is hereby authorized to enter into and upon all houses, or other buildings and premises wherein he may have suspicion, and of the sufficiency of such suspicion the officer shall be the sole judge, that spirituous liquors may have lately been or are being distilled, extracted, or manufactured, without license, or without the duties imposed by this or any other act, having been paid or secured therefor, or wherein he may suspect any goods, articles, or spirituous liquors liable to duty under this act or any other act of the legislature of this island, and illegally manufactured, distilled, or extracted, imported or landed are, and if, on investigation, he shall find such to have been or to be the case, he shall, and he is hereby authorized and required to seize and carry away the same, and sell the same at public auction, within fifteen days after such seizure, unless the owner of the spirits or other dutiable articles shall prove, to the satisfaction of the officer making the seizure, that no breach of this or any other act in force relating to the importing, distilling, extracting, or manufacturing of spirituous liquors, has been made, or that the duties payable in respect thereof have been paid; and the officer making the seizure shall be entitled to the same proportion of the amount of the sale as in the fifty-fourth section of the act nineteenth Victoria, chapter one, is awarded preventive officers and landwaiters making seizures; and a similar amount to that also pointed out in the said section of the said last recited act shall be paid into the treasury of this island for the use of her Majesty's government thereof.

XXII. Any distiller, or his agent, or servant, or other person, who shall be convicted of having wilfully and fraudulently made a return short of the real quantity of liquor made by him, or shall make a false return of the substances from which the same has been made, or who shall be convicted of having refused to account, or pay, or secure the duties at the times prescribed by law, or who shall have delayed his return, or payment, or security therefor, for more than ten days after the expiration of the two months from the day wherein he last accounted, shall, on conviction thereof, over and above the aforesaid penalty, be held not entitled to distil for six months from and after the day of such conviction, under the penalty of five pounds for each and every day he, or those employed by him, shall so distil after such conviction.

XXIII. The treasurer shall publish a list of the persons licensed to distil spirituous liquors, in the Royal Gazette newspaper, once in each and every month, instead of quarterly, as prescribed in and by the sixty-fifth section of the hereinbefore recited act of the nineteenth Victoria, chapter one.

XXIV. That any person or persons who shall, after the passing of this act, give to any collector of excise or preventive officer, or to any justice of the peace in this island, information of any unlicensed distillation being carried on within this island, or if any spirituous liquors which have not paid the duty imposed upon the same by the laws of this island, and which shall be liable to seizure, such person or persons shall, on the conviction of the parties so carrying on unlicensed distillation, or of the condemnation and sale of any such spirituous liquors which shall have been seized in consequence of the non-payment of the duties payable thereon, be entitled to receive the half of the fine which shall be imposed upon any such distiller, or one-half of the proceeds of any spirituous liquors which may be condemned and sold as aforesaid.

XXV. From and after the passing of this act, instead of the credit mentioned in the seventy-eighth section of the said recited act of the nineteenth Victoria, chapter one, to be given for duties on goods, wares, and merchandise to the importer thereof, as therein mentioned, the following terms of credit for duties shall be given—that is to say: If the said duties shall exceed the sum of ten pounds, and not amount to more than thirty pounds, a credit of three months shall be given therefor; and if the said duties shall exceed thirty pounds, a credit of six months shall be given for the payment thereof, and no longer time than six months shall in any case be given; and all bonds and recognizances hereafter to be entered into for securing the payment of duties on goods, wares, and merchandise of any kind whatsoever, shall bear interest on the amount thereof at the rate of six pounds per centum per annum; and such interest shall be computed and paid and payable from the day of the date of such bond or recognizance until the payment thereof: provided always, that nothing in this or any other act contained shall be held or construed to entitle or give any person or persons any right or claim to a longer term of credit for the amount of any bond or recognizance than the time therein mentioned for the payment thereof.

XXVI. The warrant of attorney by law required to be taken by collectors of impost, in addition to the recognizances directed to be entered into as security for the payment of duties of impost and excise, shall, as well as the defeazance thereon to be indorsed, be in the form in the schedule to this act annexed, marked (B,) or in such other form as the lieutenant governor, or other administrator of the government of this island for the time being, in council, may, from time to time, direct.

XXVII. It shall be competent and lawful for any of her Majesty's Queen's counsel in this island, when called upon so to do, in the absence, or in the event of the incapacity from illness of the attorney general or solicitor general, or when either of those offices shall be vacant, to sign all necessary declarations, pleas, bail pieces, and other papers required to be signed in order to enter up judgment in her Majesty's supreme court of judicature, on any warrant of attorney heretofore taken by collectors of impost and excise, in addition to the recognizance by law directed to be taken as security for the payment of duties of impost and excise, notwithstanding that such warrant of attorney shall be directed to the attorney general and solicitor general only; also, to issue execution on the same, to take all necessary steps to perfect execution, and to acknowledge satisfaction under any such circumstances as aforesaid when payment has been recovered or received.

XXVIII. All warrants of attorney which have heretofore been taken by collectors of impost and excise, in addition to the recognizance by law directed to be taken as security for payment of duties of impost and excise, shall, notwithstanding that the same shall not in all cases be found to have been strictly taken in accordance with the directions contained in the statutes in force respecting the same, or the taking or form of such warrants of attorney, be held and deemed to be good and valid, and to be sufficient to enable and authorize judgment to be entered up thereon in her Majesty's supreme court of judicature, as of the term of the said supreme court in Queen's county next preceding the date of entering up judgment or otherwise, as the case may be, and execution to be issued thereon for the recovery of the amount purporting to be secured thereby, and by the recognizance taken at the same time therewith.

XXIX. The tenth, twenty-fourth, forty-fourth, fifty-third, fifty-fourth, sixty-first, sixty-second, sixty-seventh, sixty-eighth, and eighty-first sections of the said hereinbefore recited act of the nineteenth Victoria, chapter one, shall be, and the same are hereby, repealed.

XXX. Any collector of impost and excise who shall neglect or omit to administer any of the oaths prescribed in and by the twenty-fifth, thirty-seventh, forty-ninth, seventieth, and seventy-second sections of the hereinbefore recited act of the nineteenth Victoria, chapter one, and in and by any of the sections of this act, shall, for each and every such neglect or omission, forfeit and pay into the treasury of this island the sum of fifty pounds for the use of her Majesty's government, to be recovered in the supreme court of judicature in her Majesty's name, in an action of debt, on the oath of a credible witness.

XXXI. It shall be unlawful for any person or persons to import into this island any indecent or obscene paintings, books, cards, lithographic or other engravings, or any other indecent or obscene articles; and if imported, the same shall be seized and destroyed by any collector of impost and excise, or preventive officer.

XXXII. All fines, penalties, and forfeitures, imposed under or by virtue of any of the provisions contained in the hereinbefore recited act of the nineteenth Victoria, chapter one, or of this act, may be prosecuted and sued for by information of her Majesty's attorney general, filed in the supreme court of this island.

XXXIII. This act shall go into operation and be in force immediately on the passing thereof, and from thence shall continue and be in force until the first day of May, in the year of our Lord one thousand eight hundred and sixty-five.

XXXIV. So soon as this act shall go into operation, the act of the twenty-sixth Victoria, chapter two, entitled "An act for raising a revenue," shall be, and the same is hereby, repealed.

DEMERARA—C. G. HANNAH, *Consul.*

APRIL 5, 1864.

I have the honor to send enclosed a condensed statement of the imports from the United States into this colony during the quarter just expired. I have compiled it from the best sources of information at my command.

Statement showing the quantity and value of the imports from the United States into Demerara for the quarter ended March 31, 1864.

Beef, 68 barrels, 530 ½-barrels, 65 ¼-barrels.
Pork, 943 barrels.
Potatoes, 357 hampers, 2,212 barrels.
Candles, 7,411 boxes.
Hams, 2,775 number and 69 tierces.
Lard, 3,245 tins and 200 pails.
Paper, 3,650 reams.
Corn, 2,461 bags.
Cornmeal, 1,648 barrels, 100 boxes.
Flour, 14,585 barrels.
Peas, 490 barrels, 100 bags.
Bread, 3,680 barrels.
Cheese, 1,700 boxes.
Bran, 500 bags.
Lard oil, 80 barrels.
White-oak staves, 204,064.
White-oak shingles, 1,620.
Shooks, 4,301.
Red-oak staves, 195,572.
Kerosene, 100 boxes.

Potash, 78 barrels.
Tobacco, 50 cases, 1 hogshead, 4 kegs.
Buckets, 150 dozen, 100 cases.
Wooden hoops, 200 bundles, 11,500 number.
Spruce scantling, 36,688 feet, 326 pieces.
White pine lumber, 126,563 feet.
Pilot bread, 148 barrels.
Mackerel, 49 barrels.
Hay, 188 bales.
White-oak headings, 7,600.
Matches, 101 cases.
Crackers, 35 barrels.
Oil meal, 6 puncheons.
Tallow, 25 kegs.
Vinegar, 50 barrels.
Butter, 32 tins.
1 suction engine.
Ice and provisions.

Total value, $259,730 22.

H. Ex. Doc. 60——7

JULY 14, 1864.

I have the honor to forward enclosed the following documents, viz:

Condensed statements of imports from the United States for the quarter ending Ju .e 30, 1864—enclosure No. 1.

Condensed statements of exports to the United States for the same time—enclosure No. 2.   *   *   *   *   *   *

No exchange rates are published here except those on England.   These have not been received since I have been here.   *   *   *   *

Statement showing the description, quantity, and value of the exports from Demerara to the United States, with the names of the ports where shipped, during the quarter ended June 30, 1864; also the number, tonnage, and nationality of the vessels.

No. of vessel.	Nationality.	Where to.	Tonnage.	SUGAR.			MOLASSES.		OLD METAL.		COCOA-NUTS.	HIDES.	COFFEE.	CANVAS AND ROPE.	SUNDRIES.	TOTAL.
				Hhds.	Tcs.	Bbl.	Pun.	Casks	Tons.	Pounds.						
1	British	Baltimore	529	942		358	53									807,432 72
1	American	New York	555	159	31	358	38									90,778 13
1	Do.	Bangor	137			50										674 84
1	British	New York	251			13					1,000	785	39 bbls.	4,616 lbs.		14,780 69
1	Do.	Baltimore	194	194		905	99			56,351						91,729 83
1	American	New York	901	64		190				141,068						11,131 31
1	British	New York	94						58	53,714		3,185 lbs.			6,148 lbs. old copper, 72 empty casks.	3,104 92
1	Do.	Baltimore	597	920		610	78		920							34,169 99
1	Do.	Baltimore	154	156		288	88								Clothing, plate, &c.	92,433 35
1	Do.	New York	913			9			139 19-20	91,746						3,117 94
1	Do.	New York	251				108	416				528	25 bbls.			10,983 70
1	Do.	New York	134													7,393 73
12			3,421	1,077	31	1,988	356	416	447 19-20	963,099	1,000		64 bbls.	4,616 lbs.		177,394 85

Statement showing the description and quantity of the imports into Demerara from the United States, with the names of the ports whence shipped, during the quarter ended June 30, 1864; also, the number, tonnage, and nationality of the vessels.

Nationality	Where from	Number of vessels	Tonnage	Flour (Barrels)	Corn meal (Bbls.)	Bread (Bbls.)	Corn (Bags)	Candles (Boxes)	Lard (Tins)	Lumber (Feet)	Ice (Tons)	Pork (Pounds)	Pails (Dozen)	Potatoes (Bbls.)	Cheese (Boxes)	Beef (Bbls.)
British	Baltimore	1	238	1,481	300	400	700	1,000	400							
American	Boston	1	335								318		†100			125 half
British	New York	1	350	409	100	150		1,000	300			100		300	300	900 do.
American	do	1	255	502	150	300	400	100	900			543		280	100	
British	do	1	140	550		50		100	150			100		50	50	
British	Do	1	171	200				50								86 bbls.
American	Boston	1	137				300			93,000		5				50 do.
British	New York	1	913	500	25	308		600	560			25				45 do.
American	Baltimore	1	194	1,323	234	300	400	600	400			477			900	
British	New York	1	201	2,480		500	700	900	900			251	50	283*	900	350 half
British	do	1	297		100			700	900			128				
American	do	1	96	700	966	400	400	500	900	15,106		50			100	100 do.
British	Baltimore	1	948	1,384		300		400	400			100				130 do.
Do	New York	1	154	850				700	500			443	100		150	
Do	do	1	141	1,175			900	685	500			128				300 do.
American	Boston	1	251	935					900	108,172						70 bbls.
Do	Bangor	1	976		150				596	155,000						
Do	New York	1	237	560		225	900	500	100	12,588						335 half
Do	Boston	1	296						100	139,290			†10)			
British	New York	1	390	225		900		100	900	15,056		900		900	304	900 do.
American	do	1	984	980		350	50		900			100		170	100	300 do.
British	Baltimore	1	134	1,017	150	275	375	600	400							
British	do	1	255	1,529	300	400	500	700	400							
		25	**5,605**	**17,085**	**1,625**	**4,058**	**4,926**	**8,775**	**6,376**	**538,212**	**318**	**9,654**	**350**	**1,263**	**1,504**	

* Besides large quantities of iced provisions.   † Together with ice and iced provisions.

Statement showing the description and quantity of the imports into Demerara—Continued.

Nationality	Where from	Number of vessels	Tonnage	Hams Quantity	Oil Gallons	Tobacco Hhds	Peas Quantity	Matches Cases	Paper Reams	Hoops Quantity	Staves Bbl. oak	Bran Bags	Brooms Doz.	Tallow Kegs	Hay Quantity	Shooks Quantity	Shingles Quantity
British	Baltimore	1	928	16 tierces	500						5,040						
American	Boston	1	335			12											
British	New York	1	250	6 tierces			25 bbls.	100									
American	do.	1	255	150 hams			45 bbls.			30,000	22,390	30					
British	do.	1	140				25 bbls.		600		16,000				2 planks and 1 car riage		
Do	do.	1	171														
American	Boston	1	137	10 tierces	25 casks	10	30 bbls.				21,600		25	60			
British	New York	1	213	10 tierces	26 bbls.	3		30			98,000						
Do	Baltimore	1	194	10 tierces			150 bbls.		1,000	250 bund.	5,000						
American	New York	1	201						500		6,000				113 truss	3,400	
British	Baltimore	1	397				105 bbls.				43,000	100					
Do	New York	1	96	374 hams					1,500		15,600					339 bund.	40,000
American	Baltimore	1	248		50 cases										50 bales	300 bund.	
British	do.	1	154														
Do	New York	1	141														
American	Boston	1	251	30 boxes			50 bbls.				17,700						308 bund.
Do	Bangor	1	276														
Do	New York	1	527														
Do	Boston	1	296					75	100	12,300	2,400 hds.					350 bund.	
British	New York	1	370	3 tierces			61 bags				4,600	100				900 bund.	
American	do.	1	284													300 bund.	
British	Baltimore	1	134	10 tierces													
Do	do.	1	255														
		22	5,605			25		195	3,700			220					

OCTOBER 8, 1864.

In accordance with the regulations of the Department of State, I forward herewith my annual report on the trade of my consular district for that portion of the year ending on the 30th of September last, which comprises all the time I have filled the office of consul at this port.

I enclose herewith six schedules, viz:

No. 1 comprises a statement of imports and exports for the years 1862 and 1863, with the respective increase and decrease of the same for the latter year.

No. 2 comprises a statement of exports of colonial products for the same time with the respective increase and decrease on the same for the latter year.

No. 3 comprises a list of the customs duties at this port.

No. 4 comprises a statement of the imports of produce, and the exports of produce not colonial, since the first day of January last.

No. 5 comprises a statement of the exports of colonial produce for the same time.

No. 6 comprises a statement of all the exports to the United States for the same time.

It is impossible for me to arrive at the exact amounts of all the imports from the United States, nor have I any means of arriving at the values thereof.

I give herewith, however, the amounts of some of the chief staples of exportation, as far as I have been able to ascertain them. They are, at least, approximatively correct:

Flour, 47,569 barrels; beef, 8,487 barrels; candles, 20,808 boxes; staves, 900,413; bread, 11,228 barrels; paper, 11,150 reams; lumber, 1,083,608 feet; pork, 7,295 barrels; lard, 14,624 tins; corn, 9,458 bags; corn-meal, 5,356 barrels.

This forms but a portion of the infinite variety of articles imported from the United States of America.

These imports were brought in 48 English vessels of the registered tonnage of 10,668 tons, and 28 American vessels of the registered tonnage of 5,488 tons. The chief, in fact almost the only articles of importation from the United States are provisions and lumber. I think it not too much to say that four-fifths of all the articles of food of any kind whatever imported into the colony come from the southern States of America. Large quantities of lumber are also imported from the eastern States. The greater part of the lumber used here, however, comes, I think, from the British provinces of North America.

The chief articles of importation from the United States are provisions. These are of all kinds. Not only flour and corn, and the other great staples of life, but large quantities of meats and vegetables, arrive by almost every vessel. Large quantities of ice and iced provisions are also imported chiefly from Boston.

In this connexion it may be as well for me to say that the duty on kerosene and coal oils, heretofore one of the chief articles of import from the United States, has been increased to two dollars per gallon. This, however, not without violent opposition in many quarters. It has been proposed to prohibit their importation altogether; but that measure could, I think, have no chance of success.

The chief articles of export are sugars, rum, and molasses. These, together with cocoa-nuts, seem to be almost the only articles raised in the colony for exportation. Occasionally a small quantity of coffee is exported, but this is of rare occurrence. Large quantities of the Wallaba shingle are also exported, but not to the United States. Almost the only articles of export to the United States are sugars and molasses. Within the last few months, however, large quantities of old metals, the refuse of the recent fires, have been sent thither.

I regret to say, however, that whether owing to the increased rate of duty, or from some other cause, the exportation of sugars to the United States seems, for the present to have entirely ceased.

For some years past the high prices of labor and the low prices of sugar have materially interfered with the prosperity of the planters. Many of them have been ruined, and many fine estates have been abandoned, from a combination of these two causes. During the last year, however, labor has been more plentiful, owing to an increased immigration, not only from China and India, but also from Barbadoes and other places. This fact, combined with the advanced prices of sugar in England and elsewhere, has given a new impulse to its culture. Large fortunes have been made and are being made daily, and the natural prosperity of the colony seems to be on the increase.

Comparative statement showing the imports and exports into and from the ports of Georgetown and Berbice, in the colony of British Guiana, for the years 1862 and 1863.

[Compiled from the best authorities.]

IMPORTS.

Articles.	From Jan. 1 to Dec. 31, 1862.	From Jan. 1 to Dec. 31, 1863.	Increase in 1863.	Decrease in 1863.
Beef ....barrels..	4,705	4,069	....	636
Bread ....do....	24,850	25,357	507	....
Bricks ....number..	1,867,400	1,868,635	1,235	....
Butter ....pounds..	565,625	56,798	....	4,827
Candles, tallow........do....	390,857	328,140	....	62,717
composition........do....	139,064	183,671	44,607	....
Cheese ....do....	304,834	252,346	....	52,488
Cigars ....number..	1,116,415	1,299,637	183,222	....
Coals ....hogsheads..	26,853	24,583	....	2,270
Do.....................tons..	19,887	19,598	....	289
Cocoa ....pounds..	94,931	228,759	133,828	....
Coffee ....do....	51,283	2,552	....	49,271
Confectionery ....do....	18,104	41,771	23,667	....
Cordage ....cwt..	1,841	1,948	107	....
Corn ....bags..	33,012	22,777	....	10,235
Corn-meal and oat-meal ...pounds..	2,714,900	3,311,922	597,022	....
Fish, dried ....quintals..	64,902	67,474	2,572	....
Salmon ....barrels..	332	249	....	83
Mackerel ....do....	4,189	5,578	1,389	....
Herring, &c. ....do....	5,048	5,964	916	....
Fish, smoked ....pounds..	39,224	18,011	....	21,213
Flour ....barrels..	86,567	80,590	....	5,977
Ground feed ....bags..	5,179	5,000	....	179
Gunpowder ....pounds..	5,940	15,566	9,626	....
Hams and bacon ....do....	336,348	32,384	....	43,034
Hay ....do....	913,640	667,290	....	246,350
Hoops, wood ....number..	1,023,126	1,224,470	201,344	....
iron ....cwt..	7,969	6,342	....	1,627
Horses ....number..	69	98	29	....
Lime, building ....hogsheads..	1,149	1,125	....	24
temper ....perches..	2,087	1,678	....	409
Lard ....pounds..	453,722	500,617	46,895	....
Lumber ....feet..	7,356,454	6,323,856	....	1,032,598
Malt liquor ....hogsheads..	1,999	1,880	....	119
Do. ....dozens..	93,624	45,257	....	48,367
Matches ....gross..	3,223	1,539	....	1,664
Mules ....number..	179	97	....	82

Comparative statement showing the imports and exports, &c.—Continued.

Articles.	From Jan. 1 to Dec. 31, 1862.	From Jan. 1 to Dec. 31, 1863.	Increase in 1863.	Decrease in 1863.
Oats ....bushels..	34,559	44,355	9,796	....
Oils ....gallons..	68,106	80,602	12,496	....
Onions ....pounds..	957,066	795,547	....	161,519
Pitch and tar ....barrels..	943	1,083	140	....
Pork ....barrels..	15,702	9,825	....	5,877
Potatoes ....bushels..	45,149	42,931	....	2,198
Rice....................bags..	124,619	164,084	39,465	....
Salt......................pounds..	585,193	1,069,930	484,747	....
Shingles ....number..	537,748	692,000	154,252	....
Shooks ....packages..	35,703	51,077	5,374	....
Slates..................number..	71,200	173,400	102,200	....
Soap ....pounds..	1,943,325	542,775	....	1,400,500
Staves, white-oak ....number..	866,834	334,522	....	32,312
, red-oak .....number..	357,105	451,721	94,616	....
Sugar refined................cwt..	353	501	148	....
foreign..........hogsheads..	770	251	....	519
Tea ....pounds..	18,945	29,433	10,488	....
Tobacco, leaf.............do....	382,952	273,234	....	109,718
manufactured......do....	25,261	41,833	16,572	....
pipes.............gross..	5,192	3,479	....	1,713
Brandy ....gallons..	40,275	61,081	20,806	....
Gin ....do....	27,789	56,957	29,168	....
Rum ....puncheons..	177	120	....	57
Whiskey ....gallons..	31	82	51	....
Liquors, &c ....gallons..	1,233	1,746	513	....
Wine ....gallons..	28,442	17,032	....	11,410
Do. ....dozens..	2,647	2,154	....	493

EXPORTS.*

Articles.	From Jan. 1 to Dec. 31, 1862.	From Jan. 1 to Dec. 31, 1863.	Increase in 1863.	Decrease in 1863.
Beef......................barrels..	871	865	....	6
Bread ....do....	935	1,695	760	....
Bricks ....number..	40,000	2,500	....	37,500
Butter ....pounds..	18,818	19,921	1,103	....
Candles, tallow.............do....	16,580	46,880	30,300	....
composition........do....	4,197	5,812	1,615	....
Cheese.....................do....	16,161	3,333	....	12,828
Cigars ....number..	29,000	49,800	20,800	....
Coals ....hogsheads..	....	240	230	....
Do. ....tons..	220	217	....	3
Cocoa ....pounds..	5,370	126,085	120,715	....
Coffee ....do....	1,610	112,707	111,097	....
Confectionery ....do....	117	10,570	10,453	....
Cordage ....cwt..	3	1	....	2
Corn ....bags..	1,236	1,480	244	....
Corn-meal and oat-meal...pounds..	353,612	371,740	18,128	....
Fish, dried.............quintals..	2,363	946	....	1,417
Salmon ....barrels..	36	23	....	13
Mackerel ....do....	372	416	44	....
Herring, &c..............do....	1,609	719	....	890
Fish, smoked ....pounds..	6,720	....	....	6,720
Flour....................barrels..	13,316	10,714	....	2,602
Ground feed.................bags..	35	8	....	27
Gunpowder ....pounds..	4,750	1,500	....	3,250
Ham and bacon.........do....	1,178	13,570	12,392	....
Hay.......................do....	14,488	59,892	43,454	....

* Of produce not colonial.

Comparative statement showing the imports and exports, &c.—Continued.

Articles.	From Jan. 1 to Dec. 31, 1862.	From Jan. 1 to Dec. 31, 1863.	Increase in 1863.	Decrease in 1863.
Hoops, wood............number..	47,730	7,920	....	39,810
iron ....cwt..	3	42	39	....
Horses ....number..	5	....	....	5
Lime, building ......hogsheads..	....	4	....	....
temper ....perches..	30	26	....	4
Lard ....pounds..	48,695	27,350	....	21,345
Lumber ....feet..	268,755	489,140	220,391	....
Malt liquor ....hogsheads..	314	41	....	273
Do. ....dozens..	2,616	5,127	2,511	....
Matches..............gross..	510	....	....	510
Mules..............number..	2	2	....	....
Oats ....bushels..	888	18	....	870
Oils..............gallons..	2,370	9,024	6,654	....
Onions ....pounds..	82,876	65,327	....	17,549
Pitch and tar ....barrels..	6	92	86	....
Pork ....do..	1,191	1,998	807	....
Potatoes ....bushels..	855	856	1	....
Rice..............bags..	32,073	49,622	17,549	....
Salt ....pounds..	95,981	89,818	....	6,163
Shingles ....number..	60,000	225,000	165,000	....
Shooks ....packages..	2,966	924	....	2,042
Slates ....number..	9,710	22,820	13,110	....
Soap ....pounds..	200,773	223,179	22,406	....
Staves, white-oak ....number..	....	....	....	....
red oak ....do....	80,040	22,365	....	57,675
Sugar, refined ....cwt..	70	73	3	....
foreign........hogsheads..	514	250	....	258
Tea..............pounds..	1,263	6,708	5,445	....
Tobacco, leaf............do....	3,100	12,332	9,232	....
manufactured......do....	16,401	6,743	....	9,658
pipes ....gross..	939	37	....	902
Brandy............gallons..	2,055	3,342	1,287	....
Gin ....do....	288	296	....	8
Rum ....puncheons..	177	94	....	83
Whiskey ....gallons..	478	....	....	478
Liquors, &c..............do....	667	355	....	312
Wine ....do....	1,250	2,761	1,511	....
Do. ....dozens..	139	312	173	....

Statement of exports of colonial produce from the ports of Georgetown and Berbice, in the colony of British Guiana, for the years 1862 and 1863.

Articles.	1862.	1863.	Increase in 1862.	Dec'se in 1863.
Sugar ....hogsheads..	58,193	65,326	7,133	....
Do. ....tierces..	2,619	4,205	1,586	....
Do. ....barrels..	13,581	15,884	2,303	....
Do. ....bags..	21,783	46,942	25,159	....
Rum ....puncheons..	23,801	27,486	3,685	....
Do. ....hogsheads..	3,308	3,958	650	....
Do. ....barrels..	2,304	2,361	57	....
Molasses ....casks..	3,377	5,704	2,327	....
Timber ....feet..	652,122	407,839	....	244,283
Charcoal ....barrels..	27,521	23,091	....	4,430
Cocoa-nuts ....number..	558,965	532,322	....	26,643
Shingles ....do....	5,951,400	7,859,150	1,907,750	....

Custom-house duties.

Jamaica, free.

Beef................	$3 00 per barrel.
Beer................	24 per dozen.
in hogsheads	5 00 per hogshead.
Brandy	2 00 per gallon.
Bread	50 per 100 pounds.
Bricks, building	30 per 1,000.
fire	30 per 1,000.
Butter	2 per pound.
Candles, tallow......	3 per pound.
composition.	5 per pound.
Cheese................	2 per pound.
Coals, in hogsheads ..	24 per hogshead.
loose	30 per ton.
Cocoa	1½ per pound.
Coffee	1½ per pound.
Corn	5 per bushel.
Corn-meal	25 per 100 pounds.
Crackers	50 per 100 pounds.
Fish	50 per quintal.
Flour	1 00 per barrel.
Geneva	2 00 per gallon.
Hams	2 per pound.
Hay	10 per 100 pounds.
Herrings	75 per barrel.
Hoops, iron	10 per 112 pounds.
wood	1 50 per 1,000.
Horses................	7 00 per head.
Lard	2 per pound.
Lime	25 per hogshead.
tempér	25 per puncheon.
Lumber, white-pine ..	2 00 per 1,000 feet.
pitch-pine...	2 00 per 1,000 feet.
Mackerel............	1 00 per barrel.
Matches	1 00 per gross.

Mules	$5 00 per head.
Oats................	5 per bushel.
Oils, excepting the mineral oils hereafter mentioned and essential, perfumed, and castor oils	15 per gallon.
Paraffine, kerosene, coal oils, and other mineral oils, of an explosive nature...	2 00 per gallon.
Patent fuel	30 per ton.
Peas, bird's-eye.....	5 per bushel.
split	5 per bushel.
Pork	3 00 per barrel.
Porter, in hogsheads.	5 00 per hogshead.
Potatoes	8 per bushel.
Rice	25 per 100 pounds.
Salmon	2 00 per barrel.
Soap	1 per pound.
Salt	½ per pound.
Staves, red-oak	1 50 per 1,000.
white-oak ...	2 00 per 1,000.
Shooks	8.
Tar................	50 per barrel.
Pitch	50 per barrel.
Tobacco	18 per pound.

All other goods 10 per cent. ad valorem.

Trade allowances.

There is an allowance of 5 per cent. on white-pine lumber, for splits. No allowance for pitch-pine.

Statement showing the imports and exports into and from the ports of George-town and Berbice, in the colony of British Guiana, from the 1st of July to the 30th of September, 1864.

Articles.	Imports.	Exports.	Articles.	Imports.	Exports.
Beef ....bbls.	4,157	506	Lumber ....feet.	6,599,919	277,438
Bread...........bbls.	13,645	1,085	Malt liquor ...hhds.	1,726	21
Bricks............no.	1,347,992	15,000	Do. ....doz.	51,896	1,667
Butter ....lbs.	466,801	16,849	Matches ......gross.	9,380	128
Candles, tallow ..lbs.	474,598	7,810	Mules ....no	200	....
Do. comp'n..lbs.	106,169	4,326	Oats ....bush.	67,151	....
Cheese ....lbs.	180,858	373	Oils ....galls.	68,942	5,653
Cigars .... no.	925,450	23,975	Onions ....lbs.	557,920	82,243
Coals ....hhds.	18,800	145	Peas and beans.bags.	7,632	406
Do. ....tons.	14,451	269	Pitch and tar...bbls.	1,729	89
Cocoa............lbs.	104,451	72,300	Pork ....bbls.	10,025	1,163
Coffee............lbs.	27,605	42,400	Potatoes......bush.	22,629	1,029
Confectionery....lbs.	22,669	268	Rice ....bags.	81,567	17,158
Cordage ....cwt.	5,216	18	Salt ....lbs.	945,769	2,210
Corn ....bags.	14,614	1,902	Shingles ....no.	845,400	561,000
Corn-meal and oat-			Shooks ....bundles.	52,880	1,039
meal ....lbs.	1,696,013	142,990	Slates ....no.	265,315	23,886
Fish, dried.. quintals.	54,265	560	Soap ....lbs.	682,803	76,089
Salmon ....bbls.	138	10	Staves, w.oak...no.	462,434	....
Mackerel.......bbls.	4,704	564	red-oak..no.	618,098	5,003
Herrings ....bbls.	4,206	342	Sugar, refined..cwt.	21,641	125
Fish, smoked ....lbs.	19,129	450	foreign. hhds.	569	561
Flour ....bbls.	51,028	11,259	Tea. ....lbs.	16,471	701
Ground feed....bags.	2,682	36	Tobacco, leaf... lbs.	213,141	17,716
Gunpowder . ....lbs.	21,250	6,320	man'f ..lbs.	11,320	7,829
Hams, bacon ....lbs.	219,920	3,676	pipes.gross.	3,800	113
Hay ....lbs.	823,461	103,937	Brandy, forg'n.galls.	28,271	2,807
Hoops, wood.....no.	1,355,086	14,400	Gin... " galls.	18,546	514
iron ..... cwt.	8,503	7	Rum... " punch.	171	95
Horses ....no.	68	7	Whiskey, " galls.	50	....
Lime, building .hhds.	1,288	....	Liquors,&c. "galls.	513	594
Do. temper..punch.	1,854	7	Wine.. " galls.	22,906	2,424
Lard ....lbs.	475,083	38,125	Do... " galls.	1,318	308

Exports of colonial produce from the ports of Georgetown and Berbice from the 1st of January to the 30th of September, 1864.

Sugar ....hogsheads..	37,729	Molasses ....casks..	7,096
Do. ....tierces..	3,298	Cotton............. ...bales..	182
Do. ....barrels..	10,153	Timber...............feet..	643,462
Do. ..:....... ....bags..	34,397	Charcoal ....barrels..	18,725
Rum ....punch..	16,478	Cocoa-nuts...........number..	417,909
Do. ....hogsheads..	2,702	Shingles...........number..	6,395,005
Do. ....barrels..	1,563		...

Exports to the United States from the colony of British Guiana from the 1st of January to the 30th of September, 1864.

Sugar, 2,951 hogsheads, 4,399 barrels, 123 tierces; molasses, 1,647 puncheons, 931 casks, 12 barrels; coffee, 5 tierces, 158 barrels; peanuts, 700 bushels, 350 bags; cocoa-nuts, 1,000; besides large quantities of old metals. Total value of the same, $390,364 83. Carried in 30 British vessels, registered tonnage 5,900 tons; carried in 12 American vessels, registered tonnage 1,753 tons.

Statement showing the description and value of the exports from Calcutta, the production of Bengal, and the ports where shipped, during the quarter ended December 31, 1863, (compiled from official invoices.)

Where shipped.	Description.	Value, including costs and charges.		
		R.	*A.*	*P.*
New York	Cotton	19,544	12	5
New London	Hemp, twine, and India-rubber	34,063	14	0
New York	Jute and linseed	133,582	0	0
Do	Coir, matting, and saltpetre	20,645	10	8
Boston	Indigo, shellac, gunny cloth, &c	73,407	13	11
New York	Linseed	8,562	11	1
Boston	Goat skins, saltpetre, India-rubber, &c	53,902	9	7
Do	Linseed, gunny cloth, and jute cuttings	28,927	2	0
Do	Lac dye, goat skins, cow and buffalo hides	15,019	7	0
Do	Cow and buffalo hides, goat skins, linseed, &c	102,512	8	6
Do	Saltpetre, goat and sheep skins, gunny cloth, &c	53,160	14	9
Do	Lac dye, goat skins, linseed, &c	172,932	6	3
New York	Buffalo hides	5,460	5	6
Boston	Linseed, shellac, lac dye, &c	28,128	9	0
Do	Castor oil, cow hides, and rice	46,393	12	7
Do	Linseed, saltpetre, hides, &c	212,910	12	3
Do	Saltpetre	60,358	8	8
Do	Linseed, saltpetre, shellac, &c	173,022	0	6
Do	Linseed and shellac	45,702	9	4
New York	Linseed	8,644	4	6
Boston	Cow hides	2,080	5	4
Do	Linseed, shellac, lac dye, &c	66,693	6	10
Do	Rice, dry ginger, shellac, &c	201,609	9	6
Do	Linseed and buffalo hides	19,936	13	9
Do	Saltpetre and buffalo hides	10,752	0	2
Do	Saltpetre, linseed, hides, &c	146,211	5	7
Do	Saltpetre, linseed, hides, &c	38,134	13	2
New York	Lac dye	6,693	13	9
Do	Saltpetre, linseed, and buffalo hides	65,683	7	9
	Total rupees	1,854,678	8	4
	Total in dollars	$927,339 00		

Statement showing the description and value of the exports from Calcutta, the production of the East Indies, and the ports where shipped, during the quarter ended June 30, 1864, (compiled from official invoices.)

Where shipped.	Description.	Value, including costs and charges.		
		R.	*A.*	*P.*
Boston	Indigo, 40 chests	22,714	4	11
New York	Gunny bags, 150 bales	7,386	14	6
Boston	Goat skins, saltpetre, lac dye, linseed, and rugs	43,158	1	8
Do	Saltpetre, linseed, buffalo and cow hides	33,853	10	9
Do	Tragacanth gum, India-rubber, and senna leaves	2,960	15	5
Do	Saltpetre, linseed, goat skins, and castor oil	97,170	2	0
New York	Saltpetre, 1,296 bags	34,463	12	3
San Francisco	Gunny bags, 150 bales	9,657	0	0
Boston	Jute, 559 bales	12,948	8	4

Statement showing the description and value of the exports, &c.—Continued.

Where shipped.	Description.	Value, including costs and charges.
		R. A. P.
Boston	Saltpetre, 1,531 bags	49,175 14 6
New York	Saltpetre, 1,030 bags	32,838 8 6
Boston	Jute, 441 bales	10,215 3 2
New York	Gunny bags, shellac, and jute	31,796 4 0
Boston	Saltpetre, 1,038 bags	32,587 4 3
Do	Saltpetre, hides, skins, and linseed	93,377 13 11
Do	Gunny bags, 50 bales	2,123 4 0
New York	General goods and merchandise	183,499 6 11
Boston	Goat skins, 20 bales	4,400 7 3
New York and Boston	General goods and merchandise	187,657 14 6
New York	Jute, 386 bales	3,184 2 9
Boston	Cow hides and linseed	9,966 2 6
Do	General goods and merchandise	54,818 5 10
Do	Saltpetre, linseed, lac dye, and skins	17,014 13 6
Do	General goods and merchandise	101,950 11 6
Do	Jute, linseed, and cow hides	32,449 5 0
Do	Indigo, linseed, cotton, lac dye, and gunny bags	39,739 10 1
Do	Jute, ginger, and India-rubber	17,867 3 2
Do	Jute, 50 bales	1,158 3 0
Do	Goat skins, 12 bales	4,900 7 4
Do	General goods and merchandise	134,244 8 9
Do	India-rubber, 185 bags	4,124 2 2
Do	India-rubber, 53 bales	1,136 8 9
Do	Lac dye, gunny bags, linseed, and jute	15,588 5 3
Do	General goods and merchandise	57,850 11 8
Do	Buffalo hides, 30 bales	6,636 13 9
New York	Indigo, 10 chests	4,712 11 0
Boston	Shellac and lac dye	3,576 3 0
San Francisco	Gunny bags, 250 bales	12,766 9 5
New York	Jute and linseed	121,491 10 3
Boston	Indigo, 78 chests	38,055 3 0
Do	Castor oil, 200 cases	6,085 8 7
Do	Linseed and gunny bags	49,152 5 11
Do	General goods and merchandise	177,110 0 0
Do	Jute and jute cuttings	6,112 5 6
Do	Indigo, 14 chests	6,708 0 0
New York	Indigo, 51 chests	33,982 6 0
Boston	Saltpetre, India-rubber, cow hides, dry ginger, &c.	67,475 3 6
Do	Saltpetre, linseed, hides, and gunny bags	37,310 1 3
Do	Linseed and ginger	125,161 11 7
San Francisco	Ginger and gunny pockets	3,263 11 6
New York	Linseed, 1,000 bags	4,832 10 0
Do	Linseed, 1,000 bags	4,832 10 0
Boston	Goat skins, 20 bales	6,976 15 0
Do	Saltpetre, indigo, linseed, hides, skins, and India-rubber.	118,067 13 9
New York	Castor oil and ginger	6,741 15 3
Do	Linseed, 500 bags	4,770 2 0
Do	Shellac, coir matting, and door mats	21,603 12 6
Do	Cashmere goods, 1 package	4,304 3 0
Boston	Linseed, goat skins, and buffalo hides	31,144 7 6
Do	Saltpetre, linseed, jute, gunny bags, and rags	53,985 9 0
Do	Saltpetre, 1,060 bags	28,269 8 0
New York	Table rice, 1,228 bags	9,614 1 8
	Total rupees	2,382,712 0 0
	Total dollars	$1,191,356 00

ANTIGUA—M. GALODY, *Consular Agent.*

SEPTEMBER 30, 1864.

In conformity with section 153 of consular regulations, I send by this mail an annual report, in tabular form, of the commerce and shipping of this island for the last year.   *   *   *   *   *   *   *

I have nothing of moment or any change to report, save the fresh impulse given to the planting of cotton. But, as the result cannot be known till the gathering of the crop, which will only take place next year, I refrain for the present from expressing any opinion.   *   *   *   *

Statement showing the general imports into the colony of Antigua in the year 1863.

ARTICLES.	Countries whence imported.	QUANTITIES IMPORTED.			Quantities entered for home consumption.	Value in sterling of total imports.	Average price fixed for the value, (if calculated officially.)	DUTY.	
		In British vessels.	In foreign vessels.	Total.				Gross amount received in sterling.	Rate, and when imposed.
						£ s. d.	£ s. d.	£ s. d.	
Ale and beer .... dozen	United Kingdom	2,044½	......	2,044½	......	1,067 8 9	0 7 6	......	9d. per dozen, 30 per cent additional to 16th June, 30 per cent additional from 16th June to 16th July—the percentage abolished on the latter date.
	Barbadoes	405½	......	405½	......	150 18 9			
		3,949	......	3,949	356½	1,218 7 6		155 13 6	
Ale and beer .... tun	United Kingdom	49½	......	49½	......	792 0 0	16 0 0	......	£3, as above.
	Barbadoes	5	......	5	......	80 0 0			
		54½	......	54½	56½	872 0 0		135 5 0	
Bread and biscuits ...... bbl.	United Kingdom	5½	......	5½	......	3 3 0		......	1s. 6d. per barrel, as above.
	Barbadoes	33	......	33	......	19 16 0			
	Hamburg	......	15	15	......	9 0 0	19 0		
	Dutch Colonies	......	5	5	......	3 0 0			
	United States	515	......	515	......	309 0 0			
		553½	20	573½	549½	343 19 0		53 6 9	
Bread and biscuits ...... 100 lbs.	United Kingdom	308	......	308	......			......	9s. per 100 lbs. from 16th July.
	Barbadoes	18,100	......	18,100	......				
	Dominica	300	......	300	......				
	St. Kitts	1,000	......	1,000	......				
	United States	94,354	3,000	87,354	......				
		104,662	3,000	107,662	90,960	1,076 12 4	90 19 2	......	
Beef and pork .... bbl. of 200 lbs.	United Kingdom	11½	......	11½	......	58 0 0	40 0 0	......	
	Barbadoes	596	......	596	......	1,178 0 0			
	St. Kitts	585	......	585	......	450 0 0			
	Anguilla	1	......	1	......				

Statement showing the general imports into the colony of Antigua in the year 1863—Continued.

ARTICLES.	Countries whence imported.	QUANTITIES IMPORTED.			Quantities entered for home consumption.	Value in sterling of total imports.	Average price fixed for the value. (If calculated officially.)	Gross amount received in sterling.	DUTY. Rate, and when imposed.
		In British vessels.	In foreign vessels.	Total.					
Butter ....lbs.	British North America........	2		2		£4 0 0			
	United States...............	1,952	229	2,181		4,396 0 0			
	Danish Colonies............	54		54		110 0 0			
	Dutch Colonies.............	4		4		3 0 0			
	French Colonies............		10	10		90 0 0			
		2,864	229	3,075½	2,744½	6,151 0 0		2,569 2 11	
............lbs.	United Kingdom.............	21,754		21,754		815 15 6			
	Barbadoes..................	8,687		8,687		325 15 3			
	Trinidad...................	5,250		5,250		96 17 6	9		
	British North America.....	175		175		6 11 3			
	Dutch Colonies............	250	130	380		14 5 9			
	French Colonies...........	6,890	14,185	21,045		89 3 9			
	United States.............	38,445	3,735	42,180		1,561 15 0			
		81,421	18,050	99,471	999,982	3,730 3 3		469 16 9	
Bricks and tiles........	United Kingdom.............	209,100		209,100		470 9 6			
	Demerara..................	18,000		18,000		40 10 0			
	Danish Colonies...........		8,000	8,000		18 0 0			
		227,100	8,000	235,100	235,100	528 19 6		59 10 2	
Candles, tallow ....lbs.	United Kingdom.............	489		489		12 4 6			1d. per lb., 30 per cent. additional to 18th June, 30 per cent. additional from 18th July—the percentage abolished on latter date.
	Barbadoes..................	13,000		13,000		395 10 0			
	United States.............	104,500	6,760	111,260		2,781 10 0	6		
		117,989	6,760	124,759	130,554	3,118 14 6			
Candles, other than tallow....lbs.	United Kingdom.............	5,281		5,281		308 12			3d. as above.
	Barbadoes..................	1,214		1,214		70 16 4	1 2		
	St. Kitts.................	800		800		46 13 4			

Heading	Description									Rate of duty
Coffee	United Kingdom	7,835	437	7,972	7,913	465 0 8		119 4 9		1d., as above.
	Barbadoes	13,504		13,504		312 12 0				
	Dominica	11,071		11,071		276 11 8				
	Montserrat	13,989		13,989		0 12 0				
	Danish Colonies	94		94		98 11 6				
	Swedish Colonies	1,149		1,149		53 7 6				
	French Colonies	935	76	935		1 18 0				
Cocoa	United Kingdom	38,696	78	38,734	43,369	908 7 0	6	907 4 1		1d., as above.
	Barbadoes	51		61		1 5 6				
	Demerara	21,453	549	22,002		550 1 0				
	Swedish Colonies	18,876	700	19,576		489 10 0				
	French Colonies		100	100		2 1 0				
			50	50		1 0 0				
Cheese	United Kingdom	40,380	1,399	41,799	35,941	1,044 9 6	9 6	165 18 5		1d., as above.
	Barbadoes	4,994½		4,994½		186 18 7	9 6			
	St. Kitts	6,006½		6,006½		150 3 3				
	British North America	1,169		1,169		39 4 6				
	United States	1,736	2,165	1,736		43 8 0				
	Dutch Colonies	46,894½		49,059½		1,286 9 9				
	French Colonies	118	120	118		2 16 0				
				120		3 0 0				
Cigars	United Kingdom	60,902½	2,285	63,187½	61,981½	1,649 0 1		980 1 11		10s., as above.
	St. Kitts	1,175		1,175		4 14 0				
	Dominica	919		919		3 12 11				
	Montserrat	900		900		0 16 0	80 0 0			
	Hamburg	5,100		5,100		20 8 0				
	Swedish Colonies		50,200	50,200		200 16 0				
	French Colonies	17,835	3,960	21,795		87 7 1				
	Danish Colonies	1,774		1,774		7 1 11				
		30,400		30,400		131 19 0				
Cattle		57,396	54,160	111,556	84,156	446 4 5		48 18 6		10s., with 20s. to 18th June, 20 per cent. additional to 16th July—the per centage abolished on latter date, and then 4s. 2d. per head.
	Montserrat	64	34	64		256 0 0	4 0 0			
	French Colonies		9	34		136 0 0				
	Dutch Colonies			9		36 0 0				
Fish, dried		64	43	107	107	428 0 0		61 17 0		1s. per quintal, as above.
	United Kingdom	65 1 0		65 1 0		43 13 6	14 0			
	British North America	5,141 3 15		5,141 3 15		3,329 6 4				

Statement showing the general imports into the colony of Antigua in the year 1863 – Continued.

ARTICLES.	Countries whence imported.	QUANTITIES IMPORTED.			Quantities entered for home consumption.	Value in sterling of total imports.	Average price fixed for the value, (if calculated officially.)	DUTY.	
		In British vessels.	In foreign vessels.	Total.				Gross amount received in sterling.	Rate, and when imposed.
		£ s. d.	£ s. d.	£ s. d.		£ s. d.	£ s. d.	£ s. d.	
Fish, dried.	Barbadoes	2,720 0 0		2,720 0 0		1,904 0 0			
	St. Kitts	81 3 0 0		81 3 0 0		57 0 6			
	Montserrat	8 0 0		8 0 0		5 12 0			
	United States	709 3 4	20 0 0	729 3 4		510 17 0			
		8,796 2 19	20 0 0	8,746 2 19	7,930 2 7	6,129 13 4	90 0	473 1 10	2s. per barrel, as above.
Fish, pickled.	United Kingdom	90		90		90 0 0			
	Barbadoes	596		596		596 0 0			
	St. Kitts	187¼		187¼		187 5 0			
	British North America	2,636¼		2,636¼		2,636 5 0			
	Madeira		30	30		30 0 0			
	United States	2,986	100	3,086		3,086 0 0			
	French Colonies	67		67		67 0 0			
		6,494¼	130	6,624¼	5,888	6,629 10 0	22 0	690 5 7	5s, as above.
Flour.	St. Kitts	143		143		157 6 0			
	Trinidad	901		901		901 2 0			
	Montserrat	100		100		110 0 0			
	Barbadoes	5,359		5,359		5,887 4 0			
	Anguilla	3		3		3 6 0			
	United States	12,309½	1,452	13,761½		15,137 13 0			
	Dutch Colonies	30	25	55		60 10 0			
	Swedish Colonies	192		192		911 4 0			
	Danish Colonies	50	129	179		196 18 0			
		18,380½	1,606	19,986½	19,332½	21,985 3 0			
Fruits, dried.	United Kingdom	5,165		5,165		93 13 0	9	5,477 7 0	2d per lb., and 30 per cent. to 18th June, 30 per cent. additional to 18th July,—the percentage abolished on latter date.
	St. Kitts	35		35		13 1 0			
	Barbadoes	356		356		1 7 0			
	Muslim.		250	260		9 15 0			
	Danish Colonies	48		48		1 16 0			

Hams, bacon, tongues, &c.	United Kingdom	18,343		6,151	5,866	587 17 3		1d. per lb., as above.
	United States	34,808		18,208		907 11 0		
	British North America	653		653		16 6 6	8 8	
	St. Kitts	1,137		1,137		98 8 6		
	Barbadoes	10,048	1	10,048		251 1 0		
	Danish Colonies	1,163		1,163		99 1 6		
	Dutch Colonies	900		900		5 0 0		
		66,346	1,494	67,840	64,223	1,925 5 9		306 18 2
Horses	United Kingdom	1		1		30 0 0	30 0 0	
	Barbadoes	94		94		790 0 0	10 0 0	
	Montserrat	2		2		10 0 0		
	Anguilla	1		1		60 0 0		
	Spanish Colonies	6		6		10 0 0		
	Dutch Colonies	0	1	1				
	Buenos Ayres	1		1		10 0 0		
		35	1	36	36	890 0 0		66 2 0
Kerosene and other fluids	United Kingdom	90		90		2 10 0	2 6	
	United States	40	15	40		5 0 0		
	Danish Colonies			15		5 17 6		
	Barbadoes	208		208		25 5 0		
		208	15	977	492	34 12 6		6 3 0
Lard .... cwt.	United States	2 2 3	22 1 9	2 2 3		7 1 6	56 0	
	St. Kitts	139 2 18		161 3 27	175 2 20	453 11 6		56 13 4
		142 0 21	22 1 9	164 22 0		460 13 0		
Lard .... lbs.	United Kingdom	77		77		1 18 6	6	
	United States	9,175	2,860	12,035	13,180	300 17 6		54 18 4
	Dutch Colonies	300		300		7 10 0		
		9,552	2,860	12,412		310 6 0		
Mules	United Kingdom	26		26		260 0 0	10 0 0	
	Barbadoes	31		31		310 0 0		54 18 4
	Buenos Ayres	84		84		840 0 0		
	French Colonies		15	15		150 0 0		
		141	15	156	156	1,560 0 0		202 16 0

Statement showing the general imports into the colony of Antigua in the year 1863—Continued.

ARTICLES.	Countries whence imported.	QUANTITIES IMPORTED. In British vessels.	QUANTITIES IMPORTED. In foreign vessels.	QUANTITIES IMPORTED. Total.	Quantities entered for home consumption.	Value in sterling of total imports.	Average price fixed for the value, (if calculated officially.)	DUTY. Gross amount received in sterling.	DUTY. Rate, and when imposed.
						£ s. d.	£ s. d.	£ s. d.	
Meal	United Kingdom	28½	....	28½	....	22 13 4	16 0	....	2s., with 30 per cent. to 18th June, 20 per cent. additional to 18th July—after latter date percentage was abolished.
	Trinidad	100	....	100	....	80 0 0	....	....	
	Barbadoes	5,239	....	5,239	....	4,191 4 0	....	....	
	Montserrat	15	....	15	....	12 0 0	....	....	
	Dominica	100	....	100	....	80 0 0	....	....	
	Swedish Colonies	143	....	143	....	114 8 0	....	....	
	Danish Colonies	20	....	20	....	16 0 0	....	....	
	St. Kitts	284	....	284	....	227 4 0	....	....	
	St. Vincent	250	....	250	....	200 0 0	....	....	
	United States	7,933	134	8,067	....	6,453 12 0	....	....	
	Dutch Colonies	75	20	95	....	76 0 0	....	....	
		14,187½	154	143,41½	13,214½	11,473 1 4	....	1,445 10 11	
Meal, oil-cake ....cwt..	United Kingdom	871 3 27	....	871 3 27	....	348 16 0	8	....	1s. per cwt., as above.
	Barbadoes	89 1 4	....	89 1 4	....	35 14 4	....	....	
	United States	610 3 27	107 0 16	718 0 15	....	287 5 0	....	....	
	Hamburg	....	10 1 0	10 1 0	....	4 2 0	....	....	
		1,572 1 2	117 1 16	1,689 2 18	1,588 1 0	675 17 4	....	100 11 4	
Meal, oil-cake..... .....100 lbs..	United Kingdom	38,938	....	38,938	....	137 18 1½	7 1	....	10d. per 100 lbs. only.
	United States	125,004	15,000	140,004	....	495 16 11½	....	....	
	St. Kitts	2,500	....	2,500	....	8 17 1½	....	....	
	Barbadoes	54,250	....	54,250	....	192 2 8	....	....	
	Dutch Colonies	2,500	....	2,500	....	8 17 1½	....	....	
		223,192	15,000	238,192	238,192	843 11 11	....	99 4 11	
Oils ....gals..	United Kingdom	5,000¼	....	5,000¼	....	1,000 2 0	4 0	....	6d., as above.
	Barbadoes	872	....	872	....	174 8 0	....	....	
	St. Kitts	20	....	20	....	4 0 0	....	....	
	Trinidad	1,293	....	1,293	....	258 12 0	....	....	
	Montserrat	1	....	1	....	0 4 0	....	....	

Onions	cwt.	St. Vincent .... Madeira .... French Colonies .... United States	30 901¼ 1,004½	3 600	30 901¼ 8,306½			6d. per cwt.
			8,006½	603	9,609	6,967½	219 18 0	
							219 5 5	
Onions	100 lbs.	St. Kitts .... Bermuda .... Madeira	3 3 0 33 1 0	46 2 0	3 3 0 33 1 0 46 2 0	9 2 0	6 0 40 6 0 441 14 0	6d. only.
			37 0 0	46 2 0	83 2 0	83 2 0	33 8 0	
							7 1 9 14 3	
Peas, corn, oats, &c.	bush.	United I .. m. Barbadoes .... St. Kitts .... United States .... French .... do. Madeira .... British Domini..	679 670 5,036 10,658 9,090 1,308 280	3,125 60 1,308	679 670 5,036 13,777 9,040 1,306 980		9 7 0 2 6 11 17 12 4½ 48 4 4 31 15 7½ 4 11 6½ 0 19 7½	6d. only.
			96,330	4,493	30,283	30,823	107 17 7	
							77 1 2	
Peas, corn, oats, &c.	bush.	United Kingdom .... Trinidad .... Anguilla .... Barbadoes .... Dominica .... British North America St. Kitts .... Grenada .... United States .... Hamburg .... Madeira .... Swedish Colonies .... Dutch Colonies .... French Colonies .... Danish Colonies	7,968½ 1,040 12½ 16,054 596 458 607 3 37,888½ 40 163 768 70 100	3,815 163 600 98 2,348	7,968½ 1,040 12¼ 16,054 596 458 607 3 41,643¾ 40 163 1,368 96 3,958 100		1,593 13 0 208 0 0 2 10 0 3,910 0 0 119 4 0 87 12 0 121 8 0 0 12 0 8,328 13 0 8 0 0 32 12 0 273 12 0 19 4 0 791 11 0 50 0 0	3d., with 30 per cent. to 18th June, 30 per cent. additional to 18th July, after that date 3d. only.
			67,084½	6,992	74,087½	67,909½	14,817 10 0	
							4 0 975 6 4	
Potatoes and yams	cwt.	United Kingdom .... British North America Buenos Ayres .... Bermudas .... Barbadoes .... Dutch Colonies .... Dominica .... St. Kitts	47 3 0 351 0 0 5 0 0 151 2 0 25 2 0 10 0 0 1 0 0 3 0 0		47 3 0 351 0 0 5 0 0 151 2 0 25 2 0 10 0 0 1 0 0 3 0 0		11 18 9 87 15 0 1 5 0 37 7 6 8 7 6 2 10 0 0 0 50 0 0 150	1s., as above.
							5 0	

Statement showing the general imports into the colony of Antigua in the year 1863—Continued.

ARTICLES.	Countries whence imported.	QUANTITIES IMPORTED. In British vessels.	In foreign vessels.	Total.	Quantities entered for home consumption.	Value in sterling of total imports.	Average price fixed for the value, (if calculated officially.)	DUTY. Gross amount received in sterling.	Rate, and when imposed.
						£ s. d.	£ s. d.	£ s. d.	
Potatoes and yams ......cwt.	Montserrat	9 0 10		9 0 10		2 15 6			
	French Colonies	2 0 0		2 0 0		0 19 0			
	Swedish Colonies	12 0 0		12 0 0		3 0 0			
	Anguilla	7 2 0		7 2 0		1 17 6			
		625 3 10		625 3 10	625 3 10		156 9 2	40 27	
Potatoes ......bbl.	United Kingdom	109½		109½		95 12 6			1s. 6d. per barrel only.
	British North America	107		107		96 15 0	5 0		
	St. Vincent	90		90		5 0 0			
	Barbadoes	149		149		37 5 0			
	United States	328½	66	394		98 10 0			
	St. Kitts	4		4		0 6 3			
	Dutch Colonies			1½		0 0 0			
	Madeira		63	63		15 15 0			
	French Colonies		125	125		31 5 0			
Rice ......cwt.		711½	954	965½	965½		12 6	7s 8 7	2s., and 30 per cent. to 18th June, 30 per cent. additional to 18th July.—percentage abolished on latter date.
	United Kingdom	1,196 1 16		1,196 1 16		747 14 10			
	Barbadoes	579 0 10		579 0 10		361 18 10			
	St. Kitts	114 1 0		114 1 0		71 8 1			
	United States	280 1 22		280 1 22		175 5 5			
		2,170 0 20		2,170 0 20	1,967 3 22	1,356 7 2		948 1 6	
Rice ......100 lbs.	United Kingdom	342,900		342,900		1,889 2 0	11 0		2s. per 100 lbs., as above.
	Barbadoes	23,862		23,862		130 18 2			
	Danish Colonies	1,700		1,700		9 7 0			
		367,702		367,702	299,616			989 12 3	

Ships, goods, pigs, &c.

Finished		3	107			107			
Anguilla		107	114			114			
Montserrat		104	119	119		119			
Dutch Colonies		10	6			6			½d., as above.
Danish Colonies		8	9			9			
Dominica		9	9			9			
Buenos Ayres		4	4			4			
Nevis		39	39			39			
Swedish Colonies		10	10			10			
St. Kitts									
		293	405	119	405	405	90 0	92 16 4	
Soap....................lbs.	United Kingdom	192,079	192,079		192,745	1,017 6 6			
	Barbadoes	3,976	3,976		90	33 2 8	2		2s. 6d., and 30 per cent. to 18th June, 20 per cent. additional to 18th July, after which date 2s. 6d. only.
	French Colonies	90	90		3,600	0 15 0			
	Danish Colonies	3,600				30 0 0			
		129,745	129,745	119	129,745	1,081 4 2		274 11 10	
Spirits, brandy....gal.	United Kingdom	3,658 8 10	3,658 8 10		3,658 8 10	1,889 8 0	10 0		
	Barbadoes	224	224		224	119 10 0			
	St. Kitts	75	75		75	37 10 0			
	Swedish Colonies	29 9 10	29 9 10		29 9 10	14 19 0			
		3,967 7 10	3,967 7 10		3,967 7 10	1,993 17 0		663 3 8	
Spirits, gin.........gal.	United Kingdom	3,818½	3,818½		3,818½	477 6 3	9 6		9s., as above.
	Barbadoes	1	1		1	6 2 6			
	St. Kitts	125	125		125	15 12 6			
	Montserrat	1	1		1	2 2 0			
	United States	250	250		250	31 10 7			
	Hamburg			204½	204½	25 10 1			
	Danish Colonies	308½	308½	350	658½	82 7 3			
	Swedish Colonies	18½	18½		18½	2 16 3			
	Dutch Colonies	48½	48½		48½	6 1 3			
		4,737½	4,737½	554½	5,291½	661 8 11		500 16 1	
Spirits, sweetened	Barbadoes	2½	2½		2½	2 10 0	20 0		4s., as above.
	Hamburg			12	12	12 0 0			
	French Colonies			3	3	3 0 0			
	Swedish Colonies	2	2	90	92	22 0 0			
		4½	4½	35	39½	39 10 0		6 15 2	
Sugar, refined.......	United Kingdom	21,782	21,782		21,782	544 11 0	6		½d., as above.

Statement showing the general imports into the colony of Antigua in the year 1863—Continued.

ARTICLES	Countries whence imported	In British vessels	In foreign vessels	Total	Quantities entered for home consumption	Value in sterling of total import	Average price fixed for the value, (if calculated officially.)	Gross amount received in sterling	DUTY. Rate, and when imposed.
Sugar, refined	Barbadoes	1,073		1,073		26 16 6			
	United States	1,985		1,985		49 12 6			
		94,840		94,840	25,081	621 0 0		59 10 1	
Tea ...... lbs	United Kingdom	6,927		6,927		622 14 0	9 0		4d., as above.
	United States	91	50	91		9 2 0			
	Danish Colonies	162	50	212		91 4 0			
		6,480	50	6,530	6,666	653 0 0	9 0	127 18 0	
Tobacco, manufactured	United Kingdom	4		4		0 8 0			4d. per lb., as above.
	Barbadoes	168		168		16 16 0			
	Danish Colonies	7		7		0 14 0			
		179		179	377	17 18 0		6 6 4	
Tobacco, unmanufactured ...lb.	United Kingdom	7,168		7,168		179 4 0	6		3d., as above.
	Barbadoes	11,548		11,548		988 14 0			
	Demerara	1,354		1,354		33 17 0			
	Trinidad	18		18		0 9 0			
	St. Kitts	6,501		6,501		168 10 0			
	Swedish Colonies	7,683		7,683		198 1 0			
	Danish Colonies	1,031		1,031		25 15 0			
	United States	34,720	8,167	42,887		1,072 3 0			
	French Colonies	90		20		0 10 0			
		70,043	8,167	78,210	65,188	1,955 5 0		933 5 6	

Wine		5 10 57	4	5 10 61	5 9 57	1,826 5 6		465 1 6	15 per cent. and 20 per cent. to 18th June, 20 per cent. additional to July 18th—percentage abolished on latter date.
	United Kingdom					167 18 3			
	Madeira					61 1 8			
	Barbadoes					8 0 0			
	St. Kitts					10 10 8			
	Dominica					90 16 8			
	Swedish Colonies	3				5 5 10			
	Dutch Colonies	1				163 9 5			
	Danish Colonies					384 18 4			
	French Colonies	7							
	United States								
Wood, pitch pine							26 per M.		13s. 6d. per M, as above.
	Barbadoes	100		100		12 0 0			
	United States	2,000		3,000		12 0 0			
		2,100		2,100	2,100	12 12 0		1 13 9	
Wood, white pine and spruce ...ft.		738		738		2 4 3	3 per M.		3s. 4d., as above.
	United Kingdom	1,319,155		1,319,155		3,957 9 3			
	British North America	5,600		5,600		16 16 0			
	United States	400				1 4 0			
	Barbadoes								
		1,325,893		1,325,893	151,000	3,977 13 6		656 7 11	
Cypress and Wallaba shingles			101,000	101,000		101 0 0	1 per M.		6s. 3d., as above.
	Demerara	24,000		24,000		24 0 0			
	Dominica	90,000		90,000		90 0 0			
	Barbadoes		6,000	6,000		6 0 0			
	French Colonies								
		44,000	107,000	151,000	151,000	151,000		56 3 11	
Cedar and pine shingles		1,297,584		1,297,584		309 7 11	5s. per M.		
	British North America	85,000		85,000		91 5 0			
	Barbadoes	2,000		2,000		10 0 0			
	French Colonies								
		1,384,584		1,384,584	1,384,584			183 15 4	
Wood, wood hoops		309,850		309,850		1,514 5 0	25 per M.		6s. 3d. per 1,200, seabove, to 18th July, and then 5s. per 1,000 only.
	United Kingdom	5,400		5,400		27 0 0			
	British North America	3,000		3,000		15 0 0			
	Barbadoes								
		311,250		311,250	299,250	1,556 5 0		96 3 8	
Wood staves		297,073		297,073		948 5 10	24 per M.		10s. 5d., as above.
	British North America	4,000		4,000		24 0 0	6		
	Barbadoes	1,000		1,000		4 0 0	4		
	French Colonies								

Statement showing the general imports into the colony of Antigua in the year 1863—Continued.

ARTICLES.	Countries whence imported.	QUANTITIES IMPORTED.			Quantities entered for home consumption.	Value in sterling of total imports.	Average price fixed for the value, (if calculated officially.)	Gross amount received in sterling.	DUTY.
		In British vessels.	In foreign vessels.	Total.					Rate, and when imposed.
Wood staves	Montserrat	2,400		2,400	244,473	£ s. d. 14 8 0	£6 per M.	£ s. d. 159 13 2	9d., as above.
		244,473		244,473					
Shooks	United Kingdom	2,926		2,926		428 18 0	3s. per M.		
	British North America	95		95		14 5 0			
	French Colonies	556	400	956		143 8 0			
	Barbadoes	2,337		2,337		350 11 0			
	United States	250	210	460		69 0 0			
	Montserrat	95		95		3 15 0			
	St. Vincent	900		900		30 0 0			
		6,389	610	6,999	6,799	1,049 17 0		322 6 6	
Non-enumerated articles	United Kingdom	£ s. d. 50,315 15 4	£ s. d. 44 3 0	£ s. d. 50,359 4 5		£ s. d. 50,359 4 5			12½ per cent. ad valorem, to 18th June 5 per cent, with 20 per cent additional to 18th July, and after latter date to December 31, 1863, 5 per cent only.
	Barbadoes	5,570 14 10	13 10 10	5,584 5 8		5,584 5 8			
	Montserrat	67 13 3		67 13 3		67 13 3			
	Trinidad	99 2 5		99 2 5		99 2 5			
	St. Kitts	452 11 9	10 0 0	462 11 9		462 11 9			
	Anguilla	53 7 3		53 7 3		53 7 3			
	Dominica	90 1 6	10 10 8	100 12 2		100 12 2			
	Nevis	7 19 0		7 19 0		7 19 0			
	British North America	39 3 3		39 3 3		39 3 3			
	United States	1,302 4 1	250 6 1	1,552 10 2		1,552 10 2			
	Danish Colonies	143 16 8	80 15 10	223 12 6		223 12 6			
	Madeira		10 18 10	10 18 10		10 18 10			
	Swedish Colonies	86 16 2	58 10 10	147 7 0		147 7 0			
	Dutch Colonies	363 13 4		363 13 4		363 13 4			
	French Colonies	52 4 9	153 18 7	206 3 4		206 3 4			
	Buenos Ayres	77 10 0		77 10 0		77 10 0			
	Spanish Colonies	12 9 4		12 9 4		12 9 4			
	St. Vincent	66 18 8		66 18 8		66 18 8			

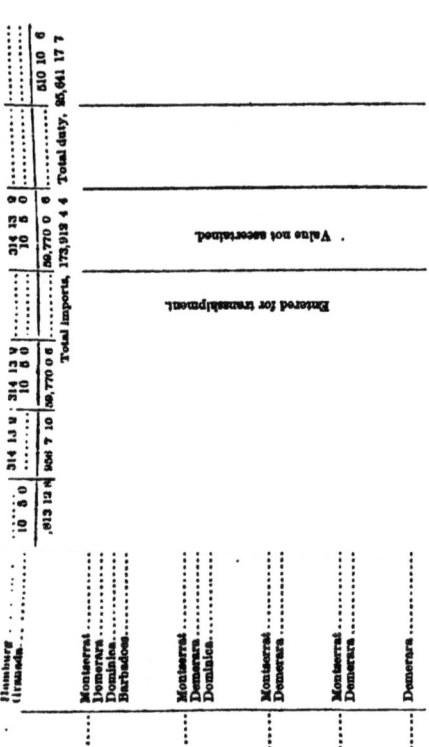

No. 3.—*Statement showing the general exports from the colony of Antigua.*

ARTICLES.	To which country exported.	Produce and manufacture of colony. In British vessels.	In foreign vessels.	Total.	British, foreign, and other colonial produce and manufacture.	Produce & manufacture of the colony.	Total.	British, foreign, and other colonial produce and manufacture. £ s. d.	Produce and manufacture of the colony.	Total. £ s. d.	Average price fixed for the value, if calculated officially.
Ale and beer ....bbl.	Montserrat	10			156			78 0 0		90 0 0	40s.
	St. Kitts				34			18 0 0			
	Barbadoes							2			
	Danish Colonies						196			98 0 0	10s. £5.
Beef and pork	United Kingdom				95			195 0 0			
	Montserrat				90			190 0 0			
	Barbadoes				105			525 0 0			
	United States				90			100 0 0			
	French Colonies				9			45 0 0			
	St. Kitts				24			120 0 0			
	Spanish				2			10 0 0			
Bread and biscuits	Barbadoes				95		305	95 0 0		1,925 0 0	20s.
	St. Kitts				95			95 0 0			
	Montserrat							0 10 0			
Bricks and tiles	Montserrat				4		50½			50 10 0	60s.
							300			0 18 0	
Butter	Barbadoes				9,650					132 10 0	1s.
	St. Kitts				875					43 15 0	
	Montserrat				25					1 5 0	
	Danish Colonies				1,250		4,800			62 10 0	
Candles	Nevis				1,580		1,600	59 5 0		60 0 0	70s.
	Dominica				90		513	0 15 9		17 19 1	
Coffee and cocoa	British North America										
Cigars	British North America				11,500		12,500	34 10 0		37 10 0	60s.
	St. Vincent				1,000			3			
Cattle	Montserrat				12		38	120 0 0		380 0 0	£10.
	French Colonies				90			200 0 0			

Article	Destination					Value
						1s. 9d. 10s. per quintal.
Candles other than tallow						8 2 0
Fish, dried	St. Vincent					
	Dominica					
	Montserrat					
	St. Kitts					
	Dutch Colonies					
	Oranain					
	Madeira	134		10 12 0		970 12 0
						94s.
Fish, pickled	Barbadoes	100		180 0 0		
	Montserrat	340		418 16 0		
	St Kitts	419		505 16 0		
	Turk's Island	60		72 0 0		
	British North America	58		69 12 0		
	French Colonies	10		12 0 0		
	Dominica	14		16 16 0		
	Danish	134		160 16 0		
	St. Vincent	8		9 12 0		
	Dutch Colonies	5	1,213	6 0 0		
Flour	bbl.					30s.
	United Kingdom	39		48 0 0		
	British North America	4		6 0 0		
	United States	7		10 10 0		
	Barbadoes	23		34 10 0		
	St. Kitts	288		432 0 0		
	French Colonies	125		187 10 0		
	Dutch Colonies	113		169 10 0		
	Lisbon	400		600 0 0		
		101		151 10 0		
	Anguilla	3		4 10 0		
	Nevis	50		75 0 0		
		16		24 0 0		
		150	1,319	225 0 0		1,388 8 0
Fruits	Barbadoes	719		35 19 0		
	St. Kitts	168	887	8 8 0		1,966 0 0
						9d.
Hams, tongues, bacon	French Colonies	4,726		177 12 0		
	Barbadoes	619	5,355	23 4 3		44 7 0
Horses	Montserrat	11				200 16 3
Kₐ wine and other fluids	Barbadoes	985				220 16 0
Mules	Montserrat	14				42 15 0
						350 0 0
Meal	Montserrat	10		10 0 0		
	Dutch Colonies	174		174 0 0		
	Nevis	62		62 0 0		
	St. Kitts	100		100 0 0		
	Dominica	143		143 0 0		
	Danish	2		9 0 0		
		50	541	50 0 0		541 0 0

No. 3.—*Statement showing the general exports from the colony of Antigua—Continued.*

ARTICLES.	To which country exported.	QUANTITIES. Produce and manufacture of colony.			QUANTITIES. British, foreign, and other colonial produce and manufacture's.	QUANTITIES. Total.	VALUE IN STERLING. Produce & manufactures of the colony.	VALUE IN STERLING. British, foreign, and other colonial produce and manufactures.	VALUE IN STERLING. Total.	Average price fixed for the value, if calculated officially.
		In British vessels.	In foreign vessels.	Total.					£ s. d.	
Meal, oil-cake, &c.	Montserrat				4 2 0	49 2 0		5 13		29s.
	St. Kitts				45 0 0			50 12 6	85 13 9	
Oils	St. Kitts				617	901		154 5 0 0	225 5 0	
	Montserrat				5			1 5 0 0		
	Nevis				111			27 15 0 0		
	Danish Colonies				165			41 10 0 0		
	Dominica				2			0 10 0		
Molasses ...... puncheons	United Kingdom	5,094				5,050	15,973			30s.
	United States	312				312	896			15s.
	Lisbon	903				903	906			
	Swedish Colonies	8				8	94			
	Dutch Colonies	94				94	72			
	Turk's Island	2				2	6			
	Danish Colonies	2				2	6			
	Anguilla	1			96	1	3	78 0 0		
	Bermuda	90				90	60			
	Madeira	59				59	117			
	St. Kitts	1				1	3			
	British North America	312				312	936			
		5,908			96	5,994	17,904 0 0	78 0 0	17,982 0 0	
Molasses ...... hhds.	United Kingdom	99			95	99	6 15 0		43 10 0	
Molasses ...... bbls.	British North America					9	6 10 0			
	St. Kitts					2				
	Dutch Colonies					94	1 17 0			
	Swedish Colonies					1	0 15 0			
						£ s. d.	£ s. d.			
Onions	St. Kitts				40 0 90			28 9 8	10 17 6	16s. per cwt.
	French Colonies				139 1 4			103 8 7		

Oats, peas, beans, &c							
St. Vincent	2						
United Kingdom	1,144						
Barbadoes	312						
Montserrat	284						
St. Kitts	726						
French Colonies					394 10 0	791 0 0	16s. 8d.
Dutch Colonies	6				105 10 0		
Danish Colonies					100 0 0		
	90				1 0 0		
Potatoes							
Montserrat	2		4,968	1 13 4		134 3 4	£6.
French Colonies	20		18	16 13 4			
Swedish Colonies	5		60	4 3 4			
United States	130		138	108 6 8			
St. Kitts	4		60	3 6 8			
			30				
Rum ... puncheons	13	161	5,274	78 0 0			£3.
United Kingdom		841					
British North America		3					
Madeira		10					
Dutch Colonies		93					
Danish Colonies		10					
St. Kitts		5					
Rum ... hhds	13	892	£ s. d.	78 0 0	5,325 0 0		
United Kingdom	112½	121¼	364 10 0			364 10 0	30s.
British North America	8						
St. Kitts	1						
Rice	£ s. d.	£ s. d.					
Montserrat	96 2 0	131 3 16		96 10 0	135 17 10		30s.
Barbadoes	35 16 0			35 7 10			
St. Kitts	70 0 0			70 0 0			
Spirits, brandy	159	169		189 0 0	169 0 0		6s.
Montserrat	4			4 0 0			
United Kingdom	6			6 0 0			
Allied States							
Spirits, gin							
United Kingdom	4	398¼		1 4 0	119 12 6		
Dominica	85½			25 13 0			
British North America	130½			45 1 6			
St. Kitts	43			12 18 0			
Turk's Island	2			0 12 0			
Spanish Colonies	24			7 4 0			
United States	14			4 4 0			
St. Vincent	72			21 12 0			
French Colonies	4			1 4 0			

No. 3.—*Statement showing the general exports from the colony of Antigua—Continued.*

ARTICLES	To which country exported.	QUANTITIES — Produce and manufactures of colony. In British vessels.	In foreign vessels.	Total.	British, foreign, and other colonial produce and manuf's.	Total.	VALUE IN STERLING — Produce & manufacture of the colony.	British, foreign, and other colonial produce and manufactures.	Total.	Average price fixed for the value, if calculated officially.
Sugar ....hhds.	United Kingdom	11,911	......	11,911	330	122,41	£ s. d. 165,754 6 0	£ s. d. 4,680 0 0	£ s. d.	£14
	British North America	13	......	13	......	13	182 0 0			
	United States	5	......	5	......	5	70 0 0			
				330	330	12,259	167,066 0 0	4,680 0 0	171,686 0 0	
Sugar ....tierces	United Kingdom	1,336	......	1,336	464	1,800	13,469 6 8	4,330 13 4		£9 6s. 8d.
	United States	3	......	3	......	3	28 0 0			
	British North America	1	......	1	......	1	9 6 8			
					464	1,804	13,506 13 4	4,330 13 4	16,837 6 8	
Sugar ....bbls.	United Kingdom	5,471	......	5,471	372	5,83	9,574 5 0	651 0 0		35s.
	British North America	278	......	278	......	278	486 10 0			
	United States	105	......	105	......	85	183 15 0			
	Turk's Island	10	......	10	......	10	17 10 0			
	Danish Colonies	45	......	45	......	45	78 15 0			
	Swedish Colonies	17	......	17	......	17	99 15 0			
	Madeira	80	......	80	......	80	140 0 0			
	Lisbon	105	......	105	......	105	183 15 0			
	Anguilla	4	......	4	......	4	7 0 0			
	St. Kitts	9½	......	9½	......	9½	16 12 6			
		6,124½	......	6,124½	372	6,496½	10,717 17 6	651 0 0	11,368 17 6	
Spirits, sweetened	Yarmouth, (B. N. A.)				9				7 0 0	10s.
	St. Kitts				12	14		1 0 0	7 0 0	1s.
Tobacco, manufactured	Dominica				1,580			79 0 0		
	Montserrat				2,095	3,675		104 15 0	183 15 0	5s.
	Montserrat				3,000			0 15 0		

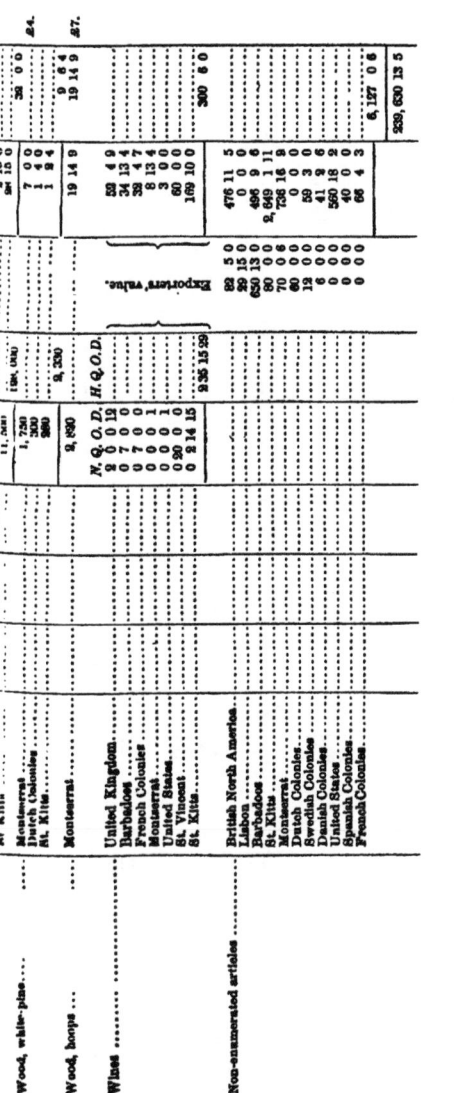

Wood, white-pine ....

Wood, hoops ...

Wines ....

Non-enumerated articles ....

Number, tonnage, and crews of vessels entered at ports in the colony of Antigua from each country in the year 1863.

Countries whence arrived.	BRITISH, (flag.) With cargoes			BRITISH In ballast			BRITISH Total			FOREIGN With cargoes			FOREIGN In ballast			FOREIGN Total			TOTAL With cargoes			TOTAL In ballast			TOTAL Total		
	Vessels	Tons	Crews	Vessels	Tons	Crews	Vessels	Tons	Crews	Vessels	Tons	Crews	Vessels	Tons	Crews	Vessels	Tons	Crews	Vessels	Tons	Crews	Vessels	Tons	Crews	Vessels	Tons	Crews
EUROPE.																											
Great Britain	94	6,508	981	1	981	10	95	6,769	991										94	6,508	981	1	981	10	95	6,760	991
Hamburg	1	298	9				1	298	9	1	74	10				1	74	10	1	74	10				1	74	10
Italy	1		7		178	7													1	298	9				1	298	9
Spain	1	174	7	1	178	7	2	352	14										1	174	7	1	178	7	2	352	14
AFRICA.																											
Sierra Leone				9	341	14	9	341	14													9	341	14	9	341	14
St. Michael				3	354	13	9	354	13													3	354	13	9	354	13
Madeira				1	285	3	1	285	9	1	106	8				1	106	8	1	106	8	1	285	9	2	384	17
Cape de Verde	1	966	11	2	455	16	3	723	57										1	966	11	2	455	16	3	723	57
AMERICA.																											
British North America	34	2,770	166		980	115	34	2,770	166										34	2,770	166		980		34	2,770	168
British West Indies	216	6,633	972	37	980	115	243	7,613	1,087	7	250	35				7	250	35	223	6,883	1,007	27	980	115	250	7,863	1,122
United States	39	3,199	168				39	3,199	168	6	533	39				6	533		35	3,739	207				35	3,739	207
FOREIGN WEST INDIES.																											
Swedish	12	232	43	1	8	3	13	940	45	5	35	20				5	35	20	17	287	62	1	8	3	18	275	65
Danish	15	115	21	4	904	23	9	319	44	4	31	13				4	31	13	9	146	34	4	904	23	13	350	57
Dutch Colonies	5	110	30	1	8	3	6	118	53	4	108	24		4		4	108	24	9	918	44	1	8	3	10	526	47
French Colonies	13	211	46	6	953	47	19	1,160	93	17	447	94	9		6	19	451	100	30	658	140	8	953	53	38	1,611	193
REPUB. SOUTH AMER.																											
Buenos Ayres	1	921	9				1	921	9										1	921	9				1	921	9
Total	343	30,739	1,759	48	3,924	260	390	24,663	2,012	45	1,586	243	2	4	6	47	1,590	949	387	32,325	1,995	50	3,928	266	437	96,923	9,201

*Only two vessels under the American flag.

Number, tonnage, and crews of vessels cleared at ports in the colony of Antigua to each country in the year 1863.

Countries to which departed	BRITISH									FOREIGN									TOTAL								
	With cargoes			In ballast			Total			With cargoes			In ballast			Total			With cargoes			In ballast			Total		
	Vessels	Tons	Crews	Vessels	Tons	Crews	Vessels	Tons	Crews	Vessels	Tons	Crews	Vessels	Tons	Crews	Vessels	Tons	Crews	Vessels	Tons	Crews	Vessels	Tons	Crews	Vessels	Tons	Crews
EUROPE.																											
Great Britain	48	12,970	514				48	12,970	514										48	12,970	514				48	12,970	514
Portugal										1	174	6				1	174	6	1	174	6				1	174	6
AFRICA.																											
Madeira										1	150	8				1	150	8	1	150	8				1	150	8
AMERICA.																											
British North America	19	1,327	67	3	316	16	22	1,643	103										19	1,327	87	3	316	16	22	1,643	103
British West Indies	158	6,514	781	97	1,920	280	255	8,434	1,150	9	315	58	1	13		10	328	57	167	6,689	833	98	1,933	374	265	8,762	1,207
United States	6	499	38	3	943	16	9	671	48										6	499	38	3	943	16	9	671	48
FOREIGN WEST INDIES.																											
Swedish Colonies										16	313	65	7	152		23	465	98	16	313	65	7	152		23	465	98
Dutch Colonies																			16	400	71	9	397	51	24	888	129
Danish Colonies										6	200	6	4	91	12	10	300	17	14	306	83	7	372	53	21	665	106
French Colonies										55	198	67	4	21	7	59	219	67	30	455	97	20	188	49	35	1,583	146
Spanish										9	46	9	1	9	1	9	46	9	7	46	9	8	776	39	8	882	48
Mexico																			7		39	9	250	13	9	250	13
Total	276	32,279	1,606	135	4,130	556	411	36,409	2,162	37	1,486	206	11	456	52	48	1,942	258	313	33,765	1,812	146	4,576	608	459	38,351	2,420

Number, tonnage, and crews of vessels of each nation entered at ports in the colony of Antigua, in the year 1863.

NATIONALITY OF VESSELS.	ENTERED.								
	WITH CARGOES.			IN BALLAST.			TOTAL.		
	Vessels.	Tons.	Crews.	Vessels.	Tons.	Crews.	Vessels.	Tons.	Crews.
British	342	20,739	1,752	48	3,924	260	390	24,663	2,012
American	2	250	13				2	250	13
French	19	393	97	2	4	6	21	397	103
Dutch	6	151	32				6	151	32
Danish	2	117	16				2	117	16
Swedish	13	319	61				13	319	61
Portuguese	2	282	14				2	282	14
German	1	74	10				1	74	10
Total	387	22,325	1,995	50	3,928	266	437	26,253	2,261

Number, tonnage, and crews of vessels of each nation cleared at ports in the colony of Antigua, in the year 1863.

NATIONALITY OF VESSELS.	CLEARED.								
	WITH CARGOES.			IN BALLAST.			TOTAL.		
	Vessels.	Tons.	Crews.	Vessels.	Tons.	Crews.	Vessels.	Tons.	Crews.
British	276	22,282	1,604	135	4,190	556	411	26,402	2,160
American				2	250	13	2	250	13
French	16	375	88	4	21	12	20	396	100
Dutch	2	76	11	4	78	19	6	151	32
Danish	1	10	8	1	107	8	2	117	16
Swedish	13	319	61				13	319	61
Portuguese	3	432	22				3	432	22
German	1	74	10				1	74	10
Total	313	23,768	1,810	166	4,576	608	459	28,341	2,420

Total value in sterling of the imports and exports of the colony of Antigua from and to each country in the year 1863.

Countries.	Imports.			Exports.		
	£	*s.*	*d.*	£	*s.*	*d.*
United Kingdom	69,946	2	7¼	219,207	3	9
BRITISH COLONIES.						
Barbadoes	27,910	5	1	2,637	15	11
Dominica	1,189	1	2	173	16	0
St. Kitt's	2,201	8	4½	5,516	5	9
Anguila	180	0	9	14	10	0
British N. America	11,803	10	4	2,395	10	8
Trinidad	1,067	2	11			
Demerara	141	10	0	24	0	0
Montserrat	617	0	2	2,844	3	5
St. Vincent	307	18	8	102	14	0
Grenada	10	17	0	10	12	0
Nevis	11	19	0	262	0	0
Bermuda	51	3	6 ·	60	0	0
Turk's Island				96	2	0
Total	115,437	19	6¼	233,338	13	6
FOREIGN COUNTRIES.						
Hamburg	599	11	7			
Dutch Colonies	786	2	11½	515	5	6
United States	51,071	12	5¼	2,010	13	10
Danish Colonies	957	1	11	738	13	6
French Colonies	2,600	10	0¼	1,040	16	9
Swedish	1,165	18	10	129	16	4
Madeira	290	12	7¼	377	0	0
Spanish	72	9	4	57	4	0
Buenos Ayres	930	15	0			
Lisbon				1,422	10	0
Total	173,912	4	4	239,630	13	5

Statement showing the principal exports from Penang to Great Britain, from January 1 to November 30, 1864.

Articles.	From Jan. 1 to Oct. 31, 1864.	November 26.	Total to November 30, 1864.	Same period in 1863.
Sugar ....piculs..	60,133	1,943.75	62,077	38,175
White pepper.....................piculs..	1,232	159.91	1,392	1,529
Black pepper ....piculs..	64,653	2,918.13	67,571	38,864
Tin ....piculs..	33,585	5,151.92	38,737	27,008
Cutch ....piculs..	1,371	....	1,371	223
Ratans ....piculs..	8,136	508.97	8,645	4,577
Buffalo hides ....piculs..	2,312	161.50	2,474	1,383
Cow hides........................piculs..	849	34.39	883	218
Buffalo horns....................piculs..	423	59.74	483	414
Rice..............................piculs..	....	....	....	17,304
Gum Benjamin ....piculs..	290	....	290	1,361
Tortoise shell ....catties..	261	....	261	135
India-rubber ....piculs..	2,013	87.98	2,101	2,478
Gutta-percha ....piculs..	1,195	15.99	1,211	777
Nutmegs..........................piculs..	3,093	472.95	3,566	1,110
Mace ....piculs..	230	10.61	241	171
Cloves ....piculs..	174	....	174	187
Rum ....gallons..	143,805	4,900.00	148,705	127,875
Fish maws ....piculs..	242	20.66	263	90
Tapioca...........................piculs..	11,042	1,061.48	12,103	12,515
Coffee ....piculs..	19	....	19	91
Tea...............................boxes..	4	....	4	6
Essential oil ....dozens..	40	....	40	82
Cocoanut oil.........../...........piculs..	....	....	....	148

Statement showing the principal exports from Penang to the United States of America, from January 1 to November 30, 1864.

Articles.	From Jan. 1 to Oct. 31, 1864.	In Nov., 1864.	Total to November 30, 1864.	Same period in 1863.
White pepper......................piculs..	....	....	....	145
Black pepper......................piculs..	2,141	....	2,141	9,80
Tin................................piculs..	2,981	....	2,981	10,06
Cutch ....piculs..	....	....	....	1,64
Ratans ....piculs..	....	....	....	66
Buffalo hides.......................piculs..	220	....	220	17
Cow hides..........................piculs..	....	....	....	44
Gum Benjamin.....................piculs..	....	....	....	10
India-rubber........................piculs..	451	....	451	1,33
Gutta-percha ....piculs..	....	....	....	12
Nutmegs...........................piculs..	879	....	879	1,05
Mace ....piculs..	16	....	16	1
Tapioca............................piculs..	....	....	....	84

Statement showing the principal exports from Penang to the continent of Europe, from January 1 to November 30, 1864.

Articles.	From Jan. 1 to Oct. 31, 1864.	November 20.	Total to November 30, 1864.	Same period in 1863.
White pepper................................piculs..	102	....	102	00
Black pepper...............................piculs..	16,853	1,900.13	18,753	9,811.00
Tin ....piculs..	3,924	....	3,924	1,066.00
Ratans ....piculs..	301	....	301	....
Buffalo horns...............................piculs..	110	....	110	53.17
Gum Benjamin ....piculs..	136	329.82	466	....
India-rubber ....piculs..	201	....	201	....
Tapioca......................................piculs..	218	....	218	.92

Comparative summary of exports from Bombay, as per ships' manifests, during November, 1864, with the total of eleven months, and of the same period during 1863, 1862, 1861, 1860, 1859, *and* 1858. *(Cotton and wool in bales; everything else in cwts.)*

Vessels.	Destination.	Sailed.	COTTON. Great Britain.	COTTON. Cowes, &c., for orders.	COTTON. Foreign Europe.	COTTON. America.	COTTON. China, &c.	COTTON. Total.	WOOL. Great Britain.	WOOL. Cowes, &c., for orders.	WOOL. Foreign Europe.	WOOL. America.	WOOL. Total.	SEEDS. Linseed. Great Britain.	SEEDS. Linseed. Cowes, &c., for orders.	SEEDS. Linseed. Foreign Europe.	SEEDS. Linseed. America.	SEEDS. Linseed. Total.	SEEDS. Gingelly. Great Britain.	SEEDS. Gingelly. Cowes, &c., for orders.
Indore	Hong Kong	Nov. 5																		
Tiverton	London	5	11					11						3,384½				3,384½		
Elizabeth Kate	Liverpool	10	6,189					6,189	193				193	500				500		
Contest	Liverpool	13	5,077					5,077	58				58	208½				208½		
South Carolina	Liverpool	13	4,472					4,472	2,220½				2,220½	210				210		
Queen of the Clyde	Liverpool	14	4,598					4,598	614				614	600				600		
Elgin	Hong Kong	18																		
Catherine Rankin	Liverpool	22	6,102					6,102	392				392	2,058½				2,058½		
City of Dublin	Havre	24			4,096			4,096												
Malmerby	Liverpool	28	2,420					2,420	58				58							
Charger	Liverpool	29	5,200½					5,200½	324				324	1,564				1,564		
Lancastrian	Liverpool	30	5,559					5,559	736				736	1,808½				1,808½		
Total for the month			39,628½		4,096			43,724½	4,595½				4,595½	10,334				10,334		
Previously exported this year			779,251½		49,925½	706		829,883	55,542		396	3,871	59,809	358,777½	14,575½	3,496½	111,919½	488,769	11,721½	
Total for eleven months			818,880		54,021½	706		873,607½	60,137½		396	3,871	64,404½	369,111½	14,575½	3,496½	111,919½	499,103	11,721½	
Exported same time 1863			797,336	2,867	37,707	3,394		841,304	50,694½	1,263		824½	52,782	400,258½	68,512½	7,655½	29,019½	505,445½	26,790½	
" 1862			850,864½	3,757½	18,724		7,934½	881,280½	52,972		5	374	53,351	525,159½	382	2,564½	94,335	622,440½	38,469	
" 1861			853,746	18,560½	8,426½		56,132½	936,865½	47,814		85	1,575	49,474	850,377½	10,150	21,513½	72,835	954,876½	23,178½	
" 1860			405,304½	2,701	15,257½		196,153	619,416	50,301		113	1,712	52,126	898,767½	34,023½	10,673	221,657½	1,165,121½	6,566	
" 1859			486,794	23,125	4,700		136,858	651,477	76,462		962	3,885	81,309	1,038,425		12,041	37,842	1,088,308	27,381	
" 1858			276,340	13,993	19,542		96,381	406,256	81,721		1,893	135	83,749	585,323	20,006	23,266	48,151	676,746	41,705	4,490

Comparative summary of exports from Bombay, as per ships' manifests, during November, 1864, &c.—Continued.

Vessels.	Destination.	Sailed.	SEEDS. Gingelly. Foreign Europe.	Gingelly. America.	Gingelly. Total.	Rape and mustard. Great Britain.	Rape and mustard. Cowes, &c., for orders.	Rape and mustard. Foreign Europe.	Rape and mustard. America.	Rape and mustard. Total.	Groundnuts.	Other seeds.	Cardamoms.	Coffee.	Hemp.	Ivory and teeth.	Munjeet.	Myrabolams.	Pepper.	Saltpetre.
Indore	Hong Kong	Nov. 5														133				
Tiverton	London	5				1,533¼				1,533¼		249½	22½	2,417½		10				
Elizabeth Kate	Liverpool	10				250				250										
Contest	Liverpool	13				203½				203½		49½			285					
South Carolina	Liverpool	13													150					
Queen of the Clyde	Liverpool	14																		
Elgin	Hong Kong	18				216½				216½						66				
Catherine Rankin	Liverpool	22																139		
City of Dublin	Havre	24												795						
Malmerby	Liverpool	28				406½				406½										
Charger	Liverpool	29																		
Lancastrian	Liverpool	30																147½		
Total for the month						2,609¾				2,609¾		298¾	22½	3,212½	435	209		286½		
Previously exported this year			18,406½		30,128	100,494½				100,494½		8,717½	382¾	55,109	34,830	4,514	10,445¼	25,655	5,620¾	3,622¼
Total for eleven months			18,406½		30,128	103,104				103,104		9,016¼	405¼	58,321¾	35,265	4,723	10,445¼	25,941½	5,620¾	3,622¼
Exported same time 1863			3,523¼	12,351¼	42,665½	296,102¼		1,009	21	297,132¼	6,293¼	15,720½	418½	34,984½	22,674	2,820½	9,753¼	46,676½	8,283	6,743
" 1862			11,249½		49,718	147,430¾				147,430¾	8,251	18,155½	337	35,237½	33,885½	3,158¾	15,901¼	41,454¾	13,984½	30,728
" 1861			78,357		101,535½	160,119½	3,750		578	164,447½	3,171	4,452¾	632¾	37,036	5,136¼	3,397½	22,587	30,162½	9,185	38,719¾
" 1860			112,680	14	119,260	293,301½			3,095	296,396½	2,153	8,186½	462¾	37,030¼	10,848	3,063¼	15,869	28,015¾	8,171¼	56,300¾
" 1859			315,807		343,188	575,896	9,480		1,126	586,502	13,473	19,108	297	24,704	38,285	3,702	13,806	19,429	4,281	95,558
" 1858			267,997		314,192	443,262	12,785	14,112		470,159	85,003	48,317	635	16,615½	23,478	3,651	19,294	19,608	17,750	54,057

Comparative summary of imports of piece goods into Bombay from Great Britain during October, 1864, with the total of ten months, and of the same period during 1863, 1862, 1861, 1860, 1859, and 1858.

Date.	Shirtings, Longcloths, and Printers.		Jaconets.		Madapolams.		Cambrics.	
	Grey.	White.	Grey.	White.	Grey.	White.	Grey.	White.
	Pieces.	*Pieces.*	*Pieces.*	*Pieces.*	*Pieces.*	*Pieces.*	*Pieces.*	*Pieces.*
From 1st to 31st October, 1864	185,053	13,368	40,308	57,757	60,425	13,225	......	2,889
Previously imported this year	1,787,071	131,996	1,065,258	541,455	596,196	22,387	1,550	45,394
Total for ten months	1,972,124	145,364	1,105,566	599,212	596,621	35,692	1,550	48,213
Imported same time 1863	1,811,633	196,468	389,447	443,489	555,448	12,748	5,394	54,407
Imported same time 1862	1,918,853	176,399	446,428	671,137	394,990	11,143	2,999	125,749
Imported same time 1861	2,689,761	222,002	490,981	614,669	1,094,865	53,965	12,746	59,171
Imported same time 1860	2,975,875	138,775	923,899	551,410	1,881,613	54,403	10,138	9,180
Imported same time 1859	2,682,749	941,432	1,063,536	695,134	787,250	29,605	9,350	13,719
Imported same time 1858	1,660,419	179,434	534,101	337,599	730,303	69,670	11,555	73,885

Date.	T. Cloths.	Domestics.	Mulls.		Figured or fancy shirtings.	Lappets.	Dhoties.	
	Grey.	White.	Grey.	White.	White.	White.	Grey.	White.
	Pieces.	*Pieces.*	*Pieces.*	*Pieces.*	*Pieces.*	*Pieces.*	*Pairs.*	*Pairs.*
From 1st to 31st October, 1864	93,831	1,650	20,104	36,443	1,965	9,000	41,018	90,999
Previously imported this year	351,568	59,166	387,762	932,532	44,093	175,182	150,088	168,431
Total for ten months	445,399	60,816	407,866	968,975	45,356	184,189	191,106	188,710
Imported same time 1863	409,510	34,472	255,017	361,061	34,301	109,716	145,988	6,743†
Imported same time 1862	827,042	126,766	153,763	504,711	81,094	179,398	194,035	135,872†
Imported same time 1861	791,997	83,319	127,414	182,729	173,963	165,494	204,078	457
Imported same time 1860	1,015,885	188,923	233,600	924,418	171,783	167,551	130,455	698†
Imported same time 1859	661,575	134,895		306,355	178,447	923,194	118,784	688
Imported same time 1858	755,135	146,710	110,028	374,504	194,399	972,238	91,807	75,712†

Comparative summary of imports of yarns into Bombay from Great Britain during October, 1864, with the total of ten months, and of the same period during 1863, 1862, 1861, 1860, 1859, and 1858, and totals for the years 1855 to 1863.

Date.	Mule.									Water.			Total grey.	Colored.			
	9s.	30s.	40s.	50s.	60s.	70s.	80s.	90s.	100s. and upwards.	90s.	30s.	40s.		Turkey red.	Orange.	Green.	Other Dyes.
	Lbs.	Lbs.	Lbs.	Lbs.	Lbs.	Lbs.	Lbs.	Lbs.	Lbs.	Lbs.	Lbs.	Lbs.	Lbs.	Lbs.	Lbs.	Lbs.	Lbs.
From 1st to 31st Oct., 1864	75,740	119,655	71,740	51,735	3,905		46,745	17,770	93,685	954,565	89,790	94,190	429,675	85,895	18,000	14,000	4,000
Previously imported this year	981,140	980,585	1,147,400	949,995	107,445	51,670	46,745	17,770	93,625	954,565	1,496,345	365,425	4,274,650	300,070	279,690	165,985	86,505
Total for ten months	398,890	410,180	1,219,140	301,730	111,350	51,670	46,745	17,770	93,625	954,565	1,579,125	349,545	4,704,325	375,965	297,690	179,985	90,505
Imported same time 1863	903,810	999,410	980,390	997,310	113,075	94,925	18,720	7,515	91,270	611,170	954,960	917,385	3,511,890	449,485	139,480	85,940	55,080
Imported same time 1862	110,430	997,350	490,960	131,780	33,410	10,300	4,500	4,900	12,545	63,340	1,133,900	378,380	2,920,535	471,451	485,300	187,650	85,100
Imported same time 1861	389,270	597,250	390,675	988,985	108,695	4,605	3,700	600	600	592,940	1,178,380	304,145	4,465,640	412,505	301,300	85,300	71,830
Imported same time 1860	388,550	430,090	546,945	988,415	100,470	28,610	8,305	2,505	9,830	1,988,450	1,682,606	355,437	4,060,613	943,185	193,319	211,285	107,459
Imported same time 1859	458,595	740,185	2,251,377	457,798	192,255	30,110	36,525	18,080	97,945	1,239,635	2,469,645	792,595	8,691,543	947,910	909,215	78,325	100,196
Imported same time 1858	558,900	755,211	767,130	140,815	42,910	9,115	4,010	600	96,000	1,068,480	1,898,130	985,670	5,497,971	239,665	371,900	86,455	198,150
In the year 1863	903,810	997,970	1,138,540	315,060	108,160	63,689	30,135	13,315	83,370	891,170	1,104,000	963,695	4,099,064	455,485	168,980	112,740	75,980
In the year 1862	156,340	792,740	678,785	156,380	42,410	10,900	4,500	4,900	12,545	132,560	1,381,500	381,900	3,729,720	617,081	615,300	217,650	89,100
In the year 1861	389,370	650,915	1,210,925	395,005	190,700	19,610	8,905	4,905	10,725	385,540	1,432,500	416,989	5,040,905	473,915	462,500	99,680	89,840
In the year 1860	396,370	495,940	590,465	313,635	103,470	92,610	8,900	21,330	99,680	1,385,680	1,768,546	278,997	5,446,378	385,685	909,319	284,085	169,058
In the year 1859	444,640	495,085	985,700	490,005	929,355	91,920	7,195	1,110	8,645	1,443,905	954,385	954,353	9,641,940	318,183	985,092	105,085	
In the year 1858	503,550	341,900	896,175	191,450	76,175	7,150	6,750	1,705	3,700	953,510	1,061,920	979,320	3,362,335	430,425	478,015	104,610	
In the year 1857	341,700	727,300	173,450	33,300	7,180	10,715	5,810	10,650	610,540	737,980	188,769	3,078,985	175,605	275,105	91,000		
In the year 1856	712,450	851,500	1,389,900	509,300	211,300	44,925	10,300	2,000	13,700	1,468,385	1,530,775	359,735	6,905,525	149,954	566,080	38,450	
In the year 1855	911,385	988,400	643,060	990,640	101,900	13,125				1,467,910	771,980	91,600	2,873,570	145,491	147,100	18,000	

SEPTEMBER 2, 1864.

I beg leave to hand you herewith certain tables, numbered from I to IX, setting forth to some extent the commercial condition and prospects of this island

* * * * * * * * * *

They have all been compiled, at no inconsiderable labor, from official sources, and are as thoroughly trustworthy as any such statistics can be.

I do not perceive that these tables require any explanation, unless it be the remark that the large quantity of oil reported in table V, as shipped to the United States, was wholly the "catch" of American vessels brought to this port for shipment.

Comparative statement showing the value of the imports and exports of Mauritius for the years 1862 and 1863, with the names of countries whence derived and whither sent.

Countries.	Imports.		Exports.	
	1862.	1863.	1862	1863.
United Kingdom...........	$3,110,729 89	$2,845,420 83	$5,123,571 91	$5,948,858 56
BRITISH POSSESSIONS.				
Australasia................	1,956,486 16	1,133,244 45	2,740,910 39	3,281,820 25
Cape of Good Hope	364,422 25	263,951 00	746,163 12	521,008 35
Ceylon....................	56,929 25	148,454 91	90,431 25	160,171 00
Continental India .....·....	3,396,507 70	4,249,004 23	907,802 91	1,302,153 25
Dependencies of Mauritius..	22,574 54	15,100 25	....	....
Prince of Wales island.....		3,379 00		
Hong Kong	....	....	13 25	
Nova Scotia	13,993 75	13,234 00		
St. Helena			15,175 00	14,500 00
Singapore	96,187 27	71,333 79	41,225 04	7,405 00
Trinidad	....	....	22 00	....
EUROPE.				
Denmark			23,505 00	
Holland...................				60 50
France....................	1,951,870 90	2,067,395 98	2,388,982 10	1,754,330 98
Italy		8,692 50	....	38,175 00
Hanseatic Towns	25,059 50	....		
Spain		....·.....	....	119,052 50
Sweden	14,173 00	6,855 83	....	....
AFRICA.				
Ichaboe	33,163 25	5,202 50	....	....
Gabon		555 50		
Johanna	....	26,983 31	....	1,936 00
Madagascar	353,536 68	515,630 38	288,574 95	113,273 83
Mozambique		707 64		
Reunion island	90,572 54	162,517 90	80,142 56	109,982 70
Zanzibar..................	....	....	17,072 00	6,090 00
ASIA.				
Bussorah..................	46,607 75	....	....	....
Java.....................		8,142 65	....	75 00
China.....................	4,736 41	75 00	....	
Lombock		4,412 33		
Muscat	23,502 06	19,291 50	10,455 00	7,091 33
Nicobar islands	....	....	25 00	....

Comparative statement showing the value of the imports, &c.—Continued.

Countries.	Imports.		Exports.	
	1862.	1863.	1862.	1863.
ASIA.				
Sandal Wood islands		$2,500 00		$730 50
Persia	$15,021 12			17,045 00
Siam		79 81		
Phillippine islands	699 68	1,172 16		
Pondicherry	155,728 81	144,058 62	$88,073 27	115,718 38
Sava	540 00			
Timor	12,483 75	10,280 00		
AMERICA.				
United States	67,335 58	103,316 38	23,671 25	82,013 50
St. Pierre	21,394 16	25,150 00		
Brazil	10 00			
Mexico	11,288 00			
Peru	272,848 50	479,711 88		
Rio de la Plata	52,680 50	101,620 27		
The fisheries	22,976 87	225,548 50		
Total	12,194,059 87	12,703,023 14	12,586,441 00	13,600,491 65

Comparative statement showing the description, quantity, and value of merchandise imported into Mauritius in the years 1862 and 1863.

Articles.	1862.		1863.	
	Quantity.	Value.	Quantity.	Value.
Asses ... no	21	$550 00	29	$800 00
Cows and oxen ... no	10,934	283,205 00	14,557	358,370 00
Dogs ... no	34	620 00	56	975 00
Goats ... no	19	105 00	20	87 50
Horses ... no	201	24,525 00	596	51,455 00
Mules ... no	1,194	124,300 00	1,725	145,150 00
Sheep ... no	1,269	6,220 00	1,812	7,877 50
Tiger ... no			1	100 00
Swine ... no	539	2,850 00	1,985	5,595 00
Tortoises ... no			292	258 00
Apparel		120,297 00		114,756 04
Apothecary wares		46,763 81		45,527 58
Army carbines ... no	101	251 00		
Fowling-pieces ... no	47	1,920 00	124	4,077 75
Muskets ... no	15			
Ordnance, iron ... cwt	10	30 00		
Pistols ... no	6	130 00	15	312 54
Rifles ... no	11	375 00		
Swords and cutlasses ... no	2	109 25		
Gunpowder ... lbs	34,445	6,596 50	88,096	13,182 25
Shot lead ... cwt	212½	1,135 00	114	699 00
Arrow-root ... cwt	4	412 50	10	94 25
Artificial flowers		2,721 75		4,780 25
Asphaltum ... tons	181½	1,683 75	223½	1,639 50
Bacon and hams ... cwt	859½	16,689 00	1,376	31,350 50
Bags, empty gunny ... no	72,935	3,157 20	318,843	14,505 25
linen ... no	1,102	42 00	31,960	1,270 50

Comparative statement, &c.—Continued.

Articles.	1862.		1863.	
	Quantity.	Value.	Quantity.	Value.
Bags, straw ... no..	$1,102	42 00	31,960	$1,270 50
vacoa ... no..	47,525	4,490 50	325,337	30,309 75
Bark, tanner's ... cwt..	500	430 00	849	736 25
Baskets and basket-work ...	....	561 25	....	489 00
Beef, salted ... cwt..	10,715	59,672 50	14,366½	87,823 56
Beer and ale ... hhds..	1,938 }		1,550 }	
Do. ... galls..	39 }	134,594 25	.... }	91,768 50
Do. ... doz. or bottles..	64,166 }		43,052 }	
Bellows, smith's ... no..	95	901 50	322	1,335 75
Betel-nuts ... cwt..	1,530½	3,407 00	1,286½	3,556 50
Blacking ...	....	3,260 25	....	3,482 25
Blocks for ship-rigging ... no..	773	702 00	25	....
Boats ... no..	8	1,341 00	15	....
Books, printed ...	....	24,865 12	....	....
Bran ... cwt..	1,585	28,694 25	25,246½	....
Bread and biscuits ... cwt..	467	670 75	842½	....
Do. ... cwt..	789	2,069 06	....	....
Bricks and tiles ... no..	864,569	16,667 50	1,164,476	26,418 00
Brushes and brooms ...	....	4,356 75	....	4,671 00
Bunting ... yds..	242	214 50	....	....
Butter ... cwt..	590½	11,792 45	1,960½	40,901 04
Cabinet wares, &c ...	....	40,325 30	....	31,035 20
Candles, composition ... lbs..	393,659	30,412 50	192,048	36,102 75
tallow ... lbs..	9,295	900 50	23,582	2,421 65
wax and sperm ... lbs..	83,256	11,057 25	35,077	5,325 75
Canes and sticks ...	....	680 00	....	734 75
Caoutchouc, manufactures of ...	....	287 50	....	1,316 00
Cards, playing ...	....	416 50	....	878 25
Carriages ... no..	118	36,645 75	103	21,856 00
Carts and wagons ... no..	109	4,110 00	91	25,725 00
Casts of statues, &c ...	....	224 00	....	135 00
Cement ... cwt..	8,319	6,994 25	5,666½	4,262 25
Charcoal, animal ... cwt..	224	955 00	224	698 50
Cheese ... cwt..	1,732	26,801 00	1,495¼	21,740 48
Chocolate and cocoa ... lbs..	24,492	5,190 00	13,363	2,499 50
Cider and perry ...	....	....	....	300 00
Clocks and watches ... no..	723	7,399 75	1,075	6,277 00
Coals ... tons..	19,243¾	89,139 75	27,176½	117,604 75
Coffee ... cwt..	5,351½	83,650 88	8,644¾	139,321 67
Confectionery ...	....	19,346 06	....	21,044 50
Copper, sheets, and nails ... cwt..	5,245½	143,012 68	4,247¾	147,171 20
Cordage, coir ... cwt..	3,360¾	10,947 10	1,874	8,990 79
hemp ... cwt..	4,193¼	35,047 50	3,862¼	40,834 20
Cordials and liquors ... galls..	6,832¼	13,825 57	7,963⅝	19,922 06
Corks and bungs ... gross..	61,166¾	7,107 00	115,868	15,747 50
Corn, barley ... qrs..	318	2,450 00	114⅝	1,370 50
beans ... qrs..	699½	7,900 50	925⅞	8,615 60
dholl ... cwt..	75,293	141,997 06	105,360	195,855 00
grain ... cwt..	171,261	326,785 81	252,059½	478,044 50
maize ... cwt..	129	187 00	484	1,003 00
oats ... qrs..	32,818⅞	209,958 50	49,640⅝	366,958 50
oat meal ... cwt..	6¾	74 50	4½	76 00
peas ... qrs..	500	4,734 75	605⅞	3,545 25
pollard ... cwt..	1,184	2,780 00	604	1,015 00
rice ... cwt..	1,109,603¾	2,100,883 23	1,284,790½	2,621,584 56
wheat ... qrs..	38,801⅝	311,000 00	38,718⅞	349,279 50
wheat flour ... cwt..	29,459½	103,283 75	34,205½	106,057 00
Cotton goods—				
Plain ... yds..	4,102,659	413,768 50	2,168,184	105,261 50
Colored ... yds..	3,106,562	304,530 04	3,678,984	212,808 10

Comparative statement, &c.—Continued.

Articles.	1862.		1863.	
	Quantity.	Value.	Quantity.	Value.
Cotton goods—				
Counterpanes and quilts.no..	8,832	$3,848 50	7,327	$6,226 87
Hosiery..........	....	23,103 50	....	14,412 75
Cotton for sewing ......lbs..	11,017	4,105 00	22,678	11,303 50
Wicks ....lbs..	69	63 00	114	69 00
Wool..........cwt..	31½	14,443 08	246¾	8,332 83
Drawings..........	....	40 00	....	5 00
Earthern and chinaware..pieces..	1,124,851	21,124 70	1,233,583	33,911 75
Feathers, ornamental..........	....	845 00	....	267 00
Fire-works	....	1,013 25	....	2,395 25
Fish, dried or salted..........cwt..	43,518¾	126,815 25	42,163½	118,802 25
herring ....cwt..	187½	748 75	547½	1,660 40
pickled ....bbls..	581	3,326 50	398½	1,402 50
mackerel ....bbls..	225	1,800 00	733	3,285 00
salmon .... ½-bbls..	25	100 00	63	334 00
not otherwise desc'bed.bbls..	674½	2,275 00	1,177½	6,072 00
Fishing tackle..........	....	142 00	....	70 00
Fruits, dried, almonds ..... cwt..	146¾	1,090 49	34½	517 50
apples ....cwt..	4	20 00	18½	147 50
cocoa-nuts ....no..	57,502	957 75	114,451	2,196 00
dates ....cwt..	8,591	21,168 68	2,431¼	8,088 75
figs ....cwt..	20	607 50	15¾	260 09
pistachio nuts.cwt..	370¾	568 25	1,279¾	1,664 75
prunes ....cwt..	70½	1,143 50	47	1,127 00
raisins ....cwt..	124	1,736 75	251¾	2,206 92
walnuts .... bush..	27½	734 50	18	73 00
of all other sorts....	....	460 00	....	342 50
fresh..........	....	411 75	....	561 50
Ghee ....cwt..	1,570	15,645 75	2,623 00	26,370 00
Ginger ....cwt..	32¼	1,175 25	111¾	420 16
Glass, window ....panes..	104,060	8,279 00	32,770	2,891 75
bottles, imp'ted, full.gross..	9,683⅛	30,682 70	7,763 8/11	29,285 88
bottles, imp., empty.gross..	67¾	147 75	37 4/11	119 25
Glassware ....pieces..	215,012	15,488 64	169,529	13,103 00
Glasses, looking, and mirrors.no..	20,134	3,611 00	20,849	3,888 00
Glue ....cwt..	55¾	143 00	39½	401 50
Grease..........cwt..	....	....	114	1,400 00
Groceries	....	8,997 50	....	12,279 00
Gum arabic ....cwt..	19¼	155 00	95	692 75
copal ....cwt..	13¾	73 00	68½	645 00
not otherwise described....	....	5 00	....	....
Gutta-percha, manufactures of....	....	401 00	....	25 00
Haberdashery, millinery, &c....	....	281,401 48	....	446,896 70
Hair, horse..........cwt..	49¾	448 00	28½	214 50
ornamental..........	....	74 50	....	34 00
Hardware and cutlery	....	458,223 56	....	284,867 68
Hats, beaver ....no..	178	460 00	18	74 00
felt ....no..	28,119	25,540 50	35,931	30,978 75
silk..........no..	3,242	6,295 00	4,550	8,867 88
solar..........no..	100	15 00	435	97 50
straw ....no..	65,366	18,408 75	97,988	22,355 88
Hay and straw..........bales..	507	1,127 50	1,201	1,864 50
Hides, raw..........no..	500	2,421 00	2,622	2,453 81
Honey..........	....	10 00	....	19 75
Horns, cow or ox ....no..	200	2 50	760	29 88
Hulls of vessels abandoned	5	4,065 00	10	11,200 00
Ice ....tons..	420	1,000 00	870	5,000 00
Indigo ....cwt..	27¼	549 75	35	880 75
Iron, bar ....tons..	1,680¾	52,480 20	536¼	17,491 75
cast ....tons..	1,103½	71,548 66	3,307 18/20	110,740 12

Comparative statement, &c.—Continued.

Articles.	1862.		1863.	
	Quantity.	Value.	Quantity.	Value.
Iron, wrought, anchors, &c. cwt..	72½	$386 50	98	$536 25
nails .... cwt..	9,244½	42,532 45	8,016	32,690 75
of other sorts. cwt..	1,904½	4,567 25	5,995	20,279 00
Jewelry....................	....	38,436 25	....	36,701 00
Juice of lemons or limes... galls..	405	74 50	58	13 50
Jute.................... cwt..	....	....	7	250 00
Lard .... cwt..	1,091½	135,268 66	17,951	230,062 35
Lead, sheet, and pipes...... cwt..	3,645	19,339 50	3,456½	17,549 88
Leather—				
Unwrought .... cwt..	1,744½	33,691 50	970½	22,063 96
Wrought, boots & shoes. prs..	178,439	153,650 36	175,254	142,626 62
Gloves............ doz. prs..	2,147 9/12	7,040 75	1,470½	5,519 75
of other sorts............	....	10,484 62	....	10,676 75
Leeches .... no..	47,400	502 00	32,000	185 00
Lentils .... cwt..	840½	2,547 25	2,214½	4,711 00
Lime .... cwt..	5,412	4,700 00	2,747	2,424 00
Linen, manufactures of plain. yds..	122,233	22,380 00	44,868	9,650 00
colored .... yds..	981	263 75	1,612	723 50
sail-cloth .... yds..	171,382	12,377 62	133,380	28,110 00
sails .... no..	....	....	1,931	2,781 20
tents .... no..	49	250 85	....	....
thread .... lbs..	9,847	2,705 25	14,266	3,653 12
Machinery and mill work........	....	127,006 50	....	153,941 00
Manure, guano .... tons..	15,230 14/20	393,450 00	22,030	517,215 00
of other sorts..... tons..	90 12/20	2,060 00	20 18/20	1,020 00
Maps and charts	....	175 00	....	63 00
Mathematical and optical instruments	....	2,792 00	....	938 00
Mats and matting...............	....	3,627 62	....	4,921 00
Molasses.................. cwt..	....	....	16½	54 50
Musical instruments............	....	14,884 88	....	12,505 00
Mutton, salted............. cwt..	15½	91 50	49½	200 00
Oakum .... cwt..	150	737 25	124½	502 00
Oil-cloth .... yds..	2,420	878 50	2,048	1,132 75
castor .... cwt..	1,360	9,563 50	1,596½	14,078 75
cocoa-nut .... galls..	78,821	19,711 75	50,341½	12,737 20
gingely .... cwt..	3,930½	19,629 16	5,925½	29,627 50
mustard .... cwt..	505	2,662 25	1,719½	9,029 25
neat's-foot .... galls..	1,305	1,508 00	959½	1,022 50
olive .... galls..	14,810	18,345 25	23,269	26,914 00
pistachio .... cwt..	11,735½	59,306 50	16,934½	85,580 35
rape seed.............. galls..	9,355	4,900 00	600	500 00
sperm or fish........... galls..	779	942 59	220,293	225,714 75
of other sorts.......... galls..	6,256	3,511 25	9,999	6,550 92
Onions and garlic......... bush..	585	811 10	813	1,730 00
Painters' and dyers' material	....	85,936 44	....	51,194 70
Paper-hangings .... rolls..	63,872	9,445 12	58,940	11,992 00
Pearl and Scotch barley .... cwt..	87½	443 25	83	366 20
Perfumery	....	27,101 90	....	35,268 04
Phosphate of soda	....	212 50	....	125 00
Pickles and sauces..............	....	11,067 73	....	16,622 06
Pictures—oil paintings	....	7,245 00	....	172 00
Pitch and tar .... bbls..	3,996½	5,596 25	3,544	9,279 50
Plants and roots	....	1,822 00	....	1,385 50
Plaster of paris................	....	79 00	....	244 75
Plate, wrought, of silver ..... oz..	1,713	3,025 50	1,243	2,145 00
Plated and gilt wares............	....	4,013 50	....	3,786 25
Plaiting for straw hats..........	....	23 00	....	....
Poonac.................. cwt..	32	52 50	....	42 50
Pork, salted............... cwt..	5,712½	56,084 52	5,585½	41,574 90

Comparative statement, &c.—Continued.

Articles.	1862.		1863.	
	Quantity.	Value.	Quantity.	Value.
Potatoes ....cwt..	5,691¾	$13,707 50	3,427½	$9,302 50
Prints and engravings..........	....	1,369 50	....	832 50
Printing types, &c..........	....	398 75	....	1,882 00
Provisions, preserved..........	....	31,695 16	....	15,050 94
Rabannas ....pieces..	99,853	7,448 25	79,077	5,578 25
Ratans ....cwt..	2,190¾	4,744 00	1,722½	3,049 00
Rosin, red ....cwt..	128	631 25	27	164 50
rough	....	140 62	70½	422 50
Saddlery and harnesses..........	....	12,973 88	....	17,671 75
Sago ....cwt..	598½	1,880 50	199½	380 50
Sal ammoniac........cwt..	70½	470 25	43¾	391 75
Salt........tons..	20,937½	16,478 04	143½	6,094 45
Saltpetre........cwt..	25	100 00	277	205 80
Sand ....cwt..	84	40 50	197	137 50
Sausages ....cwt..	166½	2,818 25	154	4,108 25
Sculptures, stone or marble	....	560 00	....	325 00
Seeds, garden	....	2,177 25	....	2,911 58
unenumerated........	....	6,956 35	....	13,558 20
Sheathing paper, or felt........	....	3,628 75	....	2,898 25
Silks, satins, and ribbons...yds..	14,741	6,955 25	8,589	3,442 33
Sewing silk........lbs..	10	85 00	....	....
Silk hosiery	....	....	....	11 50
Slops and negro clothing	....	7,725 00	....	3,167 50
Soap ....cwt..	9,281	45,803 20	13,957½	67,463 00
Specie	....	2,560,781 55	....	1,508,789 77
Specimens, natural history........	....	142 50	....	267 50
Spelter, or zinc, unwrought.cwt..	....	....	73½	72 50
Spices—cinnamon ....cwt..	14¾	313 00	13	103 00
cloves ....cwt..	17	233 00	8½	42 50
nutmegs ....lbs..	50	2 00	100	10 00
pepper ....cwt..	468¾	2,340 50	1,572½	10,598 25
of other sorts ....cwt..	25½	59 75	70½	129 00
Spirits—brandy ....galls..	59,033	102,250 45	54,849¾	169,416 23
Geneva ....galls..	4,468	4,725 88	6,836¾	11,665 38
rum ....galls..	8,100	11,923 75	34,366½	51,941 62
whiskey ....galls..	96	253 12	185	455 62
of wine ....galls..	1,694½	1,580 00	422½	613 00
Sponge........lbs..	189	401 75	306	343 00
Starch........cwt..	743	2,477 50	293¾	871 50
Stationery	....	52,987 73	....	57,418 92
Steel, unwrought ....cwt..	65½	657 00	264	2,276 75
Stones, filtering ....no..	287	945 00	165	567 50
grindstones ....no..	816	482 75	1,064	795 50
marble ....slabs..	82	605 00	73	1,274 00
millstones........no..	4	230 00	....	....
paving ....no..	5,700	880 00	4,400	500 00
slates........no..	3,333	310 38	....	....
tomb ....no..	....	....	1	10 00
Sugar ....cwt..	1,183½	4,394 68	7,292¾	26,555 50
candy........cwt..	64½	618 75	2½	25 00
refined ....cwt..	74	724 00	432¾	2,914 00
Tallow ....cwt..	2,057½	18,390	½	11,882 75
Tamarinds ....cwt..	5,853½	6,665		5,983 25
Tea ....lbs..	20,774¾	7,823	[illegible]	17,830 10
Tin, unwrought ....cwt..	213	2,329	385	7,607 50
plates	....	43,719	....	24,524 25
Tobacco, unmanufactured...lbs..	1,328,198½	66,659	1,049,887	119,699 50
manufactured ....lbs..	52,740½	2,539	131,388¾	23,448 40
cigars ....lbs..	6,551½	9,533 00	13,857¾	11,078 70

Comparative statement, &c.—Continued.

Articles.	1862.		1863.	
	Quantity.	Value.	Quantity.	Value.
Tobacco, snuff..............lbs..	877	$70 83	314	$70 16
pipes ....gross..	147½	470 50	170½	585 25
Tongues ....cwt..	43¼	477 88	114¼	1,718 25
Tortoise shells ....lbs..	156	215 75	1,018	457 50
Toys	....	10,837 00	....	13,099 33
Turmeric ....cwt..	790¼	1,282 77	2,866½	5,417 50
Twines.....................lbs..	59,033½	5,746 16	47,418	5,725 25
Umbrellas, cotton	....	5,088 00	....	5,990 25
silk	....	14,233 25	....	18,566 00
Vegetables, fresh	....	120 00	....	10 00
Vermicelli and maccaroni...cwt..	311½	2,620 25	361½	2,759 90
Vinegar............ ......galls..	34,398	8,396 83	14,394	4,026 73
Wax, bees'..................cwt..	129	599 50	78½	934 25
Whalebone......................	....	....	....	300 00
Wine.....................hhds..	23,926	⎫	29,455	⎫
Do. ....galls..	46½	⎬ 677,187 12	40	⎬ 683,196 92
Do. ....doz. bottles..	23,660⁹⁄₁₀	⎭	32,319	⎭
Wood, boards and plank ..run. ft..	3,666,946	115,175 94	3,252,552	86,752 94
casks, empty..........no..	4,505	6,052 70	3,291	4,092 75
fire-wood..........cords..	6	91 25	16	57 50
houses	....	....	2	2,107 00
masts and spars......no..	196	2,663 25	2,489	3,096 75
oars ....no..	383	250 00	302	195 50
shingles..............no..	1,926,295	11,355 50	2,556,366	11,641 46
spokes and wheels....no..	....	....	....	30 00
timber............cub. ft..	70,340	42,345 00	72,691	27,084 00
Wooden ware.................	....	27,749 75	....	96,927 65
Woollen manufactures—				
cloth ....yds..	18,893	17,257 00	125,880	38,149 75
blankets ....no..	15,495	4,906 65	13,920	4,097 75
carpets and carpeting...yds..	790	348 00	934	1,102 00
hosiery	....	10 00	....	....
shawls ....no..	5,543	7,818 25	7,433	8,739 45
thread ....lbs..	88	139 00	448	25 00
Woollens mixed with cotton				
and silk, &c.... ....yds..	120,308	31,314 00	43,312	15,126 00
Wool, sheep and lamb......cwt..	....	....	168¼	1,847 31

*Comparative statement showing the description, quantity and value of the ex-
ports from Mauritius in the years* 1862 *and* 1863.

Articles.	1862.		1863.	
	Quantity.	Value.	Quantity.	Value.
Animals, cows and oxen.....no..	2	$50 00	....	....
horses ....no..	16	5,400 00	1	$100 00
mules............no..	28	4,200 00	....	....
Apothecary wares................	....	902 00	....	435 00
Apparel.........................	....	9,523 75	....	7,695 00
Arms and ammunition—				
fowling-pieces ....no..	29	385 00	49	1,080 00
muskets..............no..	869	2,172 50	....	....
swords and cutlasses...no..	1	107 75	....	....
gunpowder ....lbs..	164,786	9,749 88	17,910	3,150 00

Comparative statement, &c.—Continued.

Articles.	1862.		1863.	
	Quantity.	Value.	Quantity.	Value.
Arrowroot .... cwt..	58½	$597 50	49	$275 00
Bacon and hams .... cwt..	½	5 00	12½	362 50
Bags, empty, gunny .... no..	48,800	1,497 00	60,225	3,794 00
vacoa .... no..	21,500	1,130 00	73,005	4,865 00
Baskets and basket work	....	....	....	15 00
Beads, ornamental	....	60 00	....	....
Beef, salted .... cwt..	82	410 00	593	3,935 00
Beer and ale, all sorts .. doz. bot...	1,044	1,993 00	1,108 }	2,366 00
Do. do. .... hhds..	....	....	4 }	
Betel nuts .... cwt..	7	17 50	157	1,105 00
Blacking	....	....	....	12 50
Books, printed .... cwt..	109½	1,118 75	12½	330 00
Bran .... cwt..	....	....	152	407 50
Bread and biscuit .... cwt..	1	15 00	13	70 00
Bricks and tiles .... no..	2,000	120 00	5,000	150 00
Butter	1	51 00	1½	60 00
Cabinet and upholstery ware	....	255 00	....	2,071 25
Candles, composition .... lbs..	724	159 00	2,575	765 00
wax and sperm .... lbs..	784	130 00	822	302 00
Caoutchouc .... lbs..	80	15 00	....	25 50
Carriages .... no..	7	2,350 00	1	300 00
Cheese .... cwt..	15	451 00	7	190 00
Chocolate and cocoa .... lbs..	326	70 00	....	....
Clocks and watches .... no..	6	120 00	1	40 00
Coals .... tons..	178	815 00	72	375 00
Coffee .... cwt..	941½	9,517 50	32	512 50
Confectionery	....	915 50	....	524 00
Copper, old, for manufacture . cwt..	5,106⅓	70,364 81	6,918¾	105,151 70
Cordage, coir .... cwt..	215⅓	1,107 50	757	3,480 00
hemp .... cwt..	66	660 00	14½	135 00
Cordials and licorice .... galls..	506½	1,016 00	528⅝	917 50
Corks and bungs .... gross..	20	40 00	1,647 5/12	169 50
Corn, grain and beans .... qrs..	96	375 00	138½	730 00
dholl .... cwt..	....	....	375	690 00
grain .... qrs..	8,333	16,285 00	3,742	7,000 00
maize .... qrs..	30	30 00	....	....
oats .... qrs..	....	....	1	5 00
peas .... lbs..	30	5 00	....	20 00
rice .... cwt..	10,310½	31,735 00	31,848½	74,498 75
wheat .... qrs..	9,586	86,952 50	630⅓	5,005 00
flour .... cwt..	8,232½	24,503 75	149	440 00
Cotton, manufac'd, plain .... yds..	2,410,069	131,657 00	387,410	19,033 50
colored .. yds..	539,884	34,941 67	384,857	31,123 25
counterpanes .... no..	....	....	3,929	2,455 62
wool .... cwt..	1,290⅓	12,616 00	635	6,272 70
Earthen and China ware .. pieces..	27,102	3,282 00	30,018	2,651 00
Feathers, ornamental	....	680 00	....	....
Fish, dried or salted .... cwt..	158	235 00	4,439	16,048 00
herring .... cwt..	1	10 00	1½	20 00
pickled do. .... bbls..	....	....	48	222 00
not otherwise described	....	....	105	500 00
Fruits, dried almonds .... lbs..	25	5 00	....	....
cocoa-nuts .... no..	1,706	90 00	1,316	284 00
dates .... cwt..	13,793	16,357 00	5,230½	6,917 75
pistachio nuts .... cwt..	....	....	165	350 00
Glue .... cwt..	....	....	15	150 00
Ginger .... cwt..	222½	1,112 50	22	110 00
Glass bottles, empty .... gross..	4	60 00	4½	7 00
broken .... cwt..	72	140 00	255	240 00
ware .... pieces..	677	165 00	1,167	235 00

Comparative statement, &c.—Continued.

Articles.	1862.		1862.	
	Quantity.	Value.	Quantity.	Value.
Glass, looking, and mirrors....no..	2,624	$675 00	4,815	$185 00
Grease................... ....cwt..	28	140 00	68	260 00
Groceries	....	611 00	....	189 00
Gum copal................ ...cwt..	....	....	140¼	1,222 50
Gutta-percha . ...cwt..	49¼	755 00	....	....
Haberdashery, &c.	....	63,697 50	....	10,808 75
Hardware and cutlery.............	....	4,391 50	....	6,771 00
Hats, felt................ ...no..	48	416 00	192	90 00
silk. ....no..	366	576 00	....	....
straw................no..	385	150 00	....	....
Hay and straw........bales..	20	100 00	40	40 00
Hemp, undressed........cwt..	95	182 00	....	....
Hides, raw................no..	10,000	21,193 25	16,986	36,971 50
Horns, cow and ox..........no..	13,402	882 25	22,699	836 25
Ice.................... ....cwt..	....	....	1	5 00
Indigo.....................lbs..	....	....	25	12 50
Iron, cast.................cwt..	20	150 00	....	....
bar ....cwt..	....	....	170	220 00
old, for remanufacture.cwt..	7,398	19,535 00	6,970	7,595 75
wrought nails.........cwt..	13	95 00	4½	187 50
of other sorts.cwt..	....	....	178½	692 25
Jewelry............................	....	1,120 00	....	650 00
Lard ....cwt..	....	....	2,043½	23,480 00
Lead, old, for remanufacture.cwt..	56	90 00	199	525 00
sheet and pipes...........	....	....	6	55 00
Leather, unwrought.............	57	880 00	103	2,583 75
wro't boots & shoes.prs..	1,969	2,162 50	700	1,650 00
of all other sorts.......	....	370 00	....	50 00
Lentils ....cwt..	....	....	337	655 00
Lime......................cwt..	....	....	1,123	1,133 00
Linen, manuf'd, plain.......yds..	....	....	3,991	925 00
sail cloth..yds..	808	225 00	360	20 00
sails........no..	....	....	20	1,500 00
Machinery and mill work.....	....	300 00	....	16,500 00
Manure, guano..........cwt..	....	....	1	6 00
other sorts.........cwt..	110	50 00	15	30 00
Mats and matting..............	....	597 50	....	332 50
Molasses.................cwt..	2,283	3,740 00	6,406½	7,991 50
Musical instruments............	....	1,868 00	....	....
Oil, castor ....cwt..	2½	42 00	....	....
cocoa-nut...........galls..	9,665	500 50	4,396	2,481 50
ginger..............cwt..	....	....	22	115 00
mustard ....cwt..	....	....	19	220 00
olive..............galls..	3,606	4,562 50	135	209 00
pistachio..............cwt..	....	....	28	140 00
sperm or fish.........galls..	27,528	34,550 62	621,418	194,228 50
of other sorts.........galls..	....	....	20	50 00
Opium............................	....	....	182	586 00
Painters' and dyers' materials.....	....	755 00	....	2,586 20
Paper manufactures............	....	260 00	....	....
hangings...........rolls..	575	455 00	....	....
Perfumery......................	....	100 00	....	70 00
Pickles and sauces.............	....	1,282 50	....	362 50
Picture and oil paintings.........	....	5,025 00	....	....
Pitch and tar ....bbls..	....	....	12	55 00
Plants and roots...............	....	....	....	10 00
Plaster of Paris..........cwt..	20	150 00	....	....
Plate, wrought of silver..ounces..	39	1,415 50	....	....
Plated and gilt wares............	....	320 00	....	420 00
Poonach................cwt..	....	....	10	10 00

Comparative statement, &c.—Continued.

Articles.	1862.		1863.	
	Quantity.	Value.	Quantity.	Value.
Pork, salted..........cwt..	100	$500 00	686	$4,845 00
Paintings and engravings..........	....	625 00	....	....
Printing type and material..........	....	200 00	....	....
Provisions, preserved..........	....	922 75	....	1,680 50
Rebannas..........pieces..	6,250	565 00	15,801	1,030 00
Ratans..........cwt..	1,367	6,849 00	....	....
Rosin, red..........cwt..	1	5 00	7½	70 00
Sago..........cwt..	5	51 00	90	310 00
Salt..........tons..	452¾	4,473 08	1,211½	3,440 50
Seeds, garden..........	....	25 00	....	23 00
unenumerated..........	....	....	....	1,752 35
Sheathing paper, or felt..........	....	250 00	....	....
Silk, manufactured..........yds..	293	586 00	900	1,500 00
Slops, and negro clothing..........	....	2,700 00	....	....
Soap..........cwt..	44¾	424 00	46	423 00
Specie..........	....	533,750 00	....	295,900 00
Specimens, illus. of natural history	....	15 00	....	220 00
Spices, cinnamon..........cwt..	9¾	137 50	43lbs	5 00
cloves..........cwt..	178	1,030 00	74	193 00
pepper..........cwt..	½	5 00	11	110 00
other sorts..........	....	....	20lbs	5 00
Spirits, brandy..........galls..	1,276¾	1,711 50	1,218¼	2,417 50
rum..........galls..	1,208,576¾	128,093 40	358,399¾	112,435 75
of wine..........galls..	223	278 75	....	....
Sponge..........	....	50 00	....	....
Straw ware..........	....	....	....	10 00
Starch..........cwt..	22	130 00	8	80 00
Stationery..........	....	1,017 00	....	521 25
Stones, marble..........no..	....	....	4	20 00
grindstones..........no..	5	10 50	....	....
mill..........no..	....	....	2	5 00
Sugar..........lbs..	268,377,039	11,161,247 50	275,319,210	12,472,680 10
refined..........cwt..	....	....	1	10 00
candy..........lbs..	10	5 00	....	....
Tallow..........cwt..	56	420 00	....	....
Tamarinds..........cwt..	29	68 50	238	363 00
Tea..........lbs..	6,719	1,462 54	50	20 00
Tin plates..........lbs..	....	1,750 00	....	1,197 50
old, for remanufacturi'g.cwt..	....	....	3	5 00
Tobacco, unmanufactured...lbs..	....	....	4,696	589 50
manufactured.....lbs..	36,422	3,610 67	8,015	1,419·16
cigars..........	8,655½	6,801 00	9,385½	8,076 95
Toys..........	....	35 00	....	60 00
Tortoise shells..........lbs..	3,910	5,160 00	1,828	7,600 00
Turmeric..........cwt..	....	....	42	155 00
Twines, of all sorts..........lbs..	....	....	504	70 00
Umbrellas and parasols, silk..........	....	63 75	....	....
other sorts..........	....	3 00	....	360 00
Vanilla..........lbs..	53	150 00	1,470	3,540 00
Vermicelli and maccaroni...cwt..	¾	8 50	49	252 00
Vinegar..........galls..	392	119 00	872	248 75
Wine..........hhds..	1,368	....	730	
Do. ....galls..	48	41,411 50	11	22,987 20
Do. ....doz. bot..	2,043	....	1,431	
Whalebone..........cwt..	....	....	4	300 00
Wax, bees'..........cwt..	....	....	18	500 00
Wood, boards and plank....feet..	728	39 00	5,353	490 25
casks, empty..........no..	1,544	2,238 50	3,201	4,470 00
ebony..........tons..	84½	3,206 00	7	100 00
shingles..........no..	....	....	11,200	225 00

Comparative statement, &c.—Continued.

Articles.	1862.		1863.	
	Quantity.	Value.	Quantity.	Value.
Wood, spokes and staves....no..	2,070	$1,035 00	....	....
timber.........cubic feet..	230	280 00	2	$25 00
Wooden ware...................	....	281 50	....	128 75
Wool, sheep and lambs......cwt..	336¼	4,444 08	156	2,000 00
Woollen manufactures, cloths.....	390	412 56	363	285 00
blankets...............	2	12 00	....	....
Total....................	....	12,580,669 50	....	14,080,589 48

Comparative statement showing the description, quantities, and value of the exports from Mauritius to the United States during the years 1862 and 1863.

Description.	1862.		1863.	
	Quantity.	Value.	Quantity.	Value.
Rice ....cwt..	286	$715 00	3,132	$5,875 00
Oil, sperm or fish ....galls..	18,141	22,816 00	75,738	75,743 00
Grease...........................cwt..	....	....	32	80 00
Iron, wrought.....................cwt..	....	....	40	20 00
Cocoa-nut oil.................galls..	....	....	102	45 50
Painters' materials.................	....	....	....	250 00

Comparative statement showing the description, quantity, and value of the imports into Mauritius from the United States in the years 1862 and 1863.

Articles.	1862.		1863.	
	Quantity.	Value.	Quantity.	Value.
Apothecary wares				$150 00
Apparel				200 00
Bacon and hams ....lbs..	6,426	$525 00	9,632	2,130 00
Beef, salted ....lbs..	17,696	1,342 50	96,544	5,340 00
Blocks, ships' ....no..	138	702 00	25	6 00
Boats ....no..			3	80 00
Books, printed ....no..	20	20 00		10 00
Bread and biscuits ....lbs..	21,632	741 25	34,048	1,735 00
Bricks and tiles ....no..			50,000	1,000 00
Brushes and brooms		47 50		64 00
Butter ....lbs..	546	135 00	1,120	155 00
Beans		74 00		5 00
Cabinet and upholstery wares		573 75		2,922 00
Candles, composition ......lbs..	3,026	450 00		
Candles, wax and sperm .....lbs..	160	233 00	784	175 00
Carriages ....no..	3	500 00	45	7,535 00
Cheese ....lbs..	2,296	300 00		
Cider ....galls..			380	247 50
Chocolate and cocoa ....lbs..	880	174 75		
Clocks and watches ....no..	300	550 00	496	1,431 75
Cocoa-nut oil ....galls..			182	45 50
Coals ....tons..	13	107 25	11	105 00
Coffee ....cwt..			1½	17 50
Confectionery		5 00		62 50
Copper sheets and nails ....cwt..			136½	1,837 30
Cordage, hemp ....cwt..	690	6,353 00	353½	3,400 00
Peas				2 50
Oats ....bush..	12,488	11,072 00		
Flour ....cwt..	1,117	8,145 50	2,787½	10,485 00
Cotton cloth, plain ....yds..			206	25 75
Cotton wick ....no..	10	49 00		
Earthen-ware ....pieces..			24	3 00
Fish, dried or salted........cwt..	57	193 75	638	3,581 00
herrings ....cwt..	184	650 00		
pickled ....bbls..	100	200 00		
mackerel ....bbls..	125	550 00	286	1,000 00
salmon..........half bbls..	25	100 00	20	50 00
other kinds ....bbls..	250	850 00	944	4,492 00
Apples, dried ....cwt..	4	20 00	18½	147 50
Fresh fruit		100 00		275 00
Glass, window..........panes..	764	147 00		
Glass-ware ....pieces..	2,568	248 00	662	665 00
Glue..............cwt..			1	10 00
Groceries		94 00		278 50
Haberdashery, &c		25 00		20 00
Hardware, cutlery		1,396 75		2,266 25
Hulls of vessels abandoned .....no..	1	570 00		
Ice ....tons..	420	1,000 00	870	5,000 00
Nails, wrought ....cwt..	63	215 00	82½	412 50
Leather				55 00
Lard ....cwt..	486	5,361 75	1,286½	17,292 50
Linen, plain ....yds..			20	10 00
Linen sails...........no..	4	54 50	5	13 00
Maps and charts				15 00
Guano.............tons..	1,002	15,100 00	1,324	13,240 00
Oil ....galls..	2,000	900 00	3,991	1,421 25
Paints, &c.		213 00		92 50
Pickles and sauces		50 00		2 50

Comparative statement, &c.—Continued.

Articles.	1862.		1863.	
	Quantity.	Value.	Quantity.	Value.
Pitch and tar ....bbls..	....	....	1	$7 00
Pork, salted............ ....cwt..	218	$1,745 00	108	847 50
Provisions, preserved	....	....		169 50
Salt.....................................	....	59 00	....	1 25
Saddlery and harness.................	....	....	....	885 00
Soap ....cwt..	10	80 00	80	400 00
Slops and negro clothing				30 00
Spirits, brandy ....galls..	114	....	....	
Spirits of wine.................galls..	1,065	....	....	....
Specimens natural history	....		....	5 00
Grindstones ... .no..	10	20 00	4	4 00
Tallow............................cwt..	237	1,100 00	....	....
Tea ....lbs..	....	....	12	5 00
Tobacco, manufactured.............lbs..	8,968	561 33	20,786	3,464 33
Vinegar ....galls..	3,204	286 00	1,015	134 50
Wood: boards...................feet..	80,472	931 50	228,496	2,854 75
casks ....no..	....	....	242	439 50
masts and spars ....no..	16	470 00	372	923 00
houses ....no..	....	....	1	1,357 00
oars ....no..	306	180 00	290	187 00
shingles..................no..	380,000	1,044 50	730 600	1,468 00
Wooden ware....................:	....	135 00	....	542 00
Mathematical instruments ....⌣...	....	....	....	17 50
Molasses ....cwt..	....	....	16½	54 50
Woollen cloth ....yds..	....	....	20	16 00
Total	....	67,751 58	....	103,322 13

Statement showing the number, tonnage, and nationality of the vessels arrived at Mauritius during the years 1862 *and* 1863.

Countries whence arrived.	1862						1863.					
	CARGOES.		BALLAST.		TOTAL.		CARGOES.		BALLAST.		TOTAL.	
	Vessels.	Tons.	Vessels.	Tons.	Vessels.	Tons.	Vessels.	Tons.	Vessels.	Tons.	Vessels.	Tons.
United Kingdom	79	36,745	3	972	82	39,717	95	42,549	....	......	95	42,549
BRITISH POSSESSIONS.												
Australasia	41	12,143	4	1,036	45	13,179	54	15,737	4	1,190	58	16,927
Cape of Good Hope	60	14,112	26	6,202	86	20,314	77	16,961	23	5,708	100	22,669
Ceylon	5	456	....	......	5	456	11	3,196	....	......	11	3,196
Continental India	147	97,640	4	2,463	151	100,103	145	103,237	3	1,803	148	105,040
Dependencies of Mauritius	10	1,175	....	......	10	1,175	8	692	....	......	8	692
Nova Scotia	1	169	....	......	1	169	1	150	....	......	1	150
Rangoon	6	3,632	....	......	6	3,632	5	5,206	....	......	5	5,206
Singapore	13	5,730	....	......	13	5,730	10	4,936	....	......	10	4,936
EUROPE.												
France	54	23,594			54	23,594	60	24,595	1	415	61	25,010
Hanseatic Towns	1	238	....	......	1	238	1	276	....	......	1	276
Italy							1	321	....	......	1	321
Sweden	5	1,866	1	180	6	2,046	2	647	....	......	2	647
AFRICA.												
Gaboon							....	......	2	726	2	726
Ichaboe	4	1,153	....	......	4	1,153	2	302	....	......	2	302
Johanna							1	280	....	......	1	280
Madagascar	72	19,295	1	283	73	19,578	117	28,413	....	......	117	28,413
Isle of Bourbon	45	6,333	8	2,382	53	8,715	38	5,577	4	1,601	42	7,178
Mozambique							1	201	....	......	1	201
Suez	11	6,910	....	......	11	6,910	11	7,427	....	......	11	7,427
Zambese River			1	189	1	189						
Xont-Bé							1	214	....	......	1	214
ASIA.												
Bushire	1	368	....	......	1	368	....	......	....	......	....	......
Bussorah	3	1,519	....	......	3	1,519	....	......	....	......	....	......
China	3	2,537	....	......	3	2,537	....	......	....	......	....	......
Java	1	349	....	......	1	349	4	3,267	....	......	4	3,267
Mascat	3	827	....	......	3	827	2	544	....	......	2	544
Philippine Islands	1	516	....	......	1	516						
Pondichery	9	2,692	....	......	9	2,692	11	4,452	....	......	11	4,452
Lombok							1	254	....	......	1	254
Penang							1	286	....	......	1	286
Nervo Islands	1	254	....	......	1	254	....	......	....	......	....	......
Aden							1	851	....	......	1	851
Timor	1	273	....	......	1	273	1	294	....	......	1	294
AMERICA.												
United States	8	3,868	....	......	8	3,868	7	5,706	....	......	7	5,706
St. Pierre, Newfoundland	2	559	....	......	2	559	1	239	....	......	1	239
Brazil			1	369	1	369	1	444	2	626	3	1,070
Mexico	1	631	....	......	1	631						
Peru	15	8,981	....	......	15	8,981	26	14,234	....	......	26	14,234
Buenos of La Plata	7	3,942	4	1,372	11	5,314	12	4,864	6	1,840	18	6,704
The Fisheries							7	2,631	....	......	7	2,631
Total	610	258,807	53	15,448	663	274,255	716	298,983	45	13,909	761	312,892

Comparative statement showing the number and tonnage of vessels departed from Mauritius during the years 1862 and 1863, and the name of country to which cleared.

Countries to which departed.	1862.						1863.					
	CARGOES.		BALLAST.		TOTAL.		CARGOES.		BALLAST.		TOTAL.	
	Vessels.	Tons.	Vessels.	Tons.	Vessels.	Tons.	Vessels.	Tons.	Vessels.	Tons.	Vessels.	Tons.
United Kingdom	121	64,445	....	....	121	64,445	129	66,499	....	....	129	66,499
BRITISH POSSESSIONS.												
Australasia	97	28,603	....	....	97	28,603	91	24,234	1	65	92	24,299
Cape of Good Hope	46	8,140	....	....	46	8,140	43	6,816	....	....	43	6,816
Ceylon	12	4,464	28	14,901	40	19,365	12	3,967	25	17,487	37	21,454
Continental India	59	35,953	65	44,336	194	80,289	54	29,888	67	51,289	121	81,171
Hong Kong	....	....	3	1,797	3	1,797	1	276	....	....	1	276
Prince of Wales Island	....	773	....	....	1	773	....	....	....	....	....	....
Rangoon	1	665	1	492	2	1,157	....	....	2	1,470	2	1,470
Singapore	4	1,539	3	1,390	7	2,929	3	1,157	3	2,642	6	3,799
Trinidad	1	1,348	....	....	1	1,348	....	....	....	....	....	....
EUROPE.												
Denmark	1	282	....	....	1	282	1	434	....	....	1	434
France	59	22,788	....	....	59	22,788	44	17,755	....	....	44	17,755
Holland	....	....	....	....	....	....	4	3,267	....	....	4	3,267
Spain	....	....	....	....	....	....	3	864	....	....	3	864
AFRICA.												
Johanna	1	184	....	....	1	184	2	511	....	....	2	511
Madagascar	61	16,418	22	5,087	83	21,505	66	15,956	42	10,089	108	26,045
Nossi-Bé	....	....	....	....	....	....	1	42	1	214	2	256
Isle of Bourbon	35	5,934	14	1,510	49	7,444	57	13,765	7	1,917	64	15,682
Suez	11	6,910	1	613	12	7,523	10	6,622	1	808	11	7,430
Zanzibar	6	2,276	1	345	7	2,621	5	2,251	2	580	7	2,831
ASIA.												
Bushire	....	....	....	....	....	....	1	250	1	87	2	337
Bussorah	....	....	1	544	1	544	....	....	....	....	....	....
China	4	3,275	2	210	6	2,485	....	....	....	....	....	....
Java	1	330	....	....	1	330	....	....	4	1,934	4	1,934
Lombok	....	....	....	....	....	....	....	....	1	347	1	347
Maldive Islands	....	....	1	84	1	84	....	....	....	....	....	....
Muscat	2	414	....	....	2	414	3	1,110	....	....	3	1,110
Nicobar Island	....	....	....	....	....	....	....	....	2	1,856	2	1,856
Pondichery	18	6,996	2	781	20	7,777	20	8,020	1	348	21	8,368
Sandalwood Islands	....	....	....	....	....	....	1	281	....	....	1	281
Timor	....	....	....	....	....	....	....	....	1	170	1	170
AMERICA.												
United States	1	561	....	....	1	561	2	987	....	....	2	987
Guadaloupe	....	....	....	....	....	....	1	705	....	....	1	705
St. Thomas	....	....	....	....	....	....	2	1,136	....	....	2	1,136
Fisheries	....	....	....	....	....	....	....	....	1	288	1	288
Total	535	213,298	144	72,090	679	294,388	556	206,814	169	91,564	718	298,378

Comparative statement showing the quantity and destination of the sugar crops of Mauritius for the years 1861–'62, 1862–'63, 1863–'64.

Countries.	Crops.		
	1861–'62.	1862–'63.	1863–'64.
	Pounds.	*Pounds.*	*Pounds.*
United Kingdom	82,718,588	170,709,066	118,255,069
France	50,047,715	41,248,788	32,968,963
Cape of Good Hope	12,835,521	13,817,204	9,364,230
Australia	67,207,552	69,916,628	59,397,235
Sundry places	7,607,891	20,630,590	23,457,008
Total	220,417,267	316,322,276	243,432,525

Comparative statement of quarterly average prices and total value of the sugar crop from 1856–'57 to 1863–'64.

Crops of—	Quantity exported.	Average price.	Value.
	Pounds.		
1856–'57	231,451,053	$628	$13,358,890 52
1857–'58	215,397,729	619	13,356,656 45
1858–'59	237,898,969	577	13,812,171 60
1859–'60	226,966,182	579	12,890,186 45
1860–'61	271,167,312	544	14,460,496 52
1861–'62	220,417,237	503	11,029,355 45
1862–'63	316,322,276	426	13,476,609 00
1863–'64	243,432,525	562	13,680,907 90

VICTORIA, V. I.—A. FRANCIS, *Consul.*

JANUARY 18, 1864.

I have the honor of making the following report in relation to the commerce, navigation, and other matters connected with this port, from the year 1858 to 1863, inclusive. Victoria, V. I., being the principal depot for the northern coast of the Pacific, and as little heretofore has been known of its trade and commerce, I have, as leisure permitted, collected from the best sources possible the statistics herewith submitted.

VICTORIA, V. I., 1863.

During the past year the trade of Victoria has been moderately prosperous. The city has gradually improved. Nearly one hundred buildings, including dwelling and business houses, have been erected. Its population is now estimated at between five and six thousand permanent residents. The importations during the year 1863, and preceding years from 1861, will be found in the tables of imports, marked A, and consisted principally of dry goods, liquors, provisions, and farming implements. The exports from this port, until within the last six months, were small, and no definite data as to the amount can be ascertained. The exports of merchandise for the last six months, ending December 31, 1863, will be found in table of exports, marked B.

The year 1862 was marked by a great rush of adventurers to the gold mines of British Columbia. Over fifteen thousand persons are reported having passed up to the mines. Thousands were disappointed. Provisions were sold at famine prices, and the consequences were great suffering, destitution, and rushing back and reporting the mines as a failure and a humbug.

During the year 1863 the number of miners in the British Columbia gold mines was reported at thirty-five hundred. Provisions the past season were cheaper, and the mines have been more remunerating; several instances of fortunes having been and the parties returning to the United States.

The export of gold during the past year, as obtained from reliable sources, amounts to $2,935,170 16. It is computed that an equal amount has been taken away in the hands of private individuals. I enclose statement of the exports of gold from the year 1858 to 1863, inclusive, furnished at my instance by parties therein named, marked C.

SHIPPING.

Reference is made in relation to the amount of tonnage and number of crew entering and clearing at this port during the six months ending December 31, 1863, to statement marked D.

It will be noticed that the amount of American tonnage entering exceeds that clearing 1,018 tons. This is accounted for in the transfer to English subjects of quite a number of small vessels, prohibited by the collector of Port Angelos from importing goods subject to duty which heretofore had been running between this port and ports on Puget's sound.

AGRICULTURE.

But little attention is given to farming on Vancouver's island. For beef, pork, bacon, and provisions generally, as well as hay, oats, and barley, the people are almost wholly dependent on California, Oregon, and Washington Territory. During the year 1863 there were received from California alone 30,097¼ barrels of flour, 3,899 sacks of wheat, 28,939 sacks of barley, and 6,252 sacks of oats.

MINES OF VANCOUVER'S ISLAND.

The business of prospecting for copper the past season on the island was quite a mania, and resulted in the discovery of several mines, which are attracting considerable attention. Companies have been organized, and are now working to develop their extent and value. His excellency the governor of Vancouver's island some months since offered a reward of £1,000 for the discovery of any paying gold fields on the island. Several parties immediately commenced prospecting, and late in the fall it was reported that mines had been found some twelve miles from the city. Quite a number of persons rushed to the spot and found gold, but not in sufficient quantities to pay for the labor. The miners, however, struck several quartz ledges, assays from which are encouraging. The quartz rock is now being raised, crushers manufactured, and it is predicted that this branch of business will open a new field for enterprise, and have a salutary effect upon the prosperity of Victoria.

MANUFACTURES, ETC.

Aside from the foundry and machine business little is doing in manufacturing. One large foundry and machine shop has been erected during the past season.

and is now in successful operation. There have been two steamboats built during the past season.

The wages of mechanics, carpenters, and stone-masons, during the working season, have been from $5 to $6 per day.

The principal business of this part of the world appears to be digging from the earth gold. Every branch of industry seems dependent upon the success of gold-miners. As new discoveries are made and become known, the tide of adventurers turns, and now the gold and silver mines of Washington, Idaho, and Nevada Territories are attracting all attention, and on the opening of spring two-thirds of the miners who labored in British Columbia the past season will turn their steps towards these new gold fields. This fact causes a sort of doubt to hang over the prospects of Victoria and British Columbia for the approaching season.

Comparative tabular statement showing the value of the imports into Victoria during the years 1861, 1862, and 1863.

Countries.	1861.	1862.	1863.
From San Francisco	$1,288,359	$2,345,066	$1,860,117
From Washington Territory	228,250	224,793	242,781
From Oregon	216,603	75,370	108,603
From England	516,041	694,278	1,432,521
From Sandwich Islands	54,382	112,108	113,486
From British Columbia	31,454	32,424	65,870
From Melbourne		32,170	
From China		22,268	45,434
From Valparaiso		17,000	
Total imports	2,335,069	3,555,477	3,867,812

Statement showing the exports from the port of Victoria, V. I., during the six months ending December 31, 1863.

Months.	San Francisco. Value.	Port Angelos. Value.	Astoria. Value.	New York. Value.
July	$20,673 00	$5,970 00	$945 00	
August	25,015 00	6,804 00	1,727 00	$349 00
September	16,650 00	6,187 00	637 00	
October	28,112 00	8,863 00	4,208 00	
November	23,217 00	3,988 00	2,586 00	
December	25,456 00	10,412 00	361 00	
Total	139,123 00	42,224 00	10,464 00	349 00

Statement showing the export of gold from Victoria, Vancouver's island, from 1858 to 1863, inclusive.

1858, Wells, Fargo & Co.	$337,765 17
1859, Wells, Fargo & Co.	823,488 41
1860, Wells, Fargo & Co.	1,298,466 00
1861, Wells, Fargo & Co.	1,340,395 72

1862, Wells, Fargo & Co.................................	$1,573,096 18
1863, Wells, Fargo & Co.................................	1,373,443 39
McDonald & Co., from 1858 to December 31, 1861.........	1,207,656 00
1862, not included in Wells, Fargo & Co.'s statement.......	335,379 00
1863, Bank British North America......................	585,617 85
1863, Bank British Columbia	824,876 92
Hudson Bay Company and others, from 1858 to 1863, inclusive.	500,000 00
	10,200,184 64

Shipment of gold by express and on freight during the year 1862	$2,167,183 18
Same for the year 1863	2,935,170 16

Statement showing the tonnage and number of crews of American and foreign vessels entered at and cleared from Victoria during six months ended December 31, 1863.

Nationality.	Tonnage entered.	No. crew.	Tonnage cleared.	No. crew.
American............................	47,075	2,412	46,057	2,343
Foreign.............................	43,800	1,516	47,048	1,711

APRIL 6, 1864.

The total imports from California, Oregon, and Washington Territory, during the quarter just closed, amount to $547,205, a falling off of more than $100,000 from California as compared with the same period last year.

The imports from England have more than doubled that of the corresponding quarter for last year.

The exports from this port to San Francisco, Portland, Oregon, and Port Angelos, Washington Territory, during the quarter, amount to $124,220, which is a greater increase over the corresponding quarter of last year.

The exact amount of gold and gold dust shipped from this port during the quarter I am unable to furnish at present. It is estimated that at least $250,000 have been forwarded to San Francisco by express and in private hands.

In the mining prospects of Vancouver's island and British Columbia nothing new has been announced. The Frazer river to Yale has been open all winter, and since the 20th of March between eight and nine hundred miners have left this city for the Carriboo mines; but a large majority of the miners wintering here have gone to the Boise country, leaving as early as the first of March.

The weather during the last five months has been ruled by storms of wind and rain unprecedented in the knowledge of the "oldest inhabitant."

JULY 5, 1864.

During the last quarter the importations from California have fallen off, as compared with the previous quarter, $110,020.

From Oregon the importations have increased $9,243, and from Washington Territory $10,985.

The importations from foreign countries to this port during the last quarter are as follows: from England, $171,297; from British Columbia, $22,514; from Sandwich Islands, $8,288.

During the quarter there has been a decrease in the importations from England, as compared with the last quarter, of $391,429, and an increase from British Columbia of $18,904, and from the Sandwich Islands of $5,643.

The imports from California, Oregon, and Washington Territory, embraced flour, bacon, pork, beef, mutton, wheat, barley, lumber, live stock, agricultural implements, machinery, dry goods, and groceries.

The imports from England were principally dry goods, hardware, iron, liquors, &c.

From the Sandwich Islands the imports were sugar, molasses, and coffee, and from British Columbia furs, hides, and skins.

·The exports from this port were furs, hides, skins, wool, coal, copper ore, dry goods, hardware, iron, and liquors.

There has been no change in the commercial regulations of this port since the previous quarter. A pilot bill, however, passed the colonial legislature, and has been approved by the governor, which levies a charge of four dollars per foot pilotage on vessels entering and leaving the harbor of Victoria and Esquimalt.

St. Helena—G. Gerard, *Consul.*

June 6, 1864.

* * * In answer to No. 44, (no date,) I would say that there exists no tax of any description at St. Helena, except on landed property, and the law makes no exception. The only courtesy extended to foreign consuls residing here is the exemption to perform military duty—an order to that effect having been published by the authorities a year ago.

Malta—Wm. Winthrop, *Consul.*

March 10, 1864.

I have the honor to make my twenty-ninth annual report.

The number of arrivals (American) during the year 1863 was eleven, as follows: 2 in January, 3 in March, 2 in April, and 1 in July, August, September, and December. One was a ship, eight were barks, and two schooners—and all of four thousand seven hundred and forty-three tons burden—four came from Boston, two from Gibraltar, two from Alexandria, in Egypt, one from New York, one from Soulina, and one from Marseilles.

During the year several vessels, under foreign flags, with valuable cargoes, have stopped at this port on their way to the United States. * * *

August 20, 1864.

I have the honor to make my consular report for the first half year of 1864, the number of arrivals during this period being eight—five barks and three ships—in all of four thousand four hundred and thirty-six tons burden.

Of these vessels three came from New York with general cargoes, two from Boston with the same description of merchandise, and three were loaded with coal from Cardiff.

On their departure five vessels were bound to Sicily, one to the Black sea, one to Smyrna, and one to Callao. * * * * *

GIBRALTAR—HORATIO J. SPRAGUE, *Consul.*

OCTOBER 6, 1864.

* * * You will perceive, by the present returns, that the number of arrivals of American vessels at this port falls considerably short of that of previous quarters ; still the importations of produce from the United States have fully kept pace with those of former quarters—with this difference, however, that the largest portion of the merchandise was brought in foreign bottoms, principally under British and Italian flags. The preference given to foreign bottoms is in consequence of the advanced rates of insurance charged, both in Europe and in the United States, on property shipped under our flag. * * With the exception of the coal business, I have to report a decrease in the trade of this port.

As for the coal trade, it is daily becoming more important as the arrivals of steamers increase. During the year ended the 30th ultimo no less than 1,536 steamers, of all nations, have entered this port for the purpose of replenishing their supplies of coal, which are obtained from private companies having hulks in the bay.

HOBART TOWN—D. M. PHASON, JR., *Consul.*

JANUARY 20, 1864.

I have the honor to enclose a copy of the new tariff of customs duties for this colony, and which is now in force here, and supersedes the " ad valorem." It was rather unpopular at first, but is now getting more liked and is found to work better than the former one, and is therefore likely to be continued for some time.

TARIFF OF TASMANIA.

SCHEDULE No. 1.

	s.	*d.*
Ale, beer, and porter, of all sorts, in wood, per gallon..............	0	6
Ale, beer, and porter, of all sorts, in bottle, reputed quarts, per bottle.	2	0
Ale, beer, and porter, of all sorts, in bottle, reputed pints, per dozen..	1	0
Hams, bacon, lard, butter, cheese. candles, nuts, walnuts, ginger, almonds, pepper, pimento, licorice, mustard, blue, arrowroot, maccaroni, vermicelli, tapioca, sago, per pound............................	0	2
Cigars, snuff, per pound--	4	0
Coffee, cocoa, chocolate, chicory, per pound	0	3
Perry and vinegar, per gallon....................................	0	4
Cinnamon, cloves, mace, gunpowder, (except blasting,) tartaric acid, citric acid, nutmegs, spices, mixed spices, ground spices, and cassia, per pound....	0	4
Hops, per pound...	0	2
Fruits, dried, per pound............—............................	0	1½
Malt, per bushel..	1	0
Oil of all kinds, (except fish oil,) turpentine, varnish, per gallon.....	0	6
Pickles in bottles, reputed quarts, per dozen	3	0
Pickles in bottles, reputed pints, per dozen	2	0
Rice, pearl barley, white lead, red lead, paints of every description, carbonate of soda, soda crystals, per pound	0	0½
Spirits—brandy, rum, whiskey, and perfumed spirits, per gallon....	12	0

	s.	*d.*
Rum, per gallon	12	0
Whiskey, and all other spirits, cordials, liqueurs, or strong waters, the degree of strength of which cannot be ascertained by Sykes's hydrometer, per gallon	12	0
Perfumed spirits, per gallon	12	0
Wine, containing more than 25 per cent. of alcohol of a specific gravity of .825 at the temperature of 60° of Fahrenheit's thermometer, for every gallon in proportion to the strength, in wood, per gallon	2	0
Ditto, in bottle, per dozen, reputed quarts	8	0
Ditto, in bottle, per dozen, reputed pints	4	0
Wine, not containing more than 25 per cent. of alcohol, &c., per gallon	2	0
Tobacco, per pound	2	6
Tobacco, cigars, and snuff, destroyed for sheep wash, per pound	0	3
Sugar, refined, per cwt	8	0
Sugar, unrefined, per cwt	6	0
Molasses, per cwt	3	6
Tea, per pound	0	6
Soap, per pound	0	1
Starch, per pound	0	1
Shot, per pound	0	1
Sauces, reputed pints, per dozen	3	0
Sauces, reputed half-pints, per dozen	2	0

And so in proportion for all spirits, cordials, and strong waters, for any greater or less quantity than a gallon, not being less than one-eighth part of a gallon; for ale, beer, and wines, in bottle, for any greater or less quantity than a dozen reputed quart or pint bottles; for all sugar and molasses, for any greater or less quantity than a hundred weight, not being less than a quarter of a hundred weight.

SCHEDULE No. 2.

	s.	*d.*
Manufactures of silk, cotton, linen, and woollen, and all articles manufactured therefrom, drapery, hosiery, haberdashery, millinery, furs, hats, boots, shoes, confectionery, bottled fruits, preserves, oilman's stores of all kinds, (except pickles and sauces,) plate, crown, and sheet glass, and all other goods, innenumerated, measuring outside the package, per cubic foot, and all packages of the foregoing, measuring outside the package less than one cubic foot	2	0
Glassware, crockery, per crate, cask, packet, or other package	10	0
Brushware, cutlery, hardware, hollow ware, plated ware, ironmongery of all kinds, per cwt., or any portion thereof	3	0
Wool bags, each	0	2½
Corn sacks, each	0	0½
Gunny bags, each	0	0¼
Bagging, per bale of 1,000 yards	8	4
Deals, manufactured or unmanufactured, per load of 50 cubic feet	8	0
Tubs and buckets, per dozen	2	0
Matches, per case of not more than 50 gross	10	0
Blacking, per cask	5	0
Toys, per cubic foot	0	6
Coir matting, per cubic foot	0	6

SCHEDULE No. 3.—TABLE OF EXEMPTIONS.

Agricultural implements and tools of all kinds.
Guano and other manures of every description.

Wheat, oats, barley, maize, hay, bran, beans, peas, oranges, lemons, pine-apples, green fruit, and vegetables of every description.

Salt.

Flour, oatmeal, bread, biscuit.

Trees, plants, shrubs, bulbs, and seeds of every description.

Horses, pigs, poultry, dogs, sheep, cattle, and living animals.

Empty casks, cases and boxes, of wood.

Empty bottles, corks.

Galvanized iron—sheet or piping.

Zinc, sheet, or piping.

Anchors, chains, and cables, of every description.

Copper, or yellow metal, rod, bolts, or sheathing.

Felt for sheathing.

Oakum and junk.

Sail canvas, rope, and twine.

Pitch, tar, and resin.

Fish oil, whalebone, and whale fins.

Whaling implements and gear of every description.

Ships' blocks, binnacle lamps, signal lamps, compasses, shackles, sheaves, dead-eyes, dead-lights, boats' oars.

Beef, pork, and lime-juice.

Printed books, printed paper, paper, and books of every description, except room papers.

Ink, printing presses, printing type.

Maps, charts, and globes.

Organs and bells specially imported for churches and chapels.

Passengers' baggage and cabin furniture, arriving in the colony with owner.

Coke, coals, hides and skins, raw and unmanufactured, of every description.

Timber of all kinds, unmanufactured, except deals.

Firewood.

Lead, sheet or piping.

Chaff-cutters and machinery for agricultural purposes.

Cart and carriage axles, arms, and boxes.

Carriage shafts, spokes, and felloes.

Iron pipes, iron tanks.

Gunpowder, for blasting.

Slates for roofing, cement of all kinds, plaster of Paris.

Tallow, soda ash, caustic soda.

Whiting, chalk.

Wool, flax, hemp, tow, unmanufactured.

Works of art, viz: statues, busts, casts of marble, bronze, alabaster, or plaster of Paris, paintings, drawings, prints, engravings, lithographs, photographs, specimens of sculpture, cabinets of coins, medals, gems, and all collections of antiquities.

Specimens of natural history, mineralogy, or botany.

Ores of all kinds of metals.

Gold dust, gold bars, bullion, and coin.

Philosophical instruments and apparatus.

Fire-engines, steam-engines, pumps, and other apparatus for raising water.

Coir, bristles, and hair, unmanufactured.

Fire-bricks, cotton waste, candle cotton, saltpetre, iron bridges, iron fencing, draining tiles, and draining pipes.

Empty tin cases for jam.

Unmanufactured tin, tin plates.

Millstones and machinery for mills.

Bath bricks, grindstones.

Blacksmiths' bellows and anvils.
Rod, bar, hoop, sheet, plate, and pig iron, share moulds.
Unmanufactured steel of all kinds.
Lime and bark.
Ice.
All goods imported for the use of her Majesty's government.

CAPE TOWN—WALTER GRAHAM, *Consul.*

MAY 19, 1864.

I beg leave to inform you that the colonial parliament has just increased the duties on imports twenty-five (25) per cent., specific as well as ad valorem duties.

Previous to the passage of this act, and before the nature of it was known, the governor telegraphed to the collectors of customs to exact a bond from all persons desirous of taking goods out of the bonded warehouses that they would pay the increased duties *whatever they might be.* This was pronounced illegal by the supreme court; but parliament subsequently passed an act indemnifying the governor and refusing the plaintiff's costs, when the supreme court succumbed. This matter has caused a great excitement among importers, and business was nearly suspended for ten days. The subject will go before her Majesty's home government on appeal.

In answer to circular 44, from your department, I would say that consuls in this colony and the other British possessions in South Africa, embraced in my district, are not exempt from taxation in any way.

The colonial taxes are raised chiefly from duties on imports, which are ultimately paid by the consumer, whether he is a British subject or a foreign consul. The other taxes are laid upon stamps, transfer of real estate, &c., and are paid by all alike, and so with the municipal taxes.

SEPTEMBER 1, 1864.

I have the honor to submit my annual report on commerce.

The British possessions in South Africa on the seaboard consist of Cape Colony, British Kaffraria, and Natal, all of which are within my district, but under separate governments. For this reason I am obliged to collate the commercial statistics of each colony separately, beginning with Cape Colony.

The following table, compiled from the Blue Book for 1863, just issued, exhibits the movements of commerce generally in this colony, and the growing importance of the American trade in particular.

	Imports.	Exports.
Great Britain	£1,427,088	£1,345,067
British colonies	372,076	270,256
United States	187,604	533,481
All other countries	289,065	75,642
	2,275,833	2,224,446
Balance of trade against the colony		51,367
		2,275,833

The following table shows the aggregate value of all exports and imports of the colony in the 6½ years named therein :

	Imports.	Exports.
1850	£2,277,043	£1,747,632
1859	2,579,359	2,021,371
1860	2,665,902	2,080,398
1861	2,605,305	1,972,700
1862	2,785,853	1,957,686
1863	2,275,833	2,224,441
1864, (6 months)	1,113,861	1,319,139

The balance of trade against the colony for the five years ending with 1863 was £2,655,651, but the balance of trade in favor of the colony for the first six months of the present year is £205,278.

The following table shows the growth of imports from and exports to the United States in the years named :

	Imports.	Exports.
1830	£19,859	£5,416
1850	39,747	18,971
1859	147,111	295,445
1860	177,867	357,713
1861	75,836	171,287
1862	249,023	280,200
1863	187,604	533,481
1864, (6 months)	Not known.	499,852

Wool, skins, and hides still continue the chief articles of export to the United States, and the aggregate value of them was greatly increased during the first six months of the present year, or before the character of the present tariff of the United States was known here.

The following table will show the growth of this branch of commerce with America :

Years.	To United States.	To all other countries.	Total value.
1859	£210,190	£990,658	£1,201,348 Wool.
1860	281,606	1,167,023	1,448,629 "
1861	149,313	1,311,471	1,460,784 "
1862	239,007	1,044,129	1,283,136 "
1863	467,891	1,036,770	1,504,661 "
1864*	468,422	568,069	1,035,491 "
1859	79,383	84,454	163,837 Skins and hides.
1860	71,095	63,744	134,839 " " "
1861	17,862	79,222	97,084 " " "
1862	36,962	92,682	129,544 " " "
1863	55,983	84,588	140,571 " " "
1864*	43,779	24,513	68,292 " " "

* First six months only.

The foregoing tables merely show the volume of *direct* trade between this colony and the United States; but during the early part of this year, and on former occasions, a large quantity of Cape wool was shipped from England to America. The same is true with regard to imports, as sewing and other useful machines of American manufacture are frequently imported into this colony from England.

The relative prominence of the several ports in the colony, and the manner in which the foreign trade is distributed amongst them, is illustrated by the table below.

Names of ports.	Value of imports.	Entered for consumption.	Colonial produce exported.
Cape Town............................	£1,154,588	£995,774	£613,990
Port Elizabeth.....................	1,057,366	976,631	1,361,423
Simon's Bay...........................	29,050	17,971	5
Mossel Bay............................	27,660	27,660	22,483
Port Beaufort.......	4,718	4,718	None.
Port Alfred...........................	2,451	2,451	None.

NEW TARIFF.

At the last session of the colonial parliament the duties on imports were increased twenty-five per cent. all around, or, in other words, the duties were still computed by the old tariff, and twenty-five per cent added to the amount thereof. The following is the free list:

Live animals; books and music, except foreign reprints of works copyrighted in the United Kingdom; glass bottles, or contents of which a specific duty is levied; bullion, coin, and diamonds; guano and ice; maps, charts, and pictures; seeds, bulbs, plants and specimens of natural history and certain other articles for the use of her Britannic Majesty's forces in the colony.

The following is the specific list under the old tariff, to which twenty-five per cent. must be added.

Specific list.

		£	s.	d.
Coals, coke, and patent fuel...................per ton...........		0	0	6
Cheese..per cwt. (112 lbs.)..		0	10	0
Coffee....................................do......do.....		0	12	6
Currants, raisins, and figs (dried)...............do.............		0	5	0
Meats, (salted or cured).....................do.............		0	3	0
Pepper.....................................do.............		0	10	0
Rice..do.............		0	2	0
Sugar (unrefined)...........................do.............		0	3	6
Sugar (refined).............................do.............		0	5	0
Cinnamon and cassia.......................per lb...........		0	0	3
Cloves......................................do.............		0	0	4
Ginger.....................................do.............		0	0	1
Ginger preserved, or chow-chow..................do.............		0	0	2
Gunpowder..................................do.............		0	0	6
Mace.......................................do.............		0	0	9
Nutmegs....................................do.............		0	0	6
Tea..do.............		0	0	6
Tobacco (unmanufactured).....................do.............		0	1	0

	£	s.	d.
Cigars per 1,000, £1 5s. 0d., or at the option of the collector.......	0	2	6
Ale, beer, and porter, in bottles................per gallon..........	0	0	3
Ale, beer, and porter, not in bottles...............do..............	0	0	2
Spirits and cordials.............................do..............	0	5	0
Wine in bottles............................do..............	0	3	6
Wine not in bottles...........................do.....	0	3	0
Flour..per barrel..........	0	3	0
Wood (unmanufactured)....................per cubic foot.......	0	0	0
Guns, or gun barrels, each........................do............	1	0	0
Pistols, or pistol barrels...........................do............	0	10	2

Ad valorem duties.

There is no list of *ad valorem* duties, because they are levied on *all* articles not included in the two foregoing schedules, except foreign reprints of books copyrighted in Great Britain, which pay a duty of 20 per cent. By the old tariff, $7\frac{1}{2}$ per cent. was levied on all articles not already enumerated, and 10 per cent. of that amount was added for packages, making $8\frac{1}{4}$ per cent. in all. By the *new* tariff just passed, 20 per cent. of the $8\frac{1}{4}$ per cent. is added to it, making $10\frac{5}{16}$ per cent. in all.

IMPORTS FROM THE UNITED STATES, 1863.

The principal articles imported from the United States in 1863, (and the value of each) are as follows :

Agricultural implements......................................	£8, 342
Bread and biscuit..............................	1, 988
Wheat and maize...	7, 604
Flour..	77, 185
Butter..	2, 242
Cabinetware	3, 861
Candles	1, 826
Carriages	1, 637
Glassware..	1, 347
Hardware	2, 807
Tobacco	55, 171
Lard	1, 408
Meat (salted or cured)..	5, 983
Kerosene oil..	3, 175
Whale oil	1, 290
Oilmen's stores...	2, 228
Soap	1, 833
Other articles	7, 848
Total...	187, 604

Some of the " other articles " in the above list are apothecary ware, apparel, ale, basket ware, books, copper and brass manufactures, brushes, cement, cheese, cider, confectionery, cordage, bran, dried fruit, haberdashery, millinery, hats, hops, spars, cables, hoops, rivets, jewelry, clocks, leather manufactures, machinery, malt, musical instruments, perfumery, resin, seeds, plants, spirits, stationery, wooden ware, and staves.

PORT DUES.

There have been no tonnage or port dues levied since 1854, except for wharfage, and the proceeds collected under this head are exclusively devoted to the construction of the new breakwaters and docks, on which 500 convicts and 300 free laborers are employed. These wharfage dues are comparatively light, but it is expected that they will be reduced as soon as the harbor improvements are completed. As it is, from the low price of fresh provisions and other ship's stores, the ports of the colony continue a favorite resort for ships calling in for supplies.

NAVIGATION, 1863.

ENTERED WITH CARGOES.		CLEARED WITH CARGOES.	
British....410	From United States.....11	British....417	To United States.......34
Foreign...181	From United States.....27	Foreign...131	To United States........19

NATIONALITY OF SHIPS.

ENTERED WITH CARGOES.			CLEARED WITH CARGOES.		
Nationality.	No. ships.	Tons.	Nationality.	No. ships.	Tons.
British........	323	153,568	British....	297	143,276
Colonial......	87	13,816	Colonial.	120	19,625
American.....	40	19,625	American	34	16,945
Other countries........	141	49,742	Other countries......	97	32,388

DISTRIBUTION OF SHIPPING.

Ports cleared from.	BRITISH SHIPS.		FOREIGN SHIPS.		Total.
	With cargoes.	Without cargoes.	With cargoes.	Without cargoes.	
Cape Town......	252	29	85	25	391
Port Elizabeth ...	145	11	26	12	194
Simon's Bay.	15	6	19	6	46
Mossell Bay.	5	1	1	0	7

COASTING TRADE.

Nationality.	ENTERED.		CLEARED.	
	Ships.	Tons.	Ships.	Tons.
British..........	272	41,219	275	43,880
Foreign............	13	3,558	23	6,818
Total........	285	44,777	298	50,698

INTERNAL AND OTHER IMPROVEMENTS.

The ground has been broken for a new railway from Wellington, the terminus of the present line to Worcester, 60 miles further inland, which will open up to commerce the most fertile region in the western part of the colony.

A telegraph line has been put in operation within the present year from Cape Town, through Port Elizabeth, to Grahamstown, a distance of 600 miles. Another line from thence to Natal, nearly as long, is now being constructed.

A company has been organized to furnish Port Elizabeth with a better supply of water.

A light-house has been erected at the entrance of Mossel bay, which is now an excellant port of refuge for ships coming from the eastward in the four winter months, when it is difficult to double Cape Agulhus by reason of the strong northwesterly gales.

A new system of lights for Table and False bays is to be put in operation on the 1st of January, 1865, and the new sailing directions corresponding have been already promulgated. I will transmit copies to the Light-house Board at Washington.

The patent ship-docks at Simon's bay and at Table bay (the port of Cape Town) have been repaired, and are now in good working order.

The harbor improvements at the mouth of the Kowie river (Port Alfred) are nearly at a standstill, but the works at Table bay are progressing finely.

BRITISH KAFFRARIA.

This colony is governed by the governor of Cape Colony, without any parliament or constitution. It contains many rich sheep farms, and its only port of entry is East London, though much of its commerce with foreign nations flows through Cape Colony. The following table, therefore, but partially shows the volume of trade of the colony, as it is merely a return of imports and exports at East London, at which no American vessels with cargoes have yet called :

	Imports.	Exports.
1863	£153, 013	£29, 979
1864, (6 months)	91, 843	22, 947

The tariff on imports is made by the governor to correspond with that of Cape Colony, so as to prevent smuggling. His excellency has proposed to annex the colony to Cape Colony, but the people are much averse to it.

The seaboard between this colony and Natal has always been occupied by independent Kaffre tribes, ruled by their own chiefs; but the governor has recently pushed his authority beyond its precincts, and proposes to open the whole of the Transkein territory to white settlers, by offers of grants of land on certain conditions, and this proposition has raised a commotion among the neighboring chiefs. At present there is little trade on this part of the coast, but it will increase as colonization progresses, unless interrupted by another Kaffre war.

NATAL.

This is a young, vigorous, and very progressive colony. Its customs duties are considerably lower on many articles than those of Cape Colony, and hence there is some fear in the latter that its port will draw off the trade of the Transvaal republic and the Orange River Free State, (another interior republic,) which now flows through Port Elizabeth mainly. The following table gives the imports and exports of Natal for 1863 :

	Imports.	Exports.
1863 :		
Great Britain	£308, 147	£113, 520
United States	2, 879	....
Other countries	162, 307	45, 045
	473, 333	158, 565
1862		118, 286
Increase		40, 279

The imports set down in the above table as from the United States all came . through Port Elizabeth; but there were, no doubt, many other American goods imported from England to Natal, and I know that others were shipped from that colony to Cape Town, of which no account is taken in the table. No cargoes that I am aware of have ever been sent to Natal directly from America.

The following will show the growth of the *new* articles of colonial export for the first six months of 1863 and 1864, respectively:

	1863.	1864.
Sugar	£6, 219	£26, 845
Cotton	136	485
Wool	17, 600	23, 277
Tobacco	0	10
	23, 955	50, 617

The other articles of export are arrowroot, coffee, butter, ostrich feathers, ivory, hides, skins, horns, pepper, and Indian meal. Indigo and other products of tropical climates have been introduced, but as yet none except those already mentioned figure among the exports. The cotton culture is carried on under the auspices of a company in Manchester, England, and an excellent staple has been produced. Coolies from India are being imported into the colony to raise this article, as well as the coffee and sugar, because Kaffre labor has been found not so reliable.

The harbor improvements are suspended for the present, on account of the failure of the contractor in England.

The colonial parliament has granted a tract of land and other privileges to a company to induce it to build a railway to the coal mines, which are located 100 miles inland, and are not worked. When this project is carried out it will be a great benefit to Cape Colony, Mauritius, and steamers proceeding to or from India, China, Australia, &c., as well as Natal, because all the coal used in this part of the world comes from Europe.

Many improvements are being made by the colonists in other respects. American ploughs have been generally introduced, and on a cotton plantation a steam plough has been tried. At one of the stations of the American missionaries, among the Kaffres, a sugar mill has been erected to manufacture sugar, grown in small quantities by the natives themselves. These missionaries are doing a good work in promoting civilization, which is duly appreciated by the government.

BELIZE—CHARLES A. LEAS, *Commercial Agent.*

APRIL 4, 1864.

In answer to your circular No. 44, I have to say that there is no taxation whatever in this colony, except the import tax of 4 per cent. upon all articles brought into the colony, save ice and a few other articles, which enter free; but all persons, it matters not to what position they belong, must pay this tax if they import or receive articles from a foreign country. There is, also, a dog and horse tax collected within the town of Belize; but here again all persons must pay the tax who keep a horse or dog. And no foreign consuls are exempt from this tax whether they are allowed to trade or not.   *   *   *

MAY 7, 1864.

I have the honor to inform you that the colonial assembly has just adjourned. and among the acts passed was one declaring that the currency of this colony shall be dollars and cents, the dollar to be equal to four English shillings, and the cents equal to the hundredth part of a dollar, hence the dollar of British Honduras will be $2\frac{1}{2}$ per cent. less in value than the United States dollar. This demission of the currency has been brought about in consequence of the fact that the bulk of the trade of this colony is with the United States. The law provides, also, that book accounts shall also be kept in dollars and cents.

An act was also passed levying an additional impost duty of one per cent., to pay interest upon a loan for the improvement of the lawn of Belize; hence the duties now are, in the aggregate, five per cent. ad valorem, that is, according to the foreign value or cost, with charges added.

MAY 24, 1864.

I have the honor herewith to transmit a commercial exhibit for the year 1863, showing that the trade movements to and from this colony for the above named period, amounted in the aggregate to $3,497,755—of which the imports were $1,154,540, and the exports $1,943,215. The following tabular statement will exhibit the imports and exports from and to the various countries that carry on trade with British Honduras, and also the total commercial movements with the same, viz:

Imports and exports.

Countries.	Imports.	Exports.	Total trade movement.
United Kingdom	$739,045	$1,176,020	$1,915,065
Jamaica	13,410	....	13,410
United States	460,235	267,435	727,670
Spanish Honduras	262,085	137,730	399,815
Guatemala	10,140	55,585	65,725
Yucatan	39,735	227,200	266,935
Mexico	27,995	74,145	102,140
Cuba	1,895	2,000	3,895
Mosquito coast	....	3,100	3,100
Total	$1,554,540	$1,943,215	$3,497,755

The following will show the various articles imported, the quantity of each, and the countries that furnish the same, viz:

IMPORTS.

Articles.	Countries.	Quantity.	Total.
Bricks................M..	United Kingdom........	252,944	
Do....................do...	United States..........	66,400	
			319,344
Cattle..............head.	Spanish Honduras	1,210	
Do....................do...	Guatemala	390	
Do....................do...	Yucatan	305	
			1,905
Coffee.............pounds.	Jamaica...............	88,854	
Do....................do...	Spanish Honduras	100	
Do....................do...	Guatemala	11,066	
Do....................do...	United States..........	1,188	
			101,208
Cacoa.................do...	United Kingdom........	4,070	
Do....................do...	United States..........	15,272	
Do....................do...	Jamaica...............	3,165	
Do....................do...	Guatemala.............	40	
			22,547
Cigars.................M..	Jamaica...............	1,100	
Do....................do...	Spanish Honduras	41,700	
Do....................do...	Yucatan...............	573,945	
Do....................do...	Guatemala	64,500	
Do....................do...	Cuba........	4,500	
			685,745
Cotton.............pounds.	United States..........	647,475	
Do....................do...	Mexico............	120,645	
			768,120
Cotton seed.........barrels.	United States...........	27	
Do...do..............do...	Jamaica...............	26	
Do...do..............do...	Mexico............	29	
			82
Drugs..............pack's.	United Kingdom........	44	
Do....................do...	United States..........	682	
Do....................do...	Jamaica..............	9	
			735
Earthen-ware.........do...	United Kingdom........	....	324
Furniture............do...	...Do.....do	64	
Do....................do...	United States..........	78	
			142
Glass-ware...........do...	United Kingdom........	469	
Do....................do...	United States..........	864	
			1,333
Hay...............pounds.	United Kingdom........	11,676	
Do....................do...	United States..........	24,751	
			36,427
Horses..............head	Spanish Honduras	19	
Do....................do..	United States..........	4	
Do ....do..	Other countries.	102	
			125
Malt liquors...........gallons.	United Kingdom........	11,284	
Do....................do...	Spanish Honduras	2	
Do....................do...	United States..........	2,267	
			13,553
Merchandise.........pack's.	United Kingdom........	10,649	
Do....................do...	United States..........	5,167	
Do....................do...	Jamaica..............	384	
			16,200
Machinery............do...	United Kingdom........	467	
Do....................do...	United States..........	82	
			549
Oars..............	United States...........	....	334

Importations—Continued.

Articles.	Countries.	Quantity.	Total.
Provisions—			
Beef ....barrels.	United States............	....	267
Bread.....................do...	Do...do............	....	1,831
Flour.....................do...	Do...do............	....	12,516
Pork......................do...	Do...do............	....	2,506
Vegetables............pack's.	Do...do............	....	858
Slates....................	United Kingdom........	36,000	
Do.	United States............	13,000	
			49,000
Soap....................cwt.	United Kingdom........	3,496	
Do.......................do...	Yucatan	28	
Do.......................do...	Cuba...................	2	
Do.......................do...	United States...........	599	
			4,125
Spirits and cordials.........gallons.	United Kingdom........	12,348	
Do.......do.............do...	Jamaica...............	299	
Do.......do.............do...	Spanish Honduras	1	
Do.......do.............do...	Guatemala	2	
Do.......do.............do...	United States............	271	
			12,921
Sugar....................pounds.	United Kingdom........	7,479	
Do.......................do...	Spanish Honduras	100	
Do.......................do...	United States...........	34,036	
			41,615
Tea.......................do...	United Kingdom........	5,710	
Do.......................do...	Jamaica	3	
Do.......................do...	United States...........	2,167	
			7,880
Turpentine...............barrels.	United States............	....	418
Tobacco..................pounds.	Spanish Honduras	1,792	
Do.......................do...	Yucatan	3,384	
Do.......................do...	Guatemala	438	
Do.......................do...	United States...........	52,923	
			58,537
Wine....................gallons.	United Kingdom........	3,492	
Do.......................do...	Jamaica...............	13	
Do.......................do...	Spanish Honduras	921	
Do.......................do...	Guatemala	10	
Do.......................do...	Yucatan...............	47	
Do.......................do...	Cuba..................	27	
Do.......................do...	United States...........	1,415	
			5,925
Lumber..................feet.	United Kingdom........	4,418	
Do.......................do...	Spanish Honduras.......	14,101	
Do.......................do...	United States...........	1,097,220	
			1,115,739
Shingles..................	United States............	1,443,500	
Do.	Spanish Honduras	160,000	
			1,603,500

The following will exhibit the various articles of export, the quantity of
each, and the countries to which the same were sent, viz:

EXPORTS.

Articles.	Countries.	Quantity.	Total.
Bark....................seroons.	United Kingdom........	139	
Do....................do...	United States..........	12	
			151

Exports—Continued.

Articles.	Countries.	Quantity.	Total.
Cochineal....................seroons..	United Kingdom........	724	
Do......................do....	United States...........	82	
			806
Cocoa-nuts	United Kingdom........	436,340	
Do.	United States...........	30,250	
Do.	Spanish Honduras	40,800	
			507,390
Coffee....................bags..	United Kingdom........	....	57
Cotton....................bales..	Do.....do........	1,194	
Do.......................do...	United States...........	1,118	
			2,312
Cigars....................cases..	United Kingdom........	2	
Do.........................M...	United States...........	19,800	
Hammocks................bales..	United Kingdom........	2	
Indigo....................seroons..	Do.....do........	112	
Merchandise.............pack's.	Cuba..................	88	
Do.....................do ...	Mexico	1,235	
Do.....................do...	Yucatan	2,982	
Do.....................do...	Guatemala	1,843	
Do.....................do...	Spanish Honduras	1,673	
			7,821
Metal—old copper ....tons..	United Kingdom........	5	
Do.......do..............casks..	United States...........	18	
Powder....................pack's.	Spanish Honduras	262	
Do.......................do...	Yucatan	161	
Do.......................do...	Guatemala	524	
			947
Rags.......................do...	United States...........	....	8
Rosin....................barrels..	Do... do........	....	7
Turpentine ....do...	Do....do........	....	29
India-rubber..................bales..	United Kingdom........	5	
Do. ....do...	United States...........	4	
			9
Sarsaparilla................do...	United Kingdom........	115	
Do....................do...	United States...........	726	
			841
Shell, tortoise...............pack's.	United Kingdom........	12	
Do.......................do...	United States...........	7	
			19
Silver-ore bags...............	United Kingdom........	....	60
Skins—deer.................bales..	United States...........	....	164
hides..................	Do....do............	....	266
Specie....................dollars.	United Kingdom........	165,150	
Do.......................do...	United States...........	23,376	
			$188,526.
Spirits....................gallons.	United Kingdom........	3,351	
Do.......................do...	United States...........	400	
Do.......................do...	Spanish Honduras	748	
Do.......................do...	Mexico................	1,181	
			5,680
Sponges....................dozen..	United States.............		13
Sugar....................pounds..	United Kingdom........	299,544	
Do.......................do...	United States...........	65,980	
Do.......................do...	Spanish Honduras	21,010	
Do.......................do...	Mexico................	65,432	
			451,966
Tobacco....................bales..	United Kingdom........	810	
Do.......................do...	United States...........	22	
			832

Exports—Continued.

Articles.	Countries.	Quantity.	Total.
Turtle............ :	United Kingdom.........	....	38
Mahogany .... sup. feet.	United Kingdom.........	6, 035, 264	
Do...................... do....	United States............	161, 206	
			6, 196, 470
Logwood .... tons..	United Kingdom.........	7, 141	
Do...................... do...	United States............	1, 285	
Do...................... do...	Guatemala.............	45	
			8, 471
Fustic.................... tons..	United Kingdom.........	126	
Do...................... do...	United States............	4	
			130
Ziricote................... tons..	United Kingdom.........	26	
Do...................... do...	United States............	6	
			32
Lignumvitæ................ tons..	United Kingdom.........	....	9
Pitch-pine................. logs..	......do................	69	
Do...................... do...	United States............	492	
			561

Vessels that arrived during the year 1863 from foreign countries were 101, of the aggregate tonnage of 29,072. And there were from the United States 41; from the United Kingdom, 17; from Mexico, 9; from Cuba, 4; from Gibraltar, 2; from France. 3; from Spain, 8; from Italy, 3; from Brazil, 2; from St. Thomas, 5; from Bahamas, 1; from Teneriffe, 2; from Medina, 1; from Fernando, 2.

The nationalities of the vessels that entered were as follows: British, 64; American, 5; Norwegian, 19; Swedish, 2; Danish, 2; Russian, 2; Hamburg, 1; Central America, 1; Sardinia, 1.

The above shows only five vessels as having entered the port under the flag of the United States, but this is explained from the fact that nearly all the regular traders to Belize changed their flags from American to English to avoid capture.

The following will exhibit the average price of provisions in this market for 1863:

Wheat flour.......................................per barrel....	$10	00
Horned cattle.....................................each	15	00
Horses..each	60	00
Sheep ....each	8	00
Goats...each	6	00
Swine...each	8	00
Milk ....per pint......		12
Butter, fresh......................................per pound....		50
Cheese ....per pound....		25
Beef..per pound....		15
Mutton ....per pound....		28
Pork..per pound....		15
Rice...per quart		12
Coffee ....per pound....		25
Tea...per pound....	1	75
Sugar ....per pound....		9
Salt...per pound....		3

Wine...per dozen....	$8	00
Brandy..per gallon....	6	00
Beer ....per dozen	3	00
Tobacco ....per pound....		30

Though cochineal, indigo, and sarsaparilla form articles of export from Belize, yet they are the products of Spanish Honduras, Guatemala, San Salvador, and Yucatan. The cotton which is stated as imported from Yucatan was mainly from the southern States, though they are commencing to cultivate that article both in Yucatan and British Honduras.

The amount of gunpowder that the foregoing statement represents as having been exported is altogether incorrect, though taken from the custom-house returns. I know, of my own knowledge, large quantities of powder taken on board the blockade-running vessels in not only a disguised form, but in the original packages. And I informed the authorities of the fact at the times, but the captains were allowed to call it candles, pork, or anything else they pleased upon their manifests.

AUGUST 26, 1864.

I have the honor to communicate the following as the wholesale prices that are prevailing at this date for the principal articles that are exported to the United States from this colony. Also the rates of exchange and freights, viz:

Cochineal ....per pound........	$0	75
Cocoa-nuts ....per thousand	12	00
Copper, old..............................per pound........		18
Cordage, old.............................per pound........		
Cotton, upland...........................per pound........		45
Cotton, Sea Island.......................per pound........		
Deerskins, Spanish Honduras..............per pound........		40
Deerskins, Yucatan ....per pound........		40
Hides, dry ....per piece.........	1	75
Hides, green.............................per piece.........		
India-rubber.............................per pound........		20
Indigo ....per pound... 1 to 1		25
Iron, old ....per pound.........		¼
Oil, cocoa-nut ....per gallon........		
Oil, cahoun ....per gallon........		
Sarsaparilla, Spanish Honduras...........per pound........		17
Sarsaparilla, British Honduras...........per pound........		17
Sarsaparilla, Guatemala..................per pound........		17
Sarsaparilla, Mexican ....per pound........		17
Sugar, brown ....per pound........		10
Cigars ....per thousand	8	00
Sponges ....per dozen		37½
Tobacco, leaf ....per pound........		
Turpentine, sap ....per barrel	10	00

Woods :

Cedar ....per thousand feet..	40	00
Fustic ....per ton	16	00
Logwood ....per ton	13	00
Mahogany ....per thousand feet..	40	00
Rosewood ....per ton	17	00
Pitch pine lumber ....per thousand feet..	70	00

EXCISE DUTY.

Sugar is subject to an excise duty of three shillings per hundred pounds, which is entitled to drawback if exported from the colony.

FREIGHTS TO THE UNITED STATES.

Logwood	per ton	$5 00, in gold.
Mahogany	per thousand feet..	15 00 do.
Cedar	per thousand feet..	15 00 do.
Rosewood	per ton	5 00 do.
Light freight	per bale	$1 50 to 2 00 do.
Cotton	per pound	1½ do.

Common custom has made the cost of lighterage a charge upon the vessel, and not the shipper, and which is about fifty cents per ton.

SHIPPING COMMISSIONS.

The usual shipping commissions are 2½ per centum.

EXCHANGE.

On England, $5 to the £.

On New York, payable in currency, no transactions.

On New York, payable in gold, par.

The general rate of exchange on England is five Central American dollars to the pound sterling, equal to twenty shillings, and equal to 487½ cents United States gold currency.

The Central American dollar has been decreed to be worth 2½ per centum less than the gold dollar of the United States; hence the par of exchange on New York when expressed in dollars and cents here means 2½ per centum premium.

IMPORT DUTIES.

The duty on all goods imported from foreign countries is 4½ per centum, estimated upon the amount of invoice, with charges and freight.

TONNAGE DUES.

The tonnage dues are two shillings per ton registered measurement.

HOSPITAL DUES.

All vessels arriving from foreign ports, outside of the coasting limits, are required to pay for each man six shillings.

SINGAPORE—ALEXANDER HUTCHINSON, *Acting Consul.*

NOVEMBER 19, 1861.

Thinking that you may be pleased to hear how the cultivation of cotton is progressing in the Straits settlements, I take the liberty of communicating to you some particulars concerning its growth at Washington estate, in Prince Wellesley, under the management of J. B. Hayne, esq., ex-United States consul at Turk's Islands. In the month of June last Mr. Hayne reached this port, and spoke to me on the subject of raising cotton, and wished me to assist

'him in lands and funds, informing me that he was practically acquainted with
its culture. I introduced him to the governor, who received him very cordially,
and offered to do everything that depended upon the government towards its
success.

Mr. Hayne then went to Penang, carrying letters to the lieutenant governor,
and was sent into the province by this gentleman with an armed escort, and at
the expense of the Straits government, to look for lands suitable to the culture
of cotton. He took the precaution to select ground that had previously been
cleared, cropped, and abandoned by Malays, so that a little turning up was
alone required to prepare the land for seed.

· The sea island seed has only recently arrived, but about fifty thousand
plants, collected chiefly from the seed sent out to Bombay by the Manchester
Cotton Supply Association, have been above the ground now some time, and
are doing very well.

Indeed it is as yet uncertain whether the latter will not in the end prove best
adapted for the soil and climate in the province, for the cultivation cannot but
be profitable if the crop can only be collected without damage.

Cotton planters in the province will have a great advantage over those of the
United States in being able to obtain any amount of labor required at particular
seasons, the native population being always ready to accept temporary employment when not exclusively occupied with their own pursuits, such as planting
and getting in the paddy crop.

Fifteen trees, growing near a police station in the province, that were planted
some nine months ago, have upon them, respectively, 156, 178, 125, 110, 100,
189, 215, 105, 90, 80, 59, 40, 35, 20, 45 pods, giving, as an average, 103 pods
to the tree, or about one-third of a pound of clean cotton, as it is computed that
for one pound of clean cotton it requires of Pernambuco pods 288. Mr. Hayne
has now 111 men at work, at $3 *per mensem per man.*

The estate contains about nine hundred acres of first-rate land, and so confident is Mr. Hayne of success that he has applied for another large grant of land
in the province of Malacca, about three hundred miles to the southward of province Wellesley.

FRENCH DOMINIONS.

PARIS—JOHN BIGELOW, *Consul.*

FEBRUARY 24, 1864.

The census of France for 1860 is now being published, under the superintendence of M. Legoyt, chief of the bureau of statistics in the ministry of agriculture and commerce. The first part has just appeared, and is, I presume, by
far the most minute and careful analysis of the movement of the population of
France that has ever been made. As these volumes are not printed for general
use, their contents receive but a limited circulation even in France, and in
the United States next to none at all. I have, therefore, thought it worth
while to prepare for the State Department a pretty full analysis of the most
important results revealed by them, both to show the minuteness with which
these investigations have been conducted by the French government and to
render more intelligible some of the elements both of its weakness and of its
power.

SUPERFICIES OF FRANCE.

The territory of France, exclusive of the colonies and Algeria, of which no
account is made in the statistics, which follow measures 54,239,679 hectares, or
542,397 kilometres square.

POPULATION.

The following table gives the population of the eighty-six departments of France, leaving out the department of Savoy and Nice, recently annexed, of which full returns have not yet been received:

	Population, 1860.	Mean duration of life.
Department of the Seine....................................	1,856,091	32 years.
Other cities than Paris....................................	8,461,532	34.6 "
Rural departments.......................................	26,204,781	40 "
	36,522,404	

The mean duration of life has experienced the following variations since the year 1817:

1817—1824: 31.8.	1847—1854: 37.4.
1824—1847: 34.4.	1854—1860: 37.8.

These tables show a gradual though feeble lengthening of life for the last forty years. It is estimated to have increased about six years within the last half century.

RATIO OF BIRTHS AND DEATHS.

The excess of births over deaths is greater in the country than in the cities. Thus, in 1860, when there was neither war nor famine nor pestilence, the increase per hundred inhabitants was in the cities 0.3843, or a little more than one-third per cent., while in the rural districts it was 0.5026, or about one-half per cent. Since 1855, however, in the department of the Seine (which is another name for Paris) the increase has been greater, even, than in the country—0.5937 in 1860—which is attributed to the immigration of adults, among whom the ratio of mortality is relatively small, and also the extensive municipal improvements, which have greatly promoted the health of the metropolis.

RATIO OF MARRIAGES.

The proportion of marriages is slightly on the increase. The whole number in 1860 was 288,936. From 1800 to 1850 the proportion was one to every 127 inhabitants. From 1851 to 1861 the proportion was one to 126 inhabitants.

The number of marriages is in a direct ratio to the density of the population. Thus, in 1860 there was in the department of the Seine one marriage to every 100 inhabitants, one to 122 in the other cities* than Paris, and one to 129 in the rural districts. The largest proportion of marriages is in the agricultural districts, and the smallest in the mountainous departments.

Out of 100 marriages there are 83.29 between persons never married before, 3.73 between bachelors and widows, 9.38 between widowers and maidens, and 3.60 between widowers and widows.

The mean age of the marrying parties is pretty uniform. It was 30 years and 2 months for the man and 26 for the woman in 1853; 30.5 and 26 in 1860. It is higher in the city than in the country. Thus, in 1860 the men married at an age of 31 years and 10 months and the women at 27 years and 1 month in

* Under the denomination of cities are included all towns having an aggregate of 2,000 inhabitants.

the department of the Seine, at 31 years and 26 years 6 months in other cities than Paris, and 30 years 1 month and 25 years 10 months in the rural districts. But in the rural population there is a greater disproportion of years between married people than in the cities; but it does not appear except among those married over 30 years of age. Below that age the disproportion is less than in the cities.

In comparing the sexes it is found that the men generally marry later in life than the women. The only exception to this rule is in the case of bachelors who marry widows. The statistics of births go to show that where there is least disproportion in the ages of the marrying parties there will be found the largest proportion of male offspring.

The mean duration of the marriage state is on the increase. From 23 years 2 months in 1836, it had reached 25 years in 1856. This is attributed to the average lengthening of life in France.

Epochs corresponding to certain religious usages, and also to certain extraordinary demands for labor, have a sensible influence upon the number of marriages. For example, the minimum occur in lent, and the maximum during carnival. A notable diminution is also to be remarked during harvest. Out of a hundred married persons, the number who could not sign their names to the marriage contract was in 1860 37.56. In 1855 it was 39.92.

The number of marriages between blood relations, out of 10,000, was 127 in 1858, 130 in 1859, and 121 in 1860.

From 1851 to 1855 there was one birth to every 38 inhabitants; from 1855 to 1860, one to every 37. Here, again, the density of population affects the rate of fecundity. For example, in the department of the Seine in 1860 there was one birth to every 32 inhabitants; in the cities, not including Paris, one to every 35, and one to 40 in the rural districts.

But the most remarkable fact connected with marriages in France is the constant tendency to infecundity. Towards the end of the last century the average number of children to a marriage was 4.5. For the period between 1855 and 1860 the average was not above 3.10. This average is lower in the department of the Seine. From the returns of 1856, it appears that there was one legitimate birth for every 5 women married between the ages of 15 and 45, and one illegitimate to every 57 unmarried adult females. Returns of the previous census give about the same result.

In the rural districts marriages were formerly more fruitful than in the cities, other than Paris; but they no longer possess this advantage.

The proportion of boys to girls was as 106.75 to 100 at the commencement of the century. It steadily fell to the proportion of 104.80 to 100 in 1860. According to an average taken for the period from 1853 to 1860 there were 103.84 boys to 100 girls in Paris, 104.49 to 100 in the other cities, and 105.77 in the rural districts, which shows that the predominance of boys is on an increase ratio to the density of the population.

It has been observed that the predominance of boys is less marked among legitimate than among illegitimate children.

The proportion of legitimate to illegitimate has not varied sensibly for the last ten years. It was 7.19 to 100 in 1851; it was 7.24 in 1860.

From 1852 to 1860 there was an average of 26.62 to 100 illegitimate births in the department of the Seine, 12.03 in cities other than Paris, and only 4.17 in the rural districts, showing that the number of illegitimates is proportioned to the density of population. Next to Paris, in the large cities, such as Lyons, Bordeaux, Marseilles, Rouen, Lille, where there are permanent garrisons or seaports, the largest number of natural children is begotten. In general, about one-third of the natural children are recognized by their parents; in the rural districts, about 40 per cent.

The number of children born dead in France is on the increase. From 3.91

to the 100 between 1851 and 1855, the number reached 4.30 to the 100 between 1856 and 1860. The proportion of boys born dead is very large—145 to the 100 girls.

The number of illegitimate children born dead is much greater than of legitimate, and, of course, in the cities, where there are more illegitimate births than in the country. For example, out of 100 births between 1853 and 1860, 53 were born dead in the department of the Seine, 5.16 in cities other than Paris, and 3.65 in the rural districts.

Out of 990,966 confinements in 1860, 9,943 produced two children, and 133 produced three children. Of children born dead, 4.15 out of every 100 were in single, 14.55 in double, and 32.28 in triple accouchments, showing that a single birth has more than three times as many chances of life as a double and about eight times as many as a triple birth.

The greatest number of conceptions take place in the months of May, June, and July, allowing nine months for the period of gestation; the fewest in the months of August, September, October, and November. The maximum is generally in May, and the minimum in September. The greatest number of female births correspond to the period of the maximum of conception.

DEATHS.

The average mortality for the five years from 1855 to 1860, inclusive, was for the male sex 1 death to every 41.67 inhabitants; female sex, 1 death to every 42.48 inhabitants; both sexes, 1 death to every 41.86 inhabitants.

The tables show that one-fifth of the male children and one-sixth of the female children in France die the first year; a second fifth of the males before the 15th, and of the females before the 20th year. Between 25 and 30 half of the males survive; between 60 and 65 a quarter; a sixth only survive the 70th year. Half of the females live to 35, a quarter to between 65 and 70, and a sixth between 70 and 75.

In 1860 the average mortality to every 100 inhabitants was as follows:
Department of the Seine, 2.53; other cities than Paris, 2.50; rural districts, 2.00.

This shows that the rate of mortality is more or less proportionate to the density of the population.

The following table shows some of the effects of matrimony upon mortality at different ages:

Ages.	MALE SEX.			FEMALE SEX.		
	Unmarried.	Married.	Widowers.	Unmarried.	Married.	Widows.
15.20........	0.80	9.01	14.90	0.85	1.34	8.76
20.30........	1.91	0.78	2.30	0.90	0.92	1.80
30.40........	1.31	0.73	1.74	1.02	0.95	1.30
40.50.......... ..	1.78	1.02	1.88	1.42	1.07	1.45
50.60.......... ..	2.83	1.85	2.98	2.39	1.66	2.18

The great mortality among married people under 20 is a striking commentary upon the dangers of premature marriages. It is worthy of remark in this connexion that the marriages late in life are most fruitful. After twenty the mortality among the married is less than among the unmarried. The loss of the husband or wife seems to shorten life. The mortality is also greater among the unmarried than the married, after the 20th year.

The mortality of natural children in 1860 was 1.99 to 1 legitimate child, or almost double.

The maximum of mortality occurs in the month of February and the minimum in the month of June. The minimum of deaths occurs at the period of the maximum of conception, and it is ascertained that the months which show an increase of conception show a corresponding decrease of mortality, and *vice versa*.

The influence of the seasons upon mortality is most sensibly felt in infancy and old age, and is least apparent between the ages of 20 and 50. The old suffer most from the rigors of winter, and infants from the heats of summer. Except between the ages of 5 and 15 the proportion of mortality is greater in the department of the Seine than in any other part of France. The greatest mortality is in the first year.

There were 31 men and 28 women who died over 100 years in 1860. The number of deaths among persons of this age has steadily diminished since 1853, when there were 143.

Three-fifths of the boys born are living at 20, the age for military service. It is found that the proportion which passes that age is in an inverse ratio to the density of the population.

The following table gives the average life which a person who has attained any of the ages named may be expected to live in France :

Ages.	MALES.		FEMALES.	
	Years.	Months.	Years.	Months.
Birth	35	2	37	8
1 year	42	2	44	9
5 years	46	10	48	1
10 "	44	8	45	10
15 "	41	2	42	6
20 '	37	11	39	5
30 '	32	4	33	3
40 '	25	6	26	8
50 '	18	10	19	10
60 '	12	10	13	3
70 '	7	11	8	2
80 '	4	8	4	10
90 '	3	6	3	6

It appears by this table that the average chances of life at any age before 90 are greater with the female than with the male sex.

CAUSES OF DEATH.

Out of 145,354 deaths from ascertained causes occurring during the year 1860, in cities of more than 10,000 inhabitants, it appears that 26.52 per 10 resulted from diseases of the respiratory organs, which proved most fatal to children under 5 and men over 60 years of age. Next come diseases of the organs of digestion, 14.50 per hundred ; then diseases of the brain, 7.93 per cent. ; then fevers, 5.76 per cent. ; then diseases of the organs of circulation, 5.26 per cent. ; then the nervous diseases, at 4.44 per cent. ; then eruptive fevers, 2.69 per cent. ; then diseases of the genital organs, 1.18 ; and virulent and contagious diseases and diseases of the lymphatic system, 0.53 per cent.

SUICIDES.

There has been an increase of suicides for the last 33 years of 5.63 to every 100,000 inhabitants, or an annual increase of 0.17.

There have been, on an average, about three times as many suicides among males as among females. The maximum of suicides among males is found between the ages of 40 and 50, and among females before their 21st year. The number of suicides is on the increase from January to June, inclusive, and then decreases, reaching its minimum in December. The largest number occur in the warm months and the smallest in cold months. More than two-thirds of the suicides are perpetrated by drowning and strangulation. The next agencies most in use are fire-arms of all kinds and asphyxia by charcoal. Nine-tenths of all the suicides in France are perpetrated by one of these three agencies. Two-thirds of those who resort to charcoal are to be found in the department of the Seine. One-tenth resort to poison, sharp weapons, or throw themselves from elevated places.

DEAF MUTES.

The Baron Watteville, inspector general of the first class of institutions of benevolence, in his last report, gives the following census of deaf mutes in France:

Men 12,325
Women.. 9,251

Total 21,576

The proportion of women to men in this category is as 27 to 100. They are classified according to their ages as follows:

	Men.	Women.	Total.
Under five years	573	430	1,003
From five to fifteen years	2,765	2,038	4,803
Over fifteen years	8,987	6,783	15,770
Total	12,325	9,251	21,576

There is on an average one deaf mute to every 1,669 inhabitants, that is, 1 to every 730 men, and 1 to every 939 women.

In the mountainous departments the proportion is 1 to every 1,158 inhabitants, while in the more prosperous agricultural departments the proportion is 1 to every 2,285, or about one-half.

There are 47 institutions for deaf mutes in France situated in 44 different communes, and giving shelter to 2,446 children—1,251 boys and 1,195 girls. Of these 334 only pay for their board; the rest are supported by private or public charity.

BLIND.

There were 30,214 blind persons in France in 1860—16,460 men and 13,745 women. The number of blind from 5 to 15 years of age was 1,224 boys and 989 girls; in all, 2,213.

There are 10 institutions for the blind in France, which, however, contain in the aggregate but 307 out of 1,600 children needing instruction, leaving 1,300 without means of instruction; only one-ninth of the girls and one-sixth of the boys have access to these institutions. Of 307 admitted but 37 pay.

MARCH 18, 1864.

Comparative statement of the material progress of France since the downfall of the last monarchy.

In my recent report on the consular system of the United States, I spoke of the consular organization of France as superior in nearly every respect to any other. Before I came to that conclusion it occurred to me as strange, not to say impossible, that a state which has always held a secondary rank among the commercial powers of the world should have an advantage over Great Britain and the United States in its consular service.

The fruits of a service are, at least, a presumptive proof of its quality; and I was suspicious, as doubtless some will be who read my report, that after all, in the practical operation of our system there was latent advantages for which the scientific precision of the French system did not provide. To satisfy myself more fully on this point I have endeavored to ascertain the ratio of progress which France has made for a series of years past, both as a commercial and maritime power, in order to see how far the apparent merits of her consular service are vindicated by the results.

My examination has confirmed the correctness of my first impressions, and but for my unwillingness to add to the inordinate proportions of that document, I should have given the results in my report. I concluded, instead, to enlarge the scope of my investigation a little and send you a separate communication about the material growth of France, under the conviction that the facts I have to present will serve to correct misapprehensions quite prevalent in the United States in regard to the additions which the French people are annually making to their national influence and to the wealth of the world.

I propose to give, in the first place, a comparative statement of the progress of France since the overthrow of the last monarchy, wherever statistics are accessible, or as far back as they are accessible, relying entirely upon official authorities, and mainly upon the statistics published by the government in the "Annales des Commerce Exterieur," the census returns of 1860, as edited by M. Ligoyt.

TERRITORIAL SURFACE AND POPULATION OF FRANCE, PROPER.

In order to render these statistics intelligible it will be necessary to give the territorial surface and population of France, for, whether greater or less, they constitute an all-important element in determining the productive power of a nation.

The total population of France proper was, in 1846, 35,400,000; 1851, 35,783,000; 1856, 36,205,000, distributed over a territory of 530,280 kilometres square; 1861, 37,382,000, over a territory of 542,397 kilometres square. Mean density of the population, 69 inhabitants to the square kilometre (1.)

The population of Algeria and the colonies is about 4,000,000; consisting mostly of people of African origin, and of only about 200,000 Europeans. They are distributed over a territory of about 500,000 kilometres square.

AGRICULTURAL PARTITION.

The agricultural distribution of the 86 departments of France in 1852, and before the annexation of Savoy and Nice, which make three new departments, was as follows:

	Hectares.
Arable land	*26,204,225
Natural meadows	5,057,232
Vines	2,191,162

* Of which, in cereals, 15,364,367; in other culture, 2,571,351; in artificial meadow, 2,563,490; fallow, 5,705,017.

	Hectares.
Culture	999, 078
Pasturage and heath	6, 579, 983
Forests, waters, roads, building grounds, and uncultivated land	11, 996, 496
Total	53, 028, 176

Of course the agricultural product of France cannot be very rapidly increased; for there is comparatively little land to be reclaimed, while the tillable ground is divided up into such small holdings as to render any very rapid improvement either in the amount of production or economy in tillage impossible; I shall not, therefore, dwell upon this subject, because the new returns do not vary enough from those of former years, which are everywhere accessible to make it worth my while. I will direct my attention to such industries as have more capacity for expansion and development; first, considering the domestic productive industry of France, and afterwards her commercial and maritime industry.

DOMESTIC INDUSTRY AND COMMERCE.

By the following statement it will appear that the production of coal and iron has steadily increased for many years, and that in 1859 the amount of coal produced was nearly three and one-fourth millions of tons more than in 1848, and about three millions more than in 1851; that the production both of pig and puddled iron had doubled since 1857.

Years.	Production in metrical tons.			Average price per metrical ton.				
	Combustible mineral.	Cast iron.	Puddled iron.	Of coals at place of production.	Of cast iron smelted by wood.	Of cast iron smelted by other fuels.	Of puddled iron smelted by wood.	Of puddled iron smelted by other fuels.
				f. c.	*f. c.*	*f. c.*	*f. c.*	*f. c.*
1848	4, 000, 000	472, 000	276, 000	....	142 00	117 00	402 00	298 00
1849	4, 049, 000	414, 000	243, 000	⎱	133 00	114 00	378 00	273 00
1850	4, 434, 000	406, 000	246, 000	⎰ 9 50	127 00	108 00	369 00	253 00
1851	4, 485, 000	446, 000	254, 000	⎰	136 00	105 00	370 00	266 00
1852	4, 904, 000	523, 000	302, 000	9 53	147 00	113 00	423 00	270 00
1853	5, 938, 000	661, 000	451, 000	10 05	174 00	126 30	434 60	302 10
1854	6, 827, 000	771, 000	511, 000	10 96	182 60	133 80	442 00	322 90
1855	7, 453, 000	849, 000	557, 000	12 17	187 40	147 00	465 60	346 60
1856	7, 926, 000	923, 000	569, 000	12 87	191 30	140 60	465 50	336 20
1857	7, 902, 000	992, 000	560, 000	12 60	178 40	131 50	451 00	322 90
1858	7, 353, 000	872, 000	530, 000	12 46	156 90	117 30	432 50	288 30
1859	7, 483, 000	856, 000	520, 000	12 69	147 30	112 10	424 00	274 10

SALT.

In 1851 France produced 560,000 tons of salt; in 1862, 631,000.

SUGAR.

The production of sugar manufactured in 1848 amounted to 56,281,000 kilogrammes; in 1855 it had more than doubled, and in 1862 it amounted to 161,747,000; while the duties levied upon it amounted in 1848 to 22,824,000 francs, and in 1863 to 60,848,000.

The following table gives the production since 1848 :

Years.	Quantities of sugar.		Tax levied.
	Manufactured.	Consumed.	
	Kilogrammes.	*Kilogrammes.*	*Francs.*
1848	56,287,000	48,103,000	22,824,000
1849	44,551,000	50,073,000	23,675,000
1850	67,297,000	59,760,000	30,596,000
1851	75,234,000	62,082,000	32,504,000
1852	86,795,000	64,128,000	31,046,000
1853	74,178,000	73,814,000	34,730,000
1854	53,900,000	66,464,000	30,724,000
1855	67,708,000	56,508,000	27,818,000
1856	94,808,000	88,522,000	45,510,000
1857	111,599,000	79,208,000	41,577,000
1858	158,676,000	119,664,000	63,871,000
1859	131,663,000	102,154,000	57,585,000
1860	108,782,000	106,078,000	37,606,000
1861	140,902,000	109,315,000	32,795,000
1862	161,747,000	132,752,000	50,451,000
1863	142,933,000	144,876,000	60,848,000

The sale of tobacco is conducted entirely by government. The following table shows the growth of this branch of commerce since 1847 :

Years.	Sales in France.	Gross proceeds.	Expenses to deduct.
	Kilogrammes.	*Francs.*	*Francs.*
1847	18,753,000	117,700,000	34,902,000
1848	18,275,000	116,258,000	31,325,000
1849	18,124,000	117,133,000	28,493,000
1850	18,937,000	122,114,000	26,489,000
1851	19,718,000	126,597,000	31,493,000
1852	20,334,000	131,239,000	33,754,000
1853	21,314,000	139,291,000	27,899,000
1854	22,570,000	145,703,000	45,275,000
1855	23,658,000	153,197,000	53,746,000
1856	25,434,000	164,218,000	38,269,000
1857	27,219,000	174,257,000	47,127,000
1858	27,884,000	178,075,000	59,227,000
1859	28,279,000	179,748,000	65,632,000
1860	29,280,000	195,325,000	58,207,000
1861		216,139,000	52,793,000

STEAM ENGINES.

The following table gives the number of steam-engines used in all kinds of private industry, on railroads and in navigation, for the years 1848 to 1859 inclusive. It will be seen that in ten years the number of engines increased nearly three times, and the amount of power increased four times:

Years.	Steam-engines of every kind.	
	Number.	Horse-power.
1848	6,465	158,282
1849	6,357	170,772
1850	6,832	186,363
1851	7,232	197,707
1852	7,779	216,456
1853	9,029	243,232
1854	10,421	292,212
1855	11,620	341,067
1856	13,306	405,686
1857	14,989	449,421
1858	16,490	487,354
1859	17,873	513,092

The following table will show the principal industries in which steam-power is employed, and the amount for each, for the years 1852 and 1859 :

Industries.	1852.			1859.		
	Number of establishments.	Steam-engines.		Number of establishments.	Steam-engines.	
		Number.	Horse-power.		Number.	Horse-power.
Coal mines	289	453	12,306	333	748	27,232
Other mines	10	15	337	58	80	1,496
Iron manufactories and forges	161	368	12,354	322	1,040	30,116
Metallurgy	64	94	1,354	143	222	2,850
Stone and slate quarries	18	32	455	56	87	1,019
Water engines	95	105	1,062	148	181	2,228
Threshing mills	61	91	364	899	937	4,011
Sawing mills	139	142	1,180	381	422	3,486
Oil mills	119	128	1,338	251	250	2,688
Breweries	54	49	232	166	161	813
Distilleries	39	23	105	351	271	2,170
Sugar refineries	406	515	5,193	424	849	8,915
Flour mills	34	32	203	69	93	692
Chocolate mills	54	53	204	143	151	703
Tanneries	57	52	266	163	139	849
Manufactories of chemical products	86	62	313	206	167	915
Locksmithing	48	58	453	131	136	940
Glass works	32	73	620	61	115	1,725
Porcelain works	25	27	296	47	54	543
Brick and tile works	15	15	95	82	88	557
Joining and carriage making	34	40	273	115	121	877
Ship-yards	41	40	611	52	64	660
Foundries and machine shops	431	539	3,791	982	1,194	8,268
Spinning	1,438	1,179	16,495	1,965	1,820	29,492
Weaving	101	97	1,733	197	212	3,938
Laundries	242	95	707	391	225	1,430
Dyeing establishments	270	192	1,395	441	391	2,780
Preparation of dry goods	134	80	552	187	142	1,002
Printing of dry goods	148	122	1,285	179	151	1,623
Cloth manufactories	99	93	1,194	136	132	1,741
Paper mills	179	50	552	241	159	2,244

PATENTS.

In 1848 the number of patents taken out was 853, and the extensions 338; in 1852, 2,469 patents and 810 extensions; in 1860, 4,606 patents and 1,516 extensions. For the ten years succeeding 1848 there were 27,970 patents and 9,084 additions. For the five succeeding years there were 21,931 patents and 7,258 additions. Of the patents granted in France from 1844 to 1861, 407 were for five years, 1,100 for ten years, 51,130 for fifteen years, and 4,147 to foreigners, for periods determined by the duration of their original privileges.

RIVER NAVIGATION.

The number of steamers employed in river navigation in 1848 was 187, tonnage 20,301, which transported 2,045,000 passengers and 578,000 tons of merchandise. In 1859 the number of steamers was 194, the tonnage 33,690, the number of passengers 1,851,000, while the merchandise amounted to 2,616,000. The diminution in the number of passengers is obviously attributable to the increased facilities of travel by rail.

RAILWAYS.

The following table shows the progress of railway enterprise in France since and including 1847. It will be seen that in the five years following 1854 the length of road, the number of locomotives and passengers, and the weight of merchandise more than doubled:

Years.	Length of railway in process of construction December 31.	Number of locomotives.	Number of passengers.	Weight of merchandise.
	Kilometres.			
1847	1,839	646	12,778,000	3,597,000
1848	2,222	729	11,907,000	2,921,000
1849	2,861	875	14,812,000	3,419,000
1850	3,013	973	18,741,000	4,271,000
1851	3,558	1,006	19,936,000	4,627,000
1852	3,872	1,114	22,610,000	5,378,000
1853	4,063	1,204	24,685,000	7,173,000
1854	4,660	1,500	28,070,000	8,865,000
1855	5,532	1,855	32,961,000	10,648,000
1856	6,197	2,298	36,384,000	12,865,000
1857	7,445	2,607	41,533,000	15,605,000
1858	8,687	2,941	45,364,000	17,673,000
1859	9,084	3,048	53,405,000	19,948,000
1860	9,413	....	....	....
1861	10,096	....	....	....
1862	....	....	....	....

On the 31st of December, 1861, there were, besides 7,509 kilometres of railroads constructing, charters for 630 kilometres more, besides 153 kilometres of special railroad for industrial enterprises.

The following table shows the actual receipts and net revenue of the French railways from 1847 to 1860, inclusive: .

Years.	Gross receipts.	Net profit.	RECEIVED PER KILOMETRE.	
			Gross.	Net.
1847	65,206,000	33,875,000	42,425	22,040
1848	61,183,000	26,689,000	30,080	13,121
1849	75,175,000	36,881,000	30,000	14,706
1850	95,618,000	50,853,000	32,282	17,168
1851	106,144,000	58,568,000	32,175	17,754
1852	134,824,000	79,890,000	36,425	21,627
1853	168,924,000	97,825,000	42,465	24,591
1854	198,847,000	114,855,000	45,732	26,415
1855	258,965,000	147,953,000	51,402	29,367
1856	282,849,000	183,899,000	48,317	26,289
1857	312,334,000	169,800,000	45,483	24,726
1858	337,076,000	182,624,000	41,665	22,573
1859	389,085,000	216,365,000	44,019	24,478
1860	411,068,000	226,690,000	44,862	24,740

There is no country in the world in which railway property has proved so uniformly productive as in France; while the average cost of transportation of passengers is but a trifle if at all higher than in the United States.

ELECTRIC TELEGRAPH CORRESPONDENCE.

On the 1st of January, 1862, there were 24,665 kilometres of telegraph lines in France, and 454 stations, without counting 600 railway telegraph stations, equally open to the public.

The following table gives the amount of correspondence through which they were the medium from 1851 to 1862, inclusive:

Years.	Private despatches.	Proceeds.
	Number.	*Francs.*
1851	9,014	77,000
1852	48,105	543,000
1853	142,061	1,512,000
1854	236,018	2,605,000
1855	254,532	2,487,000
1856	360,299	3,191,000
1857	413,616	3,333,000
1858	463,973	3,517,000
1859	598,701	4,023,000
1860	711,652	4,144,000
1861	920,614	4,920,000
1862	1,518,044	5,302,000

Of these despatches 591,531 were French, yielding 2,339,000 francs, and 149,121 were international, yielding 1,805,000 francs.

POSTAL CORRESPONDENCE.

The amount of correspondence by letter in France has more than doubled since 1848, while the production of printed matter has exhibited but a moderate annual increase, though steady, since 1854. As the population of France has increased but very little since 1848, the increase in correspondence must be attributed to a more general use of the facilities afforded, in consequence partly of the reduced rates of postage, and partly of a wider diffusion of intelligence.

The following table, rightly interpreted, presents a curious scholium on the history of France since 1848.

Years.	Number of letters.	Proceeds from letters.	No. of journals and printed matter.	Proceeds from same.
		Francs.		*Francs.*
1848	122,140,000	43,941,000	129,193,000	3,876,000
1849	158,268,000	32,186,000	146,528,000	4,396,000
1850	159,500,000	35,623,000	94,622,000	2,839,000
1851	165,000,000	38,589,000	33,968,000	1,019,000
1852	181,000,000	40,633,000	94,864,000	2,846,000
1853	185,542,000	42,900,000	99,537,000	2,987,000
1854	212,385,000	46,544,000	115,774,000	3,476,000
1855	233,517,000	45,835,000	123,647,000	3,709,000
1856	252,015,000	47,883,000	127,321,000	3,683,000
1857	252,454,000	48,042,000	144,295,000	3,968,000
1858	253,234,000	48,874,000	151,298,000	4,161,000
1859	258,900,000	52,018,000	165,300,000	4,671,000
1860	263,500,000	53,479,000	179,138,000	5,177,000
1861	274,000,000	55,600,000	189,000,000	5,600,000

SAVINGS BANKS.

The following table gives the number of banks for savings, in France, in the year 1847, and from 1850 to 1862, inclusive, with the amounts of deposits and withdrawals, and the number of accounts.

Years.	Number of banks.	No. of open accounts, December 31.	Deposits rec'd during the year.	Paym'ts in specie, (capital and interest.)	Balance due depositors, December 31.
			Francs.	*Francs.*	*Francs.*
1847	345	736,951	127,000,000	156,000,000	358,000,000
1850	340	565,995	98,000,000	40,000,000	135,000,000
1851	340	611,086	97,000,000	73,000,000	158,000,000
1852	341	742,889	152,000,000	66,000,000	245,000,000
1853	350	844,949	144,000,000	106,000,000	286,000,000
1854	363	865,478	112,000,000	129,000,000	272,000,000
1855	365	893,750	120,000,000	120,000,000	272,000,000
1856	370	936,188	127,000,000	122,000,000	275,000,000
1857	383	978,802	120,000,000	115,000,000	279,000,000
1858	401	1,042,305	131,000,000	100,000,000	301,000,000
1859	415	1,121,405	147,000,000	118,000,000	336,000,000
1860	433	1,218,122	162,000,000	124,000,000	377,000,000
1861	459	1,300,521	164,500,000	139,500,000	401,500,000
1862	478	1,379,180	164,500,000	148,000,000	424,000,000

Of the 220,204 accounts opened in 1860, I make the following classification of depositors as compared with 1850 :

77,097 workmen for.............................. 44,666 in 1850.
37,441 servants for.............................. 26,609 "   "
10,679 clerks for .... 7,949 "   "
 9,782 soldiers and sailors for..................... 10,892 "   "
49,710 of various callings for .... 44,224 "   "

35, 226 mariners for	21, 093	in 1850.
269 mutual aid societies for	372	" "
220, 204 accounts.*	. 155, 865	accounts.†

FOREIGN COMMERCE.

It is in her foreign commerce that the recent growth of France is most noticeable. The following table gives the ratio of her imports and exports from 1847 to 1862, inclusive, by millions of francs.

Years.	GENERAL COMMERCE.		SPECIAL COMMERCE.‡		SPECIE BULLION.	
	Imports.	Exports.	Imports.	Exports.	Imports.	Exports.
For 5 years, from 1847 to 1851, inclusive...	5, 233. 5	6, 210. 8	3, 770. 1	4, 574. 0	1, 261	458
Yearly average.......	....	1, 242. 2	742. 0	914. 8	252	91
For 5 years, from 1852 to 1856, inclusive...	9, 793. 0	10, 512. 4	7, 061. 0	7, 663. 4	2, 372	1, 788
Yearly average.......	1, 958. 6	2, 102. 5	1, 412. 2	1, 532. 7	474	358
For 5 years, from 1857 to 1861, inclusive...	12, 961. 0	14, 065. 3	9, 416. 0	10, 222. 9	3, 348	2, 346
Yearly average.......	2, 590. 2	2, 813. 1	1, 883. 2	2, 044. 6	669	469
1862..............	2, 899. 2	3, 049. 9	2, 198. 6	2, 242. 7	576	495

* Representing a credit of 42,668,000 francs.
† Representing a credit of 26,554,000 francs.
‡ That is, articles imported for consumption or export as French.

It will be seen by this table that both the imports and exports of merchandise, for the five years ending 1861, were more than doubled, and the movement of specie and bullion about trebled, while the aggregate imports and exports of 1862 exceed the average of the five preceding years over a thousand million of francs.

The following table, showing among what countries the commerce of France was distributed in 1862, and in what proportions, is worth examining in this connexion.

Names of countries.	Importations.— Values in millions of francs.		Exportations.— Values in millions of francs.		Exportations and importations united.	
	General commerce.	Special commerce.	General commerce.	Special commerce.	General commerce.	Special commerce.
England	656. 1	525. 7	834. 2	619. 5	1, 490. 3	1, 145. 2
Russia........................	94. 8	72. 9	43. 3	31. 5	138. 1	104. 4
Sweden......................	23. 0	19. 6	2. 9	2. 6	25. 9	22. 2
Norway......................	27. 8	27. 8	3. 3	3. 0	31. 1	30. 8
Denmark.....................	0. 5	0. 5	2. 2	2. 2	2. 7	2. 7
German Commercial Association and Hanover	220. 8	129. 7	232. 7	209. 8	453. 5	339. 5
Mecklenburg-Schwerin	0. 0	0. 0	0. 6	0. 6	0. 6	0. 6
Hanseatic Cities............	14. 4	11. 0	29. 1	22. 5	43. 5	33. 5
Netherlands.................	49. 5	30. 4	40. 0	26. 1	89. 5	56. 5
Belgium.....................	321. 3	259. 3	229. 9	206. 4	551. 2	465. 7

Countries in which the commerce of France was distributed, &c.—Continued.

Names of countries.	Importations.— Values in millions of francs.		Exportations.— Values in millions of francs.		Exportations and importations united.	
	General commerce.	Special commerce.	General commerce.	Special commerce.	General commerce.	Special commerce.
Switzerland	238.8	58.6	295.0	137.8	533.8	196.4
Portugal	10.0	8.1	23.8	14.5	33.8	22.6
Spain	71.7	55.0	201.8	137.4	273.5	192.4
Austria	34.4	30.8	6.9	5.3	41.3	36.1
Italy	229.3	193.7	290.0	182.9	519.3	376.6
Greece	3.9	3.0	11.9	8.6	15.8	11.6
Turkey	177.2	139.4	82.6	50.0	259.8	189.4
Egypt	45.5	37.8	21.0	16.0	66.5	53.8
Barbary States	17.4	17.4	13.0	7.7	30.4	25.1
Western coast of Africa	16.0	15.2	4.5	2.5	20.5	17.7
Isle of France and Cape of Good Hope	19.4	18.8	13.5	12.4	32.9	31.2
Other African countries	2.5	1.6	0.2	0.2	2.7	1.8
British India	74.5	74.1	12.5	10.9	87.0	85.0
Dutch India	6.3	6.1	0.7	0.6	7.0	6.7
Philippines	1.9	1.6	0.3	0.3	2.2	1.9
China, Cochin China, and Oceanica.	7.2	7.4	10.7	10.1	17.9	17.5
United States	92.5	96.2	121.3	99.9	213.8	196.1
Mexico	3.9	3.6	20.5	16.1	24.4	19.7
Guatemala	0.7	0.7	0.4	0.4	1.1	1.1
United States of Colombia	1.1	1.0	2.3	2.0	3.4	3.0
Venezuela	9.3	6.4	4.7	3.9	14.0	10.3
Brazil	89.6	45.5	92.2	63.1	181.8	108.6
Uruguay	27.7	24.6	19.2	14.8	46.9	39.4
Rio de la Plata	33.8	31.5	33.7	26.7	67.5	58.2
Ecuador	1.4	0.6	1.1	0.7	2.5	1.3
Peru	16.4	22.1	36.3	25.3	52.7	47.4
Bolivia			0.5	0.5	0.5	0.5
Chili	9.2	8.5	24.6	18.5	33.8	27.0
Hayti	28.0	21.1	12.1	9.1	40.1	30.2
Spanish possessions	59.2	43.8	29.8	20.3	89.0	64.1
British possessions	1.9	1.4	2.6	2.3	4.5	3.7
Danish possessions	0.7	0.1	9.9	9.1	10.6	9.2
Dutch possessions	0.2	0.1	0.1	0.1	0.3	0.2
Isle of Bourbon	35.5	33.5	31.5	28.3	67.0	61.8
French Guiana	0.9	0.8	7.4	6.5	8.3	7.3
Martinique	22.2	20.8	21.3	19.5	43.5	40.3
Guadaloupe	21.9	20.1	17.6	14.9	39.5	35.0
Algeria	41.5	40.8	133.8	124.8	175.3	165.6
Senégal	8.1	7.5	11.1	6.9	19.2	14.4
St. Maria de Madagarta	1.2	1.2	0.6	0.6	1.8	1.8
French India	11.5	4.9	1.2	0.9	12.7	5.8
St. Peter's, Miquelon, and Grand Peche	16.0	15.9	6.5	6.1	22.5	22.0
Waifs and Strays	0.6	0.4	1.0		1.6	0.4
Total	2,899.2	2,193.6	3,049.9	2,242.7	5,949.1	4,441.3

Movement of specie and bullion in 1862—values in millions of francs.

Names of countries.	Imports.	Exports.
Great Britain	287.5	76.2
Belgium	32.7	59.6
Germany	105.3	10.0
Italy	52.9	109.8
Spain	41.7	29.4
Switzerland	8.1	20.4
Turkey	33.4	67.1
Egypt	0.0	29.7
Barbary States	3.0	1.6
Algeria		7.2
Isle of Bourbon		0.7
Other islands and coasts of Africa		1.4
British India		69.3
Java		0.6
China and Indo China		3.9
United States	0.9	0.0
Greece	0.3	1.6
Russia	0.0	2.9
Other countries	10.2	3.2
General imports and exports	576.0	494.6
Special imports and exports	536.4	455.9

NAVIGATION.

In 1848 the total number of vessels using sails and steam together was 14,353, with an aggregate tonnage of 683,298. In 1858 the number had increased to 15,187, with a tonnage of 1,049,844. These aggregates have slightly diminished since 1858, the use of sails having been discontinued to some extent, as will appear hereafter.

The following table gives the number of vessels propelled by steam and sail combined, of 800 tons and upwards, of from 200 to 300 tons, of 30 tons and under, together with the total number of vessels thus propelled and their tonnage for the years 1848, 1853, 1858, and 1862:

Years.	Of 800 tons and upwards.		200 to 300 tons.		30 tons and under.		Total of all classes.	
	Ships.	Tons.	Ships.	Tons.	Ships.	Tons.	Ships.	Tons.
1848			500	119,187	8,852	68,232	14,353	683,298
1853			591	141,363	8,915	69,702	14,719	762,705
1858	28	30,672	763	183,710	8,854	71,314	15,187	1,049,844
1862	35	39,984	640	157,580	9,164	76,581	15,132	982,571

VESSELS PROPELLED BY STEAM ALONE.

By the following table it will appear that the tonnage of vessels propelled by steam alone has increased nearly six times since 1848:

Years.	Steam-ers.	Tonnage.	Horse-power.
December 1, 1848	118	13,152	....
1849	119	13,391	....
1850	126	13,925	....
1851	139	19,460	....
1852	151	22,171	14,013
1853	174	26,399	15,595
1854	197	35,098	19,102
1855	225	45,493	23,902
1856	275	64,339	29,425
1857	330	72,070	34,208
1858	324	66,587	32,362
1859	324	65,006	31,530
1860	314	68,025	32,691
1861	327	73,267	35,085
1862	338	78,981	36,470

Of this tonnage, in 1861 19,112 were registered in ports on the Mediterranean; in 1862 21,300 were registered in ocean ports and 57,681 in Mediterranean ports. Of the 338 steamers in 1862, 69 were of 200 horse-power and above, 76 were from 100 to 200, 85 were from 60 to 100, 64 of from 30 to 60, and 38 of 30 or less horse-power.

The total tonnage propelled by sails and steam entering and leaving French ports for the colonies and foreign countries under all flags was—

In 1847 5,785,000
In 1848 4,009,000
In 1853 5,874,000
In 1858 8,171,000
In 1861 10,174,000
In 1862 9,589,457

The number of sailors employed in this navigation of all nationalities increased from 455,786 in 1847 to 675,328 in 1862.

The total tonnage entering and leaving French ports under the French flag was—

In 1847 1,930,000
In 1853 2,314,000
In 1858 3,380,000
In 1862 3,956,400

The number of sailors employed was 175,637 in 1847 and 306,266 in 1862.

The following table gives the French as well as foreign tonnage propelled by steam alone and engaged in commerce between France and foreign countries and Algeria since 1848 :

Years.	FRENCH.		FOREIGN.		TOTAL.	
	Ships.	Tons.	Ships.	Tons.	Ships.	Tons.
1847	1,973	354,000	4,342	633,000	6,315	987,000
1848	1,980	322,000	3,769	508,000	5,749	830,000
1849	1,811	302,000	3,883	497,000	5,694	799,000
1850	1,817	307,000	4,928	691,000	6,745	998,000
1851	2,040	329,000	5,727	855,000	7,767	1,184,000
1852	2,210	389,000	4,931	759,000	7,141	1,148,000
1853	2,505	409,000	5,778	904,000	8,283	1,313,000
1854	2,347	452,000	5,590	930,000	7,937	1,382,000
1855	2,798	666,000	6,486	1,276,000	9,284	1,942,000
1856	3,436	855,000	6,359	1,302,000	9,795	2,157,000
1857	4,146	941,000	6,941	1,412,000	11,087	2,353,000
1858	3,889	842,000	6,969	1,372,000	10,858	2,214,000
1859	3,708	822,000	7,754	1,475,000	11,462	2,297,000
1860	3,837	1,013,000	7,880	1,517,000	11,717	2,530,000
1861	4,601	1,101,000	8,251	1,628,000	12,852	2,729,000
1862	5,724	1,342,295	9,270	1,913,995	14,994	3,256,290

By this table it appears that the steam tonnage of France is more than four times what it was in 1848, and that it has inwardly increased more rapidly than the foreign tonnage of the same description in French ports.

FISHERIES.

The whale fishing has almost entirely ceased in France, as in most other countries, since petroleum oil has come into general use. In 1856 eight vessels, with an aggregate capacity of 3,812 tons, were engaged in this business. In 1862 but one vessel is reported, of 637 tons.

COD AND HERRING FISHING.

The cod fishing also has been rather on the decrease for some years past, while the herring fishing has thrived.

The total of fish taken in 1862 was more than double the number taken in 1856, as will appear by the following table :

Years.	Quantity of fish taken and brought home.		
	Salt.	Fresh.	Total.
	Tons.	Tons.	Tons.
1856	6,692	4,594	11,286
1857	8,423	4,757	13,180
1858	7,614	8,849	16,463
1859	7,771	8,611	16,382
1860	8,611	7,365	15,976
1861	7,902	7,481	15,382
1862	12,095	14,849	26,944

The coast fishery also is rather on the increase. It was represented by a capacity of 48,436 tons in 1847, 59,541 tons in 1861, and 61,933 tons in 1862. Of this tonnage, in 1862 53,725 were employed in ports on the ocean, and 8,208 in ports on the Mediterranean.

When it is considered that France has no imperial domain of public lands with which to tempt a peaceful emigration; that her territory is so densely settled as to render the acquisition of land by the poor almost an impossibility; that she is surrounded by great military powers against whose predatory propensities she is obliged to provide by a large standing army recruited from the best class of her laboring population, it must be conceded that her material prosperity for the last fifteen years has been remarkable, and the credit of it must be ascribed in a great measure to a system of civil administration so admirably contrived and perfected as to protect her industry from the dynastic and other political vicissitudes which, under a less perfect civil organization, would have left her by this time a third or fourth rate power in Europe instead of the first.

In the papers annexed, and marked, respectively, A and B, you will find a classified statement of the movement of merchandise from this consular district to the United States, and its declared value for the first two quarters of the year 1864. These statements sum up as follows :

First quarter.

		Francs.		Francs.
January		11, 327, 465 73		
February		10, 891, 824 74		
March		9, 181, 287 09		
				31, 400, 577 56

Second quarter.

April		7, 734, 017 87		
May		9, 772, 790 91		
June		11, 918, 211 85		
				29, 425, 020 63
Total for six months				60, 825, 598 19

The following statement, which I give for convenience of comparison, has already been communicated to the department for the preceding six months :

Third quarter 1863.

		Francs.		Francs.
July		8, 958, 503 00		
August		7, 826, 116 00		
September		9, 065, 452 00		
				25, 850, 071 00

Fourth quarter.

October		9, 509, 391 00		
November		7, 261, 119 00		
December		12, 172, 832 00		
				28, 943, 342 00
Total for six months				54, 793, 413 00
				60, 825, 598 19
Aggregate for year ending June 30, 1864				115, 619, 011 19

I may mention here that the net income to the government from this office for the past year over and above all expenses has been $23,968 06. It deserves to be remarked that the shipments from this consular district for the past half year exceed those of the preceding half year over six million of francs, and that the shipments for the month of June, just terminated, exceed those of any other month of the twelve except that of December last, which exceeded the June shipments about 150,000 francs.

From this statement it would appear that the depreciation of the currency has had a tendency rather to increase than to diminish the exports from France to the United States. It will surprise no one to learn from the annexed tables that a very large proportion of the shipments from this district are articles of luxury; but few will be prepared to find that, notwithstanding the peculiar trials through which our country has been passing for the past three years, we should have imported since the first of January last gloves to the declared value (which is but about one-quarter the price at which they are sold in the United States) of 2,529,245 francs, and ladies' dress goods to the amount of 18,615,402 francs for the same period. This is exclusive of other dry goods, artificial flowers, and jewelry, of the declared value of not less than 27,000,000 francs.

The movement of wine to the United States from this district—champagne almost exclusively—has increased the last six months.

	Francs.
The declared value of the wine shipped the last half year of 1863	1,076,540 53
The same for first half of 1864	1,207,093 20
Aggregate for the year	2,283,633 73

Increase, 130,553 67 francs.

I am indebted to the courtesy of our consuls at Havre, Lyons, and Nantes for statements of the movement of merchandise from their districts for the same period, which are annexed, and marked, respectively, C, D, E, F, G, H, I, K.

	Francs.
By these statements it appears that the declared value of the merchandise from these consular districts for the last two quarters amounted in the aggregate to	26,849,759 28
Amount invoiced at these consulates the last six months of 1863	22,261,258 49
Total for the year	49,111,017 77
Total for the year from Paris consulate	115,619,011 19
Making for the last year from these four consulates	164,730,028 96

The exports from the Lyons consulate the last two quarters were 2,184,289 less than for the two preceding quarters, but for the month of June, just past, were considerably more than for the preceding months since February.

The exports from Nantes the last six months were 15,521 55 francs more than for the six months preceding.

*　*　*　*　*　*　*　*　*

Movement of merchandise from consular district of Paris for the quarter ended March 31, 1864.

Articles.	January.	February.	March.	Total.
Artificial flowers and feathers	459,787 25	362,239 84	184,740 15	1,006,767 24
Bronzes and works of art..	64,515 75	70,356 30	56,975 90	191,847 95
Books	19,101 85	31,689 15	53,497 85	104,288 85
Clocks and watches	8,274 65	24,407 45	22,332 90	55,015 00
Chemicals	61,727 85	58,080 30	143,272 76	263,080 91
Dry goods	1,777,807 96	1,639,260 22	1,059,825 07	4,476,893 25
Dress goods	4,782,364 09	4,096,325 86	2,389,177 59	11,268,867 54
Fancy goods	762,881 61	840,078 69	880,306 86	2,483,267 16
Flower, grass, and garden seeds	25,335 90	4,509 88	1,041 05	30,886 83
Gentlemen's and ladies' furnishing goods .'.	613,562 00	565,173 04	604,802 73	1,783,537 77
Gloves	372,333 03	447,711 70	466,234 09	1,286,278 82
Gold and silver-plated ware.	2,989 40	419 25	457 40	3,866 05
Glass, porcelain, &c	113,568 27	170,926 02	242,784 90	527,279 19
Hatters' goods	277,464 88	558,392 61	543,883 10	1,379,740 59
Jewelry and precious stones	167,500 83	390,407 40	363,089 76	920,997 99
Leather	330,806 70	471,963 80	480,207 95	1,282,978 45
Merinoes and bombazines..	199,316 34	229,040 94	158,148 06	586,505 34
Military goods	11,282 10	....	8,226 80	19,508 90
Miscellaneous goods	95,343 45	149,143 71	252,641 56	497,128 72
Optical and surgical instruments	15,483 35	24,302 55	39	39,785 90
Perfumery	34,924 90	69,411 10	30,655 00	134,991 39
Pianos and musical instruments	37,028 01	19,420 14	40,844 26	96,592 41
Ready-made clothing	183,291 02	132,664 70	48,857 95	364,813 67
Stationery	36,018 58	52,717 77	46,620 87	135,357 22
Trimmings	527,535 26	238,280 29	152,135 56	917,851 11
Woollen cloths	255,144 70	82,248 68	129,515 60	466,908 98
Wines	92,176 00	162,653 35	821,710 98	1,076,540 33
Total	11,327,465 73	10,891,824 74	9,181,287 09	31,400,577 56

Movement of merchandise from consular district of Paris for the quarter ended June 30, 1864.

Articles.	April.	May.	June.	Total.
Artificial flowers and feathers	162,734 30	81,364 81	195,684 90	439,784 01
Bronzes and works of art..	118,935 95	79,064 63	98,544 77	296,555 35
Books	28,839 38	25,173 45	25,785 31	79,798 14
Clocks and watches	36,614 30	45,582 30	42,183 40	124,380 00
Chemicals	119,595 95	117,142 35	123,395 41	360,133 71
Dry goods	828,147 44	920,326 68	1,257,320 65	3,005,794 77
Dress goods..............	1,340,927 95	2,102,474 10	3,904,133 36	7,347,335 41
Fancy goods	1,003,638 19	1,110,115 80	1,107,362 89	2,221,116 88
Ladies' and gentlemen's furnishing goods........	474,493 43	393,386 94	518,516 26	1,386,396 63
Gloves	451,660 37	376,939 54	414,366 82	1,242,966 73
Glass, porcelain, &c.......	240,090 09	237,497 80	155,687 79	633,275 68
Hatters' goods...........	425,063 21	457,293 35	348,715 51	1,231,072 07
Jewelry and precious stones	570,131 67	634,178 35	242,247 15	1,446,557 17
Leather..................	422,425 01	421,183 70	339,928 00	1,183,536 71
Merinoes and bombazines..	400,658 16	1,668,487 07	1,873,706 29	3,942,851 52
Miscellaneous	149,104 17	135,762 40	58,609 45	343,476 02
Perfumery	92,920 18	40,972 11	56,509 02	190,401 31
Pianos and musical instruments	63,850 99	37,634 90	46,795 95	148,281 84
Ready-made clothing.......	41,063 85	42,891 05	33,643 90	117,598 80
Stationery	76,984 55	92,537 60	74,154 95	243,677 10
Trimmings	79,703 40	120,831 41	246,275 65	446,810 46
Woollen cloths	50,962 85	136,264 15	231,646 25	418,873 25
Wines	555,472 48	495,676 42	522,998 17	1,574,147 07
Total...............	7,734,017 87	9,772,790 91	11,918,211 85	29,425,020 63

HAVRE—JAMES O. PUTMAN, *Consul.*

JANUARY 25, 1864.

I have the honor to transmit herewith the annual statement of imports from the United States into the port of Havre for 1863.

There is nothing particular to report in connexion with our American trade for the past year which is of a local character. Our tonnage and importations owing to the general causes which are every where affecting our commerce, have been constantly decreasing until our flag has become, if not a stranger, a comparatively rare visitant at this port.

The carrying trade between this and the northern ports of the United States, which heretofore has been wholly done by regular lines of American sailing packets, is now performed almost exclusively by ships under the French or the Bremen or Hamburg flags.

The impossibility, owing to the war risks, of competing with foreign flags for the carrying trade has led to the sale of many of the finest American bottoms which have entered this port during the year. They generally pass under the English or the Bremen or Hamburg flags.

Havre has suffered more than any other seaport in France from the effects of our war. The American has been its great trade, and the principal reliance of that portion of its labor which looks to the business connected with the shipping interest for its support.

Large fortunes have been realized by cotton operators, but with that exception the town has been a great sufferer.

The cotton trade, alone, formerly afforded the means of subsistence to thousands of laborers and small tradesmen. From its relations it must necessarily revive with peace and the return of our trade, but it is too dependent upon our commerce to realize much relief from any other quarter.

*   *   *   *   *   *   *   *   *

Statement showing the imports into the port of Havre from the United States during the year 1863.

Cotton.—1st quarter, 335 bales; 2d quarter, 695 bales; 3d quarter, 1,070 bales; 4th quarter,———. Total, 2,100 bales.

Breadstuffs.—Wheat: 1st quarter, 66,633 bushels; 2d quarter, 121,007 bushels; 3d quarter, 279,886 bushels; 4th quarter, 21,042 bushels. Total, 488,568 bushels.

Flour.—1st quarter,———; 2d quarter, 7,146 barrels; 3d quarter, 13,597 barrels; 4th quarter, 2,785 barrels and 590 cases prepared flour. Totals, 23,528 barrels and 590 cases prepared flour.

Potash.—1st quarter, 1,073 barrels; 2d quarter, 1,458 barrels; 3d quarter, 242 barrels; 4th quarter, 867 barrels. Total, 3,640 barrels.

Pearlash.—1st quarter, 20 barrels; 2d quarter, 124 barrels; 3d quarter, 160 barrels; 4th quarter, 226 barrels. Total, 530 barrels.

Tallow.—1st quarter, 672 casks; 2d quarter, 8,998 casks, 55 hogsheads, and 1,019,188 pounds; 3d quarter, 997 casks, 195 hogsheads, and 31,082 pounds; 4th quarter, 1,406 casks, 20 hogsheads, and 1,631,158 pounds. Totals, 12,073 casks, 270 hogsheads, and 2,681,428 pounds.

Lard.—1st quarter, 13,841 barrels; 2d quarter———, 1,904 cases and 1,609,877 pounds; 3d quarter, 4,258 barrels; 4th quarter, 6,965 barrels, 67 cases, and 1,294,417 pounds. Totals, 25,064 barrels, 1,971 cases, and 2,904,294 pounds.

Petroleum.—1st quarter, 6,481 barrels; 2d quarter, 26,093 barrels; 3d quarter, 7,061 barrels; 4th quarter, 3,903 barrels and 82,736 gallons. Totals, 43,538 barrels, and 82,736 gallons.

Whale oil.—1st quarter, 420 casks; 2d quarter, 446 casks and 1,428 gallons; 3d quarter, 84 casks and 80 cases; 4th quarter,———. Totals, 950 casks, 1,428 gallons, and 80 cases.

Tobacco.—1st quarter, 1,987 hogsheads and 559 bales; 2d quarter, 663 hogsheads and 10 bales; 3d quarter, 2,092 hogsheads; 4th quarter, 2,737 hogsheads, 87 bales, and 18 cases. Totals, 7,479 hogsheads, 656 bales, and 18 cases.

Salted pork.—1st quarter, 67 casks, 82 cases, 163 hogsheads, and 4,965 barrels; 2d quarter, 12 casks, and 183 cases; 3d quarter, 540 cases; 4th quarter, 633 casks. Totals, 712 casks, 805 cases, 163 hogsheads, and 4,965 barrels.

Bacon and other salted provisions.—During the year 5,298 barrels, 1,102 casks, 40 hogsheads, 4,923 cases, and 413,289 pounds.

Clover-seed.—1st quarter, 4,206 sacks; 2d quarter, 659 sacks and 80 hogsheads; 3d quarter, 1,797 sacks; 4th quarter,———. Totals, 6,662 sacks and 80 hogsheads.

Hops.—During the year, 128 bales.

Alcohol.—During the year, 1,755 barrels and 648 casks.

Quercitron bark.—First quarter, 661 bags; second quarter, 659 bags and 88 hogsheads; third quarter, 1,400 bags; fourth quarter, 650 bags and 66 hogsheads. Totals, 3,370 bags and 154 hogsheads.

Fish-eggs.—During the year, 518 barrels.

Grease.—During the year, 525 cases and 910 casks.

Goldsmiths' dust.—Second quarter, 112 barrels, 40 cases, and 19 casks third quarter, 133 barrels; fourth quarter, 90 barrels. Totals, 335 barrels, 40 cases, and 19 casks.

Sewing machines.—2d quarter, 48 cases; 3d quarter, 14 cases; 4th quarter, 47 cases. Total, 109 cases.

Staves.—During the year, 420,839.

Oars.—2d quarter, 2,986; 3d quarter, 1,214; 4th quarter, 3,609. Total, 7,809 oars.

Deals.—During the year, 27,949 and 1,216 pieces.

Laths.—During the year, 33,102 packages.

Staves for making casks.—During the year, 508 packages.

Shoe pegs.—40 casks.

Pigs' bristles.—30 bales.

Goat skins.—28 bales.

India-rubber.—71 sacks.

Sausage skins.—55 casks.

Salted fish.—50 cases.

Cocoa.—60 sacks.

Cod-liver oil.—24 cases.

Kerosene oil.—During the year, 24 cases.

Sponge.—50 bales.

Rosin.—34 barrels.

Ostrich feathers.—4 bales.

Whalebone.—3,077 bundles.

Silk waste.—203 bales.

Hams.—7,108 pounds, 15 barrels, and 1 case.

Candles.—2 cases.

Japan ware.—3 cases.

Indian corn.—5 barrels.

Capstan bars.—During the year, 487 unwrought.

Moss.—662 bales.

Leather.—66 casks.

Rice.—53 tierces.

Spermaceti.—7 casks.

Salted beef.—53 casks and 18 cases.

Salted hides.—100.

Benzine.—4 casks.

Anise-seed—1 case.

Wine.—During the year, 17 casks and 88 cases.

Absinthe.—45 casks.

Copaiba.—166 boxes.

Tar.—38 barrels.

Copper.—67 barrels.

Silver ore.—17 casks.

Mint.—46 casks and 30 cases.

Jalap.—18 bales.

Chrome ore.—756 bags.

Brandy.—24 casks.

Lima wood.—During the year, 20 cases.

Maple wood.—1,166 logs.

Cedar.—1,488 logs.

Mahogany.—326 logs.

Bark.—80 seroons.

Sarsaparilla.—34 bales.

Black walnut.—153 logs.

JANUARY 25, 1864.

There has lately been published an official document relating to French emigration, and emigration from other European states through France, containing some interesting statistics and observations which I have thought might possess some interest. I refer more particularly to its *exposé* relative to French emigration. It is from the commissioner of emigration to the minister of the interior.

The following table shows the emigration from France from 1856 to 1862 :

Years.	For foreign countries.	For Algeria.	Total.
1856	9,433	8,564	17,797
1857	10,317	7,992	18,809
1858	9,004	4,809	13,813
1859	6,786	2,378	9,164
1860	7,443	2,644	10,087
1861	6,334	2,418	8,752
1862	5,036	1,764	6,800

About one-fifth of the whole emigration from France is from the department of the Lower Pyrenees.

The agricultural element is about 27 per cent. of the whole to foreign countries and 35 per cent. to Algeria.

The following table exhibits the destination of French emigration in 1861 and 1862 :

Destination.	1861.	Destination.	1862.
Algeria	2,418	Algeria	1,764
South America	2,818	South America	2,322
United States	828	Spain	984
Spain	1,066	United States	575
Switzerland	223	Italy	210
Other countries	1,399	Cuba	133
		Egypt	127
		Other countries	685
Total	8,752	Total	6,800

The report attributes the diminution of emigration to the flourishing condition of the country, and the demand for labor created by Imperial enterprises.

Additional to these reasons, I think there are other causes founded on the institutions of the country, and in the character of the people, which will always make France a non-emigrating country compared with other states of Europe.

The peasant is the proprietor of the land he tills, and although the lands are infinitely subdivided the instinctive desire for such proprietorship is universally gratified. The revolution which transferred the proprietorship of the soil from an aristocracy of three hundred thousand to a peasantry of five or six millions removed from the masses one of the strongest motives for expatriation. There is, besides, a more easy contentment with a present possession, less of that restless desire for improved "well-being," than is found in the German races.

The French peasant is contented with a small freehold, small gains, and simple pleasures. He is religious, and will not forego the enjoyment of the ceremonials and ordinances of his church and familiar associations. And when he does seek his fortunes in a foreign land it is generally with purpose of sooner or later returning. A few thousand francs satisfy him, and he returns to enjoy his moderate acquisition.   *   *   *

Whether it be the result of philosophy or temperament, the French peasant and artisan appear to be more happy with very moderate possessions in their native land, than with all the property and consideration which are so easily won in new countries.

If they contribute little to the building up of home colonies or new foreign states, they realize a rare and happy contentment with very moderate possessions in their own land.

It appears from the report that Havre is the chief port in France for the embarcation of German emigrants to the United States and South America.

That emigration *via* Havre during 1860, –'61, and –'62 was as follows:

    1860... 21,186
    1861... 11,416
    1862.. 8,393

mostly to the United States.

The diminished emigration from Germany is attributed in the report to our war, which it is suggested can be but temporary, and that " nothing can permanently check the current of German emigration to the United States, which exists as a normal fact."

The emigrant agencies established by law in France are as follows:

At Havre... .... 6 | At Bordeaux.... 6
" Paris .... 5 | " Bayonne................. 2
" Wissembourg............. 1 | " Marseilles.............. 1
" Whart Coze .... 1 |

The system adopted for the protection of emigrants against frauds in the purchase of tickets here over American railroads is spoken of as perfect, and that but one instance of wrong occurred during the last year, which was promptly redressed by the emigration commissioners.

The report fully appreciates the great inducements held out to labor by the demands for every species of manual service in the United States, and to agriculturists for cheap lands in the midst of our " armed struggle," and adds:

"The immense extent of the federal States and the vast distance which divides some of them from the theatre of war justify, to a certain extent, the expectations of emigrants."

Statement showing the description and quantity of imports into Havre from the United States during the quarter ending June 30, 1864.

Cotton, 1,879 bales. | Salt beef, 25 barrels.
Tobacco, 215 hogsheads. | Petroleum oil, 2,000 barrels.
Tallow, 1,946 casks. | Sausage skins, 103 barrels.
Lard, 7,814 casks. | Fish-eggs, 307 barrels.
Potashes, 966 barrels. | Ochre, 74 casks.
Pearlash, 65 barrels. | Candles, 40 cases.
Goldsmiths' dust, 210 barrels. | Fur, 1 case.
Hops, 39 bales. | Cheese, 12 cases.
Hides, 4,810 hides. | Hemp, 15 bales.
Pigs' bristles, 190 barrels and 5 bales. | Butter, 5 kegs.
Buckskins, 6 cases. | Wine, 25 cases.

Wax, 10 cases.
Cigars, 11 cases.
Cod-liver oil, 8 cases.
Whale oil, 382 barrels.
Staves, 25,610.
Oars, 938.
White pine, 638 planks.
Wood, dyes, drugs, &c., &c., 125 hogsheads, and 3,353 sacks quercitron bark, 213 logs maple wood, 679 logs cedar wood, and 44 logs mahogany.
Sugar, 1,581 cases.
Whalebone, 244 packages.
Moss, 2 bales.
Hams, 32 cases.
Grease, 281 casks.
Flour, 2 barrels.
Essence of mint, 3 cases.

* * * I have supposed the information called for to be, not a summary, but the exact law, or ordinance, or decree, in *hæc verba*, imposing the duties.

After several days' examination, I find very little that meets the requirement. The authorities here act in accordance with a general book of instructions of several hundred pages, which does not contain the decree or regulation itself, but a memorandum instruction, out of which has grown, as practiced, the system so elaborately detailed in my report accompanying despatch No. 24, (1863.) This book of instructions does not give the exact method of plumbing or leading goods or wagons. That has grown into a system by arbitrary adoption of the customs.

I did find, however, a convention made between France and Belgium and Holland, regulating the transportation upon railroads of .goods crossing the frontiers of the respective countries, which seems to furnish what is desired, at least in part.

Also, a regulation of the French government defining the customs' formalities to be observed at the railway stations of the empire in regard to goods forwarded in transit.

I have had translations prepared of the same, which accompany this despatch. * * * * * * *

By an imperial decree, under date the 25th of January, 1853, the following convention between France, Belgium, and Holland in regard to the transit of goods by railway was ratified and promulgated:

Rules and regulations governing the international service between France, Belgium, and Holland, in its relation with the customs of these respective countries.

TRAINS OF GOODS.

ARTICLE I. All goods placed in wagons, closed by sliding doors or covered with tarpaulins, and duly sealed or leaded, (*plombés*,) upon arrival, either by night or by day, on the frontiers of the respective countries, shall, under the following conditions, be exempt from verification by the customs authorities.

ARTICLE II. This exemption provisionally applies for trains destined for or coming from Mons, Brussels, Antwerp, Ghent, Liege, Bruges, Ostend, Courtai, and Louvain, in Belgium; Lille, Valenciennes, Paris, Rouen, and Havre, in France; and Rotterdam and Amsterdam, in Holland.

The contracting parties shall have, however, the right of extending the privilege above named to such other places as may be put in communication with the above cities by railway.

ARTICLE III. All cases of merchandise weighing less than 25 kilos (50 lbs.) shall be put into a closed wagon with sliding doors. This rule is not absolute, and cases exceeding the weight above specified, with the permission and approval of the customs authorities, and when placed in a basket, or other cover, and leaded or sealed, may be forwarded in like manner; but only one case for each destination by one train can so be sent.

ARTICLE IV. The customs officers of the contracting parties shall respect each other's leadings, seals, and padlocks of whatever nature or kind, providing they are placed and made in conformity to the requirements of the laws. This article applies wholly to wagons and trains destined for or coming from those places above designated.

ARTICLE V. For every train a distinct and separate recapitulatory statement of the goods, of same tenor, shall be made by the respective countries.

This statement, prepared by the railway administration, shall be handed to the customs authorities at the place of the departure of the goods for their signature and approval, and shall, moreover, designate the number of the wagons and their respective numbers; and there shall be annexed to the same all the declarations and other documents prescribed by the customs of each of the contracting parties.

ARTICLE VI. Every train shall be escorted or accompanied by several custom-house officers, and the railroad company being only bound to furnish them accommodations as near the wagons containing goods as possible.

ARTICLE VII. The officers escorting the goods shall accompany the train on the territory of the respective countries to the first customs bureau, and shall not leave the train until they have delivered all the documents connected therewith into the hands of the officers of that station.

ARTICLE VIII. Before crossing the frontiers the wagons shall all be well closed or covered with tarpauline, so that the customs may only have to attach thereto their padlocks, seals, or leads.

ARTICLE IX. The padlocks of the three respective countries must be of a uniform model, and the leads or seals shall bear the name of the customs bureau from whence the goods are forwarded.

RELATING TO TRAINS CONVEYING PASSENGERS.

ARTICLE X. The privilege accorded by the 1st article of the present convention shall likewise be extended to trains conveying passengers.

ARTICLE XI. All passengers' luggage which is not inspected by the customs at the frontier shall be accompanied by a specific statement and customs document, and shall be placed in closed cars, leaded, or sealed, or padlocked.

ARTICLE XII. Luggage, however, shall in general be inspected at the frontier, except that of passengers going from France to Brussels by the way of Quievrain; or from France to Rotterdam or Amsterdam through Belgium, via Quievrain and Antwerp; or from Belgium to Valenciennes or Paris via Quievrain; or from Belgium to Rotterdam or Amsterdam via Antwerp; or from Holland to Valenciennes or Paris through Belgium by the way of Antwerp, Brussels, and Quievrain; and that said passengers so travelling shall have the right of causing their luggage to be inspected, either at the frontier customs or at the place of their destination.

This regulation shall also apply to such other places as may hereafter be appointed and put in communication by each of the contracting parties by rail, and where the customs shall permit of it.

ARTICLE XIII. Travellers shall not be allowed to take with them in the cars any article or case subject to duty or of a prohibitory character.

ARTICLE XIV. All dutiable merchandise transported by passenger trains are subject to the same conditions and formalities as laid down for the forwarding of the same by special trains.

GENERAL STIPULATIONS.

ARTICLE XV. The departures of trains of goods or passengers leaving Belgium for Paris, *via* the branch railroad, touching at Lille, shall be so regulated as, on reaching Douai, they may be united to those arriving under escort from Holland and Belgium by the way of Valenciennes; Douai being the station appointed for the purpose.

ARTICLE XVI. As a principle, the number of trains daily crossing the frontiers of the respective countries shall be limited, but the number determined upon may be exceeded, providing it is to the interest of the railroad company, and if the customs there established shall deem it essential or necessary.

ARTICLE XVII. On the arrival of the trains at destination the goods shall be deposited in such warehouses as the railway company may designate, but which must meet the approval of the customs officials, and be so built as to admit of being locked or closed securely. Here they shall remain under the custody of the customs officers, the delay accorded by the law, or until they (the goods) are entered for the consumption, or for re-exportation, or placed in bond upon declarations in detail, and after the accomplishment of the prescribed formalities. Goods withdrawn from these warehouses for re-exportation in transit under this convention shall be exempt from all verification upon leaving the territory. The unloading the wagons must take place immediately after arrival.

ARTICLE XVIII. At such railway stations as do not possess the warehouses prescribed by the foregoing regulation, the discharge of the wagons must be made in thirty-six hours after the arrival of the train, and if this is not done the goods forfeit their rights under this convention.

ARTICLE XIX. The railway administration is held to give at least eight days' previous notice of their intention or desire to alter the hours of the departures of the trains, and of their passage or arrival at the frontier by night or by day, under penalty of subjecting the goods to all the ordinary formalities of the customs.

ARTICLE XX. A division of a train, when it is rendered necessary and applied for, and permission granted by the customs authorities, may take place at the frontier, but the number of the wagons added or taken therefrom shall not exceed ten. Yet in a case of extreme urgency the chief customs officer at the frontier may authorize a larger division, but only at the following places can this be done: Quievrain, Monscreu, and Antwerp, in Belgium, and at Valenciennes and Lille, in France. For Holland, the frontier station cannot be determined upon until after the termination of the Antwerp and Holandschdiep railroad.

ARTICLE XXI. There shall be accorded to all trains of passengers or goods from France, *via* Belgium, for Holland, and *vice versa*, the same facilities and privileges under the conditions and formalities regulating the entry or exit of trains from one country into another.

ARTICLE XXII. All merchandise arriving at Paris, under this convention, can there be landed and afterwards forwarded to other destinations on the following conditions:

1. Goods comprised in one declaration can take but one destination, and may be entered for the consumption, or placed in bond, or declared for re-exportation.

2. The re-exportation for another destination shall take place thirty-six hours after arrival, or the goods will lose the rights accorded them by the present convention, and will, moreover, be immediately put in bond at the expense of the railroad company which conveyed them to Paris.

3. The sheds or warehouses at the railway depots where these formalities are

to be observed, must be especially reserved for the purpose, and suit the convenience and meet the approval of the customs authorities.

ARTICLE XXIII. All goods and luggage expedited under the convention from Hollandsch-diep to Rotterdam, and which shall continue their journey by rail to Amsterdam, or which may be forwarded from either of these two cities for Belgium or France by the way of Antwerp, shall enjoy all the rights defined above, provided they do not change wagons.

If they are taken out of the wagons to be afterwards shipped by water they shall be put into cases or baskets duly sealed or leaded, and then stowed into a particular part of the vessel, whose hatches shall likewise be leaded. The cases of baskets and the vessel itself shall all first be inspected and approved of by the custom officers.

For goods so forwarded the railroad will be held to make a separate and distinct statement of the said goods for each destination of the same, which must be accompanied by a declaration and the other documents prescribed by the customs.

Thirty-six hours after the arrival of the goods at Rotterdam or at Roodevaart, they must be discharged; if not, they will be immediately placed in bond at the expense of whom it may concern, and thereby lose all their privileges under this convention.

ARTICLE XXIV. The customs officers accompanying trains of goods or passengers shall be admitted into second-class cars, and in the places reserved for the conductors thereof, or on board the vessels carrying the goods.

ARTICLE XXV. It is hereby mutually understood, that the present rules and regulations are of no effect as concerns the punishing of fraud, or the inflicting of fines therefor, or in regard to any restrictions on the importation or exportation of goods, the laws of the country of each of the contracting parties wholly governing these matters, and that the customs authorities of the three countries further reserve to themselves the right of examining all goods on their arrival on the frontiers, or at the port of their embarcation or departure, should they have the slightest reason to suppose that fraud is intended.

ARTICLE XXVI. The customs agents and officials of the three countries shall further communicate to each other the circulars and instructions addressed to them by their respective governments concerning the carrying out of this convention.

They shall concert together and adopt such necessary measures in regard to the working hours of their officials as they may deem fit, and which may conduce to the better fulfilment of these presents and meet the exigencies of the railroad service.

ARTICLE XXVII. The countries whose railways join those which are subject to the present convention shall be admitted to participate in all the rights and privileges accorded by the same, and any stipulations or agreement of either of the contracting parties with such countries shall be applicable to the other two.

ARTICLE XXVIII. If either of the contracting parties shall desire to cancel this convention, they will be held to give six months' previous notice of their intention.

PROVISIONAL STIPULATIONS.

ARTICLE XXIX. Provisionally, and until the railroad from Antwerp to Hollandsch-diep shall be completed, and under the reserves contained in article 25, all goods and luggage sent from France, or from Belgium, by virtue of this convention, and forwarded from Antwerp by water to Holland, and coming by water from Holland, destined for Belgium or France, shall be exempt from all verification at the frontier, as well on their entry as on their exit from Belgium and Holland, under the following conditions, viz:

1st. All cases of goods must either be leaded or stowed in particular parts of the ship, which shall likewise be leaded or sealed.

2d. The declarations in detail of the same and the customs permits and other documents remain obligatory.

ARTICLE XXX. All merchandise and luggage forwarded conformably to the conditions contained in article 29 shall enjoy all the rights and immunities accorded by this convention on their entry into Belgium from Holland, and on their arrival in Holland, *via* the river Scheldt, to the place of their destination, if there is there established a custom bureau open to importations by that route.

This convention was signed on the 4th day of December, 1853, in triplicate, at Paris, by the commissioner of the contracting parties.

OF RAILWAY STATIONS COMMON TO FRANCE AND BAVARIA.

It has been agreed between the French and Bavarian governments, in order to facilitate the transportation of goods and travellers on the Strasburg and Newstadt railroad, that at the depot at Wissembourg, (in France,) common to both countries, the Bavarian government shall there establish, alongside of the French customs bureau, or as near the same as possible, an office or station, for the purpose of superintending the fulfilment of certain formalities hereinafter specified. (Art. 1, convention of the 3d of July, 1857.)

The necessary grounds for the offices, warehouses, barracks, &c., for the Bavarian officials shall be granted by the railway company and situated at the railway depot itself.

The hire or rent of the premises shall be settled by the French Custom Railroad Company and that forming a junction with the same, unless the Bavarian government should see fit to arrange or settle the matter with their own railroad company. (Art. 2, same convention.)

The premises thus occupied by the Bavarian government officials shall be designated by the Bavarian arms.

The officers in the discharge of their duties shall wear the uniform of their government, and during their sojourn in France shall be subject to French law and held to the payment of all indirect taxes, in like manner as other foreigners. They shall not, however, either themselves or their families, be liable to the conscription or to serve in the militia, and shall be exempt from all local or commercial taxes, or direct or personal taxes; and in regard to their duties, they shall account for the same to their own government. (Art 5, same convention.)

All the materials which shall be necessary for them to have, as well as their furniture, &c., when accompanying them, shall be exempt from import or export duty on their entering or leaving France with the same. They will be held, however, to go through the formalities prescribed in like cases by the customs.

The officials of the respective governments, when obliged, in the discharge of their duties, to cross the frontiers, when in uniform, or upon presentation of their commissions, shall enjoy all the immunities accorded them by their respective national laws.

The same privileges shall be reciprocally extended to their railway officials.

The two governments engage themselves to exclude from their employ any person having committed an offence against the laws of either country, or who may have been imprisoned for fraud, &c.

The authorities of both countries, in their relations with each other, shall be on a footing of perfect equality; and in the execution of their several duties, all aid and assistance possible, consistent with the laws and regulations of their own countries, shall be afforded.

The railroad between Wissembourg and the first Bavarian station is hereby declared an international railway, and shall be open to both countries for the importation or exportation of merchandise in transit or otherwise. (Art. 11 same convention.)

Regulations of the French government, under date of the 27th of June, 1857, defining the customs formalities to be observed at the different railway stations of the empire in regard to goods forwarded in transit.

ARTICLE 1. Every railroad company at each station or depot will be held to appoint a general agent, (fondé de pouvoirs,) who alone, when goods are there deposited, shall be authorized to act in their behalf and discharge the formalities prescribed by the customs in regard to the forwarding of goods or their withdrawal on arrival.

ARTICLE 2. The platforms at these several depots shall so be made that the discharge and loading of the wagons can take place immediately opposite the customs office there established.

The operation of loading and unloading shall not take place simultaneously, and a distinct place must be set apart for the one and the other, every precaution being taken to guard against the goods to be loaded becoming mixed with those to be unloaded.

That at these stations, where the same may require it, two distinct warehouses shall be made, one for goods arriving and the other for those departing. (Art. 2 continued.)

ARTICLE 3. The warehouses shall have two locks, the key of the one to be held by the general agent of the railway administration and the other to remain in the hands of the customs authorities, who shall, whenever they see fit, cause the respective warehouses to be watched day and night.

ARTICLE 4. The printing of the forms prescribed by law must be made at the expense of the railroad company.

ARTICLE 5. Those stamped shall be furnished by the government. These latter, upon the payment of the value of the stamp by the general agent of the railway administration, shall be delivered to him at all times upon his request.

ARTICLE 6. The labor in regard to the handling of the cases, or the opening and closing of the wagons containing them, must be done by the workmen in the employ of the railroad company.

ARTICLE 7. The sealing or leading of wagons shall be made by the customs packers alone, and they will be charged with all the verification or examination of the seals or leads of the same when arriving. The number of seals to be attached should not exceed two, but more may be used if the particular construction or build of the cars should require it.

ARTICLE 8. All customs formalities to be observed at depots situated in seaports shall take place under the immediate superintendence of the director of "roadstead;" but he is, in turn, held accountable to the chief inspector of the customs for the discharge of his duties.

ARTICLE 9. The price of the leading or sealing is fixed at 50 centimes, (10 cents,) and must be paid into the office of the cashier of the railroad company.

ARTICLE 10. The presentation of all goods, their examination, &c., their leading, and discharging of the same, cannot take place but between the hours of eight in the morning and four in the afternoon, unless special permission be granted by the head officer of the customs.

ARTICLE 11. The warehouses reserved for goods in transit must have but one entrance, and a customs officer will be there placed for the purpose of preventing any case or bale of goods leaving the premises without the proper permits and papers.

H. Ex. Doc. 60——14

JULY 16, 1864.

I have had the honor duly to receive despatch No. 57, instructing me to examine the system adopted in this country to prevent frauds upon the revenue in connexion with goods crossing frontiers.

I find, upon inquiry and examination, that there is comparatively little which I can add to the report accompanying despatch No. 24 of 1863 and the later despatch, No. 17, of the present year.

I am indebted to the same official to whose kindness I have been so often a debtor for a written report upon the question submitted.

There is great clearness and precision, which I hope are not wholly lost in the translation, in the original.   *   *   *   *   *   *

SUMMARY OF THE MEASURES ADOPTED IN FRANCE TO PREVENT SMUGGLING ACROSS THE NATIONAL FRONTIER.

The measures adopted by the French customs are of two distinct kinds. The first consists of certain laws and conditions regulating the circulation of merchandise within a fixed frontier limit. The second in the organization of a special customs service for the carrying out of these laws and conditions, and for effecting the seizure of all goods imported otherwise than in accordance with the prescribed restrictions and conditions.

By a "frontier limit" (rayon frontiere) is meant all that portion of territory comprised between the extreme boundary and another fixed limit in the interior of the country of four leagues or twelve miles therefrom and running parallel therewith.

Goods of French origin cannot circulate within the frontier limit without a special customs permit styled "passavant." This document contains a full description of the merchandise, the date and hour of the departure thereof, declares the road or route to be taken by the same, and the time allowed for its transportation. If the merchandise comes from without the prescribed limit or circuit, it is at the first customs depot therein that the permit must be applied for. When the goods are of the growth or manufacture of the frontier limit, then the permit must be obtained at the nearest customs bureau, and must take the most direct route to their destination.

The officers employed at these depots, prior to delivering the permits above described, verify and inspect the goods very minutely. The permit or "passavant" being instituted principally with the view of preventing the fraudulent importation of goods manufactured in foreign countries, is not obligatory and can be dispensed with wholly for products of the French soil destined for consumption at the neighboring markets, for the transportation of cereals and vegetables from the fields to the farm-houses, and for all small packages of manufactured goods in the possession of persons living within the circuit and evidently destined for their own use.

In respect to these last articles, however, when they are to be employed in that portion of the t rritory comprised between the last office of the customs and the extreme frontier, their purposed destination must be certified to by the mayor of the commune or district from whence they emanate.

The following documents are held to supply the place of the permit under certain circumstances: ·

1st. When goods are of foreign origin and imported into France, the receipt of the nearest customs depot of the payment of the entry duties is sufficient.

2d. When the goods are of French origin, and are intended for exportation, the receipt of the customs officers of the station nearest the interior limit of the payment of the export duties also suffices. It may not be amiss to state here that the receipts in question contain all the data of the permit itself.

3d. "Acquits à caution," or certificates of guarantee, accompanying goods in transit, whether withdrawn from bonded warehouses or coming from seaports and merely passing through the country, likewise supply the place of a permit. In which case, however, the customs depot on the extreme interior limit indorse on the "acquit à caution," or certificate of guarantee, the date and hour of the entry of the goods within the circuit, and the delay accorded for their transportation to the extreme boundary line.

In consequence of these divers measures it follows that all goods found within the specified circuit without permits, or which may even be accompanied by a permit whose time is expired, are considered as foreign goods and to have been fraudulently introduced, leading to their immediate seizure, with a fine of 500 francs, if the same are of a prohibited character, or of 100 francs if admissible to entry. The seizure of the merchandise carries with it the confiscation of the vehicles, &c., used in the transportation thereof, and the penalty of from three days to one month's imprisonment.

No manufacturing establishment can be erected within the customs limits without the authorization of the government. That authorization is preceded by an inquiry into the character of the petitioner, the situation of the projected establishment, and the facilities it offers for surveillance by the customs service.

When the authorization is granted, (which is never done when the establishment is upon the extreme frontier,) an open account is kept at the customs depot of the raw material destined for the factory, and which is subject to all the rules and regulations imposed upon the circulation of merchandise generally.

Manufactured articles cannot leave the establishment but by a permit grant only upon a declaration of the manufacturer.

The merchandise accompanied by that declaration goes by the most direct route to the nearest customs bureau, which then delivers the permit after verification of the merchandise, and an account taken of the raw material employed in the article manufactured withdrawn from the factory.

The service of the customs from time to time visit these establishments. If there is found an excess of raw material in the manufactory above what was represented it is seized, and if the same is of a prohibited character a fine of 500 francs is imposed, if not of 100 francs; additional to the fine of 500 francs is the penalty of imprisonment from three days to one month. In case of a second violation of law the manufactured license is rescinded. There is no fine when the stock falls below that represented.

Merchants, except small retailers, are required to declare their amount of manufactured goods (subject to heavy entry duties) upon their entry at the office of the customs nearest their place of trade, and the same forms are observed as in the case of the manufacturer.

All depots of merchandise of each character are subject to visitation by the service of the customs, and if an excess above that reported by the owners is found, the same penalties are imposed as upon manufacturers in like circumstances, except that their right or license of trade cannot be withdrawn.

In addition to the manufactories and depots of merchandise, the customs have the right of visitation of private dwellings or other enclosed places, if it suspects the presence of fraudulent goods; but in that case, out of respect to private rights, they can enter private dwellings only when accompanied by one of the municipal authorities, (mayor, commissary of police, &c.,) who is required to aid the customs officials.

The result of the search is drawn up in the presence of the municipal officer, and is signed by him. If goods are discovered whose origin cannot be justified, the party who hold them is considered as having committed a fraud, and is punished accordingly.

The penalties are the same as those above described; confiscation of the goods and a fine of from 100 to 500 francs, according to the circumstances.

The agents of the customs in whose district are observed fraudulent parties with goods arriving otherwise than by the high road, and direct to the nearest customs bureau, must arrest and conduct them, together with the effects found upon them, to their station, where a written report of the seizure is drawn. This document, signed by the capturers and the chief of the bureau, states the circumstances of the arrest, describes the merchandise, states the penalties incurred, and serves as a basis of prosecution in the courts.

Should the parties make their escape with the merchandise, they can be pursued even into closed private dwellings without the aid or presence of a municipal officer, and there arrested.

In such cases the proprietor of the place to which the fugitive parties have fled incurs no responsibility, but in order to enter his premises it is necessary that the agents of the service do not lose sight of the agents.

The customs officers are not allowed to use their arms unless they are attacked by armed force. All merchandise circulating within the customs circuit, without a permit, even upon the high roads, are subject to immediate seizure, and to be conducted, with those who are transporting them, to the nearest customs depot, where the trespass is formally declared as above indicated. The objects thus seized are kept in the custody of the chief officer of the customs bureau until the controversy is brought to an issue.

The customs being invested with the discretionary power of settling its own rights without going into a court of law, when they see fit, may waive prosecution with the consent of the accused. In such case, after payment of the fine imposed, the merchandise, if not of a prohibited character, may be surrendered to its owner upon the payment, besides, of the entry duties; but if of a prohibited character they remain confiscated.

The bureau of the customs where the declarations are received and where permits are delivered are established upon all the principal roads, some on the extreme frontier, others at the commencement of the prescribed interior limits. In certain cases, depending upon the nature of the country, intermediate stations are established to facilitate the operations of manufacturers.

Independently of the offices where are verified goods regularly declared, and where the entry and export duties are received, are established other stations whose officers have, for special duty, to guard the frontiers and to prevent smuggling.

The interior fixed customs limit and the extreme boundaries are thus guarded by an unbroken line of men detached on this special duty, and who form, as it were, a sort of cordon, all in communication one with the other. Further, between the two limits are likewise detached a certain number of men (varying according to the exigencies of the service) whose service consists in going from place to place, and watching particularly those places offering the greatest facilities for smuggling.

The chiefs of the different stations communicate their observations in a way to best combine preventive measures. Every depot, independently of its regular service, has certain supernumeraries attached, who are likewise sent on tours of observation. During the night the service is increased. At daybreak the chief officer also starts on duty, and, at some determined point, meets his brother chief of the neighboring station, and exchanges observations with him. The object of this surveillance is to obtain traces of the movements of any smugglers who might have escaped detection during the night. If any traces are discovered, a party is detached to follow them up; and if they lead to a private house, to guard it provisionally until inquiry can be made, or the aid of a municipal officer obtained in accordance with the forms indicated.

Each depot consists of 10, 15, or 20 men, according to the extent of territory attached to it, besides two chiefs to superintend the service and to register the official orders given, as well as the results of all operations.

Finally, there are superior officers whose duty it is to go from depot to depot to see that the service is well distributed, and that the men faithfully discharge their duties.

Above these last is general chief officer, who has charge of the whole service within the circuit, and who is answerable for the same to administration at Paris.

In order to complete the system for the prevention of frauds, French legislation (recently modified, however, in consequence of the almost entire abolition of prohibitory duties) permits the seizure, even in the interior of the country outside of the prescribed circuit, of all threads and manufactured cotton and woollen goods whose owners cannot give their origin. It may be well here to enumerate the methods adopted for the purpose of distinguishing all manufactured goods, and the means employed to enforce the law. French manufacturers are held to put upon their threads or twists and their woollen and cotton goods a special mark, called the manufacturer's mark, and which is applied at the two extremities of each piece. It is either woven, embroidered, or printed, (the printed, the least used, is indelible by the use of chloric of magnesia.)

If the manufacturer sells his goods by retail, each piece sold must bear the mark. The mark indicates the name of the manufacturer or some equivalent designation adopted by him, the name of the place where his establishment is situated, and a number showing the order of the manufacture, which must be inscribed upon his account sales book, or on the register kept by him for the entry of all raw material purchased by him.

In regard to twist or threads, the mark consists of a label pasted or sealed upon each parcel in such a manner as to prevent any portion of the same being extracted without destroying the label. This mark indicates the name of the manufacturer, his place of residence, and the quality and weight of each parcel. The law authorized the making up of the parcels into five or ten pounds each.

Twists and manufactured goods of foreign origin, admitted for use, receive at the moment of their having passed the customs, by the payment of the duties, a special mark indicating their origin, which is applied by the customs and in the manner already described.

It results from these different measures that all twists and manufactured goods not bearing the marks of their origin are considered as having been fraudulently introduced, and liable to immediate seizure.

For the discovery of fraud, the officers of the customs, although they have the right of search over the whole circuit, yet they cannot enter private dwellings except when attended by a municipal officer, and then only during the day. These domiciliary visits can be made only with extreme caution, and under circumstances amounting to almost absolute proof of fraudulent concealment of dutiable goods. In the manufacturing districts is an organized corps belonging to the customs department, but without uniform or any distinctive badge, and who are charged with observing and watching generally all suspicious individuals.

At places without the customs limits this service is executed by the municipal police, either at their own option or on the suggestion to them by the customs officers that fraud is intended. Twist and manufactured goods found without mark of origin are submitted to a special jury attached to the bureau of the ministry of commerce at Paris, and composed of persons appointed by the government. Upon the decision of the jury in regard to the nationality of the goods, action is commenced, and the law is put in force.

If the merchandise is found to be of French origin, it is at once restored after the affixing of its mark of manufacture, but the holder is subject to a fine of six per centum ad valorem. If the origin is found to be foreign, the merchandise is confiscated, and the fine imposed is equal to the value thereof, but under no circumstances is it less than five hundred francs. Such are the measures adopted in France for the prevention of fraud, and, as will be perceived, being for the most part of rather a delicate character, require in their execution considerable tact in order to mitigate their severity. It is especially in domiciliary visits that the greatest circumspection is needed.

In cases where there is a suspicion of concealment of contraband goods in dwelling-houses or enclosed premises, without any direct proof of the fact, the customs officers are called upon to exercise all their ingenuity in discovering whether or not such is really the case, by strict vigilance and watchfulness of the premises themselves, without attracting attention, by following the persons leaving the house with packages, and cautiously making inquiries right and left to ascertain the character of the people, and, in short, by other adroit and indirect means, to arrive finally at the certain conviction of the existence of fraud.

These observations, however, in relation to search, &c., are not suggested by the letter of the law. The right of search being fully accorded to the customs, it is only out of respect for civil liberty that it is exercised in the manner indicated. This report is limited more particularly to the action upon the land frontier, being the most vulnerable point.

The surveillance of the sea-coast forms another branch of the service, and consists in the placing of customs officers along the same from the nearest customs bureau. Officers are in like manner stationed on the banks of all the large rivers of the empire running into the sea.

There is in reality no fixed customs limits for the seaboard. The customs are supposed to seize all goods attempted to be smuggled on their landing. The service, however, possess the right, providing they do not lose sight of the goods landed, to seize them in the interior of the country.

Trade is in every respect unrestricted along the whole coast, the inhabitants being exempted from all those formalities prescribed for the purchase, sale, and circulation of goods on the land frontier.

Statement showing the description and quantity of the imports into the port of Havre from ports of the United States during the year ended September 30, 1864.

Cotton	bales	870
Tobacco	hogsheads	2,371
Tobacco	bales	30
Tallow	casks	877
Lard	casks	3,646
Flour	barrels	4,670
Potash	barrels	875
Pearlash	barrels	294
Copper	casks	131
Pigs' bristles	casks	100
Hides	number	1,725
Wax	cases	198
Quercitron bark	hogsheads	134
Quercitron bark	sacks	555
Hair for mattresses, &c.	bales	122
Sewing machines	number	42
Goldsmiths' dust	barrels	111
Petroleum oil	barrels	45,833
Whale oil	barrels	6,783
Sugar	casks	1,404
Sugar	hogsheads	415
Sugar	tierces	40
Wheat	sacks	2,287

Whalebone	packages	96
Hams	casks	217
Wool	bales	254
Indigo	cases	27
Silk goods	cases	6
Palm leaves	packages	196
Maple wood	logs	62
Staves for making casks	packages	204
Cabinet woods	logs	855
Black walnut	logs	35
Cigars	cases	7
Sausage skins	casks	20
Preserved meats	cases	43
Hops	bales	50
Coffee	sacks	5,335
Ginger	bales	2
Whiskey	casks	2
Pine apples	cases	2
Turtle meat	cases	2
Candles	cases	110
Gutta-percha	case	1
Hemp	bale	1
Cacao	packages	2
Logwood	logs	3
Quinces	case	1
Rum	keg	1
Staves		287,664

BORDEAUX—C. DAVISSON, *Consul.*

OCTOBER 10, 1864.

The population of Bordeaux in December, 1862, as estimated, was 163,750 since which time it has continued to increase notwithstanding the temporary paralysis of its commerce; and it is in many respects admitted to be the second city of the empire.

The deepening of the river channel, the Gironde, and Lower Garonne, has been nearly completed, by which means an average of $3\frac{1}{4}$ feet has been added to the depth of the channel in the most difficult passes. A pair of light-houses, called the Twins, were completed and lighted the past year at a cost of about $75,000, between the lights of Cordonan and Arcachon, at Hourtius. They are 656 feet apart, 5,900 feet from the shore, on a small hill, and 108 feet above high water, or with the hill 180 feet above the sea, and are visible a distance of 27 miles.

Vertical quays have been very much needed by the shipping interest of Bordeaux, there being only about 3,000 feet of such quay yet built, causing most of the vessels to anchor in the middle of the river, and load and discharge by means of lighters. Some 689 feet additional are now being added to the vertical quays, which will probably be further extended when this portion is completed.

In addition to the excellent hospitals of Bordeaux, to which our seamen are admitted at 30 cents per day, a new one has been recently erected by the efforts of the English clergymen for the benefit of Protestant seamen, and a new building for a lazaretto is nearly completed at Trompeloup, near Pauillac, at a cost of $32,000.

The manufacturing, commercial, and agricultural character of this consular district is gradually improving. Neither this city nor district have been heretofore very much noted for manufactures. There are a few cotton mills in the southern part of my district at Tarbes, and also in the Pyrenees, which received their cotton through Bordeaux, from our southern ports, before the war; but they have been mostly closed for some time for want of supplies. There is one large manufactory in this department which has during the last two years attracted some notice. I refer to the steel manufacturing establishment called Les Scieries de Saint Suerin, on the river l'Isle. In addition to the old process of treating the metal, the new system of Bessuner is used. Here some 400 workmen are employed, turning out 80 to 100 tons a month. In addition to the manufacture of railroad and other carriage springs, they are also engaged on conical bolts and balls for the French ordnance department. About 2,000 tons of English pig iron and 12,000 tons of English coal per annum are used; but French coal and iron will hereafter be largely substituted, being of lower price. There is a capital represented in this establishment of $240,000.

There is also in Bordeaux a large pottery or porcelain establishment, employing six to seven hundred hands. But the principal works of this character are at Limoges, a town in this consular district, some 125 miles northeast of Bordeaux. Its wares are shipped from this port quite extensively to San Francisco. The total amount of porcelain shipped from Bordeaux to the United States the last two fiscal years is as follows:

	1862-'63.	1863-'64.
To New York	913 packages.	1, 314 packages.
To San Francisco	475 casks.	843 casks.
To New Orleans	45 casks.	14 casks.

or a total of 1,433 packages and casks against 2,171 for the present year, which, estimating the value of a case at 300 francs, gives a total value of 429,900 francs for the year 1862–63, and 651,300 francs for the past year.

There are about a dozen small sugar refineries in Bordeaux, and it is proposed to erect a more extensive one in order to compete successfully with Nantes, which city has attracted much sugar commerce by its large refineries.

There are a few metallurgical establishments; also some glass-blowing establishments, chiefly for the fabrication of common glass bottles, and a limited number of manufactories of carpets and blankets. The French government has also here a large establishment for manufacturing its tobacco, and another for purifying saltpetre, from which it is afterwards sent to its powder manufactory near St. Medard, a few miles in the country.

Ship-building occupies the increased attention of the merchants here; and at the several ship-building yards of Bordeaux there were built in 1861 eighteen vessels, measuring 5,391 tons; in 1862, thirty-five, measuring 10,895 tons; in 1863, forty-five vessels, measuring 16,025 tons, besides several iron floating batteries for the French government, a large iron-clad frigate of 700-horse power for the Italian government, together with four vessels-of-war for the so-called Confederate States.

In agriculture, with the exception of the vine culture, (which is here carried to the highest state of perfection,) there is no branch within this district which is making much progress, owing principally to the prejudices and routine of the peasantry. But I repeat that the cultivation of the vine is the most important of all in this department, where every means is employed to perfect it. The quantity of land cultivated in France with vines is about 5,000,000 acres; and the annual average produce in wine is 56,782,233 hectolitres, or 1,249,231,126 gallons; and in brandy 1,088,802 hectolitres, or 23,953,624 gallons. The total annual value of the wine is estimated at 419,029,152 francs, and of brandy at 59,059,150 francs. The home consumption of wine is in the proportion of 70 liters of wine and 12 of brandy for each inhabitant; being about three gallons of the former and one-half gallon of the latter. This (the Gironde) wine department is divided into six districts, Bordeaux, Lesparre, Libourne, La Reole, Bazos and Blaye. The principal one of which, that of Bordeaux, contains a little over a million acres, one-tenth of which, or 100,000 acres, are devoted to the cultivation of wine.

The results of the vintage in the Gironde alone, in 1862, were estimated at 260,000 tuns, or 66,000,000 gallons. The vintage of 1863 was about the same, or on an average crop estimated at 230,170 tuns, or 38,000,000 gallons, distributed as follows over the district:

Classed red wines of Medoc:	Tuns.
First growth, about	200
Second growth, about	670
Third growth, about	650
Fourth growth, about	460
Fifth growth, about	690
Unclassed red wine of Medoc, about	30,000
District of Blaye and Bourg, about	12,000
District of Libourne, about	25,000
Other districts':	
Ordinary red and white wines, about	160,000
Superior white wines, about	500
	230,170

For the vintage of 1864, I give the following information gathered from leading gentlemen, as the wines are not yet "made up," and it is impossible to give anything of an official character as to the full amount of the crop. The total production of red and white wine in the Gironde district is about

350,000 tuns, or 3,150,000 hectols, or 84,000,000 gallons for 1864, against 230,000 tuns, or 2,070,000 hectols, or 53,200,000 gallons in 1863.

120,000 tuns, or 1,080,000 hectols, or 30,800,000 gallons difference, or one-third greater than last year. The Medoc (that is, that portion of Gironde district between the left bank of the river and the Gulf Gascogne) has been peculiarly favored this year. About 50,000 tuns were produced, of which 5,500 to 6,000 tuns are reckoned as classed wines. The "Cotes and Palus," usually quite productive, show also a satisfactory crop this year.

The wines of 1864 will also prove generally superior in quality to those of last year, though it cannot be said whether they will prove as good as those of 1858 and 1862, wines which, on account of their excellence, were as types of comparison at present. Prices for this year's wines are not yet established. But judging from some purchases of "cargo" wines, like Blaye, Boug, Busscus, and ordinary "Cotes," like those shipped to America, it is thought will rule from 200 to 250 francs per tun. I speak of the ordinary, not of the superior or classed wines, not much called for in the United States, the prices of which vary according to the classification.

An important change has taken place since the American war in the production of resinous matter in the Landes, a country commencing a few miles south of Bordeaux and extending along the sea-coast nearly to the edge of Spain, about 150 miles to the southward, and in some respects resembling North Carolina. Orders for resin first began to be received by Bordeaux wine-merchants in 1862, and became so urgent that many merchants turned their attention to this substance. The demand first came from Glasgow, and was soon followed by others from London, Liverpool and Hamburg, and the interior of France. Prices of resin before the American war ruled at 9 francs per 100 kilos for Brui noir, and 20 francs for first quality. The highest rates reached since have been 60 francs per 100 kilos for Brui noir, 95 francs for 100 kilos virgin resin. Spirits of turpentine have also been affected, but have never exceeded in price 22 francs per 100 kilos. The exportation of these products from Bordeaux to London alone, in 1863, reached about 220 casks of crude turpentine, 3,337 tuns spirits turpentine, and 34,324 casks resin of the different qualities. The shipments to Liverpool and Glasgow are estimated at about half the above amount; and to other British ports at about one-third of the above figures. These increased prices and new markets for this resin awakened such an interest in the subject as to cause an improvement in the manufacture, the adoption of a better system of collecting the resinous products, &c. Formerly rude holes at the foot of the trees were made, in which the resinous matter collected, from which it was scooped into wooden tanks. Now the system called "Hughes's" has generally superseded this, which collects it in earthen pots suspended below the fissures in the trunks of the trees. The original proprietors do not manufacture the resin and turpentine, but confine themselves to collecting the resinous matter, called "gemme," and selling it to manufacturers, who have recently invested large capitals in the purchase of steam and other apparatus for improving their works of distilling the turpentine and producing the resin. Dealers inform me that though only a very inferior dark article of resin was produced here before our war, the French manufacturers at present have every facility for producing a pale, clear, transparent resin, equal to the finest American, but not so good because lacking the balsamic odor of American. It is thought that the French will succeed in improving in this particular by the extraction of certain gases. France formerly furnished large quantities of a mixture of resin and water, heretofore used almost exclusively for house-light by the peasantry. This is still so used to some extent, though the advance in price brings it up to about the price of oil or candles. Considerable quantities of this matter were also shipped to England for use in paper-making, but lately a finer quality has displaced it.

As a natural consequence of the increased price of resin and turpentine, the Landes, which had heretofore remained in a state of primitive wilderness, have been very much improved in character and value. The seventy communes or parishes which owned and in which were situated these dreary and uncultivated wastes, amounting to 321,248 acres, sold a large portion of them, in order to improve the remainder by draining, ploughing, and planting it with the maritime pines, which produce the best turpentine, resin, &c. The *dunes* or sand-hills extending along the coast from the mouth of the Gironde to Bayonne, and owned by the French government, are also covered by the same maritime pines to the extent of 210,000 acres. The primary object of planting these pines along the coast was to fix the sands and prevent the inundation of the sea. The new incentive is causing great improvement to be made in the manner of planting and cultivating the pine, and these forests have acquired great increased value. The government has taken advantage of the excitement and sold many thousand acres of these *dunes*, realizing some millions of dollars. Government also encourages the communes in planting the pine. Originally all the management of the trees and producing the resin was left by the proprietors to the *ouvrier resinier*, or working peasant, who received one-half of the product as wages, which then amounted to two or three francs per day. Since the increase in the price of resin the workers have insisted on receiving half, which now gives them fifteen to twenty francs per day; and, as a consequence, it is said that the formerly poor peasants of the pine forests have now each from 7,000 to 10,000 francs in gold stored under their cabin hearths. Indeed the whole country extending from the Pyranees to Bordeaux may now be considered one of the richest portions of France, while a few years ago it was occupied by a miserable people, only devoted to grazing a few sheep and goats, who wandered over its dreary wastes in search of a precarious existence.

The numerous little lakes and ponds situated at the foot of the *dunes* have been drained during the last few years, under the superintendence of government engineers, and some 25,000 acres of land have thus been reclaimed and made excellent meadows.

Tobacco-growing is now an important branch of the agriculture of this district, but greatly restricted by governmental action. In 1862 about 2,000 acres were devoted to tobacco, producing 2,204,621 pounds, while in 1863 only 1,500 acres were planted.

With the exception of cattle-breeding, which is improving, as indicated by their appearance at the annual cattle shows here, all branches of farming remain comparatively stationary, notwithstanding government patronage.

It is almost needless to remark that the commerce of Bordeaux continues to be sensibly and injuriously affected by the American war. The trade of Bordeaux with the United States in our vessels, formerly so active and prosperous, has dwindled down about to the vanishing point. During 1861, 77 American vessels entered this port; in 1862, 45; in 1863, only 22; and up to September 30 of this year only 3, two only of which cleared for United States ports. There have, however, been 52 foreign vessels which took cargoes from Bordeaux to different United States ports during the last nine months, or since January 1, 1864, showing really, so far, little decrease in the number of vessels in our trade with this port, but only a change from American to foreign bottoms. Under our present tariff there will, of course, be a large falling off in foreign vessels, also, engaged in this trade. Very few of these foreign vessels got return cargoes, the favorable grain harvests of France the last year rendering it unnecessary to import cereals from America, and the trade in cotton and rice being cut off, while staves are now furnished cheaper from Trieste, and there is only an occasional cargo of American tobacco. Petroleum is consumed to some extent, and has been adopted in preference to gas in the new public gardens of this city, and its consumption is likely to increase as the French become more acquainted with its advantages; but no cargo shipments are made direct to Bordeaux yet.

The leading articles exported to the United States from Bordeaux are wines, brandies, sardines, preserved fruits, olive oil, porcelain, walnuts, corks, &c. The shipments of brandy fell off very greatly last year, and must do so still more hereafter under the heavy specific duty of $2 50 per gallon. Indeed, New York and Philadelphia merchants are making inquiries at what rate they can sell the brandy in bond in those cities should they reship it here.

Sardines, which are nearly all obtained on the coast of this district, have been in great demand in the United States during the war, to supply the army; and during the short season of last fall about a million dollars' worth were shipped to New York, yielding half a million of revenue to the United States treasury from this insignificant article. Shipments still continue large, but the demand is not equal to last year.

Olive oil comes from the neighborhood of Marseilles by rail, and is bottled in Bordeaux, and often mixed with *arachide*—pea-nut oil—which deteriorates its quality.

The general commerce of Bordeaux with the French colonies, and with foreign nations other than the United States, has been comparatively small during the general stagnation caused by our civil war. Considerable imports of coffee, molasses, rum, &c., have taken place from the colonies. Trade with Great Britain has been the largest, mostly in the exportation of wine, brandy, and fruits, and in the importation of coal for the railways and manufactories. In 1862 there were 243 small British steamers trading to Bordeaux, 97 of which were bringing coal, reaching in that year 241,321 tons; but owing to the decreased consumption of coal in Bordeaux manufactories, and French coal being increasingly used on railroads, only 150,331 tons were received here in 1863, being a falling off of 90,990 tons.

In addition to these steamers, Bordeaux has the coasting steamers to Bayonne and the Spanish coast, northwardly a weekly line to London, a semi-monthly to Dublin and Glasgow, a tri-monthly to Liverpool, and every twenty days to Bristol. There is also a packet or mail line of large trans-Atlantic steamers, called the *messageries imperial*, running monthly from Bordeaux to Rio Janeiro, touching at Lisbon, &c. The steamers on this line are first-class, very popular, and unexpectedly successful in receipt of patronage. Similar lines, by the same company, subsidized by the French government, are in contemplation between Bordeaux and some port or ports in the United States. With the various railroads now fully open, and connecting this port with Paris and the north, and with the Mediterranean and the Rhone to the east, and across the Pyrenees to Madrid, in Spain, such a line of steamers would be well supplied with freight and passengers and much preferred to the old-fashioned sailing ships.

The new Medoc railroad, now connecting Bordeaux with Verdon, at the mouth of the Gironde, some 60 miles in length, is a great convenience, as it runs through the heart of the Medoc wine country.

The fluctuations in exchange between Bordeaux and London are very small. The range during the year is for sight drafts, say, from lowest to highest, 25 francs 12 centimes to 25 francs 25 centimes per pound sterling, to 25 francs 26 centimes to 25 francs 32 centimes per pound sterling.

MARSEILLES—GEORGE W. VAN HORNE, *Consul.*

OCTOBER 17, 1864.
Commercial report for 1864.

The present commercial and industrial situation of France is apparently one of great prosperity. Go where he may, the observer is struck with what appears to be a general and defined system of internal improvements, effecting a complete renovation of the whole country.

The Emperor is recognized as the originator, and to a great degree the patron, of the wonderful improvements and embellishments now occupying the French mind. Beginning at the capital, he has made, in the language of Thiers, the Paris of Louis XIV, and of Napoleon I, to blush for itself. It is now thought to be *presentable.* Had the Emperor confined his attentions here, France might have regarded him as a second Louis XIV. But everywhere, in all the principal cities of France, has he encouraged, if not directed, the same taste which has beautified Paris, and the same humanitarian plans which have made the French capital the healthiest and the best provided city of its class. New hotels de ville, new palais de prefecture, palais de justice, churches, opera houses, museums, libraries, quays, basins, docks, canals, boulevards, hospitals, &c., adapted to the wants and taste of the present age, are in process of construction all over the country. This enterprise on the part of the government has begotten a kindred spirit in the breast of the citizen. Costly hotels, stores, mansions, are lining the handsome boulevards, and associations for commercial or industrial ends are multiplying daily.

The following list of public buildings in Marseilles, all commenced since my arrival here, will give some idea of the prevailing mania:

	Francs.
Palais de Justice cost	2,400,000
Palais de Prefecture, estimated cost	12,520,000
Palais Imperiale cost	2,000,000
Archiepiscopal Palace cost	600,000
Cathedral cost	5,000,000
Museum cost	1,600,000
Exchange, since 1856, cost	5,000,000
Aggregate cost	29,120,000

The question arises, is the renewed prosperity of the country commensurate to this suddenly and enormously increased public expenditure? It is not so pretended. It is true that private enterprise has received an impetus from the public movement, and that the commerce and industry of the country are surely improving; but I have not heard of any important discoveries of new sources of wealth. Free trade with England is doing something for France; but there is much dissatisfaction in its train. There are great expectations entertained in regard to the India trade; but the Suez canal is not yet open. Algiers is still more a source of disappointment than of wealth to the empire. The other colonies, by reason of the emancipation in 1850, do not contribute as much wealth as formerly. * * * * * * * *

Among the works prosecuted and the enterprises fostered by the government are some of more than national importance.

COAST BEACONS.

At the close of this year the number of *balises* (indicating sunken rocks, shoals, &c.) installed upon the French littoral will be 1,340. This number is to be increased to 1,576 by the end of next year. The number of light-houses is to be equally augmented. There are now 263 on the French coast. By the first of January next there are to be 303. These new beacons will comprise 5 of the first class, 5 floating lights, 7 of the third class, and 24 of the fourth class. When these projected works are completed, France may truly boast of having this important part of her maritime service better and more completely organized than that of any other country. * * * *

THE SUEZ CANAL.

The award of the Emperor as referee in the differences arising between Nubar Pacha, special mandatory of the viceroy of Egypt, and Mr. Lesseps, acting president of the canal company, has removed all difficulties in the way of the rapid achievement of this gigantic work. Mr. Lesseps says, "The end of 1867 will mark the opening of the maritime canal to the commerce of nations."

ADOPTION OF THE ANGLO-FRANÇAISE MARITIME CODE OF SIGNALS.

A commission composed of Rear-Admiral Ronciére le Noury, president, Captain J. E. Commeville, of the royal marine, and Lieutenants Julien and Sallandwaze de la Mornaix, of the French marine, having edited a maritime code of signals, and reported in its favor, the same has this year been adopted by the French and English governments.

This code is, with slight modifications, the same as compiled and recommended by a committee appointed by the Board of Trade in 1855. The changes introduced are such as to facilitate signalizing at great distances, and to lessen the difficulties of communication between ships at sea and the coast telegraphs.

In a report upon the results of the commission, the French minister of marine says: "By means of eighteen flags, combined two with two, three with three, and four with four, there are obtained more than seventy-eight thousand combinations, a number more than sufficient for expressing all the necessary communications at sea; finally, for signalizing at great distances, a number of combinations equally sufficient is obtained by the employment of three balls and two flags." The cost of all the *materiel* for the signals provided for by the new code is estimated at one hundred and fifty francs.

As is known to the department, the principal maritime nations of both hemispheres had already, by convention, agreed upon certain regulations affecting signalizing by lights. There remains but a common adoption of the new code to furnish navigation with a language as perfect as it will be universal.

INVENTIONS

New process of tanning.—A new process of tanning, discovered by M. Pierre Tonneni, member of the Institute du Quirité of Rome, has excited considerable interest in industrial circles.

By this new process leathers are tanned in seventy-five days. Independently of this first and important advantage, (since by the old method an entire year does not suffice oftentimes for tanning,) the system of Mr. Tonneni is distinguished by an economy of two per centum on the first material, and of one-third in labor. It is added that the qualities of the leather are excellent, and of a weight five per centum superior to leathers tanned by the present processes.

Mixture ferro-manganique.—This is the name given to the composition invented by Mr. Vian, ship-builder, at Toulon. It appears to be the only composition yet invented which, when applied to iron bottoms, successfully resists oxidation and the attachment of submarine adherences. Most of the steamers' companies of Marseilles have used, and continue to use, Mr. Vian's composition for the bottoms of their vessels, and I am assured by members of these companies that they are well satisfied with the results attained.   *   *   *

AMERICANS IN BUSINESS AT MARSEILLES.

We have three American houses doing business at Marseilles. They are engaged, respectively, in a commission business, ship-chandlery, and rice cleaning. The last business is a very important one   It employs a capital of 250,000 francs, and, though started only last spring, it already receives rice from Italy, Africa, and all parts of France. This process of cleaning leaves the rice perfectly free from the hull, clean and without bruise—a process vastly superior to the manner of cleaning in the southern States, which generally results in breaking the kernel.

COMMERCE.

Cotton.—Marseilles is not disposed to complain of the American war while she sees the trade in cotton transferred from the bourse of Havre to the bourse of Marseilles. As the position of Havre made her fortune in the prosperous times of American cotton, so does the position of Marseilles insure the latter's prosperity now that this article is received from Algiers and the Levant.

The following table, made up from the custom books of Marseilles, illustrates—

1. The relation of the American war to the culture of cotton in foreign countries.

2. The prosperous relation of Marseilles with the new trade.

Importations of cotton at Marseilles during the last seven years.

	1857.	1858.	1859.	1860.	1861.	1862.	1863.
	Kilo's.	*Kilo's.*	*Kilo's.*	*Kilo's.*	*Kilo's.*	*Kilo's.*	*Kilo's.*
Egypt	2,947,492	3,379,815	3,816,050	3,662,235	6,136,167	5,147,913	9,649,015
Turkey	958,579	261,581	615,661	1,815,156	1,547,119	4,327,645	7,761,143
United States	865,433	276,973	235,608	1,049,714	75,195		
Greece	1,313	2,997				4,588	72,792
British Indies	386,758	713,194	34,795	109,878	18,800	200,776	393,629
French Indies		120,981	6,577	8,820		131,934	3,775
China							1,147
Hayti	2,372	17,455			2,911		335
St. Thomas	272	3,424		881			
Havana						1,128	2,465
Venezuela			9,330	1,000			
Newfoundland			272				
Martinique				32			
Guyana	94						
Brazil						612	
West coast of Africa				2,165		393	37
Senegal						185	
Algiers	40	21,606	24,083	5,907	176,900	130,670	156,733
Barbary States						9,307	13,355
Two Sicilies				404			
Sardinian States		13,000	650	7,701	213,946	265,605	664,439
Tuscany				5,134			
England	6,637	24,607	36,468	61,699	17,990	65,820	790,208
Russia						67,781	10,556
Austria				3,214		25,327	
Spain						33,200	23,099
Portugal							
Total	5,168,990	4,835,563	4,779,494	6,773,940	8,189,098	10,412,884	19,542,728

The importations the present year promise to be astonishingly large. In the first four months there were imported 19,042,179 kilogrammes—being nearly equal to the total probable receipts of cotton in Europe during the present year:

	Bales.
From America	100,000
" Brazil, West Indies, Peru, Mediterranean	430,000
" Egypt	300,000
" East Indies, Japan, &c.	1,700,000
Total	2,530,000
The stock in divers markets December 31, 1863, was	345,170
Probable total bales for the year 1864	2,875,170

Notwithstanding the success which seems to crown the prodigious exertions put forth by England and France to grow cotton in every available country, that their manufactories may be independent of the southern States, the conditions imposed by the new trade raise a dark form on the face of Europe. There is no pleasant and lucrative exchange characterizing the present commerce in cotton. England manages to send back to India, Turkey, &c., considerable quantities of her manufactures, but not in such measure as to prevent the drain of specie eastward, always great, from augmenting fearfully. Every steamer, leaving for the east, carries out more or less of the precious metals, never to be returned. The other day the Said, belonging to the Messageries Imperiales, took out 5,000,000 francs in gold for Alexandria, and 14,000,000 francs in silver for Indo-China. I have often remarked like exportations. The banks, whose average rate of discount for the years 1858, 1859, 1860, 1861, was 4.34 per cent., have averaged 6.83 per cent. for 1864.   *   *   *

Wool.—The war has favorably affected the Franco-American commerce in this article. The following figures will show the relative increase in the exportations since 1860 :

In the year 1861, 1,638,214 kilogrammes; in 1862, 499,490 kilogrammes; in 1863, 4,536,819 kilogrammes; 1st quarter 1864, 1,112,170 kilogrammes.

In the first three months of the present year there were exported 1,112,170 kilogrammes. In May the new tariff made itself felt, and the shipment fell off to 148,128 kilogrammes. Since May not a bale of wool has left Marseilles for the States. Undoubtedly the high price of gold has affected the trade to some extent.   *   *   *   Petroleum continues to command an important place in the importations of this port. Against 14,308 barrels, the importation of the year ended August 31, 1863, we have 53,000 barrels for the year ended August 31, 1864.   *   *   *   I hear that some inconsiderable shipments of petroleum have arrived from Wallachia.

Beet sugar.—No agricultural subject presents such interesting statistics as the one under consideration. A comparison of the production of beet sugar of 1830 with that of 1864 will show the growing demand for this sugar :

1830.		1864.	
Kilogrammes.........	5,000,000	Kilogrammes.......	525,000,000
Pounds	11,050,000	Pounds............	1,160,250,000

The following table exhibits the relative results in sugar of the cultivation of the beet in Europe during the last four years. The figures of 1864-'65 are purely of estimation, and those of 1863-'64 approximation. Those of the other years give the real production :

Countries.	1864-'65.	1863-'64.	1862-'63.	1862-'61.
Zollverein	175,000	155,000	138,042	122,839
France	200,000	107,000	173,577	146,415
Austria	80,000	60,900	72,998	54,397
Russia, Poland, and Sweden	45,000	40,000	35,000	53,484
Belgium	22,500	77,500	21,960	17,854
Holland	2,500	2,500	1,899	1,500
Tons of 1,000 kilogrammes	525,000	382,900	443,476	396,489

The French product now supplies one-half of the saccharine wants of the empire. The importations of cane sugar to June 30, 1864, amounted to 66,631,340 kilogrammes. This would give only 133,862,680 kilogrammes of cane sugar for the year, against the generally estimated product of 200,000,000 kilogrammes of beet sugar.

Mr. Thiers, in one of his late speeches, says : "There is no person who is not struck with this probability, that the native sugar will, in time, expel the exotic." Struck with the growing French independence of colonial sugar, I have asked myself what is to prevent a similar independence being achieved in America. Our climate and soil are both favorable to this culture, would the manufacturer be wanting?

Wine vs. *beer.*—This case is not without interest. Both parties complain of not having a fair trial, and it is difficult for an outsider to arrive at the relative merits.   *   *   *   But it is amusing that the English have been counting upon free trade for the *deplacement* of the wine in France by their beer, at the same time that the French felt sure of carrying the conquests of their *Bordeaux* and *vin ordinaire* into England to the expulsion of the English beer. It is to be remarked that, notwithstanding the known partiality of the French for their wine, breweries are on the increase in France, and beer is becoming the "fashion."

The Semaphore (of Marseilles) says, "The marked predilection of the *Marsellais* for beer appears to be partaken of by all France."

The Courier de Lyons states that "the Lyonnais have been taken with such an infatuation for breweries (at which places, alone, beer was sold formerly) that all the cafés of the city, in order to prevent an imminent ruin, have been obliged to convert their establishments into beer shops under the vocable of the cities of Germany and Holland, the most renowned for the manufacture of beer."

From the already general use and unceasing popularity of this beverage, it is about time to concede the justice of the claim put forth by the beer-drinkers of Bavaria, that beer takes rank as the fifth element.

The vintage this year has been very abundant, the application of sulphur having effected an almost perfect cure of the vine.

Importations from the United States at this port for the year ended August 31, 1864:

	Value.
Alcohol	$64,607 00
Bacon	1,500 00
Beef	4,096 00
Flour	8,000 00
Lard	1,101,780 00
Logwood	18,400 00
Pepper	32,040 00
Petroleum	1,276,416 00
Pork	2,000 00
Quercitron bark	7,000 00
Rum	55,500 00
Staves	57,680 00
Tobacco	1,214,500 00
Aggregate	3,873,519 00

Exports from Marseilles to the United States for the year ended August 31, 1864:

	Value.
Almonds	$32,763 00
Cork	24,620 00
Chloride of lime	35,764 00
Cream of tartar	67,205 00
Essences	9,471 00
Filberts	5,147 00
Garancine (extract of madder)	237,745 00
Gum	78,454 00
Groundnuts	18,767 00
Lead	432,942 00
Lemons	16,870 00
Liquors	2,457 00
Licorice root	13,460 00

H. Ex. Doc. 60——15

	Value.
Licorice juice	$873 00
Madder	339, 924 00
Oil	91, 163 00
Pickles and preserves	7, 437 00
Rags	18, 289 00
Seeds	8, 383 00
Soap	105, 654 00
Sponges	14, 886 00
Sulphur	2, 790 00
Varnish	5, 911 00
Verdigris	20, 725 00
Walnuts	33, 612 00
Wine	75, 193 00
Wool	633, 999 00
Sundries	18, 245 00
Aggregate	2, 351, 749 00

Table showing the number, nationality, and tonnage of the vessels arrived at and departed from Marseilles from January 1 to August 31, 1864.

Nationality	ARRIVALS.		DEPARTURES.	
	No. of vessels.	Tonnage.	No. of vessels.	Tonnage.
Russian	72	25, 786	69	22, 86
Sweden	24	5, 982	24	5, 91
Norwegian	15	5, 077	17	5, 12
Danish	5	470	5	4
English	162	62, 609	163	66, 0
German	43	10, 000	34	8, 0
Mecklenburgian	14	4, 221	13	3, 5
Hanseatic Towns	9	3, 711	9	3, 7
Dutch	18	5, 642	22	6, 8
Belgian	1	118	1	1
Portuguese	5	914	6	1, 0
Spanish	380	69, 295	350	58, :
Austrian	163	58, 650	144	49,
Italian	658	101, 860	655	103,
Roman	2	141	2	
Greek	92	22, 834	102	24,
Turkish	6	1, 779	4	
Egyptian	7	4, 625	7	5
United States	14	6, 096	13	5
Brazilian	4	1, 500	2	
Buenos Ayres	8	2, 163	6	1
Ionian	4	896	4	
Jerusalem	4	738	8	
Moldo-Wallachian	1	280	1	
Sarniot	1	280	1	
French from foreign countries	1, 359	379, 022	1, 114	39
French from French colonies	372	106, 782	444	12
French coasting trade	2, 589	235, 963	2, 570	25
Aggregate	6, 011	1, 117 054	5, 787	1, 0

CETTE.

Statement showing the description and value of the import and export trade of Cette with the United States during the year ended September 30, 1864.

EXPORTS.

	Value in francs.
13,090 casks, 985 boxes of wine..........................	985,339 55
20 casks lees of wine................................	4,037 35
48 casks crystal of tartar	43,730 55
61 casks cream of tartar.............................	79,060 40
21 casks refined tartar..............................	25,646 95
50 barrels of olives	1,800 00
3 casks of olive oil.................................	543 35
6 boxes essential oils	2,147 00
20 casks verdigris	21,568 15
209 bales of almonds................................	30,312 80
920,000 kilogrammes of salt	9,200 00
200 bales, 1 box nuts................................	3,773 40
27 bales wool.......................................	1,423 00
23 bales lavender flowers............................	799 80
Dry goods..	6,906 60
20 boxes extract of absinth..........................	400 00
9 bales of drugs....................................	800 95
Total.....................................	1,217,489 85

IMPORTS.

	Value.
1,457 hogsheads, 5 barrels of tallow...................	$161,000 00
20 tierces, 50 barrels of lard.......................	1,900 00
51 boxes of hams..................................	660 00
500 boxes of petroleum oil..........................	2,200 00
846,876 staves......................................	120,000 00
Total.................................	285,760 00

LYONS—JAMES LESLEY, *Consul.*

JUNE 30, 1864.

The amount of invoices verified at this consulate during the quarter ending this day is ten million five hundred and forty-four thousand seven hundred and eleven francs ninety centimes, (francs 10,544,711 90.)

LOUIS W. VIOLLIE, *Vice-Consul.*

JULY 3, 1864.

A general statement of the amount of the invoices verified at this consulate has been sent to you at the end of each quarter. I thought, however, it might be interesting to your department to have some details of the business transacted during this half year at this consulate, as to the division of the exports, their destination, &c., &c.   I have, therefore, prepared a detailed table of the monthly exports, which will be found enclosed.   Allow me to offer some remarks in relation to the table.

The first column includes all silk piece goods, taffetas, velvets; moires, colored and black; plain and figured silk goods.

Column No. 2. Tulles, laces, crépe, gauze, and other light goods of which silks is the chief material.

Column No. 4. Pure and false gold and silver threads and trimmings, church ornaments, partly silk, partly metal.

Column No. 10. Dyestuffs.

Column No. 12. Prepared calf skins.

Column No. 13 Sundry articles, such as hardware, books, corks, blacking, drugs.

Column No. 14. Raw silk, crépe, organzine for manufacturing purposes in the United States.

All the above are manufactured or produced in the city of Lyons and its immediate vicinity.

Column No. 3. Lacets, soutaches, trimmings.

Column No. 7. Plain and figured velvet ribbons.

Column No. 8. Taffetas and satin ribbons of all kinds, plain and figured.

The above articles are manufactured mostly in St. Etienne and the neighborhood.

Column No. 5. Kid gloves.

Column No. 6. Silk gloves, manufactured mostly in Grenoble and Nismes.

Column No. 9. Cotton goods, principally tarlatains and muslins of fine quality, manufactured in France.

Column No. 11. Wines produced a little north of Lyons; Macon and Chalon, Burgundy wines.

	Francs.
The total amount of the invoices verified is	23, 273, 711
For the same period of 1863 it was only	12, 120, 726
Silk goods proper, six months, 1864	15, 479, 659
Silk goods proper, same period, 1863	7, 636, 671
Ribbons, velvet, and taffetas, six months, 1864	5, 771, 155
Ribbons, velvet, and taffetas, same period, 1863	3, 727, 670

The other articles of export show a proportionate increase in 1864 over 1863.

A new article of export has appeared during those six months—silk prepared for manufacturing purposes grege and organzine of fine quality amounting to 112,005 francs.

The exports can be divided as follows:

Articles under the general designation of silks, of which silk is the principal component material	22, 436, 052
Other manufactures	744, 406
Wines	93, 253
	23, 273, 711

These amounts, however large, do not really represent the full exports from this consulate to the United States.

1. Many invoices of silk goods manufactured in and shipped from Lyons have been verified in Paris.

2. It is asserted, I cannot say with what truth, that some heavy lots and

staple silks purchased and forwarded to London are then shipped to the United States direct.

3. The general opinion is that a certain quantity of silk goods is fraudulently introduced into the United States for English account through Canada.

I shall in the course of this report allude to the above.

The increase in the exports has, of course, produced a corresponding increase of labor. *   *   *   The exports of these six months on 23,273,711. francs can be approximately decided, as follows:

	Francs.
1. Amounts of invoices of commission merchants or exporters, acting as such to their American customers, about	11,100,000
2. Invoices of exporters established in this district to their own firms in the United States, about	9,400,000
3. Invoices of manufacturers shipping goods consigned for their own account to their agents	2,800,000

I call your attention to the importance of the first item, and, compared with the third, I consider it as an excellent symptom. In previous years, even in 1863, as far as I can see from my registers, the amount of goods consigned by the manufacturers was proportionately much larger. The respectable commission merchants complained of the scarcity of orders from their American customers, the jobbers, who could buy their goods in New York, principally from the agents of the manufacturers, much cheaper than they could honestly import them.

I believe, therefore, that the increase in the business of commission merchants, in spite of the war, shows that frauds against the revenue are not as frequent as they were. I have frequently stated that, in my opinion, the revenue officers have most particularly to guard against the manufacturers consigning their own goods, and against exporters sending goods to their own firms in New York, as being the parties most likely to defraud the revenue. So far I see no reason for changing this opinion, and I shall be glad whenever I shall be able to report an increase of exports by commission merchants *   *   *   In the last two years the English buyers have purchased here, and principally in Zurich, large quantities of black silk, in width (22 to 28 inches) and qualities suited for the American market, and which do not sell well in the English market.

These purchases, made besides their regular purchases for the supply of their home trade, have attracted attention, and it is generally believed that these goods ultimately find their way to our principal markets without paying duties. *   *   *   The goods cannot be traced from the place of manufacture to the real shipping port, which they do not reach directly.

The result of my researches, both here and in Zurich, is, that the manufacturers or commission merchants of these places are not directly interested in these operations *   *   *   I have stated above that many invoices of Lyons goods were reissued in Paris; I was very anxious to bring them here where they could be examined thoroughly.

I went to Paris for that purpose, and our consul, Mr. Bigelow, gave me the kindest assistance.

I examined all the invoices of this year on file at the consulate, and took the names of all the firms improperly invoicing goods not manufactured in Paris; a circular was issued and sent announcing that in future shippers would have to procure the verification of their invoices at the place where the goods were manufactured or began their journey to the United States.

This circular has already had an effect. Since my return I have received here a number of invoices which were before verified in Paris. Three of these invoices, after a close examination, were found to be undervalued. *   *   *

The firms residing in Paris used to receive from their correspondents in Lyons, Zurich, or Brussels, invoices for goods shipped from those places. These invoices were added by the firm to those of their Paris goods, and only one fee was paid.

A very important measure was adopted at this consulate early in the year. I allude to the order requiring shippers to produce samples of the goods invoiced with their invoices.

I have already reported to you on the subject. A longer experience enables me now to state that, under the present system of duties, I see no possible measure so well calculated to protect the revenue. * * * Most of the time the invoices, made out without details, and in technical terms, are scarcely intelligible. For some kinds of merchandise, an intelligent business man may, by seeing the invoice, ascertain approximately whether the prices are correct. But this is not the case for dry goods, and epecially for the kinds of silk goods manufactured in this district. The invoice alone is of no use whatever. The consul never saw the goods; and, from a description, however clear and detailed, he could form no idea as to the correctness of the prices. No prices current of manufactured silk goods are published or can be published, on account of the immense variety of prices of the same article. For instance, goods under the correct designation of taffetas, near 26 inches, vary in prices from 5f. to 8f. Black cotton velvets, 20 inches, vary from 7f. to 11f., according to their quality, finish, and weight. Under these circumstances the consular service rendered to shippers in certifying to their invoices was not the "*verification of their invoices,*" but merely the legalization of the signature of *the shippers* to the invoices and declarations.

The goods are generally shipped before the invoice is produced; and even if the consul could see them at the store of the shipper, (which would be impossible for want of time,) he could not compare them with other goods of the same kind shipped by other parties.

The sample measure, if properly enforced, enables the consul to verify the prices, and to compare those of the different shippers; the service becomes really the "*verification of invoces.*"

The measure was enforced in this district in the month of February; and, although the regulations adopted by me are very strict as to the size and arrangement of the samples, no positive opposition was made.

Two points are worthy of remark: The honest exporters and commission merchants, as soon as the purpose of the measure was explained to them, gave it their full support and declared themselves fully satisfied. The only parties which complained, and tried to bring about a protest, are firms open to suspicion, and whose invoices have since been subjects of reports to the revenue agent. These two facts show, I believe, the value of the measure. The moral effect produced has been very perceptible; shippers have seen that the government intends to use all the means in its power to protect the revenue; they realise that the presentation of the invoice to the consul is no more a mere formality; the invoices are more clearly made out. Some parties show an evident anxiety, and do their best to know what ultimately becomes of the samples.

The regulations first adopted have not been materially altered; they continue in force, but had to be much particularized, both for silks and ribbons. So far they have covered every case.

As soon as samples are received, they are compared with the invoice, carefully examined, and compared with other samples, the prices of which are known to me to be correct. When this investigation gives me cause to suspect the correctness of some prices, the sample is detached from the card and shown to one or several good judges, without indication of names or prices, with a request to state what price the goods could be purchased at in the market, for cash, in large quantities, and under the most favorable circumstances. If the appraisement, so obtained, shows that the invoice is undervalued, I at once make out a note, giving the names of the shippers, consignees, marks, and numbers of the cases and invoice, designation of the goods, prices invoiced, prices appraised, and any other detail deemed necessary.   *   *   *

This examination and appraisement of suspicious samples fulfil the intent of our revenue laws, for it enables the consuls to determine and to keep the custom-house officers advised of the market value of goods shipped to the United States, at the place where said goods have been manufactured or prepared for export.   *   *   *   The appraisements obtained here, although the greatest care be taken to guard against errors, cannot in all cases be absolute; they are based on the samples delivered by the shippers. These samples are small, frequently cut at the end of the pieces. The real value of silk goods frequently can be correctly appreciated only after a view of a whole piece, or even of the full assortment. The reports, in consequence, always suppose that the sample appraised really represents the goods invoiced. The attention of the appraisers is called to any invoice deemed under value; they are put in possession of the opinion of reliable judges, as to the market value of the sample produced; once examined, it becomes their duty to examine the goods themselves, and to see if the suspicions of the consul are founded,   *   *   *   *

The full benefit of the sample measure cannot yet be felt; I speak, at least, for this consulate.   *   *   *   I do not hear of any serious and well-grounded complaints being put forward in the places where the measure has been adopted. The consuls regard it as a valuable reform; the honest exporters generally do not only submit, but they indorse it.   *   *   *

France, by her treaties with us, is placed on the footing of the most favored nations. Several merchants, well disposed for the measure, told me that ill-intentioned parties, having an interest to defeat this measure, might cause the French government to interfere on the ground that rival markets and manufacturing districts are not submitted to the same regulations and formalities adopted in Lyons or Paris.

I allude here to Switzerland, Zurich, (for silk goods,) Basle for silks and ribbons, (where I understand no samples are required.) If I am properly informed, the proportion of goods shipped from these two places, for account of the manufacturers, is much larger than it is in this district. Most of the goods are consigned by manufacturers or shipped by exporters to their own firms; and if my opinion in regard to these two classes of shippers is correct, you will admit that the sample measure is wanted in Zurich and in Basle fully as much as it is in Lyons. It will also be more effective in Zurich than it can be in Lyons, because the goods manufactured there are more similar; there is not the same variety as to price and qualities.   *   *   *   Two points are important: First, that samples of good size (at least 10 by 30 centimetres for silks) be required for such quality of goods invoiced, and with every invoice, although the firm may always ship the same quality of goods. Second, that the card on which the samples are pasted give all necessary indications, such as width, number of pieces, designation of goods, price per ounce or metre; discount if variable.

JULY 27, 1864.

I take the liberty of calling your attention to some remarks suggested to me by the perusal of a copy of the tariff sent to me by a friend.

I have seen with great pleasure that all unmanufactured silk goods would in future be taxed equally at 60 per centum duty. The former differential rates of 30 and 40 per centum, according to the cost of the goods, were, I believe, a strong inducement to frauds, many goods worth from 5 to 15 per cent. above the limit of the low duty were undervalued, so as to be entered at 30 per cent. This differential duty was also against the Lyons goods, and in favor of the cheaper Zurich and German silks. It is calculated that four-fifths of the Zurich exports, at least, were invoiced so as to pay 30 per cent., whilst not over one-fourth of the goods manufactured here could lawfully be entered at the same rate. This explains the importance of the registered Zurich exports for the first six months of this year.

In the enumeration of silk goods paying a duty of 60 per centum, *silk cravats* of all kinds have been forgotten. What duty will be levied—60 or 50 per cent.?

The duties on silk threads are as follows:

Grege, (silk thread single, as it is taken from the cocoon,) 25 per centum; organzine, (two threads twisted together, so as to join them and give them greater strength,) tram, (several threads joined and slightly twisted,) both 35 per centum.

The cost of preparing these two kinds is as follows:

Organzine, which requires a fine kind of silk, regular and strong, 33 per cent., about, added to the cost of the raw grege; tram from 8 to 15 francs the kilo, according to quality and fineness.

Deeming the subject of great importance to our country, I have been led to study the probable effects of the new tariff (in regard to the above articles) on the establishment of silk manufactures in the United States.

I believe that under this new tariff the prosperous establishment of this important industry is impossible. Allow me to explain the reasons of my belief, and to state the alterations wanted to bring about this very desirable result.

In all large silk-manufacturing districts, such as Lyons, Zurich, Basle, Crefeld, experience has demonstrated that division of work alone can produce cheapness. The foundation of the prosperity of all these places is the completeness of the arrangements for the manufacture of goods. Each process of the manufacture (and there are many) is intrusted to special factories, which, being worked on a very large scale, can be satisfied with a slight remuneration. The cocoons producing the silk are bought by the "marchands de soie"—raw silk merchants— who in their factories prepare the grege. The mouliniers in their establishments buy the grege or receive it from the silk merchants and manufacturers to be converted into organzine or tram. The dessmateurs, liseurs, metteurs en cartes, monteurs, &c., each in their turn are called upon by the manufacturers to contribute to the manufacture of his goods.

This great facility of finding at a moment's notice all the articles or branches of workmen necessary to the perfection of goods, without having to keep a large stock of raw material or a number of workmen frequently unemployed, reduces the prices.

No manufacturer would think of setting up a moulinage, or any other of the branches above mentioned, for his own special use. He knows that by giving his work to one of the large special factories he can have it done cheaper and better than he could do it himself. He can give all his attention to his looms and to the finish of the goods.

The high duty on silk dress goods, the present premium on gold, would induce many manufacturers to emigrate to the United States to establish there their industry. The moment would be highly favorable, and their success would be for our country a source of great future wealth. All kinds of silk goods could not at once be manufactured. Lyons, for instance, for many years would preserve a kind of monopoly for its rich goods; but plain, ordinary goods, and small, cheap figures, or checked silks, could easily be manufactured in the States—such as those exported from England, Zurich, Basle; taffetas, colored and black lastings, gros du Rhin, foulards, checked and striped silk ribbons, &c. The manufacturers, however, are unwilling to make the experiment without some protection. The conditions made to them by the tariff are too unfavorable. Such is the opinion of a number of manufacturers and merchants whom I consulted on the subject. A manufacturer going to the United States would have to spend a very large amount of money and to contend with many difficulties. He would be obliged to buy here a number of looms and all the instruments necessary for the finishing of his goods, to bring over with him several workmen to begin to work, and to teach to our native mechanics the secrets of silk manufacture. Besides the weavers, other workmen would be required to prepare the silks, tram, and organzine for the looms, to put them in working order, and to finish, prepare, and fold the silks, after weaving. The manufacturer would also have to set up the special kinds of buildings required by his looms. All these would demand a very large capital and a year of profitless work. Still some manufacturers would be willing to try if two fundamental objections were removed. They argue that paying a duty of 35 per cent. on the trams and organzine they would have to import would make the cost price of the goods manufactured at home higher than the cost price in New York, duty paid, of the European goods imported. As for preparing themselves their trams or organzines in the United States from greges they would import at a duty of 25 per cent., I am assured that none would do it. None would invest another large capital in machinery and installations for moulinage which for a long time, and until the weaving has taken a large development, would be idle half of the time. The only course to be taken by manufacturers, for the present, would be to import their own trams and organzines and to confine themselves to the weaving of their goods. To enable them to do so, and to establish in a permanent manner the silk manufacture in the United States, the following conditions seem necessary: Allow the free introduction of looms and other machinery connected with the silk manufacture; the introduction, with a very light duty, of the undyed trams and organzines imported directly by the manufacturer for his manufacturing purposes. Later—when the number of looms at work would warrant the establishment of moulinages—a duty would be put on tram and organzine, which would cause mouliniers to build factories.

I am persuaded that silk manufacturing cannot successfully be attained in our country unless it be introduced from Europe by European workmen or manufacturers who from youth have acquired the experience and ability necessary to make perfect goods.

SEPTEMBER 30, 1864.

The amount of the invoices verified at this consulate during the quarter ending this day is four million one hundred and thirty thousand six hundred and eleven francs and thirty-five centimes, (frs. 4,130,611 35.)

VISIT TO ST. ETIENNE.

DECEMBER 15, 1864.

RIBBONS.

I have visited St. Etienne, a large city in which all the taffetas and velvet ribbons, exports from this consular district, are manufactured. My motive in doing so was to obtain positive information on the state of the market, the value of different kinds of goods, and particularly to take some measures to enable me to obtain for St. Etienne goods the same facilities for appraisements that I have secured for Lyons goods in connexion with the sample measure, which continues to be enforced at this consulate.

The following reports contain the different points of information I have obtained from different reliable sources, and mention some measures I have taken for the protection of the revenue, which I hope will meet with the approbation of the department. It is also proper to state that, in addition to the results shown below, I have used with profit every hour of my stay in St. Etienne, and I return with a much better knowledge of the goods, the process of manufacture, the custom of the trade, and standing of the principal firms doing business with our country. These I believe are very important points, and will, I hope, enable me on future occasions to promote the interest of the revenue.

THE STATE OF THE MARKET

For many years has not been so dull in St. Etienne as it has been this season; the manufacturers and the commission merchants are unanimous in their complaints. The principal markets of Europe, as well as those of the United States, are over-stocked; no new orders are received; the manufacturers have large quantities of goods unsold in their stores. More than half the looms are idle or work at half-time, and with a loss to the manufacturers. The large advance in raw silk has had no or very little influence on manufactured goods, and the manufacturers who generally have stocks on hand, bought at low prices, continue to work only to keep their best workmen and to prevent the destruction of their looms and other material.

There is a general hope that business will somewhat revive at the beginning of next year. If such be the case, prices will certainly advance from 15 to 20 per centum, probably more, for certain kinds of goods—at all events, owing to the shortness and inferiority of the last silk crop, and the light stocks of raw silk. The prices for several months at least cannot fall under the present rates. The last demand for Europe, or the prospects of a speedy peace in the United States, would at once be felt on the market.

Such has been the case. About six weeks ago some very trifling orders for re-assortments having been received; an improvement of from 3 to 5 per centum has taken place on some goods; and although these orders have not been continued, prices have not receded. The present prices, therefore, can be taken with certainty as the lowest limit for next season.

I have now to review the different kinds of goods, exports from St. Etienne, and make some remarks on the invoices of the principal shippers. Some of the observations now presented have already been laid before the department in previous reports. I wish, however, to make this communication very complete, so as to be able on future occasions to refer to it for details. I shall therefore endeavor to give a full description of the rules, customs of the trade, and conditions of sale for each kind of goods exported from St. Etienne.

VELVET RIBBONS.

These goods formed about one-quarter of the exports of St. Etienne; it is believed that before the war the shipments to the United States amounted to about ten million francs a year.

The quarterly returns of this consulate show the influence of the war on these goods. These goods are not manufactured in large factories. Each of the manufacturers—and some are very important—owns the looms, and places a number (5 or 6) in the care of a chef d'attelier, who receives a certain amount for each piece he returns, the manufacturer furnishing the cotton and silk. The ribbons were furnished cut, folded, and put in the cartons at the store of the manufacturer. The trade with the United States was formerly in the hands of the commission merchants, at least in great part. It has changed—now the manufacturers consigning to their own agents, and one importer monopolizes it almost entirely. Honest houses dared not deal any more in that article, as they cannot compete with the manufacturers who invoice their goods below the selling prices.

Some years ago all the manufacturers of velvet ribbons, wishing to correct some irregularities in the conditions of sale, and to establish a tariff of widths, met and bound themselves to observe and follow several invariable rules in all their future transactions in black cotton-back plain velvet. These rules, usually called general tariff, have never been reported, and are adopted, without exception, in all the sales made in St. Etienne. This tariff, being an established custom of the St. Etienne trade, ought to be adopted in all the invoices for the United States. In consequence, I shall have to explain it in detail. A scale of widths has been agreed upon. All the manufacturers and dealers have adopted it. The different widths are designated by numbers. The French numbers usually used go from 0 to 700. Very few goods, however, are manufactured wider than No. 200. The numbers used in the American trade are different— No. 1 to 20. They, however, correspond exactly as to width of the goods to the French numbers from 0 to 200. All the manufacturers make and sell their goods according to the established scale of widths. The prices given in the tariff for each number or width are invariable, whatever may be the quality or real comparative value of the goods. These prices are for full pieces of 27.60— twenty-seven metres sixty centimetres. A margin is allowed for short measure—3.33 per centum for each metre short from the tariff measure. The New York market requiring only half pieces of about ten metres, they are generally invoiced as full pieces, but at half the prices given in the tariff. In calculating the margin, however, they are considered as half pieces. The lengths most usual for our markets are 10 metres, 10.10, 10.20, 10.40 metres. The calculation for margin is invariably made as follows :

Pieces measuring 10 *metres.*

	Metres.
Prices given for pieces of........................	27 60
Two half pieces of the 10 together................	20.00
Actual short measure..............................	7.60

Margin, 25.30 per centum.

Pieces measuring 10.20 *metres.*

	Metres.
Prices given for pieces of........................	27.60
Two half pieces of 10.20 together.................	20.40
Actual short measure..............................	7.20

multiplied by 3.33 give margin 23.97, or 24 per centum.

According to this invariable rule the margin for the most usual lengths are half pieces of—

10	metre ....margin 25.30 per centum.
10.10	do	do.	24.64	do.
10.20	do	do.	24	do.
10.30	do	do.	23.31	do.
10.40	do	do.	24.64	do.

General tariff for cotton-back black velvet ribbons of all qualities. Prices for pieces of 27.60, *or half pieces of* 13.80, *margin* 3.33 *per centum per metre short.*

WIDTHS.		PRICES FOR—		WIDTHS.		PRICES FOR—	
French.	American.	French piece, 27.60 m.	American piece, 13.80 m.	French.	American.	French piece, 27.60 m.	American piece, 13.80 m.
No.	*No.*	*Francs.*	*Francs.*	*No.*	*No.*		
0	1	2 70	1 35	60	5½	12 90	6 45
2	1⅛	2 90	1 45	70	6	14 30	7 15
4	1¼	3 20	1 60	80	6½	15 65	7 82½
6	1⅜	3 50	1 75	90	7	17 25	8 62½
8	1½	3 90	1 95	100	8	19 00	9 50
10	1¾	4 20	2 10	110	9	21 25	10 62½
12	2	4 75	2 37½	120	10	23 50	11 75
14	2¼	5 30	2 65	130	11	25 50	12 75
16	2½	6 00	3 00	140	12	27 50	13 75
18	3	6 50	3 25	150	13	29 50	14 75
20	3¼	7 50	3 75	160	14	31 50	15 75
24	3½	8 50	4 25	170	16	33 50	16 75
30	4	9 50	4 75	180	17	35 50	17 75
40	4½	10 55	5 27½	190	18	37 50	18 75
50	5	11 65	5 82½	200	20	39 50	19 75

WIDE NUMBERS.

210	....	44 00	....	350	....	92 00	....
220	....	47 00	....	400	....	108 00	....
230	....	50 00	....	450	....	125 00	....
240	....	53 50	....	500	....	142 00	....
250	....	57 00	....	600	....	185 00	....
300	....	75 00	....	700	....	220 00	....

The same tariff is used for black cotton-back velvet ribbons with white and colored satin or satin edges. Each firm has particular conditions or tariffs for cotton-back velvets. As a general rule, however, it can be stated that the prices made are for pieces of 13.89 metres. The margin is proportional to the real length of the pieces of common colors. The pieces of fine colors (being much more expensive) and the margin is made as if they had the same length as the common color pieces, but to compensate for the higher cost the manufacturer cuts them shorter, according to their color and shade:

Blue, Mexico, pink, lilac	7	per cent.
Blue imperial, pensee, fuchsia, rubio, cherry, ponceau, mi fin....	13	do.
Ponceau, fin	20	do.

For instance, on an invoice, pieces of which measure (common colors) 10 metres, the margin would be on the whole 27½ per cent., but the pieces ponceau fin would really measure only 8 metres. Lilac and Mexico measure 9.30 metres. Black cotton-back velvets, as indicated by the name, are mixed goods; the tram and chain being cotton, the velvet and a few threads of the edges silk, the proportion between the cotton and the silk, the closeness of the texture of the ground, the length and quantity of the velvet (silk) constitute the difference of qualities and prices. Each manufacturer makes one quality, (very seldom two,) to which he confines himself, never altering it; this is so well known that, when a purchase is made, samples of the goods are seldom shown by the manufacturer, it being understood that the goods are to be of his make and similar to this regular quality. (This is not the case for any other silk goods, ribbons, piece goods.) This circumstance greatly facilitates the verification of most of the invoices, and it would be very desirable that, in their invoices, the commission merchants and the exporters should indicate the name or the brand of the black velvet ribbons they export. The prices for the different numbers and the margin for short measure being the same for all the manufacturers of black velvet ribbons—whatever may be the quality and real value of the goods, their real market value—the prices of sale are determined by the rate of discount, which varies for each manufacturer in consequence of the state of the market and the quality of the goods.

The rate of discount, which is from 25 to 50 per cent., is, therefore, the principal point to which the attention of the appraisers ought to be directed. The finer qualities, on which the discount is now from 25 to 35 or 36 per cent., are never sent to the United States; they are specially manufactured for the Paris market.

The exports to the United States—the bulk of the goods sent in a regular way—can be divided into three great classes, samples of which I procured and shall forward with this report.

Quality No. 1.

This can be taken as a type of the best quality exported to our markets. Three or four firms only manufacture such goods—wealthy and important houses—which have a large capital and regular customers, direct the market, keep up their prices, and never sacrifice their goods. The prices for this class of goods are at present thirty-eight per cent. discount at 90 days, and two per cent. extra for cash on delivery.

Quality No. 2.

Still a good quality, generally designated as "bonnequalite courante," generally purchased for account of jobbers and retailers. The prices are also well kept, and no plotting lots are found in the market offered at a sacrifice. The price at present for such a quality is 40 to 41 per cent., say 41 per cent. extra, for cash.

Quality No. 3.

A lower quality. Present value, 46 per cent. discount net for cash, or from 44 to 45 per cent. discount at 90 days, and 2 per cent. extra.

The large firms generally make no concessions in their prices; they make their rate of discount known to their purchasers in the beginning of the season, and, unless there is a change in the state of the market or in the price of silk, they keep the same rate on all their transactions. There is also a kind of tacit agreement between the large houses; the comparative value of their several regular qualities being well known, the changes in the rate of discount are generally adopted simultaneously by the principal firms in proportion to the value of their goods.

There are, however, in St. Etienne some small manufacturers who generally make goods similar to quality No. 2 or 3, who, not having the means of the large houses, are sometimes in want of money, and are obliged to sell at lower prices—from 2 to 3 per cent. The following remarks are to be made:

These are not regular sales, and do not influence the state or rates of the market. These sales are always for cash on delivery, and, in ordering seasons, they are not very frequent. The goods so sold are generally irregular—the names or brands of the manufacturers are not known—and it frequently happens to help the sale. False labels or marks of well-known manufacturers are put on the goods; or even, sometimes, large manufacturers purchase these floating lots and pass them as their own goods. These goods, as above stated, may sometimes be purchased two or three per cent. below the prices of the corresponding well-known qualities. The exports to the United States being, in great part, composed of goods consigned by the manufacturers, few of these floating lots are likely to reach our market. A simple house may purchase some, as will be stated below. The prices indicated above are for good assortments, composed in the usual proportion, of all the principal numbers or widths.

An order for narrow goods, from No. 1 to 3 or 5, without any wide numbers, could not be placed at the same price. An advance of from 5 to 10 per cent. would be claimed. It sometimes happens that a special margin (different from the tariff) is made when the pieces are cut of irregular lengths—such as 8 metres or 12 metres. Such cases, however. are not frequent.

I think it may be useful, in connexion with the above general information, to review the principal shippers of velvet ribbons and their most recent invoices. For this purpose I had taken with me to St. Etienne a number of the samples, provided with the invoices, and caused them to be appraised by competent judges, without, of course, saying anything about the names or prices.

I can state that, in many cases, the parties to whom I applied have been able to tell me the name of the manufacturer of the goods and the rates of discount allowed at the time of shipment.

Mr. ⸺

is the principal partner of a firm of ⸻⸻⸻, and has, on his own account, a manufacture of velvet ribbons. None of these goods are offered for sale in St. Etienne; he appears to dispose of them to the customers of his firm.

He uses the prices of the general tariff. Margin 4.15. His pieces measuring 10.20 metres, the margin ought to be only 24 per cent. Discount 50 per cent. Several of his samples are carefully examined and compared with quality No. 3, as far as could be seen; although differing somewhat in the make, they are of the same value or very nearly.

Such goods could not be found in the market for cash net for less than 47 to 48 per centum for a good assortment.

The last invoices of ⸺ are composed only of narrow numbers. I have reasons to suppose that they are consigned, and therefore not paid in cash. These two circumstances induced me to believe that they are under value. And I see no reason to alter the opinion expressed on these invoices on the 21st of November last, to the general appraiser, Boston. A discount of 43 or 44 per cent. to 2 per cent. if paid cash would be cheap.

Mr. ⸺

is the agent, in St. Etienne, of a certain house. He invoices taffetas as well as velvet ribbon; for the present I shall only notice his velvet invoices. His velvet ribbons are very regular; they are supposed to come all from the same manufacturer. His prices and margin are correct.

Discount 50 per centum ought not to be allowed. The quality is precisely that of sample No. 2; there is not a difference of one per cent. in the real value of these two qualities. Bearing in mind that ——— consigns for account of the manufacturer, the discount ought not to be allowed to exceed 42 or 43 per cent. net. He has invoiced at 25 per cent. discount some black velvet, colored edges, which appear to be at about their real value.

Messrs. ——— ———,

manufacturers, consign to ——— ———, New York. No invoices of black velvets produced lately. Quality No. 3 of samples, with 46 per centum discount for cash, is purchased from them. It is their lowest price for large lots. Have invoiced at 40 per cent. discount some few cases of colored velvet ribbons of an inferior quality.

The goods are cheap at that price, and the general appearance of the goods ought to be considered in the appraisement. Some sales of inferior goods, however, have been made at these prices.

Mr. ———,

a commission merchant of Lyons, consigns, for account of a St. Etienne, manufacturer, to ——— ——— in New York. His invoices are generally correct. His quality of goods is between samples, Nos. 2 and 3, or with about 44 per centum cash. He produced, on the 10th instant, an invoice to one case of goods with a discount of 45 per centum. The case is entirely composed of small numbers, and is therefore more valuable. I believe that the discount granted in St. Etienne, if the goods were purchased for cash, (the same indorsement,) would not exceed 41 or 42 per centum.

Messrs. ——— ———,

the most important manufacturers in St. Etienne—they had the market—consign to ——— ———, in New York, their agent. They manufacture several kinds of goods. Samples No. 1 are of their manufacture.

They make two qualities of black velvet ribbons; the first for their European customers, the second (like the samples) for the United States. Their mark is well known and enjoys a great favor. Their last invoice (24th September, 1864) was as follows: Prices of general tariff, margin 4.15, or 26.66 per cent. Their pieces measuring 10.10 metres, the margin ought to be only 24.64 per cent. Discount 46 per cent.

During last season that firm has never given more than 42 per cent. discount for cash. Black cotton-back velvet ribbons, satin or corded white edges. They only make one quality for sale; they, however, sometimes mark some cases "2d quality," being the imperfect pieces of their manufacture. They sell these goods in St. Etienne at the usual tariff prices, except for the following numbers :

For pieces of 27.60 metres.

				Francs.
No. 4 French,	No. 1¼	American	....	3,50
6 "	" 1⅜	"	....	3.90
8 "	" 1½	"	....	4.20
10 "	" 1¾	"	....	4.75
12 "	" 2	"	....	5.30
16 "	" 2½	"	....	6.50

Margin as per rule given above. They now ask for these goods 22 and 2 per cent. discount, with very few sales. These being fancy goods are now likely to fluctuate; if they received an offer for a large lot, it is supposed they would accept 25 per cent. discount for cash. For colored plain velvet ribbons and for colored velvets, white edge, they use a special tariff.

Prices for metres 13.80.   *Proportional margin.*

American.	Francs.	French.	Francs.
No. 1¼	2.40	No. 6	10.25
" 1⅜	2.75	" 6½..................	11.50
" 1½	3.15	" 7	12.25
" 1¾	3.45	" 8	14.
" 2	3.90	" 10	16.
" 2½	4.40	" 12	18.
" 3¼	5	" 14	21.
" 4	6.20	" 17	24.
" 4½	7.25	" 20	26.
" 5	8.25		
" 5½	9.25		

Discount not regular; fluctuation, for reason given on previous page, from 20 to 25 per cent. Details on margin and length of pieces of fine colors are given before in this report. A small sample, the only one I could procure, of black velvet ribbon, white edge, of —— ——, is annexed to the samples.

Mr. ————,

a very important manufacturer, makes the same quality, or very nearly, as —— ——.

His black velvet ribbons will be mentioned in a subsequent part of this report. He does not invoice them directly.

Black velvet ribbons, satin, white edge. Invoices to ————————, New York, does not ship frequently.

I have been able to procure and annex to the other samples a sample of these goods taken out of a lot purchased from —— —— during my visit to St. Etienne; the conditions obtained were a full assortment.

Prices of general tariff; margin, as per rule, (10.20 metres, 24 per cent.) Discount twenty-seven, and two per cent. for cash. He refuses any lower offer.

Messrs. —— ——,

exporters, shipping to their own firm in New York, the largest exporters of St. Etienne. I beg to enclose a confidential communication in reference to that firm about their invoices of velvet ribbons.

There are some other shippers of velvet ribbons, but they are not regular or important; and, for the present, I have no remarks to offer on their invoices.

I enclose, with the samples, the official scales of widths used in St. Etienne. I would recommend that the width be frequently verified by the appraisers, as undervaluations by false numbers are said to be very frequent. The samples are all properly labelled and the prices given. I believe that they are a fair representation of the principal qualities manufactured and reported, and I can vouch for the correctness of the prices given. Any change in these prices will be reported without loss of time.

OCTOBER 15, 1864.

I have the honor to advise you that during the year ended September 30, 1864, the exportations from this consular district to the United States were as follows:

Olive oil, of the value of	$7,676,18
Perfumery	4,502,12
Lemons	28,000,00
Miscellaneous	175,50
Total	40,353,80

During the same year not a single American vessel has entered the port of Nice, and not a single vessel has cleared for the United States. This remark is equally applicable to the preceding year.

The harbor of Nice is not a good one, having only about fifteen feet of water, and in bad weather is quite difficult of entry.

The harbor of Villefranche, about two miles from Nice, is, perhaps, the finest natural harbor upon the Mediterranean, and is the constant resort of French vessels of the largest class. Owing to the difficulties in reference to the harbor to which I have adverted, and the comparatively small amount of exportation to foreign countries, the direct commerce of Nice is principally carried on in small vessels, and mostly with other ports or the French and Italian coasts. "The olive oil, mostly of the inferior qualities, and the perfumery, destined for the United States, are sent from here either to Genoa or Marseilles, principally to the latter port, and from thence shipped directly to New York or Philadelphia. The lemons sent from this district to the United States are all shipped from Mentone, a small city twenty miles from Nice, in the direction of Genoa, and almost entirely in foreign bottoms, only one American vessel having cleared from that port for the United States within the past two years.

The entire exports of olive oil, perfumery, lemons, and lemon and orange peel from this consular district were as follows:

*Olive oil, valued at	$562,514,00
Lemons	155,171,00
Perfumery	18,486,00
Lemon and orange peel	7,714,00
Total	743,885,00

The season of 1863 was very unfavorable for the olive, and the product was not more than one-third to one-fourth as large as usual. Nearly two-thirds of the above amount of oil was manufactured in what was formerly the kingdom of Naples, thence imported into Nice, and after undergoing the refining preparation was exported.

The remaining exportation from Nice and Mentone, and other small ports, are mostly of articles sent to ports along the coast, and quite unimportant.

The olive oil manufactured at Nice is of a very superior quality, and ranks, I believe, at the head of olive oils in all the markets of commerce.

---

*During ordinary seasons the figures above given would represent about the value of the oil manufactured at Nice

H. Ex. Doc. 60——16

The olive is largely cultivated upon the coast of the Mediterranean for over twenty miles in each direction from Nice; but oils of the first quality are obtained only from the olives grown in the more immediate vicinity of Nice. The oil is expressed from the olives during the winter and spring months in small and roughly constructed mills scattered upon the small streams. In this crude state it is brought to Nice in skin sacks, where, after undergoing the refining process, it is fit for exportation.

There are some thirty varieties of the olive, but of these only five are cultivated in the environs of Nice. The olive tree is ordinarily from seven to twelve inches in diameter, though instances occur in which it attains to a very large size and a very great age. There is one in the vicinity of Nice called the "patriarch," of which the circumference is twenty-three feet, and which is probably more than eight centuries old. The olive supports a temperature of 18° to 20°, but its sprouts are killed by a temperature of 22° to 24°. I see no reason why the olive may not be successfully cultivated in parts of the United States.

The perfumery exported from this consulate district is also of a superior quality. The "violette de parme," the jasmine, the rose, the jonquille, the tubereuse, the lavender, the geranium, and the orange for its blossoms, are largely cultivated for purposes of perfumery, and at certain seasons of the year, and in certain localities, the atmosphere is literally redolent with their perfumes. There are fields of "violette" which produce a revenue of from six to eight thousand dollars.

The exportations both of olive oil and perfumery to the United States were much larger before the rebellion, and with the return of peace will, I have no doubt, largely increase.

In the absence of more extended commercial information, it has occurred to me that a statement of facts in reference to the advantages offered in Nice as a winter residence for invalids, especially for those suffering from pulmonary complaints, (of which class, unfortunately, a large number is to be found in the United States,) may not be uninteresting.

Nice is situated in latitude 43° 45′ north. It is distant 656 miles from Paris, and 138 miles from Marseilles, and can now be reached by railroad from Paris in about twenty-six hours, (that portion from Marseilles to Nice being just completed,) and passing through Toulon, the great naval seaport of France, also Hyeres and Cannes, both of which small cities owe their prosperity very largely to the annual influx of visitors to this favored coast. From Nice to Genoa, 129 miles, the trip is made either by sea or along the coast over the macadamized cornice road, one of the most delightful routes in Europe, and one of the most splendid triumphs of engineering skill to be found in the world. The railroad is to be pushed vigorously from Nice to Genoa, but it will be several years before this immense work can be completed. From Genoa, in the direction of Nice, some thirty miles of it is finished.

The district of territory stretching from Hyeres to Nice (and the same description is applicable to Menton and other localities, stretching a distance of thirty miles or more along the coast in an easterly direction from Nice) is thus truthfully described by Mr. Martin, a French author, in the "Annuaire Meteorologique" of France for 1850:

"There is a province, a privileged district, extending from Hyeres to Nice, situated at the base of the Alps, (maritime.) Removed from the course of the Misteal, it enjoys a milder climate than Rome or Naples. It is there that persons with delicate lungs go to seek the mild atmosphere, the constant temperature, the calm existence which retards the progress of the most inexorable of diseases, and would sometimes avert it, did not neglect or a fatal blindness prevent patients from seeking in time a possible cure or divert their attention to less favored localities."

Nice has a resident population of about 44,000, the largest portion of whom subsist, directly or indirectly, upon the money spent by visitors, amounting to about two millions of dollars annually. The number of visitors who remain what is called the season, that is, from October to April, or May, averages 2,000, while the average for the three winter months is 8,000

The city is divided into the old and new part, the former dating from the days of the Roman power, the latter of more modern growth. In the former the houses are high and the streets so narrow that through many of them a wheeled vehicle cannot pass. In the latter the streets are wide and the houses spacious and well built. Thus a step transports you from the bustling present back to the years before the birth of Christ. The city is situated upon the sea, at the bottom of a large and beautiful but not very deep bay, and describing very nearly the arc of a circle. The plain extending back from the sea from one to three miles, and dotted over with beautiful villas, (of which many are also to be seen upon the side of the first range of hills,) is protected from the north and northwest winds by a triple girdle of mountains rising one above the other. Those nearest the city have an altitude of from 600 to 2,000 feet, and the more remote of 3,000 feet. The highest of the latter, the chain of the maritime Alps, about twenty miles distant, is, during the winter, the seat of fierce storms, and, covered with snow, offers a striking contrast to the almost perpetual sunshine below, and to the hills and plain nearer the city covered with the olive, the orange, the lemon and the fig.

Nice is also sheltered on the east and northeast by several high mountain peaks, and on the west is protected to a great extent from the influence of the Misteal (the much dreaded wind which occasionally sweeps our province with great fury) by hills and the great mountain chain of the Estrelles. The sea, at the distance of leagues from the shore, is often seen tossed by this fierce wind, while nearer land it remains as calm as a lake. Thus protected, Nice during the winter months enjoys a climate of unparalleled excellence, and for more than two thousand years having never ceased to attract invalids to her shores.

Speaking of her delightful location, M. de Saussure, in his voyage "Aux Alpes Maritimes," says "high mountains protect Nice from northern winds, and lower hills, enclosing the little circle in which the town and garden are comprised, concentrate within it the sun's rays, and cause a perpetual spring to reign."

The following table, the result of thirteen years of observations, will show the mean temperature (Fahrenheit) of the fall, winter, and spring months at Nice, Rome, and Paris:

Months.	Nice.	Rome.	Paris.
	°	°	°
October	63	66	51
November	57	58	41
December	54	47	36
January	48	44	37
February	50	45	41
March	51	49	43
April	58	56	51
May	63	65	57

The following table gives the mean temperature for the year and for each season at Nice and various other places of winter resort:

Places.	Year.	Winter.	Spring.	Summer.	Autumn.
	°	°	°	°	°
Nice	61	49	64	73	55
Paris	51	38	50	64	52
Florence	59	44	59	75	60
Pisa	61	47	57	75	62
Rome	60	47	57	73	63
Naples	61	49	58	74	63
Palermo	63	52	59	74	67
Malta	68	58	63	78	71
Madeira	65	62	64	70	64
Cairo	73	58	74	85	71

The thermometer at Nice rarely descends to freezing point. During the winter of 1863–'64, a winter of unusual severity in all Europe, ice formed at night, three or four times, of the thickness of window glass, while at Florence and Pisa the Arno was frozen over; and at Naples the cold was very severe; accompanied in all these cities by an atmosphere of greater or less humidity, an atmospheric condition extremely trying to pulmonary patients, and from which Nice is remarkably exempt. But while the ice was thus formed, the roses in full bloom, owing to the warm temperature of the earth and the extreme dryness of the atmosphere, remained untouched.

It will be perceived by the first table that January, having a mean temperature of 48°, is the coldest month in the year. Once since my residence here a few flakes of snow fell during this month, but they immediately melted, while, as I have observed, it not unfrequently occurs that the distant hills and mountains are entirely covered for weeks. Before the first of February the almond tree puts forth its blossoms, and is rapidly followed by the hyacinth, violet, &c. The transition from winter to spring some years is hardly perceptible unless marked, as it is occasionally, by winds of a longer or shorter duration. As may be well imagined, the vegetation of Nice is extremely luxuriant. The almond, the orange, the lemon, the fig, the pomegranate, the grenadine, the palm, and other trees and shrubs unknown to the United States, cover the fields. The flora of Nice is also extremely rich. It is the dryness of the atmosphere of Nice which gives it so great a superiority over Florence, Rome, Pisa and Naples as a resort for invalids. This is so at least up to the month of February or March, at which time the climate of these latter places becomes ordinarily fine. Thus many persons who remain at Nice with great benefit through the winter months find it to their advantage to proceed into Italy upon the approach of spring, particularly (as is not unfrequently the case) if the spring is ushered in at Nice by trying winds. The proportion of electricity is very large in the atmosphere of Nice and often exerts a happy influence upon persons who have become debilitated by disease or by a long residence in low, damp, and miasmatic localities. But notwithstanding the excess of electricity, thunder-storms are of very rare occurrence. The summer temperature of Nice, that is, from June to the middle of September, is not healthy for strangers, owing not so much to the heat (for in the shade the temperature rarely reaches a higher point than 88°, with a gentle sea-breeze almost invariably during the day) as to the even range of the thermometer day and night, ranging for weeks from 84° to 88°. This is also attributable to the extreme dryness of the atmosphere—no rain; it frequently occurs, no rain falling from May to September.

Hence foreigners, especially from a more humid climate, cannot pass the summer at Nice with impunity. Many of the natives, even, find it desirable then to seek a cooler and more variable climate.

It must not, however, be inferred that there are no rainy days at Nice. The annual average number of partially or entirely rainy days at Nice, as well as I can ascertain from tables kept for a series of years, is sixty; and those more or less cloudy one hundred and fifteen, and of clear one hundred and ninety. From October to April the average number of days partially or entirely rainy is thirty-seven. During the same period the days more or less cloudy are sixty and the clear eighty. During the same months the average fall of rain is 13.53 cubic inches; during the entire year 25.80 cubic inches. In many latitudes this quantity of rain would produce a very humid atmosphere. The annual quantity at London is 21 cubic inches, and at Paris 20. But at Nice the evaporation is very rapid and great, and the moisture soon disappears. Besides, the intervals between the rains are frequently very long—half an inch, sometimes, not falling in a month. Again, in the equinox great and continued rains sometimes produce five cubic inches in twenty-four hours, and occasionally half an inch in ten minutes.

Such is a general description of Nice and its climate, a climate indicated by meteorological observations made at different periods for upwards of a century not materially to have changed, and doubtless the same when resorted to in the days of the Roman occupation.

NANTES—JOHN DE LA MONTAGNIE, *Consul.*

APRIL 25, 1864.

I have the honor to enclose (enclosure 1) a numeration of the "fixed tax" on records.

I also enclose (No. 2) a resumé of the proportional or per cent. tax on records. I found it scattered over a large surface of books, and have aimed to put it into comprehensible shape. You will be struck with the erroneous absorption to the state of all mutations of property in the form of donations, whether by will or among people yet living.

The "fixed tax" covers *all* records outside of those which are written in enclosure No. 2.

Proportional tax levied on recorded acts.

1. Abandonment of property under a policy of insurance, *in time of peace*—the tax is levied on the value of the property abandoned—1 per cent.; in time of war, for the same, $\frac{1}{2}$ per cent.

2. Adjudications, sales, resales, cessions, retrocessions, and all other civil and judicial acts for the transfer of or usufruct of real estate, (there is a proportional tax as the formality of copying the transfer,) 5$\frac{1}{2}$ er cent.

NOTE.—When the act of transfer comprises both real and personal property, the tax is levied on the whole value as if it were real estate, unless a stipulated value is put on the personal, which must be estimated article by article in the contract. In such case the personal property pays the tax on that kind of property.

3. Adjudications of real estate of an inheritance, the heirs reserving the benefit of the inventory—"that is, the right to accept or refuse after a certain time given for examining into the value of the inheritance"—(the tax is put on the formality of the transcription,) 1$\frac{1}{2}$ per cent. on the value transferred.

There is a further tax on the inheritance.—(See "Mutations of Property by Decease.")

4. Adjudication of personal property when outside bidders run the property beyond its value; but this tax is only for the price bid over the previous adjudication, provided the tax on the first adjudication has already been paid—2 per cent.

5. Adjudication of real property under the same conditions as in No. 4, 5 per cent.

6. Adjudications, sales, resales, cessions, retrocessions, bargains, agreements, or other acts, civil or judicial, transferring property or personal estate of actual value, standing crops for the year, standing forest trees, or other movable property whatever—even sales of that nature made by the state—2 per cent.

7. Adjudications of real estate of an inheritance, the heirs taking advantage of the "inventory," $1\frac{1}{2}$ per cent. The tax is levied on the whole value.

8. Adjudications upon deductions and bargains for building, repairing, and supplying with furniture or provisions, the price of which is to be paid by the local authorities or state, 1 per cent.

9. Adjudications upon deductions and bargains for building, repairing, and keeping in order or repair, and on all other objects the values of which are susceptible of extinction made between the individuals, which contains neither sale nor promise to deliver merchandise, provisions, or other movable objects of property, 1 per cent.

10. Annuities, either perpetual or for life, and pensions, 2 per cent.

11. Auction sales of inseparable personal property, 2 per cent.

12. Auction sales of inseparable real estate, 4 per cent.

13. Adding the right of usufruct to the property by act of cession, donation, or renunciation, (independent of the fixed duty of 3 per cent. for transcribing,) $1\frac{1}{2}$ per cent.

14. Bills to order and all other negotiable papers of individuals or companies, with the exception of bills of exchange drawn between two places, $1\frac{1}{2}$ per cent.

15. Bills to bearer, $\frac{1}{2}$ per cent.

16. Bills of exchange drawn between two places, and those coming from abroad or from French colonies, when they are protested for non-payment, (they cannot be presented for record unless with the assignment,) $\frac{1}{4}$ per cent.

17. Bonds for military substitutes, 1 per cent.

18. Boot given in partitions of personal property, 2 per cent.

19. Boot given in exchange of real estate, $5\frac{1}{2}$ per cent.

20. Boot given in partition of real estate, 4 per cent.

21. Cessions of stock or promises of stock or bonds in a society, company, or enterprise, whether financial, industrial, commercial, or civil, whatever may be the date of its creation, $\frac{1}{2}$ per cent. tax on the value negotiated.

NOTE.—This tax on bonds or stock to bearer, and for those whose transfer may be made without transfer upon the companies' books, is converted into an annual and obligatory tax of 12 centimes to the 100 francs of the capital of the stock or bonds, estimated by their average market value during the preceding year.

22. Cessions of stock or bonds not yet due, 1 per cent.

23. Cessions of interest in companies or societies whose capital is not divided into stock or bonds of interest, 2 per cent.

24. Cessions, transfers, and delegations of income of all kinds, 2 per cent.

25. Cessions and transfers of government bonds, 3 per cent.

26. Concessions of lands, cemeteries, if perpetual, 4 per cent.; if temporary, $\frac{1}{2}$ per cent.

27. Contracts, compromises, and all other acts or writings containing obligations for sums, where they are not a gift, and when the obligation is not the price of a conveyance of real or personal estate, nor registered, 1 per cent.

28. Counter deeds, made under private signature, having for their object an augmentation of the price stipulated in a private act or deed, or under a private signature previously recorded, triple tax, 5½ per cent.

29. Counter deeds, showing a deception upon the price expressed, concession of office, double tax, 2 per cent.

30. Cancelling, by judgments, of sales of real estate, from failure to pay any part of the payment due, in cases where the buyer has entered upon possession, 4 per cent.

NOTE.—Where the buyer has *not* entered on possession, the record pays five francs for the transcription only, which is the *fixed* tax.

31. Cancelling, by compromise between the parties, of contracts of sales of real estate, 5½ per cent.

32. Donations between persons living, (outside of a marriage contract,) if in a direct line, personal estate pays 2½ per cent.; real estate pays 2½ per cent.

NOTE.—The tax of transcription of 1½ per cent. is not included above, it being levied in addition.

In collateral line:

Between sisters and brothers, uncles and aunts, nephews and nieces, of real and personal property, 6½ per cent.; between great uncles and great aunts, nephews and nieces and first cousins, real and personal property, 7 per cent.; between relations from the fourth to the twelfth degree, real and personal pay 8 per cent.; between persons not related, real and personal property pay 9 per cent. The tax of transcription is here included.

NOTE.—The value of the objects given is determined for the tax as follows, viz: For personal property, according to the estimation value declared by the parties, without deducting changes; for real property, according to 20 times, if it is in fee and simple, and 10 times if it is in usufruct, of the current revenue or rents, without deducting changes.

33. Donations between persons living, by marriage contract, of real estate, 1½ per cent.; of personal, 3½ per cent.

34. Donations during marriage, of personal property, 3 per cent.; of real property, 3 per cent.

NOTE.—This tax is independent of the transcription tax, which is 1½ per cent.

35. Marriage *donations,* when they are made in the contract of marriage, when they convey actual dispositions, by fathers and mothers and grandparents, real and personal property, 1¼ per cent., (independently of the tax for transcribing the hypothecation at 1¼ per cent. for personal property.)

In collateral line:

By brothers and sisters, uncles and aunts, nephews and nieces, for real estate and personal property, 4½ per cent.; by great uncles, aunts, nieces and nephews, and first cousins, real and personal, 5 per cent.; by relations beyond the fourth degree to the twelfth degree, real or personal, 5½ per cent.; by persons not related, 6 per cent.

36. Donations between persons living of government stocks, same taxes as for all other property.

37. Donations between persons living of foreign public funds and stock of manufacturing companies and finances, profiting Frenchmen, same tax as for all other property of a like nature.

NOTE.—The value of the gift is estimated according to the current value quoted on change the day of the donation; if not quoted on change, according to the estimated value declared by the parties.

38. Donations between persons living of real and personal property, by fathers, mothers, and grandparents, with division among the children and descendants, 1 per cent.

39. Drafts, 1 per cent.

40. Deposit of sums with individuals, 1 per cent.

41. Damages fixed by court in a civil case, 2 per cent.

42. Damages fixed by court in a criminal case, 2 per cent.

43. Extensions of payment between debtors and creditors, (the tax is levied upon the sums which the debtor binds himself to pay,) ½ per cent.

44. Exchanges of personal property. The tax is levied on one of the parts exchanged—upon the smallest part if boot is given—at 2½ per cent., independently of the "tax of sale," at 5½ per cent., levied on the boot paid.

45. Contracts of *insurance*, other than acts of maritime insurance, not fixed by a judicial decision, *in time of war,* ½ per cent.; *in time of peace,* 1 per cent.

46. Judgments, ½ per cent.

47. Judgments and decisions, contradictory or by default, of judges of peace, civil courts, of commerce and arbitration, of police courts, of courts of sessions, and the *higher courts,* bearing condemnation, investment of sums and movable values, interests and expenses, between individuals, except the damages allowed, ½ per cent.

48. Leases, subleases, transfers, cessions, retrocessions of leases on personal or real estate—even those of the state; of pasturages; feeding animals, when the cattle are taken without counting or so much a head; agreements for the sustenance of persons, when the time is limited; upon the aggregate price of all the years together, ½ per cent.

49. Leases of long continuation, cessions or retrocessions of these leases, 5½ per cent.

50. Leases of workmanship or skill, 1 per cent.

51. Leases of perpetual income on real estate, 5½ per cent.

52. Leases of real estate of unlimited durations, if they remain in the form of rent. 4 per cent.

53. Leases of movable property for an unlimited time, 2 per cent.

54. Life leases of real estate, if they remain in the form of rent, 4 per cent.

55. Mortgaging of personal property, 3 per cent.

56. Chattel *mortgages* and indemnities of personal property, ½ per cent.

57. Mutations (or change) of property by *decease,* in a direct line, real and personal, 1 per cent.

NOTE.—Children born out of marriage, when called to the succession by failure of heirs, are to be considered, as to the tax, as persons not related.

Between husband and wife, for real and personal estate, 1 per cent.

NOTE.—When the surviving husband or wife is made heir through relations, in the regular succession, he or she is to be considered, in regard to the tax, as if not kin.

In collateral line :

Between brothers and sisters, nephews and nieces, uncles and aunts, real and personal, 6½ per cent.; between great uncles, great aunts, great nieces and nephews, and first cousins, for real and personal property, 7 per cent.; between relations beyond the fourth and as far as the twelfth degree, for real and personal, 8 per cent.; between persons not related, real and personal property, 9 per cent.

NOTE.—Distant relations, beyond the twelfth degree, are considered as not of kin, as to the tax they pay, in receiving inheritances.

The value of the property transmitted by decease is determined, for the payment of the tax, upon the same basis as for donations between persons living.—(See "Donations between persons living," No. 37, page 7. Note.)

58. Mutations (or changes) by decease of inscriptions upon the great book of the public debt, same tax as for other property of the same nature.

NOTE.—The capital used for the liquidation of taxes is determined by the market value on change the day of decease.

59. Mutations by decease of public funds and stock of foreign manufacturing companies, and those of finance, dependent on or subject to an inheritance governed by the French law, same taxes as for other property of like nature.

Note.—The capital used for the liquidation of this tax is determined by the average market value of the stock on change the day of the decease. If the property involved is not quoted on change, the capital value is determined by the declared estimative value of the parties concerned.

60. Simple *notes*, 1 per cent.

61. Promises to pay, 1 per cent.

62. Quittances, reimbursements and recovery of income and rents of all kinds, and all other acts and writings bearing discharge of claims and values of personal property, $\frac{1}{2}$ per cent.

63. Receipts for deposit of arms with individuals, 1 per cent.

64. Redemption after the expiration of the delay agreed upon by the contracts of sale under the power of redemption, or after that of 5 years, counting from the day or date of the contract, $5\frac{1}{2}$ per cent.

65. Retrocessions of personal property, 2 per cent.; of real estate, $5\frac{1}{2}$ per cent.

66. Redemption, withdrawing a power of, by public act, within the time of delay stipulated, or private agreements presented for record before the expiration of the time of delay stipulated. and before that of five years, $\frac{1}{2}$ per cent.

67. Security on leases of all kinds, of limited duration, $\frac{1}{10}$ per cent.

68. Security of persons to state accounts, $\frac{1}{2}$ per cent.

69. Security to appear, either in person or through a third person, in case of being set at liberty temporarily, in civil or criminal cases, $\frac{1}{4}$ per cent.

70. Security of sums and movable property, guarantees of movable property and indemnities of like nature, $\frac{1}{2}$ per cent.

71. Security for the charter of a vessel for the round voyage or for the return voyage, $\frac{1}{2}$ per cent.

72. Security on sums of any kind, 1 per cent.

73. Settlement, agreement of, by children, of a certain sum for the support of parents, with abandonment of all rights to personal property by the parents to the children, $\frac{1}{4}$ per cent.

74. Substitutions by compromise, where they have the effect of a transfer of debt, 1 per cent.

75. Legal *substitutions* from a credit or holding a mortgage to another creditor, who assumes it, $\frac{1}{2}$ per cent.

76. Public sales of goods on change and at auctions by brokers or other public officers, by authority of the Chamber of Commerce, $\frac{1}{2}$ per cent.

77. Voluntary *sales* at auction at wholesale, made without the authority of the Chamber of Commerce, in places specially set apart therefor, $\frac{1}{10}$ per cent.

78. Sales of real estate, $5\frac{1}{2}$ per cent.

79. Sales of personal estate, 2 per cent.

80. Sales of real estate, in the name of the state, by public officers, agents of the government, 2 per cent.

81. Sales of new merchandise, other than that fixed at $\frac{1}{2}$ per cent., 2 per cent.

82. Sales, private, of real estate, 4 per cent.

83. Transfer of debts not yet due, 7 per cent.

84. Wills, when they contain a legacy of real estate or trust, $1\frac{1}{2}$ per cent.

Fixed tax on acts recorded in France.

There are about 160 acts subject to the fixed tax, when recorded, distributed as follows, viz:

				Francs.
27 acts with a tax fixed for recording at			....	1
68	do.	do.	do.	2
20	do.	do.	do.	3
3	do.	do.	do.	4

				Francs.
17 acts with a tax fixed for recording at			....	5
6 do.	do.	do.	....	10
3 do.	do.	do.	....	15
3 do.	do.	do.	....	20
3 do.	do.	do.	....	25
1 do.	do.	do.	....	40
2 do.	do.	do.	....	50
1 do.	do.	do.	....	100
3 do.	do.	do.	....	0 10
3 do.	do.	do.	....	0 50

It will be seen that the greatest number of acts (68) bear a fixed record tax of 2 francs; the next greatest number bear a fixed tax of 1 franc; the third greatest number bear a fixed tax of 3 francs; the fourth greatest number bear a fixed tax of 5 francs. There is but one record which bears a tax of 100 francs.

NOVEMBER 12, 1864.

I have the honor to enclose statements of the exports from, imports to, and also of the navigation of the port of Nantes for the year ended September 30, 1864.

Statement showing the exports from the port of Nantes from October 1, 1863, to September 30, 1864.

Description.	Weight or measure.	Quantities.
Cereals, (grains)	Quintals	421,641
Flour	....do	145,849
Refined sugar	....do	93,065
Lumber	....do	11,460
Building materials	....do	69,296
Salted meat	....do	11,161
Salted butter	....do	632
Preserved meats and fish	....do	3,031
Mules	Number	1,333
Wines, (ordinary table)	Hectolitre	7,615
Woollen tissues	Quintals	123
Cotton tissues	....do	640
Manures	....do	5,549
Machinery	....do	1,270
Oleaginous grains	....do	19,615

Statement showing the imports at the port of Nantes from October 1, 1863, to September 30, 1864.

Description.	Weight or measure.	Quantities.
Sugar from French colonies	Quintals	348,234
Sugar from other countries	....do	233,651
Coffee	....do	24,314
Ordinary lumber	....do	219,325
Cabinet-makers' wood	....do	1,413
Dye-wood	....do	6,352
Coral	....do	1,336,928
Pig-iron	....do	28,796
Bar and sheet iron	....do	1,315

Statement showing the imports at the port of Nantes, &c.—Continued.

Description.	Weight or measure.	Quantities.
Lead	Quintals	21,532
Oils	do	15,865
Guano	do	106,859
Other manures	do	65,178
Pepper	do	2,948
Bacon	do	4,107
Rice	do	26,406
Cereals	do	3
Flour	do	
Cotton	do	1,308
Machinery	do	471
Woollen tissues	do	27
Cotton	do	9
Linen	do	2

Statement showing the nationality, tonnage, number of vessels, and seamen arrived at and departed from Nantes from October 1, 1863, to September 30, 1864.

Nationality.	ARRIVALS.			DEPARTURES.			No. of tons for each seamen.
	No. of vessels.	Tonnage.	No. of seamen.	No. of vessels.	Tonnage.	No. of seamen.	
Russia	10	1,449	74	3	463	22	20
Sweden	34	5,040	269				19
Norway	94	9,853	570	48	6,121	302	15
Denmark				6	1,245	57	24
German States	25	3,806	186	5	680	35	16
Hanover				1	79	6	13
Hanseatic cities	7	543	42	5	470	32	14
England	1,057	90,042	6,058	879	86,524	5,232	16
Holland	14	1,246	79	9	790	51	16
Belgium	11	928	62	3	234	19	15
Spain	42	4,372	260	35	3,171	189	17
Portugal	4	608	45				14
Kingdom of Italy	6	726	41	27	3,516	276	13
Austria	1	135	8				17
Algiers	4	516	26	1	126	6	20
West coast of Africa, (Senegal not included)				1	74	4	18
Brasil	4	402	20	1	230	18	18
Uruguay, (Montevideo)	1	399	15	1	399	15	26
Spanish possessions	1	301	16				19
Guadalupe	3	600	32	1	199	10	19
Martinique	2	377	20	2	374	18	20
China	2	252	42				6
Hayti	1	154	10				15
Cod fishery	6	517	63	1	72	7	8
French coasting trade	1,472	58,228	7,052	1,761	105,695	10,612	13
Senegal	1	64	9				7
Egypt	5	711	38	8	1,074	56	19
Barbary States				1	70	4	15
French colonies in India	1	206	12				17
Aggregate	2,808	181,475	15,049	2,795	211,606	16,965	....

St. Pierre, (Martinique)—Wm. F. Given, *Vice-Consul.*

January 9, 1864.

I have the honor to transmit herewith a comparative statement of the exportation of the two principal articles of export from this island for the years ending December 31, 1862, and December 31, 1863, respectively, from which it will appear that the decrease in the amount of sugar exported for the year just closed, as compared with the preceding, is 1,626,343 kilogrammes, and that of rum, for the same period, 417,303 litres.

Comparative statement showing the exportation of sugar and rum from Martinique for the years ended December 31, 1862, and December 31, 1863, respectively.

	Kilogrammes.
Sugar in 1862	32, 101, 447
Sugar in 1863	30, 475, 104
Decrease	1, 626, 343

	Litres.
Rum in 1862	5, 865, 635
Rum in 1863	5, 448, 332
Decrease	417, 303

Comparative statement showing the exportations from Martinique and Guadaloupe for the year ended December 31, 1863.

Description.	Martinique.	Guadaloupe.
Sugar .... hogsheads *..	60, 918	60, 532
Molasses .... litres..	84, 928	257, 696
Rum and tafia............................ litres..	5, 455, 051	1, 423, 237
Coffee. .... kilogrammes..	32, 161	409, 059
Cotton .... kilogrammes..	1, 600	32, 502
Cacao........................... kilogrammes..	258, 127	67, 995
Cassia .... kilogrammes..	362, 589	129
Logwood........................... kilogrammes..	731, 556	822, 027
Roucou .... kilogrammes..	....	124, 400

* 500 kilogrammes each.

Statement showing the number of vessels cleared from Martinique to the United States, also the description of their cargoes and value in francs, during the quarter ended December 31, 1863.

No. of vessels.	Destination.	Productions.	Value in costs and charges.
			Fr. C.
25	New York......	Sugar	396,606 19
	Do	Tamarinds..................................	902 20
	Not known.....	Sugar and tamarinds.......................	*33,820 83
	New York......	Tamarinds and confitures..................	250 00
	Do	Confitures	18 00
	Do	Sugar and molasses........................	75,249 46
	Do	Old lead..................................	98 00
	Do	Liquors...................................	250 00
			507,194 68

* All the merchandise enumerated in the above list was the product of Martinique, and shipped in French vessels, with this exception, which was British.

MAY 18, 1864.

I have the honor to enclose herewith a comparative statement of the exportations from Martinique and Guadaloupe from January 1 to May 1, 1864.

Comparative statement showing the description and quantity of exports from Martinique and Guadaloupe from January 1 to May 1, 1864.

Description.		Martinique.	Guadaloupe.
Sugar, (refined)..........................	kilogrammes..	....	18,179
Sugar, (raw).............................	kilogrammes..	9,667,846	3,946,655
Molasses	litres..	76,982	1,357
Rum.....................................	litres..	1,036,431	96,621
Coffee	kilogrammes..	7,209	209,681
Cacao	kilogrammes..	164,232	52,015
Cassia	kilogrammes..	90,363	229
Logwood................................	kilogrammes..	202,046	85,780
Cotton	kilogrammes..	875	15,431
Roucou	kilogrammes..	....	49,800
Vanilla	kilogrammes..	....	295

JUNE 1, 1864.

*　　*　　*　　*　　*　　*　　*　　*

I will also state that, according to the "*Annuaire de la Martinique*" for the year 1864, just issued, the total population of the island of Martinique is stated to be 135,017—males, 61,613; females, 73,404—of which there are 15,576 immigrant laborers, divided as follows: Coolies, 7,676; Chinese, 675; Africans,. 7,225.

POINTE À PETRE—H. THIONVILLE, *Consul.*

APRIL 26, 1864.

In conformity with my letter of the 10th instant, (No. 6,) I have the honor to give a statement of importations of American produce by vessels of the following nationalities from 1st January, 1864, to the 15th instant:

Nationality.	Number.	Tonnage.	Value.
In British bottoms	34	4,685	$251,029
In Danish bottoms	2	309	17,679
In Swedish bottoms	2	251	20,000
In Dutch bottoms	1	112	14,000
Total	39	5,357	302,708

ALGIERS—EDWARD L. KINGSBURY, *Consul.*

JANUARY 20, 1864.

I have the honor to present to the department a report upon the commerce, agriculture, and industry of Algeria, which, on account of illness, I have been compelled to defer until this date.

Since the beginning of my residence here no merchant vessel of the United States has entered this port, and until the resources of the country are better developed, and its agricultural interests extended, we cannot reasonably hope for any important commerce with this colony. The amount of produce at present offered for exportation to foreign countries is not sufficient to guarantee a full cargo to large vessels bound to foreign ports.

The transportation between France and Algeria is reserved to vessels under the French flag, and vessels of all other nations coming to the ports of the colony are subject to a tax of about seventy-five cents per ton upon the amount of cargo discharged or received, consequently the competition for the trade of Algeria is almost entirely confined to the countries of Spain and Italy, where small vessels can be advantageously employed.

The following statement shows the value of the commerce of Algeria for the years indicated:

Importations in 1861................................... $22,397,218
Exportations in 1861................................... 9,426,071

Total 31,823,289

Importations in 1862...................................... $19,970,971
Exportations in 1862...................................... 6,788,913

Total 26,759,884

The decrease of importations has been caused partly by the high price of cotton goods, (the principal article of importation,) and the reduction of the army about 10 per centum, while the most evident cause of the difference in exportations is the falling off in the productions of the country. The people of the colony complain bitterly of the illiberality of the laws which govern them, and the source of this complaint, the dangers of acclimation and the natural aversion of Frenchmen to emigrate, are probably the chief reasons why, after a period of more than thirty years' occupation of the territory by the French, the statistics of its commerce and its population do not evince a more flattering degree of prosperity.

The principal articles of exchange with Europe are grain, wool, cattle, leather, oil, and tobacco; the products of the forests, iron and lead. The productions of grain and cattle, however, constitute the principal richness of Algeria.

Exportation of grain in 1861, 2,125,000 bushels; value, $1,324,500. Exportation of grain in 1862, 659,000 bushels; value, $580,200. Value of flour exported in 1861, $112,576; value of flour exported in 1862, $41,160.

In the year 1861 about 5,000,000 acres of land were sown with wheat, barley, and corn. The European cultivators obtain about 24 bushels to the acre; the natives only about 6 bushels. The hard wheat (blé dur) of Algeria is highly valued in Europe for the manufacture of alimentary pastes, but for general uses I see no reason to believe that it would find favor in competition with the varieties now cultivated in our country.

CATTLE.

Number exported in 1862, 55,262; value, $558,912.

WOOL.

Amount exported in 1862, 8,084,454 pounds; value, $705,552. In the year 1861 the amount exported was 13,500,000 pounds. I can get no satisfactory explanation of this remarkable diminution of the exports of the succeeding year.

The number of sheep belonging to the natives and to the Europeans may be reckoned at about 10,000,000. The weight of the fleece, unwashed, varies from 3 to 4 pounds. According to these facts Algeria produces from 30 to 40,000,000 pounds of wool; though I suspect that purchasers would experience some difficulty in finding this amount. The general commercial importance of this article, and the interest which its production excites at the present time in our country, warrant a report of all the information upon the subject which I am able to give. I therefore translate the following brief and interesting extract from a report made by a gentleman who is extensively engaged in the purchase of wool in the south of Algeria:

"My business amounts to $200,000 or $240,000. Before 1857 all the commerce of the south, beyond Boghar, was carried on by the Mozabites and the native Jews. They did not pay more than five dollars per hundred-weight, the price that I paid myself in 1857. In 1858 my presence in the south, and the large purchases which I made, raised the price at the beginning of my journey to eight dollars per hundred-weight, and, finally, to eleven dollars per hundred-weight. The province of Algiers alone could produce eleven or twelve million pounds of wool, instead of eighteen hundred thousand pounds which it now produces, if the natives would provide for the nourishment of their sheep during the period comprised between the end of the warm season and the beginning of the rainy season."

The information given by this gentleman upon the commerce of wool in the province of Algiers does not differ from the reports from the provinces of Oran and Constantine.

The chief wool market of Algeria is at the town Tlemeen, in the province of Oran, near the boundary of Morocco. In 1860 and 1861 the quantity exported from this place each year was about 700,000 pounds. The price averaged $20 per hundred weight. The Algerian wool is of excellent quality for coarse fabrics. It is long and coarse, very strong and brilliant; but the immense frauds practiced by mixing sand and salt with the wool and saturating the whole with milk has rendered it extremely unpopular, and, indeed, almost unsalable in the north of Europe. In view of this great depreciation of one of the principal products of the colony, the government has taken some measures to prevent the fraud, while purchasers are recommended to aid in the accomplishment of the object, and save themselves from loss by positively refusing to purchase any wool which is not entirely exempt from fraud.

TOBACCO.

Although the agriculturists of Algeria are giving much attention to the cultivation of this article, it will be seen by the following figures that the colony does not yet produce as much as it consumes.

Leaf tobacco.—Importations in 1862, 3,729,136 pounds; exportations in 1862, 4,348,553 pounds.

Manufactured tobacco.—Importations in 1862, 1,147,146 pounds; exportations in 1862, 549,553 pounds.

The following table shows the comparative production of tobacco during the three years designated.

Provinces.	1860.		1861.		1862.	
	No. of planters.	Area of land cultivated.	No. of planters.	Area of land cultivated.	No. of planters.	Area of land cultivated.
		Acres.		*Acres.*		*Acres.*
Algiers	1,303	7,800	7,160	3,429	1,290	7,355
Oran	562	1,063	374	654	168	1,307
Constantine	2,183	1,714	2,962	1,662	693	3,038
Total	4,048	10,577	10,496	5,745	2,151	11,700

About seven-tenths of all the tobacco produced in Algeria is purchased by the government. In 1862 the prices paid were, for "extra quality," 14 cents per pound; for first quality, 13 cents per pound; for unmerchantable, 4½ cents per pound. There were also several intermediate qualities and prices. About 1 per cent. of the crop of 1862 was "extra," 9 per cent. of "first quality," and 40 per cent. of "unmerchantable."

The planters, in their eagerness to increase the quantity, have sacrificed the quality of their tobacco by immoderate irrigation.

COTTON.

The French government has for several years past endeavored to encourage the cultivation of cotton in Algeria; but if the result has satisfied those interested, it certainly has no importance in the commerce of the colony. The chief cause of failure appears to be the want of information and experience on the part of the planters; but if the cultivation of cotton cannot be made successful in Algeria with the extraordinary inducements offered at the present time, one may reasonably think there is not much probability that any remarkable results will be obtained in the future.

Table showing the result of operations for the two years 1861 *and* 1862.

No. of planters.	Area of land cultivated.		Gross weight of crops obtained.		Weight after ginning.		Quantity exported.		Amount of premiums paid to planters by government.
	Long staple.	Short staple.	Long staple.	Short Staple.	Long staple.	Short staple.	Long staple.	Short staple.	
311	*Acres.* 3,650	*Acres.* 20	*Pounds.* 1,136,583	*Pounds.* 14,348	*Pounds.* 257,844	*Pounds.* 4,873	*Pounds.* 257,580	*Pounds.* 2,923	$60,445

In the year 1863 the cotton plantations in the province of Algiers covered about 1,000 acres. In the province of Oran the cultivation is reported to be somewhat more extensive, as the climate and nature of the soil seem better adapted. A company has recently been formed by the authority of the French government, with a capital of several hundred thousand dollars, to promote the cultivation of cotton in Algeria.

MINERALS.

There are 15 mines situated near Bona, in the province of Constantine, covering an area of 75,000 acres, employing 500 workmen and two steam machines of 25 horse power. During the year 1863 there was extracted 230,249 cwt. of minerals, viz: iron, 172,624 cwt.; sulphur of mercury, 3,500 cwt.; argentiferous lead, 26,834 cwt.

OLIVE OIL.

Total number of olive trees in Algeria in 1862, 1,696,173. Amount of olives harvested, 40,448,551 pounds. Number of oil mills, 5,386. The improvements which have been made in the mode of triturating and refining the oil give some reason to hope for an important extension of this branch of commerce. In very favorable years the export of olive oil has attained a value of $600,000. Several European factories have been established in Algeria for the trituration of oil. The most important of these triturates an average of 400,000 pounds of olives annually. The oil is said to compete fairly with the best oils of Nice.

TRADE WITH THE INTERIOR.

In the year 1862 a treaty was signed between the French government and the Tonareg chiefs at Ghadames, designed to guarantee the security of caravans; but this branch of trade has not yet attained any very important influence upon the commerce of the country.

The foregoing statistics of the productions and commerce of Algeria have been gathered from official sources, and while they are the most reliable that can be obtained, one may be assured that the facts have in no instance been underestimated. The chief interest apparently of the French government in regard to this territory is to make it a nursery for its army and a convenient and important station for its navy. And while every exertion is made for the promotion of this purpose, the interests of colonization are not only neglected, but obstacles are thrown in the way of its progress.

The chamber of commerce of Algiers, Oran and Constantine have unanimously declared in favor of the abrogation of the ordinance which established the principle of reserved navigation between France and Algeria. While this principle accords a privilege to French vessels by preventing foreign competition, it raises the price of transportation and does not profit the Algerian marine. They have also proclaimed against the differential taxes which are levied upon various kinds of merchandise destined for consumption in the colony, and which are in consequence of these taxes turned from its ports to Marseilles and the entrepots of France. For example, coffee coming from France to Algeria is subjected to a duty of only $1 20 per cwt. If it arrived at Algiers or Oran from the countries where it is produced, even by French vessels it pays about $1 75, or if by foreign vessels the duty is about $3; consequently, coffee from Brazil, Havana, and other producing countries, goes to Marseilles instead of coming to Algiers. Indeed, the duty is reduced on these goods when they pass by the entrepots of France, and they do not pay any tonnage tax. A similar differential tax is levied upon tobacco. Imported from the entrepots of France, it pays only about $2 per cwt.; imported from the countries where it is produced, it pays $2 50 by French vessels and $2 65 by foreign vessels, besides the tonnage tax.

It is the same with raw sugars; coming from France the duty is $2 50 per cwt.; from the countries where they are produced, other than French colonies, the general tariff is levied; that is, $4 or $4 28 according as they are transported by French or foreign vessels. Refined sugar coming from any country but France is prohibited in Algeria.

The coasting trade on the coast of Africa is reserved to the French marine and the local marine of Algeria, though foreign vessels are admitted to the same privileges by a system of *frenchification* (franciser). French steamboats ply between different ports of the coast, but the coasting is done principally by the Algerine feluccas, which measure from ten to one hundred tons. The number of these vessels is 133, measuring 3,365 tons. This navigation employs from five to six hundred marines.

The coral fishery on the coast of Algeria is valued at $1,200,000; the official documents show that 239 boats are engaged in this fishery; 235 are manned by foreigners, principally Italians; only four are manned by Algerians. The coral fishery gives employment to about 1,500 to 2,000 sailors.

In concluding this report, the following information concerning the port of Algiers may not be considered unworthy of notice. The improvements which have been made in the harbor of Algiers must prove of valuable importance to vessels engaged in the Mediterranean trade. The extensive breakwaters, which have been constructed since the French conquest, render the harbor safe in all weathers, while it is sufficiently commodious to receive any number of vessels likely to seek its protection. Two magnificent dry-docks have just been completed, capable of accommodating the largest men-of-war now afloat. Other appliances are provided for "heaving down" vessels not exceeding three or four hundred tons.

The ordinary port charges at Algiers are, pilotage inward and outward, three cents per ton register.

Health fees, two cents per ton, and twenty-five cents for bill of health; but small vessels wishing to make a harbor in stress of weather, or seeking a market, and not wishing to incur the expense of entering the port, may pass around to the eastward of the mole and anchor in the bay, as near as possible to the mole, where they will be sheltered from the north winds.

Table showing the European population of Algeria, December 31, 1862.

| | PROVINCES. | | | |
	Algiers.	Oran.	Constantine.	Total.
French	49,960	34,561	34,283	118,804
Spanish	24,124	25,016	2,488	51,628
Portuguese	2	27	66	95
Italians	4,316	2,044	7,011	13,371
Anglo-Maltese	2,572	85	7,231	9,888
Belgians	222	265	184	671
Germans	1,407	2,066	2,357	5,830
Poles	164	66	83	313
Swiss	967	95	687	1,749
Greeks	5	17	11	33
Various countries	559	1,444	486	2,489
Total	84,298	65,686	54,887	204,871
Religion—Catholics	82,206	63,023	52,795	198,014
Protestants	2,092	1,463	2,092	5,647
Total	84,298	64,486	54,887	203,661

Native population in 1861.

Arabs in villages 358,760
Arabs in tribes 2,374,091
Jews.................. 28,097

Total.. 2,760,948

SPANISH DOMINIONS.

BARCELONA—JOHN ALLEN LITTLE, *Consul.*

JANUARY 20, 1864.

I beg to enclose herewith my report of commerce and navigation for the quarter ended December 31, 1863. I also submit the following

Tabular statement showing the number and tonnage of vessels that entered the port of Barcelona for the quarter ended December 31, 1863.

Description.	No.	Tons.	Description.	No.	Tons.
American	1	535½½	Mecklenburg	2	553
Belgian	1	228	Portuguese	4	544
Danish	9	1,781	Prussian	7	3,644
English	44	11,246	Russian	4	1,800
French	14	2,447	Spanish	614	74,131
Hanoverian	1	72	Swedish	13	5,649
Dutch	4	747			
Italian	22	4,962	Total	740	108,329½½

Tabular statement showing the amount of cotton entered at the port of Barcelona during the quarter ended December 31, 1863.

Where from.	Bales.	Where from.	Bales.
Alicante	50	Marañon	1,031
Bahia	1,054	Marseilles	10,361
Cadiz	3,703	Mayaguez	450
Cette	1,519	Palma	107
Gibraltar	80	Pernambuco	533
Havana	1,267	Santander	281
Liverpool	1,040	Tarragona	11
London	428		
Malaga	390	Total number of bales	22,305

IMPORTS.

The amount of imports from the United States for the same quarter at the port of Barcelona was 57,000 pipe staves, 107 boxes of furniture, and 2 barrels of delft.

At the port of Tarragona 32,000 pipe staves and 24,600 hogshead staves.

EXPORTS.

The exports from the port of Barcelona to the United States for the same quarter were 352 bales of corks; and for the port of Tarragona 128 pipes of wine, 150 tierces, 610 quarters, and 250 eighths; 13 bags of almonds, 2,397 bags hazel-nuts, and 3,500 quintals licorice root.

APRIL 16, 1864.

I have the honor to enclose to you herewith my returns of "arrivals and departures of American vessels" and "navigation and commerce" for the quarter ended March 31, 1864.   *   *   *   *   *

Statement showing the imports and exports from and to the United States at the ports of Barcelona and Tarragona during the quarter ended March 31, 1864.

PORT OF BARCELONA.

Imports.

None.

Exports.

1,163 bales of corks, valued at $24,556 18.

PORT OF TARRAGONA.

Imports.

89¾ thousand staves, viz: 73 thousand pipe, 8¾ thousand hogshead, and 8 thousand barrel—value, $12,750.

Exports.

410 quarter, 50 half casks of wine	$8,334 00
52 half, 122 quarter, 41 eighth, 450 different sized casks wine, 400 bundles licorice root, 10 bags hazel-nuts, and 10 bags almonds	9,000 00

358 different sized casks wine...............................	$3, 655 00
100 cases licorice paste......................................	4, 667 95
992 bundles licorice root.....................................	1, 745 35
193 bags almonds..	1, 351 65
200 boxes broken almonds....................................	716 45
	29, 470 40

Total exports to the United States from this consular district during the quarter ended March 31, 1864, $54,026 58.

Amount of cotton entered at the port of Barcelona during the quarter.

	Bales.		Bales.
From Alicante	512	From Malta.............	243
Bahia	200	Manzanillo...........	20
Cadiz	2, 600	Marseilles........'........	16, 293
Carrill...............	398	Matamoras...........	771
Cette ·..............	3,·217	Marañon............. ...	559
Cienfuegos	21	Mayaguana	23
Falmouth.......	54	Nassau	227
Gibraltar.............	176	Pernambuco	8, 420
Havana..............	1, 563	Puerto Cabello........	482
Ibiza............·....	100	Santander............	539
Liverpool	1, 793	Santiago	105
London...............	27	· Smyrna..............	634
Malaga.............	687		
		Total number of bales.............................	39, 664

Statement showing the number, nationality, and tonnage of vessels entered at the port of Barcelona from January 1 to March 31, 1864.

Nationality.	No.	Tonnage.	Nationality.	No.	Tonnage.
Austria	1	119	French	11	1, 815
Danish	4	915	Prussian	36	12, 917
Greek....................	1	196	Russian...............	12	5, 459
Holland	6	631	Spanish................	666	81, 947
Italian	40	5, 956	Sweden and Norwegian..	22	8, 059
Portuguese	4	423			
English	26	7, 417	Total	829	125, 854

OCTOBER 1, 1864.

It will be seen by my quarterly reports that, during the year ending September 30, 1864, only two American vessels have arrived at the port of Barcelona, and three at the port of Tarragona. This is attributed to the injury caused to our mercantile navy by the rebel privateers, and also, to a great extent, to the financial and industrial crisis from which the whole of Spain has been and still is suffering. The cotton factories of Catalonia have again almost entirely ceased work, and the manufacturers are unable to dispose of the goods with which their warehouses are filled, on account of the immense increase of smuggling into this country of English and French goods ; the market is full of these smuggled goods, which, not having paid duties, can be sold much cheaper than those of Spanish manufacture. As stated in my despatch No. 65, a committee from Catalonia was lately sent to

Madrid to represent to the government the present condition of the manufactories of Catalonia, and to devise some means for protecting the interests of the provinces; this committee has returned convinced that the government will take some measures for their protection, but of what nature these measures will be has not as yet been made known.

Cork manufactories of Catalonia.

The cultivation of cork trees and the manufacture of this article is increasing rapidly in Catalonia, and also the exports of the same to the United States. During the year ending September 30, 2,987 bales, containing 71,319,941 corks of different sizes, and valued at $65,965 80, have been exported to the United States from this consular district. The annual production of the manufactories of Catalonia is about 1,162,800,000 corks, valued at $2,325,600.

List of imports and exports from and to the United States for this consular district from October 1, 1863, to September 30, 1864.

IMPORTS FROM UNITED STATES AT BARCELONA.

	Quantities.
Pipe staves	253,000
Hides	1,000
Furniture ....boxes..	107
Perfumery ....boxes..	154
Glass ware ....cases..	200
Delft ....bbls..	2

IMPORTS FROM UNITED STATES AT TARRAGONA.

	Quantities.
Pipe staves	625,800
Guano ....tons..	1,393

Exports to the United States from Barcelona.

Articles.	Quantities.	Value.
Corks	2,987 bales	$65,965 80
Red wine	90 quarter casks	709 80
Brandy	6 eighth casks	61 56
Red wine	24 dozen bottles	24 00
	Total value	66,761 16

Exports to the United States from Tarragona.

Articles.	Quantities.	Value.
Tarragona Oporto	128 pipes	$4,056 00
Do....do	150 ¼-casks	2,250 00
Do.....do	1,382 ¼-casks	25,859 80
Do....do	411 barrels	8,885 73
Ordinary red wine	52 hogsheads	842 80
Do....do	448 ¼-casks	6,607 61
Do....do	808 barrels	8,628 00
Do....do	35 ¼-casks	330 00
Tarragona sherry and Madeira	837 ¼-casks	14,642 70
Do.....do.......do	689 barrels	11,554 37
Licorice root	3,561 quintals	9,912 95
Licorice paste	100 cases	4,667 95
Almonds, soft-shell	2,585 bags	14,709 55
Almonds, broken	200 boxes	716 45
Almonds, in shells	11 boxes	38 50
Hazel-nuts	83 bags	569 50
Olive oil	50 ¼-casks	1,800 00
	Total value	116,071 91

The total value of exports to the United States from this consular district during the year ending September 30, 1864, is therefore $182,833 07.

Amount of cotton entered at the port of Barcelona from October 1, 1863, to September 30, 1864.

Where from.	Bales.	Where from.	Bales.
Alicante	562	Matamoras	771
Azama	17	Mantanzas	867
Bahia	1,736	Mayaguez	1,181
Cadiz	9,790	Matril	7
Cardenas	19	Nassau	227
Cardiff	340	Noya	10
Carril	498	Palmer	297
Cette	7,277	Parahibo	1,168
Cienfuegos	24	Pernambuco	15,834
Falmouth	54	Puerto Cabello	1,992
Gibraltar	356	Puerto Rico	290
Havana	8,044	Ruan	72
Isla Carmen	8	Santander	1,164
Iviza	100	Santiago	105
Liverpool	4,993	Seville	6
London	1,040	Smyrna	934
Malaga	1,138	Tarragona	11
Malta	243	Trinidad	24
Manzanillo	20	Valencia	58
Maranon	2,439		
Marseilles	35,023	Total number of bales	98,739

Number, nationality, and tonnage of vessels entered at the port of Barcelona from October 1, 1863, to September 30, 1864.

Nationality.	No.	Tonnage.	Nationality.	No.	Tonnage.
American	2	1,106	Holland	14	1,880
Austrian	6	1,541	Italian	163	26,273
Belgian	4	699	Muhlenburg	4	1,136
Danish	18	3,462	Portuguese	12	1,381
English	133	43,691	Prussian	104	38,770
French	49	7,284	Russian	21	8,881
Greek	1	196	Spanish	2,979	355,113
Hanover	4	334	Sweden and Norwegian	49	18,192
Hamburg	1	342	Total	3,564	510,281

The works of improvement in the port of Barcelona, as described in my yearly report of September 30, 1863, are progressing slowly, and will still require about three years before completion.

The railway from Barçelona to Valencia is completed from this city to Tarragona, and will be opened to the public during the month of November next. Very little progress has been made during the last year upon the railway to connect Catalonia with France.

MALAGA—JOHN R. GEARY, *Vice-Consul.*

NOVEMBER 5, 1863.

I have the honor to acknowledge the receipt of circular No. 40, which has received my particular attention, and to the 12th paragraph I beg most respectfully to submit the following reply:

No law, nor usage, through courtesy existing, or has ever existed, in this city and province, which imposes taxes of any description on consuls, nor on any public employé of any nation, unless they become engaged in the least commercial operations, or purchasing or holding real or personal property, in which case they are taxed. Consuls engaged in commercial operations are treated as merchants in their mercantile intercourse.

Every description of commerce is taxed on the assessed or supposed profits of industry, from the muleteer on the road to the merchant that trades with all the ports of the world.

Statement showing the description, quantities, and value of exports from Malaga to the United States in American vessels, together with the total in American and foreign vessels, during the quarter ended December 31, 1863.

Description of exports in American and foreign vessels.	Value.	Description of exports in American vessels.	Value.
Raisins......boxes..	$359,400	Raisins......boxes..	$98,922
Raisins......kegs and barrels..	9,874	Raisins......kegs and barrels..	1,816
Raisins......frails..	7,659	Raisins......frails..	2,614
Almonds......frails..	3,697	Almonds......frails..	991
Almonds......bags..	762	Almonds......bags..	200
Almonds......boxes..	3,624	Almonds......boxes..	313
Almonds......barrels..	1,787	Almonds......barrels..	....
Wines......qr. casks..	407	Wines......qr. casks..	277
Figs......boxes..	1,400	Figs......boxes..	250
Olive oil......casks..	280	Olive oil......casks..	280
Lead......quintals..	7,500	Lead......quintals..	465
Licorice root......bales..	396	Licorice root......bales..	280
Grapes......barrels and kegs..	8,000	Grapes......barrels and kegs..	2,600
Oranges......boxes..	1,137	Oranges......boxes..	418
Lemons......boxes..	15,242	Lemons......boxes..	4,174
Mats......bales..	185	Mats......bales..	100
Esparto......bales..	161	Esparto......bales..	161
Wool......bales..	343	Wool......bales..	343
Olives......barrels..	225	Olives......barrels..	100
Total......	422,079	Total......	114,304

Statement showing the number and nationality of vessels entered at the port of Malaga during the year 1863, including sailing vessels and coasters.

SAILING VESSELS AND COASTERS.

United States	26	Prussian	6
Spanish	1,800	Russian	5
British	141	Greek	1
French	15	Neapolitan	1
Italian	46	Roman	1
Swedish	45	Hamburg	3
Norwegian	24	Austrian	3
Danish	36	Oldenburg	1
Hanoverian	5	Lubeck	1
Mecklenburg	3	Belgian	5
Dutch	6		
Total......			2,181

Tonnage entered, 146,775; crews, 22,236.

MERCHANT LINE OF STEAMERS.

Spanish	620	Mecklenburg	1
British	32	Dutch	1
French	6		
Total......			660

Tonnage entered, 828,500; crews, 13,225; horse-power, 62,525.

WAR STEAMERS.

Spanish, 11; British, 2; French, 1; total, 20; crews, 1,800; horse-power, 11,200; guns, 206.

VESSELS-OF-WAR.

Spanish, 2; British, 1; Dutch, 1; total, 4; crews, 1,300; horse-power, 62; guns, 105.

Statement showing the description, quantities, and value of exports from Malaga to the United States in foreign * vessels during the quarter ended March 31, 1864.

Description.	Quantities.	Value.
Raisins	Boxes	$119,698
Do	Frails	338
Do	Casks	603
Almonds	Boxes	298
Do	Seroons	213
Wines	½-casks	376
Do	¼-casks	100
Wool	Bales	276
Corks	Bales	69
Mats	Bales	49
Licorice paste	Boxes	50
Licorice root	Bales	881
Oranges	Boxes	192
Orange-peel	Bales	263
Olives	Pipes	10
Olive oil	¼-casks	75
Lead	Tons	1,097
Esparto (grass)	Tons	124
	Total value	272,469

* No exports in American bottoms this quarter.

Distribution by nationality.	Amount.	Distribution by ports.	Amount.
British	$106,818	New York	$238,534
Bremen	102,862	Boston	33,935
Norwegian	62,789		
Total	272,469		272,469

Statement showing the description, quantities, and aggregate value of the exports from Malaga to the United States in foreign vessels during the quarter ended June 30, 1864, together with distribution by flags and ports.

Description.	Quantities.	Amount.
Raisins	Boxes	$71,801
Almonds	Bales	519
Lemons	Boxes	283
Olive oil	Pipes	40
Esparto grass	Tons	33
Lead	Tons	947
Palm leaf	Quintals	43
Wines	½ casks	225
Corks	Bales	35
Licorice paste	Pipes	80
Licorice root	Bales	1,354
Orange peel	Bales	120
	Total value	187,379

DISTRIBUTION.

By nationality:

British	$61,491
Mecklenburg	38,602
Prussian	87,285
	187,378

By ports:

New York	$123,838
Boston	63,540
	187,378

SEPTEMBER 30, 1864.

The vintage season has commenced, and the trade with the United States from this consular district has been very limited during the present quarter.

The value of imports of American produce (staves) by American vessels amounted to $105,600.

The shipments to the United States during the same quarter have been unusually small, the total value of exports by American vessels amounting to $81,993.

Large shipments of raisins are made for Montreal in foreign bottoms, though cleared for New York.

The following are the quotations of the market on board:

Boxes raisins, layers, $1 15; do. bunch, $1 05; casks, sun raisins, per 25 lbs., 95 cents.; boxes lemons, according to quality, $2 65 to $3; frails of softshell almonds, per fanega, $5; kegs grapes, $2 10; lead, per quintal, $2 40; wines, (inferior class,) Malaga dry, per quarter cask, $17 45 to $19 45.

Exchange.—On London, 90 days, 50.35; Paris, 5.28; Hamburg, 44.85.

Freights.—To the United States, for fruit, $10 to $11; for lead, $5 to $6.

Statement showing the description, quantity, and value of exports from Malaga to the United States in American vessels, together with the total in American and foreign vessels, during the year ended September 30, 1864.

DESCRIPTION OF EXPORTS IN AMERICAN AND FOREIGN VESSELS.

(No exports in foreign bottoms.)

DISTRIBUTION.

By flag:
United States $81,993

DESCRIPTION OF EXPORTS IN AMERICAN VESSELS.

Raisins, boxes	14,474
Raisins, casks	404
Lemons, boxes	7,789
Grapes, kegs	800
Almonds, frails	100
Wool, bales	86
Lead, quintals	16,392
Licorice root, bales	1,004

Value, $81,993.

DISTRIBUTION.

By ports:
New York	$55,845
Boston	26,148
	81,993

By nationality:
United States	$186,584
British	369,780
Danish	45,601
Russian	19,423
Hamburg	13,754
Norwegian	13,807
Hanover	26,317
Swedish	20,514
	695,780

By ports:
New York	$400,822
Boston	124,244
Philadelphia	67,824
Baltimore	54,896
San Francisco	47,994
	695,780

For the following despatch the department is indebted to the courtesy of Robert W. Taylor, esq., First Comptroller of the Treasury:

OCTOBER 13, 1864.

The vintage season came in late this year, and shipments to that quarter have been unusually small during the past month. As the weather is dry and fine, and the muscatel crop abundant, a reduction in prices will unquestionably take place, consequently I anticipate that shipments to the United States will be more active. A large quantity of box raisins has been sent by British bottoms to Montreal and Halifax, though cleared for the United States.

The following appear to be the current rates:

Raisins.—Layers, $1 10; bunch, $1 05; casks, sun, $3 40 to $4; kegs, $2 25 to $2 30; frails, $2 26.

Almonds.—Soft-shell, $3 90 to $4 50 per fanega; Indian, $5 per box of 25 pounds.

Figs, 60 to 70 cents per frail of 25 pounds.

Grapes.—Almeria, $2 70 to $3 per keg.

Olive oil, $2 40 per arroba.

Mats, $2 50 to $3 50 per dozen.

Lead, $4 20 to $4 30 per quintal.

Lemons, selected, $2, $2 50 to $3 per box; second quality, $1 35 to $1 45; refused or residues, 95 cents to $1 10.

Wines, inferior Malaga, sweet, $18; dry, $17; Mentilla, $24 per cask; red Baldepenas, $24; red Catalonia, $11 to $11 25.

Freights to the United States for fruit, $10 to $11; for lead, $5 to $6.

Exchanges.—London, 90 days, 50.30; Paris, 5.29; Hamburg, 44.80.

The transactions in Malaga have always been conducted, as regards the fruit trade, which is the main staple of this province, in the most obscure and mysterious manner; hence an impossibility (sometimes, notwithstanding the practice of this consulate, which has always been to enforce an advance of rates on invoices) to find out with certainty the rate or value, particularly of green fruit. Lemons, no doubt, have declined in price within the last six days—which, however, it is difficult to quote with any accuracy the real market value; this is chiefly owing to the way in which the business is transacted. Fruit traders, in combination with carpenters, sole purchasers of this article, brought in from the country, fix the prices, which are strictly adhered among them.

The printed price-current herein is the one in circulation within this locality, and generally conducted by merchants owning part in the fruit trade. There is no price-current of green fruit except of grapes, and even the prices fixed cannot be much depended upon. There are no printed sales published.

The value for packing, covering, &c., of a box of lemons, such as those sent to the United States, is from 60 to 70 cents. It is estimated that about 24,000 boxes of lemons are sent from this quarter to the United States, principally to New York and Boston.

The cost of one iron-bound quarter cask of wine is $2 to $2 25; lighterage on board is 25 cents.

The shipments lately made amount, viz:

In September ultimo, boxes raisins	15,000
Up to 11th instant, boxes raisins	65,000
Total boxes	80,000
Boxes lemons, about	6,200

The bulk, I am glad to say, have been carried by our bottoms.

BILBAO—DANIEL EVANS, *Consul.*

Commercial report upon the trade of Bilbao and of this consular district for the year ended December 31, 1863:

Exports of 1862 and 1863 compared.

Total exports.
1862.. $975, 000 00
1863.. 668, 215 00

Notwithstanding a decrease in the aggregate of the exports for the year 1863 of $306,785 from that of the previous year, yet, when the transient cause of this reduction is considered, the export trade has been remarkably active, as the following table and analysis will show:

Year.	Wheat and flour.	General exports.	Aggregate.
1861	$661, 120	$226, 665	$887, 785
1862	728, 745	232, 060	960, 805
1863	261, 555	406, 660	668, 215

The exports of wheat and flour are subject to considerable fluctuation, depending upon the yield and foreign demand.

An indisposition on the part of farmers to sell maintained prices so high that the exportation of these two articles fell off from the previous year $466,190. Of the entire amount exported for the year 1863 all was sent to the Havana, except $9,411 in value, which was shipped to England.

It will be seen that there has been an increase of $175,000 in the general exports over the previous year.

The following table exhibits in detail the exports for 1863:

Articles.	Countries to which exported.	Quantities.	Values.
Flour	Cuba and England................	3, 669 tons	$261, 550
Chestnuts...........	England, Holland, and Belgium...	1, 011 cwt.......	6, 310
Preserved food	England, France, and Cuba.......	217 cwt.......	114, 455
Lamb and goat skins.	France	11 packages..	8, 100
Beans	England, Cuba, and South America.	30 cwt.......	585
Madder root.........	England	50 tons	8, 000
Madder powder......	England	850 tons	153, 000
Licorice	England and United States........	30 tons	7, 745
Common salt........	Norway, Sweden, and Denmark...	250 tons	3, 555
Wines and spirits....	France and Holland..............	45, 500 gallons....	21, 510
Guns.	Cuba and South America........	713 pieces.....	5, 080
Straw paper.........	England, Cuba, and South America.	5 tons	3, 190
Minerals	England, France, Belgium, and Holland	36, 566 tons	73, 185

Imports.

The following table shows the aggregate imports for the before-named three years, but does not embrace railway materials, which, for the Bilbao, Tadela, Del Norte, and other lines, have been immense:

Years.	Total imports.
1861	$6, 807, 045 00
1862	7, 066, 505 00
1863	7, 385, 885 00

The following table is an analysis of the import trade for 1863:

Articles.	Countries from whence imported.		Quantities.	Value.
Salted codfish	Great Britain 1, 375, 711 Norway and Sweden.. 6, 609, 369	kilo's	7, 965 tons..	$1, 254, 100
Cocoa	Cuba 50, 834 United States 9, 000 Venezuela and Ecuador 948, 128	..do..	1, 015 tons..	708, 300
Timber, deals, and spars.	France 321, 364 Norway 2, 371, 580 Sweden 50, 879	cub. ft.	3, 085, 841 cub. ft.	179, 800
Hides	France 68, 600 Venezuela and Ecuador 96, 840	kilo's	165 tons..	93, 230
Sugar	Cuba and France 18, 768	..do..	1, 959 tons..	489, 500
Cinnamon	Great Britain and colonies 56, 079	..do..	56 tons..	86, 425
Tea	Great Britain 4, 894	..do..	5 tons..	* 8, 415
Coffee	France 15, 436 Cuba 35, 269	..do..	51 tons..	30, 310
Coal	Great Britain 13, 996, 846	....do..	13, 997 tons..	84, 010
Iron nails	Great Britain 76, 340 France 12, 268 Holland, Belgium, and Germany 23, 560	..do..	112 tons..	10, 890
Pig iron	England		1, 643 tons..	62, 500
Hoop and sheet iron	England		1, 032 tons..	103, 200
Locks, &c	England 4, 563 France 18, 927 Holland, Belgium, and Germany 6, 265	kilo's	30 tons..	12, 060
Brass manufacture.	England 812 France 6, 231 Holland, Belgium, and Germany 3, 101	..do..	10 tons..	14, 360
Steel, wrought and cast.	England 40, 651 Holland, Belgium, and Germany 6, 519	..do.		
Buttons	England 1, 864 France 8, 169 Holland, Belgium, and Germany 2, 161	..do..	12 tons..	18, 935
Spirits of all sorts..	England 10, 630 France 45, 307 Cuba 13, 741 United States 10, 000	galls.	79, 678 galls .	238, 910
Yarns	Great Britain 718, 482..	kilo's.	718 tons..	631, 650
Woollen manufactures.	Great Britain 48, 261 France 23, 127	..do..	71 tons..	447, 000
Linen	Great Britain 46, 661 France 12, 330	..do..	69 tons..	207, 065

Analysis of the import trade for 1863—Continued.

Articles.	Countries from whence imported.		Quantities.	Value.
Silk..............	Great Britain	503 ⎱ kilo's.	4 tons..	$98,300
	France	3,101 ⎰		
Cotton manufactures.	England............	99,203 ⎱ ..do..	130 tons..	354,700
	France	30,759 ⎰		
Cotton mixed with other material.	England............	61,720 ⎱ ..do..	77 tons..	226,620
	France	15,170 ⎰		
Cotton yarn and thread.	Great Britain	.2,100 ⎫	13 tons..	64,550
	France............	6,311 ⎬ ..do..		
	Holland, Belgium, and Germany.....	4,200 ⎭		
Tin plates ...,.....	England............	236,000 ....do..	236 tons..	64,950
Tobacco...........	France	46,332 ⎫	375 tons..	498,895
	Holland, Belgium, and Germany.....	315,960 ⎬ ..do..		
	Cuba	3,200		
	United States.......	9,140 ⎭		
Perfumery........	Great Britain	2,130 ⎱ ..do..	15 tons..	23,300
	France	l5,245 ⎰		
Clocks and watches	France	1,123 ..No	....	33,690
Hardware and cutlery.	Great Britain.......	47,291 ⎫	207 tons..	257,560
	France	135,211 ⎬ kilo's.		
	Holland, Belgium, and Germany.....	24,142 ⎭		
Drugs and medicines.	Great Britain.......	12,310 ⎱ ..do..	432 tons..	432,250
	France	420,131 ⎰		
Guns and powder.	Great Britain......	1,782 ⎱ ..do..	22 tons..	32,200
	France	21,060 ⎰		
Machinery........	England............	4,120 ⎱ pieces.	4,623 pieces	284,480
	France	507 ⎰		
Haberdashery.....	France	29,879 ⎫	45 tons..	59,400
	Holland, Belgium, and Germany.....	18,789 ⎬ kilo's.		
Wire of all kinds..	Great Britain.......	134,250 ⎱ ..do..	180 tons..	94,503
	France	45,952 ⎰		
Raw cotton	Great Britain.......	121,000 ....do..	121 tons..	167,310

The increase of the imports of 1863 over the previous year, although in the aggregate amounting to only $319,380, shows a satisfactory augmentation of commercial activity, as a decrease of the importation of cocoa to the extent of $830,000, and of codfish to the sum of $275,000, from transient causes, must not be overlooked in estimating the state of this trade.

The following table shows the relative amount of imports from different countries :

	Value.
Great Britain..	$2,823,970 00
France...	1,350,810 00
Norway and Sweden	1,197,970 00
Cuba....	818,420 00
Venezuela and Ecuador................................	719,425 00
Holland, Belgium, and Germany.......................	442,090 00
United States	35,200 00

The custom-house returns do not indicate the full extent of either the exports to or the imports from the United States.

The articles which are sent to the United States or imported therefrom by way of Liverpool and other ports, are set down as going to a country from Great Britain. It is estimated that the amount of merchandise smuggled into the country along the French frontier, and by coasting vessels, is equal to one-fourth of the whole imports which pass through the custom-house.

RAILWAY MATERIALS.

In addition to the articles embraced in the foregoing tables an immense amount of railway materials, locomotives, coaches, machinery, &c., for the different roads, now in course of construction, adds greatly to the business of this port.

The following table exhibits the amount of customs collected at this port for the years therein named:

	U. S. currency.
1853	$636,671 21
1854	846,688 72
1855	921,541 70
1856	954,088 41
1857	978,607 30
1858	867,394 35
1859	995,435 56
1860	1,102,499 68
1861	1,410,633 67
1862	1,201,963 61
1863	1,305,345 21

SHIPPING.

The following table embraces the returns of the port for the years 1862 and 1863, the shipping of all nations included:

Years.	ENTERED.		CLEARED.	
	Ships.	Tons.	Ships.	Tons.
1862	590	52,617	535	50,017
1863	798	83,177	785	77,351

ENGAGED IN THE COASTING TRADE.*

1862	1,154	37,384	1,070	33,320
1863	1,574	49,969	1,270	42,481

* There are no foreign ships engaged in the coasting trade.

STEAMSHIPS.

There is regular steam communication between this port and London, Liverpool, Antwerp, St. Nazaire, and the chief towns of Spain. The steamers number about twenty-four, and are generally under the Spanish flag.

H. Ex. Doc. 60——18

SHIP-BUILDING.

The following are the statistics of this trade for the years 1862 and 1863:

Years.	Ships.	Tons.
1862	15	2,340
1863	7	2,200

In former years ship-building was carried on extensively, but at present it shows little activity.

The mountains of the provinces, which formerly furnished oaks in great abundance for home constructions and also for exportation, have very generally been stripped of their trees, and no pains have been taken to secure new growths upon them.

AGRICULTURE.

The poverty of the soil and the mountainous character of the country are not favorable to the cultivation of wheat and maize. Indian corn yields poorly even in the richest valleys, as it is rare that more than one ear grows upon a stalk; yet it is much used as an article of food by the peasantry, and sells for about half the price of wheat flour.

The yield of wheat and maize in the Basque provinces and in the Castiles, the great grain-growing section of Spain, was an average one. The yield, also, for the present year, 1864, is excellent, and the prices of wheat in consequence have been about 15 cents a bushel.

Potatoes, raised in this district, are of a very inferior quality and are always dear, selling from twenty to thirty-five cents the arroba.*

The grape disease has been much less destructive this year than in preceding years, and, with favorable weather, a large quantity of wine has been secured. The wine made in the north of Spain is of a very inferior quality, and the manner of preserving the skins, which are filthy, gives it a disgusting taste. The common wine, which is in general use, costs about fifty cents the gallon.

A superior mode of manufacturing wine is being introduced by some wealthy proprietors, who substitute casks and barrels for the skins, in immemorial use for that purpose. The results of this change are a very great improvement in the quality of the common wines of the country.

The climate is excellent for apples, peaches, plums, and many other kinds of fruit, which are abundant, but generally of an inferior quality; farmers appearing to have sought only to obtain the largest yield instead of improving the quality. They have heretofore made no efforts to improve the quality of any kind of fruit they cultivate.

FAIRS AND CATTLE SHOWS.

Fairs and cattle shows are now becoming frequent in the provinces, at which liberal premiums are awarded for excellence.

The rude modes of agriculture, the indifference to improvement in fruits, in the breeds of their cattle, &c., will doubtless give way before the stimulus excited by these generous competitions.

A *Franco-Español* exhibition, in which the industries of the two nations are brought into comparison, is now being held at Bayonne, which furnishes evi-

---

* 25 lbs. English.

dence, in the Spanish products exhibited, of a capability which, when stimulated by such rivalries, will not leave Spain far behind the foremost nations.

MANUFACTURES.

The iron manufactories are in a flourishing condition, having the protection of a high tariff. A suspension occurred for a short time in consequence of a doubt as to the continuance of the high duties, but the iron interest triumphed. The following table shows the manufactories of iron in and near Bilbao :

Manufactories.	QUANTITIES.		Value.
	Quintals.	Tons.	
Harra company	125,000	5,800	$375,000
Bolueta	105,000	4,900	420,000
Castrojana	40,000	1,800	140,000
Alousategué	30,000	1,350	100,000
Totals	300,000	13,850	1,035,000

The removal of the prohibition against the exports of iron ore has encouraged mining. New mines have been opened and the old ones worked with greater activity.

Thirty-seven thousand tons were exported during the year 1863, thereby aiding other interests in giving freight to vessels that previously were obliged to leave in ballast.

The cost of the ore delivered in town and ready for shipment is from $175 to $225 per ton.

PUBLIC WORKS.

Extensive embankments and walls are being made along the river side, and its channel is being dredged to improve its navigation to the Barat Portugalete.

It is in contemplation to build a railway from Bilbao to the mouth of the river, seven miles from the city, so that vessels may discharge their cargoes without ascending the river.

Several methods have been proposed for the removal of the obstructions to navigation caused by the bar at the mouth of the river; but the difficulty and expense of the enterprise will defer its completion a long time.

The Bilbao and Tudela railway was opened in August, 1863, through its whole extent, which with its connexions forms a continuous line from Bilbao to Barcelona.

The great northern line, the Del Norte, which has been in construction for ten years, and which connects Paris with Madrid, was opened in August, 1864.

The opening up of these several railway communications has been very marked in its effect upon Bilbao. Set down in the midst of mountains, communicating with adjoining valleys by roads always difficult, and often impracticable, its daily markets supplied with provisions carried along paths in high baskets on the heads of market women, it remained for ages stationary in population and dilapidated in appearance; but since the completion of the railways the population has rapidly increased, houses are difficult to be obtained, rents are high, the prices of provisions have trebled, while real estate within the city and neighborhood has risen one, two and three hundred per cent. during the last six years.

The state of education in Spain is at a very low ebb, and is even below what might be expected from the limited provisions made for public instruction. The public schools are of two classes: primary and secondary. In the colleges throughout the country is generally a school of primary instruction, and in many of the large towns there are schools of both classes.

I forward, also, a report upon the trade and commerce of San Sebastian, in the Basque provinces, for the year 1863. These provinces are three in number: Alava, Guipuzcoa, and Biscaya, of which San Sebastian, in Guipuzcoa, and Bilbao, in Biscaya, are the only seaport towns of importance. These provinces contain nearly half a million of inhabitants, industrious, frugal, and devoted chiefly to agriculture. They are considered to be the descendants of the aborigines of Spain, and have lived immemorially among the mountains, enjoying a political liberty of which they have always been jealous, and of which, also, they have retained a large portion in their present union with the crown of Spain, such as exemption from tariffs upon salt and tobacco, freedom from conscription, with local parliaments to watch over their interests, and with a power, in former days, to nullify a law of the kingdom if it conflicted with their *fueros* or local privileges.

Statement showing the principal exports from San Sebastian, together with their values, and the names of the countries to which sent, for the year 1863.

Description.	Countries.	Value.
Wool	France	$248,340
Flour	Cuba and France	130,675
Wine	France and Cuba	73,320
Hatchets	Cuba	29,130
Fire-arms	Cuba and France	20,240
Copper ore	England	15,940
Lead	England	11,565
Licorice	France	8,460
Cotton	England	5,545
Cement	France and England	4,300
Lime	France	2,045
Eggs	France	1,760
Cocoa—shell	England	1,740
Fruit	France	1,465
Hones (sharpening)	France	990
Iron ore	France and England	890
Garlic	France	700
Almonds	France	295

Statement showing the description and value of the imports at San Sebastian for the year 1863, *together with the names of the countries whence derived.*

Description.	Countries.	Value.
Salted codfish	Norway, Newfoundland, and Scotland	$462,030
Sugar	Cuba and France	350,525
Silk (manufactured)	France and England	233,625
Cocoa	Ecuador, Venezuela, France, and Cuba	220,795
Machinery	England and France	174,865
Cotton (manufactured)	England and France	157,230
Coffee	Venezuela, Cuba, Ecuador, and England	149,320
Timber	Norway and France	144,000
Linen, hemp	England and France	143,175
Chains, wire, nails	England and France	113,375
Drugs, chemicals	France and England	87,395
Wine and spirits	France and England	61,490
Wax, raw and manufactured,	Cuba, France, and England	45,475
Hides and prepared skins	Ecuador, Venezuela, France, and England	35,800
Earthenware and glass	France and England	30,605
Coal	England	25,695
Yarn	France	25,000
Haberdashery	France and England	18,395

Statement showing the description and value of the railway materials imported at San Sebastian during the year 1863, *and the names of countries whence derived.*

Description.	Country.	Value.
Coal, coke, wagons, and articles of iron	England	$100,655
Locomotives, sleepers, creosote oil	France	1,089,665
Rails, wagons, carriages, turntables	Belgium	1,030,200

Statement showing the number and tonnage of vessels which entered and cleared at the port of San Sebastian during the year 1863, *as compared with the returns of* 1861, *there being no return for* 1862.

Year.	ENTERED.		CLEARED.	
	No. of vessels.	Tonnage.	No. of vessels.	Tonnage.
Foreign shipping:				
1861	171	18,440	163	17,465
1863	363	42,119	340	39,815
Coasting trade:				
1861	814	35,626	741	35,217
1863	709	35,493	701	35,047

STEAM COMMUNICATION.

About twenty-nine steamers ply between San Sebastian and foreign and home ports, as follows :

London and San Sebastian	3
Liverpool and San Sebastian.......................................	2
St. Nazaire and San Sebastian	3
Bordeaux and San Sebastian......	2
Bayonne and San Sebastian...	5
Bilbao and San Sebastian.......... -	5
Santander and San Sebastian	5
Coasts of Spain..	3

SHIP-BUILDING.

This industry may be said to have almost disappeared. Formerly it was very flourishing. In the year 1660, at the Passages was constructed the largest ship to that date built in Europe.

The following are the statistics of this trade :

Years.	No. of vessels.	Tonnage.
1861...	2	220
1862...	1	49
1863...	3	531

AGRICULTURE.

The staple production of the province of Guipuzcoa is Indian corn. It grows vigorously in the valleys and up the slopes of the mountains, which are cultivated at great heights, their forbidden ruggedness yielding to the industry of the peasantry. The average annual yield of corn is 92,625 quarters, valued at three-quarters of a million of dollars. The quantity of wheat grown yearly is estimated at 39,000 quarters, and worth half a million of dollars. This amount is inadequate to the requirements of the inhabitants. A considerable quantity is therefore imported. 59,347 quarters of potatoes are yearly grown, but of a very inferior quality, as far as I am able to judge. Flax is grown to the amount of 66,300 quarters, valued at $27,500.

Apple orchards abound in the Basque provinces; and it is estimated that 1,114,500 gallons of cider, valued at $95,000, was made in Guipuzcoa alone for the year 1863.

Great quantities of cider are drank by the peasantry; and it is believed that cider-drinkers were much less subject to attacks of cholera during the prevalence of that disease in 1852-'53.

The northern part of Spain is a fine fruit-growing country; but no effort is made to improve the quality. The agricultural operations are exceedingly simple and primitive.

INDUSTRIES.

The following is a statement of the number and description of the mines in the province of Guipuzcoa:

Description.	No.
Lead	12
Iron	14
Calamine	21
Lignite	15

In proportion to the number, the total yield of these mines is small; but they are generally very imperfectly worked.

Statement showing the number and description of the manufactories in this province.

Description.	No.	Description.	No.
Flour mills	256	Fire arms factories	9
Cloth factories	2	Chocolate..do	29
Linen..do.	1	Porcelain..do	1
Cotton .do.	5	Wax lucifer match factories	9
Paper ..do.	6	Ropewalks	36
Cement .do.	5	Potteries	3
Gun-barrel factories	7	*Cap factories	15

* " Boinas," a sort of cap, generally worn, and woven without a seam.

The following statement shows the population of the province at the several periods of 1800, 1832, 1842, and 1861, and the number of births and deaths during the year 1862:

Year.	Population.	No. of births in 1862.	No. of deaths in 1862.
1800	100,000	5,972	3,509
1-32	105,000		
1-42	113,000		
1-61	162,547		

PUBLIC WORKS.

The great northern railway—linea del norte—was opened the 20th of August, 1564, for passengers and merchandise, from Madrid to Irun, on the French frontier, where it connects with the railway to Paris. The line has been operated through Castile and other sections for a considerable period; but the heavy character of the work—the engineering difficulties of carrying the line over and under the Pyrenees, which here break up into detached spurs—has delayed for a long while the enterprise just so happily completed. The longest tunnel in Guipuzcoa is 2,970 yards in length, and is 1,869 feet above the sea level. Besides this there are 22 other tunnels, measuring in all six miles. The viaduct of Orinostiqui is 1,120 feet long, and is carried over five arches, each having a span of 150 feet.

The construction of this road is a grand tribute to engineering skill, and with other railways built and being built will place Madrid within 35 hours of Paris, and do much to redeem Spain from the stagnation into which she has so long fallen, by putting her in communication with ideas, agencies, and influences.

PORT MAHON—H. B. ROBINSON, *Consul.*

OCTOBER 22, 1864.

I have the honor to forward to the department commercial report of the Balearic islands for the year ended December 31, 1863.

Ivica, situated near the main land, produces salt in great abundance; also fruits, some of which are shipped to the United States under foreign flags. The culture of cotton has been commenced, which, from the present high price of the raw material, will be remunerative.

Majorca is esteemed next to Cuba for productiveness. Wheat, fruits, oil, and various other articles, are shipped to the Spanish-American colonies and, coast-wise, to Spain. The wealth of this island is very great. It has no direct communication with the United States. The imports and exports are made mostly under the Spanish and English flags. Heretofore, when American cotton was manufactured to a considerable extent, the raw material was received coastwise from Spanish ports.

No American citizens are registered at Ivica and Majorca.

Minorca, the most central point in the Mediterranean, and in constant communication with all parts of the world by telegraph and steam, is celebrated throughout Europe for the production of superior wheat, sought after for seeding, and shipped to the continent. The commerce of the island is very limited. The cotton mills formerly manufactured considerable quantities of American cotton, brought here coastwise.

The vexatious annoyances persons meet with in passing through Spain have measurably prevented that intercourse which might lead to an extensive interchange of commodities. The baggage of passengers going from one Spanish port to another is subjected to a close inspection.

I know of no country in Europe with which, I think, exchanges could be made to greater advantage to the United States than Spain.

An article has recently been discovered in Spain which, from experiment, it is said, produces vegetable silk. So soon as I can procure samples, I will forward them to the department.

Statement showing the number, tonnage, and cargoes of the vessels entered and cleared at the island of Minorca during the year 1863.

ENTERED.			CLEARED.	
Description of cargoes.	No. vessels.	Tonnage.	Description of cargoes.	No. vessels.
Coal and lumber	14	3,414	Vessel in ballast	18
Steamer employed on the sub-marine cable.......	1	....	Steamer employed on the sub-marine cable.......	1

Statement showing the value of the exports and imports at the island of Majorca during the year 1863.

Exports to foreign countries.. $242, 280 40
"   American colonies 1, 234, 526 40
"   Manilla 33, 753 60
"   Spain—Majorcan goods......................... 1, 765, 480 00
"   "   foreign   do...................... 514, 497 60

      Total value 3, 790, 538 00

Imports from Spain—Spanish goods....................... 3, 144, 668 00
"   "   foreign   do.... .... 404, 400 00

      Total value................................. 3, 549, 068 00

Statement showing the description, quantity, and value of the exports to the United States from the island of Ivica for the year 1863.

Description.	Quantities.	Value.
Mats	162 bundles	$425, 42
Almonds...	1, 497 sacks..............	7, 233, 89
Salt	50 measures..............	126, 66
	Total value	7, 785, 97

Many vessels are quarantined here which are reported at other Spanish ports.

Not one American vessel is included in the above statement.

Seed wheat and cattle are shipped coastwise from Minorca.

HAVANA—W. T. MINER, *Consul General.*

Revised tonnage dues.

The following is a free translation of the' order issued by our intendant general, under date of the 2d instant:

His excellency the intendant general of the treasury, by virtue of royal authorization, dated 21st December last, has been pleased to resolve that, from the 1st of July next, the different port charges at present in force on all vessels arriving at this island shall be substituted by one sole duty, as follows:

	Foreign.	National.
1st. All vessels entering and clearing with cargo shall pay per ton measurement.......................................	$2 35	$1 35
2d. All vessels entering with cargo and leaving in ballast....	2 30	1 30
3d. All vessels arriving in ballast and clearing loaded.......	2 00	1 00
4th. All vessels with coals to the extent of or exceeding the number of their register tons, even when loaded with other cargo..		50

	Foreign.	National.
All vessels with coal only, but less than their register tonnage, shall pay on the quantity of coals they carry	$0 50	$0 50
And for every ton unoccupied	1 50	62
All vessels with less coal than their register tonnage, and, moreover, other goods, whatever the extent thereof, shall pay on the number of tons coals	1 35	73
And on the rest of the cargo	2 35	1 35
5th. All vessels entering in ballast and clearing loaded with a full cargo of molasses	50	37
6th. All vessels arriving in ballast and only loading produce of the country, per ton of cargo	2 00	1 00
And for every ton unoccupied	5	5
7th. All vessels coming and leaving in ballast	5	5
8th. All vessels arriving in transit or in distress	5	5

9th. All steamers engaged in the regular trade with this island, of whatever flag or place of departure, shall be exempt from all dues, provided that neither bring nor take away more than 6 tons of cargo, and, when carrying a mail, they are to have all preference in clearance.

10th. All steamers under the foregoing circumstances, but bringing or taking away cargo exceeding the prescribed six tons, shall pay, per foreign flag, $1 60, and 62½ cents per national flag.

11th. The Spanish mail steamers shall pay tonnage in accordance with their special contracts with the government.

12th. All steamers not coming within schedules 9, 10, and 11, shall pay tonnage according to flag and place of departure, deducting the number of tons occupied by the engines and coal-bunkers from the total tonnage.

Of which the commercial community is informed for general intelligence.

HAVANA, *June* 2, 1864.

Statement showing the description of the importation into Havana.

From 1st January to December 31.	1864.	1863.	1862.	1861.	1860.	1859.	1858.	1857.	1856.	1866.
Jerked beef, South America..quintals..	299,208	278,891	316,177	926,802	421,333	353,161	158,737	369,002	229,572	218,069
Codfish, America..............do....	34,627	39,596	36,530	38,793	45,662	62,794	101,964	53,536	0850	87,541
Europe.........do....	42,455	34,448	21,789	36,360	36,460	33,675	26,561	36,246	25,030	17,726
Flour............barrels..	231,696	211,533	231,108	247,971	196,603	262,684	249,610	213,584	166,313	163,563
Rice, China.......quintals..	105,224		675	47,549	98,234	89,313	86,951	79,144	9820	102,549
Spain.........do....	319,874	57,503	94,968	52,838	60,097	39,030	73,499	70,829	70,100	90,049
East India.......do....	129,361	283,269	5815	261,615	219,601	123,251	129,647	140,472	81,495	41,063
Lard............do....	64,025	113,342	171,304	162,554	90,509	117,726	87,043	63,514	68,823	40,975
Wine............pipes..	322,172	48,979	44,947	49,718	51,659	43,748	44,758	35,347	31,061	32,865
Oil, (olive)........jars..	45,552	350,592	475,192	479,740	369,834	502,647	638	273,645	587,869	517,987
Hogshead shooks......number..	569,080	69,660	48,330	47,436	52,269	74,253	51,908	86,674	97,354	109,742
Box nas.........do....	11,185	368,075	452,903	468,247	470,256	497,061	434,983	475,633	465,747	640,138
Boards...........M feet..	142,884	8,162	10,551	15,747	28,375	29,587	24,084	21,567	15,732	14,743
Coals.............tons..		110,038	95,565	138,872	94,291	61,422	80,473	62,798	45,989	63,718

Comparative statement of the exports of the principal articles of produce from Havana from January 1, 1864 and 1863.

DESTINATION.	SUGAR. 1864. Boxes.	1864. Hhds.	1863. Boxes.	1863. Hhds.	MOLASSES. 1864. Hhds.	1863. Hhds.	COFFEE. 1864. Arrobas.	1863. Arrobas.	HONEY. 1864. Tierces.	1863. Tierces.
United States	123,328	6,763	172,847	7,323	12,651	6,843	132	281	226	172
United Kingdom and a market	467,974	9,457	376,383	3,229	70	750	16	4		
Russia	3,577		13,111	2						
Norway, Sweden, and Denmark	11,634	175	33,782		120			80	91	81
Hamburg and Bremen	13,618		19,478				65	72	815	800
Holland	4,366		4,472						114	
Belgium	22,422		4,386				16		302	836
France	203,541		135,996	177	157	1,699	117	83	5	
Spain	217,560	54	185,651			493	2,877	8,362	192	153
Gibraltar, Italy, Adriatic, and Mediterranean ports	9,625		14,677		673		6	4		
British possessions in North America	2,710	415	904	263	25	962	967	596	3	
Mexico, South America, &c.	20,378		17,941				42,423	44,265		
Total to December 31, inclusive	1,120,633	16,804	979,538	10,994	13,696	10,740	46,619	53,747	1,838	2,042

Comparative statement of the exports, &c.—Continued.

DESTINATION.	WAX. 1864. Arrobas.	1863. Arrobas.	RUM. 1864. Pipes.	1863. Pipes.	CIGARS. 1864. Mille.	1863. Mille.	TOBACCO. 1864. Pounds.	1863. Pounds.
United States		255	16	105	24,533	15,192	1,460,718	676,252
United Kingdom and a market			4	1,678	47,748	30,514	146,435	150,310
Russia				20	354	1,035	101,781	
Norway, Sweden, and Denmark				4	149	487		
Hamburg and Bremen				10	14,939	22,141	1,158,565	1,035,383
Holland			62		1,510	1,763	50,759	10,853
Belgium	531		110		3,274	3,127	422,985	141,919
France		2,329	190	64	3,127	27,109	975,985	380,618
Spain		12,861	7,024	16,366	46,041	13,158	2,449,071	1,803,479
Gibraltar, Italy, Adriatic, and Mediterranean ports	14	28	15	42	14,357	158	120,971	4,300
British possessions in North America	17,087	23,221	141	290	789	699	3,000	
do. South America, &c.	114		2,246	2,954	365	4,738	38,625	100,145
	97,663				9,425			
Total to December 31, inclusive	45,409	38,754	9,896	20,753	165,363	120,105	6,928,819	4,312,239

Table showing the production and cost of sugar and molasses during the last five years, taken on the last quarter ending December 31.

Havana and Matanzas.	1864.	1863.	1862.	1861.	1860.
SUGAR IN BOXES.					
Exports from Jan. 1 to Dec. 31...	1,360,259	1,233,092	1,286,751	1,181,115	1,136,199
Of previous crop on Jan. 1...	15,486	25,426	12,079	29,000	13,000
Of new crop	1,344,773	1,207,666	1,274,672	1,152,115	1,123,199
Stock on Dec. 31 at both ports...	43,261	15,486	29,124	8,000	25,000
Production total............	1,388,034	1,223,152	1,303,796	1,160,115	1,148,199
Price: Basis No. 12...per arroba.	7½ reals.	10 reals.	6¾ reals.	8¼ reals.	8¼ reals.
Freight....sterling pr. ton.	40s. -5 p. c.	45s. -5 p. c.	40s. -5 p. c.	40s. and 5 p. c.	45s. and 5 p. c.
Exchange...... premium.	12 p. c.	10 p. c.	13 p. c.	14 p. c.	13 p. c.
Cost: f. o. b., including freight, sterling per cwt	25s.	31s. 6d.	22s. 4d.	25s. 7d.	27s. 3d.
SUGAR IN HOGSHEADS.					
Exports from Jan. 1 to Dec. 31...	69,559	66,046	79,812	86,319	68,502
Of previous crop on Jan. 1...	962	1,378	2,569	1,960	2,190
Of new crop	68,597	64,668	77,243	84,359	66,312
Stock on Dec. 31 at both ports ...	1,920	962	1,604	2,701	3,500
Production total............	70,517	65,630	78,847	87,060	69,812
Price: Good refining..per arroba.	7 reals.	7½ reals.	5¼ reals.	6¼ reals.	6 reals.
Freight...sterling per ton.	40s. and 5 p. c.	45s. and 5 p. c.	40s. and 5 p. c.	40s. and 5 p. c.	45s. and 5 p. c.
Exchange...... premium.	12 p. c.	10 p. c.	13 p. c.	14 p. c.	13 p. c.
Cost: f. o. b., including freight, sterling per cwt	21s. 5d.	23s. 2d.	17s. 8d.	19s. 10d.	19s. 1p.
MOLASSES IN HOGSHEADS.					
Exports from Jan. 1 to Dec. 31...	97,647	91,090	93,879	91,941	92,648
Of previous crop on Jan. 1...	2,077	1,923	1,835	2,210	3,005
Of new crop	95,570	89,167	92,044	89,731	89,643
Stock on Dec. 31 at both ports ...	6,198	1,777	3,595	4,738	3,500
Production total............	101,768	90,944	95,639	94,469	93,143
Price: Good clayed .....per keg.	5¼ reals.	5 reals.	3¼ reals.	3½ reals.	4 reals.
Freight...sterling per ton.	42s. 6d. -5 p. c.	47s. 6d. -5 p. c.	42s. 6d. & 5 p. c.	42s. 6d. -5 p. c.	47s. 6d. -5 p. c.
Exchange...... premium.	12 p. c.	10 p. c.	13 p. c.	14 p. c.	13 p. c.
Cost: f. o. b., including freight, sterling per cwt	10s. 6d.	10s. 8d.	8s. 6d.	8s. 9d.	9s. 5d.

Comparative statement showing the export of sugar from Havana and Matanzas from January 1 to December 31, 1864, '63, '62.

DESTINATION.	BOXES.						HOGSHEADS.					
	Havana.			Matanzas.			Havana.			Matanzas.		
	1864.	1863.	1862.	1864.	1863.	1862.	1864.	1863.	1862.	1864.	1863.	1862.
New York	83,852	123,003	43,240	18,686	20,783	10,557	4,611	5,202	6,903	22,055	23,139	29,697
Boston	15,633	35,763	17,545	4,119	6,759	9,305	920	643	1,111	3,857	1,059	5,904
Portland	5,472	5,505	2,840	841	1,460	2,319	316	1,090	460	1,337	2,225	3,728
Philadelphia	7,827	7,702	5,675	285	1,630	100	547			773	2,843	641
Baltimore	8,506	874	640	1,483	3,158	80	409	388	362	1,228	638	448
Other ports											371	
Total to United States	121,790	172,847	69,940	25,414	33,780	22,361	6,803	7,323	8,836	29,250	30,273	40,408
British provinces	1,499	904	97	2,084	206	47	415	263	605	2,350	1,027	624
Mexico and South America	21,457	17,941	22,472	7,927	9,028	8,773				266	25	
Total	22,956	18,845	22,569	10,011	9,234	8,820	415	263	605	2,616	1,052	624
British Channel for orders	390,260	358,719	368,814	94,059	79,964	97,407	8,229	2,688	4,140	14,729	15,095	6,774
Cork and Queenstown	50,290	7,825	6,192	24,826	22,122	23,061	700			4,908	7,114	6,198
Greenock and Glasgow	40,306	9,749	30,904	4,259	4,925	5,584	435	541	1,132	725	801	4,691
London and Liverpool												
Total to Great Britain	481,416	376,293	405,910	123,144	106,311	126,052	9,357	3,229	5,272	20,362	23,010	17,663
Russia, Norway, Denmark, and Sweden	13,271	46,893	57,275	2,759	2,101	6,690	175	2	45	401		428
Hamburg, Bremen, &c	13,368	19,478	21,364		700	2,356			103			
Belgium	22,422	4,386	14,993			1,356						
Holland	4,472	4,472	5,816									
Total to north of Europe	55,967	75,229	99,448	2,759	2,801	10,282	175	2	148	401		428
Havre, Dieppe, &c	75,512	38,032	44,086	5,817	572	1,350				126		708
Bordeaux, B. Isle, Nantes	35,559	34,489	48,708	32,787	34,675	14,361						1,460
Marseilles	92,446	63,475	113,015						580			
Total to France	203,517	135,996	205,669	38,604	35,247	15,711			580	126		2,168
Spain	215,427	185,651	207,966	48,670	64,923	60,864	54	177	290		115	2,001
Gibraltar, Malta, &c												
Trieste, Venice, &c												769
Leghorn and Genoa	9,614	14,677	25,056	1,740	1,258	5,903						
Total to south of Europe	225,041	200,328	233,022	50,410	66,181	66,767	54	177	290		115	2,770
Grand total	1,109,917	979,538	1,038,758	250,342	253,554	249,993	16,804	10,994	15,731	52,755	55,052	64,061

Comparative statements showing the quantity and destination of molasses exported from Havana and Matanzas from January 1 to December 31, 1864, '63, '62.

	HAVANA.			MATANZAS.			CARDENAS.		
DESTINATION.	1864.	1863.	1862.	1864.	1863.	1862.	1864.	1863.	1862.
	Hhds.	Hhds.	Hhds.	Hhds.	Hhds.	Hhds.	Hhds.	Hhds.	Hhds.
Portland	3,785	1,427	2,736	18,443	13,742	19,293	36,849	31,606	25,588
Boston	3,643	749	929		8,336	6,942		14,683	18,453
Providence	35	226							
Bristol	50	344	479		680	639			
New York	2,293	2,967	762	19,741	10,249	8,966	16,179	13,740	6,970
Philadelphia	1,150	358		9,455	5,918	2,587	4,077	8,981	7,764
Baltimore		1,444	40	2,258	688	503	358	577	1,443
Other ports	1,721	44	498	8,181	5,760	1,706	8,060	3,035	4,602
Total to United States	12,677	6,859	5,444	58,078	45,373	40,636	65,523	72,629	40,636
Cork, &c		550		6,702	18,930	27,843	8,116	16,063	22,464
River Clyde				4,028	4,926	5,301			
Leith									
Liverpool	70		861	5,770	2,818	4,160			
Cowes for orders		200		1,674	668				
Total to Great Britain	70	750	861	18,174	27,342	37,304	8,116	16,063	22,464
British provinces	673	962	135	5,396	2,805	2,324	457	107	615
France		1,692	2,861	1,032	4,793	2,353		469	298
Spain	157	493	195	8	37	1,666			
Other ports	120		100	1,262			1,211		276
Total	950	3,147	3,291	7,698	7,635	6,343	1,668	576	1,189
Grand total	13,697	10,756	9,596	83,950	80,350	84,283	75,307	89,261	84,015

Statement showing the importations at Havana and Matanzas during the year ended December 31, 1864.

Articles.	IMPORTATIONS FROM—	
	America.	Europe.
Ale .....casks..	2,330	23,854
Bacon.....boxes..	1,204	
Beans.....bbls..	6,842	
Do.....bags..		1,547
Beef.....bbls..	3,211	
Butter.....bbls. and kegs..	14,934	120
Candles (composition).....boxes..	1,416	32,814
Coals.....tons..	5,257	142,884
Coal oil.....bbls..	5,133	
Do.....boxes..	14,381	
Cheese.....boxes..	3,661	29,119
Chickpeas.....bbls. and bags..		16,547
Codfish.....casks..	1,234	
Do.....drums..	22,516	
Do.....boxes..	1,546	42,455
Coffee.....bags..	35,988	
Corn.....bags..	12,582	

Statement showing the importations at Havana and Matanzas, &c.—Continued.

Articles.	IMPORTATIONS FROM—	
	America.	Europe.
Cotton ....bales..	31,297	....
Figs ....boxes..	....	25,412
Flour...bbls..	1,578	213,112
Do ....bags..	....	34,011
Gin ....demijhons..	....	138,837
Do ....cases..	....	25,229
Hams ....tcs. and bbls..	4.540	....
Do ....No..	....	14,791
Hay ....packs..	20,497	5,315
Hides ....No..	23,979	....
Jerked beef ....qtls..	299,268	....
Lard ....tcs. and bbls..	30,335	....
Do ....kegs..	16,042	....
Lumber. { Boards ....M. ft..	11,185	164
{ Box shooks.........................No..	569,080	....
{ Hhd. shooks.........................No..	45,552	....
Olives ....kegs..	....	73,853
Olive oil ....jars..	....	322,172
Do..cases..	....	10,467
Onions ....bbls..	7,691	....
Do ....strings..	77,075	150,462
Pork..bbls..	6,664	....
Potatoes.......................................bbls..	84,394	....
Do ....hampers..	....	56,301
Raisins ....boxes..	....	41,969
Rice.. { E. India.............................bags..	11,444	130,722
{ Spanish ....bags..	....	52,612
Salt ....bags..	14,714	10,794
Sardines a l'huile ....boxes..	....	13,634
Soap ....boxes..	2,578	33,440
Tallow..bbls..	2,482	1,064
Vermicelli ....boxes..	....	108,407
Wheat...bags..	11,662	....
Wine, Spanish ....pipes..	....	60,370
Do ....bbls..	....	14,217
Do ....boxes..	....	6,336
Wine, French...................................casks..	....	1,063
Do ....boxes and hampers..	....	19,538

MATANZAS—H. O. HALL, *Consul.*

Pro forma disbursements account of a vessel of 450 tons entering with cargo other than coal, and clearing with cargo other than molasses, previous to July 1, 1864.

Interpreter's fees (custom-house and government)..................	$8	00
Hospital fee, $2; health visit, 3 cents per ton, $13 50	15	50
Tonnage dues, 450 tons, at 1½ cent per ton and 1 per cent..........	681	75
Pontoon dues, 450 tons, at 1¾ cent per ton and 1 per cent..........	99	38
Light dues, 450 tons, at ½ cent per ton and 1 per cent.............	28	37
Extract of manifest ......,..	1	00
Visit discharging ( ) at 5 cents per ton.......................	55	00
Opening register and visit to loading.............................	13	50
Stamp for outward manifest.......................................	8	00

Captain of the port fee and pass..................................	$7 00
Pilotage in and out.......................................	12 00
	929 50

Under the new regulations for a vessel of same tonnage the charges are as follows:

Government interpreter's fees	$4 00
Hospital fee...	2 00
Tonnage, 450 tons, at $2 35 per ton....	1,057 50
Pilotage in and out.......................................	12 00
	1,075 50

Pro forma disbursements account of a vessel of 450 tons entering in ballast and clearing with molasses previous to July 1, 1864.

Interpreter's fees, custom-house agent.............................	$8 00
Hospital fees, $2; health visit, 3 cents per ton, $13 50....	15 50
Pontoon dues, 450 tons, 1¾ cent per ton....	99 38
Light dues, 450 tons, ½ cent per ton and 1 per cent................	28 37
Extract of manifest	50
Visit inward, $2 75; outward, $5 50	8 25
Opening register..	8 00
Stamp for outward manifest.......................................	8 00
Captain of the port fee and pass.................................	7 00
Pilotage in and out.......................................	12 00
	195 00

Under the new regulations the same vessel would pay as follows:

Government interpreter's fee...................................	$4 00
Hospital fee......................................	2 00
Tonnage dues, 450 tons, at 50 cents per ton.....................	225 00
Pilotage in and out..	12 00
	243 00

H. Ex. Doc. 60——19

Statement showing the description, destination, and value of the exports from Matanzas to the United States in American and foreign vessels from October 1, 1863, to September 30, 1864.

DESTINATION.	SUGAR.		MELADO.	MOLASSES.			HONEY.	TOBACCO.	CIGARS.	PINE APPLES.	OLD IRON.	OLD COPPER.	SUNDRIES.	INVOICES.
	Hhds.	Boxes.	Hhds.	Hhds.	Tierces.	Bbls.	Tierces.	Bales.	Mille.	Dozen.	Pounds.	Package.	Bags.	Amount.
In American vessels.														
New York	13,314	8,857	1,932	16,951	9,172		414	96	146½	20,536		8 casks		$1,796,458 45
Boston	6,733	18,968	987	3,882	406		182		28	4,715		96 casks		1,071,540 47
Boston	1,376	372		5,390	653									272,015 61
Portland	338	3,940	10	310	17	22	1		632					95,797 02
	281	689		7,115	798			60	166					269,946 17
Philadelphia	232	1,355		1,685	249		29		12					72,828 69
Philadelphia	974			11,339	1,122		7				1,455,648	11,609 lbs.	4 coffee	500,654 08
	40			866	101									59,123 30
In foreign vessels.														
New Orleans				1,068	65	2,886								95,097 94
Baltimore, R. I.	1,164	296		1,398	49	90	39							124,760 85
Bristol, R. I.		63		929	4	9								35,759 49
Fall River				44										7,669 41
Belfast, Me.				413	54	12	25							1,460 67
Newport, R. I.				279	38	21								13,493 76
Bangor, Me.				943	40									8,682 61
Providence, R. I.														6,896 95
Total	94,452	33,790	2,929	50,442	5,768	3,970	683	163	986½	25,251	1,455,648	11,609 lbs. / 34 c'ks	4 bags	4,335,057 80

Statement showing the commerce of the United States in foreign vessels at Matanzas from October 1, 1863, to September 30, 1864.

CARGOES INWARD.

Where from	Number and class of vessels	Ton'ge.	Cargoes.	Values.
New York	11 barks, 11 brigs, 4 schooners	6,486	General cargoes, provisions, furniture, drugs, machinery, &c.	$378,480
Boston	1 ship, 2 barks, 4 brigs	9,241	General cargoes	64,000
Philadelphia	3 brigs	769	do	19,400
Baltimore	1 bark, 2 brigs	687	Box shooks, lumber	17,980
Portland	1 bark, 41 brigs, 1 schooner	3,924	Box shooks, lumber, cooperage, and general cargoes	81,480
Bangor, Me.	1 bark	445	Box shooks	11,200
Bath, Me.	1 brig	230	Lumber	4,800
New Orleans	1 ship, 1 brig	820	Ballast	
	59 vessels	15,657		567,340

CARGOES OUTWARD.

Where bound.	Number and class of vessel.	Ton'ge.	Sugar Hhds.	Sugar Boxes.	Melado Hhds.	Molasses Hhds.	Molasses Tier.	Sundries.	Values of cargoes outward.
New York	16 barks, 16 brigs, 2 schooners	9,023	6,733	18,988	267	3,882	405	182 tierces honey, 26 M cigars, 4,715 dozen pine-apples, 35 casks old copper.	$1,071,540 47
Boston	1 bark, 11 brigs	9,867	338	3,940	10	310	17		272,015 61
Philadelphia	3 brigs	546	40			995	101	4 hhds. coffee.	98,183 90
Baltimore	1 brig	178	232			1,685	249	Ballast.	72,538 69
Portland	2 barks, 6 brigs	1,563						156 M cigars.	
Providence	1 brig	129				943	40		6,896 00
	59 vessels	14,305	7,343	22,228	277	8,986	813		1,452,113 97

RECAPITULATION.

Nationality.	No.	Tons.
Great Britain	56	13,285
Hanoverian	1	390
Prussian	1	480
Belgium	1	150
Total	59	14,305

Statement showing number and tonnage of vessels of all nations arrived at Matanzas from October 1, 1863, to September 30, 1864.

Nationality.	Steamers.	Ships.	Barks.	Brigs.	Schooners.	Total vessels.	Total tonnage.
United States	2	7	69	126	36	240	71,829
Great Britain	3	19	71	89	20	202	57,159
Spain	3	......	36	153	3	195	*43,556
France	......	5	6	......	......	11	4,471
Holland	......	......	......	1	1	2	289
Hanover	......	......	1	......	......	1	343
Sweden and Norway	......	......	3	4	......	7	2,173
Prussia	......	......	2	......	1	3	949
Denmark	......	......	......	3	......	3	535
Russia	......	......	2	2	......	4	1,523
Belgium	......	......	......	1	......	1	240
Uruguay	......	......	......	1	......	1	318
Total	8	33	191	377	61	670	223,385

*Ships included with barks and polaccas with brigs.

Statement showing the number and description of British vessels in the direct and indirect trade of Matanzas, together with the names of the countries where from and whither bound during the year ended September 30, 1864.

	Steamers.	Ships.	Barks.	Brigs.	Schooners.	Tonnage in ballast.	Tonnage with cargoes.	Total vessels.	Total tonnage
Where from:									
Great Britain direct	1	10	31	8	....	....	18,329	50	18,329
British colonies	1	2	9	23	10	4,247	4,765	45	9,012
Other parts of the island	....	5	13	13	4	5,993	5,609	35	11,602
Mexico, South America, &c.	1	....	2	9	1	2,559	....	13	2,559
United States	....	2	16	36	5	820	14,827	59	15,657
Total	3	19	71	89	20	13,619	43,240	202	57,159
Where for:									
Great Britain direct	1	10	13	6	....	....	11,336	30	11,336
Cowes, Falmouth., &c, for orders.	....	9	29	18	....	....	20,369	56	20,369
British colonies	....	....	3	18	14	483	4,060	35	4,549
Other parts of the island	2	....	7	8	3	1,160	4,078	20	5,240
Hamburg	....	....	....	1	....	....	247	1	247
United States	....	....	18	36	2	....	13,285	56	13,285
Total	3	19	70	87	19	1,645	53,381	198	55,026

Statement showing the number and description of Spanish vessels in the direct and indirect trade of Matanzas, together with the names of the countries where from and whither bound.

	Steamers.	Brigs and barks.	Brigs and polaccas.	Schooners.	Total vessels.	Tonnage.	Nature of cargoes.
Where from:							
Spain direct	....	10	49	2	61	12,843	Flour, wines, oil, rice, &c., &c.
Spanish islands and Coast isle.	3	15	42	......	60	14,887	General cargoes and cargoes in transit.
South America, Mexico, &c.	....	7	57	......	64	13,252	Jerked beef, hides, &c., &c., &c.
North of Europe......	....	4	5	1	10	2,574	Hardware, machin'ry, &c.
Total	3	36	153	3	195	43,556	
Where for:							
Spain direct	....	6	63	3	72	14,852	Sugar.
Spanish island and Coast isle.	....	13	36	1	50	10,525	Sugar coastwise in ballast and cargoes in transit.
South America, Mexico, &c.	....	15	17	......	22	4,820	Sugar to Mexico in ballast.
North of Europe	....	19	24	3	46	11,873	Sugar.
Total.	....	43	140	7	190	41,070	

MANZANILLO—M. R. ECAY, *Consular Agent.*

FEBRUARY 4, 1864.

Statement showing the number of British vessels cleared from the port of Manzanillo for the United States during the quarter ended December 31, 1863, together with the description and total value of their cargoes.

Total number of vessels.	Description.	Value.
18	Melado, honey, fustic, cedar, mahogany, palm-leaf, leaf-tobacco, sugar, hides, mats, molasses, coacowood, cigars, cedarwood, granadilla, and lancewood.........................	$191,460 68

Of the above, 16 vessels cleared for New York, and 2 for Philadelphia.

Tabular statement showing the number, description, and value of cargoes of foreign vessels cleared for ports of the United States from Manzanillo for the six months ended June 30, 1864.

No.	Port of destination.	Description of cargoes.	Amount.
15.	New York	Timber, lancewood spars, cotton, honey, leaf tobacco, palm leaf, sugar, molasses, and melado.	$124,395 34
3	Boston	Molasses, melado, sugar, timber, and palm leaf..	16,107 91
	Total		140,503 25

GUANTANAMO—FRANCIS BADELL, *Consular Agent.*

SEPTEMBER 30, 1864.

I am happy to inform you that the export of sugar during the past shipping season has been greater than in any previous year. Besides sugar, which is the principal article of exportation, there is also a large quantity of coffee exported, for the most part shipped to Europe.

The coffee crop of the coming year promises to be large. Owing to the dry weather we have experienced, I am afraid the coming sugar crop will not exceed the past one.

The growing of cotton in the district is largely on the increase, and the crop for the coming year promises well. One drawback to the culture here is a sort of insect which eats the cotton before it reaches maturity. Some years this insect is more prevalent than at others. At the present there is a very little appearance of it.

The imports of this port consist chiefly of cooperage, with a small cargo of machinery every year to supply the wants of the different estates.

Freights, during the present season, have varied greatly, and only a very few American vessels have loaded here. Of 49 arrivals at this port since September 30, 1863, but 9 were under the American flag.

As the railroad brings the cargoes alongside the vessels, this port is one of the most convenient for loading. The wharf, at present, is capable of accommodating five vessels; and as the government has announced the intention of lengthening it by fifty yards, that improvement will give increased accommodation.

This port is in daily communication by mail, and weekly by steamer with that of St. Jago de Cuba.   *   *   *   *   *

PORTO RICO.

Summary statement showing the description and quantities of the exports of Porto Rico for the year ended October 31, 1864, together with the names of the countries of destination.

Countries of destina-tion.	Sugar.	Molasses.	Coffee.	Tobacco.	Hides.	Cotton.	Rum.
	Pounds.	*Gallons.*	*Pounds.*	*Pounds.*	*Pounds.*	*Pounds.*	*Quarts.*
United States	33, 032, 774	2, 421, 065	493, 384	....	71, 732	339, 885	15, 000
Great Britain........	56, 972, 174	....	21, 238	....	....	548, 175	....
British North Ameri-can provinces	6, 162, 780	287, 559	233, 916	4, 920	....	....	....
Spain...............	1, 396, 876	1, 368	453, 215	83, 300	369, 775	261, 147	2, 435
France...............	9, 291, 565	....	853, 171	199, 926	....	....	....
Germany	....	....	....	4, 050, 899	....	....	....
Italy...............	....	....	595, 845	....	....	....	....
Cuba	....	....	1, 958, 036	....	....	....	....
St. Domingo	2, 080	....	....	....	....	....	2, 315
St. Thomas	105, 494	....	3, 822	....	....	....	....
Other countries......	4, 660, 270	26, 971	5, 841, 402	189, 177	118, 158	422, 974	12, 805
Total	110, 914, 013	2, 736, 963	10, 454, 029	4, 528, 222	559, 665	1 572, 181	32, 555

Summary statement showing the exports from the several ports of the island of Porto Rico for the year ended October 31, 1864.

Names of ports whence shipped.	Sugar.	Molasses.	Coffee.	Tobacco.	Hides.	Cotton.	Rum.
	Pounds.	*Gallons.*	*Pounds.*	*Pounds.*	*Pounds.*	*Pounds.*	*Quarts.*
San Juan	17, 149, 994	379, 273	3, 467, 383	896, 356	328, 125	250, 780	8, 897
Manate and Torta-guero	....	....	....	663, 476	....	....	....
Arecibo	5, 686, 205	126, 712	....	2, 707, 352	....	....	....
Mayaguez	22, 362, 005	806, 289	5, 783, 686	13, 369	176, 318	231, 937	....
Ponce.	21, 476, 362	889, 488	1, 790, 926	211, 528	6, 264	472, 250	....
Arroyo	11, 944, 356	620, 709	72, 956	119, 933	....	62, 935	17, 315
Humacao, &c	18, 576, 782	734, 110	....	29, 865	....	....	....
Guayanilla and Gua-nica	6, 903, 498	115, 185	1, 030, 885	46, 461	8, 158	181, 285	....
Aguadilla............	6, 325, 800	64, 310	2, 858	....	50, 800	376, 000	5, 843
Total	110, 425, 022	3, 741, 076	14, 993, 836	4, 678, 333	569, 665	1, 575, 187	32, 055

Comparative tabular statement showing description and quantities of the exports from the island of Porto Rico from 1857 to 1864, inclusive.

Years.	Sugar.	Molasses.	Coffee.	Tobacco.	Hides.	Cotton.	Rum.
	Pounds.	*Gallons.*	*Pounds.*	*Pounds.*	*Pounds.*	*Pounds.*	*Quarts.*
1864	110, 425, 022	3, 732, 076	14, 993, 836	4, 678, 333	569, 665	1, 575, 187	32, 055
1863	146, 467, 283	4, 972, 645	20, 980, 475	6, 024, 593	627, 681	396, 810	363, 305
1862	150, 584, 626	4, 987, 252	13, 861, 586	8, 591, 720	396, 246	123, 861	1, 092, 024
1861	145, 965, 816	4, 616, 108	14, 446, 956	9, 394, 845	279, 997	166, 398	393, 066
1860	127, 944, 749	4, 231, 772	13, 505, 518	2, 337, 921	545, 775	265, 976	....
1859	91, 732, 084	3, 089, 632	13, 456, 637	2, 825, 485	359, 299	96, 985	....
1858	121, 319, 374	3, 730, 511	9, 811, 225	4, 907, 844	405, 982	38, 962	....
1857	80, 969, 188	2, 707, 740	8, 244, 664	4, 035, 134	612, 430	276, 310	....
Total........	974, 751, 194	32, 367, 756	109, 294, 897	42, 795, 875	2, 796, 905	2, 872, 389	1, 880, 450

TENERIFFE—W. H. DABNEY, *Consul.*

DECEMBER 31, 1863.

* * * These islands being free ports, it is almost impossible to obtain any statistics from the Spanish officials of imports and exports of the island or islands, as, under any circumstances, the Spaniards do not pay that atter

tion to that important branch which we do. I forward a synopsis of imports from, and exports to, the United States from this island during the year 1863. Since the failure of the vines, which have been nearly destroyed by the oidium, commerce with the United States has declined very much, and is now limited to the importation of less than half a dozen cargoes of lumber, provisions, flour, tobacco, &c., a year, while the exportations are very trifling; the principal reason is that the great article of exportation, cochineal, is but little consumed in the United States, but is exported to England and France. From conversations held with the principal merchants here, the amount of this article exported is perhaps 1,000,000 pounds, of the value of $600,000. The price here fluctuates very much, having in the spring been as low as half a dollar a pound, while at present it commands from eighty to eighty-five cents. The culture of tobacco has been lately introduced with some success, and it is of good quality, but at present no great quantity is raised. Cotton also has been introduced, and is of fine quality, but it cannot be profitably cultivated here when it returns to its ordinary price in other countries. A small quantity of barilla, orchilla, and moss are likewise exported. The island produces some wheat and corn, but not enough for the consumption of its inhabitants, and considerable quantities of both are imported mostly from Barbary. Large quantities of potatoes and onions are raised, and exported principally to Cuba and Porto Rico. The island is supplied with dry goods, iron, and all manufactured articles from England and France, and colonial produce from Cuba, with which there is a direct trade carried on by island vessels. This island is an important coal depot, the only one in the islands, and many steamers going south and west come here to replenish their stocks; and the importation of this article from England gives employment to a large amount of tonnage. The usual price for coals to steamers is ten dollars per ton. I subjoin some statistics of population of these islands, which may be interesting. It will be perceived that nearly one-seventh are over fifty years of age, which proves the great salubrity of this climate, which is one of the very finest known, and admirably adapted to invalids who have to seek a warm region in winter; and in this connexion I subjoin some statistics of the temperature made by a Frenchman, who came to this island for his health, and has found it so fine that he has taken up his abode in the favored valley of Orotava. These statistics show that this is one of the most equable climates in the world; and it is superior to Madeira, being dryer, and not liable to high winds.

The gross amount of importations into the rest of the Canary islands from the United States during the past year may be set down at about $40,000, and the exports at about $5,000—say, importations into Grand Canary $28,000, into Lanzerota $5,000, and into Palma $7,000. The exports consisted of barilla from Grand Canary to New York, via Havana. This island enjoys unusual mail communications with Europe; there is a weekly steamer from Cadiz, the alternate one proceeding on to Cuba, and the other returning to Spain, and a monthly mail to and from Liverpool by the West Africa packet. Light-houses of second and third classes are being constructed, one on each island—seven in all, and one of the sixth class has been built on the mole of this place, and which will be lighted to-night for the first time. A fine road is being built which will, eventually, extend around the island, and a mole intended in time to enclose a part of the harbor and form a dock is in process of construction. The facilities for doing business in this place are not good, there being no bank; private money lenders charge from 1 to 2 per centum per month for money, and discounting bills is scarcely known. The commission charged by merchants for selling by wholesale is $2\frac{1}{2}$ per centum. There is no paper money, and currency consists of Spanish gold and silver and French napoleons, or five-franc pieces; the latter form the larger part of the money in circulation, and pass for 15 reals vellon, or $\frac{95}{100}$ Spanish dollar. With the exception of some rude pottery and coarse cloth, made in hand looms, there are no manufactures of any kind made on the island, and there is not a single steam-engine on the island. The true resources of the island are but partially developed in the hands of the Spaniards, and the cultivation of many new articles could no doubt be successfully introduced. Fully one-half of the island, occupying all that part turned to Africa, is for the most part uncultivated for want of water to irrigate, and which could be extracted with ordinary engineering skill from the mountains, where many springs are found which are allowed to run to waste. Fish abound in these waters, and on the neighboring coast of Africa forms a very important fishery, which is frequented by a large number of vessels from Spain and the Balearic islands. A large fleet of island vessels are employed, which keep the islands supplied with salt fish, which is sold very low, and which, with potatoes and gofio, (wheat toasted and ground, and eaten raw, moistened with goats' milk or water,) forms the only food of the poorer classes.

The port charges are very trifling at this place; a vessel calling and remaining only twenty-four hours pays nothing, unless she takes a pilot, which is optional; and if she remains in port longer, or discharges or loads any cargo, a light tonnage duty of one real per kilolitre from America, and one-half from Europe is levied.

Statement showing the imports from the United States into the island of Teneriffe during the year 1863.

Nation.	Class.	Name.	Port of shipment.	Cargo.	Value.
American	Bark ..	Azor	Boston.....	General cargo.	$6,000 00
Do	Brig ..	Monte Cristo .	... do	.... do.	1,200 00
English.................	Bark ..	Fredonia	... do	.... do.	8,000 00
Do	Brig ..	Pioneer......	New York..	.... do.	5,000 00
				Total value..	20,200 00

Statement showing the exports from the island of Teneriffe to the United States during the same period.

Nation.	Class.	Name.	Destination.	Cargo.	Value.
English.................	Sch'r ..	Alice T	New York..	Almonds and goods	$3,000 00
Spanish.................	Brig ..	Guanche	New York..	Barilla	4,750 00
				Total value..	7,750 00

Statement showing the population of the seven islands composing the Canary group, extracted from the census report of 1860.

	Males.	Females.	Total.
Fuerteventura	5,369	5,627	10,996
Gomera	5,310	6,050	11,360
Canary	30,995	37,975	68,970
Hierro	2,281	2,745	5,026
Lanzerota	7,457	8,380	15,837
Palma	13,264	17,874	31,138
Teneriffe	42,661	51,048	93,709
Total	107,337	129,699	237,036

Number of those who can read and write.......................... 23,431
Number of those who can read, but cannot write 7,391
Number of those who can neither read nor write.................. 206,214

         Total... 237,036

Of those who can neither read nor write 90,301 are males and 115,913 are females.

Statement of the population above fifty years of age.

From 50 to 60..................... 16,837   From 85 to 90..................... 399
       60 to 70..................... 10,413   90 to 95..................... 87
       70 to 80..................... 4,030   95 to 100..................... 37
       80 to 85..................... 729   Over 100 3

         Total.. 32,544

AUGUST 20, 1864.

I would now make a few additions to the said report of statistics, &c., which I have, after a very long delay, succeeded in obtaining.

1. Under the head of agriculture, I forward herewith a statement of the superficial area of all the Canary islands, (No. 1.)

2. Under the same head. Deeming that possibly some information in regard to the introduction and progress of the culture of the cochineal (introduced, comparatively, quite recently into these islands) might be interesting, and possibly of use and assistance in case this insect could be introduced successfully into any part of our own country, I have carefully prepared a sketch of the rise and progress of the cultivation of this article of commerce in these islands, to which I have added what statistics I have been able to obtain relating to same, and also a sketch of the manner of cultivating the nopal plant and raising the insect, and enclose it herewith, (No. 2.)

3. Under the head of navigation and trade, I enclose the following papers: First, a return of shipping of all nations which have entered and left the port of Santa Cruz, Teneriffe, for the five years ending December 31, 1862, with the value of imports and exports by these vessels, to which is added also the value of the imports and exports for 1863, (No. 3.)

Secondly, under the same head, a statement of the value of all the imports into all the Canary islands during the last five years ending December 31, 1864, (No. 4.)

Thirdly, under same head, a return of shipping of all nations which have entered and cleared at Grand Canary during the year 1863, with the value of the imports and exports by same, to which is added a statement of the article cochineal exported from the same during the same period, (No. 5.)

4. Under the head of fisheries, a statement of the vessels engaged in the fishery of the coast of Africa belonging to Grand Canary, with value of catchings, (No. 6.)

These islands being free ports, only the small duty of 1 real per 1,000 is exacted on importations, excepting tobacco and cereals, and their products. The former pays in leaf one real vellon (5 cents) per pound, and manufactured 4 reals vellon (20 cents) per pound. Grain pays according to a sliding scale, which I enclose herewith, (No. 7.)

Several articles when introduced into the place pay a municipal duty. I enclose herewith a tariff of the same, as also of new articles subjected to this tax since July 1 of this year, which were before free, (Nos. 8 and 9.) Several of these articles are allowed to be deposited, and if re-exported pay nothing, while others do not enjoy this privilege. Merchandise introduced in Spanish vessels pay one-half duty of customs, but no difference is made in the flag in the municipal duty.

Statement showing the superficial area of the Canary islands in fanegadas, a fanegada being about $1\frac{1}{16}$ English acre.

Area mountains and hills (wild.)	Area uncultivated (wild.)	Area cultivated.	Total area.
124,000	650,000	349,000	1,129,000

Statement showing the superficial area of all the Canary islands in square leagues.

Islands.	AUTHORITY.	
	Spanish.	Humboldt.
	Sq. leagues.	Sq. leagues.
Teneriffe	62	73
Canary	51	63
Palma	45	60
Lanzerota	25	26
Fuerteventura	24	27
Gomera	10	14
Hierro	4	7
Total	221	270

Sketch of the progress of the culture of the cochineal in the Canary islands, and description of the manner of raising it, and of cultivating the nopal on which it subsists.

The first cochineal was introduced into Teneriffe about the year 1828, by a native of this island, who brought it from Mexico by way of Havana. No attention was paid to it by any one but the introducer for some years, who persevered in cultivating it, unmindful of the ridicule of his friends and others. In the year 1834 1,882 pounds were exported, and it began to be found out that it could be cultivated successfully, and other persons began to pay attention to it, and the following year, 1835, 5,658 pounds were sent away; the next two years the increase was not much, but in 1838 it took a rapid jump, and in that year more than three times the quantity of the previous years—say 24,548 pounds—were produced. It began now to excite general attention, and about that time the Teneriffe wines began growing in disfavor abroad and the demand to diminish, and as these declined the cochineal came forward. About the year 1848 the destructive vine disease, the *oidium tuckery*, made its appearance, and made rapid progress, threatening to exterminate the vine, which, in three years, it did almost entirely. From that time the cochineal grew rapidly into favor, taking the place of the extinct vine, and ever since has been constantly increasing, and is yet susceptible of large development, but the demand being limited, a larger crop would most likely tend to reduce the price and make it less profitable to the growers.

I will here submit a statement showing the increase from year to year up to the present time since its introduction in 1828.

Years.	No. of pounds.	Years.	No. of pounds.
1831	8	1848	373,385
1832	120	1849	386,518
1833	1,319	1850	782,670
1834	1,882	1851	368,109
1835	5,658	1852	806,254
1836	6,008	1853	790,524
1837	7,020	1854	681,562
1838	24,548	1855	935,912
1839	28,642	1856	1,334,996
1840	77,041	1857	873,845
1841	100,566	1858	897,142
1842	74,589	1859	1,119,530
1843	78,994	1860	1,087,654
1844	139,950	1861	2,244,007
1845	221,350	1862	1,673,823
1846	232,338	1863	776,645
1847	292,495		

The great variation in amounts produced in different years is owing to the excessive heat of those years, or to early or heavy rains, both of which are very injurious.

Below is a statement showing the value of cochineal exported during five years ending December 31, 1862, showing also what proportion goes to Spain and what to foreign countries; though it is probable most of that sent to Spain is re-exported.

Tabular statement showing the exports of cochineal from Teneriffe, for five years ending December 31, 1862, where to and value of same.

Years.	To Spain.	Value.	To foreign.	Value.	Total value.
1858	£248,733	$149,239 80	£648,409	$368,608 95	$517,848 75
1859	141,421	84,852 60	978,109	354,615 15	639,407 75
1860	129,548	76,628 80	958,106	552,682 90	629,311 70
1861	273,400	143,192 95	1,970,586	1,069,685 00	1,212,877 95
1862	153,100	76,580 00	1,540,723	814,836 40	891,416 40
Total	946,202	530,494 15	6,095,933	3,160,428 40	3,890,922 55

It will be seen from the above that the average value of the crop of cochineal for the five years ending 1862 was $778,184 51; this includes only that of Teneriffe. The value of the same exports from the other islands during the same period may be calculated at $950,000, making the total value of the crop in all the Canary islands to be at an average rate of $1,728,184 51.

The crop of 1863 was very much injured by the excessive heat of that year, which, as I have before said, has a most injurious effect upon the insect.

The exports from all the islands for that year was as follows:

Tabular statement showing the exports of cochineal from all the Canary islands for 1863.

Islands.	No. of pounds.	Value.
Teneriffe	776,645	$582,485 75
Grand Canary	793,196	537,455 00
Lanzerota	350,000	245,000 00
Palma	390,000	273,000 00
Total	2,309,841	1,637,940 75

These islands are the only ones open to foreign commerce, and the productions of the other three are brought to these for shipment, but they do not produce much cochineal. The prices have ruled very much higher during the last year, and the crop of 1863 has been very remunerative to the growers in proportion to the quantity raised in consequence.

The crop of Teneriffe has been exported as follows:

	Pounds.	Value.
To Bremen	9,380	$7,035 00
To England	280,120	210,090 00
To France	452,375	339,281 25
To Mogadore	1,490	1,117 50
To Italy	950	712 50
To Spain	32,330	24,247 50
Total	776,645	582,483 75

From these data it will be seen that the cultivation of this article has assumed large proportions of late years, and is a source of much prosperity to these islands. It has supplanted successfully the vine, the production being superior in value to that of the wine crop during the last few years before the appearance of the wine disease, and it does not occupy more than half the amount of ground, releasing the other half for cultivation in wheat, corn, potatoes, &c., and were the *oidium* to disappear altogether, the vine would not be cultivated to any extent in lands suitable for raising cochineal.

It may be interesting to compare the production of wine in former years with that of cochineal at the present time. I have selected the production of 1830, that having been a good year for wine, and I have given also the crop of cereals and other productions for that year, which have been augmented since the failure of vines and introduction of cochineal, for reasons above stated, and which may be interesting.

Tabular statement showing the principal productions of the Canary islands for the year 1830.

Productions.	Teneriffe.	Canary.	Palma.	Gomera.	Hierra.	Langarote.	Fuerteventura.	Total.	Value in dolls.
Wine, (pipes)	25,000	9,000	5,000	4,000	3,000	4,000	200	53,200	$1,064,000
Wheat, (fanegas)	90,000	60,000	20,000	10,000	500	80,000	100,000	360,000	900,000
Corn	35,000	140,000	8,000	5,000	400	20,000	4,000	212,400	494,800
Barley	25,000	55,000	18,000	10,000	6,000	140,000	100,000	354,000	494,800
Rye	10,000	5,000	12,000	2,000	1,000	10,000	1,000	41,000	61,500
Pulse	18,000	12,000	8,000	4,000	500	6,000	2,000	50,500	50,500
Potatoes, (quintals)	400,000	200,000	80,000	20,000	10,000	60,000	12,000	782,000	782,000
Barilla, (quintals)	30,000					100,000	200,000	330,000	330,000
Orchilla	500	300	200	200	200	900	300	1,900	19,000
Total for 1830									4,056,600

Value of wine crop in 1830 ....$1,064,000 00
Value of cochineal crop in 1863.......................... 1,637,940 75

Manner of cultivating the nopal and of raising the cochineal.

The nopal *(opuntia funa)* is apparently indigeneous in these islands and very large quantities have always been cultivated for its fruits, (prickly pear,) which, for three or four months of the year, forms a large item in the food of the lower and poorer classes. It has been found that to cultivate it for cochineal successfully, it must be supplied with water and manure, guano being the best for this purpose, and as it does not rain here from May to October, water must be supplied by irrigation, and this can be done only in certain localities.

It is planted by setting out leaves of the plant in rows four feet from each other. When two years old the insect is placed upon it, the young insect having been deposited upon strips of cloth; these are fastened upon the plant, and in four or five days the young insect will have transferred itself to the plant, when the cloths are removed. On getting on the leaf it inserts its proboscis into the leaf and commences sucking the juices and to grow, and scarcely moves during its whole life; and as it grows it surrounds itself with a fine white powdery substance, which in time almost hides it from view, and which causes the insect when dried to assume the peculiar silvery appearance which it has. At the end of three months in favored localities, and four months in those less favored, it is ready for gathering, which is done by brushing it off the plant with a small brush into a tin vessel; it is then taken to the drying room and placed in trays made of straw, and these placed on shelves around the room, and in the centre of the room is a stove which is heated 140° Fahrenheit. In 48 hours it is dry, and is then sifted through two sieves, one extracting the perfect insect, the other the dust from the broken insect; these two siftings produce what is called granilla, worth about half as much as the perfect insect, say thirty-seven and a half cents, and polvillo, which is worth about twelve and a half cents, or less; these three are then ready for sale and shipment. In some very favored localities two crops are made, but generally only one can be made annually.

The insects on the leaves are apparently all females; the male is a small fly which makes its appearance at the season of the maturity of the females, when they become impregnated, and the young insects almost immediately begin to appear around them alive. When it is desired to collect the mothers for seed, they are watched, and on the appearance of the young they are gathered and placed upon pieces of white cotton cloth, which they soon cover with the young insect, and which is not much larger than a grain of mustard seed. The cloths when covered are put out, as before mentioned, on the plant, insect side down.

The raising of seed is made a specialty of by certain persons and on certain parts of the island, the south side. And those wishing to put out cochineal on their plants purchase of these persons the quantity they may require.

The mothers, after depositing their young, are dried also. They are known in commerce as madres, are of a black color, and are more valuable than the silvered because they produce more coloring matter to the pound.

I am informed, on good authority, that a fanegada of ground (equal to one acre, sixteen perches, and six yards) in a good locality, sufficiently watered and manured, will produce the third year after planting 250 pounds clean cochineal, worth say $187 50; that the expenses may be called one-fifth, leaving clear production of a fanegada $150. While the plant is growing the first two years a good crop of potatoes can be made without injuring the plant, but not after the insect is put out, as the plant must be then kept carefully clean and free from spiders, earwigs, and other insects which destroy the young cochineal.

The plant after four or five years becomes exhausted, and requires renewing to produce a good return.

Statement showing the shipping of all nations which have entered and left the port of Teneriffe for the five years ending December 31, 1862, with the value of imports and exports by same, and countries whence from and where to.

Year.	No. of vessels.	Nation.	Tons.	Where from and to.	Value imports in dollars.	Value exports in dollars.
1858......	133	Spanish	27, 664	Spain	$86, 365 81	$46, 937 00
				Spanish West Indies........	64, 090 80	57, 623 80
	52	French	18, 049			
	77	English........	33, 507		591, 478 60	616, 599 20
	42	Italian	11, 071			
	11	Other nations..	2, 213			
Total...	315	....	92, 504	....	741, 935 20	721, 160 00
1859......	127	Spanish	29, 978	Spain	110, 619 20	53, 070 80
				Spanish West Indies	99, 878 80	106, 066 80
	40	French	9, 903			
	81	English........	23, 218		620, 925 00	654, 815 00
	33	Italian	7, 832			
	16	Other nations..	3, 332			
Total...	297	....	74, 263	....	831, 423 00	813, 953 60
1860......	119	Spanish	25, 267	Spain	86, 706 00	74, 633 75
				Spanish West Indies........	115, 512 25	69, 946 65
	33	French	9, 558			
	86	English........	29, 078		567, 347 85	489, 203 65
	38	Italian	9, 841			
	15	Other nations..	3, 098			
Total...	291	....	76, 842	....	764, 666 10	633, 784 05
1861......	143	Spanish	36, 186	Spain	129, 579 30	111, 567 75
				Colonies..................	71, 603 35	57, 636 90
	33	French	7, 023			
	81	English........	29, 975		514, 171 20	637, 400 00
	50	Italian	13, 549			
	18	Other nations..	3, 869			
Total...	325	....	90, 602	....	715, 153 85	806, 606 65
1862......	131	Spanish	43, 397	Spain	113, 537 85	49, 594 60
				Colonies..................	104, 530 35	74, 740 00
	33	French	10, 716			
	120	English........	38, 419		479, 624 00	439, 997 25
	47	Italian	13, 423			
	29	Other nations..	5, 956			
Total...	360	....	111, 911	....	697, 692 20	564, 321 85

Statement showing the value of imports and exports of Santa Cruz, Teneriffe, for the year 1863.

Where from and to.	Value imports in dollars.	Value exports in dollars.
Spain	$76,966 30	$61,917 80
Spanish West Indies	53,734 50	30,223 80
Foreign	406,474 30	490,408 50
Total..	537,175 10	582,550 10

Statement showing the value of all imports into all the Canary islands for the five years ending December 31, 1863.

Years.	Spain.	Spanish West Indies.	Foreign.	Total.
1859	$214,240 05	$162,238 65	$1,121,199 55	$1,497,678 25
1860	197,503 10	228,309 15	1,171,823 90	1,594,636 15
1861	148,595 00	160,393 50	1,142,084 50	1,451,073 00
1862	150,520 00	170,042 50	1,194,228 50	1,517,791 00
1863	158,335 00	160,071 00	1,139,623 00	1,458,029 00
	869,193 15	881,054 80	5,768,959 45	7,519,217 40

Statement showing the arrivals and departures of vessels at the island of Grand Canary during the year 1863, including coasters, with the values of imports and exports, not including coastwise, for the same period; and also the statement of export of cochineal during same year.

INWARD.

Where from:	No. of vessels.	Tonnage.	Crews.	Value of imports.
Spain..............⎱ Spanish West Indies ⎰	483	50,074	5,388	{ $57,612 05 { 71,605 95
Foreign............................	185	40,016	7,521	470,430 00
Total............................	668	90,090	12,909	599,648 00

OUTWARD.

Where to:				
Spain ....⎱ Spanish West Indies ⎰	518	54,712	5,415	{ 31,329 95 { 52,360 90
Foreign............................	198	40,748	7,688	545,240 00
Total............................	716	95,460	13,103	628,930 85

The exports to Spanish West Indies consist of flagstones and vegetables. The exports to foreign countries consist almost entirely of cochineal, as may be seen in the following:

Statement of the exportation of cochineal from the island of Grand Canary during the year 1863.

To what places exported.	No. of kilo-grammes.	Value.
Spain	13,640	$14,826 75
London	295,635	349,750 10
Marseilles	57,557	70,794 70
Hamburg and Bremen	23,690	36,050 00
Other places	747	1,091 00
Total	391,269	472,512 55

Statement showing the tonnage and number of vessels, with their crews, engaged in the fisheries on the coast of Africa near these islands, and hailing from and belonging to Grand Canary.

Number of vessels 20
Tonnage 1,079
Crews 679
Value of vessels $70,000
Amount of catchings ....quintals.. 80,000
Value of catchings $23,000

The islands of Teneriffe, Lanzarote, and Fuerteventura, have, perhaps, as many more vessels engaged in these fisheries as the above from Grand Canary.

Scale of duties exacted on all foreign grains and flour introduced into the Canary islands.

WHEAT.

Duty.

When worth 58 reals vellon and under (equal to $2 90) per fanega, (125 lbs.,) each fanega pays.................. 20 reals vellon.
When worth 59 to 61 reals vellon, each fanega pays...... 25 " "
" " 62 to 70 " " " " ...... 20 " "
" " 71 to 80 " " " " ...... 16 " "
" " 81 to 90 " " " " ...... 12½ " "
" " 91 to 100 " " " " ...... 8 " "
" " 100 reals vellon and over, " " ...... 4 " "

RYE.

When worth 38 reals vellon and under (equal to $1 90) per fanega, each fanega pays........................... 15 " "
When worth 39 to 41 reals vellon, each fanega pays...... 25 " "
" " 42 to 50 " " " " ...... 20 " "
" " 51 to 60 " " " " ...... 16 " "
" " 61 to 70 " " " " ...... 12 " "
" " 71 to 80 " " " " ...... 8 " "
" " 81 reals vellon and over, " " ...... 4 " "

H. Ex. Doc. 60——20

BARLEY.

Duty.

When worth 28 reals vellon and under (equal to $1 40) per fanega, each fanega pays........................... 12 reals vellon.
When worth 29 to 31 reals vellon, each fanega pays...... 25 "   "
"   "   32 to 40 "   "   "   "   .... 20 ..   ..
"   "   41 to 50 "   "   "   "   16
"   "   51 to 60 "   "   .   "   "   12   ..
"   "   61 to 70 "   "   "   "   8
"   "   71 reals vellon and over,   "   "   4   ..   ..

OATS.

When worth 28 reals vellon and under (equal to $1 90) per fanega, each fanega pays...................... 12   ::   ::
When worth 29 to 31 reals vellon, each fanega pays...... 25   --   "
"   "   32 to 40 "   "   "   "   20   --   "
"   "   41 to 50 "   "   "   "   16   --   "
"   "   51 to 60 "   "   "   "   12   --   "
"   "   61 to 70 "   "   "   "   8   --   --
"   "   71 reals vellon and over,   "   "   4   --   --

CORN.

When worth 48 reals vellon and under (equal to $2 40) per fanega, each fanega pays...................... 18   .
When worth 49 to 51 reals vellon, each fanega pays...... 25   .
"   .   "   52 to 60 "   "   "   "   20   .
"   "   61 to 70 "   "   "   "   16   .
"   "   71 to 80 "   "   "   "   12   ..   ..
"   "   81 to 90 "   "   "   "   8   ..   .
"   "   91 reals vellon and over,   "   "   4   ..   ..

FLOUR.

When wheat is worth 58 reals vellon and under, (equal to $2 90,) the quintal flour (100 lbs.) shall be estimated worth 62 reals vellon, (equal to $3 10,) and pays each quintal.......... 22   ..
When worth 62 reals vellon, (equal to $3 10,) the quintal of flour shall be estimated at 64 reals vellon, (equal to $3 20,) and pays...................................... 25   ..   ..
When worth 61 to 70 reals vellon, 5 reals are added to each quintal of flour, and pays........................... 20   ..
When worth 71 to 80 reals vellon, 6 reals are added to each quintal of flour, and pays........................... 16   ::   ::
When worth 81 to 90 reals vellon, 7 reals are added to each quintal of flour, and pays........................... 12   --   ..
When worth 91 to 100 reals vellon, 8 reals are added to each quintal of flour, and pays........................... 8   ..   ..
When worth 101 reals vellon and over, 9 reals are added to each quintal of flour, and pays........................... 4   ..   ..
Imported in Spanish bottoms, ½ only is paid.

Tariff of municipal duties exacted on certain articles imported into Teneriffe.

Duty.

Wine, common Spanish.................per 25 lbs....	4	reals	vellon.
good Spanish....................per 25 lbs....	6	"	"
foreign ....per 25 lbs....	14	"	"

		Duty.
Vinegar, all kinds.......................per 25 lbs....	1½	reals vellon.
Cider, all kinds.........................per 25 lbs....	2	" "
Brandy, to 20°, inclusive................per 25 lbs....	14	" "
20° to 27°, inclusive...........per 25 lbs....	16	" "
27° to 34°, inclusive...........per 25 lbs..:..	22	" "
34° and upwards...............per 25 lbs....	26	" "
Liquors, all kinds........................per 25 lbs....	28	" "
Oil, olive...............................per 25 lbs....	8	" "
Soap, hard ....per 25 lbs....	6	" "
soft ....per 25 lbs....	3½	" "
Pork: salted hams..	$0\frac{48}{100}$	" ..
pigs' feet, sausages, } ....per 2 lbs.... lard, &c. }	$0\frac{48}{100}$	" "
Beef, salted, &c..	$0\frac{36}{100}$	" ..
Ale and porter, all kinds.................per 25 lbs....	6	" "

The first seven articles are allowed to be deposited, and if re-exported no duty is exacted; but the last three are not allowed this privilege.

Supplementary tariff of municipal duties exacted on the three articles of kerosene and all coal oils, butter, and ice, since July 1, 1864, they having been before that date exempt from taxation.

		Duty.
Coal oil...............................per 25 lbs....	6.18	reals vellon.
Butter................................per lb.......	0.50	" "
Ice ....per 25 lbs....	0.76	" "

The first article is allowed to be deposited, and if not consumed in the place pays no duty; but the last two are not allowed this privilege.

TRINIDAD DE CUBA—WILLIAM H. RUSSELL, *Consul.*

OCTOBER 1, 1864.

*   *   * The probable total amount of exports from this entire consulate, for the current year, comprising Cienfuegos and Santa Espiritus or Zuza, will probably reach the sum of seven millions of dollars.

The largest amounts, perhaps, approximating to fifty per cent., have been shipped or exported from Cienfuegos.   *   *   .   *

The agricultural, commercial, and monetary condition of this part of the island remain almost identical as at the same period last year.

There has been no particular change in commercial operations, or with anything else within my consulate, growing out of new treaties or construction of old ones—everything remains upon the precise basis as I found them on my arrival three years ago. I am pleased to be enabled to state that, under the strict vigilance of the present captain general of her Catholic Majesty at Havana, the infamous traffic in the African race has been materially abridged. I have heard of no arrival of slaves on this part of the island for a considerable length of time, and the last resulted in the recapture of the unfortunate kidnaps.

I also report, with much satisfaction, that no injury has been done to our commerce by privateers, or casualties of any kind, since the date of my last annual report; and I do not consider our merchantmen in the slightest danger in their transits to and from any part of the United States and the southern side of Cuba.   *   *   .   *   *   *

From the 1st of July, 1864, the different port charges at present in force on all vessels arriving at this island shall be substituted by one sole duty, as follows :

	Foreign.	National.
1. All vessels entering and clearing with cargo pay per each ton Spanish measurement	$2 35	$1 35
2. All vessels entering with cargo and leaving in ballast	2 30	1 30
3. All vessels arriving in ballast and clearing loaded	2 00	1 00
4. All vessels with coals to the extent of or exceeding the number of their register even when loaded with other cargo	50	
All vessels with coal only, but less than their registered tonnage, shall pay on the quantity of coal they carry		
And for every ton unoccupied		
All vessels with less coal than their tonnage, and, moreover, other goods, whatever the extent thereof, shall pay on the number of tons of coal	1 35	73
And on the rest of the cargo	2 35	1 75
5. All vessels entering in ballast and clearing loaded with a full cargo of molasses	50	37
6. All vessels arriving in ballast, and only loading fruits of this country, per each ton of cargo		
And for every ton unoccupied	5	5
7. All vessels coming and leaving in ballast	5	5
8. All vessels arriving in transit or in distress	5	5

9. All steamers engaged in the regular trade with this island, of whatever flag or place of departure, shall be exempt from all dues provided they neither take away nor bring more than six tons of cargo; and, when carrying a mail, they are to have all preference in clearance.

10. All steamers, under the foregoing circumstances, but bringing or taking away cargo exceeding the prescribed six tons, shall pay, per foreign flag, $1 62 and 62½ cents national flag.

11. The Spanish mail steamers shall pay tonnage in accordance with their special contracts with the government.

12. All steamers not coming within schedules 9, 10, and 11, shall pay tonnage, according to flag and place of departure, deducting the number of tons occupied by the engine and coal-bunkers from the total tonnage.

PORTUGUESE DOMINIONS.

LISBON—C. A. MUNRO, *Consul.*

DECEMBER 31, 1863.

Statement showing the description and value of the exports of Lisbon to New York, and where produced, during the quarter ended December 31, 1863.

(Compiled from an official document.)

EXPORTS.		
Production.	Where produced.	Value, including costs and charges.
12 hogsheads and 20 fifths pipes white wine...	Portugal	£200 0 0
14......do ......65....do........do......	Portugal	400 0 0
33 bags orchil, or archil	Portuguese Possessions	Rs 56,800
26 bags black wool........................	Portugal	615,000
149 bags unwashed wool....................	Portugal	4,524,000

Statement showing the description and value of the exports of Lisbon, where produced, and whither sent, during the quarter ended March 31, 1864.

(Compiled from an official document.)

EXPORTS.

Whither sent.	Production.	Where produced.	Value, including costs and charges.
New York..	1 case, 42 bottles, sherry wine, and 1 case with 36 bottles Oporto wine....	Spain and Portugal..	Reis. 81,400
Philadelphia	8 quarter casks and 8 octaves with wine.	Portugal	£96 0 0
New York..	40 bags white and 60 bags of black wool.	....do..............	Rs. 2,021,400
	24 bags archil.......................	Portuguese colonies.	563,040
	5 pipes and 25 fifths pipes red wine and 1 hogshead geropiga	Portugal	£190 0 0
	7 pipes and 25 fifths pipes white wine..	....do..............	240 0 0
	119 bags corks, 531 bundles white and 1 parcel black corkwood	....do..............	1,395 2 0
	148 moyos salt and 18 packages gum copal	Portuguese colonies.	Rs. 716,000
	318 bundles and 1 parcel corkwood....	Portugal	£527 3 9
	58 bags black and 150 bags white wool.	....do..............	Rs. 6,205,480
	134 moyos salt	....do..............	259,000
	10 barrels of white Lisbon wine........	....do..............	150,000
	97 bags of unwashed wool	....do..............	2,636,000
	4 barrels containing argols	....do..............	350,000
	13 barrels, 16 bags, and 2 cases gum ..	Portuguese colonies.	457,188
	100 bundles corkwood	Portugal	$458 95
	414 moyos salt and 1,190 mats....... ..	....do..............	Rs. 486,900
	42 bags black and 2 sacks white wool..	....do..............	903,660
	50 bundles corkwood	....do..............	$195 30
	44 ..do......do......	....do..............	184 24
	18 sacks .....do......	....do..............	162 20
	50 bundles ...do......	....do..............	Rs. 231,129
	81 bags wool	....do..............	1,877,495
	35 bundles corkwood	....do..............	277,830
	60 bundles corkwood and 22 bags corks.	....do..............	677,497
	140 packages of gum	....do..............	875,065
	88 bags of wool......................	....do..............	4,317,200
	16 bundles of corkwood...............	....do..............	289,400
	1 barrel red Lisbon wine	....do..............	£7 1 0
	26 bales of corks....................	....do..............	78 18 3
	580 bundles of corkwood, 6 bales do. in pieces, and 377 bags of corks.....	....do..............	2,217 16 7
	36 bags of wool.....................	....do..............	$418 36
	20 barrels and 4 boxes containing white Lisbon wine......................	....do..............	£124 10 0
	31 moyos of salt in bulk	....do..............	Rs. 55,955
	123 balks timber	Brazil	810,022

St. Paul de Loando—John T. Bradberry, *Commercial Agent.*

DECEMBER 31, 1863.

   *   *   *   I have the honor to state that clearing vessels from this port is a perplexing operation. First, notice of eight days must be given; second, a bond with two sureties (merchants) in the sum of four thousand milreis francos ($2,675 59,) must be entered into as a guarantee that the vessel will not engage in the slave trade. This is well where suspicion attaches to any vessel, but it is exacted indiscriminately previous to granting a clearance, not that there is

any fear that a well-known vessel will engage in the slave trade, but that the merchants who sign the bonds may realize the fee, which is forty-five pounds, or one hundred and twenty-five dollars, for so doing.   *   *   *

The merchants established here sign the bond for each other, but an American vessel arriving here for the first time encounters much trouble and expense in consequence of such bond.

She must also select a consignee, if not previously consigned, which obliges her to pay a further sum of one hundred milreis a mark-bancos, or $66 66⅔.

*   *   *   I have not succeeded in obtaining a copy of duties on imports for this province. The present duties are based upon the tariff law of 1842, modified for colonial purposes, but I have the assurance that on the first of February next a new tariff will be published, based on the tariff of 1863, with colonial modifications, which will, I understand, increase the duties on both imports and exports. I will forward it as soon as possible.

At Benguela, Messamidis, and Loando, duties must be paid; all other trading stations are free.

I feel it to be my duty to mention the fact that the iron lighters here, belonging to the government, are nearly valueless, being rusted through in many places. Cargoes that would sink (coal, for instance) cannot be transported in them with safety. In fact, they are not well adapted to this navigation either in model or material. Lighters for this harbor should be of wood, forty-five to fifty feet long, and coppered—the models such as are used at Havre de Grace, Maryland—very strong, cheap, light draught of water, burdensome, easily managed, and will sail well when sail is put upon them. I have no doubt such lighters could be sent here—all parts precisely fitted, and put together here—for one thousand dollars each. I am informed that freights alone on one of these lighters now here amounted to twelve hundred dollars, and her term of service has been very short. For two years last past, trade with the interior has been much obstructed in consequence of a war between the Portuguese and the King (Guga) of Cassango, one of the most powerful potentates of the interior of Africa, and whose dominions border on the Portuguese possessions. On the 29th of August last a treaty of peace was entered into between the belligerents, the Guga of Cassango agreeing to pay the whole expenses of the war. On the 26th of September the ambassador of the Guga was received at the palace of the governor general, when the treaty was ratified; in consequence, it is expected that trade with the interior will revive and importation increase.

Our own unhappy civil war has a very depressing effect upon American trade here, in consequence of the high price of cotton, heretofore the most profitable article of American manufacture imported into this country; also an important auxiliary to all other articles of sale or barter. Under present circumstances the English, who have only one house here, sell goods for at least 30 per cent. less than the same article can be bought for in the United States.

   *   *   *   *   *

DECEMBER 31, 1863.

Export duties, &c.

		Duty.
Almude of palm oil (34 pounds)		$0 03
" peanut oil "		5
" fish oil "		3
Arroba of beeswax (32 pounds)		8
" hides, dry, "		1½
" copper, old, "		½
" copper ore, "		24

	Duty.
Cotton	free.
Ivory, under 25 pounds, each pound	$0 02
" 25 pounds and upwards	3
Cazingale of peanuts (28 pounds)	3
Arroba of urzula, a red dye, (32 pounds)	27
" gum copal, (32 pounds)	1⅔
" coffee, (32 pounds)	5

Local duty on imports, 3 per cent. on amount of invoice.

Other expenses.

Cooperage, average on 1 pipe, (950 pounds)	$1 67
Porterage, average on 1 pipe, (950 pounds)	20
Bags, capacity of 1 arroba (32 pounds)	20
" straw " "	9

Exchange, freights, &c.

England, naval and commercial, none, par.
Lisbon, " " " "
Paris, " " "
Hamburg " " "
United States, commercial 15 per cent.
Brokerage, none.
Commission on sales, 5 per cent.
" on returns, 4 per cent.
" on sales and returns, guaranteed, 10 per cent.

Freights—England, on coal, £1 12*s.*; on merchandise, £3; United States, no fixed rates, worth about the same as English—say, on coal, $8; on merchandise, $15.

Custom-house, port, and provincial charges at St. Paul de Loando for an American vessel of three hundred and one tons register.

Register of entry	$1 07
Bill of health, per ton, 1⅓ cent; visa, per ton, ⅔ cent	3 33⅓
Certificates, necessary to be obtained: Of entry, 41 cents; of bond, $1 87; of clearance, 41 cents	2 69
Custom-house guards on board: two men, each 26⅔ cents; in some cases only one man—40 days while in port	21 34
Each boat load of cargo bonded, (about 15 tons per load,) 33⅓ cents, 300 tons of cargo	67 00
Entrance and clearance, both included	5 34
Hospital fees, obligatory: Each officer, up to two, $2: each sailor, $1 34—twelve men, all told	17 40
Pilotage in and out	8 57
Tonnage fee in secretary's office: 50 tons and under, 67 cents; 50 to 100 tons, $1 34; 100 to 200 tons, $2 01; 200 to 300 tons, $2 68; over 300 tons, $5 36; 301 tons	5 36
Stamps upon papers used: Official bill, 4¼ cents; hospital bill, 4¼ cents; bill of health, 4¼ cents; clearance, 4¼ cents	17
Broker's fees, (obliged to employ one,) clearing vessel, $5; making manifest of outward cargo or in ballast, $2	7 00
Consignment fees, (obligatory:) Each master (3) $66 66⅔ to procure signers to bond not to engage in the slave trade, $217 80	417 80

his consignee.. $662 94
Total cost with permanent consignee, who is an established merchant,
signing bond reciprocal 245 14

Sand is the only ballast to be obtained here, and costs eighty-eight cents a
ton, (launch hire included.) Launch hire, for loading and unloading cargo, is
about eight dollars a day for each one employed.

---

* MACAO—W. P. JONES, *Consul.*

SEPTEMBER 30, 1864.

I have the honor to submit my annual report for the year closing as above.
Macao is a short, irregular, narrow peninsula of the great island of Keang-Shan,
constituting almost the entire southwestern shore of the Gulf of Sintin, (the
estuary of the Canton or Pearl river.) A flat sandy isthmus, more than a mile
long, though scarcely forty paces broad, connects it with the main island.
Across the middle of this isthmus lie the ruins of an ancient barrier wall,
marking the Portuguese limits. The city is situated in north latitude 22° 12′,
longitude 113° 31′ east from Greenwich, and is thus almost due south from
Canton, distant about ninety miles, and due west from Hong-Kong some forty
miles. Immediately west of it the great West river (Si-Kiang) enters the sea
freighted with immense traffic, which should find here its most natural communication with foreign commerce. Under present restrictions but a small portion
of it comes hither, and that, for the most part, illicitly. This grand island of
Keang-Shan, lying between the wealth-laden Canton and West rivers, and
upon the sea, should certainly, under good government, become the Manhattan
of southern China.

Situated barely within the northern tropic, a picturesque promontory pro-
jecting boldly into the sea, and fanned by the southwest and northwest mon-
soons, Macao enjoys a salubrious and generally delightful climate that renders
it the sanitarium of China. The equability of the temperature is remarkable;
the mercury never, so far as I have experienced, rising to above Fahrenheit
100° in the shade, or falling below 36°. The mean maximum (in a series of
years) for July, the warmest month, was 87°; the minimum for January, the
coldest month, 46°.

Geologically, Macao, like all the southern coast of China, belongs to the
primitive formation, presenting seven unwooded, barren-faced hills, composed
of a coarse disintegrated feldspathic granite, cut vertically by numerous parallel quartz veins of from one to fifteen inches thick, crossing the entire peninsula in right lines from northeast to southwest. This rotten granite is easily
dug with pickaxe and spade, and gullied by the rains, which latter, carrying
down the decaying feldspar into what was once, no doubt, a tide-water bay,
have, with the joint action of the West river depositing here its rich alluvium,
created a low basin of, perhaps, 600 acres area of exceeding fertile land, which,
until very lately, has been for centuries the one spot for European garden produce in all China.

The entire population of the Macao peninsula, by calculation based on a late
census, is estimated at 105,800—classed as Europeans, 800; Creoles and Mesti-
zos, 5,000; Chinese, 100,000.

With such a climate and such a system of manuring as produce four crops
per year, it is still wonderful what an amount these frugal and industrious natives gather from the small area of arable land within this petty territory.

Of course Macao is too insignificant in extent to render its agricultural products of any commercial importance. Like Hong-Kong, this is a consuming, not a producing colony—a mere coast station for distribution into and collection of exports from China proper; as such its market abounds with all the fruits and staples of this fertile tropical clime, from the neighboring shores and island, while its own gardens supply it bountifully with European vegetables, and contribute of the same to the markets of Hong-Kong and the open ports north.

The industrial energies of Macao are employed principally as follows, viz: In drying, sorting, firing, and boxing tea, (a large business;) preparing aniseseed and cassia, and their oils, for exportation, (bottling and casing it;) in gold beating and sugar refining; in making Chinese cigarettes for the coast and straits trade, (a large business;) making vermilion, umbrellas, fire-crackers, incense sticks, camphor-wood trunks, desks, and bureaus, bamboo and ratan work. It is impossible to ascertain the amount of capital invested in these employments; but it is safe to say they engage fully one-fifth of the Chinese population, or about 20,000 persons.

In the early part of the seventeenth century, immediately preceding the exclusion of foreigners from Japan, the commercial prosperity of Macao excited the wonder and envy of all Europe. Many of the mansions of the merchant princes of those days, almost palatial in their extent, still remain to attest the opulence of their first masters, and maintain some air, at least, of the city's ancient importance and glory.

It cannot be denied that the impolicy of the Macao authorities in persistently demanding heavy import and export levies, long after they had good reason to know that these very duties were impelling the English and other traders to run the risks of smuggling rather than submit, had much to do with hastening and aggravating their misfortune. On the other hand, the existing abolition of all imposts, the extreme liberality of the present authorities, together with low rents and exemption from taxes, the much greater security to life and propert here than in the other China ports, (under the superior police force and regula tions of this colony,) are now promising to effect a favorable reaction in its favor. Since the closing of the custom-house little or no effort has been made to collect the statistics of trade, until since the accession of the present governor. Since the first of January last all masters of vessels have been required to furnish the captain of the port manifests of inward and outward cargoes, with estimated value. Of course, while the Macao government has no direct pecuniary interest in the correctness of these figures, and the jealousies of merchants induce them to conceal their transactions from each other, the manifests can be regarded as mere approximations, much below the actual values. From these data, to which the truth would, I am fully persuaded, add at least a third, we learn that the imports, during the first six months of 1864, amounted to—

In foreign-rigged vessels	$3,336,296
Chinese junks.......................................	379,358
Total imports for the half year.....................	3,715,554

Or, at an average rate of seven and a half millions per annum; being three times the imports of all China in 1815–'16, and twice the same of 1825–'26.
The exports for the same period amounted to—

In foreign-rigged vessels	$2,302,097
Chinese junks.......................................	207,982
	2,510,079

Or, an average rate of above five millions per annum; being more than the exports of all China in 1830 or any year previous that I find reported, except 1805, which were about the same. So that, were the profits of this trade what they once were, Macao might still be opulent.

The inner harbor of Macao is one of the safest havens on the China coast, being perfectly land-locked, but, unfortunately, a sand-bar renders its entrance impossible to vessels of heavy burden. The Macao roads are entirely safe and commodious, but some four miles distant, which, when a high sea is running, proves a serious disadvantage. His excellency the present governor promises to dredge the bar hindering entrance to the inner harbor, which it is hoped will be accomplished at an early day.

There is no American capital employed at Macao except in merchandising, and this is done at present principally through agents of firms at Hong-Kong, what direct American trade may have hitherto existed at Macao having been totally arrested by the accidents of war. The purchases of American houses made at this port during the preceding year probably reached the sum of $350,000, entirely for European trade, or, if for shipment to the United States, to be delivered at Hong-Kong, whence they were invoiced. I have no doubt that, would several enterprising American firms, taking advantage of the present liberal policy of this government, resolve to establish houses at Macao, they might transact a very profitable business.

Tabular statement showing the nationality, tonnage, and number of vessels, with their crews, and aggregate value of their cargoes, entered at the port of Macao during the first six months of the year 1864.

Nationality.	WITH CARGO.			IN BALLAST.			TOTAL.			Value.
	No.	Tons.	Crews.	No.	Tons.	Crews	No.	Tons.	Crews.	
Austrian	....	....	....	1	763	19	1	763	19	....
Bremen	1	314	14	....	....	....	1	314	14	$18,421
Belgian	....	....	....	1	832	21	1	832	21	....
Chilian	....	....	....	1	301	11	1	301	11	....
Dutch	3	729	74	4	887	69	7	1,616	143	30,109
Danish	5	1,327	57	2	454	18	7	1,781	75	55,916
British	13	5,217	205	4	2,471	137	17	7,688	342	2,515,359
French	6	2,237	93	3	1,082	25	9	3,319	118	96,473
Hamburg	11	2,626	194	5	1,196	64	16	3,822	188	207,708
Oldenburg	1	322	12	1	340	14	2	662	26	22,000
Peruvian	1	1,215	24	5	2,402	78	6	3,617	102	95,000
Portuguese	4	912	88	2	696	17	6	1,608	105	65,896
Prussian	1	380	11	1	200	10	2	580	21	10,700
Siamese	1	250	20	....	....	....	1	250	20	111,242
Swedish	1	268	11	1	206	11	2	474	22	20,102
Spanish	20	4,988	371	4	1,411	73	24	6,399	444	87,380
Chinese junks	....	....	....	....	....	....	....	....	....	379,358
Total	68	20,785	1,104	35	13,241	567	103	34,026	1,671	3,715,654

Tabular statement showing the nationality, tonnage, and number of vessels, with their crews, and aggregate value of their cargoes, cleared from the port of Macao during the first six months of the year 1864.

Nationality.	WITH CARGO.			IN BALLAST.			TOTAL.			Value.
	No.	Tons.	Crews.	No.	Tons.	Crews	No.	Tons.	Crews.	
Austrian	1	763	19				1	763	19	
Bremen				1	314	14	1	314	14	
Chilian	1	301	11				1	301	11	
Danish	3	539	30	3	777	33	6	1,316	63	
Dutch	6	1,617	106	1	350	15	7	1,967	121	
English	8	3,707	210	4	1,117	46	12	4,824	256	
French	5	1,581	69	2	788	29	7	2,369	96	
Hamburg	6	1,935	83	7	1,432	75	13	3,367	158	
Oldenburg	2	662	26				2	662	26	
Peruvian	9	4,071	148				9	4,071	148	
Portuguese	3	2,181	73				3	2,181	73	
Prussian	1	200	10				1	200	10	
Siamese	1	297	32				1	297	32	
Swedish	1	206	11				1	206	11	
Spanish	9	2,400	174	8	1,964	179	17	4,364	353	
Total	56	20,460	1,002	26	6,742	391	82	27,202	1,393	2,510,079

Comparative statement showing the aggregate number of vessels and their crews, together with their tonnage, arrived at and departed from the port of Macao during the years 1860, 1861, 1862, 1863, and 1864.

Years.	ARRIVED.			DEPARTED.		
	Number of vessels.	Number of crews.	Tonnage.	Number of vessels.	Number of crews.	Tonnage.
1860	287	5,513	104,613	298	5,898	120,398
1861	231	4,245	84,992	220	4,469	94,145
1862	195	3,333	75,819	198	3,619	75,422
1863	172	2,809	63,280	171	2,854	62,075
1864 *	206	3,342	68,052	164	2,786	54,404
Total	1,091	19,242	396,756	1,041	19,626	406,444
Average 5 years	218⅕	3,848⅖	79,351⅕	208⅕	3,925⅕	81,288⅘

* By doubling the returns sent you for the first six months.

Statement showing the number of coolies shipped from Macao during several eight months of the year 1863, with their respective ports of destination.

Months.	Port of destination.	Number.
January	Callao, 925; Havana, 256	1,181
February	Havana	121
March	do	373
April	Callao	317
August	do	132
October	Havana, 638; Callao, 700	1,338
November	Callao, 424; Havana, 926	1,350
December	Havana, 608; Callao, 1,240	1,848
	Total	6,660

Statement showing the average market price of imports and exports at Macao during the year 1864.

IMPORTS.

Opium, New Patna	$5 02
Malwah	6 26
New Benares	4 40
Turkey	5 24
Cotton, Shanghai	$27\frac{1}{2}$
Ningpo	28
Rice, Bengal, new cargo	3
Bengal, old cargo	$2\frac{82}{100}$
Java and Saigon, cargo	$2\frac{94}{100}$
Java and Saigon, old	$2\frac{94}{100}$
Yloe, new	$2\frac{94}{100}$
Yloe, old	$2\frac{78}{100}$
Siam, new	$2\frac{84}{100}$
Siam, old	$2\frac{90}{100}$
Bassein, Rangoon, and Aracan	$2\frac{10}{100}$
Bassein, Rangoon, and Aracan, old	$2\frac{45}{100}$
Pepper, white, per picul	12 00
black, per picul	7 25
Betelnut, new, per picul	3 40
old, per picul	3 00
Ratan, Benzemissing, per picul	3 50
Straits, per picul	3 10
Sapanwood, Siam, per picul	2 25
Manila, per picul	1 75
Sulphur, per picul	2 00
Saltpetre, per picul	11 00
Gunpowder, superfine, per pound	20
coarse, per 20-pound keg	3 50
Tin, Banca, per picul	28 00
Straits, per picul	27 00
Pig lead, per picul	6 00
Quicksilver, per picul	68 00
Alum, per picul	2 60
Tea, per picul	$32 70 to 37 50
Flour, California, per barrel	8 40
Beef, per barrel	$16 00 to 20 00
Pork, per barrel	$25 00 to 30 00
Yellow peas, per picul	2 30
Black dates, per picul	5 75
Silk, per picul	420 00
Nos. 16 to 24 cotton yarn, per pound	2 30
No. 56 white shirtings, per bolt	4 50
Tury, red, per bolt	3 00
Plain crape, per bolt	6 20
Assorted crape, per bolt	14 50
S. S. assorted camlets, per bolt	22 50
Assorted lasting, per bolt	19 50
H. H. long ells, per bolt	8 50
Black velvet of 22 inches	30 cts. to 1 00

EXPORTS.

No. 1 white sugar, per picul	$8 50
No. 2 white sugar, per picul	7 25
Cassia, per picul	16 25
Cassia oil, per picul	206 00
Star anise-seed, per picul	19 00
Star anise-seed oil, per picul	150 00
Galangal, per picul	1 85
Vermilion, per 50-ctts. box	35 00
Copper cash, per picul	17 00
Gold-leaf, per tael weight	22 70

OPORTO—HENRY W. DIMAN, *Consul.*

APRIL 7, 1864.

*   *   *   *   *   *   *   *   *

I beg to state to the department that no American vessels have sailed or entered this port during the past quarter, the trade with America having been carried on in vessels under the Portuguese, Norwegian, and Italian flags.

DECEMBER 31, 1864.

I have the honor to transmit herewith my annual report on the trade and commerce of Oporto for the year ended September 30, 1864.

* * * General trade in Oporto is in a flourishing condition, and the city is increasing in wealth and population every year. The census of the city, taken on the first of January, 1864, shows a population of 97,796, without including the suburbs, which being added shows a total of 141,408.

The commerce of the place, although quite extensive, as shown by the annexed tables, would doubtless be much greater were it not for the exceedingly dangerous, and oftentimes impassable, bar at the mouth of the Douro. Large sums of money have been expended by the government, and the best engineering talent employed, but thus far all endeavors to improve it have proved fruitless. At the present time surveys are being made near Seca, about four miles north of the mouth of the river, in reference to a contemplated harbor of refuge. But it is found that the outlay would be too great to warrant the undertaking.

The steam traffic is constantly increasing, there being at present regular steamers plying between this port and London, Bristol, Liverpool, Glasgow, Dublin, and Nantes, and a line is about being established to Havre.

During the past year the railway between Oporto and Lisbon, distance about two hundred miles, has been opened to the public, thus giving daily communication with the capital, a wonderful advance on the old lumbering stage coach or diligence, which was 36 hours in making the journey. When the railway is completed between Madrid and Badajos, Oporto will be in communication with all Europe. With this great improvement, of course, comes the usual stimulating influences to trade and commerce which such advances are in all countries sure to effect.

Fine macadamized roads are being constructed throughout the country, especially in the northern provinces. Bridges are being built, and other and more important improvements are in contemplation.

The following is a statement of the revenue collected at the Oporto custom-house during the four years ended June 30, 1864:

1861	82, 296, 362
1862	2, 574, 750
1863	2, 742, 980
1864	2, 902, 960

The statistics of emigration from this port are not so exact as they might be, there being no distinction made between those who leave the country with the intention of remaining abroad and those who go away on business or for pleasure with the intention of returning. During the year 1863, 3,709 passengers left this port for Brazil, the larger part, if not all of them, going as emigrants.

The wine trade, which far exceeds in importance all other branches of commerce, and the shipments of which constitute more than three-quarters of all the exports from the Douro, is fast recovering from the influence of the vine disease which a few years ago threatened to be as fatal to the vineyards of the Upper Douro as it was to those of Madeira. Greater care in cultivation, and a general use of sulphur as a remedy against the disease, have had the effect of increasing the crops, so that the exportation has increased from 16,690 pipes in 1858 to 35,619 pipes in 1864. The odious and unpopular laws regulating the cultivation and exportation of wine still exist, but it is anticipated that the new Cortez, which meets in January, will make some important modifications in the present laws.

In my despatch of August 17, I transmitted a royal decree permitting, for a specified term, the importation of foreign cereals on deposit. Many merchants, both here and in other countries, acting on the supposition that the first decree would be followed by a second, admitting the grain so imported for consumption, imported large quantities of cereals, but up to the present time none has been allowed to be entered for that purpose. Since the issuing of that decree ten cargoes of flour and wheat have been imported from the United States, some of which has been re-exported to the Brazils and other countries, but most of it still remains here on deposit. The importers and owners have suffered very heavy losses in consequence of this delay of government in not allowing the grain to be admitted. The new Cortez meets on the 2d of January, and it is supposed that during the session a law permitting the importation of foreign cereals at a fixed duty will be passed.

The most important legislation during the past year affecting the interests of commerce was the abolition of the tobacco monopoly, commonly known as the "tobacco contract." For upwards of 250 years the importation and sale of tobacco and its products in Portugal have been a monopoly. It was first sold at the rate of $47 per annum, and from this trifling sum it has gone on increasing until the year 1864, when the monopoly was sold for the enormous sum of $1,640,000. And at this high rate the profits of the company were said to have been very great; and the country was furnished, as might be supposed, with tobacco at a very high price, and of a very poor quality. This law abolishing the monopoly was passed in May last, and goes into effect on the 1st of January, 1865.

The following are its principal provisions as affecting foreign commerce: The importation, manufacture, and sale of tobacco are declared free to all. The cultivation of tobacco is prohibited on the main land of the kingdom, but is permitted in the islands. The importation of tobacco can only take place through the custom-houses of Lisbon or Oporto. The duties levied on its importation are as follows:

For tobacco in the roll, per kilogramme of 8 ounces .... 1,100 reis.
      in the leaf   "   "   .... 1,300 "
      in cigars .... 2,000 "
      in all other forms, per kilogramme of 8 ounces ..... 1,600 "

Trade between Oporto and the United States during the past year has been dull. This is owing in part to the war, but more especially to the present high tariff on goods which are exported from this point. There is reason, however, to believe that the free importation of tobacco, and the probable passage of a permanent law admitting cereals, will, with the re-establishment of peace at home, largely increase the American trade at this port.

A summary statement of exports from Oporto for the fiscal years 1860-'61 and 1861-'62 in reis.

Description.	1861-'62.	1860-'61.
	Value.	Value.
Live animals	374,486,000	383,207,100
Hides, hoofs, &c	101,929,300	116,006,300
Fish..	3,194,000	1,980,200
Wool and skins	132,422,000	239,159,500
Silks	39,241,000	52,692,800
Cottons	81,733,000	23,981,350
Linen	33,196,800	34,858,360
Timber and wood...................................	93,042,800	90,296,060
Farinaceous products...............................	78,945,800	68,095,280
Colonial products	11,531,600	14,898,540
Fruits, seeds, &c	221,867,400	171,006,390
Metals	323,044,400	435,560,820
Minerals	5,171,000	2,528,240
Wines and liquors..................................	4,441,379,600	4,338,510,500
Glass, pottery	8,018,300	11,939,990
Paper and its various fabrics......................	5,807,000	4,923,440
Chemical products..................................	79,930,000	63,686,000
Sundry articles.....................................	8,654,500	8,156,000
Various manufactures	50,003,600	46,641,600
Total	6,093,598,100	6,128,128,470

A summary statement of imports into Oporto for the fiscal years 1860–'61 *and* 1861–'62.

Description.	1861–'62. Value.	1860–'61. Value.
	Reis.	*Reis.*
Live animals	1,858,500	3,164,600
Fish and their products.	551,678,900	849,562,455
Wool and skins	598,892,470	514,871,440
Hides, hoops, &c.	432,107,500	385,171,136
Silk	307,230,000	339,376,940
Cotton	1,633,727,500	1,747,710,125
Linen	387,802,500	374,149,525
Timber and lumber	256,830,300	113,267,695
Farinaceous products	682,352,000	299,203,230
Colonial products	1,022,072,000	1,092,492,805
Seeds, fruits, and plants	81,344,700	75,896,360
Metals	914,835,558	922,176,015
Minerals	439,490,500	205,986,705
Liquors	1,180,326,520	682,370,945
Pottery and glassware.	85,939,150	76,168,050
Paper and its various fabrics	51,364,700	48,117,710
Chemical products	76,638,790	92,434,805
Various manufactures	167,316,280	161,957,250
Sundry articles	64,450,100	56,793,215
Total	8,936,258,268	8,040,863,006

Statement showing the number of vessels entered and cleared the ports of the Oporto consular district during the year 1863.

Ports.	ENTERED.			CLEARED.		
	No. vessels.	No. vessels.	Total.	No. vessels.	No. vessels.	Total.
	Portuguese.	*Foreign.*		*Portuguese.*	*Foreign.*	
Oporto	753	359	1,112	749	369	1,118
Caminha	91	2	93	87	2	89
Vianna	152	25	177	151	26.	177
Esposenda.	49	2	51	49	2.	51
Povoa	10		10	10		10
Villa do Conde	62	2	64	67	2	69
Aveiro	371	17	388	381	17.	398
Figueira	374	48	422	372	46	418
Total	1,862	455	2,317	1,866	464	2,330

Statement showing the number and class of vessels owned in Oporto, with their tonnage, January 1, 1864.

Class.	Number.	Tonnage.
Ships	13	6,627
Barks..	44	12,875
Brigs	11	2,319
Schooners...	15	2,440
Luggers	1	97
Hiates	23	2,521
Rascas...	4	390
Steamers..	2	140
Total	113	27,409

Statement showing the number, nationality, and tonnage of vessels cleared from the port of Oporto during the years 1861-'62-'63.

Nationality.	1861.		1862.		1863.	
	No. of vessels.	Tonnage.	No. of vessels.	Tonnage.	No. of vessels.	Tonnage.
America	4	852	12	2,841	7	2,481
Belgium	1	146	....	......	....	......
Brazil	6	1,249	6	1,295	6	1,204
Denmark.....................	3	362	4	310	3	402
France	2	155	4	589	23	4,056
Hanover	2	226	15	1,661	10	1,062
Spain	10	966	28	4,505	23	2,361
Holland......................	16	1,777	32	3,853	20	2,030
England......................	187	50,547	177	58,219	233	62,206
Norway	5	636	....	......	2	333
Oldenburgh	....	......	3	334	....	......
Portugal	712	108,074	626	94,512	749	99,860
Prussia	6	1,460	3	962	5	1,076
Russia	10	1,763	12	3,366	20	4,270
Sweden	10	1,883	16	2,843	12	2,036
Turkey	....	......	....	......	1	100
Total	974	170,096	938	175,290	1,114	183,479

Statement showing the annual exportation of port wine at Oporto to the United States from 1809 to 1864 inclusive.

Years.	Pipes.	Years.	Pipes.	Years.	Pipes.	Years.	Pipes.
1809	140	1823	115	1837	860	1851	3,933
1810	....	1824	648	1838	2,628	1852	4,452
1811	64	1825	344	1839	3,471	1853	1,658
1812	162	1826	473	1840	1,400	1854	326
1813	13	1827	337	1841	1,164	1855	683
1814	....	1828	787	1842	1,005	1856	1,813
1815	176	1829	361	1843	647	1857	439
1816	677	1830	327	1844	3,591	1858	193
1817	71	1831	206	1845	3,241	1859	424
1818	122	1832	858	1846	3,628	1860	398
1819	36	1833	418	1847	2,383	1861	57
1820	181	1834	206	1848	5,174	1862	150
1821	216	1835	2,745	1849	4,921	1863	143
1822	20	1836	1,363	1850	6,220	1864	131

Statement showing the quantity of port wine exported from Oporto during the years 1861, 1862, 1863, and 1864, also the countries where shipped.

Countries.	1861.	1862.	1863.	1864.
	Pipes.	Pipes.	Pipes.	Pipes.
Australia	631	1,064	294	....
Belgium	....	2	....	....
Brazil	1,735	2,079	2,746	3,331
Canada	135	221	234	415
Hanseatic cities	244	562	476	620
Denmark	101	191	222	87
United States	57	150	142	131
France	17	20	57	38
Gibraltar			4	8
Great Britain	22,955	24,843	30,044	29,942
Spain	2	1	49	1
Holland	68	69	101	138
Montevideo	1		15	22
Italy	....	....	¼	... .
Nova Scotia	150	5	7	246
Prussia	11	2	¼	... .
Portugal and possessions	237	233	313	263
Russia	176	51	68	83
Sweden and Norway	281	142	79	190
Newfoundland	96	64	45	98
Total	26,897	29,699	34,836¼	35,616

Statement showing the description and value of the exports of Oporto, where produced, and whither sent, during the quarter ended March 31, 1864, (compiled from an official document.)

Whither sent.	Production.	Where produced.	Value, including costs and charges.
New York...........	Corks and cork wood	Portugal...........	$8,583 18
Do.............	Crude argols	....do.............	4,265 97
Do.............	Dried fruit	....do.............	195 65
Do.............	Almonds....................	....do.............	102 72
Do.............	Port wine....................	....do.............	11,164 17
San Francisco	Port wine....................	....do.............	454 96
Total...........	....	....	24,766 65

FAYAL—C. W. DABNEY, *Consul.*

Statement showing the imports and exports at the port of Fayal during the quarter ended December 31, 1863.

IMPORTS.

Great Britain :
Coal, goods, tea, sugar, liquors, soap, iron, spices, &c...... 8,814,400

Lisbon, St. Michael's, Terceira, Gracioza, St. Jorge, and Flores :
Dry goods, liquors, furniture, tobacco, olive oil, grain, paper, iron work, sundries, &c............................. `53,930,190

United States :
Lumber, grain, coal, provisions, oils, glass, furniture, and sundries 11,035,000

Production of whale fishery :
Sperm oil, common oil................................. 34,387,200

108,166,790

EXPORTS.

Great Britain :
Fruit, old metal, and sundries 14,056,850

Lisbon, St. Michael's, Terceira, Gracioza, St. Jorge, and Flores :
Butter, iron work, liquor, spices, coffee, sugar, old metal, glass, paper, tobacco, sundries...................... 19,610,430

United States :
Sperm oil, straw hats, braid, old ropes.................. 60,533,140

94,200,420

Statement showing the description and value of the exports of Fayal, produced at Fayal, and the places where shipped, during the quarter ended March 31, 1864.

Where shipped.	Productions.	Value.
New Bedford	Fruit, baskets, &c	118,750
Philadelphia	Fruit	236,200
Boston	Straw hats and braid	551,230
Do	Straw hats and aloe work, &c	2,067,440
Do	Yellow metal baskets, fruit, &c	353,460
Total reis		3,327,080

Statement showing the description and value of imports and exports at the port of Fayal, together with the names of the countries or places whence or where shipped, during the quarter ended March 31, 1864.

IMPORTS.

Countries or places.	Description.	Value.
Great Britain	Coal, goods, teas, sugar, soap, paint, liquors, iron, and sundries	31,643,000
Lisbon, St. Michael's, St. Jorge, Terceira, Gracioza, and Flores.	Goods, grain, tobacco, paper, brandy, wine, olive oil, iron-work, hides, furniture, vegetables, and sundries	77,562,900
United States	Cheese and grain	1,896,700
Gibraltar	Corn	7,700,000
Whaling	Sperm oil	270,000
Total reis		119,072,600

EXPORTS.

Great Britain	Oranges and sperm oil	2,804,190
Lisbon, St. Michael's, St. Jorge, Terceira, Gracioza, and Flores.	Butter, old metal, goods, paper, tobacco, liquors, lumber, &c	20,747,140
United States	Sperm oil, oranges, straw hats, and sundries	76,675,150
Total reis		100,226,480

Statement showing the description and value of the imports and exports at the port of Fayal during the quarter ending June 30, 1864, together with the names of countries of production and destination.

IMPORTS.

Countries.	Description.	Value.
Great Britain..............	Coal and flax......................	331,140
St John's, N. B............	Lumber and hemp canvas	1,748,130
Lisbon, St. Michael's, Terceira, Gracioza, St. Jorge, Flores, and St. Maria.	Goods, tobacco, sugar, paper, liquors, olive oil, furniture, dried fruit, rice, vinegar, leather, grain, coarse earthenware, potatoes, lime, meat, and sundries.	47,127,420
United States..............	Soap, bread, iron work, vinegar, petroleum, matches, hams, glass, furniture, flour, leather, &c.	14,491,000
Teneriffe	Iron work, glass, whiskey, olive oil, and sundries.	244,500
	Total reis	63,942,190

EXPORTS.

Countries.	Description.	Value.
Lisbon, St. Michael's, Terceira, Gracioza, St. Jorge, and Flores.	Butter, tallow, crockery, glass, wine, hides, empty casks, lamps, goods, straw hats, coffee, cheese, tea, sugar, tobacco, iron work, gin, leather, salt, soap, flour, &c.	21,612,820
United States..............	1 piano, straw hats, wine, and sundries	2,105,500
Havre	Baskets, &c............................	90,000
	Total reis....................	23,808,320

Statement showing the description and value of the imports into and exports from Fayal during the quarter ending September 30, 1864, together with the names of the countries whence and where shipped.

IMPORTS.

Countries.	Description.	Value.
Great Britain..............	Coal, soap, cheese, paint, oil, ropes, corn, iron work, liquors, paper, tea, sugar, rice, dry goods, piano, and sundries.	27,840,000
Lisbon, St. Michael's, St. Maria, Terceira, Gracioza, St. Jorge, and Flores	Leather, soap, furniture, candles, crockery, corn, wheat, iron work, starch, limestone, flour, cheese, liquors, olive oil, petroleum, paper, medicines, dry goods, and sundries.	42,914,300
United States..............	Tea, corn, flour, bread, beef, pork, dry goods, blacking, clocks, glass, petroleum, starch, furniture, sundries, &c.	14,397,500
St. John's, N. B	Lumber, spars, and oak	3,650,000
Rio de Janeiro.............	Coffee, sugar, oars, rice, soap, and sundries..	2,415,600
Whaling	Sperm oil, common oil, and whalebone......	92,706,300
	Total reis....................	183,983,700

EXPORTS.

Countries.	Description.	Value.
Lisbon, St. Michael's, Terceira, Graciosa, St. Jorge, and Flores.	Hides, coffee, tea, sugar, flour, bread, vinegar, liquors, butter, cheese, straw hats, empty casks, ropes, matches, beef, soap, blacking, dry goods, paper, old metals, lumber, and sundries.	25,211,000
United States..............	Sperm oil, common oil, whalebone, clothing, cotton, straw hats, braid, &c.	84,190,000
		109,401,000*

BELGIUM.

TREATY WITH THE UNITED STATES.

Whereas a convention between the United States of America and his Majesty the King of the Belgians, to complete by new stipulations the treaty of commerce and navigation between the United States and Belgium, of the 17th of July, 1858, was concluded and signed by their respective plenipotentiaries, at Brussels, on the twentieth day of May, eighteen hundred and sixty-three, which convention, being in the English and French languages, is word for word as follows: [The English version only is here given.]

The President of the United States of America, on the one side, his Majesty the King of the Belgians on the other side, having deemed it advantageous to complete, by new stipulations, the treaty of commerce and navigation entered into by the United States and Belgium on the seventeenth day of July, eighteen hundred and fifty-eight, have resolved to make a convention in addition to that arrangement, and have appointed for their plenipotentiaries, namely:

The President of the United States, Henry Shelton Sanford, a citizen of the United States, their minister resident near his Majesty the King of the Belgians; his Majesty the King of the Belgians, the Sieur Charles Rogier, grand officer of the Order of Leopold, decorated with the iron cross, grand cross of the Order of the Ernestine Branch of Saxony, of the Polar Star of St. Maurice and St. Lazarus, of Our Lady of the Conception of Villa Vicosa, of the Legion of Honor, of the White Eagle, &c., a member of the Chamber of Representatives, his minister of foreign affairs; who, after having communicated to each other their full powers, found to be in good and proper form, have agreed upon the following articles:

ARTICLE I. From and after the day when the capitalization of the duties levied upon navigation in the Scheldt shall have been secured by a general arrangement—

1st. The tonnage dues levied in Belgian ports shall cease.

2d. Fees for pilotage in Belgian ports and in the Scheldt, in so far as it depends on Belgium, shall be reduced twenty per centum for sailing vessels, twenty-five per centum for vessels in tow, thirty per centum for steam vessels.

3d. Port dues and other charges levied by the city of Antwerp shall be throughout reduced.

ARTICLE II. In derogation to the ninth article of the treaty of the seventeenth of July, eighteen hundred and fifty-eight, the flag of the United States shall be assimilated to that of Belgium for the transportation of salt.

ARTICLE III. The tariff of import duties resulting from the treaty of the first of May, eighteen hundred and sixty-one, between Belgium and France, is extended to goods imported from the United States, on the same conditions with which it was extended to Great Britain by the treaty of the twenty-third of July, eighteen hundred and sixty-two.

The reduction made by the treaties entered into by Belgium with Switzerland on the eleventh of December, eighteen hundred and sixty-two, with Italy on the ninth of April, eighteen hundred and sixty-three, with the Netherlands on the twelfth of May, eighteen hundred and sixty-three, and also with France on the twelfth of May, eighteen hundred and sixty-three, shall be equally applied to goods imported from the United States.

It is agreed that Belgium shall also extend to the United States the reductions of import duties which may result from her subsequent treaties with other powers.

ARTICLE IV. The United States, in view of the proposition made by Belgium to regulate, by a common accord, the capitalization of the Scheldt dues, consents to contribute to this capitalization under the following conditions:

A. The capital sum shall not exceed thirty-six millions of francs.

B. Belgium shall assume for its part one-third of that amount.

C. The remainder shall be apportioned among the other states, pro rata to their navigation in the Scheldt.

D. The proportion of the United States, to be determined in accordance with this rule, shall not exceed the sum of two millions seven hundred and seventy-nine thousand two hundred francs.

E. The payment of the said proportion shall be made in ten annual instalments of equal amount, which shall include the capital and the interest on the portion remaining unpaid at the rate of four per centum.

The first instalment shall be payable at Brussels, on the first day of April, eighteen hundred and sixty-four, or immediately after the Congress of the United States shall have made the requisite appropriation. In either event, the interest shall commence to run on the date of the first of April, eighteen hundred and sixty-four, above mentioned.

The government of the United States reserves the right of anticipating the payment of the proportion of the United States.

The above-mentioned conditions for the capitalization of the Scheldt dues shall be inserted in a general treaty, to be adopted by a conference of the maritime states interested, and in which the United States shall be represented.

ARTICLE V. The articles I and IV of the present additional convention shall be perpetual; and the remaining articles shall, together with the treaty of commerce and navigation made between the high contracting parties on the seventeenth of July, eighteen hundred and fifty-eight, have the same force and duration as the treaties mentioned in article III.

The ratifications thereof shall be exchanged with the least possible delay.

In faith whereof, the respective plenipotentiaries have signed the present convention, and have affixed thereto their seals.

Made in duplicate, and signed at Brussels the twentieth day of May, eighteen hundred and sixty-three.

H. S. SANFORD. [SEAL.]
CH. ROGIER. [SEAL.]

And whereas the said convention has been duly ratified on both parts, and the respective ratifications of the same were exchanged at Brussels on the twenty-fourth of June last:

Now, therefore, be it known, that I, Abraham Lincoln, President of the United States of America, have caused the said convention to be made public, to the end that the same, and every clause and article thereof, may be observed and fulfilled with good faith by the United States and the citizens thereof.

In witness whereof, I have hereunto set my hand, and caused the seal of the United States to be affixed.

Done at the city of Washington, this eighteenth day of November, [SEAL.] in the year of our Lord one thousand eight hundred and sixty-four, and of the independence of the United States of America the eighty-ninth.

ABRAHAM LINCOLN.

By the President:
WILLIAM H. SEWARD, *Secretary of State.*

BY THE PRESIDENT OF THE UNITED STATES OF AMERICA.

A PROCLAMATION.

Whereas a treaty between the United States of America and his Majesty the King of the Belgians, for the extinguishment of the Scheldt dues, was concluded and signed by their respective plenipotentiaries at Brussels on the twentieth day of July, eighteen hundred and sixty-three, which treaty being in the English and French languages, is word for word as follows: [The English version only is here given.]

The United States of America and his Majesty the King of the Belgians, equally desirous of liberating forever the navigation of the Scheldt from the dues that incumber it, to assure the reformation of the maritime taxes levied in Belgium, and to facilitate thereby the development of trade and navigation, have resolved to conclude a treaty to complete the convention signed on the twentieth of May, eighteen hundred and sixty-three, between the United States and Belgium, and have appointed as their plenipotentiaries, namely: The President of the United States of America, Henry Shelton Sanford, a citizen of the United States, their minister resident to his Majesty the King of the Belgians, and his Majesty the King of the Belgians, Mr. Charles Rogier, grand officer of the Order of Leopold, decorated with the iron cross, &c., &c., &c., his minister of foreign affairs, who, after having exchanged their full powers, found to be in good and due form, have agreed upon the following articles:

ARTICLE I. The high contracting parties take note of, and record—

1st. The treaty concluded on the twelfth of May, eighteen hundred and sixty-three, between Belgium and the Netherlands, which will remain annexed to the present treaty, and by which his Majesty the King of the Netherlands renounces forever the dues established upon navigation in the Scheldt, and its mouths, by the third paragraph of the 9th article of the treaty of the nineteenth of April, eighteen hundred and thirty-nine, and his Majesty the King of the Belgians, engages to pay the capital sum of the redemption of those dues, which amount to 17,141,640 florins.

2d. The declaration made in the name of his Majesty the King of the Netherlands on the fifteenth of July, eighteen hundred and sixty-three, to the plenipotentiaries of the high contracting parties, that the extinguishment of the Scheldt dues consented to by his said Majesty applies to all flags, that these dues can never be re-established under any form whatsoever, and that this suppression shall not affect in any manner the other provisions of the treaty of the nineteenth of April, eighteen hundred and thirty-nine, which declaration shall be considered inserted in the present treaty, to which it shall remain also annexed.

ARTICLE II. His Majesty the King of the Belgians makes, for what concerns him, the same declaration as that which is mentioned in the second paragraph of the preceding article.

ARTICLE III. It is well understood that the tonnage dues suppressed in Belgium, in conformity with the convention of the twentieth of May, eighteen hundred and sixty-three, cannot be re-established, and that the pilotage dues and local taxes reduced under the same convention cannot be again increased.

The tariff of pilotage dues and of local taxes at Antwerp shall be the same for the United States as those which are set down in the protocols of the conference at Brussels.

ARTICLE IV. In regard to the proportion of the United States in the capital sum of the extinguishment of the Scheldt dues, and the manner, place, and time of the payment thereof, reference is made by the high contracting parties to the convention of the twentieth of May, eighteen hundred and sixty-three.

ARTICLE V. The execution of the reciprocal engagements contained in the present treaty is made subordinate, in so far as is necessary, to the formalities and rules established by the constitutional laws of the high contracting parties.

ARTICLE VI. It is well understood that the provisions of article 3 will only be obligatory with respect to the state which has taken part in, or those which shall adhere to, the treaty of this day, the King of the Belgians reserving to himself expressly the right to establish the manner of treatment as to fiscal and customs regulations of vessels belonging to states which shall not be parties to this treaty.

ARTICLE VII. The present treaty shall be ratified, and the ratifications thereof shall be exchanged at Brussels, with the least possible delay.

In faith whereof, the respective plenipotentiaries have signed the same in duplicate, and affixed thereto their seals.

Done at Brussels, the twentieth day of July, eighteen hundred and sixty-three.

H. S. SANFORD. [SEAL.]
CH. ROGIER.   [SEAL.]

[Translation.]

Treaty of May 12, 1863, between Belgium and the Netherlands, annexed to the treaty of July 20, 1863.

His Majesty the King of the Belgians and his Majesty the King of the Netherlands, having come to an agreement upon the conditions of the redemption, by capitalization, of the dues established upon the navigation of the Scheldt, and of its mouths, by paragraph 3 of the 9th article of the treaty of the 19th April, 1839, have resolved to conclude a special treaty on this subject, and have appointed for their plenipotentiaries, namely :

His Majesty the King of the Belgians, M. Aldephonse Alexander Felix, Baron du Jardin, commander of the Order of Leopold, decorated with the iron cross, commander of the Lion of the Netherlands, chevalier grand cross of the Oaken Crown, grand cross and commander of several other orders, his envoy extraordinary and minister plenipotentiary near to his Majesty the King of the Netherlands;

His Majesty the King of the Netherlands, Messrs. Paul Vander Maesen de Sombreff, chevalier grand cross of the Order of the Nichan Iftihar of Tunis, his minister of foreign affairs ; M. Iran Rudolph Thorbecke, chevalier grand cross of the Order of the Lion of the Netherlands, grand cross of the Order of Leopold of Belgium, and of many other orders, his minister of interior, and M. Gerard Henri Betz, his minister of finance;

Who, after having exchanged their full powers, found in good and due form, have concluded upon the following articles.

ARTICLE I. His Majesty the King of the Netherlands renounces forever, for the sum of 17,140,640 florins of Holland, the dues levied upon the navigation of the Scheldt, and of its mouths, by virtue of paragraph 3 of article 9 of the treaty of 19th April, 1839.

ARTICLE II. This sum shall be paid to the government of the Netherlands by the Belgian government, at Antwerp, or at Amsterdam, at the choice of the latter, the franc calculated at 47½ cents of the Netherlands, as follows:

One-third immediately after the exchange of ratifications, and the two other thirds in three equal instalments, payable on the 1st May, 1864, 1st May, 1865, and 1st May, 1866. The Belgian government may anticipate the above-named payments.

ARTICLE III. From and after the payment of the first instalment of one-third, the dues shall cease to be levied by the government of the Netherlands.

The sums not immediately paid shall bear interest at the rate of four per cent. per annum in favor of the treasury of the Netherlands.

ARTICLE IV. It is understood that the capitalization of the dues shall not in any way affect the engagements by which the two states are bound in what concerns the Scheldt by treaties in force.

ARTICLE V. The pilotage dues now levied on the Scheldt are reduced—

20 per cent. for sailing vessels; 25 per cent. for towed vessels; and 30 per cent. for steam vessels.

It is, moreover, agreed that the pilotage dues on the Scheldt can never be higher than the pilotage dues levied at the mouths of the Meuse.

ARTICLE VI. The present treaty shall be ratified, and the ratifications shall be exchanged at the Hague, within four months, or earlier if possible.

In faith whereof, the plenipotentiaries above named have signed the same and affixed their seals.

Done at the Hague, the 12th May, 1863.

BARON DU JARDIN.	[SEAL.]
P. VANDER MAESEN DE SOMBREFF.	[SEAL.]
THORBECKE.	[SEAL.]
BETZ.	[SEAL.]

[Translation.]

Protocol of July 15, 1863, annexed to the treaty of July 20, 1863.

The plenipotentiaries undersigned, having come together in conference to determine the general treaty relative to the redemption of the Scheldt dues, and having judged it useful, before drawing up this arrangement in due form, to be enlightened with respect to the treaty concluded the 12th of May, 1863, between Belgium and Holland, have resolved, to this end, to invite the minister of the Netherlands to take a place in the conference.

The plenipotentiary of the Netherlands presented himself in response to this invitation, and made the following declaration:

"The undersigned, envoy extraordinary and minister ·plenipotentiary of his Majesty the King of the Netherlands, declares, in virtue of the special powers which have been delivered to him, that the extinguishment of the Scheldt dues, consented to by his august sovereign in the treaty of the 12th May, applies to all flags; that these dues can never be re-established in any form whatsoever; and that this extinguishment shall not affect in any way the other provisions of the treaty of the 19th July, 1839.

"BARON GERICKE D'HERWYNER.

"BRUSSELS, *July* 15, 1863."

Note has been taken and record made of this declaration, which shall be inserted in or annexed to the general treaty.

Done at Brussels, the 15th July, 1863.

BARON GERICKE D'HERWYNER.	[L. S.]
BARON DE HUGEL.	[L. S.]
T. C. DE AMARAL.	[L. S.]
M. CARVALLO.	[L. S.]
P. BILLE BRAHE.	[L. S.]
D. COELLO DE PORTUGAL.	[L. S.]
H. S. SANFORD.	[L. S.]
MALARER.	[L. S.]
HOWARD DE WALDEN ET SEAFORD.	[L. S.]
VON HODENBERG.	[L. S.]
CTE. DE MONTALTO.	[L. S.]
MAR YRIGOYEN.	[L. S.]
V'TE DE SEISAL.	[L. S.]
SAVIGNY.	[L. S.]
ORLOFF.	[L. S.]
ADALBERT MAUSBACH.	[L. S.]
C. MUSURNS.	[L. S.]
GEFFEKEN.	[L. S.]
CH. ROGIER.	[L. S.]
BN. LAMBERMORT.	[L. S.]

And whereas the said treaty has been duly ratified on both parts, and the respective ratifications of the same were exchanged at Brussels on the twenty-fourth of June last:

Now, therefore, be it known that I, Abraham Lincoln, President of the United States of America, have caused the said treaty to be made public, to the end that the same and every clause and article thereof may be fulfilled with good faith by the United States and the citizens thereof.

In witness whereof, I have hereunto set my hand and caused the seal of the United States to be affixed.

[SEAL.] Done at the city of Washington, this eighteenth day of November, in the year of our Lord one thousand eight hundred and sixty-four, and of the independence of the United States of America the eighty-ninth.

ABRAHAM LINCOLN.

By the President:

WILLIAM H. SEWARD, *Secretary of State.*

GHENT—MARINUS LEVISON, *Consul.*

OCTOBER 22, 1864.

* * I have the honor to enclose herewith my report for the year 1863. * *
No American vessels arrived in this port during the years 1863-'64.

•   •   •   •   •

General report upon the commerce and industry of the arrondissement of Ghent for the year 1863.

GENERAL SITUATION.

Commerce has been languishing during all the year 1863. The continuance of the American war, and the fear of peace being disturbed in some parts of

Europe, seriously checked business and put a stop to all kinds of enterprise. Consequently the trade confined itself to the wants of consumption, and completely gave up all remote operations. The situation of the cotton industry contributed largely to general uneasiness. The district of Ecloo, more agricultural than manufacturing, may be excepted from this general unfavorable situation. The crops in general have been very abundant in 1863; the flax culture, largely encouraged by the high prices obtained for this article during the year 1862, was affected on an enormous scale, and the expectations of the farmers, with regard to quantity, were even surpassed. As to the industry of the said district, it is little important, and consists chiefly of wool and flax, both articles, to a certain measure, substituted for cotton. The situation of the working classes was not quite so bad as could be expected. Before the American crisis Ghent had twelve thousand workmen engaged in the cotton mills. The first year of the war the labor was suddenly reduced to about one-third, and the measures taken in favor of the working classes, however energetic, could only be a faint palliative for such general distress.

The year 1863, without putting an end to the sufferings of the working population, saw them greatly lessened. The labor in cotton rose to about 50 per centum of an ordinary year; besides, several manufacturers transformed their works to the use of flax, and many unemployed hands emigrated to the manufacturing towns to the north of France.

At the beginning of the year money was abundant, and good bills could easily be disposed of; later, the rate of discount gradually ascended from 3 to 6 per cent., the highest legal rate; in neighboring countries it went up to 7 and 8 per cent.

MARITIME COMMERCE.

The tonnage of the vessels which entered the port of Ghent in 1863 shows an increase of 3,959 tons against 1862. The regular steam navigation between this and the English ports has not varied. We received in 1863:

Arrivals from Goole... 60
Arrivals from London 24

Total.. 84

The following is the statement of arrivals in 1863 compared with those of the preceding year :

Cargoes.	1862.		1863.		DIFFERENCE IN 1863.	
	No.	Tonnage.	No.	Tonnage.	More.	Less.
Wood	66	14,847	89	20,383	5,536	
Oleaginous grains........	11	1,023	16	1,727	704	
Flax, hemp and tow......	26	4,082	23	3,890	....	192
Oil cakes	6	353	6	412	59	
English coals	....	....	2	179	179	
Grain....................	6	1,344	4	617	....	727
Rice....................	5	357	6	443	86	
Wine	12	946	9	615	....	331
Raw salt................	17	3,648	7	1,639	....	2,009
Raw sugar	6	1,437	6	1,618	181	
Portugal fruit...........	7	645	9	745	100	
Stock fish and liver oil....	6	346	....	....	....	346
Cast iron................	12	904	18	1,816	912	
Various merchandise	100	16,134	107	15,702	....	432
In ballast without freight .	1	73	4	312	239	
Total	281	46,139	306	50,098	3,959	4,037

These vessels carried the following flags :

Countries.	No.	Tonnage.
Great Britain...............................	125	17,725
Belgium................................	37	5,107
Denmark...............................	7	523
Spain..................................	3	846
France	9	615
Hanover	41	5,602
Mecklenburg	19	4,825
Sweden and Norway	29	5,416
Prussia................................	27	7,748
Russia.................................	3	707
Mecklenburg and Schwerin	2	490
Holland...................	4	434
Total......	306	50,098

Notwithstanding the importance of our flax crop the importations of flax were almost as large as the preceding year.

TIMBER.

On account of the difficulties in Poland, and of the absence of snow in the north of Europe, the arrivals during the winter 1862–'63 were not so large as might have been anticipated. This trade, however, is steadily increasing.

Linseed for sowing has been imported largely, (820,000 kilogrammes declared for consumption.) The culture of flax having been considerable, linseed has been much inquired for. For crushing the importations have been limited.

Of raw sugar, this port has received some cargoes from Havana; those that arrived the latter part of the year turned out profitable. The returns of the custom-house of Ghent state an amount of 2,797,373 kilogrammes raw sugar for consumption.

There has been a large trade in petroleum, the use of which is increasing daily. The construction of a special entrepot for this article has been recently decided, and will allow direct importation.

Cotton spinning factories.—In 1862 the consumption of cotton in Belgium from about 15,000,000 kilogrammes, as it was before the American crisis, was reduced to 5,417,000 kilogrammes. In 1863 it reached 7,318,000 kilogrammes, showing an increase of about 50 per cent.

Weaving.—The manufactured goods made of pure cotton sold with difficulty, on account of their high prices, and were only produced for the immediate wants of the consumption. The printing of pure cotton goods was nearly left off.

Mixed goods of cotton and flax or cotton and wool are now made, to a great extent, both for home consumption and exportation.

Flax industry—preparing of flax.—The high prices commanded by this article in 1862, induced farmers to sow considerably. Notwithstanding a very abundant crop, prices remained high, and the working classes in the country earned a very good salary by preparing flax. Ghent is an important centre for the flax trade; its weekly market generally attracts a great many buyers.

Spinning factories for flax, hemp, and tow.—The year 1863 has been one of the most prosperous that ever has been witnessed in this industry. A considerable and almost daily increasing demand for yarn, both flax and tow, has prevailed with the greatest activity all the year round. About October an increase of orders from abroad, as well as for the home trade, gave a new impulse to prices, which at that period attained their highest point. This extraordinary activity was of great assistance to the laboring classes; many families, formerly engaged in cotton mills, found their principal support in the high wages by one or two of their members earned in the flax mills.

Weaving.—An extraordinary demand during all the year, chiefly in low-priced cloth of yarns from No. 12 to No. 30. Fine linen and sail-cloth did not find a sale quite so ready.

Laces.—Political events, both in America and Europe, weighed heavily upon the sale of fine lace. Common small lace sold rather freely.

Construction of machines and mechanism.—The important establishment for the construction of steam engines, &c., had some large orders from abroad, and were actively employed during the year 1863. The establishments of less importance, generally occupied for the interior, were of course affected by the cotton crisis.

Distilleries.—Some increase of activity is to be noticed in this industry; the taxes for this district are 501,707 hectolitres, or 61,533 hectolitres more than in 1862. Several causes account for this activity; increase of consumption, low prices, abundance of grain, short crop of beet-root, &c.

Sugar refineries.—About the month of July the short crop of beet-root produced a total perturbation in this branch of industry; prices of raw sugar, especially of beet-root sugar, rose considerably, whereas refined sugar did not rise in the same proportion. This induced the refiners to lessen their production—some of them ceased altogether.

The oil industry.—The crop of rape and linseed was of very good quality and very abundant—about a third above an average year; consequently the importation of oleaginous grains was inferior to that of 1862. The campaign commenced under very unfavorable circumstances; the financial crisis prevented speculation, and the always increasing consumption of petroleum limited that of other oil, owing to heavy exportation; some activity was, however, maintained in the factories. The crushers expect much benefit from the reduction of duty in Germany and Switzerland.

Chemical products.—The slackening of work in the cotton manufactories, and the progressive importation of English crystals of soda, though generally of inferior quality, weighed heavily on this branch of industry. The manufacturing, by chloridic acid, of *colle d'os*, has totally disappeared from this district. The use of petroleum has almost put an end to the clarifications by sulphuric acid of rape oil; and with the dying and printing of cotton goods, disappeared also, to a great extent, the use of nitric acid. Great activity was shown in the fabrication of discoloring chlorines, greatly consumed by the flax industry for the bleaching of yarns, &c.

Ultramarine blue met with a regular sale during the year. White lead shared in the general stagnation.

The manufactories of chicory had to submit to some heavy losses, the prices not having been in proportion with those of the root, and the demand for exportation having failed altogether.

The preparing of rabbit-skins.—Dyed and dressed skins met with an active and continued demand for exportation.

Horticulture.—A great activity prevailed all the year round in this branch, which is very important here; however, exportation to the United States and to the north of Europe was reduced next to nothing.

Sundry industries.—Most of them, being principally engaged for the home consumption, shared in the general uneasiness.

ANTWERP—A. W. CRAWFORD, *Consul*.

JANUARY 29, 1864.

I have the honor to enclose you a statement of the trade of the port of Antwerp during the past year.

The unnatural rebellion which exists in a section of our country has had more or less influence upon the commerce of Europe. Perhaps the kingdom of Belgium has suffered as little as any other portion. Iron, nails, glass, cloth, and lace, are the principal articles manufactured and exported. The manufactories are all in successful operation, and are sending a large amount of goods to the United States. On account of the piratical vessels of the so-called Confederate States, these goods are, unfortunately, shipped on board of neutral vessels, confidence being impaired in our flag, although it has heretofore enjoyed the advantage of most of the carrying trade between Belgium and the United States. The shipping interest has suffered much during the past year, there being no arrivals of American vessels at this port direct from the United States during the last eight months. We have had fifty-eight arrivals of American vessels from foreign ports during the past year; with but few exceptions they came from the Chinchas, freighted with guano. Notwithstanding they were loaded with neutral cargo they were compelled to pay heavy war risks, which gives neutral flags a decided advantage. I have just learned that the Peruvian government has given orders to its agents in Spain, Hamburg, and Rotterdam to charter our ships free of war risks. Being larger and better ships, other things being equal, they get the preference. Some now lying in our port are chartered on those conditions.

The treaty for the abolition of the Scheldt dues, negotiated by General H. S. Sanford, minister at Brussels, during the past summer, and which went into operation on the first of last, will prove of great importance to our trade with this port as well as advantageous to our vessels, by relieving them from the payment of a large amount of the onerous charges to which they have heretofore been subjected. The law of last winter in regard to triplicate invoices works well, and will do much both to prevent frauds on the treasury and make the consulates, in many places, self-supporting. This consulate has received comparatively little advantage from it, as the new consular districts of Brussels, Liege, and Verviers embrace the principal manufacturing provinces of the kingdom of Belgium. On my arrival at Antwerp, in the fall of 1861, petroleum was unknown as an article of commerce. Having become familiar with its properties in Pennsylvania, I called the attention of commercial men to its superiority over the rapeseed or colza oil (the illuminating fluid then in use) both in point of economy and beauty of light. In the year 1862, one million five hundred thousand gallons were sold. During the past year, four million five hundred gallons have been imported and sold at an average of 57 cents per gallon—making an aggregate of $2,565,000. Its advantages over all other burning fluids are now being appreciated; and at no distant day it will assume a commercial importance that will startle the most sanguine. Antwerp is now the largest petroleum market in Europe. In consequence of the very abundant crops in Belgium last year the importation of grain has fallen off considerably. On the other hand, a portion of bacon, which our western States would, in peaceful times, have sent to the south, has found a new market in this kingdom, and this article, once a luxury to the Belgian peasantry, is now, owing to its cheapness, becoming a valuable addition to his ordinary diet of brown bread and vegetables. In 1863, 1,500 hams, a considerable number of shoulders, and 33,000 boxes of sides were received, against 17,000 boxes only during the year 1862. Its importance and value, as an article of food, are beginning to be realized, and it may now be said to have taken a permanent place among Belgian imports.

In the matter of emigration I have to report that upwards of two thousand emigrants have left this port in sailing vessels during the past year. A large proportion of them were Germans, carrying with them considerable means with which to purchase homes on our broad prairies.

Notwithstanding Belgium is the most densely populated part of Europe, comparatively few have emigrated to the United States, to seek homes, where, instead of cultivating their little patches with the spade, our western prairies would afford them farms sufficiently large to reward their industry. Being patient and industrious, accustomed to be governed rather than to govern, they would be a desirable class of emigrants, and operate as a check on the more excitable and ambitious classes who are now emigrating to the United States from other countries. * * * *

DOMINIONS OF THE NETHERLANDS.

ROTTERDAM—GEORGE E. WISS, *Consul.*

APRIL 15, 1864.

As you will perceive by my returns, international commerce and navigation between Holland and the United States were still decreasing more than formerly, owing not only to our civil war, but also to the hard winter we had here, the river Maas, which connects this city with the sea, having been frozen up for seven or eight weeks. Besides, there were many circumstances depressing commerce and enterprising spirit through all Europe, and consequently working their influence also upon this city: the war broken out between Germany and Denmark, injurious to commerce, not so much by its extent as by its neighborhood, the fears of a general European war threatening from the loud complaints of several oppressed European nations; above all, the high rate of exchange and discount of the great banks of France and England during December, 1863, January and February, 1864. The latter fact cannot well be attributed to the uncertain political affairs of Europe and America, for in such times supplies of money would seek investments in banks rather than in business, but it is especially owing to the necessity for France and England paying specie for their supplies of cotton imported from such other countries as are not able to accept of manufactured articles in exchange as the United States.

As to the internal improvements of this country made during the past quarter, there is but little to report. By instruction of the department of the marine, storm signals were ordered to be erected at the seaports Flushing, Nieuwedeip, and Hellevoet, in order to let the vessels in port know from what direction a storm is threatened, as would appear from the official meteorological telegrams; these signals being given by black cylinders in the day time, and by lamps in the night time.

A most important improvement in trade and commerce is the abolition of the duty on coal and turf, once so high as to double the price of those articles, so necessary in a country already denuded of its forests; this law was published December 31, 1863, and takes effect March 1, 1864. The duty on distilled liquors was, however, increased.

There are two treaties to be mentioned—the one entered into between the governments of the Netherlands and Belgium for opening the canal of Slius and Brugge, February 5, 1864, and the other with Hanover for building a railroad from Almil as far as Saltzbergen, March 1, 1864.

Annual report of merchandise exported from Rotterdam to the United States from October 1, 1863, to September 30, 1864.

Articles.	Where produced.	Packages.	October 1 to December 31, 1863.	January 1 to March 31, 1864.	April 1 to June 31, 1864.	July 1 to September 30, 1864.
Arrack	Java	Casks	$1,088 24		$495 15	$340 34
Anchovy	Holland	Kegs	710 00			
Cheese	Holland	Cases	2,578 95	$1,024 52	795 93	647 88
Chicory, (ground)	Holland	Casks				
Chicory root	Holland	Casks and bags				
Cinnamon	Java	Packages				
Coffee	Java	Bags	6,851 73	25,733 91	7,813 33	13,109 08
Drugs	Holland	Bags and casks	186 77		780 80	
Flax	Holland	Bales	13,360 30	46,454 01	40,960 91	
Flower roots	Holland	Cases	320 72			4,924 20
Glycerine	Holland	Casks		3,470 00	8,721 63	4,251 20
Gin	Holland	Casks and cases	23,566 89	41,035 14	15,130 64	1,306 84
Herrings	Holland	Kegs	15,841 67	1,112 00	3,087 69	7,489 80
Lead	Germany	Slabs			19,843 23	2,394 96
Liquors and wines	Holland and Germany	Casks and cases	1,234 50	1,482 72	353 44	335 14
Madder	Holland	Casks	33,792 88	41,651 64	68,457 49	
Nutmegs	Java	Casks	2,809 82	9,067 58	16,565 41	2,371 90
Pipes, (tobacco)	Holland	Cases and baskets	1,304 30	1,288 63	919 00	1,032 38
Pipe-clay	Germany	Casks	4,284 69	2,490 72	6,740 56	1,135 06
Ratans	Java	Bundles	649 95	4,063 17	1,352 14	
Seeds	Holland	Bags and casks	2,070 11	347 40	1,339 30	334 00
Cigars	Germany	Cases			511 45	
Stockfish	Holland	Bundles	424 00			
Tin	Banca	Slabs	1,439 49	787 71	1,771 46	1,754 76
Tow	Holland	Bales	536 00		9,600 00	
Water, (mineral)	Germany	Baskets	23,809 09		275 75	
Total			126,099 03	187,090 55	205,515 31	41,351 84

Annual prices current of American merchandies in United States currency at Rotterdam from October 1, 1863, to September 30, 1864.

ARTICLES.		1863.			1864.		
		October.	November.	December.	January.	February.	March.
Ashes—pearl, American	50 kn.	$7 80 to $7 90	$7 40 to $6 00	$7 40 to $6 60	$6 40 to $6 70	$6 60 to $6 70	$6 60 to $6 80
pot, United States, in bond	"	7 00 7 10	7 00 7 20	7 00 7 20	7 00 7 20	7 10 7 20	7 20 7 40
Cotton—Inferior	½ kn.	44 cts. to 48 cts.	48 cts. to 54	44 cts. to — cts.	44 cts. to 50	44 cts. to 50	44 cts. to 50
Virginia ordinary	"	48	52	48	48	48	48
New Orleans good ordinary	"	52	54	52	50	50	52
Mobile low middling	"	56	56	58	58	54	54
Alabama middling	"	66	66	66	66	58	58
Tennessee good middling	"	70	68	64	70	64	64
middling fair	"	74	74	70	70	70	70
Dyes and dry salteries—Bark, quercitron, Philadelphia, in bond	50 kn.	$2 10 to $2 20	$2 10 to $2 20	$2 20 to $2 20	$2 10 to $2 20	$2 10 to $2 20	$2 20 to $2 20
Baltimore, in bond	"	1 50 1 70	1 30 1 90	1 30 7 90	1 50 7 90	1 30 7 90	1 55 7 90
Rosin—brown American	"	7 40 8 00	7 40 8 00	7 40 8 00	7 40 8 00	7 40 8 00	7 40 8 00
transparent and yellow	"	9 60 10 00	9 60 10 00	9 00 10 00	9 00 10 60	10 00 10 80	10 00 10 80
Lard, American prime	120 ps.	8 60 16 00	8 00 16 00	8 00 16 00	7 80 14 80	7 80 14 80	8 00 15 30
Staves—pipe	"	5 60 15 00	5 60 15 00	5 60 15 30	5 80 16 00	5 60 16 00	5 30 11 10
hogshead	"	3 60 6 00	3 60 6 00	3 30 6 00	3 30 7 30	3 30 7 30	3 30 6 00
barrel	"						
Tobacco—Maryland colored, fine yellow	½ kn.	16 cts. to 17 cts.	16 cts. to 17 cts.	16 cts. to 17 cts.	16 cts. to 17 cts.	16 cts. to 17 cts.	16 cts. to 17 cts.
brown, fair and good	"	13 14	13 14	13 14	14 14	13 14	14 14
ordinary	"	11 13	11 13	10 13	11 13	11 13	11 13
Virginia heavy and fine leaf	"						
middling	"						
ordinary	"						
Kentucky	50 kn.	14 15	14 15	14 15	14 15	14 15	14 15
Stems, in hogsheads, Virginia	"	13 18	13 18	13 18	13 18	13 18	13 18
Kentucky	"	$4 80 to $5 60	$4 80 to $5 60	$4 80 to $5 60	$4 80 to $5 60	$4 80 to $5 60	$4 80 to $5 60
in packages	"	3 60 4 80	3 60 4 80	3 80 4 80	3 60 4 80	3 60 4 80	3 60 4 80
home shipped	"	4 00 4 80	4 00 4 80	4 00 4 80	4 00 4 80	4 00 4 80	4 00 4 80

Annual prices current of American merchandise in United States currency at Rotterdam, &c.—Continued.

ARTICLES.		1864.					
		April.	May.	June.	July.	August.	September.
Ashes—pearl, American	50 kt.	$9 60 to $9 80	$9 60 to $9 80	$8 80 to $9 20	$9 00 to $9 20	$9 00 to $9 20	$9 00 to $9 20
pot, United States, in bond	¼ kt.	7 30 7 50	7 30 7 50	7 30 7 80	7 60 7 80	7 40 7 60	7 40 7 60
Cotton—inferior	"	44 cts. to — cts.	44 cts. to — cts.	44 cts. to — cts.	44 cts. to 46 cts.	44 cts. to 46 cts.	40 cts. to 44 cts.
Virginia ordinary	"	48	48	48	50	50	43
New Orleans good ordinary	"	54	54	54	52	52	44
Mobile low middling	"	58	58	58	58	58	48
Alabama middling	"	64	64	64	64	64	52
Tennessee good middling	"	70	70	66	70	68	58
middling fair	"	72	72	70	72	72	64
Dyes and dry salteries—Bark, quercitron, Philadelphia, in bond	50 kt.	$9 10 to $4 —	$9 10 to $4 —	$1 80 to $1 85	$1 80 to $1 85	$1 75 to $1 80	$1 80 to $1 85
Bark, quercitron, Baltimore, in bond	"	1 50 1 80	1 50 1 80	1 30 1 80	1 40 1 60	1 40 1 60	1 40 1 60
Rosin—crown American	"	7 00 7 80	7 00 7 80	7 00			
transparent and yellow	"	7 40 8 00	7 40 8 00	7 40 8 00			
Lard, American prime	"	10 40 11 00	10 00 11 20	10 40 10 80	10 20 10 80	10 20 10 60	10 80 11 80
Staves—pipe	120 pc.	8 00 11 80	8 00 11 80	8 00 11 80	8 00 15 20	8 00 15 20	8 00 15 20
hogshead	"	5 90 11 20	5 90 11 20	5 10 11 80	5 20 15 00	5 20 16 00	5 20 16 00
barrel	"	3 90 6 00	3 90 6 00	3 90 6 00	3 90 6 00	3 90 6 00	3 90 6 00
Tobacco—Maryland colored, fine yellow	¼ kt.	14 cts. to 18 cts.	14 cts. to 15 cts.	14 cts. to 15 cts.	14 cts. to 15 cts.	14 cts. to 15 cts.	14 cts. to 15 cts.
brown, fair and good	"	12 15	12 11	11 13	11 13	11 13	11 13
ordinary	"	10 12	9	10	8	9	8
Virginia heavy and fine leaf	"						
middling	"	12 15	12 15	12 14	12 13	12 13	12 13
ordinary	"	11 18	11 15	9 13	9 12	9 15	8 10
Kentucky	50 kt.	$4 80 to $5 60	$4 80 to $5 60	$3 60 to $5 60	$3 60 to $4 40	$3 60 to $4 40	$3 60 to $4 40
Stems, in hogsheads, Virginia	"	3 60 4 80	3 60 4 80	2 40 4 80	2 40 4 00	2 40 3 20	2 40 3 20
Kentucky	"	4 00 4 80	4 00 4 80	2 20 4 80	2 20 4 00	2 20 4 00	2 20 4 00
in packages							
house shipped							

AMSTERDAM—JOSEPH E. MARX, *Consul.*

SEPTEMBER 30, 1864.

*   *   *   *   *   *   *   *   *

Navigation between this port and the United States has not improved since my last report, but among the arrivals is now an American ship at Nieuwediep, outport of Amsterdam, having lately arrived from Bassein with a cargo of rice. In connexion herewith, I might call the attention of your honor to an inconvenience most of the American ships are subjected to at this port in consequence of their large size and heavy draught of water. This prevents them from coming up to this place, as the canal regulation only admits ships of 16 feet draught, but compels them to discharge at Nieuwediep in lighters, the cargo to be brought here by them. This fact seems not much known in the United States, at least the charter-parties never contain a provision as to which party shall pay the lighterage, the ship-owner or the merchant receiving the cargo. I understand that this neglect has created, for several years, troubles between the captains and merchants. The former maintaining to have fulfilled his contract by having arrived at Nieuwediep, that place being as near as the ship can safely get to Amsterdam, (the general term of the charter-parties,) the latter asserting that the ship can get up to this place after discharging part of her cargo, and that he (the merchant) is entitled to receive his goods here, the ship being ordered to Amsterdam and not to Nieuwediep. The same troubles arose with the Richard III, now at Nieudeep; and not to commence a tedious and costly lawsuit, they were settled, like former charters, by dividing the cost of lighterage; but this could be avoided entirely by altering the charter-parties so as to read, "or as near as she can safely get *without breaking bulk and lay afloat.*" This would settle the whole question in all cases where the charterer is not willing to pay any part of the lighterage; when, however, the same shall be borne by both parties, it should be noticed in the charter-party. The lighterage amounts to 50 cents United States currency in coin per ton. As quiet as the trade is between this place and the United States as regards produce and merchandise, it is lively in United States bonds and other United States securities. The sale of them for investment and speculation outruns by far that of any other kind; were it not for the latter there might not be bought as many, but the value might be enhanced and less fluctuating.

*   *   *   *   *   *   *   *   *

I cannot close this report without taking notice of some reforms in this country, which, when executed, will show themselves to be decided improvements, some of them, especially, to commerce, industry, and education, not only benefiting the citizens of this state, but also foreigners. They are the abatement of the municipal taxes, which are, at some places, as for instance here, very heavy; a postal treaty with England, going into force on the 1st of October, 1864, whereby the postage between the two countries is materially diminished, and provision made for the abolition of the stamp duty on newspapers and periodicals, which is yet in existence in this country, and greatly enhances the prices of all such publications, and a treaty of commerce with France based on free trade principles.   *   *   *   *

The imports at this place from the United States during this quarter were as follows:

From Baltimore, per English ship Mozart:
    1,175 hogsheads tobacco.
    485 bags quercitron.
    15 tons wood and staves.

From Baltimore, per Dutch galley Fosca Helena:
    272 hogsheads tobacco and staves.
    per Dutch brig Maelstrom:
    390 hogsheads tobacco and staves.
From Boston, per Italian brig Concettino:
    1,336 barrels petroleum.
    per Dutch bark Vereeniging:
    1,584 barrels flour.
      25 casks bread.
      10 do. tallow.
    275 barrels beef and pork.
 11,520 pieces pipe and hogshead staves.
      29 barrels honey.
      57 do. palm oil.
      60 boxes soap.
       9 do. tobacco.
    225 barrels herring.
      25 do. salmon.
      21 boxes lobsters.
       7 do. sundries.
From New York, per Dutch brig Susanna:
    710 barrels flour.
      60 do. ashes.
       5 hogsheads tobacco.
    500 boxes extract of logwood.
    100 barrels lard and staves.
    per schooner Peterdina Martina:
    150 bags cocoa.
    130 barrels beef.
  1,040 oars.
  1,260 pipe staves.
      50 hogsheads tobacco.
    100 barrels pot ashes.
      13 do. wax.

PARAMARIBO—H. SAWYER, *Consul.*

FEBRUARY 13, 1864.

I beg to inform you of the manner by which the recently emancipated negroes are kept at work, and so far with success, considering all circumstances. On the first of July, 1863, the slaves of this colony, about 37,000, (thirty-seven thousand,) were proclaimed free, with the proviso that they should " be under the surveillance of the government for the term of ten years;" that is, they were obliged to make a contract with their former owners for a term of months, and, on the expiration of the time specified in the agreement, they should renew the same, or with other planters, at their option.

At first they all objected to the contract, and wished to commence work on their own account, by taking a small piece of land and live in a state of independence, or, in other words, laziness.

Men-of-war steamers were sent up the rivers near the plantations; the negroes were called before the magistrate, ("of which there is one in each division,") and had their choice either to abide by the law, " which was explained to them," or at once be taken from the plantations and sent to the government estates.

Nearly all have contracted and remain on the same plantations, with but few exceptions.

The stipulations of the contract are that wages are paid for the amount of work performed, there being a tariff. A common field hand can earn from one to two guilders per diem; and, at the cheap rate of clothing and provisions, they can lay up one-half of their wages.

The laborer has a book, duly signed by himself and the planter before the magistrate, and, in case a dispute should arise between them, it is settled before that officer. If the planter should violate the stipulations of the contract, he is liable to a heavy fine; and, on the other hand, if the laborer does not fulfil his part thereof, he or she is punished by being sent to the chain gang, or on government works.

The planter finds horses and medical attendance gratis.

If the United States government should decide to send destitute negroes here, they would probably be obliged to come under the same regulations, which is certainly all that could be desired, and is beneficial to both planter and laborer, and also prevents vagabondage.

If a planter hires a laborer otherwise than by the aforementioned manner he is subject to a heavy fine.

The only trouble at the moment is, the negroes do not work regular, as the amount of wages earned in three days provides for all wants during the rest of the week.

I understand that a treaty has been concluded between the Netherlands and the United States government relating to the immigration of the free colored people of the United States to this colony.

I beg to make one or two remarks, knowing the state of the colony well at the moment.

There are many planters here who could employ thousands of the immigrants and pay them well for their work, but there are others who would willingly take them trusting to their crop for the payment of their wages, they not having the means otherwise; and, in case of the failure of the crop, the hands would be destitute. I beg to suggest that it would be the safest way to have the planters individually give security to the government for the payment of their wages before they are sent here.

I have been a resident of this colony now nearly fifteen years, and can say that I am well acquainted with the standing of nearly, if not quite all, of the planters here. As I before informed you, I will attend to the interests of the emigrants here if required by the United States government.

As some one must bear the expense of passage, &c., I think it could be so arranged that the planters would pay the same, and afterwards be allowed to deduct it from the wages gradually.

The enclosed tables show what this colony has produced in former years, and could now, with emigrants and labor-saving implements, produce double the quantity.

The great drawback on business of all kinds in this colony is, that there is nothing in the shape of a bank, and all affairs here are carried on in hard currency, (the Dutch guilder,) which is gradually leaving the colony in the shape of remittances to Holland.

Exportations from Surinam from 1771 to 1774, inclusive.

Years.	Sugar, lbs.	Coffee, lbs.	Cocoa, lbs.	Cotton, lbs.	Value.
1771	19,494,000	11,135,132	416,821	203,945	....
1772	19,260,000	12,267,134	354,935	90,035	....
1773	15,741,000	15,427,298	332,229	135,047	....
1774	15,111,000	11,016,518	506,610	105,126	....
Amount....	69,606,000	49,846,082	1,610,595	534,153	$10,439,219 95
Annually...	....	....	....	....	2,609,804 98

Exportations from Surinam from 1859 to 1862, inclusive.

Years.	Sugar, pounds.	Coffee, pounds.	Cotton, pounds.	Cocoa, pounds.	Molasses, gallons.	Rum, gallons.	Value.
1859..	25,275,219	665,214	544,108	451,757	622,811	100,454	....
1860..	33,375,667	488,069	516,580	507,465	870,173	167,510	....
1861..	31,753,369	139,735	478,875	504,208	673,723	191,001	....
1862..	32,775,681	126,021	451,920	657,177	775,233	166,039	....
Am't.	123,179,936	1,419,039	1,991,483	2,120,607	2,941,940	625,004	$5,181,253 23
Annually..	....	....	....	....	....	....	1,295,313 30

OCTOBER 10, 1864.

In accordance with instructions, I have the honor to submit a recapitulation of the trade of this port with the United States for the year ended September 30, 1864:

SHIPMENTS.

Nearly all the shipments to and from the United States for the past year have been made under foreign flags, although the cargoes were owned by American parties.

The value of imports, consisting of provisions, have amounted to $439,514 75. The value of exports, $551,199 95. Aggregate tonnage 8,191$\frac{44}{91}$ tons.

PLANTATIONS.

The plantations have now been carried on more than one year by paid labor, and at the high rates of sugar they have paid their way; but as a general thing have given no profit, the rates of wages being about forty cents, American currency, per diem, the laborers furnishing their own provisions.

The great difficulty experienced by the planters at present is that the hands will not work regularly.

The revenue from the estates thus far since the emancipation, which took place the first of July, 1863, is from the cane planted previously, which requires from fifteen to eighteen months to ripen. The ensuing twelve months will decide whether free labor will warrant the continuing the culture of sugar. The general opinion of planters is that it will not; and in consequence many of them will change the culture to that of cocoa, which requires but very little labor after the tree becomes two years old.

COFFEE.

The coffee estates are nearly all abandoned or changed into cocoa plantations.

IMMIGRANTS.

About 500 immigrants have arrived here from Barbadoes during the past year, and were at once employed on the estates.

GOLD MINING.

The gold mines discovered some four years since have so far not been properly worked, or at least merely prospected, and, of course, the result of these researches cannot be given. However, a small company has recently been formed, and about 30 laborers are now engaged working them. They left town for the mines on the 25th of September. Undoubtedly these mines will prove as lucrative as those of Cayenne and Demarara, which are on each side of this colony, and the same range of mountains runs through the three. These mines are about 150 miles up the Surinam river and are quite easy of access by water. I have sent to the United States some specimens of the gold, which proves to be very pure.

VALATA, OR GUTTA PERCHA.

This is a sort of gum which oozes from the valata, or balla tree, and resembles very much the gutta percha when dried. I have forwarded to the New York Gutta Percha Company samples of the same to experiment upon for covering telegraphic marine cables. The colony abounds with these trees, and the wood is used for building purposes. It is tapped the same as the maple for sugar, and the pine for turpentine, without any injury to the tree, as the gum comes only from the bark.

IMPORT DUTIES.

The import duties are quite low, being about 3 per cent. on the appraised value here. This appraisement here, however, leads to a great deal of trouble to the importers, as the market fluctuates to such a degree that nearly every cargo has a different valuation affixed, and the original invoice is not accepted by the custom-house authorities. The government also retains the right to take all cargoes at 12 per cent. above the invoice price, and the importer is not allowed to make any correction after he has once cleared his cargo in, or to make a so-called port entry in case of omissions, as in the United States.

A CUSTOM-HOUSE REGULATION.

If it shall be found that any goods have been left out of the clearance, (entering,) and that such leaving out did happen by omission or neglect, which must appear clearly, the master or commander shall pay a fine of not less than $100 and not more than $1,000, in the discretion of the judge. But if any duties are due on such goods, or if they are prohibited from being imported, they shall be confiscated; and in case it should appear that they were left out with intent to escape the payment of duties in, or on exportation of the same, or in fraud of the prohibitory laws, the ship and cargo are to be confiscated.

This law is certainly very extraordinary, and does by no means agree with our treaty on the reciprocity of navigation and commerce with the Netherlands.

The planters here are greatly disappointed that the proposed convention between the United States and the Netherlands, relating to the immigration of free colored people from the United States to this colony, was not ratified. As I have already stated in my former reports, they would have had good care, ample employment, and fair wages. Two thousand could at once be employed. This colony remains perfectly healthy, and the quarantine laws are observed very rigidly.

IMPROVEMENTS.

Government is about building a fine wharf near the warehouses, in order that vessels may discharge and take in their cargoes instead of lightering, as at present.

BATAVIA—M. P. PELS, *Vice-Consul.*

DECEMBER 31, 1863.

Statement showing the description, quantity, where produced, and value of exports from Batavia during the quarter ended December 31, 1863.

Description.	Quantity.	Where produced.	Value.
Sugar ....Piculs..	12, 068. 78	East India	$167, 172 03
India-rubber .... Cases..	182	....do............	26, 187 98
India-rubber ....Piculs..	72. 82	....do............	7, 379 48
Ratans ....Piculs..	1, 770. 18	....do............	26, 541 70
Pepper ....Piculs..	344. 78	....do............	6, 165 14
Cloves...........................Piculs..	39. 98	....do............	1, 890 18
Coffee ....Piculs..	4, 400. 77	....do............	209, 007 63
Coffee Padang bags	30	....do............	810 40
Rice ....Piculs..	216. 95	....do............	2, 123 40
Tin ....Piculs..	113. 04	....do............	8, 792 70
Total........................	....	....	456, 070 64

SEPTEMBER 30, 1864.

During the year ending September 30, 1864, the business between Java and the United States has somewhat revived, and at present the imports and exports are approaching to what they were before the war. As yet, however, American bottoms are not in favor, and owners are obliged either to load on their own account or employ their vessels in making short coasting voyages. The tables which accompany this report show the course of trade, and also the proportion which is in the hands of private merchants and government under the name of the Dutch Trading Company.

In regard to the internal affairs of Java there is but little to report. A railroad was commenced at Samarang a few months ago which is to extend into the interior, but not enough progress has been made to have any influence as yet. This is the first railroad in the island, or in the Dutch possessions in the east; and its commencement is regarded as a sign that a more improving policy will prevail in the future in the development of these islands.

Statement showing the description and quantities of the private exports from Java during the years 1861, 1862, and 1863, and also the names of the countries whither shipped.

Articles.	Year.	Holland.	England.	France.	Other European ports.	United States.	China.	Australia.	Other places.	Total.	Dutch Trading Company.	Grand total.
		Piculs.	*Piculs.*	*Piculs.*	*Piculs.*	*Piculs.*	*Piculs.*	*Piculs.*	*Piculs.*	*Piculs.*	*Piculs.*	*Piculs.*
Coffee......	1861	85,585	638	33,507	......	......	192	5,117	902	125,941	811,240	937,181
	1862	126,047	......	30,253	293	800	185	1,531	720	161,829	877,241	1,039,070
	1863	144,155	......	67	18,255	13	7,150	196	1,271	1,557	172,664	734,858	907,522
Sugar......	1861	896,943	143,727	21,833	7,651	......	111	66,317	50,733	1,186,615	831,563	2,018,178
	1862	1,138,367	25,163	34,149	14,237	1,833	111	105,444	71,050	1,390,354	939,544	2,329,898
	1863	839,487	14,806	22,283	4,287	15,933	28,804	46,159	54,549	1,026,308	986,449	2,012,757
Rice........	1861	201,875	24,663	5,045	4,316	......	70,242	13,631	145,935	464,117	2,941	467,058
	1862	133,523	41,553	......	4,369	8,746	69,864	18,072	192,357	468,477	......	468,477
	1863	194,058	84,312	......	......	6,000	101,072	11,574	301,143	597,859	......	597,859
Ratans......	1861	17,872	2,310	1,638	555	......	5,873	1,127	1,619	30,974	20,801	51,775
	1862	19,379	901	1,196	190	494	3,416	1,007	1,737	38,250	21,870	50,120
	1863	24,171	3,444	659	150	2,354	5,553	37	5,301	61,669	18,652	60,321
Pepper	1861	4,104	2,288	1,915	......	......	171	853	603	9,204	4,901	14,135
	1862	4,019	422	722	4	73	81	1,165	417	6,896	1,615	8,511
	1863	5,493	......	2,422	......	1,960	80	855	1,159	11,289	2,909	14,178
India-rubber	1861	10,219	301	69	......	......			39	10,021	100	10,721
	1862	5,930	364	167	119	73			1,123	7,769	......	7,769
	1863	6,435	435						153	7,093	189	7,212
Tobacco ...	1861	81,127								81,127	......	81,127
	1862	98,011						30	7,540	105,581	3,821	109,402
	1863	142,100					741		13,707	156,548	4,128	160,676
Indigo	1861	2,254	......	163						2,417	3,902	6,319
	1862	2,538	2		19				3	2,553	4,176	6,729
	1863	2,813		24						2,837	2,982	5,819
Gum damar	1861	3,549	511	100	716					4,876	......	4,876
	1862	4,107	276	864	445					5,692	932	6,624
	1863	4,885	683	850					305	6,723	403	7,126
Tin	1861	3,114								3,114	72,182	75,296
	1862	950	8	518						1,476	63,274	64,750
	1863	4,516				25				2,552	73,065	80,158
Oil cakes...	1861	......					86,443		4,294	90,727	......	90,727
	1862	......					85,063		27,748	102,811	......	102,811
	1863	......					67,179		3,000	70,170	......	70,170

REMARKS.—Picul = 136 lbs. English.

A large proportion of the sugar under the heading "other places," goes to the Persian Gulf. The large figures for rice under the same heading include all the rice which leaves Java for the neighboring islands in native vessels and coasters. The figures by no means show the superfluous production of Java, for much of this rice is probably consumed by persons whose home is Java.

Principal private imports into Java.

	Holland.	England.	France.	Other European ports.	United States.	Australia.	Other places.	Dutch Trading Co.
Cotton goods:	*Pkgs.*	*Pkgs.*	*Pkgs.*	*Pkgs.*	*Pkgs.*	*Pkgs.*	*Pkgs.*	*Pkgs.*
1861	46,855	33,239	....	117	190	....	1,155	11,263
1862	53,793	30,275	4	290			1,386	8,759
1863	15,389	11,167					1,666	968
Iron, band:								
1861	23,509	90,108		38,857			2,000	8,344
1862	116,160	121,147		56,310			161	5,525
1863	44,803	63,744		27,155		15,180	....	....
Metallic:								
1861	*	*	*	*	*	*	*	*
1862	26,846	5,106			1,400			1,435
1863	2,909	1,804			2,024	400		4,230
Machinery:								
1861	2,798	5,170	3,592	197	16		104	388
1862	3,866	4,784	35		105			
1863	1,514	2,509						
Coal:	*Tons.*	*Tons.*	*Tons.*	*Tons.*	*Tons.*	*Tons.*	*Tons.*	*Tons.*
1861	25,210	6,046	2,248				4,633	12,975
1862	42,115	21,196	1,075	120		6,757	165	8,494
1863	26,140	23,591	115	180		2,460	1,030	
Flour:	*Bbls.*	*Bbls.*	*Bbls.*	*Bbls.*	*Bbls.*	*Bags.*	*Bags.*	*Bags.*
1861	1,420	50	190		4,064		704	
1862	4,669	20			3,712	12,171	72	
1863	1,298	50	40		4,685	4,320	6,860	
Wines:	*Kegs.*	*Kegs.*	*Kegs.*	*Kegs.*	*Kegs.*	*Kegs.*	*Kegs.*	*Kegs.*
1861	13,459	3,200	183				1,159	61
1862	11,907	1,365	3,523				80	
1863	17,098	814	2,500		51		427	

* REMARKS.—In addition to the articles of import mentioned in the table, provisions, liquors, ship-chandlers' stores, &c., are imported in moderate quantities.

Statement showing the description and quantity of imports into Java from the United States from the year 1856 to 1863, inclusive, and to July 1, 1864.

Years.	Cotton goods, bales.	Drills, cases.	Flour, barrels.	Pitch, barrels.	Tar, barrels.	Rosin, barrels.	Beef, barrels.	Pork, barrels.	Bread, barrels.
1856	25	1,187	1,070	276	100	607	40	125	60
1857		350	1,345	200	112	100	80	......	272
1858		812	1,310	162	125	125	250	......	670
1859		765	1,634	350	100	650	236	15	338
1860	136	351	5,221	445	100	759	433	·153	400
1861	26	90	4,064	500	50	2,076	595	300	706
1862	......	....	3,712	......	......	300	900	50	650
1863	......	....	4,685	......	......	1	100	100	800
1864, six months	......	....	2,352	......	......	....	167	71	200

Statement showing the description and quantity of imports, &c.—Continued.

Years.	Furniture, cases.	Soap, boxes.	Planks, pieces.	Provisions, cases.	Clocks, cases.	Ice, tons.	Oars, pieces.	Tobacco, cases.	Carriages, pieces.
1856............	1,374	200	4,000	241	20	717	....	9	......
1857............	2,450	700	....	170	224	1,516	600	10	......
1858..........*..	2,033	500	298	......	81	1,478	......	......	......
1859............	3,766	....	12,105	......	......	1,420	400	270	......
1860............	4,992	300	21,000	400	220	2,237	1,004	72	12
1861............	1,014	1,878	1,514	525	119	3,428	3,158	55	107
1862............	1,339	....	13,496	420	247	2,798	901	......	67
1863............	1,917	200	100	70	86	1,368	......	......	28
1864, six months.	292	....	5,868	95	39	502	375	......	11

Statement showing the description and quantity of exports from Java to California from the year 1856 to 1863, inclusive.

Years.	Coffee, piculs.*	Sugar, piculs.	Rice, piculs.	Pepper, piculs.	Cassia, piculs.	Nutmegs, piculs.	Mace, piculs.
1856....................	10,271	17,535	18,649	788	16	103	14
1857....................	1,020	13,185	13,672	396	......	24	1
1858....................	4,609	4,378	12,627	290	......	......	......
1859....................	3,940	14,617	12,698	82	......	60	10
1860....................	2,995	1,970	9,818	10	......	......	......
1861....................							
1862....................	736	....	2,746	73	......	14	2
1863....................	7,150	1,625	3,796	912	......	26	......

* A picul = 136 lbs. English.

Statement showing the description and quantity of exports, &c.—Continued.

Years.	Ratans, piculs.	Cubebs, piculs.	Sago, piculs.	Cloves, piculs.	Arrack, leaguers.†	Tin.
1856 .....:...........	350	8	39	......	2	......
1857	128	......	40	60	15	......
1858	50	......	......	......	65	......
1859	375	......	350	......	65	......
1860	287	8	......	......	3	......
1861						
1862	56	......	......	14	......	......
1863	102	......	14	60	20	25

† A leaguer = 133 imperial gallons.

Statement showing the description and quantity of exports from Java to the Atlantic ports of the United States from the year 1856 to 1863, inclusive, and to July 1, 1864.

Years.	Coffee, piculs.	Sugar, piculs.	Rice, piculs.	Ratans, piculs.	Pepper, piculs.	Nutmegs, piculs.	Mace, piculs.	Cassia, piculs.	Gum damar, piculs.
1856...........	5,951	5,005	200	1,037	1,044	261	41	3	1,074
1857...........	2,475	12,754	....	5,965	354	148	15	370	640
1858...........	7,099	3,541	....	19,519	154	66	11	....	130
1859...........	1,066	1,927	....	12,015	49	39	......	....	200
1860...........	1	42,425	105	4,537	....	104	31	....	200
1861...........	....	....	....	....	....	....	......	....	....
1862...........	64	1,833	6,000	438	558	....	......	....	....
1863...........	....	13,308	2,204	2,252	....	....	......	....	....
1864, six months.	219	9,732	....	7,453	348	....	......	....	....

Statement showing the description and quantity of exports, &c.—Continued.

Years.	India-rubber, piculs.	Gutta-percha, piculs.	Indigo, u.*	Hides, pieces.	Sapanwood, piculs.	Cubebs, piculs.	Tin, piculs.	Gambier, piculs.
1856....................	2,798	430	1,965	5,000	102	44	200	171
1857....................	1,256	70	1,091	1,000	......	50	....	......
1858....................	1,605	......	....	....	......	45	....	......
1859....................	1,835	8	....	5,870	......	91	630	......
1860....................	1,378	......	....	....	100	48	....	......
1861....................	....	......	....	....	......	......	....	......
1862....................	....	......	....	....	......	......	....	......
1863....................	73	......	....	....	......	......	....	......
1864, six months..........	47	......	....	....	......	......	....	......

* Amsterdam pound (u) = 1¼ lb. English.

ST. MARTIN—CHARLES REY, *Consul.*

JULY 5, 1864.

 * * * The salines here have furnished during the last six weeks of gathering 600,000 bushels salt of superior quality, which is held here at from 8 cents to 8¼ cents per bushel. No other item of interest to communicate.

DANISH DOMINIONS.

Elsinore—George P. Hansen, *Consul.*

FEBRUARY 23, 1864.

I have the honor herewith to enclose to you a proclamation relating to the blockade of the eastern ports of Holstein and Sleswig by the Danish government.

I have also to inform you that a few changes have been made in the present tariff and also in the tariff of July 4, 1863, which will go into effect on the first of April next.

An addition to the duty now collected has been ordered on the following articles, to be in force from the 1st to the 31st of March next.

1. On spirits manufactured of grain, potatoes, grapes, &c., all kinds, whiskey as well as liquors, 50 per cent.

2. Chiccory roots, raw, 50 per cent.

3. Cider, &c., 50 per cent.

4. Coffee, raw as well as burnt, ground and unground, also on chiccory and on all other burnt substitutes of coffee, ground or unground, 50 per cent.

5. Sugar, all kinds, refined and unrefined, also molasses and sirups, 33⅓ per cent.

6. Tea, all kinds, 33⅓ per cent.

7. Tobacco, leaves and stems, also manufactured tobacco of all kinds, 33⅓ per cent.

8. Wines, also wine of raisins and liquid mother of wine, 50 per cent.

From the 1st of April an addition to the duty then to be collected according to the tariff of July 4, 1863, which then goes into operation, will be collected on the following goods:

On wine, liquid mother of wine, cider, wine of raisins, and other fruit wines, also on liquid fruit juice, without addition of spirits, or with no more than is necessary to its preservation, also on lemonade, 50 per cent.; other kinds of spirits, 50 per cent.

Chiccory roots or other roots which can be used as substitutes for coffee, per pound, 0.5 skillings.

Coffee, per pound, 2 skillings.

Coffee, burnt, also chiccory, and all other kinds of burnt substitutes for coffee, also essence of coffee, per pound, 2 5 skillings.

Sugar candies, loaf sugar, whole or broken, white crushed sugar of a lighter quality than the specimen furnished the collectors, and nearest to the Amsterdam standard proof, No. 18, per pound, 11.25 skillings.

Sugar, other kinds, pulverized, and not so light as the above enumerated specimen No. 9, also liquid kinds of sugar, including cane juice, from which the sugar has not been separated; further, white sirup and honey, also grape and starch sugar and grape and starch sirup, per pound, 0.9 skillings.

Molasses, common brown sirup and brown honey, &c., per pound, 0.55 skillings. Tea, per pound, 4 skillings. Tobacco and substitutes for tobacco, leaves and stems, per pound, 2 skillings. Cigars, per pound, 8 skillings; all other kinds, per pound, 2 skillings.

On spirits imported after the first of March, and on which duty has been paid, an indemnification of 50 per cent. will be made on exportation, on satisfactory proof that the duty has been paid since the first of March.

ALTONA—W. MARSH, *Consul.*

AUGUST 20, 1864.

* * * The wisdom of a government favoring the development of national institutions commercially, fraternally, and politically, begins to manifest itself in a number of ways, showing that prejudice was the only drawback to the extension of commerce at this port. Building operations are going on here to a large extent; upwards of two hundred dwelling-houses are in course of erection and several manufactories; one, a hat manufactory, is the largest in Europe.

In railroads much is being done. A new loop through Hamburg to connect the terminus of the Berlin road with the Altona depot is in course of construction and will soon be in operation. This connexion has long been needed, owing to the immense traffic of the two roads having to be transshipped on drays from from one point to the other.

The lines of railroad penetrating Holstein and Schleswig have a large foreign traffic, aside from their own products, gathered from the ports of Kiel, Neustadt, Eckenfoird, Rendsburg, Schlessing, Flensburg, Touning. Much of these goods undergo a further process of manufacture, either at Altona or Hamburg, previous to being forwarded to their destination. Since the Hamburg and American Steamship Company have adopted Gluckstadt as their, port of embarcation all the goods intended for these steamers are carried on drays to the Altona depot, and forwarded by rail in winter, and in flat-boats in summer, to Gluckstadt. But when the Loop line is finished Altona will become the great junction and terminus of the two roads.

Another line of railroad is now being laid through the duchy of Lunenburg to Lubec, Travemund, and Neustadt. These ports are open to the East sea and Baltic trade, which, in a few months, will find over these new roads a natural outlet here.

The Prussian government are making a survey for a great ship canal over the isthmus of Holstein; but I am credibly informed that they will ultimately adopt Hansen's route, which is most in favor, as it is purely a commercial undertaking. This canal will open a way from Gluckstadt, on the Elbe, to Neustadt, economizing the distance in freights leaving the North sea for the Baltic, to the extent of forty-eight hours; making the voyage less risky than through the Cattegut.

Other internal arrangements are meditated whenever a permanent government for the duchies shall be determined. Capitalists here are so prejudiced against the Danish government that they will not invest their money freely until they have an executive composed, at least, of their own countrymen.

Altona, as a commercial and manufacturing town, will then rise to the level of Hamburg. This, at the first glance, may appear presumptuous, but, viewed by unprejudiced minds, it elucidates itself in plain practical facts easy to be understood. For years the commerce of Hamburg has suffered immensely for want of territory on the Elbe westward. But, this being the location of Altona, it has been crowded eastward into a labyrinth of narrow streets, in lofty warehouses, to economize space and keep their wares within dray-distance of the harbor.

In this the city of Altona has every advantage over Hamburg. The town is two hundred years old, has fifty thousand inhabitants, and commands as fine a position for trade and commerce as any out-port of Germany. It has a regular harbor three-fourths of a mile long, with a river frontage of several miles, all of which is eligible for the extension of trade, commerce, and manufactures, with all the superior advantages. Altona, while regarded as a Danish port, has ever been the victim of a prejudice destructive to its general interests; and, although a free port, it has remained in comparative *statu quo* for these many years.

Now this prejudice is about to be removed, or at least the cause of it, by a change in the administration of these duchies. Thus their commercial, agricultural, and marine advantages, under a friendly national government, will be encouraged; the enterprise of the people will be developed in numerous ways; they will open up avenues of trade and commerce with us, and the whole world, in fact, and their cities and harbors become generally prosperous. * * *

SWEDEN.

STOCKHOLM—GEORGE V. TEFFT, *Consul.*

APRIL 28, 1864.

In reply to circular No. 44, I have the honor to inform you that, in Sweden, consuls of the United States who are not engaged in business are not taxed by the Swedish government, provided they have no Swedish servants in their employment and possess no real estate.

If they are engaged in business, or owners of real estate, or have Swedish servants in their employment, they are subject to taxation in the same manner and to the same amount as Swedish citizens are, except that consuls of foreign birth are not taxed for their persons or personal property.

Every Swede is liable to a personal tax; and if a man employs one or a number of servants he is by custom required to pay this tax for them.

Such real estate as pertains to agriculture is taxed at the rate of 3 ore for every full one hundred riksdaler, and all other real estate at the rate of 5 ore for every full one hundred riksdaler.

On all incomes, whether from capital or labor, a tax of one per cent. is levied. The personal tax is 40 ore for a man and 20 ore (or 5½ cents) for a woman.

NOVEMBER 29, 1864.

Herewith I have the honor to transmit a succinct report of invoices certified at this consulate during the quarter ended September 30, 1864.

The whole number of such invoices is nineteen (19,) containing 76,867 bars of iron, weighing 33,069 centner, and valued at 287,578.27 riksdaler, including all charges and commissions, which is in excess of those of the corresponding quarter of 1863.

Three invoices containing 33,892 bars of iron, weighing 3,858.61 centners, and valued at 184,931.15 riksdaler, including all charges and commissions.

There has been no exportation direct to the United States during this quarter, all exports having been shipped hence to Lubec, thence to Hamburg, and reshipped thence to New York, or, as in the case of the steamer Ernst Uerck, *via* England to Ireland, and then to New York.

The law imposing a tax on the exportation of iron from Sweden having been rescinded, it is supposed it will increase the amount of the exportation of that article in the coming summer.

GOTTENBURG—J. P. M. EPPING, *Consul.*

FEBRUARY 16, 1863.

I have the honor to acknowledge the receipt of your circulars Nos. 29 and 30, dated November 20 and December 24, 1862. They both reached me but

H. Ex. Doc. 60——23

a few days ago, and I have, as requested in circular No. 29, forthwith made the necessary inquiries, and ascertained, from the first legal authorities of this city, that the laws of Sweden do not prohibit foreign consuls to administer oaths. Such oaths would, however, have only a moral and not a legal force. They would not be taken in evidence before any Swedish tribunal, nor do I believe before any tribunal on the continent of Europe. There are, however, among the Germanic nations two forms of verifications : one the oath proper, which, to be binding, can only be administered under certain legal and religious forms ; and the other, called a declaration upon oath, does not require the oath to be actually administered—answering about to our mode of taking affirmations ; in fact, being a legal and solemn mode of declaration, which the laws allow to be administered by all notarial and magisterial officers, and which is, in all trivial matters, admitted in the courts as evidence, and if proved to be false is severely punishable, but an action for perjury cannot be brought in consequence. This form of declaration upon oath, if administered by or taken before a United States consular officer, would be perfectly legal and binding.

Perceiving the difficulties concerning the taking of the oath from subjects of Sweden upon my arrival here, and an affirmation to an invoice being equally binding and lawful, I have ever since only taken a solemn affirmation from the shippers of iron here, and attached a certificate to that effect to the invoices.

Most of the iron shipped from this port to the United States is shipped in small parcels, from 5 to 25 tons, indirect by the way of Hamburg, Bremen, or London ; and if the shippers here, who are all highly respectable persons, should be compelled to make an oath to every one of these small invoices in proper form of Swedish law, it would be extremely burdensome and embarrassing to our commerce with this country.

.   *   *   *   *   *   *   *   *   *

W. W. THOMAS, JR., *Consul.*

NOVEMBER 10, 1863.

I have the honor to acknowledge the receipt of circulars Nos. 40 and 42 from the Department of State.

In answer to the questions contained in section 12, of circular No. 40, I have the honor to inform the department that the consuls of all foreign powers, except Holland, not engaged in business, are exempt from all taxes of a personal nature in Sweden. Foreign consuls engaged in business, or Swedes becoming consuls for a foreign power, are not exempt.

This exemption from taxation is in accordance with a Swedish law which was promulgated in the King's letter of October 7, 1818.   *   *   *

Report on the shipping and commerce of Gottenburg, Sweden, for the year 1863.

GOTTENBURG MERCHANT MARINE.

There are owned in Gottenburg 124 vessels, of a capacity of 47,063 tons. In 1863 3 vessels were built here of a net capacity of 432 tons, and 14 vessels bought, capacity 5,148 tons. In the same year were lost 5 vessels, capacity 876 tons, and sold 16, capacity 4,032 tons. Ninety out of the 124 vessels belonging to Gottenburg are insured in the Gottenburg Marine Insurance Company for a net sum of $956,267.

FREIGHTS.

During the spring of 1863 the freights ruled about the same as in the previous years, but in the summer and autumn there was an increased demand for ships, and freights rose steadily.

The freights on iron per ton to the United States in 1863 were as follows:

	New York.	Boston.
Spring.........		$4 84 and 5 per cent.
Summer	$4 84 and $5 44 in fall	$4 84 and 5 per cent. ; $6 05 in fall.
Autumn	$7 26 and 5 per cent......	$6 84 and $7 26 and 5 per cent.

SHIPPING.

Entered at Gottenburg from foreign ports in 1863 2,142 vessels, of 323,844 tons capacity, which exceeds the previous year by 174 vessels and 4,464 tons. But two of these vessels, of a capacity of 2,005 tons, belonged to the United States. They both arrived in ballast.

Cleared from Gottenburg for foreign ports in 1863 1,826 vessels, of 317,314 tons capacity ; of this number there were 275 steamers, capacity 92,027 tons. Out of the sailing vessels 17 cleared for the United States. In 1862 the number of vessels cleared at Gottenburg was 1,779, with a capacity of 310,958 tons.

EXPORTS.

The export of iron, the great business of Gottenburg, and, indeed, of Sweden, is steadily increasing. The export of this metal from Gottenburg in 1863 was greater than that of any previous year, amounting to 44,362 tons. This gratifying result is owing partly to the improved communication between Gottenburg and the interior by means of the extension of railways, canals, &c., and partly to the increased foreign demand for Swedish iron, which I believe is admitted to be the most tenacious, if not the best, iron in the world. It is an interesting fact that every horseshoe nail driven in the United States is made from iron taken out of the mines of Sweden.

The following table shows the amount of iron exported from Gottenburg to each foreign country in 1863, estimated in Swedish centners, of which 24 equal 1 ton:

	Centners.
England..	588, 136. 81
United States	148, 145. 80
Germany...	112, 614. 32
West seas	78, 146. 87
France	46, 670. 69
Denmark	44, 051. 30
Holland	26, 710. 09
Belgium	8, 340. 48
Africa...	6, 659. 21
Mediterranean sea......................................	3, 178. 30
West Indies...	995. 32
Norway	681. 38
Spain	360. 00
Total	1, 064, 690. 57
Sent into the interior, or used on the spot.................	93, 500. 24
Grand total	1, 158, 190. 81

DEALS.

The exports from Gottenburg in 1863 of planks, deals, and boards amounted to 329,078 dozen, being about the same as in 1862. Nearly two-thirds of this quantity was shipped to Great Britain, consisting principally of 3 by 7 and 2½ by 7 deals, together with boards adapted for shipping purposes.

GRAIN.

Sweden both exports and imports grain. The chief grain exported is oats, the annual shipment of which from all Sweden amounts to about 4,000,000 bushels, together with very small quantities of wheat and barley. On the other hand, rye bread being the "staff of life" to the Swede, the rye crop, although large, is not sufficient to supply the home demand, and Sweden is forced to eke out her own crop of rye with importations from abroad.

The total exportation of grain from the Gottenburg district during 1863 reached 3,323,888 bushels, of which 3,256,584 bushels were oats, exceeding the amount of oats exported in 1862 by about 1,000,000 bushels. During the same year there were imported into the city of Gottenburg 520,606 bushels of rye.

IMPORTS OF GOTTENBURG IN 1863.

Brandy.—The import of this article for the last three years is as follows:

	Pounds.
1861	4,414,040
1862	2,822,355
1863	4,328,241

Coffee.—The following table shows the amount of coffee imported for the last three years; also the amount on hand at the close of each year:

	Import.	On hand December 31.
1861	pounds.. 5,577,306	1,659,084
1862	do.... 7,437,599	2,716,585
1863	do.... 6,351,662	3,288,807

Cotton.—The following table of the importation of this article gives us an example of the descending scale:

	Pounds.
1861	11,173,079
1862	2,127,071
1863	1,635,227

Dried fish.—1,275,000 pounds of dried fish were imported in 1863, against 950,000 pounds in 1862.

Herring.—About 350,000 bushels of herring were imported from Norway in 1863, against 400,000 bushels in 1862.

Hides and skins.—During 1863 were imported 2,948,290 pounds of hides and skins, against 2,416,031 pounds in 1862.

Salt.—420,794 bushels of salt were imported in 1863, against 527,022 bushels in 1862.

Sugar.—The following table shows the number of pounds of sugar imported from 1861 to 1863, and also the amount left on hand at the close of each year:

	Import.	On hand December 31.
1861	pounds.. 16,895,152	3,486,515
1862	do.... 18,229,670	6,116,754
1863	do.... 15,974,946	4,663,948

The falling off in the importation from over eighteen millions of pounds in 1862 to less than sixteen millions in 1863 is the natural result of the overstrained importation of 1862, which left over six millions of pounds on hand at the close of that year. Nine-tenths of the sugar imported is brown sugar of an inferior quality, which is refined by extensive establishments in Gottenburg.

Tobacco.—Less tobacco was imported in 1863 than in any year since 1850. The following table shows the amount of tobacco leaves and stems imported during the last three years:

		Tobacco leaves.	Stems.
1861	pounds..	901,779	247,854
1862	do....	1,023,971	186,222
1863	do....	690,144	200,381

APRIL 20, 1864.

SIR: In accordance with the request contained in your despatch No. 28, I have the honor to forward you, herewith enclosed, a "schedule of the stamp duties of the kingdom of Sweden" and a "schedule of the excise and poll taxes of the kingdom of Sweden."

These schedules I have extracted principally from a mass of official documents, the size of which nearly appalled me when I first broke ground upon it. Some of the information I have also obtained verbally from government officers. The enclosures have, however, been prepared from the best official sources, and with such care that I am able to certify they are accurate and complete:

POLL AND EXCISE TAXES OF THE KINGDOM OF SWEDEN.

	Rd.
Banks, private, have the right to issue bank notes for every thousand riksdalers issued	2 00
Discoveries, the value of which amounts to 1,000 riksdalers, 4 per cent	
Estates, for every soldier's farm	0 30
Foreigners doing business for first three months	100 00
Foreigners continuing, for every additional month	40 00
Foreigners doing business without paying the above tax are fined 500 riksdalers, and, besides, must pay	100 00
Foreigners, men or women, who with permission travel about exhibiting menageries, panoramas, theatres, concerts, circuses, &c., are open to the public in Gottenburg and Stockholm, per day	3 00
Gifts of real estate with the full right to the property, 5 per cent.	
Income tax is not assessed on incomes less than 400 riksdalers.	
Income derived from capital or labor is subject to a tax of 1 per cent., and on incomes not exceeding 1,800 riksdalers, 300 are free from taxation.	
Legacies of annual revenues or interest without right to the property from which the revenue or interest is derived, for the first year, 2 per cent.	
Legacies of feoffment, in trust or entail, of the value of estate given in fee, 5 per cent.	
Legacies in fee simple of all real and personal estate, capital, or claims, 5 per cent.	
Mines of Dylla, for every cwt. of sulphur	0 31
" " vitriol	0 08
" , " red ochre	0 06
Poll tax for men	0 40
Poll tax for women	0 20
Possession in land for every riksdaler of 100 valuation	0 03
Real estate of all other kinds, for every 100 riksdalers of valuation	0 05

NOTE.—These soldiers' farms are allotted according to the so-called "Indelta" system. This system was established by Charles XI, and is peculiar to Sweden. The country is divided into military districts, and the holders of crown lands within these districts provide, in proportion to their holdings, the troops form-ing the Indelta. In fact, both officers and men are permanently quartered upon and paid by the holders of the crown lands. Both have a certain portion of land, with a dwelling, &c., upon it, assigned to them. In time of peace, and while not called out for the annual review, they cultivate this land themselves, otherwise the crown holders must cultivate it for them. The men are also employed in making roads and other public works. During their leisure time they are bound to work at the usual rate of wages for the crown holders. Both men and officers provide their own clothing, and, in addition, the officers provide their arms and horses.

SCHEDULE OF STAMP DUTIES OF THE KINGDOM OF SWEDEN.

	Rd.
Appointments, held at the pleasure of the king	6 00
Appointment of a clergyman to be pastor of a congregation....	15 00
Appointment of a clergyman to a higher grade, on difference of salary, 5 per cent.	
Appointment of town porters and others whose salary is above 20 riksdalers, 5 per cent	
Bill of exchange..	1 00
Bill of divorce or separation...............................	0 25
Bill of sale, for every 100 riksdalers......................	0 60
Certificate, iron wharf, for obtaining a loan on iron held........	0 25
Certificate of master mechanic in Stockholm, Gottenburg, and towns of 1st class	3 00
In towns of 2d and 3d class	1 50
In towns of 4th and 5th class....	1 00
Certificate of minister of justice at first publication of a news-paper...	5 00
Certificate of measurers to measure Swedish ships....'........	0 75
" " " foreign ships	1 50
Certificates of notary publics, when given to Swedish subjects, per sheet...	0 25
Foreigners, per sheet...............................	0 50
Certificate for burghers in Stockholm or Gottenburg— For merchants..	33 00
Manufacturers..................................	25 00
Sea captains	12 00
Mechanics	10 00
Other tradesmen................................	9 00

Certificates for Burghers.

	Class of towns.				
	First.	Second.	Third.	Fourth.	Fifth.
For merchants................riksdalers..	20	15	10	8	5
manufacturers.................do	15	10	8	5	4
sea captains ....do.....	8	6	5	4	3
other tradesmen ....do.....	6	4	3	2	1
mechanics ....do.....	7	5	4	3	2

Rd.

Charts or maps used by the general surveyors, or by the surveyors in the country, per Swedish mantal	0 20
Charts, less than one and greater than ¾ mantal	0 15
Below ¾ mantal	0 10
Charter parties, for every 100 riksdalers worth of freight	0 30
Commission, held at pleasure	3 00
Commissions, warrants, or letters patent, by which offices or appointments at the royal court are given, on the amount of salary, 5 per cent.	
Commissions or appointments to the civil, military, ecclesiastical, or other departments, appointed by his royal Majesty, and besides on the amount of salary, 15 per cent.	
Commissions to any higher honor or dignity of office in the same branch of service, on difference of salary, 15 per cent.	
Commissions in any other branch of service, as, for example, a military man receiving a civil appointment, or the reverse, on difference of salary, 35 per cent.	
Commission, letter patent, or appointment for any one not previously having been in the service of the crown, on the amount of salary, 65 per cent.	
Commission of county sheriffs given by the chancellor of justice	9 00
Commission for parish clerks	1 00
Commission for town sheriffs in Gottenburg and towns of first class	9 00
In all other towns of the kingdom	6 00
Commission of notary publics in Stockholm and Gottenburg . . .	24 00
In all other towns	6 00
Contracts, reservations in, when vised by a judge	0 70
Contract, on every 100 riksdalers paid	0 30
Contracts, reservations in marriage contracts	3 00
Crown duties, on payment of	0 40
Decision on pension	6 00
Diploma, for doctors without previous examination	80 00
Diploma, for agents, consuls general, consuls, who receive salary, on amount of salary, 5 per cent.	
Discharges, in case his Majesty permits, the whole or part of the salary to be retained	6 00
Documents, showing a person's right to property, for every 100 riksdalers valuation	0 15
Insurance, letter of	0 25
Insurance, marine policy, up to 200 riksdalers	0 10
For every 100 riksdalers above	0 05
License of ship-brokers in Stockholm and Gottenburg	50 00
In all other towns of the kingdom	13 00
License of sworn brokers in Stockholm and Gottenburg	150 00
In all other towns	40 00
License for keeping public houses in Stockholm and Gottenburg (without spirits)	6 00
In towns of 1st and 2d class	4 00
In remaining towns and in the country	2 00
License to build foundries, manufactories, paper and saw mills . .	15 00
License to trade, without the other privileges of a citizen	8 00
Legal documents issued, King's judgment in cases of contested property less than 3,000 riksdalers in value for every copy . . .	13 00

	Rd.
King's judgment in cases of desertion and confirmations, in cases of reconciliation when the sum is fixed at a value above 3,000 riksdalers	16 00
9,000 riksdalers	22 00
15,000 riksdalers	26 00
30,000 riksdalers	50 00
For every full 100 riksdalers more	1 50
Documents of this kind, taking up more than one sheet, for every additional sheet	2 00
Document of safe conduct and person	6 00
Summons, warrants, &c., per sheet—	
From first-class courts	0 25
From second class courts	0 50
From third-class courts	2 00
Judgments, sentences and resolutions, per sheet—	
From first-class courts	0 25
From second-class courts	0 50
Documents of all other kinds issued from first-class courts	0 25
From second and third class courts	0 50
Legal documents delivered in, deductions submitted and deductions in offset	5 00
For every additional sheet	2 00
Applications, actions, and declarations, per sheet	0 25
Legal inventory on estate of a deceased person, ¼ of 1 per cent. When value of estate is less than 1,000 riksdalers, free.	
Letters of free passage for ships	0 40
When bond is given	0 20
Passport for Sweden or Norway, for two or more persons	0 40
One person	0 20
For foreign countries two or more persons	1 50
For one person	1 00
Pass, custom-house, for boats trading abroad	0 15
For decked ships	0 50
For foreign ships	1 00
Patent, (privilege exclusive)	23 00
" of nobility	250 00
" of barons	500 00
of counts	1,000 00
" to which any one is added, privileges, titles of honor and prerogatives above other subjects, as senators	1,000 00
" of nomination as knight of the royal order of the Seraphim	100 00
" of nomination as commander of the great cross of the royal order of the Sword	50 00
" " North Star	50 00
" " " Wasa	50 00
Patent of nomination as a commander of the royal order of King Charles XII	50 00
Patent of nomination as knight or member of the royal order of the Sword	12 00
" of nomination as knight or member of the royal order of the North Star	12 00
" of nomination as knight or member of the royal order of the Wasa	12 00
Promissory notes, for every 100 riksdalers	0 30

Rd.

Ship articles	0 75
Stamped paper, whole sheets	0 25
" "	0 50

Stamps, single and double, 10, 15, 20, 25, 30, 40, 50, and 75 ores, and 1, 2, 3, 4, 5, 6, 7, 8, 9, 10, 13, 15, 25, 50, 75, and 100 riksdalers.

SEPTEMBER 7, 1864.

I have the honor to forward the department the following report of the commerce and shipping of Sweden for 1862, which I have condensed from the latest available statistics :

IMPORTS.

The principal imports of Sweden are coffee, cotton, salt, spirits, sugar, tobacco, wine, and wool. During the year 1862 there were imported of these articles the following amounts :

Coffee ....pounds*..		15, 891, 498
Cotton ....do....		3, 064, 285
Sugar, refined ....do....		3, 717, 696
brown ....do....		34, 803, 184
Salt ....cubic feet†..		1, 939, 744
Spirits: Arrack...................................pounds..		1, 079, 552
Rum ....do....		665, 066
Cognac ....do....		267, 839
Alcohol ....do....		175, 587
Tobacco leaves ....do....		3, 038, 532
stems......................................do....		600, 339
manufactured ....do....		54, 421
Wine in barrels......................................do....		3, 429, 554
in bottles......................................do....		62, 595
Wool ....do....		2, 715, 751

The importation of cotton during 1860 and 1861 amounted to nineteen millions of pounds per annum, while in 1862 it did not reach four millions. This great falling off is due to the American blockade.

EXPORTS.

Iron is the one great export of Sweden. There are also exported considerable quantities of planks, deals, &c., oats, and some steel and copper. The quantities of these articles exported in 1862 are as follows :

Iron in bars ....centner*..		2, 099, 389
manufactured ....do....		414, 131
other sorts.....................................do....		155, 329
Steel ....do....		152, 892
Copper...do....		31, 038
Planks and deals ....tolft†..		1, 603, 869
Staves of beech ....number..		5, 021, 098
oak ....do....		3, 677, 292
Oats ....bushels (about)..		4, 000, 000

* 100 Swedish pounds, equal 95½ English.
† 100 Swedish cubic feet, equal 92¾ English.

The following table shows the value of the imports and exports from and to each country during the year 1862. These values are reckoned in Swedish riks-dalers, riksmynt, of which $3\frac{15}{100}$ equal $1:

Countries.	Value of imports.	Value of exports.	Overplus of imports.	Overplus of exports.	Total.
Norway	5,784,000	2,253,000	3,531,000		
Finland	2,771,000	2,167,000	604,000		
Russia	4,420,000	169,000	4,251,000		
Danish States	8,201,000	7,739,000	462,000		
Prussia	4,873,000	1,368,000	3,505,000		
Lubeck	26,301,000	4,310,000	21,991,000		
Hamburg	3,684,000	1,528,000	2,156,000		
Bremen	4,287,000	275,000	4,012,000		
Netherlands	3,472,000	2,020,000	1,452,000		
Austria	58,000	17,000	41,000		
West Indies	3,035,000	....	3,035,000		
Brazil	6,304,000	759,000	5,545,000		
					50,585,000
Mecklenburg	51,000	725,000	....	674,000	
Hanover and Oldenburg	....	150,000	....	150,000	
Belgium	1,514,000	1,525,000	....	11,000	
Gr't Britain and Ireland	19,814,000	39,519,000	....	19,705,000	
France	1,845,000	9,801,000	....	7,956,000	
Portugal	452,000	1,937,000	....	1,485,000	
Spain	575,000	3,825,000	....	3,250,000	
Gibraltar and Malta	....	182,000	....	182,000	
Italy	547,000	1,494,000	....	947,000	
Turkey	....	167,000	....	167,000	
Egypt	....	64,000	....	64,000	
Algiers	....	934,000	....	934,000	
Rest of North African coast	....	295,000	....	295,000	
United States	162,000	1,083,000	....	921,000	
Rest of America	....	47,000	....	47,000	
Cape of Good Hope	....	638,000	....	638,000	
E. Indies and Australia	370,000	1,647,000	....	1,277,000	
					38,703,000
Total	98,520,000	86,638,000			
Excess of imports	....	....	....	....	11,882,000

The total importation of Sweden for 1862 is thus seen to amount to $26,107,800; and the total exportation to $22,959,070—leaving an overplus of imports to the amount of $3,148,730.

The following table shows the value of the imports and exports of Sweden to and from each country for each year from 1853 to 1862, inclusive, reckoned in Swedish riksmynt:

---

* 24 centners equal 1 ton.
† 1 tolft equal 15 cubic feet English.

Value of imports in riksdalere, riksmynt.

	1853.	1854.	1855.	1856.	1857.	1858.	1859.	1860.	1861.	1862.
Norway	4,239,000	6,048,000	8,435,000	8,735,000	8,851,000	5,102,000	5,394,000	5,554,000	5,641,000	5,784,000
Finland	668,000	2,179,000	3,372,000	2,886,000	1,668,000	1,447,000	1,746,000	1,846,000	3,652,000	2,771,000
Russia	4,776,000	473,000	207,000	9,373,000	7,550,000	1,945,000	2,304,000	2,921,000	7,669,000	4,420,000
Danish States	3,174,000	3,941,000	4,697,000	6,690,000	4,777,000	4,385,000	4,741,000	5,872,000	7,221,000	8,201,000
Prussia	713,000	1,747,000	3,327,000	3,079,000	3,198,000	1,061,000	1,042,000	963,000	3,097,000	4,873,000
Mecklenburg, Hanseatic cities, Hanover, and Oldenburg	16,955,000	39,040,000	27,357,000	27,377,000	20,603,000	18,612,000	22,033,000	25,974,000	27,154,000	34,383,000
Netherlands	589,000	939,000	1,866,000	2,693,000	1,547,000	1,299,000	1,565,000	3,296,000	4,714,000	3,472,000
Belgium	147,000	271,000	310,000	307,000	253,000	437,000	865,000	581,000	943,000	1,514,000
Great Britain and Ireland	8,509,000	13,896,000	18,495,000	19,217,000	14,853,000	10,696,000	15,733,000	16,549,000	23,362,000	19,814,000
France	713,000	1,099,000	1,230,000	1,383,000	1,361,000	1,091,000	2,374,000	1,792,000	1,505,000	1,845,000
Portugal	247,000	692,000	480,000	712,000	373,000	286,000	387,000	516,000	504,000	452,000
Spain	306,000	756,000	985,000	775,000	759,000	408,000	566,000	677,000	551,000	575,000
Gibraltar and Malta				1,000			1,000		1,000	
Italy	246,000	309,000	378,000	307,000	465,000	311,000	470,000	578,000	647,000	547,000
Austria			79,000	148,000	180,000	96,000	90,000	249,000	81,000	58,000
Turkey										
Egypt										
Algiers and remaining coast of North Africa										
United States	3,674,000	4,875,000	2,911,000	6,996,000	6,405,000	2,902,000	5,518,000	6,438,000	6,425,000	162,000
West Indies	907,000	901,000	1,194,000	1,800,000	2,285,000	2,357,000	2,130,000	2,203,000	4,419,000	3,035,000
Brazil	4,324,000	7,607,000	7,242,000	9,575,000	6,633,000	786,000	5,413,000	4,459,000	6,762,000	6,304,000
Other lands in North and South America			3,000							
Cape of Good Hope										
East Indies	2,103,000	889,000	2,357,000	3,360,000	3,568,000	3,669,000	1,849,000	1,991,000	2,224,000	370,000
Total	51,580,000	78,655,000	84,841,000	105,844,000	85,290,000	56,920,000	74,241,000	82,469,000	106,570,000	98,520,000

Value of exports in riksdalere, rikmynt.

	1853.	1854.	1855.	1856.	1857.	1858.	1859.	1860.	1861.	1862.
Norway	923,000	3,362,000	6,258,000	4,023,000	2,650,000	2,297,000	3,642,000	4,485,000	3,097,000	2,253,000
Finland	1,014,000	414,000	317,000	2,505,000	1,851,000	1,494,000	1,241,000	1,312,000	2,666,000	2,167,000
Russia	244,000	199,000	88,000	1,172,000	308,000	250,000	1,138,000	441,000	201,000	169,000
Danish States	7,159,000	10,652,000	11,547,000	9,116,000	8,152,000	5,405,000	6,761,000	7,067,000	6,629,000	7,739,000
Prussia	2,666,000	3,954,000	7,093,000	6,053,000	2,355,000	2,358,000	2,310,000	1,758,000	1,530,000	1,366,000
Mecklenburg, Hanse-towns, and Oldenburg	5,268,000	7,851,000	7,440,000	17,333,000	17,905,000	6,013,000	10,381,000	5,994,000	5,055,000	6,988,000
Islands	1,110,000	2,072,000	8,586,000	2,935,000	1,053,000	1,850,000	1,981,000	2,753,000	2,049,000	2,020,000
Belgium	333,000	583,000	1,271,000	649,000	911,000	861,000	1,784,000	2,124,000	2,627,000	1,525,000
Great Britain and Ireland	23,900,000	34,639,000	39,758,000	39,886,000	24,579,000	23,646,000	39,400,000	41,710,000	35,612,000	39,519,000
France	3,971,000	4,553,000	5,360,000	6,256,000	8,445,000	5,561,000	7,679,000	7,705,000	10,423,000	9,801,000
Portugal	1,144,000	2,088,000	1,389,000	1,410,000	1,572,000	1,301,000	1,385,000	1,397,000	2,024,000	1,937,000
Spain	643,000	1,622,000	1,002,000	1,083,000	1,362,000	1,301,000	1,656,000	2,835,000	3,875,000	3,825,000
Gibraltar and Malta	10,000	111,000	51,000	27,000	291,000	145,000	153,000	263,000	204,000	182,000
Italy	156,000	535,000	456,000	388,000	492,000	450,000	359,000	996,000	608,000	1,494,000
Austria	192,000	379,000		34,000	58,000	70,000	129,000			17,000
Turkey					44,000	38,000	40,000	25,000	27,000	167,000
Egypt			4,000		10,000	23,000		61,000	27,000	64,000
Algiers								892,000	373,000	934,000
Remaining coast of North Africa	390,000	543,000	621,000	700,000	765,000	849,000	639,000	156,000	130,000	295,000
United States	1,745,000	3,260,000	2,859,000	3,471,000	2,952,000	1,996,000	2,878,000	2,660,000	841,000	1,083,000
West Indies	640,000	939,000	667,000	513,000	752,000	845,000	763,000	653,000	835,000	759,000
Brazil					6,000					
Other lands in North and South America	90,000	270,000	36,000	141,000	265,000	68,000	503,000	72,000		47,000
Cape of Good Hope	357,000	472,000	313,000	249,000	629,000	944,000	843,000	625,000	1,345,000	638,000
E. Indies and Australia	309,000	726,000	801,000	1,659,000	729,000	1,119,000		582,000	901,000	1,647,000
Total	51,705,000	79,215,000	95,847,000	92,433,000	78,434,000	58,894,000	78,667,000	85,496,000	81,084,000	85,638,000

DUTIES.

The total revenue derived by the Swedish government from duties on imports and exports amounted in 1862 to the sum of $3,655,913, as follows:

Duties on imports..	$3,591,736
" exports..	64,177
Total	3,655,913

There are no longer export duties in this kingdom, the act abolishing them having gone into effect on January 1, 1864.

SHIPPING.

Table showing the number and tonnage of vessels with cargoes entered and cleared at Swedish ports in 1862.

Countries.	ENTERED.		CLEARED.	
	No.	Tons.	No.	Tons.
Sweden........	2,736	356,208	3,875	416,724
United States...................	1	2,333	2	768
Other flags...................	3,054	392,735	3,716	920,484
Total	5,791	750,276	7,593	1,337,976

The Swedish merchant navy is very large in comparison with the size and population of the country. There are owned in Sweden 3,108 vessels of all classes, of an aggregate tonnage of 347,211 tons, and navigated by 11,339 men.

The following table shows the number and capacity of foreign vessels of every flag, *with* or *without* cargoes, entering any Swedish port for each year from 1858 to 1862, inclusive. The capacity is reckoned in Swedish lasts, one of which equals 2⅘ tons:

Countries.	1858.		1859.		1860.		1861.		1862.	
	No.	Last.	No.	Last.	No.	Last.	No.	Last.	No.	Last.
Norway..............	1,290	129,443	1,588	166,763	1,841	199,304	1,718	198,085	2,051	239,865
Finland...............	619	25,152	750	34,621	676	32,125	880	40,590	818	40,739
Russia	20	293	37	378	41	657	55	1,177	26	691
Prussia..............	211	23,512	162	15,949	58	5,524	192	13,516	230	13,396
Denmark	985	18,981	1,100	25,704	1,272	30,082	1,074	30,245	857	23,136
Mecklenburg	47	4,589	141	15,776	64	6,994	90	10,064	84	8,945
Lubeck..............	1	63	5	510	3	158	8	776	2	136
Hamburg..............	15	2,280	19	1,896	17	1,274	25	3,760	24	2,936
Bremen	6	1,737	4	734	3	460	8	2,379	2	333
Hanover	82	4,370	171	8,018	199	8,848	176	8,552	155	7,239
Netherlands	133	11,240	131	7,574	139	8,466	222	15,734	202	14,616
Belgium..............	1	60	.....	......	2	192	1	141	2	193
Great Britain........	357	36,462	366	30,848	332	37,729	490	51,558	482	60,027
France..............	55	4,544	85	5,876	101	6,922	143	9,676	192	12,325
Spain	2	247	1	82	4	509	5	597	1	123
Portugal	.....	......	1	96	.....	......	.....	......	.....	......
Italy.................	.....	......	.....	......	1	114	.....	......	1	138
United States.........	10	2,701	19	5,596	18	5,118	51	15,570	10	2,386

The great falling off in American shipping from 51 in 1861 to 10 in 1862 will at once attract attention. This decrease is but a natural result of our blockade. The American vessels remain away because there is no cotton to bring, and it does not pay to make the voyage for the sake of the home freight on iron.

DIRECT TRADE BETWEEN THE UNITED STATES AND SWEDEN.

On account of the blockade of the harbors of the cotton-producing States, the imports of Sweden from the United States, which in 1860 and 1861 reached a value of nearly $1,750,000, have in 1862 dwindled away to the paltry sum of $43,000.

Of cotton, the importation of which article in 1860 amounted to 10,659,456 pounds, there was imported in 1862 *not a single pound.* It would be well for those croakers who worry themselves and their neighbors with the idea that our blockade is not effective to ponder on these figures.

The direct imports of Sweden from the United States in 1862 were all brought in two vessels—one Swedish, with cargo worth 51,000 riksdalers, and one American, worth 111,000 riksdalers. Total value of imports 162,000 riksdalers, or $43,200.

The direct export from Sweden to the United States in 1862, though larger than in 1861, was yet much larger than usual, and reached a value of but $288,800. These goods were carried to the United States by the following vessels: 2 American, with cargoes worth 118,000 riksdalers; 7 Swedish, worth 638,000 riksdalers, together with 2 English, 2 Hamburg, and 1 Danish, worth 327,000 riksdalers. Total number of vessels 14; total value of cargoes 841,000 riksdalers, or $288,800.

DIRECT IMPORT.

The following table shows the amounts of the principal direct imports of Sweden from the United States for each year from 1860 to 1862, inclusive:

Description.	1860.	1861.	1862.
Tobacco leaves ....pounds ..	633,541	651,996	....
Tobacco stems...................................do	462,188	2,250,532	51,466
Rice ....do	16,402	1,049	....
Train oil ....do	....	24,420	....
Dyewoods ....riksdalers..	2,080	16,725	8,100
Pepper...pounds..	15,116	10,940	35,040
Cotton ....do	10,659,456	7,439,531	....

There was also imported from the United States in 1862 331,185 pounds turpentine, 1,479 pounds rum, 84 centners dry untanned hides, 506 pounds coffee, also seed to the amount of 655 riksdalers.

DIRECT EXPORT.

The following table shows the amounts of the direct exports from Sweden to the United States for each year from 1860 to 1862, inclusive:

Description.	1860.	1861.	1862.
Bar iron ....centner..	328,146	95,270	116,829
Hoop iron ....do....	3,609	....	74
Blooms ....do....	380	....	....
Plate iron ....do....	884	....	....
Steel...do.....	288	....	....

It must be remembered that this table gives only the amounts of the *direct* exports. Nearly an equal amount of iron and steel is exported to the United States *indirectly*, *via* Hamburg, Bremen, and London, and is called "German manufactured iron," "Lancashire iron," &c.

In 1862 there were exported, directly and indirectly, to Boston alone 6,030 tons Swedish iron, worth $348,047. The asking prices were for the so-called German manufactured iron $75 to $80; for the so-called Lancashire iron $85 to $92 50; and for stamps of the choicest quality $107 50 to $112 50 per ton, in gold coin, at 6 to 8 months' credit.

SWEDISH VESSELS IN AMERICAN WATERS.

The following table shows the number and capacity of all Swedish vessels arriving at and clearing from ports in the United States (except California) for each year from 1858 to 1862, inclusive:

Arrivals of Swedish vessels in the United States.

Years.	From Sweden.		From foreign ports.				Total.	
	With cargoes.		With cargoes.		In ballast.			
	No.	Last.*	No.	Last.	No.	Last.	No.	Last.
1858	6	1,106	19	3,130	3	587	28	4,323
1859	7	1,166	22	3,444	4	836	33	5,446
1860	8	1,175	12	2,258	5	901	25	4,334
1861	9	781	27	4,635	13	2,840	46	8,256
1862	7	1,182	19	1,995	5	910	31	4,087

* Equal to 2⅓ tons English.

Departures of Swedish vessels from the United States.

Years.	To Sweden.		To foreign ports.				Total.	
			With cargoes.		In ballast.			
	No.	Last.	No.	Last.	No.	Last.	No.	Last.
1858	2	312	19	3,207	2	354	23	3,873
1859	5	928	21	3,225	6	1,035	32	5,118
1860	6	870	14	2,527	1	322	21	3,719
1861	5	741	36	6,551	6	1,157	47	8,450
1862	1	125	33	4,402	....	.....	34	4,528

ANNUAL REPORT.

SEPTEMBER 30, 1864.

Gottenburg, (Swedish Götheborg,) the second city in Sweden, is situated on the left bank of the Göta river, four miles from its mouth. Gottenburg was founded in 1618, by the great Gustavus Adolphus, whose statue stands on the market place, still pointing out, with finger of bronze, the site of the city. Wide canals, frequently spanned by tasteful bridges of granite and iron, run through the centre of the principal streets, giving a Venetian aspect to the town and greatly facilitating its traffic. The houses all stand on piles, but are very solidly built of stone or brick, and the streets well paved and lighted.

The population, including the suburb of Majorne, which is in fact a part of the city, amounts to 50,000, a considerable portion of whom are of Dutch, German, or English descent.

CLIMATE.

The climate is mild, and not liable to great variations; the temperature in summer scarcely ever exceeding 75 degrees Fahrenheit, and in winter seldom descending to zero.

During the entire winter of 1863–'64, the only one I have passed in Sweden, the thermometer did not fall to 15 degrees above zero. Indeed the ice consumed here in the summer has frequently to be imported from Norway. Yet Gottenburg is situated in latitude 57 degrees 42 minutes north, or within 2½ degrees of the parallel of Greenland.

A still more remarkable fact is that the harbors along the entire coast of Norway, even up to the North cape, 4 degrees within the Arctic circle, are never frozen in winter, while all summer potatoes and barley are raised along the banks of the Altenfiord, in 71 degrees north latitude, the highest cultivated land in the world. The gulf stream, which flows *by* America and *on to* Northern Europe, explains all this, while it floats wood from the sunny groves of tropical America on to the arctic coast of Norway in sufficient quantities to greatly assist the inhabitants, who cling to those rugged rocks, in keeping warm when the long night of winter comes on.

LENGTH OF DAYS.

The following table shows the length of day and night at Gottenburg on the longest and shortest day of the year:

Date.	Sun rises.	Sun sets.	Length of day.	Length of night.
December 23..	8. 45 a. m ..	3. 13 p. m ..	6 hours, 28 minutes ...	17 hours, 32 minutes.
June 23......	3. 2 a. m ...	9. 2 p. m ...	18 hours	6 hours.

In summer the northern sky is aglow throughout the short six hours of night, while everything is lighted up by a pale twilight; there is, in fact, no night at all. In winter the sun simply slides along the southern horizon, reaching an altitude of but 10 degrees at high noon, and sliding under soon after 3 o'clock.

SWEDISH CROPS FOR 1864.

In the early part of the season the fields gave good promise of a bounteous harvest, but heavy rains in the latter part of August and throughout September made it almost impossible to get the grain dry, and the greater portion of the crop has been secured in a damaged condition. The crop of 1864 will thus fall considerably below the average, at least in quality.

FACTS FOR CAPTAINS PROPOSING TO SAIL FOR GOTTENBURG.

Port charges, including pilotage, light and beacon dues, amount to about $275 for a vessel of 600 tons, or nearly 50 cents per ton; this also includes the discharging of ballast.

Wharfage.—None to pay.

Quarantine.—There are no quarantine charges, neither is there any hospital where sailors are received free of expense.

Printed port regulations are handed to all ships on arriving.

Insurance to New York or Boston during the spring and summer is generally 1½ to 2 per centum, and in the autumn 3 to 3½ per centum.

Freights to New York or Boston have averaged about $7 50 per ton, iron; this, however, is rather more than the usual rates.

Depth of water.—Vessels can carry 17 feet up the Göta river as far as Klippan, a suburb of Gottenburg, 2½ miles further down the river, but only 14 feet to the city itself. Vessels drawing more than 14 feet finish their loading at Klippan by means of lighters. Ships can lie at Klippan with perfect safety.

Winter on the *west* coast of Sweden seldom sets in before the 1st of January, and rarely lasts more than two months; on the east coast, however, winter generally commences in the month of November and continues till April; sometimes in the Gulf of Bothnia even till the latter end of May.

The harbor of Gottenburg, although fresh water, is sometimes navigable all winter; such was the case last winter, that of 1863–'64.

AMERICAN SHIPPING.

But two American ships have visited this port during the consular year ending September 30, 1864. The first, "General Butler," 1,095$\frac{57}{95}$ tons, of Bath, Maine, arrived in ballast from London on October 16, 1863, and sailed on November 16 for Melbourne, Australia, with 508$\frac{117}{168}$ standard deals, worth $20,347. The second, "Free Trade," 1,284$\frac{11}{95}$ tons, arrived on June 2, 1864, in ballast, from Hamburg, and sailed on June 30 for Boston, with 1,509 tons iron, worth $86,543 82, and 210 emigrants.

TRADE BETWEEN UNITED STATES AND GOTTENBURG.

Shipping.—During the year 24 vessels have cleared from Gottenburg for the United States—14 for Boston and 10 for New York. Only one of these was American; the remaining were mostly Swedish and Nova Scotia vessels. But one vessel has arrived from the United States, the Swedish brig "Susannah," from New York, with a cargo of petroleum.

Exports.—The following table shows the amount and value of all merchandise exported from this port to the United States for each quarter of the year ending September 30, 1864:

Quarter ending.	IRON AND STEEL.		OTHER ARTICLES.		Total.
	Tons.	Value.	Amount.	Value.	
1863. December 31	2,356	$130,270 03	....	....	$130,270 03
1864. March 31	1,142	65,591 30	100 bushels oats.	$97 86	65,689 16
June 30	2,984	166,334 85	Anchovies	78 73	166,413 58
September 30	8,622	530,856 14	....	....	530,856 14
Total	15,104	893,052 32	....	176 59	893,228 91

H. Ex. Doc. 60——24

I would call particular attention to the large amount of iron and steel exported during the last quarter of the year, it being no less than 8,622 tons, worth $530,856 14. This is a much larger amount than has been exported in any previous quarter since the establishment of this consulate.

The 100 bushels of oats exported in the first quarter of 1864 were sent by me to the Department of Agriculture for seed.

Imports.—The imports of Gottenburg from the United States during the year were 791 barrels refined petroleum, 200 boxes ditto, and 15 boxes spirits, (naphtha,) worth, together, $12,000. These articles were all brought from New York in one vessel—the Swedish brig "Susannah."

The petroleum met with a quick sale, at high prices, and paid a handsome profit to the importers.

Several agencies for American sewing machines have been established here this year. These machines are selling rapidly at good prices.

Additional articles which the United States might export to Gottenburg.— American fruits and vegetables, preserved in hermetically sealed cans, especially pine apples, peaches, peas, and corn, would, I believe, sell well here, with great profit, also fresh and dried apples.

STEAM PILE-DRIVER.

The houses of Gottenburg are almost all built upon piles, yet there is not a steam pile-driver in the city. The piles are all driven by hand; a gang of 15 men clutch as many ropes and bob up and down an iron weight, with cries as wild as when all hands are bracing up the yards in a blow at midnight; then they rest, and then bob and sing again, till sometimes the hour closes before the pile is fairly driven into its place.

An enterprising American could make his fortune by introducing and work- ing one or two small steam pile-drivers of moderate power, so constructed that they could be used either on land or water.

A LINE OF STEAMSHIPS BETWEEN NEW YORK AND GOTTENBURG.

The project of establishing a line of steamers to sail once a month between New York and Gottenburg has been lately introduced by myself to the atten- tion of the merchants of Gottenburg, and has been received with favor. Two screw steamers of 800 to 1,000 tons would be sufficient to begin with.

To ascertain whether it would pay, let us look at the volume of trade flowing between Gottenburg and the United States:

First, as to exports: There were exported during the past year to the United States 15,104 tons iron, at an average freight of $7 50 per ton, which gives $113,280 as the freight on iron. Also, 2,500 immigrants, which, at $30 per capita, gives $75,000; total, $188,280. The mails, some Russian trade *via* Stockholm, and extra trade created by steam, would bring the amount of freight on exports from Gottenburg up to at least $200,000 per annum.

Second, as to imports: Sweden imported before our rebellion nineteen million pounds of cotton, six million pounds of tobacco a year, and will doubtless im- port at least an equal amount after the rebellion is quelled. There will also be in the future a considerable importation of petroleum.

A great portion of these imports would undoubtedly be brought by the steamers proposed.

I present this project as being worthy the careful consideration of American merchants.

DECEMBER 31, 1863.

I have the honor herewith to transmit an abstract of the report on commerce and navigation of the kingdom of Norway in the year 1862, (enclosure No. 1,) which has just been received.   *   *   *   *   *   *

In submitting this report, I would respectfully renew my suggestion respecting the reduction of duty upon fish and herring. I have since my arrival used every influence in my power to establish direct trade between this country and the United States, and have in a measure been successful. The only products which this country can export, besides small quantities of iron and copper, are fish and herring, and the market in the west for those articles promises fair; but there is now a new obstacle in the way of exporting some into the United States besides the existing high revenue tariff, namely, by the section of the Norwegian passenger act of the 25th of May, 1863, which takes effect on the 1st day of January, 1864, which provides that herring carried in vessels having passengers on board must be put up in double tight casks or barrels, which, besides being impracticable, makes the herring too expensive for exportation to the United States, which will, so long as this state of things exist, destroy the prospects of direct trade. From the within report might be seen that the import of Norway is large in proportion to its population, and worthy of attention, and to secure any considerable portion of this trade it is necessary to prepare the way for reciprocal commerce, and the introduction of Norwegian products into the United States.   *   *   *   *   *   *   *   *

Abstract of the tables exhibiting the commerce and navigation of Norway in 1862, published by the Department of the Interior, at Christiana, 1863, in kind.

EXPORTS.

(The most important articles.)

Cod and and other salted dried fish	pounds..	65, 450, 328
Herrings, salted	barrels..	928, 536
Spawn	do....	26, 165
Cod-liver and other fish-oil	gallons..	1, 911, 449
Bar iron	pounds..	2, 725, 536
Copper, crude	do....	1, 020, 739
Timber and lumber	Petersburg standard..	725, 536

IMPORTS.

(The most important articles.)

Grain of all kinds	bushels..	5, 814, 760
Beef, salted and fresh	pounds..	846, 483
Pork and lard	do....	1, 838, 397
Cheese	do....	686, 138
Butter	do....	3, 463, 855
Salt	bushels..	3, 112, 044
Coffee	pounds..	11, 532, 222
Sugar	do....	12, 742, 876
Tobacco	do....	3, 153, 777

Wines	gallons..	177, 436
Spirituous liquors	do....	284, 784
Coal and coke	bushels..	4, 997, 252
Cotton	pounds..	1, 197, 784
Manufactures of cotton	do....	877, 344
Flax and hemp	do....	7, 311, 168
Manufactures of flax and hemp (excepting cordage)	do....	1, 374, 431
Cordage	do....	250, 685
Wool	do....	313, 088
Manufactures of wool	do....	1, 068, 801

Articles exported direct to the United States from Norway in the year 1862.

Iron in bars and herrings.

Articles imported direct from the United States to Norway in the year 1862.

Beef, salted	pounds..	8, 916
Bread of wheat	do....	11, 321
Beans	bushels..	92
Butter	pounds..	2, 574
Castings	do....	925
Chains	do....	22
Cheese	do....	80
Cigars	do....	797
Coffee	do....	368
Coal oil	do....	1, 151
Corn	bushels..	1, 392
Flour, wheat	barrels..	437
Glassware	pounds..	192
Japanned ware	do....	30
Leather	do....	95
Machines manufactured from iron	do....	47
Metals, manufactured	do....	38
Pork, salted	do....	41, 688
smoked	do....	566
Skins for furriers, dried	do....	730
Skins for furriers, green	do....	1, 652
Sugar	do....	863
Spirits	gallons..	16
Rye	bushels..	47, 188
Staves (valued)	specie dollars..	29
Tobacco, manufactured	pounds..	10
manufactured into snuff	do....	14
Tallow candles	do....	1, 301
Star candles	do....	614
Vinegar	gallons..	88
Wheat	bushels..	2, 132
Wine	gallons..	597
Soap	pounds..	732
Wool, manufactured	do....	20
Machines (value)	specie dollars..	240
Paper and books	pounds..	42

Arrivals.

	Loaded.		In ballast.		Total, together.	
	No.	Tonnage.	No.	Tonnage.	No.	Tonnage.
Norwegian.....	2,888	334,144	3,952	762,934	6,840	1,097,078
Foreign........	2,155	152,612	2,333	236,401	4,488	389,013
Total........	5,043	486,756	6,285	999,335	11,328	1,486,091

Departures.

Norwegian.....	6,378	886,928	690	264,997	7,068	1,151,925
Foreign	4,106	352,967	402	46,911	4,508	399,878
Total........	10,484	1,239,895	1,092	311,908	11,576	1,551,803

At the close of the year 1862 the commercial navy of the kingdom of Norway consisted of 5,541 vessels, of aggregate tonnage of 795,021, navigated by 34,817 sailors.

OCTOBER 1, 1864.

The commerce of the city of Bergen has, during the period from October 1, 1863, to September 30, 1864, been nearly the same as the foregoing year; there is but little difference in the amount of imports which was furnished by the same countries in about the same proportion.

The commerce with Sweden has been somewhat heavier, and that with Denmark, on account of the war, considerably less. The commerce in the ports of the Baltic sea was much interrupted by the Danish-German war, besides the herring fisheries of last spring being much less than in 1862, and estimated at 900,000 barrels, consequently the quantity exported was, in some proportion, much less. The export of salted and dried codfish was heavier than in the foregoing year. There were two cargoes of round-dried codfish exported to China; two cargoes of coffee were imported direct from Brazil, and the importation of this article has been much larger than in the former year. The importation of spirits has, since the change in the law, which took effect on the 1st of January, 1864, been much less, although it appears to be about the same. Great quantities were imported in the month of December, so as to escape paying the additional duty. Of sugar, two cargoes have been imported from the West Indies. The importation of cotton was much less, but of manufactured cotton considerable heavier.

The direct trade with Chicago, which was introduced under such promising aspects, I fear will have to be discontinued, the last year's operations having been carried on at a considerable loss to those engaged in it; but when the war shall have closed, and commerce assumed a more steady character, it is to be hoped that this trade will be renewed, as the direct communication with the west has great influence upon the emigration from this country. The main obstacle was the fluctuation in the exchange, the grain prices in the Baltic and Black seas having, the past year, been uncommonly low, particularly rye, and American productions and manufactures have been purchased nearly as low in the European markets as in the United States. The import duty on fish products in the United States makes exportations of that commodity unprofitable. fish products being the chief export from this city.

One vessel cleared for Chicago in the spring with a cargo of iron, fish, and passengers, but having experienced rough weather at sea, and been damaged by the ice, had to discharge her cargo at Montreal. A small shipment of pickled herring and dried codfish was made to Chicago *via* Montreal. No American vessels have visited the ports of this consulate during the past year.

Statement showing the description and quantities of the principal imports of the city of Bergen from October 1, 1863, to September 30, 1864.

Ale and porter	barrels..	6, 485
Beef, salted	do....	6, 856
Bread	do....	4, 923
Bricks and tiles		175, 147
Butter	pounds..	64, 264
Candles, stearine	do....	9, 421
tallow	do....	2, 015
Cheese	do....	39, 506
Chiccory root	do....	213, 678
Coal and cinders	barrels..	151, 351
Coffee	pounds..	1, 450, 790
Cotton	do....	147, 130
Cotton goods	do....	303, 715
Cork-wood	do....	80, 109
Cork-wood, manufactured	do....	3, 933
Farina	do....	43, 186
Feathers	do....	22, 715
Flax and hemp	do....	2, 708, 188
Flax yarn and thread	do....	120, 823
Flax cordage	do....	14, 741
Flax other fabrics	do....	315, 192
Flour, wheat	do....	228, 188
rye	do....	26, 407
Fruit, dried	do....	26, 834
in bottles	do....	8, 871
Glass	do....	84, 758
Grain, wheat	bushels..	62, 141
barley	do....	1, 189, 000
rye	do....	849, 388
oats	do....	21, 928
grits	do....	10, 616
peas	do....	31, 444
Hops	pounds..	49, 706
Hides, dried	do....	171, 740
salted	do....	587, 131
Hoops		1, 433, 194
Leather	pounds..	31, 652
Liquors	do....	102, 422
Logwood, logs	do....	183, 651
other forms	do....	46, 113
Machines	do....	17, 093
Metals, pig iron	tons...	611
manufactured	pounds..	1, 483, 600
lead, tin, pewter	do....	13, 545

Oils, fatty...pounds.. 526,000
   ethereal ....do.... 120,960
Paper..do.... 156,534
Pork, salted and smoked.............................do.... 28,668
Pottery...do.... 56,217
Paints, white and zinc lead.........................do.... 124,942
Rice and rice flour ....do.... 156,632
Salt ....do.... 181,729
Silk, all kinds.....................................do.... 4,818
Soap...do.... 29,153
Staves 715,243
Sugars, sirup, and molasses ....pounds.. 2,538,589
Tallow...do.... 8,842
Teas...do.... 10,577
Timber and lumber...................................value... $527 27
Tobacco..pounds.. 563,684
Vinegar..do.... 11,000
Wines..do.... 127,455
Wool...do.... 120,625
Wool fabrics.......................................do.... 208,896

Statement showing the description and quantities of the principal exports from the city of Bergen during the years, respectively, ended September 30, 1863, and September 30, 1864.

Description.	1863.	1864.
Anchovies ....kegs..	5,369	2,640
Boats, (value)................................	$360	$167
Bark, tanning ....tons..	....	5,295
Bone...pounds..	724,000	960,000
Codfish, (clepfish)...........................tons..	321,862	577,723
Copper ore	60,800	....
Copper and brass, (old)	13,904	63,400
Dried fish, all kinds.........................	595,776	597,364
Fish oil.....................................	928,800	1,053,895
Fish manure...................................pounds..	....	403,500
Glue ....do....	39,200	23,460
Hair...do....	28,036	10,940
Iron in bars	6,850	128 tons,818 pounds.
Iron castings ....pounds..	1,295	707
Oats...bushels..	25,700	1,867
Kerosene oil ....gallons..	4,000	3,472
Spawn ....barrels..	24,134	22,472
Tallow.......................................pounds..	1,320	860¼
Tar ....barrels..	2,190	1,094¼
Wool ....pounds..	6,300	7,690

The import and export duty collected at the custom-house of the city of Bergen for the years ending, respectively, September 30, 1863, spd. 421,603 $\frac{65}{120}$, September 30, 1864, spd. 421,421 $\frac{100}{120}$.

Statement showing the average wholesale prices of merchandise (unusually exported from the United States) sold in this market during the year ended September 30, 1864, and the import duty thereon, for the convenience of shippers, calculated at American standard of weight, measures, and values.

Merchandise.	Average prices.	Import duty.
Alcohol, (90 per cent) .... per gallon..	$1 60	$0 15
Axes... per dozen..	12 00	1
Barley.......................................200 pounds..	....	....
Beef, mess..do......	11 00	Free.
Beeswax ....per pound..	33	5¼
Brooms ....per dozen..	4 25	2⅞
Butter..per pound..	18¼	1
Cheese ....per pound..	18	1¼
Corn, shelled ....bushels..	90	3⅞
Cotton, China...............................per pound..	42	Free.
New Orleans, (none in market)	....	....
Mobile middling...........................per pound..	53	Free.
Brown shirtings ....per pound..	68	5¼
Bleached shirtings ....per pound..	71	13
Fruit, dried apples ....per pound..	14	2¼
pears and peaches ....per pound..	15	2¼
Flour, wheat, first quality ....per barrel..	9 56	1 43
second quality ....per barrel..	8 35	1 43
Rye flour ....per barrel..	5 25	34
Hides, dried ....per pound..	29	⅛
salted ....per pound..	15¼	¼
Hams, smoked ....per pound..	14	1
Hogs' lard ....per pound..	11	1
Hops, American..............................per pound..	37	6¼
Leather, sole ....per pound..	27	4½
cowhide ....per pound..	43	8
Manila rope ....per pound..	13¼	1
Molasses, common ....per pound..	3¼	1
sugar-house.........................per pound..	5¼	1
Logwood, Tampico ....per pound..	3	Free.
St. Domingo ....per pound..	1½	Free
extract of ....per pound..	11	5¼
Oats, (32 lbs)..............................per bushel..	60	2 ¹⁄₁₀
Oil, coal, refined.............................per gallon..	75	7
castor, refined........................per pound..	36	4½
Pork, called mess ....per barrel..	17 00	Free.
prime ....per barrel..	14 00	Free.
Quercitron bark ....per pound..	3	¼
Rice, shelled ....per pound..	9	1¼
Rye...per bushel..	....	5¼
Soap, brown ....per pound..	13	1¼
Stearine candles ....per pound..	22	3½
Staves, oak, for barrels.........................120 ft..	2 14	22⅞
Wheat ....per bushel..	....	11¼
White lead, in oil ....per 100 pounds..	....	1 37
dry ....per 100 pounds..	....	1 37

NOTE.—To the duty should be added two per cent., which is paid into the harbor fund for the building of a breakwater in this harbor. Dried American pork in cases is imported duty free.

Statement showing the merchandise exported from this city direct for Chicago as per invoices certified at this consulate in kind, quantity, and value, according to the declaration of shippers, for the year ended September 30, 1864.

Merchandise.	Quantity.	Value.
Codfish....................................	29,106 pounds..........	$1,170 00
Herring, pickled.............................	580⅛⅝ barrels...........	2,449 00
smoked	102 cases	123 74
Iron in bars..............................	128 tons, 118 pounds....	9,337 84
Mackerel, salted...........................	48½ barrels	219 72
Steel	1,886 pounds...........	85 50
Cod-liver oil................................	14 barrels	341 32
	Total..............	13,727 12

All the iron and steel, and part of the fish, were sold at Montreal.

The whole number of vessels arrived at the city of Bergen from foreign countries during the year ended September 30, 1864, was 1,189, with an aggregate tonnage of 105,956.09 tons, of which number 548 were foreign, from the following countries:

	Vessels.	Tonnage.
From Sweden...............................:	168	16,608.22
Denmark.......	149	14,973.44
Holland................................	99	32,833.07
Belgium................................	17	1,635.11
Great Britain..........................	13	'1,871.36
Prussia	31	3,693.39
Spain..................................	25	3,589.58
Bremen	1	133.65
Russia	9	1,555.95
Hanover	9	798.11
Hamburg...............................	1	72.67
France	20	1,944.03
Mecklenburg...........................	3	782.44
Oldenburg..............................	1	177.78
Portugal...............................	1	377.64
Lubeck................................	1	195.95

Of the whole number, 15 foreign, with an aggregate tonnage of 1,985.56 tons, and 3 Norwegian, arrived in ballast. The whole number of vessels cleared from the city of Bergen for foreign countries during the same period was 1,192, with an aggregate tonnage of 105,955.09 tons, of which 548 were foreign, with an aggregate tonnage of 80,142.28 tons. Of the whole number 60 were Norwegian, with an aggregate tonnage of 13,421.27 tons, cleared in ballast.

The whole number of vessels owned in the city of Bergen on the 30th September, 1863, was 725, with an aggregate tonnage of 62,980 tons; purchased the present year 10, with an aggregate tonnage of 3,789.42 tons; new built 6, with an aggregate tonnage of 3,291.09 tons; wholly rebuilt 3, with an aggregate tonnage of 272.38 tons; making the whole number of vessels owned in the city of Bergen on the 30th September, 1864, 744, with an aggregate tonnage of 70,332.87 tons, manned by 3,632 sailors.

EMIGRATION.

The emigration to the United States from this consular district the past year has been considerably larger than that of the year ending 30th September, 1863, namely, 2,835 persons to 418 last year. The greater portion of the emigrants was from this city.

Statement showing the principal articles exported from the city of Drontheim in kind and quantity from July 1, 1863, to July 1, 1864, reported by Mr. Just V. M. Finne, consular agent for that place.

Articles.	Quantity.	Articles.	Quantity.
Codfish, round dressed...tons..	36.04	Herring, salted ......barrels..	17,959
Clipfish ....do...	855.02	Fish oil ....gallons..	37,005
Chromsaltz..........pounds..	2,032,123	Spawn .... barrels..	230
Chromium ore	292,052	Timber and lumber ....tons..	9,156
Copper ore.................	583,072	Mundi (pyrites)........do...	4,346

Statement showing the imports of the city of Drontheim from July 1, 1863, to July 1. 1864, in kind and quantity, as reported by Mr. Just V. M. Finne, consular agent.

Articles.	Quantity.	Articles.	Quantity.
Barley ....bushels..	336,334	Sugar, refined......pounds..	728,535
Castings, hollowware.pounds..	59,279	Sugar, brown.........do....	384,401
Clay pipes ....do....	1,441	Sirup and molasses ....do....	287,775
Cheese ....do....	18,503	Teas ....do....	2,783
Coffee ....do....	1,189,936	Tiles and brick...hogsheads..	20,518
Farina ....do....	55,091	Tobacco ....pounds..	363,050
Linseed and rape oil ....do....	109,506	Wheat............bushels..	102,15¼
Rye ....bushels..	304,158¼	Wheat flour ....pounds..	721,579
Salt................do....	159,848	White lead and zinc white,lbs.	41,847
Staves for barrels..hogsheads..	144,925	Venetian red........pounds..	42,141

Timber is calculated after two tons to one Norwegian commercial last; otherwise, the calculation is 10 commercial lasts = 2,995.55 tons; one Norwegian pounds = 1.098 pounds, avoirdupois. All the reductions in this report are in this proportion.

The commercial navy of the city of Drontheim on the 1st January, 1864, consisted of 129 vessels, with an aggregate tonnage of 12,261 tons, no vessels having been built during the past year; two ships, with an aggregate tonnage of 504 tons, have been added by purchase from foreign countries, making the total amount of shipping of Drontheim on the 1st of September, 1864, 131, with an aggregate tonnage of 12,765 tons.

No American vessels have arrived at this port during the past year, nor have any direct shipments been made from this city to the United States.

Statement showing the principal articles exported from the city of Stavanger, in kind and quantity, from the 1st September, 1863, to and including September 1, 1864, according to the report of Mr. Thomas S. Falk, consular agent:

Anchovies ....barrels..	273
Bone..tons...	130
Calfskins...pounds..	20,128

Cranberries...bushels.. 236
Herrings...barrels.. 230, 612
Lobsters... 232, 505
Old rope..pounds.. 93, 000
Oysters ....bushels.. 76
Seal oil ....gallons.. 3, 720

Statement of imports of the city of Stavanger, in kind and quantity, from the 1st of September, 1863, to and including September 1, 1864, as per the report of the consular agent.

Brandies..pounds.. 16, 131
Butter...do.... 376, 317
Cabbages ....heads... 15, 871
Coal ....tons.... 6, 618. 25
Cork-wood..pounds.. 115, 640
Coffee...do.... 367, 519
Clocks ....do.... 2, 591
Cotton, crude ....do.... 13, 021
    dyed ....do.... 8, 723
    bleached...do.... 9, 346
    brown..do.... 19, 146
    other goods of.......................................do.... 27, 821
Feathers...do.... 6, 278
Fruit, raisins..do.... 28, 316
Glass bottles..do.... 9, 098
Glass, other fabrics.......................................do.... 2, 897
Grain, barley ....bushels.. 119, 111
    rye ....do.... 437, 650
    peas...do.... 9, 108
    wheat..do.... 12, 584
    malt...do.... 7, 878
Wheat flour...pounds.. 305, 070
Hemp flax..
Hemp yarn..do.... 58, 546
Hemp sail-cloth ....do.... 79, 622
Hemp rope, tarred..do.... 67, 552
    untarred...do.... 10, 233
Hides, salted ....do.... 79, 860
    dried..do.... 17, 588
Hoops for barrels... 2, 779, 575
Metals, implements..do.... 14, 149
    hinges, &c..do.... 13, 480
    pots and kettles......................................do.... 3, 184
    other castings..do.... 1, 810
    bar and bolt iron.....................................do.... 213, 684
    anchors and chains...................................do.... 96, 673
    tin ....do.... 4, 376
    yellow metal...do.... 315, 813
    sheathing nails ....do.... 4, 742
Oils ....do.... 91, 021
Paints and dyestuffs.......................................do.... 9, 374
Paper...do.... 29, 322
Rice ....do.... 86, 800
Salt..bushels.. 713, 718
Silk goods ....pounds.. 1, 068

Sugar	pounds..	413, 926
Sirup and molasses	do....	130, 575
Soap	do....	8, 445
Tar	barrels..	1, 373
Tea	pounds..	14, 780
Tobacco and cigars	do....	36, 584
Staves under 4 feet		3, 661, 692
Barrel heads		1, 184, 809
Wool, yarn	pounds..	2, 090
Wool, other fabrics	do....	58, 045
Wine, in casks	do....	62, 111
Wine, in bottles		553

The commercial navy of the city of Stavanger, on the 1st day of January, 1864, consisted of 420 vessels, with an aggregate tonnage of 54,505½ tons; during this year no additions have been made by building, but 10 vessels have been purchased, with an aggregate tonnage of 12,977½ tons, of which number five were American, making the commercial navy of Stavanger, on the 1st September of the present year, 430 vessels, with an aggregate tonnage of 67,482 tons. No American vessels have arrived at this port during the past year.

It appears that the consulate of Bergen is among the oldest of the United States consulates, having been established before 1808; but from the archives of this office it does not appear that any commercial report was ever sent to the Department of State by any of my predecessors. For the purpose of supplying this defect as regards Norway, I take the liberty of making the following appendix to this annual report. It is rather voluminous, but I could not make it complete in a more concise form

In the middle ages the Norwegian commerce of any importance was confined to the cities of Bergen and Drontheim. The fisheries induced the Hanseates to give their attention to Bergen, and soon seized upon and monopolized the whole trade of that city, and established a factory for this, in those days, powerful Hanseatic association. Drontheim also received part of the fish trade; the other six Norwegian cities, Stavanger, Tonsberg, Opslo, (now Christiania,) Skien, Sarpsburg and Hammer, were established more with a view of political importance than for commerce. Stavanger, Tonsburg, Opslo and Hammer were seats of bishops and in the possession of powerful clergy, and with their power those cities fell into insignificance. Sarpsburg had a natural advantageous situation for commerce, but was removed to Frederickstadt where, in the meanwhile, commerce did not flourish; wherefore, at a later period, they have endeavored to build up Sarpsburg anew. (The distance between the two places is 14 miles.) At this time the southern cities of Norway had no products for export of any importance; timber was not known as an object in the market of foreign countries, and the Norwegian mining operations were in their very infancy. The Dutch, being the rivals and successors of the Hanseates, commenced the timber trade, and during the sixteenth and seventeenth centuries they got out great quantities of timber from the forests of Norway and shipped to Holland, and manufactured lumber at their own saw-mills, and shipped to distant markets. The trade at the commencement was forced; they purchased direct from the producers and took timber where they found it most convenient, and paid no duty nor any other imposts. To facilitate the trade, the timber was brought to particular landing places, where they had established their agencies. These purchased the timber from the producers who had to deliver it at the landing places. After a time the agents and owners of timber were attentive to their own interest, and established at the different places of landing their own timber trade, which, however, for a long time remained feeble. In this way were the towns of Frederickstadt, Moss, Soon, Drobak, Bragernaes,

Risver and Arendal founded, and several of those landing places have grown into flourishing cities; saw-mills were erected, and the timber thus converted into lumber was exported to the markets of Holland. Ships were built and the timber and lumber trade of Norway ceased to be passive and in the possession of the Dutch. The mineral wealth of Norway was developed, and considerable quantities of iron were introduced into foreign markets. In the seventeenth century the Norwegian commerce was progressing, and if left to itself would have continued prosperous, but for the ruinous political measures of Christian IV and his successor, which favored some particular towns and hindered those first established from commercial development. This was the case with the new established city of Christiana, (Opslo,) a royal decree compelling the merchants of Bragernæs, Moss and Soon, under the penalty of losing their privilege to trade, to establish themselves at Christiana; the like force was used in favor of Christiana and to the detriment of all the smaller towns in the neighborhood, and even the old city of Stavanger was stricken out of the list of Norwegian cities. Christiansand and Molde were also deprived of their charters for the purpose of building up Drontheim. The commercial navy was not well calculated for the trade. In the reign of Frederick the Third there were only fifty large vessels. At the close of the century the commercial navy had grown to some importance; the stift or commercial district of Aggershuus had, in the year 1692, 140 large ships, and the city of Bergen in 1699, 125. The size of the ships was then calculated by commercial lasts and timber lasts; until the year 1666 the measurement was by commercial lasts in all calculations, but in that year a treaty of commerce was entered into with Holland in which it was stipulated that for the calculation of the export duty on timber and lumber the commercial last should be equal to 5,200 pounds, and the timber last 4,000 pounds, (about two English tons;) the proportion between the commercial and timber lasts should be 13 to 10, and the timber last calculated to contain 120 cubic feet. At a later period, by closer calculation, it was found to be 125 cubic feet. In the first half of the foregoing century the commerce of Norway did not progress; the long war under Frederick the Fourth with Sweden brought the cities to decline, and the people suffered much from conscriptions; a greater part of the commercial navy was captured by the enemy, so that the district from Frederickshald to Langesund, which, in the year 1692, had 131 vessels, with an aggregate tonnage of 27,099.61 tons, in the year 1723 had only 96 vessels, of 18,830.25 tons. Bergen lost, in the period from 1710 to 1713, 55 vessels, with an aggregate tonnage of 7,895 tons. The revenue from the customs was also considerably diminished. In the first ten years of the eighteenth century this income amounted to 252,000 rix-dollars yearly, and in the period from 1713 to 1746, to only 220,000 rix-dollars yearly. The royal decree of September 16, 1735, prohibiting the importation of all kinds of grain excepting from Denmark, worked much to the disadvantage of the Norwegian commerce. The commercial navy of Norway in the years 1740 and 1748 was as follows:

Years.	Total.	Under 25 tons.	From 25 to 60 tons.	From 50 to 78 tons.	From 78 to 130 tons.	From 130 to 260 tons.	Over 260 tons.
1740......	699	147	137	97	109	106	103
1748......	565	108	115	74	91	86	94

Of the foregoing number 277 belonged to the stift or district of Aggershuus; 177 to the stift of Christiansand; 51 to the stift of Bergen, and 33 to the stift of Drontheim. In the third quarter of the previous century the commerce of Norway was visibly on the increase, which was particularly attributable to the very profitable fisheries, especially of herring, which, in the periods of 1750 and 1770, was extraordinary in quantity. The shipments of copper products assumed greater importance, and the iron works had reached a higher proficiency. The treaty of commerce with Tunis, Tripoli, and Algiers of 1746, 1751, and 1752, procured for the Norwegian shipping a profitable carrying trade in the Mediterranean. The trade with the West Indies was free, and in 1754 and 1755 was of some profit to the commerce of Bergen; and to what extent the commerce of Norway increased can best be seen by the increasing revenue of the customs, which, according to the statement of Nathanson, was as follows:

In the years 1747–1751 average yearly 270,289 rix-dollars.
"   "   1752–1756   "   "   322,243 "   "
"   "   1757–1761   "   "   341,142 "   "
"   "   1762–1766   "   "   392,383 "   "
"   "   1767–1771   "   "   409,088 "   "
"   "   1772–1776   "   about   442,000 "   "

Notwithstanding this progress, the value of the Norwegian exports in the middle of the past century was but three millions of rix-dollars. The number of merchant ships in 1767 was 594, with an aggregate tonnage of 65,910.12 tons, and the population of the cities 64,747. The period including the last quarter of the past century, until the breaking out of the war of 1807, was by far the most prosperous for the Norwegian commerce during the union with Denmark. The American war of independence commenced, and the Norwegian shipping received great advantage from the neutrality. The western powers—England, France, and Holland—were engaged in war, which secured to the Norwegian shipping a prosperous carrying trade; the Norwegian products found profitable markets, and the neutrality of the Norwegian harbors caused extensive exchange of commerce; the greatest advantage was realized by the carrying trade, and the growth of the commercial navy was the immediate result, which in the year 1792 reached the number of 860 vessels, with an aggregate tonnage of 115,528.30 tons. Until the year 1770 all the timber and lumber was transported from Norway to Holland in Dutch vessels; at this period larger ships were built, and the timber products were carried to Holland in Norwegian ships, thus securing a considerable carrying trade to the Norwegian shipping. The wars of the French revolution were of great advantage to the commerce of Norway, during which Norway enjoyed perfect neutrality until the year 1807; the Norwegian timber and lumber trade had been extended to Great Britain, where they found good market at high prices. The commercial navy of Norway in 1802 consisted of 990 vessels with an aggregate tonnage of 139,516 tons, and at the breaking out of the war in 1807 it amounted to 1,514 vessels, with an aggregate tonnage of 160,983.5 tons, distributed as follows:

		Vessels.	Tons.
To the stift of Aggershuus		626	78,666
" " Christiansand		497	53,098
" " Bergen		241	19,563
" " Drontheim		150	9,656½

The influence of commerce was visible by the relative increase of the population. The population in the land districts had, in the period from 1770 to 1801, been increased 22 per cent., and that of the cities in the same time 40 per cent. The prosperity and increase of commerce are more fully shown by the revenue of imports, which in the period amounted to, yearly average:

	Rix-dollars.
From 1777 to 1781	461,747
1782 to 1784	548,549
1789	563,697

	Rix-dollars.
From 1790 to 1794	631,972
1795 to 1799	655,046
1800 to 1802	782,005
1803	980,917
1804	1,055,303
1805	1,110,348
1806	1,292,275

The increase of the revenue was not wholly attributable to the increase of commerce, but in part to the additional imposts in the latter years of the period on commerce and shipping. In the year 1796 an extra tax was laid upon freights, which amounted yearly, from 1797 to 1803, to 20,000 rix-dollars, and later, in 1804, this impost was increased so as to be estimated at 50,000 rix-dollars annually. In the year 1796 a tax was laid upon the naturalization of vessels purchased from foreign countries, amounting to 4,800 rix-dollars yearly; and from 1799 to 1802 the import and export duty was increased to about 25,000 rix-dollars yearly, and in the year 1803 the ship charges and import duty were increased 12½ per cent., whereby the imposts were increased about 100,000 rix-dollars. That this period was the most profitable for the Norwegian commerce cannot be denied, nor were the merchants of this country at any former time in possession of such considerable wealth. Legislation became actuated by more liberal principles, as, for instance, the abolition of unnatural prohibition of the importation of foreign grain; the tariff was revised and established on a more liberal basis, and the commerce upon the east and west Fenmarken was made free, but this was not the immediate cause, although it in some degree contributed to the result. The large profit of the commerce had also its advantages; the prices of all kinds of property rose to an unnatural height. The agricultural pursuits were neglected, and the attention of all were directed to articles of export.

From 1807 to 1814 was an unfortunate period for the whole country, when commerce assumed a very uncertain and gloomy aspect. The war with England, in August, 1807, unexpectedly broke out. A great number of Norwegian ships, lying in English ports and on the seas before the declaration of war, were confiscated and condemned as lawful prizes, besides a great deal of Norwegian merchandise and money in the hands of British merchants; and though partially restored after the peace, the capital was withheld from the free disposition of the owners, and the people were under the penalty of capital punishment from having any dealings or intercourse with England, and a complete stoppage was put to all business connected with commerce. In 1808 and 1809 all the Norwegian harbors were closed, and the English cruisers were so vigilant that no vessel ventured to seek the Norwegian ports. The complete ruin of the export trade, and the shipping which had escaped being captured by the English, were lying idle in the harbors. The grain trade was carried on upon a very limited scale, with smaller vessels, and of these but few escaped the vigilance of the English cruisers. Towards the close of 1809 the unfortunate license system was introduced. England could not do without the Norwegian products, and gave Norwegian ships the liberty to carry timber products to England, and the shipping was again brought into activity. Timber products commanded the highest prices and freights beyond all limits. A commercial period now took place which appeared flourishing, but the consequences proved to be disastrous. The ships were cleared to France, with which country there was no prohibition of commercial intercourse. In fact, the whole trade was based on cheat, as it was forbidden by the laws of Denmark to have any intercourse with England. And yet this license traffic was tolerated by the Danish government. But in a short time England, in consideration of the license, made it obligatory that the vessels, as a return cargo, should take considerable English manufactured goods.

Great quantities of extravagant articles were in this way imported, and thereby theretofore unknown luxuries were introduced into the country, which, by the high prices of timber products, were accessible. The deranged money system assisted much in spreading the evil. Paper money was issued in boundless quantities and without guarantee, and its value fell with the increase of its issue. The year 1812 completed the general confusion. A wet and cold summer, succeeded by an early and rainy fall, destroyed the crops throughout all parts of Norway; and although they had an abundant supply of all sorts of manufactured and colonial goods, the people were threatened by a general famine. Numbers died from starvation; and in many districts bark was substituted for corn, and baked into bread. The consequences of this unfortunate year extended to the years 1813 and 1814, and the period of Norwegian independence commenced under very distressing auspices. The fluctuations of commerce in the afore-named years cannot well be exhibited by any public documents. The clandes-tine and irregular course of trade evaded all public control. With the change of government and the adoption of a constitution, commenced a new and happier period for Norwegian commerce. England, the most important market for Norway, was, by the new and, for the Norwegian trade, very pressing revenue system, nearly closed, and it required time to seek a new channel for the Nor-wegian export trade, which was finally found in France. But notwithstanding all this, the commercial progress went forward with sure steps, and at the present time is of greater importance than at any former time, and it is so much more satisfactory, as it is not so much the result of contingent circumstances, but has its foundation in the development of material wealth. The first year after the close of the war it was less prosperous, as the relations had not resumed their natural channel; and the great shipments which took place in 1815 were more from necessity to dispose of old stocks than for actual profit. Above all, the timber and lumber trade was precarious. The fishing districts were more fortunate, as they had enjoyed prosperous and increasing drafts of spring herring. From the year 1823 the timber products commenced a more prosperous trade, when the market price rose and higher freights could be paid. In the year 1826 the prospects for Norwegian products were darkened, at which time the commercial crisis in England was felt very severely in Norway. Not-withstanding a provisional decree of the storthing of February 27, 1826, reducing the export duty upon timber products twenty-five per cent., and upon mineral products fifty per cent., the prospects had become so discouraging that the storthing in 1828 had to take up a loan of two hundred thousand dollars in specie to assist the several branches of industry. The fisheries became promising in 1829, and have since that time met with no particular derangement. The timber trade, on the contrary, did not revive until 1833, since which it has, upon the whole, been lucrative. There was some depression in this trade in the year 1839 and the succeeding years, but since the year 1843 the market prices have been good, and in later years have reached a height before unknown. The carrying trade since 1823 has made steady progress. The prospects of this branch of commerce have been particularly advantageous; and, upon the whole, the commerce and shipping of Norway have made steady progress, though at some periods less profitable than at others. Whether the commerce of Nor-way has increased since 1814 can best be ascertained by the following statement, containing the impost of revenue. The column headed silver contains the im-port duty, transit and storage imposts, and the sums headed bills contain import duty, naturalization of purchased foreign vessels, tonnage, light-house dues, and quarantine charges. In 1842 the value of paper money was made equal to silver, when the difference between paper and coin ceased. The first two years are set forth in Danish rix-dollars, being at that time the currency of the country.

Years.	Silver.	Bills.	Years.	Silver.	Bills.
1815 ......ruble ..	....	7,777,621	1839 ....sp.d...	1,303,514	526,308
1816........do ...	....	7,569,370	1840 ......do ..	1,566,890	515,895
1817...... sp.d...	....	688,898	1841 ......do ..	1,404,430	444,563
1818........do ..	....	811,382	1842 ......do ..	1,535,070	446,283
1819........do ..	....	1,022,556	1843 ......do ..	....	2,056,906
1820........do ..	....	1,002,532	1844 ..:....do ..	....	1,875,752
1821........do ..	90,190	1,119,086	1845 ...•..do ..	....	2,405,437
1822........do ..	337,770	534,508	1846 ......do ..	....	2,099,427
1823........do ..	540,493	586,256	1847 ......do ..	....	1,886,158
1824........do ..	742,672	667,502	1848 ......do ..	....	1,907,065
1825........do ..	699,558	719,802	1849 ......do ..	....	2,036,765
1826........do ..	735,098	552,544	1850 ......do ..	....	2,196,953
1827........do ..	706,324	527,433	1851 ......do ..	....	2,257,865
1828........do ..	631,432	550,862	1852 ......do ..	....	2,074,277
1829........do ..	720,182	509,833	1853 ......do ..	....	2,080,579
1830........do ..	808,754	502,945	1854 ......do ..	....	2,318,027
1831........do ..	742,081	465,840	1855 ......do ..	....	2,236,200
1832........do ..	739,189	483,394	1856 ......do ..	....	2,613,342
1833........do ..	947,104	539,316	1857 ......do ..	....	2,654,756
1834........do ..	360,670	504,931	1858 ......do ..	....	2,114,882
1835........do ..	1,071,761	537,653	1859 ......do ..	....	2,656,398
1836........do ..	1,477,235	521,114	1860 ......do ..	....	2,854,408
1837........do ..	1,355,443	484,737	1861 ......do ..	....	2,842,700
1838........do ..	1,343,760	456,166	1862 ......do ..	....	....

Although the increase of this income, in part, might be attributed to the increased vigilance of the customs, it does not fully exhibit the progress of commerce and shipping, for in the years 1826, 1830, 1833, 1836, 1839, 1842, 1845, 1848, 1851, 1854, 1857, 1860, and 1863, great reductions were made in the export and import duty and ship dues. The quarantine imports were repealed in 1842, and by this reduction the revenue was reduced at least one-half million specie-daler yearly. By observing the foregoing statement, it will be seen that the income in paper money decreased after the reduction, while the income in silver is steadily increasing. The transit duty was abolished in 1842. On the other hand, the storthing has made some reduction in the import duty on some important articles. The raising of the import duty on different occasions might exceed the reduction, but the overplus is far from being as large as the deductions in other imposts.

A powerful agency for the development of the Norwegian shipping are reciprocity treaties. Although by this arrangement the carrying trade between Norway and some foreign countries might be done by foreign shipping, yet, upon the whole, Norway has by far the greatest advantage, and has been placed in the position for carrying on a very extensive shipping trade; and it is this carrying out the principle of reciprocity to its fullest extent which has in the main contributed to the success and advancement of Norwegian commerce. Norway can in this respect compare favorably with any nation of Europe. Norway has entered into reciprocal treaties with Sweden, Russia, Prussia, Mecklenburg Schwerin, Lubec, Denmark, Hamburg, Bremen, Hanover, Oldenburg, Holland, Belgium, Great Britain, France, Portugal, Italian States, Austria, Greece, Turkey, United States, China, and Venezuela. In Brazil Norwegian ships are enjoying the same privileges as their own with respect to impost duty and ship dues, although there is no existing treaty to that effect; and vessels of all nations with which there are no existing treaties of commerce with Norway enjoy in the main the same privileges as the Norwegian.

Statement showing the commercial navy of Norway from 1800 to 1862.

Years.	Number of vessels.	Tonnage.	Crews.
1800	1,156	151,078	....
1803	1,267	153,453	....
1806	1,650	194,203	....
1809	1,363	139,467	....
1814	1,651	179,328	....
1815	1,673	184,519	....
1818	1,658	172,753	....
1821	1,674	151,162	....
1824	1,743	141,306	....
1825	1,761	140,711	....
1828	1,919	156,976	....
1831	2,067	172,978	....
1834	2,165	185,070	....
1837	2,303	208,263	8,819
1840	2,606	254,201	13,471
1841	2,237	254,321	12,447
1842	2,772	269,511	12,661
1843	2,710	275,696	13,888
1844	2,693	276,918	13,284
1845	2,735	285,853	13,398

During the years 1841–1845 the yearly average number of vessels wrecked was 55, with an aggregate tonnage of 4,990 tons, or about $\frac{1}{15}$ of the whole number.

Statement showing the commercial navy of Norway, &c.—Continued.

Years	No. of vessels	Tonnage	No. of crews	Vessels wrecked. No.	Tonnage	Vessels cut up. No.	Tonnage	Vessels built. No.	Tonnage	Vessels purchased. No.	Tonnage
1845	3,521	312,915	17,683	38	3,613	16	401.98	98	14,492	19	3,534
1847	3,526	328,335.97	17,754	34	3,440	14	416.14	75	11,080	30	3,116
1848	3,573	356,575	17,980	41	4,563.75	16	728	85	12,497.88	12	3,431.19
1849	3,624	380,639	18,499					85	9,760 bbls.		
1850	3,696	364,703.75	19,037	48	7,607.41	17	1,020.	96	12,995.67	4	7,462.61
									19,440 bbls.		
1851	3,762	372,769	21,654	35	4,617	13	313	98	10,283	19	3,797
									52,025 bbls.		
1852	4,089	413,383.05	23,180	67	7,968	13	586	138	19,521	27	6,696
1853	4,200	403,338	24,458	67	7,876	10	895	81	17,767 bbls.	31	8,812
								105	16,860		
								64	12,870		
1854	4,309	487,694	25,473	95	14,801	9	956	14	(No tonnage.)	77	19,995
								183	30,207		
								64	17,250 bbls.		
1855	4,464	595,123	26,105	69	9,392	21	454	14	(No tonnage.)	64	18,272
								159	98,325		
								10	4,770 bbls.		
1856	4,851	599,063	28,937	55	7,296	5	78	14	(No tonnage.)	70	25,955
				11	(Not given.)			157	26,044		
								53	9,025 bbls.		
1857	5,159	609,406	31,149	71	941	5	757	1	(No tonnage.)	37	14,494
						7	(Not given.)	249	40,557		
1858	5,247	661,667	31,878	50	7,969	3	5,490	58	15,010 bbls.	15	6,070
1859	5,278	672,356	32,406	68	12,069	11	1,906	171	21,495	53	7,399
								168	92,392		
1860	5,287	693,143.08	33,014	190	24,739	27	801	25	5,640 bbls.	96	13,557
								127	13,516		
1861	5,493	716,557.08	33,963	94	13,913.05	12	274	40	8,950 bbls.	46	16,733
								111	14,619+		
								25	7,980 bbls.		
1862	5,541	812,638	34,817	198	20,800	11	144	123	16,555	66	24,452
								41	11,670 bbls.		

In the oregoing statement are not included the smaller vessels belonging to the north and west districts, which are only employed in the inland and coasting trade, of which only of late years there has been any official statement made ; they amounted, (according to Mr. Forthe,) in 1845, to 1,995 vessels, with an aggregate tonnage of 40,269 tons, manned by 7,496 men; smaller vessels and boats, under five tons, are not included in this statement. According to the government statistics of 1855, the number of smaller coasting vessels was stated to be 751, carrying 148,432 barrels of fresh herring, manned by 2,455 men ; and, in 1860, 673 vessels, carrying 142,160 barrels fresh herring, manned by 1,723 men ; in 1862 to 568 vessels, carrying 226,500 barrels fresh herring, manned by 1,763 men. It is probable that all vessels measuring over five tons are in the statement after the year 1850, as I can find no statement corresponding with that of Mr. Forthe, in his statistics of Norway, published in 1848, and considered authentic.

The proportion between the larger and smaller vessels, at different times, will be seen by the following tabular statement:

Years.	Vessels under 20 tons.		Vessels over 20 and under 50 tons.		Vessels over 50 and under 130 tons.		Vessels over 130 tons and under 260 tons.		Vessels over 260 tons and under 590 tons.		Vessels over 590 tons.	
	No.	Tonnage.	No.	Tonnage.	No.	Tonnage.	No.	Tonnage.	No.	Tonnage.	No.	Tonnage.
1806.....	325	3,964	948	8,633	494	39,530	287	71,652	186	666,54	.....	....
1825.....	611	7,067	387	13,194	360	29,724	293	63,013	110	37,689	.....	....
1835.....	670	8,149	580	19,829	469	38,094	382	89,956	171	59,823	.....	....
1845.....	593	7,793	763	27,155	576	45,814	487	92,218	316	120,846	.....	....
1855.....	905	10,915	1,513	49,601	700	183,334	601	116,295	656	260,813	89	54,257
1860.....	964	12,218	1,846	59,878	759	59,698	674	132,657	884	313,278	160	80,769
1862.....	986	12,480	2,022	53,418	756	53,347	669	129,974	913	338,941	202	130,894

How large a proportion of the shipping is employed in the inland, coast, and river trade cannot be estimated with any degree of certainty, but it is evident that the number of smaller vessels, stated (by Mr. Forthe,) in 1846, to have been 1,995, with an aggregate tonnage of 40,364 tons, was not intended to include the whole tonnage engaged in the inland, coasting, and river trade; but if to this number be added the vessels belonging to the sound, near Fahrsund, and of Staten, near Christiana, a large portion of the smaller vessels from Bergen and the small towns of Rounsdale and Drontheim, which are engaged in the inland fish transportation from the island of Lafoden, and the vessels engaged in carrying ore from the mines of Redenes to the above-situated iron-works, and were the smaller vessels trading with the Swedish and Baltic ports, and from the western cities exporting herring, and from the timber districts of Denmark, to be excepted, it might with safety be concluded that vessels under 50 tons are not employed in foreign trade; consequently a large portion of this class of vessels might be included in the number carrying on the inland trade, and the tonnage engaged therein might be safely estimated at 60,000 tons. Since 1814 the inland commerce has been steadily on the increase, as may be seen by the considerable increase of the number of vessels under 50 tons. The inland commerce of Norway, compared with the foreign, is, upon the whole, unimportant; the nature of the country, the difficulties of transportation to and from the interior, and the want of domestic industry, are the prime causes of such a comparatively large foreign commerce. This country has but few industrial pursuits, but several of those produce more than is consumed in the country ; others, on the contrary, are largely insufficient for the demand. For these reasons, large quantities of breadstuffs, provisions, and manufactured goods are imported from abroad. The easy commercial intercourse with foreign nations, the difficulties of inland communication, and a sparsely settled country, make it easier to procure necessaries from abroad. The importance of the city of Copenhagen as a central point for the commerce of Norway has vanished, and Christiana has in part taken its place, but a great part of the Copenhagen-Norwegian trade has been transferred to the cities of Hamburg and Altona, between which and this country there is an extensive trade. In addition to the fact that Christiana is the central point of the inland trade of Norway, it is also the political capital. In 1814 it had 14,000 inhabitants, and in 1860 it had 38,958. Christiana is to the south and east what Bergen is to the north and west. The mountainous nature of the country will ever prevent any extensive railroad communications. The influence of the great commercial crisis of this continent in 1856–'57 reached this country in November, 1857, and caused the failure of a number of influential mercantile houses which had been largely connected with Hamburg after a period of inaction in trade. These, with a few exceptions, sustained their credit, and have been since as prosperous as before. The city of Bergen, which, before the crisis, had the greatest trade with Hamburg, had its credit much shaken by the crisis. It received a great blow and lost much of the commercial influence it had enjoyed for centuries, yet so great is its advantage of position that it will always be the emporium for the Norwegian fish trade and shipping. The growing cities of Stavanger and Christiansund will eventually cut off the coast trade north and south, and being surrounded by mountains, Bergen will forever be deprived of railroad communications with the interior. It may be said that this old and renowned city is on the decline.

Telegraphic lines are extended over all parts of the country; and Norway, considering its limited resources, is keeping pace with the other Scandinavian countries in the way of internal improvements, as far as its mountainous nature will admit. Steamboats were first introduced into Norway in the year 1823, when two were purchased by the government and employed in the coast trade. In 1828 a government steamer was put on the route between Christiana and Copenhagen; the same year the first private steamer was purchased in Norway and plied between Bergen and Christiana, but, found to be unprofitable, was discontinued. In 1838 steamers were put upon the large fiords. In the year 1846 Norway had 16 steamboats in active employment, of which five belonged to the government. They ran between Christiana and Copenhagen, and carried the mails along the coast from Christiana to Fenmarken. In the year 1852 the steamship association of Bergen was incorporated, and two steamships were put on the route to run weekly between Bergen and Hamburg. Another association was formed at Drontheim two years later for the same purpose, and thus weekly steam communication was extended between Drontheim and Hamburg. In 1865 it will be extended to Hammerfest. In 1857 a Holland steam navigation company put one steamer on the route between Rotterdam and Bergen, *via* Hull; and, in 1859, increased that line with another steamer, running regular every other week. There are also lines of steamers between Christiana and Hull, also between Christiana and Hamburg; and, during the present year, a steamer was put on the direct route between Christiana and London, but with little encouragement. On the 31st day of September Norway had, in all, 36 steam vessels, owned by private individuals and associations, besides a number owned by the government, of which four are employed in carrying mails.

The mountainous nature of the country will always be a barrier to railroad communication between the west coast of Norway and the interior, consequently steam navigation will, in the main, have to be relied on for the transportation of the mails. Steam navigation to the interior is rendered easy by the deep bays and fiords and navigable rivers, which, along the whole coast of Norway, are generally free from ice in the winter, and navigable far into the interior. There will be complete railway communication between Drontheim and Christiana, and from thence to the Swedish boundary, which will be the extent of railroads in this country of any importance.

NORWEGIAN FOREIGN SHIPPING.

There is no country, in proportion to its population, that has as large a commercial navy as Norway. At the close of the year 1860 it consisted of 5,287 vessels, with an aggregate tonnage of 693,143 tons; at the same time its population was 1,600,000, making $2\frac{31}{100}$ persons to the ton; when in the United States, having the largest commercial navy of any nation in the world, there are $4\frac{22}{100}$ persons to the ton. The following tabular statement will exhibit the population and commercial navies of the principal maritime nations, and the relative proportion to the number of inhabitants at the time therein stated:

Countries.	Tonnage.	Population.	Ratio of tonnage to population.
United States.............1860..	7,361,639	31,000,000	1 ton to $4\frac{14}{100}$
Great Britain.............1859..	5,840,000	29,000,000	1 ton to $4\frac{96}{100}$
France....................1859..	1,297,750	37,000,000	1 ton to $28\frac{46}{100}$
Norway ....1860..	693,143	1,600,000	1 ton to $2\frac{31}{100}$
Holland...................1859..	651,470	3,500,000	1 ton to $5\frac{36}{100}$
Greece....................1857..	415,280	1,100,000	1 ton to $2\frac{65}{100}$
Sweden....................1859..	340,000	3,800,000	1 ton to $11\frac{17}{100}$
Denmark...................1858..	321,000	2,600,000	1 ton to $8\frac{9}{100}$

Although the commercial navy of Norway is so extraordinarily large in proportion to its population, and greater than the commerce of the country demands, yet it maintains its strength by engaging in the carrying trade of other nations, and thus adding very considerably to the wealth and prosperity of the country. So great is the demand for first-class vessels that the ship-yards have been unable to meet it, and they have had to be purchased from abroad. The ownership of these vessels is divided among a great many joint partners; the profits are thus enjoyed by the greatest number.

The profits of the Norwegian shipping are estimated at two specie dollars per month per ton during the period of navigation, which is eight months— amounting to sixteen specie dollars per year; the net profits per ton, after deducting all charges and expenses, are twelve specie dollars. The total tonnage at the close of the year 1862 was 812,638 tons, which, at twelve specie dollars per ton, gives an aggregate net profit of $9,751,656.

THE TIMBER AND LUMBER TRADE.

The export trade in timber and lumber is mainly confined to the southern part of Norway, or to the stifts of Christiana and part of the stift of Drontheim. On the coasts of the stifts of Bergen and Drontheim the forests do not produce timber suitable for export. Plank, boards, square timber, and smaller material for building, are exported. The lumber is manufactured at saw-mills propelled by water power, and partially by whip-saws. In former times the exclusive privilege of owning and running saw-mills was, by grant from the Danish kings, awarded to certain individuals, such as merchants and proprietors of large landed estates. After the change in the government this system was found to be detrimental to the development of the timber trade, and was abolished by law, and every owner of timber was, on paying a reasonable tax to the government, allowed to erect and run a saw-mill for the manufacture of his own timber and lumber. The law was passed June 8, 1818. The number of saw-mills in the country in 1835, 3,898; in 1845, 3,296; in 1855, 3,265; in 1860, 3,258.

The most extensive timber regions are found in the interior of the country, and are mostly owned by farmers, who cut and prepare the logs and square timber during the autumn and winter, and transport them to the banks of the mountain streams for market, where it is purchased by merchants, who then receive and mark their respective lots. Great quantities are exported to Holland to be manufactured into lumber and square timber; to Great Britain, for building and mining purposes. Inferior qualities are sent to Denmark. The exportation of timber first commenced in the seventeenth century. In the year 1664 it amounted to 562,200 tons.

Statement showing the export of timber.

		Tons.
From 1776 to 1783	average	245,504.00
1804 to 1806	"	520,000.00
1815 to 1819	"	322,704.00
1820 to 1824	"	341,276.00
1825 to 1829	"	382,682.00
1830 to 1835	"	397,566.00
1836		465,638.00
1837		456,884.00
1838		483,138.00
1839		544,414.00
1840		533,198.00
1841		533,488.00
1842		527,944.00
1843		534,514.00
1844		531,428.00
1845		572,678.00
1846		568,702.00
1847		439,892.00
1848		355,672.00
1849		390,504.00
1850		457,714.00
1851		514,332.00
1852		539,621.78
1853		586,812.50
1854		584,344.00
1855		803,602.16
1856		609,554.28
1857		608,614.13
1858		628,880.00
1859		628,796.00
1860		589,180.00
1861		697,554.00
1862		702,098.00

The timber and lumber trade has in the last fifty years undergone several changes. Formerly England and Ireland were the most important and surest markets for the Norwegian timber products. In return, the English manufactures were introduced into Norway. Commerce with France was at first unimportant; with Germany there was none. In the year 1809 Great Britain, for the purpose of protecting the owners of timber in Canada, levied an import duty upon the timber products of all countries except the Canadas; in consequence

of which the commerce with Great Britain greatly fell off. New markets for
these products were sought, which were in time found in France, when the condition of the middle classes becoming greatly improved, they were in a condition to build comfortable dwellings, thus creating a market for the timber and
lumber of Norway. The timber trade with England declined; the importation
of English manufactures also declined. Commercial relations, at this time, were
opened with Hamburg and many other German cities; in consequence of which
German manufactures crowded out of Norwegian markets those of the English.
The loss to England by this system of prohibition, and the grave question it
involved, engaged the serious attention of the British government. But the influence of the land-owners of the Canadas, and of the English ship-owners engaged
in the trade with the East and West Indies, was so great that no essential change
could be brought about. At later times some changes were made which had
an important influence on the timber and lumber trade of Norway, which will
appear more fully by the following statement of the export of timber and lumber
to England and France from 1805 to 1863; since 1850 the shipments of these
articles to England have greatly increased. The increased consumption of coal,
iron, cotton, and other manufactured goods now imported from England have
made the trade with that country at this time very active:

Years.	England.	France.	Years.	England.	France.
	Tons.	Tons.		Tons.	Tons.
1805	295,422	11,022	1844...............	135,274	163,642
1815	197,952	24,950	1846...............	121,342	198,263
1819	138,896	52,896	1852...............	163,178	137,218
1824	158,016	74,106	1856...............	133,216	104,082
1829	95,318	98,026	1860...............	226,972	137,252
1834	102,624	120,610	1861...............	251,108	146,020
1838	128,886	143,908	1862...............	207,616	115,944
1842	100,254	80,294	....		

The export of timber products to Holland compared with that to England is
about the same or a little less in tonnage, but the difference consists principally
in squared timber, and therefore of less value. The export to Denmark is somewhat less, being 85,000 tons annually, it also being of inferior qualities. The
timber of Norway, though smaller in dimensions, is in quality superior to that
of any other country. It is impossible to calculate with any degree of certainty
the value of the products of the forests of Norway; their value varies in different parts of the country. It would be safe to estimate the value of fire-wood at
one-half specie dollar per cord.

	Specie dollars.
The value of the fire-wood in the country is estimated at 2,200,000 cords annually, at one-half specie dollar per cord.............	1,100,000
300,000 tons annually made into coal for silver, copper, and iron works, at two-fifths specie dollar per ton....................	120,000
350,000 tons timber annually exported to England, France, and Belgium, at five specie dollars per ton......................	1,750,000
230,000 tons to Holland, Denmark, and northern Germany, an-nually, at three and one-fourth specie dollars per ton.........	748,000
16,000 tons oak bark, at one specie dollar per ton.............	16,000
Total annual value................................:	3,734,000

The value of the timber products is estimated by their valuation at the places of shipment. To the value of that used in the country for other purposes should be added one-fourth of a million of specie dollars. Thus the entire annual value of the products of the forests of Norway may be set down with safety at four millions of specie dollars; the cost of preparing them for shipment may be stated at less than 25 per cent. on that sum. There are no forest laws in Norway, but during the period of its union with Denmark a bureau for the regulation and protection of the forests was established. In 1771 it was abolished; on the 12th of October, 1857, an act was passed placing the forests on the crown lands under the protection of superintendents.

MINING.

Skilful mining and manufacture in Norway commenced 300 years ago, and it is asserted that as early as in the fifteenth century copper mines were in operation, but it is not probable that they were worked in a skilful manner. During the reformation King Christian the Third imported miners from Germany. In 1539 an act was passed introducing the German regulations for operating the mines. A copper mine was worked in the district of Telemarkin. No mines are worked at the present time, except the iron-works at Fossum, opened in the 16th century. It was not until one hundred years later that the silver mine of Konigsburg, and the copper mines of the North mountains, were first worked, and mining generally carried on with any degree of success. This country possesses great mineral wealth—iron in the south, and copper in the north and west; in the west the mines appear to be less valuable, though some have been worked there. The want of timber and cheap fuel has been the main obstacle in working many mines, and has caused the mines of Eidsvold, Dikkemarks, Odalere, and Lessoc to be stopped; the richest ore is found along the coast of the Arnt of Bræstsburg and the district of Redevus, where firewood commands very high prices. Most of the iron-works are situated near the coast in order to avoid the transportation of the ore, which is very expensive.   *   *   *   *   *

The following table exhibits the yearly products of all the iron-works in Norway from the year 1781 to 1860:

Years.	Pig iron.	Castings.	Bar iron.	Spikes and nails.
	Tons.	Tons.	Tons.	
1781..................	6,248.00	1,777.54	4,649.9	2,702,000 st.—1,988 tons.
1792..................	5,789.00	1,426.76	4,249.58	4,597,000 st.—293 tons.
1813—1817, yearly av'ge.	2,136.23	1,236.15	1,708.98	Not given.
1821—1825......do.....	3,963.00	1,210.55	3,080.29	Do.
1827—1829......do.....	4,618.25	1,545.00	3,705.65	Do.
1830—1835......do.....	4,738.79	1,423.19	3,737.14	Do.
1836—1840......do.....	5,625.16	1,713.48	3,925.90	9,233,000 st.—67.95 tons.
1841—1845......do.....	7,634.76	2,358.70	3,866.42	3,674,000 st.—40.90 tons.
1846—1850......do.....	6,831.78	2,730.60	4,279.88	6,677,868 st.—71.31 tons.
1851—1855......do.....	7,266.78	2,357.14	4,748.74	5,423,000 st.—18.74 tons.
1856—1860......do.....	6,675.74	2,427.40	5,077.91	5,083,748 st.—55.92 tons.

There are nine spike and nail factories located near the Swedish frontiers, which turn out yearly fifteen millions of spikes and sixty-nine tons of nails, for the making of which they use Swedish iron. Castings are made at the iron-works at Drontheim, Christiana, Bergen, Drummen, and Sarpsberg, which procure their pig iron mainly from England and Scotland. The amount of their productions cannot be ascertained. Notwithstanding the depression caused by the separation from Denmark in 1814 the iron manufacturers of Norway have been steadily on the increase; this is principally owing to the improvement and better economy introduced into the works, as well as to the increased demand from foreign markets, especially from the United States, since the year 1843. A considerable portion of the iron manufactures are exported, though at present the exportations are somewhat diminished; the great developments in the different branches of industry having caused larger quantities to be used within the country. Exportation has not been in proportion to production. The following table will show the quantity of iron exported from Norway from 1815 to and including 1862:

Years.	Bar iron.	Castings.	Spike and nails.
	Tons.	Tons.	Pounds.
1815—1819	1,122.5	....	....
1820—1824	1,907.4	....	....
1825—1826	3,154.6	....	....
1827—1829	2,804.4	....	48,000
1830—1835	2,459.2	....	17,980
1836—1840	1,720.6	.49	13,440
1841—1845	2,314.4	222.5	13,120
1846—1850	2,313.61	273.66	14,037
1851—1860	2,573.00	109.09	6,240
1856—1860	2,046.8	60.64	39,186
1861—1862	1,321.00	58.35	13,165

The most important market for Norwegian castings has been Denmark, but since the establishment of iron foundries in the latter country, protected by an import duty, it has greatly fallen off. Great Britain has proved a good market for castings; Denmark for nails, spikes, and bar-iron. In consequence of the superior quality of the Norwegian bar-iron the United States of America have taken precedence of Denmark as consumers of this important article.

The following table will exhibit the quantities of bar-iron exported to Denmark and the United States from the year 1841 to 1862, both inclusive:

Years.	Denmark.	United States.
	Tons.	Tons.
1841	1,578.7	24.52
1842	1,569.1	27.33
1843	1,485.9	670.57
1844	1,013.7	1,487.6
1845	903.76	1,379.7
1846	802.09	1,544.1
1847	643.00	940.55
1848	989.3	954.6
1849	810.6	1,265.00
1850	960.5	532.00
1851	948.6	1,221.00
1852	955.6	1,179.00
1853	839.00	1,028.5
1854	647.00	826.6
1855	719.2	571.6
1857	676.4	....
1858	297.9	328.00
1859	338.2	776.3
1860	377.2	1,139.54
1861	266.6	402.7
1862	298.8	695.8

The export duty on pig-iron in the year 1836 was reduced from one specie dollar to sixteen shillings per 320 Norwegian pounds. The average yearly export from 1836 to 1840 was 181.21 tons; 1841 to 1845, 106.89 tons; 1851 to 1856, 67.35 tons; and in 1857 to 1862, 25.04 tons. It is to be hoped that hereafter the entire production will be consumed within the country. The great cost in its manufacture prevents the exportation of iron from Norway to any great extent. In quality and value it excels the Russian sable and Swedish bar-iron. In many instances the cheaper Swedish and English iron successfully competes with that of Norway. In those countries engaged in the manufacture of iron, Norway has to encounter high protective tariffs, which render competition very difficult. Notwithstanding considerable quantities of iron were exported, yet, previous to the year 1842, some pig and old iron was imported, though in no very great quantities, and machine shops were being established in the country. In that year the importation of pig-iron amounted to 109.24 tons; in 1843, 1,068.69 tons were imported; this increase was caused by the low price of pig-iron in Scotland. On the 4th of December, 1843, a provisional import duty was laid upon foreign pig-iron of three-fifths of a specie dollar per 320 Norwegian pounds, which was reduced by the storthing, January 1, 1846, to three-tenths of a specie dollar; in 1857 this duty was entirely abolished, since which time the importation of pig-iron has steadily increased. From 1845 to 1850, 2,091.95 tons; 1851 to 1855, 3,006 tons; 1857 to 1862, 3,709.15 tons yearly. There being no cannon foundries in Norway, large quantities are imported from Sweden.

Hollow-ware made at the works at Dyuldorf are imported from Holland. Great improvements having been made in the manufacture, a greater portion of the hollow-ware is now made in Norway. The importation of bar, bolt, and band-iron is on the increase. The yearly average for the years 1844 to 1846, 1,110.82 tons; 1847 to 1850, 1,179.38 tons; 1851 to 1854, 1,635 tons; 1855 to 1858, 4,189.05 tons; 1859 to 1862, 3,890.05 tons; these importations are made from Sweden and England. Sheet-iron is also imported from Great Britain and in small quantities from Sweden and Altona. In 1843 the iron works at Lanwig for manufacture of rolled iron plate, bar, and sheet iron were established. The importation of these articles has therefore ceased. Chains, anchors, and ship-knees are largely imported from Great Britain. In 1844 and 1845 factories for the manufacture of these articles as well as of anchors were established at Lanwig; that the importations continue to increase may be accounted for from the great increase of Norwegian shipping, the cheapness of the foreign fabrics, and there being no import duty to protect the home manufacturers, who, under these circumstances, are unable to compete with those of England where labor and materials are so much cheaper. The imports of spikes, nails, and rivets are on the increase, notwithstanding the large quantities made in the country. The importations from 1856 to 1862 averaged yearly 388,559 lbs.; this amount does not include large quantities imported from Sweden by land, all goods thus imported being free of duty. A comparison shows that the exports of iron exceed the imports, yet the latter are far more valuable. Copper is the next mineral in importance, but no great degree of success has attended the efforts to develop this source of national wealth.

The following table will show the operations in this mineral from the year 1781 to 1861 :

Names of copper mines and works in Norway, and years when established.	1781.	1791.	1821.	1829.	1836–'40. Yearly average.	1841–'45. Yearly average.	1846–'50. Yearly average.	1851–'55. Yearly average.	1855–'60. Yearly average.
	Tons.	Tons.	Tons.	Tons.	Tons.	Tons.	Tons.	Tons.	Tons.
Vinoren, established 1838...					L. 56	6. 89			
Fredrickagift.* estab'd 1748..	51. 99	54. 77	......	9. 06	329. 27	349. 19	317. 70	894. 04	285. 73
Roras,* established 1684....	478. 80	326. 57	353. 96	277. 88					
Queeken or Indral,† 1629...	22. 56	17. 20							
Licken,‡ established 1655...	49. 00	29. 80	18. 66	19. 99	26. 08	12. 65	60. 00	1, 305. 00	......
Selbo, established 1717......	33. 55	55. 08	22. 65	39. 20	63. 45	60. 70	60. 98	64. 26	57. 99
Tydal,§ established 1835.....	......	......	......	......	11. 40	4. 53		3. 12	17. 64
Alten, established 1826.....	......	......	......	232. 55	219. 51	169. 61	69. 83	118. 47	45. 45
Ovenanger, estab'd 1842....	......	......	......	......		11. 79		70. 91	......
Eger, established 1848......	......	......	......	......			6. 34	85. 91	21. 10
Other mines..............							105. 72	6, 000. 00	121. 57
Total productions	635. 90	483. 42	394. 57	568. 68	651. 27	615. 36	613. 47	8, 971. 71	549. 41

* These mines were unclosed in 1826.   † Discontinued.   ‡ Discontinued in 1843.
§ Discontinued in 1844, and reopened in 1859.

Great quantities of mundic or iron pyrites are found, but the lack of capital is an impediment to their being made productive; the want of fuel for smelting the ore has been another difficulty to be encountered, for which cause many mines have had to be abandoned. Stone coal is advantageously used at the copper-works at Alton; 200,000 pounds of sheet copper are yearly made at the works in Drontheim. Copper ore and mundic are exported to Great Britain. Cleaned copper is more or less exported to Holland, Great Britain, Altona, Belgium, Spain, Denmark, and Sardinia. Rolled sheet copper is principally sent to Altona.

The following table exhibits the kind, quality, and quantity of copper exported from Norway from 1815 to 1862, inclusive :

Years.	Copper ore.	Copper, cleaned.	Rolled and sheet copper.	Mundic or iron pyrites.
	Tons.	Tons.	Tons.	Tons.
1815–1819, yearly average.	....	264. 02	....	.....
1820–1826......do........	....	364. 06	....	.....
1827–1829......do........	....	325. 75	3. 81	.....
From works at Alton:				
1828–1829, exported yearly.	446. 58	....	....	.....
1830–1835........do......	846. 13	474. 00	13. 06	.....
1836–1840........do......	968. 87	429. 58	16. 30	.....
1841–1845........do......	12. 34	499. 28	41. 72	.....
1846–1850.	{ 169. 50 } 36. 05	497. 66	21. 33	116. 05
1851–1855	503. 00	509. 00	68. 55	250. 03
1856–1858	91, 000 s. dol	....	....	.....
1856–1860	606. 69	511. 76	27. 60	127. 33
1860	....	....	....	700 lbs
1861	....	....	....	1, 028. 64
1861–1862	749. 91	502. 59	....	.....
1862	....	....	....	5, 514. 16

In addition to cleansed and old copper, there are about 23,000 pounds in sheets, bars, bolts, nails, tacks and wire, imported yearly from Great Britain.

The silver mine at Konigsberg, discovered in 1623, has been worked on government as well as private account, in the main unprofitably, and was abandoned in 1805, and again worked in 1816, but not productively. The Norwegian storthing made the following annual appropriations for the working of this mine, viz:

In 1815 to 1824, the sum of........................ 24, 000 specie dollars.
   1824   do.   .... 28, 000   do.
   1827   do.   .... 26, 000   do.

Notwithstanding this aid the mine had incurred a debt of 80,000 specie dollars.

A rich vein of silver was discovered in what is called the ring mine, which, with the exception of the period from 1841 to 1846, was worked to advantage. The following are its results from 1831 to and including 1860:

1831..	9, 220$\frac{2}{3}$	marks fine silver.
1832..	21, 565$\frac{1}{4}$	do.
1833..	48, 843$\frac{1}{4}$	do.
1834..	27, 216$\frac{1}{4}$	do.
1835..	17, 353	do.
1836..	28, 202$\frac{1}{2}$	do.
1837..	24, 974$\frac{1}{4}$	do.
1838..	20, 031$\frac{1}{4}$	do.
1839..	26, 302$\frac{1}{4}$	do.
1840..	31, 474$\frac{3}{4}$	do.
1841..	25, 097$\frac{3}{4}$	do.
1842..	21, 518$\frac{1}{4}$	do.
1843..	17, 261$\frac{1}{2}$	do.
1844..	17, 689	do.
1845..	17, 085$\frac{1}{4}$	do.
1846..	16, 079$\frac{3}{4}$	do.
1847..	25, 183$\frac{1}{4}$	do.
1848..	36, 398$\frac{1}{4}$	do.
1849..	34, 003$\frac{1}{4}$	do.
1850..	22, 877$\frac{3}{4}$	do.
1851..	18, 359$\frac{1}{2}$	do.
1852..	19, 672$\frac{1}{2}$	do.
1853..	17, 858$\frac{1}{4}$	do.
1854..	25, 410$\frac{1}{4}$	do.
1855..	40, 566$\frac{1}{4}$	do.
1856..	23, 971$\frac{3}{4}$	do.
1857..	24, 235$\frac{1}{4}$	do.
1858..	41, 121$\frac{1}{4}$	do.
1859..	20, 515$\frac{1}{4}$	do.
1860..	18, 139$\frac{2}{3}$	do.

Since 1860 the products have declined. On the whole it appears that the mine has used up several millions of silver more than it has produced; it has had the effect to call into existence the city of Konigsberg, which in 1769 had a population of 8,068. In 1855 it had only 4,417 inhabitants; the cause of this decline will be found in the fact that since the union of Norway and Sweden the great manufactories have been removed to Christiania. It is admitted that Konigsberg has been the school for the development of the mechanical genius of this country. Other silver mines in various parts of the country, and gold mines at Eidsvold, have been discovered, but their operations have been so unimportant as scarcely to deserve notice; the working of them was abandoned many years ago.

Cobalt was first discovered in this country in the year 1772. The first manufactory of cobalt blue was established at Modum, in the year 1778; its operations were not very important till several years later. It has been much improved since 1822, when it became private property. The yearly productions of smalt are 450,000 pounds. Since the year 1832 the manufacture of smalt and zaffer has been less profitable, by reason of the establishment of factories for the refining of cobalt, in England; in consequence of which a protective import duty was imposed upon foreign cobalt, since which time double the quantity of cobalt, in the shape of zaffer, has been exported yearly, nearly all to England, for many years the most important market for smalt. From 1836 to 1840 Holland was the largest consumer; during those years the exportation of smalt to that country averaged yearly 147,600 pounds, against 50,000 pounds to England during the same period; but during the period from 1841 to 1845 this was reversed; the yearly exportation to England was 128,900 pounds, against 49,490 pounds to Holland during the same period. Belgium, latterly, has been the best market. However, the exportation of this article is on the decline.

Chromium was first discovered in this country in the beginning of the present century; large quantities were exported at a very small profit. Since the establishment at Drontheim, in the year 1834, of a factory for making chrome yellow and sulphuric acid, great quantities of the ore are used in the country. From 1858 to 1862 the yearly consumption of this article amounted to 316,582 pounds; about one-quarter of this quantity was exported to Altona and Holland. Since the year 1837 the exportation of the ore has been on the increase, and almost exclusively to England. In the year 1862, 606,855 pounds were exported to England, particularly from the stift of Drontheim.

There are no important lead mines in the country; those worked in the 17th and 18th centuries have been abandoned. The various kinds of stone used for mechanical and building purposes are found in this country. No coal has yet been discovered.

The mineral wealth of Norway may be stated as follows:

	Specie dollars.
15,000 skpd. of cast-iron, (1 skpd. equal 320 Norway pounds,) at 7 specie dollars per skpd.	105,000
25,000 skpd. bar iron, at 10 specie dollars per skpd.	250,000
3,800 skpd. copper products, at 65 specie dollars per skpd.	247,000
220,000 skpd. smalt, at 30 specie dollars per 100 pounds.	66,000
110,000 pounds zaffer, at 18 specie dollars per 100 pounds.	19,800
20,000 marks silver, at 10 specie dollars per mark.	200,000
5,500 tons mundic, (iron pyrites,) at 5 specie dollars per ton.	27,500
Total	915,300

THE FISH TRADE.

This trade is confined to the cities and towns along the coast of Norway from Lindesnaes to Hammerfest; the city of Bergen holding the first rank. Salted and dried codfish, (stock-fish and clep-fish,) fish-oil, spawn, pickled herring, and lobsters are largely exported to and used by Catholic countries.

Tabular statement showing the exports of the fisheries from Norway, as far as reliable statements have been received.

Years.	Round dry fish. Tons.	Dried salted fish. Tons.	Oil. Barrels.	Spawn. Barrels.	Remarks.
1756–'60	7,921.39	....	14,000	8,000	The yearly average of exports from 1756 to 1846
1776–'83	8,147.78	....	15,000	......	is calculated for the cities
1804–'06	7,197.60	....	17,930	10,000	of Bergen, Christamund,
1815–'19	7,652.88	1,337.60	19,193	8,545	and Drontheim.
1820–'24	8,969.77	4,270.08	27,265	......	
1825–'29	14,199.05	5,664.06	40,458	22,146	
1830–'35	14,988.84	6,451.54	27,468	21,742	
1836–'40	14,523.83	8,822.93	38,564	21,356	
1841–'45	11,128.21	8,056.50	49,004	22,883	
1846........	14,356.81	10,389.38	60,504	21,149	
1847........	13,682.65	9,598.81	53,932	21,583	
1848........	12,255.62	12,031.45	55,500	25,657	
1849........	15,017.83	10,443.76	59,910	23,957	
1850........	13,816.79	10,455.04	54,730	21,262	
1851........	18,698.54	13,299.94	39,509	31,233	
1852........	15,910.42	9,712.91	45,571	24,429	
1853........	13,490.36	11,954.43	53,127	25,230	
1854........	14,568.51	10,401.54	49,487	23,215	
1855........	13,433.10	20,552.62	78,804	30,668	
1856........	17,706.55	17,961.32	76,694	39,816	
1857........	13,972.00	21,776.15	55,296	19,739	
1858........	10,893.86	14,167.42	36,562	24,109	
1859........	8,982.87	17,238.64	56,894	24,954	
1860........	11,823.28	17,297.10	72,634	34,064	
1861........	10,971.46	17,600.38	67,551	30,591	
1862........	12,060.04	15,051.99	63,181	26,165	

The above stated quantities are set down in the public statistics in Voger, one vog equals 39.5 pounds avoirdupois; 1 ton, 2,240 pounds avoirdupois. The quantity of oil is by no means in proportion to the number of fish caught; that depends upon the quality. The quantity of fish consumed in the country is very large, and the consumption increases with the population; this quantity is of course not included in the above statement of exports, nor is the quantity caught on the coast of Finmark and sold to Russia in exchange for meal, hemp, sail-cloth, &c., included in that statement. It is remarkable that the winter herring periodically disappear from the Norwegian coast. In 1559 such vast quantities were caught that they were sold for four cents per barrel, but in 1567 they had disappeared entirely, the precise period of their reappearance is uncertain. The spring herring fishery commenced to some extent in 1669 or 1670; it would from this appear that the herring were absent from the coast of Norway for the period of one hundred and two years—a remarkable circumstance, and one which challenges the investigation of the ichthyologist.

The following tabular statement shows the annual exportation of spring herring from 1752 to 1757 from Bergen alone, and from the latter year to 1862 from the whole country :

Years.	Barrels.	Years.	Barrels.
1752, winter herring from Bergen alone..	123,570	1840......................	648,619
1755.......do......do......do........	53,490	1841......................	487,554
1756......do......do......do........	111,220	1842......................	567,922
1757.......do......do......do........	82,900	1843......................	368,947
1816—1820............................	95,850	1844......................	732,960
1821................................	269,195	1845......................	584,142
1822................................	337,355	1846......................	712,565
1823................................	296,409	1847......................	556,180
1824................................	172,281	1848......................	431,868
1825................................	244,508	1849......................	698,747
1826................................	260,912	1850......................	493,591
1827................................	359,459	1851......................	659,996
1828................................	450,906	1852......................	516,156
1829................................	347,870	1853......................	514,488
1830................................	260,095	1854......................	427,759
1831................................	416,870	1855......................	469,868
1832................................	523,151	1856......................	480,852
1833................................	622,368	1857......................	415,831
1834................................	632,797	1859......................	606,577
1835................................	430,712	1860......................	685,384
1837................................	643,959	1861......................	366,571
1838................................	322,144	1862......................	744,658
1839................................	346,930		

In addition to the spring herring, large quantities of summer herring are caught on the Norwegian coast. The yearly value may be stated as follows :

Specie dollars.

Average yearly export of spring herring at 600,000 barrels, at 3 specie dollars per barrel...................................	1,800,000
Summer herring, at 5 specie dollars per barrel.................	500,000
100,000 barrels spring herring for home consumption, at 2½ specie dollars per barrel..	250,000
100,000 barrels summer herring, at 3 specie dollars per barrel...	300,000
20,000 barrels bristling, at 2 specie dollars per barrel.........	40,000
20,000 kegs anchovies, average yearly quantity, at ½ specie dollar per keg..	10,000
Total	2,900,000

RECAPITULATION.

Average yearly value of timber products......................	4,000,000
" " mineral products	915,300
" " dried salted cod.....................	1,400,000
" " dried round cod.....................	814,000
" " dried round cod (used in the country)..	200,000
" " fish-oil	840,000
" " fish-oil (used in the country)..........	200,000
" " fish spawn	150,000
" " freights on fish	70,000
" " herring............................	2,900,000

	Specie dollars.
Average yearly value of freight on herring	200,000
" " lobsters	134,267
Aggregate value	11,823,567

DECEMBER 13, 1864.

I have the honor herewith to transmit an abstract of the public statistics of the commerce and shipping of the kingdom of Norway for the year 1863, published by the royal department of interior in 1864, (enclosure No. 1.)

IMPORTS.

Breadstuffs of all kinds	bushels..	5,015,724
Beef of all kinds	pounds..	1,222,947
Pork and lard of all kinds	do....	4,904,192
Cheese of all kinds	do....	830,229
Butter of all kinds	do....	4,427,382
Salt of all kinds	bushels..	3,045,560
Coffee of all kinds	pounds..	11,981,885
Sugar, sirup, and molasses of all kinds	do....	10,740,884
Tobacco of all kinds	do....	2,866,014
Wines	gallons..	204,292
Liquors and spirits	do....	303,863
Coal and coke	tons..	76,617
Cotton	pounds..	503,871
Cotton manufactures of all kinds	do....	756,519
Flax and hemp of all kinds	do....	7,001,461
Flax and hemp, manufactures of, (except cordage)	do....	1,740,127
Cordage of all kinds	do....	274,094
Wool of all kinds	do....	312,403
Manufactures of wool	do....	1,229,386

EXPORTS.

Fish, salted and dried, all kinds	tons..	26,518.27
Herring, pickled	barrels..	917,822
Spawn	do....	31,456
Cod-liver and other fish oil	gallons..	1,397,678
Iron in bars	tons..	2,118.92
Copper	pounds..	889,312
Timber products	tons..	759,076

EXPORTS DIRECT TO THE UNITED STATES IN 1863.

Anchovies	kegs..	300
Books, (value)	specie dollars..	20
Cod-liver oil	gallons..	173
Herring. pickled	barrels..	483
smoked	pounds..	2,134
Iron in bars	tons..	44.22
Liquors (cornbrendenn)	gallons..	250
Tar	barrels..	18

H. Ex. Doc. 60——26

IMPORTS DIRECT FROM THE UNITED STATES IN 1863.

Beef, salted	pounds..	88
tongues	do....	80
Bread	do....	1,798
Butter ...	do....	223
Cast-iron goods	do....	1,129
Cheese	do....	38
Coffee	do....	1,052
Corn, Indian	bushels..	3,112
Cotton manufacture	pounds..	15
Glass in connexion with metal	do....	134
other	do....	123
Hides, dried	do....	3,097
salted	do....	11,941
Machines (valued)	specie dollars..	8
Petroleum	pounds..	1,420
Rye	bushels..	19,560
Star candles	pounds..	12
Peas	bushels..	54
Tobacco	pounds..	16,176
Tools and implements	do....	180
Wheat	bushels..	2,280
flour	pounds..	236,823

The foregoing statement of the exports direct to the United States is incorrect, and does not contain all the merchandise shipped thereto during the year. The following contains the merchandise shipped direct from the city of Bergen to the city of Chicago during the year 1863, as appears by the invoice certified at the consulate, viz:

Anchovies	kegs..	300
Books (valued)	specie dollars..	235
Codfish	pounds..	2,971
Cod-liver oil	barrels..	5
Herring, pickled	do....	694½
smoked	do....	8¾
brestling	do....	21
Liquors	gallons..	564¼
Salt	barrels..	470
Tar	do....	250

The reason for this discrepancy was probably that the sloop Skjóldmoërs cleared at this port for England to receive orders, and some goods were shipped in vessels for Montreal, there to be transhipped to Chicago.

The exports of Norway in the year 1863 were somewhat heavier than in the foregoing year, particularly that of bar-iron, which was exported to the following countries:

Countries.	1862.	1863.
	Tons.	*Tons.*
Denmark	298.80	215.71
Great Britain and Ireland	194.15	575.41
Hamburg	121.21	1,270.53
United States	695.80	44.22
France	....	4.69
Other countries	....	8.34
Total	1,309.96	2,117.90

The imports have been greater, particularly of breadstuffs and provisions. Of cotton the importation has been reduced to less than one-half the quantity imported in 1862. Cotton in manufacture has been somewhat less; nearly all the cotton factories of the country were in operation during the year, but on a very limited scale.

There were considerable shipments of ice made from various ports of the south of Norway. The first shipment of importance was made in 1857, and until 1862 they were exclusively made to Great Britain and Ireland, and in the year 1863 were extended to nearly all the countries of northern Europe. The statement below shows the extent of the exportations of this natural product of Norway. The numerous glaciers in the different parts of this country lying near the coast, where this commodity might be had at all seasons of the year, might yet prove to be an inexhaustible source of wealth for Norway.

Countries.	1860.	1861.	1862.	1863.
	Tons.	Tons.	Tons.	Tons.
Sweden	....	....	....	1,321
Finland	....	....	....	83
Prussia	....	....	....	820
Denmark and Schleswig	....	....	86	1,474
Holstein	....	....	....	278
Hamburg	....	....	....	3,066
Lubeck	....	....	....	36
Bremen	....	....	....	446
Oldenburg	....	....	....	553
Hanover	....	....	....	981
Holland	....	....	....	911
Belgium	....	....	....	639
Great Britain and Ireland	13,390	8,106	26,414	39,797
France	....	....	....	1,570
Total	13,390	8,106	26,500	51,975

Statement showing the number, tonnage, and nationality of vessels entered and cleared the ports of the kingdom of Norway during the year 1863.

Vessels.	ENTERED.		CLEARED.	
	No.	Tons.	No.	Tons.
Norwegian, freighted	3,012	321,468	6,280	865,540
ballast	3,960	762,117	572	194,957
Foreign, freighted	2,378	153,139	4,728	380,360
ballast	2,744	163,612	403	35,377
Total	12,094	1,400,336	11,983	1,396,238
With freight	5,399	474,607	11,008	1,145,900
In ballast	6,704	925,729	975	250,338
Total	12,094	1,400,336	11,983	1,396,238

Statement showing the number and tonnage of vessels owned in the kingdom of Norway, also the number of their crews, on the 31st December, 1863.

Vessels under 20 tons :

Number of vessels	930
Tonnage	11, 542
Number of crews	2, 409

Over 20 tons and under 50 :

Number of vessels	2, 042
Tonnage	67, 327
Number of crews	7, 806

Over 50 tons and under 130 :

Number of vessels	796
Tonnage	61, 991
Number of crews	4, 865

Over 130 tons and under 260 :

Number of vessels	655
Tonnage	186, 315
Number of crews	5, 588

Over 260 tons and under 520 :

Number of vessels	959
Tonnage	357, 659
Number of crews	11, 246

Of 520 tons and over :

Number of vessels	239
Tonnage	158, 429
Number of crews	3, 786

Making the total number of vessels 5,621, with aggregate tonnage of 843,263 tons, manned by 35,700 sailors. Number of vessels built during the year 1863 was 141, with aggregate tonnage of 2,561 tons. Number of vessels purchased in foreign countries in the same period was 91, with aggregate tonnage of 38,984 tons. Number of vessels wrecked during the year was 10, with aggregate tonnage of 19,603 tons. Number of vessels cut up during the year was 35, with aggregate tonnage of 1,028 tons.

PORSGRUND—C. J. KRABY, *Consul.*

DECEMBER 31, 1863.

In compliance with the requirement of the consular regulations of the United States, I have the honor to submit herewith a brief statement and report concerning this consulate during the year ended the 31st day of December, 1863.

1st. Since my last annual report no vessel belonging to the United States has been in this nor the nearest ports within this consular jurisdiction. The commerce and direct trade by Norwegian vessels between the United States and ports of this consulate during the year have, however, been of a more increasing prosperity than last year; and there is good reason to believe that the trade and direct communication between the United States and this nation will hereafter be more important and of greater interest for both nations. The navigation at the several seaports in this consulate has up to this time been undisturbed, as the ports are yet free from ice.

2d. The exports from this consulate to the United States have been principally bar-iron. The certificates to invoices issued from this office on iron shipped to the United States during the year are 248½ tons, amounting in value to $16,195 52.

*   *   *   *   *   *

4th. The emigration to the United States from this district during the year is about equal to the emigration of 1862, although there was an impression prevalent that immigrants on their arrival in the United States would be liable to be drafted for soldiers, and obliged to serve in the national army, as long as the present rebellion shall last, or until peace is restored. But all this unfounded fear has ceased since my publication of circular No. 42 from the Department of State, which circular I caused to be circulated through this district. I have done all in my power to stimulate a large emigration from this country into our western States; and I am satisfied that during the next year there will be a larger emigration from this district than ever heretofore. Here are thousands of good, strong, laboring persons, who would not hesitate a moment to emigrate to the United States if they only had means to pay their passage thereto. But poverty keeps the greatest number of hardy laborers chained to their fatherland.

*   *   *   *   *   *

8th. No changes or alterations relative to light-houses have been made in this consular district since my last report to the department; but one new light within the common jurisdiction of Bergen has been established since the first day of October last, by the name of "Koppernaglen," under 59° 17¼′ latitude north and 5° 19¾′ longitude east of Greenwich.

*   *   *   *   *   *

11th. According to a request in circular No. 40, section 12, I have the honor to inform the department that, in reply to inquiries addressed to the authorities of the country, I have received the following information:

According to the law of August 28, 1851, section 2, "every individual over ten years of age, and residing in the kingdom, shall pay poor taxes to that community or place in which he may be a resident; and the tax shall be according to the ability."

Consuls of foreign governments residing within this kingdom are exempt from all government and local taxation, except the poor tax, provided that the consul is not engaged in trade or commerce and not receiving any benefit from this country. The salary or compensation which consuls receive from their own respective governments cannot be taxed. No person, native or alien, is permitted to engage in trade or commerce until he has received a license from the government to become a free burgher of the kingdom.

*   *   *   *   *   *   *

16th. The population of the twenty-four ports within this consular district is as follows:

1. The population of the city of Christiania, the capital of this kingdom, at the close of this year is 55,080, besides a population of 5,000 in the several suburbs, outside the old city limits, which makes an aggregate population of a trifle over 60,000 inhabitants. The exports are iron and lumber.

2. Drammen has 10,300 inhabitants. Its export is lumber.

3. Christiansund has 9,800 inhabitants, and has an excellent harbor.

4. Frederickshald east, 7,500 inhabitants.

5. Laureig has a population of 5,200 and the largest iron works in the kingdom.

6. Arendal, 4,800 inhabitants, and is noted for its iron works.

7. Horten, on the bay of Christiania, has 4,700 inhabitants. Here are located

the government mechanic and machine shops, cannon foundries, the navy yard, arsenals, and navy station.

8. Moss, population 4,300. It has one iron foundry.

9. Skeen, population 4,150, and it has two iron foundries.

10. Fredericksstad, population 3,550,

11. Kragero has 3,500 inhabitants.

12. Tonsberg, 3,000 inhabitants, and has large shipping.

13. Porsgrund, 2,600 inhabitants and one iron manufactory.

14. Oster Reisor, 2,250 inhabitants.

15. Sarpsborg, 2.200 inhabitants.

16. Brevig, 1,880 inhabitants.

17. Holmestrand, 1,850 inhabitants.

18. Drobak, 1,600 inhabitants.

19. Sorlvig, 1,500 inhabitants.

20. Sannefjord, 1,300 inhabitants, and has a celebrated sulphurous bath.

21. Frederickswarn, 1,300·inhabitants. It is a harbor for men-of-war.

22. Grimstad, 1,200 inhabitants.

23. Lillesand, 800 inhabitants.

24. Langesund, 700 inhabitants.

The inland towns are:

1. Kongsberg, only four miles from Drammen, has a population of 4.500. The government has here silver mines and works, a manufactory of arms, a mint, &c.

2. Roraas, north, on the highlands, has 1,900 inhabitants, where are situated Norway's largest copper mine and works.

3. Hamar, 1,400 inhabitants.

4. Lillehammer, 1,300 inhabitants.

5. Grinage, on Lake Mjosen, north of Christiania; and

6. Honefos, 800 inhabitants.

RUSSIA.

The following notification was officially communicated to the department by Mr. Stoeckl, the envoy extraordinary and minister plenipotentiary of his Majesty the Emperor of Russia:

On the 17th February last, his Majesty the Emperor deigned to sanction a decision of the council of the empire, of which the following are the provisions:

1. All merchant vessels, as well masted and sea-going as coasters, and without masts, arriving at the port of Cronstadt, must pay to the benefit of the municipal revenues of Cronstadt a special tax for their cleansing and the removal of their filth, to wit: on each voyage, masted sea-going vessels, fifty. copeks each mast, and vessels not masted and coasters, ten copeks each vessel

2. The arrangements relative to the cleansing and removal of filth from vessels, as well as for the collection of the duty for which they are liable on this head, are made in the general order in force, by the municipality of Cronstadt, either by means of letting out by public auction or by a commission, as it shall judge proper.

3. In virtue of the laws in force, the military governor of Cronstadt is charged, as the immediate head of the city of Cronstadt, to attend to the execution of the present regulation.

EPITOME OF THE RUSSIAN EXCISE LAW.

Commerce, trade, and manufactures are divided into two guilds.

First guild.

Is confined to transactions at wholesale, is unlimited as to amount, and may extend its operations over the entire empire.

In consideration of these privileges a "patent" must be obtained from the crown, costing.. 265 roubles.
Additional tax to city of St. Petersburg .... 319 "
Tax upon each depot and store .... 30 "

In whatever city of the empire the merchants of the first guild establish a bureau or place of business, an additional tax is imposed by such city, regulated according to the necessities of the municipality.

Unlimited foreign commerce, contracts with government, and the establishment of manufactories, and other industrial institutions, are likewise granted, on payment, however, in each case, of 30 roubles additional for certificate.

Second guild.

Tax to the crown.. 65 roubles.
Tax to the city of St. Petersburg .... 90½ "
Tax to each depot or store .... 20 "

The other cities of the empire are classified into five categories, according to their size and importance, and taxed as follows :

First category... 65 roubles.
Second category... 55 "
Third category.. 45 "
Fourth category.. 35
Fifth category 25

The foregoing are payable to the crown.

The city tax is assessed according to the necessities of the municipality.

Merchants of the second guild confine their transactions to retail, both in Russian and foreign articles ; may establish manufactories and other industrial institutions upon taking out a certificate, costing 20 roubles for each establishment, and may make operations, both with the state and individuals, to the amount of 15,000 roubles at a time.

Stock and insurance companies, banking and commission houses, agencies for the transport of merchandise, and steamboats, belong to the first guild.

Proprietors of pharmacies, lithography, and typography do not belong to either guild, and only take out a certificate of second guild—20 roubles.

Proprietors of restaurants and other eating-houses, who pay an excise tax of more than 200 roubles annually, are obliged to provide themselves with a patent of the second guild; but those whose excise tax falls short of that sum are exempt from this obligation, but are, notwithstanding, required to procure a certificate of the second guild.

Small shopkeepers.

These pay for their certificate as follows :

St. Petersburg and all cities of the first category.............. 20 roubles.
Cities of the second category .... 18 "
Cities of the third category .... 15 "
Cities of the fourth category............................... 10
Cities of the fifth category................................. 8

And have the privilege of selling in the places where they have taken out their certificate, the following merchandise, viz:

Ordinary cotton goods, handkerchiefs, and ties, for the use of the lower classes; stockings and gloves; cord, laces, and ribbons; rags, thread; delph ware, but not porcelain; window glasses, lamp-chimneys, ploughs, scythes, needles, pins, and knives and forks and pen-knives of Russian manufacture; axes, locks, nails, and all articles of iron necessary for housekeeping and in the construction of rustic buildings, carts, &c.; coarse cloth and other stuffs for the use of peasants; belts and boots for the same; hardware, tanned skins, and sheep-skins, except morocco; paper, and everything necessary for writing; roots, seeds, and herbs of all kinds; salt, sal ammonia, alum, potash, sulphur, chalk, resin, bitumen, glue; harness, without ornaments in metal; small bells, sleighs, and wagons without springs; string and cord, mats, sacks, pack-cloth, fruits, vegetables, and pot-herbs; sacks; fish, and all kinds of meat and fowls; old furniture and other utensils; holy images, with their trimmings; old books and engravings, and all kinds of trifles.

Moreover, they are permitted to keep Russian baths and restaurants, provided their excise tax does not exceed 200 roubles; likewise to conduct industrial establishments of every sort where steam machinery is not employed, nor more than sixteen persons engaged; and, finally, to make contracts not exceeding 1,200 roubles in amount.

Costermongers.

Hawkers of articles in the streets are obliged to provide themselves with a certificate as follows:

With a cart or other wheeled vehicle......................... 15 roubles.
Foot pedler.. 6 "

Workmen and laborers

Must be provided with a certificate of 250 roubles cop.

Merchants' clerks

Are required to take out a certificate after the following manner:
Head clerks in all the cities of the empire pay for certificate.... 20 roubles.
Assistant clerks of three first categories .... 5 "
Under clerks of fourth and fifth categories.................. 2½ "

Peasants

May sell at the bazaars, markets, and railway stations the workmanship of their own hands without certificate or tax of any sort.

Remarks.

It will be seen by the foregoing that, although the Russian excise laws are based upon a theory of aggregation, each and every branch of industry is taxed.

These statistics were furnished me by Prince Obolensky, minister of international commerce, which I have carefully translated, and have the honor respectfully to submit.

ST. PETERSBURG—W. E. PHELPS, *Consul.*

DECEMBER 31, 1863.

I have the honor to transmit herewith a cursory account of the commerce of St. Petersburg, for the year 1863, together with some tabular statements, showing the character and amount of the principal transactions, the amount of duties received by the custom-house, the arrival and departure of shipping, and sundry other items which seem worthy of notice. Business of almost all descriptions has been reasonably active during the past year, notwithstanding the disturbed political condition of Europe and the constant fear of war; yet there has been everywhere apparent a disposition to run little risk, and realize as quickly as possible. The energetic naval and military preparations of the imperial government have given a great impetus to many branches of industry and trade. Immense quantities of war materials, coals, &c., have been imported on government account. It appears to be the intention to keep a large stock of coals in reserve against contingencies, the experience of the Crimean war having demonstrated that necessity.

A good idea of the resources and the wants of this district may be formed from the general export and import lists, showing the character and quantity of various articles handled on private account during the navigation of the last four years:

General list of goods cleared for exportation at the custom-house of St. Petersburg during the navigation of the last four years.

Articles.	1860.	1861.	1862.	1863.
Bristles: cut .... pds..				
okatka .... do..				
first sort........... do..	70,463	58,387	64,036	76,340
second sort......... do..				
suhoi .... do..				
other sorts .... do..				
Cantharides .... do..	771	424	623	132
Caviare................... do..	39	50	38	1,142
Copper .... do..	24,807	47,291	21,632	7,252
Cordage: new.............. do..	171,515	86,626	100,663	147,534
old.............. do..	280,051	140,849	200,085	168,040
Down: eider down........... do..	....	....	2	12
goose down........... do..	1,848	2,270	2,916	2,510
goat's down .... do..	3,768	8,689	5,747	4,034
Feathers .... do..	35,794	29,152	29,917	36,807
Flax: 12-head............... do..				
9-head.............. do..	1,028,251	912,043	1,297,429	1,064,499
6-head.............. do..				
codilla .... do..	186,221	385,138	368,447	377,481
yarn .... do..	....	15	15,408	5
Furs: ermine............... do..	....	....	....	77,405
squirrel ....do..	2,798	312	1,674	752,757
Galls .... do..	....	....	....	....
Glue .... do..	789	701	1,188	1,716
Grain: barley .... chtwt..	....	2,500	....	....
oats..... .... do...	482,761	158,601	35,810	204,616
rye................ do...	411,826	518,778	140,221	127,351
wheat .... do...	262,352	280,723	109,407	224,542
Gum: ammoniac..........pds	....	....	....	....
galbanum .... do..	....	....	....	....
Hair: camel hair............ do..	....	293	5,279	12,949
goat's hair............ do..	4,514	201	3,523	696
ox and cow hair........ do..	1,829	3,145	5 156	12,984

General list of goods cleared for exportation, &c.—Continued.

Articles.	1860.	1861.	1862.	1863.
Hemp: clean................pds.				
out-shot..............do..	1,748,317	1,591,278	1,761,460	1,552,270
half-clean.............do..				
codilla................do..	3,701	8,491	3,908	9,059
yarn..................do..	202,229	207,829	293,882	239,027
Hides: raw cow............do..	11,653	10,060	8,711	1,034
ox...................do..			125	
horse.................do..	8,704	108		
red..................do..	12,622	15,700	12,270	7,734
white................do..	1,908	2,228	1,864	1,929
black................do..	48	23	67	28
dressed..............pcs.				5
Horse-manes..............pds	17,863	13,460	15,795	11,507
tails.................do..	9,869	8,377	9,480	7,707
Iron: in bars.............do..	208,898	130,966	382,178	150,877
in blocks.............do..	3		31	
in sheets.............do..	71,000	30,838	108,458	35,259
old..................do..	9,056		264	13,180
Isinglass.................do..	3,094	2,668	3,217	3,438
Samovy...............do..	1,694	418	1,875	1,637
Licorice.....................	5,518	1,726	3,265	4,835
Manufactures: flems........pcs	701	1,429	2,601	1,340
ravens duck...do..	10,098	3,214	8,991	8,531
sail-cloth.....do..	22,448	18,609	51,396	26,061
Diaper, broad.............arsch.	27,370	8,900		13,980
narrow..............do..	8,924			
linen, broad.........do..				
narrow..............do..				
drillings............do..	4,056	5,928		
crash................do..	5,187,000	3,440,000	6,276,250	4,414,500
Meal: rye meal...........chwt.	10,866	102,532	16,878	11,717
wheat meal...........do..	8,120	10,002	2,193	1,670
Oil: aniseed oil.........pds..	165	115	82	4
hempseed oil.........do..	721	38,859	150,545	844
linseed oil..........do..	25		5,644	16,013
Pot ashes................do..	369,276	585,364	573,373	448,265
Quills.................thousand.	76,428	593	14,271	18,436
Rhubarb..................pds..	363	108	211	
Seeds: aniseed............do..	3,252	383	149	53
cuminseed............do..	7,549	1,647	4,236	3,740
hempseed............chwt.	1¼	1¼		5
linseed...............do..	289,262	179,379	345,429	317,159
wormseed............pds	13,895	25,139	22,420	31,578
Skins: calf...............do..		3,775	3,401	11,129
dressed..............pcs.				23
badger...............do..	21,953	709	6,108	22,845
cat..................do..				1,000
ermine...............do..	9,823	187,247	133,667	111,622
hare, gray ....do..	241,507	7	19,761	20,500
white................do..	125,989		15,938	5,000
sable................do..	9,811	8,925	981	650
squirrel.............do..	1,519,857	1,511,077	1,053,198	1,204,868
Soap....................pds..	615	440	911	541
Sole leather.............do..				
Squirrel tails............pcs..	2,137,042	1,891,500	3,537,245	1,183,405
Tallow...................pds.	3,302,823	2,215,353	1,682,262	1,992,490
Candles..............do..	33	156	10	4
Wax: white...............do..				
yellow...............do..				
candles ....do..				
Woods: battens...........pcs..				

General list of goods cleared for exportation, &c.—Continued.

Articles.	1860.	1861.	1862.	1863.
Woods: beams .... pcs..	....	76	....	....
do .... do..	555	150	48	1,190
lathwood .... do..	....	....	....	....
Wool : sheep wool .... do..	235,039	242,610	354,460	228,532
woollen yarn .... do..	1,409	652	396	466
Sundries............. per value ro..	8,215,204	8,149,135	11,523,922	43,229,066
Total value	52,854,041	47,051,923	60,657,399	80,943,372

General list of principal goods imported to St. Petersburg during navigation of the last four years.

Articles.	1860.	1861.	1862.	1863.
Cheese........................ pds..	19,522	23,426	21,733	26,163
Cacao......................... do..	2,271	5,448	1,872	2,997
Coals.................... chaldr's..	96,594	100,712	112,200	125,319
Coffee........................ pds..	224,186	240,712	275,169	214,942
Corkwood...... .... do..	32,883	44,796	18,409	7,670
Corks...................... bales..	1,084	980	675	652
Cotton wool................. pds..	2,086,103	2,097,825	178,176	426,156
yarn undyed........... do..	50,396	60,534	18,825	24,237
dyed............... do..	6,159	8,836	3,380	6,542
Cotton goods................. do..	23,294	28,549	11,286	8,637
Drugs and dry salteries:				
Acids, sundry............... do..	8,935	4,730	. 5,086	4,486
Aloes......................... do..	407	26	212	279
Alum......................... do..	44,043	65,939	72,484	36,360
Annatto...................... do..	2,985	1,643	4,577	1,271
Antimony.................... do..	4,911	2,548	1,580	5,281
Argol........................ do..	2,578	1,298	5,960	2,432
Arsenic...................... do..	7,531	5,860	3,837	1,190
Bay leaves................... do..	1,681	1,584	2,135	3,767
Bleach'g powder or chlorochalk. do..	69,583	58,169	49,830	31,192
Borax........................ do..	3,945	4,139	4,961	2,653
Brimstone...... .... do..	50,393	106,934	257,917	428,633
Camphor.... .... do..	488	1,067	774	1,110
Chalk........................ do..	32,366	59,281	46,797	41,785
Cinnabar .... do..	978	2,800	401	1,586
Cobalt : smalts .... do..	875	450	699	511
zaffres .... do..	38	24	30	45
Cochineal.................... do..	9,403	10,722	14,736	8,104
Crystal Tartary.............. do..	1,797	2,983	3,531	5,536
Cudbear... .... do..	....	213	1,236	620
Emery........................ do..	9,821	4,248	263	1,737
Gum : Arabic and Senegal..... do..	10,898	21,696	18,475	8,381
benjamin: ....do..	144	397	276	977
copal..... .... do..	1,969	1,150	1,295	2,303
elastic or India-rubber.. do..	3,186	7,851	4,044	5,447
gamboge .... do..	589	371	259	236
gutta-percha........ do..	9	124	166	8
olibanum. .... do..	4,780	5,867	11,565	15,332
schellac .. .. do..	298	2,259	7,315	9,730
Garancine................. do..	66,614	70,073	37,604	27,904
Indigo : Bengal.......... ......do.. }	33,621	29,647	13,567	22,425
Java .... do..		20,021	9,520	14,961
Lemon juice................ pipes..	15	3	....	10
Madder...................... pds..	44,705	67,810	25,757	9,812

General list of principal goods imported to St. Petersburg, &c.—Continued.

Articles.	1860.	1861.	1862.	1863.
Magnesia........ ....pds..	1,121	1,313	988	1,522
Manganese...................do..	17,543	17,965	15,893	12,362
Manna.......................do..	53	129	168	108
Minium......................do..	14,084	6,481	4,511	5,175
Musk........................do..	2	4	4	4
Natrum nitricum ....do..	15,142	55,697	25,669	93,226
Ochre.......................do..	77,709	49,875	40,170	30,288
Opium.......................do..	5	36	2	5
Orchella ....do..	1,049	1,285	479	262
Peel, lemon and orange........do..	1,773	1,650	2,382	3,365
Peruvian bark................do..	372	881	804	1,188
Pumice stone.................do..	· 12,142	21,852	15,963	3,145
Quercitron bark..............do..	19,981	16,748	17,436	10,585
Red ochre....................do..	5,349	18,390	8,970	5,268
Rosin............... ....do..	....	74,165	2,128	6,096
Roots: galanga...............do..	4,998	1,813	43	957
gentian...............do..	167	84	....	9
jalap. ....do..	31	71	47	89
ipecacuanha ....do..	3	15	10	24
ireos.... ....do..	858	91	283	191
salep..................do..	1	19	10	18
sarsaparilla...........do..	4,005	3,047	4,073	3,055
snake ....do..	....	....	....	....
Safflower ....do..	5,189	3,409	762	769
Saffron ....tb..	269	1,108	316	425
Sago...... ....pds..	511	284	186	528
Salamoniac ....do..	7,755	6,902	8,362	10,403
Senna leaves.................do..	427	520	185	544
Soda.........................do..	380,974	270,693	329,021	428,600
Sumach ....do..	38,124	14,732	44,433	19,184
Star aniseed.................do..	1,607	905	184	343
Turmeric....................do..	9,832	5,145	561	1,024
Turpentine...................do..	760	1,599	409	1,449
Ultramarine ....do..	2,103	3,046	932	1,066
Verdigris........ ....do..	3,159	1,352	1,762	2,088
Vitriol.......................do..	6,200	2,706	2,899	116
Water, mineral...........pitcher..	265,860	286,748	238,648	280,912
White leak and white lead....pds..	5,288	14,982	6,669	11,468
Wood: mahogony..............do..	21,287	14,718	2,011	6,209
Braz., Nicar., and St.				
Mart...............do..	90,307	35,843	99,234	15,300
fustic................do..	11,538	13,319	33,697	22,987
logwood ....do..	176,085	122,278	295,889	198,272
dye, rasped...........do..	9,727	19,799	17,055	6,642
Extracts, sundry..............do..	36,672	56,322	48,665	29,200
Elephants' teeth..............do..	162	90	83	145
Fruits: almonds.. ....do..	18,513	14,815	32,232	46,614
currants...............do..	3,256	3,658	1,213	1,564
figs.... ....do..	1,078	2,568	8,824	6,808
prunes... ....do..	17,964	40,575	21,672	16,936
raisins.................do..	10,708	15,851	19,856	10,196
nuts ....do..	29,401	47,619	50,535	77,456
dry, other sorts........do..	21,918	54,928	12,908	67,715
capers.................do..	325	1,122	1,094	491
olives ....do..	1,118	1,179	1,183	1,361
lemons.... ....boxes..	44,538	45,468	41,493	46,243
oranges, sweet ....do...	50,536	60,233	39,661	44,011
oranges, bitter. ....do...	559	164	80	315
lemons, salted......pipes..	2	1	1	1
Gloves, leather..............doz..	6,535	8,638	2,622	1,652
Herring, white...........barrels..	86,369	45,755	81,853	93,259
Linen goods: cambric and cambric				
handk'fs .....pds..	2,597	1,574	4,052	1,661

General list of principal goods imported to St. Petersburg, &c.—Continued.

Articles.	1860.	1861.	1862.	1863.
Linen goods: linen ....pds..	17,996	1,448	15,312	7,374
handk'fs ...doz..	36,805	43,600	28,959	25,076
Metals: iron ....pds..	629,633	395,933	273,164	1,023,084
pig-iron................do..	400,528	186,125	317,327	387,145
lead, pig.............do..	391,510	279,830	266,223	470,061
sheet ....do..	45,982	27,599	20,834	35,406
litharge............do..	7,866	14,067	4,127	5,267
quicksilver...........do..	2,695	736	1,784	1,709
steel ....do..	30,003	33,844	23,107	37,683
tin.................do..	46,102	33,608	32,957	38,840
tinfoil ....do..	40	95	194	183
tin plates .....half boxes..	6,763	5,339	11,340	12,955
zinc................pds..	67,924	108,852	95,807	207,253
Oils: olive................do..	510,378	479,093	614,175	502,931
ethereal.............do..	15,265	421	2,215	744
Paper: drawing ....do..	2,602	1,662	1,286	815
cord ....do..	241	316	570	246
writing ....do..	6,177	4,826	3,152	2,361
Pencils in wood..............do..	436	465	535	317
Perfumery: oils..............do..	1,437	283	454	469
waters..........do..	363	292	168	222
eau de Cologne...doz..	3,612	4,120	2,568	18,358
Porter ....hhds..	544	604	727	663
Porter. ....bottles..	170,185	121,209	103,164	169,387
Ale......................do....	72,026	44,705	30,463	38,337
Rice......................pds..	92,720	143,286	122,737	143,793
Salt......................do..	806,857	846,844	934,277	440,082
Silk......................do..	2,538	1,947	395	1,428
Silk and half-silk goods........do..	3,201	5,723	2,997	2,306
Skins: bear.................do..	68	106	20	24
fox ....do..	1,995	2,102	1,304	668
raccoon.... ....do..	3,284	2,256	1,381	1,113
Spices: cardamons............do..	87	51	16	77
cinnamon Cas. Lign...do..	1,109	914	1,011	1,663
cloves...... .....do..	78	126	99	135
ginger............do..	227	133	240	711
mace...............℔..	1,854	1,471	....	185
nutmegs .. ..pds..	317	226	11	214
pepper ....do..	13,756	13,258	4,198	5,455
pimento ....do..	422	1,158	1,194	948
vanilla ....℔..	903	1,198	1,120	567
Spirits: arrack ....ank..	18	39	43	62
brandy ....do...	1,945	2,450	2,893	1,745
rum ....do...	4,997	6,179	3,189	4,095
Sugar: Havana.............pds..	459,502	670,060	725,858	849,382
other sorts ....pds..	324,604	186,398	798,404	2,369,197
Tea......................do..	....	....	111,679	61,884
Teasals..................thous..	14,800	15,731	7,640	22,680
Tobacco: leaves ....pds..	60,560	51,332	31,875	62,034
stalks.... ....do..	8,716	....	....	....
cut ....do..	176	123	58	122
cigars ....thous..	6,640	7,880	6,249	4,944
snuff..............pds..	214	258	138	201
Tortoise shell................do..	19	117	12	149
Vinegar.... ....hhds..	29	20	12	67
Whalebone. ....pds..	1,009	237	136	192
Wine: French ....hhds..	7,077	10,716	7,407	5,488
Portug'se and Span'h.pipes..	5,386	4,062	4,835	5,405
Rhenish.............awm..	518	498	373	364
Champagne........bottles..	620,268	521,413	545,297	659,581
other sorts.... ......do....	127,639	126,359	84,227	102,627
Wool yarn....................	67,116	74,190	43,201	35,864
Woollen goods....................	17,459	20,529	10,250	17,354

Imports cleared during the year 1863, as per custom-house reports.

Articles.	Quantity.	Value.	COMPARED WITH 1862.		Additional in transit for Moscow.
			More.	Less.	
	Poods.	*Roubles.*	*Poods.*	*Poods.*	*Poods.*
Sugar, raw and in lumps	1,931,915	15,452,597	866,048		45,657
Tea	81,853	3,613,363	9,730		38
Coffee	233,201	3,132,939		9,681	2,593
Tobacco	41,893	1,315,980		9,809	3,674
Grape wine in casks	224,935	2,850,351		25,469	50,164
Grape wine in bottles	532,696	1,521,349	86		207,829
Oile oil	566,122	6,219,208	68,61		5,135
Dye wares	544,808	6,526,818		242,804	4,710
Salt	839,092	353,955		44,743	
Unmanufactured iron	2,238,535	4,005,350	1,643,81		
Cast-iron in pigs	667,050	405,495	365,91		
Cotton	436,032	7,598,020	91,63		2,62
Cotton twist	24,873	1,052,090	8,28		5,049
Woollen yarn	31,287	1,440,388	6,37		63
Silk, raw and spun	1,304	331,969	81		375
Cotton manufactures	6,157	545,571		3,964	8
Flax manufactures	3,723	307,943		168	74
Silk manufactures	2,208	1,213,798		270	064
Woollen manufactures	11,579	1,063,801		1,054	
Other manufactures in value		34,029,791			
Total silver roubles		92,980,776			

Goods cleared for export in the year 1863.

Articles.	Quantity.	Value.	COMPARED WITH 1862.	
			More.	Less.
	Poods.	*Roubles.*	*Poods.*	*Poods.*
Hemp	1,552,270	4,657,734		209,190
Flax	1,064,499	4,257,714		232,930
Potash	448,265	1,344,706		125,108
Tallow	1,992,490	9,971,545	310,228	
Raw hides	12,359	106,812		1,605
Red leather	9,837	98,799		4,365
Wrought-iron	199,317	571,682		291,615
Copper	7,252	72,524		14,380
Bristles	76,340	3,026,307	12,304	
Cordage	315,574	1,216,481	14,826	
Linen manufactures in pieces	35,932	356,370		27,056
Breadstuffs in chetwerts	569,905	3,694,392	192,346	
Sundry goods in value		12,415,649		4,605,918
Total silver roubles		41,790,715		

Arrivals and departures of vessels in 1863.

Nationality	Wintered from 1862	Added since	ARRIVALS			Of which		DEPARTURES			NOW WINTERING	
			With goods	In ballast	Total	To St. Petersburg	To Cronstadt	With goods	In ballast	Total	In St. Petersburg	In Cronstadt
American			12	4	16	2	14	15	1	16		
English			1,082		1,082	176	906	750	333	†1,083		
Brazilian			1		1		1	1		1		
Bremen			4	1	5		5	4	1	5		
Belgian			8		8	4	4	8		8		
Hamburg			8	1	9	4	5	9		9		
Hanoverian			102	1	103	97	6	99	3	102		
Dutch	1		348		348	320	28	316	31	347		
Danish			105	3	108	91	17	99	8	107	1	
Italian			13		13		13	13		13		
Lubeck			67		67	63	4	65	2	67		
Norwegian			8		8	2	6	6	2	8		
Oldenburg			108		108	71	37	87	21	108		
Prussian	2		41		41	39	2	39	1	40		
Russian	10		112		112	93	19	104	6	110		
Rostock	1	4	84	4	88	47	41	25	4	29	1	1
French			85		85	41	44	7	1	8	1	
Swedish			47	7	54	36	18	44	42	86	2	6
Total	14	4	2,243	21	*2,264	1,089	1,175	1,735	466	2,201	5	7
Lasts, (1 last = 2 tons)					229,925					220,284		
Passengers arrived					2,821							

* Of which 909 vessels are coal laden.   † Including one Russian vessel sailing under the English flag.

Navigation opened April 10, (O. S.)—closed December 10, (O. S.)   Trips.

English 154
Italian 2
Prussian 42
French 19
Dutch 21
Belgian 9
Portuguese 1
Swedish 3
Lubeck 51
Rostock 5
Spanish 1
Russian and Finnish.. 196

Total 504

TRAFFIC IN GOLD AND SILVER.

Imported in 1863—647,632 roubles, being less than the amount imported in 1862 by 272,785 roubles.

Exported in 1863—39,152,656 roubles, being more than the amount exported in 1862 by 23,466,037 roubles.

Summary of the value of trade in the year 1863.

	Imports.	Exports.	Total.
Amount of duty-paying goods handled by Russian merchants........	89,900,175	41,789,763	131,689,938
Amount of duty-paying goods handled by passengers and captains................	15,599	952	16,551
Total for 1863...................	89,915,774	41,790,715	131,706,489
Total for 1862...................	76,173,418	44,970,781	121,144,199

Confiscated goods sold by auction, articles prohibited....... 19,942 roubles.
    Do.   do.   do. allowed........ 12,038 do.

GENERAL RESULTS.

I. *Of receipts.*

1. Duty and other dues levied more than in 1862, 2,948,970 roubles 56 kop's.
2. Duty levied on goods going to Moscow, 732,511 roubles.
3. Amount of duty on goods uncleared, 6,900,397 roubles.
4. Machinery and other articles admitted duty free, to the value of 427,383 roubles 12 kopecks.

II. *Of trade balance.*

Value of imports above the value of exports for the year 1863, 48,125,059 roubles.

III. *Of commerce.*

Compared with 1862, excess of imports, 13,742,356 roubles.
Deficit of exports, 3,180,066 roubles.

H. Ex. Doc. 60——27

IV. *Of the precious metals.*

The exports exceeded the imports by 38,505,024 roubles.

V. *Of shipping.*

1. The navigation of 1863 lasted longer by 54 days than that of 1862.
2. The vessels arriving with cargoes in 1863 exceed those of 1862 by 343.
3. Fifty-six more passengers arrived in 1863 than in 1862.

The annexed table gives the average price of a number of the leading articles of Russian produce during the year, together with the duty at present charged upon their exports. By comparing these with prices of the same articles in the United States, it will be seen how large a sum is used up in freights, commissions, exchanges, profits, &c.

Average price current of leading articles of Russian produce with the export duty thereon.

Name of article.	Price.		What quantity.	Duty.
Hemp, clean...........	S. R. 33.50 to	36	per 10 poods...........	55 copecks and 5 pr. ct. additional.
Do..out-shot........	33 to	35	.....do............	Do. do.
Do..half clean........	29 to	32	.....do.................	Do. do.
Flax, 12-head...........	41 to	48	.....do.................	Do. do.
Do..9-head........	38 to	46	.....do.................	83 copecks and 5 per cent. additional duty.
Red leather.............	30.50 to	—	per pood.................	duty free.
Sheet iron.............	3.50 to	4	.....do............	Do.
Junk	1.15 to	1.25	.....do............	Do.
Bolt rope...............	4.75 to	—	.....do............	Do.
Cordage	3.85 to	4.75	.....do............	Do.
Crash..................	51 to	69	per 1,000 arebims......	Do.
Bristles, Okatka........	230 to	272	per pood, bank note*..	15 copecks per pood, and 5 per cent additional duty.
Do... Suhay.........	58 to	117	.....do............	Do. do.
Do... 1st sort........	125 to	172	.....do............	Do. do.
Do... 2d sort	30 to	68	.....do............	Do. do.
Rags....................	90 to	1.60	per pood.................	60 copecks per pood and 5 per cent. additional duty.
Sail cloth made of hemp.	16 to	20	per piece	Duty free.
Sail cloth made of flax..	8 to	19	.....do............	Do.
Ravens duck............	6.25 to	9.50	.....do............	Do.
Flour, brown, common..	8.75 to	9.	.....do............	Do.
Wheat.................	7.50 to	11	per chetwert...........	Do.

* One rouble silver is equal to three and one-half roubles bank note.

The following list exhibits the gross value, in silver roubles, of the exports and imports at this port during the last five years:

Year.	Exports.	Imports.
	Silver roubles.	*Silver roubles.*
1859...	61,075,440	105,389,144
1860...	52,854,021	101,772,183
1861...	47,051,923	108,537,832
1862...	60,657,399	80,754,391
1863...	80,943,372	94,254,127

This, of course, does not include the immense importations upon government account, of the amount of which the public are not yet advised.

It will be observed that the imports very much exceed the exports. The reason of this will be apparent when it is recollected that St. Petersburg is the port through which all the northern provinces of Russia receive those articles which it is impossible as yet for them to produce themselves. Immense quantities of light goods are even imported for the trade with Siberia, Tartary, and the region watered by the Volga. But the products of the country, on the other hand, are largely exported from the small ports near which they are produced. For instance, lumber, tar, and fish are sent from Finland and Archangel, and flax from the Baltic provinces, whilst the immense grain-growing districts of the south find their outlet by way of the Black and the Mediterranean seas. Besides, it must be remembered that St. Petersburg being the capital, and consequently the residence of the court and principal nobility, as well as of a whole army of government officials, is, of necessity, a large consumer of the wealth produced in other parts of the country. This will be the better illustrated by giving a summary of the value of trade for the whole empire at the last published date, viz: for the year 1862.

	Roubles.
Goods exported	173,278,891
Goods imported	150,107,858
Excess of exports	23,171,033
Gold and silver exported	39,297,968
Gold and silver imported	5,016,393
Excess of exports	34 281,575

Thus it appears that while there is a balance of trade in favor of Russia of twenty-three millions of roubles, she has, nevertheless, been obliged to send thirty-four millions abroad. This is accounted for by the heavy importations of the war and navy departments, and by the fact that large sums of money have been borrowed both on government and on individual account, the interest of which must be paid in specie. It will be seen that while at the port of St. Petersburgh even, the exports have been gradually gaining upon the imports; in the whole empire the change has been far greater.

For example, in the year 1858 the amount of goods imported was 148,799,752 roubles, while the amount of goods exported was 148,396,628 roubles; leaving a balance of 403,124 roubles against the country, which, added to the excess of 1862, gives a total gain in four years of 23,574,157 roubles.

Russia, of course, in common with all young nations, must import heavily, but when her vast agricultural and mineral resources shall be rendered more productive by modern appliances, and her manufacturing talent shall gain education and experience, she will, from the very nature of her position and capabilities, increase her exports very much more rapidly than her imports, leaving each year a heavy balance to augment the wealth of the country.

The trade of this port with the United States has been much curtailed by the civil war. Formerly large amounts of cotton and sugar were imported direct in American vessels; but now these staples either come from different places or seek other means of transportation, so that the import trade is reduced to a few unimportant articles scarcely worthy of mention. The export business also has been much injured, although new demands, growing out of the necessities of the war, have, to some extent, made good the place of former customers.

The following lists, published by Mr. Alexander Wilkins, the consular agent at Cronstadt, show the amount of export and import trade with the United States by sailing vessels.

Account of goods exported in American vessels from St. Petersburg, also in foreign vessels, to the United States, in 1863.

For—	No. of vessels		Tonnage.	Sheet iron.	Clean hemp.	Flax.	Flax tow.	Cordage.	Junk.	Rags.	Oakum.	Bones.
	American.	Foreign.										
				Pds.	Pds.	Pds.	Pds.	Pds.	Pds.	Pds.	Pds.	Pds.
Boston	7	....	3,548	18,944	34,858	1,300	17,038	7,915	34,039	19,012	567	......
New York	3	....	1,872	13,354	10,109	1,299	654	11,564	15,938	22,806	....	......
			5,420	32,298	44,967	2,599	17,692	19,479	49,977	41,818	567	......
Boston	....	3	1,092	6,440	13,546	......	....	7,493	22,698	....	1,500	......
New York	....	1	480	....	7,488	1,950	....	....	530	17,875	....	......
Total to U. States.	10	4	6,992	38,738	66,001	4,549	17,692	27,502	90,550	41,818	2,067	......
London	2	....	678	....	4,011					10,982		
Gloucester	1	....	336									
Aberdeen	1	....	108									4,057
Husum	1	....	632	} Ballast.								
Wyburg	1	....	422									
Total	16	4	9,168	38,738	70,012	4,549	17,692	27,502	90,550	52,800	2,067	4,057

Account of goods exported, &c., from St. Petersburg—Continued.

For—	No. of vessels		Tonnage.	Bristles.	Horse-manes.	Horse-hair.	Red leather.	Crash.	Broad diapers.	Sail-cloth.	Ravens duck.	Mats.	Deals.
	American.	Foreign.											
				Pds.	Pds.	Pds.	Pds.	Arshs.	Arshs.	Piec.	Piec.	Piec.	St. Dz.
Boston	7	....	3,548	362	......	344	116	832,000	4,480	4,230	1,720	5,530	......
New York	3	....	1,872	145	......	2,056	235	784,000	....	1,941	605	1,350	......
			5,420	507	......	2,400	351	1,616,000	4,480	6,171	2,325	6,880	......
Boston	....	3	1,092	288	......	....	......	370,000	10,219	1,258	220	1,450	......
New York	....	1	480	....	....	....	47	100,000	....	....	200	1,585	......
Total to the U. S.	10	4	6,992	795	......	2,400	398	2,086,000	14,699	7,429	2,745	9,915	......
London	2	....	678	....	537	....	......	500,000	....	....	....	250	......
Gloucester	1	....	336										1,174
Aberdeen	1	....	108										
Husum	1	....	632	} Ballast.									
Wyburg	1	....	422										
Total	16	4	9,168	795	537	2,400	398	2,586,000	14,699	7,429	2,745	10,165	1,353

For Boston: In American vessels, 2,075 pounds lignumvitæ, 24 pounds tea, 2 pieces sheeting, 1 case caviar, 1 case dry plants; in foreign vessels, 1 box papyros cigars and 1 box pressed caviar. For New York: In American vessels, 2 packages sable skins and 3 packages sundries. For London: 3 boxes and 1 parcel sundries.

Goods imported in American vessels and in foreign vessels from the United States to St. Petersburg in 1863.

Where from.	No. of vessels (American)	No. of vessels (Foreign)	Tonnage.	Logwood. Pds.	Fustic. Pds.	Quercitron bark. Pds.	Sarsaparilla. Pds.	Logwood extract. Pds.	Sugar. Pds.	Coal. Pds.	Coke. Pds.	Soda crystals. Pds.	Cement. Pds.	Gas pipes. Pds.	Railroad iron. Pds.	Iron castings. Pds.	Fire-bricks. Pieces.	Wooden pails. Piec.	Petroleum oil. Casks.	Sewing machines. Cas.	Lamps and glass-ware. Cas.	Agricultural implements. Cas.	Sundries. Cas.
Boston	3	..	1,394	58,881	5,187	1,600	370	749								53				32	3	3	..
New York	..	2	516	4,890				8,301										1,800	2,200		52		9
Total from the U. S.	3	2	1,840	63,771	5,187	1,600	370	8,950								53		1,800	2,200	32	55	3	9
Newcastle	5		2,304							129,341	24,255												
Glasgow	1		500									2,394	4,599										
Cardiff	1		639							8,820				12,726	39,690								
Havre	1		108	} Ballast																			
London	3		1,480							3,150							110,000						
Hull	1		556														60,000						
Havre	1		692						5,176														
Total	16	2	8,112	63,771	5,187	1,600	370	8,950	5,176	141,311	24,255	2,394	4,599	12,726	39,690	53	170,000	1,800	2,200	32	55	3	9

As there are a great many goods sent by steamer *via* Hamburg and London, a more correct idea of the export trade to the United States may be formed from the annexed list, which gives the value in silver roubles of the various invoices certified at this consulate during the last two years.

Statement showing the description and value of the merchandise exported from St. Petersburg to the United States during the years 1862 and 1863, as appears by consular returns.

Description.	1862.			1863.		
	No. invoices.	Roubles.	Copecks.	No. invoices.	Roubles.	Copecks.
Bolt-rope and cordage	3	33,329	22	21	130,269	96
Sheet iron......................	14	299,055	02	18	146,011	11
Red leather	1	19,146	24	7	23,330	47
Oakum	....	....	....	2	6,486	61
Junk	2	15,501	82	15	99,283	78
Flax-tow.......................	2	43,052	53	8	74,935	37
Clean hemp	1	4,797	50	14	264,643	23
Wool	1	6,781	50	....	....	....
Insect powder and worm seed......	1	905	21	6	6,276	12
Bristles	11	50,662	33	38	118,353	96
Tar............................	4	4,996	81	....	....	....
Sail-cloth......................	7	83,044	94	22	141,418	53
Mats...........................	7	992	76	....	....	....
Flax...........................	1	6,239	09	2	10,081	55
Crash	9	91,413	72	25	210,134	84
Horse-hair	....	....	....	4	21,741	42
Diapers	....	....	....	1	1,420	86
Ravens duck	....	....	....	7	20,062	09
Bobbin flax....................	....	....	....	2	11,447	01
Rags	....	....	....	2	109,029	43
Sable-skins....................	....	....	....	2	9,402	30
Isinglass......................	....	....	....	2	2,375	....
Lignumvitæ....................	....	....	....	1	2,189	....
Sundries, merchandise, &c........	9	35,228	32	3	801	50
Total	67	695,147	01	202	1,408,694	14

The following extracts from the shipping lists of the port of Cronstadt show the effect the civil war has had in diverting our mercantile marine from the trade with that place:

Years.	Whole number of ships entering port.	No. of American ships.	No. sailed with cargoes for the United States.
1859	2,424	50	16
1860	2,159	33	16
1861	2,210	33	7
1862	1,999	10	8
1863	2,275	16	14

It is somewhat difficult to state the exact cost of freights to the United States, as the merchants are usually in the habit of chartering ships for the voyage for a round sum, and then loading them with such goods as they think fit. The following rates, however, have been paid to sailing vessels during the past year, viz:

Cordage	$15 per ton.		Junk	$12 per ton.
Sheet iron	10 "		Rags	22 "
Crash	16 "		Horse hair	36 "
Flax	24 "		Sail cloth	16 "
Flax tow	36 "		Bristles	16 "

payable in gold, with five per cent. primage.

A new regulation has been made, to go into effect the coming year, by which all foreign ships arriving at Cronstadt or St. Petersburg are to be measured, and all port charges and tonnage dues paid according to the Russian lastage. The restrictions formerly imposed upon the importation of tea have been removed, and the article is now allowed to be brought by sea direct from China. Although the overland teas are preferable, yet they are so much more expensive that it is believed they cannot compete with those brought by sea. Hence, as the demand is very great, this trade is likely to prove lucrative. At present the greater portion of these teas are reshipped from England. However, had it not been for the dangers to American shipping from the so-called Confederate privateers, there is little doubt that they would have been largely brought direct in United States vessels; and it is thought that eventually this trade will furnish much and profitable employment for American shipping.

Owing to the unusual demand in the United States, considerable quantities of rags have been exported the past season. However, this trade is very much injured by a heavy export duty, which as yet the merchants interested have not been able to get remitted.

During the year a great change has taken place in the material used for lights—a matter, of course, of great importance in this latitude, where in winter there are scarce six hours of daylight. Formerly tallow, in its various preparations, was wholly relied upon; now the use of kerosene is fast becoming universal. There have been various oils brought here from Scotland, Bremen, and other places; but they are unable to compete with the American oil, being much inferior in quality and equally expensive. The American lamps are also the most popular.

Kerosene not being mentioned in the Russian customs lists, was at first classed with other burning oils, and charged one rouble per pood duty. Then, owing to the great demand, a temporary arrangement was made, by which the stock for the present winter was cleared at twenty-five copecks. The imperial ministry have now fixed the duty at fifty copecks per pood, or about seven and one-half cents per gallon.

Petroleum has been discovered in some parts of southern Russia, particularly in the neighborhood of Kertch; but whether it can be profitably worked has not yet been demonstrated. Indeed, it is the opinion of those best informed that such are the difficulties of interior transportation, and the lack of proper facilities for working and refining, that unless the government should make a heavy protective distinction in its favor it will be impossible for it to compete with American oil for many years. One thing is now certain, kerosene has been fairly introduced into Russia. The people are becoming accustomed to it, and they will not do without it in the future. It is, therefore, at least safe to calculate upon a large annual increase of the demand from the United States for several years to come.

Since the expiration of the contract of Messrs. Winans, Harrison & Winans, for the running of the Nicholi railroad, there remains but little American capital in St. Petersburg. The American mechanics formerly in the employ of Messrs. Winans, Harrison & Winans have nearly all left St. Petersburg, and as they constituted the majority of the United States citizens here, of course the present number is very small.

From the foregoing facts, and, what is more, from the nature and condition of the Russian people, their social, political, and commercial tendencies, together with the varied resources and wants of this great country, it is but fair to expect a very large increase of the trade with the United States.

The most casual observer cannot have failed to notice that the Russians have a decided preference for articles of American manufacture. Our machinery, implements, and inventions are very popular throughout the empire. But the chief reason is that these articles, particularly agricultural implements and machinery, having been constructed and adapted to answer new and great exigencies, growing out of the immense territory, sparse population, and meagre capital of the United States, are just suited to the necessities of this crude, undeveloped, but vast and growing nation.

It is, then, reasonable to presume that with the return of peace, when the prices of materials and labor again find their true level, the American manufacturer will possess very great advantages over his English and French competitors in supplying the demands of the ever-increasing mechanical wants of this great country.

And permit me, sir, in closing this report, to express the hope that the attention of our manufacturers, particularly of agricultural implements and machinery, may be so directed to this matter that they will avail themselves of these golden opportunities.

HENRY BERGH, Vice-Consul.

APRIL 13, 1864.

I have the honor to acknowledge the receipt of despatch No. 21, of the date of March 21 ultimo.

Since my last communication I have been industriously engaged seeking the information required by the department in relation to excise duties in Russia; and although I have succeeded in procuring already much that is interesting and valuable, I refrain from forwarding it until I shall have exhausted the material within my reach.

In the mean time, however, I have thought proper, in view of the vast importance and urgency of the matter, to prepare and send along with the present some statistics concerning the excise duty on tobacco, marked A.

I have no doubt of my ability to furnish the government with many minor details should it determine on the adoption of the European system of revenue to be derived from this one of the most fruitful fields of American production and consumption.

I have also translated and enclosed the substance of the law upon patents, (marked B,) which may be found useful to those of our countrymen desirous of availing themselves of this privilege in Russia.

STATISTICS OF EXCISE TAX UPON TOBACCO IN RUSSIA.

An excise tax on tobacco was first imposed in Russia in the year 1838.

Siberia, Finland, and the governments of trans-Caucasia are exempt, and in Poland the impost is leased or farmed out to a private administration.

The tax is imposed only upon manufactured tobacco—such as snuff, cut, plug, cigars, cigarritos—and not on leaf, which may be sold upon the plantation, or at the markets, or elsewhere, on the simple taking out of a license.

The excise duties are indicated by means of stamped paper bands, completely encircling the box or parcel, which are sold to the manufacturers at the treasury of the district, and are stuck or pasted thereon. All tobacco sold or offered for sale without this "banderole" is considered fraudulent, and the vendee punished by fine and confiscation.

The "banderoles" bear upon them the price regulated according to the quality of the article.

Manufactories of tobacco can only be established in cities upon sufficient guarantee and a previous permit obtained from the minister of finance.

Every manufacturer, besides the special license, must be provided with a certificate that he belongs either to the first or the second guild, which costs 265 and 65 roubles, respectively.

At first the "banderoles" or impost was fixed upon a basis of 20 per centum upon the sales; in 1854 it was raised to 26. According to the tariff of 1838 the inferior qualities bore a tax of 35 per cent., whilst the superior paid only $17\frac{3}{4}$ per cent. The consequence of this was, that first-class foreign tobacco came into competition with indigenous, and, finally, at the revision of the tariff in 1861, the excise tax was rendered more uniform, as may be seen by the following table:

SNUFF.

4th quality,	at 12 copecks and less the pound (Russ.)............	4	copecks.
3d "	13 to 24 copecks and less the pound (Russ.)......	8	"
2d "	25 to 48 " " " "	16	"
1st "	63 and upwards the pound (Russ.)	30	

SMOKING TOBACCO.

5th "	10 copecks and less the pound (Russ.)............	3
4th "	11 to 22 copecks and less the pound (Russ.).......	6
3d "	23 to 40 " " " " ...	12
2d "	41 to 80 " "	25
1st "	92 and upwards	36

PAPER CIGARRITOS.

5th "	30 copecks and less per 100....................	9	..
4th "	30 to 46 copecks	14	..

CIGARS.

3d "	46 to 1 rouble	30	..
2d "	1 rouble to 2 roubles........................	65	"
1st "	2 to 36 copecks and upwards	1 rouble.	

By an *ukase* published in the year 1854 manufacturers of tobacco are obliged to purchase at least 500 roubles' worth of " banderoles " per annum. And in 1861 and '62 this minimum was increased to 3,000 roubles for the cities of St. Petersburg, Moscow, Riga, and Odessa, and all other cities 1,500 roubles.

Smoking in the streets is punishable by a fine, but it is permitted while riding or driving, and generally upon the public promenades.

The privilege of smoking in public houses is granted upon the payment of 20 roubles for hotels, restaurants and wine shops.

20	do.	for cafés and other inferior analogous places.
10	do.	for buffets of theatres, clubs, and railroad stations of first class.
5	do.	for steamboats.
1	do.	for street peddlers (foot.)
2	do.	for street peddlers (wheel) for native leaf only.

All trades people, provided with a "patent" or license, are allowed to sell at retail indigenous tobacco in leaf without "banderoles."

The following table shows the gradual increase in patents taken out, banderoles, and total revenue:

Years.	Patents.	Banderoles.	Total rev'ue.
	Roubles.	Roubles.	Roubles.
1838–1839	27,554	734,116	761,670
1840	24,403	628,397	652,800
1841	25,429	791,239	816,668
1842	26,711	731,034	757,745
1843	28,690	828,439	857,129
1844	25,180	886,567	911,747
1845	45,160	905,149	900,309
1846	51,748	959,689	1,011,437
1847	52,830	983,181	1,036,011
1848	112,287	1,072,040	1,184,327
1849	128,824	1,167,606	1,296,430
1850	129,808	1,205,500	1,335,308
1851	142,565	1,334,138	1,476,703
1852	146,168	1,360,668	1,506,836
1853	146,343	1,358,363	1,504,706
1854	142,104	1,701,381	1,843,485
1855	130,802	1,491,151	1,630,953
1856	150,705	2,169,004	2,319,709
1857	162,863	2,192,117	2,354,980
1858	170,334	2,198,352	2,368,686
1859	173,723	2,209,337	2,383,060
1860	200,718	2,286,460	2,487,178
1861	308,997	2,695,185	3,004,182
1862	421,882	2,944,890	3,366,772
1863, (1)	482,960	3,457,820	3,940,780

I am informed that these returns would have been far more considerable were it not for the frauds committed during the first twenty years of the excise by reason of its imperfect imposition.

If smoking were permitted in the streets the revenue would be greatly enhanced.

Enormous as these results are seen to be from *one* article of commerce alone, they fall short of what they would have been had the surveillance been more rigid. Such, however, as they are, the return is claimed to be five millions of silver roubles annually at the present time—sufficient to pay the expenses of the following departments, viz:

Roubles.

The council of the empire, chancellor of the Emperor, and commission of requests... 1,165,375
Ministry of foreign affairs.................................. 2,102,532
Registry general of the empire............................. 232,889

3,500,796

Moreover, the revenue is constantly increasing, and when those portions of the empire now exempt shall also be subjected to the excise, and the indigenous leaf tobacco taxed, the return will not fall short, it is thought, of the subjoined revenues of the following nations:

France, 32,000,000 of roubles.
England, 30,000,000 of roubles.

Austria, 14,000,000 of roubles.

The monopoly on tobacco in the latter-named country reaches 100 per cent., and in France 250 per cent. !

In addition to the foregoing Russian excise duties, there exist also the customs.

Should our government, under such circumstances, hesitate about adopting a similar system of revenue, yielding such prodigious returns, and that, too, upon a luxury ?

Goods imported in American vessels and in foreign vessels from the United States to St. Petersburg in 1864.

Where from.	No. of vessels.		Tonnage.	Logwood.	Logwood extract.	Fustic extract.	Sarsaparilla.	Sewing machines.	Petroleum.	Chloride of lime.	Thistles.	Lamps and glassware.
	American.	Foreign.										
				Pds.	Pds.	Pds.	Pds.	Cases.	Bbls.	Bbls.	Casks.	Pack.
Boston	3	....	1,392	42,755	370	.....	3,712	.....	150	.....	.....	.....
New York	5	....	2,823	30,041	8,267	165	590	409	3,639	.....	.....	366
			4,215	72,796	8,637	165	4,302	409	3,789	.....	.....	366
New York	....	3	958	.....	2,926	.....	.....	302	6,335	.....	.....	238
Philadelphia	....	2	662	.....	.....	.....	.....	.....	4,979	.....	.....	.....
Total from the U. S.	....	....	5,835	72,796	11,563	165	4,302	711	15,103	.....	.....	604
Marseilles	1	....	336	.....	.....	.....	.....	.....	.....	250	107	.....
Total	9	5	6,171	72,796	11,563	165	4,302	711	15,103	250	107	604

Account of goods exported in American and foreign vessels from St. Petersburg to the United States in 1864.

For—	No. of vessels — American	No. of vessels — Foreign	Tonnage	Sheet iron	Hemp	Flax	Flax tow	Cordage	Junk	Rags	Oakum	Tar	Felt	Bristles	Feathers	Horsehair	Red leather	Crash (Archines)	Diapers (Archines)	Sail-cloth (Archines)	Ravens duck (Pieces)	Flems (Pieces)	Mats (Pieces)	Deals (St. Dz.)
Boston	4		1,896	25,845		653	11,324	1,888	34,231	1,575	900	4,500		654		672		90,000	17,959	2,904	1,550	50	3,790	
New York	4		2,242	24,404	15,799	1,301		3,041	41,303	19,533	630		130	626		1,377		547,000		5,797	3,380	100	3,660	
			4,138	50,249	15,799	1,954	11,324	4,929	75,534	21,108	1,530	4,500	130	1,280	325	2,049	310	637,000	17,959	8,701	4,930	150	7,450	
Boston	1		259						4,156	14,943								127,000		100	140			
New York		2	842						98,355	14,117										506			1,470	
Total to the U. S.	8	3	5,332	50,249	15,799	1,954	11,324	4,929	106,045	50,168	1,530	4,500	130	1,280	325	2,049	310	764,000	17,959	9,307	5,070	150	8,920	
Penarth Roads f. O.		1	413																	9,307				1,466
Total	9	3	5,745	50,249	15,799	1,954	11,324	4,929	106,045	50,168	1,530	4,500	130	1,280	325	2,049	310	764,000	17,959	9,307	5,070	150	8,920	1,466

For Boston: In American vessels, 141 pds. flax-seed, 2,830 pds. Lima wood, 27 pds. tortoise shell, 60 chtv. linseed, 8 packages sundries, and 100 pieces cotton robes; in foreign vessels, 1,000 archines cotton robes. For New York: In American vessels, 363 pds. oak wood.

ODESSA—TIMOTHY C. SMITH, *Consul.*

DECEMBER 31, 1863.

* * * I am sorry to report that no American vessels have visited Odessa during the year. Some other ports in the Black sea and sea of Azoff have been, however, I have understood, favored with a sight of our national colors.

The work upon the railway towards Kiro is progressing with considerable rapidity, and it is expected that about fifty miles of it will be finished by the middle of May.

Business continues to be dull and mercantile failures are not uncommon. The Bank of State has been forced to suspend specie exchanges again and coin is no longer given out for the government paper, even at its former depreciated rate.

An English sovereign is worth about 7 to $7\frac{30}{100}$ roubles of the government paper.

APRIL 4, 1864.

In answer to circular No. 44, of the department, I would say that I have not been required nor requested to pay taxes of any description to the Russian government during my residence here as consul.

The local authorities, without any special law or regulation on the subject, are in the habit of considering the exequatur of the consul as equivalent to a ticket or permit of residence, and the consul is therefore exempt from the payment of a tax for the privilege of residing in the empire, which all other foreigners are charged with.

This tax is two or three roubles a year and answers nearly to the poll-tax in our country. In all other respects consuls are regarded and treated as other foreigners, and are subject to taxation like them.

Consuls who engage in commerce or other business pay the regular license, and if they have property it is taxed as that of other persons.

It may be proper to state, however, that in Russia there is no tax for personal property, money at interest, nor income against anybody; real estate and the different occupations and trades being alone taxed. * * *

MARCH 12, 1864.

I have to inform you that an American company of about twelve persons have arrived in this city on their way to the petroleum lands in the vicinity of the sea of Azoff. * * * Their object is to explore the lands, a large tract of which they have leased for a term of years, and if they prove successful in discovering the oil (as they have good reason to expect they shall be) they are prepared with all machinery and men for refining and barrelling great quantities of it. They intend to make Kertch their headquarters. The company has already entered into engagement, or some members of the company have already contracted, to light the cities of St. Petersburg and Moscow with petroleum.

Colonel Gowen, the American who raised the vessels sunk in the harbor of Sebastopol, and who has a contract with the Russian government to build and run a line of steamers on the Kooban river, which flows into the sea not far east from Kertch, has also formed a petroleum company in London, and has leased lands in the same vicinity for the purpose of exploring and operating, and already has men at work, it is said, with success.

Captain Pierce, the American contractor for supplying railway ties at Marseilles for the French railways, is still at work on the east coast of the Black sea, with a large party of men near Poti, and is said to be making money fast.

The ice is now mostly out of the port of Odessa, and some forty or fifty vessels, which have been waiting out beyond the ice for some time, are nearly all safe in port.

The winter may be considered past, and the spring commerce about to commence. The ice which has blocked up the port rather later than usual has been drift ice blown in by southerly and easterly winds.

The municipal government lately conceded to the city of Odessa by the Emperor is now organized and in satisfactory operation, to the great joy of some of the inhabitants, who rejoice as they feel it in unaccustomed liberty.

JULY 1, 1864.

Another quarter of this year is ended, and no American vessels have appeared in the port of Odessa. It is now a year and three-quarters since the Parthian sailed, and no vessel carrying the flag of the United States has since that day been seen here. Some other ports of the Black sea and even of the sea of Azoff, I have heard, have been more favored in this respect. * * * At present the Italian, Austrian, Russian, and British ships are the birds of commerce most often met with in all these eastern waters, and their superiority in numbers is in the order named.

The season this year has been thus far unusually favorable for agriculture in southern Russia. There have been frequent and plentiful rains, and wherever other causes have not interfered, the prospect is good for abundant crops. In the neighborhood of Yalta, on the south coast of the Crimea, a severe hailstorm, several weeks ago, is said to have done some damage to the crops, and in a district of Azoff, for a distance of many miles around Berdiansk, a kind of beetle is said to have appeared upon the ground in great numbers and to have destroyed entirely all vegetation, not a new but rather wonderful thing in this country. These causes have affected only comparatively little of the general prospect.

The commerce of Odessa also seems to be reviving just now, if one can judge by the number of carts and wagons loaded with grain and other articles of export and import which throng the streets at all hours. I think for the last two years there has not appeared so great activity as now. Still, the number of vessels in port is not unusually large, although there is a slight rise in freights.

The railroad towards Kiev is now ready for trains to run about forty miles, and at the end of another year it is expected to be opened half the distance to that city.

THE GRANITE PAVING.

The paving of the streets with granite blocks progresses well; and a curious feature of the work is, that much of the granite is brought from Scotland as ballast, although great quarries are worked on the borders of the Bug, not far from Ackolaif, and only about one hundred miles from Odessa by sea. But a still more curious feature is that all the blocks, as well as the sewers, are laid with American cement.

AMERICAN IMPLEMENTS AND MACHINES.

Agricultural implements and machines are beginning to be introduced here from America; McCormick's reapers, Grover & Baker's sewing machines, petroleum lamps, &c., &c.

OCTOBER 29, 1864.

I herewith enclose (No. 1) a statement showing the value in roubles of imports and exports to and from foreign countries at this port during the year ended September 30, 1864.

I also enclose (No. 2) a table showing the number of sailing vessels of each nation cleared from this port during the year, and their destination.

From the first it appears that the total value of imports has been 11,200,000 roubles, or about 300,000 less than last year, and the total value of exports has been 34,000,000 roubles, or about 4,750,000 more than last year. Of the imports there have been—

	Roubles.
Of coffee	380,000
tea	500,000
sugar	26,000
oil	748,000
wine and spirits	243,000
fruit	816,000
tobacco	664,000
cotton and cotton yarn	110,000
iron	495,000
cotton goods	223,000
silk goods	263,000
woollen goods	358,000
linen goods	117,000
coals	530,000

Sugar is not used so freely in this country as in the United States, and it is manufactured in quantities nearly sufficient for the wants of commerce from the beet root. Hence the quantity imported has been very small, as is seen in the statement.

Coals are found of a superior quality and in great abundance near the sea of Azoff, but they are so hard that it is difficult to burn them without mixing them with the softer coals of England, when they make a better fire than English coals alone, while the Russian coals unmixed make too hot a fire for the safety of boilers and stoves; hence there have been considerable importations of coals.

The chief article exported, it will be seen, is grain of different kinds, amounting to two-thirds of all the exports; and of the different grains wheat has been the principal; nearly one-half of the whole amount of exports has been wheat, of the value of 16,500,000 roubles. The next article of export in importance has been wood, and its value nearly one-fourth of all the exports, or 7,628,000 roubles.

	Roubles.
Of Indian corn	2,537,000
linseed	1,759,000
flour and meal	988,000
tallow	815,000
barley	596,000
oats	278,000
cordage	224,000
hides	164,000
peas	130,000
rye	28,000
flax and linseed	22,000
leather	18,000
beans	5,000
iron	5,000

From the excess of exports over imports it would naturally be expected that exchanges on western Europe, which is the principal mart for the sale of Russian products, would be low. But unfortunately for Odessa, she has always to help pay the debts contracted by other cities of the empire, and when the balance sheet of imports and exports for the whole country is drawn, the excess is found to be on the other side, and the country is brought in debt to western Europe. This state of things has existed so long that the country has been almost completely drained of gold and silver to pay the foreign debt. Last April the government contracted a loan in England and in Germany of ten millions of pounds to draw against in order to relieve the financial condition of the country and keep up 'the value of the paper currency. But the relief was only temporary and partial, and now, for the past three months, a time of profound peace, the exchanges have risen to a point never before reached—eight roubles for the pound sterling, and the paper currency of Russia is depreciated to the extent of twenty to twenty-five per cent., the rouble being worth in federal money, therefore, only about sixty cents.

The number of sailing vessels cleared for foreign ports during the year has been 555, of which 169 have been Austrian, 89 Russian, 65 British, 129 Italian, and 9 French. 38 have cleared for ports in the Adriatic, 175 for Mediterranean ports, (except French,) 198 for Great Britain, 48 for France, and 8 for the United States. The British vessels have every one cleared for the United Kingdom. Only one United States vessel has visited this port during the year. * * * Eight vessels have sailed from Taganrog, in the sea of Azoff, during the year, with cargoes for the United States, the invoices of which have been certified at this consulate, making, with the eight from this port, sixteen cargoes for the United States from this consular district during the year. Forty-two triplicate invoices in all of goods for the United States, representing a value of nearly a million roubles, have been certified at this consulate during the year.

The heaviest export trade, however, has been to England. Perhaps nearly one-half of all the exports have found their market in Great Britain.

A considerable trade has during the last few years been carried on with Egypt.

Besides the regular weekly or semi-weekly line of steamers which run from Odessa to different ports in the Black sea and sea of Azoff, connecting with those upon the Danube, the Dneiper, the Borg, and the Don, there have been for several years, also, regular lines of steamers monthly to Alexandria, Marseilles, and London, touching at Constantinople, thereby forming a weekly line to Constantinople. These Alexandria steamers have been the means of opening the trade with Egypt, which is increasing and which will be encouraged. The trade from this port consists mostly of flour, grain, butter, cattle, and horses. Cattle, horses, and sheep are cheaper here than in the United States.

The total population of Russia, according to the census of 1858, recently published, is 74,271,205, distributed in square miles as follows: In Poland, 2,110; in Russia in Europe, 687; in the Caucasus, 532; in Siberia, 15.

The crops this year have been good, both in quality and quantity; and at this time the amount of grain stored at Odessa is greater than for many years previous at this season. This fact argues well in favor of free labor, this being the second year of emancipation. There never has been a time when wages were so high and when all kinds of labor were so well rewarded, and when the demand for laborers was so great. During the wheat harvest farmers in this vicinity were obliged to pay as high as a rouble and a half a day for workmen, who in other years could have been had for half a rouble a day.

The land in the vicinity of Kertch, between the sea of Azoff and the Black sea, is to a great extent saturated with petroleum to such a degree that a small hole or well, three to five feet deep, in almost any part, will fill, by filtering, at the rate of a gallon or more in a week. In this way oil has been obtained and used for lights and other purposes by the Tartars for centuries. It is believed that by boring deep into the earth in those regions immense reservoirs of oil may be discovered. Two American companies have been at work during the past spring and summer, and are still at work, boring for oil. They have already bored about two hundred feet in different places, but have not yet obtained any large quantities. *   *   *   *   *

The railway from Odessa north is now in running ·order about sixty miles, and is progressing with rapidity. In two or three years it is hoped that it will be opened as far as Kiew, on the Dnieper, which will be at least one-third the distance to Moscow or to Warsaw. Surveys have lately been made with the view of connecting this road with those now building in the Danubian principalities, and, through them, with the network of European railways.

Summary statement of the principal articles imported into Russia and entered at the St. Petersburg custom-house for the year 1864.

Description.	Quantity in poods.	Value in roubles.	Compared with 1863.	
			More.	Less.
Sugar, raw and crushed	1,582,878	12,205,273	....	349,037
Tea	75,363	2,721,095	....	6,490
Coffee.	208,186	2,766,600	....	25,015
Tobacco.	46,277	1,480,388	4,384	....
Wine................................|.....	211,809	2,409,149	....	13,126
Wine in bottles	497,882	1,252,467	....	34,814
Oil, olive	555,853	5,667,635	....	30,269
Paints ..·.............................	567,851	6,064,188	23,043	....
Salt	830,115	478,382	....	7,977
Iron	1,074,215	1,638,539	....	1,164,320
Iron, cast	832,671	493,934	165,621	....
Cotton, raw	676,795	17,597,355	240,763	....
Cotton yarn...........................	48,051	2,552,735	23,178	....
Wool, spun............................	37,784	2,067,652	6,497	....
Silk, raw and spun	945	231,574	....	359
Fabrics, cotton........................	5,025	554,863	....	1,132
Do...linen	7,368	360,905	3,645	....
Do...silk	857	467,054	....	1,351
Do...woollen........................	7,209	783,065	....	4,370
Other goods, in value.................	....	29,547,284	....	1,417,405
Total..............	....	91,340,137	467,131	3,055,668

H. Ex. Doc. 60——28

Summary statement of the principal articles entered for export at the St. Petersburg custom-house for the year 1864.

Description.	Quantity in poods.	Value in roubles.	Compared with 1863.	
			More.	Less.
Hemp	1,624,022	4,868,379	71,752	....
Flax	975,158	3,866,415	....	89,341
Potash	662,510	1,921,318	214,245	....
Tallow	1,532,008	6,718,329	....	460,482
Skins, undressed...................	21,560	180,635	9,201	....
Russia leather	12,462	129,864	2,625	....
Iron	290,943	655,400	91,626	....
Copper	38,658	360,269	31,406	....
Bristles	73,958	3,092,193	....	2,382
Cordage	306,083	871,745	....	9,491
Linen piece goods	48,621	510,712	12,689	....
Breadstuffs	1,204,773	7,264,546	634,868	....
Other goods......................	....	15,314,095	2,898,446	....
Total	....	45,753,900	3,966,858	461,696

Statement showing the value in roubles of the imports into Odessa for the year ended September 30, 1864.

	Roubles.
Coffee	380,286
Sugar..	21,347
Oil..	747,946
Spirits and wine	241,879
Fruit	817,160
Tobacco	552,669
Cotton and cotton yarn	110,794
Dyestuffs	45,624
Iron	490,952
Pewter and lead	64,320
Silk and wool...	13,178
Cotton goods	222,134
Silk goods..	262,515
Woollen goods	357,406
Linen goods	43,164
Coals...	529,652
Machines and models......................................	797,460
Sundries	366,634
Tea	502,296
Money	1,928,779
Total value..	8,496,195

Statement showing the value in roubles of the exports from Odessa for the year ended September 30, 1864.

	Roubles.
Rye..	20,850
Wheat..	16,017,369
Peas	129,751

	Roubles.
Oats	275, 814
Barley	595, 698
Flour and meal	989, 562
Corn	2, 385, 966
Rape and linseed	1, 885, 466
Tallow	4, 766, 618
Wool	8, 598, 637
Hides	154, 310
Leather	19, 090
Iron	5, 050
Cordage	234, 547
Linen	28, 447
Wood	2, 726
Furs	1, 930
Beans	5, 130
Sundry products	2, 310, 733
Money	302, 838
Total value	38, 730, 532

Comparative statement showing the number and nationality of vessels cleared from the port of Odessa during the year ended September 30, 1864, also their ports of destination.

Nationality.	DESTINATION.						
	Adriatic ports.	Mediterranean ports.	British ports.	French ports.	United States ports.	Ports of other countries.	Total.
Austrian	32	70	50	17	......	1	169
Belgian	......	......	......	......	......	8	8
Bremen	......	......	1	......	......	......	1
English	......	......	65	......	......	......	65
French	......	......	......	8	1	......	9
Greek	3	12	......	1	......	2	18
Hanoverian	......	......	1	......	......	......	1
Dutch	......	......	......	......	......	1	1
Italian	3	59	39	5	4	18	128
Mechlenburg	......	9	12	......	1	1	23
Norwegian	......	6	7	......	2	......	15
Prussian	......	6	9	1	......	......	16
Russian	......	13	13	16	......	47	89
Swedish	......	......	......	......	......	1	1
Turkish	......	......	......	......	......	8	8
United States	......	......	1	......	......	......	1
Maldo-Wallachian	......	......	......	......	......	1	1
Total	38	175	198	48	8	88	554

HELSINGFORS—R. FRENCKELL, *Vice-Consul.*

DECEMBER 31, 1863.

*   *   *   *   *   *   *   *

The statement of the commercial movement of the Grand Duchy in the year 1862, recently published in official way, shows a considerable increase on that of the foregoing year.

The export trade in 1862 amounted to roubles 10,013,061, against roubles 7,278,747 in 1861.

The following return will specify the principal articles exported, and their value :

	Silver roubles.
Timber, deals, battens, &c	2,671,173
Firewood	304,044
Tar	1,283,811
Pitch	21,317
Iron, steel, and copper	752,457
Butter	988,761
Fish	251,786
Woven goods and thread	632,534
Cattle	151,625
Meat	51,365
Corn and other grains	259,916
Candles	145,267
Furs	34,671
Sundries	2,464,334
Total	10,013,061

The annual increase of the exports from Finland will be seen by the following table, viz :

	Silver roubles.
In 1858	3,302,167
1859	4,615,833
1860	6,588,525
1861	7,278,747
1862	10,013,061

The imports during the same year, 1862, consisted principally of the following articles, viz :

	Silver roubles.
Cotton, raw	215,224
Cotton twist	54,736
Tobacco	473,875
Sugar	1,308,270
Coffee	1,428,649
Salt	393,738
Corn	6,264,981
Spirits and wines	880,191
Fish	124,653
Iron and steel	981,431

	Silver roubles.
Fruits and spices	136, 655
Colors	201, 235
Coals	165, 407
Woven goods (cotton, linen, and silk)	1, 786, 511
Grain	178, 940
Candles	133, 975
Leather and leather works	360, 812
Tallow	209, 414
Sundries	266, 920
Total	15, 565, 617

The value of the imports to the country has been in the last five years as follows, viz :

	Silver roubles.
1858	5, 462, 201
1859	8, 952, 880
1860	10, 836, 967
1861	8, 318, 179
1862	15, 565, 617

The Grand Duchy of Finland had a population of 1,746,227, all professing the Lutheran religion. There were, moreover, about 40,000 professing the Greek religion.

The aggregate number of vessels belonging to the merchant fleet was 532, measuring 67,723 Swedish lasts, or 162,535 tons, not including vessels employed in the coasting and internal trade, and 33 steamers. I have to mention but one American vessel arrived in ballast, and left with a cargo of 2,099 dozen planks.　＊　＊　＊　＊　＊　＊　＊

APRIL 15, 1864.

I have the honor to inform you that such foreign consuls in Finland as are not Finnish subjects are exempt from taxes of every description.

There exists no proper law upon this subject. It is to be believed that it has become a rule, derived from mutual international courtesy. The treaties with foreign powers do commonly only engage to a kind of reciprocity with regard to the privilege of the respective consuls—so the Article VIII of the treaty between Russia and the United States of December 6, (18,) 1832.

A foreign consul, being the subject of a foreign power, is, no more than any other foreign subject, allowed to trade in this country in his proper name. Nor do such foreign consuls in Finland as are Finnish subjects pay any taxes in their capacity of consuls, but only as tradesmen, proprietors, &c., if being such. I, for instance, who am not engaged in business, pay taxes only in my capacity of house-owner.

AMOOR RIVER—H. G. O. CHASE, *Vice-Commercial Agent.*

MARCH 30, 1864.

I have the honor of submitting to the department this report concerning trade and mercantile affairs upon the Amoor river, together with the accompanying statistics for the year 1863.

＊　　＊　　＊　　＊　　＊　　＊　　＊　　＊　　＊

Since my last report previous to this to the department, upon the subjects herein brought to notice, it can be safely said that no perceptible favorable progress has been made in increasing or extending the mercantile or trade intercourse of our countrymen with the inhabitants of the Amoor country and the adjacent provinces and regions and the more distant parts of the "maritime province of East Siberia."

The fundamental difficulties (in a measure, however, heretofore explained in former reports to the department) appear to be at present various. First, the difficulties, dangers, and expense of transportation of merchandise, particularly *from* Nicolaifsky *up* the Amoor, and especially if its destination points beyond the mouth of the Schilker. Difficulties are caused by the frequent delays encountered in ascending the Schilker, that river at times being, from its shallowness, quite unnavigable for steamboats of the lightest draught, which occurrence completely stops all transportation of merchandise, as there is no land route, the nature of the country being in the main an unbroken wilderness of rugged, precipitous, and lofty hills with intermediate valleys. From such difficulties are formed part of the *dangers* to be encountered, as in case of a stoppage of merchandise (intended for the Trans-Baikal province) at the mouth of the Schilker river until navigation closes, and which only is open about five and a half months in the year, from May 15 to September 30. The parties to whom such merchandise belongs by such a misfortune are subjected to a greatly increased expense and no little risk of loss or damage to articles of a perishable nature from the severity of the climate in the winter season, and are thereby much deterred from making purchases in Nicolaifsky of merchandise destined for points beyond the sources of the Amoor. Besides which the rates for transportation by steamboat to headwaters of navigation on the Amoor and its sources remain until this time so comparatively great, viz., roubles 2.50, equal to $2 per pood of 36 pounds English, avoirdupois weight, or $120 per ton of 2,240 pounds, as to be a serious drawback to the development of trade and commercial intercourse with the Trans-Baikal and other surrounding provinces, and has up to this time partly prevented those pursuits from becoming of any importance on the Amoor.

The principal explanations to be offered for the high rates for such transportation are, the great wages paid here to mechanics of all kinds, particularly machinists and mechanical engineers, also to masters and other employés on steamboats. Again, the want of constant employment for private steamboats, even during the season of navigation, (which for the entire length of the Amoor only lasts about five months, leaving about seven months in which steamboats are frozen in, and during which time the master and other principal employés must be kept at full pay.) Further, the exorbitant prices sometimes paid for wood, considering its plentifulness, although very abundant, and usually not difficult to get at, and also for other articles required for running steamboats; the great difficulties and cost of making repairs and obtaining proper material for such purposes, except at a great expense, (particularly at Nicolaifsky,) and yet more the dangers of the navigation, which in some seasons are not inconsiderable, and can only be insured against at a very high per centum, together with the value of the sums which the steamboats themselves cost—all these particulars combined make it quite plain here why rates of transportation still continue so high, and these high rates of freight must reduce the chances for a successful competition of merchandise carried into the Trans-Baikal and other surrounding provinces, &c., with that which reaches these places through West Siberia from Russia and other parts of Europe, unless we except some of the so-termed "colonial goods"—for instance, sugar; also a few kinds of wines, porter, ale, cigars, &c., but these in quite limited quantities, and only to be disposed of in any case to advantage on the east side of the Lake Baikal, as upon crossing that lake towards Iskritsk City all merchandise imported into the Amoor and destined for that city and places west of it is subjected to a duty which has, as was anticipated, effectually prevented the opening of any demand for merchandise from Nicolaifsky for those places. As concerns the nearer trade upon the Amoor and other parts of the maritime province, other difficulties are, the comparatively limited number of the inhabitants along the Amoor and its tributaries, &c., easily accessible from Nicolaifsky, and which places are mainly dependent upon that town for their supplies of foreign goods, such as they purchase; also the fact of the great bulk of the Russian population being either in the naval or military or civil service of the imperial Russian government, or peasants, or released convicts, and other people exiled to Siberia, and the greater part of which have but little means of purchasing anything besides the bare necessaries of life, for which they have always been accustomed to depend upon, and be content with articles of the commonest and coarsest kinds, produced in Siberia in sufficient abundance for their wants, and to better advantage than any, where else; further than this, the absence of any known (and until quite recently permitted) profitable articles of export of any importance adds another difficulty, perhaps more important than all others. To all this must yet be added that in the trade of Nicolaifsky itself, and the immediate vicinity, parties engaged in the business have up to this time been obliged to compete with the government in retail sales of "ardent spirits," the most extensive and most profitable article of commerce here, and during the year last past, 1863, the government entered into the wholesale trade in that article, and that in a manner which did not permit of the entire trading communities having an opportunity to benefit themselves by the government operations, which in such a limited business as this makes an important difference. It has been proposed by the administration of this province to the general government of East Siberia to impose an import duty (said to be equal to one rouble, or seventy-five cents, per gallon) upon all strong liquors imported into this port. If this is done, the effect will probably be much to diminish foreign trade to this place, as that article, *now the basis* of all the trade here, will not bear the imposition of such a tax. It is believed that since last report from this agency, (January, 1863,) no significant changes concerning number of inhabitants upon the Amoor, and in the maritime province generally, have taken place, as no information of any has been received.

*   *   *   *   *   *   *   *

The government steam vessels on the Amoor, for river navigation, have been increased in number by one, the largest and most powerful one of all, and intended particularly for towing barges, of which the government has now three large iron ones. Private steamers have not at all increased, and at present there is no reason to expect any increase. Parts of the Amoor, from the mouth of Keege lake (not more than 200 English statute miles above Nicolaifsky) to its headwaters, and some of its tributaries, particularly the Ousuree, and most of the small streams between the head of that river and the sea-coast of the Gulf of Tartary, in the same latitude, have, during the summer last past, again suffered an inundation which created much loss, especially on the Ousuree, and in that direction, towards the sea-coast. In places whole crops were destroyed, houses swept away, and the country, for many versts, on either bank of those swollen streams, remained for a long time submerged.   *   *   *

Permission has finally been granted for the cutting and shipment of timber, lumber, &c., by any one so disposed, upon compliance with certain regulations and the payment of a tax to the government, the amount of which is fixed and specific. The place designated for such operations at present is "Emperor's bay," and application for especial permission to engage in such a business must be made to the governor of this province, who has a spot selected for each applicant's use. The governor has also discretionary power to permit the cutting and shipping of timber from other points of the maritime province should he find it advisable, and in several instances he has granted such permissions;

and it is expected that, during the coming year, the general shipment, &c., of timber, &c., from places on the Amoor will be allowed upon same conditions as from Emperor's bay. One foreign house (German) established at Nicolaifsky has already engaged in that business, and application has been made to the general government by the same parties to permit the formation of a joint-stock company for a like purpose.

The lead mine in Olgh bay (mentioned in former reports) during the year last past has been re-examined by an engineer in the imperial service, and who is of the opinion that it is very rich and could be easily worked, in the first instance, with a quite limited capital. No known progress whatever has been made in regard to finding purchasers for Sughalein coal; the probable difficulties have been referred to in former reports.

During the year last past, (1863,) the arrivals of merchant vessels of all descriptions, with merchandise for sale here, have much decreased, in comparison with former years, which will be found by reference to table No. 1 sent herewith, and that of last year, concerning this subject; and as the quantity of tonnage has been much reduced, such, of course, has also been the case with the quantity of merchandise arrived; although, still, probably more than sufficient (if properly proportioned of such articles as are required) to supply the demand here for one year, or until the arrival of fresh supplies. The estimated amount of merchandise received in 1863, both in quantity and value, can be seen from table No. 2 enclosed herewith. This agency has been supplied with some statistics from private sources in relation to the exportations from Nicolaifsky up the Amoor to different points, but these statistics must also, probably, be received with many allowances, as private parties are not usually disposed to give accurate particulars of their own operations in business. Besides these statistics concerning exports, (enclosures Nos. 3 and 4,) &c., and others on same subject, (furnished by the department of the local government here, which has been herein before referred to,) enclosure No. 5, by comparing, it will be observed a great discrepancy exists between the two as to the amount of value of these exports, &c. Enclosure No. 6 is a statement of the amount of supplies, &c., received at Nicolaifsky, down the Amoor, from various points, principally from the Trans-Baikal provinces and the Chinese settlements on the Amoor, nearly opposite the mouth of the Zea river. Enclosure No. 7, statistical information concerning the quantity or value of fares received at Nicolaifsky from different parts of the Amoor, its branches, and from Kamschatka during that time. Enclosure No. 8, statistics in relation to the kinds and value of merchandise exported to foreign countries from Nicolaifsky. Enclosure No. 9, the same of merchandise shipped to the more distant ports of the maritime province. Enclosure No. 10, return of amount of money remitted by foreign merchants through the government bank during the year 1863.   *   *   *   *   *

The great difficulty in this trade now is, that the extension and increase of it by no means keep pace, or have done so, with the increased supply of foreign imported merchandise received at this place, and the result is that the very limited business is entirely overdone. No better proof of the insignificance of the trade here considered as mercantile or commercial operations can, perhaps, be presented, than simply to state that it does not yet permit of particular branches of business being engaged in exclusively—for instance, exclusive dry-goods, hardware, crockery ware, or other separate establishments, all branches of business being united in one concern and conducted in one establishment; and in addition to this, there is not a single mercantile or trade establishment here which finds it an object to do an exclusively wholesale or even jobbing business, and which is not considerably dependent upon its retail sales (and these, especially this year, in general, of the most minute description) for support. Such obstacles and difficulties as are hereinbefore mentioned do much at this time to prevent a desirable or growing trade in this country.   *   *   *   *

From the increased cost of merchandise, cotton manufactures in particular, increased insurance, (war risks, and other detrimental effects from the same cause,) arises a quite general dissatisfaction of the foreigners engaged in the business.

*　　　*　　　*　　　*　　　*　　　*　　　*　　　*　　　*

Although it is generally understood, outside of Russia, that it has always been the intention and desire of the central government at St. Petersburg to promote and encourage trade, commerce, &c., (especially foreign trade,) in these parts of the imperial Russian possessions, still, it cannot be doubted that no general marked advance in these matters has taken place since the sudden and unhealthy influx of foreign merchandise, forced attempts at reciprocal trade, and extension of mercantile relations made in 1857, mainly in response to the inducements offered and invitations extended by the representatives of the imperial Russian government about that time; but which inducements, &c., it may be safely asserted, have not served to realize the expectations of a majority of the foreigners engaged in this business, and it is, at least, an open question whether, on the whole, the movements made in these particulars, (of trade, &c.,) have not been rather retrogressive than progressive since that date; and whatever may have been the intentions of the local authorities here, they certainly have not, to a remarkable degree, either privately or officially, succeeded in seconding the views generally credited to the central government concerning the matters now referred to as applicable to the Amoor. The Amoor company, with all of its especial privileges and advantages, and the general very favorable disposition of the local authorities, has, after a number of years of mistakes, misunderstandings, accidents, &c., finally been obliged to wind up its affairs, and their property here will probably be sacrificed for less than one-half of its real cost. It is generally supposed the government will purchase, as no other parties, who are able to do so, will find it an object to compete for it. It would, perhaps, not be out of place to note here, that any foreign concern here owning real estate will hardly be able to dispose of it for more than one-half of its actual cost, if as much.

JULY 22, 1864.

I enclose herewith, for the information of the department, a statement of the imports and exports per American vessels at this port the present season, up to this time, (enclosure No. 1,) and of the arrivals of other merchant vessels, with cargoes for sale, here. The particulars given in the said statement cannot be said to be strictly correct, *i. e.*, particularly concerning the amount and value of imports and exports, but may, nevertheless, be of some interest and value. Most of the foreign concerns engaged in this trade are abandoning it. *　* *

Of the American concerns in the trade, only four now remain, and there is reason to believe that, from a feeling of dissatisfaction, next year there may be only one, and perhaps not any American concerns remaining.

AUSTRIAN DOMINIONS.

VIENNA—T. CANISIUS, *Consul.*

MARCH 6, 1864.

Having not yet received an official answer to the question whether our consuls in Austria have to pay taxes, I propose to answer you the question without waiting any longer for an official communication.

I have never been asked to pay taxes of any kind except a house tax to the local government, which amounts to 80 florins per annum, payable half yearly in advance. The rate of this tax is 8 per cent., which the tenant has to pay, and which is collected by the house owner, and by him transferred to the city treasury. Nobody is excepted from this tax as far as I know.

* * * The total amount of taxes already paid by me, during the time I have held my official position here, is 240 florins.

Besides this house tax the residents of this city have to pay an indirect tax on all necessaries of life, as for every article that comes into the city a certain amount of taxes has to be paid before it crosses the city limits. All this makes living in Vienna extremely expensive, and the paper currency has made it still more so. * * * * * * * *

In answer to your despatch, No. 29, I have the honor to transmit herewith a schedule of the Austrian "stamp duty tax," prepared by me with great care and labor, from the official works. The "Reichsrath" has changed the duties in many respects, but the schedule contains all the changes made, and may be regarded as entirely correct, and in conformity with the new law of February 29, 1864.

You will observe that the Austrian stamp duty law is more comprehensive than ours, and if Congress would pass anything like the Austrian law, it would yield an immense sum to the United States treasury.

The law concerning "stamp duties" has engaged the ablest financiers of Europe for a long time. How remunerative a good, or, at least, perfect system can be made, is clearly seen by a comparison of the amount yielded by the old Austrian law of January 27, 1840, and the one of 1851. The first never brought over 6,531,411 florins, and the last adds more than 44,000,000 to the state treasury annually. The law of February last will still increase this sum.

Austrian stamp duties according to the law of February 29, 1864.

Scale I.—For bills of exchange, orders from merchants and on merchants; bills of debt of public money institutions; for money advanced, for bonds or goods, loaned only for three months.	Rate of stamp duty, Austrian currency.		Additional rate of stamp duty, Austrian currency.		Total, Austrian currency.	
	Fl.	*Kr.*	*Fl.*	*Kr.*	*Fl.*	*Kr.*
Up to the amount of 60 florins		4		1		5
Over 60 to 120 florins		8		2		10
120 to 240 florins		16		4		20
240 to 360 florins		24		6		30
360 to 480 florins		32		8		40
480 to 600 florins		40		10		50
600 to 720 florins		48		12		60
720 to 840 florins		56		14		70
840 to 960 florins		64		16		80
960 to 1,080 florins		72		18		90
1,080 to 1,200 florins		80		20	1	00
1,200 to 2,400 florins	1	60		40	2	00
2,400 to 3,600 florins	2	40		60	3	00
3,600 to 4,800 florins	3	20		80	4	00
4,800 to 6,000 florins	4	00	1	00	5	00
6,000 to 7,200 florins	4	80	1	20	6	00
7,200 to 8,400 florins	5	60	1	40	7	00
8,400 to 9,600 florins	6	40	1	60	8	00
9,600 to 10,800 florins	7	20	1	80	9	00
10,800 to 12,000 florins	8	00	2	00	10	00
12,000 to 13,200 florins	8	80	2	20	11	00
13,200 to 14,400 florins	9	60	2	40	12	00
14,400 to 15,600 florins	10	40	2	60	13	00
15,600 to 16,800 florins	11	20	2	80	14	00
16,800 to 18,000 florins	12	00	3	00	15	00

And so on from each 1,200 florins 1 florin more. A fraction of 1,200 florins has to be taken as full; accordingly, from each 120 up to 1,200 florins 10 kreutzers have to be paid, taking fractions always for full; and from each amount, not over 60 florins, a stamp duty of 5 kreutzers has to be paid. Each 1,200 additional, 1 florin more.

Scale II.—For all legal business for which the stamp duty has to be paid according to this scale, and which is not classed under scales I and III, as, for instance, relative amount of insurance.	Rate of stamp duty, Austrian currency.		Addition'l duty, Austrian currency.		Total, Austrian currency.	
	Fl.	*Kr.*	*Fl.*	*Kr.*	*Fl.*	*Kr.*
To 20 florins....		5		2		7
Over 20 to 40 florins		10		3		13
40 to 60 florins		15		4		19
60 to 100 florins		25		7		32
100 to 200 florins		50		13		63
200 to 300 florins		75		19		94
300 to 400 florins	1	00		25	1	25
400 to 800 florins	2	00		50	2	50
800 to 1,200 florins	3	00		75	3	75
1,200 to 1,600 florins	4	00	1	00	5	00
1,600 to 2,000	5	00	1	25	6	25
2,000 to 2,400 florins	6	00	1	50	7	50
2,400 to 3,200 florins	8	00	2	00	10	00
3,200 to 4,000 florins	10	00	2	50	12	50
4,000 to 4,800 florins	12	00	3	00	15	00
4,800 to 5,600 florins	14	00	3	50	17	50
5,600 to 6,400 florins	16	00	4	00	20	00
6,400 to 7,200 florins	18	00	4	50	22	50
7,200 to 8,000	20	00	5	00	25	00

From every 400 florins over 8,000 florins, an additional duty of 1 florin 25 kreutzers, and a fractional amount of 400 florins has to be regarded as full.

Austrian stamp duties, &c.—Continued.

Scale III.—For loan agreements, if the bond is drawn to bearer; agreements for service to be rendered; stock companies chartered for more than ten years; moneys deposited in public establishments and branches, if the same are chartered for more than ten years; lottery prizes and tickets; agreements of purchasing and exchanging personal property; for contracts of supplying; agreements of income for life-time, if personal property is exchanged.	Rate of stamp duty, Austrian currency.		Addition'l stamp duty, Austrian currency.		Total, Austrian currency.	
	Fl.	Kr.	Fl.	Kr.	Fl.	Kr.
From 10 florins		5		2		7
Over 10 to 20 florins		10		3		13
20 to 30 florins		15		4		19
30 to 50 florins		25		7		32
50 to 100 florins		50		13		63
100 to 150 florins		75		19		94
150 to 200 florins	1	00		25	1	25
200 to 400 florins	2	00		50	2	50
400 to 600 florins	3	00		75	3	75
600 to 800 florins	4	00	1	00	5	00
800 to 1,000 florins	5	00	1	25	6	25
1,000 to 1,200 florins	6	00	1	50	7	50
1,200 to 1,600 florins	8	00	2	00	10	00
1,600 to 2,000 florins	10	00	2	50	12	50
2,000 to 2,400 florins	12	00	3	00	15	00
2,400 to 2,800 florins	14	00	3	50	17	50
2,800 to 3,200 florins	16	00	4	00	20	00
3,200 to 3,600 florins	18	00	4	50	22	50
3,600 to 4,000 florins	20	00	5	00	25	00

For each 200 florins over 4,000 florins, 1 florin 25 kreutzers more has to be paid as stamp duty.

	Fl.	Kr.
Absolutory, concerning studies or bills of indebtedness, given by private persons or by judicial persons or other officers, each sheet		50
Accounts of merchants and business men, each sheet		5
below 10 florins		1
balanced, per sheet		5

Agreements of companies:
1. If the company does not derive any pecuniary profit by it, per sheet 2
2. If the object of the company is not the gain of material benefit, per sheet 5
3. When the members unite their labor and property, forming stock companies and branch houses, according to scale III.

In all other cases, scale II.

Agreement by which a person receives permission to have the use and benefit of certain real estate, scale II.

when the object in question is not valuable, per sheet.... 50

if the consequence of it is a transfer and acquisition of real estate, each sheet of the document.............. 50

The agreement itself, however, according to the value of the object, 1, 1½, 2, 2½, 3, 3½ per cent. (additional duty 25 per cent.) The percentage depends upon the time when the property has been last sold, corresponding with 2, 4, 6, 8, 10 and over ten years.

Agreements of companies—Continued.

    In all other cases, according to the object in question, scale
        II.

Advertisements :

    Placards, measuring not over 180 Vienna □ ' ....each sheet 1

        "   measuring over 180 Vienna □ " ....   "   2

        "   in newspapers, every insertion   30

Almanacs..each   6

Appeals for revision of judgment :

    If, in the first instance, 5 florins stamp duty have been paid for ren-
    dering the judgment, the same amount has to be paid in the sec-
    ond instance; in every other case, for the first sheet............ 10

Apprentice's indenture................................each sheet   50

Appraisement...   "   50

    In lawsuits, if the object in question is not worth over 50 florins,
    each sheet..   12

Assignments, gratuitous, are subject to the same duty as the docu-
    ments for donations...............................per sheet   50

    Of parents not separated; of parents and children in proportion to
    the value of 1 per cent.; of other relatives, including first cousins,
    in proportion to the value of 4 per cent.; in all cases, 25 per cent.

    Recompensated but not with debts, like all other transactions of buy-
    ing and selling, if the object is personal property, in proportion to
    the amount paid, scale III; if real estate, each sheet of the docu-
    ment..   50

    Bills of exchange, indorsed; of State bonds and other similar
    securities, subject to scale I, or to the fixed rate of 5 per cent.; of
    checks, are duty free.

    Of bills of lading, of bills of storage, of bottomry, and of marine
    insurance, each session.....................................   5

Bail—donation and commission—documents, according to the value,   .
    scale II.

Banks, taking money on deposit for a fixed time or giving the privi-
    lege to withdraw it at any time, 2 per cent. of the interest derived
    from the money.

Bills of complaints....................................each sheet   36

    If the object of complaint is not worth over 50 florins....per sheet   12

Bills for sold goods, etc., according to scale II.

    If the value is below two florins, free.

Bills of lading, of storage, of warrants .... each 1

Bills of purchase of personal property, according to amount paid,
    scale III.

    Of real estate for stamp duty, each sheet   50

    For fees, however, has to be paid, according to the value of the ob-
    ject, 1, 1½, 2, 2½, 3, 3½ per cent. (additional 25 per cent.) The
    amount paid has to be considered as the value.

Bonds of state are free.

    Personal, for the payment of money, according to value, scale II.

    If payable to bearer, scale III ; but if payable at a fixed time, not
    over 10 years, scale II.

Bonds, or bills of debt, according to the value of the loaned object,
    scale II ; payable to bearer and not redeemable in less than 10
    years, scale II ; if the time is prolonged and not redeemable in 10
    years, or if the time is not fixed, scale III.

Fl. Kr.

Bills of exchange:

    Drawn in the inland and payable at the longest in six months; drawn in foreign countries, but transferred to the inland and payable at the longest in 12 months, according to the value, scale I.

    All others, according to scale II.

    Drawn in a foreign country and payable there, free.

    Sight, when drawn in the inland and payable within six months, or drawn in a foreign country and payable within 12 months from the day of date, not presented for payment, according to scale II.

    Second and third are subject to the same duty as first.

    Prolongation of, are considered as new bills of exchange, and are consequently subject to scale I.

    If the prolongation is over six months for the inland or 12 months for the foreign country, the duty is to be paid according to scale II.

Cards, playing...each set   15

Certifying to signatures, as by officers of the courts ....each   1

    When there is more than one signature to be certified to, every subsequent signature only.....................................   50

    (b) By a notary public......................................   50

    Every second or other.......................................   25

Checks..each   2

Codicil..per sheet   1

Coupons, of inland and foreign state securities, free.

        of private, as per scale II, the amount is paid by the stock company.

Copies, official, from an officer of a court.................per sheet   36

    If the value of the object in question is not worth over 50 florins, per sheet......................................   25

    From other authorities......................................   50

    Legalized by a court...   1

    If the object in question is not worth over 50 florins......per sheet   30

Copies, official, procured by the party and subsequently legalized before a court or a notary public...................per sheet   50

    simple, procured by the party, are free of stamp duty.

    several documents on one sheet require all the stamp duties of each of the rubrics...........................per sheet   15

Courts, public, with the exception of the courts for the real estate of the empire and for industrial enterprises subsisting by the state treasury, are duty free.

Documents of adoption, i. e., agreements concerning the adoption of a child...per sheet   50

Donations are subject to double duties : 1, to scale or percentage duty; and 2, without regard to the object of donation, to stamp duty.

    Concerning the stamp, when donations are made between living persons...per sheet   50

    In case of death..   1

    The duties are according to the value of the object of donation, when made between living persons, whether it be personal property or real estate, as follows :

    1. Between married persons living and not separated, between parents and legitimate children, as also illegitimate children or their descendants, between adopted parents and children, 1 per centum, (additional duty is 25 per cent.)

Fl.   Kr.

Donations—Continued.

2. Between other relations, including first cousins, 8 per cent. (additional duty is 25 per cent.)

The duties have to be paid as soon as the property comes into the possession of the parties.

Enclosures of documents are subject to stamp duty (excepting certificates of poverty)....................................per sheet   15

For legal business, when the object in question is below the value of 50 florins ....per sheet   10

Exemption from conscription, duty free.

Petition for..per sheet   50

Extracts from record-books...........................each sheet   1

Insurance policies and agreements, in proportion to the premium, scale II.

Lease of lands or tenements, according to the amount paid, scale II.

Letter addresses or freight letters for packages, &c., sent by mail or otherwise ....each   5

Loan business, commercial, *i. e.*, advancement of money for a certain time, if the money is advanced only for eight days, and if this time is prolonged, but not over eight days ....each sheet   10

Lottery tickets, in proportion to the amount paid for it, scale II, to be paid before the tickets are given out.

Tickets, drawing a prize larger than the amount staked upon the number, scale III.

Prizes below two florins are free.

Other lotteries have to pay 5 per cent. of the prizes, after deducting the amount paid in.

For benevolent purposes, free.

Lists of exchange of brokers..............................each   5

Matrimony, contracts made with regard to the disposition of the property, subject to scale II.

Memorials to be presented in legal proceedings............per sheet   36

If the value of the object in question is not over 50 florins   "   50

Mortgage, in proportion to the amount for which it is given, scale II.

If it does not consist in a valuable object or document..each sheet   50

Marriage license......................................   "   50

Newspapers, inland................................each number   1

foreign...............................   "   2

Notices, for instance, to quit a dwelling or land, or for recall of capital, if legalized............. ....per sheet   36

Orders of merchants or on merchants, if the payment consists in money, scale I; for bills of exchange, if the order be payable within eight days from the day of date ....each   5

Passports, for the laboring and poorer class ....each   15

for others...   1

Petitions for an appointment to office, or for a grant.......each sheet   50

for license to carry on a free or privileged business or private agency in the city of Vienna ....each sheet   6

in cities not over 50,000 inhabitants.....................   4

in cities of 5 and 10,000 inhabitants.....................   2

in all other places...................................   1   50

for all other licenses....................................   1

to a civil authority requesting a decree, as for issuing licenses

. for import, export, transit, and all other permissions required by the custom-house regulations......................   1

	Fl.	Kr.

Petitions—Continued.

for granting, approving, transferring titles of nobility, titles, honors, distinction, &c....................each sheet 5

for conferring industrial and other privileges......per sheet 3

to receive citizenship of state or community.......per sheet 2

for recording real estate in the books of record, whether it is done to establish real or conditional ownership, or for any other purpose, if the value exceeds not 50 florins..each sheet   36

exceeding 50 florins, but not 100 florius.......... "   1   50

for registering existing or altered firms or partnerships, and of branch houses..........................each sheet 10

for procuration.............................every person 5

for liquidation ....each sheet 5

for registration of the rights which a wife of a merchant acquires, in consequence of a contract of matrimony, on the property of the husband....................each sheet 5

for remittance of punishment.................. "   1

Pawner checks...each   50

If by a public pawn institution certain sums of money are advanced for goods or papers of value, as, for instance, state securities, &c., for three months, or every prolongation, scale I.

All others according to scale II.

Proposals...each sheet   50

Protests upon note, bill of exchange, checks, drafts, &c., when made before a notary public....................each sheet 1

made before a court, up to 200 florins 2

over 200 florins.......... 3

Railroad and steamboat passage tickets, if the price is not above 50 kreutzers, for each...   1

When above 50 kreutzers, for each 50 kreutzers one kreutzer more, but never above 15 kreutzers.

Receipts, as an acknowledgment of having received a certain amount of money due, &c., (when not of merchants and business men,) in accordance to scale II.

of merchants, if not used for legal proceedings, free.

on bills of lading, when not used for legal purposes, free.

Reciprocal bonds, if the object be one of value, according to scale II; when not ....per sheet   50

Rejoinder, in civil law suits...........................each sheet   36

If the matter in dispute is worth less than 50 florins .... "   12

Religious corporations, concerning their documents, are free.

Security, documents of :

If the security for which the document is given is not valuable, each sheet...   50

If it is valuable, according to scale II.

Signature, legal, of officers, free, excepting signatures to copies, visas, passports, protocols, judgments, decrees, and duplicates.

Stock companies, according to the amount of stock, scale III. The duties have to be paid before the shares are issued.

For the real estate the company has to pay 1½ per cent.

Suits...each sheet   36

If the object in dispute is not worth over 50 florins ..... "   12

Testimonials, written by government officers or courts......per sheet 1

Of other officers or courts or of private persons.... .....each sheet   50

For the laboring and serving class.................... "   15

	Fl.	Kr.

School and studies ....each sheet   15

Concerning the examination in common schools, free; but testimo-·
   nials of absolutory of studies are subject to stamp duty, each sheet   50

Transfer of property in consequence of death:

   1. From parents to children 1 per cent. of the value of the property,
      (additional 25 per cent.)

   2. To persons who have been in a serving condition or relation to
      the deceased, and if the annual rent for life or for a number of
      years is not more than 50 florins, or if the capital sum is not over
      500 florins, 1 per cent.

   3. To other relations, including first cousins, of the value of the in-
      herited property, 4 per cent.

   4. In all other cases, from the value of the inherited property, 8 per.
      cent., (additional 25 per cent.)

   Is the property real estate? then the duty of $\frac{1}{2}$, 1, $1\frac{1}{2}$ per cent. has
   also to be paid, (additional duty 25 per cent.)

The document of..................................each sheet   1

Translation, official.................................per sheet   1

Will, last, documents of ....each sheet   1

   This amount has only to be paid in case a transfer of property is the
   consequence of the will.

   Concerning the duty to be paid from the transfer of the property,
   · (see *Donations.*)

The following were omitted in the list:

Books:

   Printed works, free.

   Used by merchants, mechanics, manufacturers, and business men
   generally as main-conto, corrent-saldo, corrent books, having the
   highest measure of 726 Vienna □ ''...................each sheet   25 ·

   All others, bound or stitched or in single sheets or leaves, each sheet
   not over 380 Vienna □ ''......................................   5

   Over 380 □ '', but not more than 726 □ ''....   10

   Over 726 □ ''...... ....   15 ·

   Copy, for commercial correspondence and letters, are free, if the
   same are not used for legal proceedings.

Judgments:

   Of first instance, concerning suits of rights of possession, of legality,
   of notices to quit lodgings or lands......................each   2   50

   In liquidations of bankruptcy.........................each sheet   1   25

   First instance, concerning incidence; suits, if the value of the object in question is not worth over 50 florins...............each   1

   In all other cases...   2   50

   First instance, in the main points, concerning a value not over 50
   florins...   1   00

   50—200 florins...   2   50

   200—800   "   5

   Over 800 florins of the value, $\frac{1}{2}$ per cent.

   Final judgments, if the object in question is real estate and the value is
   over 50 florins, and if the right of getting possession is in consequence of
   the legal process, and not of the possession of a legal title, $3\frac{1}{2}$ per
   cent. of the percentage duty, (additional 25 per cent.)

Fl. Kr.

Judgments—Continued.

Of classification of the active property of a bankrupt ½ per cent.

If the object in question is not valuable....................each 12

Powers of attorney:

If the same are for no valuable object...................per sheet   50

If the same are for a valuable object, according to the value, scale II.

APRIL 24, 1864.

I have the honor to transmit to-day the Austrian system of taxation and rates.

It was not possible to give the rates of the taxes in a schedule-like form, as you have sent, because the Austrian system is so very different from ours. But I believe that the enclosed exposition will be satisfactory. I had to get first all the laws of Austria concerning the tax system, to be enabled to work this exposition out in the manner I have done. The Austrian secretary of treasury who was kind enough to send me the Austrian tax laws, requested me to beg you to send him all our laws concerning our tax system.

*   *   *   *   *   .   *   *   *

TAX SYSTEM OF AUSTRIA.

GENERAL REMARKS.

The Austrian system of taxation is so different from ours that it is impossible to give you the rates of the taxes paid here in schedule-like form, as you have transmitted to me with your despatch No. 29. Class A, for instance, in your schedule, seems to be a tax to be paid for articles or goods in the hands of the inhabitants. This kind of tax does not exist in Austria. For the stock of goods on hand no tax is paid. Nos. 8, 32, 33, 62, 63, and 69, in this class, are in Austria subject to the income tax. Nos. 43 to 47, inclusive, in this same class, are subject to the stamp-duty tax, which I have already transmitted to you.

Class B of your schedule is in Austria subject to the excise law of occupations *and* income. It is not possible to give the rates of this class in the form as I find it in the schedule, as the amount of the tax to be paid depends upon the location and extent of the business. With regard to Nos. 63, 64, and 65 of this class, it must be remarked that the tobacco traffic is a monopoly of the government.

In class A of your schedule it appears to me that articles subject to the excise law of consumption, of luxury, and of articles in the possession of the inhabitants, are all mixed up. The excise of consumption is here a special branch of the tax system, and differing in the different provinces and towns. Nos. 5, 7, 8, 9, and 10, also 105, 106, and 107, in this class, are articles of luxury, and not subject to a tax in Austria, because no tax law for luxuries is in existence. The government tried in the last session of the reichrath (congress) to have such a law passed, but it failed in being successful.

By the foregoing remarks you will perceive that the system of taxation is entirely different in Austria; and I will now proceed to give you her tax classification and rates in as short a space and as complete as possible.

The Austrian system of taxation is divided into direct and indirect taxes. The direct taxes are derived—

1. From the land tax.
2. From the house tax.
3. From the tax of occupations.
4. From the income tax.

The indirect taxes are derived on articles:

1. From the tax of consumption.

2. From custom-house duties.
3. From the tobacco monopoly and salt monopoly.
4. From the stamp duty tax.

DIRECT TAXES.

I. *Land tax.*

The land tax in Austria is not paid from the value of the land itself, but from the value of the produce raised on the land—that is to say, from the net profits derived from the land. As our system is so different in this respect, it is but necessary to state that the rate of this tax is 16 per cent. from the net profits of the products of every kind of land in the empire. Under this class belongs, also, the house tax, which is classified as follows:

a. House-class tax.
b. House-rent tax.

1. *House-class tax.*

All houses, whether situated in so-called closed cities or in the country, are subject to the house tax, and the person having the permanent use of the house (owner) has to pay the taxes. Exempt from this tax are churches, state buildings, barracks, hospitals, poor-houses, institutions for benevolent purposes, buildings used for official purposes if the same are not rented, police-houses, public school-houses and institutions for education, houses of teachers kept exclusively for a dwelling of the same, city halls for the use of the city officers, dwellings of priests and bishops if exclusively kept for this purpose, convents.

The house tax is subdivided into two classifications: *a*, house-rent tax; *b*, house-class tax.

1. *House-rent tax.*

The house-rent tax is to be paid from the real amount of the rent taken in for the rented house. In this case the rent taken in is taxed. The rate of this tax is 21½ per cent. after having deducted 15 per cent. from the rent for keeping the house in repair.

2. *House-class tax.*

All houses not rented out come under this classification. The rate of the house-class tax is according to the real or possible income from the house, differing only from the house-rent tax in respect to the rate of taxation, namely, while the rate of the house-rent tax is according to the real or possible amount of the rent, the house-class tax is measured according to the rooms and stories of the house.

No. 1.

Declaration of the amount of rent of house No. —, which it brings during the year 18—, situated in the place, (city or town,) classified under house-rent tax.

Province. }
County. }

I.	II.	III.	IV.	IN THE 1ST QUARTER.		IN THE 2D QUARTER.		IN THE 3D QUARTER.		IN THE 4TH QUARTER.		IN THE 5TH QUARTER.		VI.	VII.
No. of the house, or of the parts of the house, rented out.	Situation of the house.	The different parts of the house.	Family and given name of the party.	In W.W.	In C. W.	In W.W.	In C. W.	In W.W.	In C. W.	In W.W.	In C. W.	In W.W.	In C. W.	Signature of the party certifying to the correctness of the amount of rent paid.	Remarks.
				Fl. kr.	Fl. kr.	Fl. kr.	Fl. kr.	Fl. kr.	Fl. kr.	Fl. kr.	Fl. kr.	Fl. kr.	Fl. kr.		
								Annual rent.							

No. 2.

Description of house No. —, in the place belonging to the house-rent tax, (city or town.)

Province. }
County. }

I.	II.	III.	IV.	V.	VI.	VII.
	Number		Rooms.		No. of the dwelling of which the rooms are rented or used.	Remarks.
Of the parts of the house.	Yard.	Stairs.	Situation.	For what used.		

Register of the house-class tax of the township.

Province. }
County. }

Number.	Names of the places.	Number of the house.	Name of the house owner.	Name of the former owner.	Description of the house.			Houses over 35 rooms.	The house belongs to the—						Annual house-class tax to the double amount of the original estimation.	Remarks
					Kind.	Different parts of the house.	Style of building.		1 / 7	2 / 8	3 / 9	4 / 10	5 / 11	6 / 12		
									Class to—							
									30	25	20	16	12	8		
									6	4	3	2	1	20		
									Florins.							
									Kr.	fl.	krs.					

If the houses are not rented out, or kept for that purpose, the rates of the house-class tax are—

Class.	Fl.	Kr.
I	80	00
II	66	40
III	53	20
IV	42	40
V	32	00
VI	21	20
VII	16	00
VIII	10	40
IX	8	00
X	5	20
XI	2	40
XII	0	$53\frac{1}{2}$

The classification of the houses is made according to the following scale:

Number of rooms and apartments of the houses.	Class to which the houses belong.	
	One story.	Several stories.
35 to 30	II	I
29 to 28	III	II
27 to 25	IV	III
24 to 22	V	IV
21 to 19	VI	V
18 to 15	VII	VI
14 to 10	VIII	VII
9 to 8	IX	VIII
7 to 6	X	IX
5 to 4	XI	....
3 to 1	XII	....

It will be seen by this scale that houses with stories having less than five rooms are classed as having no stories, but when any other house has one or more stories it is transferred to the next highest class.

All houses having more than thirty-five rooms, but only one story, remain in class II; when they have one or more stories then they are transferred to class I. For every additional five rooms over thirty-five 2 florins 40 kreutzers, or, relatively, 5 florins 20 kreutzers more have to be paid. Blank forms 1 and 2 are used for establishing the different facts with regard to the house-rent tax and house-class tax.

II. *Tax of occupations.*

All occupations (excepting the common day laborer) are taxed as such. They are divided into four principal classes:
1. Prime production.
2. Manufacturing industry.
3. Commercial industry.
4. Rendering of personal services.

But as the prime production is reached by the land tax, there are but three principal classes.

The rate of the tax is according to the number of inhabitants of the places. The rates are given in the annexed schedule, No. 3.

No. 3.

Schedule of occupations subject to the Austrian excise laws.

Rates of taxes, from the lowest to the highest rates of the classification.

Occupations	Valid for—	I		II		III		IV		V		VI		VII	VIII		IX	X	XI	XII
		Fl.	Kr.	Fl.	Kr.	Fl.	Kr.	Fl.	Kr.	Fl.	Kr.	Fl.	Kr.	Fl.	Fl.	Kr.	Fl.	Fl.	Fl.	Fl.
Factories	All provinces of the empire	42		84		105		315		525		735		1,050	1,575					
Wholesale houses	do ... do	315		525		735		1,050		1,575										
Mercantile enterprises	In the capital, Vienna	105		137		210		315		430		525		735	1,050					
Do ... do	In places of 4,000 inhabitants and more	42	50	84		105														
Bankers	In places of 1,000 to 4,000 inhabitants	31		63		84	40													
Do	In places of less than 1,000 inhabitants																			
Common professions	In the capital, Vienna	5		10		21		31		42	50	52	50	63	73	50	84	105	210	315
Do	In places of 4,000 inhabitants and more	5		8		15	75	16	80	42		52	50							
Shop-keepers	In places of 1,000 to 4,000 inhabitants	3		5		10	50	31	50	31										
Traders, &c	In places of below 1,000 inhabitants	2		4		8	40	21	16											
Pedlers	In the capital, Vienna	5				21														
Services	In the capitals of the provinces	2																		
Instruction	In the capital, Vienna	52		105		137		315												
Do	In the capitals of the provinces	42		63		105		210												
Intelligence offices	Cities of 4,000 inhabitants and over	26	25	42		63														
Do	Cities of 1,000 to 4,000 inhabitants	10	50	15	75	21														
Expeditions of persons and goods.																				
Do	Cities of below 1,000 inhabitants	5	25	10	50	13	73													
Do	In the capital, Vienna	10		21	75	52	50	105												
Do	In the capitals of the provinces	8	40	15	50	31	50	52												
Do	Cities of 4,000 inhabitants and over	5	25	10	40	21	73													
Do	Cities of 1,000 to 4,000 inhabitants	3	15	8		15	40													
Do	Cities of below 1,000 inhabitants	2	10	4	20	8														

For some larger provincial towns, especially for capitals of the provinces, there exists a special tariff of taxes. Besides the tax of occupation, the bankers at Vienna have to pay an income tax. This amounts to a large sum. The highest has to pay 30,000 florins.

III. *Income tax.*

The object of taxation of this class is the net income of the inhabitants from their personal business or their property in Austria, in so far as certain regulations do not establish exceptions.

1st *class of income.*

To the first class belong the incomes derived from the different occupations. The rates and classification will be seen by schedule No. 3.

The following occupations belong also to this classification:

a. The incomes from mining and forges.

b. The profits derived by the renter from an estate.

When an enterprise subject to the excise law of occupations is let, a double income arises—1, to the lessor, which is represented by the amount of rent, and, 2, the profit left to the renter after having deducted the amount of the rent paid by him to the lessor; and both kinds of income are also subject to the income tax under class I, the first, because it is an income from an occupation, subject to the excise law of occupations, and the second, because this law, rule III, prescribes it. The profits derived by contractors from the building of roads, from contracts of supplying of different objects, are also subject to class I of the income tax, because in such cases not only the condition of renting takes place, such enterprises are also subject to the excise law of occupations.

The profits derived by renters of road and bridge tolls are subject to the income tax of class 2, which class will be specified hereafter, because they are exempt from the tax of occupations.

2d *class of income tax.*

To this class belong the incomes derived—

a. From such labor or occupation not subject to the excise law of occupations. To this class are also added the salaries of government or private officers and pensions of every description; contributions paid to religious orders out of the state treasury, public funds, or by communities; the income of journalists, of artists, physicians, surgeons, and midwives, and of such persons occupied in healing diseases of man and beast; of private teachers, proprietors of institutions of education, and of persons occupied in tuition in places not over 4,000 inhabitants.

The following persons also belong to this class:

1. Persons keeping tobacco shops.
2. Persons selling stamped paper.
3. Persons selling lottery tickets.
4. Postmasters.

Declaration for the tax of occupation.

Number of the house.	Family and given name.	Kind of occupation of business or enterprise.	Place of the business and where executed.	Amount of capital used by the manufacturer.	Number of machines, forges, &c., in use.	Number of workmen and apprentices.

[*Date.*]

[*Signature of the person subject to the tax.*]

Members of the university receiving incomes from taxes and fees for lectures. The income of all these persons is subject to the 2d class and not to the first, because they are exempt from paying the tax of occupations.

b. From incomes received from life insurance companies or establishments of sustenance, for which money has been deposited in such establishments.

Stock companies and private railroad companies are subject to the income tax of class 1, because they are also subject to the excise law of occupation.

3d class of income tax.

While the income tax under the foregoing classifications (1 and 2) are derived from labor, with or without the application of capital, the 3d class comprises only such not depending upon labor, namely, interests from capital or indebtedness, annuities, &c. To this class belong, consequently, the interests of all such capital not subject to a deduction from the side of the debtor, as state securities of every description; also the income of associations are subject to this class of taxation. All rents, (even life rents,) whether received by private persons, by the state, or by institutions, either in money or natural products, are subject to this class of tax.

Rates of the income tax.

The rates of the income tax from the incomes sub-class 1 and 3 amount to 5 from every hundred—*i. e.,* 3 kreutzers each florin.

The rates from the incomes sub-class 2 have to be paid according to the following scale:

From an income over	600 florins to 1,000 florins, inclusive...				1 per cent.
" "	1,000 " 2,000 "		..		2 "
" "	2,000 " 3,000 "	•	...		3
" "	3,000 " 4,000 "				4
" "	4,000 " 5,000 "		...		5
" "	5,000 " 6,000 "		...		6
" "	6,000 " 7,000 "		...		7
" "	7,000 " 8,000 "		...		8
" "	8,000 " 9,000 "		...		9
" "	9,000 "		...		10

Schedule of the tax of consumption for the city of Vienna.

No.	Names of articles.	Amount of the articles.	Amount of tax in Austrian currency.			
			Tax of consumption.		Additional city tax.	
			Fl.	*Kr.*	*Fl.*	*Kr.*
1	Liquor of every variety	per eimer	0	00	0	63
2	Vine	do	1	75	0	44
3	Vine—must	do	1	31½	0	33
4	Apple-vine, 2 musts	do	0	70	0	17½
5	Mead	do	0	70	1	50½
6	Beer, imported*	do	0	84	0	23
7	Vinegar	do	0	35	0	9
8	Cattle, oxen, bull, cows, and calves over one year old.	each	7	87½	1	5
9	Calves not over one year old	do	1	40	0	28
10	Sheep, rams, goats	do	0	52½	0	12½
11	Lambs to 25 lbs., kids, sucking pigs	do	0	35	0	7
12	Pigs from 9 to 35 lbs	do	1	5	0	21
13	Hogs over 35 lbs	do	2	10	0	42
14	Beef	Vienna cwt.	1	54	0	21
15	Meat, fresh, all other without difference, whether it be salted, smoked, pickled, or sausage meat.	do	2	75	0	69
16	Poultry, as geese, turkeys, ducks	each	0	10½	0	3
17	Chickens, pigeons	do	0	3½	0	2
18	Game—deer	do	2	10	0	52½
19	wild hogs over 30 lbs	do	1	57½	0	42
20	young deer, chamois	do	0	52½	0	13½
21	hares	do	0	10½	0	3
22	fasars, prairie chickens	do	0	21	0	5¼
23	hazel-hens, wild ducks, snipes	do	0	10½	0	3
24	other small birds	per dozen	0	3½	0	1
25	Fish and shell-fish of every kind, fresh, dried, pickled, &c., &c., &c.	Vienna cwt.	2	10	0	52¼
26	All kinds of sea-fish, oysters, craw-fish, frogs, &c.	do	0	70	0	17½
27	Rice	do	2	10	0	52½
28	Flour of every description	do	0	35	0	9
29	Grain, as wheat, rye, Indian corn, buckwheat, &c.	do	0	26½	0	7
30	Pulse: beans, horse, peas, &c	do	0	31½	0	8
31	Oats	do	0	28	0	9
32	Hay, straw, bran, chopped straw	do	0	10½	0	5½
33	Vegetables	do	0	21	0	5½
34	Fresh fruit	do	0	31½	0	8
35	Fruit dried	do	0	63	0	16
36	Butter	do	2	10	0	45½
37	Candles, every kind	do	2	10	0	52½
38	Tallow and grease	do	0	87½	0	52½
39	Lard, marrow, pork	do	1	40	0	35
40	Soap, common and fine	do	2	71½	0	68
41	Cheese	do	1	57½	0	17½
42	Eggs	do	0	10½	0	3
43	Wax, bleached and yellow, and wax candles and all other fabrics of wax.	do	2	62½	0	87½
44	Hemp, linseed and rapseed oil, &c	do	0	87½		
45	Other lamp oil, and olive oil, almond oil, &c.	do	1	75	0	44
46	Wood, fire	klafter	0	87½	0	42

*The brewers have to pay a special tax of consumption specified in schedule No. —.

No.	Names of articles.	Amount of the articles.	Amount of tax in Austrian currency.	
			Tax of consumption.	Additional city tax.
			Fl. Kr.	Fl. Kr.
47	Coals	Vienna cwt.	0 7	0 3¼
48	Honey	do .	0 59¼	
49	Train oil	do .	0 7	0 2
50	Brick and tile bricks	per 1,000...	1 36¼	0 34¼
51	Quarry stones	cwt. klafter.	3 78	0 94¼
52	Paving stones	per 100	0 42	0 10¼
53	Sand for building	per load	0 7	0 2
54	Lime	do .	0 31¼	0 8
55	Plaster	Vienna cwt.	0 7	0 2

INDIRECT TAX.

The indirect tax is divided into two principal branches:

1. The tax on articles of consumption.
2. Stamp-duty tax.

The taxes from articles of consumption are derived—

1. From the consumption of meat in the country.
2. From articles of consumption brought into so-called closed cities.
3. From wine, beer, and liquor.
4. From sugar refineries.
5. From custom-house duties.
6. From tobacco and salt monopoly.

The rates of the taxes of consumption for articles brought into the cities are somewhat differing in different provinces, but not very materially; and I therefore produce only the schedule No. 4, for the city of Vienna.

This schedule gives also the rate of the tax to be paid by the open country and small towns.

Distillers of liquor have to pay an extra tax for every eimer of liquor distilled. The rate of the tax differs according to the strength of the liquor and according to the material from which the liquor is distilled. The rates are also differing in the different provinces.

The rates of the tax.

1. When the liquor is distilled from produce containing flour, corn, potatoes, &c., 56 kreutzers per "dust," eimer, in Lombardy and Venice; but in all other countries 31½ kreutzers.

2. When it is distilled from the skins of pressed grapes, 28 kreutzers in Lombardy and Venice, and 16 kreutzers in all other countries.

3. When distilled from fruit, as apples, pears, berry-like fruit, roots, and waste of breweries, 37½ in Lombardy and Venice; 21 kreutzers in all other countries.

4. From cherries, plums, vine, vine must, 56 kreutzers in Lombardy and Venice; 31½ kreutzers in all other countries.

5. From sugar, wastes of the refineries of sweet sugar potatoes, and grain sirup, or other concentrated liquids of a higher percentage of sugar-stuff than of

the articles mentioned in rule 103, and from starch, 5 florins 56 kreutzers in Lombardy and Venice; in all other provinces 3 florins 15 kreutzers.

The foregoing rates have to be paid when the percentage of alcohol is below $52\frac{1}{2}°$. But when the percentage is $52\frac{1}{2}°$ and below 65°, 6 florins 95 kreutzers in Lombardy and Venice, and 3 florins 94 kreutzers in all other provinces.

When 65° and below $77\frac{1}{2}°$, 8 florins 34 kreutzers in Lombardy and Venice, and 4 florins $72\frac{1}{4}$ kreutzers in all other provinces.

When $77\frac{1}{2}°$ and below 90°, 9 florins 83 kreutzers in Lombardy and Venice, and 5 florins $51\frac{1}{2}$ kreutzers in all other provinces.

When 90° and below 100°, 11 florins 12 kreutzers in Lombardy and Venice, and 6 florins 30 kreutzers in all other provinces.

Brewers of beer pay also a certain tax for every cimer produced. The tax is likewise different in the different provinces, and is fixed according to the percentage of alcohol contained in the beer. The annexed schedule No. 5 gives the rates of the different provinces, which have to be paid by the brewers. The supervision of the breweries by the government is very strict.

Sugar refineries.—The sugar refiners have to pay for each Vienna cwt. of manufactured sugar from the fresh sugar beets $31\frac{1}{2}$ kreutzers; from dried beets 1 florin $73\frac{1}{2}$ kreutzers.

From glucose in a liquid state and manufactured from other material than beets, $17\frac{1}{2}$ kreutzers; in a crystallized state, 1.75.

Stamp-duty tax.

The schedule of this tax has been already forwarded to you by me with despatch No. 35.

This completes the Austrian system of taxation. I have already remarked it is not possible to give the whole system in a schedule-like form, as you have transmitted to me, because the whole system and division and the principle of taxation are so very different from ours. But I think I have been successful in giving the system and rates in such a clear and condensed manner that our able Secretary of the Treasury will at once see the system and the rates of this country. The rates of Austria are at least three times as high as ours. It was very difficult to get the Austrian system of taxation in such a short space and at the same time accurate, because the tax-laws are so very voluminous. The many amendments, additions, repeals, and corrections made it necessary to go over the whole material. Schedules like those you have transmitted do not exist in Austria.

Schedule of the beer tax, for brewing beer—valid for the whole empire except Trieste and Dalmatia.

In—	To 12°.		To 13°.		To 14°.		To 15°.		To 16°.		To 17°.		To 18°.		To 19°.		To 20°.		For each additional degree.
	Fl.	*Kr.*	*Fl.*	*Kr.*	*Fl.*	*Kr.*	*Fl.*	*Kr.*	*Fl.*	*Kr.*	*Fl.*	*Kr.*	*Fl.*	*Kr.*	*Fl.*	*Kr.*	*Fl.*	*Kr.*	*Kr.*
Lombardy and Venice	1	09 3/5	1	15 2/5	1	21 1/5	1	27	1	32 4/5	1	38 3/5	1	44 2/5	1	50 1/5	1	56	05 4/5
The city of Venice	2	25	2	30 4/5	2	36 3/5	2	42 2/5	2	48 1/5	2	54	2	59 4/5	3	05 3/5	3	11 2/5	05 4/5
Other closed cities in Lombardy	1	47 3/10	1	53 1/10	1	58 9/10	2	04 7/10	2	10 5/10	2	16 3/10	2	22 1/10	2	27 9/10	2	33 7/10	05 4/5
Galicia, Cracow, and Bukowina	0	30	0	30 1/2	0	35	0	37 1/2	0	40	0	42 1/2	0	45	0	47 1/2	0	50	02 1/2
Hungary, Transylvania, Servia, Banat, Croatia, Slavonia, and Military Corderlars.	0	36	0	39	0	42	0	45	0	48	0	51	0	54	0	57	1	00	03
The cities of Lemberg and Cracow	0	46 1/4	0	48 3/4	0	51 1/4	0	53 3/4	0	56 1/4	0	58 3/4	1	01 1/4	1	03 3/4	1	06 1/4	02 1/2
Prenburg, Post-ofen, and Oltopen	0	36	0	39	0	42	0	45	0	48	0	51	0	54	0	57	1	00	03
Bohemia	0	39	0	42 1/4	0	45 1/2	0	48 3/4	0	52	0	55 1/4	0	58 1/2	1	01 3/4	1	05	03 1/4
Prague	1	00 1/8	1	03 3/8	1	06 5/8	1	09 7/8	1	13 1/8	1	16 3/8	1	19 5/8	1	22 7/8	1	26 1/8	03 1/4
The other German and Slavonian provinces.	0	52	0	45 1/2	0	49	0	52 1/2	0	56	0	59 1/2	1	03	1	06 1/2	1	10	03 1/2
Vienna	1	27 1/2	1	31	1	34 1/2	1	38	1	41 1/2	1	45	1	48 1/2	1	52	1	55 1/2	03 1/2
Linz, Brunin, Gratz, Laibach, and Innsbruck.	1	04 3/4	1	08 1/4	1	10 3/4	1	15 1/4	1	18 3/4	1	22 1/4	1	25 3/4	1	29 1/4	1	32 3/4	03 1/2

REMARKS.—The amount of the tax of consumption which has to be paid by the brewers is in proportion to the quantity and strength of the beer produced. The strength refers to the amount of sugar-stuff contained in the beer. The quantity is measured according to the Austrian eimer. 1 eimer beer equal 13½ gallons. The per cent. of sugar-stuff is measured according to Baume.

VENICE—W. D. HOWELL, *Consul.*

MARCH 31, 1864.

Statement showing the description and value of the exports of Venice to the United States for the quarter ended March 31, 1864; also the names of the countries or places where produced and whither sent.

[Compiled from official documents.]

Where produced.	Description.	Whither sent.	Value, including costs and charges.
Venice	Glass beads	New York....	15,205 74 florins.
Do.............	.....do.....	....de..	1,191 14 old florins.
Do....	.....do.....	Philadelphia .	493 22 florins.
Do....	.....do.....	New York....	25,121 48 zwanzingers.
Do....	.....do.....	....do..	8,142 29 francs.
Vallonara.......	Straw goods..............	....do..	56,097 30 francs.
Venice	Photographic views	....do..	170 00 francs.
Do....	Photographic views and one oil painting.	Boston	3,063 30 francs.
Total value in American currency............		....	$23,624 24

JUNE 30, 1864.

Statement showing the description and value of the exports of Venice to the United States for the quarter ended June 30, 1864; also the names of the countries or places where produced and whither sent.

[Compiled from official documents.]

Where produced.	Description.	Whither sent.	Value, including costs and charges.
Venice	Glass beads	New York....	4,491 54 florins.
Do....	.....do.....	Baltimore....	£30 3 7
Do....	.....do.....	....do..	15,959 33 florins.
Do....	.....do.....	....do..	22,435 45 zwanzingers.
Do....	Stereoscopic instruments	....do..	368 50 francs.
Do....	Photographic views	....do..	360 00 francs.
Do....	Stereoscopic instruments and photographic views.	Boston	580 00 francs.

SEPTEMBER 30, 1864.

Instead of presenting the usual annual report of transactions in a commerce growing every year less interesting and important, I propose here to review very succinctly the whole history of Venetian commerce, and to develop as far as possible the causes of its rise and decline. I think this will be more useful to those who look upon commerce as a means of civilization, and not merely a system of mercenary transactions, than a dry exhibit of the present meagre affairs of Venice. And I believe that the analogy which must always exist in the careers of republican nations struggling from small beginnings to great national prosperity cannot be without peculiar instruction to Americans.

The commercial history which shall present all the facts of Venetian grandeur and decay in a philosophical light has not yet been written; and at this time even the material data for such a work is inaccessible, the documents concerning the imports and exports of the republican times having been removed from the archives in Venice and deposited in the Austrian capital. I have been obliged, therefore, to content myself with such authorities as I have found in print; and I have adopted as a basis for the following relation the history sketched in the interesting but too brief "Treatise of the Commerce of the Venetians," by Fabio Matinelli, formerly director of the imperial royal archives in Venice.

The new cities formed by the fugitives from barbarian invasion on the Italian mainland had hardly settled around a common democratic government on the islands of the lagoons, in the fourth century, when they began to develop great maritime energies and resources; and long before this government was finally established at Rialto, (the ancient seaport of Padua,) and Venice had become the capital of the young republic, the Venetians had thriftily begun to turn the wild invaders of the mainland to account—to traffic and to make treaties of commerce with them. Theodric, the king of the Goths, had fixed his capital at Ravenna, in the sixth century, and would have been glad to introduce Italian civilization among his people. But this warlike race was not yet prepared to practice the useful arts; and although they inhabited one of the most fruitful parts of Italy, with ample borders of sea, they were neither sailors nor tillers of the ground. The Venetians supplied them with the salt made in the lagoons and with wines brought from Istria. They continued to extend and confirm their commerce with these helpless and hungry warriors, and were ready, also, to open a lucrative trade with the Longobards, when they descended into Italy, about the year 570. The Venetians had, in fact, abetted the Longobards in their war with the Greek Emperor Justinian, (who had opposed their invasion,) and in return the Longobards gave them the right to hold great free marts or fairs on the shores of the lagoons, whither the people resorted from every part of the Longobardic kingdom to buy salt of Venice, grain from Istria and Dalmatia, and slaves from every country. The traffic in these unhappy beings formed then one of the most lucrative branches of Venetian commerce, as now it forms the greatest stain upon the annals of that commerce. Not only the Venetian, but other Italian states, were guilty of this infamous trade, and made profit by it. The trade may be said to have been all but universal. The Venetians, however, were the most deeply involved in it, pursued it most unscrupulously, and relinquished it the last. * * * It is not very easy to fix the dates of the rise or fall of the slave trade, but slavery continued in Venice as late as the fifteenth century. * * * While this baleful and enormous traffic in man was growing up, the Venetians enriched themselves by many other more blameless and legitimate forms of commerce, and gradually gathered into their power that whole trade of the east with Europe which passed through their hands for so many ages. After the dominion of the Franks had been established in Italy, in the eighth century, the Venetians began to supply that people—more luxurious than the Lombards—with the rich stuffs, the jewelry, and the perfumes of Byzantium, and held a great annual fair at the imperial city of Pavia, where they sold to the Franks the fabrics of the polished and effeminate Greeks, and whence, in return, they carried back to the east the grain, wine, wool, iron, lumber, and excellent armory of Lombardy.

From the time when they had assisted the Longobards against the Greeks, the Venetians found it to their interest to cultivate the friendship of the latter, until, in the twelfth century, they mastered the people so long caressed, and took their capital, under Enrico Dandalo. The privileges conceded to the wily and thrifty republican traders by the Greek Emperors were somewhat extraordinary in their extent and value. The Venetians had beaten the pirates of Dalmatia, and at their request the Greeks recognized Venetian rule all over Dalmatia, thus securing to the republic every port on the eastern shores of the Adriatic. Thus, having aided the Greeks to repel the aggressions of the Saraccns and Normans, all the ports to the empire were made free to Venetian commerce; and the Venetians were allowed to trade without restriction in all the cities, and to build warehouses and depots throughout the dominions of the Greeks, wherever they chose. When the Crusaders had taken the Holy Land, the kings of Jerusalem bestowed upon the Venetians, in return for important services against the infidels, the same privileges conceded by the Greek emperor; and when, finally, Constantinople fell into the hands of the Crusaders, nearly all the Greek islands fell to the share of Venice and the Latin emperors, who succeeded the Greeks in dominion, and gave her such privileges as made her complete mistress of the commerce of the Levant.

From this opulent traffic the insatiable enterprise of the republic turned, without relinquishing the old to new gains in the farther Orient. The Venetians, against whose trade the exasperated infidels had closed the Egyptian ports, did not scruple to coax the yet more barbarous prince of the Scythian Tartars newly descended from the shores of the Black sea. Having secured his friendship, (without imparting their purpose to their Latin allies at Constantinople,) they proceeded to plant a commercial colony at the mouth of the Don, where the city of Azof stands. Thenceforward, through this entrepot Venetian enterprise, with Tartar favor, directed the entire commerce of Asia with Europe and incredibly enriched the Venetian people. The vastness and importance of such a trade, even at that day, when the wants of the people of Europe were far simpler and fewer than now, could hardly be overstated, and one nation then monopolized the traffic which is now free to the whole world. The Venetians bought their wares at the great marts of Samarcand, and crossed the country of Tartary in caravans to the shore of the Caspian sea, where they set sail and voyaged to the river Volga, which they ascended to the point of its closest proximity to the Don. Their goods were then transported overland to the Don, where they were again carried by water down to the mercantile colony of Venetians at the mouth of the river. The national ships having free access to the Black sea there received their cargoes and set sail direct to Venice. The products of every country of Asia were carried into Europe by these dauntless traffickers.

The partial civilization of the age of chivalry had now reached its climax, and the class which had felt its refining effects was the opulent class, best able to gratify the wants still unknown to the great mass of the ignorant and impoverished people.   *   *   The Venetians, who seldom did merely heroic things, turned the crusaders to their own account, made money out of the Holy Land, and whom one always fancies as having half a scorn of the noisy grandeur of chivalry were very glad to supply the knights and ladies with the gorgeous stuffs, precious stones, and costly perfumes of the east. Now, also, they began to establish manufactories and to practice the industrial arts at home. The Venetian jewellers and workers in precious metals soon became famous throughout Europe; the glass-works of Murano rose into a celebrity and importance never since lost, (for they still supply the whole world with beads,) and they began to weave stuffs of gold tissue at Venice, and silks so exquisitely dyed that no noble of perfect fashion was content with any other.

Besides this, the Venetians gilded leather for tapestry of walls, wove carpets, and wrought miracles of ornaments in wax, a material that modern taste is apt to disdain; while Venetian candles in chandeliers of Venetian glass lighted up the palaces of the whole civilized world.

The private enterprise of citizens was, in every respect, protected and encouraged by the state, which did not fail to make due and just profit out of it. The ships of the merchants always sailed to and from Venice in fleets at stated seasons, and some of these fleets departed annually, one for Romania, a second for Azof, a third for Trebisond, a fourth for Cyprus, a fifth for Armenia, a sixth for

Spain, France, and England, and a seventh for Egypt. Each squadron of traders was accompanied and guarded from corsairs and other enemies by a certain number of the state galleys, manned and armed by the state, the equipage of each amounting to three hundred men, embracing officers. The state, also, appointed a captain of the whole squadron, with absolute authority to hear complaints, decide controversies, and punish offences. While the republic was thus careful for the protection and discipline of the citizens who traded upon the seas, it was no less zealous for their security and its own dignity in the traffic with the continent of Europe. In that rude old time neither the life nor the property of the merchant who visited the ultramontane countries was safe. * * The Venetians, therefore, were forbidden by the state to trade in those parts, and the Bohemians, Germans, and Hungarians, desirous to buy Venetian wares, were obliged to frequent Venice and purchase at the great marts held in different parts of the city, thus subserving a triple purpose; the Venetian merchants were protected in their lives and goods, their national honor saved from insult, and many an honest sequin turned to the inn-keepers, who entertained the customers of the merchants. Five of these great fairs were held every week in Venice and its vicinity, the chief market being at the Rialto. The transactions in trade were carefully supervised by the servants of the state. Among the magistrates especially appointed for the orderly conduct of the foreign and domestic commerce were the so-called mercantile consults, whose special duty was to see that the traffic of the nation received no hurt from the individual schemes of any citizen or foreigner, and to punish offences of this kind with exile, and even graver penalties. They measured every ship about to depart, to ascertain if her cargo exceeded the lawful amount; they guarded the respective rights of debtors and creditors, and punished thefts sustained by the merchants.

It is curious to find, contemporary with this beneficent magistracy, a charge of equal dignity exercised by the college of reprisals. A Venetian injured abroad, either in person or property, demanded justice of the country where the injury was committed. If the demand was refused, it was repeated by the republic; if still refused, then the Venetian government (though at peace with the nation from which the offence came) seized any citizen of that country whom it could find, and, through the college of reprisals, spoiled him of sufficient property to indemnify the Venetian citizen. Finally, besides several other magistracies, resident in Venice, the republic appointed consuls in its colonies and some foreign ports, to superintend the traffic of its citizens and compose their controversies. These consuls were nobles, acted with the advice and consent of twelve other Venetian nobles, or merchants, and were paid out of duties levied on the merchandise.

At this time, and indeed throughout the existence of the republic its great lucrative monopoly was the salt manufactured in the lagoons. The salt is forced into every market, and sold at such rates that no other could compete with it. When alien enterprise attempted rivalry, it was instantly discouraged by Venice. There were troublesome salt mines, for example, in Croatia, and in 1381 the republic caused them to be closed by paying the King of Hungary an annual pension of seven thousand crowns of gold. What was the exact income of the state from the monopoly of salt, or from the various imposts and duties levied upon merchandise, it is impossible to state. Venetian commerce reached the acme of prosperity just before the time of Tourmaso Mocenego Doge, from 1414 to 1423. From his dying speech to the senators and other chiefs of the state, as well as from some other desultory data, the value of this commerce may be approximately computed. There were then three thousand and three hundred vessels of the mercantile marine making annual voyages and bringing to Venice each an average value of one hundred thousand zecchins. The zecchin was worth $2.30 of our money, and the yearly value thus brought to Venice was 330,000,000, or about $800,000,000. This was merely the commerce by sea. Some idea of the inland trade of Venice may be gathered from the amount of traffic with the Duchy of Milan, alone of the yearly value of $100,000,000. When it is remembered that this is only a fragmentary exhibit of the whole national commerce, that the population never greatly exceeded three millions, and that the number of dollars is multiplied by the vastly greater value of money in that day, the immense commerce and enormous wealth of Venice in the fifteenth century will be partially appreciated. Then when the greatness of this commerce is contrasted with the meagre totals of the present day, the extent of the decline of Venetian prosperity will be apparent. In 1423 the commerce, as far as we are able to learn, amounted to $900,100,000; in 1863, by the careful statistics of the Chamber of Commerce, to $60,229,740. The number of vessels now owned in Venice is one hundred and fifty. The old commercial prosperity of Venice was based upon the monopoly of the most lucrative traffic in the world, upon her exclusive privileges in foreign countries, the indefatigable industry and intelligent enterprise of her citizens, the enlightened zeal of her government, the imperfect knowledge of geography, and the barbarism of the rest of Europe. America was yet undiscovered; the overland route to India the only one known; the people of the continent outside of Italy unthrifty serfs, ruled by a multitude of unthrifty masters. The whole world's sloth, ignorance, and misery were Venetian gain; and the very superstitions of the day, gross as they were, and embodying perhaps the noblest and most hopeful sentiment of the time, were a source of incalculable profit to the sharp-witted mistress of the Adriatic. It was the age of penances, pilgrimages, and relic-hunting, and the harvest which the Venetians reaped from the devotion of others was exceedingly rich. Venetian ships carried the p lgrims to and from the Holy Land; Venetian adventurers ransacked Palestine and the whole Orient for the bones and memorials of the saints, and Venetian merchants sold these precious relics throughout Europe at an immense advance on first cost.

But the foundations of Venetian prosperity were at last sapped by the tide of wealth which poured in from every quarter of the globe. The merchant imported the vices as well as the rich stuffs, perfumes, and jewelry of the debauched Orient. It is needless to rehearse the stories of old Venetian magnificence and immorality. At the time when the hardy, hungry people of other nations were opening paths to prosperity by sea and land, the Venetians, gorged with the spoils of ages, relinquished their ancient habits of enterprise and fell into luxury and idleness. The incessant wars with the Genoese began, and, though Venice signally defeated the rival republic in battle, Genoa finally excelled her in commerce. A Greek prince had arisen to dispute the sovereignty of the Latin emperor whom the Venetians had helped to place upon the Byzantine throne, and the Genoese, seeing the favorable fortunes of the Greeks, threw the influence of their arms and intrigues in his favor, and the Latins were expelled from Constantinople in 1271. The new Greek emperor had promised to give the sole navigation of the Black sea to his allies, together with the churches and palaces possessed by the Venetians in his capital, and he bestowed also upon the Genoese the city of Smyrna. It does not seem that he literally fulfilled all his promises, for the Venetians still continued to sail to and from their colony of Tana, at the head of the sea of Azof. But it is certain that they had no longer the sovereignty of those waters, and the Genoese founded on the shores of the Black sea three large and important colonies to serve as entrepots for the trade usurped from the Venetians. The Oriental traffic of the latter was maintained through Tana, however, for nearly three centuries later, when, in 1410, the Mogul Tartars, under Tamerlane, fell upon the devoted colony, took, sacked, burnt, and utterly destroyed it. This was the death-blow to the most magnificent commerce which the world had ever seen, and which had endured for ages. * * * After that the Venetians humbly divided with their ancient foes the possession and maintenance of the Genoese colony of Caffa, and continued with greatly diminished glory their traffic in the Black sea till the Turks having taken Constantinople, and the Greeks having acquired under their alien masters a zeal for commerce unknown to them during the time of their native princes, the Venetians were finally, on the first pretext of war, expelled from those waters in which they had latterly maintained themselves only by payment of heavy tribute to the Turks. In the mean time industrial arts, in which the Venetians had hitherto excelled, began to be practiced elsewhere, and the Florentines and the English took that lead in the manufactures of the world which the latter still retain. The league of the Hanseatic cities was established and rose daily in importance. At London, Bruges, Berne, and Novogorod special favor was shown to the cities of the league. Their ships were preferred to any other; and the tide of commerce setting northward, the Hanseatic towns persecuted the foreigners who would have traded in those ports. On the west of Venice the city of Barcelona, in Spain, began to dispute her pre-eminence throughout the Mediterranean, and Spanish salt was brought to Italy itself and sold by the enterprising Catalans. Their corsairs vexed Venetian commerce everywhere.

The Portuguese, also, began to extend their commerce, once so important, and, catching the rage for discovery, (then so prevalent,) infested every sea in search of unknown land. One of their navigators, sailing by a chart, (which a monk named Fra Mauro, in a convent on the island of St. Michele, (now the cemetery,) at Venice, had put together from the stories of travellers and his own guesses at geography,) discovered the Cape of Good Hope. The trade of India with Europe was turned in that direction, and the old overland traffic perished. * * * It remained for Christopher Columbus, by the discovery of America, to give the last blow to the commercial supremacy of Venice. While all these discoveries were taking place the old queen of the seas was weighed down with many and unequal wars. Her naval power had everywhere been crippled, her revenues reduced, her possessions one after another lopped off; and, at the time Columbus was on his way to the New World, the Old, united in the league of Cambree, was attempting to crush the republic of Venice. The whole world was now changed, commerce sought new channels, and the feeble remains of Venetian prosperity, year by year, are crumbling away, and it is melancholy to discern in the future no prospect of amended fortunes.

STATES OF THE ZOLLVEREIN.
PRUSSIA.
STETTIN—CHARLES J. SUNDELL, *Consul.*

APRIL 30, 1864.

In reporting upon the trade, commerce, and shipping of this place for 1863, it must again be stated, at first, that its direct relations with the United States are still but very insignificant, (only four American cargoes having arrived direct during that period,) and that articles of American production and export are continually being shipped to this the principal port of Prussia by the importers of Great Britain, Hamburg, and Bremen, &c., &c. * * *

The general trade of this place during 1863 assumed larger proportions than ever before, and its shipping surpassed any of the previous years.

This, in itself, very encouraging circumstance, did, nevertheless, not produce proportionally remunerative results to those engaged, finding its cause in the fact that most of the increase in trade fell to the lot of the forwarding business, where profits, from a very lively competition, are rather small. And again, some of the chief branches, as, for instance, operations in grain, from a continual fall in the foreign markets, were attended with occasional losses. The marine insurance companies also, from turbulent storms prevalent during the fall, found their gains considerably lessened.

But, on the other side again, the mechanical works, the manufactories, and the mills, &c , gave very satisfactory results. When the progress of Stettin undoubtedly must be ascribed to its favorable location, which makes it the commercial depot for a large extent of territory, so should it not be forgotten that its further aggrandizement greatly depends upon the improvement of its essential communications.

First and foremost deserving of earnest and immediate attention is the river Oder, the upper part of which, leading into the grain-producing districts and the coal region, (Silesia,) from its small depth of water was, during the larger part of the year, unnavigable even for canal boats. On the Vorpomersche railroad, which was opened to its full length during last fall, the traffic is commencing to develop itself satisfactorily; and when this road, as is anticipated, will be in connexion with the Mecklenburgische. now under construction, its earnings will undoubtedly be large, and the trade of this place greatly benefited, as thereby coming in direct railroad communication with the ports of Rostock, Wismar, Lubeck, and Hamburg. &c., &c.

The principal exports of Stettin during 1863 were—

Wheat	80, 972	wispels, of 37½ American bushels.			
Ba ley	44, 143	"	"	"	"
Rye	40, 363	"	"	"	"
Peas	9, 439	"	"	"	"
Potatoes	7, 320	"	"	"	"
Oats	5, 544	"	39	"	"
Flour and mill products	236, 457	zoll-centners, of 110 American lbs.			
Rapeseed	182, 433	"	"	"	
Clover and timothy seed	23, 287	··	··	"	
Spirit and alcohol	187, 987				
Beet-root molasses	31, 153	··			
Zinc	380, 838				
Rapeseed and other oil	40, 732				
Oil cakes	15, 293				
Chemical products	12, 246				
Iron ware	67, 525	·			
Oak and pine timber and lumber	468, 504	pieces.			

The cereal prices were on a constant fall during the year, wheat opening in March with 7½ thalers per wispel of 2,100 zoll pfund, and closing in December with 52 thalers, Prussian currency. Most of the articles went to England, namely : 63,241 wispels of barley exported; 34,071 wispels also went to England, the price varying from 40 to 30 thalers per wispel of 1,750 zoll-pfund For rye the price varied from 45½ in spring to 33 thalers in December, per wispel of 2,000 zoll-pfund. Of this grain the largest quantities went to Sweden, Norway, and Holland. All the oats exported were to England, the price keeping steady during the whole season at from 23 to 24 thalers per wispel of 1,200 zoll-pfund. Peas had, in consequence of a very good crop, an active demand, chiefly from England, whence 7.675 wispels were sent at a price varying from 45 to 33 thalers per wispel. Two successive extraordinary crops of potatoes, bringing the price down as low as 8 thalers per wispel, led to a very extensive fabrication of spirits and alcohol, so that quantities three times larger than the year before were exported at prices varying from 16 to 14 thalers per 100 quarts, equal to about 30 American gallons, of 80 per cent. alcoholic strength. Out of the grand total exported, 3,150,000 quarts went to Italy, and 2,092,000 quarts to France. Prices for cloverseed were, in February, 17½ to 16½ thalers for red, and 21 to 19 thalers for white per zoll-centner, but as, with opening of navigation, several large shipments of the American red seed arrived from England, prices commenced falling, and a decline of 2 thalers per zoll-centner took place within a few weeks. White clover kept steady at former rates, and timothy varied from 5½ to 7¾ thalers per zoll-centner.

The total value of all the exports of Stettin during 1863 is stated at 26,454,711 Prussian thalers.

The principal imports (mostly transits) of Stettin in 1863 were—

	Zoll-centners.
Cotton, raw	94,465
Cotton, twist	19,154
Coffee	146,684
Rice	85,676
Wine	63,849
Loaf sugar and candies	24,771
Brandy, cognac, arrack, and rum	11,242
Pepper and different spices	20,365
Foreign fruits, fresh and dried	21,954
Almonds and nuts	5,150
Lard (mostly American)	19,857
Sirups	34,888
Palm, cocoa, olive and other oils	209,107
Tallow and stearine	88,371
Linseed	85,673
Tar, pitch, and asphalt	66,048
Guano (mostly Baker's island)	45,485
Soda	89,589
Brimstone	80,993
Potash	42,755
Lubricating and other grease	72,558
Petroleum	4,582
Saltpetre	11,412
Dye and logwood	60,049
Flax and hemp	56,349
Rosin	38,131
Sulphuric and other acids	10,450
Thran, or blubber oil	50,357
Copper, ingots and pig	28,193
Iron in pigs	811,370
Iron in bars and fashioned	206,264
Coal	3,207,966
Total	5,719,292

The imports of herring, pickled, from Scotland and Norway were again exceedingly large, amounting to 235,538 barrels, or about 56.000,000 pounds of that particular fish, besides 7,009 zoll-centner of other kinds, salt and dried. The forwarding merchants of Stettin, although doing a large and extensive business during the year, are still complaining, and with right, of existing obstacles to the free development of their (for this place) so very essential branch of trade, and that the American civil war continues to exercise its baneful influences on them, the transit trade of cotton, twist, rosin, turpentine, &c., being thereby greatly reduced, and partly cut off altogether.

The chief hindrances to a fuller extension of their business are stated to be, the irregularity of the Oder, the high railroad freights to and from Saxony, the difficulty of prepaying through freights to some important stations on railroads in connexion with this place, the lack of a railroad line to Swinemünde, cu'ting off all shipping from here for that part of the year when the river is frozen; and last, not least, the burdensome proceedings at the custom-house, by which much of the business man's time is lost, and many annoyances created. The forwarding business, they say, can only then flourish properly when all local hindrances are first removed, and as yet many obstacles to its free development still exist here, but which, in the course of a few years, will certainly be remedied.

The total value of the imports of Stettin during 1863 is stated at 47,022,887 Prussian thalers. Fabrication of beet-root sugar within the Zollverein proves to have increased considerably, so that during last year the total quantity of beet-root on which sugar tax was paid from the 1st of September, 1862, to the 31st of August, 1863, amounted to 36,719,258 zoll-centners, or 5,026,864 centners more than the year before. Out of this 31,783,088 zoll-centners were for consumption in Prussia alone, where 216 refineries are in operation; the whole number of refineries within the Zollverein being at present 247. This increase of production was occasioned not so much by a larger home consumption as by the fact of a larger export chiefly to France, where the crop of beet-root for the year proved almost a total failure.

In a former report I made mention of the high harbor, river, and navigation dues, &c., for vessels entering and clearing at Swinemünde and Stettin, and which has been frequently complained of by charterers and shipmasters. During the last year, however, the Prussian government saw fit to reduce some of them, so that the expenses for a vessel of 150 lasts, or about 320 tons, (by a new measurement lately adopted,) for entering and clearing at the two ports, are now as follows:

AT SWINEMÜNDE.

	Thalers.	Silver gros.
Harbor dues, inward, at 8 silver groschens per last	40	00
outward " " "	40	00
Navigation dues	5	00
Declaration and bills, inward	6	20
outward	6	20
Sea poor rates	1	7½
Pilotage to Stettin	9	15
from Stettin	9	15
Boat assistance	2	15
Commission for clearing, in and out	30	00
Total	151	2½

AT STETTIN.

	Thalers.	Silver gros.
Declaration and bills	6	20
Sea poor charges	1	7½
Port charges	7	15

Total 50   12½

On the other hand, again, steam towage, if required, has been raised a trifle, namely, from sea to Swinemünde from 2⅜ silver groschens to 2⅝ silver groschens per last, and from Swinemünde to Stettin, and *vice versa*, from 10⅜ silver groschens to 11¼ silver groschens per last. At the same time it should be stated that the new measurement for vessels which has been ordained by the government, and already carried into effect, makes the Prussian *last* now about seven per centum larger than formerly, and consequently all the above stated dues are thereby being still further reduced. Having applied for information as to the principles of and the rules for this new measurement, I shall have the honor to report more fully in regard thereto at some future day.

The maritime trade and shipping of Stettin during the year may be summed up thus:

Arrivals from abroad by sailing vessels 1,720
                by steam vessels 622

Out of those arrivals only four were direct from the United States, and of them only one American vessel, the three-mast schooner Arzac, Captain Baas, of which I had the honor to report under July 6 and October 3, 1863.

Arrivals from off the coast and the roads, &c., by sailing vessels, 2,773. The number of arrivals by flat and canal boats, engaged in carrying freight on rivers and canals, was 7,543. Departures for abroad by sailing vessels, 1,671. Departures for abroad by steam vessels, 618. Departures from off the coast and the roads, &c., by sailing vessels, 2,786. Departures by flat and canal-boats, 7,609. To this will be added 2,305 arrivals and departures by steamboats plying up and down the river and along the coast, besides 40 arrivals and departures by steamers carrying the mail from and to Sweden. At the beginning of 1863 the Prussian merchant fleet numbered 1,420 vessels, of together 183,960 lasts. During the year 93 new vessels were being built and completed, and 18 added through purchase from other nations. In the same period 79 vessels were lost, wrecked, or condemned, and 13 sold to other nations, so that by the 1st of January, 1864, the grand total of merchant vessels under the Prussian flag was 1,439, of together 186,560 lasts, out of which 946 were what is termed sea-going, or larger sailing vessels, 26 were sea-going steamboats, 389 were smaller sailing crafts and coasters, and 78 were river and coasting steamers; of this number 213 vessels are owned in Stettin, of together 29,224 lasts, namely, 165 sea-going sailing vessels, 5 sailing coasters, 18 sea-going steamboats, and 25 river and coasting steamers. At the commencement of this year 80 new vessels were under construction within the kingdom, namely, 74 for Prussian, and 6 for foreign account, and of those 4 sailing vessels and 10 steamers are being built at this place.

The income from customs collected at the Stettin custom-house during 1863 amounted to 1,583,068 thalers 24 silver groschens on imported goods, and 911 thalers 2½ silver groschens on exported goods, or together 1,583,979 thalers 26½ silver groschens, being 174,758 thalers 4½ silver groschens over the amount collected in 1862.

SWINEMÜNDE

Had, as usual, all the preliminary and concluding business of the shipping of Stettin to attend to besides its own, a considerable import of English coals, and some exports of timber and lumber to France and Britain. The total number of arrivals at that port during 1863 was 2,149 by sea-going sailing vessels, of which 1,839 were in lading and 310 in ballast; 796 by sea-going steamers, of which 781 were in lading and 15 in ballast; and 536 by smaller crafts and coasters, of which 519 were in lading and 17 in ballast, or together 3,481 arrivals.

The departures were 2.214 by sea-going sailing vessels, of which 1,663 were in lading and 551 in ballast; 798 by sea-going steamers, of which 764 were in lading and 34 in ballast; and 697 by smaller crafts and coasters, of which 666 were in lading and 31 in ballast, or together 3,709 departures.

Out of the above numbers 43 sailing vessels and 1 steamer came to the port for relief or in distress, besides which 10 arrivals and 8 departures by Prussian vessels-of-war, and 1 arrival and departure of a Danish man-of-war, are to be noted.

The already excellent harbor of Swinemünde is being still further improved and deepened, with a view, it is thought, of making it a principal station for the Prussian navy, which at present consists of 69 vessels-of-war, of together 392 guns; besides which, 1 iron-clad, 2 corvettes, and 2 first-class gunboats, of together 51 guns, are now under construction and to be completed by the 1st of July next.

The mercantile tonnage owned at that port on the 1st of January last consisted of 49 vessels, of together 5,489 lasts, of which 30 were sea-going sailing vessels, and 19 smaller sailing crafts; at the same time 5 new vessels were on the stocks and being built there.

The United States consular agent in the place, A. Radmann, esq., reports of only one American vessel having passed there, (the same one as reported upon from here,) and of no fees having been received at his agency during 1863.

DANTZIC,

The large grain warehouse of Prussia, also complains of but small remunerative results of the year's trade, notwithstanding very considerable exports and extended shipping. The causes ascribed are the insurrection in the neighboring Poland, the low water stand of the Vistula, and, chiefly, the unfavorable state of the foreign markets. In their report the merchants of Dantzic express their earnest desires for some long-needed improvements necessary for the prosperity of that important commercial point, such as regulating the Vistula, widening the harbor, completion of several railroads, additional depot grounds for the timber trade, extension of the custom warehouse and adjacent yards, abolishing the import duty on cereals and seeds, sundry other reductions of the tariff, and also simplifying the way of proceedings at the custom-house offices. This, as I take it, proves a high spirit of progress and expansion pervading the mercantile class of that community, and which, as such, in its report, further ascribes the deplorable discord existing between the state government and the chosen representatives of the land as being the main cause of some continued defects with which their place has to contend.

From a detailed statement of the year's trade it is found that the principal exports of Dantzic in 1863 were—

	Prussian thalers.
Wheat, to the value of	10,643,000
Rye	4,900,000
Barley	510,000
Peas	850,000
Timber and lumber of all kinds	5,300,700
Total	22,203,700

The grand total of all exports amounting in value to 23,022,761 Prussian thalers.

As usual, England received most of the wheat, or about seven-eighths of the whole quantity exported, and so likewise with barley; most of the rye was taken to Holland and Scandinavia; timber and lumber to different foreign lands.

The principal articles imported were—

	Prussian thalers.
Coffee, to the value of	748,374
Wine	291,878
Wrought iron and rails	543,258
Cast-iron goods and cast steel	271,566
Scraps and pig iron	216,846
Raw hides	246,550
Herring, pickled	600,000
Salt	117,880
Loaf sugar and sirup	123,220
Olive, palm, and cocoa oil	139,468
Cotton and cotton goods	182,980
Copper and brass ware	105,540
Coals	482,434
Total	4,069,886

The grand total of all imports amounting in value to 5,226,081 Prussian thalers.

The shipping of the place comprised 3,103 arrivals by sailing vessels and steamers from abroad; 3.065 departures by sailing vessels and steamers for abroad; 4,123 arrivals and departures by river crafts and steamboats; besides which there arrived from up the Vistula and its tributaries 1,472 rafts of timber, &c.

Of tonnage, Dantzic owns a larger share than any other Prussian port, and on the 1st of January last it consisted of 123 sea-going sailing vessels, of together 33,996 lasts; 2 coasters, of together 49 lasts; 3 sea-going steamers, of together 445 lasts; and 12 river steamers and tugs, of together 317 lasts. Some of the largest merchantmen under the Prussian flag are owned in Dantzic.

The United States consular agent at that port, Peter Collas, esq., reports two arrivals and departures of American vessels, and consular services rendered at his agency during 1863, as per statement hereto.

KOENIGSBERG,

From where the present United States consular agent sends some very full and elaborate tables and statements of its commerce and shipping, appears to enjoy an unabated increase of business, although the year's profits were not quite satisfactory to its merchants, as declared in their report on the last year's trade and shipping of that place. The state of the foreign markets is also complained of here, and the abundant crops all over Europe, with exception only of some parts of Hungary, had a dwindling-down effect upon the profits of the otherwise large sales of grain. England itself, the report says, had a good wheat crop; and what a mighty influence such a fact exercises in a region like this, where that very grain is the chief article of export, the observer of commercial matters will have no difficulty to perceive.

The state of the weather also, constantly drying up the water-courses which connect Koenigsberg with Prussia, was another misfortune, goods having to be brought in and out at costs considerably higher than usual; and added thereto came the threatening aspects of the "Schleswig-Holstein" quarrel, which pro-

duced unsteadiness and fear among holders and operators.   Nature and politics,
the report goes on to say, have in the past year operated equally to make our
trade extensive it is true, but at the same time little remunerative.   The following are the chief imports of the place during 1863:

	Prussian thalers.
Tea, to the value of	7,599,000
Coffee, to the value of	855,000
Indigo, to the value of	459,000
Cotton, raw, to the value of	282,000
Spices of all kinds, to the value of	217,000
Southern fruits, to the value of	106,000
Rice, to the value of	98,000
Coals, to the value of	170,000
Potash, to the value of	213,000
Chemical products, to the value of	200,000
Raw mineral products, value	150,000
Cast and pig iron, value	138,000
Wrought and fashioned iron, rails, and tin (sheet)	696,000
Steel and iron ware, to the value of	584,000
Shelf goods, to the value of	560,000
Spirits, arrack and rum, to the value of	1,063,000
Wine, to the value of	504,000
Pickled herring, to the value of	967,000
Tobacco and cigars, to the value of	402,000
Raw sugars, to the value of	474,000
Refined sugars, to the value of	2,766,000
Total	18,503,000

Among the principal exports were—

	Prussian thalers.
Wheat, to the value of	3,315,000
Rye, to the value of	2,970,000
Barley, to the value of	389,000
Oats, to the value of	463,000
Peas, to the value of	653,000
Beans, to the value of	134,000
Vetch, to the value of	169,000
Hemp and linseed, to the value of	684,000
Rape, clover, and other seeds, to the value of	430,000
Hemp and flax, to the value of	557,000
Wool, to the value of	101,000
Raw hides, to the value of	231,000
Rags, to the value of	241,000
Total	10,337,000

It should here be remarked that the above statement of imports and exports
is of such portions thereof only as arrived to and went out of the place by sea,
and that the total amounts, according to the corporation report, are much
larger—the Koenigsberger, as therein appears, thinking it best, in order to
make a big show, to include everything coming in and going out under those
respective heads, whether it comes from or goes to the next village, or from and

to a foreign country. Even among those items here enumerated are large proportions of some having come from and gone to the western provinces of Russia by sea over Stettin, as the forwarding place, as, for instance, sugar, tobacco, arrack, rum, potash, and chemical products among the imports, and hemp, flax, wool, and rags among the exports.

Consequently, and although the general trade of Koenigsberg was very considerable during the year, showing, according to the tables, a grand total of 42,083,000 Prussian thalers' worth of imports, and 30,370,000 in exports, the genuine transactions under those heads would, by examination, dwindle down not a little, becoming smaller and less than the merchants' report would have it appear.

The same wishes and desires, the same demands for reforms as those coming from Dantzic and Stettin, are expressed in this report—improvement of harbors and rivers, enlargement of custom warehouse and yards, abolition of income duty on cereals, rice, and coals, and the export duty on rags. The salt monopoly is also bitterly complained of as contrary to all late principles of state economy. On the other hand, again, the great advantages secured for Koenigsberg through extended railroad communications are cheerfully acknowledged, the merchants closing their report in predicting for their place an important and bright future, with which is chiefly and, I think, justly combined the mighty beneficent influences which must be derived from the serf emancipation in the neighboring empire of Russia.

The maritime trade of Koenigsberg during the year comprised 1,560 arrivals by sailing and steam vessels, among which 248 were in ballast; 1,560 departures by sailing and steam vessels, among which 31 were in ballast. And the tonnage owned on the first of January last consisted of 20 sea-going sailing vessels of, together, 3,706 lasts, one coaster of 21 lasts, and six steamboats, of, together, 176 lasts. Of new vessels under construction there was only one, namely, a bark of 380 lasts burden.

The United States consular agent at this place, J. H. Brockman, esq., reports no arrivals or departures of American vessels, and sundry fees received at his agency during 1863, as per statement heretofore transmitted.

MEMEL,

with its splendid harbor and fine location, is still being comparatively neglected, and in shape of communications with the inland but step-motherly provided for, as the commercial report sent by the United States consular agent from there asserts. True, a few branches of trade have during 1863 experienced some increase, but the total business proves to have again fallen below that of the year before, as successively the case from year to year during several of the preceding ones.

From there also come the same pleadings for reductions in the tariff, taking off import duties on cereals, &c., abolishing monopolies, and so on, just as from the places above reported on; so it appears that the demands for those governmental reforms are very generally participated in by the commercial interests of the kingdom, and that they will be complied with by and by is very probable, as in such respects the Prussian government has always of late proved itself susceptible of all well-founded wishes. The total exports of Memel during the year amounted in value to 6,578,700 Prussian thalers, and among the chief articles were oak and pine timber and lumber, staves and sleepers, rye, linseed, linseed oil, barley, flax, and rags. The total imports amounted to 3,212,900 Prussian thalers, and the principal articles were salt, coals, iron and ironware, rails, pickled herring, sugar, sirup, and chemical products.

Compared with the list for 1862, the above would show an increase in favor of this year, but the merchants in their report positively assert that the figures of last year were erroneous, and prove their assertion by the facts that this year's shipping comprises 6,000 lasts less of incoming, and 4,200 lasts less of outgoing goods. The number of arrivals by sailing and steam vessels in 1863 was 904, of together 101,802 lasts, against 107,809 lasts in 1862. The number of departures during the same period was 930, of together 106,539 lasts, against 110,722 lasts in 1862.

On the first of January, 1864, Memel owned in tonnage 84 sea-going sailing vessels, of together 19,420 lasts, one coaster of 14 lasts, and five steamboats of together 230 lasts.

At the same time there were under construction and being built five large sea-going sailing vessels. Among industrial branches at Memel, and also at Dantzic, are the fishing and digging for yellow amber, which is being found along the eastern coast of the Baltic, and principally at those places where the quantities collected are at periods very considerable, amounting to 20,000 or 30,000 barrels in a year, at a value of from 4 to 40 thalers per zoll-pfund, and the most of which is being exported to Constantinople, the Orient, and to China.

The United States consular agent at Memel, Henry Fowler, esq., reports no arrivals or departures of American vessels and no consular services rendered at his agency during 1863.

AUX-LA-CHAPELLE—WILLIAM H. VESEY, *Consul.*

MAY 10, 1864.

In obedience to the instructions of the department of the first of March last, I have the honor to transmit herewith a report, with translation, in schedule form, of the revenue duties now imposed by the Prussian government.

SCHEDULE OF THE PRESENT REVENUE DUTIES IN PRUSSIA.

A. *Indirect duties and taxes.*

	Rate of duty or tax. Thalers.		
1. Custom and excise duties on foreign goods, as per custom-house tariff annexed. Transit duties have been abolished.			
2. Mashing duty, or duty on distilling brandy:			
For every 20 quarts of mashing—tun space...........	0	3	0
3. Malt-brewing tax:			
For every hundred weight of malt	0	20	0
4. Duty on growing wine:			
1st class growth, every eimer (60 quarts Prussian) of must from the wine-press..............................	1	0	0
2d class growth, every eimer of must from the wine-press.	0	25	0
3d " " " "	0	17	6
4th " " " "	0	12	6
5th " "	0	10	0
6th " "	0	7	6
5. Duty on growing tobacco:			
1st class soil, of every area of 6 ruthen, (180 ruthen equal 1 morgen)	0	6	0
2d class soil, of every area of 6 ruthen...............	0	5	0
3d " " "	0	4	0
4th " " "	0	3	0
6. Stamp duty:			
According to the law and tariff annexed.			

Rate of duty or tax.
Thalers.

7. **Saltduty.** (The sale of salt is a monopoly of the government:)
   200 pounds—equal 100 kilogrammes—cost 6 10 0
8. **Newspaper stamp duty:**
   Gazettes, periodicals, and advertisers, for every copy of
   400 square inches 0 0 1
   Gazettes, periodicals, and advertisers, foreign, pay one-
   third of the subscription price of the place where they
   appear.
9. **Duty on beet-root sugar:**
   Per cwt. of raw beets, (periodically fixed,) at present.. 7 6 0
10. **Tolls:**
    a. Vehicles, including sledges—
       For conveying persons, each horse per mile, equal
       2,000 ruthen............................ 0 1 0
       For conveying loads, carrying more than 200 pounds,
       each horse or beast.......... .... 0 1 0
       For unladen wagons, per beast 0 0 8
       For land-carts, per beast 0 0 4
    b. Beasts not put to—
       For a horse or mule, with or without horseman or
       charge 0 0 4
       For an ox, or cow, or ass..................... 0 0 2
       For five foals, calves, sheep, lambs, swine, or goats. 0 0 2
    Vehicles in public service, and such as carry dung and
    materials for building roads, are free.
11. **Milling tax,** (merely exacted in 83 towns:)
    1 cwt. of wheat................................ 0 20 0
    1 cwt. of any other kind of corn or leguminous plants.. 0 5 0
12. **Tax on slaughtering cattle,** (merely exacted in 83 towns:)
    Every cwt. of flesh, including bones and grease....... 1 0 0
    Every cwt. of slaughtered flesh brought into town 1 10 0
    Feet, entrails, and fat of the latter, are free.
    Tax at Aix-la-Chapelle per head of cattle:
    1. Of an ox or cow 7 0 0
    2. Of a cow of 5 cwt. at the most 4 0 0
    3. Of a heifer................................. 2 0 0
    4. Of a calf of 1 cwt. or more.................... 1 0 0
    5. Of a calf of less than 1 cwt.................... 0 20 0
    6. Of a pig.................................... 1 10 0
    7. Of a mutton, sheep, or goat, of less than 1 cwt..... 0 15 0
    8. Of a mutton of 1 cwt. and more................. 0 20 0.
    9. Of a sucking pig or lamb....................... 0 7 6
13. **International removal duty:**
    This duty exists merely in the states belonging to the .
    German Union of Customs.
14. **Navigation duty:**
    This duty amounts in Prussia to 220,733 thalers. For
    every river, canal, or inland water, exist particular
    tariffs.

B. *Direct duties or taxes.*

1. **Duties on railways:**
   Railway companies with a capital of 1,000,000 thalers—
   Annual net proceeds not exceeding 10,000 thalers.... 250 0 0

		Rate of duty or tax. Thalers.		
Annual net proceeds not exceeding 20,000 thalers....		500	0	0
" " " 30,000 thalers....		750	0	0
.. .. " 40,000 thalers....		1,000	0	0
" . " 45,000 thalers....		1,250	0	0
" 50,000 thalers....		1,500	0	0
" 55,000 thalers....		2,000	0	0
" 60,000 thalers....		2,500	0	0
" 65,000 thalers....		3,500	0	0
" " " 70,000 thalers....		4,500	0	0

For every 5,000 thalers, in addition to the net proceeds,
1,000 thalers duty more.

2. Duties on buildings:

1st degree, value of usufruct per annum	4 thalers : 1st class	0	4	0
	2d class	0	2	0
2d	6 thalers : 1st class	0	6	0
	2d class	0	3	0
3d	8 thalers : 1st class	0	8	0
	2d class	0	4	0
4th	12 thalers : 1st class	0	12	0
	2d class	0	6	0
5th , "	15 thalers : 1st class	0	18	0
	2d class	0	9	0
6th	20 thalers : 1st class	0	24	0
	2d class	0	12	0
7th	25 thalers : 1st class	1	0	0
	2d class	0	15	0
8th	30 thalers : 1st class	1	6	0
	2d class	0	18	0
9th	35 thalers : 1st class	1	12	0
	2d class	0	21	0
10th "	40 thalers : 1st class	1	18	0
	2d class	0	24	0
11th "	45 thalers : 1st class	1	24	0
	2d class	0	27	0
12th "	50 thalers : 1st class	2	0	0
	2d class	1	0	0
13th '	60 thalers : 1st class	2	12	0
	2d class	1	6	0
14th "	70 thalers : 1st class	2	24	0
	2d class	1	12	0
15th "	80 thalers : 1st class	3	6	0
	2d class	1	18	0
16th "	90 thalers : 1st class	3	18	0
	2d class	1	24	0
17th '	" 100 thalers : 1st class	4	0	0
	2d class	2	0	0
18th '	" 120 thalers : 1st class	4	24	0
	2d class	2	12	0
19th "	" 140 thalers : 1st class	5	18	0
	2d class	2	24	0
20th '	" 160 thalers : 1st class	6	12	0
	2d class	3	6	0
21st '	" 180 thalers : 1st class	7	6	0
	2d class	3	18	0

Rate of duty or tax.
Thalers.

					Thalers		
22d degree, value of usufruct per ann.	200 thalers :	1st class	8	0	0
			2d class	4	0	0
23d	"	225 thalers :	1st class	9	0	0
			2d class	4	15	0
24th "	"	250 thalers :	1st class	10	0	0
			2d class	5	0	0
25th "	"	275 thalers :	1st class	11	0	0
			2d class	5	15	0
26th "	"	300 thalers :	1st class	12	0	0
			2d class	6	0	0
27th "	"	325 thalers :	1st class	13	0	0
			2d class	6	15	0
28th " "	"	350 thalers :	1st class	14	0	0
			2d class	7	0	0
29th "	"	375 thalers :	1st class	15	0	0
			2d class	7	15	0
30th "	"	400 thalers :	1st class	16	0	0
			2d class	8	0	0
31st "	"	450 thalers :	1st class	18	0	0
			2d class	9	0	0
32d	"	500 thalers :	1st class	20	0	0
			2d class	10	0	0
33d	"	550 thalers :	1st class	22	0	0
			2d class	11	0	0
34th "	"	600 thalers :	1st class	24	0	0
			2d class	12	0	0
35th "	"	650 thalers :	1st class	26	0	0
			2d class	13	0	0
36th "	"	700 thalers :	1st class	28	0	0
			2d class	14	0	0
37th "	"	750 thalers :	1st class	30	0	0
			2d class	15	0	0
38th "	"	800 thalers :	1st class	32	0	0
			2d class	16	0	0
39th "	"	850 thalers :	1st class	34	0	0
			2d class	17	0	0
40th "	"	900 thalers :	1st class	36	0	0
			2d class	18	0	0
41st "	"	950 thalers :	1st class	38	0	0
			2d class	19	0	0
42d	"	1,000 thalers :	1st class	40	0	0
			2d class	20	0	0
43d	"	1,100 thalers :	1st class	44	0	0
			2d class	22	0	0

Up to 2,000 thalers every degree rises 100 thalers; from 2,000 thalers upwards every degree rises 200 thalers. Should the value of usufruct lie between two grades, the duty of the lowest is to be paid. Public buildings, and such buildings as are used for churches and schools, are exempted from the duty.

3. Ground rent, (amounting to 10,000,000 thalers for the whole state:)

1st class land, of 4 thalers 18 kreutzers net proceeds per annum, pays actually per morgen 0 17 9

	Rate of duty or tax.
	Thalers.

	Thalers		
2d class land, of 3 thalers 24 kreutzers net proceeds per annum, pays actually per morgen	0	14	8
3d class land, of 2 thalers 18 kreutzers net proceeds per annum, pays actually per morgen	0	10	0
4th class land, of 1 thaler 24 kreutzers net proceeds per annum, pays actually per morgen	0	6	11

4. Poll tax—(is to be paid by all inhabitants of 16 years old:)

	Thalers		
Of an income up to 150 thalers per annum............	1	0	0
" " 200 " "	2	0	0
" " 250 " "	3	0	0
" " 300 " "	4	0	0
" " 350 " "	5	0	0
" " 400 " "	6	0	0
" " 450 " "	8	0	0
" " 500 " "	10	0	0
" " 650 " "	12	0	0
" " 800 " "	16	0	0
" " 900 " "	20	0	0
" " 1,000 " "	24	0	0

When the income exceeds 1,000 thalers, then the income tax takes place.

	Thalers		
Workingmen and domestics, with an income of less than 150 thalers, pay..............................	0	15	0

5. Income tax—3 per cent. of the income per annum:

	Thalers		
1st grade—income of more than 1,000 thalers, not exceeding 1,200 thalers, per annum..................	30	0	0
2d grade—income of more than 1,200 thalers, not exceeding 1,400 thalers, per annum..................	36	0	0
3d grade—income of more than 1,400 thalers, not exceeding 1,600 thalers, per annum..................	42	0	0
4th grade—income of more than 1,600 thalers, not exceeding 2,000 thalers, per annum..................	48	0	0
5th grade—income of more than 2,000 thalers, not exceeding 2,400 thalers, per annum..................	60	0	0
6th grade—income of more than 2,400 thalers, not exceeding 2,800 thalers, per annum..................	72	0	0
7th grade—income of more than 2,800 thalers, not exceeding 3,200 thalers, per annum..................	84	0	0
8th grade—income of more than 3,200 thalers, not exceeding 3,600 thalers, per annum..................	96	0	0
9th grade—income of more than 3,600 thalers, not exceeding 4,000 thalers, per annum..................	108	0	0
10th grade—income of more than 4,000 thalers, not exceeding 4,800 thalers, per annum..................	120	0	0
11th grade—income of more than 4,800 thalers, not exceeding 6,000 thalers, per annum..................	144	0	0
12th grade—income of more than 6,000 thalers, not exceeding 7,200 thalers, per annum..................	180	0	0
13th grade—income of more than 7,200 thalers, not exceeding 9,600 thalers, per annum..................	216	0	0
14th grade—income of more than 9,600 thalers, not exceeding 12,000 thalers, per annum..................	288	0	0
15th grade—income of more than 12,000 thalers, not exceeding 16,000 thalers, per annum..................	360	0	0

Rate of duty or tax.
Thalers.

16th grade—income of more than 16,000 thalers, not exceeding 20,000 thalers, per annum..................	480 0 0
17th grade—income of more than 20,000 thalers, not exceeding 24,000 thalers, per annum..................	600 0 0
18th grade—income of more than 24,000 thalers, not exceeding 32,000 thalers, per annum..................	720 0 0
19th grade—income of more than 32,000 thalers, not exceeding 40,000 thalers, per annum..................	960 0 0
20th grade—income of more than 40,000 thalers, not exceeding 52,000 thalers, per annum..................	1,200 0 0
21st grade—income of more than 52,000 thalers, not exceeding 64,000 thalers, per annum..................	1,560 0 0
22d grade—income of more than 64,000 thalers, not exceeding 80,000 thalers, per annum..................	1,920 0 0
23d grade—income of more than 80,000 thalers, not exceeding 100,000 thalers, per annum..................	2,400 0 0
24th grade—income of more than 100,000 thalers, not exceeding 120,000 thalers, per annum..............	3,000 0 0
25th grade—income of more than 120,000 thalers, not exceeding 140,000 thalers, per annum..............	3,600 0 0
26th grade—income of more than 140,000 thalers, not exceeding 160,000 thalers, per annum..............	4,200 0 0
27th grade—income of more than 160,000 thalers, not exceeding 180,000 thalers, per annum..............	4,800 0 0
28th grade—income of more than 180,000 thalers, not exceeding 200,000 thalers, per annum..............	5,400 0 0
29th grade—income of more than 200,000 thalers, not exceeding 240,000 thalers, per annum..............	6,000 0 0
30th grade—income of 240,000 thalers and more	7,200 0 0

6. Tax for carrying on a trade:

Great manufacturers, joint-stock companies, and important commercial establishments, in the principal towns, per annum	96 0 0
Id. in the other towns, per annum...................	72 0 0
Small manufacturers and merchants: 1st class, per annum	24 0 0
2d class, per annum	16 0 0
3d class, per annum	10 0 0
4th class, per annum	10 0 0
Hotel and tavern keepers: 1st class, per annum........	18 0 0
2d class, per annum........	12 0 0
3d class, per annum........	8 0 0
4th class, per annum........	4 0 0
Bakers and butchers: 3d class, per annum.............	6 0 0
4th class, per annum.............	4 0 0
Peddlers: 1st class, per annum	16 0 0
2d class, per annum	8 0 0
3d class, per annum	4 0 0
4th class, per annum	2 0 0
Shopkeepers and dealers in victuals: 1st class, per annum	8 0 0
2d class, per annum	6 0 0
3d class, per annum	4 0 0
4th class, per annum	2 0 0
Craftsmen of every kind: 1st class, per annum	8 0 0

H. Ex. Doc. 60——31

	Rate of duty or tax.		
	Thalers.		
Craftsmen of every kind: 2d class, per annum	6	0	0
3d class, per annum	4	0	0
4th class, per annum	4	0	0
Brewers: for the first 96 thalers of brewing malt tax, per annum	2	0	0
for any further 64 thalers of brewing malt tax, per annum	2	0	0
Carriers and horse-courses, per horse, yearly..........	1	0	0
Id. possessing only *one* horse are exempted from the tax.			
Shippers, for the space of their ships, every space for 24,000 pounds..................................	0	20	0
Steamboats, per horse-power	0	7	6

MAY 21, 1864.

I have the honor to refer to my letter to the department, No. 39, and to state that the regulations concerning the inspection and revision of railroad cars conveying goods from out of Prussia into some other foreign country emanate from the minister of state at Berlin. They are as follows:

"Railroad freight and baggage cars must be secured by locks provided by the custom-house authorities, combination locks. The secret word upon locking is made known to the officers of the customs along the line of transit, who may open the cars and examine the goods at such stations as are named in the way-bill accompanying them. The cars, when divided into more than one compartment, must be marked and numbered on the outside opposite each compartment. Goods are sometimes accompanied by an officer, and in such case he is entitled to a seat in the second passenger cars. Whenever the time-bill of the road is altered, the company is bound to notify the custom-house. Where goods and luggage cannot be examined, they are put into a public warehouse, and are examined the next day in presence of the owner, carrier, and custom-house officers. No goods can be sent out of Prussia into some other foreign country without a declaration being made at the custom-house at the point of departure, giving a description of the goods, the marks, numbers, and weight of each package. In cases of insignificant value, the key of the car is sealed up in a bag and delivered to the conductor of the train, who hands it to the proper officer of the frontier. '

Statement showing the description and value of exports from the Aix-la-Chapelle district to the United States during the year ended December 31, 1864.

Description.	1st quarter.	2d quarter.	3d quarter.	4th quarter.	Total.
	Thal. Gr. Pf.	*Thal. Gr. Pf.*	*Thal. Gr. Pf.*	*Thal. Gr. Pf.*	*Thal. Gr. Pf.*
Woollen cloth, cassimeres, satins, &c.	482,330 17 07	496,761 19 06	297,123 03 09	144,949 24 11	1,421,165 05 09
Woollen gloves	2,547 06 06	12,256 19 00	6,675 08 07	4,058 00 09	25,537 04 10
Woollen flocks	17,238 08 00	15,245 29 03	17,459 08 06	15,577 23 06	65,521 09 03
German wool		7,350 16 00			7,350 16 00
Tapes	142 20 00				142 20 09
Lead and zinc	159,817 28 03	256,095 05 03	48,215 19 05	141,242 06 06	605,300 29 05
Needles and pins	14,244 17 00	14,453 27 06	8,936 24 06	5,068 29 00	42,704 08 00
Glass buttons	2,811 29 00	3,086 14 06	657 27 00	449 18 00	7,005 28 06
Agath buttons			1,185 02 00		1,185 02 00
Window glass	5,787 21 04	194 05 06	795 00 00		6,776 26 10
Enamel	505 00 00		300 00 00	416 20 00	1,221 20 00
Paper			2,294 00 00	1,763 00 00	4,057 00 00
Wine	518 00 00	588 00 00			1,106 00 00
Kid gloves		22,980 26 09	14,751 20 04	4,910 09 06	42,642 19 07
Alizarine ink		29 05 00			29 05 00
Empty bottles	110 12 00				110 12 00
Velvets and velvet ribbons	2,305 28 03		639 25 00		2,945 23 03
Total	688,360 07 11	828,979 18 03	399,033 19 01	318,436 05 02	2,234,802 20 05
Of which were exported by the way of—					
Antwerp, via Hull & Liverpool	584,632 24 08	501,809 02 05	297,861 15 04	150,308 18 11	1,534,612 01 04
Antwerp, direct	35,810 15 09	195,215 23 06	37,767 10 01	55,690 26 03	324,354 15 07
Havre	33,770 20 00	76,076 09 04	24,598 29 10	11,544 27 09	145,990 26 11
Hamburg	16,032 12 06	15,302 00 03	9,098 14 01	7,058 11 06	47,491 08 04
Bremen	14,015 21 00	39,563 27 09	28,801 03 09	30,846 28 00	113,227 20 06
Rotterdam	1,733 22 00	1,005 15 00		63,056 12 09	65,795 19 09
Marseilles	2,364 12 00		966 06 00		3,330 18 00
Total	688,360 07 11	828,972 18 03	399,033 19 01	318,436 05 02	2,234,802 20 05

Statement showing the description and value of merchandise exported from the consular district of Cologne to the United States during the year 1864.

	Thalers.	Grs.	Pfs.
Books, printed	939	1	3
Brandy	103	10	6
Brass ware	741	25	0
Cigars	1,342	13	0
Cologne water	5,574	3	0
Clothes, &c	130	0	0
Copy-books and copying paper	2,957	9	4
Fancy articles	778	1	0
Felt shoes	264	22	6
Frames, gilt	250	0	0
Glaze ore, in powder	1,002	5	10
Glycerine	180	0	0
Hams	122	3	0
Hardware	11,109	25	11
Instruments, musical	900	0	0
Instruments, surgical	48	0	0
Iron wire chains	11,845	28	9
Iron furnace grates	63	0	0
Knitting wares	733	29	4
Lead, sugar of	2,193	0	0
Lead, white	337	3	8
Leather (calfskin)	143	11	6
Lithography	716	25	0

	Thalers.	Grs.	Pfs.
Oil paintings	9,605	22	6
Porcelain ware	95	21	3
Paper	10,287	2	5
Perfumeries	143	8	6
Percussion caps	6,306	23	9
Pharmaceutical chemicals	355	1	8
Pipes, earthen	1,036	25	0
Pipes, smoking	339	18	0
Potash, muriate of	2,305	7	10
Sacred vessels	178	28	0
Salt, crude mineral	2,275	14	3
Saltpetre, refined	4,872	11	0
Seeds and bulbs	552	10	0
Snuff	20	25	0
Steel, cast	77,647	16	0
Steel, manufactured	33,881	28	9
Stomach bitters, (liquors)	1,468	22	6
Succory, ground	179	25	6
Sundries	52	16	0
Taffetas, (ribbons)	43,217	4	9
Ultramarine	10,535	0	0
Utrecht velvet	12,154	8	9
Velvets and velvet ribbons	85,206	29	6
Waistcoat buttons	537	19	0
Wine	12,122	17	4
Wool	255	24	0
Total	358,111	19	10

Statement showing the description and value of the merchandise exported from the consular district of Barmen (Prussia) for the year 1864:

	Thalers.	Grs.	Pfs.
Woollen cloths, cassimeres, &c.	1,211,762	23	8
Ribbons of all kinds, trimmings, tapes, and other small articles	1,678,708	29	11
Silk and half-silk goods, worsted, cotton, and mixed dress goods	358,289	11	7
Iron, steel, brass-ware, cutlery, needles, and other hardware	513,755	24	10
Buttons, button stuffs, and clasps	137,121	10	4
Dyestuffs, drugs, and bleaching powders	87,314	5	1
Nickel	45,562	16	8
Oil paintings	28,862	15	0
Cigars	1,400	0	0
Shoddy	4,091	8	11
Cologne water and wine	777	19	0
Dyed cotton yarn and hosiery	371	9	0
Hosiery	960	21	4
Books	1,319	3	8
Musical instruments	85	0	0
Looms	186	6	0
Pipes	98	20	0
Total	4,070,667	15	0

Of the above articles were exported by way of—

	Thalers.	Grs.	Pfs.
Amsterdam	673	14	0
Antwerp	147,540	27	3
Bremen	557,615	12	8
Hamburg	556,329	19	2
Havre	65,230	15	8
Liverpool	2,898,086	26	10
London	960	21	4
Rotterdam	43,502	17	5
Southampton	719	10	8
Total	4,070,667	15	0

Statement showing the description and value of merchandise exported from Crefeld to the United States during the year 1864.

	Thalers.	Grs.	Pfs.
Silk goods	414,344	28	4
Silk goods mixed with cotton, &c	373,353	24	5
Do. do. do.	231,547	0	1
Worsted goods	1,499	0	0
Worsted goods mixed with silk, &c	1,747	19	0
Cotton goods	1,673	20	0
Cotton goods mixed with silk, &c	1,920	18	3
Sundry woven goods	28,105	13	11
Liquors	4,176	0	0
Paper and manufactures of paper	4,885	0	0
Musical instruments	1,414	1	6
Chemical preparations	852	0	0
Manufactures of metal and sundries for church use....	1,634	16	0
Books and prints	186	17	0
Dolls and sundries	541	17	0
Total	1,067,881	25	6

Of which were exported by way of—

	Thalers.	Grs.	Pfs.
Havre, Havre to Southampton, and Havre to Liverpool..	831,535	16	1
Liverpool and Antwerp to Liverpool	25,054	11	8
Antwerp	78,047	29	0
Hamburg	49,103	26	0
Bremen	68,946	1	7
Altona	1,675	18	0
Not stated and Rotterdam	1,540	4	0
Total	1,055,903	16	4

BAVARIA.

NUREMBERG—C. GILBERT WHEELER, *Consul.*

SEPTEMBER 30, 1864.

The state of trade during the past year has been in the main very flourishing, and the general material condition of the entire kingdom may be said to be highly prosperous. Prices of labor are everywhere increased; opportunities for the profitable investment of capital are abundant; facilities of transportation have been improved; and last, but not least, Bavaria is gradually giving her citizens *liberty of trade.* For the last three or four years measures have been in operation having for their end the abolishing of the antiquated guild privileges, ("zureft-rechte,") which, though not the most speedy, are perhaps, on the whole, as judicious as any the government could have adopted. The sentiment of the Bavarian people, with the exception of a small and not entirely disinterested minority, is fully ripe for this important enlargement of their liberties, and the government would long before this have granted the most unrestrained freedom of trade but for the difficulty that presented itself with regard to the extinguishment of a certain class of privileges bearing a peculiar character. Their nature may be illustrated by the following: The sole right of carrying on the business of a cabinet-maker in a given district of the city has, for example, been given to A, who resides at No. 1 Main street. He, and after him his heirs, conduct the business for many years, which, increasing with the growth of the population of the district, becomes quite prosperous, perhaps, finally, to the extent that the heir-at-law, having acquired a competency, chooses to retire, and, removing to a finer part of the city, sells out the former residence, and with it the right of carrying on the cabinet business in that particular district, for the "right" (das realrecht) is inseparably connected with the house, and is sold and purchased with it; the value of the former being often far the greatest. The property is purchased by B, who is, however, without sufficient ready means to pay for the same, and at the same time provide himself with the necessary material to carry on the business. To obtain the latter he mortgages his right to C, whose security is, therefore, based upon the assumed market value of B's exclusive privilege to prosecute in a given district his occupation of cabinet-maker, and, of course, were the restrictions heretofore existing to be all at once removed and perfect liberty granted to any rival of B, who might wish to enter upon the same business within the district referred to, the security given by the latter to C would become quite worthless.

Unfortunately, there is in Bavaria an exceedingly large class of debtors and creditors, occupying to each the relationship represented by B and C in the above case, and the amount of capital therein involved is quite enormous. Though much more frequent in the southern part of the kingdom than here, yet they are more or less general in nearly all of the cities and towns; and in giving freedom of trade it was, therefore, necessary to provide for the extinguishment of these rights in such a manner as to prevent the ruin that would inevitably ensue to many thousands were this reform, unaccompanied by proper safeguards, to be at once generally introduced. The only method by which this desirable measure could be at once entered upon, without prejudice to the interests of so many, appeared to be by securing to the possessors of these exclusive privileges, which in course of centuries had come to have so great a value, indemnification by the government, the necessary means to be raised from general taxation. This method met with, however, much opposition; it was urged that these claims for indemnification, being of local interest, should be met by those only who would have derived a direct benefit by their adjustment. Why should the residents of Kof or Aschaffenburg be heavily taxed to lighten the burdens that would come upon the city of Munich because of the abolishment of their mediæval "zureft-rechte," and to whom their existence or non-existence could be of very little direct interest? Upon the whole, it appeared that in protecting the interests of one class those of another were in danger of being almost equally encroached upon, and the immediate introduction of freedom of trade seemed incompatible with a due regard to the interests of the whole people. The policy was, therefore, resolved upon which during three or four years has been in operation, and with very general satisfaction is rapidly attaining the desired result, and which consists in gradually, and with judicious care, lessening the exclusive character of the "zureft-rechte," having in view their entire extinguishment. For instance, in a given district where previously only a single baker might be permitted to establish himself, another is allowed to commence business; after the lapse of a year or two the permission is granted to still another, and thus it continues until, eventually, the trade of a baker is for the district in question entirely without the former restrictions. In like manner increased freedom is extended to other trades, until the district, and finally the whole city, enjoys the benefit of liberty of trade, and this is effected in so quiet and gradual a manner that the interests of the few are sacrificed but very slightly to the advantage of the many. In like manner other restrictions upon trade are being gradually removed. The cabinet-maker may now possess a turning lathe; may employ a wood-carver, and a varnisher and polisher, and thus, without infringing on the rights of other mechanics, is able to complete for use any article of furniture upon which he may be engaged. However, as yet, the barber cannot cut his customer's hair, nor may the hair-dresser, under penalty, wield the razor, and many like antiquated regulations still prevail, but by degrees they are being abolished. On the whole, in view of the many difficulties that render the undertaking an arduous one, the Bavarian government is introducing a most important internal reform in a manner that must be considered most sound and politic. Labor during the past few years has been in steadily increasing demand, and, though still as cheap or cheaper in Bavaria than in other German states, there is, nevertheless, abundant work for all, at prices much higher than formerly prevailing. This is particularly true in the consular district, in which are located a much larger share of the industrial interests of Bavaria than in the southern portion of the kingdom. Here mechanics in the cities obtain from 45 kreutzers to 1½ florin per day, and common laborers 30 kreutzers to 1 florin; in the country the latter are usually paid 30 to 42 kreutzers. These wages are 20 to 50 per cent. higher than those obtained five to ten years ago. This increase, together with the good harvests of late years, and the gradual introduction of free trade, has exercised a restraining influence upon emigration during the past three to ten years.

Since 1860 the war in the United States has naturally had a tendency to still further reduce the number of emigrants, as to the United States by far the largest number directed their steps, commonly 70 to 90 per cent. of the whole.

It should be stated that the administrative year in Bavaria ends with the 10th of September.

The state of commerce in this consulate has been very prosperous on the whole during the past year. The local trade receives due stimulus from the general good harvests of last year, and it, as well as the foreign trade, has been not a little benefited by the completion of new lines of railroad communication. Of new railroads there have been opened—

1. The line from Nördlingen to Stuttgart, which, though mainly a Wirtemburg road, is of great importance to this section, giving, as it does, direct railroad communication with Stuttgart, Strasburg, and Paris, instead of the former very circuitous route, via Augsburg and Ulm.

2. The line from Ansbach to Würzburg, opened last June, reducing the time from Munich to Frankfort-on-the-Main, via Gunzenhausen, by about two hours;

a further reduction of about one hour and a half is anticipated on completion of. the road from Munich to Gunzenhausen, *via* Ingolstadt, which is now being built.

3. The road from Nuremberg to Würzburg, which is just completed, and reduces from one and a half to two hours the time between these two cities, as also by the same amount the most direct route from Frankfort to Frankfort-on-the-Main and Cologne. This road is also important as connecting the two cities of Nuremberg and Fuerth, distance about three miles, having, as they do, more extensive manufacturing interests and greater foreign commerce than all other Bavarian cities combined. They are already connected by a railway in operation since 1835, the oldest, the poorest equipped, and at the same time the best paying in Germany, its stock ranging commonly from 300 to 350. Under these circumstances an opposition railway communication is to the business community of the two cities an undertaking most heartily welcomed.

4. Weiden to Millerteich, opened the 15th of August, to be extended to Eger, possibly to Carlsbad, next year.

A great depression has rested for months upon the minds of the business community in this portion of Bavaria, fearing, as there seemed good reason to, that the Zöllverein, which has been to Germany so great a blessing, would be dismembered; but two days since this incubus was removed, it having become known, though at the eleventh hour, that Bavaria had consented—last of all the participating states—to renew her previous relations.

Concerning the general trade of this consulate, other than with the United States, there can be no reliable statistical data obtained, though the writer had made the most strenuous endeavors to this end; the government has none, and makes no provision for collecting any. From the chambers of commerce in the various cities only general information may be obtained—figures few or none; the substance of what they have to offer is herewith given.

Exportation to England, for home consumption, has been less than ordinary the past year, owing to the loss of employment of so large a proportion of the working classes, who are the principal consumers of Bavarian manufactures, while the business *through* England to the East Indies has greatly increased. To France exportations have been small on account of high duty, while to Spain, but particularly to Italy, they have been very large; this is also the case with regard to the Orient. Commerce with Russia has suffered somewhat, owing to the difficulties in Poland and the state of Russian finance.

To the United States the exportations have been very large during the first nine months of the year now closing—very nearly or quite equalling with some articles the amount exported previous to the war.

At the commencement of the present quarter the business began rapidly to diminish, in consequence of the high rate of exchange and increased duties, until at the present it is quite at a standstill.

· Subjoined are tables of exports during the several quarters of the entire year, and, for comparison, also of last year. Details concerning the various classes of goods are added, as it would seem that such have never been transmitted from this office.

Comparative statement showing the description, quantity, and value of the exports from Nuremberg consular district to the United States during the several quarters of the year ended September 30, 1864.

QUARTER ENDED DECEMBER 31, 1863.

To—	Looking-glass plates.	Toys and fancy goods.	Cloths.	Lead pencils.	Bronze powder, Dutch and silver leaf metal.	Baskets.	Hosiery.	Drugs and paints.	Lithographic stones.	Sundries.	Total florins.
New York	161,573 94	109,068 50	28,847 09	44,663 13	55,539 38	32,149 19		8,534 38		21,458 00	464,854 11
San o.		27,197 46								44,174 09	71,371 55
Philadelphia	10,004 34	5,050 50								2,617 09	8,362 98
Baltimore		2,643 59		560 45	228 12	260 00				502 12	4,199 08
Cincinnati	1,206 59	2,161 36	1,011 03		412 00	2,733 51				17,105 07	24,630 59
Boston										3,293 53	3,293 53
Chicago						1,570 06					1,570 06
St. Louis		1,510 55									1,510 55
New Orleans										149 41	149 41
ther os										1,155 59	1,155 59
Total florins	172,814 50	140,653 36	29,858 12	45,243 58	56,183 50	37,403 11		8,534 38		90,456 10	591,128 45

QUARTER ENDED MARCH 31, 1864.

To—	Exiting-glass plates.	Toys and fancy goods.	Cloths.	Lead pencils.	Bronze powder, Dutch and silver leaf metal.	Baskets.	Hosiery.	Drugs and paints.	Lithographic stones.	Sundries.	Total florins.
New York	135,809 06	102,814 24	65,048 37	45,431 02	50,294 25	44,512 53		6,027 23		16,926 16	467,940 01
San Francisco	2,937 49	6,057 49	960 41			727 97	13,253 09	942 05		17,885 53	43,064 53
Philadelphia	13,402 16	5,335 26		463 87		5,704 19				405 25	25,350 53
Baltimore				1,139 05							473 92
Cincinnati	928 33	356 16	11,438 50	1,157 00	647 37	6,457 14		314 17		187 09	21,372 41
Boston		3,497 96	795 50			3,006 59				1,956 32	3,226 07
Chicago		2,787 41	468 17			14,373 09					17,619 07
St. Louis											
New Glass		250 43									250 43
ther] ass									375 55	473 90	473 90
Total florins	152,377 44	121,315 45	78,705 54	48,230 34	50,942 09	74,782 01	13,253 09	7,283 45	375 55	37,814 28	585,081 17

Comparative statement showing the description, quantity, and value of the exports, &c.—Continued.

QUARTER ENDED JUNE 30, 1864.

To—	Looking-glass plates.	Toys and fancy goods.	Cloths.	Lead pencils.	Bronze powder, Dutch and silver leaf metal.	Baskets.	Hosiery.	Drugs and paints.	Lithograph stones.	Sundries.	Total florins.
New York	216,980 30	111,713 58	104,576 49	44,556 58	57,224 23	40,821 43		9,801 49	3,434 25	13,099 58	602,210 30
San Francisco	2,646 00	30,094 23			1,028 14	5,514 05		3,158 45		11,459 56	53,901 22
Philadelphia	14,650 23	21,093 58		797 15		6,009 30				7,293 23	50,654 29
Baltimore		23,017 50		401 33		1,718 02					25,137 25
Cincinnati	17,769 39	9,029 38				8,639 28					46,004 56
Boston		11,991 54	5,843 51		647 36	13,876 04	3,774 25			100 19	13,111 55
Chicago		11,989 30								1,130 01	13,139 34
St. Louis		4,745 23									25,745 23
New Orleans	453 00					767 23					4,250 23
Other places		5,362 07	2,100 00			646 80				3,480 39	11,589 06
Total florins	252,529 32	229,121 40	112,520 33	45,755 46	58,900 23	78,199 35	3,774 25	12,960 34	3,434 25	36,554 10	833,744 03

QUARTER ENDED SEPTEMBER 30, 1864.

To—	Looking-glass plates.	Toys and fancy goods.	Cloths.	Lead pencils.	Bronze powder, Dutch and silver leaf metal.	Baskets.	Hosiery.	Drugs and paints.	Lithograph stones.	Sundries.	Total florins.
New York	70,879 00	48,527 13	8,268 49	30,358 17	42,843 31	17,899 13		8,521 14	676 26	10,106 53	328,083 06
San Francisco	4,776 24	19,052 42	6,895 22	1,022 30		2,431 53				12,777 59	46,956 43
Philadelphia	6,719 11	3,819 59		320 24		119 02				1,098 24	12,070 00
Baltimore		2,971 29		377 29							3,348 58
Cincinnati			1,250 03								3,900 98
Boston		1,753 48	634 15		647 36	1,302 47					3,090 31
Chicago		11,677 30				1,908 43				197 00	17,311 05
St. Louis						4,999 80					
New Orleans		3,069 13									3,069 13
Other places		7,950 12				251 00	1,831 00			3,746 18	13,778 30
Total florins	82,374 35	98,815 06	17,048 29	32,078 38	43,490 67	28,212 58	1,831 00	8,534 14	676 26	27,855 57	340,908 30

Comparative statement showing the description, quantity, and value of the exports from Nuremberg consular district to the United States during the years ended September 30, 1863 and 1864.

YEAR ENDED SEPTEMBER 30, 1863.

To—	Looking-glass plates.	Toys and fancy goods.	Cloths.	Lead pencils.	Drugs and paints.	Dutch leaf metal and bronze powder.	Sundries.	Total florins.
New York	478,396 11	130,534 47	110,559 30	117,467 30	6,489 48	87,146 33	35,566 52	966,094 11
San Francisco	2,467 30	27,233 37	4,346 06		1,600 65		32,544 14	68,182 23
Philadelphia	32,048 34	10,680 34	769 30	996 27			11,294 26	55,699 40
Baltimore	13,162 35	1,954 13	856 30			412 00	16,978 34	33,572 50
Cincinnati		6,399 58	2,394 94				2,362 27	8,691 04
Chicago		6,067 18		1,279 53				7,885 18
St. Lis		5,690 52				1,218 00		7,690 52
New Orleans		476 35						5,476 05
Other places		4,289 33	356 57				1,559 00	5,849 05
Total florins	586,074 50	198,885 49	119,315 57	119,743 50	8,090 44	88,763 33	99,514 03	160,401 49

YEAR ENDED SEPTEMBER 30, 1864.

To—	Looking-glass plates.	Toys and fancy goods.	Cloths.	Lead pencils.	Baskets.	Drugs and paints.	Hosiery.	Dutch leaf metal and bronze powder.	Lithograph stones.	Sundries.	Total florins.
New York	583,249 00	365,134 95	206,741 17	165,099 30	135,373 08	22,889 04		205,909 07	4,486 46	61,590 31	1,767,377 48
San Francisco	9,660 13	82,402 39	7,856 03	1,092 80	8,673 25	4,100 50	13,253 09	1,028 14		26,297 50	214,594 53
Philadelphia	4,966 34	36,123 13		1,691 36	12,592 46					11,415 21	106,469 50
Baltimore		5823 18	19,543 56	9,498 02	1,978 02	314 17		529 12		502 12	34,948 51
Cincinnati		11,747 30	495 20	1,157 00	19,333 20		3,774 25	2,334 49		17,399 48	95,908 52
Boston	1985 34	17,943 08	1,096 32		916 49					6,477 26	98,732 36
Chicago		2941			34,818 39						62,638 52
St. Louis		6,256 18								149 41	6,256 18
New Orleans	183 00	3,319 56			767 53		1,813 00			856 16	4,720 00
Other places		13,312 19			897 20						24,878 55
Total florins	660,096 41	590,976 27	236,033 08	171,308 56	218,580 45	37,303 11	18,840 34	209,517 92	4,486 46	192,689 05	2,339,925 55

Looking-glass plate.—Nine-tenths of the glass exported from this consulate comes from Fuerth, the balance chiefly from this city, with a small quantity from Erlangen.

Reliable statistics, later than 1857, with regard to this branch of manufacture in Fuerth, are not to be obtained. However, though it has expanded somewhat since that time, yet the statistics of that year are not very far from expressing its present state, and I therefore take the liberty of subjoining them, previously, however, giving some general statements with reference to the same.

The glass used is chiefly blown glass, and is ground, polished, silvered, and framed in Fuerth, being obtained in its rough state from the Bavarian forest on the borders of Bohemia, where it is made on a very extensive scale. Considerable quantities of cast glass are also imported from Belgium, but it is chiefly looking-glass. plates made from blown glass that are shipped to the United States, and principally small sizes—thirty-six by twenty inches is most commonly the maximum.

The glass as delivered from the furnace in the Bavarian forest has a rough wavy surface, and is, on that account, not transparent. At Fuerth and vicinity it is ground, polished, and silvered for transportation beyond the sea; the plates are not framed. The grinding and polishing are effected by water-power mainly, though the last finish is performed by hand. It is the comparatively slight expenditure at this stage of preparation that enables the exporters in Fuerth successfully to compete, as to price in foreign markets, with the Belgium manufacturers, who grind and polish by steam-power.

The mercury used in silvering is mostly questrian from Idria, though Spanish is sometimes employed. The average price is 150 florins per cwt. Bavarian, (123.5 lbs. English;) at least 1,200 to 1,400 cwt. are used per year, necessitating an outlay of 180,000 to 200,000 florins.

The tinfoil is for the most part manufactured in Nuremberg and Erlangen. The price varies with the width, but at the lowest calculation at least 335,000 to 375,000 florins' worth is used annually. Silver instead of mercury, as a reflecting surface in the mirrors, is made use of only at Erlangen, and but in a single factory. The glass dealers in Fuerth and adjacent towns employ about 3,000 persons, and bring their manufactures into the market as follows :

I. Ground and polished glass, but unsilvered, for window glass, for photographers, &c.
II. Silvered, but not framed.
III. Silvered and framed.

The first is sometimes exported to the United States; the third never.

	Florins.
Amount of first produced	1,800,000
Amount of second produced	500,000
Amount of third produced	490,000
Total	2,790,000

Of this total, one-third is exported to America—United States, West Indies, Brazil, &c.; one-third to the Orient and Spain, Italy, North Africa, Denmark, Sweden, and Norway; and one-third to different states of the Zollverein. It will be seen by the table that the exports of looking-glass plates to the United States, for the year just closed, amounted, as shown by invoices authenticated at this office, to 660,096 florins and 41 kreutzers; and as there is satisfactory reason for believing that the exportations in this branch have been nearly as large as previous to the rebellion, it is not too high an estimate if the annual export to the United States, under ordinary circumstances, be stated at 700,000 florins.

Toys and fancy goods.—Of the former, those of metal and papier-mache are made in Nuremberg and Fuerth, while other toys, at least those carved out of wood, are chiefly the work of the peasants, particularly of those inhabiting the forests where material is abundant. There are no large factories, but the work is performed at home, and shared by all members of the family. In any one household but a few varieties are made, often only a single one from year to year. The tools used are but few and simple, and there prevails a general aversion to such improvements in style and utility as may make necessary any considerable outlay for additional ones. Excessive cheapness is mainly aimed at in the production of the so-called "Nuremberg toys;" and in this characteristic they are surpassed by no others, though there is commonly more taste displayed in those of the Paris manufactures, and the latter are more and more becoming successful competitors with those of this city in foreign markets. Also, in the United States, particularly in Connecticut, there are now many extensive manufactories of such toys as can be made of sheet-tin, which, by the introduction of labor-saving machinery, furnish wares of such excellent quality and moderate price as very largely to prevent the importation of this class of toys from Germany.

Yet Nuremberg maintains its ancient reputation in most departments, at least, as the toy-shop of the world, and particularly in the manufacture of children's games, of optical, mathematical, and musical toys.

The manufacture of fancy goods is principally carried on in Nuremberg, and is very extensive. Almost every imaginable article coming under this head, whether of metal, wood, ivory, bone, horn, or glass, is manufactured in this city. There are over a thousand varieties, and to go into especial details with regard to this branch would be too tedious. Here, also, the inexpensive character of the goods produced is the more especial recommendation. Vienna, Paris, and Birmingham are the chief competitors of Nuremberg in the European market.

The communication between the manufacturers of Nuremberg toys and fancy goods and the foreign purchaser is almost invariably through the medium of commission houses or brokers, who receive the orders, distribute the same among the various manufacturers, and collect, pack, and ship the goods, as soon as they are ready, there being no stock on hand. For their service they make a charge of from 3 to 10 per cent. Three months is the usual credit given.

Cloths.—Woollen and half woollen, from the Voightland, the northeastern corner of Bavaria, bordering on Saxony. The goods are similar to those produced in the latter country, and are exported largely to the United States from the towns of Hofgrafengehaig and Munchberg.

Baskets, chiefly willow, have rapidly attained to a very prominent position among the exports from this district. Lichtenfels and Hochstadt are the principal centres of this branch of manufacture, in which there is an almost endless variety; though ladies' fancy baskets are most largely exported. The willow is obtained in the vicinity, partially, though a very considerable quantity is imported from Prussia.

The basket-makers of Bavaria compete very successfully with those of France in foreign markets, and besides to the United States, export also very largely to Great Britain. As in the manufacture of toys, so here also the workmen are mostly the peasants. In the neighborhood of Lichtenfels and Hochstadt about 10,000 persons are employed in this branch.

Bronze powder, Dutch and silver leaf.—The exportation of that article is confined to the cities of Nuremberg and Fuerth, which produce a very large proportion of the entire amount consumed upon the continent, besides exporting largely to all parts of the world. The silver leaf exported to the United States is chiefly used for coating picture and mirror frames, the latter of which afterwards, on receiving an application of suitable varnish, have much the appearance of gilded frames. Genuine gold leaf is also extensively manufactured here, though but little exported to the United States.

Lead pencils.—This branch of manufacture is one of the most important in Nuremberg, and that which, above all others, is characteristic of this city. To merely mention the names of some of the leading manufacturers, is all that is necessary to give evidence of the very general distribution through all lands of this product of Nuremberg industry.

There are here and in the vicinity, Stein and Fuerth, twenty lead-pencil manufactories, employing 5,000 persons; about two million gross are made annually, having a value of four million florins. In quality, they vary from "Faber's best," made from Siberian graphite, to the commonest, having a price of half a florin (twenty cents) a gross. The graphite comes mostly from Passau and Siberia; the Siberian is by far the best, and has a value in its unprepared state of 1,000 florins per cwt.

The cedar came, previous to the present rebellion, exclusively from Florida. This source of supply cut off by the war, the price has risen as the stock became exhausted, until a few weeks ago it stood over 100 per cent. higher than that prevailing in 1861. Cedar is commonly bought and sold here by the cwt., which is usually about three cubic feet. Under ordinary circumstances the price is about twelve florins per cwt. At present there is no Florida cedar in market, and scarcely any of the manufacturers have a supply for more than a month or two. What they will do when this is exhausted cannot now be determined. The high price has caused several attempts to be made to imitate cedar by coloring other woods, and in a communication last spring I had the honor of giving a somewhat detailed account of a large factory established here last winter for he purpose of the treatment of the common timber of the country to give it the appearance of cedar and other valuable woods. As yet this and other imitation cedars have not been generally used by the pencil manufacturers.

Extensive search has been instigated in almost every land for the purpose of finding a substitute for the Florida cedar, but as yet without satisfactory results. There appears to be nowhere in the world a wood so well adapted for pencils. Considerable quantities of cedar have been imported from Tennessee, but the quality has been found too poor to make its employment profitable.

The greater cost of manufacturing consequent upon the insufficient supply of cedar wood, and more particularly the high rate of duty upon lead pencils, has prevented for the past year the exportation to the United States of the very large quantities of lead pencils, formerly sent thither. Only the better qualities are now sent, inasmuch as the cheaper ones could not bear with profit the payment of one dollar per gross duty for this kind of goods; it acts as an entirely prohibitory tariff.

One of the largest manufactories here has, however, established a factory in New York, and ships there large quantities of prepared leads for the same. Leads for pencils are also sent from other houses here.

Drugs and paints.—From 100,000 to 150,000 florins' worth of vegetable medicines and coloring substances, the latter used in the United States are annually collected in the vicinity of Nuremberg. The exportation to the United States in this line amounted during the last year to about 20,000 florins.

Considerable quantities are also exported to other countries, as several of the vegetable substances here collected are found nowhere else.

The paints are mostly ultramarine and vermillion; the former was here discovered, and since 1840 extensively manufactured. One manufactory, the largest in Europe, employs 200 to 250 workmen, and produces 15,000 to 20,000 cwt. annually, worth 500,000 to 700,000 florins.

Hosiery is principally from the "Voightland"—woollen and cotton—and in the United States is exported mainly to California.

Lithographic stones are from the famous quarries of Solenhofen, producing stones superior for lithographic purposes to any other in the world. Here they find application also as table tops for silvering-tables in looking-glass manufactories; they are much liked for flooring, and the very thin slabs are used instead of slate for roofing. During the past two years but small quantities of lithographic stones have been exported to the United States, the market having been previously overstocked.

FRANKFORT-ON-THE-MAIN—WILLIAM W. MURPHEY, *Consul.*

FEBRUARY 10, 1864.

I have the honor of reporting that the usury laws hitherto in force in this city were repealed on the 2d of this month, and a new law of interest enacted instead; of which the following is a faithful translation:

Law relating to interest.

We, the burgomaster and council of the free city of Frankfort, hereby ordain, in pursuance of a decree of the legislative body of the 20th of January, 1864, as follows:

SECTION I. The legal restrictions on rates of interest agreed on are withdrawn.

SEC. II. The maximum legal interest, especially back interest, shall be six per cent. per annum.

SEC. III. If there is a fixed day for demand of payment the creditor shall be entitled, with or without agreement, on warning, to claim back interest from the day on which the debt became due.

SEC. IV. The provisions of article 291 of the code of commercial law, that— 1. Any person having a surplus due to him at the close of the account is entitled to claim interest on the whole amount, and also on the interest due on it from the day of closing the account; and, 2. The close of the account takes place once a year, unless otherwise agreed on—are applicable in every case in which there is a running account (account current) between the parties.

SEC. V. Interest on arrears of interest, with the exception of the case provided for in section 4, shall only be exacted—

(*a.*) Where an agreement has been made to that effect.

(*b.*) In a legal suit, out of the interest in dispute, from the day of the commencement of the suit; and in the case of *a*, at the rate agreed on; in the case of *b*, at the legal rate of interest, even though a lower rate may have been agreed on.

SEC. VI. The aggregate amount of interest may exceed the principal.

SEC. VII. Claims for arrears of interest, and for interest on interest, lapse after a period of five years.

The period of limitation commences from the expiration of the 31st day of December of the year immediately following the day fixed for payment, and if no particular day has been fixed for payment, then from the expiration of the 31st day of December of the year in which the demand has been made.

In claims for interest which may be already due at the time of the promulgation of this law, the period of limitation is to be calculated from expiration of the 31st of December, 1864.

Should, however, the period of limitation be completed earlier, by the previous laws, it shall abide by the same.

Done, at our meeting of council, this second day of February, one thousand eight hundred and sixty-four.

MARCH 17, 1864.

Having just received the official tabular statements of the statistics of commerce of the free city of Lubeck for the year 1863, I hasten to transmit an extract of them, with two tables, marked A and B.

Although the direct maritime communication between Lubeck and the United States is, of course, very limited at present, I think it desirable to furnish a report at once, and to direct the immediate attention of the department to the commercial activity of that little republic, as it may become of some importance to the United States if the Dano-German war is continued, or perhaps extended.   *   *   *   *   *   *

The transatlantic cargoes destined for Hamburg would then, probably, be ordered to Lubeck, and the shipments from Hamburg to America be made also from Lubeck, which would thus obtain a lively and direct intercourse with the United States.

As regards the maritime traffic of Lubeck in 1863, which was chiefly with Russia, Sweden, Norway, and Denmark, it may be stated to have improved, although no particularly propitious influences have been exercised on it, and the troubles which have arisen in the Polish provinces of Russia and unfavorable harvests in a part of Finland might rather be said to have had a prejudicial effect. The staple articles of northern trade—timber, wares, tar, and pitch—have especially sought a market in Lubeck, and the necessity for increased warehousing accommodations has become more pressing as the contemplated extension of railway communication will give a still greater impulse to trade in these articles, and promises to open new markets for the northern timber, and wares in particular. The arrangement for crossing the Elbe at Lunenberg, which has been delayed by so many circumstances, is now so far completed that the communication may be expected to be opened shortly. The works commenced last spring on the Lubeck and Hamburg railway line have also made rapid progress, and if not trammelled by the prevailing political complications, we may hope to see this important line of communication, between the German ocean and the Baltic established by the end of this year. The plan undertaken by English promoters in consequence of these new communications, of a railway from Lubeck to Kleinen, having obtained the requisite concession from all the governments interested in it, is also soon to be realized. When carried into effect it will not only afford considerable facility for the traffic of Lubeck and Hamburg with the neighboring state of Mechlenberg, but will also establish a direct tramway communication with the further railway branches projected along the whole of the German sea-coast, as Russia, and thus prove to be of great advantage to the transit traffic.

As regards navigation, the greater number of Lubeck vessels were, as usual, employed in foreign voyages. Only a small number of sailing vessels can be used for the Baltic, so much merchandise falling to the share of the numerous steamers which navigate it from Lubeck. Two vessels from thence were unfortunately wrecked and sold; two sailing vessels, also, and three steamers, found purchasers to England, Hamburg, and Rostock. The number of vessels entered again exceeds that of the preceding year by about 50, with about 3,200 freights, as appears from the annexed list, marked A.

The number of sailing and steam vessels that arrived this year was

1,302, with 91,644 cargoes, (at 4,000 lbs.)

against 1862 .... 1,251 " 88,437 "   "
        1861 .... 1,074 " 85,975 "   "
        1860 .... 1,134 " 83,455 "
        1859 .... 1,056 " 79,086 "
exclusive of open coasting vessels.

The two steamboats employed for some years past in foreign navigation, and belonging to the St. Petersburg and Lubeck Steam Packet Company, have this year been engaged in navigation from Lubeck, the company having sold two boats to England. Riga had also one boat in regular employ, that company, too, having sold one boat to England. Almost all the steamers from Lubeck obtained good cargoes, and had to make many additional voyages in the autumn in order to convey the goods. The steam navigation traffic was carried on this year by five steam vessels, to and from Petersburg, of 103, 115¼, 135, and 170¼ loads, respectively; one steam vessel, to and from Riga, of 85½ loads; one steam vessel, to and from Helsingfors and Revel, of 145 loads; two steam vessels, to and from Stockholm, Calinar, and Ystad, 196½ and 247½ loads; two steam vessels, to and from Stockholm, Varrkoping, Calinar, and Ystad, 167½ and 129 loads; one steam vessel to and from Stockholm, Gefle, and Sundsvall, 184 loads; one steam vessel, to and from Athens, Solvesberg, Carlshamn, Carlscrona, and Westervik, 81¼ loads; one steam vessel, to and from Copenhagen and Malmo, 81¼ loads; two steam vessels, to and from Copenhagen, Helsingborg, Halinstadt, and Gottenburg, 72½, 85½, and 89½ loads; one steam vessel to and from Holstein ports, 35 loads; one steam vessel, to and from Hull, 122¼ loads. Many steamboat communications took place also in the course of the year with other trading places.

The traffic of the Lubeck and Buchen railway has considerably increased again this year, and the transport of goods was about 10 per cent. increase on the preceding year. The receipts show a surplus of 18,000 thalers.

The transport of goods in the year 1863 amounted to about 2,056,627 quintals
against 1862... 1,853,680 "
      1861... 1,699,645 "
      1860... 1,778,139 "
      1859... 1,745,809 "

The total receipts for passengers and goods were—
      in 1863............................about per cr. 219,781 thalers,
against 1862............................. " 201,781
      1861............................. " 195,231
      1860............................. 200,618
      1859............................. " 191,875

The harvest this year, as last year, was a good one, and in seed a very rich one; and the farmer, notwithstanding declining prices, was able to obtain satisfactory remuneration for his husbandry, while the results of trade in those articles were, in Lubeck as elsewhere, sad enough, and it was thought favorable even if there was no loss.

The decrease in imports of rye and oats by sea is worthy of remark, because just at that time there was less need of them, while those of wheat and seed steadily increased. The latter, indeed, consisted, for the most part, only of transit shipments from Holstein ports, which either go by Lubeck and Hamburg to the German ocean, or else remain in Hamburg.

Prices, especially since American exportation in proportion to its flourishing state in late years is at a minimum, have now reached a standard below which they can hardly be expected to fall further; at the close of the year they marked
Wheat, 128 lbs. Dutch.................................. 116 rix thalers.
Rye, 123 lbs. Dutch..................................... 84 "
Barley... 74 "
Oats... 64 ..
Peas, for cooking.................................... 96 ..
Peas, for feed... 84 ..
Buckwheat... 76 ..
the stock on hand being considerable.

H. Ex. Doc. 60——32

Amount of imports.

	Wheat.	Rye.	Barley.	Oats.	Buckwh't.	Peas.	Vetch.	Rape.	Total.
By land carriage, about.	54,163	21,834	6,843	10,862	1,820	3,078	1,787	14,018	166,905 ag't 134,065 in 1862.
By boats, about........	18,000	3,000	1,000	....	....	....	500	30,000	49,614 ag't
By sea, about..........	13,833	5,311	9,478	2,258	....	2,376	....	16,358	109,595 in 1862.
Total........	85,996	30,145	17,321	13,120	1,820	5,454	2,287	60,376	216,519
Against 1862........	76,234	56,406	18,576	29,498	2,417	9,182	1,179	50,168	243,660

Lübeck has a steam corn-mill, on which the unfavorable course of commercial business this year exercised an injurious influence, and even when it was in constant activity the business was not sufficient to develop its full power. The consignments outwards have further increased in extent and are still kept up during the continuance of open water.

The amount of timber wares from Sweden and Finland is more particularly stated in table marked B, from which it may be seen that a considerably larger quantity of boards and planks, viz., about 42,000 dozen more, is quoted than in the preceding year. Of beams and spars there were about 9,500 fewer; on the other hand, of laths a quantity double that of the preceding year. The decrease in beams and spars was chiefly in the North Swedish sorts, of which large stores were still lying in the warehouses in spring. The sale maintained itself during the spring, summer, and beginning of autumn, till perhaps the early part of November; but in the middle of November a serious stagnation took place, which constantly increased till the close of the year, so that finally the sale fell to zero. This was to be accounted for, probably, by the pending solution of the Schleswig and Holstein question, and by the uncertainty, even, of the most immediate prospects. The demand for Schleswig, Holstein, and Lunenburg had almost entirely ceased during the last two months of the year. The condition of the warehouses at the end of the year was not essentially better than on the 31st December of the preceding year. The demands in the course of the year were for Hamburg, Altona, Mecklenburg, Lunenburg, Holstein, Schleswig, Denmark, Hanover and Bremen. The consumption in the city itself and the immediate vicinity has decreased, if not considerably, at least in some degree, in comparison with the year before; but on the other hand a quantity of goods went off to the earthworks of the Lubeck and Hamburg railway line. The present state of political affairs does not allow me to form an approximatively correct judgment of the prospects for trade next year. The imports of 1863 consisted of about 139,000 dozen boards and planks against 1862, about .... 96,200 dozen.

  1861, about .... 93,400 "

  1860, about .... 114,350 "

Further, in 1863 of about 46,000 beams and spars—

against 1862, about..................................... 56,465

  1861, about 60,385

  1860, about 52,740

In 1863 of about .... 105,000 laths.

ag'nst 1862 of about .... 54,817 "

  1861 of about .... 117,250 "

  1860 of about .... 72,000 "

The stock of Russian hemp-oil on the 1st of January, 1863, was about 680 casks. In January of this year the price was about 35½ to 36 marcs, at which many sales were realized, and as there arose a heavy demand, especially for Holstein, the price rose, and as early as February the quotation was 37 marcs per 100 pounds, and in March rose to 38 marcs, at which price some good sales took place. In April and May owners sent away large quantities, and the stock was considerably diminished; in the middle of May 40 marcs per 100 pounds were asked, at which price, however, only small quantities were taken. In the beginning of June the warehouses were completely cleared. The article had reached such a high price in Russia that it was impossible for Lubeck to draw it from thence, and in the latter half of the year it had to be supplied mostly by linseed oil, although that had also risen to a high price both in Russia and in England; only at the close of the year was a small quantity of hemp-oil received from Petersburg, which was eagerly bought upon its arrival. The quotation for the small stock is 40 to 41 marcs per 100 pounds.

Stock on hand 1st January, 1863, was about	680 casks.
Import in 1863 amounted to about.........................	200 "
Against 1862 about.......................................	2,538 "
Against 1861 about.......................................	1,384 ..

The stock on the 31st December, 1863, was about 50,000 pounds.

Of rapeseed oil the mill produced this year about.........	450,000 pounds.
Against 1862 about..................................	500,000 "
Against 1861 about..................................	450,000 "

which was partly bought up in its raw state, and partly refined for home consumption.

Of rapeseed cake the mill produced about 360 tons, of which 280 tons were shipped off, and the rest bought for home consumption.

The small stock of linseed oil of the beginning of the year was cleared in the course of January and February at 35½ and 36 marcs per 100 pounds:

In contrast of the preceding year, people were this last year recommended to make their stock from England, as the prices in Petersburg and Riga returned only by the autumn, and one single importation was produced from Flushing by a higher price agreed on.

The following course of the English market prices rose in the course of the summer to 40 and 41 marcs ct. per 100 pounds, at which unimportant sales were made. In autumn, naturally, a reaction took place, and English linseed oil fell to 34 marcs ct. per 100 pounds. By the close of the year, however, the article became more firm again, and owners are no longer willing to take low prices.

The imports in 1863 amounted (from Hull) to about	230 casks.
From Riga and Petersburg about........................	130 "
Stock on 31st December, 1863, about...................	100,000 pounds.

At the very beginning of the year a brisk demand arose, and considerable purchases were made at 22¼ and 22½ marcs per 100 pounds. This price maintained itself almost until summer, and both by important shipments and purchases the warehouses were pretty well cleared by the time the new supplies arrived. In July the price became more moderate, and there were purchases to some extent. In August, September, and October, again, there was much done at 22 and 22½ marcs per 100 pounds; considerable sales were made in November at advanced prices, as it happened that the importation was so far short of that of the preceding year, and large quantities were taken at 23, 23½, 24, and 24½ marcs per 100 pounds. The fixed price asked now is 24¾ to 25, and even at these prices no large quantity could be obtained.

The stock on the 1st January, 1863, was about.............. 1,300 casks·
Importation in the year 1863............................ 1,641 "
Against 1862 about..................................... 2,900 " ·
    1861 about...................................... 1,463 "
    1860 about...................................... 1,686 "
Stock on the 31st December, 1863, about................. 750 "

Of Finland potash no stock was carried over from the preceding year. The importation was larger this year than the last, and supplies were all taken up immediately on their arrival. At first 22 marcs and something more was paid, but later only 21 marcs 10 batzens were to be obtained, and in October prices were had at 21 marcs 8 batzens.

The importation in 1863 was about.......................... 497 casks.
Against 1862 about.................................... 164 "
    1861 about....................................... 236 "
    1860 about....................................... 733 "
Stock on 31st December, 1863, about....................... 50 "

Yellow Russian tallow for candles : Stock on 1st January, 1863, about 400 casks. The demand was slack during the whole of the year, and only moderate sales were made; only single casks went off at 37 to 38 marcs per 100 pounds, and in May prices were to be had at 35 marcs per 100 pounds. In summer the market was exceedingly flat, and it was only towards the end of September that some important business was done at 34 marcs 8 batzens per 100 pounds. The price asked now is 35 to 36 marcs.

Of Petersburg soap tallow there is only a very small stock, which is also at about 35 marcs per 100 pounds.

The stock on 1st January, 1863, was about................. 400 casks.
The importation this year amounted to about................ 667 "
Against 1862 about..................................... 1,205 "
    1861 about...................................... 1,058 "
    1860 about...................................... 1,125 "
Stock on 31st December, 1863, about...................... 360 "

St. Petersburg and Riga hemp : Stock on 1st January, 1863, was about 980,000 pounds. The position of this article is not only good, but it has even partially surpassed the expectations formed of it. Successively rising prices in Russia combined with the gradual improvement in Russian value, which latter, however, retrograded considerably at the close of navigation in November, had produced an essential improvement in the price of hemp. The sale in Lubeck was satisfactory, and whatever good samples came into the market till September found purchasers immediately. When the prices in Russia rose still higher, the Lubeck dealers thought they had sufficient stock, and even at those prices had no great confidence. In consequence imports almost wholly ceased for some time, and it was not until nearly the close of navigation that some single lots were again brought in from St. Petersburg and Riga. In the present state of politics it is impossible to hazard a conjecture on the probable amount of business of the coming year.

Quotations on the 31st December, 1863, were—

Petersburg best hemp.................. 36 to 37 marcs per 100 pounds.
Petersburg refuse .... 34½ to 35 " "
Petersburg second quality.............. 31½ to 33½ " "
Riga, best quality..................... 36½ to 37½ " "
Fine Riga, best quality................ 38½ to 39 " "
Fine Riga, refuse..................... 36 to 36½ " "

Fine Riga, refuse	$37\frac{1}{2}$ to 38	marcs per 100 pounds.
Riga pass hemp	$35\frac{1}{2}$ to 36	" "
Fine pass hemp	$36\frac{1}{2}$ to 37	" "
Riga long black pass hemp	$35\frac{1}{2}$ to 36	" "
Riga, common sort	34 to 35	" "

The stock on the 1st January, 1863, was about	980,000 pounds.
Importation in the year 1863 amounted to (from Petersburg) about	1,500,000 "
Against 1862 about	1,000,000 "
1861 about	1,200,000 "
1860 about	1,112,000 "

Importation from Riga about	1,800,000 pounds.
Against 1862 about	2,000,000 "
1861 about	2,200,000 "
1860 about	2,000,000 "
Stock (of all sorts) on 31st December, 1863, about	950,000 "

Of Swedish iron, the stock on 1st January amounted to about 1,200,000 pounds. It was almost exclusively in the hands of Lubeck dealers, who have a considerable sale to Mecklenburg, the Holstein and Lunenburg country, Hamburg, &c. Owing to the war in America the supply to that country was sensibly affected. The quantity stated below was chiefly imported from Stockholm, and but little was sent from the other Swedish ports. During the whole of the year prices have changed very little, and at the present quotation of $9\frac{1}{2}$ marcs per 100 pounds several holders are not in the market, as they are of opinion that Swedish iron, in consequence of the rise in English, will also advance.

Stock on 1st January, 1863, was about	1,200,000 pounds.
Imports of this year were about	8,000,000 "
Against 1862 about	6,650,000 "
1861 about	6,000,000 "
1860 about	7,000,000 "
Stock on 31st December, 1863, about	2,200,000 "

Of English iron, the stock on 1st January was about 2,200,000 pounds. This year as well as last year the article was all appropriated to Lubeck dealers, who sold their stock to the forges of the place or those of the neighboring country. In the course of the year iron rose in England about 30 per centum, and Lubeck holders kept pace with those prices. At the end of the preceding year the quotation was $6\frac{1}{2}$ marcs per 100 pounds, and is now 8 marcs per 100 pounds.

Stock on 1st January, 1863, was about	1,200,000 pounds.
Imports this year about	2,600,000 "
Against 1862 about	1,800,000 "
1861 about	1,400,000 "
1860 about	1,500,000 "
Stock on 31st December, 1863, about	2,400,000 "

Of tar, which is a principal article of traffic in Lubeck, the stock on the 1st January, 1863, was about 26,100.1 and 4,850.2 tons. Owing to the large stock in warehouse at the close of the year prices were nominal, and the value per ton for their middling and thick was quoted at $21\frac{1}{2}$, 21, and $20\frac{1}{4}$ marcs per ton. In the middle of January there was a demand for Holland, and at the same time from Hamburg and London for Italy, in consequence of which a few thousand tons were bought at the price of 20 marcs per ton, and shipped partly direct and partly by Hamburg. The price became a fixed one in the market, and 1,000 tons at 20 marcs 4 batzens per ton, 1st quality, and a load of Christianstadt at 21½, 21, and 20¼ were sold; at which prices, also, orders given in February were executed. In the mean time consignments came from Stockholm for Sweden and Finland, and 3,000 tons were bespoken for summer; first at 20¼, 20, and 19½, and later at 1 marc per ton less. In March the prices maintained themselves with slack sales, and when the first direct consignments came in from Finland, in April, they met with the greater attention, as England came forward early as a buyer. Some thousands of tons were done at 12½ marcs banco to 12¼ free on board from Uleaborg and Wasa. At the same time in May three shipments were made for London, Liverpool, and New Castle, while the home market was very dull. At the end of May came the first direct imports from Christianstadt and Wasa, but to be warehoused, as no satisfactory prices could be expected, owing to the want of steady demand and confidence in the article at the existing prices. 18 marcs were given for thin Christianstadt, and in June several samples of thick at 16 marcs per ton. In June, with the continued importation, some thousands of tons of thin tar found buyers for Lisbon and Spain at 14½ marcs per ton, and the Weser and Elbe countries were purchasers also at those reduced prices. At the same time two ship-loads of Finland were sold for Italy at 10 marcs banco, free on board, and sales in the market kept pace with the supply. In September the demand became sensibly less, and a portion of the arrival was cleared off at 14 marcs per ton, first quality. In the course of October there was again a demand, and several thousand tons were taken from the market at advancing prices—15, 14¾, and 14¼ marcs being for the three sorts paid. At the end of the month, after the first clearance, 16 marcs per ton was paid for thin Christianstadt to order; and as Stockholm now entered into account several thousand tons were bought there and sold to Wrake at 16¼, 16¼, and 16 marcs. For home, 17 marcs per ton were paid for thin sort, a brisk demand having arisen in Bremen owing to improved accounts from New York. In December it was again very dull as regards this article, and the arrival of many imports caused the year to close with a tolerably large stock. The quotation for their middling and thick sorts was 17, 16¾, and 16¼ marcs per ton. The stock on 1st January, 1863, amounted to about 26,000.1 and 4,850.2 tons. The imports this year were about 38,341.1 and 5,149.2.

Against 1862 about.. 55,000 tons.
        1861 about.. 40,253 "
        1860 about.. 26,521 "
Stock on 31st December, 1863....................25,345.1 and 1,950.2 "

Finland and Stockholm pitch: Stock on 1st January, 1863, was about 626.1 and 387.2 tons. There was a good demand for this article in the spring, and though prices were high, there were occasionally large sales. The prices in Stockholm for pitch boiled there were pretty satisfactory, and considerable orders were made in the course of the year, particularly as the article was so much in favor. On the arrivals from Finland the desire for the former considerably slackened and holders had to content themselves with more moderate prices. Several lots were sold at 27 marcs 8 batzens to 29 marcs 8 batzens per ton, according to quality. The demand being kept up, prices improved again later, and there were some high sales though the importation was greater that year than it had ever been before. At the present advanced period of the season it is dull; mean time the prices may be confidently quoted at from 32½ to 33 marcs per ton; and, as long as resin is so dear, pitch cannot be expected to be at so low a standard as in other years.

Stock on 1st January, 1863, was about..........   626.1 and   387.2 tons
Imports in the year about .... 6,058.1 and 1,290.2 tons

Against in 1862 about............ .... 1, 300 tons.
in 1861 about..................................... 520 tons.
in 1860 about .... 2, 458 tons.
Stock on 31st December, 1863, about............ 1, 921.1 and 1, 290.2 tons.

Finland caraway, (cummin:) Stock on the 1st of January, 1863, was about
235,000 pounds. In the first months of the year single purchasers were made
here and there, at the market prices, 18½ to 19 marcs per pound. A brisker
demand occurred later, and there were some extensive dealings, without, however, affecting the prices. When the news arrived, late in the summer, of a
good crop in Finland the prices could not be kept up; and, on the arrival of
the first supplies, various allotments took place at 16½ marcs per 100 pounds.
At these reduced prices many large purchases were made also, both on the spot
and to order. The Danish dealers were great buyers, but, as there were some
speculators, prices rose rapidly, and 18 marcs and more were paid. Business latterly was slack, but there is much salable stock in the market, as so much is
lying in the hands of the shippers. The quotation at present is 18½ to 19
marcs per 100 pounds.

Stock on 1st January, 1863, was about.................. 235, 000 pounds.
Imports in 1863 was about............................ 370, 000 "
Against in 1862 about............................... 170, 000 ::
in 1861 about.............................. 320, 000 ::
in 1860 about.............................. 500, 000 ··
Stock on 31st December, 1863, about.................. 120, 000 "

Of Russian anise-seed : The stock on 1st January, 1863, was about 25,000
pounds. This trifling store was cleared in the course of the summer, and prices
being so high in Russia this year, no orders were given in that quarter, as there
would be a great uncertainty of finding purchasers in the market at such an
advance of price.

Of Finland butter there was no stock at the beginning of the year, and the
price of the article being constantly higher in Sweden and Russia than at
home. Only small supplies came, from time to time, which were speedily
bought up on arrival. The last lots sold at about 65 marcs per 100 pounds.

The supplies of Riga linseed (for sowing) of 1862 were...... 8, 680 tons.
The spring of 1863....................................... 3, 325 "

In the early part of the year several dealings were made at 39 to 38¾ marcs
per ton; but, owing to high prices, business was, on the whole, not very brisk,
so that holders were induced, in April, to sell at 37 marcs per ton. After these
sales there was a lull, and dealers could not dispose of their stock for the sowing time. Considerable lots remained on hand, which were partly sold, late in
the autumn, for cruising.

Riga linseed, (1863, for sowing:) Supplies, up to the end of the year,
amounted to 8,470 tons, which quantity, for the most part, intended for the
home market, and but a small portion for transit, 4,290 tons are expected,
which, it is hoped, will arrive safely. Quality ordinary, and the price asked
29½ to 30 marcs per ton. There had been no sales up to the end of the year.

A.

Comparative statement showing the arrivals and departures of sea and coasting vessels at Lubec from the year 1858 to 1863, inclusive.

Countries.	1863.				1862.			
	Arrived.		Left.		Arrived.		Left.	
	Number of vessels.	Lasts of 4,000 lbs., met. weight.	Number of vessels.	Lasts of 4,000 lbs., met. weight.	Number of vessels.	Lasts of 4,000 lbs., met. weight.	Number of vessels.	Lasts of 4,000 lbs., met. weight.
Vessels, steamships included—flag.								
Lubec	87	9,993	87	10,066	117	15,784	127	16,630
Belgium								
Denmark	362	9,745	362	9,925	374	9,332	373	9,946
England	24	2,677	27	3,223	21	2,251	21	2,251
France	6	366	6	366	7	403	7	403
Hamburg	4	117	5	1,195	6	218	10	957
Hanover	25	733	26	732	19	548	19	548
Mechlenburg	75	8,446	77	8,763	66	7,709	69	8,256
Netherlands	16	937	16	937	11	638	11	638
Norway	5	162	5	162	6	219	6	219
Oldenburg	2	91	1	60	2	143	2	143
Prussia	74	3,203	71	2,981	70	2,428	74	2,611
Russia	210	17,321	211	17,475	200	16,156	199	16,065
Sweden	412	37,851	412	37,968	352	32,608	352	32,660
Total	1,302	91,644	1,306	93,873	1,251	88,437	1,270	90,627
Steamer trips between Lubec and—								
St. Petersburg	46	6,046	45	5,870	52	8,940	49	8,531
Reval, Narva								
Stockholm, Calmac, Ystadt	42	9,324	43	9,520	36	7,890	36	7,941
Riga	21	1,978	21	1,978	30	3,106	30	2,997
Narrköping, Stockholm, &c	35	4,889	35	4,889	29	4,056	29	4,056
Solvitsberg, Carlshamn, &c	19	2,265	19	2,265	20	2,556	20	2,556
Copenhagen, Malmö	39	3,290	39	3,290	39	3,169	39	3,169
Copenhagen, Gothenburg	73	6,514	73	6,514	66	5,590	66	5,590
Copenhagen							1	104
Helsingfors	11	1,595	11	1,595	9	1,299	10	1,444
Wyburg								
Stettin	1	138	1	115	2	223	2	270
Konigsberg			3	606			2	350
Hull	13	1,884	11	1,489	11	1,441	11	1,441
Stockholm			1	104	2	233	1	115
Narrköping								
Westerwick								
Gefle	2	113	1	51				
Malmö	1	104						
Neustadt, Tehmern, Kiel	66	2,359	66	2,359	53	2,073	53	2,073
Sundry ports	4	421	8	1,029	8	931	8	944
Total	373	40,920	377	41,674	357	41,507	357	41,581
Coasting vessels—under Lubec flag..	10	317	10	317	6	181	6	181
Coasting vessels—under foreign flag..	254	646	254	646	247	641	247	641
Total	264	963	264	963	253	822	253	822

A.—*Comparative statement showing the arrivals and departures of sea and coasting vessels at Lubec, &c.*—Continued.

Countries.	1861.				1860.			
	Arrived.		Left.		Arrived.		Left.	
	Number of vessels.	Lasts of 4,000 lbs., met. weight.	Number of vessels.	Lasts of 4,000 lbs., met. weight.	Number of vessels.	Lasts of 4,000 lbs., met. weight.	Number of vessels.	Lasts of 4,000 lbs., met. weight.
Vessels, steamships included—flag.								
Lubec	126	16,220	116	15,318	115	14,363	126	15,655
Belgium					1	148	1	148
Denmark	241	5,686	242	5,923	303	8,170	302	8,919
England	18	2,038	18	2,038	12	990	12	990
France	2	90	2	90	4	206	4	206
Hamburg	5	173	5	260	6	280	8	763
Hanover	14	555	15	573	21	604	21	642
Mechlenburg	75	8,721	59	6,516	30	2,911	28	2,709
Netherlands	16	867	16	867	15	751	15	751
Norway	5	151	6	391	12	702	12	702
Oldenburg	1	20	1	20	1	31	1	31
Prussia	66	3,779	64	3,660	48	2,192	51	2,630
Russia	190	16,216	190	16,129	208	17,437	212	17,814
Sweden	315	31,459	316	31,451	358	34,670	358	34,463
Total	1,074	85,975	1,050	83,166	1,134	83,455	1,151	85,723
Steamer trips between Lubec and—								
St. Petersburg	52	9,042	43	7,790	47	8,186	47	8,159
Reval, Narva	1	170	1	170	4	417	4	417
Stockholm, Calmac, Ystadt	40	8,880	40	8,829	44	9,768	43	9,571
Riga	29	2,955	29	2,955	30	3,075	30	3,075
Narrköping, Stockholm, &c.	32	4,349	32	4,349	35	5,108	35	5,108
Solvitsburg, Carlshamn, &c.	19	2,372	19	2,372	25	3,246	25	3,246
Copenhagen, Malmö	41	3,331	41	3,331	38	3,097	38	3,097
Copenhagen, Gothenburg	63	5,193	63	5,193	37	3,123	37	3,123
Copenhagen	1	170						
Helsingfors	10	1,450	10	1,444	11	1,589	12	1,734
Wyburg								
Stettin	2	198	3	330			2	270
Konigsberg			1	212			1	212
Hull	11	1,347	11	1,347				
Stockholm	2	177	2	177	3	450	2	324
Narrköping								
Westerwick								
Gefle					1	62	1	62
Malmö								
Neustadt, Tehmern, Kiel								
Sundry ports	8	804	11	1,327	3	401	4	392
Total	311	40,438	306	39,826	278	38,522	281	38,790
Coasting vessels—under Lubec flag	12	375	12	375	11	325	12	325
Coasting vessels—under foreign flag	251	646	251	646	173	455	173	455
Total	263	1,021	263	1,021	184	780	185	780

A.—*Comparative statement showing the arrivals and departures of sea and coasting vessels at Lubec, &c.*—Continued.

Countries.	1859.				1858.			
	Arrived.		Left.		Arrived.		Left.	
	Number of vessels.	Lasts of 4,000 lbs., met. weight.	Number of vessels.	Lasts of 4,000 lbs., met. weight.	Number of vessels.	Lasts of 4,000 lbs., met. weight.	Number of vessels.	Lasts of 4,000 lbs., met. weight.
Vessels, steamships included—flag.								
Lubec................................	114	13,095	119	13,414	111	11,412	122	12,318
Belgium.............................	.....	.....	.....	.....	.....	.....	.....	.....
Denmark............................	252	6,038	252	6,079	251	5,756	250	5,663
England.........	13	1,049	13	1,049	4	306	4	306
France..............................	4	299	4	299	2	108	2	108
Hamburg............................	4	116	7	332	9	361	11	457
Hanover.............................	19	647	18	590	13	379	16	496
Mechlenburg........................	57	6,033	59	6,211	45	4,395	49	4,969
Netherlands........................	12	575	13	643	25	1,309	26	1,357
Norway.............................	5	235	5	235	1	31	2	122
Oldenburg..........................	.....	.....	.....	.....	1	31	2	109
Prussia.............................	32	1,607	32	1,431	27	1,718	25	1,632
Russia..............................	205	16,440	202	16,239	173	13,967	171	13,847
Sweden.............................	339	33,022	341	33,150	278	26,406	279	26,387
Total............................	1,056	79,086	1,165	79,672	940	66,179	959	67,771
Steamer trips between Lubec and—								
St. Petersburg......................	43	6,651	43	6,651	41	5,305	42	5,409
Reval, Narva.......................	1	108	1	108	.....	.....	.....	.....
Stockholm, Calmac, Ystadt..........	44	9,666	44	9,666	48	8,998	48	9,117
Riga................................	30	3,075	30	3,075	29	3,009	28	2,893
Narrköping, Stockholm, &c..........	39	5,664	40	5,793	26	3,706	26	3,706
Solvitsberg, Carlshamn, &c..........	27	3,004	27	3,004	5	881	5	881
Copenhagen, Malmö.................	40	3,250	40	3,250	24	1,950	24	1,950
Copenhagen, Gothenburg............	33	2,756	33	2,756	32	2,553	32	2,553
Copenhagen.........................	.....	.....	1	105	1	148	1	148
Helsingfors.........................	10	1,450	10	1,450	8	1,160	9	1,275
Wyburg.............................	4	619	4	619	2	309	2	309
Stettin.............................	2	206	.....	.....	.....	.....	.....	.....
Konigsberg.........................	.....	.....	.....	.....	.....	.....	.....	.....
Hull................................	.....	.....	.....	.....	.....	.....	.....	.....
Stockholm..........................	2	319	2	319	2	223	3	333
Narrköping.........................	.....	.....	.....	.....	1	247	.....	.....
Westerwick.........................	.....	.....	.....	.....	1	81	1	81
Gefle...............................	.....	.....	.....	.....	4	265	3	154
Malmö..............................	1	105	.....	.....	.....	.....	.....	.....
Neustadt, Tehmern, Kiel............	.....	.....	.....	.....	.....	.....	.....	.....
Sundry ports.......................	2	427	1	103	4	516	2	251
Total.........................	278	37,300	276	36,899	228	29,351	226	29,060
Coasting vessels—under Lubec flag...	12	356	12	356	9	266	9	266
Coasting vessels—under foreign flag...	234	581	234	581	237	586	237	586
Total............................	246	937	246	937	246	852	246	852

B.

Statement showing some of the most important articles imported by sea into Lubeck during the year 1863.

Alum from Sweden	casks	65
Alkali from England	casks	20
Bed feathers from Riga and Petersburg	bales	3,664
Bristles from Petersburg	casks	346
Butter from Finland	casks	11,000
" " Denmark	barrels	1,103
Cement from England	casks	5,242
" " Stettin	casks	20
Chiccory from Rostock	casks	480
Cash from Petersburg { imperials		33,900
{ roubles		338,152
Cash from Stockholm { rixdaler, rent		147,900
{ sl. sp. rixdaler		16,720
Drugs: Isinglass from Petersburg	colas	16
Semen cynac from Petersburg	colas	1,047
Insect powder from Petersburg	colas	190
Lycopodium from Petersburg	colas	47
Cantharides from Petersburg	colas	272
Licorice from Petersburg	colas	292
Iron from Sweden	pounds	8,000,000
against 1862	pounds	6,650,000
1861	pounds	6,000,000
Plates	pounds	170,000
Steel	pounds	368,000
Nails	boxes	296
Nails from England	pounds	2,600,000
against 1862	pounds	1,800,000
1861	pounds	1,400,000
Flax from Russia	bales	104
" " Finland	bales	131
Grain: Rye from Denmark	tons	2,391
Rye from Prussia	bushels	7,291
Rye from Rostock	tons	400
Wheat from Denmark	tons	13,553
Wheat from Finland	tons	163
Wheat from Russia	tschetworts	80
Barley from Denmark	tons	9,478
Oats from Denmark	tons	1,565
Oats from Sweden	tons	693
Peas from Denmark	tons	2,376
Glassware from Belgium { boxes		2,030
{ boxes		171½
{ boxes		495¼
Hemp from Petersburg	pounds	1,500,000
against 1862	pounds	1,200,000
1861	pounds	1,200,000
Hemp from Riga	pounds	1,800,000
against 1862	pounds	2,300,000
1861	pounds	2,200,000
Herrings from Norway	tons	3,270

Calf, lamb, and sheep skins, from Denmark..........bundles..   1, 172
    "   "   "   Sweden ....bundles..   445
    "   "   "   Petersburg.... ....bundles..   675
                     Riga..............bundles..   1, 181
    "   "   "   Finland ....·.....bundles..   30
White hares' skins....................................   50, 000
Lumber: Boards and plank from Sweden ....dozen..   89, 000
        Boards and plank from Finland ....dozen..   41, 000
          against 1862 from Sweden ....dozen..   65, 630
              1861 from Sweden ....dozen..   60, 523
              1862 from Finland ....dozen..   30, 571
              1861 from Finland ....dozen..   25, 218
        Spars and beams from Sweden..............pieces..   25, 600
        Spars and beams from Finland..............pieces..   21, 100
          against 1862 from Sweden ....pieces..   30, 835
              1861 from Sweden ....pieces..   32, 927
              1862 from Finland ....pieces..   25, 631
              1861 from Finland ....pieces..   27, 458
        Laths from Finland......................pieces..   105, 000
          against 1862...........................pieces..   54, 817
              1861...........................pieces..   117, 250
Lime from Sweden.................................tons..   18, 000
Cheese from Amsterdam ....pieces..   7, 024
Copper from Sweden ....pounds..   2, 000, 000
  against 1862 ....pounds..   1, 600, 000
       1861 ....pounds..   1, 700, 000
Copper from Petersburg ....blocks..   950
  "   " Finland ....blocks..   1, 160
Cumin from Finland...............................pounds..   370, 000
  against 1862 ....pounds..   170, 000
       1861 ....pounds..   320, 000
Linen from Petersburg: Ravens duck.................boxes..   510
               canvass ....boxes..   5, 430
Linseed from Riga: for 1862.........................tons..   3, 225
            for 1863.........................tons..   8, 470
Linseed used for oil from Finland ....bags..   140
Candles, stearine, from Petersburg.....................boxes..   44
  "   "   " Finland.....................boxes..   73
Rags from Sweden.................................bales..   684
  " " Denmark ....bales..   133
  " " Petersburg ....pounds..   650, 000
  " " Riga ....bales..   344
  " " Finland ....bales..   67
Mats from Russia ....pieces..   15, 000
Mineral water from Amsterdam.............. { stone bottles..   16, 900
                        { stone bottles..   11, 600
Oil, hemp, from Petersburg and Riga................. { casks..   44
                        { casks..   193
Linseed oil from Riga ....casks..   105
  "   " Petersburg ....casks..   31
  "   ·" Hull ....casks..   223
  "   " Flensburg...........................casks..   20
Pitch from Finland and Sweden................. { tons..   6, 058
                        { tons..   1, 290
  against 1862.......................................tons..   1, 300
       1861.......................................tons..   582

Paper from Sweden		reams	380
" " Copenhagen		bales	35
Potash from Petersburg		casks	1,641
against 1862		casks	2,894
1861		casks	1,463
Potash from Finland		casks	497
against 1862		casks	164
1861		casks	236
Horsehair from Petersburg		bales	621
" " Revel		bales	221
" " Liban		bales	990
" " Finland		bales	706
Rapeseed from Denmark		tons	16,358
Fur from Petersburg		colas	26
Rice from Copenhagen		bags	1,682
" " Bremen		bales	980
" " England		bales	113
Soda from Newcastle		casks	355
" " Hull		casks	349
Sirup from England		casks	60
" " Nantes		casks	980
" " Havre		casks	69
" " Itzehoe		casks	203
" " Glückstadt		casks	133
Spirits from Stettin, (alcohol)		barrels	613
" " Cette, (alcohol)		barrels	15
Rum from Bremen		barrels	132
" " London		barrels	63
" " Amsterdam		barrels	63
" " Liverpool		barrels	20
" " Hull		barrels	19
Arrack from Amsterdam		barrels	70
" " Rotterdam		barrels	30
" " Bremen		barrels	13
Stearine from Petersburg		boxes	155
" " Wyburg		boxes	50
Salt from Liverpool		tons	355
Stone coal from England		tons	285,000
against 1862		tons	265,000
1861		tons	343,000
Stoneware, &c., from England		colas	430
Train oil from Copenhagen		barrels	60
Tallow from Petersburg		casks	667
against 1862		casks	1,205
1861		casks	1,058
Tackling from Petersburg		colas	11,542
Tar from Finland and Sweden	{	tons	38,341
	{	tons	5,149
against 1862		tons	55,000
1861		tons	40,000
1860		tons	26,500
Cart-grease and fat from Antwerpen		casks	843
" " " Hull		casks	1,100
Wine from Bordeaux		hogsheads	5,143
" " Cette		barrels	988

Wool from Petersburg ....bales..   **946**
"   "   Riga ....bales..   **30**
"   "   Reval ....bales..   **34**
"   "   Copenhagen ....bales..   **50**
Sugar from Nantes ....loaves..   **75,000**
"   "   Itzehoe............................loaves..   **43,200**
"   "   Bremen............................loaves..   **20,000**
"   "   Glückstadt ....loaves..   **9,000**
"   "   Havre................................loaves..   **4,100**
"   "   Hull, (candies) ....boxes..   **450**
"   "   Antwerpen, (candies)............ .....boxes..   **300**
"   "   Itzehoe, (candies) ....boxes..   **70**

Tabular statement showing the exports from the consular district of Frankfort-on-the-Main to the United States during the quarter ended December 31, 1863, in florins and kreutzers.

Description.	Frankfort.	Hesse Darmstadt.	Hesse Cassel.	Hesse Homburg.	Nassau.	Brunswick.	Total.
	Flor. Kr.	Flor. Kr.	Flor. Kr.	Fl. Kr.	Flor. Kr.	Flor. Kr.	Flor. Kr.
1. Hares' fur	173,908 54	17,076 40	24,203 30	....	....	....	215,189 04
2. Leather	104,445 38	28,962 57	....	....	....	....	133,408 35
3. Leather goods	53,095 31	35,713 11	....	....	....	....	88,808 42
4. Cloth..................	20,019 36	20,495 39	....	....	....	....	40,515 15
5. Hosiery	40,616 21	....	....	....	....	....	40,616 21
6. Cotton goods	4,060 45	....	....	....	....	....	4,060 45
7. Lace goods	4,393 20	....	....	....	....	....	4,393 20
8. Fancy goods...........	6,029 31	....	....	....	....	....	6,029 31
9. Raw silk	23,666 44	....	....	....	....	....	23,666 44
10. Wine	12,806 45	84,777 22	....	319 45	11,311 11	....	109,215 03
11. Cigars...............	4,798 35	....	....	....	....	....	4,798 35
12. Drugs and chemicals....	1,912 07	24,059 17	....	....	....	....	25,971 24
13. Paper................	1,912 09	6,974 21	....	....	....	....	8,886 30
14. Toys................	2,868 23	....	5,630 13	....	....	....	8,498 36
15. Glassware	2,540 04	8,362 06	....	....	....	....	10,902 10
16. Hardware	3,669 30	....	....	....	....	....	3,669 30
17. Pipes................	....	....	6,092 24	....	8,955 45	....	15,048 09
18. Jewelry..............	....	....	15,291 08	....	27,477 31	....	42,768 39
19. Optical instruments.....	....	....	....	....	....	11,976 04	11,976 04
20. Chiccory	....	....	....	....	....	8,240 45	8,240 45
21. Sundries..............	17,682 26	25,320 25	16,182 48	....	2,880 11	....	62,065 50
Total.................	478,426 19	251,741 58	67,400 03	319 45	50,624 38	20,216 49	868,729 42

Statement of exports from the States of Frankfort consular district to the United States during the quarter from January 1, 1864, to April 1, 1864.

Articles.	Frankfort.		Hesse Darmstadt.		Hesse Cassel.		Nassau.		Total.	
	Fl.	*Kr.*	*Fl.*	*Kr.*	*Fl.*	*Kr.*	*Fl.*	*Kr.*	*Fl.*	*Kr.*
Hares' fur	188,806	02	30,390	29	27,439	49			246,636	20
Leather	92,643	08	41,279	21					133,922	29
Leather goods	25,688	35	14,743	46					40,431	54
Cloth	38,380	35	63,954	03	6,622	25			108,957	03
Hosiery	72,453	41							72,453	41
Woollen goods	5,254	32							5,254	32
Cotton	2,371	21							2,371	21
Linen					12,048	25			12,048	25
Raw silk	23,828	35							23,828	35
Fancy goods	11,376	09	4,725	15					16,101	24
Glass	6,280	14	4,435	58					10,716	12
Wine	1,218	15	92,043	10			6,992	54	100,254	19
Cigars	10,297	06							10,297	06
Paper	4,341	26	6,374	50					10,716	24
Pipes					8,752	02			8,752	02
Toys					10,057	26			10,057	26
Drugs and chemicals	1,370	40	3,172	34					4,543	14
Jewelry							7,159	12	7,159	12
Sundries	20,622	45	25,242	06	6,582	47	4,582	40	57,030	18
Total	504,932	37	286,361	40	71,502	54	18,734	46	881,531	57

JUNE 30, 1864.

* * * The exports to the United States during the quarter ending June 30, 1864, amount to f. 156,826 19, consisting of—

Hares' fur	37,844	57
Toys	79,549	06
Pipes	10,694	28
Cast-iron goods	3,967	50
Silk goods	8,458	06
Woollen goods	4,257	30
Linen	2,748	26
Jewelry	5,920	59
Cotton goods	2,096	42
Sundries	1,290	15
	156,826	19

The produce and manufacture of the Electorate of Hesse Cassel.

JUNE 30, 1864.

The exports to the United States for the quarter ended this day amount to f. 278,653 20, consisting of—

	Francs.	
Wine	92,215	04
Leather	47,824	10
Leather goods	33,335	33

	Francs.
Cloth...	30,380 12
Hosiery...	17,859 53
Fancy goods..	5,038 04
Hares' fur..	5,213 57
Drugs and chemicals...	14,015 31
Paper...	7,588 54
Mineral water..	7,501 29
Cigars..	1,845 33
Sundries..	15,835 00
	278,653 20

The produce and manufacture of the Grand Duchy of Hesse Darmstadt.

Statement showing the exports from Frankfort consular district of the United States during the quarter ending June 30, 1864.

Articles.	Frankfort.	Hesse Darmstadt.	Hesse Cassel.	Nassau.	Hesse Homburg.	Brunswick.	Total.
1. Hares' fur....................	259,483 59	5,213 57	37,844 57				302,541 73
2. Leather	102,156 09	47,824 10					149,980 19
3. Leather goods	51,379 00	33,335 33					84,714 33
4. Cloths......................	19,393 36	30,380 12					49,773 48
5. Hosiery	96,063 00	17,859 53					113,922 53
6. Sundry wool and cot. goods	12,860 03			6,354 12			19,214 15
7. Linen				2,748 26			2,748 26
8. Silk goods..................	14,243 32			8,458 06			22,701 38
9. Fancy goods................	14,456 17	5,038 04					19,494 21
10. Raw silk	24,186 43						24,186 43
11. Wine	12,510 07	92,215 04			14,197 07	10,038 06	129,020 24
12. Paper......................	10,424 16	7,588 54					18,012 70
13. Cigars.....................	8,319 08	1,845 33					10,164 41
14. Pipes......................				10,694 28	6,378 55		17,072 83
15. Toys.......................	3,362 23			79,549 06			82,911 29
16. Drugs and chemicals.......	2,748 25	14,015 31			1,050 00		17,813 56
17. Mineral water.............		7,501 29				360 00	7,861 29
18. Jewelry				5,920 59	20,123 10		26,043 09
19. Chicory						2,005 51	2,005 51
20. Sundries	15,677 23	15,835 00	5,258 05	9,365 46			46,135 74
Total	647,262 01	288,651 20	157,826 99	51,114 18	10,458 06	2,005 51	1,146,317 35

SEPTEMBER 30, 1864.

 *   *   * Finally, I have the honor to give a statement of the exports to the United States from the district of Frankfort-on-the-Main during the quarter ending this day, which will be found to agree with the returns of fees made to your department for this period.

The exports amounted to f. 166,146 59—consisting of

	Francs.
Hares' fur..	57,079 01
Leather...	16,307 00
Leather goods..	15,705 51
Hosiery...	29,277 22
Cloth...	6,956 58
Fancy goods..	7,989 11
Paper stationery...	3,874 41
Toys..	11,182 58

	Francs.
Wine	830 00
Sundries	16,944 02
Total	166,145 39

Tabular statement showing the exports to the United States from all the States embraced in the consular general district of Frankfort-on-the-Main for the quarter ended September 30, 1864.

Articles.	Frankfort-on the-Main.	Darmstadt.	Hesse Cassel.	Nassau.	Bruns- wick.	Total.
	Flor. Kr.	Flor. Kr.	Flor. Kr.	Flor. Kr.	Flor. Kr.	Flor. Kr.
Hares' fur	57,079 01	17,410 46	23,585 45			98,075 32
Leather	16,307 00	9,742 43				26,049 43
Leather goods	15,705 51	19,251 09				34,957 00
Hosiery	29,277 22	2,691 20				31,968 42
Cloth	6,956 53		4,822 25			11,779 18
Fancy goods	7,989 11	1,484 51				9,474 02
Wine	830 00	43,376 37		14,808 07		59,014 44
Toys	11,182 58		30,875 50			42,058 48
Paper and stationery	3,874 41	7,509 49				11,384 30
Drugs and chemicals		5,172 07		3,771 43		8,943 50
Pipes				6,553 04	917 00	7,470 04
Jewelry			11,984 06	2,598 06		14,582 12
Sundries	16,944 02	92,236 52	6,001 10	1,256 42	42 44	33,481 30
Total	166,145 39	115,874 14	77,268 36	28,987 02	959 44	389,239 55

Total exports from the states included in this consular district to the United States during the financial period from October 1, 1863, to September 30, 1864, compared with those during the same period in the preceding year.

Articles.	Frankfort-on-the-Main.		Hesse Darmstadt.		Hesse Cassel.		Hesse Homburg.	
	1864.	1863.	1864.	1863.	1864.	1863.	1864.	1863.
Hares' fur	679,277 56	391,249 18	70,091 52	16,828 55	113,074 01	47,265 42		
Leather	315,551 55	192,559 52	127,809 11	132,862 56				
Leather goods	145,868 30	50,022 44	103,043 39	73,209 56				
Cloth	84,750 40	78,062 23	114,829 54	25,186 07	11,444 50	1,076 24		
Hosiery	238,410 24	273,747 35	20,551 13	20,552 56				91 58
Woollen and cotton	24,546 41	4,567 23			6,354 12			
Linen				4,197 43	14,796 51			
Raw silk	71,689 02	40,498 25						
Fancy goods	39,851 08	31,413 15	11,248 10			5,972 27		
Glass goods	8,820 18		12,798 04					
Wine	27,365 07	8,218 37	312,412 13	240,779 29			10,417 51	1,378 21
Cigars	23,414 49	9,888 26	1,845 33	8,901 09				
Paper	20,552 38	7,766 20	28,448 02	19,506 38				
Pipes		5,950 56		541 08	25,538 54	3,369 42		
Toys	17,413 44	14,187 25			126,112 33	54,435 16		
Drugs & chemicals	6,031 19	1,679 39	46,419 29	19,515 48				
Jewelry		9,800 05		4,996 55	33,196 13	3,091 24		
Chicory						1,177 00		
Optical instruments								
Sundries	93,233 08	61,211 25	83,135 52	60,671 24	42,482 56	37,327 53	360 00	
Total	1,796,770 06	1,180,753 48	932,633 12	627,751 04	373,000 32	153,715 48	10,777 51	1,470 19
In favor of	616,016 18		304,882 08		219,284 44		9,307 32	

Total exports from the States, &c.—Continued.

Articles.	Nassau.		Brunswick.		Total.		1864.	
	1864.	1863.	1864.	1863.	1864.	1863.	More.	Less.
Hares' fur....					862,443 49	455,343 45	407,099 54	
Leather					443,361 06	325,422 48	117,938 18	
Leather goods...					248,912 09	123,232 40	125,679 29	
Cloth....					211,025 24	104,324 54	106,700 30	
Hosiery		5,795 21			258,961 37	300,107 50		41,226 13
Wollen & cotton.					30,900 53	4,567 23	26,333 30	
Linen					14,796 51	4,197 43	10,599 08	
Raw silk....					71,682 02	40,428 25	31,253 37	
Fancy goods					51,099 18	37,385 42	13,713 36	
Glass goods					21,618 22		21,618 22	
Wine....	47,309 19	45,464 01			397,504 30	295,840 28	101,664 02	
Cigars....					25,260 22	18,789 35	6,470 47	
Paper....					49,000 34	27,272 58	21,727 36	
Pipes....	21,887 44	34,965 47	917 00		48,343 38	44,827 33	3,516 05	
Toys					143,526 19	68,622 41	74,903 38	
Drugs & chem'ls.	4,891 43			999 46	57,272 24	22,195 13	35,077 11	
Jewelry	57,357 59	15,021 90			90,554 12	32,939 44	57,644 28	
Chicory....			10,226 36	13,941 13	10,264 36	15,118 13		4,871 37
Optical Ins'ts..			11,976 04	20,711 42	11,976 04	20,711 42		8,735 38
Sundries....	18,085 19	1,144 06	42 44	2,619 44	237,339 59	162,974 32	74,365 27	
Total	149,462 04	102,390 35	23,182 24	38,272 25	3,285,896 09	2,104,353 59	1,236,305 38	54,833 28
In favor of	47,071 29				15,090 01	1,181,472 10		

Statement showing the exports from Hesse Darmstadt to the United States, together with the description, value, and place of production for the quarter ended September 30, 1864.

Place of production:	Articles.	Value.
Mayence	Wine......................	$23,808 00
Darmstadt	.. do.......................	7,040 46
Welgesheim	.. do.......................	391 05
Bingen	.. do.......................	281 06
Biebelsheim.	.. do.......................	307 45
Budesheim	.. do.......................	264 46
Offenbach	Leather goods	10,727 77
Mayence	Leather....................	18,619 18
Do	Mechanical utensils	1,636 60
Darmstadt	Chemicals	4,007 57
Offenbach	Drugs ...:	104 00
Grimberg	...do	953 30
Offenbach	Fancy goods	919 39
Mayence.............................	Sundries	60 00
Nicde Ramstadt	...do	593 39
Herrnhang...........................	Hosiery....................	2,691 20
Offenbach	Hares' fur	9,472 11
Do	Paper	2,702 09
Aschaffenburg.......................	...do	840 00
Offenbach...........................	Fiddle strings, &c	1,783 14
Mayence	Mineral	494 13
Offenbach	Woollen goods..............	565 12
Mayence	Books	105 00
Do	Musical works..............	600 51
Offenbach	........do	1,143 47
Do	Machinery	1,175 00
Do	Hooking needles............	670 36
Mayence	Musical works.	673 52
	Total....................	92,629 53

SEPTEMBER 30, 1864.

The exports to the United States during the quarter to date amounted to f. 28,987 42—consisting of

	Florins.
Wine	14, 808 07
Pipes	6, 553 04
Agate ware	2, 098 06
Colors	3, 771 43
Sundries	1, 256 42
	28, 487 02

The produce and manufactures of the Duchy of Nassau.

SEPTEMBER 30, 1864.

The exports to the United States during the quarter to date amounted to f. 77,269 16—consisting of

	Florins.
Hares' fur	23, 585 45
Cloth	4, 822 25
Toys	30, 875 50
Jewelry	11, 984 06
Sundries	6, 001 10
	77, 268 36

The produce and manufactures of the Electorate of Hesse Cassel.

SEPTEMBER 30, 1864.

The past twelve months have been remarkable for a number of events which have exercised the most important influence on the commercial activity of Europe generally, and more especially on the states belonging to the German Zollverein. In the commencement, from the prevailing insecurity of political relations, the commercial relations suffered materially, and, indeed, seriously, from the bloody strife carried on in our country, as well as from the lamentable disturbances in Poland. If, then, under these circumstances, speculation faltered, and the means of commerce were limited for the greater part to the supply for the most indispensable consumption, the political apprehensions were soon increased by the outbreak of the Dano-German war, and, as regards the commercial interests and relations of Germany specially, more so by the feverish apprehensions for the continued existence of the German "Zollverein." These were the four principal points which would not free commerce and industry from those fluctuations, some of which are still exercising their prejudicial influence on the developments of the future. Apprehensions with regard to the Polish question have entirely ceased. The reorganization of the Zollverein, about which I shall not fail to furnish particular remarks in this report, is obtained at last from the decision of Wurtemburg, Bavaria, Hesse Darmstadt, and Nassau to join the newly organized commercial league, as planned by Prussia, on the basis of the commercial treaty with France, and to the partial exclusion of Austria, which met with the most energetic opposition on the part of the four latter states. The consequences of the Dano-German war cannot be rightly ascertained and determined yet, as the settlement of the matter is still under consideration at Vienna. It can only be accepted as certain that peace is secured; that, therefore, in this respect there is no danger of any further disturbance of German commerce by an apprehended interference of foreign powers; on the contrary, that the borders of the Zollverein may be extended by the accession of the duchies of Sleswig, Holstein, and Lunenberg to the same.

Irrespectively, however, of these particular events and their influences, the general state of the political affairs of Europe is so complicated and unsettled at present that there are no flattering prospects whatever in the future of commerce and industry—the restraining position of an armed peace, or rather of a continued war readiness, which consumes much cash capital and strength without any real utility; the prolonged discussion of political affairs, which evolves a series of inquiries from year to year which fail to indicate the possibility of peace.

As regards the extent and importance of the exchange business of Frankfort, I refer to my monthly and weekly reports on the subject. Commercial activity, as stated upon several former occasions, is best judged from the extent of the business of the two annual fairs, although it is to be remarked that they have for several years past lost much of their former importance. In olden times the fairs had a very peculiar character, by reason of the means of communication being very difficult and troublesome. The journey was expensive, and he who had the means had his competitors on the spot, both as regards choice and price, a matter of no small advantage. At the present time things are different, owing to the more easy means of transit. The dealers receive so many offers from travelling agents throughout the year that there is no difficulty in ordering any article they need. The travelling agents of wholesale houses generally return a few days before the commencement of the fair. Under these circumstances the German retailers, who were in the habit of attending this fair, have now no great need to do so. They come chiefly to convince themselves whether the fair does not afford them still greater novelties in articles of fashion than they had been supplied with some days before by the agents, and thus the fair is attended to select a supplementary stock—in this respect the Frankfort fair is not peculiar. The wholesale merchants, who ten years ago supplied their wants at Leipzig, do not now find in that town the fashionable goods they may want. Thus, the leading houses, who pride themselves on their carefully selected stocks, now purchase their goods at the manufacturer's before the commencement of the fair, or receive from them at the fair patterns of such goods as are not supplied by the Prussian merchants at the Leipzig fair. The Frankfort fair this time presented a different aspect. By reason of the high price of wool the traders in woollen and mixed woollen goods have not been able fully to supply the market; this great advance in price was occasioned less by the scarcity of the raw material than from their inability to fill the heavy orders pressing on them. The financial power of this place enables the wholesale dealers at an early day to contract with the manufacturers for a large delivery of such goods on which it was foreseen that at the end of the year a great advance would be realized. For this reason those merchants who entered the field at a later day found the market too high. In this city they could have bought at usual prices the calicoes, linens, woollen and mixed woollen goods they had ordered from the factories. In such articles, as also in fashionable fabrics, there were extensive sales. In fashionable goods those of Dambreth Caro excelled all others, both in quantity and colors, so that the body-stuffs and shawls always found purchasers; but for the more ordinary articles there is less demand from year to year, and the purchasers give a decided preference to the more beautiful class of fabrics than to others of a lower grade. The same remarks apply to the cloth department; there was a ready sale at high prices for the medium fine cloths, buckskins, and serges; for the finer coat and pantaloon cloths of new designs there was a great demand, to no great stock on hand. The production is not equal to the consumption; the latter has increased very much in consequence of the almost exclusive use of the improved cheap yarns made of Indian cotton to the injury of the linen trade, which, for want of stock, cannot meet the demand, and it is supposed that the cheaper class of goods will disappear in the course of three months. Since the Easter fair the prices of linen have advanced 30 per cent., and are yet far below the standard prices of yarn. The public are of opinion that instead of giving 200 per cent. more for shirting and other cotton goods, which are much inferior and less durable than before, it would be much more economical to pay a few more kreutzers per ell for good substantial linen fabrics. Cotton goods are always in demand, and good yarns find a profitable market. In consequence of the deficiency of the stock the linen manufacturers are unable to meet the demands on them for goods; they have in consequence advanced their prices. The raw materials, flax and hemp, are only a trifle dearer, and still bear no proportion to the prices of yarn; the latter maintain their position in consequence of the difficulty of obtaining American cotton. In consequence of the new importation tariff on the raw materials the sales of fine silks were more active. The markets in the above-named goods were, as a whole, satisfactory. Leather took its usual place in the fair. The most profitable business was done in upper-leather, of which considerable quantities sold rapidly, and at good prices. Light leather and oxskins sold at rather moderate prices. Cowhides (vache leather) of fine quality maintained about the former prices, while inferior kinds were very plentiful, and, according to quality, brought a few dollars per hundred weight less than at the last fair. Brown and black calfskins were in great demand, and higher prices were readily realized. Sheepskins were higher than before, and sustained their prices throughout.

The following prices were paid for good polished leather of first quality sold in lots of 5 or 6 skins:

Wild cattle soling leather, per cwt............................	62 to 66
Wild cattle, light quality, 1st class goods.....................	52 to 58
Wild cattle, lower quality.....................................	37 to 50
Tame cattle soling leather, heavy goods........................	57 to 60
Tame cattle soling leather, light goods........................	50 to 56
Cowhides, as per quality......................................	46 to 55
Oxhides	52 to 65
Calfskins, (brown,) as per quality............................	108 to 130
Calfskins, (black,) as per quality............................	92 to 108

American customers were fewer at the fair this year than ever, which finds its explanation in our high tariff and the overstocked state of the American market, which does not justify importations at prices double the usual rates. The few purchases made were of articles of luxury, the buyers being persons who occasionally visited Frankfort, but who had not come for the special purpose of buying. The horse fair which has lately been connected with this fair was attended by results similar to those on former occasions. Sellers as well as buyers were satisfied with their business, and this market may be said to be one of the best ever held. Many dealers have left, and others partly sold out. Some had so many demands for their fine horses that they sent for more during the market. Of the 1,260 horses brought to the market 962 were sold. The most important sales were made in fancy horses, while the sale of working horses was even greater as regards numbers, but their prices did not range so high. The demand for chances in the lottery connected with the market was so great that the committee were obliged to purchase 18 horses, which, together with some other smaller prizes, were valued at 11,400 florins, or about $4,560

The following is an official statement of the traffic of the Frankfort cattle market from May to October, 1864, compared with the same period for the year 1863:

Description.	1863.			1864.		
	Import.	Export.	Remained here.	Import.	Export.	Remained here.
Oxen............	9,081	5,671	3,410	11,010	6,198	4,812
Cows and neats......	5,048	4,841	207	6,047	5,846	201
Swine	12,729	638	12,091	14,928	1,606	13,322
Calves.........	13,138	1,448	11,690	16,584	1,750	14,834
Wethers	12,913	4,031	8,882	16,125	6,514	9,611
Lambs	27	....	27	537	134	403
Total.	52,936	16,629	36,307	65,231	22,048	43,183

RECAPITULATION.

Years.	Import.	Export.	Remained here.
1864.........	65,231	22,048	43,183
1863......	52,936	16,629	36,307
In favor of 1864...........................	12,295	5,419	6,876

It may be of some interest to know the whole number of patents granted by the governments of all the states belonging to the German Zollverein for new inventions, in order to be able thereby to judge of the inventive genius of the nation. The whole number during the past year amounted to 640, viz: in Saxony, 176; Bavaria, 91; Hanover, 54; Wurtemberg, 85; Prussia, 71; Baden, 33; Hesse Darmstadt, 24; Nassau, 17; Electoral Hesse, 11; Brunswick, 10; Coburg Gotha, 9; Anhalt, 8; Saxe Weimar, 7; Bamberg, 6; Oldenburg, 4; Altenburg, 4; Frankfort, 8; Schwarzburg Sondershausen, 3; Schwarzburg Rudolstadt, 2; Saxe Meiningen, 2; Luxemburg, 2; Lippe, 2; Waldeck, 1; Hesse Homburg, none. Of course these 640 patents do not represent so many new inventions, but are for the most part patents granted in the smaller states for inventions which had already been patented in other parts. Such instances are, however, less frequent than might be supposed. On a rough calculation, there are about 60 patents which may be regarded as such, the validity of which extends beyond three German states.

The following is an official statement of the coinings which have taken place at the mint of Frankfort since the conclusion of the mint treaty of the 25th of August, 1837, up to the end of 1863; from which it appears that the total amount coined during that period amounted, exclusive of 1,786 gold ducats, to f. 21,844,904 11, or $8,737,960.

Amount of coin produced at the mint of Frankfort since the treaty of coinage of August 15, 1837, to the end of 1863.

Years.	Gold-coin pieces.	SILVER CURRENT COIN.				
		Two-thaler pieces.	One-thaler pieces.	Two-florin pieces.	One-florin pieces.	Half-florin pieces.
	Ducats.	*Florins.*	*Florins.*	*Florins.*	*Florins.*	*Florins.*
1838 to 1862, inclusive..........	1,786	12,490,758	4,188,359	2,192,876	1,843,586	395,101¼
1863..................................	....	....	72,663½	....	55,334	....
Total	1,786	12,490,758	4,261,022½	2,192,876	1,899,120	395,101¼

Years.	SMALL SILVER COIN.			COPPER COIN.	Total, except gold coin.
	Six-kreutzer pieces.	Three-kreutz'r pieces.	One-kreutzer pieces.	Hellers.	
	Florins. Kr.	*Florins. Kr.*	*Florins. Kr.*	*Florins. Kr.*	*Florins. Kr.*
1838 to 1862, inclusive..........	306,844 18	78,662 18	179,953 34	28,843 03	21,704,985 43
1863..................................	....	....	10,179 33	1,541 25	139 918 28
Total	306,844 18	78,662 18	190,133 07	30,384 28	21,844,904 11

For Frankfort specially the past year has been remarkable for many changes of great importance favorable to the progress of its commercial and industrial relations.

On the 2d of February last the usury laws hitherto in force in this city were repealed, as I specially reported on that occasion, when I transmitted a translation of the new law in relation to interest. The law of the "free exercise of a trade, profession, or business," respecting which I reported more fully in my last annual report, went into operation on the 1st of May last, and has produced important results for the local and social intercourse of Frankfort. Before, the city was surrounded by walls and ditches, and was furnished with gates, which were closed at night, and the rural and city populations were in consequence so entirely separated from each other that there existed an excise duty on all articles imported from the outer district of Frankfort territory into the city proper. This antiquated system has now been abolished; walls and gates have been removed, and the excise officers placed at the frontiers of the .Frankfort territory. This step of real progress has led to some more important advances in political and social matters. Formerly, for instance, all the citizens of this little republic were not entitled to equal rights and privileges. The full right of citizenship was only enjoyed by the Christian citizens residing in the city itself. The rural population, as well as the Jews, were subject to all the duties of citizens, without enjoying equal rights. The restriction hitherto existing with regard to the rights of citizens of the Jewish religion and the citizens of the rural community are abolished. The law will take effect on the 7th of this month. The citizens of Frankfort are still divided into three classes, the first including all the members of the senate; the nobility who do not occupy themselves with any kind of business which would entitle them to votes under any of the other heads; the learned of all classes or faculties, under which head come all the public officers and clergy, the notaries included; all those citizens, not belonging to the rank of the learned, who are appointed to public offices either by the senate or according to constitutional dispensation of .the same, or those who are appointed "representatives of the city," and who receive an annual salary or emolument out of the state funds; military officers, of all ranks;

land-owners; those citizens registered as living on their property; the school-teachers, teachers of languages, and teachers of other sciences; and all artists whose business has not been included in the above-named classes. To the second division belong all business people, without distinction; bankers; whole-sale and retail dealers; hotel-keepers; book-keepers and clerks; the sworn brokers; the store-keepers, and all landlords who do not carry on a business belonging to any of the classes hitherto named; those servants and persons in office, not belonging to the learned professions, who are not included in the first division, and who, through other avocations, belong to the second division. To the third division belong those whose business has hitherto been incorporated as a guild; those persons in office, and servants, not belonging to the learned professions, who are not included in the first division, and by avocation belong to the third division; all citizens, not enumerated in the former divisions, who carry on any legal or other business here. Upon any votings or elections the citizens have to vote according to these three classes, so that the majority of the votes of each class and the majority of the two classes are decisive as to the result of the election. It is singular that although all citizens have been made equal with regard to religious profession and residence, there should still exist a difference as to the pursuit of business or the possession of wealth.

In an industrial point of view Frankfort last year made an important step in advance, in originating and opening, on the 4th of July last, a so-called "exhibition of fine arts and industry," which remained open two months. This exhibition was so far different from the "world exhibitions" held at New York, Paris, and London, that it was a mere local undertaking—that is to say, only those articles were admitted for exhibition that were the products of the industry of Frankfort citizens, or of such persons residing in the city and who were engaged in business there.

The artistic branch of the exhibition was rendered very interesting by the fact that the productions of Frankfort artists from the earliest to the present time were so exhibited that the spectators were enabled to take in at one view the history of the fine arts in Frankfort. The articles exhibited were divided into seven groups. The first comprehended the metallurgic products and chemical objects; the second, provisions and kindred objects, (confectionery, wine, liquors, oil, tobacco, and cigars;) third, clothing materials and articles made of the same, leather products and textures and similar articles of dress; fourth, tools, instruments and machines, wood, stone, hardwares, &c.; fifth, polygraphy and its auxiliary branches, printing, paper-making, type foundry, engraving, &c., stylography; sixth, scientific horticulture, porcelain painting, photography, plastic and galvanic copying, &c.; seventh, groups of sculpture, plastic drawing, &c.

The senate had appointed a special committee to award prizes, &c.

A few words must also be said on another branch of industry, which had its origin in our country, and has lately become of great importance in Frankfort. I mean the manufacture and sale of American machines. The past year was very favorable to the export of many articles of American manufacture, but especially machinery, which found an ever-increasing sale in Germany. The great American sewing-machine manufacturers send great quantities of their machines to Germany, partly in exchange for other commodities and partly to extend their business. Heretofore the American houses established themselves in Hamburg only, and had agents in other parts of Germany; but in that year they came here also, in which they acted very wisely, Frankfort being the great metropolis of southern Germany and the centre of many populous cities, through which business can easily be transacted with the whole of southern Germany. Business has also been much facilitated by the German steam navigation between Bremen, Hamburg, and New York. The freight from New York to Bremen or Hamburg comes almost as cheap as to Liverpool, on account of the high warehouse expenses there, so that the entire freight from Liverpool to the German ports is saved, which, of course, is in some degree prejudicial to the trade of England.

The American machines are also imitated here, and although these imitations are not equal to the real American ones, still the American manufacturers ought to take care that they do not lose the market by the *much cheaper price of the German machines.*

* * * * * * * * *

The business is extending here in the same degree as in the United States. As formerly the spinning wheel, so will shortly the sewing machine be seen in every house. It may be calculated on with certainty that in the next ten years from 300,000 to 400,000 machines will be sold in Germany and Austria. Therefore, there is here a large field open for speculation where machines are only made by small mechanics who are not supplied with the proper machinery for their work, and where no large factories are in existence yet.

The house of Wirth & Sountag, here, who has established the said permanent exhibition of machines, have, as stated already in my last annual report, through the medium of Messrs. Lee & Co., also introduced the steam fire-engine of the Amoskeag company of New York and Manchester. The engine has been tried on several occasions and found to work excellently, but, on account of its very large size, not yet found a purchaser. Although the success for the whole of Germany has not been so great as might be expected, still the construction of steam fire-engines in Munich, Chemnitz, Hanover, and Hamburg demonstrate that the time is not far distant when they will become very general also in Germany. It is generally acknowledged by all authorities that the American machines are the best of all. Mr. Maffei, the celebrated manufacturer of Munich, for instance, has already taken the American engines as model for his own.

One kind of machines, which has been introduced here this summer by the same firm of Wirth & Sountag, and which has given universal satisfaction, is the grass-mowing and reaping machines of McCormick, Wood & Allen. The said gentlemen, in order to bring the machines into notice, lent several for mowing trials to farmers and others, and have thereby sold many. It may be calculated on with confidence that an important business in these machines will be done here next year. The success of the American washing machines has not been so favorable, and their sale has been very limited. Those, however, who have made a trial with these machines are very well satisfied with them, and there is no doubt but they will, by degrees, become very much used. The same thing may also be said with respect to other American household machinery. It is, therefore, desirable that the American machine-manufacturers should not fail to send specimens of their machines to the exhibitions which are so common in this part of the world. Among other places, there have been such exhibitions at Hoechst, for the Duchy of Nassau; at Okarben, Offenbach, Gross-Gerau, and Gaualgesheim, for the Grand Duchy of Hesse; and the machines which were exhibited partly by industrial and agricultural societies and partly by private individuals were nearly all sold. It is very desirable that in all exhibitions there should be specimens of our American agricultural, household, and wood-cutting machinery, especially of the last-named kind, which is very much in demand, as there is so much building going on that there are scarcely sufficient workmen to be found. A builder here has, in consequence of this, fitted up his workshop with machinery. For the industrial department, good wood-cutting and working machines, small hand machines as well as large ones to be worked by steam power, are much wanted, and a good market might be opened in the sale of them with all south Germany. But the German mechanics cannot be induced to try a machine they have not seen previously. To meet this difficulty the industrial societies have therefore begun to make experiments with the machines, and then buy the same for the resale. Manufacturers would, therefore, do well to send either to the societies or to the United States consuls prospectuses or designs of their machinery in order to establish business relations. The bringing into notice, and introduction of machines, is here considerably facilitated by the said machine exhibitions, and by the industrial newspapers, of which there are many in circulation. There is one of this kind published here under the title of "Der Arbeitgeber," (The Employer,) which contains every week a list of all new inventions and patents, American ones included. There is connected with this paper (like the "Scientific American") an agency for the medium of patents in all Germany and the continent, a combination which acts very well, as the agency is acquainted with all new inventions and improvements, through the paper, and can therefore give the inventor the best of advice. This agency not only procures patents in Europe for American inventions, but also procures patents in America for German inventions. Of the other American machines which were remarked in the exhibition, the following may be mentioned: Root's rotating steam-engine, which was unknown here before; Aikens & Soffe's knitting machines, of which the former has already become more known; implements of trade of American construction, very little known here heretofore; a new wooden hay-rake; ice-boxes; ice-press; small agricultural implements, &c. In general, machinery here meets with a ready sale, as there are in many districts a want of workmen, and people are obliged to use machinery. American machine-manufacturers might, therefore, very safely speculate in sending many other kinds of machines to this market.

With respect to the efforts of the "*Frankfort Emigration Society*" it appears from the last annual reports of the same that during the period from 1st of February, 1862, to 31st January, 1864, 1,537 persons emigrated, with a cash capital of 430,000 florins, after they had called for advice at the office of the society. The ports for which they embarked were the following:

For Rio de Janeiro and Porto Alegre..............................   231
    Quebec..   307
    Adelaide, Melbourne, and Sidney   342
    New York..   657

The professions of the 1,165 male emigrants were as follows:

Apothecaries	3	Miners	11
Architects	2	Merchants	12
Bakers	2	Masons	5
Barbers	3	Millers	2
Blacksmiths	14	Manufacturing workmen	6
Beer brewers	4	Painters	3
Butchers	10	Saddlers	3
Chemists	3	Stone-masons	2
Cabinet-makers	12	Shoemakers	7
Coopers	4	Shepherds	12
Carpenters	11	Tanners	2
Engineers	3	Tailors	20
Farmers and husbandmen	969	Vine-dressers	17
Iron-founders	5	Watchmakers	2
Locksmiths	9	Wheelwrights	3
Mechanicians	4		

The native place, sex and age of these emigrants are given in the following list:

States.	Males.	Females.	Children, 1—19.	Infants.	Total.
Baden	85	11	6	1	103
Bavaria	233	40	26	7	306
Hesse Darmstadt	202	59	27	4	292
Hesse Cassel	244	64	16	3	327
Nassau	219	51	10	....	280
Prussia	40	4	6	1	51
Wurtemberg	142	22	11	3	178
Total	1,165	291	102	19	1,537

These statistical statements of the society make their appearance accompanied by some explanatory remarks, of which a few seem to be interesting enough for a translation. Among other things it is said that the frequent and not inconsiderable announcements which have lately appeared of members of the community emigrating even out of the more happy districts of Germany, give reason to suppose that emigration will shortly be much greater than hitherto; so much the more as new colonies are opening, culture is gradually extending to the remotest parts of the world, and the passage to the newer colonies is assisted by the respective governments.

   *   *   *   *   *   *   *   *

Before going over to the statistical report respecting the activity of the " German Zollverein " of which Frankfort and the other states belonging to this consular district (excepting the three Hanseatic towns of Lubeck, Hamburg and Bremen) are members, it may be of interest to give a short sketch of the history, tendency and former activity of that commercial league, which, by its being now reorganized on the basis of the treaty of commerce with France, has taken a considerable step of advancement on the territory of free trade. I beg to remark that I have taken the principal details of this sketch from a very valuable work by Professor Otto Michaelis, " on the Zollverein and the French treaty of commerce."

The princes of the German empire had found the 16th century had so extended the power against that of the Emperor that the latter might be said only to hold the empire together nominally. In reality the empire had already fallen into several hundred smaller or larger territories, which, jealous of each other's power, had become rigidly isolated one from another. This isolation showed itself in an economical point of view. The last remains of the restrictions imposed on those who wished to settle down and carry on their profession in another part of the country extend even down to the present time; and there are many yet living who remember the tolls and custom-houses on the borders of the different larger and smaller states upon the time of the fall of the German empire down to the foundation of the Zollverein.

Having shaken off the yoke of the Napoleonic government, it happened that many of the new states instituted toll-laws and customs entirely different from one another. In Vienna they had no time to demolish in newly founded Germany the turnpikes between the different states. They put off the occasion, with the urgency of which they were well acquainted, like so many other things, for an indefinite period, and confined themselves to deciding in article 9 of the federal act, (Bundes act,) " that the members of the confederation intend at the first meeting of the Diet in Frankfort to enter into conference respecting the business and traffic among the different states of the confederation." Although this determination was repeated in article 69 of the Vienna treaty, it never came into execution.

In the year 1818 Prussia first arranged within her own territory the customs, tolls, &c.; and by a simple comprehensive code of custom laws dispensed with the toll restrictions within the different divisions of the country. A few of the other states endeavored to make custom regulations between themselves, but Austria entirely excluded herself from participating in these regulations. The idea of the toll alliance of the German states was first broached in the conference of ministers held at Vienna in 1818 and 1819, in pursuance of which it was agreed between Bavaria, Wurtemberg, Baden, Grand Duchy of Hesse, the Saxon Duchies and Nassau, that commissaries should be sent to Darmstadt in order to conclude a custom and commercial treaty. The conference really took .place on the 13th September, 1820, in Darmstadt, and in the year 1821 Electoral Hesse, Hohenzollern, Reuss, and Waldeck also joined it. But when the conference began to discuss the tariff, the division of revenue, the organization of government, and the right of votes, they became divided, and the negotiations entirely ceased on the 1st of July, 1822.

In the year 1824 Wurtemberg and Bavaria endeavored to reorganize a conference, and they succeeded in uniting at Stuttgart commissaries from Baden, the Grand Duchy of Hesse and Nassau. But here, also, the tariff was the point of quarrel, and nothing was effected. On the 18th January, 1828, a toll alliance was concluded between Bavaria and Wurtemberg, and on the 14th of February, 1828, a toll alliance was concluded between Prussia and Hesse Darmstadt. The basis of this last treaty was the system proposed by Prussia in 1818.

On the 27th of May, 1829, the toll alliances, that of Bavaria and Wurtemberg, and that of Prussia and Hesse Darmstadt, concluded between themselves a commercial treaty. After this treaty had been joined by Saxe Gotha, Electoral Hesse, and a few of the very small states, a treaty was concluded in 1833, whereby the Prusso-Hessian and the Bavaro-Wurtembergian toll alliances entered into a toll treaty, which soon after was also joined by the kingdom of Saxony and the Thuringian states. The latter had already concluded a commercial and toll alliance, consisting of the Saxonian Duchies, Schwarzburg, Reuss, a few districts of the province of Erfurt, and the Electoral Duchy of Schmalkalden, and entered therefore the new toll treaty as the Thuringian toll alliance.

The following is a chronological table of the principal events, and the dates when the German states entered the German Zollverein:

1818. New code of custom laws in Prussia.

1828, January 18. Custom alliance between Bavaria and Wurtemberg.

1828, February 14. Custom alliance between Prussia and Hesse Darmstadt.

1829, May 27. Commercial treaty between Prussia and Darmstadt on the one part, and Bavaria and Wurtemberg on the other.

1833, March 2. Foundation of the Zollverein between Prussia, Bavaria, Wurtemberg, and Hesse Darmstadt.

1833, March 30. The kingdom of Saxony joined the same.

1833, May 11. The Thuringian states joined.

1835, May 12. The Grand Duchy of Baden joined.

1835, December 10. The Duchy of Nassau joined.

1836, January 2. The free city of Frankfort joined.

1841, October 18. The principality of Lippe joined.

1841, October 19. The Duchy of Brunswick joined.

1851, December 7. The kingdom of Hanover joined.

1852, March 1. The Grand Duchy of Oldenburg joined.

1853, February 19. Commercial and customs treaty between Austria and Prussia respecting the Zollverein.

1853, April 4. Renewal of the general customs treaties.

1856, January 26. Conclusion of a treaty of traffic with the free city of Bremen.

At present there remain out of the Zollverein the Grand Duchies of Mecklenburg, the free cities of Hamburg, Bremen, Lubeck, and the Duchy of Holstein; Lauenburg-Mecklenburg remains isolated to the prejudice of its own interests. Whether the Hanseatic cities will join the Zollverein or not depends, perhaps, partly on the final solution of the Sleswick-Holstein question. To this short sketch of the history of the Zollverein it is only necessary to remark that the same was renewed for the first time in 1841, and the second time in 1853. The last twelve-year period commenced on the 1st of January, 1854, and will terminate on the 31st December, 1865.

It appears, from what has been before said, with what difficulties since the year 1820 the several German states have had to battle with regard to an agreement respecting a joint custom-house tariff, the attempt to establish business regulations were more than once frustrated with the question of a tariff. It also appears that Prussia formed, in the year 1818, a uniform tariff for the whole of her territory, and that this tariff formed the base of the treaty of 1833, as well as of the present Zollverein.

It is therefore of importance to examine this tariff a little more closely, and to estimate it in its importance for the period at which it was issued, as otherwise an understanding of the so-much-discussed "Zollverein-confusions" is impossible. When Prussia came forward with her new tariff, France, England, Russia, and Austria were surrounded with import prohibitions, or duties greatly resembling prohibitions. The Prussian tariff, therefore, in contrast with the tariff legislations of the said states, an immense progress, as its object was not so much the exclusion of foreign products from the inland markets, as the placing of the inland mguufacturers in a position to compete at home with the foreign markets. When, therefore, the Prussian tariff is discussed with regard to the protective duty, it must be distinguished between this and the protective duties of other states of the same period.

The rates of the tariff of 1818 protect, it is true, the inland industry, but not by entirely excluding foreign imports; they only protect it so far as to strengthen it and place it in a position to compete with foreign imports. The Prussian tariff has, therefore, for its object, in the first place, free trade, and the efforts of the Prussian legislation to institute a protective system for the home industry, which should consist not so much in high duties as in its adaptation to further and render more easy competition; these efforts made the Prussian tariff suitable both for Prussia herself and for a general German toll treaty, the foundation of which was, therefore, much furthered by it. The Prussian, as well as the Zollverein tariff, however, besides affording a protection to inland industry and rendering it thereby more capable of competition, has also its financial side, as it is intended to procure at the same time, for the states of the confederation, as large a revenue as possible. The Prussian tariff of 1818 gives as its object "to protect the inland luxury by a moderate taxation of external commerce, and the consumption of foreign articles, and to insure to the state a revenue which business and luxury can afford, without impeding commerce." It was, therefore, laid down as a principle, that the duty on foreign manufactures should not exceed 10 per cent. on an average, and that the duty should be lightest, if the same could be done without injuring the home industry.

Since the establishment of the Zollverein an age has passed away. By the progress of natural science, and science generally by the new means of communication and by the introduction of machinery, many of the articles subjected to duty are much lower in price. Thus calico which in 1825 cost 15 to 20 silver groschen for seven-eighths wide, can now be bought nine-eighths wide for 4 silver groschen.

In consequence of such great revolution in price it now happens that certain duties which then were 10 per cent. now exceed 50 per cent. So that the same regulations which then only imposed a moderate duty, which business and luxury could well pay, now impose on many articles, viz: those of a coarse nature of the same class a tax which amounts to a prohibition. The constitution of the Zollverein is such that the most glaring faults in the tariff, in the way of custom legislation, cannot be remedied. For instance, the constitution prescribes for all conclusions of the tariff conferences *unanimity*. It gives, therefore, to every little state of Germany the power to prevent, by its vote, every reform, and renders the reduction of the tariff impossible. Thus the tariff modifications proposed by Prussia during the last few years have failed through Bavaria, Wurtemberg, and Hesse Darmstadt voting against the same.

The inconvenience of this antiquated tariff made itself, however, during the present tariff period, (begun on the 1st January,) 1854, so much the more sensible, as, at this period, other nations have altered their systems of customs, and have gone over to liberal tariff principles. England has taken the prohibition tariff quite away, and Austria has approached the system of the protective duties. Belgium, Holland, Italy, even Russia, have reformed their tariffs; and at last France, who had longest upheld the prohibition, was led by the treaty concluded between England and Belgium to enter the path of a liberal tariff policy. The Zollverein alone has remained in its former stagnation, with its antiquated tariff. It was, therefore, evident that with the termination of the twelve-yearly period a considerable change must take place. The present crisis of the Zollverein is nothing further than the severe and extended conflict caused by a stagnation of the tariff legislation through the resistance of the minority, while the necessity of a reform was universally acknowledged. The German Zollverein is an alliance of German states, the joint territories of which are forming a closed girdle of land.

The object of this alliance is the introduction of a common custom and commercial system. Every one of the allied states cannot, however, represent itself by a deputy of its own in the said alliance. By the renewed treaty of 1853 there are only twelve members provided with a full vote, viz: Prussia, Bavaria, Saxony, Hanover, Wurtemberg, Baden, Electoral Hesse, Grand Duchy of Hesse, the Thuringian states, Oldenburg, Nassau and Brunswick. The representative of Nassau has also to give his voice for the free city of Frankfort. Still Frankfort has the right of sending a special commissary, to be present at the conference, but this commissary has not the right to vote.

There are, in all, twenty-seven German states of the confederation which have an interest in the Zollverein ; that is to say, all except Austria, Holstein, Lauenburg-Mecklenberg, Lichtenstein, Lubeck, and Hamburg.

The toll and custom revenue realized by the import, export, and transit duties, according to the general tariff, forms the first and most important of the common revenues of the Zollverein. To secure this revenue, the borders of the Zollverein have been marked with as exact a toll line as possible. In the different states there exist the same laws for the levying of the duties. Also, the organization of the board of customs is as much as possible placed on the same footing in the different states. The legislation of the Zollverein, in so far as the financial side is held in view, comprehends the custom law, the custom tariff, the arrangement of the customs, the regulation of the fines, the law respecting the taxation of beet-root sugar, the agreement respecting the levying and controlling of inland (transit) imposts. The principal taxation is laid on such objects of consumption as are not absolute necessities, and which are used chiefly by the better classes of the population, such as coffee, sugar, tobacco, and wine. The duty is regulated according to rather extensive classes of goods, so that as a rule it is not necessary to make a distinction in the contents of a case. The amount of duty is regulated according to weight, measure, and number, so that it is not necessary to ascertain the value of the goods. As immediately after the introduction of the Zollverein, people in Germany began to produce sugar out of inland beet-root, and as the industry connected with the same soon became very flourishing, financial respects made it necessary to subject beet-root sugar to a corresponding duty. The revenue of beet-root sugar, therefore, although produced and consumed within the limits of the Zollverein, forms a general revenue of the Zollverein, and is divided amongst the several states according to the same principles which have been agreed upon for the distribution of the import duties. Excepted from the general taxation are salt and *playing cards*, which belong to the *state monopolies*. Salt is taxed in all the states of the Zollverein with rather a high and yielding duty in proportion to its value and its indispensability. The import of salt, and of all objects out of which common salt is extracted, into the Zollverein, is prohibited unless a government of one of the states should import it into its own magazine for sale.

Each state has the power to tax the following articles with an inland duty; viz: brandy, vinegar, beer and malt, wine, fruit juice and cider, tobacco, meal and other ground articles, meat, articles made of meat, and fat. Still it is endeavored in the several states of the Zollverein to have, as far as possible, certain general principles respecting the duty on these articles, which are not allowed to be exceeded. Those states which have laid a tax on the production or preparation of an article of consumption can levy the legal amount of the same when the same article is imported from other states of the Zollverein, and also, when the article is exported to other states, claim the same duty, or part of the same, at pleasure. For the levying of transit duties there are certain offices prescribed on certain transit roads.

With regard to the monopoly of salt, before stated, the following statistical remarks may be of interest:

Salt is not produced in all the states of the Zollverein, but *rock salt* only, principally in the Prussian province of Saxony, in Thuringia, and in the states in the neighborhood of the Neckar; and *salt waters* in Electoral Hesse, Hanover, and on the Rhine.

The annual production of salt in Germany, with the exception of Austria, is said to amount to 5,500,000 of zollcentners, which is contributed in the following ratio:

a. Prussia	46 per cent.	*f.* Hesse Darmstadt...	4 per cent.
b. Bavaria	14 per cent.	*g.* Hesse Cassel.:....	3 per cent.
c. Wurtemberg	14 per cent.	*h.* Thuringia	2½ per cent.
d. Hanover	9½ per cent.	*i.* Brunswick and Old-	
e. Baden	6½ per cent.	enburg	1½ per cent.

The following states of the union produced no salt at all, viz: the kingdom of Saxony, Luxemburg, Nassau, and Frankfort.

The consumption of salt in the states of the Zollverein is computed to have amounted, in 1849, to 5,555,998 zollcentners, or 18 lbs. per head. According to the present state of population in the Zollverein, the aggregate demand would now be calculated at 18 lbs. per head, at 6,087,644 zollcentners. According to that the production of salt has been about half a million zollcentners less than the consumption.

The salt monopoly has for its foundation the royal salt prerogative, which has developed itself out of the royal mining prerogative. The royal salt prerogative evinces itself in two ways: First. That no private individual can carry on salt works without a royal permission. Secondly. That no one can sell salt unless authorized by the state. The latter statute has led to the salt monopoly. As the state has secured for itself the exclusive right of selling salt, it has become sole sovereign of the price of salt throughout the state.

In my despatches, No. 342, of May 28, No. 344, of June 2, and No. 368, of

21st July last, I entered more fully into the subject of the treaties, tendency, and tariff of the new Zollverein. In addition I beg to annex an official and printed German copy, marked A, of all the treaties in full, up to the latest date, with reference to the continuance of the Zollverein as well as the new tariff, with its additions, as proposed by the several German governments interested.

After these preliminary remarks, I pass over to the transactions of the Zollverein in 1863–'64. The total receipts of the Zollverein for *import* and *export* duties in the year 1863, compared with those of 1862, show a decrease of 105,108 thalers, thus:

	Thalers.
The decrease on the import duties amounted to	128, 356
Whilst the increase on the exportation amounted to	23, 248
Leaving the above	105, 108

So that the decrease of the receipts of 1863 amounts to about half per cent. against those of 1862, as appears more fully from the annexed table, marked B.

The table C exhibits a comparison of some of the principal articles imported and exported in 1862 and 1863. The following remarks will serve better to explain the different branches of the receipts:

	Thalers.
The joint gross receipts of the impost duties amounted in 1862, to	25,703,236
1863, to	25,574,880
Which shows a decrease, in 1863, of	128,356

With respect to the result which hereby appears in import duties, in comparison with the result of the preceding year, it may be remarked that, although in the beginning of the year business appeared lively, and there were prospects that the same would increase during the course of the year, these prospects have not been realized.   •   •   •   Not only has speculation been stagnated under these circumstances, and business been limited to the supply of the most urgent wants; but, also, during the last months of the year has been added the growing political uneasiness, as well as the uncertainty which the crisis of the Zollverein has produced.

It must, however, be remarked, that the result of the revenue on import duties, at the close of the third quarter showed an increase of more than two per cent., and as, at the end of the year, this result has shown a decrease of one-half per cent., it may be inferred from this circumstance that the result of the receipts of the last quarter, against the corresponding portion of the former year, has again become more favorable. As regards the result of the revenue with respect to the import duty in the different states of the Zollverein, it appears from a comparative review that the decrease of receipts was, in 1862, about ten in a hundred in Wurtemberg; in the Grand Dutchy of Hesse Darmstadt it only reached the amount of six per cent.; in Oldenberg, three; in Hanover, two per cent.; and in Prussia, Bavaria, Electoral Hesse, and Frankfort-on-the-Main, it is even less important. As regards the increase of receipts, it was most important in Luxemburg, though the result of the revenue of 1859 has not been reached again there. In Baden and Nassau the receipts exceed the result of the preceding year by about seven or six in a hundred; in the Thuringian states, about two per cent.; and in Saxony and Brunswick the receipts have remained about the same.

A survey of the articles imported shows that the decreased import of bleached and unbleached cotton yarns and cotton articles has had great influence on the sinking of the receipts. Next to these articles the diminution of imported raw sugar for boiling must be considered. It must be remarked that with this article, it was attempted the former year to make a competition with beet-root raw sugar, which, however, had not a very advantageous result. Nevertheless, in the year 1862 the import of raw sugar, not only on account of the unfavorable beet-root harvest, but also through the decrease of duty imposed, had risen to almost three times the amount of 1861. In the year 1863 the importation had diminished more than ten per cent. at the close of the third quarter.

Against the decreased importation of the above-mentioned articles, the decreased importation of other articles, such as raw coffee, cattle, woollen goods of all kinds, and unworked tobacco leaves, has been of less importance. It must not, however, be omitted to be remarked that the minor differences, as they showed themselves at the close of the third quarter, have, through the result of importation during the last quarter, been frequently as much and partly much more diminished. This has been the case more especially with regard to cotton yarn, sirup, unworked tobacco leaves, and wool goods. Increased importation has taken place, more especially in wine in bottles, railway rails, fresh and dried southern fruits, herrings, meats, spices, and other articles of less importance. With regard to the increased importation of wine, it may be stated that the wine wholesale dealers, by the unfavorable vintage in France, and in the supposition that the treaty of commerce with France would come into existence earlier, had limited their wine imports as much as possible. In order, however, to complete their stores, or on account of the favorable prices, they have again imported large quantities. Herrings, on account of the very productive season, and southern fruits and spices, on account of the good harvest and cheap prices, have reached a high rate of importation. With regard to the again increasing importation of meat, it must be stated that the consumption of bacon and fat from America, on account of the cheapness of these articles, in comparison with the inland prices, has greatly increased. The increase of the export duties of 1863, over those of 1862, amounts to 23,248 thalers.

Thus, whilst the western states show an increase of 26,041 thalers, the eastern states, as appears from the annexed table D, show a decrease of 2,793, or 23,248 thalers.

The above increase of the receipts of the western states was principally caused by the increased exports of raw skins from Frankfort-on-the-Main to France and Belgium. The decrease of the receipts of the eastern States was partly caused by the diminished export of several articles, in consequence of the disturbed state of affairs in Poland.

The total gross receipts of import and export duties for the first half of the present year, up to the 1st of July last—   Thalers.
Amounted to... 11, 476, 372
Whilst they amounted during the same period of 1863 to...... 11, 968, 348

Showing a decrease for 1863 of......................... ·491, 976

In the present year the circumstance which has had the most influence on the result of the receipts is, that navigation was, in the months of January and February, quite closed by the severity of the winter, while in the spring months it was carried on uninterruptedly. Besides this, the blockade of the harbors of the North sea and Baltic, caused by the war with Denmark, the war in our country, as well as the disturbances in Poland, also the presentiment of still greater European embarrassments, which have long impeded commerce and industry, in conjunction with the uncertainty respecting the result of the cities of the Zollverein, all have had a prejudicial influence on the development of commercial intercourse.

Important decrease of importations have taken place, principally in raw

H. Ex. Doc. 60——34

sugar, unworked iron, and wine; also, although in a less degree, in unbleached single and two-fold cotton yarn, cotton goods, meat, herrings, silk, and half-silk goods, and in several other articles.

With respect to the two first-named articles, I must here refer to what has been before said, and only mention, with respect to the increased importation of wine, that the good quality of the wines of 1862 causes the same to be bought up in the spring, so that, during the last six months, less has been imported.

The increase of importation has chiefly taken place in raw coffee and unworked tobacco leaves; this circumstance, with respect to the first-named article, has been explained in the foregoing remarks. It here remains to be said, with respect to the latter, that the cigar manufacturers have caused the same by pushing the sale of their articles.

The following statement furnishes the exact number of all the industrial establishments and factories in the Zollverein in the year 1861:

In the year 1861 there existed in the Zollverein 223 factories for carding wool by the hand, spinning-mills, and mills for spinning hair and wool of all kinds.

1,777 carded yarn half-wool (vigogne) spinning-mills, with 1,117,862 fine spindles; 146 combed yarn spinning-mills, with 251.897 fine spindles. Further, 94 silk-reeling mills; 215 spun-silk mills, floret silk spinning-mills, and silk throwsters' establishments; 310 cotton spinning-mills, with 2,235,195 fine spindles; 221 wadding and wick yarn factories; 295 establishments for preparing flax and hemp; 38 flax and hemp and tow spinning-mills, with 78,064 fine spindles for flax yarn, with 396 for hemp yarn and 56,032 fine spindles for tow yarn and 419 factories for making, knitting, stitching, and darning yarn out of wool, cotton, and linen. The weaving, the fancy, and ribbon manufactories are as follows: 1,067 cloth factories, with 2,592 machines; 622 factories for other wool, and half-wool articles, (excepting shawls and carpeting,) with 3,655 machines; 1,072 fulling-mills; 940 factories for cotton and half-cotton fancy articles, with 23,941 machines; 301 factories for linen articles—with 350 and 314 factories for silk, half-silk, velvet-silk ribbon and velvet ribbon manufactured, with 1,270 machine stools; 60 shawl factories, with 867 machines and 1,229 hand machines; 45 carpet manufactories, with 250 machines and 293 hand machines; 354 factories for ribbons, cords, trimmings, lace, and fancy buttons, (not including the factories for silk and leonine worked ribbons and laces,) in which there are at work 2,843 machines, and machines worked by the hand, and 1,619 regular ribbon and trimming machines; lastly, 279 establishments for making stockings, with 4,236 machines and 103 factories, with tulle, bobbinets, and laces, (including the lace making,) with 50 machines worked by the hand. The numbers of machines at work in the Zollverein, both hired and owned property, are as follows: 32,882 in silk, half-silk, velvet, silk ribbon, and velvet ribbon; 151,451 machines for cotton and half-cotton; 120,229 for linen; 39,833 for wool and half-wool; 29,944 in stocking-making and weaving; 5,014 for linen, cotton, and cotton bands or tapes; 14,966 machines are at work in the other branches of industry; besides, as kindred branches, there are 370,970 machines for linen cloth or canvas; 6,284 machines for coarse wool fabric, and 10,715 for other textures.

In addition to my remarks in my last year's annual report respecting beetroot, and the substances manufactured from it, and respecting sugar, I beg to annex table marked E, which exhibits the receipts of the Zollverein for duty on beet-root sugar, and the distribution of them from 1st September to 31st December, 1863; the table marked I, which exhibits the amount of duty on foreign sugar and beet-root sugar in the Zollverein, from 1st April, 1862, to 30th of March, 1863. Table marked C exhibits the quantity of raw beet-root manufactured into beet-root sugar from 1st September, 1863, to 31st of August, 1864.

From the foregoing it appears that the fabrication of beet-root sugar during the said period, exhibits again some considerable increase. Against 257 factories, in the preceding period, there were last year 253 factories in activity, and the consumption of raw beet-root of 39,911,520 cwt. In 1863-'64 against 36,719,258 cwt. in 1862-'63, is shown an increase in favor of the former period of 3,192,262 cwt.

The annexed table, marked H, contains a tabular statement of the products of the mining, smelting, and salt works of the Zollverein in 1862, from which it appears that the total amount of works numbered 6,615, and the total quantity of produce amounted to 399,983 quintals.

  *   *   *   *   *

The annexed table, marked K, exhibits the number of German railroads, together with the total receipts for the month of August last, and from the period from the 1st of January to the last of August, 1864, compared with those for the same period of 1863.

The following statement furnishes a synoptical view of the lines and stations of all the German-Austrian telegraph union, as extracted from the official reports of the same.

The number of stations and the length of lines and wires at work, arranged according to the different states, were, on the 1st of January, 1864, as follows:

Countries.	Number of stations.	Geographical miles of lines.	Geographical miles of wires.
Austria	300	2,208.1	3,904.2
Prussia	296	1,524.3	4,740.8
Bavaria	73	379.5	775.2
Saxony	26	138.6	204.6
Hanover	46	239.4	481.9
Wurtemberg	81	214.7	283.3
Baden	79	194.7	425.6
Mecklenburg	17	58.3	73.2
Netherlands	63	248.0	617.7
Total	981	5,205.6	11,506.5

At the beginning of the year 1863 there were 775 stations, 4,496.9 miles of line, and 9,633.2 geographical miles of wires. There is, therefore, now an increase of 226 stations, 710.7 geographical miles of line, and 1,873.3 geographical miles of wires.

This increase distributes itself among the separate states of the union in the following manner:

Countries.	Stations.		Geographical miles of lines.	Geographical miles of wires.
	Opened.	Removed.		
Austria	63	˙2	284.1	612.3
Prussia	99	....	215.3	846.9
Bavaria..	24	....	91.8	101.2
Saxony	....	....	0.7	0.7
Hanover	10	....	37.9	61.1
Wurtemberg	16	....	38.0	41.9
Baden ....:.	14	....	16.4	114.9
Mecklenburg	2	....	1.5	5.5
Netherlands	1	....	25.0	88.8
Total..	226	2	710.7	1,873.3

To each station there are in—

	Miles of line.	Miles of wire.
Austria........................	7.36	10.62
Prussia........................	5.15	7.87
Bavaria........................	5.20	10.48
Saxony........................	5.33	3.50
Hanover........................	5.20	5.39
Wurtemburg........................	2.65	4.31
Baden........................	2.46	9.80
Mecklenburg........................	3.43	13.00
Netherlands........................	3.94	16.02

Yielding to an average for each single station in the whole net, 5.31 miles of line and 11.72 miles of wire.

The development of the telegraph net in the Zollverein, during the last seven years, is shown in the following tabular view:

At the beginning of the year—	No. of stations.	Total length, geographical miles.		Geographical miles on one station.		Average length of wire for 100 miles of line.
		Lines.	Wires.	Lines.	Wires.	
1856	234	2,317.7	3,889.8	9.90	16.62	167.8
1857	307	2,644.6	4,772.9	8.61	15.55	180.5
1858	357	2,857.3	5,501.4	8.01	15.41	192.5
1859	425	3,255.8	6,348.0	7.61	14.94	195.0
1860	480	3,534.8	7,104.0	7.36	14.80	201.1
1861	545	3,864.1	7,869.4	7.09	14.44	203.7
1862	627	4,125.3	8,590.5	6.58	13.70	208.2
1863	755	4,494.9	9,633.2	5.97	12.76	214.3
1864	981	5,205.6	11,506.5	5.31	11.72	221.0

In the course of eight years, therefore, the length of line has increased 124¼ per cent., but that of wires almost three-fold; that is, in the proportion of 1 to 2.96. The increase in the number of stations was still greater, viz: in the proportion of 1 : 4.19; consequently, as the foregoing table shows, on the one hand, the proportion of length of wire to the length of the line, (and therefore the average number of wires on the line,) has steadily increased, and, on the other hand, the proportion of length of line, as well as that of length of wire to the number of stations, has regularly and steadily decreased.

*   *   *   *   *

Before concluding the commercial part of the report, I may be permitted to show, by two very striking instances, of what great and injurious influence the war in our country has been in this part of Germany. The following figures show, with regard to the traffic and navigation of the Rhine, in what great degree the importation of goods and raw materials from the United States to Germany, and the exportation of goods, &c., from Germany, &c., to the United States, have decreased during the first years of the war.

There passed the custom-house office at Emmerich *up* the Rhine—

Cotton raw, 1860	450, 043	ctrs*
1861	518, 282	"
1862	284, 983	"
Pitch and rosin, 1860	251, 047	"
1861	73, 204	"
1862	38, 579	"
Tobacco (unmanufact'd) 1860	120, 256	"
1861	91, 801	"
1862	72, 038	"
Turpentine oil, 1860	20, 678	"
1861	12, 890	"
1862	2, 117	"

There passed the same office *down* the Rhine—

Tobacco, manufactured, 1860	26, 059	cwt.
1861	3, 339	"
1862	1, 516	"
Mineral water, 1860	69, 775	"
1861	53, 275	"
1862	50, 194	"
Hardware, 1860	18, 567	"
1861	17, 533	"
1862	16, 375	"

Another instance is furnished in the decrease of commercial intercourse between the Grand Duchy of Hesse Darmstadt and the United States.

As the port of Bremen is the natural medium of that intercourse, the result of the traffic between Bremen and the said Grand Duchy may be considered as the criterion whereby to judge of the total traffic between the latter and the United States. Now the *export* from Hesse Darmstadt to Bremen amounted—

	Louis d'ors.
In 1855 to	245, 933
1856 to	298, 475
1857 to	404, 494
1858 to	425, 690
1859 to	573, 860
1860 to	433, 807
1861 to	181, 330
1862 to	229, 947
1863 to	181, 316

Whilst the *import* from Bremen amounted in—

		Louis d'ors.
1855 to		165,474
1856 "		314,573
1857 "		327,320
1858 "		279,374
1859 "		360,734
1860 "		448,019
1861 "		457,039
1862 "		438,487
1863 "		444,272

It is seen by the foregoing that the exports to Bremen, until the commencement of our present war, went on increasing every year; but that, since then, they have decreased in an extraordinary degree. Among the exports to Bremen, there are, according to value, articles of consumption to an amount of 61,336 Louis d'ors; raw material, 21,253 Louis d'ors; half manufactures, 41,183 Louis d'ors; manufactured goods, 7,644 Louis d'ors; and other products of industry, 49,258 Louis d'ors.

A few remarks remain to be made respecting the result of the *crops* of the present year in this neighborhood and in Germany generally.

The price of provisions remained pretty firm until the present harvest, which not only here but in all the other districts of Germany, and in Europe generally, has been rather favorable. On an average the prices of grain were from 1st October, 1863–'64, as follows:

Wheat, 10½ florins per 200 pounds.
Rye,   7¾   "   "
Barley, 7½   "   "
Oats,   6¾ . "

The production of red clover-seed is generally very important in Silesia, Saxony, Rhenish Bavaria, and Manheim, from where, especially, the great amount consumed in England is obtained. This year, however, in these districts, the harvest is scarcely worth mowing, and it is believed there will be much imported of this article from the United States, provided the result of the crops there has been more favorable, and allows a greater import than the former regular shipments, especially to England.

The importation of petroleum from the United States, also, is continually increasing, on account of the very considerable increase of the consumption here. The average price has been, during the last twelve months, 20 f. per ctnr.

Last year's plentiful tobacco crop is followed by one still more abundant this year. It is supposed the result will amount to above 450,000 ctnr., and a good middle quality is expected. Since about three months a new market has been opened in Portugal (through altered rates of duty) for the Palatine cigars, as also the consumption of the finer sorts, used for cigar covers, has risen in England. Of Palatine cigars there has also been much sold for Canada, and this branch of manufacture has thereby become rather lively.

The result of the vintage this year is very unfavorable both as regards quantity and quality.

First. There came very unfavorable weather, while the vine was in bloom, which shows itself in the irregular ripeness of the fruit, and has much injured the quality of the wine. The weather was also very unfavorable as the fruit was ripening, being very cold. A very low quality of wine is, therefore, expected, (perhaps, like that of 1863,) as also high prices, which would even now be felt if the exportation were as lively as formerly, and if the money market did not fetter speculation. The prices of wine in Rhenish Bavaria have been on an average during the last twelve months—

For low quality, 80 florins—120 per 1,000 litres,
" middle quality, 150 florins—200 per 1,000 litres,
" best quality, 250 florins—400 per 1,000 litres,

taken directly from the producers and without casks.

The wine of the Rhine countries is generally sold by wholesale auctions in spring, and about this season of the year. The auctions of wines of former years, which were recently held in the Palatinate and neighboring wine countries, were accompanied with very satisfactory results. There were throughout good prices obtained for such produce, which met a steady sale, and is now in safe hands. As Bavaria has now joined the Zollverein, and the transit duties through that country are abolished, it is generally expected there will be a lively trade with northern Germany. At the auctions held at Bingen, Röidesheim, &c., wine of 1863 was sold at 275 florins—400 per "stuck," (a cask of 15 kilderkins or 600 litres,) without casks; wine of 1862 at 345—1,200 florins; wine of 1861 at 340—1,100 florins; wine of 1859 at 400—1,200 florins; wine. of 1858 at 450—800 florins; and wine of 1857 at 400—1,000 florins per "stuck."

The fruit harvest has been exceedingly favorable. A great many cultivators have such a large quantity that they are able to use a deal for cider and fruit-brandy, which, in some districts of Baden, &c., has not been the case for a long time.

The potato harvest has been good in every respect, which, being an article of general consumption, greatly influences the prices of other provisions, and causes also brandy to be cheap, the production of which is very important, especially in Rhenish Bavaria. The price of potatoes is not yet fixed. It is expected, however, to be about 36 to 48 kreutzers per ctnr. for potatoes used iu manufacture, (including starch and grape-sugar productions,) and for edible potatoes, 1 florin to 1½ florin per cwt.

Hops, which have been much cultivated for many generations in the Baden part of the Pfalz, between Carsule and Manheim, and have gone under the name of schwezingerhops, scarcely pay this year for cultivation in that district. In the inferior qualities of this harvest, 65 to 75 florins per cwt. are asked. The same complaints are reported from other countries where hops are extensively cultivated. Thus a correspondent from Bavaria writes that the hopes of a yielding crop and good quality have not at all been fulfilled. The warm weather, in the middle of August, was of very short duration, and the lack of sunny weather, together with the cold stormy weather, was very prejudicial to the ripening hops and destroyed all hopes of a good harvest, either as regards quantity or quality. Under these circumstances the hop districts have been taxed, according to the result of the harvest, thus: Bavaria produces half a harvest, of which Bohemia yields a scanty half harvest, of which the Saazer district is most productive. Prussia, Poland, Brunswick, and Altmark are not more fortunate. Wurtemberg is favored with a full half harvest, against which Baden only has a one-third harvest. France, Elsace, and Loraine can only reckon on a one-third harvest, while Belgium expects one-half a harvest. England realizes about £180,000 to £200,000 old duty, therefore about 100,000 cwt. more than last year. The quality is not satisfactory in any country. Not more than a third of the continental crop consists of a good first quality, and even this best portion is inferior to that of former years.

The produce of the harvest this year has been injured partly by the stormy weather, and partly by the defective development of the umbel and dim color. On account of these circumstances the hop business will be much impeded, as the same difficulty of choice exists in all kinds of hops, from the best qualities for beer down to the inferior qualities. The greatest knowledge of the article is therefore needed, and the greatest precaution necessary in order to select, even out of the best stores, such hops as will prove satisfactory when applied to brewing purposes. On a general survey, however, in spite of the increased beer consumption, the produce of this year is considered sufficient for the continental consumption. Since ten years, the production of hops on the continent has increased nearly two-fold; and England having, this year, the best harvest she has had since 1859, will leave the continental market unnoticed, and not exercise that influence to which that trade is accustomed. The scarcity of hops of the former years, and the late harvest of the present year, caused fast purchases during the gathering, and an increase of price, occasioned by speculation, in almost all countries. Half-dried common country quality is bought at 82 florins. Hops of Hallastan as high as 100 florins, and Landspalter Sigel hops at 140 florins.   *   *   *

Finally, in accordance with the consular regulations, I beg to annex a table, marked L, which exhibits the total exports from the states included in this consular district to the United States during the financial period from the 1st of October, 1863, to the 30th September, 1864, compared with those during the same period of the preceding year. From the same, it appears that the total export from this district in 1862–'63 amounted to f. 2,104,354.59; and in 1863 –'64, to f. 3,285,826.09, which exhibits an increase in favor of the financial period, just expired, of f. 1,181,472.10 ; and, at the same time, the gratifying fact that the principal part of the decrease of the export of the present year refers to articles of luxury. The decrease of the export of optical instruments and chiccory is explained by the circumstance that, not in entire accordance with the proper law, the invoices of the Brunswick exporters of these articles have been verified at the United States consulate at Hanover, notwithstanding the Duchy of Brunswick is included in my consular district.

B.

Statement showing the import and export duties of the Zollverein of 1863, compared with those of 1862.

States	Population	Import duties 1863	Import duties 1862	Export duties 1863	Export duties 1862	Total 1863	Total 1862	Increase, 1863	Decrease, 1863
		Thalers.	*Thalers.*	*Thalers.*	*Thalers.*	*Thalers.*	*Thalers.*	*Thalers.*	*Thalers.*
Prussia	18,867,061	14,642,908	14,900,764	68,294	66,999	14,901,202	14,967,763		66,561
Luxemburg	197,731	135,901	118,778	2,139	1,603	138,190	120,383	17,737	
Bavaria	4,695,494	1,445,536	1,452,883	21,766	13,767	1,467,302	1,467,590		288
Saxony	2,225,240	2,563,108	2,553,630	9,559	8,148	2,572,667	2,561,778	10,889	
Hanover	1,908,631	2,945,573	2,311,668	8,154	6,025	2,953,727	2,317,693		63,996
Wurtemberg	1,720,708	485,280	538,119	1,574	1,550	487,394	540,689		53,275
Baden	1,365,739	1,178,001	1,102,538	15,169	15,890	1,193,170	1,118,488	74,742	
Hesse Cassel	710,680	349,433	353,974	685	651	350,118	354,625		4,507
Hesse Darmstadt	674,168	548,714	585,810	9,870	3,287	551,561	589,097		37,513
Thuringia	1,069,681	297,029	290,987	68	31	297,117	291,018	6,099	
Brunswick	287,634	274,329	272,980	233	51	274,562	273,931	1,531	
Oldenburg	328,568	255,612	280,167	948	165	256,660	285,332		8,475
&c.	454,398	98,294	92,904	550	470	98,841	93,382	6,502	
Frankfort	397,477	853,502	861,794	45,305	25,039	898,807	886,833	11,974	
Total	34,913,185	25,574,880	25,703,226	166,634	143,386	25,741,514	25,846,622	129,474	224,589 / 129,474
									105,108

Comparative statement showing some of the principal articles imported and exported in 1862 and 1863.

IMPORTS.

Articles.	1863.	1862.	1863. Increase.	1863. Decrease.
Cotton and cotton goods—				
Raw cotton ....cwt..	1,008,697	1,063,791	4,906	....
Cotton goods ....do ..	167,350	280,390	....	113,040
Lead and leaden ware ....do ..	5,504	6,436	....	932
Drugs and dyestuffs..............	2,746,090	2,334,323	411,767	....
Iron and steel ware—				
Pig iron and unwrought steel ..	4,127,945	3,265,958	861,987	....
Forged wrought iron	163,270	138,722	24,548	....
Iron and steel ware	290,157	320,411	....	30,354
Ore..........................	776,006	940,823	....	163,817
Flax, oakum, and hemp	357,305	427,685	....	70,380
Grain, pulse, and seeds—				
Wheat .. ..scheffle..	3,194,440	8,082,407	....	4,887,967
Rye ....do....	7,442,857	10,951,984	....	3,509,127
Hemp-seed...............cwt..	1,202,357	1,372,184	....	169,827
Clover-seed ....do ..	146,146	144,060	2,106	....
Glass and glass ware	46,888	43,226	3,662	....
Hides, skins, and hair.............	577,394	561,739	15,656	....
Wood and wooden ware—				
Wood..................cord..	29,097	31,707	....	2,700
Wooden ware ....cwt..	363,391	412,744	....	49,353
Hops	18,633	13,052	5,581	....
Copper and brass and copper and brass ware	117,055	103,037	14,018	....
Leather and leather goods	14,511	11,804	2,707	....
Linen and linen ware	276,170	230,400	45,770	....
Rags and paper ware	83,266	52,526	30,740	....
Groceries, confections, and articles of consumption—				
Beer........................	14,378	10,725	3,653	....
Brandy	44,824	45,714	....	890
Wine	247,873	341,528	6,345	....
Butter	29,843	45,953	....	16,110
Tropic fruits ....tierces..	373,922	342,845	31,067	....
Spice ....cwt..	49,545	44,845	4,700	....
Herrings ....tons..	489,314	426,234	63,080	....
Coffee ....cwt..	1,334,743	1,348,262	....	13,519
Cocoa ....do ..	18,920	18,964	....	44
Cheese ....do ..	42,741	38,918	3,823	....
Rice ....do ..	582,487	173,411	9,076	....
Salt ....do ..	613,918	479,294	134,624	....
Sirup ....do ..	90,998	102,219	....	11,321
Tobacco.................do ..	572,985	583,914	....	10,929
Tea ....do ..	15,842	14,829	1,013	....
Sugar...................do ..	430,531	464,569	....	34,038
Oil ....do ..	935,624	964,306	....	28,682
Paper and pasteboard	19,935	17,437	2,641	....
Silk and silk goods	35,445	38,861	....	3,416
Stone coal	18,367,743	17,897,864	69,879	....
Tallow and stearine	63,601	86,852	....	23,251
Tar and pitch....................	262,684	192,701	69,983	....
Earthen-ware....................	248,564	41,790	6,774	....
Cattle...................number..	708,549	788,119	....	83,166
Wool and goods ....cwt..	701,028	644,643	66,380	....
Pewter and ware ....do ..	46,440	44,104	2,336	....
Fish ....do ..	69,682	54,170	15,512	....
Dried fruit..................do ..	184,689	190,007	....	5,418
Oil dregs and train oil	184,048	242,899	....	58,851

Statement showing the principal articles imported and exported, &c.—Cont'd.

EXPORTS.

Articles.	1863.	1862.	1863.	
			Increase.	Decrease.
Cotton ---- . ---------------cwt..	179,536	274,697	----------	95,161
Flax, oakum, and hemp ----------	194,226	266,129	----------	71,903
Raw skins and hides ------------	51,393	41,070	10,323	----------
Rags for paper------------------	2,291	871	1,420	----------
Raw and carded wool . ----------	153,914	151,440	2,474	----------
Raw silk ------ ----------------	1,906	2,626	----------	720

D.

Total receipt of import and export duties during the first half of 1864 up to July 1, compared with those of the same period of 1863.

States.	Population.	IMPORT DUTIES.		EXPORT DUTIES.		TOTAL.		FIRST HALF, 1864.	
		First half, 1864.	First half, 1863.	First half, 1864.	First half, 1863.	First half, 1864.	First half, 1863.	More.	Less.
		Thalers.	Thalers.	Thalers.	Thalers.	Thalers.	Thalers.	Thalers.	Thalers.
Prussia	18,867,061	6,460,661	6,875,149	31,336	26,387	6,491,997	6,901,536	------	409,539
Luxemburg	197,731	70,504	63,319	1,143	807	71,647	64,026	7,621	------
Bavaria	4,695,424	645,415	645,390	5,566	11,586	650,981	656,966	------	6,005
Saxony	2,225,940	1,256,332	1,222,742	5,262	5,562	1,261,549	1,228,304	33,290	------
Hanover	1,906,631	940,097	1,040,447	4,681	2,862	944,778	1,043,309	------	98,531
Wurtemberg	1,720,708	213,757	215,637	1,467	704	215,224	216,341	------	1,117
Baden	1,365,732	525,755	520,025	8,659	8,192	534,414	528,217	6,197	------
Electoral Hesse	710,680	188,815	171,711	561	415	189,376	172,126	------	2,750
Hesse Darmstadt	874,166	237,960	260,726	1,231	1,328	239,191	262,064	------	22,863
Thuringia	1,069,821	149,036	137,064	35	74	149,071	137,158	11,913	------
Brunswick	257,624	133,919	141,152	49	103	133,968	141,255	------	7,287
Oldenburg	238,562	103,696	124,569	111	172	103,797	124,741	------	20,944
Nassau	454,326	46,091	45,349	97	528	46,188	46,377	------	189
Frankfort	397,477	437,465	421,206	26,681	24,712	464,146	445,918	18,228	------
Total	34,913,185	11,389,493	11,884,906	96,879	83,442	11,476,372	11,968,348	77,249	569,225
									77,249
									491,976

E.

Receipts of the Zollverein for duty on beet-root sugar, and the distribution of them, from September 1 to December 31, 1863.

States.	No. of factories.	Population.	Quantity of beet root worked into sugar from Sept. 1 to Dec. 31.	Amount of duty on beet-root sugar, deducting refining and cost.	Portion of each state in proportion to population.	To pay.	To receive.
			Zollcentner.	*Thalers.*	*Thalers.*	*Thalers.*	*Thalers.*
Prussia......................	221	18, 867, 061	20, 084, 613	4, 767, 967	2, 878, 136	1, 889, 831	
Luxemburg..................	......	197, 731	....	....	30, 163	....	30, 163
Bavaria.....................	6	4, 695, 424	234, 599	56, 854	716, 278	....	659, 424
Saxony......................	1	2, 225, 940	47, 785	11, 438	339, 457	....	328, 019
Hanover.....................	1	1, 906, 631	90, 300	22, 148	365, 617	....	343, 469
Wurtemberg.................	6	1, 720, 708	657, 909	161, 573	262, 491	....	100, 918
Baden.......................	1	1, 365, 732	323, 163	77, 890	208, 340	....	130, 450
Hesse Cassel................	......	710, 680	....	....	108, 413	....	108, 413
Hesse Darmstadt............	......	874, 168	....	....	133, 353	....	133, 353
Thuringia...................	2	1, 069, 821	125, 597	27, 959	163, 199	....	135, 240
Brunswick..................	14	257, 624	1, 370, 311	283, 881	39, 301	244, 580	
Oldenburg..................	......	238, 562	....	....	45, 699	....	45, 699
Nassau	......	454, 326	....	....	69, 307	....	69, 307
Frankfort-on-the-Main	......	327, 477	....	....	49, 956	....	49, 956
Total..................	259	34, 913, 185	22, 934, 277	5, 409, 710	5, 409, 710	2, 134, 411	2, 134, 411

F.

Amount of duty on foreign sugar and beet-root sugar in the Zollverein from April 1, 1863, to March 31, 1864.

STATES	Loaf sugar.		Brown or raw sugar.		For home refineries.		Sirup.		Quantity of beet root.	Amount of duty.	Total amount of duty paid.	Bonifications for sugar exported.	Balance after deduction of said bonifications.
	Quantity of importation.	Amount of duty 477¼ per cwt.	Quantity of importation.	Amount of duty.	Quantity of importation.	Amount of duty.	Quantity of importation.	Amount of duty.					
	Zolls. Bs.	*Thalers.*	*Cwt. Bs.*	*Thalers.*	*Cwt. Bs.*	*Thalers.*	*Cwt. Bs.*	*Thalers.*	*Cwt. Bs.*	*Thalers.*	*Thalers.*	*Thalers.*	*Thalers.*
1 Prussia	398 55	2,992	520 60	1,383	295,178 97	1,254,510	49,152 7	105,380	34,189,599 50	8,547,399	9,911,557	274,731	9,636,806
2 Luxemburg	83	6	3				157 56	7			350		350
3 Bavaria	415 5	3,043	58 7	348			1,817 23	4,543	465,304 00	101,323	109,961		109,961
4 Saxony	155 31	1,128	17 97	103			108 64	25,271	60,070 00	98,017	46,819		46,819
5 Hanover	550 1	4,033	79 8	474	67 58	987	10,116 11	60,290	143,455 00	33,613	372,655	*2,480	370,175
6 Wurtemburg	944 00	1,791	4 13	94	64,057 17	272,242	24,437 18	1,082	1,184,793 50	296,198	909,108		299,108
7 Baden	985 55	2,094	1 80	10			935 15	2,337	987,303 00	246,825	315,131		315,131
8 Hesse Cassel	20 88	153		1,035	15,026 47	63,862	94 66	236	13,790 00	3,447	3,838		3,838
9 Hesse Darmstadt	83 26	610	172 57				1,047 37	2,618	243,959 30		4,264		4,264
10 Thuringia	25 51	187	37	2			2,336 12	5,840	2,490,721 50	60,999	65,930		65,930
11 Brunswick	6 40	46	2 89	17			2,250 94	5,625		605,180	67,030	1,100	439,695
12 Oldenburg	942 00	1,774	4 70	98			3,587 9	8,967			610,870	151,185	10,324
13 Nassau	42 58	312	1 95	11			457 18	1,149			10,771		324
14 Frankfort-on-the-Main	55 66	408	1 96	5							1,557		1,557
Total	2,925 83	18,517	564 46	3,380	374,330 19	1,590,901	89,476 68	293,664	39,667,997 50	9,916,999	11,753,506	429,494	11,324,010

G.

Quantity of raw beet root worked into beet-root sugar from September 1, 1863, to August 31, 1864.

States	No. of factories	BEET ROOTS PAID DUTY FOR.				
		From Sept. 1 to Dec. 31, 1863.	1st quarter, 1864.	2d quart'r, 1864.	July and Aug. 1864.	Total.
		Zoll. pounds.	*Zoll. pounds.*	*Z. pounds.*	*Z. pounds.*	*Zoll. pounds.*
Prussia	221	20,064,613 00	19,933,897 50	166,285	2,495	34,187,290 50
Luxemburg						
Bavaria	6	234,599 00	169,510 00	18,335	....	422,944 00
Saxony	1	47,785 00	32,285 00	....	....	80,070 00
Hanover	1	90,300 00	52,155 00	....	....	142,455 00
Wurtemberg	6	648,208 14	560,440 00	82,639	....	1,247,287 14
Baden	1	323,163 00	291,504 00	350,325	179,480	1,44,472 00
Electoral Hesse	1	....	13,790 00	3,570	....	17,360 00
Hesse Darmstadt						
Thuringia	2	125,597 00	118,362 00	1,551	....	245,510 00
Brunswick	14	1,370,311 50	1,050,411 00	3,910	....	2,424,631 50
Oldenburg						
Nassau						
Frankfort						
Total	253	22,924,576 64	16,178,353 50	626,615	181,975	39,911,510 14
Total in 1862-'63	247	21,740,040 30	14,398,833 56	428,393	151,992	36,719,258 86
In favor of 1863-'64	6	1,184,536 34	1,779,519 94	198,222	29,983	3,192,261 28

H.—*Statement showing the products of the mining,*

States.	I. MINES.					
	No. of works.	Stone coal.	No. of works.	Peat.	No. of works.	Iron ore.
		Zollcentner.		*Zollcentner.*		*Zollcentner.*
Prussia	428	261,767,816	443	76,140,999	1,079	24,277,221
Anhalt Dessau			9	4,080,057		
Anhalt Bemburg			5	2,738,550		17,648
Waldeck					1	11,592
Luxemburg						7,890,000
Bavaria	131	4,494,402	49	911,403	279	1,032,957
Saxony	85	34,621,436	166	7,672,903	166	1,002,199
Hanover	35	7,206,759	2	108,314	87	2,370,387
Hanover Brunswick Com					25	45,790
Wurtemberg					17	640,542
Baden	3	187,519			77	274,042
Hesse Cassel	1	283,239	26	2,524,660	21	341,154
Hesse Darmstadt			8	639,371	38	590,594
Thuringia	4	484,369	93	3,466,424	49	
Brunswick			4	2,388,352	6	
Oldenburg	1	20			2	
Nassau			28	1,019,651	500	5,352,946
	688	311,525,560	833	101,687,984	2,347	44,390,414

States.	I. MINES.					
	No. of works.	Tin ore.	No. of works.	Cobalt ore.	No. of works.	Arsenic ore.
		Zollcentner.		*Zollcentner.*		*Zollcentner.*
Prussia				313	3	6,642
Anhalt Bemburg						
Bavaria			4	1,907		
Saxony	49	4,319		4,060		25,140
Hanover Brunswick Com						
Wurtemberg					1	1,841
Baden						
Hesse Cassel			2	709		
Hesse Darmstadt			1	75		
Thuringia			2	22,003		
Nassau						
	49	4,319	9	29,067	4	33,623

States.	I. MINES.					
	No. of works.	Asphaltum.	No. of works.	Fluor spar.	Total works.	Total weight.
		Zollcentner.		*Zollcentner.*		*Zollcentner.*
Prussia			4	87,834	2,288	372,797,699
Anhalt Dessau					9	4,080,057
Anhalt Bemburg			1	2,943	9	2,776,959
Waldeck					1	11,592
Luxemburg					2	7,890,723
Bavaria			4	32	567	6,437,952
Saxony				4,734	655	43,901,554
Hanover	2	10,400			152	11,578,451
Hanover Brunswick Com					26	371,221
Wurtemberg					18	642,042
Baden			3	11,021	91	536,808
Hesse Cassel			1	1,466	57	5,793,964
Hesse Darmstadt					53	1,333,030
Thuringia			3	1,175	263	4,165,277
Brunswick					11	2,688,450
Oldenburg					3	19,060
Nassau					613	6,748,368
	2	10,400	16	109,205	4,818	471,773,227

smelting, and salt works of the Zollverein in 1862.

I. MINES.

No. of works.	Gold and silver ore.	No. of works.	Mercurial ore.	No. of works.	Lead ore.	No. of works.	Copper ore.	No. of works.	Zinc ore.
	Zollcentner. 5		*Zollcentner.*	154	*Zollcentner.* 920,607	85	*Zollcentner.* 2,247,508	62	*Zollcentner.* 6,522,197
3	19,279						275		
				1	683	1	100		
20	698	5	70	8	3,000	5	735		
189	541,758				160				8,005
5	88,314			17	1,739,999	2	21,528		25,400
				1	218,723		96,255		
				2	2,696	1	65,089	2	59,000
				2	2,625	2	30,000		
						7	10,385		
						1	228		
				18	97,676	19	4,927		57,438
217	649,356	5	70	203	2,986,109	123	2,477,030	64	6,671,964

I. MINES.

No. of works.	Antimony ore.	No. of works.	Manganese ore.	No. of works.	Alum ore.	No. of works.	Vitriolic ore.	No. of works.	Graphite.
2	*Zollcentner.* 1,556	9	*Zollcentner.* 35,559	3	*Zollcentner.* 337,584	14	*Zollcentner.* 446,241	2	*Zollcentner.* 5,687
							964		
1	320					8	50,627	53	12,499
							3,907		
							10,453		
						1	1,500		
		3	689						
		4	1,977			1	25,690		
		2	68,440					1	2,000
1	1,891	103	45,197			2	1,329		
		46	193,733						
4	3,767	169	365,878	3	337,584	26	540,711	56	20,186

II. COKE.

No. of works.	Raw iron.	No. of works.	Raw steel iron.	No. of works.	Castings from ore.	No. of works.	Castings from pig ir'n.	No. of works.	Iron in bars, wr't iron.
134	*Zollcentner.* 9,836,496	4	*Zollcentner.* 155,353	26	*Zollcentner.* 529,683	199	*Zollcentner.* 1,973,269	298	*Zollcentner.* 6,619,987
1	10,706				27	3	14,229	2	3,543
1	6,300				1,064			7	5,260
6	262,800			1				1	2,500
64	600,021				118,617	12	114,303	29	694,421
7	417,598			6	33,608	13	82,398	20	339,453
11	605,991			2	11,101	26	210,437	29	37,293
		1	19,090						
6	124,833	1	2,829	4	78,205	4	48,730	17	170,364
5	68,209			6	32,513	13	52,099	21	88,041
10	104,910				39,235	21,526		1,835	24	30,572
6	96,671			4	43,023	8	28,853	17	45,656
10	51,701	2	2,765	2	15,059	3	16,549	19	34,776
7	153,337				36,337		31,083		26,957
				1	11,658	4	43,886		131,886
15	362,807				12,259	80,706	3	12,903	16	42,754
303	12,682,410	8	231,454	52	1,013,131	281	2,638,574	500	8,263,465

H.—*Statement showing the products of the mining,*

States.	II. COES.					
	No. of works.	Iron plate.	No. of works.	Iron wire.	No. of works.	Steel.
		Zollcentner.		*Zollcentner.*		*Zollcentner.*
Prussia	29	1,017,869	86	523,470	164	794,574
Anhalt Bemburg					1	23
Bavaria	1	12,879	6	11,860	3	2,692
Saxony	4	4,286			2	1,368
Hanover			1	854	1	1,124
Hanover Brunswick Com						
Wurtemberg					4	8,372
Baden	2	7,239	4	20,800		
Hesse Cassel			7	800	7	7,507
Hesse Darmstadt	1	30	1	2,300		
Thuringia					3	2,134
Brunswick						533
Nassau	2	14,054				
	39	1,056,357	105	560,084	185	818,327

States.	II. COES.					
	Copper.				No. of works.	Brass.
	No. of works.	Rose copper.	No. of works.	Wrought copper.		
		Zollcentner.		*Zollcentner.*		*Zollcentner.*
Prussia	9	51,640	22	34,663	39	39,001
Saxony		686	1	7,108		
Hanover		1,315				
Hanover Brunswick Com	1	2,569	1	1,723	1	460
Hesse Cassel	1	1,629	1	1,891	1	707
Hesse Darmstadt	1	201				
Brunswick			1	108		
Nassau	1	607				
	13	58,651	26	45,493	41	40,668

States.	II. COES.					
	No. of works.	Arsenic.	No. of works.	Antimony.	No. of works.	Alum.
		Zollcentner.		*Zollcentner.*		*Zollcentner.*
Prussia	3	4,468	1	1,200	9	60,802
Anhalt						
Waldeck						
Luxemburg			1			
Bavaria			1		1	16
Saxony		2,290				
Hanover					1	200
Hanover Brunswick Com						164
Wurtemberg					1	40
Baden						
Hesse Cassel						
Hesse Darmstadt						
Thuringia			1	414		
Brunswick						
Oldenberg						
Nassau						
	3	6,758	4	1,614	12	61,222

smelting, and salt works of the Zollverein in 1862—Continued.

II. COES.

No. of works.	Gold.	No. of works.	Silver.	No. of works.	Lead for sale.	No. of works.	Litharge.	No. of works.	Wrought lead plates.
	Zollcentr.		*Zollcentner.*		*Zollcentner.*		*Zollcentner.*		*Zollcentner.*
	380	4	46,156.923	10	416,122		41,309	1	5,497
1		1	1,110.219		455		6,014		
	10,106	2	51,169.394		74,836		6,502	1	1,783
		4	20,587		87,439		4,620		
1	9,213		2,011.290		6,609		3,257		1,996
		1	551.178			1	1,130		
		3	6,386		36,222		12,819		
2	19,619	15	127,971.934	13	621,683	1	75,671	2	9,276

II. COES.

No. of works.	Zinc in bars.	No. of works.	Zinc in plate.	No. of works.	Pewter.	No. of works.	Smalt, house produce.	No. of works.	Nickel.
	Zollcentner.		*Zollcentner.*		*Zollcentner.*		*Zollcentner.*		*Zollcentner.*
46	1,195,257	7	263,825	1	40,599			4	5,511
1	29			7	2,708	2	7,346		553
	61					3	5,460		201
						1	3,695		338
								2	2,023
47	1,195,347	7	263,825	8	43,307	6	16,501	7	8,626

II. COES.

No. of works.	Vitriol of copper.	No. of works.	Green copperas.	No. of works.	Mixed vitriol.	No. of works.	Sulphur.	Total works.	Total weight.
	Zollcentner.		*Zollcentner.*		*Zollcentner.*		*Zollcentner.*		*Zollcentner.*
1	800	2	37,942		2,693	1	7,469	1,100	23,660,463
				1	244			9	35,252
								8	265,306
								9	1,265,306
		1	7,275		1,457			139	1,563,541
	10,518		576					66	1,000,167
	800		400		200			78	947,440
1	7,181		3,162	1	5,337	1	780	11	52,339
1	50		200					38	433,653
								53	270,040
								52	214,508
								39	217,076
								43	193,798
		2	140		152			7	230,257
								5	177,430
								42	577,211
3	19,349	5	49,695	2	10,083	2	8,249	1,699	29,801,099

H.—*Statement showing the products of the mining, smelting, and salt works of the Zollverein in 1862—Continued.*

States.	No. of works.	Rock salt.	No. of works.	Common salt.	No. of works.	Black or yellow salt.	No. of works.	Dung gypsum.	Total works.	Total weight.
		Z'centner.		*Z'centner.*		*Z'centner.*		*Z'centner.*		*Z'centner.*
Prussia..............	3	1,063,456	18	2,461,499	....	....	....	....	21	3,524,955
Anhalt..............	1	89,000	1	21,325	....	1,791	....	1,500	2	113,616
Lippe...............	....	....	1	22,170	....	1,153	....	480	1	23,803
Waldeck............	....	....	1	2,500	....	80	....	625	1	3,905
Luxemburg.........	....	....	....	....	....	....	7	240,000	7	240,000
Bavaria............	1	56,623	7	890,060	....	37,946	....	25,124	8	1,009,453
Hanover............	....	....	16	713,029	....	19,519	....	1,407	16	733,955
Wurtemberg........	2	493,579	6	376,992	....	8,917	1	78,054	9	957,542
Baden..............	....	....	2	372,851	....	17,270	....	5,531	2	395,652
Hesse Cassel.......	....	....	3	194,190	....	9,262	....	579	3	204,031
Hesse Darmstadt ...	....	....	3	247,348	....	9,104	....	....	3	256,452
Thuringia..........	....	....	7	212,319	....	40,579	17	25,435	24	278,333
Brunswick..........	....	....	1	93,272	....	24,093	....	....	1	116,465
	7	2,702,658	66	5,606,655	....	169,714	25	378,735	98	7,857,762

RECAPITULATION.

States.	Total works.	Total weight.
		Cwt.
Prussia...	3,409	399,983,117
Anhalt..	29	7,005,884
Lippe...	1	23,803
Waldeck	10	27,421
Luxemburg	18	8,396,123
Bavaria...	714	9,011,246
Saxony...	721	44,901,721
Hanover..	246	13,279,846
Hanover Brunswick Com	37	423,560
Wurtemberg......................................	60	2,033,237
Baden..	146	1,202,500
Hesse Cassel	112	6,212,523
Hesse Darmstadt.................................	95	1,806,558
Thuringia	320	4,567,408
Brunswick	19	3,035,172
Oldenburg.......................................	8	196,490
Nassau...	655	7,325,579
	6,615	509,432,088

DUCHY OF BADEN.

CARLSRUHE—B. O. DUNCAN, *Consul.*

DECEMBER 8, 1864.

I have the honor to transmit herewith my annual report for the year ending September 30, 1864:

Report on the commerce, industry, and agriculture of the Grand Duchy of Baden and Rhenish Bavaria for the year ending September 30, 1864.

Commerce and other branches of industry in this consular district, in common with others in Germany, have suffered considerably from the threatening aspect of political affairs during the last twelve months. The American war still exerts an unfavorable influence on some branches of industry, such as cotton manufactories, &c. But this is no longer so keenly felt as formerly. Supplies are partly obtained from other sources, and the industry is partly turned in other channels. Notwithstanding the continuance of the war and the high rates of exchange, exportation was pretty active up to the beginning of July last, especially in wine, as will be seen from table No. 1. The difficulties with Denmark, and the uncertainty how the affair would be finally settled, has had a more immediate influence on business.

The pretty generally prevailing fear of a great crisis in the money market has also had a tendency to prevent speculation. This fear has rather been increased by the failure of large houses at London, Liverpool, Paris, Vienna, &c. One of the principal reasons for this is, that so much gold has been sent to the United States to purchase our bonds. Since the 1st of July last, exportation has fallen off immensely, and so long as the duty is so high this condition of things will continue.

The new harvest of breadstuffs has been a very favorable average, not only in this region, but generally all over Europe. The prices have remained the same—quite moderate all the year. The average price of cereals, at present, is about as follows:

Wheat.....................................per 100 kilos.. 10¼ florins.
Rye.................................... "   .. 7¾ "
Barley...... .... "   .. 7½ ..
Oats........... .... 6¾

The crop of potatoes has been extraordinarily favorable both in quantity and quality. This article of food is extensively used by all classes. It may be said to constitute at least half the living of the poorer classes, so that an unfavorable crop is severely felt by them. Other breadstuffs, on account of the higher prices, cannot well be substituted. The potato is also extensively used for making starch, sugar, and an inferior kind of brandy, or schnapps. The price of esculent potatoes is 1–1¼ florins per cwt., and for manufacturing purposes, 36–48 krs. per cwt. Hops, from time immemorial, have been very extensively cultivated in the district between Carlsruhe and Manheim, and are known in commerce as the "Schwatzinger hops." This season the crop has been very poor, scarcely sufficient to cover the expenses of cultivation. The inferior article produced sells at an average of 65 florins per cwt. The unfavorable crop here, however, will be counterbalanced by the very favorable one in Bavaria, the eastern portion about Nuremburg, Bohemia, &c. Clover-seed is a very important product of Rhenish Bavaria, Silesia, and Saxony. In each of these regions the crop has almost entirely failed. The principal markets of England were, to a great extent, supplied from these sources, and, as they have failed, the supply for the next year will probably have to come from America, assuming the crop to have been better there.

The tobacco crop has been extraordinarily large, greater even than that of last year. It will not fall short of 450,500,000 centners. In quality it is a very fine average. The continued failure of Virginia tobacco to appear in the market, together with the new tariff regulations in Portugal, gives promise of new markets for the tobacco of the Palatinate, so that it is now in much greater demand than formerly. Hitherto it has been sent principally to the lower Rhine and North Germany. Now there is a prospect of considerable quantities being sent to England, and some large orders have been made for Canada. Recently a few shipments of cigars have been made to the United States, but the high duty prevents it from being a profitable business. Some years ago, before the duty was increased, the cigar trade with the United States was very important. Very little old tobacco is now on hand in the Palatinate. This causes a very brisk sale of the new crop at good prices, ranging from 13 to 17 florins per centner. The finer qualities of Palatinate tobacco are also growing in demand for the purpose of manufacturing better cigars. The present prospects, therefore, are favorable for the cultivation of greater quantities, as well as finer qualities, in this region. Hitherto "Pfaltzer" Palatinate tobacco and cigars were almost synonymous with poor or cheap quality. The wine crop of this year has turned out very indifferent, both in quality and quantity. This was attributable, first, to the cold wet weather in the blooming season, which gave a great backset to the young grapes. Then, in the autumn, the frosty weather came on very early. In many localities the grapes were frozen before they matured. Notwithstanding the very poor quality of the wine, it commands, however, a pretty fair price on account of the scarcity. The price would be yet greater but for the tariff regulations and the high rates of exchange, which, to a great extent, prevent exportation to the United States. So different are the qualities of the same wine that it is very difficult to specify prices. This difficulty gives the exporter the best opportunity of defrauding the government with impunity when duties are collected ad valorem. For instance, an exporter may send a fine Deidesheimer at a low price, and, if the invoice is questioned, can easily prove that Deidesheimer may be bought at the price he has given. The only safeguard is the taste of the taxer or valuer of the wines in the custom-house. In this the finest taste may be deceived, and immense frauds practiced if the exporter is sharp enough not to attempt to gain too much at a time. The prices of wines in Rhenish Bavaria (from which province most wines are shipped to the United States) may be classified as follows:

Inferior quality.........................per 1,000 litres.. 80–120 florins.
Second   "   ....   "   .. 150–200   "
First   "   ....   "   .. 250–400   "

Eighty florins seem an exceedingly low price, but a mixture called wine can be purchased for that, and frequently finds its way to the United States. The qualities mostly sent range in price from 90 to 130–140 florins. We receive very little over 400 florins per 1,000 litres. These cheap wines are usually shipped by small wine dealers here to German dealers in New York, Philadelphia, Cincinnati, St. Louis, Chicago, &c., and, no doubt, are mostly consumed by Germans. Much finer wines are produced in the vicinity of Deidersheim, selling as high even as from 3,000 to 5,000 florins per 1,000 litres. But such qualities find sale in European markets. The export of sparkling wines will probably be entirely prevented, the duty of $6 per dozen bottles being over 100 per cent. for the qualities usually shipped.

The use of petroleum is constantly becoming more general, and is rapidly driving oil and oil lamps from the market. The average price for the last year was about 12 florins per 50 kilos. All the petroleum yet used comes from America. Springs have been discovered in the Danubian principalities, but I have heard nothing of the oil appearing in the market.

Tables Nos. 2 and 3 show the exports and imports of the ports of Manheim and Ludwigshafen for the year ending October 1, 1864. The port of Ludwigshafen are now being considerably enlarged, and the business and population of the town is on the increase. Some large manufacturing establishments are to be erected soon. A railroad bridge is in process of reconstruction across the Rhine, between Manheim and Ludwigshafen, which will contribute much to attract travel and traffic through both places. This will be the fifth railroad bridge across the Rhine, below the Swiss frontier. No railroads have been opened in Baden for the last twelve months. Several, mostly short ones, are in process of construction, and will be completed during the next year.

Statement showing the description and value of the exports from Baden and Rhenish Bavaria to the United States during the fiscal year 1863 and 1864.

Products.	4th quarter, 1863.	1st quarter, 1864.	2d quarter, 1864.	3d quarter, 1864.	Total.
	Fl. Kr.	*Fl. Kr.*	*Fl. Kr.*	*Fl. Kr.*	*Fl. Kr.*
Wines and brandy ...	185,908 34	122,529 45	202,428 28	45,539 11	556,405 58
Dry-goods and cloth-ing	43,777 37	37,347 44	89,657 26	37,532 37	208,315 24
Leather	44,774 26	28,147 06	55,182 04	25,153 54	153,257 30
Tobacco and cigars...	27,943 02	20,011 53	37,315 18	3,425 47	88,696 00
Drugs and chemicals..	9,799 22	40,948 52	27,652 59	6,345 33	84,746 46
Fancy articles	21,920 42	22,967 49	25,351 06	6,493 34	76,733 11
Straw goods	19,261 19	38,274 15	882 00	....	58,417 34
Miscellaneous	26,699 51	23,555 26	28,224 00	13,681 52	92,161 09
Total..........	380,084 53	333,782 50	466,693 21	138,172 28	1,318,733 32

Statement showing the quantity of imports and exports of the port of Ludwigshafen from October 1, 1863, to October 1, 1864.

IMPORTS.

	Quintals.
Ascended the Rhine....................................	570,394
Descended the Rhine...................................	312,916
Per railway...	1,962,940
Total...	2,846,250

At 50 kilogrammes per quintal.................. 142,312,500 kilogrammes.

EXPORTS.

	Quintals.
Ascended...	502,882
Descended..	402,969
Per railway...	1,932,738
Total...	2,838,589

At 50 kilogrammes per quintal................ 141,929,450 kilogrammes·

Statement showing the description and quantity of some of the imports and exports of the port of Manheim, during the year ended September 30, 1864; also the totals of imports and exports during the same period.

Some of the products.	Imports.		Total imports.	Exports.		Total exports.
Cotton ....cwt..	177,500	....	177,500	2	750	752
Petroleum ....do ..	22,242	....	22,242	6	3,186	3,192
Lard ....do ..	3,517	164	3,681	219	184	403
Tobacco ....do ..	5,045	....	5,045	93,726	288	94,014
Cigars...............do ..	3,340	54	3,394	4,840	74	4,914
Wine ....do ..	3,014	2,905	5,919	26,360	92	26,452
Total	214,658	3,123	217,781	125,153	4,574	129,727

Total imports and exports.

IMPORTS.

Rhine river, up the stream	cwt.	4,981,781
" " down the stream.........................	do	347,518
Neckar river.......................................	do	635,609
Total.......................................		5,964,908

EXPORTS.

Rhine river, up the stream.............................	cwt.	2,908
" " down the stream..........................	do	990,326
Neckar river...........................	do	289,343
Total.......................		1,282,577

HANSEATIC FREE CITIES.

BREMEN—CHARLES BOERNSTEIN, *Consul.*

NOVEMBER 11, 1863.

In accordance with your invitation, as contained in section 12 of circular No. 40, to inform you, "if and how far foreign consuls are subject to taxation in the state of Bremen," I have the honor to report:

1st. There is very little direct taxation in the state of Bremen, and the state taxes consist only in a semi-voluntary proportional tax on property and income levied upon their own assessment by the citizens themselves.

From this state tax foreign consuls, if they have no real estate in Bremen, and if they do not exercise any trade or other professional avocation, are exempted.

Trading consuls, or those who possess real estate in Bremen, have to pay that tax like all other citizens.

2d. There are other commercial and municipal taxes in Bremen like as follows, "a tax for cleaning and lighting streets," which all foreign consuls residing in Bremen have to pay.   *   *   *   *   *   *   *

And, up to to-day, the commercial taxes are paid by the United States consuls at Bremen.

3d. All indirect taxes, like excise tax, &c., are borne by foreign consuls in common with all Bremen citizens.

JANUARY 12, 1864.

    *   *   *   *   *   *   *   *

The total emigration from January 1 to December 31, 1863, amounted to 17,952 passengers in 87 ships, viz:

To New York...................	16,379	passengers in	70 ships.
Baltimore	1,085	do	13
Quebec	401	do	2
Rio Grande do Sul.............	86	do	1
St. Jago	1	do	1

From the above 17,952 passengers, the Bremen Steamship Company, North

German Lloyd, forwarded 6,231 passengers, while 10,206 passengers were forwarded in 48 sailing vessels.

The emigration from Bremen to different parts from 1832 to 1863 is shown in the following statement:

1863	17,952	1847	33,682
1862	14,710	1846	32,372
1861	17,261	1845	31,822
1860	30,128	1844	19,857
1859	22,098	1843	9,927
1858	23,095	1842	13,619
1857	49,399	1841	9,594
1856	36,511	1840	12,806
1855	31,550	1839	12,412
1854	76,875	1838	9,312
1853	58,111	1837	15,087
1852	58,551	1836	14,137
1851	37,493	1835	6,185
1850	25,776	1834	13,086
1849	28,629	1833	8,891
1848	92,947	1832	10,344

JUNE 15, 1864.

I have the honor to submit herewith a general statement of commerce and navigation at the port of Bremen in the year 1863, accompanied by tables, showing the export and import of products and manufactures and other interesting commercial items.

The total results of the Bremen commerce in 1863 give, in general, satisfactory evidence of the great expansion of the Bremen trade. The value of the total commercial intercourse has been about the same as in the last year.

The total import amounted, in 1863, to 67.1 million thalers against 67 millions in 1862, and the export of 1863 to 60.4 millions against 61.3 million thalers in 1862. Of great importance is the undiminished transatlantic import which makes Bremen a world-trading emporium.

It has increased in the last year from 29.1 million thalers in 1862 to 31.1 million thalers in 1863, an increase of two million thalers. The signification of those figures is to be appreciated better when we remember the obnoxious effects of the American war on the Bremen trade.

Bremen's total import from the United States represented in 1860 the value of 16.3 million thalers and increased in 1861 to 19 million thalers. From the import of the year 1860, the amount of 10.7 millions came from the rebel States. Bremen received at that time from New Orleans only a value of 5.9 million thalers and about the same amount from Charleston, Savannah, Galveston, Mobile, and Richmond together. In the year 1861 the Bremen imports from New Orleans raised to 6.06 million thalers, and the total import from the rebel States amounted yet to 9.7 million thalers. Those great import values have vanished completely from the Bremen import lists since the blockading of the rebel ports. In 1863 Bremen received from New Orleans goods for the value of 484,218 thalers only.

Notwithstanding the falling off of the products from southern ports, which amounted in former years to one-third of the whole transatlantic import of Bremen, we see now the figures rise instead of falling. While Bremen in 1860 imported from transatlantic places, together, 28.4 millions, (of this amount 10.7 millions from rebel States,) the transatlantic import in 1863, notwithstanding the falling off of the last 10 million thalers, reached the height of 31.1 million thalers. The increase of the import from transatlantic places comes specially from New York, New Granada, Brazil, British East Indies, Burmah, and the Sandwich Islands. Let us again take for comparison the year before the blockade of the rebel ports, and we will find that Bremen imported from New York in 1860 3.7 million and in 1863 8.7 million thalers; from New Granada, in 1860 2.4 and in 1863 5.2 million thalers; from Brazil, in 1860 2.6 million and 1863 4.03 million thalers; from the British East Indies, in 1860 1.2 million and in 1863 2.6 million thalers; from Cuba, in 1860 2.2 million and in 1863 3 million thalers; from Japan, in 1860 nothing, and in 1863 85.052 thalers.

The transatlantic export has fallen one million thalers, and has never reached the height of former years, as 1859 and 1860. The export of Bremen to other transatlantic places, excluding the United States, has increased, as the tables show, especially to China, New Granada, Brazil, Venezuela, and the Sandwich Islands.

The navigation, against last year, has increased enormously. While in 1862, 2,775 vessels arrived with 269,803 lasts, there arrived in 1863, 2,947 vessels with 282,119 lasts. The number of departed vessels in 1862 amounted to 3,146 with 286,343 lasts, against 3,437 vessels with 308,556 lasts in 1863, the highest figure known in the Bremen navigation list. As to the destination of the vessels we find an increase of vessels going from this port to other European ports. While at the end of the year 1862 only 277 vessels with 90,935 lasts sailed under Bremen flag, the Bremen mercantile marine increased up to the end of 1863 to 302 vessels with 103,162 lasts.

The Bremen maritime insurance business increased in the same way. In the year 1861 there were insured for 69.6 million thalers, in 1862 for 79.3, and in 1863 for 85.4 million thalers. The emigration over Bremen amounted in 1863 to 18,175 persons against 15,187 in 1862. The financial results of the Bremen commerce in 1863 have not been so favorable as in 1861 and 1862, in which the Bremen merchants speculated under always advancing prices, while in 1863 the prices of goods fell, and the merchants, having large stocks on hand, had to suffer great losses, especially on tobacco.

The above figures show the prosperity of Bremen commerce, although it lost a part of the transatlantic business, which was partly recovered by the trade in the East Asiatic waters.

Imports.

Imports from—	BARLEY.			
	Quantity in 1860.	Quantity in 1861.	Quantity in 1862.	Quantity in 1863.
	Lasts. Schff.	*Lasts. Schff.*	*Lasts. Schff.*	*Lasts. Schff.*
Hanover	284 2	72 4	257 13	227 39
Oldenburg	158 34	50 39	48 23	145 19
Brunswick	74 29	4 21	27 31	29 25
Prussia	620 19	826 38	844 6	768 24
Anhalt	4 13	37 00	125 20	238 30
Zollverein	23 39	19 2	23 19	24 5
Austria			174 03	147 15
Hamburg	149 3	156 38	....	....
Schleswig Holstein	103 9	112 24	....	....
Russia	13 20	25 00	....	102 00
Denmark	8 17	27 26	....	....
Turkey	....	330 9	....	....
Other imports	10 00	2	....	....
Quantity	1,450 25	1,661 83	1,500 35	1,683 37

	RICE.			
	Pounds.	*Pounds.*	*Pounds.*	*Pounds.*
Hanover	645,479	366,296	147,591	95,326
Hamburg	461,240	36,151	125,984	124,688
Great Britain	4,664,193	9,681,401	10,105,963	1,692,741
Holland	168,443	....	....	440,228
New York	479,533	1,007,509	....	400
Charleston, S. C	2,304,522	1,872,954	....	....
Savannah	110,355	59,615	....	....
British East Indies	17,184,040	16,219,004	35,587,109	38,239,294
Burmah	4,682,315	21,718,847	26,516,744	36,126,055
Siam	56,033	2,588,480	....	....
Netherland East Indies	6,837,619	5,761,400	5,766,968	4,011,404
Sandwich Islands	....	....	....	69,773
Other imports	1,122	3,446	....	200
Net weight	37,594,894	59,315,103	78,250,359	80,800,109

	OATS.			
	Lasts. Schff.	*Lasts. Schff.*	*Lasts. Schff.*	*Lasts. Schff.*
Hanover	1,436 19	1,529 10	1,754 26	1,836 39
Oldenburg	903 26	643 17	917 28	1,386 24
Schaumburg Lippe	19 25	3 14	87 5	7 20
Brunswick	215 32	663 8	224 12	303 26
Prussia	333 33	225 29	312 21	310 10
Kur Hesse	364 25	176 25	101 2	98 10
Austria	....	19 24	183 33	....
Hamburg	....	....	....	212
Schleswig Holstein	5 9	....	....	66 10
Other imports	37 31	12 34	23 19	1 25
Quantity	3,317	3,274 01	3,604 26	4,223 4

Imports—Continued.

RYE.

Imports from—	Quantity in 1860.		Quantity in 1861.		Quantity in 1862.		Quantity in 1863.	
	Lasts.	*Schff.*	*Lasts.*	*Schff.*	*Lasts.*	*Schff.*	*Lasts.*	*Schff.*
Hanover	660	38	1,570	13	489	20	309	9
Oldenburg	523	27	664	10	219	18	287	36
Brunswick	3	16			9	17	92	14
Prussia	9,125	26	4,637	18	4,847	11	6,593	12
Hamburg	199	32			158	14	448	6
Schleswig Holstein	332	35	256	25	10	28		34
Mecklenburg	483	21	364	35			337	10
Russia	8,319	31	2,712	28	5,091	27	2,589	34
Sweden	180	5						
Denmark	90	11	53	32	1	30		
Turkey	779	20	524	20	944	26		
New York			879	21	2,363	10	2,681	17
Baltimore					141	3		
Other imports		4		25	14	14	2	34
Quantity	20,699	26	11,664	27	14,291	18	13,342	46

WHEAT.

Imports from—	Quantity in 1860.		Quantity in 1861.		Quantity in 1862.		Quantity in 1863.	
	Lasts.	*Schff.*	*Lasts.*	*Schff.*	*Lasts.*	*Schff.*	*Lasts.*	*Schff.*
Hanover	1,297	34	1,694	22	453	21	642	6
Oldenburg	46	7	5	35		30		10
Brunswick	76	11	573	20	224	20	140	22
Prussia	302	39	176	25	62	13		2
Kur Hesse	10	16			2	10	4	27
Bavaria			10	32	21	16		
Austria			466	11	369	29		
Hamburg	24	11					12	19
Schleswig Holstein			84	5		12		
Mecklenburg			7	13				
Russia					32	25		
New York	544	38	700	31	559	32	1,292	3
Baltimore			24	20	55	8		
Sandwich Islands	17	7						
Other imports	7	30		5			5	3
Quantity	2,327	33	3,744	19	1,782	16	2,097	12

TOBACCO—HAVANA.

Imports from—	*Pounds.*	*Pounds.*	*Pounds.*	*Pounds.*
Hamburg	186,741	106,473	147,671	199,287
Great Britain	5,820	1,586	1,836	7,001
Holland		14,115	2,191	311
Belgium		10,244		1,581
New York	405,572	46,843	458,429	209,286
New Orleans	4,147			
Cuba	607,090	596,462	1,884,830	896,333
Other imports	2,273	6,310		134
Net weight	1,211,643	782,033	2,494,957	1,313,933

Imports—Continued.

Imports from—	TOBACCO—CUBA.			
	Quantity in 1860.	Quantity in 1861.	Quantity in 1862.	Quantity in 1863.
	Pounds.	*Pounds.*	*Pounds.*	*Pounds.*
Hamburg	101,251	86,420	20,059	114,864
Sweden	....	37,199	....	....
Great Britain.....................	23,204	14,677	4,117	12,355
Holland	8,628	44,900	337	13,249
Belgium	....	....	25,492	10,152
New York.........................	125,758	138,618	5,528	145,021
Cuba	3,225,654	4,399,064	4,269,350	2,425,451
Other imports	1,437	2,621	3,247	1,716
Net weight...............	3,485,932	4,723,497	4,327,130	2,722,808

Imports from—	TOBACCO—ST. DOMINGO.			
Hamburg	229,135	432,129	679,580	911,462
Holland	....	....	....	7,429
New York.........................	21,760	40.990	133,225	135,045
Baltimore	....	....	....	6,377
Hayti	2,031,314	3,868,018	3,708,139	2,529,911
Other imports	7,826	5,879	249	98
Net weight...............	2,290,034	4,347,016	4,521,193	3,590,322

Imports from—	TOBACCO—COLOMBIA.			
Hamburg	111,827	13,563	65,239	19,735
Great Britain.....................	282,290	99,094	620,592	79,948
Belgium ....•	....	....	....	9,501
New York.........................	248,274	226,131	175,005	152,465
New Granada......................	6,404,021	5,451,296	8,722,166	13,227,446
Ecuador	....	53,469	....	....
Peru	10,806	....	5,362	....
Venezuela.........................	4,324	....	7,256	2,890
Other imports	541	562	1,224	2,446
Net weight...............	7,062,083	5,844,115	9,596,844	13,494,431

Imports from—	TOBACCO—PORTO RICO.			
Hamburg	104,367	39,953	26,420	761,298
Holland	....	62,581	....	900
Porto Rico	1,701,859	4,892,141	5,649,656	1,951,105
Net weight...............	1,806,226	4,994,675	5,676,076	2.713,303

Imports—Continued.

Imports from—	TOBACCO—BRAZIL.			
	Quantity in 1860.	Quantity in 1861.	Quantity in 1862.	Quantity in 1863.
	Pounds.	*Pounds.*	*Pounds.*	*Pounds.*
Hamburg	372,545	11,853	528,365	506,684
Great Britain	708	1,870	36,677	109,569
Holland		,16,519	4,176	12,000
France	76,015	48,909		
Brazil	7,115,949	2,747,589	10,104,490	17,579,145
Other imports			2,588	700
Net weight	7,565,217	2,826,740	10,676,296	18,208,098

	TOBACCO—CANASTER, (VARINAS.)			
Hamburg	5,838			1,292
New York			4,385	200
Venezuela	9,708	17,319	2,974	149,456
Other imports	275			
Net weight	15,821	17,319	7,359	150,948

	TOBACCO—FLORIDA.			
Hamburg	2,042	562		
New York	386,570	135,362	62,139	6,300
Baltimore	5,625			
New Orleans	8,126	1,483		
Galveston	1,579	5,889		
Other imports		188		
Net weight	403,942	143,484	62,139	6,300

	TOBACCO—KENTUCKY.			
Zollverein	15,403			13,227
Hamburg	1,836	41,753	1,440	271
Sweden and Norway			58,885	7,645
Great Britain	86,336	33,172	111,184	110,738
Holland	23,960	82,144		1,620
Belgium	7,675		40,338	
France			133,882	
New York	522,096	6,265,775	13,578,483	15,039,334
Baltimore	775,912	2,552,829	2,481,604	456,950
New Orleans	18,861,677	8,168,109	956,663	2,007,350
Other imports	25	4,919	5,194	9,392
Net weight	20,295,520	17,148,701	17,367,783	17,646,527

Imports—Continued.

Import froms—	TOBACCO—MARYLAND.			
	Quantity in 1860.	Quantity in 1861.	Quantity in 1862.	Quantity in 1863.
	Pounds.	*Pounds.*	*Pounds.*	*Pounds.*
Great Britain		5,715	6,039	78,295
France		3,366		
New York			28,125	33,300
Baltimore	14,107,797	19,300,613	7,910,990	5,656,586
Other imports	1,539	2,381	3,443	1,814
Net weight	14,109,336	19,312,085	7,948,597	5,769,995

	TOBACCO—OHIO.			
Hamburg		238,353		
Great Britain	45,182	114,835	2,692	36,974
France		5,082		
New York		385,667	12,364	23,215
Baltimore	2,387,246	3,820,299	1,093,942	1,259,912
Net weight	2,432,428	4,564,236	1,108,998	1,320,101

	TOBACCO—SEED-LEAF.			
Hamburg	90,004	2,786	1,899	19,914
New York	4,319,189	12,384,584	3,735,712	787,571
Baltimore	133,858	682,779	6,757	
Other imports	554	2,988	4,105	7,198
Net weight	4,543,605	13,073,137	3,738,473	814,683

	TOBACCO—VIRGINIA.			
Kur Hesse				36,662
Sweden			2,352	2,745
Great Britain	68,184	2,451		
Holland	26,400	14,374		30,056
Belgium			55,639	270
New York	207,016	1,290,808	127,854	3,654
Baltimore	263,651	1,451,737		991
Richmond, Va	3,459,104	4,905,737		
Net weight	4,024,355	7,665,107	185,845	74,288

	STEMS—KENTUCKY.			
Italy	247,485	1,107,227	610,673	
Various European ports	57,355	3,100	31,050	49,852
New York	892	1,076,690	1,919,950	4,449,664
Baltimore		41,621	380,302	1,043,554
New Orleans	888,392	1,611,317	18,064	589,431
Other places in the United States				23,970
Net weight	1,194,124	3,839,955	2,960,039	6,147,471

Imports—Continued.

Imports from—	STEMS—VIRGINIA.			
	Quantity in 1860.	Quantity in 1861.	Quantity in 1862.	Quantity in 1863.
	Pounds.	*Pounds.*	*Pounds.*	*Pounds.*
Prussia		40,837		
Holland		151,886	108,446	
New York	180,304	469,600	936,751	96,141
Baltimore	769,365	317,430	11,898	
Richmond, Va	7,844,211	3,402,275		
Other imports		1,423		
Net weight	8,793,880	4,383,451	1,058,095	96,141

	TRAIN OIL.			
	Tons.	*Tons.*	*Tons.*	*Tons.*
Hanover	557⅛	385⅛	175¼	885¼
Oldenburg	402	271½	377	62
Hamburg	990¾	2,497	1,567	1,266⅝
Norway	3,311	2,852	2,323	1,175¾
Great Britain	1,092¼	34¾	43	98
Holland			154	257⅛
Greenland	779¼	352⅜	665	368⅝
New Bedford			10,460	
New York		8,909½	11,975	2,725
Sandwich Islands	13,626	7,358¾	7,689	9,986
Other imports		9	9⅝	4
Quantity	20,758⅞	22,670¾	35,438½	16,827⅞

	SUGAR, UNREFINED—EAST INDIES.			
	Pounds.	*Pounds.*	*Pounds.*	*Pounds.*
Great Britain	2,591,030	546,681		15,456
Holland	36,632	601	227	
Mauritius	28,180	768,581		836,926
British East Indies	243,159	884,284	170,687	
Siam	788,451	33,788		
Netherland East Indies	138,410	2,057,579	1,464,798	1,556,998
Manila			293,635	
China		630,300	236,698	
Net weight	3,825,862	4,921,814	2,166,045	2,409,380

	SUGAR—BRAZIL.			
Great Britain		11,165	21,082	
Brazil	976,585	2,994,418	3,101,834	1,656,567
Net weight	976,585	3,005,583	3,122,916	1,656,567

Import from—	HAVANA AND CUBA MUSCOVADO, MELADO, AND MOLASSES.			
	Quantity in 1860.	Quantity in 1861.	Quantity in 1862.	Quantity in 1863.
	Pounds.	Pounds.	Pounds.	Pounds.
Hamburg	17,460	283,545	....	398,491
Great Britain	15,446	412,466	1,994,624	560
Holland	551,933	....	....	....
Belgium	....	....	17,924	....
France	513,725	....	....	....
New York	324	7,432,574	346,896	185
Central America	....	....	....	78,315
Cuba	4,541,723	9,488,197	12,958,848	18,900,174
Jamaica	15,029	798	807	....
Porto Rico	204,131	1,637,093	1,338,893	1,042,516
British East Indies	....	65,049	....	....
Other imports	939	1,045	7,870	830
Net weight	5,860,710	19,320,767	16,665,862	20,421,071

H. Ex. Doc. 60——36

MANUFACTURES.

NAMES OF THE ARTICLES.

From—	Pieces	Packages	Cottons.	Linen sail-duck, and other linen goods.	Silk and half silk wares.	Woollen cloth.	Other woollen and half woollen goods.	Other manufactured articles.	Total value of manufactures.
	Pieces.	*Packages.*	*Louis d'or.*	*Louis d'or.*	*Louis d'or.*	*Louis d'or.*	*Louis d'or.*	*Louis d'or.*	*Louis d'or.*
Hanover	17,455	3,956	30,169	117,009	5,525	12,256	114,379	142,144	481,462
Dukedom of Lippe	646	102	189	7,886	170			89	8,904
Brunswick	1,119	912	2,005	11,963	164		10,946	7,884	34,983
Prussia	6,152	8,988	526,731	188,064	320,164	1,118,232	458,571	178,453	2,500,555
Oldenburg	391	784	74,121	3,537	786	529	19,110	4,448	102,571
Saxony, { kdm of.	3,480	11,734	1,807,565	100,225	64,967	257,065	956,629	228,004	3,494,515
, duchy of.		318	1,022	584			98,315	180	30,350
Saxony (principality)	2,638	290	16,814	34,900	145	4,479	60,525	1,563	79,302
Reuss (principality)		300	3,074	8	15		11,221	6,194	60,013
Kur-Hesse		66	330				3,023	4,368	7,644
Hesse-Darmstadt		302	5,105	1,474	7,729	2,900	25,936	1,132	43,546
Frankfort		140	11,333	1,724	1,260		13,541	132	97,990
Bavaria		331	46,637	2,131		3,148	32,471	2,684	97,101
Wurtemburg		43	2,997	182		402	2,442	2,275	7,298
Baden		58	840	25	98	298	2,165	1,948	5,364
Oer Sies in the Zollverein		483	84,707		9,060	56,402	38,853	47,777	226,499
Austria		753	115,468	1,277	19,625			2,692	139,302
Switzerland	3,199	9,443	112,892	75,464	53,532	19,383	168,762	472,667	982,679
Hamburg	13,615	2,053	151,053	122,298	4,012	10,944	174,930	90,632	553,709
Great Britain	29	232		1,418	15	6,800	11,387	1,296	21,708
Holland	903	198	7,228	18,549		3,637	1,161	2,648	36,546
Belgium		364	10,504	80	38,912		13,298	36,146	102,977
Fra use		85	1,339	189	3,448		3,393	2,599	10,903
Europe (per State)		32					70	7,929	8,069
New York &c.		7						30	580
Oer imports			40		510				
Total........1863	48,847	41,784	2,759,143	688,840	589,993	1,505,407	2,151,829	1,216,754	8,814,365
Total........1862	65,239	46,850	3,091,692	672,359	364,187	2,337,145	1,449,597	1,704,255	9,619,298
Total........1861	51,522	41,967	1,828,438	669,464	279,073	2,115,343	1,406,970	1,554,989	7,853,577
Total........1860	61,755	56,712	4,421,851	888,919	430,155	3,968,980	2,382,384	1,549,045	12,841,327

Total export seaward in the year 1863.

TO—	Articles of consumption.	Raw productions.	Half manufactured articles.	Manufactured articles.	Other industrial productions.	Coins and precious metals.	Total export seaward.
	L. d'or.	*L. d'or.*	*L. d'or.*	*L. d'or.*	*L. d'or.*	*L. d'or.*	*L. d'or.*
Hanover	433, 023	273, 348	20, 221	11, 532	46, 659		784, 783
Oldenburg	1, 103, 600	963, 499	116, 874	276, 210	228, 656		2, 688, 839
Heligoland	820	20			15		855
Hamburg	729, 064	493, 494	6, 227	4, 444	96, 184		1, 329, 413
Schleswig-Holstein Lunenburg	393, 811	52, 394	8, 558		6, 153		460, 916
Lubeck	63, 523	2, 132		70	113		65, 838
Mecklenburg	111, 461	9, 306		34	360		121, 161
Prussia and Zollverein	833, 002	399, 339	3, 010		18, 330		1, 253, 681
States, (via Hamburg, &c)	6, 834	27, 311					34, 145
Russia, European	433, 593	26, 068	250	948	199, 714		660, 573
Sweden	990, 083	27, 670		216	6, 245		1, 024, 214
Norway	642, 912	14, 801		1, 806	4, 143		663, 662
Denmark	896, 356	38, 701		144	4, 416		939, 617
Great Britain and Ireland	1, 988, 923	1, 445, 012	26, 947	135, 971	396, 925	33, 560	4, 027, 338
Holland	689, 514	199, 625		258	3, 766		893, 163
Belgium	41, 661	56, 519			6		98, 186
France	383, 360	25, 132			160		408, 500
Spain	277				2, 163		2, 440
Portugal	8, 102			3, 721	910		12, 733
Italy	677, 025			74	166		677, 265
Austria	716, 951	9, 170					726, 121
Switzerland	70						70
Ionian Islands	430						430
Greece	628						628
Turkey, European	216						216
British North America	13, 929			12, 082	16, 311		42, 322
Boston	20	1, 056	3, 200	15, 006	1, 187		20, 469
New York	763, 600	568, 246	549, 504	4, 817, 523	1, 560, 866		8, 259, 739
Philadelphia	401	4, 049	1, 675	102, 297	36, 546		144, 968
Baltimore	29, 662	8, 668	1, 234	84, 055	79, 276		202, 895
New Orleans	108						108
San Francisco	11, 128	527			2, 481		14, 136
St. Louis, Mo	50			1, 916	17, 295		19, 261
Other places in the United States	1, 520	457	260	7, 807	11, 422		21, 466
Mexico	24, 102	1, 387	3, 955	72, 698	12, 514		114, 656
Central America	17, 111	4, 460	8, 215	36, 980	42, 304		109, 070
United States of Columbia	51, 400	2, 605	1, 113	89, 673	36, 398		181, 189
Ecuador				1, 640	360		2, 000
Peru	13, 348	349		16, 746	6, 900		36, 636
Chili	35, 636	180			4, 686		40, 502
Buenos Ayres	121, 520	3, 351		1, 408	9, 160		135, 439
Uruguay	2, 285				140		2, 425
Brazil	108, 621	8, 207		21, 790	15, 751		154, 369
Guayana—Netherlands	98						98
Venezuela	39, 773	4, 615	4, 714	224, 615	50, 451		324, 168
Cuba	313, 566	8, 346	7, 419	57, 832	40, 550		427, 713
Jamaica	77, 272	531		10, 684	6, 011		94, 498
Hayti	31, 094	669	330	108, 968	15, 721		156, 782
Porto Rico	158, 692	8, 425	2, 945	60, 127	26, 528		256, 717
St. Thomas	7, 299				1, 170		8, 469
Egypt	13, 171	13		778	2, 847		16, 809
Algiers	195						195
Canary Islands	23, 266	7, 659	1, 871	12, 333	10, 582		55, 711
Africa—west coast	41, 976	11, 242	2, 979	36, 695	29, 437		122, 399
Cape Colony	3, 073	2, 843	558	930	2, 518		9, 922
Mauritius	418			1, 100	90		1, 190
Turkey—Asiatic	418						418
British East Indies	20, 174	22, 722			9, 490		52, 386
Burmah	9, 009	872			937		10, 818
Netherland, East Indies	10, 013	4, 861		450	2, 649		17, 973
Manila	1, 892						1, 892
China	44, 326	19, 984	633	55, 873	14, 751		135, 567
Japan	32				119		151
Russia, Asiatic	158						158
Australia	49, 722	1, 026		935	252		51, 935
Sandwich Islands	36, 172	19, 360	9, 788	169, 874	62, 360		297, 554
For equipment of commercial fleet	370, 923	153, 765	5, 670	89, 762	118, 430		738, 550
Total	13, 591, 842	4, 864, 009	788, 150	6, 548, 005	3, 262, 874	33, 560	29, 088, 440

Statement showing the exports from Bremen to several places in the United States during the year 1863.

BOSTON.

			Louis d'or.
Human hair	pounds net..	107	600
Clay	do.....	58, 773	436
Woollen yarn from Zollverein	do.....	2, 440	3, 200
Cotton goods—Zollverein	packages..	46	10, 506
Manufactured goods—Austrian	do.....	8	4, 500
Books and music	do.....	5	1, 162
Other articles	for..	....	65
Total			20, 469

NEW YORK.

			Louis d'or.
Starch	pounds net..	1, 500	116
Beer	barrels..	9	298
Coffee	pounds net..	193, 759	43, 139
Chiccory	do.....	2, 234, 190	100, 039
Vinegar	...	20 ohm. 10 vrtls	396
Fish : herring	barrels..	49½	704
lamprey	casks..	208	2, 063
anchovies—12 anker	pounds net..	2, 434	438
Fruits, dried : prunello	do.....	1, 400	252
nuts	do.....	2, 689	175
prunes	do.....	272, 834	15, 412
other	do.....	2, 680	172
Fruit juice	1, 422 oxhofts 25 vrtls.		31, 148
Lentils	pounds net..	349, 640	16, 651
Beans	do.....	38, 632	1, 132
Spice cloves	do.....	9, 966	1, 150
Hops	do.....	782	250
Articles of consumption : meat—hams	do.....	7, 449	1, 523
sausages	do.....	1, 801	562
grain	do.....	10, 339	461
sago	do.....	21, 872	1, 365
other articles	do.....	35, 014	2, 141
Mineral waters { bottles		1, 600 }	1, 266
{ half-bottles	..	76, 864 }	
Fruit, dried	pounds net..	76, 864	5, 433
Rice	do.....	2, 944, 299	129, 626
Salt	lasts..	6	186
Seeds : anise	pounds net..	2, 241	206
coriander	do.....	28, 742	1, 701
cumin	do.....	7, 590	651
Spirits : cognac	4 oxhofts	2 vrtls	709
gin	5 oxhofts	2 vrtls	385
corn brandy	24 oxhofts	5 vrtls	1, 344
rum	2 oxhofts	10 vrtls	262
Liquors : foreign	3 oxhofts	24 vrtls	328
of this place	3 oxhofts	8 vrtls	229
Tobacco : Havana	pounds net..	29, 755	12, 608
Cuba	do.....	9, 602	3, 620

Louis d'or.

				Louis d'or.
Tobacco:	Florida	pounds net..	41,964	11,526
	Kentucky	do.....	2,825	470
	seed-leaf	do.....	1,052,754	190,041
	manufactured	do.....	1,552	324
Cigars:	Havana	mille..	4.2	175
	from Zollverein	do...	2,525.5	12,510
	from this place	do...	724.9	8,518
Tea		pounds net..	6,404	2,639
Wine:	French	150 oxhofts 15 vrtls		1,668
	Spanish	1 oxhofts 27 vrtls		517
	Tokay	21 oxhofts 12 vrtls		961
	Champagne { bottles......		464 }	414
	{ half-bottles ..		120 }	
	Rhenish	1,052 ohm. 13 vrtls		41,612
Sugar:	Muscovado	pounds net..	708,091	53,509
	Melado	do....	1,391,595	60,425
Other articles of consumption		for....	....	177
Building materials		packages..	20	486
Cotton		pounds net..	21,306	14,070
Lead		do.....	416,012	25,793
Leeches		tubs..	4	174
Drugs: (a.) crude alum		pounds net..	4,400	106
	gum-elastic	do.....	19,219	6,265
	rhubarb	do.....	60	168
	shellac	do.....	2,415	1,140
	other drugs	do.....	280,585	55,489
	(b.) prepared vitriol	do.....	31,824	613
	prepared chemicals	do.....	20,365	3,471
	(c.) mineral arsenic	do.....	7,468	920
	manganese	do.....	108,371	1,301
	cobalt	do.....	1,850	185
Iron, crude		do.....	404,368	4,050
Pigments, wood		do.....	5,424	271
Other pigments		do.....	5,808	91
Colors:	blue	do.....	3,681	670
	white paint	do.....	4,526	421
	ultramarine	do.....	66,788	19,385
	vermilion	do.....	16,958	12,282
	other colors	do.....	38,034	16,380
Deer-skins		do.....	7,082	4,720
Other skins		do.....	34,074	113,967
Hair, human		do.....	935	4,539
Hares' wool		do.....	28,368	56,927
" bristles		do.....	5,199	3,951
Other hair		do.....	7,830	1,801
Hides, dried		do.....	136,495	27,962
Staves		pieces..	10,500	800
Rags		pounds net..	197,124	7,062
Natural curiosities		packages..	19	394
Oil of poppies		pounds net..	1,730	301
Oil, olive		do.....	2,128	325
Oil of lard		do.....	45,266	4,604
Oil, medical		do.....	5,488	5,486
Plants		packages..	89	722
Saltpetre		pounds net..	46,173	5,310

		Louis d'or.
Seeds: rapeseed .... scheffels..	30	135
other seeds .... pounds net..	21, 834	2, 456
Wool .... do.....	90, 132	43, 623
Shearings . ... do.....	956, 393	100, 835
Animals, living .... head..	6, 803	1. 352
Clay .... pounds net..	2, 364, 000	16, 367
Train-oil .... barrels..	9	261
Other raw productions .... value..	....	595
Iron wire—Zollverein .... pounds net..	2, 864	150
" bar—Sweden .... do.....	5, 157, 977	208, 888
Steel—Zollverein .... do.....	178, 730	24, 598
Copper .... do.....	435, 065	123, 351
Nickel .... do.....	20, 301	31, 670
Zinc in sheets .... do.....	702, 307	43, 565
Yarn, cotton, from Zollverein .... do.....	2, 580	1, 933
Woollen yarn from Zollverein .... do.....	67, 131	76, 724
" " " Hamburg .... do.....	463	528
Twine .... do.....	286	323
Leather: tanned ....:................ do.....	13, 838	11, 883
patent .... do.....	12, 019	22, 234
Other half-manufactured articles .... do.....	2, 987	3, 657
Ribbon, cotton, from Zollverein .... packages..	260	83, 861
" silk—Austria .... do.....	1	1, 100
" silk—Swiss .... do.....	2	1, 910
" silk—Zollverein .... do.....	11	5, 356
" woollen—Zollverein .... do.....	43	18, 880
" mixed—Zollverein .... do.....	20	10, 115
Cottons from England .... do.....	2	266
" " Austria .... do.....	230	73, 929
" Swiss .... do.....	77	19, 236
" from Zollverein .... do.....	6, 721	1, 728, 088
Hair-cloth from Zollverein .... do.....	68	39, 666
Linen from Belgium .... pieces..	20	340
" " Zollverein .... packages..	90	17, 168
Drillings from Zollverein .... do.....	10	3, 243
Bags .... { pieces	6, 547 }	2, 819
{ packages..	12 }	
Silk and half-silk ware from Austria ..... do.....	8	6, 412
" " " Swiss .... do.....	1	213
" " " from Zollverein ... do.....	290	312, 361
Laces—Zollverein .... do.....	33	39, 738
Woollen cloth from Austria .... do.....	34	46, 350
" " " Zollverein .... do.....	1, 405	1, 060, 549
Woollen and half-woollen ware—		
from England .... do.....	11	4, 388
" Austria .... do.....	35	21, 582
" Zollverein .... do.....	2, 049	1, 116, 977
" Holstein .... do.....	1	645
Other manufactures from England .... do.....	13	4, 189
" " " Holland .. do.....	2	1, 456
" " " Austria .... do.....	70	40, 685
" " " Zollverein ...... do.....	318	156, 181
Books and music .... do.....	300	62, 035
Hardware—nails .... pounds net..	16, 839	1, 155
Steel-ware—Zollverein .... packages..	84	25, 207

			Louis d'or.
Arms—Zollverein	{ piece..... / packages..	1 } 158 }	49,286
" other	do.....	2	260
·· Austria	do.....	1	250
" Zollverein	{ pieces .... / packages..	13 } 794 }	97,535
Fancy goods from Austria	do.....	152	28,740
" Swiss	do.....	4	397
" from Zollverein	do.....	1,597	215,382
" " Hamburg	do.....	9	807
" " this place	do.....	9	251
Paintings	do. ...	126	56,392
Furniture, household	do.....	35	1,206
Other furniture	{ piece..... / packages..	1 } 16 }	412
Glassware, bottles, from Zollverein	bottles..	157,536	5,680
Demijohns from Zollverein	demijohns..	21,128	5,750
Window-glass from Zollverein	packages..	60	614
Looking-glasses from Zollverein	do.....	1,665	246,712
Other glassware from Bohemia	do.....	368	30,952
" " Zollverein	do.....	221	9,304
Gun-ware from Zollverein	do.....	52	12,127
Thread	pounds net..	1,349	500
Willow-ware from Zollverein	{ stz....... / packages..	7,941 } 1,476 }	90,301
Toys from Zollverein	do.....	1,213	56,385
Wood-ware, fancy, from Austria	do.....	157	13,873
" " Swiss	do.....	10	816
" " from Zollverein	do.....	65	5,131
Piano-fortes from Zollverein	pieces..	5	1,017
" " this place	do...	1	280
Optical instruments from Zollverein	packages..	15	1,473
Musical instruments from Austria	do.....	9	1,703
" " " Zollverein	do.....	487	73,313
Clothing, new	do.....	243	101,945
Corks	mille..	6,634	7,482
Leather-ware from Zollverein	packages..	82	33,864
" " Hamburg	do.....	3	358
Candles, wax	pounds net..	835	542
Machines from Zollverein	do.....	37,022	5,070
Brass-ware from Zollverein	packages..	32	4,063
Metal-ware from Zollverein	do.....	61	13,427
Paper	do.....	234	30,914
Perfumery	do.....	28	1,499
Chinaware from England	do.....	1	90
" " Zollverein	do.....	1,526	92,291
Sealingwax	pounds net..	964	124
Cards (playing) from Zollverein	packages..	4	606
Stoneware, fine, from Austria	do.....	70	3,000
" " Zollverein	do.....	57	1,703
Stoneware, common, from Zollverein	do.....	463	6,411
Marble-ware	do.....	32	7,409
Slates and slate pencils from Zollverein	do.....	735	13,577
Straw goods from Austria	do.....	161	68,207
" Swiss	do.....	25	15,023

		Louis d'or.
Straw goods from Zollverein ....packages..	93	37,635
Earthenware from Zollverein............do.....	17	335
Clay-pipes from Zollverein ....do.....	18,340	7,875
Crucibles from Zollverein ....do.....	228	3,003
Watches—Swiss ....do.....	3	975
" Zollverein ....do.....	4	2,336
Tin-foil............................do.....	4	324
Tin-ware...........................do.....	7	1,003
Matches......................... ....do.....	10	220
Other industrial products ....do.....	40	4,408
Total....		8,260,025

Or, in regard to kind of goods—

		Louis d'or.
Articles of consumption ....ctr. gross..	117,996	763,600
Raw productions.......................do.....	58,053	568,246
Half manufactured articles..............do.....	67,017	549,504
Manufactured articles..................do.....	35,907	4,817,523
Other industrial products................do.....	59,878	1,560,866
Total	338,856	8,259,739

In the year 1862—

		Louis d'or.
Articles of consumption...............ctr. gross..	119,811	748,841
Raw productions.......................do.....	93,479	1,156,080
Half manufactured articles ....do.....	31,516	325,104
Manufactured articles.................do.....	47,087	5,408,469
Other industrial products...............do.....	58,290	1,653,328
Total.................................	350,183	9,291,822

PHILADELPHIA.

		Louis d'or.
Articles of consumption...............lbs. net..	306	87
Liquors....................... ....oxhofts..	2	200
Wine, Rhenish.................................	2 ohm 11 vtl.	114
Drugs : manganese...................lbs. net..	168,221	1,996
soda ....do.....	2,068	175
other drugs ....do.....	4,005	675
Oil, medical...........................do.....	143	306
Clay, (pipe).........................do.....	120,000	833
Other raw products ....value..	....	64
Woollen yarn from Zollverein..........lbs net..	1,342	1,675
Ribbon, cotton, from Zollverein........package..	1	460
Cotton goods from Zollverein............do.....	339	79,207
Linen...... ....do.....	3	707
Silk and half silk goods from Zollverein..do.....	6	2,815
Laces................................do.....	5	1,671
Woollen cloth from Zollverein..........do.....	3	3,600
Woollen and half-woollen goods, Zollverein . do.....	26	7,510
Other manufactures from Zollverein......do.....	10	6,327
Books...... ....do.....	4	1,353
Hardware, arms, from Zollverein........do.....	17	6,820
Other hardware from Zollverein ....do.....	1	95

		Louis d'or.
Fancy goods from Zollverein..........package..	19	4, 243
Paintings ....do.....	21	8, 528
Glassware, Bohemian...................do.....	5	1, 063
Glassware from Zollverein ....do.....	2	97
Wooden-ware, common, from Zollverein...do.....	98	4, 673
Wooden-ware, fine, from Zollverein .....do.....	9	563
Corks...............................miHe....	301	128
Leather-ware from Zollverein.........package..	1	706
Metal-ware from Zollverein.............do.....	2	1, 400
Paper ....do.....	7	666
Musical instruments....................do.....	19	2, 360
Chinaware from Zollverein.............do. ...	47	3, 274
Stoneware, fine, from Austria..........do.....	5	136
Stoneware, common, from Zollverein .....do.....	6	100
Slates and slate-pencils from Zollverein...do.....	8	199
Watches ....do.....	1	142
Total	...	144, 968

Or, in regard to kind of goods—		Louis d'or.
Articles of consumption...............ctr. gross..	36	· 401
Raw productions.......................do.....	3, 103	4, 049
Half manufactured articles ....do.....	15	1, 675
Manufactured articles...................do.....	977	102, 297
Other industrial products................do.....	861	36, 546
Total	4, 992	144, 968

In the year 1862—		Louis d'or.
Articles of consumption...............ctr. gross..	605	4, 090
Raw productions.......................do.....	5, 440	8, 295
Half manufactured articles..............do.....	86	9, 967
Manufactured articles...................do.....	2, 376	188, 978
Other industrial products...............do.....	3, 237	91, 873
Total.................................	11, 744	303, 203

BALTIMORE AND WASHINGTON.

		Louis d'or.
Chiccory.........................lbs. net..	6, 527	294
Vinegar.............................oxhofts..	45	528
Fish : herrings.......................barrels..	32	459
lampreys......................casks ..	18	150
Lentils............................lbs. net..	10, 370	480
Articles of consumption................do.....	7, 524	239
Mineral waters .... { bottles	1, 236 }	198
{ half-bottles..	50 }	
Fruit, dried....................pounds net..	18, 077	1, 405
Rice ....do.....	551, 731	22, 612
Spirits : cognac	2 oxh's 15 vrtls	245
other spirits....................	1 oxh. 25 vrtls	129
Wine of France	15 oxh's 19 vrtls	699
" Tokay	17 oxh's 5 vrtls	687 ·

		Louis d'or.
Wine, Rhenish............................ohm..	33	1, 401
Other articles of consumption.............value..	....	136
Drugs.........................pounds net..	18, 201	3, 363
Colors.............................do.....	934	128
Hares' fur............................do.....	2, 016	3, 149
Oil, medical..........................do.....	218	272
Clay, (pipe)...........................do.....	246, 374	1, 647
Other raw productions..................value..	....	109
Cotton yarn from Zollverein........pounds net..	477	360
Woollen yarn from Zollverein..........do.....	720	874
Ribbons, cotton, from Zollverein......packages..	12	2, 380
" woollen, from Zollverein........do.....	5	2, 526
" mixed, from Zollverein........do.....	2	460
Cotton goods—Swiss....................do.....	4	525
" Zollverein ....do.....	243	51, 824
Sail-cloth ....pieces..	96	1, 188
Woollen cloth from Zollverein........packages..	32	21, 601
Woollen and half-woollen goods from		
Zollverein ....do.....	12	3, 551
Books and music.......................do.....	13	1, 389
Fancy goods from Austria...............do.....	5	1, 037
" " Zollverein...........do.....	168	14, 067
" " this place............do.....	4	255
Glassware, bottles, from Zollverein......bottles..	25, 920	897
Demijohns from Zollverein..........demijohns..	12, 830	3, 881
Other glassware—Bohemian..........packages..	4	442
India-rubber manufactures...............do.....	5	1, 829
Willow-ware, from Zollverein ...... { baskets ... / packages..	4, 353 } / 8 }	4, 510
Toys from Zollverein....................do.....	324	10, 895
Wooden-ware, fine, from Austria........do.....	4	337
" " Zollverein .....do.....	3	294
Musical instruments from Zollverein......do.....	37	6, 498
Clothing..............................do.....	3	1, 338
Leather-ware from Zollverein............do....	3	694
Candles, wax ....pounds net..	2, 057	1, 275
Paper ....packages..	8	294
Chinaware from Austria.................do.....	2	200
" " Zollverein ....do.....	206	11, 143
Stoneware, common ....do.....	113	1, 402
Marble...............................do.....	1	189
Slate and slate-pencils..................do.....	27	516
Straw manufactures.....................do.....	20	4, 521
Earthenware ....do.....	510	259
Watches ....do.....	6	750
Tin-ware ....do.....	10	532
Other industrial products...............do.....	29	9, 292
Total	....	202, 355

Or, in regard to kind of goods—

		Louis d'or.
Articles of consumption..............ctr. gross..	6, 750	29, 662
Raw productions.......................do.....	2, 906	8, 668

		Louis d'or.
Half-manufactured articles ....ctr. gross..	14	1, 234
Manufactured articles...................do.....	794	84, 055
Other industrial products...............do.....	4, 539	79, 276
Total...............................	15, 003	202, 895

In the year 1862—

		Louis d'or.
Articles of consumption.............ctr. gross..	23, 838	113, 727
Raw productions......................do.....	1, 607	5, 386
Half-manufactured articles..............do.....	32	3, 070
Manufactured articles...................do.....	677	69, 257
Other industrial products...............do.....	4, 833	63, 408
Total...............................	30, 987	254, 848

NEW ORLEANS, VIA NEW YORK.

		Louis d'or.
Mineral waters.......................bottles..	900	108

SAN FRANCISCO.

		Louis d'or.
Fish: herrings.......................barrels..	110½	2, 291
anchovies ....anker..	72¾	1, 031
Spice ....pounds net..	7, 292	2, 023
Articles of consumption: meat—hams....do.....	13, 329	2, 946
sausages.......do.....	334	112
cheese.........do.....	2, 812	508
Mineral waters .... { bottles ..... / half-bottles..	2, 240 } / 120	186
Fruit, dried.....................pounds net..	14, 253	1, 181
Salt	2 lasts 22 scheffels.	128
Cigars ....mille..	22	337
Wine, Rhenish	1 ohm 4 vrtl.	260
Other articles of consumption............value..	....	125
Gum-arabic ....pounds net..	1, 077	135
Vitriol ..:.......................do.....	2, 724	345
Books ....packages..	2	213
Paintings ....do.....	1	183
Willowware...... .... { satz ...... / packages..	584 } / 20	706
Candles, wax ....pounds net..	1, 140	773
Strings ....package..	1	500
Other articles....................value..	....	153
Total		14, 136

ST. LOUIS, MISSOURI.

		Louis d'or.
Cotton goods ....packages..	4	1, 408
Woollen goods ....do.....	5	508
Arms ....do.....	3	1, 297

			Louis d'or.
Fancy goods	packages..	35	4,702
Paintings	do.....	2	398
Looking-glass	do.....	4	676
Toys	do.....	109	5,735
Hardware	do.....	2	536
Musical instruments	do.....	6	1,965
Corks	mille..	164	328
China-ware	packages..	16	1,053
Stoneware, common	do.....	18	291
Slate and slate pencils	do.....	6	171
Other articles	value..	....	166
Total			19,234

OTHER PLACES IN THE UNITED STATES.

			Louis d'or.
Chiccory	lbs. net..	11,878	535
Cigars	mille..	62.9	927
Drugs	lbs. net..	1,202	380
Woollen yarn	do.....	228	260
Cotton goods	packages..	16	2,008
Hair-cloth	do.....	2	1,200
Silk and half-silk goods	do.....	2	3,151
Woollen and half-woollen goods	do.....	4	1,352
Other manufactures	do.....	1	96
Books	do.....	13	2,623
Steel-ware	do.....	1	650
Arms	do.....	1 and 2 pcs.	463
Hardware	do.....	3	218
Fancy goods	do.....	10	3,942
Paintings	do.....	1	250
Toys	do.....	16	1,026
Wooden-ware, fine	do.....	1	77
Machines	lbs. net..	5,380	576
Chinaware	packages..	20	1,237
Other articles	value..	....	295
Total			21,466

Imports in 1863 from various places in the United States.

PORTLAND.

			Louis d'or.
Petroleum	pounds net..	924,205	38,506

NEW YORK.

			Louis d'or.
Starch	pounds net..	67,354	4,267
Cacao	do.....	47,977	7,096
Coffee	do.....	213,462	48,280
Fruits	do.....	3,371	883
Grain: maize	180 lasts* 19 scheffels		16,415
rye	2,681 lasts 17 scheffels		268,626

* 40 scheffels = 1 last = 4,000 pounds.

Louis d'or.

Grain: wheat		1, 292 lasts 3 scheffels	149, 289
Spice: cassia lignea	pounds net.	11, 445	2, 665
pimento	do....	95, 914	6, 770
vanilla	do....	64	• 235
Honey	do....	185, 677	16, 294
Hops	do....	380, 025	51, 575
Articles of consumption: butter	do....	1, 884, 488	438, 108
meat	do....	1, 166, 076	104, 347
hams	do....	621, 929	61, 384
pork	do....	3, 605, 998	355, 532
cheese	do....	2, 158, 290	264, 107
flour, rye	do....	4, 240	170
" wheat	do....	2, 468, 014	96, 302
grease	do....	3, 745, 099	449, 203
sundry provisions	do....	5, 601	1, 150
Fruits: fresh	quarts..	129	178
dried	pounds net..	358, 045	27, 492
Liquors: gin		41 hhds. 15 quarts	1, 150
rum		6 hhds. 24 quarts	682
spirits		351 hhds. 28 quarts	9, 819
other liquors		24 quarts	102
Tobacco: raw Havana	pounds net..	209, 286	105, 966
Cuba	do.....	145, 021	54, 743
Domingo	do.....	135, 045	24, 768
Columbia	do.....	152, 465	49, 676
Florida	do.....	6, 300	1, 618
Kentucky	do.....	15, 039, 334	3, 118, 775
Maryland	do.....	33, 300	3, 635
Ohio	do.....	23, 215	3, 100
seed-leaf	do.....	787, 571	167, 997
Virginia	do.....	3, 654	1, 200
manufactured	do.....	137, 277	36, 398
cigars		130, 000$\frac{8}{16}$	5, 775
stems, Kentucky	do.....	4, 449, 664	277, 208
" Virginia	do.....	96, 141	8, 033
Tea	do.....	22, 906	8, 108
Animals	head..	10	147
Wine		2 hhds. 10 quarts	194
Sundry articles	value..	....	176
Drugs, raw: ashes, pearl, stov?	pounds net..	1, 139, 577	100, 300
balsam	do.....	13, 440	6, 435
gum	do.....	470	178
other drugs	do.....	7, 894	5, 277
prepared spermaceti	do.....	1, 000	346
Iron, unwrought	do.....	88, 210	827
Dye-woods: logwood	do.....	1, 641, 908	22, 298
quercitron	do.....	55, 151	1, 103
logwood, extra	do.....	2, 388, 226	232, 170
yellowwood, extra	do.....	1, 212	230
redwood, extra	do.....	4, 712	1, 182
quercitron, extra	do.....	21, 425	2, 043
gambier	do.....	22, 011	1, 472
cutch	do.....	23, 482	1, 923
Indigo	do.....	10, 591	24, 571
Varnish	do.....	17, 805	1, 807

			Louis d'or.
Feathers for beds ....pounds net..	169	110
Skins, sheep ....do.....	2, 250	800
Furs, raw ....do.....	94, 235	269, 175
Hair, horse ....do.....	507	188
" bristles ....do.....	1, 076	818
Hides................................do.....	2, 560	404
Rosin ....do.....	3, 273	262
Wood: oak..........................cubic feet..	4, 690	3, 096
fir............................do.....	310	250
staves ....pieces..	425, 512	45, 026
cedar ....square feet..	128, 858	10, 399
wood ....pounds net..	107, 723	1, 775
walnut....................square feet..	115, 336	8, 833
Metals ....pounds net..	1, 531	230
Natural products ....packages..	53	1, 765
Oil: palm........................pounds net..	364, 734	35, 400
petroleum ....do.....	6, 201, 826	433, 914
of lard ....do.....	2, 863, 326	283, 157
of tallow.......................do.....	17, 661	1, 968
medicinal ....do.....	10, 780	43, 444
for machinery...................do.....	2, 451, 748	226, 826
Moss ....do.....	20, 126	1, 815
Seeds: clover-seed ....do.....	805, 684	99, 851
linseed ....barrels..	148	1, 875
other seeds..............pounds net..	10, 026	2, 011
Shears..................................do.....	3, 659	384
Tallow.................................do.....	1, 629, 683	193, 655
Tar ....barrels..	250	1, 887
Bladders ....pounds net..	34, 124	2, 938
Train oil.............................barrels..	2, 725	65, 338
Wax ....pounds net..	5, 068	2, 170
Whalebone ....do.....	59, 041	95, 061
Other raw productions...............value..	....	579
Leather ....pounds net..	382	188
Leather cloth........................packages..	12	2, 047
Manufactured articles...................do.....	20	5, 962
Books and music ....do.....	58	7, 450
Hardware: cast-iron ....pounds net..	1, 707	127
nails ....do.....	2, 819	438
hardware ....packages..	6	545
arms ....do.....	52	7, 040
other hardware .... { pieces	3 }	2, 510
{ packages..	37 }	
Fancy goods ....do.....	397	29, 729
Pictures—paintings ....do.....	13	2, 052
Furniture, household ....do.....	33	2, 062
Wagons ....pieces..	12	3, 196
Other furniture .... { pieces	845 }	1, 107
{ packages..	24 }	
Glassware ....do.....	84	3, 200
Gun-ware ....do.....	99	29, 424
Ship nails, wooden...................pieces,.	10, 800	541
Shoes nails ....lbs. net..	1, 911, 094	77, 571
Other manufactures of wood. ...... { pieces	482 }	743
{ packages..	30 }	

			Louis d'or.
Instruments : musical............pieces..	3	645
mathematical.........packages..	20	1,965
Brazier's ware.............lbs. net..	320	201
Candles, spermaceti............do.....	2,663	1,005
Machines.............do.....	91,316	27,326
Brass-wares...........packages..	60	3,561
Hardware, metallic............do.....	14	766
Paper { reams	100 }	1,974
{ packages..	158 }	
Soap ....lbs. net..	1,900	194
Watches { pieces	3 }	6,604
{ packages..	517 }	
Caps.............do.....	2	335
Other industrial productions.........for..	....	389
Coins............packages..	24	36,995
Copper.............lbs. net..	10,378	2,387
Total..........		8,747,513

Or, in regard to kind of goods—

		Louis d'or.
Articles of consumption.........ctr. gross..	622,512	6,249,668
Raw productions.............do.....	287,510	2,237,566
Half manufactured articles..........do.....	108	2,575
Manufactured articles.............do.....	85	8,009
Other industrial productions........do.....	26,392	212,700
Coins.............do.....	13	36,995
Total.................	936,620	8,747,513

PHILADELPHIA.

		Louis d'or.
Hams............lbs. net..	7,550	842
Lard.............do.....	1,687	200
Petroleum.............do.....	1,146,355	49,773
Arms............package..	1	168
Other articles............	....	140
Total..........		51,123

BALTIMORE.

		Louis d'or.
Fruits............lbs. net..	703	167
Maize............	11 lasts 35 scheffels	1,187
Meat............lbs. net..	4,550	511
Pork............do.....	6,180	659
Wheat flour............do.....	57,619	2,379
Lard............do.....	160,229	18,460
Tobacco: Domingo............do.....	6,377	1,772
Columbia............do.....	908	170
Kentucky............do.....	456,950	75,915

*ctr. gross = 100 weight gross.

			Louis d'or.
Tobacco: Maryland................lbs. net..	5, 656, 586	779, 734
Ohio......................do.....	1, 259, 912	169, 773
Virginia.....................do.....	901	210
manufactured................do.....	173	120
Stems: Kentucky.....................do.....	1, 043, 554	76, 158
Other consuming articles.................for..	....	129
Drugs............................lbs. net..	47, 548	1, 144
Quercitron.........................do.....	881, 485	15, 869
Wood: oak.......................cubic feet..	10, 620	6, 154
fir..........................do.....	1, 606	950
staves ....pieces..	5, 962	572
Tar..............................barrels..	100	725
Other raw productions.....................for..	....	236
Hardware.......................packages..	15	142
Paintings ....do.....	1	300
Ship nails, wooden...................pieces..	134, 199	4, 087
Musical instruments ....do.....	2	525
Candles, spermaceti................lbs. net..	3, 520	1, 062
Hardware, metallic ....package..	1	108
Other industrial productions...............for..	....	271
Total..		1, 159, 488

Or, in regard to kind of goods—

		Louis d'or.
Articles of consumption...............ctr. gross..	99, 739	1, 127, 344
Raw productions......................do.....	16, 446	25, 650
Industrial productions ....do.....	4, 194	6, 495
Total.................................	120, 379	1, 159, 489

NEW ORLEANS.

		Louis d'or.
Tobacco: Kentucky ....lbs. net..	2, 007, 350	443, 753
manufactured................do.....	216	300
Stems, Kentucky ....do.....	580, 431	37, 548
Cotton ....do.....	231	154
Staves...............................pieces..	18, 392	2, 247
Other articles......................packages..	3	216
Total..		484, 218

Or, in regard to kind of goods—

		Louis d'or.
Articles of consumption...............ctr. gross..	28, 428	481, 617
Raw productions ....do.....	1, 474	2, 401
Industrial productions ....do.....	......	200
Total.................................	29, 902	484, 218

GALVESTON, VIA MATAMORAS.

		Louis d'or.
Cotton............................lbs. net..	1, 050, 022	480, 581

ST. LOUIS, MO.

		Louis d'or.
Petroleum ....lbs. net..	1,155	90

OTHER PLACES IN THE UNITED STATES.

		Louis d'or.
Articles of consumption : pork.........lbs. net..	28,584	2,546
rye flour.......do.....	12,910	443
wheat flour ....do.....	23,400	947
lard ....do.....	107,504	12,195
Tobacco: Kentucky ....do.....	9,392	3,134
seed-leaf....................do.....	4,367	619
Stems, Kentucky ....do.....	23,970	1,650
Ox and cow horns ....pieces..	36,930	1,094
Lard-oil...........................lbs. net..	1,908	217
Clover-seed..........................do.....	4,120	536
Tallow..............................do.....	33,094	4,131
Wax ....do.....	655	250
Machinery...........................do.....	295	141
Other articles ....value..	....	287
Total...		28,190

General summary of total imports in the years 1861, 1862, and 1863, gross weight, value, percentage, and average value.

Imports.	1861.					1862.					1863.				
	Ctr. gross, at 100 lbs.	Per cent.	Value in Louis d'ors.	Per cent.	Average value.	Ctr. gross, at 100 lbs.	Per cent.	Value in Louis d'ors.	Per cent.	Average value.	Ctr. gross, at 100 lbs.	Per cent.	Value in Louis d'ors.	Per cent.	Average value.
Seawards:					_G. R._					_R. R._					_R. G._
Articles of consumption	3,135,342	41.77	25,311,886	51.50	8.05	3,233,725	45.05	28,692,856	65.62	8.61	3,269,164	49.24	28,141,80	62.02	8.44
Raw productions	4,069,605	54.49	17,355,908	35.32	4.18	3,660,586	51.00	10,269,707	23.55	2.58	3,068,429	46.29	13,046,84	28.75	4.18
Half-manufactured articles	184,180	2.45	4,798,82	9.76	26.04	166,903	2.33	3,015,099	6.92	18.05	173,061	2.61	2,208,63	4.87	12.55
Manufactured articles	13,345	.18	779,320	1.59	58.39	11,224	.16	759,895	1.74	67.49	9,543	.14	657,81	1.43	68.66
Other industrial productions	63,155	1.11	861,69	1.75	10.26	104,963	1.46	904,463	2.07	8.44	118,944	1.39	1,057,362	2.31	8.64
Coins and precious metals	8		39,274	.08		5		43,550	.10		33		263,15	.58	
Total Louis d'ors	7,505,635	100.00	49,149,499	100.00		7,177,456	100.00	43,691,370	100.00		6,639,173	99.60	45,375,997	100.00	
Landwards:															
Articles of consumption	908,202	18.92	4,763,304	25.84	5.18	744,784	14.45	4,822,105	22.34	6.34	704,791	16.60	4,218,435	21.03	5.71
Raw productions	3,623,143	75.48	2,020,064	10.96	.40	4,115,866	79.86	3,010,633	13.95	.53	3,369,199	76.93	2,922,501	14.57	.62
Half-manufactured articles	94,029	1.50	950,961	5.16	39.41	22,286	.43	866,893	4.01	38.67	20,182	.46	768,410	3.83	38.05
Manufactured articles	69,580	1.45	7,044,530	38.22	101.18	86,281	1.71	8,828,229	40.90	100.00	69,888	1.58	8,129,645	40.52	116.93
Other industrial productions	175,018	3.65	3,652,660	19.82	91.63	182,901	3.55	4,057,407	18.80	22.13	221,560	5.03	4,021,156	30.04	18.11
Coins and precious metals											1		1,650	.01	
Total Louis d'ors	4,799,972	100.00	18,431,519	100.00		5,154,098	100.00	21,565,267	100.00		4,405,551	100.00	20,062,817	100.00	
By river:															
Articles of consumption	256,832	7.92	460,018	23.23	1.57	176,566	5.33	993,412	16.17	1.48	223,131	7.12	372,069	21.80	1.48
Raw productions	2,938,822	89.41	1,072,003	54.13	.36	3,040,800	91.85	1,172,250	64.61	.24	2,824,351	90.49	975,978	57.37	.35
Half-manufactured articles	1,959	.06	10,768	.54	5.26	269	.01	1,745	.10	6.33	906	.03	503	.96	.70
Manufactured articles	758	.02	29,717	1.50	39.15	1,178	.04	31,404	1.73	26.47	925	.03	27,149	1.59	29.17
Other industrial productions	88,432	2.69	407,979	90.60	4.44	91,841	2.77	315,415	17.39	3.31	85,549	2.73	305,793	18.98	3.57
Coins and precious metals															
Total Louis d'ors	3,286,803	100.00	1,980,85	0.00		3,3,64	100.00	1,814,226	100.00		3,134,862	100.00	1,706,392	100.00	
Total:															
Articles of consumption	4,300,376	27.58	30,535,908	43.90	7.07	4,155,075	28.56	33,724,373	50.33	8.08	4,197,086	29.60	32,732,394	48.75	7.58
Raw productions	10,651,570	68.11	20,450,975	29.40	1.66	10,817,252	68.16	14,452,590	21.57	2.24	9,284,909	65.46	16,949,433	35.24	1.59
Half-manufactured articles	210,168	1.35	5,760,911	8.28	27.29	189,438	1.21	3,883,737	5.80	20.36	194,149	1.37	2,981,578	4.44	15.28
Manufactured articles	83,683	.54	7,853,577	11.29	93.61	100,683	.64	9,619,298	14.36	95.39	80,356	.57	8,814,333	13.12	109.50
Other industrial productions	346,605	2.22	4,922,358	7.07	14.14	379,725	2.43	5,277,985	7.88	13.65	426,053	3.00	5,043,211	8.05	12.49
Coins and precious metals	8		39,274	.06		5		43,505	.06		33		265,165	.40	
Total Louis d'ors	15,592,410	100.00	69,561,503	100.00		15,642,178	100.00	67,000,083	100.00		14,179,598	100.00	67,145,146	100.00	

Comparative statement showing the emigration from Bremen from 1858 to 1863, inclusive.

TO—	1858 Ships	1858 Passengers	1859 Ships	1859 Passengers	1860 Ships	1860 Passengers	1861 Ships	1861 Passengers	1862 Ships	1862 Passengers	1863 Ships	1863 Passengers	Total Ships	Total Passengers
Quebec	1	154	1	62	...	......	1	199	2	197	2	408	7	1,013
New York	71	12,457	65	12,767	75	15,556	74	12,048	65	12,477	71	16,428	491	81,733
Philadelphia	6	262	7	403	6	390	1	196	...	......	...	......	20	1,251
Baltimore	22	3,721	23	3,626	36	7,023	21	3,190	18	2,251	13	1,110	133	20,921
Charleston	3	304	2	179	4	258	2	12	...	......	...	......	11	683
New Orleans	27	5,046	22	3,949	25	5,407	5	692	...	......	...	......	79	15,194
Galveston and Indianola	8	532	6	683	11	1,496	...	......	...	......	...	......	25	2,711
Mexico	...	......	...	......	...	......	...	1	3	4	1	1	5	6
Costa Rica	...	......	...	......	...	......	...	......	1	2	...	......	1	2
U. States of Columbia	...	......	...	......	...	......	...	......	...	......	2	2	2	2
Venezuela	2	7	2	5	...	......	...	......	1	1	3	6	8	19
Brazil	1	28	2	278	5	80	6	139	5	162	4	90	23	777
Buenos Ayres	3	16	5	23	5	38	4	36	7	54	4	72	28	239
Chili	...	......	1	7	...	......	...	......	...	......	...	......	1	7
Peru	1	3	...	......	...	......	1	1	...	......	...	......	2	4
West Indies	12	36	5	12	6	9	6	11	13	19	13	15	55	102
Africa	1	6	1	6	1	9	1	7	2	10	3	8	9	46
Capetown	...	......	2	5	...	......	1	1	...	......	1	12	4	18
Burmah, China, Russia, Asia	...	......	...	......	...	......	1	10	3	6	1	1	5	17
Australia	4	675	...	......	...	......	...	......	...	......	1	3	5	678
Honolula	...	......	2	6	...	......	1	4	2	4	2	19	7	33
Total	162	23,177	146	22,011	174	30,296	126	16,540	122	15,187	121	18,175	...	......
Total from 1858 to 1863, inclusive													851	125,388
Total from 1832 to 1857, inclusive													4,739	685,768
Thus since 32 years, from 1832 to 1863, inclusive													5,590	811,156

Statement showing the description, quantity, and value of exports from Bremerhaven into the United States, together with the port of destination, for the two quarters ended March 31 and June 31, 1864.

QUARTER ENDED MARCH 31, 1864.

Description.	Quantity.	Destination.	Value.
Cigars	1 case	New York ....guilders..	147 09
Toys	3 cases	....do ....do....	109 50
Accordeons	....do	....do ....do....	467 41
Marbles	6 boxes	....do ....do....	222 57
Crockery ware	2 cases	....do ....do....	70 46
Meerschaum pipes	1 case	....do ....do....	80 50
Lead	4 molds	....do ....l. d'or..	523 00¼
Drugs	2 cases	....do ....guilders..	120 00
Toys and China ware	....do	....do ....do....	72 66
Prunes	37 casks	....do ....do....	251 61

Statement showing the description, quantity, and value of exports from Bremerhaven into the United States, &c.—Continued.

QUARTER ENDED JUNE 31, 1864.

Description.	Quantity.	Destination.	Value.
Toys	1 case	New York.......... gold r. d..	76 57
Prunes	19 casks	...do .... do..	521 15
Do	30 casks ....'.	...do .... do..	826 00
Accordeons.............	1 case	...do .... do...	216 15
Hams	3 cases	...do .... Prus. r. d..	341 17
Drugs	8 casks	...do .... gold r. d..	187 03
Bagging	5 bales	Baltimore .... do..	433 18
Canes and pipes	3 cases	New York .... do..	558 16
Musical instruments ...	1 case	...do .... do*...	560 33
Corks	2 bales	...do .... do..	48 00
Rice................	790 bags	...do .... do..	6,481 53
Pipes.................	184 cases	Philadelphia .... do..	355 06
Toys ....·.	9 cases	...do .... do..	611 60
Fancy goods	47 cases	...do .... do..	2,576 49
Do	1 case	New York .... do..	32 59
Cloth........	3 bales	...do .... Prus. r. d..	998 06
Toys and crockery.....	16 cases	...do .... gold r. d..	1,087 60
Melting pots	24 casks	...do .... Prus. r. d..	285 20
Prunes	35 casks	...do .... gold r. d..	2,359 04
Cigars, loose	5,000	...do .... dollars..	50 00
Succory meal	50 casks	...do .... gold r. d..	1,096 30
Drugs	5 cases, 4 casks, 12 bales	Baltimore .... do..	788 21
Torsk-liver oil..........	2 barrels	New York .... do..	77 39
Furs	1 cask	...do .... do..	293 00
Drugs	37 bales, 3 casks.. }		
Bones	1 case .... }	Baltimore.............. do..	638 17
Envelopes	8 cases .... }		
Hardware.............	1 case	...do .... do..	212 04
Crockery and hardware.	23 cases	New York .... do..	1,318 50
Crucibles	28 casks .... }	.... do .... Prus. r. d..	492 21
Apothecary bones......	12 casks .... }		

Statement showing the description and value of the exports from Hamburg into the United States, together with the place of production for the quarter ended September 30, 1864.

Country of production.	Description.	Value.
Germany	Glassware .... banco fl..	1,588 03
Do.....	Earthenware............................Prus. fl..	361 27
Do	.....do .... do....	598 24
Do	Gilt table, watches, and toys.............. banco fl..	122 00
Russia.................	Bristles .... s. rbl..	633 00
Germany	Buttons and pearls.................... Aust. fl..	1,300 25
Do....	Woollen and worsted goods............... Prus. fl..	11,123 03
Do....	Dirt and refuse of rags...................... £..	44 6 09
Africa	Ostrich feathers .... banco fl..	7,968 12
Germany...............	Tartar, linsey, &c .... do....	1,274 12
Do	Scrap iron................................ £..	50 12 02
Do	.....do................................. £..	79 3 04
Do	Dry goods .... banco fl..	1,945 13
England and Germany.	Pig-iron and spelter, in sheets.............. do....	9,048 10
Germany	Watches and boddles .... do....	12,075 00
Do....	Cream of tartar....................... do....	3,871 05

Statement showing the exports from Hamburg, &c.—Continued.

Country of production.	Description.	Value
Germany............	Whalebone, brushes, and leather	719 12
Do	Musical instruments ....Prus. fl..	685 05
Do	Knives ....do....	5 97
Do	Tools and cigars.................banco fl..	116 04
Do	Horse-hair ....do....	6,489 10
Do	Pearls ....Aust. fl..	237 88
Do	Lead pencils ....fl..	1,576 27
Do	Pearl sago.................banco fl..	1,227 09
Do	....do.	1,208 13
Do ....·.......	Dry goods.................Prus. fl..	124 00
Do	Cotton and woollenware..............banco fl..	2,533 14
Do	Cotton hose ....do....	5,623 00
Do	Samples ....do....	366 14
Do	....do ....frs..	1,665 00
Do	Trimmings....................frs..	4,488 50
Do	Toys ....banco fl..	3,086 05
Do	Succory flour..............do....	2,397 00
Do	....do...............Prus. fl..	1,621 12
Do	Stoneware..................do....	6,179 07
Do	Porcelain ware ....fl..	888 00
Do	Toys ....fl..	688 48
Do	Hair-cloth ....banco fl..	2,206 03
Do	Rhubarb..................do....	250 10
Do	Piano nails, &c............do....	509 14
Do	Fancy goods............Prus. fl..	25,429 06
Do	....do...................do....	1,102 86
Do	Woollen and half woollen goods....... .....do....	12,592 17
Do	Leather ....banco fl..	1,254 00
Do	Tin.......................do....	2,099 12
Different countries	Sundries ....do....	14,954 01
Germany	Glassware ....do....	3,013 09
Do	Cotton goods.........Prus. fl..	735 05
Do	Lace and trimmings ....frs..	18,901 75
Do	Schnapps..............banco fl..	3,075 00
Do	Woollen goods................do....	4,928 14
Do	Pocket handkerchiefs ....fl..	451 12
Do	Cloth ....banco fl..	3,222 00
Do	Succory flour................do....	2,442 05
Do	Gloves ....frs..	6,949 50
Do	Sundry goods.............banco fl..	10,656 10
Do	Trimmings..................frs..	3,721 00
Do	Cloth ....banco fl..	5,398 06
Do ......,........	....do ....Prus. fl..	6,943 02
Do	Woollen goods................do....	6,437 28
Do ....,..	Half woollen goods.............do....	256 10
Do	Toys ....do....	420 27
Do	Drugs ....do....	153 10
Do	Fancy goods ....do....	6,061 26
Do	Porcelain ware ....fl..	348 06
Do	Toys ....fl..	2,433 53
Do	..do........................fl..	1,452 45
Do	Scissors....................Prus. fl..	121,618 03
Do	Fancy goods............banco fl..	1,910 12
Do	Woollen goods ....fl..	745 30
Do	Hardware, &c ....banco fl..	1,868 12
Do	Woollen yarn................do....	4,933 08
Do	Black lead ....do....	2,560 07
Do	....................frs..	1,524 40
Do	Flocks.....................Prus. fl..	746 20
Do	...do.......................do....	16,069 21
Russia............	Russia leather ....banco fl..	263 04
Germany ....·........	Samples ....Prus. fl..	74 00

Statement showing the exports from Hamburg, &c.—Continued.

Country of production.	Description.	Value.
Germany	Linen thread ....fl.,	1,045 42
Do	Hair-cloth ....banco fl..	5,402 00
Do	Lithographic stones, &c....................do....	263 14
Do	Cloth.........................Prus. fl..	9,759 15
Do	Feathers ....banco fl..	1,551 04
Do	Glass and porcelain ware ....do....	1,273 10
Do	Woollen goods........................	1,277 10
Different countries	Sundries	5,370 12
Do	Nutmegs and candy......................	911 05
Do	Sundries ....banco fl..	9,413 08
Germany	Cherry juice...........................do....	1,494 10
Do	Fancy ware...........................do....	752 00
Do	Hair-cloth..........................do....	2,211 01
Do	Sausage ....do....	187- 01
Do	Strings ....Prus. fl..	388 12
Do	Canes.........................banco fl..	1,308 02
Do	Canvas ....Prus. fl..	472 10
Do	Pipes ....banco fl..	948 13
Do	Toys............................do.....	5,396 03
Do	Smoked hams....................Prus. fl..	358 27
Do	Fancy wares.........................banco fl..	130 00
Do	.................................fl..	700 23
Do	Pipes, &c.........................Aust. fl..	102 65
Do	Musical instruments..........banco fl..	653 06
Do	............do...........do....	855 00
Do	Pipes, &c.......................Prus. fl..	7,051 73
Do	Golden-ware ....fl..	1,995 52
Do	Trimmings.........................frs..	3,043 15
Do	Drugs.........................banco fl..	1,019 03
Do	Matches and glass ....do....	5,209 13
Do	Pig-iron, lead, and wine.............do....	6,175 14
Do	Buttons and pearls......................Aust. fl..	502 45
Different countries	Sundries ....banco fl..	9,821 00
Germany	Pianos.........................do....	800 00
Do	Chinaware ....fl..	1,285 29
Do	Glassware.........................Prus. fl..	9,692 26
Do	Corsets.........................banco fl..	366 12
Do	Cloth.........................Prus. fl..	782 00
Do	..do.........................do....	1,914 20
Do	....	2,471 25
Do	Stockings and woollen goods........banco fl..	3,542 07
Do	Woollen ware ....do....	1,120 04
Do	Black lead ....do....	1,251 12
Do	Books and lithographies ....do....	578 00
Do	Golden trimmings....................do....	600 00
Do	Trimmings ....frs..	3,257 80
Do	Enamel...........................fl..	812 00
Do	Soaps and perfumeries. ....banco fl..	732 14
Do	Spelter in sheets.....................do....	1,008 00
Do	Mineral waters....................Prus. fl..	284 00
Do	Percussion caps ....do....	1,267 00
Do	Books ....do....	80 00
South America	Wool.........................banco fl..	863 15
Germany	Books and lithographic stones.............do....	1,077 12
Do	Succory flour.........................do....	2,416 14
Do	Canes, &c.........................do....	496 12
Do	....	927 11
Do	Woollen and glass ware.............Prus. fl..	1,239 13
Do	Tin.........................banco fl..	2,075 86
Do	Woollen ware ....do....	588 06
Do	Cloth.........................do....	3,605 00
Do	Bristles ....do....	886 12

Statement showing the exports from Hamburg, &c.—Continued.

Country of production.	Description.	Value.
Germany	Spirits ....£..	31 10 06
Do	Pearls ....Aust. fl..	320 93
Do	Black lead ....banco fl..	271 10
Do	Hair-cloth ....do....	3,210 00
Do	....do ....do....	2,233 09
Russia	Russia leather......................do....	2,126 00
Germany	Pipes ....Prus. fl..	31,323 06
Do	Bristles ....do...	387,528 04
Do	....do ....do...	17,891 16
Do	Pipes................................fl..	193 48
Do	Canes ....banco fl..	275 00
Do	Porcelain ware..................Prus. fl..	148 26
Do	Fancy goods ....do....	4,711 76
Do	Sundries ....banco fl..	196 12
Do	Hams ....Prus. fl..	324 39
Do	Machinery.......................banco fl..	302 00
Do	Glass ware........................do....	2,590 01
Do	Glass, porcelain, earthenware, &c..........do....	4,740 00
Do	Cherry juice.........................do....	2,307 11
Do	Black lead ....do....	2,490 06
Do	Salt ....do....	40 05
Do	Furs ....do....	512 03
Do	Trimmings ....frs..	7,322 35
Do	Manufactured succory.............Prus. fl..	431 02
Do	Drugs ....$..	266 08
Do	Bristles ....Prus. fl..	402 05
Do	Toys ....do....	1,582 26
Do	Strings.............................£..	107 18 04
Do	Glassware.........................O. W. fl..	1,795 26
Do	Porcelain ware..................Prus. fl..	109 00
Do	Cotton hose ....banco fl..	2,174 04
Switzerland	Cotton handkerchiefs...................do....	1,403 15
Germany	Gloves.............................frs..	12,748 50
England	Extracts ....£..	187 17 10
Germany	Succory flour ....banco fl..	2,371 01
Do	....do.........................Prus. fl..	1,718 03
Do	Worsted goods...................banco fl..	2,250 08
Do	Woollen goods ....do....	1,037 12
Do	Trimmings ....frs..	7,059 25
France	Silk ware ....frs..	3,181 70
Germany	Brushes......................Prus. fl..	1,402 66
Do	Fancy goods ....£..	37 16 00
Do	Stationery and aigrettes.........banco fl..	1,236 01
Do	Glass and porcelain ware..................do....	247 14
Do	Piano nails..........................do....	475 11
Do	Cloth ....do....	1,853 10
Do	Toys ....fl..	1,141 34
Do	Hair-cloth ....banco fl..	2,334 08
Do	Sail-cloth...........................do....	5,800 00
Do	Russian leather, and fancy goods...........do....	1,246 14
Do	Cloth.........................Prus. fl..	2,452 05
Do	Canes ....banco fl..	1,087 04
Do	Clothes.......................Prus. fl..	1,150 24
Do	Trimmings...........................frs..	905 25
England	Pig-iron.......................banco fl..	7,129 11
Germany	Cotton ware..........................do....	3,371 13
Do	Woollen and worsted goods............Prus. fl..	428 46
Do	Marble ware and lithographies.........banco. fl..	163 13
Do	Sundries ....do....	1,142 14
Different countries	....do.............................do....	5,314 13
Do	....do.............................do....	29,180 13
Holland	Stearine candles ....do....	2,431 10

Statement showing the exports from Hamburg, &c.—Continued.

Country of production.	Description.	Value.
Germany	Woollen goods......................banco fl..	910 00
Do	Worsted and cotton goods..................do....	2,732 04
Do	Silk goods.................................frs..	4,789 55
Do	Color cases.................................fl..	.170 46
Do	Scheidam schnapps.................banco fl..	3,075 00
Do	Glassware.............................Prus. fl..	376 28
Do	Worsted goods...................banco fl..	2,892 15
England	Hessians.................................do....	6,064 12
Germany	Window glass.........................do....	2,023 15
Do	Twines and perfumeries ....do....	915 03
Do	Twines, furniture, &c.....................do....	893 03
Do	Hair-cloth ....do....	2,862 06
Do	Wine......................................do....	2,350 12
Do	Succory flour.......................Prus. fl..	1,764 21
Do	Cane ....do....	1,261 76
Different countries....	Horse-hair and cotton..................banco fl..	22,888 00
Do	Horse-hair, feathers, &c............do....	453 55
Germany	Hair-cloth ....do....	2,764 00
Do	.....do............................do....	2,310 04
England	Pig-iron ....do....	574 59
Germany	Pipes ....Prus. fl..	36 63
Do	Fancy goods ....do....	749 69
Do	Cloth....................................do....	451 18
Do	Button forms............. *.........banco fl..	178 03
Do	Cherry juice............................do....	2,301 14
Do	Anchovies ....do....	206 10
Do	Camillen...............................do....	200 10
Do	Worsted goods.........................do....	2,329 08
Do	Musical instruments ....Prus. fl..	718 15
Do	Canes, &c ....do....	64 12
Do	Books, &c ....banco fl..	3,546 05
Do	Woollen goods......................Prus. fl..	13,868 10
Do	....	369 24
Do	Hair-cloth and flannel...............banco fl..	179 19
Different countries.....	Sundries ....do....	9,171 11
Germany	Flocks....................................do....	1,239 11
Do	Notions	288 12
Do	Shoes...................................Prus. fl..	1,155 77
Do	Mineral salt............................do....	889 16
Do	Gloves ....frs..	12,572 10
Do	Cod-liver oil ....banco fl..	276 05
Do	Piano nails.............................do....	480 06
Do	Fancy goods ....do....	448 66
Do	Trimmings...............................frs..	1,380 30
Do	Feathers, horse-hair, and bristles ....banco fl..	6,835 07
Do	Hair-cloth..............................do....	241 45
Do	Half-woollen goods.... ....Prus. fl..	491 15
England	Pig-iron...........................banco fl..	6,437 11
Germany	Succory flour........................do....	2,481 15
Do	.....do...............................do....	2,511 12
Do	.....do.............................Prus. fl..	1,143 01
Do	Soaps ....banco fl..	401 05
Do	Scrap-iron ....do....	1,049 14
Do	Anchovies ....do....	333 07
Do	Woollen goods.........................do....	1,275 01
Do	Wool ....Prus. fl..	366 10
Do	Lentils............................banco fl..	1,705 04
Do	...do...................................do....	7,829 04
Do	Woollen goods......................Prus. fl..	7,200 28
Do	Clocks.............................banco fl..	683 08
Do	Cotton goods......................Prus. fl..	814 16
Do	Tar................................banco fl..	231 43

Statement showing the exports from Hamburg, &c.—Continued.

Country of production.	Description.	Value.
Germany	Mineral water........................Prus. fl..	284 26
Do	Cloth ....banco fl..	1,890 09
Do	Currants................................do....	2,069 03
Do	Hams...............................Prus. fl..	419 12
Do	Worsted ware.......................banco fl..	9,971 36
Do	Drugs ....do....	1,320 00
Do	Cloth.................................do....	2,457 13
Do	Pearls ....do....	556 14
Do	Gloves.................................frs..	5,886 00
Do	Corsets ....fl..	7,450 09
Do	Pipes and fancy goods..............banco fl..	3,064 04
Do	Calendars	238 00
Do	Button moulds...........................	117 00
Do	Feathers and bristles	9,545 10
Do	Iron and steel ware.....................	2,448 00
	Total in marcs banco.....................	804,288 02
	or......	$297,586 56

HAMBURG—J. H. ANDERSON, *Consul.*

Comparatire statement showing the description, quantity, and value of the principal articles imported into Hamburg during the years 1862 and 1863.

Description.	1862.		1863.	
	Quantity.	Value.	Quantity.	Value.
	Centners.	*Marcs-banco.*	*Centners.*	*Marcs-banco.*
Lard ....,	93,823	2,778,790	55,671	1,406,280
Beef and pork, salted		2,716,920		1,154,920
Butter	148,319	8,590,310	164,492	9,129,820
Honey...........................	28,192	549,280	26,030	473,920
Cheese..........................	40,880	1,336,490	43,993	1,588,250
Cigars	119,266	3,393,440	133,986	5,031,270
Copper	39,307	2,478,040	54,318	3,234,090
Whalebone.......................	4,179	1,022,200	1,594	549,050
Potash..........................	15,394	286,340	15,169	288,450
Tobacco	236,491	13,628,270	213,464	9,685,610
Machines and parts of	20,735	5,220,170	33,296	6,449,440
Furs............................		6,281,840		7,036,130
Guano	716,240	6,142,000	1,069,208	8,599,081
Total	1,462,326	54,424,090	1,811,221	54,626,311

Statement showing the value in marcs-banco of the imports into Hamburg for the year 1863, together with the names of the principal countries whence derived :

	Marcs-banco.
Great Britain and dependencies	230,488,420
United States	13,937,150
China...	2,363,710
Holland and dependencies...................	10,801,960
Spain and dependencies.................................	12,704,060

		Marcs-banco.
Africa (east and west coast)...........................		1, 078, 690
Uruguay and Argentine republic		642, 110
Ecuador, Peru, and Chili.............................		10, 560, 000
German states.......................................		398, 312, 180
France..		13, 571, 630
Italy		2, 877, 120
Austria...		267, 180
Greece and Ionian islands............................		320, 690
Asia Minor..		793, 400
Sandwich islands....................................		256, 000
Shippers' islands		182, 180
Mexico..		1. 494, 830
Central America.....................................		849, 340
Brazil...		10, 474, 080
Venezuela...		6, 735, 390
Denmark and dependencies...........................		356, 920
Russia..		706, 430
Norway and Sweden..................................		3, 125, 240
Belgium...		6, 439, 690
Portugal..		760, 460
Hayti...		3, 580, 850
Total		733, 680, 510

Statement showing the nationality, tonnage, and number of vessels, with their crews, arrived at the port of Hamburg during the years 1862 and 1863.

Nationality.	1862.				1863.			
	Number of vessels.	Tonnage in lasts of 6,000 pounds.	Number of crews.	Number of lasts to each seaman.	Number of vessels.	Tonnage in lasts of 6,000 pounds.	Number of crews.	Number of lasts to each seaman.
United States.........................	11	2, 957	164	18.0	25	10, 602	529	20.0
Austria..............................					1	275	33	8.3
Belgium..............................	3	315	29	10.9	5	570	50	11.4
Brazil...............................	1	83	15	5.5	1	87	9	9.7
Bremen	46	3, 770	317	11.9	102	8, 878	743	11.9
Denmark.............................	489	16, 590	2, 284	7.2	502	17, 577	2, 406	7.3
France...............................	95	10, 816	1, 435	7.5	149	14, 582	1, 979	7.4
Great Britain.........................	1, 817	218, 069	24, 788	8.8	1, 870	234, 973	26, 122	9.0
Hamburg.............................	795	107, 538	12, 283	8.8	836	114, 383	12, 790	8.9
Hanover.............................	1, 023	19, 597	3, 065	6.5	1, 253	22, 928	3, 606	6.4
Holland..............................	430	20, 540	2, 650	7.8	373	21, 256	2, 566	8.3
Italy................................	7	716	82	8.7	4	342	41	8.3
Lubeck	2	165	18	9.2	2	202	22	9.2
Hawaiian Islands.....................					1	159	20	8.0
Mecklenburg.........................	14	1, 443	134	10.8	19	1, 760	173	10.2
Norway..............................	96	9, 311	1, 348	6.9	127	13, 067	1, 727	7.5
Oldenburg...........................	76	4, 600	557	8.2	89	2, 971	322	9.2
Peru.................................	1	143	13	11.0				
Portugal.............................	12	700	110	6.4	14	1, 035	145	7.1
Prussia..............................	47	2, 881	319	9.0	48	3, 326	344	9.7
Russia...............................	6	690	162	4.3	5	379	42	9.0
Sweden..............................	77	6, 713	847	7.9	71	6, 081	794	7.7
Siam................................	2	297	45	6.6				
Spain................................	38	5, 080	580	8.8	45	5, 709	656	8.7
Venezuela............................					1	76	9	8.4
Total	5, 083	433, 274	51, 245	......	5, 543	481, 216	55, 125	......

Statement showing the nationality, tonnage, and number of vessels, with their crews, departed from the port of Hamburg during the years 1862 and 1863.

Nationality.	1862.				1863.			
	Number of vessels.	Tonnage in lasts of 6,000 lbs.	Number of crews.	Number of lasts to each seaman.	Number of vessels.	Tonnage in lasts of 6,000 lbs.	Number of crews.	Number of lasts to each seaman.
United States......................	9	2,874	152	18.9	15	5,685	293	19.4
Austrian				......	2	411	45	9.1
Belgium..........................	3	315	29	10.9	4	320	33	9.7
Brazil............................	1	83	15	5.5	1	87	9	9.7
Bremen...........................	50	4,357	371	11.7	96	8,624	690	12.5
Denmark..........................	493	16,830	2,333	7.2	505	17,499	2,737	6.4
France	96	11,060	1,456	7.6	147	14,363	1,953	7.4
Great Britain	1,818	217,483	24,811	8.8	1,875	235,631	26,119	9.0
Hamburg..........................	790	105,832	12,045	8.8	852	118,280	13,039	9.1
Hanover	1,011	19,479	3,023	6.4	1,244	22,621	3,543	6.4
Holland...........................	419	19,683	2,460	8.0	388	22,073	2,343	9.4
Italy	6	580	70	8.3	4	342	41	8.3
Lubeck	3	261	29	9.0	2	202	22	9.2
Mecklenburg......................	8	905	80	11.3	16	1,301	141	9.2
Norway	101	10,040	1,405	7.1	132	14,100	1,832	7.7
Oldenburg........................	71	4,165	509	8.2	85	2,800	301	9.3
Peru.............................	1	143	13	11.0	......	......	......	......
Portugal..........................	11	630	100	6.3	13	933	130	7.2
Prussia...........................	46	2,932	327	9.0	48	3,556	360	9.9
Russia	5	460	148	3.1	6	624	56	11.1
Siam	2	297	45	6.6	......	......	......	......
Spain	35	4,633	523	8.9	46	5,756	658	8.7
Sweden	75	6,334	826	7.7	67	5,488	741	7.4
Total.........................	5,054	429,376	50,770	......	5,548	480,696	55,086	......

A commercial last is about three tons.

SWITZERLAND.

ZURICH—R. FAIRLAMB, *Consul.*

JANUARY 20, 1864.

I have the honor of transmitting herewith the quarterly statement of this consulate for the fourth quarter of the year 1863, showing the amount and character of the goods exported to the United States from within this consular jurisdiction during that period, together with the fees received for the verification of the invoices of the same and for other official services. For convenience of reference a summary of the said statement is hereto annexed.

Summary statement showing the description and value of the exports from Zurich to the United States during the quarter ended December 31, 1863.

	Francs.
Month of October.....................................	2,179,156 71
" November.....................................	1,563,998 13
" December.....................................	2,973,424 56
Total...	6,716,579 40

	Francs.
Silk goods...	5,698,023 89
Straw goods	422,149 09

	Francs.
Cotton goods...	393, 290 05
Curtains and embroidery................................	88, 929 49
Foulards..	29, 810 20
Ribbons...	25, 856 52
Bolting cloths...	15, 742 30
Catholic devotional articles.............................	6, 710 73
Cheese...	4, 828 72
Rags, (for making paper)...............................	3, 628 56
Miscellaneous...	27, 609 85
Total	6, 716, 579 40

JANUARY 30, 1864.

The total exports from this consular district to the United States during the year 1863 were as follows:

First quarter.

	Francs.	Francs.
January...............................	1, 890, 592 00	
February..............................	1, 518, 989 00	
March................................	1, 841, 710 00	
		5, 251, 291 00

Second quarter.

April.................................	1, 233, 825 00	
May..................................	1, 333, 562 00	
June.................................	2, 343, 084 00	
		4, 910, 471 00

Third quarter.

July..................................	2, 337, 204 41	
August...............................	2, 741, 850 60	
September............................	2, 823, 019 79	
		7, 902, 074 80

Fourth quarter.

October..............................	2, 179, 156 71	
November............................	1, 563, 998 13	
December............................	2, 973, 424 56	
		6, 716, 579 40
Total for 1863.................................		24, 780, 416 20

The character or nature of these exports is shown in the following table:

Description.	1st quarter.	2d quarter.	3d quarter.	4th quarter.	Total.
	Francs.	*Francs.*	*Francs.*	*Francs.*	*Francs.*
Silk goods	4,757,124	4,711,390	7,359,400 62	5,698,023 89	22,525,938 51
Cotton goods...........	136,677	62,948	171,360 00	393,290 05	764,275 05
Straw goods	75,733	59,771	244,737 55	422,149 09	802,390 64
Foulards	7,835	....	11,898 80	29,810 20	49,544 00
Bolting cloths	38,936	22,835	22,099 35	15,742 30	99,612 65
Curtains and embroidery.	184,820	29,678	48,587 92	88,929 49	352,015 41
Ribbons	....	....	19,371 30	25,856 52	45,227 82
Tobacco, wines, and cigars.................	....	....	483 20	....	483 20
Miscellaneous	50,166	23,849	24,136 06	42,777 86	140,928 92
Total............	5,251,291	4,910,471	7,902,074 80	6,716,579 40	24,780,416 20

APRIL 15, 1864.

I have the honor of transmitting herewith the quarterly statement of this consulate for the first quarter of the present year, showing the amount and character of the goods exported to the United States from within this consular jurisdiction during that period, together with the fees received for the verification of the invoices of the same and for other official services. For convenience of reference a summary of the said statement is hereto annexed.

It will be remembered that the shipments have been unusually large during the quarter just ended, a fact attributable to three known causes:

1st. An unusual activity in the American market and consequent increased demand for goods from abroad.

2d. A growing confidence in regard to American affairs.

3d. The rumor of an intention upon the part of the government to raise the duties upon silks.

I may be allowed to express a doubt as to whether the raising of the duties upon silks would increase the revenue from this source, as I am inclined to believe the imports of silks would fall off in greater percentage than the additional duties would amount to. I recommend, however, most strongly, the equalizing of the present duties; charging, say, 40 per cent. on all silks, instead of 30 per cent. on some and 40 per cent. on others. I am confident that the result would be eminently satisfactory.

Summary.

	Francs.
January..	3,835,828 58
February...	3,407,220 96
March..	2,930,675 82
Total	10,173,717 36

	Francs.
Silk goods...	8,950,805 20
Straw goods	220,387 61
Cotton goods...	723,748 18
Silk ribbons...	108,140 10
Taffetas...	24,452 30
Foulards...	5,389 00
Curtains and embroideries.............................	67,995 06

	Francs.
Bolting cloths	23, 013 30
Mathematical instruments	3, 192 25
Catholic devotional wares	11, 442 56
Wines and liquors	793 30
Cheese	4, 532 87
Miscellaneous	29, 825 63
Total	10, 173, 717 36

JULY 16, 1864.

I have the honor to transmit herewith the quarterly statement of this consulate for the second quarter of the present year, showing the amount and character of the goods exported to the United States from within this consular jurisdiction during that period, together with the fees received for the verification of the invoices of the same and for other official business. For convenience of reference a summary of the said statement is hereto annexed.

The exports have been steadily decreasing since the first month of the quarter, and, by reference to my report for the first quarter, it will be seen that the exports of the second quarter fall nearly 1,500,000 francs below those of the first. This falling off in exports still continues. Up to yesterday evening, the 15th instant, but forty-nine invoices had been legalized since the first half of the month, whilst during the first half of the month of June one hundred and ten invoices were legalized.

Summary.

	Francs.
Month of April	3, 619, 319 16
" May	2, 992, 684 14
" June	2, 117, 565 19
Total for second quarter of 1864	8, 729, 568 49

Specification.

	Francs.
Silk goods	7, 742, 786 29
Silk ribbons	132, 701 60
Straw goods	31, 244 71
Cotton goods	517, 046 55
Curtains and embroidery	89, 701 77
Bolting cloth	136, 918 80
Catholic articles	17, 827 00
Cheese	17, 413 31
Woollen goods	20, 416 00
Miscellaneous	23, 512 46
Total, as before	8, 729, 568 49

OCTOBER 10, 1864.

In accordance with the general instructions of the department, I have the honor to report for the year, from October 1, 1863, to September 30, 1864, inclusive, as follows.

The following tabular statement of the exportations from my consular district to the United States for the period named, exhibits at a glance not only the amount of each particular kind of goods or wares thus exported during the entire year, but the total amount of exportations and the amount of each particular kind for each separate quarter:

Tabular statement showing the exportation of merchandise during the year ended September 30, 1864, and also for each quarter.

Articles.	4th quarter, 1863.	1st quarter, 1864.	2d quarter, 1864.	3d quarter, 1864.	Total.
Silk goods	$5,698,023 89	$8,950,805 20	$7,742,786 29	$1,082,733 65	$23,474,349 03
Silk ribbons	25,856 52	132,592 40	132,701 60	146,241 05	437,391 57
Cotton goods	393,290 05	722,748 18	517,046 55	203,753 80	1,837,838 58
Curtains and embroidery	88,929 49	67,995 06	89,701 77	162,136 54	408,762 86
Straw goods	422,149 09	220,387 61	31,244 71	33,179 60	706,961 01
Bolting cloths	15,742 30	23,013 30	136,918 80	38,992 40	214,666 80
Foulards	29,810 20	5,389 00			35,199 20
Woollen goods			20,416 00		20,416 00
Catholic articles	6,710 73	11,442 56	17,827 00	19,906 50	55,886 79
Rags	3,628 56				3,628 56
Mathematical instruments		3,192 25			3,192 25
Cheese	4,828 72	4,532 87	17,413 31		26,774 90
Wines and liquors		793 30			793 30
Miscellaneous	27,609 85	29,825 63	23,512 46	7,718 20	88,666 14
Total	6,716,579 40	10,173,717 36	8,729,568 49	1,694,661 74	27,314,526 99

COMPARISON WITH PREVIOUS YEAR.

Fourth quarter, 1862 .... $2,515,074
First quarter, 1863 5,251,291
Second quarter, 1863 4,910,471
Third quarter, 1863 7,902,074

Total 20,578,910

It will be remarked, from the comparison at the end of the foregoing statement, that the exportations for the first three quarters of the year which has just closed reached an amount more than double that of the corresponding quarters of the preceding year, whilst the exportations of the last quarter (3d quarter, 1864) fell to nearly one-fifth of those of the corresponding quarter of the preceding year, and to *less* than one-fifth of those of the quarter immediately preceding, (2d quarter, 1864.) This great falling off in exportations to the United States is attributable to two reasons: First, the raised tariff; and second, the overstocked state of the American market. Nevertheless, the exportations of the past year, reaching a total of 27,314,527 francs, exceed in all probability* the exportations of any previous year. Taking this amount in round numbers in United States coin, at, say, $5,000,000, and roughly averaging the duty at 30 per cent., we have an estimated revenue to the government, from duty on imports from this consular district during the past year, of $1,500,000 in gold. I deem it but just to state, in this connexion, that after nearly two years and a half of daily close observation and experience, it is my belief that little or no attempt is made by merchants and exporters in my consular district to defraud our government by undervaluing in their invoices the goods which they export to the United States. I believe, however, that large quantities of silk goods manufactured in this district are smuggled from Canada into the United States, but I doubt if the parties here are in any way interested in these smuggling operations. A merchant or manufacturer who can find an

---

* It is impossible to speak certainly upon this point, as it is only two years and a half since consular cognizance has been taken of all exports to the United States.

English customer for his goods, be they silks of American widths or not, demands the ultimate destination of the goods, nor, as he world goes, hesitates to sell them, because he may suspect the buyer's purpose. As far as he and the buyer are concerned, in their relation to each other, the actual disposition of the goods by the one to the other constitutes a complete and perfectly legal business transaction. The most a consular officer can do in reference to such transactions is to keep the government, as far as possible, apprised of them, (though they may be very easily kept from the knowledge of the consul, if the parties concerned desire him to be kept in ignorance,) and, in order to detect the real offenders, the government must then direct its operations to the neighborhood where the smuggling actually takes place. The appointment of consuls at different points in Canada was a much-needed measure, and the benefits proceeding therefrom will, I doubt not, be soon manifest.

The United States being the principal market for Swiss silks, the falling off of exportations is severely felt by all concerned in the manufacture of silk goods. The cotton-weavers of the cantons of St. Gall, Appenzell, Thurgovia, &c., are, of course, also suffering, but many of these, I am told, have turned their attention to the manufacture of cigars, which they say yields better profits than cotton-weaving. And, apropos of cigar-making, it may be mentioned that while in some of the Swiss cantons tobacco, generally of an inferior quality, I believe, is cultivated with great success, certain parties who have experimented with American tobacco seed complain that whilst they get splendid leaves they get no new seed, the climate appearing to be unfavorable to the development of the flower.

During the past few years the number of banking institutions in Switzerland has been largely increased by the establishment of new banks of various kinds, such as credit banks, savings banks, &c., but comparatively few bank-notes are in circulation, the people at large not regarding them with particular favor. The Swiss federal bank (Eidgenössische bank) established last year at Bern, with a capital of 60,000,000 francs, and under the presidency of Mr. Stalmpfli, formerly president of the republic, is said to be doing well, but dissatisfaction is expressed by many on two accounts, viz: First, that a title should have been adopted, which is a misnomer, conveying the idea, as it does, of the bank being national, whereas it is, like all other banks in this country, simply a *private* institution. And, second, because the bank is built upon so much foreign, and particularly French, capital. In general, it may be remarked, the Swiss appear to be jealous of the French, and suspicious as to the policy and designs of the Emperor. Nevertheless, much intercourse is kept up between the two countries, and, at times, with some display of at least outward friendship.

Many, and, indeed, much-needed improvements are being made, not only in the city of Zurich, but throughout the canton, and in other sections of the country falling within my consular jurisdiction. But the spirit of enterprise seems confined for the most part to the better educated and more enlightened; it does not appear to have reached or stirred up the masses removed from the vicinity and influence of thriving cities and towns, and even *there* there are many things to show that though so much has been already accomplished, yet how much room there still remains for improvement and progress. I do not think that I have ever seen *less* than *two* men shoeing a horse; and in passing localities where building is going on, even here in the city of Zurich, one constantly sees two-handled planes and saws, two men working with the one tool. And in the country one finds the same cumbersome old-fashioned ploughs and other agricultural implements as used by the present generation's grandfathers and their fathers before them. Ninety-nine men out of a hundred it would be impossible to convince of the advantages and actual economy, notwithstanding its first cost, in the use of a modern and scientifically constructed plough or mower, and the hundredth would not buy one. I speak from actual knowledge, having been informed by an enterprising mechanic who spent many years in America, and who is now established in business here as the agent for sewing machines, that having imported some American agricultural implements, which he exhibited and explained at fairs and elsewhere, and which did not fail to attract the momentary attention of the curious, he has been unable to dispose of a single piece. The sewing machines have come greatly into favor, however. There are agencies for American sewing machines in all the principal Swiss cities, and Swiss machines are now manufactured somewhere in the neighborhood of Zurich, but do not, I conceive, meet with much success. A friend of mine, a gentleman of considerable wealth, who lived for some years in New York, has also imported a number of washing machines, which he presented, I believe, to various friends and acquaintances.

But to speak of the improvements which have been or are now being made in my consular district—and first, of the city of Zurich. A broad and beautiful bridge across the river Limmat, which runs through the heart of the city, built of granite, at an expense of some 1,500,000 francs, has recently been completed and opened to the public. It is situated opposite the railroad depot, and is at the same time an ornament to the city and of immense public service. A "boulevard" is now in course of construction from the railroad depot to the Baugarten, a public garden or square bordering on the lake. This boulevard will also be both an ornament and a convenience. It occupies the site of the "Froschen graben," an old moat which was formerly one of the western defences of the city. The quays along the eastern bank of the Limmat are being improved, and the slaughter-house, which here disfigured the city, is to be replaced by a fine market-house.

The private buildings, as dwelling-houses, stores, &c., are springing up in all directions, not only in the city itself, but beyond the city limits in the so-called "Gemeinden" or communities, and, though generally not remarkable for beauty of architecture, these new buildings all appear to be solidly and substantially built, much more so, indeed, than many if not most of our American houses. They have not the same conveniences, however, nor are they as comfortable as the dwelling-houses in our American cities, and it must, moreover, be acknowledged that particularly the middle and lower classes of the people here evince much less taste and idea of comfort in furnishing their houses than is generally to be found in America, sometimes even in the humblest dwellings. One peculiarity of Swiss houses, those at least in this section of Switzerland, which is likely to strike the American traveller as a very singular arrangement is, that almost invariably the entrance, or, to use an Irishism, the front door, is put at the back of the house. The Swiss deserve much praise for the degree of excellence to which they have brought their educational system; but it is certainly to be regretted that not only "the Word of Life," with its beneficent influences, but that, also, all religious influences are, for the most part, if not by regulations, at least by habit and custom, shut out of the public schools. The cause of this is easily found in the decline of the national church from its first faith to the rationalism whose blighting power has been unhappily felt over so much of the continent. The public schools of the city of Zurich are considered particularly good, and the "Polytechnicum," a national institution, has already become a formidable rival to the longer established and more widely known polytechnic colleges in various parts of Germany.   *   *   *   *

The Polytechnicum building, situated on an eminence, and overlooking the city, is the largest and finest public building in the canton of Zurich. It was designed by Professor Semper, one of the faculty; has accommodations for 1,000 students, and cost in the neighborhood of 2,000,000 francs. This expense is to be defrayed by the canton of Zurich, whilst the federal government is to furnish the building and provide the various and numerous mechanical and scientific apparatus complimentary to its fitting up. The present corps of polytechnicum instructors comprises 38 professors, 18 masters, (of which 13 are so-called "privatdozente," who receive no salaries, but are paid by the students who choose to study under them,) and 7 assistants—in all 63. Most of the professors are Germans, and of well-established reputations. The students, about 300 in number at the present time, are from all parts of the world; more than one-half being, perhaps, from Germany, with quite a number of Russians, and some few Americans.

The Cantonal school, an institution which in its general plan and scope covers the same ground as our grammar and high schools in America, is also well worthy of particular mention. The course of instruction is very complete and thorough, so that when finished, lads are fitted, so far as general education goes, for most of the ordinary vocations of life, whilst those whose aims are higher, and whose success is in a measure dependent upon classical attainments, are prepared to at once enter a university.   *   *   *   *

An interesting event of the past year has been the opening of the Zurich Zug Luzerne railroad, which took place on the first of June and was celebrated by a grand dinner, illuminations, music, &c. To get from here to Luzerne, one was formerly obliged to travel around three sides of a square, and the journey occupied four hours. By the new road, however, the journey is now accomplished by the express train in less than two hours. This road belongs to the Northeast Railroad Company, and its cost is estimated at 12,000,000 francs. It cannot fail to prove one of the best paying lines of railroad in Switzerland.

The principal railroad in this consular district is the Northeast railroad, the main line of which extends east-northeast from Zurich to Romanshorn on Lake Constance, and west from Zurich to the city of Aarom in the canton of Argorie. The branch or adjunct lines belonging to the same company are, besides the Zurich Zug Luzerne railroad and that from Winterthur to Schaffhausen, the iron steamers on Lake Constance plying between Romanshorn and Lindau (connecting with the railroad to Munich *via* Augsburg,) Frederickhafen, (connecting with the railroad to Stuttgard *via* Ulm;) and other points also belong to the Swiss Northeast Railroad Company. On the 31st of December, 1863, the company possessed 134 passenger cars with 6,487 seats; 528 freight cars with the capacity 91,280 cwt., and 39 locomotives, of which four were for express trains, eighteen for ordinary, thirteen for freight trains, and four for "depot service." Of the 6,487 seats in the passenger cars, 368 were first class, 2,019 second class, and 4,100 third class. The total number of passengers transmitted over the lines, or some part of them, of the Northeast Railroad Company during the year 1863, (the Zurich Zug Luzerne railroad was not then open,) was 1,767,931, of which 18,338 (or 1.04 per cent.) were first class, 417,916 (or 23.64 per cent.) second class, and 13,31,677 (or 75.32 per cent.) third class. The amount received for passenger fares was: first class, francs 90,427.18, (or 3.97 per cent.,) second class, francs 896,682.28, (or 39.35 per cent.,) and third class, francs 1,291,760.52, (or 56.68 per cent.;) total, francs 2,278,869.98. For freight of passengers' baggage were received francs 121,643 14; for freight of horses, cattle, and dogs, francs 89,250.96; for freight of carriages, francs 7,016.02, and for freight on merchandise, &c., francs 2,839,973.98. To this is to be added francs 520,767.59, received as bonus for the use of Northeast railroad cars on other roads, net profits from the Constance steamers, interest on loans, &c.; and the total receipts of the company for the year 1863 are found to have been francs 5,857,521.67. The total expense of working the entire road during the same period was francs 2,422,509. The company declared a dividend to the stockholders of francs 2,081,330 for the year. I should have stated that the total length of the Northeast railroad, branch lines included, in operation during the year 1863, was 178 kilometres, or in the neighborhood of 111 English miles. Over this ground the trains ran in the course of the year a distance of 24,490,418 kilometres, or say 15,217,790 miles. The total number of the company's regular employés was at the close of the year, 1,055, of which 49 were employed upon the Constance steamers. The company has commenced the building of a railroad from Bulach to Regensberg, the cost of which is estimated at francs 1,826,525. Quite a novelty has recently been introduced into my consular district in the shape of two screw steamers on Lake Zurich, all the other steamers on this and, as far as my observation extends, on the other Swiss lakes having side-wheels. They are well patronized, and so great is the demand for still increased facilities for travel in this neighborhood that several more steamers are to be added, I understand, to the ten or twelve in all that ply regularly, summer and winter, between Zurich and Rapperschiriel, at the further end of the lake.

Excepting the vintage, this year's harvest has been most satisfactory. But, unfortunately, at the very season for ripening the grapes an unusually cold spell of weather set in, and the vintage, in consequence, has been poor both in quantity and in quality. In western Switzerland it is said to be much better. In speaking of the trade of this consular district, I should have mentioned that the Zurich Public Silk Drying Institution ("die offenthiche Serden Trock mungs Austalt in Zurich") reports for the year ending June 30, 1864, the drying of 1,092,281 Swiss pounds (equal to about 1,202,279 English pounds) of raw silk; being 282,644 pounds (310,908 English) more than in the year immediately preceding. I have already explained in my despatch No. 12, (old number,) dated October 28, 1863, the object of drying the silk, and will only now repeat, though not all the raw material used in the manufacture of Zurich silk goods passes through the Zurich Drying Institution, its reports give a very good basis of calculating or rather of estimating "the relative amount of business done in raw silk in different years."

BASLE—A. L. WOLFF, *Consul.*

MARCH 31, 1864.

Statement showing the description and value, both in French and United States currency, of the exports from Basle during the quarter ended March 31, 1864.

Articles.	Francs.	Dollars.
Ribbons	2,375,901 80	441,917 75
Dyestuffs	8,904 60	1,656 25
Machines	1,295 80	240 80
Books	949 27	176 55
Silks	294,596 32	54,794 90
Straw goods	302,919 95	56,343 00
Watches	2,302,981 45	428,354 90
Cheese	71,714 92	13,338 95
Liquors	10,366 10	1,927 90
Total	5,369,630 21	998,751 00

596   ANNUAL REPORT ON FOREIGN COMMERCE.

Statement showing the description of merchandise exported from Basle consular district to the United States, with invoices authenticated, together with their value in francs and dollars, during the quarter ended September 30, 1864.

Description.	Francs.	Dollars.
Silk ribbons	1,249,332 57	232,375 60
Silk stuffs	34,796 35	6,470 26
Straw goods	36,962 57	6,878 87
Watches	620,383 53	115,391 91
Cheese	35,123 07	6,532 69
Liquors	9,080 00	1,688 89
Sundries	9,106 37	1,693 27
Total	1,994,794 46	371,031 48

NOVEMBER 29, 1864.

I have the honor to present herewith the annual report of the commerce of Switzerland. *   *   *   *   *

It will be observed that since the new United States tariff of July 1 went into effect the exports to the United States from all the consular districts of Switzerland are decreasing—partly on account of the high rate of exchange, partly on account of the large stocks on hand, and, it is supposed, also on account of smuggling goods, *via* Canada, into the United States.

The goods shipped from this district are mostly silk goods, watches and parts of watches.

	Francs.	Dollars.
The shipments of the quarter ended September 30, 1863, amount to	4,883,674 82	976,734 96
For the same period of 1864	1,994,794 46	398,958 89
Falling off of last quarter of 1864	2,888,880 36	577,776 07

The exports of all the consular districts of Switzerland to the United States, and of the district of Lyons, in France, have also fallen off compared with the exports of previous corresponding periods. It is, moreover, remarkable to notice so great a decrease while the general exportations of Switzerland show an increase.   *   *   *   *   *

Well-informed business men here are of the opinion that great quantities of silks, watches, and other merchandise, have been purchased on English account, and shipped to Canada, with the intention of smuggling them into the United States.   *   *   *   *   *   *

Tabular statement showing the value in francs, and also in dollars, of merchandise exported to the United States from the Basle consular district for each quarter of the year ended September 30, 1864.

QUARTER ENDED DECEMBER 31, 1863.

Description.	Francs.	Dollars.
Watches	1,645,629 62	306,067 10
Ribbons	1,870,943 77	347,995 93
Straw goods	263,475 08	49,006 00
Silk stuffs..	125,123 50	23,272 87
Liquors...	4,056 40	754 49
Cheese	42,702 80	7,942 70
Dyestuffs	24,336 30	4,526 55
Sundries	8,799 98	1,636 80
Total	3,985,067 45	741,222 44

QUARTER ENDED MARCH 31, 1864.

Description.	Francs.	Dollars.
Ribbons	2,375,901 80	441,917 75
Dyestuffs	8,904 60	1,656 25
Merlines	1,295 80	240 80
Books	949 27	176 55
Silks	294,596 32	54,794 90
Straw goods...	302,919 95	56,343 00
Watches	2,302,981 45	428,354 90
Cheese	71,714 92	13,338 95
Liquors...	10,366 10	1,927 90
Total..	5,369,730 21	998,751 00

QUARTER ENDED JUNE 30, 1864.

Description.	Francs.	Dollars.
Ribbons	2,225,176 08	422,783 44
Silk stuffs	185,282 55	35,203 69
Straw goods...	5,128 40	974 40
Watches	2,371,091 29	450,507 35
Cheese	84,905 22	16,132 00
Liquors	6,777 58	1,287 44
Sundries	5,303 70	1,007 61
Total..	4,883,664 82	927,895 93

QUARTER ENDED SEPTEMBER 30, 1864.

Description.	Francs.	Dollars.
Ribbons	1,249,332 57	232,375 60
Silk stuffs...	34,786 35	6,470 26
Straw goods...	36,982 57	6,878 87
Watches	620,383 53	115,391 91
Cheese	35,123 07	6,532 89
Liquors	9,080 00	1,688 88
Sundries	9,106 37	1,693 27
Total	1,994,794 46	371,031 68

Comparative statement showing the importations into Switzerland for the first nine months of the years 1863 and 1864.

Description.	Quantities.	Quantities.
	1863.	1864.
Cattle...number....	75,984	86,999
Smaller animals ....do......	69,717	75,490
Value of agricultural implements...................francs....	336,199	864,016
Merchandise, principally in ....quintals....	5,438,744	5,756,476
Books and music sheets ....do......	6,528	7,234
Butter and lard ....do......	45,621	32,356
Cheese. ....do......	3,787	4,167
Coffee and coffee substitutes....................do......	112,187	97,277
Cotton, raw ....do......	141,608	189,471
Cotton, yarn and cloth ....do......	16,803	26,279
Dyewoods ....do......	44,079	40,030
Drugs and druggists' wares ....do......	39,974	40,234
Flax and hemp ....do......	9,679	11,129
Flour and grain................................do'....	2,295,159	2,523,291
Furniture and glassware........................do......	47,008	252,324
Iron, crude....................................do......	165,369	169,064
Iron, unwrought ....do......	185,349	222,134
Iron, cast ....do......	34,078	35,251
Steel, manufactured...........................do......	52,271	58,230
Madder ....do......	25,055	20,474
Leather..dol.....	15,386	14,431
Linen goods....................................do......	23,606	34,613
Machinery ....do......	54,521	51,966
Metals, crude..................................do......	19,979	22,347
Oil ....do......	141,739	147,463
Paper . ...do......	8,860	9,563
Rice ....do......	57,971	55,742
Seeds ....do......	54,631	48,889
Salt ....do......	170,435	155,114
Soap...do......	26,679	23,290
Sugar ....do......	161,961	143,921
Tobacco, leaf ....do......	34,855	51,918
Tobacco, manufactured..........................do......	13,220	13,071
Tallow and fat.................................do......	19,524	14,635
Wine in barrels................................do......	485,898	54,473
Wool and its fabrics ....do......	43,448	52,541

The exports of merchandise for the first nine months of 1863 and 1864 were: 1863, 735,389 quintals; 1864, 733,326 quintals.

Comparative statement showing the principal exportations from Switzerland for the first nine months of the years 1863 and 1864.

Description.	1863.	1864.
Books and sheet music ....quintals....	3,800	3,913
Butter and lard...do......	6,866	10,468
Cheese...do......	118,539	130,532
Cotton, raw ....do......	21,763	21,894
Cotton, yarn and cloth ....do......	166,767	158,435
Dyewoods ....do......	10,853	8,489
Druggists' wares..do......	4,216	3,090
Flour and grain..do......	31,668	26,787
Furniture ....do......	10,773	8,598
Iron, crude ....do......	30,635	16,735
Iron, wrought ....do......	8,749	4,657
Steel ware ....do......	9,135	13,322
Hides ....do......	30,206	31,534
Leather..do......	201	402
Silks...do......	6,534	6,899
Silk thrown ....do......	4,262	5,408
Silk floss ....do......	4,448	3,780
Silk and half silk goods ....do......	30,954	33,068
Straw goods...do......	3,421	3,287
Watches ....do......	1,934	2,004
Transit.		
Transit of merchandise.......................................	584,006	569,698

The commerce of Switzerland with Italy before the latter became one kingdom was of great importance, and since that event it shows an annual increase. The statistics from the Swiss custom-house authorities state only the quantities of imported and exported merchandise, and it is therefore difficult to fix the value.

The commercial statistics published in Italy as late as the year 1861 show that the general commerce of that country, including imports and exports, amounts for the year 1860 to 1,084,600,000 francs; for the year 1861 to 1,482,600,000 francs; which, divided among different countries, gives the following portion to Switzerland: 1860, 246,000,000 francs, or 23 per cent.; 1861, 274,000,000 francs, or 18 per cent. The Swiss importations from Italy for 1860, 127,009,480; for 1861, 159,281,337; of which the principal articles are raw silk, cocoons, thrown silk, and silk stuffs; amounting in all, in the year 1860, to 10,200,000 francs, and in the year 1861 to 5,700,000 francs, as follows:

Wine in barrels, 1860, to............................. 100,196 quintals.
   "   "   1861, to............................. 79,259   "
   "   "   1862, to............................. 125,914   "
   "   "   1863, to............................. 140,781   "

The imports of grain, rice, flour, &c., into Switzerland in 1860 amounted to 6,000,000 francs; in 1861 to 5,200,000 francs.

Emigrants leaving Switzerland for the United States who made their passage contracts at this city during the year 1862 numbered 1,764; during the year 1863, 2,109; for the part of the year 1864 terminating November 20, 3,487; while an equal number, if not more, have gone without entering into contracts here, in order to save some expenses.

It is astonishing to see at what sacrifices people dispose of property to emigrate to the United States—the natural result of the inducements our country offers to laborers, who in their own country can earn but the scanty pay of nine francs a week, or skilled mechanics fifty francs a month.   *   *   *

In the last century the cantonal government of Basle regulated employments and the wages of labor, and issued regulations to the dyer, the weaver, and the employer; and designing to keep the manufacture of ribbons a monopoly, prohibited the sale of looms, as the Basle looms were considered the best; and none were allowed to be made, or old ones to be moved from one place to another, without special permission from the authorities; and even the laborers were not allowed to leave the country. Manufacturers residing in other countries were not allowed to manufacture ribbons here, with the exception of four houses that were in possession of four looms. Whether the laborer owned the loom or it belonged to the manufacturer, he had not the right to select his own employer; neither could he change without permission. At that time factories were not in existence, but every weaver had a loom at his residence, which was either his own or the manufacturer's property. The laborer, however, was permitted to enjoy domestic life, and to cultivate a garden during his leisure hours.

This law has been changed to a certain extent; yet of the 7,500 looms now employed in weaving ribbons 5,000 are still in the hands of the laborers, while the remaining 2,500 are in factories, besides 250 looms that, under the especial attention of the manufacturers, are employed in weaving samples.

The rooms of the factories are light and well ventilated. 6,000 looms are worked by hand, 750 by steam, and 500 by water-power. With a few exceptions the looms are owned by the manufacturers. These manufacturers, with their abundant capital, spare no pains to make their looms superior to all others.

The greatest ribbon manufactory in the world is here. It contains about 900 looms, and is the only one operated by steam.   *   *   *

The weaver who uses the loom of a manufacturer pays two per cent. of his wages for its use, and the only security he is able to give is his integrity.

The wages of a silk-winder are, per day, fr. 1 30 to fr. 1 70; the wages of a warper, fr. 2 to fr. 2 70; the wages of a weaver, fr. 2 50 to fr. 4.

Basle city is well known for making the best looms, and has seven loom manufacturers with 250 laborers, and eight with 50 laborers, turning out about 600 looms annually, of which 350 are ordered for the interior of Switzerland, 150 to foreign countries, and 100 to replace old ones.

Dyeing is of the greatest importance in the manufacture of ribbons. If the silk thread is neglected by the dyer, neither the winder, the warper, nor the weaver is able to cure the defect. There are, in all, eight dyeing establishments, with 300 workmen, which dye the silk for all our manufacturers; and to such an excellency have they attained, that silks are sent here from abroad to be dyed.

This Basle ribbon manufacture altogether employs 10,000 persons; and in 1846 the value of their products amounted to 20,000,000 francs, and that of all the ribbon manufacturers in Switzerland amount to 35,000,000 francs, and the total silk manufactures of Switzerland to 46,000,000 francs.

Basle ribbons are sent to all parts of the world, in competition with those of Lyons, St. Etienne, and Crefeld, and find a ready market at Paris, in spite of customs duties of from five to seven per cent., and in Germany, where they are subject to a duty of eight per cent.

The Basle ribbons are disposed of as follows: to Germany, thirty-eight per cent.; United States and England, forty-four per cent.; France, ten per cent.; other countries, eight per cent.

SEPTEMBER 30, 1864.

I have the honor to submit herewith my first annual report upon the trade of this consular district with the United States, together with a brief description of the manner in which watchmaking commenced and is carried on in Geneva and its environs. Also a description of a new kind of railroad, which has just been introduced here from Manchester, England, and seems to me to be worthy of mention in our southern cities. Also a statement of the exports from this district for the past year.

OUR COMMERCE WITH GENEVA.

The trade between the United States and this consular district, and, indeed, with all Switzerland, is a very one-sided business, but there is no reason why it should continue to be so. For the past year we have purchased from the Swiss between seven and eight millions of dollars of goods, principally silks and jewelry, which we have paid for in gold, they taking nothing from us directly, and but little now indirectly, although they take some of our cotton, tobacco, and petroleum, with a few of our sewing machines. Recently a direct line of steamers has been established between Havre and New York. From Havre to Geneva freight may be taken by railroad, without change of cars, in from three to fifteen days; if in the first named time, which is called *grande vitesse*, the charge for the Swiss quintal, equivalent to one hundred and ten pounds, is $3 44; by the second time, or *petite vitesse*, the charge is $1 34. By the 25th article of a treaty of commerce concluded between France and the Swiss Confederation, on the 30th of June, 1864, it is provided that (with the exception of arms and munitions of war, for which special authority is required) there shall be no transit duty whatever upon goods coming from or going to Switzerland.

The Swiss tariff is, for the most part, extremely fair, and the duties, with a few *ad valorem* exceptions, are levied upon the Swiss quintal, and vary from 3 cents to $3 the quintal. The articles which I am satisfied may find an advantageous market here are, first, hams and dried beef, duty 70 cents per quintal— good family hams. The pork of Switzerland is fattened without corn, and makes a very poor ham, which, however, retails for 22 cents per pound. Westphalia hams, which are in truth inferior to our good Cincinnati hams, cannot be bought here for less than 25 to 30 cents per pound.

Secondly. New Jersey light carriages, duty 10 per cent. *ad valorem.* I believe a market could be made for these vehicles here and elsewhere upon the continent, which would more than compensate for the loss of the southern market at home.

Thirdly. Flour and crackers, duty 10 cents per quintal.

Fourthly. Canned oysters and fruit, duty $3 per quintal.

Fifthly. Light and elegant furniture, duty $3 per quintal.

Sixthly. Articles of gutta-percha and caoutchouc, duty $1 60 per quintal.

Seventhly. Horse-rakes, churns, apple-parers, and the cheaper kind of agricultural machines, duty 40 cents per quintal.

An American hotel could be profitably established in Geneva, and this would help to open the way to a direct trade, and enable us, since our people will wear silk, to exchange pork for silk, and thus refute, in one sense, a homely adage.

WATCH-MAKING.

The first European watches were made at Nuremberg and Venice, but the earliest commerce in this article was at Paris.

Towards the end of the sixteenth century watches were an important branch of Parisian commerce, and at that time there was a corporation of master-workmen established at Paris, who had for their device a shield displaying a clock with second-hands, and underneath a scroll with these words: *Solis mendaces arquit horas*—it convicts the sun himself of error. The greater part of these workmen were Protestants, and religious persecution drove them into the neighboring countries, and many of them found shelter in and around Geneva, which became finally a great centre of the watch trade. The history of watch-making, from the period when rude contrivances of weights and wheels took the place of sun-dials and hour-glasses down to the present day, when such accuracy has been attained in the measure of time that chronometers are relied upon as one of the means of determining longitude, is both curious and instructive. Such a history will not be expected in a commercial report, but now that this industry has been transplanted to our own country, and Waltham may one day rival Geneva, some details of the manner in which the business is conducted here, about which little is generally known, if not really useful, may at least be interesting. Our common idea of manufacturing is associated with numerous workmen employed in extensive buildings, but in this sense there are but two watch manufactories in Geneva, those of Patek & Philippe and Vacherne & Constantin; yet there are all over the city signs bearing the inscription "watch-making," and may justly claim to be manufacturers of watches, whose skill enables them to put together the various parts of the machine. In the construction of watches there is almost as much diversity of labor and skill as in the building of a ship: the vessel is seldom fitted for sea in the ship-yard; the sails, rigging, chains, anchors, and machinery are all the work of separate artificers. Thus it is here with the watch. Some make the rough parts of the movements, others the more delicate; some the jewels, face, case, hands, &c., and others again put together and regulate the works, and if there be enamelling or chasing and engraving in the finish of the watch, these require still other workmen. The distribution of labor is so great that it is difficult to say who is the manufacturer, unless it be he whose skill enables him to adjust the value of the article and bring it into market. Great improvements have been made of late years in the tools used in making the various parts of watches, and these have materially lessened the cost of production. Take a single example: the jewels which are put into the works to prevent injury by rust and friction, that cost, some years ago, three or four dollars each, are now made for ten cents apiece.

Although Geneva is the great centre of the watch trade, the larger portion of the watches sold here are made in the adjoining cantons of Vaud and Neufchatel. In these cantons the mountains and valleys of the Jura are covered with towns, villages, and hamlets, whose inhabitants, peasants, and merchants are nearly all engaged in this lucrative business. The peasants are not exclusively thus employed, for, like the dwellers upon our own coast of Maine, who are farmers in summer and fishermen in winter, so these hardy and industrious sires gather their scanty crops in the short season of warmth, but so soon as the first flakes of snow fall in September, these agriculturists shut themselves in doors and return to the lathe and file, gaining a livelihood by making these pieces of machinery which are least difficult of execution. When the snow covers these sombre regions as far as the eye can reach, and rests upon them for six or seven months in the year—when a silence like that of the arctic, unbroken by the foot of man or the wheel of carriage, is around their dwellings, and they can scarcely force a path through the snow to procure things of absolute necessity, what is there left for these prisoners to break the monotony of life? Nothing but labor, and, little by little, labor became a fixed and indispensable habit.

In this labor the peasants are aided by their wives and children, and among these rude mountains and gloomy valleys have occasionally sprung men whose genius has diversified and lightened the toils of their art. The principal markets for these workmen are St. Croix, Loches, Chaux-de-fonds, and Neufchatel, but these again are chiefly tributary to Geneva for the gold cases, enamelling and carving, and other ornaments which set off the watches. The variety of work which is executed is truly wonderful, and it finds its way into every part of the world, even to China and Japan, for they have learned to imitate the Indian style of grotesque ornaments, and to make watches, which, if not accurate as time-keepers, suit the taste of the celestials. Switzerland has no law of patents or trade-marks, and thus, when any person or firm has made an improvement or achieved a reputation, it is afterwards poached upon by unscrupulous rivals. Geneva, however, endeavors to preserve her general reputation by requiring that all gold employed in the construction of watches and jewelry shall be of eighteen carats. The city has also schools of design and watch-making, the former free, and the latter opened at first for both sexes, but unfortunately confined now to boys alone.

There are annually about 20,000 watches made wholly in Geneva, and 50,000 whose works are made elsewhere, but put together and supplied with rubies and cases here. The male laborers earn from $20 to $80 per month, the female from 40 cents to $1 per day. The principal points of export are the United States, Italy, Spain, Portugal, Brazil, Greece, and the Indies; very little is sent to France and England.

A NEW HORSE RAILROAD.

An English company have recently constructed a railway from Geneva to Chene, a distance of between two and three miles, which deserves notice for its adaptability to most of our southern cities. It consists of a single track, level with the bed of the road, and in the centre a grooved rail, in which runs the *guiding wheel* of the carriage, a small iron wheel, which is attached to the forward axletree and controlled by a lever which is under the driver's foot, so that it can be instantly raised when he desires to leave the track. The wheels of the carriage have a broad tire, and are of much less circumference than the ordinary carriage wheel. This grooved rail would be useless in winter, when clogged by ice, but, with this exception, the road is a decided improvement, being much cheaper, of less obstruction, adapted to narrow streets and to carriages, which can move on or off it at pleasure.

Statement of exports from this consular district for the year commencing October 1, 1863, and ending September 30, 1864.

First quarter—from October 1 to December 31, 1863:

	Francs.	Dollars.
Watches	493,076	
Straw goods	31,420	
Cigars	17,704	
Music boxes	15,685	
Leather	14,127	
Cheese, &c., &c.	1,093	
	573,105	114,621

Second quarter—from January 1 to March 31, 1864.

	Francs.
Watches	496,591
Leather	21,010

	Francs.	Dollars.
Straw goods...............................	17, 875	
Music boxes...............................	12, 645	
Cigars, &c., &c............................	10, 341	
	558, 462	111, 692¾

Third quarter—from April 1 to June 30, 1864:

	Francs.	
Watches...............................	560, 812	
Music boxes...............................	25, 754	
Cigars...............................	19, 964	
Silks...............................	8, 839	
Cheese, &c., &c...........................	1, 201	
	616, 570	123, 314

Fourth quarter—from July 1 to September 30, 1864:

	Francs.	
Watches...............................	222, 780	
Straw goods...............................	44, 659	
Music boxes...............................	11, 139	
Cigars...............................	2, 835	
Leather...............................	1, 215	
	282, 628	56, 525¾
Total in francs and dollars.................	2, 030, 765	406, 153

Under the head of watches I have included their appurtenances, such as parts of watches, and small tools used in the manufacture and putting together of these parts.

ITALY.

GENOA—D. H. WHEELER, Consul.

NOVEMBER 18, 1864.

The port of Genoa consists of a simple indentation of the coast of the Ligurian gulf, forming a semicircular basin, open towards the south. This basin is calculated to contain about three hundred and twenty-five acres. The open side seaward is protected by two works, called, respectively, the old and new mole. The old mole extends from the eastern side of the port into the channel. It was begun very early in the history of the republic of Genoa, and in the year 1133 all ships entering or leaving paid a tax for its extension. In the ten years from 1822 to 1832 it was extended one hundred and twenty metres; a violent storm on the 28th of December, 1821, having shown the necessity of further protection to shipping in the harbor.

The present plans for the improvement of the port embrace a further extension of one hundred metres. This mole lies in a right line. The old portion of it was constructed from one to another of some sunken rocks, which stretch out from the head-land; and the latte radditions have been bent inward so as to run nearly parallel with the new mole.

The new mole was commenced in 1658, and lies on the west side of the channel. The first intention was to make it a breakwater, and a passage was left between it and the western shore; but the sea broke through the passage with such violence that it was found necessary to connect the work with the mainland. This work runs in a right line, cutting at right angles the original line of extension of the old mole, but forming, with its present extension, a channel of about 550 metres in breadth. In storms, the sea at times drives in through this channel with a good deal of violence, rendering at least one-third of the harbor an unsafe anchorage for vessels.

Both moles have an average width of fifteen metres at the top, which is about seven metres above the sea level. The depth of water inside the moles averages between four and fifteen metres. In the eastern or old part it is shallow, and the average is not more than four metres. In the western part the average is perhaps ten metres.

When, after the peace of 1815, the commerce of Genoa began to revive, it became evident that two things were necessary to render the harbor adequate to the increase of the Sardinian commerce, viz : to protect the entire space embraced inside the moles, so as to render it all safe for mooring vessels; and, secondly, to increase the depth of the harbor so as to receive vessels of a larger size than had theretofore frequented these waters. The developments of commerce and the introduction of steam vessels have rendered these reforms more urgent every year; yet, after half a century and a dozen reports of as many engineers, the work remains but half completed. Indeed, this is probably an overestimate, since the whole work completed consists of 100 metres added to the length of the old mole, and 150 to the new, and an average increase in the depth of the eastern part of the harbor of about one metre; and while it is calculated that the harbor, if fully protected, would give anchorage to three thousand vessels of medium size, it is believed that in its present condition not more than 600 can be moored so as to be entirely safe.

The number of vessels, during the winter season, sometimes amounts to 700, and they are compelled to lie in a dangerously crowded condition. * * *
In 1856 the government made a contract for excavating 946,000 cubic metres of earth, in order to increase the depth in different portions of the harbor from two to eight metres. This work is still progressing. The contractors employ steam dredges, whose minimum capacity is 500 cubic metres per day, and their maximum 1,200 cubic metres; and it is calculated that the depth of the eastern side has already been increased one metre.

The bottom of the port is a tenacious clay, covering a solid rock. There is some complaint that the excavations have laid bare the rock, and in this way impaired the anchorage. It was calculated, when this contract was concluded, that less than one-fourth of the harbor was available for anchorage, while, as I have said, a considerable portion of this one-fourth was, and is, occupied by the war marine, thus still further reducing the space available for commercial purposes.

In addition to the plans for dredging, new works for the protection of the entrance of the harbor have been found necessary. * * *
The extension of the moles since 1822 has narrowed the channel about onefourth, and complaints are made by masters of vessels that the entrance is not as easy as before the new works were undertaken; and vessels are now frequently seen outside waiting for a favorable wind for entering, a sight rarely witnessed before the extension of the moles. It is conceded, however, that mere ease and convenience of entering the harbor must be sacrificed to the safety of the anchorage within it. The new mole therefore is being carried out 300 metres to cover the new part of the old mole; and some hope that this, with

a further extension of the old mole 100 metres, will fully protect the harbor. But should the commerce of this city increase, as its merchants hope, it will be found necessary to construct a breakwater, or some equivalent work, to cover the exposed portion.

The landing and taking in cargo from larger vessels is effected almost exclusively by the use of lighters. The only apology for this course is, that hitherto, owing to the low price of labor, the cost of landing a cargo has been less than in most European ports. Since 1851 a general system of wharfage has been in process of construction. At that time there were only eight hundred (800) linear metres of wharfage, and this was in a part of the harbor accessible to small vessels. Since then, however, wharves have been built with a linear extension of 3,800 metres; but two-thirds of this increase is only available for small craft, while the wharves for large vessels are not at present entirely safe, as they lie exposed to the sea from the entrance of the port. Masters of large vessels prefer to pay lighterage rather than run the risk of greater expense from chafing of vessels and tearing out of "timber-heads" at the wharf; and an American vessel of 550 tons is at this time paying lighterage under these circumstances.

The access to the land from the harbor is obstructed by ancient walls, to the detriment of commercial interests; and all goods must pass through a few gates on the land side of the harbor, which virtually reduces it to a small portion of its total length, that is, to the aggregate width of the gates. This state of things creates embarrassments and perplexities for commercial men of a very serious character. It leads to long delays in the unloading of certain kinds of goods, and it is often necessary to leave them exposed upon the wharves.

The railway has side lines along a portion of the shore, including a line along the new mole; and goods are transferred from the vessels to the cars, or from the cars to the vessels, without the intervention of an expensive cartage.

This port has two light-houses. The principal one is located near the base of the new mole, on the west end of the harbor, and bears a Fresnel light at an elevation of 112 metres above the sea, and is visible for 20 miles seaward. The other is a small light of the fourth class, and its only purpose is to determine the point of the old mole upon which it stands.

The quarter known as the *Porto Franco* was built by the Bank of St. George about the year 1660. It consists of an enclosed quarter attached to the custom-house, which was formerly the Bank of St. George, and contains eleven buildings, each of three stories in height, and capable of containing each 36,000 tons of merchandise. These edifices, under the name of *Porto Franco*, constitute a system of free warehouses. Goods are landed and stored here, and reshipped without bond or payment of duty to foreign or other Italian ports. Merchants have stores here, and a very active wholesale trade is carried on in the street of the little burgh. Duties are paid only on the goods taken within the city without any reference to the original cases, packages, or invoices. Part of these storehouses belong to the chamber of commerce and part to private persons.

The space in the *Porto Franco* is wholly insufficient to the wants of commerce. Since 1851 the difficulty has been increasing with every year. Indeed, it is of much older date, and within a few years of its foundation it was found necessary to provide other warehouses in various parts of the city to be devoted to particular kinds of goods. These warehouses are now numerous and extensive. The suburb of San Pierdorena, on the west side of the city, has now a number of large warehouses for heavy goods not for consumption in the city as tobacco, guano, coals, &c. These are bonded warehouses on a system similar to our own.

There has long been a dry dock in this harbor appropriated exclusively to the use of the war marine. But in 1863 a private company had constructed and opened a dry dock near the old mole. It is capable of containing a vessel of 1,200 tons, or two small vessels at the same time. Since the date of its completion it has never been unoccupied for a single day.

About 4,000 men now find employment in the harbor as bargemen, lightermen, porters, &c. Formerly these laborers were organized as privileged associations with the character of monopolies, but a recent law has abolished these privileges and opened all these branches of labor to free competition. About one thousand men are employed in lightering goods; and their lighters occupy a good deal of space that ought to be appropriated to the use of vessels, as the extension of the wharfage is gradually decreasing this service with its annoyances.

The coast line embraced in the annexed tables is divided into four departments—all, however, subject to general direction at Genoa—viz., Maurizio, Savona, Genoa, and Chiavori. Within this coast line 35 ports are set down in the tables as having received entries for foreign commerce, and 51 as open to the coasting trade.

Statement showing the description, quantity, and value of the exports from the port of Genoa for the year ended September 30, 1864.

Description.		Quantity.	Value.
Wine	gallons..	370,000	$110,544
Olive oil	pounds..	2,850,184	489,930
Other oils	do....	2,500	6,428
Fruits, candied	do....	124,832	49,933
Chemical products	do....	1,116,680	443,280
Manna	do....	202,120	47,430
Soap	do....	30,620	2,134
Fruits, green	do....	572,510	13,425
Almonds	do....	212,420	17,240
Oil-seeds	do....	2,658,056	144,826
Cheese	do....	991,778	131,828
Fish, salt	do....	178,116	34,046
Hides	do....	286,112	33,360
Cordage	do....	341,056	10,430
Linen fabrics	do....	35,870	8,240
Cotton thread	do....	25,240	24,260
Cotton cloth	do....	35,430	44,560
Silk, raw	do....	124,160	637,843
Silk, manufactured	do....	36,080	432,080
Grain	bushels..	443,564	386,820
Rice	pounds..	65,023,298	1,300,564
Paste	do....	4,801,986	840,228
Paper	do....	3,690,392	247,515
Rags	do....	1,623,840	94,953
Bones	do....	3,083,570	35,260
Lead	do....	2,248,600	224,860
Sulphur	do....	627,958	13,556
Earthenware	do.	226,604	18,200
Marble	tons..	10,400	148,360
Wool	pounds..	113,700	28,425
Jewelry and ornaments		....	33,240
Sundries		....	1,840,260
Total		....	7,894,058

The articles enumerated in this list are nearly all the productions or manufactures of the country dependent upon this port for its outlet to the sea. But this exhibit by no means gives the entire exportation, since the transshipment trade, which is much the largest, does not appear at all; and it is very difficult to arrive at correct estimates of the total exportation. However, it has been estimated for the year ended September 30, 1864, at $24,000,000.

I ought to say, too, that I have no great faith in the statements of trade furnished from the custom-house. The estimates of the chamber of commerce are much more reliable, but they will not be available for some months to come. In the custom-house only a part of the goods pass under the supervision of the officers, and, as the estimates as to all those that do not pay duty are of little consequence to the government, there is not much attempt at accuracy.

Statement showing the description, quantity, and value of the imports into the port of Genoa for the year ended September 30, 1864.

Description.		Quantity.	Value.
Wines	gallons..	4,816,028	$1,489,339
Do	bottles..	3,379	548
Distilled waters	gallons..	934,970	337,800
Do ....do	bottles..	2,073	1,498
Oil, olive	pounds..	1,205,022	225,396
Other vegetable oils	do....	8,617,102	438,450
Oil, petroleum	do....	25,000	450,000
Cocoa	do....	1,142,788	182,846
Coffee	do....	10,404,268	208,084
Pepper	do....	519,334	154,520
Sugar	do....	50,956,346	4,760,340
Chemical products	do....	12,628,298	1,950,765
Dyestuffs	do....	5,194,985	55,278
Wax, crude	do....	1,593,810	206,420
Soap	do....	508,892	32,800
Seeds, oil	do....	5,162,144	163,243
Cheese	do....	588,860	88,332
Fish, salt	do....	7,907,224	841,970
Hides	do....	7,642,330	942,330
Furs	do....	70,024	50,494
Leather	do....	232,845	18,624
Leather, manufactured	do....	259,884	82,858
Hemp, crude	do....	988,100	63,200
Linen, spun	do....	268,504	448,650
woven	do....	424,248	88,250
Cotton, raw	do....	5,934,448	1,890,167
spun	do....	2,119,770	1,296,000
woven	do....	1,527,678	834,161
Wool, raw	do....	5,671,140	650,612
spun	do....	36,136	13,840
woven	do....	1,147,626	573,800
Silk, raw	do....	187,510	933,222
manufactured	do....	67,948	368,740
Grain	bushels..	6,681,427	3,886,824
Paste	pounds..	1,148,416	35,232
Furniture		....	18,840
Tapestry	pounds..	60,112	12,003
Paper	do....	59,543	23,400
Books		....	6,850
Varieties and fashionable goods		....	188,360
Machines and tools		....	5,850
Iron ore	tons...	13,597	135,973
Railway iron	do....	5,768	98,460
Wrought-iron	do....	20,736	414,740
Copper ore and brass	do....	189	19,500
Copper and brass, manufactured	pounds..	943,240	28,317
Lead ore	tons...	2,004	39,780
Tobacco, manufactured	pounds..	72,694	11,024
leaf	do....	22,485,000	3,500,000
Coal	tons..	290,868	2,128,786
Other articles		....	1,927,800
Total		....	32,324,306

The leading articles imported from different countries were as follows:

		Pounds.
Coffee from France		2,050,706
	Holland	959,754
	Belgium	570,756
	England	4,215,188
	Central America	858,888
	Spain	748,976
Sugar from France		7,815,174
	Holland	15,271,582
	Belgium	5,710,948
	England	12,188,790
	Central America	9,962,952
Cotton from Sicily		1,812,000
	Turkey	450,000
	Tunis	260,480
	England	925,240
Cotton fabrics from England		1,212,820
	France	920,460
	Holland	260,473

		Bushels.
Grain from Turkey		2,120,360
	Russia	1,950,290
	England	216,816
	Africa	820,310
	Austria	480,815
	France	380,890
	Spain	375,820

		Barrels.
Petroleum from United States		16,500
	France	8,500

		Pounds.
Tobacco from United States		11,200,000
	other countries	11,285,000

		Tons.
Coals from Great Britain		290,868

DUTIES.

Government collected on these importations a total of 14,263,303 francs, or $2,742,943.

Export duties were collected on olive oil, charcoal, and fire-arms to the amount of 15,570 francs.

GENERAL INTELLIGENCE.

The following general information with regard to the method of doing business at this port, has already been furnished to the Treasury Department; but as it is of permanent value, I embody it in this report:

CREDITS.

The usual terms on which merchandise is bought and sold are cash; but there

H. Ex. Doc. 60——39

is some variation by special usage or agreement.   Coals, for instance, are commonly paid for three months after date of invoice.

DISCOUNTS.

Discounts vary according to the state of the market.   The prices of some articles, such as raw sugar, coffee, spice, hides, &c., are regulated almost always by the discount; for instance, raw sugar of good quality commands a fixed price of forty (40) francs for fifty (50) kilogrammes, (equal to 110 pounds,) and the discount on the same varies up to 16 per cent.,according to demand and supply.   Cotton is sold at a discount of four per cent.

There are no bounties allowed on articles of export.   On gold and silver work a drawback is allowed of one-half the duties.

The customary commissions for buying and selling are 2 per cent.; for receiving and shipping from one to six francs per ton, according to bulk or weight of the merchandise.   Brokerage is usually 1 per cent. from the seller, and one-half per cent from the buyer.   On sugar and coffee, it is one-half per cent. from each party.   When brokerage bills are settled, merchants have the right of retaining ten (10) per cent., of which amount 1 per cent. is paid to the broker.   In other words, brokers' bills are paid with a discount of nine (9) per cent.

Shipping charges for landing or loading goods are from 1 to 2 per cent. for lighterage to wharf, and for discharging lighters the same.   This charge is divided invariably between buyer and seller.

The custom-house charges are insignificant.

Cooperage is reckoned according to size of packages : on barrels, 20 centimes ; on hogsheads, 1 franc ; on cases, from ten (10) to forty (40) centimes.

Storage in government warehouses is—

2 20 per ton on general merchandise.

3 00 per ton on sugar.

1 20 per ton on coffee in bags.

1 00 per ton on coffee in hogsheads.

In private warehouses the charge is according to agreement.

The commissions for selling ships are 2 per cent. from the seller.   But this is in most cases reduced by special contract between the master of the vessel and the broker.   The government taxes on transfers of vessels amount to about one and one-half per cent., which is paid by buyer or seller, or both, according to agreement.

SPEZIA—W. T. RICE, *Consul.*

FEBRUARY 29, 1864.

I have the honor to inform you that no changes of material importance have taken place in the port regulations or duties since my last annual report.

The commerce of Spezia has increased considerably within the last year, as have also its internal trade and population.   Spezia itself has been much improved during the last two years.   Private individuals, with a view to the rising importance of this place, have purchased land in and about the city and constructed residences and magazines, notwithstanding which the demand for both by far exceeds the supply.   House-rent has risen one hundred per cent., and every article of living over thirty per cent.

I herewith enclose a report comprising the leading imports of this port during the years 1861, 1862, and 1863, showing the great increase of trade.   The exports for the past year, ended December 31, 1863, have been confined to a few cargoes of marble and timber, shipped principally to France and Spain ; also, a few cargoes of olive-oil and wine; but, owing to the disease of the vine, (from which this part of the country has severely suffered,) also a bad harvest of last year's olive crop, the exports of this port have been inconsiderable. I also enclose a tabular report giving the number of arrivals and departures of all merchant ships, their nationality and aggregate tonnage, during the years 1862 and 1863. The works in connexion with the naval arsenal are being pushed forward with vigor, as are also those upon the fortifications of the gulf. About two thousand workmen are employed upon the former. The Italian company to whom the contract for the construction of the arsenal was granted has been permitted by this government to sublet a portion of the same to an English company, who are now at work, and with English engineers proceeding very well. This port being now the Italian naval depot, most of their ships-of-war are here, consisting of six large steam frigates, one iron-clad, one sailing frigate, three school-ships, and two despatch steamers, all under the command of Vice-Admiral Albini. Owing to the failure of certain contractors to carry out their agreements, the railroad from Pisa to this place has as yet only been open to Sarzana, a town within nine miles of this place; but the Italian government having taken its construction under their own supervision, I can safely announce its completion to Spezia by the first of June next. The continuation of the line to Genoa will be attended with many difficulties and great expense; the tunnelling of one mountain alone will occupy the space of four years. I cannot, therefore, predict its completion within six years at least. In the mean time large and comfortable steamers ply daily between Spezia and Genoa, and *vice versa*, heavily laden both with passengers and merchandise. The extensive lead works at Pertusola, on the eastern side of this gulf, owned and directed by an English company, are reaping a splendid harvest. Within the year ended December, 1863, the receipts of silver lead ore amounted to six thousand tons—5,970 tons from the island of Sardinia and 30 tons from Como. The exports of lead amount to 3,500 tons, principally shipped to Genoa and Naples, but considerable quantities are sent to Ancona, Trieste, and Rome. American commerce at this port has decreased during the past year, for various reasons, which (in a former despatch) I have already mentioned. * * *

Comparative statement showing the description and value of the imports into Spezia during the years 1861, 1862, and 1863, together with the names of the countries whence shipped.

Description of merchandise.	Where from.	1861. Value.	1862. Value.	1863. Value.
Wine, beer, brandy, oil, and vinegar...	England, Spain, France, and the United States of America.	$13,373 72	$20,704 30	$27,605 74
Coffee, tea, sugar, vegetable, medical extracts, and chemical products.	England, Holland, and Switzerland.	17,835 68	10,134 98	12,668 73
Green, dry, and oleaginous fruits	Spain, France, and Switzerland	1,482 00	1,660 98	2,076 23
Stearine candles, salt meats, fatty substances.	United States, Switzerland, and France.	1,631 41	2,167 14	2,708 93
Fish, pickled and salted...............	United States and Leghorn....	3,603 92	4,573 87	5,717 34
Goats	Leghorn....................	40 00	160 00	200 00
Leather of a'l descriptions..........	France	2,333 58	1,924 38	2,405 47
Hemp, flax, cordage, and canvas	England, France, and Switzerland.	942 78	8,951 66	11,189 58
Cotton, raw, spun and woven, braids and velvet ribbon.	England, United States, and Switzerland.	8,797 00	11,867 78	14,834 73
Wool, raw and manufactured, carpets..	England, Belgium, France, and Switzerland.	12,185 46	839 80	1,049 75
Silks, stamped, plain and figured, velvets.	England, Belgium, France, and Switzerland.	484 50	162,502 63	182,815 46
Grain and flour	United States and France	135,924 48	80,348 58	100,435 73
Charcoal and wood of all kinds	United States and England....	1,732 80		443 01
Paper of all descriptions............: ..	France and England	177 65	4,345 49	5,431 87
Fowling-pieces, bonnets, haberdashery, artificial flowers, and machines.	Switzerland, France, Spain, and England.	9,185 74	42,545 75	53,182 19
Iron, tin, copper, brass, and lead	Switzerland, France, Belgium, and England.	48,393 38	16,380 25	20,475 31
Marble, alabaster, coal, stone, and building materials.	United States, France, and England.	11,083 65	208,439 50	260,549 38
Pottery, glass, crystal mirrors.........	Switzerland..................	2,478 55	2,860 64	3,575 80
Tobacco and cigars	France and Roman States.....	80 00	120 00	150 00
Total....................		271,766 30	580,882 14	797,515 25

Comparative statement showing the number, nationality, and tonnage of the vessels arrived at, and departed from Spezia, during the years 1862 and 1863.

Nationality.	1862. Arrivals. No.	1862. Arrivals. Tons.	1862. Departures. No.	1862. Departures. Tons.	1863. Arrivals. No.	1863. Arrivals. Tons.	1863. Departures. No.	1863. Departures. Tons.
Italian.............	54	7,320	54	7,320	672	38,117	670	37,901
French	4	1,198	4	1,198	6	934	6	934
English	21	8,133	21	8,133	28	9,953	28	9,953
United States...........	3	1,099	3	1,099	2	1,724	2	1,724
Papal States............	7	245	7	245	6	314	6	314
Norway.................	2	351	2	351	4	589	4	589
Austria	8	1,774	8	1,774	10	2,214	10	2,214
Spain.................	......	....	......	....	1	246	1	246
Denmark	......	....	......	....	1	320	1	320
Grecian.............	......	....	......	....	2	216	2	216
Total	99	20,120	99	20,120	732	54,627	730	54,411

DECEMBER 20, 1864.

   *   *   *   Since my last annual report no change or modifications have taken place in the commercial system of this country affecting the interests of our own commerce.

I herewith enclose a report (No. 1) of imports for the year ended September 30, 1864, the exports being of little value. I also enclose a tabular statement (No. 2) of merchant vessels which have entered and cleared during the same period, as also the aggregate tonnage of vessels of each nation. No American merchant vessels have entered at this port, with the exception of the Pocahontas, (now in port,) with a cargo of coal.   *   *   *   *

I have to inform the department of the opening of the railway through from this place to Pisa, where it connects with the railway to Florence and Leghorn. The completion of this railway will be of great advantage to Spezia. Already the marble dealers of Carrara are endeavoring to charter vessels here, and design to ship their marble from this port, instead of sending it to Leghorn as heretofore, as it can be done at less expense. This change would be of material benefit to masters of vessels discharging cargoes at Spezia, who now take marble instead of returning in ballast, and small vessels can have full cargoes. And I have no doubt but that the opening of this line will be the means of creating an extensive export trade from this port, which heretofore it has not enjoyed.

The company owning the lead foundry at Pertulosa, on the east side of the gulf, have increased the number of their furnaces and have made great improvements, and their receipts of ore and shipments of lead will now be double that of last year.

No. 1.

Tabular statement showing the description and value of the imports into the port of Spezia during the year 1864, with the names of the countries whence shipped.

Description of merchandise.	Countries whence shipped.	Value.
Wine, beer, brandy, rum, oil, and vinegar	England, France, Spain, and United States....	$22,865 20
Coffee, tea, sugar, vegetable medicinal extracts, and chemical products.	England, Holland, and Switzerland...........	17,934 35
Green, dry, and oleaginous fruits..............	Spain, France, and Switzerland..............	3,690 16
Stearine candles, salt meats, and fatty substances.	United States, France, and Switzerland.......	8,540 84
Fish, pickled and salted......................	United States and Leghorn..................	5,680 12
Goats......................................	Leghorn...................................	45 00
Leather of all descriptions...................	France....................................	3,960 64
Hemp, flax, cordage, and canvas.............	England, France, and Switzerland...........	20,812 33
Cotton, raw, spun, and woven, braids and velvet ribbons.	England, United States and Switzerland......	28,516 29
Wool, raw and manufactured, and carpets.....	England, Belgium, France, and Switzerland...	9,618 43
Silk, stamped, plain, and figured, and velvets..	England, Belgium, France, and Switzerland...	140,720 92
Grain and flour.............................	United States and France...................	130,149 89
Charcoal and wood of all kinds...............	United States and England..................	2,884 16
Paper of all descriptions.....	France and England........................	7,316 97
Bonnets, haberdashery, and artificial flowers; also, fowlingpieces and machines.	France, Switzerland, England, and Spain.....	68,811 12
Iron, tin, copper, brass, and lead......	France, Switzerland, England, and Belgium...	26,593 65
Marble, alabaster, coal, stone, building material.	France, England, and United States..........	299,737 78
Pottery, glass, crystal, and mirrors.............	France and Switzerland......................	5,917 18
Tobacco and cigars...........................	France and Papal States......	418 00
Total	....	803,443 03

No. 2.

Tabular statement showing the number and tonnage of vessels arrived at and departed from the port of Spezia for the year 1864.

Nationality.	Arrivals.		Departures.	
	No.	Tons.	No.	Tons.
Italian	1,333	63,869	1,314	69,845
French..	40	3,689	40	3,689
British	16	3,374	16	3,374
United States	1	1,087	1	1,087
Papal ....: ...	1	63	1	63
Norwegian	3	694	3	880
Austrian	6	1,098	8	1,486
Spanish..	8	645	9	736
Danish..............	1	190	1	190
Grecian	......	....	1	87
Prussian	1	390	1	390
Total	1,410	75,099	1,395	81,827

FLORENCE—T. BIGELOW LAWRENCE, *Consul General.*

OCTOBER 31, 1864.

    *   *   *   The exports to the United States for the third quarter of the present year from the city and province of Florence are valued at 346,270$\frac{20}{100}$ Italian lire, equal to 67,868$\frac{95}{100}$ dollars, being much less in amount than usual, owing to the extravagantly high rates of gold and exchange prevailing in the United States, and their constant and uncertain fluctuations.

The extent to which exports have fallen off may be understood when I state that, previous to the war, the exportation from the province of Florence to the United States of straw fabrics alone amounted annually to nearly *fifteen millions* of Italian lire, equivalent to *three millions of dollars*, while this extraordinary valuable and important branch of our commerce was rapidly increasing.

The returns of the consular agency for the island of Sardinia at Cagliore for the third quarter are herewith enclosed, accompanied by two valuable views of the imports and exports of the island of Sardinia during the year 1863, and a " price current" of the articles exported, drawn up with great care and accuracy by my consular agent.   *   *   *

By the last mail I transmitted the first quarterly report and returns of the consulate at Carrara since its re-establishment in May last. The detailed report of the consul, and, considering the state of our commercial affairs, the large amount received for fees from triplicate invoices, prove, I think, the necessity and importance of this consulate.

Carrara is in the centre of the marble quarries of Italy, and all the marble shipped to the United States from the kingdom is quarried and sent from within the jurisdiction of its consul.

Return of exports from the island of Sardinia for the year 1863.

NATURE AND VALUE OF THE MERCHANDISE EXPORTED.

Countries to which exported.	Pig lead with silver.	Lead ore.	Almonds.	Live cattle.	Wheat and other cereals.	Wood for building.	Rings.	Coral.	Cheese.	Olive oil.	Wool, raw.	Cork wood.
United States	$52,004			$1,456	$256					$56		
Algiers		$61,396				$280	$419	$1,209	$4,475			
Belgium												
Austria				12,669								
England, (Great Britain and colonies)			$11,383	362,373					4,711		$539	$14,131
France		229,991			2,306	122,726		465	17,609	2,910	619	Lbs. 4
Holland		94,860							16,740			
Prussia												
Roman States				130		14						
Russia					100,553							
Spain												
Sweden			558	84					6,186	5		
Tunis									1,772		22	74
Various countries				15,093		735						
Italian Continental States	153,748	100,781	4,611	297,135	126,942	6,854	28,104	74,162	942,652	93,226	47,798	34,066
Total of values .... dollars	205,752	512,028	16,552	689,140	230,057	130,631	28,523	75,836	294,145	96,197	48,978	48,275
Total of quantities	Lbs. 3,177,655	Lbs. 21,983,104	Lbs. 99,418	Number, 90,262	Eng'sh qrs. 212,244	Value, 130,631	Lbs. 857,357	Lbs. 78,474	Lbs. 3,016,004	Lbs. 69,000	Lbs. 72,540	Lbs. 1,375,427
Values in 1862	$187,494	$621,385	$24,914	$482,000	$136,149	$8,727	$22,929	$125,537	$180,165	$120,630	$31,058	$54,706
Increase in 1863	18,328			207,140	93,908	121,904						
Decrease in 1863		109,367	8,362				5,594	49,701	113,980	34,433	17,980	6,431

Return of exports from the island of Sardinia for the year 1863—Continued.

Countries to which exported.	NATURE AND VALUE OF THE MERCHANDISE EXPORTED.										Total values per country in dollars.	Total values per country in france.
	Bacon and salt meat.	Bones and horn.	Skins, raw.	Salt.	Bartilla.	Wine.	Tongue, salt and pickled.	Salt fish.	Beans, barley, and pulse.	Articles not enumerated.		
United States	$56			$1,857						$59	$1,909	Fr. 10,308
Algeria										225	8,220	44,443
Belgium											83,396	448,338
Austria											501	2,705
England, (Great Britain and colonies)				501							28,055	151,497
France	2,640	$7,507	$177,667	2,883	$651	$15		$238	$2,113	4,040	1,033,438	5,570,654
Holland				1,222	171	3,287		193	3,115	19,917	94,889	508,565
Prussia								2			17,435	94,154
Roman States				696							94,154	601
Russia										5	601	138,215
Spain				25,688					5,720	1,767	95,688	561,216
Sweden				27,368		53					108,040	147,941
Tunis	907	37	77	5		125		37	30	3,612	10,177	54,753
Various countries	942				7,566	104,874			614	1,986	22,057	118,903
Italian Continental States	8,027	2,096	114,065	76,940			$199,024	21,175	32,237	218,118	1,994,901	10,728,805
Total of values ....dollars	11,872	9,640	291,809	137,160	8,388	106,324	199,024	21,665	43,829	Value, $12	3,457,552	18,600,277
Total of quantities	Lbs. 113,730	Lbs. 997,474	Lbs. 743,597	Lbs. 187,074,060	Lbs. 99,744	Imp. galls. 21,173	Lbs. 1,295,702	Lbs. 25,384	Imp'al grs. 7,967	Value, $12		
Values in 1862	$6,334	$1,975	$151,622	$246,616	$5,777	$105,014	$66,730	$19,691	$34,116	$ 90		
Increase in 1863			140,187			3,310	132,294	1,974	9,713			
Decrease in 1863	5,538	7,665		109,456	2,611					223,568		

Return of imports into the island of Sardinia for the year 1863.

NATURE AND VALUE OF THE MERCHANDISE IMPORTED.

Countries from which imported.	Wood of all kinds.	Coffee.	Cotton yarn.	Leather and tanned skins.	Copper, wrought and unwrought.	Drugs and spices.	Spirits.	Iron and steel.	Wool, raw.	Paper of all kinds.	Fish, salt.
America, Central	$3,894	$127,438		$20,906	$614	$58	$1,023				
Sth., South	19	135,990			30	11,286	30,171	$14,866		$2,086	$1,284
France		1,951	$1,775	51,159	166,614	53					
Holland	35										
Belgium											
England	117	6,174	3,149	4	3,450	1,410	341	21,626		5	4,558
Spain	19	1,439			996		58	1,618			2,976
Austria, &c.	5,707							2,790			
Roman States	7	9,102		1,376	251	279		376		5	
Switzerland, &c.	4			465	37				$106		
Brazil											
Russia	7,864				121	98		7,719			24
Sweden and Norway		2,206				19					
Portugal											
East Indies						23,321	818	72,374	3,943	22,035	3,147
West Indies	3,994	12,053	1,903	40,613	27,146	752	256	1,876	127	105	4,645
Italian Continental States	2,379	5,963	4,400	142	1,942	94		93		5	
Various countries	15			74	28						
Algiers											
Total of values	Value. 79,879	296,294	11,927	114,739	199,217	37,300	34,837	123,245	4,269	24,261	16,634
Total of quantities		Lbs. 1,315,159	Lbs. 30,647	Lbs. 152,438	Lbs. 1,168,209	Lbs. 646,761	Imp. galls. 2,933	Lbs. 1,810,734	Lbs. 3,649	Lbs. 11,909	Lbs. 315,451
Values in 1862	$79,597	$132,003	$26,630	$88,106	$27,574	$45,090	$53,754	$168,329	$5,969	$40,206	$17,778
Increase in 1863	282	164,251			171,643						
Decrease in 1863			15,403	26,633		7,790	18,917	45,084	1,700	15,945	1,144

Report of imports into the island of Sardinia for the year 1863—Continued.

NATURE AND VALUE OF THE MERCHANDISE IMPORTED.

Countries from which imported.	Hardware.	Soap.	Sugar, coarse and fine.	Glass and crystal.	Rope, flax, hemp, and fibre.	Cotton.	Cloths. Woollen.	Cloths. Linen.	Cloths. Silk.	Articles not enumerated.	Total values per country in United States dollars.	Total values per country in francs.
America, Central	$20,643	$11,093	$3,692	$15,267	$461	$129,047	$50,662	$12,740	$15,919	$469	$24,598	Frs 132,250
America, South	517		517							141,949	129,445	685,942
France			326,349					6		141,949	1,208,694	6,498,372
Holland			4,506								6,559	35,259
Belgium			400								441	2,378
England	585	6,204	2,578	435	182	93,511	59,146	4,287	8,134	72,138	289,630	1,557,260
Spain			60	642	8,774	301	112			43	13,714	73,723
Austria	460							184		184	8,937	48,049
Roman States		273					30			62	2,889	15,530
Switzerland	2,241			379		9,072	1,967		660	3,212	19,723	106,043
Tunis	571			264						799	2,635	13,576
Brazil											2,102	11,300
Russia					370	149				27,994	43,301	222,797
Sweden and Norway					53					76	2,431	13,070
Portugal											28	150
West Indies											12,082	64,960
Italian Continental States	46,480	22,964	58,097	11,683	7,693	90,258	40,695	231,903	58,169	845,704	1,611,500	8,663,979
Various countries	1,064	28	4,920	590		760	6,918	336	203	38,071	71,830	386,176
Algiers			3	7		5				3,144	11,161	60,010
Total of values	72,440	40,568	401,122	29,267	17,533	353,103	169,730	249,465	83,085	1,133,405	3,461,610	18,610,818
Total of quantities	*Lbs.* 52,840	*Lbs.* 252,891	*Lbs.* 4,627,893	*Lbs.* 602,880	*Lbs.* 560,012	*Lbs.* 385,149	*Lbs.* 143,732	*Lbs.* 64,597	*Lbs.* 54,893	*Value.* 1,133,405		
Value in 1862	$102,110	$50,170	$482,605	$31,193	17,553	$567,689	$296,830	$392,022	$97,714	1,279,130		
Increase in 1863					17,553							
Decrease in 1863	29,670	9,602	19,463	1,926		244,326	129,100	157,443	14,629	145,725		

LEGHORN—ANDREW J. STEVENS, *Consul.*

JUNE 30, 1864.

With this communication, I have the honor to lay before the department my report of the business and affairs of this consulate for the second quarter of the present year. Nothing of particular interest in the commercial operations of this consular district has come to my knowledge since my last report; nevertheless, the usual activity, in the way of shipments to the United States, has continued without abatement, and, as a proof of this, my receipts for consular certificates exceed those of any previous quarter, notwithstanding this consulate is now deprived of one of its largest sources of receipts, in consequence of the revival of the consulate at Carrara.

The high duty upon imports contemplated by our government, when put in force, will doubtless materially decrease the amount of exports from Italy to the United States; but few of the articles sent from this country will bear these additional rates of duty.

Considerable excitement has existed among the commercial circles of this city during the last few weeks, in consequence of the contemplated high rates of duty upon marble. It is claimed by the dealers in this article that the proposed duty will amount to a prohibition, and that the adoption of it will be an act of great injustice to the commercial interests of Italy. This question will doubtless be brought to the notice of our government through our legation at Turin, and hence I do not deem it to be necessary at present for me to do anything more than to call the attention of the department to it as a matter deserving consideration.

A more just and meritorious act of legislation has not for many a year been placed upon our statute-books than that which fixes a less duty upon imports by American ships. Unpleasant as this discrimination may be to foreigners, it will meet the hearty approval of all well-wishers of our national existence. The effect of this measure is already manifest at this port by the increased inquiry for American bottoms. * * * * * *

As will be observed by the returns herewith forwarded, but one American vessel has left this port during the present quarter, the balance of the large shipments made to the United States having been sent forward under foreign flags.

The following table shows the number and nationality of the vessels that have cleared from this port for the United States since the 1st of January, 1864, and the value of their respective cargoes, so far as the invoices of the same have been certified at or forwarded from this consulate:

No. of vessels.	Nationality.	Amount of cargoes.
4	American	$91,134 64
8	Italian..	152,739 77
4	Norwegian	68,042 00
1	Russian	23,032 33
9	British	93,054 74
3	Prussian..	33,270 11
3	Dutch	10,567 46
	Total	471,841 05

Considerable attention has been given in Italy during the past year to the cultivation of cotton, especially in the island of Sicily. I have instituted inquiry as to the extent of the growth of this article, and the prospects for the future production, and such facts as I may be able to obtain I shall promptly lay before the department. * * * * * *

PALERMO—LUIGE MONTE, Consul.

Statement showing the description and value of the exports of Palermo to ports in the United States in American vessels, also in foreign, together with the total in American and foreign vessels during the quarter ended December 31, 1863.

Destination.	Brimstone, cantaros.	Sumac, bags.	Corkwood and cork, bags and loose.	Rags, bales.	Almonds, bags or boxes.	Walnuts, bags.	Filberts, bags.	Wine, pipes.	Olive oil, barrels.	Hemp-seed, bags.	Macaroni, boxes.	Licorice, boxes.	Manna, boxes.	Figs, boxes.	Canary-seed, bags.	Oranges and lemons, boxes.	Value.
In American vessels:																	
New York	10,770	8,550	28		1,361	990	962	40		100		17	12			22,980	$111,908 00
Philadelphia	650				900	50	50								150	5,900	8,725 00
Total in American vessels	11,420	8,550	28		1,561	970	1,002	40		100		17	12		150	29,180	120,633 00
In foreign vessels:																	
New York	5,750	3,400	92	978	1,097	700	800	18		125						14,498	61,300
Boston	630	4,000	39		407	400	340	80	10		133			300	100	9,810	31,168
Philadelphia			4		150	150	100	2	5		35				130	10,045	15,980
Baltimore	900		4		290	200	200						2		25	5,000	13,145
New Orleans					162	25	24	5	20		136					11,288	15,147
Total in foreign vessels	7,250	7,400	69	978	2,116	1,475	1,464	45	35	125	304		2	300	275	43,641	135,020
Total in American and foreign vessels	19,170	15,950	97	978	3,677	2,445	2,466	83	35	225	304	17	14	300	425	72,821	255,653

Statement showing the description and value of the exports of Palermo to ports in the United States, in American vessels, also in foreign, together with the total in American and foreign vessels during the quarter ended March 31, 1864.

Destination.	Brimstone, cantaros.	Sumac, bags.	Corkwood, cantaros.	Corks, bags.	Rags, bales.	Almonds, bags.	Shelled almonds, boxes.	Walnuts, bags.	Filberts, bags.	Wine, pipes.	Lemon juice, casks.	Canary-seed, bags.	Hemp-seed, bags.	Macaroni, cases.	Olive oil, casks.	Manna, cases.	Essence of lemon, jars.	Licorice, boxes.	Oranges, boxes.	Lemons, boxes.	Value.
In American vessels:																					
New York	6,940	6,391	14		375	553	744	136	739	20	20	221	360	100					24,031	12,044	$117,073 85
Boston	2,000	2,550	30		100					50									6,200	3,000	32,588 30
Philadelphia	2,740	1,600	21	100			400	134	260			48	33	100					12,401	2,300	42,054 61
Total in American vessels	11,680	10,541	65	100	475	553	1,144	270	999	70	20	269	393	200					42,632	17,344	191,718 76
In foreign vessels:																					
New York	17,132	6,539	21	52	25	60	332	85	599	27		52	79	1,495	17	169	5	90	52,631	49,845	225,615 58
Boston	4,600	600							50										2,440	700	17,985 25
Philadelphia	520											25	10						4,109	2,161	9,489 63
Baltimore	1,284		2				25	45	25	5				175	10	23		10	5,734	1,700	16,081 44
New Orleans												5	5	69			5		1,269	1,430	4,791 33
Total in foreign vessels	23,536	7,139	23	52	25	60	357	130	674	32		82	94	1,739	27	192	5	100	66,183	55,836	273,963 23
Total in American and foreign vessels	35,216	17,680	88	152	500	613	1,501	400	1,673	102	20	351	487	1,939	27	192	5	100	108,815	73,180	465,681 99

Statement showing the description, quantity, and value of the exports from Palermo to the United States in foreign vessels, with their nationality and destination, for the quarter ended March 31, 1864.

Nationality	Sumac, bags	Corkwood, cantaros	Corks, bags	Rags, bales	Almonds, bags	Shelled almonds, boxes	Walnuts, bags	Filberts, bags	Wine, pipes	Brimstone, cantaros	Lemon juice, casks	Canary-seed, bags	Hemp-seed, bags	Macaroni, boxes	Olive oil, casks	Manna, boxes	Essence of lemons, jars	Licorice, boxes	Orange, boxes	Lemon, boxes	Value	Destination
Italian	6,039	21	23	25	60	332	85	599	27	15,960		58	79	1,495	17	171	5	90	41,109	42,363	$189,374 22	New York.
Italian		2				25	45	25		1,984		25	10	175				10	5,734	1,700	16,081 44	Baltimore.
Italian										1,820									6,790	3,061	15,986 37	Philadelphia.
Italian								50	5		90	5	5	69	10	23			1,289	1,430	4,791 33	New Orleans.
Dutch	600									600									2,440	700	9,169 03	Boston.
English	500									1,272									8,956	5,237	25,658 01	New York.
English																			1,876	1,343	8,416 20	Philadelphia.
Dutch										4,000											4,985 55	New York.
Total	7,139	23	23	25	60	357	130	674	32	23,936	90	88	94	1,739	27	194	5	100	68,183	55,836	273,862 17	

Statement showing the description and value of the exports of Palermo to ports in the United States in American vessels, also in foreign, together with the total in American and foreign vessels, during the quarter ended June 30, 1864.

Destination.	Brimstone, cantaros.	Sumac, bags.	Corkwood, cantaros.	Corks, bags.	Rags, bales.	Almonds, bags.	Shelled almonds, boxes.	Walnuts, bags.	Filberts, bags.	Argola, casks.	Lemon juice, casks.	Lemon oil, jars.	Canary-seed, bags.	Hemp-seed, bags.	Macaroni, boxes.	Olive oil, casks.	Wine, pipes.	Orange, boxes.	Lemons, boxes.	Value.
In American vessels:																				
New York	4,740	3,870	11	150	465	194			256	20			308	201	20	30	110	6,007	11,545	99,480 90
Boston	600	780		28					193	10		27		249	100		63	695	6,159	30,823 03
Total in American vessels	5,340	4,650	11	178	465	194			449	30		27	338	450	120	30	173	6,702	17,704	130,303 93
In foreign vessels:																				
New York	6,936	1,480	16		100	19	35	32	214		2	56	53	150		25	96	20,950	29,666	119,211 50
Boston	1,228	1,860	6	40									50					3,074	2,362	19,880 90
Philadelphia	1,300	1,400					200											3,672	6,888	29,525 10
Baltimore	300																	1,453	2,739	6,539 15
Total in foreign vessels	9,764	4,740	22	40	100	19	235	32	214		2	56	103	150		25	96	29,149	41,815	174,859 65
Total in American and foreign vessels	15,104	9,390	33	218	565	213	235	32	663	30	2	83	441	600	120	55	269	35,851	59,519	305,163 58

Statement showing the description, quantity, and value of the exports from Palermo into the United States, together with the port of destination, for the quarter ended September 30, 1864.

Sumac.	Cork-wood.	Corks.	Rags.	Canary seed.	Lemons.	Destination.	Value.
Bags. 5,000	*Cantars.* 13	*Bags.* 180	*Bags.* 186	*Bags.* 74	*Bags.* 527	New York..........	$32,882 10

SEPTEMBER 30, 1864.

The export trade of this consular district to the United States has been better than what might have been expected, considering the unsettled state of the American market, and the enormous loss on exchange to which merchants here are subject in their remittance through London, especially as there is but very little to import directly from America.

The following will show the number of vessels cleared from this port to the United States, and the value of merchandise, as deducted from the invoices certified at this consulate, compared with last year's report. There will be noticed a decrease of American vessels, and an increase in foreign; also a small advance in the value exported, viz :

September 30, 1863.—Number of American vessels, 46 ; number of foreign vessels, 46 ; total, 92 ; value exported, $994,375.

September 30, 1864.—Number of American vessels, 30 ; number of foreign vessels, 70 ; total, 100 ; value exported, $1,059,378 67.

The prospect for this year, however, is very unpromising; so large an amount of capital has been left in America for the last three years, awaiting a more favorable rate of exchange, which has been so often disappointed, that merchants here are no longer able or willing to invest any more, and the American traders are very slack in giving commissions. So far there have arrived none, and very few orders, from America for the coming season of export of Sicilian products, either in Palermo or Messina, and the American trade is actually at a standstill.

    *   *   *   *   *   *

To give a general idea of the trade done at this port, I have compiled the following :

Statement of vessels of all flags, and their tonnage, arrived and cleared at the port of Palermo from October 1, 1863, to September 30, 1864.

Nationality.	Class.		Class.		Class.		Class.		Class.		Class.		Total vessels.	General tonnage.
	Steamers.	Tonnage.	Ships.	Tonnage.	Barks.	Tonnage.	Brigs.	Tonnage.	Schooners.	Tonnage.	Lateen sails.	Tonnage.		
American, U. S	....	....	2	1,672	25	10,008	4	1,107	....	....	....	....	31	12,785
Austrian........	....	....	....	....	9	2,415	18	4,458	6	510	....	....	33	7,383
Belgian........	6	3,426	....	....	....	....	....	....	....	....	....	....	6	3,426
Danish.........	....	....	....	....	....	....	....	....	20	1,680	....	....	20	1,680
Dutch..........	27	9,651	....	....	....	....	....	....	21	2,886	....	....	48	12,537
English........	99	52,818	....	....	3	1,140	39	7,374	102	12,885	....	....	243	74,217
French.........	54	45,834	....	....	3	645	6	933	12	1,563	....	....	75	48,975
Greek..........	....	....	....	....	....	....	60	12,099	....	....	....	....	60	12,099
Hanoverian.....	....	....	....	....	....	....	....	....	12	1,116	....	....	12	1,116
Italian	471	134,634	6	2,367	33	9,435	180	26,007	90	11,937	780	29,337	1,560	213,717
Norwegian......	....	....	....	....	2	880	6	909	....	....	....	....	8	1,789
Ottoman........	....	....	....	....	....	....	6	1,047	9	615	....	....	15	1,662
Spanish	....	....	....	....	....	....	6	645	....	....	....	....	6	645
	657	246,633	8	4,039	75	24,522	325	54,579	272	33,192	780	29,337	2,117	392,033

Owing to several causes, but principally to the unsettled state of politics and the constant threat of a European war, and especially to the war in the United States, the general trade of the island has fallen nearly one-third, as compared with previous years. The total navigation of the island was 5,600 vessels, of the aggregate tonnage of 1,300,000 tons, viz:

	Tons.
American flag	43,000
English "	230,000
French "	150,000
Italian "	760,000
Other flags	117,000
Total	1,300,000

The following is the summary of the general trade during the year, viz:

Countries.	Import.	Export.	Total.
United States of America*	$125,090	$1,955,040	$2,080,130
Baltic, Belgium, and Germany	862,215	2,257,250	3,119,465
England and colonies	3,747,300	4,290,315	8,037,615
France	2,497,095	2,638,990	5,136,085
Italy	558,780	2,007,530	2,566,310
Other countries	876,940	721,900	1,598,840
Total	8,669,420	13,869,025	22,538,445

* This is partly American goods imported through England and France. The actual *direct* importation from the United States does not exceed $50,000.

The railroad line which is to connect this town with Messina and Catania, through the interior, and which was opened last year as far as Bagheria, has now advanced as far as Trabia, twenty-four miles from Palermo. It is a very slow progress, but, considering the rocky soil, and the mountainous topography of the country, it is as much as can be expected. Even in this short transit *along the sea-shore* it passes through five tunnels, two of them of considerable length, and now they are working in a very long one which is to carry it to the termini. The work, however, is carried on in a very solid and thorough manner, and at several places, employing about 3,000 laborers—some 1,500 at Palermo, and 1,500 more at Messina and Catania.

Another line is proposed along the southern coast to Trapani and Marsala, and large sums have already been voted by the several townships all along in furtherance of the project. It is hoped soon to see it initiated.

The harvest this year has been very fair, both of cereals and fruits; the vine disease is fast disappearing under the treatment of pulverized brimstone.

The sudden demand for cotton, caused by the entire withdrawal of the American staple from the European market for the last three years, and the enormous advance in the price of the raw material, caused an immense start in its cultivation all over the island, which, from its soil and climate, is excellently adapted for it. Add to this that the failure of the vine crop for several years back, on account of the vine disease, had left abundant fields uncultivated and unproductive.

It has been proved that in 1863 cotton paid 40 per 100 more than wheat. Before the American war cotton used to sell at about $15 a cantar. It was of very poor quality, and only used for local consumption. None at all was ever

H. Ex. Doc. 60——40

exported, and it had no marketable value. Last year's crop was sold to speculators, on an average of about $60 a cantar, and producers are now asking from $65 to $80 for this year's crop.

From information that I have been able to obtain, as there are no official statistics published, last year's exportation amounted to about 300,000 cantars, but this year (1864) it will exceed 1,000,000 cantars, with the prospect, if the demand still continues abroad, of being tripled next year.

The entire crop is exported mostly to England and France, a small quantity to Italy. None at all remains in the island, as there are no cotton factories, except one at Marsala, which had to stop work after the American crisis, and has not yet resumed it again. The shipment of cotton is done at Messina, Catania, Terranova, and Syracuse, mostly, however, at Catania. Hardly any comes to Palermo for exportation, as it is mostly cultivated on the southern side of the island of Sicily.

All the agricultural societies have taken a great interest in its cultivation, and a great deal has been published in a scientific point of view to advance and perfect its production.

The Italian government also has given particular attention to this branch of industry, and appointed a special royal commission, under the superintendence of the minister of agriculture, industry, and commerce, to promote and facilitate its cultivation in Italy, and to hold a yearly exposition of its growth and progress.

This royal commission opened an exhibition in the Royal Industrial Museum of Turin on the 1st of January, 1864, for the exposition of cottons grown in 1863. This commission has not published any general report from which I could gather any commercial information, but only—

1. A catalogue of the specimens exhibited.

2. Reports of the cultivators on the growth, expense of cultivation, and quality.

3. Reports of the several committees on awards.

*   *   *   *   *   *   *   *   *

I will quote the following general items as worthy of interest to the American traders and manufacturers :

"There were at this exhibition 302 exhibitors, representing 42 provinces and 159 communes of Italy, but mostly from Sicily, Sardinia, and the southern provinces. There were exhibited 971 specimens, viz :

Cotton with seed	296
" without seed	274
" seed	133
" pods	151
" plants	107
" oil	5
" husks	5
Total	971

"The cotton exhibited comprised eight several species, viz :

	Specimens.
1. White Siamese, (*G. siamensa V. Lana albo-nivea.*—TEN.)	487
2. Yellow Siamese, (*G. siamensa V. Lana Prufa.*—TEN.)	58
3. Grass cotton, (*G. herbaceum.*—LINN.)	112
4. Curly cotton, (*G. hirsutum.*—PROXT.)	7
5. New Orleans, La., and North Carolina, (*G. barbadense.*—LINN.)	88

	Specimens.
6. Sea island, (*G. barbadense.*—LINN.)	162
7. Macao, (*G. barbadense.*—LINN.)	31
8. Doubtful	26
Total	961

"There were also exhibited 783 specimens of experimental cultivation and botanical studies upon cotton. Also, 76 varieties of machines and agricultural implements, and 106 samples of woven cottons."

I will now quote some passages from the reports of the several committees on awards, which I consider of great importance to our cotton trade, prefacing them with the following extract from the opening address of the president of the royal commission, *Commendatore Devincenzi*, in which, after describing the favorable condition of soil and climate in the greater part of Italy for this rich cultivation, he added:

"The cotton crisis caused by the war in America brought forward this happy condition of our soil and climate, and induced the government to collect more than 150 specimens of cotton from various parts of Italy and send them to the London exhibition. These were considered of bad quality, not on account of the nature of its original fibre, *which was excellent, and such as to compete with the best American cottons, but on account of the bad method of ginning,** done with the so-called hot-press, (*mangello,*) a primitive and very imperfect implement, which breaks the fibre of the cotton, and leaves broken and crushed fragments of seed. The famous cotton association of Manchester, in judging of its quality, calculated in some of them a loss of value, caused by the bad ginning, of more than 45 per 100.

"This fact induced me to study the ginning machines in London and in Manchester, and I came to the conclusion that the most perfect ones could be reduced to two classes, viz: The American machines, which separate the cotton from the seed by a system of saws, (saw gin,) and the others, also of American invention, which perform this operation by a system of knives, (Macarthy gin.) These, instead of breaking the fibre, as is the case with the hot-press, preserve it intact. I therefore recommend them in preference to any other.

"In 1862 the cotton crop in Italy was only 25,000 bales, of 100 kilogrammes each, valued at about $3,000,000. The crop of 1863 has been quadrupled, being calculated at about 100,000 bales, and valued at $12,000,000.

"Until 1862 there was only used in Italy the rough hot-press; now there are over 500 of the best foreign machines, and the quality of the ginned cotton is considerably bettered. The lands which are expected to be cultivated for the first time with cotton in 1864 will be of very vast extension, and there are proprietors who will cultivate from 300 to 400 and even 500 acres of land. Hence, we may reasonably hope for the present year a very abundant crop.

"The exhibition of cottons has been purely national, but the section of machines and implements has, of its own nature, no limit of nationality; hence, when it was first organized, it was resolved to admit machines from any derivation. There was no great manufacturer, either English, French, or from the United States of America, that did not send machines, especially gin machines, to our exhibition.   *   *   *   *   *

"We cannot cultivate cottons except principally for exportation; therefore, it is of the greatest importance that we should equal them to foreign productions. The basis of working well and economically our lands will be the true basis of our future cultivation. *The American commerce once reopened, we will inevit-*

---

* The italics are my own.

ably lose our cotton trade if we do not take advantage of the benefits of agricultural machines and improvements.   *   *   *   *

"I avail myself with pleasure of this opportunity to make special mention that, not only many private foreigners, but also the famous cotton association of Manchester, has taken a large share in this, our first, exhibition; sending a very large collection of commercial cotton, in order that we may understand which is to be cultivated in preference; *as also, a very important collection of agricultural implements, which are used in the United States of America.*"   *   *   *

. *Compendious extracts from the report of the committee on ginning.*

"Your committee present the results of their operations in cotton ginning, by Dobson & Barlow and Pratt Brothers' machines, from samples derived from all parts of Italy. *They have come to the satisfactory conviction that Italy, especially, in her middle, southern, and island provinces, is called to occupy, both for quantity and quality, a distinct place among countries producers of cottons.*

"This branch of agriculture will be undoubtedly a fountain of immense resources to our country, and all the cares that shall be dedicated to it will be watched with great interest and satisfaction, both by our own and by the foreign traders, who, uncertain and timorous of the sad effects which may produce hereafter the civil war which is fought in America, can, even from now, hope from this cultivation of ours a large supply of raw material to their innumerable and extensive factories.   *   *   *   *   *

"The samples received from some parts of northern Italy are of good quality, but this might have been the effect of an exceptional mildness in the weather this year; therefore, to be able to decide fully, it would require three or four years of experiments.

"Judging from the strength and brilliancy of the cotton sent from the middle provinces of Italy, this cultivation can be favorably carried on there.   *   *

"The samples sent from the Neapolitan provinces, from Sicily, and Sardinia, show indisputably the gratifying fact, that the conditions, both of climate and soil, are exceedingly favorable to this cultivation, and there is no doubt that it will hold in them henceforth a foremost place above all others. And although the fabulous prices to which this staple has arrived, in consequence of the war in America, has been and is a strong incentive in order to meet and overcome the difficulties of a new cultivation, there is no fear that once introduced it can be continued with advantage, even when, this war ceasing, prices shall have fallen again to their normal state.

"Your committee is fully satisfied with its quality, especially with the samples of Sea island cotton, sent from various parts of Italy, and from the island of Sardinia.

"The Siamese and grass cottons, which comprised the greater part of the samples exhibited, and will constitute the total crop raised in the Neapolitan and Sicilian provinces, are both very good."

Compendious extracts from the report of the committee on cultivation.

"Your committee has come to the satisfactory conclusion that, both for method of cultivation, for fitness of soil and climate, for quality and quantity of production, and certain hopes of future improvements, Italy is eminently a cotton-growing country.   *

"Italy, still infant in the cultivation of this precious vegetable, has produced good and fine cotton with little expense. *Once adult, she can reasonably hope to become the supplier of Europe of the best cottons, at a moderate price.*"

Compendious extracts from the report of the committee on experimental cultivation and botanical studies.

"Beside the botanical studies, no less satisfaction has this committee derived from the successful results arrived at by the directors of botanical gardens, and experienced and learned agriculturists in the introduction of the new and superior species or varieties of cotton, both in the continent and the Italian islands. Until 1862, only two species of cotton were cultivated in our country, viz: the *Gossypium herbaceum*, (grass cotton,) and the *Gossypium hirsutum*, Linn., *Gossypium siamense*, Ten., (Siamese cotton.)

"Of these two qualities the second is a great deal better than the first, because it produces a much more abundant, whiter, finer, and longer fabric. The celebrated cottons of the United States of America, known in commerce with the names of New Orleans, Louisiana, North Carolina, and Upland, are simply varieties of these.

"The royal commission distributed the seeds of the above beautiful specimens of United States cottons, and also of other very beautiful varieties, viz: the *Gossypium barbadence*, Linn., known by the names of the Island, Georgia, Long-staple, and Egyptian.

"These being the best qualities of cottons, and therefore the most valuable in commerce, it was important to essay their cultivation, and to substitute them wherever the condition of the soil and climate were propitious to those cultivated before in Italy.

"*The experiments have demonstrated that in many parts of Italy, and especially in Sicily, the cultivation of these superior species and varieties of cottons has succeeded stupendously.*"   *   *   *   *   *

Compendious extracts from the report of the committee on machines and agricultural implements.

"Most of the gin-machines were sent from abroad, and also the greatest part of rural instruments. These latter were experimented on a farm near Turin, and the work performed by them carefully noted and measured.

"Your committee found justly worthy of praise the well-known ploughs of Lambuy & Bella, manufactured in Italy by Guthier; also several Swiss ploughs, for their lightness; *and among those sent from the United States of America, ————, and the scarificator and horse-line of ————, particularly, because these last are more than any other well adapted for most of the lands of our southern provinces where cotton is cultivated; and more especially because they can be also well adapted and used for many other agricultural uses.*

"Your committee is thoroughly convinced that the success of the cultivation depends, in a great measure, upon the goodness and fitness of the implements used, and in properly tilling the earth."   *   *   *

From the foregoing extracts it will be perceived what interest the Italian government and the agriculturists have taken in this production, and what progress they have made.

This royal commission is now organizing, and has already issued a call for a new exhibition of cottons, to be held in Naples, in the spring of next year, and which, being nearer the cotton growing region, will, without doubt, be more fully attended.

It is to be hoped that the United States may be well represented, especially in machines and agricultural implements. The attention of our manufacturers of these is particularly called to the facts noted in the foregoing reports, that there are no implements of agriculture in southern Italy but what were used at the times of the Romans. The few improvements that have been used are of oreign derivation and manufacture; *the greater part, however, of American invention, but manufactured in England or France.* Sicily, which is a very ertile agricultural island, and large grower of cotton, has not a plough or a hoe of later invention than what was used at the times of Agrigentum and Syracuse; to say nothing of machines; wheat being thrashed by *horses' feet,* and *grapes pressed by human.*

This consular district comprises four consular agencies, where considerable business is transacted, viz: in Trapani, Marsala, Girgenti, and Licata.

The arrivals of American vessels at these ports have considerably decreased, as everywhere else, since the war, being hardly one-third of what used to be. This year arrivals have only been seven at Trapani, none at Marsala, two at Girgenta, and thirteen at Licata.

The following are the general reports furnished to this consulate by the agents for this year:

TRAPANI—ONERATA TUBINO, *Consular Agent.*

*   *   *   *   *   *   *   *   *

Salt is the principal article of export, and is mostly sent to Sweden and Norway, as you will observe from the large number of vessels of that flag that have arrived at this port. Small quantities of other products, such as wine, cereals beans, nuts, &c., are also exported, but mostly to other Italian ports of shipment.

The coral fishery was once carried to a great extent, but it has lately much decreased.

Great attention has been given, since the war in America, to the cultivation, of cotton, and I hope in a few weeks, when the statistics which are being collected by our municipal government be completed, to give you an accurate report of it.

The following is a statement of vessels of all flags with their tonnage arrived at the port of Trapani, for the year ended September 30, 1864.

Nationality.	CLASSES.						GEN'L TOTAL.	
	Steamers.	Ships.	Barks.	Brigs.	Schooners.	Lateen sails.	Vessels.	Tonnage.
Unietd States of America		6	1				7	6 253
Austrian				3			3	455
Danish			1	3			4	470
English		1	4	5	6		16	3,795
Greek				7			7	1,100
Hanoverian			1	2	11	2	16	1,319
Italian	153		21	56	50	365	645	75,725
Norwegian		11	40	46	3		100	29,180
Ottoman				1			1	200
Prussian		1	4	2			7	2,127
Spanish						2	2	64
Swedish		1	4	7	3		15	4,136
Total	153	20	76	132	73	369	823	124,824

MARSALA—HUMPHREY A. HENRY, *Consular Agent.*

There have been no arrivals or departures of American vessels at this port during the past twelve months, ending September 30, 1864. The only arrival from the United States was the Italian schooner "Guilia," from New York, with a cargo of staves, alcohol and Manila ropes; the only cargo shipped to America being the Italian brig "Caroline," with 200 pipes of Marsala wine, valued at $13,632 50, for Boston.

The total exports from this port to foreign countries during the said term are as follows, viz: 14,032 pipes wine (produced here,) of the value of $1,121,760. Also, small quantities of olive and linseed oil, fruits, cheese, linseed, &c.

The aggregate tonnage of the vessels that have sailed from this port during said term was 10,970 tons, being all of the Italian and English flags.

The imports here are of little account, being principally coal, staves, hoop-iron, and small cattle from the coast of Barbary; the total amount of the same being, perhaps, about $5,000. All other necessaries consumed here are supplied from the larger Italian ports.

Formerly there was a large quantity of Marsala wine shipped direct from here to the United States, but since the war began the shipment has fallen off very much.

The cultivation of cotton has considerably increased; last year there were only 300 acres cultivated; this year it has been tripled. The production will probably amount to 6,000 quintals, and would have been more had not the plants been damaged by the worms.

A few gin-machines have been imported, but have not yet been put in operation.

If the price will keep up as at present, I am sure that next year the cultivation will greatly increase, as the land and climate are very favorable to it.

The quality of cotton produced is very good; it is true that it has not the length of the American, but it is still longer and finer than any other cotton produced on the island. This shortness might have been produced, nevertheless, by the bad system of ginning, which is here done by the hot-press (manganello;) with the machines now just imported, there is a hope that this year's crop will be much improved in that respect.

GIRGENTI—LOUIS GRANET, *Consular Agent.*

The following is a general statement of the vessels of all flags entered at this port during the year ending September 30, 1864.

Nationality.	Number.	Tonnage.
United States	2	668
Austrian	8	2,162
Belgian	2	666
Danish	3	417
Dutch	17	2,307
English	38	16,253
French	79	11,157
Greek	5	643
Hanoverian	5	606
Italian	267	30,002
Lubeck	1	116
Norwegian	4	615
Oldenburg	2	378
Ottoman	1	60
Prussian	3	540
Russian	2	963
Spanish	6	523
Swedish	1	175
Total	506	66,271

The importation at this port is limited to small parcels of sugar, coffee, pepper, rice, tobacco, petroleum, spirits, &c., so that the greatest part of vessels arrive in ballast. The exportation, on the contrary, forms the principal business, and the article chiefly shipped is brimstone, each vessel taking either the entire load or a portion of cargo. Besides this, there is exported in limited quantity grain, barley, beans, almonds, linseed, olive oil, sumac, soda, and cotton. The cultivation of this latter is increasing daily.

The total export of brimstone for the year ending as above was 970,909 cantars, valued at $1,699,000.

LICATA—JOSEPH MASTROENI, *Consular Agent.*

I enclose the following statement of the vessels of all flags that have arrived and cleared at this port, their tonnage and the quantity and value of the brimstone exported during the year ending September 30, 1864.

Nationality.	Steamers.	Barks.	Brigs.	Schoon'rs.	Latine sails.	Total vessels.	General tonnage.	Brimstone.	Value.
								Cantars.	
American, U. S.		11		2		13	5,876	30,380	$60,769
Austrian					1	1	120	1,560	2,990
Belgian				1		1	211	2,750	5,270
Bremen		1				1	590	7,680	14,730
Danish			2	2		4	874	11,364	21,781
Dutch			1	11		12	2,112	27,468	52,647
English		5	15	28		48	12,218	158,843	304,449
French		1	10	2		13	2,736	35,572	68,179
Greek				2		2	330	4,300	8,241
Hamburg				1		1	266	3,460	6,631
Hanoverian				4		4	783	10,184	19,590
Italian	mail	52	7	47	46	73	225	29,200	293,806	563,198
Prussian		2	2	1		5	1,508	19,609	37,584
Spanish			3	3	1	7	739	9,612	18,423
Swedish and Norwegian			3			3	710	9,230	17,690
Total	52	27	85	101	75	340	68,273	625,818	1,212,013

Brimstone is the principal article of export at this port, and being of a better quality than elsewhere in Sicily, obtains a higher price. Small quantities of other Sicilian products are also exported, but mostly to Italian ports.

Statement giving the description, quantity, and value of the exports from Messina, together with the nationality and destination of the vessels, for the quarter ended March 31, 1864.

Nationality.	Macaroni.	Essences.	Lemons.	Oranges.	Brimstone.	Almonds.	Rags.	Walnuts.	Filberts.	Canary seed.	Olive oil.	Hemp seed.	Pumice stone.	Tartar.	Manna.	Liquorice paste.	Sumac.	Argol.	Value.	Destination.
	Boxes.	Jars.	Boxes.	Boxes.	Cantars.	Box's.	Bales.	Bags.	Bags.	Bags.	Casks.	Bags.	Cases.	Casks.	Cases.	Cases.	Bags.	Casks.		
Italy	191	50	6,339	18,981	6,344	900			900	105	10	75							$50,790 00	New York.
Italy			3,370	14,871	3,460	75		40											38,980 00	Philadelphia.
Italy			1,550	6,930	1,916	900		60											16,460 00	Baltimore.
Italy			750	9,277															6,525 00	Boston.
England		90	3,550	9,840	1,856	980		167	900	50		46	52	4					29,760 00	New York.
England			1,289	4,040	512														9,700 00	Baltimore.
England			1,000	3,194	640	900	402												10,000 00	Philadelphia.
Bremen		40	1,000	3,525	3,840										20		1,000		32,485 00	New York.
Indirect		115													17	102		3	13,370 00	Indirect.
	191	295	18,811	64,658	17,868	935	402	967	400	155	10	131	52	4	37	102	1,000	3	210,800 00	

OTRANTO—J. S. REDFIELD, *Consul.*

JUNE 30, 1864.

* * * * * * *

In this despatch I would report that no American vessel has been within the jurisdiction of this consulate since it has been established, nor is any American capital employed here.

JUNE 30, 1864.

* * * * * * *

I enclose herewith a report of the shipments of olive oil, alone, from the port of Gallipoli for the last three years. * * * *

Gallipoli is the most important seaport in this district at present. Besides its foreign trade, it is now a stopping place for two lines of steamers from Naples, and in another twelve or eighteen months it will be connected with Naples, and all the other principal cities of the kingdom, by railroad. * * *

Statement showing the quantities of olive oil exported from Gallipoli, together with the number and nationality of the vessels in which shipped, during the years 1861–'2, 1862–'3, and 1863–'4.

Years.	Nationality.	No. of vessels.	Tons of oil.	Total.
1861–'2	English	56	6,905	
	Dutch	11	1,490	
	Italian	53	5,666	
	Other nations	4	509	14,570
1862–'3	English	30	3,360	
	Dutch	3	390	
	Italian	6	980	4,730
1863–'4	English	34	3,719	
	Dutch	11	1,345	
	Italian	7	730	5,794

These cargoes were mostly for the United Kingdom and the Baltic. The two last crops of olives have been very small, which accounts for the diminution in exports the last two years. The crop of the coming season promises to be very abundant. Casks for oil are manufactured at Gallipoli, and exported, to a large extent, to the Ionian Islands and the Levant. The last year the proprietors in this province were induced to cultivate cotton on a much larger scale than heretofore, on account of the high prices ruling, so that about 280,000 pounds of cotton have been exported from this port alone to Naples and Genoa for exportation since September last. This year it is calculated that the crop will exceed ten times that of last year. Wine and grain are shipped from this port also, though not in large quantities.

CARRARA—FRANKLIN TORREY, *Consul.*

SEPTEMBER 30, 1864.

I have the honor to transmit herewith my first report on the commerce within the jurisdiction of this consulate. * * * * * *

I will first give a brief description of the country and customs of the people, that a more correct judgment may be formed of the nature and value of its commerce.

The town, or city as it is called, of Carrara is situated in the nich of a low branch of the Apennine mountains, which nearly surround the town, leaving an aperture of less than one-eighth of a mile wide that gives a view of the Mediterranean sea, which lies about three miles distant. From the sea-coast the land rises gradually to the town, and is very fertile and highly cultivated even to the very summit of the first range of mountains, producing excellent wine and olive oil, the former the best in the kingdom. The population of Carrara proper is about 12,000; but the commerce is extended to several small towns, of which Avenza, near the sea-coast, and Torano, near the mountain, are the principal, and altogether number about 18,000 souls. Massa and Seravezza are the only other commercial towns of importance within this consular district. They are both situated, like Carrara, about the same distance from the sea, and engaged in the same commerce; but of much less extent, and, consequently, are less known as marble-producers.

Nearly the whole male population of this district is engaged in this marble business or in working for the trade; but at least seven-eighths of them either work in the quarries, saw-mills and studios, or are transporting the blocks to the sea-coast and preparing them for shipment. Even the peasant women have their part to do: one can see hundreds of them with enormous loads of sand or water, which they carry on their heads, moving in procession up the mountains to the quarries, to supply the sawyers with the means to cut the large masses of marble into transportable blocks. Other groups may be seen on the rugged peaks of the mountains gathering forage and bedding for the numerous oxen that are used in drawing the marble away from the quarries.

The marble-producing towns have a large stream of water running through each, where mills are established for sawing the blocks into slabs. The water comes from the mountains, and in sufficient quantities to run heavy machinery during the whole year. With these natural advantages, which God in his goodness has bestowed upon this people, there are few who are able to appreciate them, and the greatest ignorance and indolence prevail to an enormous extent.

In the industrial arts, the people are far behind other countries engaged in the same pursuits; and not only is it with the greatest difficulty that they can be induced to adopt the simplest modern tools and machinery, but they put every obstacle in the way to their introduction. The reason of this has been ascribed to their great jealousy of their trade; and, as all such improvements are introduced by foreigners, their hostility to both are equal.

The quarries for which Carrara is so famous lie along the ravines of the mountains, through which roads or pathways are cut for access. The excavations begin quite near to the town and continue up different ravines from one and a half to two miles. Quarrying marble is like mining for minerals. Many quickly make a fortune while others as rapidly lose one. The surface indicates only the quality of marble; the quantity and value are risked by the quarrymen.

There is no quarry so productive that it cannot contain all it produces when squared into blocks. But as the marble from many quarries is loaded on to wagons at one common landing, and is in danger of being damaged there by crowding the blocks together, and the continual falling of the debris from the higher surrounding quarries, it has been the custom to remove all the marble as fast as it is quarried.

A mérchant seldom goes to the quarries, but to the sea-shore or deposit to purchase and where he can choose from thousands of blocks of all descriptions. It is here that the marble is divided, and cargoes made up for all parts of the world; the first quality going to England, France, and Germany, and the second and third qualities to the United States. The transport to the ports of shipment for the United States is made in small craft or lighters, either to Leghorn or Genoa, at a small expense. * * * * *

The Vermont marble quarrymen can always compete successfully with the importers of Carrara marble in cost, but it is in the qualities that they fail. * * Since the passage of the tariff bill, which is so hostile to this trade, a perfect stagnation of business has prevailed; and the quantity of marble of the quality usually shipped to the United States has become so great that no market price can be established; many quarries are closed, and the workmen discharged; and all those quarrymen who continue to keep a few men employed have reduced their wages so much that it is difficult for them to support their families. As the winter approaches more men will be discharged, and great want and misery be the consequence. Under these disadvantages it is difficult for me to fix upon the average prices of marble prepared for shipment.

From my returns it will be seen that during the months of June and July I issued for invoices of marble twenty-six certificates, nine in the month of August, and five in September. The reason is as follows: Before the passage of the present tariff, merchants were looking forward to their usual amount of trade, and took engagements accordingly; but on the arrival of the news of the intended enormous increase of the duty on marble and other Italian produce, no other vessels were chartered. Those vessels already loading and chartered to arrive in Leghorn and Genoa were despatched with little more than the marble previously engaged on board, leaving thereby a great loss to the charterers. These engagements having been fulfilled, no merchant has entered into others of any importance; and until Congress reduces the duty on marble to its former rate, which was all it could bear, the trade cannot be revived, for with this and the high exchange against them the merchants cannot continue to ship their merchandise to the United States without incurring a certain loss. This marble trade must necessarily be carried on *via* Leghorn and Genoa, there being no safe anchorage for large vessels at the place of shipment. It is, nevertheless, quite independent of either port, and, I might say, controls the amount of their trade, for no vessel is chartered either in Genoa or Leghorn for the northern States without securing first a portion of the cargo in marble. * *

If a safe and convenient harbor could be constructed on this coast, Carrara would command a greater amount of trade with the United States than either Leghorn or Genoa. But this will probably never be realized on account of the movable sandy bottom all along the coast for twenty or thirty miles. The Italian government has, however, been convinced of the importance of assisting the trade, and has constructed a railroad expressly for the transport of marble to connect with the line now in construction from Leghorn to Genoa, and open to traffic as far as Spezzia.

The report of the Chamber of Commerce shows that in Carrara alone there are 400 quarries of all descriptions, of which over 100 have been, up to the present time, constantly worked, giving employment to about 3,000 workmen.

The quantity of marble quarried annually, and transported to the place of shipment, is about 60,000 tons. The exact amount drawn from the quarries in 1863, with a depressed market, was 59,790 tons; and the value of marble, wrought and unwrought, exported from Carrara to all parts of the globe was 4,000,000 francs.

Since May 19 (the time at which I entered upon the duties of this office) the value of the exportations to the United States amounted to 207,014$\frac{57}{100}$ francs, consisting entirely of wrought and unwrought marble. This is a small amount in comparison with the value of the same article usually sent in the same period of time since the year 1853. From my personal knowledge of the trade, the value of marble of all kinds shipped annually from this district to the United States since the year 1853 has averaged about 1,200,000 francs; and if Congress would establish the tariff of 1862, the value of the annual exportations would exceed 1,500,000, whilst with the present tariff they will soon cease altogether.

PONTIFICAL STATES.

ROME—W. J. STILLMAN, *Consul.*

SEPTEMBER 30, 1864.

I have the honor to report that during the year past there has been a slight change in the American trade. The Roman government is now preparing to re-open the ancient port of Ostia, and to build a railway thence to Rome, along the south side of the Tiber. Prince Torlenia has also surveyed a line from Fin-mercino, on the north side of the river, to unite with the Civita Vecchia railway. These works will doubtless much facilitate the transportation of imports, and divert the greater part of the trade of Rome from Civita Vecchia; but there is little hope of their largely increasing the foreign trade until the onerous restrictions are removed from commerce, and especially the government monopolies are abolished.

The exports to America have been somewhat diminished by the new tariff of the United States, and by the high rate of exchange. The export of silks is almost destroyed, the duty being effectually prohibition. But as it was a trade hardly established yet, it may be considered rather a prospective than an actual advantage lost.

The articles which have increased in the amount of importation are chiefly petroleum, candles—stearine and parafine—and spirits. The trade in candles has just been thrown open to competition, having been until lately a government monopoly.

Since my last report I have made an effort to inaugurate a trade in ice from the United States. But though the company organized at my suggestion offered to furnish the government monopolist of the supply with good American ice at the same price per pound, delivered in Civita Vecchia, that he now pays for the snow packed in his pits on the Alban hills, he declined the offer. The company then offered him a large sum (I think about $5,000) per annum for the monopoly. This he also refused. The failure of this effort is to be regretted, as much on account of sanitary reasons as the public convenience and comfort. * * *
I have also personally experimented, with success, in sending the Roman wines to the United States, they having made the passage in bottles during the greatest heat of summer. These wines may be obtained, perfectly pure and sweet, at from 30 to 60 cents per gallon, and might be imported into the United States in barrels, if shipped in the winter, and would most desirably displace the cheap so-called clarets and white wines of France, as well as the common grades of Rhine wines.

In the beginning of last winter there was an effort made to establish a silk trade with the United States; but, as I have intimated, it was checked by the new tariff; and as the Roman government lays an export duty of ten per cent. on raw silk, there is no present probability of much business in that direction.

In the present uncertain and unsettled condition of things in Rome, there is, indeed, little hope of any extension of commercial enterprise with reference to it. Nothing but political reform of a thorough character, and assimilation of revenue regulations, involving free interchange with the neighboring state, can reanimate the commerce of Rome. Some good might be done by the establishment of a line of steamers direct from Boston or New York to Leghorn; and in case of a customs union with the kingdom of Italy, this would give an enormous impetus to Roman production and absorption.

TURKISH DOMINIONS.

CONSTANTINOPLE—C. W. GODDARD, *Consul General.*

Statement showing the tonnage and nationality of vessels arrived at and departed from Constantinople during the year 1863.

Nationality.	Arrivals.	Tons.	Departures.	Tons.	Total of vessels.	Total of tons.
Ottoman sailing vessels................	9,263	345,869	8,989	342,987	18,052	688,856
Ottoman steamers	638	84,529	638	74,589	1,276	169,178
Total Ottoman proper..........	9,901	430,458	9,427	427,576	19,398	856,034
Dependencies—						
Moldo-Wallachian.................	228	17,989	226	17,719	454	35,708
Samian..........................	164	12,000	193	12,606	357	24,606
Servian	7	856	6	988	13	1,844
Total Ottoman and dependencies.	10,300	461,303	9,852	458,889	20,152	920,192
American.....	26	13,225	26	13,225	52	26,450
British sailing vessels...............						
British steamers.....................	1,280	446,766	1,293	451,305	2,573	898,073
Austrian sailing vessels...............	1,012	390,959	1,094	363,902	2,036	794,861
Austrian steamers	295	133,093	293	132,495	588	265,588
Belgium.............................	18	7,802	17	7,449	35	15,251
Bremen	4	1,326	4	1,326	8	2,652
Brazilian	1	319	1	319	2	638
Danish	7	946	6	800	13	1,746
French sailing vessels................	172	33,293	172	33,293	344	66,586
French steamers.	307	170,855	298	164,845	605	335,700
Hamburg............................			1	239	1	239
Hanoverian..........................	45	6,332	44	6,174	89	12,506
Greek sailing vessels	3,345	562,948	3,355	565,643	6,700	1,128,591
Dutch	52	8,237	54	8,533	106	16,770
Ionian..............................	539	92,932	548	94,480	1,087	187,412
Italian.............................	2,056	576,660	2,072	587,925	4,128	1,164,585
Jerusalem	10	2,998	10	2,998	20	5,996
Mecklenburg........................	154	52,945	167	56,760	321	109,705
Norwegian	145	39,726	160	42,790	305	82,516
Oldenburg...........................	9	1,328	9	1,320	18	2,648
Prussian............................	90	35,764	91	36,573	181	72,337
Roman..............................	2	694	2	694	4	1,248
Russian sailing vessels	461	48,300	471	48,781	932	97,081
Russian steamers.	194	42,480	207	45,718	401	88,198
Sweden	8	2,352	9	2,600	17	4,952
Total........................	20,584	1,190,365	20,238	3,145,856	40,822	4,266,269

Statement showing the number of vessels arrived at and departed from Constantinople during the year 1864, together with their tonnage and nationality.

Nationality.	ARRIVALS.		DEPARTURES.		TOTAL.	
	Number.	Tons.	Number.	Tons.	Number.	Tons.
United States	9	5,941	8	5,558	17	11,499
Austrian	10,301	472,949	10,297	471,882	20,598	944,831
Belgian	27	9,137	27	9,137	54	18,274
British	1,662	584,504	1,655	582,380	3,317	1,166,884
Danish............	2	843	2	843	4	1,685
Dutch	44	7,731	43	7,241	87	14,972
French............	557	212,675	552	210,655	1,109	423,330
Greek...............	4,628	755,848	4,590	750,443	9,208	1,506,291
Do., Ionian........:	244	40,463	251	41,646	495	82,109
Italian	2,289	643,410	2,306	562,350	4,595	1,205,760
Mecklenburg	258	51,365	259	51,569	517	102,934
Norwegian	189	53,586	189	53,586	378	107,172
Prussian	179	51,495	181	52,067	360	103,562
Portuguese	2	528	.....:......	....	2	528
Russian	727	238,577	744	252,395	14,721	490,972
Turkish............	12,504	635,502	11,312	572,709	23,816	1,208,211
Do., Maldo-Walla-chian	160	13,220	159	13,132	219	26,352
Do., Samian	244	14,878	257	16,042	501	30,920
Do., Servian	4	484	5	821	9	1,305
Swedish............	5	854	5	854	10	1,708
Total..........	34,035	3,793,990	32,842	3,655,310	66,877	7,449,306

Statement showing the imports and exports between the United States of America and the port of Constantinople during the year ended September 30, 1864.

IMPORTS.

1,700 barrels rum—69,959 gallons........................	$27,375 00
Total value of imports.................................	27,375 00

EXPORTS.

1,263 bales wool...	$57,824 00
938 bales rags...	13,835 00
Otto of roses...	12,352 00
Otto of geranium	769 00
Scammony of Aleppo....................................:	1,441 00
Total value of exports.................................	86,221 00

BEIRÛT—J. A. JOHNSON, *Consul.*

DECEMBER 29, 1863.

Referring to my despatch of the 26th of October last, I beg to state that the Ottoman government, by a decree dated July 6, 1863, require the payment of a light-house duty by all vessels entering this port, both on entry and departure, and at every port, of ten paras per ton; but this duty is reduced one-half for vessels of more than 800 tons on the excess over that number.

I have just received notice that the official description of the light-house at Rus, or Cape Beirût, is erroneous, and that it should read "for the height of 38 metres, and for the distance of about 400 metres."

DECEMBER 30, 1863.

I have the honor to submit a few remarks on the state of Syria.

The year 1863 has drawn to a peaceful close. As usual during the year, there have been outbreaks and revolts among discontented and restless tribes of Arabs, and commerce along the coast of Tyre and Acre was for a time interrupted; but in general there has been greater security for life and property than in preceding years, owing doubtless to the severity of the punishment inflicted by the authorities. For every murder there has followed an execution, until confidence has been restored along the coast. The execution of the assassin of the American missionary, Mr. Coffing, and the subsequent degradation and imprisonment of the pasha in whose district the murder was committed, have had an excellent effect throughout the country.

Commerce and agriculture have made but little progress in advance of other years, except in the cultivation and sale of cotton in northern Syria, where the attempts made to stimulate the cultivation of this staple have been quite successful.

The export duty on tobacco has been removed, and several bales of the famed Latakea smoking tobacco have already been sent to the United States.

Two light-houses have been established at Beirût during the present quarter, details concerning which have been given in another despatch. New and wider roads have been constructed in and about Beirût, and new buildings, of a better class, are in process of construction.

But one American vessel has visited Syria during the year 1863. She entered in ballast, and carried to Boston a cargo of Syrian wool.

American sailing-vessels visit annually all the principal ports of Turkey and Egypt, but I am convinced that the American-Ottoman trade admits of a much fuller development. The prospect of an early peace in the United States, and the consequent changes in the operations of capitalists, induce me to suggest that the formation of a company of American merchants for the establishment of a line of screw steamers to touch at the principal ports of Turkey and Egypt would be productive of commercial advantages and profit to the United States and to Turkey. Agents at every port could prepare cargoes of wool, madder roots, olive oil, silk, asphaltum, dried fruits and nuts, wine and oriental drugs, and manufactures generally, in exchange for sugar, coffee, flour, pimento, rope, stoves, house furniture, cotton, cotton and linen thread, alcohol, &c. And in case it should be found that American goods are not sufficiently well adapted to the Turkish, Syrian, and Egyptian markets, it would not be difficult to form combinations with United States trading companies in the Mediterranean such as would avoid the necessity of sending steamers in ballast.

I believe that if such a company should be formed for the above-mentioned purpose, commerce between the two countries would be greatly stimulated, to the advantage of both.   *   *   *   *   *

SEPTEMBER 30, 1864.

In pursuance of instructions I have the honor to lay before the department such information as I have been able to obtain relative to Syrian commerce.

*   *   *   *   *   *   *   *   *

Resident consuls have been obliged this year to restrict their commercia returns to the statistics furnished by their respective records and to such as could be gathered from their colleagues. It is much to be regretted that the Syrian authorities do not publish commercial and agricultural returns, and that they accord no facilities to those who desire to do so. The commercial transactions of France with Syria are worthy of attention. Exclusive of "groups" (of coin) they amount to 14,000,000 of francs for 1863. Syria exports to France silk and cocoons, and imports sugar 1,000,000 francs, ironmongery 700,000 francs, wines 120,000 francs, machines 300,000 francs, silks (or dupions) 600,000 francs.

FRENCH NAVIGATION.

Arrivals—vessels and steamers....	115..................tonnage		59,000
Departures—vessels and steamers..	112..................	"	58,700

ENGLISH NAVIGATION.

Arrivals—vessels and steamers....	97..................tonnage		55,184
Of which in ballast............	34..................	"	11,243
Departures—vessels and steamers..	96..................	"	54,889
Of which in ballast............	41..................	"	12,602

Syrian commerce with the United States was extremely limited. One vessel from Boston, Massachusetts, arrived here in ballast, under the British flag, and took a cargo of wool to the United States, the invoice value of which was about $60,000.

French, Austrian, and Russian steamers continue to touch regularly at Beirût; six of the French, four of the Austrian, and four of the Russian every month; and now an English coast line of freight and passenger steamers has been established, which proposes to touch at Beirût and other Syrian ports every five days, and to connect with another line of English steamers which ply regularly between Egypt and England. But one steamer of this new line has yet begun operations, and its arrivals are irregular, depending upon freights. The three first-mentioned lines carry the mails of their respective governments, for which they are heavily subsidized, and do most of the carrying trade of the Turkish coast.

The silk crop of 1863 amounted to 9,000,000 pounds of cocoons—about half the usual harvest. The grain crop was good; 1,500,000 kilos (of Constantinople measure) and 1,000,000 kilos of wheat were exported to Europe. Among other articles of export should be mentioned 2,000,000 okes of olive oil, 2,250,000 okes of sesame seed, and about 18,000,000 pounds of cotton *from the port of Beirût.* Although much progress has been made in the cultivation of cotton, owing to the stimulus of high prices and the gratuitous distribution of seed by the government, it does not equal in quality, and can never compete with American cotton. Average price, 26 cents per pound. The clip of wool has been estimated at about 504,000 okes, or about 1,386,000 pounds. Average price, in Beirût market, 21 cents for washed wool and 13 cents for unwashed per pound. The importation of powder, lead, salt, and tobacco is prohibited; but tobacco, in compensation for the prohibition, may be exported duty free. Telegraph lines have been completed between Beirût, Constantinople, Damascus, Bagdad, Jerusalem, and Egypt. Thus putting Syria into telegraphic communication with London and Paris by two routes, viz: *via* Egypt and Malta, and by way of Constantinople. Rumors prevail here that English workmen have landed at Suadiab, in the Gulf of Alexandretta, to begin operations on the proposed Euphrates Valley railroad; but Mr. Vice-Consul Levy states that the ground has not yet been broken. Surveyors are re-examining the various routes between Jaffa and Jerusalem for a carriage road, and a survey has been made with a view to bringing water into Beirût from Dog river, (the Lycus of the Romans,) about ten miles from the city.

The sum of $100,000 has been raised in the United States for the establishment, in Beirût, of a Syrian Protestant college, which will probably be opened in the spring of 1865, under the presidency of Rev. Dr. Bliss, formerly of the A. B. C. F. M. The parent society or board of trustees has been incorporated in New York.

Light-houses have been established at all the principal points on the Syrian coast, viz: at Beirût, Tripoli, Latakia, Alexandretta, Caradash, one of the ports of Tarsus, Acre, Carpha, and Mount Carmel. Details of their nature and locations have been given in previous reports. The dues are 10 paras (or the fourth of a piastre the pound sterling at 109 piastres) per ton on vessels of less than 800 tons, and for vessels of greater tonnage one-half that sum, and are payable alike for entry and departure at every port where the vessel stops. This rate is deemed exorbitant and causes great dissatisfaction in commercial circles.

Syria remains tranquil. Near Aleppo some Bedouins are fighting about water privileges on their land, but the quarrel is purely local. Just at this time a panic prevails among dealers in cotton—a fall of more than 30 per cent. having occurred within the past fortnight, owing to expectations of peace in America; and the imperial Ottoman bank, in Beirût, declines to make advances or discounts for the moment.

One American vessel has entered at Beirût during this quarter, and will take in exchange for its cargo of lumber a cargo of wool.

I enclose herewith commercial returns from the United States consular agent at Tripoli, Latakia, Aleppo, and Tarsus. Other returns will be forwarded when they come to hand.

P. S.—No commercial changes have been introduced since the date of last year's report other than those mentioned. Freight, insurance, interest, transportation are the same, but the price of labor and living is constantly increasing.

OCTOBER 1, 1864.

No commercial changes have occurred during the past quarter, except the gradual establishment of light-houses and light dues, which have been reported. Rents, the price of labor and of living, are steadily increasing; but now that a fall of 30 per cent. has occurred in cotton, a general fall in prices may be expected. The Syrian cotton crop is very much larger than that of former years; a better class of machinery has been introduced from England, and a steam factory for making cotton thread has been put into successful operation by a Moslem gentleman, who has represented the Ottoman government for many years as consul at Manchester, England. Another factory, I learn, will be started at Damascus, and will go far towards supplying the local demand for coarse thread. The French steamers "Messageries Imperiales" now touch six times every month at Beirût, and an English line of merchant steamers touch irregularly for freight. The Austrian and Russian lines touch as usual four times every month.

<hr/>

CYPRUS—J. JUDSON BARCLAY, Consul.

JANUARY 11, 1864.

Two very important measures of internal improvement have just been adopted by the British government, in connexion with this island, with which

I beg to acquaint you: 1st. The laying of a telegraphic cable between this place, and Syria, connecting with the Constantinople and Egyptian lines. 2d. The immediate completion of a carriage road similar to the Beirût and Damascus French road from Larnica to Nicosia, the capital of the island, the construction of which has already been proposed to an American engineer in this place. The construction of light-houses on the island has also been lately ordered by the Porte.

APRIL 26, 1864.

I have the honor to acknowlege receipt of circulars Nos. 44, 45, and 46, inclusive, and, in reply, beg to state that I forwarded to the department, in despatch No. 8, December 18, 1863, a circular from the Sublime Porte in regard to the privilege accorded representatives of foreign powers in the Ottoman empire. That no taxes whatever are paid by consuls who do not trade or engage in business. Those who are permitted to trade pay the regular import and export duties over the amount of 15,000 piastres in goods, provisions, &c., to vice-consuls and 20,000 piastres to consuls, respectively, accorded free of duty.

No vessels under the insurgent flag have appeared in this port, the governor general of Cyprus having given the most definite and strict orders for the various ports of the island, that in case any should appear they are to be debarred the privilege of entering or receiving any aid whatever.

JUNE 10, 1864.

I have the honor herewith to enclose tables of the exports and imports of this island for the year 1863. Also, a tabular list of the number of vessels and their nationality entering the port of Cyprus. It will be remarked that no American vessels figure in these tables. Commerce was more active in 1863 than in preceding years, and this is especially observable in the export trade. The total amount of exports for 1863 was £276,700—an increase of £88,565 upon the year 1862. Cotton alone shows an increase in the exports of £57,529. Cotton carobs, wine, spirits, grain, salt, and live stock were the principal articles of exportation. The total amount of imports in 1863 was £120,000—exceeding that of 1862 by £20,000. Greece has been the chief foreign importing country, next Austria, and then France.

Of articles of exportation cotton rose from 21 cents at the close of 1862 to 40 cents the pound at the close of 1863; wheat advanced $1 50 and barley 36 cents the quarter during the same period. Carobs ruled $3 the ton and wool $5 the cwt. higher than in 1862. Wine and spirits maintained about the same price as in the preceding year, excepting the superior quality of commanderia wine, which rose about 40 per 100 in value.

The weights and measures in use in Cyprus are those of Constantinople, viz: Weights, 1 oke $= 2\frac{3}{4}$ pounds.

Measures, 1 kilo $= 1$ bushel, weighing of Cyprus wheat 56 to 58 pounds, and of Cyprus barley 4J to 45 pounds.

The cultivation of cotton was much extended in 1863, the increase being calculated to amount to as much as 40 per cent. upon former years. The total produce of the island must have been, in 1863, about 8,000 bales of $2\frac{1}{4}$ arobas, (or 2,016,000 pounds,) of which the principal part was sent to Great Britain. The introduction of American seeds by the Manchester Cotton Supply Association has been successful. The demand for them is very great; and in future they will, no doubt, abundantly furnish the island. The improved quality of the cotton and the introduction by a resident British merchant of the Macarthy roller gin, which does not weaken the staple as the saw gins used in the island are found to do, have diverted the channel of cotton exportation from Marseilles to Liverpool.

Notwitstanding the active measures taken to destroy them, the locusts continue to multiply in Cyprus. Their presence in the island is a constant obstacle to cotton cultivation by the delay which they cause in planting. The plant does not ripen till late, and at times the pods do not open at all from want of sufficient heat in the autumnal season.

Government has made grants towards insuring their extirpation, and the local authorities have taken some pains for the same end, but the locusts are found to multiply greatly in spite of all that is done for their destruction; and, should they not be destroyed, they will, no doubt, destroy the agriculture of the island.

Statement showing the imports from the inland of Cyprus for the year 1863, through the port of Larnaca.

Name of articles.	Foreign weights and measures.	From Great Britain		From France		From Austria		From Italy		From Greece		From Turkey		Total				
		Quantity.	Value.	Quantity.	Value.	Quantity.	Value.	Quantity.	Value.	Quantity.	Value.	Quantity.	Value.	Foreign weights and measures	English weights and measures	Foreign money.	English money.
				Piast's.		*Piast's.*				*Piastres.*		*Piastres.*				*Piastres.*	*£*
Manufactures	Packages	18	18,000	10	30,000	47	141,000			12	36,000	2,300	4,200,000	*2,369	2,369	4,407,000	40,064
Hardware and machinery	Cases		4,400	25	25,000	20	20,000					310	310,000	373	†373	373,000	3,390
Earthenware and glassware	Cases				36,000		32,500		43,250				100,000			218,150	1,965
Soap	Okes											40,000	240,000	140,000	†1,000	240,000	2,188
Tobacco	Okes											70,000	220,000	71,300	†1,782	1,212,100	11,019
Rice	Okes			15,000	75,000	440	1,210	2,200	6,050	1,300	22,100	80,000	1,190,000	89,840	†2,246	247,060	2,246
Sugar	Okes			6,100	61,000	1,500	7,500			7,200	19,800	88,000	220,000	85,600	†1,940	428,000	3,890
Coffee	Okes					500	5,000			11,100	55,500	19,200	290,000	30,500	762	305,000	773
	Value				347,500					4,700	47,000		192,000		11,025	1,487,500	13,518
Beer	Okes										740,500		400,500	141,000	†221	102,500	1,532
Iron	Okes			6,000	15,000	7,000	17,500			13,000	32,500	15,000	37,500	32,500		177,000	1,609
Copper vessels	Okes					6,350	127,000			500	10,000	2,000	40,000	18,850	325	495,000	4,500
Butter	Okes					5,000	75,000					98,000	490,000	133,000		311,900	2,830
Salt fish	Okes				15,000		7,500				208,700		80,000				
	Value																
Coals	Tons	130	96,400									8,000	240,000	§120		26,400	240
Beeswax	Okes													18,000	‡200	240,000	2,183
Sundries	Value		130,500		207,500		370,740		5,700		152,100		2,086,000			2,932,590	26,660
Total			179,300		811,500		805,000		55,000		1,333,700		10,025,500			13,920,000	120,000

* Packages.   † Okes.   ‡ Cwt.   § Tons.

Statement showing the exports of the island of Cyprus for the year 1863, from the port of Larnaca.

Names of articles.	Foreign weights and measures. 1 cantar equals 180 okes.	To Great Britain. Quantity	To Great Britain. Value	To France. Quantity	To France. Value	To Austria. Quantity	To Austria. Value	To Italy. Quantity	To Italy. Value	To Greece. Quantity	To Greece. Value	To Turkey. Quantity	To Turkey. Value	Total. Quantity. Foreign weights and measures	Total. Quantity. English weights and measures	Total. Value. For'gn currency	Total. Value. English currency
					Piastres.		*Piastres.*		*Piastr's.*		*Piastr's.*		*Piastres.*			*Piastres.*	£
Locust beans*	Okes	60,800	258,400	22,800	96,900	5,000	450,000	2,300	207,000			10,000	900,000	39,800	18,955	3,582,000	32,563
Madder root	Okes	10,500	210,000	168,350	3,535,350	39,300	825,300					60,000	255,000	143,600		610,300	5,550
Cotton	Bales		4,000	162,350				12,500	292,500			167,440	3,515,000	397,550	1,113,140	8,348,550	75,986
Wool	Bales			62,500	508,000			7,200	57,600			21,000	168,000	92,900		727,600	6,705
Silk	{ Value	10,000	18,000	54,000	485,200							4,000	890,000	4,000	11,900	890,000	8,000
Cocoons	Okes			82,000	97,280								50,000	66,000	11,650	535,900	4,865
Linseed	Okes		18,000		235,750							2,000	3,600	90,000	2,250	118,800	1,080
Sesame seed	Okes	2,500	90,000	9,000	72,000	88,000	198,000	8,000	1,800			8,000	23,000	176,000	49,280	258,750	2,552
Com'd wine	Okes					250	2,000	5,000	6,250	2,000	1,500	80,000	180,000	35,750	117,910	396,000	3,600
Com'd, old	Okes					6,000	7,500			1,000	1,250	12,000	96,000	132,000	394,160	296,000	1,873
Common wine	Okes											110,000	2,637,500	160,000		652,500	5,113
Raki	Okes											55,000	560,000	69,000		560,000	94,113
Raisins	Okes	14,000	28,000	25,550	711,000	92,500	202,500	150	3,000			42,000	840,000	85,700	110,703	1,714,300	15,981
Wheat	Kilo	8,000	160,000	25,000	225,000	1,200	3,000	34,500	92,500			35,000	315,000	248,300	91,315	2,224,700	91,315
Barley	Kilo	141,000	1,271,700			30	1,500					3,200	1,600,000	3,200	14,000	1,600,000	14,545
Salt**				90,000	50,000			82,000		400	20,000	51,000	197,500	72,200	1,641	180,500	1,641
Skins												200	10,000	630		31,500	288
Hides	{ Value		70,250		30		25,600		32,150		12,750		1,800,000			1,800,000	16,385
Live stock	Value								123,000				2,814,000			3,008,350	27,350
Sundries		15,500	23,250									12,000	18,000	109,500		164,250	1,494
Rags	Okes											30,000	180,000	30,000		180,000	1,638
Oil	Okes												500,000			500,000	4,545
Manufactures‡‡																	
Total			2,063,600		6,070,000		1,715,400		930,000		50,000		175,830,000			30,437,000	276,700

* To Russia—quantity, 225,000; value, 2,025,000.   † Tons.   ‡ Cwt.   § Pounds.   ‖ Gallons.   ¶ Qr.   ** Cart loads, 1,000 okes each.   †† Packages.   ‡‡ Native and foreign.

Statement showing the nationality, tonnage, number of vessels and of crews entered and cleared at the port of Larnaca during the year 1863, together with the invoiced value of the inward and outward cargoes.

ENTERED.

Nationality of vessels.	WITH CARGOES.			IN BALLAST.			TOTAL.			Invoice value of cargoes.
	Vessels.	Tons.	Crew.	Vessels.	Tons.	Crew.	Vessels.	Tons.	Crew.	
British	9	3,868	181	11	3,241	121	20	7,109	302	£5,500
French	21	8,013	567	12	1,852	98	33	9,865	665	7,300
Austrian	62	43,863	2,196	27	6,133	243	89	49,996	2,439	72,000
Italian	6	1,083	57	11	1,905	112	17	2,988	169	500
Ionian	2	162	15	9	1,404	86	11	1,566	11	....
Greek	19	1,443	125	67	10,162	527	86	11,905	652	3,000
Turkish..............	247	12,453	1,858	327	20,406	1,512	574	32,859	4,370	25,700
Russian	....	....	....	3	645	34	3	645	34	....
Swedish	....	....	....	1	215	10	1	215	10	....
Prussian	....	....	....	1	300	11	1	300	11	....
Entered	366	70,885	4,999	469	46,563	3,754	835	117,448	8,753	120,000

CLEARED.

British	19	6,763	289	4	1,098	44	23	7,861	333	17,190
French	25	8,532	596	7	1,207	61	32	9,739	657	42,250
Austrian	82	48,656	2,379	7	1,502	62	89	50,158	2,441	93,450
Italian	15	2,652	148	4	773	44	19	3,425	192	8,700
Ionian	7	1,334	75	4	232	26	11	1,566	101	2,340
Greek	64	9,831	501	21	1,972	141	85	11,803	642	25,000
Turkish............:	447	21,789	3,307	126	10,725	1,032	573	32,514	4,339	79,420
Russian	2	445	24	1	200	10	3	645	34	1,300
Swedish	1	215	10	....	....	....	1	215	10	450
Prussian	1	300	11	....	....	....	1	300	11	600
Cleared..........	663	100,517	7,340	174	17,709	1,420	837	112,226	8,760	276,700

Commercial report of Sidon for the year 1863.

As this is my first report on the state of commerce and of the government of Sidon, I take the liberty to make a brief preliminary statement respecting that part of the country which is under the jurisdiction of Sidon. In this jurisdiction was formerly included the city of Sidon and the gardens which surround it to the distance of about thirty minutes' ride; but in the month of March, 1861, the government joined to that jurisdiction the districts of Belad, Besharah, Nèz, Felmin Heunin Cana, Sahel, Maaralee, Merng Aigun, Belad-Shukif, Iebad, Shuma, and Tyre, and sent a pasha, with the rank of a caimacan, and placed governors in every district under his order.

This political arrangement has facilitated the course of business between the merchants of this city and the inhabitants of those districts, and thereby improving the state of commerce. The present government of Sidon extends from the river Anualy, on the north, to Belad-Safed, on the south, and is bounded eastwardly by Mounts Lebanon and Herman and the Huleb. The estimated area is 1,500 square miles, with a population of about 70,000, the majority of which are of the Metamali sect. The revenue of the province of Sidon is about 7,680,000 piastres, of which 2,825,000 piastres are derived from the landed estate; 140,000 from the duty on sheep and goats; 140,000 from the war exemption tax upon the Christians; 3,900,000 from the tobacco duty; 555,000 from the custom-house duties upon silk and other articles, and 120,000 from the mports of some particular articles at Sidon and Tyre, such as fish, coffee, slaughtered animals, and goods sold at auction. The expenses are about 800,000 piastres for the payment of the caimacans, mudies, clerks, and police. The principal articles of export from the city of Sidon are tobacco, silk, grain, and some dried fruits, such as figs, raisins, &c., which are sent to Egypt, except some of the silk fibre prepared by the two silk factories and exported to France. The principal articles of import are rice, leather, sole-leather, and dates. These are imported. But the European manufactures, and such articles as sugar, coffee, iron, copper, pepper, cochineal, indigo, are brought from Beirût by the small boats which daily journey along the coast.

The artisans of Sidon are weavers, gold and silversmiths, dyers, blacksmiths, coppersmiths, shoemakers, and carpenters. Three years ago a new manufactory was opened for weaving silk fabric known as "Damascus silk."

The shipping trade of this port is carried on principally with Egypt, Cyprus, the coast, and occasionally Europe. Greek vessels take a large amount of sponge from the sea bordering on this province.

The ancient Phenician port of Sidon has become entirely filled up by the neglect of the government. According to the views of experienced persons it could be perfectly restored at the cost of about £2,000. For about £15,000 a spacious harbor, suitable for the anchorage of the largest ships, could be also made.

The increase of the exported articles in 1863 is chiefly from tobacco, of which the crop was abundant, and in demand by the inhabitants of Egypt, where it was exported, and also from the exportation of cocoons to France. But the increase in the imports in 1863 is on the rice from Egypt. The importation of the other articles was correspondent with the preceding year.

Return of the imports at the port of Sidon in the year 1863.

Articles.	From Egypt.			From Cyprus.		From Turkey.		Total quantities.		Total value.	
	Turkish weights and measures.	Quantities.	Value.	Quantities.	Value.	Quantity.	Value.	Turk. weights or measures.	Eng. weights or measures.	Turkish money.	English money.
										Piastres.	£
Rice .... okes	8,000	650,000	1,800,000	....	....	....	....	8,000	1,857,143	1 800,000	15,000
Sar .... km	2,400	2,700	940,000	....	....	....	....	2,400	2,400	8,000	2,000
Sole leather .... okes	13,000	13,000	385,000	....	....	....	....	13,000	37,143	800	2,708
Linen ...... number	1,500	1,500	30,000	....	....	....	....	1,500	1,500	30,000	250
Dry peas and dates .. okes	8,000	10,000	90,000	....	....	....	....	10,000	28,571	20,000	167
Gee .... okes	3,000	....	....	3,000	15,000	....	....	3,000	8,571	15,000	155
Indigo .... okes	80	800	160,000	....	....	....	....	800	2,287	16,000	1,333
Salt .... okes	800,000	....	....	800,000	6,000	....	....	800,000	2,285,714	600,000	5,000
Wine .... okes	8,000	....	....	10,000	9,000	....	....	9,000	25,52	9,000	167
Arrack .... okes	6,000	....	....	6,000	8,000	....	....	6,000	17,143	36,000	300
Donkeys and mules ... number	300	....	....	30	18,000	....	....	300	300	150,000	1,250
Rice .... okes	20,000	....	....	20,000	9,000	....	....	20,000	57,143	30,000	167
Garlics .... okes	1,000	....	....	1,000	2,000	....	....	1,000	2,857	2,000	16
Hiraka .... number	6,000	....	....	6,000	3,000	....	....	6,000	17,143	3,000	25
Coarse linen cloth .. number	3,000	3,000	60,000	....	....	....	....	3,000	3,000	60,000	500
Vinegar .... okes	5,000	....	....	5,000	8,000	....	....	5,000	14,86	8,000	67
Coffee .... okes	4,000	4,000	60,000	....	....	....	....	4,000	11,82	6,000	500
Woods .... okes	....	....	....	....	....	....	60,000	....	....	60,000	500
Mats .... kes	2,000	2,000	40,000	....	....	....	....	2,000	2,000	6,000	333
Total	1,538,000	686,700	2,735,000	851,300	854,000	....	60,000	1,538,000	4,377,190	3,649,000	30,408
Total imports, 1862	1,014,014	258,600	1,327,500	755,414	746,000	....	....	1,014,014	2,860,592	2,277,100	18,978

Return of the exports at the port of Sidon in the year 1863.

Articles.	Turkish weights or measures.	To France. Quantity.	To France. Value.	To Egypt. Quantity.	To Egypt. Value.	To Cyprus. Quantity.	To Cyprus. Value.	To Turkey. Quantity.	To Turkey. Value.	Total quantity. Turkish weights or measures.	Total quantity. English weights or measures.	Total value. Turkish money.	Total value. English money.
Tobacco .... okes	500,000			500,000	6,000,000					500,00	1,428,571	*Piastres.* 6,000,000	£50,000
Silk .... okes	1,600	600	240,000	1,000	300,000			1,000	300,000	1,60	45 71	540,000	4,500
Dyed silk .... okes	3,100			2,000	600,000					3,100	8,838	930,000	7,750
Dried figs .... okes	30,000			30,000	90,000	100				30,00	62 14	90,000	750
Raisins .... okes	35,000			35,000	105,000		30,000			35,00	80,000	105,000	875
Sheets of dried apricots .. okes	15,000			15,000	45,000					15,00	42,857	45,000	375
Galls .... okes	500			500	4,000					500	14 29	4,000	33
Galls ..... earth	5,000			5,000	5,000					5,00	14,286	5,000	42
Red leather .... number	3,000			3,000	15,000					5,00	3,000	45,000	375
Pomegranate peels .. okes	5,000			5,000	10,000					5,00	14,986	10,000	84
Licorice .... okes	5,000			2,000	2,000					2,00	57 14	2,000	17
Oil .... okes	35,000			20,000	120,000	5,000	30,000	10,000	60,000	35,00	100,000	210,000	1,750
Lemons .... okes	300,000									300,00	87,143	300,000	2,500
Cocoons .... okes	20,000	20,000	500,000							20,00	57,143	500,000	4,167
Pomegranates ..... okes	25,000			25,000	25,000			300,000	300,000	25,00	71,429	25,000	208
Total	980,200	20,000	740,000	643,500	7,351,000	5,100	60,000	311,000	660,000	980,90	2,795,000	8,811,000	73,426
Total of exports of 1862 ..	432,280	500	200,000	401,780	4,724,90	300,000	5,000			432,280	1,235,081	4,929,700	41,080

Shipping returns at the port of Saida in the year 1863.

Nationality of vessels.	ENTERED. With cargoes. Vessels.	Tons.	Crew.	In ballast. Vessels.	Tons.	Crew.	Total. Vessels.	Tons.	Crew.	CLEARED. With cargoes. Vessels.	Tons.	Crew.	In ballast. Vessels.	Tons.	Crew.	Total. Vessels.	Tons.	Crew.	Invoice value of cargoes.
Ottoman	39	2,510	260	7	450	59	39	2,960	319	33	2,650	271	6	310	48	39	2,960	319	73,426
Italian				1	215	9	1	215	9				1	215	9	1	215	9	....
French				1	115	7	1	115	7				1	115	7	1	115	7	....
Total	39	2,510	260	9	780	75	41	3,290	335	33	2,650	271	8	640	64	41	3,290	335	73,426
Total of 1862 ..	29	1,210	207	8	429	83	30	1,639	290	10	559	101	20	1,060	189	30	1,639	290	73,426

Approximate statement showing the imports at the port of Mersine (Tarsus) during the year 1863.

Place of origin.	Colonial.	Manufactures.	Iron.	Hardware.	Hides.	Liquors.	Tobacco.	Soap.	Fruits.	Divers.	Groups of money.	Totals in piastres.
Marseilles	2,001,976	10,323,117	351,600	500,000	982,000					110,000	13,000,000	27,987,693
Liverpool	50,000									20,000		70,000
Smyrna	160,000	10,490,000	100,000	500,000					7,280	30,000	5,000,000	16,217,280
Constantinople	70,000	10,712,000		700,000						60,000	5,000,000	16,542,000
Syria	1,190,000	10,000,000	200,000	738,000				1,306,200		110,000	15,000,000	29,263,880
Egypt	70,000		100,000		1,600,000	292,320	439,680	299,000	220,000	110,000	5,690,765	2,260,765
Greece									270,000	10,000		2,301,320
Italy	300,000	372,883		300,000						20,000		952,863
Total	3,861,976	41,827,000	751,600	2,738,000	2,582,000	292,320	439,680	1,605,200	497,280	470,000	43,690,765	98,755,821

Approximate statement of exports at the port of Mersine during the year 1863.

To what place.	Cotton.	Wool.	Oleaginous seeds.	Corn.	Yellow berries.	Madder roots.	Gums.	Leeches.	Skins.	Fruits.	Lumber.	Wax.	Divers.	Groups of coin.	Totals in piastres.
Marseilles	17,900,033	947,300	4,069,895	478,000					146,000			12,000	100,000	2,000,000	25,842,728
Liverpool	11,976,557	669,400		10,000											12,655,957
Smyrna	19,847,053	505,460	200,000		249,130	274,060	778,000	189,500		20,000			40,000	1,000,000	22,733,793
Constantinople	1,988,278		300,000							10,000			10,000	1,000,000	3,229,278
Syria			500,000	421,200						11,000	60,000	20,000	9,000	1,500,000	2,331,200
Egypt				200,000						40,000	207,864	30,000	11,000	500,000	1,458,864
Greece				519,530						10,000		40,000	11,750	500,000	1,081,280
Italy	1,978,529			150,000								23,500	20,000	84,890	2,256,919
Total piastres	53,690,450	2,122,160	5,069,895	1,778,730	249,130	274,060	778,000	189,500	146,000	91,000	267,864	125,500	201,750	6,584,890	71,569,019

Commercial report of Damascus for the year 1863.

The state of commerce is better this year than it was last year, as the inhabitants are beginning to recover from the misfortunes of 1860. Most of those who were absent from the town have come back and are carrying on their business.

It is not possible to ascertain the imports and exports of the place, as the officers of the customs are forbidden from giving the necessary information about these matters.

The fruit crop has been very good this year, and large quantities of dried apricots have been exported to Egypt and Turkey. The silk manufacture cannot be less than 500,000 pieces. Two caravans came from Bagdad last year—one in the spring, the other in the fall—with from 1,200 to 1,500 loads of tombac in 9,000 bags. It was sold in the spring at the rate of 2,800 to 2,850 piastres the cantar, and in the fall at 2,950 piastres the cantar.

Imports: Rice, 12,000 baskets, at $6\frac{715}{900}$ piastres per basket; cloth, 140,000 pieces; thick cloth, 8,000 pieces; thin cloth, 5,000 pieces; worsted, 17,000 bundles; niadam, 10,000 pieces; sugar, 400 cantars; coffee, 200 cantars.

Exportation of the port of Latakia from September 20, 1863, *to September* 15, 1864.

Articles exported.	Quantity	Vessels.	To what country.	Value in fs.
Cotton	200,000 okes of 2¼ lbs.	French	Marseilles	900,000
Do	100,000 " "	English	Liverpool	475,000
Sesame	150,000 " "	French	Marseilles	100,000
Wood	40 cargoes	Arab	do	50,000
Sponges	40 "	French	Alexandria	100,000
Wool	20,000 okes of 2¼ lbs.	do	Marseilles	40,000
Do	5,000 " "	English	Liverpool	10,000
Rags	200 bales	do	do	10,000
Total				1,685,000

Importation of the port of Latakia from September 20, 1863, *to September* 15, 1864.

Articles imported.	Vessels.	From what country.	Value in fcs.
Sugar	French	Marseilles and Beirût	30,000
Coffee	do	do	20,000
English manufactures	do	Beirût	350,000
Rice	do	Egypt	50,000
Skins of buffalo	do	do	70,000
Total			520,000

The Turkish government has sent Egyptian cotton seed here, with orders to sow it, but the farmers fearing that it will not succeed, refused to try it, and continue with the old seed, short fibre. The coming crop will be about 3,000 bales.

Commercial report of Alexandretta for the year 1863.

Four monthly and twenty irregular steamers have exported from here about 34,000 bales of wool—*i. e.*, 3,400 tons destined for Marseilles, and valued at 10,000,000 francs. Formerly Dunkirk demanded wool from North America, and Boston, Massachusetts, demanded, directly, wool by four to five ships annually, but since 1861 no American vessel has visited this port.

Notwithstanding the great difficulty of transit, and the entire absence of roads in the interior, which triples sometimes the cost of products, commerce has been developed considerably at Aleppo, for many products which were formerly consumed at home are now sent to Smyrna, Egypt, and Constantinople.

Imports have quintupled. In 1859, 36,000 bales of English manufactures were imported, but this year 42,000 bales. Marseilles and Germany send us other products, fabrics, cloths, hardware, &c. Since imports have entered the country by Bassorah, the Persian gulf by Monsul and Mesopotamia, the imports to Aleppo of sugar, coffee, indigo, and dyestuff have much diminished. The country furnishes sufficient grain for its own use, and sometimes for exportation.

The culture of cotton is not pushed in the interior as in other countries; but this year a double crop is expected. Twenty-seven thousand bales of cotton have been exported this year by French, English, and Italian steamers and sailing vessels. Two thousand bales only have been sent to England, because of the quality, which is of the short staple. The bales are valued at $1,700,000. The culture of cotton may be increased without diminishing the crop of grain.

Wax, yellow grain, scamony, tobacco, sesame seed, raisins, pistachio nuts, are the products of the country, which, with the goods of silk or mixed with cotton, furnish an exportation valued at more than twenty million of piastres.

The probability of the establishment of a port at and railroad from Suadia, to connect the Mediterranean with the Persian gulf, is one cause why nothing is done to improve this port, which is isolated, and greatly needs telegraphic communication with Aleppo.

TRIPOLI, (SYRIA)—J. AUGUSTUS JOHNSON, *Consul.*

SEPTEMBER 30, 1864.

Commercial report of Tripoli for the year 1863.

SILK.

The silk crop of this year yielded about 30,000 okes, and was sold in the beginning of the crop from 270 piastres to 280 per oke.

During the past year a great portion of the silk was exported to Europe, particularly to France and Italy, where it found ready sale, but recently, on account of high prices in this country, a very small quantity of silk has been sent to Europe, but is generally exported to Egypt, Damascus, Aleppo, Hama, Herus, and Beirût. But after the destruction of Damascus, almost all the weavers removed to Herus, where they weave the silk and send it to Alexandria, Egypt, where it finds ready sale. And as the people have increasd the number of mulberry trees, the production of silk has increased.

OIL.

The crop of oil this year was excellent; it yielded about 2,600,000 okes, which was sold in the beginning of the crop for 5½ piastres per oke, the superior, and for 4½ per oke, the inferior; subsequently the price of this article went up to 6½ piastres per oke, the superior, and 5½ piastres per oke, the inferior. A portion of this article is sold to the inhabitants for cooking and lighting, and the remainder is sold to Greek merchants, who export it to different ports of the Turkish empire, and some years one or two cargoes are sent to Marseilles, but the inferior oil is made into soap. Every alternate year the olive trees produce no crop.

SOAP.

Soap is one of the chief articles made in this town, and it proves to be the best soap made in Syria. The soap manufactures yielded this year about 1,360,000 okes, and was sold at from five to six piastres per oke, of which one-third is sold to the inhabitants, and the balance was exported to different parts of the Turkish dominions, and especially to Alexandria, Tarsus, and Cyprus.

GRAINS.

Corn, barley, lentils, beans, and all other kinds of grain, are cultivated here, the product of which supplies the inhabitants, and some years a few cargoes were sent to Europe, and to other parts of the Turkish dominions.

SPONGES.

During the months of June, July, August, and a part of September, sponge divers produce a large quantity of sponges, which is of three classes—superior, inferior, and middle—which sell for about from 1,900,000 piastres to 20,000,000 piastres.

WOOL.

The crop of wool in Tripoli is just sufficient for the inhabitants, but Herus and Hama export through this city large quantities, which are sent to Europe, especially to France, and sometimes to America.

COTTON.

Before the commencement of the civil war in the United States, cotton was not much cultivated here, but after the said war broke out, the Turkish government issued an order to the farmers to cultivate cotton, and that the ground in which cotton is cultivated shall be left free of duty. This year the crop yielded about 400,000 piastres. In the future the crop will be larger.

FRUITS AND VEGETABLES.

There are various kinds of fruits and vegetables in Tripoli, viz : sour lemons, sweet lemons, oranges, citron, potatoes, apricots, apples. peaches, jujube plums, pomegranates, figs, prickly pears, pears, grapes, quinces, sugar-cane, cucumbers, and other kinds, which yielded this year from 2,000,000 to 2,200,000 piastres.

NAVIGATION.

The French and Russian steamers touch at this port regularly at appointed times—four times monthly—where they find ready freight, and, as it is safer to send goods with steamers, sail vessels very seldom find freight here, but small boats sail generally from Tripoli to Cyprus, to Alexandria, to Tarsus, and to Beirût, during spring, summer, and autumn, and very seldom in winter.

TOBACCO.

Tobacco is divided into three classes—superior, inferior, and middle—of which is exported to Egypt from 50,000 to 60,000 okes—some years about 100,000 okes. The duty on tobacco is 16 piastres when not sent to Europe.

MINES.

Iron, copper, marble, and salt are the mines found in our country, but no effort has been made to dig them, on account of the government; for if any person discovers a mine on his property he is obliged to cover it up, because when known the government places so high a tax on that ground that the owner is obliged to sell it.

ARTS AND MECHANICS.

The artisans of this port are goldsmiths, carpenters, carpet weavers, dyers, builders, blacksmiths, tailors, coppersmiths, shoemakers, weavers, saddle-makers, tinsmiths, tanners, and potters; but these arts are not so well worked as in Europe, because there are no schools for arts in this country, and no help from the government; but the art of weaving silk girdles, which are named Tripoli girdles, and other silk goods, is very well conducted.

INCOME OF GOVERNMENT FROM TRIPOLI.

Property duty, 875,000 piastres; also, property duty, 860,000 piastres; conscription money paid by Christians, 113,000 piastres; duty paid in grains, 440,000 piastres; stamped paper, 25,000 piastres; contract paper, 10,000 piastres; trakeei for arts, 6,000 piastres; tezbarah given to every man, 9,000 piastres; passports and crime punishment by money, 12,000 piastres; total, 3,510,000; custom-house on goods, 1,315,000 piastres; tobacco duty, 1,250,000 piastres.

Male population.

Of what country.	Jews.	Moslems.	Christians.	Neseyneysh or Pagans.	Total.
Tripoli	40	7,104	3,491	....	10,635
Lafeyta	......	....	2,457	15,653	18,110
Accan	......	5,486	7,017	....	12,503
Damreyeh	......	2,491	1,127	....	3,608
Sharah	......	1,916	365	....	2,281
Tertoos	......	1,124	344	....	1,468
Coorah Tahlah	......	653	1,612	....	2,265
Eroad	......	1,204	32	....	1,236
Total	40	19,968	16,445	15,653	52,106

Tabular statement showing the exports from Tripoli, (Syria,) for the year 1863.

To what country.	Grain.	Fruits.	Raisins.	Sesame seeds.	Sponges.	Flour.	Iron.	Cotton.	Soap.	Silk.	Soda.	Tobacco.	Texture.	Beans.	Cocoons.	Various articles.	Total of values by countries.
	Fr.	Fr.	Fr.	Fr.	Fr.	Fr.	Fr.	Fr.	Fr.	Fr.	Fr.	Fr.	Fr.	Fr.	Fr.	Fr.	Fr.
France		32,200		5,000	209,000		805,000	111,000		30,000				18,000	25,000	8,000	1,193,000
England																106,000	106,000
Italy		2,000	50,200		2,000				300	48,000	2,500	1,000	408,000		900,000		52,400
Turkey	344,000															25,100	1,301,800
Egypt						51,000	60,000		103,000	300,000		1,941,000	3,000,000			30,600	4,573,600
Total	344,000	34,200	50,200	5,000	211,000	51,000	865,000	111,000	103,900	378,000	2,500	1,251,000	3,408,000	18,000	925,000	171,700	7,226,800
Total of quantities	1,640,638	354,447	172,300	12,000	16,300	195,000	500,000	30,000	133,000	98,000	30,000	620,000		41,000	8,200		
Comparison of quantities with the past year	8,237,500	1,190,000	32,000	12,000	43,600	245,000	200,000	30,000	400,000	28,000	30,000	201,100		8,000	10,000		
Excess			140,300		27,300		300,000			2,000		418,900		33,000			
Less	659,862	835,525				50,000			269,000						1,800		

Navigation of Tripoli, 1863.

ENTRY OF VESSELS UNDER FLAGS.

From what country.	Turkish (No.)	Turkish (Tons.)	From what country (No.)	From what country (Tons.)	Foreign (No.)	Foreign (Tons.)	Total of entries by countries (No.)	Total of entries by countries (Tons.)
France	3	1,800					3	1,800
England	12	8,000					12	8,000
Turkey	663	44,000	17	10,300	110	42,000	773	86,000
Greece	2	500					2	500
Total	683	44,000	17	10,300	110	42,000	790	96,300
Total of the past year	253	98,370			126	37,000	479	65,370
In excess	310	15,630	17	1,000		5,000	311	30,930
Less					16			

DEPARTURE OF VESSELS UNDER FLAGS.

	Turkish (No.)	Turkish (Tons.)	To what country (No.)	To what country (Tons.)	Foreign (No.)	Foreign (Tons.)	Total of departures by countries (No.)	Total of departures by countries (Tons.)	Total of entries and departures, together (No.)	(Tons.)
France	2	500					8	500	15	2,300
England	6	6,000					8	6,000	20	14,000
Turkey	642	40,800	12	7,000	115	45,300	757	86,100	1,530	172,100
Greece	2	500					2	500	4	1,000
Total	649	40,800	12	7,000	115	45,300	769	93,100	1,559	189,400
Total of the past year	388	23,800	11	3,314	122	36,000	461	61,514	940	126,884
In excess	314	17,600	1	4,686		9,300	308	31,586	619	62,516
Less					7					

COMMERCE OF ALEPPO.

ALEPPO—J. DE PICCIOTTA, *Vice-Consul.*

—— —, 1864.

The transactions of the year have been in general very flourishing. English manufactures take the first rank among the imports, and supply almost exclusively the bazaars, as in 1862 the merchants who speculated in them realized great profits by a prompt and easy sale. During the winter, the market is much less animated, and 4,000 bales of English manufactures are in market besides those which are expected from Liverpool. England has also furnished its usual supply of colonials, sugar, coffee, &c. France takes the second rank in furnishing colonials, sugar, coffee, lead, zinc, drugs as well as cotton, silks and cloths. Switzerland furnishes only its handkerchiefs, called Jasma, and its cotton stuffs, of which a great quantity is sold here.

Exportation has been more animated than importation, particularly in cotton. Although the harvest was partly destroyed by the locusts, which have been desolating the country for three years past, it has still yielded about 4,000 cantars, (1,000,000 kilos;) for the farmers, encouraged by the increased price of cotton, devote themselves to its culture. At the beginning of the harvest the greater part was purchased by our merchants at the rate of 3,000 piastres to 3,500 piastres the cantar of 250 kilogrammes, and sent to Marseilles, where they found ready sale. Subsequently the price of this article went up to 5,000 piastres the cantar. Now the cotton of the new harvest brings from 5,000 to 5,300 piastres the cantar from speculators for transmission to France and England.

Wool, on the contrary, has for the most part been a source of loss to all specu lators. At first merchants, encouraged by their success of the preceding year, hastened to make advances to the nomadic tribes, in order to secure the larger part of their clip. But these tribes demanded prices which were excessively dear. It is calculated that Aleppo and its environs to the Euphrates have yielded this year 8,000 bales of washed wool, which were purchased at from 22,000 to 25,000 piastres the cantar, and sent mostly to Marseilles. Mesopotamia has given also about 15,000 bales of washed wool; nearly all have been productive of loss, the prices at the place of production being too high. A large part of the wools of Bagdad and Mosul is still in the market, the first for 3,500 the cantar, the latter at 3,000. It is estimated that half the wool still remains unsold at Marseilles for the account of the speculators, who would be glad to free themselves from it with a light loss.

The harvest of gall-nuts has been bad this year, and the price which at first was 3,000 piastres the cantar, was raised by the scarcity of the article to 4,000 piastres. It is calculated that the harvest has produced this year but 1,000 cantars, of which more than half has been sent from the interior to France and England.

The grain crops have been poor on account of the ravages of the locusts, and the exportation has amounted to nothing.

Statement showing the description and value of the imports into the island of Candia during the year ended December 31, 1864.

Manufactured goods	$1,856,278
Hides, tanned, and leather	112,100
Coffee	6,420
Sugar	14,500
Spirits of all kinds	12,400
Tobacco and snuff	38,644
Salt fish of all kinds	66,250
Flour	12,500
Rice	55,875
Hardware	8,500
Butter	10,540
Soda ash	30,450
Natron	53,900
Sacks for soap	26,080
Grain of all sorts	185,200
Sundries not enumerated	44,080
Total	2,533,717

Statement showing the description, quantity, and value of the exports of the island of Candia during the year ended December 31, 1864.

Description.	Quantity.	Value.
Olive oils .... tuns..	3,040	$635,360
Soap .... cwt..	100,575	653,737
Silk .... pounds..	20,790	41,580
Wax .... cwt..	160	6,400
Honey .... pounds..	50,820	25,410
Carobs .... cwt..	78,400	58,800
Almonds .... do...	984	11,808
Valonia .... tons..	570	28,500
Cheese .... cwt..	550	8,250
Oranges and lemons .... M..	6,018	15,045
Wool .... pounds..	50,000	15,000
Linseed .... bushels..	2,225	2,225
Chestnuts		8,500
Raisins (common) .... cwt..	5,042	10,084
Lambskins .... dozen..	2,000	4,000
Total		1,524,699

Statement showing the nationality, tonnage, number of vessels and their crews, entered and cleared at the ports of Candia and Canea during the year ended December 31, 1864.

Nationality.	ENTERED.			CLEARED.		
	Tonnage.	No. of vessels.	No. of crew.	Tonnage.	No. of vessels.	No. of crew.
British	412	3	25	412	3	25
Ionian	1,195	22	156	780	12	81
Turkish.............	19,823	582	4,049	20,945	598	4,215
Hellenic.............	11,995	361	2,108	11,104	336	1,932
French.............	260	2	24	75	1	9
Austrian	75	1	7	75	1	7
Russian	280	2	14	280	2	14
Italian	1,055	16	127	1,055	16	124
Dutch	125	1	6	125	1	6
Wallachian...........	75	1	6	....	.....	....
Samiote	324	5	32	234	3	17
	35,619	996	6,554	35,085	973	6,420
Austrian: Lloyd's st'r, (mail boat)........	25,228	92	2,310	25,228	92	2,310
French steamer	320	1	23	320	1	23
Total...........	61,167	1,089	8,887	60,633	1,066	8,753

MOLDO-WALLACHIA.

GALATZ—F. WIPPERMAN, *Consul.*

JUNE 27, 1864.

SIR: I have the honor to enclose my report on commerce for the year 1863.

Annual report for the year 1863.

Galatz is the principal commercial town of the Danubian principalities; here all money transactions are made; the principal bankers have their residences here; the vessels for Galatz, Braila, Sulina, and Kustendji are chartered here, and on the exchange of Galatz the business of all these ports is transacted. Galatz contains about 80,000 inhabitants, and is, after Bucharest, which has about 300,000 inhabitants, the largest city in the Danubian principalities, whilst Braila contains only about 30,000 souls. Galatz has also some manufactories, among which a large soap and candle factory, an establishment for preserving meat for naval purposes, and a large steam flour-mill are to be mentioned. Galatz is the shipping port for almost all the merchandise that enters the principalities by sea, whilst it exports only the grain of Moldavia, and is in this respect far behind Braila, which exports Wallachian grain.

The export trade from the principalities during the year 1863 brought a little more money into the principalities than the preceding year; but the merchants made no money, as the prices here were too high in comparison with the prices in those countries where the grain is consumed, particularly in England. Several houses failed in consequence of this. As the import trade is regulated by the money which flows from the produce of the exportation, the importation for 1863 has also been heavier than the importation of the preceding year. The same increase has also, of course, taken place in the shipping, whilst the

American shipping has fallen off. There used to visit at this port eight or ten American vessels, but only two entered it during 1863. The high dues which every vessel is obliged to pay at Sulina to the European commission of the Danube according to its tonnage, and not according to the depth it draws; and the fact that the masters generally obtain in England charter-parties from dishonest speculators which subject them to losses and great annoyances, may have something to do with. the decrease of the American shipping on the Danube. Since 1855 the vessels arriving at the Danubian ports do not perform quarantine, and can commence discharging and loading at once.

The legal interest in the principalities is 10 per cent., but in business transactions the borrower is made to pay as much as 24 per cent. Galatz and Braila are free ports in regard to all goods arriving by water; those goods that are to be sent to the interior pay at the barriers of these ports an import duty of 5 per cent.; and up to the year 1862 all goods exported by water from these ports had to pay an export duty of 5 per cent.; but since the commencement of the year 1862 this export duty is not levied; instead of which all goods pay one-half per cent. export duty; the amount collected to be expended in improvements of the ports. The principalities have no coin of their own, and the money of all nations is taken; but Austrian, Russian, and French coin circulate more than any other. Money of account is the piastre, at 40 para. In Galatz all coins have a double value; one the Vestiarie value, fixed by the ministry of finance, according to which the Austrian ducat contains thirty-two piastres, and the Galatz value, which is used in all business transactions, and according to which the Austrian ducat contains forty-six piastres and the American dollar twenty piastres. Braila reckons only with the Vestiarie piastres. The "oke" is used for measuring liquids and for weights; it contains 400 drachms and is about equal to 2¾ lbs. English. The "kilo" is the measure for grain; 100 kilos of Galatz are equal to 143 imperial quarters; 100 kilos of Braila are equal to 232 imperial quarters. The yard is the measure for lengths. Six Moldavian yards are equal to five yards of Vienna.

I will divide my report under three principal heads, namely:

I. Exportation.
II. Importation.
III. Shipping.

I.—EXPORTATION.

The splendid harvest of the year 1863 brought of course to the ports of the lower Danube a very considerable quantity of grain, which was destined for exportation, and as the quality was excellent, it was expected that a great amount of money would flow into the principalities; but the continually falling markets did not encourage the merchants to export, as they had reason to fear that during the two months, which the cargo has generally to float before reaching its destination, the price of grain would be lower than at the time it was shipped. Further, the very low rate of freight was the reason that long before the freezing up of the Danube vessels were wanted, and the export trade stopped several weeks earlier than was necessary on account of the season. Nevertheless the exportation of 1863 has never been reached in any preceding year; and as a great deal of grain has remained in the country, the export of this year, especially if the harvest is good, as it promises to be, will be very considerable.

The following statement of the quantity of grain exported and the value of it according to the calculated medium price of 1863 shows, compared with the export of 1862, an excess of one-fifth, whilst the money value is only one-eighth higher, to which must be remarked that the wheat of 1862 was of very inferior quality, and the wheat of 1863 of prime quality. According to the reliable reports of the harbor-master for Galatz and Braila, there were exported during 1863:

a. Galatz.

	Galatz kilos.	G. p's.		Galatz piastres.
Wheat	244,000 at 168 per Galatz kilo....			40,992,000
Maize	249,400 at 115 " "			28,681,000
Rye	56,800 at 105 " "			5,964,000
Barley	31,800 at 72 " " :...			2,289,600
Millet	440 at 60 " "			26,400
Linseed	770 at 300 " "			231,000
Beans	810 at 75 per 100 okes			157,950
	584,020			78,341,950

100 G. k. = 143 i. qr's: 835,149 imperial q'rs. $1=20 G. p's: $3,917,097 50

b. Braila.

1. Seawards :

	Braila kilo.	B. p's.		Braila piastres.
Wheat	317,000 at 168 per Braila kilo..			52,256,000
Maize	360,000 at 115 " "			41,423,000
Rye	11,600 at 105 " "			1,218,000
Barley	112,900 at 72 " "			8,128,800
Millet	6,400 at 60 " "			384,000
Rapeseed..........	2,180 at 260 " "			566,800
Beans	890 at 75 per 100 okes....			267,600
	810,970			105,244,200

100 B. kilo = 232 i. q.: 1,881,450 $7,561,926 90

2. Up river :

	Braila kilo.	B. p's.		Braila piastres.
Wheat	40,000 at 168 per Braila kilo....			6,720,000
Maize	18,000 at 115 " "			2,070,000
Barley	12,000 at 72 " "			864,000
	70,000			9,654,000

Imperial quarters 162,400 $693,861 25

Total exportation of Galatz and Braila :
Imperial quarters 2,879,463 .... $12,172,885 65

The exceptional up-river exportation was caused by the entire failure of the harvest in southern Hungary (by drought) and the famine in consequence of this failure. Therefore about one hundred ship-loads of grain were sent up the river, whilst usually double the quantity is sent from above every year to Braila and Galatz and also to Kustendji for shipment.

Experience has shown that all the grain exported from the river towns from Turn Verein downwards to Sulina amounts to one-fourth of the quantity shipped from Braila and Galatz; whilst the money value of all the minor articles of export, as wool, tallow, preserved and salted meat, hides, salt, wood, petroleum, cantharides, bones, rags, cocoons and eggs of the silkworm, &c., and the necessary amount of provisions to supply said three thousand sea-going vessels and the numerous steamers running from here to Pesth, Vienna, Constantinople,

Odessa, and Marseilles, may be calculated at less than one-sixth of the whole exportation.

Taking these observations as a basis, it will be found that there has been exported from the ports of the lower Danube during the year 1863—

From Galatz, Braila, grain in round numbers	$12, 200, 000
From other river ports...................................	3, 050, 000
Other articles, exports except grain	2, 500, 000
Total	17, 750, 000

In regard to the minor articles of export (excluding grain) the following may be remarked: 1. That the price of wool, in consequence of the high price of cotton, is about one-fourth higher than it was two years ago; 2. That, for the purpose of obtaining petroleum, the foot of the Carpathian mountains has been explored by English speculators, and that they have commenced to export during the last year, and that this article of export promises to increase and to become important.

For the last two years the shipment of grain from Kustendji has assumed such an importance that it cannot be passed over in silence. The grain which is shipped at Kustendji is grown partly in Wallachia, and is carried on the Danube to Czernavoda, from whence it is transported by rail to Kustendji; but the greater part is grown in the region between Matschin and Silistria, and is carried by land to the railroad station, Midschidjek, and thence to Kustendji.

Kustendji exported during the year 1863—

				Galatz piastres.
72, 000	Gal. kilo.	wheat, at 168 G. p.'s		12, 096, 000
120, 000	do.	maize, at 115 do.		13, 800, 000
18, 000	do.	barley, at 72 do.		1, 296, 000
210, 000	Gal. kilo. grain...............................			27, 192, 000
or, 303, 300	imp. qrs.......................................			$1, 359, 600

The following nations participated in the export:

107 English vessels; 25 Italian vessels; 20 Austrian vessels; 18 Greek vessels; 12 Turkish vessels; 5 Russian vessels; 2 French vessels; 1 Mecklenburg vessel. Total, 190 vessels.

The price paid for freights at Kustendji is usually the same as at Sulina, and about one-third lower than at Galatz and Braila; but, as the vessels have to pay rather high harbor dues at Sulina and none at Kustendji, the vessels prefer to go to the latter port.

II.—IMPORTATION.

There being no exact tables in existence giving the imports of Galatz and Braila for the year 1863, the imports cannot be given in so certain and reliable figures as has been done with the exports. However, some importers have for many years collected all the information they were able to obtain on the subject; and the result of their labor is given, in the belief that the truth lies not very far from the figures given. According to their calculations, there were imported into Galatz during the year 1863—

	Francs.
Cotton yarn, cotton, woollen, silk, and linen manufactures........	15, 135, 200
Coffee, tea, sugar, spices.....................................	9, 960, 000
Fruits, fresh and dried, eatables, &c..........................	3, 060, 000

	Francs.
Oil	1, 040, 000
Salted fish and olives	1, 840, 000
Wine and spirits	692, 000
Tobacco and cigars	3, 800, 000
Iron and brass ware	4, 500, 000
Hardware and glassware	1, 397, 500
Sundries	987, 900
Total	**42, 412, 600**
	Or $8, 482, 520

How close the relation here is between export and import is to be seen by the proportional rise of both during 1863. For 1861 the value of imports was calculated at thirty-two million (32,000,000) francs, and in 1863 the value of the exports was one-fourth higher than the exports in 1861. If, therefore, the value of imports for 1863 is taken at 42,400,000 francs, this gives a strong proof that here the amount of importation is entirely dependent on the value of the export.

On account of the peasantry becoming more humanized, and especially the younger branches adopting successively the habits of more civilized nations in their dress and in their nutriment, the consumption of manufactures, and of tea, coffee, sugar, &c., is increasing from year to year. Not ten years have passed since the whole peasantry ate and drank scarcely anything but what the country produced, and their dress consisted of such linen, woollen, and leather material as the peasant cultivated himself, or took from his domestic animals, and spun, wove, and finished at home. This condition is changing rapidly, and the peasants use now for their dress a great quantity of cotton goods, and even silks and fine cloth are beginning to be demanded.

Formerly Hamburg used to supply the market with sugar, besides some came from Holland and Belgium; but now Marseilles supplies almost the whole amount which is consumed. In consequence of the higher prices of cotton, silk, woollen, and linen goods have been more demanded, and it is stated that, during the year 1863, $77,000 worth more of these goods have been ordered from the fairs at Leipsic and Frankfort than in 1862; in 1862 the amount was $120,000, and in 1863 $197,000.

Formerly Austria and Russia, as the neighbors, supplied this country with iron, steel, and brassware; but recently more competition has taken place, and the goods of the Westphalian industry are in increasing demand; also England has commenced to send her agents into this country, and its products find much approbation, which is based on the cheapness of the common goods, and the better quality of the finer goods. France has also sent some samples of its iron industry, which have found a ready sale; but it is Belgium particularly that drives all other competitors out of the market in certain articles.

Austria watches the commerce carefully, and has for some articles almost a monopoly; for example, in door locks. The Russian iron goods have been driven entirely from the market.

III.—SHIPPING.

The degree of activity in shipping, without regard to war eventualities, depends principally on the price paid for freight. To that place where high prices for freight are paid many vessels will be attracted. In consequence of this there will be competition, and a falling of the freight, which gives to the exporter the chance of adding to the price of the grain that amount which he pays less for freight. The greater the difference is between the price of grain in the producing country and the price in the consuming country, the higher the price which the exporter can pay for freight. The time when the exporter can operate to the greatest advantage is when freight falls on account of the numerous arrivals of vessels, and the demand for his breadstuffs is great, and when, at such a time, he had a large supply on hand. The exporters did not enjoy any such period during 1863.

Though a very fine harvest had placed a large quantity of breadstuffs at the disposal of the exporter, there was no lively demand for them from the consuming countries, and the difference in the price paid here and the price which was paid in the consuming country was so small, that, after paying freight, &c., there was scarcely any profit left to the exporter, and very often actual loss.

Under such circumstances it will be easily understood that the number of freight-seeking vessels was not sufficient to carry off all the grain that was ready for shipment. The fact that the shipping season closed several weeks earlier than the Danube froze up is a sufficient proof of this. According to the reliable report of the harbor-master of Sulina, the following vessels sailed from Sulina, including those which were laden on the roadstead of Sulina:

	Vessels.
America	6
Greece	1,073
Turkey	486
Italy	368
Great Britain	247
Austria	225
Ionian Islands	172
Russia	91
Rumania	67
Holland	30
France and Jerusalem	30
Samos	22
Hanover	19
Prussia	17
Norway	15
Mecklenburg	11
Oldenburg	5
Servia	3
Sweden	2
Bremen	1
Denmark	1
Total	2,891

In 1862, 2,842 vessels sailed from Sulina. As these figures do not correspond to the proportion of the grain exported in 1862 and 1863, it is to be remarked that the vessels in 1863 were of a larger tonnage, the tonnage of 1863 amounting to 468,919 tons, whilst in 1862 only 410,376 English tons were registered.

During the entire year of 1863 the price paid for freights did not vary much; for Galatz and Braila the freight varied from £7 6s. to £8 9s. per imperial quarter for England, and did not reach £9. These figures are to be regarded as below the medium freight.

The Sulina freights varied between £6 and £6 3s., which may be considered for large-sized vessels as a medium freight. Freight for the Mediterranean, however, improved considerably; it rose from three and a half francs per charge to five and five and a half francs for Marseilles.

Masters of American vessels cannot be sufficiently warned to use the utmost care in signing charter-parties for the Danube. Speculators are in the habit of chartering a number of vessels every winter, the vessels to arrive at the Danubian ports soon after the opening of the navigation. If freight, however, has fallen, or if there is not much demand for shipping after the arrival of these vessels, no consignee is to be found or no cargo is ready, and the masters have to re-charter at a low figure after having waited until their lay days have expired, and after great expense and vexation they receive no satisfaction, as the London or other English house which chartered them has thought it best to fail. If freight, however, rises, these speculators have their agents here who sell the charter-parties to the exporter, and in this way these speculators often succeed in making a fortune in one operation, as they often charter a great number of vessels at one time.

The depth of water on the bar of Sulina has been for the last two years steadily sixteen feet, but at the close of 1863 the depth was only fourteen feet. During the winter the bar has, however, resumed its former depth. It is very much to be regretted that the low stage of water on the banks of Argish generally causes great expense to the vessels from the middle of July to the end of the season on account of the expense they have to incur for lighterage, though they are obliged to pay very high dues, according to their tonnage and not according to their depth, to the European Commission of the Danube. These dues are, for a vessel of two hundred tons, about forty to fifty ducats, ($92 to $115,) and in the fall such a vessel has to pay about the same for lighterage.

In 1863 the European Commission of the Danube collected, at Sulina, from all vessels, including the steamers:

	Ducats.
For ordinary dues	78,304
For pilotage	7,280
For light-house	4,613
Total	90,197
	Or $207,453

The steamers running on the line Vienna-Galatz met during the year 1863 great difficulties, caused by the low stage of water, especially at the "Iron Gate." The passengers had to change steamers many times, and had even to be transported some distance by land. They were of course every time detained, and the goods could only be brought down late in the fall.

From Galatz started during 1863—

Up river, (steamers of the Vienna company:) 67 fast mail and passenger steamers, 41 passenger, 35 freight, 25 tug-boats, 19 propellers.

Down river: 30 passenger steamers for Odessa, connecting with the Vienna boats; 49 tug-boats, with barges, carrying grain to Sulina.

The steamers of the Austrian Lloyd carried most of the passengers and freight between Constantinople and Galatz, connecting at Galatz and Kustendji with the Vienna boats. Eighty-four steamers of this company, with passengers and freight, arrived from Constantinople at Galatz and Kustendji.

The steamers of the "Messageries Imperiales" carried mostly freight between Marseilles and Galatz, but latterly have also carried many passengers, as the management has improved. These steamers arrived forty-three times at Galatz.

In connexion with the Vienna boats, the steamers of a Russian company ran thirty-six times between here and Odessa, besides thirty steamboat trips mentioned which the Vienna company performed. Further, a steamer of the Vienna company made a weekly trip from Braila to Galatz, Reni, Tultscha, Ismail, and back; and made more frequent trips between Galatz and Braila.

The following companies took a share in the transportation of grain down the river from the Iron Gate to Czernawoda, Braila, Galatz, and Sulina, to supply the sailing-vessels with that amount of grain which was carried by land into the magazines of Braila and Galatz: the Danubian Steamboat Company, the Wallachian Steamboat Company, the Greek and Oriental Steamboat Company, (English,) the Bavarian Steamboat Company, the Greek House of Tocca.

The steamboat business is increasing from year to year, and on all the tributaries of the Danube steamers are now to be found. Last year there was only one steamer on the Pruth, and this year there are five.

It would be well for American capitalists who are acquainted with steamboating to consider if it would not be an excellent investment of their capital to engage in steamboating on the Danube and its tributaries, in the American style.

The Bavarian company commenced business only in the year 1863 on the Lower Danube, having since 1856 done business on the river Inn and on the Upper Danube, between Donanworth and Pesth. This company had two steamers, of fifty horse power each, and twelve barges, each carr ing from 1,000 to 5,000 hundred-weight of freight. The company transported during 1863—

Down river: 30,860 Braila kilos (71,595 imperial quarters) from Cetate to Czernawoda, Braila; 8,000 cwt. of coal from Drencova to Giurgevo; 385 passengers, and tugged several vessels.

Up river: 4,156 kilos grain; 38,299 cwt. of goods, wool, &c.

The total receipts amounted to 600,191 Braila piastres, or about $43,000. If of this amount 80 per cent. is deducted for expenses, &c., the result for the first year might be called very favorable, as the value of the above-mentioned two steamers, and of the twelve barges, does not exceed $86,000. The company has therefore added for 1864 one steamer and several barges to the others; and now also does steamboating business on the Pruth and Sereth.

REMARKS.

1. On exchange.

The price of exchange did not fluctuate much during the year 1863, as, through the continual export of grain, a steady demand for exchange, especially on London, was kept up.

Rates:

	Highest.		Lowest.		
London, three months...	94½	G. piastres.	97¼	G. piastres.	per £. sterling.
Berlin and Leipsig, 3 mos.	14	"	14 12/40	"	" Prus. thaler
Genoa, three months....	3 7/9	"	3 4/4	"	" lira.
Vienna, three months...	7 8/10	"	8 12/40	"	" florin.
Marseilles, three months.	3 4/9	"	3 4/4	"	" franc.
Hamburg, three months.	7 6/40	"	7 6/40	"	" fls. banco.

2. On railroads.

No railroad is as yet under construction in the Danubian principalities; but as the railroad from Limburg to Czernowitz (Buckowina) is to be completed in three years, a contract has been sanctioned by Prince Couza and the legislature which, if fulfilled, will complete the line from Czernowitz to Galatz in six years. The road is to run from Galatz by way of the valley of the Sereth, and to touch at Tecutsch, Berlad, Roman, and Botowchani, and to have branches to Braila, Toxchani, the Okna, and Jassy, and, if the government demands it, also a branch to the Pruth. The contractors for this road are Salamanca, Delahonti, Prince

Sapriha, Mavroyeni, Brassey, Sir Morton Peto, and Betts. The Russian line, which is already nearly completed from Odessa to Bender, is to run from Bender to Kitchaneuf, and thence to Pruth, connecting with the Galatz-Czernowitz line; contractor, Salamanca.

On the southern side of the Danube the Czernowitz-Custendje line has been completed, and is in running order; and for the line Varna-Rustchuk, Mr. Crampton, Sir Morton Peto, and Betts have contracted, and work upon it has commenced. The railroad lines in Wallachia have not yet been settled; but the papers state that a contract has been given to Mr. Ward to build a railroad from the Hungarian frontier to Braila.

It will be seen by this report that up to the present time there is no direct trade between the United States and the Danubian principalities; but there exists no reason that this should always be the case, even if there should be at first some difficulty to take from here a full cargo to the United States. The vessels might always take a cargo of grain to some continental or English port, and return from that port, with a cargo, to the United States. And it is to be remarked that these countries are, and will be for many years, entirely dependent upon foreign countries for all manufactured articles which they consume. But American merchants who desire to sell their products here must do as the merchants of other nations do—they must send agents, with samples of their goods, to this country; and before they do this no commerce of any importance can spring up, as without this there is no chance that mercantile houses which are established here will order articles from the United States.

The principalities are in great need of many articles which the United States produce, and I will only mention all kinds of hardware, axes, cooking-stoves, Yankee notions, &c. In one respect the condition of the principalities is very much the same as that of the United States—labor being very scarce, and fertile land in abundance. Therefore all kinds of labor-saving machines find a ready market. And three agents in Galatz alone supply the demand for agricultural implements, which are mostly of English manufacture. (Only Wood's reaper, for which the demand is much greater than the supply, represents American ingenuity.) One of these agents sold at Galatz during the year 1863 one hundred thousand dollars' worth of threshing machines and other agricultural implements.

There is now a great demand for a threshing machine on which linseed can be threshed. Perhaps the United States might supply this article, with innumerable others.

NOVEMBER, 1864.

The prospects which the producers entertained of realizing from a very abundant harvest rich earnings have met during the last two months with several checks, partly by the action of the elements and partly by laws which have been decreed of late.

In consequence of much wet weather during harvesting time, wheat particularly has been seriously damaged and has lost in color and weight, and a large amount is not fit for shipment at all, and has to be retained on the estates on this account; besides, from the very low prices the producer will realize much less than he had a right to expect.

On the 26th of August there appeared, further, a law for Rumania, which freed the peasants from the labor which they had to perform for the proprietors, and gave them property of their own; and though, according to the law, the peasants were to work for the proprietors until they had been invested with their own property, the near prospect of being free and proprietors themselves has interfered very much with their usual labor. As these peasants not only tilled the soil, harvested the grain, &c., but also transported the produce with their own teams to the shipping place, most of the proprietors are placed in a very unpleasant position, as not sufficient time is given to them to acquire the dead and live stock, even if they had the means to do so, which most of them have not, and in consequence of this I should judge that for the future the amount of grain sown and harvested will be considerably less than usual. Again, there appeared on the 8th September a law which re-established the export duty of five per cent. which had been abolished on the 1st April, 1862, and which has taken effect on the 13th October, 1864. This law, it is understood, was meant by the lawgivers to be levied on commerce, but as nearly all merchants buy only after the receipt of orders from England, &c., and as they have no large quantities lying on speculation, they buy from the producer, who keeps it in his warehouse until it is wanted for shipment; and it seems very clear to me that this duty falls also on the producer, and injures commerce only in so far as a quantity of grain which hitherto could only be brought with a small profit from a long distance to the place of shipment will now remain where it is grown.

The prices for grain have fallen considerably; they were in piastres or kilogrammes of Galatz—

	At the beginning of August.	End of October
Wheat, kilogrammes	155, 200	100, 160
Indian corn, kilogrammes	118, 121	105, 108½
Rye, kilogrammes.....................	112, 115	7, 081
Barley, kilogrammes..................	6, 568	5, 559½

The demand for breadstuffs is very small, and it is long since prices were as low as they are at present. Wheat is now principally shipped for Italy, rye for Holland, and barley for England and Marseilles. Indian corn is scarcely shipped at the present time, but the crop of Indian corn has been excellent. Large quantities of grain harvested this year have arrived already at the shipping places, so that the rent for warehouses has risen considerably. A great amount of the grain arrives in a wet condition and has to be worked over before it is fit for shipping, but a large quantity also arrives in a good condition, and this keeps up the demand for vessels.

Wheat, per kilogramme.........................	120, 177 Braila piastres
Rye " "	90, 100	do
Barley " "	4, 365	do
Maize " "	108, 111	do

Vessels are chartered at the following rates :

	October 16.	November 1.
Soulina for England...........£7 6 to £7 9	£6 3 to £6 9 per quarter.
Kustendji for England........ 7 6 to 7 9	6 3 to 6 9 do
Galatz and Braila for England. 9 6 to 10 0	8 6 to 9 0 do
Galatz and Braila for Marseilles 5 and 5½ pia's	4¾ and 5 pia's per charge.
Galatz and Braila for Genoa.. 4¾ and 5 pia's	4½ and 4¾ pia's do

Galatz and Braila for Constantinople 95 and 100 paras per kilogramme, (nominal.)

The expenses for lighterage amount to about £7 to £8 per 100 quarters.

The stage of water, however, has been very good during the whole summer, and the usual complaints that passengers and goods did not arrive in due time have scarcely been heard. At present, on account of the fogs and the low state of the water, the steamers are not able to be punctual.

The depth of water on the lower Danube is as follows:

	October 16.	November 1.
At the bar of Soulina	16	15¼ feet English.
At the Batmich Kavac	17	15¾ do
At the Gorgoon	16¼	15½ do
At the banks of Argish	15	13¾ do
At the Little Argish	15¾	15½ do
At the Tchatal of St. George	14¾	14½ do

The merchants anticipate a heavy spring business, as they expect large quantities of grain to be transported during the winter from the interior to the place of shipping.

The export of wool has been considerable, especially to France and Transylvania, but not as much as usual went up the river into Austria. Unwashed Zigay wool rose continually in price, and up to 60 silver roubles have been paid in Bessarabia for 8 poods, (100 okes,) and in Braila 6½ Braila piastres per oke. The wool for French account was all shipped in an unwashed condition.

The demand and price for cocoons have improved.

The export of petroleum begins to be considerable, and in the month of September five vessels laden with petroleum sailed from Braila, of which three were laden for England and two for France.

The wine crop will be good in quantity but poor in quality. In case good roads and railroads should be constructed—and there is nothing heard at present of the building of railroads—and the wine manufactured in such a careful manner that it will not spoil as soon as it gets to sea, as it does at present, the exportation of wine from here will become an important business.

As the peasants of Roumania and Bulgaria have had a good harvest, tho sale of common dry-goods and shirtings, gray leng cloth, twists, &c., has been very good, though the prices have been very high; but for the finer goods which are bought by the proprietors there has been very little demand, as this class which used to buy them cannot afford it at present.

As the merchants are of opinion that the war in the United States is drawing to a close, they are very careful not to have too many goods on hand, as they expect prices to fall suddenly.

In sugar, Austria has commenced to compete with France, which has had almost a monopoly of this article during the last two years; also Austrian champagne and Austrian and Hungarian wines commence to take the place of those of France.

The business in agricultural implements and machines has been very good, and the demand has been always greater than the supply. About seven hundred threshing machines, mostly moved by steam power, have already been sold in the principalities, and now that the peasants will become proprietors and labor still scarce, as the peasants will probably not continue to work' even for wages for the large proprietors, but on their own soil, the demand for threshing machines driven by horses or oxen will be greatly increased. Exchange has been high all summer:

London, three months,	95½ a 96¾ G. ps. in £.
Paris, "	3.32 in francs.
Marseilles, "	3.31½ a 3.32 in francs.
Italy, "	3.29½ a 3.31 in francs.
Amsterdam, "	8.5 in florins.
Hamburg, "	7.7 in banco fls.

Berlin and Leipsig, three months, 14.18 in thalers.
Vienna, (always at sight,) 7.14 a 7.16 in florins.
Austrian ducat, 46 G. ps., Napoleon d'or, 77 ps.; Turkish lira, 88½ G. ps.

EGYPT.

ALEXANDRIA—A. HALE, *Consul General.*

FEBRUARY 24, 1865.

The commercial interest of Egypt at present is engrossed by cotton, which overshadows everything else. Even the production of breadstuffs, heretofore a principal article, (Egypt was anciently "the granary of the world,") has largely declined, the exports from 1,700,000 bushels in 1863 having dwindled to only 155,000 bushels in 1864. The export of rice, rags, gums, ostrich feathers, mother-of-pearl, tortoise shell, and other articles of trade hitherto important, has likewise diminished, while the export of cotton has increased in prodigious proportions. The export of cotton from Egypt were—

	Pounds.
In 1861	60,000,000
1862	82,000,000
1863	128,700,000
1864	173,604,500

That is to say, the export of cotton has trebled in quantity within three years. If we look at the prices of the staple the augmentation has been still more remarkable.
The custom-house value of the export was—

In 1861	$7,154,400
1862	24,603,300
1863	46,782,450
1864	74,213,500

Showing that the export of cotton has increased ten-fold in value within three years.

Gold and silver have poured into the country, and many large fortunes have been quickly made. Although nothing but specie is known in business or in the common operations of trade, a rise in prices has been general, similar to that which, in our own country, has been attributed to the abundant use of paper money. Rents are doubled, and the cost of the necessaries of life augmented in an equal proportion.   *   *   *   *

Meanwhile a large European emigration has poured into Egypt. The arrivals in a single week have been sometimes counted by two or three thousand, equal numerically to the whole Frank population of Alexandria ten years ago, and now estimated at seventy-five thousand.   *   *   Many are mere speculating adventurers, while others bring capital and large business experience.

The minimum rate of interest is ten per cent. per annum. Two and three per cent. per month is often paid by parties of the first position for temporary loans. The direct communication between Egypt and the United States has, of course, fallen off in consequence of the war. There was but one arrival at and two departures from this port for New York during the year 1864. The direct commerce between this country and the United States was never very brisk, by reason of the identity in the great staple productions of both, to wit: cotton, corn, and sugar.

Comparative sta'ement showing the description, quantity, and value of the exports from the port of Alexandria during the years 1861, 1862, 1863, and 1864.

Articles, weight, and measure.	1861 Quantity	1861 Value	1862 Quantity	1862 Value	1863 Quantity	1863 Value	1864 Quantity	1864 Value
		Piastres.		*Piastres.*		*Piastres.*		*Piastres.*
Buffalo horns .... mille	1,168	692,800	1,300	620,000	970	410,000	850	380,000
Cotton, Mako .... cantar	596,200	143,088,200	820,110	494,066,000	1,297,100	935,649,000	1,740,000	1,484,970,000
Chick pease .... ardeb	4,825	337,750	4,301	318,673	4,370	315,000	1,680	113,000
Berries, Turkey .... cantar	1,199	119,900	1,300	130,000	350	37,000	280	31,000
Beeswax .... oke	96,140	1,922,800	156,000	3,120,000	83,000	2,090,000	104,400	2,998,000
Coffee .... cantar	23,203	6,964,900	34,066	11,948,380	93,000	9,780,000	98,000	9,498,000
Soda ashes .... cantar	25,393	1,014,760	36,000	914,580	19,000	690,000	10,500	490,000
Dates, divers .... cantar	38,574	1,092,954	15,248		11,000	910,000		968,000
Drugs, divers .... cole	6,797	2,732,054	6,530	2,630,000	5,800	2,300,000	4,400	1,660,000
Elephant tusks .... cantar	6,508	5,016,000	3,400	3,500,000	1,100	2,600,000	1,400	3,941,000
Beans .... cantar	607,981	39,500,000	590,000	33,400,000	310,700	38,280,000	58,000	5,452,000
Iron, assorted .... cantar	8,472	339,889	6,300	310,000	5,700	984,000	4,600	520,000
Glass, &c. .... tar	121,713	13,289,430	112,116	12,853,340	105,000	15,969,000	77,000	15,677,000
Wheat .... ardeb	938,834	67,520,680	1,293,677	86,220,374	854,400	64,380,000	87,000	8,613,000
Maize .... ardeb	89,466	4,300,000	82,033	4,101,650	132,200	6,880,000	35,500	95,000
Henna .... tar	22,687	906,680	25,000	1,200,000	21,300	885,000	19,500	890,000
Incense .... cantar	4,494	674,100	6,000	900,000	4,100	694,000	7,000	1,058,000
Wool .... cantar	91,871	4,574,300	29,380	8,774,000	18,000	5,954,000	14,000	5,220,000
Flax .... cantar	91,404	2,354,440	25,805	2,967,575	21,000	3,150,000	11,000	9,222,000
Lentils .... ardeb	53,748	4,900,400	75,185	4,058,990	62,000	3,720,000	9,700	900,000
Lupines .... ardeb	110	4,400	3,811	163,873	1,250	62,500	300	30,000
Mother-of-pearl .... tar	8,719	1,569,430	8,584	1,545,120	10,000	1,089,000	6,300	615,000
Sundry I bundles .... cola	57,633	6,442,970	18,200	7,225,000	15,400	6,970,000	14,600	6,680,000
Manufactures .... cola	2,528	10,846,533	1,800	16,730,000	950	14,700,000	720	13,200,000
Essence of roses .... ounce	90,105	644,700	21,000	650,000	19,500	580,000	23,700	685,000
Natron, divers .... cantar	37,580	1,352,880	58,000	3,134,040	49,700	1,890,000	93,500	3,464,000
Barley .... ardeb	194,176	8,600,000	279,576	11,183,040	115,900	5,680,000	5,000	443,000
gum .... oke	13,047	1,043,760	16,000	1,280,000	10,220	610,000	8,400	451,000
Pepper .... cantar	889	2,055,191	720	150,000		110,000	400	97,000
Salted hides .... number	112,323	2,982,800	174,640	3,318,160	903,600	3,665,000	365,000	5,700,000
Ostrich feathers .... rot.	19,818	2,161,680	50,000	7,500,000	42,000	6,300,000	34,000	4,800,000
Peas .... ardeb	2,121	941,536	4,977	258,804	4,750	318,000	1,970	290,000
Caviare .... oke	15,096		16,200	310,000	9,400	250,000	4,200	112,000
Rice .... ardeb	35,501	10,050,300	29,990	7,837,200	25,000	8,800,000	9,200	3,850,000
Rum .... oke								
Senna .... cantar	7,708	847,880	5,760	653,600	8,700	748,200	3,300	210,000
Ammoniac salt .... i tar	1,925	197,342	1,300	210,000	300	110,000	650	192,000
Seeds, various .... ardeb								
Cotton-seed .... 1 ℔.	306,254	12,920,100	453,519	82,675,950	788,200	47,358,000	915,000	53,665,000

Comparative statement showing the description, quantity, and value of exports, &c.—Continued.

Articles, weight, and measure.	1861. Quantity.	1861. Value.	1862. Quantity.	1862. Value.	1863. Quantity.	1863. Value.	1864. Quantity.	1864. Value.
		Piastres.		*Piastres.*		*Piastres.*		*Piastres.*
Sesamum-seed .... ardeb.	3,533	646,600	2,765	497,700	2,400	502,000	950	205,000
Linseed .... ardeb.	89,727	8,567,940	35,277	4,036,855	1,900	192,000	3,600	534,000
Maiz .... cola.	1,710	1,022,623	1,800	1,290,000	1,700	1,350,000	1,850	1,610,000
Salt .... ardeb.	15,821	128,210	16,000	1,162,000	11,900	130,000	11,850	135,000
Saltpetre .... cantar.	10,000	885,600	14,756	929,628	3,400	914,300	7,000	441,000
Silke .... cola.	94	196,800	30	925,000	98	900,000	25	280,000
Tamarinds .... cantar.	1,638	248,700	1,400	210,000	600	110,000	250	54,000
Linen cloth .... pieces.	32,369	485,535	36,000	400,000	23,000	440,000	16,000	360,000
Tortoise-shells .... rot.	1,802	360,400	2,100	420,000	1,900	380,000	1,000	220,000
Tombac .... oke.	296,408	444,611	270,000	450,000	255,000	694,000	220,000	635,000
Safflower .... cantar.	1,956	117,380	730	51,100	800	56,000	550	42,000
Sugar .... cantar.	14,184	1,609,990	33,751	3,786,385	1,000	320,000	400	140,000
Empty semblin .... cola.	18,585	1,185,078	17,300	1,050,000	15,000	1,020,000	18,000	1,370,000
Rags .... cantar.	65,644	2,138,530	108,684	3,532,230	86,000	3,100,000	80,000	2,965,000
Total		374,341,039		780,694,098		1,203,144,900		1,644,571,600

NOTE.—The values here are given in government piastres, of which twenty are equal to one dollar in American gold.

GREECE.

Piræus—H. M. Canfield, *Consul.*

September 30, 1864.

Commercial report.

I have the honor to report that a comparison of the exports and imports forming the general commerce of Greece shows, with a single exception, (the importation of hides and the exportation of leather, explained by the establishment of the tanneries at Lyra,) the production of crude material and the consumption of manufactured articles.

A similar comparison, commencing in 1857, when the first very imperfect statistics were kept, and extending to 1862, shows a constant predominance of the value of the imports over those of the exports, yet a predominance which, with the exception of 1861, has been steadily decreasing. It may be confidently anticipated that the economy necessary in consequence of the high price of cotton and other fabrics which form the principal articles of import, and the unwillingness of the merchants to expose themselves to the risks consequent upon the unsettled state of the country for the past two years, on the one hand, and the extremely fruitful season of 1863, and the still more promising one of this year, will have in the last year reduced this surplus still lower, and in this create a balance in favor of the exportations.

The total value of the commerce of Greece for 1862, including exports and imports, represents a value of 81,433,392 drachmas, composed of—

Importations.................................... 49,109,166 drachmas.
Exportations.................................... 32,323,726   "

Subtracting from the first sum the amount entered in the bonded warehouses, viz., 4,981,193 drachmas, and from the second the amount shipped from the same, viz., 4,296,078, and the remainders 44,128,473 drachmas, and 28,027,648 may be fairly supposed to represent the value entered in and shipped from the country during that time.

The principal articles of consumption were for that year—

1st. Fabrics of cotton, woollen, linen, silk, and other materials, amounting in all to 9,337,551 drachmas, in the following proportions:

	Drachmas.
Cotton fabrics	3,463,954
Woollen "	3,227,165
Linen ::	556,915
Silk "	438,317
Various other fabrics	1,641,200

The principal sources of supply were England, France, and Austria.

2d. *Unworked hides.*—The importation of this article amounts to 2,784,360 okes, worth 230,527 drachmas, over the amount imported the previous year. The principal sources of supply were England, France, Turkey, Egypt, Belgium, and Italy.

3d. *Cereal grains and breadstuffs,* amounting to 615,546 kilos, valued at 3,822,192 drachmas. As the cereals were exported to the value of 1,061,574 drachmas, only the remainder, 2,760,618 drachmas, should be allowed as the amount of the actual import. The importation of flour was 291,819 okes, valued at 139,536 drachmas.

H. Ex. Doc. 60——43

4th. *Sugar.*—Amounting to 2,182,528 okes, valued at 3,034,326 drachmas, an increase of 223,809 okes, valued at 201,629 drachmas, over the amount reported for the previous year. The sugar used is wholly beet sugar, and the principal sources of supply were France, England, and Holland.

5th. *Timber for building.*—The different kinds of which were valued at 2,168,933 drachmas, an increase of 40,589 drachmas over the amount imported in 1861.

6th. *Animals,* including horned cattle, horses, sheep, &c., valued at 2,093,116. The principal source of supply is Turkey in Europe, especially the provinces of Thessaly and Epirus, upon which the whole of continental Greece and the islands depend for their supply of fresh meats.

7th. *Iron,* unworked and manufactured, valued at 1,338,890 drachmas.

8th. *Coffee,* valued at 1,008,818 drachmas.

9th. *Salt provisions,* valued at 1,246,028 drachmas.

For all these articles, comprising a value of 29,425,292 drachmas, and nearly three-fourths of the entire value of her importations, Greece is wholly dependent upon commerce, having no resources, either natural or artificial, for their home production.

The importation from America was—

	Quantity in okes.	Value in drachmas
Colonial wares	13,465	37,727
Dyestuffs (cochineal)	18	540
Printed books	30	300
Hides	34,738	130,832
Flour	4,942	3,459
Coffee	116,456	306,787
Dried fruits	7	50
Rice	4,241	2,545
Seeds	202	23
Cotton fabrics (coarse)	571	3,105
" " (fine)	127	390
Other merchandise, raw materials		84
Total		485,842

equal to $80,973 66.

The only changes which I anticipate for future years are in the increase of the importation of petroleum, of which a small quantity was introduced in 1863; its quality was so much superior to the European varieties that it will eventually take their place. Also, the introduction of machinery, of which the country has real need, and the possible introduction of cane sugars and sirups.

The principal articles of export were for the same year, 1862—

1st. *Currants.*—The exportation amounted to 79,402,318 pounds, valued at 13,235,870 drachmas; in comparison with the previous year there was an augmentation in weight of 6,710,156 pounds, but a diminution in value of 407,923 drachmas. After the currants came—

2d. *Leather,* to the value of 2,604,609, superior to the value in 1861 by 7,111,082 drachmas.

3d. *Figs,* at 1,648,629 drachmas, 258,000 more than in 1861.

4th. *Olive oil,* 1,503,807 " 811,301 " "
5th. *Valonia,* 1,381,696 " 16,807 " ..
6th. *Cereals,* 1,061,574 " 116,997 "
7th. *Spirits,* 1,022,039 "
8th. *Cocoons,* 777,789 "
9th. *Animals,* 565,907 "
10th. *Smoking tobacco,* 464,782 drachmas.

The whole amounts exported to America were—

Dried fruits—currants	425, 494 pounds,	79, 141 drachmas.
" figs	985 quintals,	19, 692 "
Total		98, 833	..

During the past year, 1863, and the present one, 1864, the high price of cotton has given a new impulse to the cultivation of this article, which, for those years, will probably take the first rank among the productions of the country. This staple has been grown in Greece since the sixteenth century, but never in great quantities, since the difficulties attendant upon the cultivation, especially the irrigation necessary during the summer months, have prevented even the best district, Lebadea, from competing with the United States, and reduced its exportation to a comparatively insignificant amount.

The amount exported was—

In 1857.....................................	227 quintals (44 okes.)
1858.....................................	162 "
1859.....................................	35 ::
1860.....................................	183 ..
1861.....................................	714 ..
1862.....................................	3, 844 ..

Its destination was, in 1861, in the following proportions—

To England...	16, 500 okes.
Ionian islands..	10, 472 "
Austria	3, 476 ":
Turkey in Europe	924 ..
France	44 ..

The quantity exported in 1862 was sent in the following proportions:

To Austria...	48, 664 okes.
Turkey	36, 996 "
France...	31, 152 ::
Ionian islands..	28, 864 ..
England	23, 760 ..

The amount sent from the port of Piræus in 1863 was exported in the following proportions:

To England...	145, 500 okes.
France...	68, 553 "
Austria	36, 693 ::
Turkey...	24, 696 ..
Italy....	270 ..

The price per quintal of 44 okes at the Piræus in 1863 varied from 230,280 to 320 drachmas. The price was, at the commencement of this month, $1\frac{80}{100}$ the oke for Lebadea unginned, but it has commenced to fall, and ranges at this date from $1\frac{50}{100}$ to $1\frac{60}{100}$ drachmas at the place where produced. The cotton of Lebadea is of excellent quality, ranking with the first qualities American long staple; $2\frac{1}{2}$ to 3 okes unginned give 1 oak clean. The cotton of the Peloponessus is inferior in quality and would be sold proportionately cheaper, as 4 to $4\frac{1}{2}$ okes uncleaned give but 1 oke clean. Until 1862 the export duty was $1\frac{30}{100}$ drachmas per quintal, by law, of that year; this duty was removed and an "impôt foncier" of 9 drachmas the quintal substituted. In practice no difference exists between the "impôt foucier" and an export duty of the same amount. The expenses, custom-house charges, (impôt foucier,) cartage from the interior, &c., reach 80 lepta ($\frac{80}{100}$) drachmas the oke.

The currant crop of this year is unusually good, the quantity produced being estimated at about 80,000,000 pounds, and, what is quite rare of late years, comparatively uninjured by the rains, they not having fallen until the curing was generally completed. The price at the commencement of the season varied from 28 to 35 dollars per 100 pounds for the best qualities, Vostizas and Petras. The price at this date is 25 dollars per 100 pounds for the same qualities. The estimated value of the crop of this year is about 14,000,000 drachmas.

The figs of Halamas, which promise this year to form one of the principal articles of export, are inferior in quality to those of Smyrna, and comparatively cheaper in price. The crop this year (1864) was better than that of any previous one, partly because the plantations are now old enough to have nearly reached their full bearing, and especially on account of the extremely favorable season. The price at this date ranges from 170 to 180 drachmas per 100 armathas, (baskets,) weighing about 600 okes, since the armatha contains 60 figs.

The introduction of steam vessels bids fair to take the commerce of the Mediterranean from the Greeks ; they have hitherto been second only to the English in tonnage. The number of vessels is increasing, but the size decreasing, as shown by the tables annexed.

Table of general and special commerce.

Years	GENERAL			Years	SPECIAL		
	Imports.	Exports.	Totals.		Imports.	Exports.	Totals.
	Dr.	*Dr.*	*Dr.*		*Dr.*	*Dr.*	*Dr.*
1857	44,945,518	22,865,185	73,111,703	1857	36,636,235	24,362,957	60,999,192
1858	49,962,317	27,888,247	77,850,561	1858	40,405,341	25,024,008	65,429,341
1859	57,650,727	30,467,429	88,118,156	1859	46,944,855	24,431,787	70,676,643
1860	51,630,886	31,891,451	83,522,337	1860	53,979,899	26,931,413	80,911,312
1861	49,109,666	32,383,726	81,433,392	1861	47,914,036	29,107,135	76,021,171
1862				1862	44,128,473	28,027,648	73,156,181

Table of the principal articles exported from Greece during 1857–1862.

Years	CURRANTS		LEATHER.		FIGS, (dried.)		OIL, (olive.)		VALONIA.		CEREALS.		COTTON.	COCOONS.	EMERY.	MARBLE.
	No. of lbs., Venetian.	Value in drachmas.	No. of okes.	Value in drachmas.	No. of quintals.	Value in drachmas.	No. of okes.	Value in drachmas.	No. of quintals.	Value in drachmas.	No. of kilos.	Value in drachmas.	Value in drachmas.	Value in drachmas.	Value in drachmas.	Value in drachmas.
1857	62,961,050	13,474,699	396,146	2,692,097	70,646	737,743	689,650	56,590	88,088	459,295	......	......	15,641	493,934	......	......
1858	55,314,650	11,800,922	250,094	1,462,592	52,187	1,960,037	241,790	739,904	62,551	974,848	......	......	11,100	783,257	......	......
1859	79,901,660	12,557,551	......	906,664	......	754,839	......	286,350	......	644,334	......	......	1,823	872,459	2,943	......
1860	79,892,182	14,106,954	390,494	1,124,439	111,784	1,729,422	67,745	97,477	82,969	691,790	30,236	902,971	12,318	1,548,158	556,421	32,460
1861	79,462,318	13,643,733	477,671	1,699,629	84,744	1,390,627	521,336	692,506	107,771	1,364,889	86,066	471,893	36,801	983,610	391,795	22,790
1862		13,925,870		2,604,609		1,646,629		1,503,807		1,381,696		1,061,574			191,921	

Table of principal articles imported from 1857 to 1862.

Years	FABRICS. Value in drachmas.	HIDES. No. of okes.	HIDES. Value in drachmas.	CEREALS. No. of kilos.	CEREALS. Value in drachmas.	SUGAR. No. of okes.	SUGAR. Value in drachmas.	LUMBER. Value in drachmas.	ANIMALS. Value in drachmas.	IRON. Value in drachmas.	SALT PROVISIONS. Value in drachmas.	COFFEE. Value in drachmas.	ROPES AND CORDAGE. Value in drachmas.
1857	9,632,649	....	1,103,455	....	3,900,597	1,913,913	2,458,970	1,977,694	678,347	1,405,181	....	799,919	....
1858	9,962,005	1,681,043	4,255,446	680,947	3,782,919	2,141,560	2,992,549	1,468,446	1,363,032	1,404,301	1,929,978	1,025,538	1,281,454
1859	9,732,539	1,690,880	4,570,219	1,170,365	3,226,731	1,833,364	3,015,819	2,338,731	1,396,897	1,333,990	1,512,806	1,066,139	2,018,069
1860	12,367,115	2,137,736	3,801,585	1,400,587	10,164,748	1,958,719	2,667,702	2,467,001	1,942,711	1,623,155	1,901,763	1,213,401	2,906,909
1861	11,482,053	2,106,942	3,806,044	954,192	6,452,997	1,959,719	2,832,697	2,128,344	2,049,782	1,911,555	....	1,029,705	1,724,855
1862	9,377,551	2,794,350	5,135,902	615,546	3,892,198	2,182,598	3,054,326	2,166,933	2,063,116	1,338,890	1,946,098	1,106,68	....

Table of the Greek merchant marine from 1857 to 1862.

Date.	FIRST CLASS. VESSELS. No.	FIRST CLASS. Tonnage.	SECOND CLASS. VESSELS. No.	SECOND CLASS. Tonnage.	Total No. vessels.	Total tonnage.	No. of equipage.
December 31, 1857	....	....	....	....	4,339	385,000	25,000
December 31, 1858	2,660	98,567	1,258	941,697	3,893	268,600	23,198
December 31, 1859	2,504	99,875	1,480	944,605	3,984	274,480	23,918
December 31, 1860	2,857	29,193	1,913	523,892	4,070	262,675	23,848
December 31, 1861	3,008	29,927	1,150	925,900	4,153	255,977	23,943
December 31, 1862	3,181	34,556	1,153	922,613	4,335	257,318	23,839

KANAGAWA—GEORGE S. FISHER, *Consul.*

DECEMBER 28, 1863.

Our peaceful relations still continue uninterrupted, and trade and commerce of this port, anomalous as it really is, seem quite satisfactory.

The exports of raw silk to date are only about 1,300 bales, less than at the same date last year, and it is now coming in quite as freely as desired.

The exports of tea are nearly 800,000 pounds greater than at the same date last year, while the exports of raw cotton are six times greater than for the same period last year. I also note the prices of the latter staple have increased at this port over 100 per cent. within the last sixty days; now commanding the high rate of $35 per picul.

JUNE 4, 1864.

Since your last the quietness of our community has continued uninterrupted, while trade and commerce have not, if at all, improved.

As regards American business, it seems, I regret to say, rapidly declining, and our shipping and carrying trade has nearly ceased, or is transferred to and absorbed by other nationalities. This, although one of the unavoidable consequences of our long-continued domestic troubles, coupled with the impunity with which the rovers of the seas roam about, has about driven our flag from the ocean, at least on this side of the world. And such is the extreme rate of insurance, and the prejudice and misrepresentation, that our merchant marine has become utterly unable to procure a pound of freight or a charter, even at unreasonable rates, either for coasting, China, or long voyages. American vessels are, therefore, forced to be sold for what they will bring, or change their colors, or lie at anchor or at wharf rotting.

There has been of late somewhat increased business in raw silk and cotton, both having slightly given way in price. Tea remains about the same in price, but the quantity has rapidly fallen off; small samples of the new crop, however, begin to appear, and increased trade may soon be looked for, provided no new restrictions or political excitement take place.

Imports have slightly improved in a few articles, particularly round and nail rod-iron, cotton yarn, camlets, &c., and, under the new concession of duties, we hope may still more largely increase.

RESTRICTIONS ON TRADE.

In relation to restrictions upon trade, the past five months have demonstrated, beyond the possibility of doubt by the most skeptical, that this government, by its officials, does interfere in and control almost every, if not every, branch of trade, industry, and business here, and probably at all the open ports; and I now believe it susceptible of proof that all business, all trades, all mechanics, all teachers, servants, coolies, boatmen, and laborers of every kind, are compelled to pay one-quarter to one-third of their gross wages to the Japanese government for the privilege of doing business and living here; and no gardener, provision dealer, wood merchant, fisherman, or compradore of any kind can furnish even a pound of necessary supplies for the foreign consumption without a special permit and duty. All this, you are well aware, is in direct contravention of treaty rights.

THE CURRENCY OF THE COUNTRY.

Besides this, the currency of the country is depreciated far below what i ought to be, and I am so fully in the belief that it is more and more debase that I shall by the first opportunity transmit to the superintendent of the branch mint at San Francisco some of the present circulation (itzibu) for assay. One now before me, fresh from the mint, is nearly half green with verdigris, and I feel persuaded it contains much whitened copper.

AMERICAN VESSELS IN PORT.

The only shipping in port is one brig, loading tea for New York. The arrivals for the quarter so far are only three vessels.

FOREIGN MEN-OF-WAR IN PORT.

The English have in port fifteen men-of-war; the Dutch two; the French two.

TEA SHIPMENTS TO AMERICA.

The tea shipments to America for the season 1864–'65 are likely to be important, but mostly through British houses and in British bottoms.

JUNE 29, 1864.

The silk and tea season 1863–'64, now closed, has not been so unpropitious as at one time anticipated, and the business year closes probably more favorable to trade and commerce than reasonably could have been expected, considering the continued uneasiness pervading all ranks of the people of this country, as well as the unsettled condition of the political relations with all the treaty powers.

The exports of raw silk for the first quarter of 1863 and 1864 were in advance of 1862 and 1863, but since that time have steadily fallen off until the close of the season. The number of bales for the year foot up total exports to all countries 15,923 bales, against 25,891 for 1862 and 1863.

Since the opening of the port exports of raw silk have been—

	Bales.
1860–'61	7,703
1861–'62	11,915
1862–'63	25,891
1863–'64	15,923

A falling off in 1863–'64, as compared with 1862–'63, in round numbers of 10,000 bales, but not in proportionate value.

The total value of the silk exported 1863–'64 I place at 6,500,000 Mexican dollars.

The number of pounds of tea exported during the year to all countries is 5,594,655 pounds, an increase for the year of 562,499 pounds.

Since the opening of the port the exports of teas have been—

	Pounds.
1860–'61	5,796,388
1861–'62	5,847,133
1862–'63	5,032,156
1863–'64	5,594,655

The amount invoiced and shipped from this port for ports in the United States of America for 1863–'64 amounts to 1,978,878 pounds.

The comparative returns of tea shipped from this port to the United States re as follows :

Pounds.

Direct shipments of 1861–'62 were.......................... 288,948
1862–'63 " 1,172,510
1863–'64 " 1,978,878

The business in cotton has largely increased. The total exports from this port to all countries for 1862–'63 were 9,645 bales. The amount for 1863–'64 is about 74,000, with considerable quantity in store and market, and several ships loading for London with partial cargoes on board.

Political matters are apparently quiet on the surface, but highly excited and threatening underneath. Consequently trade and business are much unsettled, doubtful, and more or less hazardous and perplexing for the future.

HAKODADI—E. E. RICE, *Commercial Agent.*

DECEMBER 31, 1863.

Statement showing the description and value of the exports from Hakodadi during the year 1863.

Value in Mexican dollars:

Seaweed...	$265,642
Eryngo—Bicho de mer.......................................	10,636
Awabi—Rock sucker...	12,441
Hadadinowe—Dried clams...................................	3,945
Cuttlefish..	20,013
Cedar lumber..	8,801
Pine lumber...	7,049
Hard lumber...	5,318
Mixed lumber...	2,283
Firewood..	307
Tobacco...	5,924
Oil..	5,673
Deer-horns..	1,587
Saltpetre..	521
Wax—vegetable...	892
Ginseng...	1,063
Cotton..	750
Potatoes...	633
Iron...	100
Oars..	68
One horse...	13
	353,659
Estimated amount smuggled................................	100,000
Total exports...	453,659

NAGASAKI—J. G. WALSH, *Consul.*

JANUARY 1, 1864.

Herewith enclosed I send the returns of trade at this port for the year 1862, as follows:

Return of imports from January 1 to December 31, inclusive.
Return of exports from January 1 to December 31, inclusive.

Statement showing the description, quantity, and value of the imports into Nagasaki during the year ended December 31, 1862.

Merchandise.	January.			February.			March.		
	P.	Ps.	V.	P.	Ps.	V.	P.	Ps.	V.
Betel nuts							69	60	334
Bucades									
Camlets	88	1,023	44,970	32	302	18,440	59	1,075	165,094
Camphor	1	1	336	1	1	760			
Cassia	290	232	4,176						
Chintzes	7	550	2,239	34	1,700	12,600	32	1,696	15,397
Cloth				4	24	1,344	26	103	7,372
Cloth, Turkey red				2	40	180			
Cloves									
Coal, English									
Cotton handkerchiefs	1	400	250	9	3,275	790	21	16,000	3,200
Cotton shirts							7	1,852	4,991
Cottonets	4	194	1,669				2	132	939
Cotton yarn	162	480	69,349						
Cutch							34	49	378
Damask									
Drills							3	134	552
Drinkables	149		1,483	10		80	535		4,744
Earthenware							9		416
Fishing-lines	11	4	4,272				3	2	881
Flannel							2	30	1,596
Ginghams	26	630	19,385	4	200	2,000	156	13,196	94,001
Glassware				9		450	25		317
Gypsum							590	860	2,549
Hoofs, buffalo							45	60	555
Horns, cow	5	3	612				1	1	20
Horns, rhinoceros	2	0.39	1,172	1	0.15	480			
Ivory	9	5.40	3,226				10	1	350
Lead	110	176	1,589				688	525	10,182
Licorice root							90	108	2,318
Long ells	23	305	7,399	20	380	7,800	28	580	10,420
Medicines, Chinese	369	320	11,761	96	91	3,844	334	449	8,465
Medicines, European	14	5	90	5	2	132	446	132	26,898
Musk	1	0.8	448	1	0.7	640	1	0.8	705
Paint	43	25	3,593				12	44	2,766
Paper, Chinese	1		13				100		1,953
Prints	12	632	3,384						
Quicksilver									
Ratans									
Rhubarb	35	33	1,237				68	59	2,179
Sandal wood	26	61	1,260						
Sapan wood		80	896					104	1,004
Shark fins	11	7	455				11	10	299
Shells, tortoise	15	5	3,866	4	2	1,200	2	1	322
Ship-chandleries	107		2,399				2	16	2,490
Shirting, blue				7	350	4,200			
Shirting, gray	11	275	1,902	22	1,100	10,300	17	830	6,100
Shirting, red	19	840	7,380	2	40	180	6	104	2,140
Shirting, spotted	31	1,240	10,392	21	999	9,750	2	100	1,200
Shirting, white	222	5,208	31,148	19	1,762	3,524	140	4,182	94,693
Soap	197		808	80		200	2,000		5,000
Spanish stripes	31	296	19,867						
Spelter	482	249	27,380				1,103	85	4,351
Stores	14		587				372		3,200
Sugar-candy	97	34	976				116	55	1,573
Sugar, white	740	691	13,521	100	39	1,436	942	216	3,409
Sundries	7		238	4		1,391	180		1,069
Tin							223	145	13,750
Tin-plates	596	52	14,069	490	300	36,000	134		3,206
Unicorn (sea-horse) teeth							1	1	3,300
Velvet	2	25	400				3	36	648
Woollen blankets	22	510	3,679	20	393	5,260	5	240	3,757
Wormseed	33	17	1,335	134	323	2,667	305	85	5,421

REMARKS.

1. It should be remembered that all the statements as regards quantity and quality of the import articles were made by the custom-house.

2. *P.* signifies packages, bales, boxes, tubs, &c. ; *Ps.* signifies piculs, (Japanese,) pieces, &c. ; *V.* value in Japanese taels.

3. Machinery has been discharged for account of the Japanese government, of which no statement was made, as well as of an import cargo from Shanghai in May, per Japanese ship "Armistice."

4. English coal imported by the British ship "Britain's Pride" paid no duties, as they were for account of the Russian government.

5. The value of a Japanese tael is about seventeen cents of a dollar.

Statement showing the description, quantity, and value of the imports into Nagasaki, &c.—Continued.

Merchandise.	April.			May.			June.		
	P.	Ps.	V.	P.	Ps.	V.	P.	Ps.	V.
Betel nuts							12	15	84
Bucades				66	3,281	33,010			
Camlets	146	1,565	96,540	96	1,342	64,329	21	931	10,465
Camphor									
Cassia									
Chintzes	9	423	3,165	70	4,640	31,275	81	5,278	35,411
Cloth	57	574	8,160	4	36	12,960	3	14	1,000
Cloth, Turkey red	8	480	7,200				9	51	2,550
Cloves									
Coal, English									
Cotton handkerchiefs	3	150	225	3	700	1,464			
Cotton shirts									
Cottonets	5	400	1,899				39	2,000	14,553
Cotton yarn							20	60	9,600
Cutch	59	78	1,014				26	39	390
Damask	1	48	480						
Drills				8	160	640			
Drinkables							96		432
Earthenware									
Fishing-lines				4	3	2,747			320
Flannel									
Ginghams	36	1,710	20,460	13	796	9,628	38	3,730	41,122
Glassware				50		1,085			
Gypsum				50	35	96			
Hoofs, buffalo									
Horns, cow	2	1	228		11	198			
Horns, rhinoceros				26	33.38	7,725	3	0.51	2,053
Ivory				11	12.12	5,078	15	7.25	2,872
Lead	77	164	4,098	190	87	5,871	1,077	578	15,863
Licorice root	1		12	20	22	409	40	80	1,140
Long ells	46	935	20,861	154	2,934	79,652	4	78	1,760
Medicines, Chinese	34	33	6,854	594	660	17,272	1,216	1,165	27,711
Medicines, European				15	9	244	36	13	2,584
Musk				1	0.12	1,329	2	0.13	1,832
Paint	10	7	810	42	94	4,186	94	89	9,568
Paper, Chinese	6		27						
Prints	12	135	675				8	549	2,900
Quicksilver									
Ratans									
Rhubarb	165	261	9,502	173	238	10,236	373	509	17,688
Sandal wood				166	1,379				
Sapan wood				549	4,791			460	3,222
Shark fins	7	4	85	62	46	1,089	36	42	1,496
Shells, tortoise				11	4	3,458	13	6	5,988
Ship-chandleries				2		162	100		2,263
Shirting, blue									
Shirting, gray	181	9,000	74,781	119	5,818	54,723	202	10,100	60,800
Shirting, red	9	450	3,329	4	250	2,758	47	2,350	23,484
Shirting, spotted	58	2,815	27,052						
Shirting, white	99	4,423	37,799	554	4,100	35,433	64	3,385	27,570
Soap									
Spanish stripes	4	48	2,064	10	64	3,200			
Spelter									
Stores				31		891	80		995
Sugar-candy	99	32	782						
Sugar, white				504	500	7,200	207	226	4,570
Sundries	8		762	61		1,360	12		3,453
Tin				892	324	17,670	240	121	11,566
Tin plates							205	161	5,445
Unicorn (sea-horse) teeth				1	0.27	720			
Velvet	4	72	1,494	7	164	2,089	3	16	3,112
Woollen blankets	3	80	2,800	22	798	2,727	16	568	1,738
Wormseed				105	78	3,298	69	28	1,228

Statement showing the description, quantity, and value of the imports into Nagasaki, &c.—Continued.

Merchandise.	July.			August.			September.		
	P.	*Ps.*	*V.*	*P.*	*Ps.*	*V.*	*P.*	*Ps.*	*V.*
Betel nuts				2	3	17	68	50	500
Bucades				1	23	230			
Camlets	14	140	9,800	19	225	12,132	80	800	54,200
Camphor									
Cassia									
Chintzes	15	450	3,200	31	1,550	13,875	27	2,250	22,035
Cloth	12	72	2,880				7	39	2,310
Cloth, Turkey red									
Cloves							260	260	10,530
Coal, English									
Cotton handkerchiefs	17	3,400	6,120						
Cotton shirts									
Cottonets	17	830	3,330				14	700	4,704
Cotton yarn									
Cutch									
Damask							1		410
Drills									
Drinkables	200		900	20		165	242		2,294
Earthenware							190		3,010
Fishing-lines				5	5	6,090	2		275
Flannel									
Ginghams	13	800	6,077	35	3,500	28,000	150	10,800	53,625
Glassware				66		4,400	334		4,220
Gypsum							150		660
Hoofs, buffalo									
Horns, cow	2	3	28				80	68	5,881
Horns, rhinoceros	0	0.31	1,005	1	0.90	371	1	0.12	316
Ivory							6	2.4	1,428
Lead	360	193	6,415	534	960	31,959	2,329	1,955	44,069
Licorice root	24	35	700				243	253	4,848
Long ells				6	120	2,400	1	60	1,590
Medicines, Chinese	130	186	6,700	475	414	21,966	1,365	1,138	22,112
Medicines, European	34	19	393						
Musk									
Paint	3	3	496	9	4	714	210	35	3,097
Paper, Chinese	16		82				31		957
Prints									
Quicksilver							88	49	1,173
Ratans							9,000	150	1,050
Rhubarb	356	514	18,756	143	223	7,788	412	484	21,603
Sandal wood							2,000	20	550
Sapan wood								60	868
Shark fins	4	5	132	42	42	1,155	37	35	1,667
Shells, tortoise	5	1	547	5	2	2,775	1		100
Ship-chandleries									
Shirting, blue				1	28	280			
Shirting, gray	72	3,600	27,893	36	1,800	13,345	31	1,650	13,700
Shirting, red	4	200	3,000	6	300	3,200	7	350	3,410
Shirting, spotted				1	50	550			
Shirting, white				66	3,469	27,600			
Soap									
Spanish stripes									
Spelter	340	155	4,490	1,116	798	16,016	898	529	13,289
Stores	3		249	132		1,608	92		462
Sugar-candy							120	138	2,428
Sugar, white	60	3,000	24,000						
Sundries	29		1,389	16	616	40	40		1,996
Tin	375	408	12,387						
Tin plates	48	79	2,168	50		1,735	982	607	16,378
Unicorn (sea-horse) teeth				1	1.90	3,000	1	2.50	3,000
Velvet				7	140	1,981	2	100	160
Woollen blankets	30	810	2,430	13	700	1,751	77	3,540	12,075
Wormseed	25	23	644	306	126	4,210			

*Statement showing the description, quantity, and value of the imports into Nagasaki, &c.—*Continued.

Merchandise.	October.			November.			December.			Total.		
	P.	Ps.	V.	P.	Ps.	V.	P.	Ps.	V.	P.	Ps.	V.
Betel nuts										151	128	935
Bucades										67	3,304	33,240
Camlets	142	1,420	96,800	57	540	37,324	100	950	41,200	854	10,313	651,294
Camphor										2	2	1,096
Cassia										290	232	4,176
Chintzes	13	800	4,800				17	770	6,050	336	20,107	150,047
Cloth	2	40	405	93	793	51,550	43	187	27,690	251	1,882	115,671
Cloth, Turkey red										19	571	9,930
Cloves	23	23	920	91	86	3,625				374	369	15,075
Coal, English					420						420	
Cotton handkerchiefs				1	240	385	1	50	250	56	26,375	12,684
Cotton shirts										7	1,852	4,991
Cottonets							8	400	1,600	86	4,586	28,624
Cotton yarn										182	540	78,949
Cutch							60	48	792	172	207	2,574
Damask							10	497	2,982	12	545	3,872
Drills										11	294	1,192
Drinkables	50		100	229		1,532	236		1,545	1,767		13,273
Earthenware							86		3,320	215		6,746
Fishing-lines				9	5	5,013	18	11	6,663	52	30	26,261
Flannel										2	30	1,596
Ginghams	6	600	4,950				76	4,848	46,013	553	40,810	357,261
Glassware							5		118	489		10,530
Gypsum							22		136	812	895	3,441
Hoofs, buffalo										45	60	555
Horns, cow				6	5	621				96	92	7,318
Horns, rhinoceros	1	0.6	264	3	1.67	546	5	2.73	1,164	45	40.15	15,096
Ivory				1	1.50	577	7	2	880	59	31.31	14,411
Lead	1,506	1,400	31,800				102		2,100	7,903	6,038	153,946
Licorice root							1			9	419	9,429
Long ells				14	345	3,751	2	40	1,200	298	5,777	136,833
Medicines, Chinese	286	453	11,953	992	1,429	30,406	302	413	19,036	6,123	6,751	188,310
Medicines, European				2	1	250	12	1	420	564	202	30,911
Musk	2	0.25	2,900	6	0.52	6,747	5	0.34	4,145	19	159	18,746
Paint	11	6	302	41	38	6,882	98	75	5,677	573	350	38,093
Paper, Chinese				5		80	149		2,980	308		6,092
Prints										32	1,316	6,959
Quicksilver				40	14	2,618				128	63	14,351
Ratans				800	112	1,344				9,800	262	2,394
Rhubarb	260	371	13,027	187	290	11,242	3	3	79	2,175	2,988	113,319
Sandal wood				53	14	774	12	7	629	2,071	268	4,592
Sapan wood							60		150		1,313	10,861
Shark fins	9	6	138	4	5	240	18	9	413	241	211	7,149
Shells, tortoise	2	1	885	1		110	1		180	60	22	19,431
Ship-chandleries							20		160	229		4,984
Shirting, blue										10	394	6,970
Shirting, gray	78	3,900	39,000	31	1,530	15,363	546	29,099	349,883	1,346	68,722	667,790
Shirting, red	12	600	6,556				4	200	2,100	190	5,684	57,537
Shirting, spotted										113	5,204	48,944
Shirting, white	10	497	3,976	14	700	7,000	57	2,850	23,412	1,245	30,576	222,148
Soap										4,770		6,008
Spanish stripes				12	70	860				57	478	25,991
Spelter	175	112	3,080	1,360	310	8,100				5,474	2,168	76,699
Stores							232		1,629	956		9,621
Sugar-candy										432	259	5,759
Sugar, white	208	200	4,000	6	6	148				2,067	4,808	58,284
Sundries	11		759	204		3,076	7		440	579		16,549
Tin				362	259	6,141				2,092	1,250	61,514
Tin plates	200	170	4,000							2,705	1,369	82,991
Unicorn teeth							1	1.20	3,700	5	6,487	13,720
Velvet				13	300	8,700				41	853	18,513
Woollen blankets				58	2,110	6,050	2	9	90	276	10,158	43,567
Wormseed							106	108	5,156	1,083	788	23,889
												3,773,994

SEPTEMBER 10, 1864.

Herewith enclosed I send the returns of trade for this port for the year 1863, as follows : Imports, No. 1; exports, No. 2; and shipping, No. 3.

The treaty value of the Mexican dollar, the only foreign coin used in Japan, is its weight in native silver coins. The market value is its value in trade, and this during the year 1863 was 27¾ per cent. less than the treaty value.

The returns show a decrease of 882,697 Japanese taels in the value of exports as compared with the year 1862, and a decrease of 221,027 taels in the value of imports as compared with the same year. The falling off is to be attributed to the disturbances in the country and the fear consequent upon the demand made by the British government on the government of Japan for outrages alleged to have been committed on the persons and property of British subjects during previous years. The demand was made in the month of April, and trade did not recover from the consequent depression until September.

The export of greatest value was tea, the next vegetable wax, and the third raw cotton.

Of imports the most valuable was tin used in the manufacture of cannon and small coins. The next was camlets, and the third lead, used chiefly as a munition of war.

Of the exports about fourteen and one-half per cent. of the value went in American vessels, more than sixty per cent. in British, and the remainder in Dutch, French, Prussian, Russian, and Portuguese vessels.

Of imports about nine and three-fourths per cent. came in American vessels, more than fifty per cent. in British, and the remainder in vessels of the other treaty nations.

The American flag has had the same difficulty to contend with in these waters as in other parts of the world. Although rebel cruisers did not appear in the China or Japan seas during the year, yet reports of their expected arrival were industriously circulated by unscrupulous interested persons, which had the desired effect.

It is proper to state that the returns obtained from the custom-house do not show the true value of the imports and exports. It is probably fifty per cent. more than stated. This is caused by the imperfect way in which custom-house business is managed by the native officials in charge. But few pay the duties prescribed by the treaties.

Statement showing the description, quantity, and value of the imports into Nagasaki during the year 1863.

Description.	Quantity.	Value.	Duty.
Aloes wood ....piculs..	11	1,351	270
Betel nuts ....piculs..	2,808	16,545	3,308
Brushes, (Chinese) ....pieces..	3,000	450	90
Camlets ....pieces..	13,760	619,854	31,189
Camphor ....piculs..	3.72	4,450	889
Cassia ....piculs..	212	3,127	525
Carpets ....pieces..	1,403	4,308	215
Chintzes ....pieces..	12,260	116,504	5,824
Cigars ....pieces..	15,150	2,285	456
Cloth ....pieces..	732	61,509	3,064
Cloves ....piculs..	1,143	32,666	6,531
Coal, (English) ....boxes..	14,240	21,359	1,066
Corals ....boxes..	1	2,000	400
Cotton handkerchiefs ....pieces..	330	1,800	294
Cottonets ....pieces..	5,370	51,410	2,570
Cotton yarn ....piculs..	169	23,224	1,260
Cutch ....piculs..	1,294	22,381	3,474
Deer-horns ....piculs..	7	1,059	211
Drinkables ....boxes..	2,577	25,632	8,967
Dyestuffs ....piculs..	21	3,176	635
Earthenware ....boxes..	46,338	5,942	1,238
Fishing-lines ....piculs..	24	15,796	3,158
Gingseng ....piculs..	49.20	13,321	2,663
Ginghams ....pieces..	6,676	59,743	2,992
Glassware ....boxes..	231	5,582	1,115
Hides ....pieces..	805	1,480	296
Hoof, (buffalo) ....piculs..	126	5,248	1,048
Horn, " ....piculs..	189	7,552	1,509
Horn, (rhinoceros) ....piculs..	5.71	4,659	930
Indigo ....piculs..	244	15,058	3,010
Ivory ....piculs..	23.85	13,409	1,327
Iron ....piculs..	533	3,736	747
Lead ....piculs..	26,469	558,439	27,920
Leather ....pieces..	9,822	3,253	659
Licorice root ....piculs..	171	2,562	512
Long ells ....pieces..	1,316	33,171	1,658
Mattings ....pieces..	5,380	11,767	2,353
Medicines ....piculs..	21,913	409,593	77,671
Musk	1.12	4,351	869
Oil ....boxes..	280	3,454	690
Paint ....boxes..	97	2,757	474
Paper, (Chinese) ....piculs..	2,924	14,971	2,993
Pepper ....piculs..	441	8,186	1,637
Quicksilver ....piculs..	111	14,744	2,948
Quinine ....ounces..	100	500	100
Ratan ....piculs..	946	8,447	1,689
Rhubarb ....piculs..	774	29,358	5,870
Sail-cloth ....pieces..	170	1,480	74
Sandal wood ....piculs..	145	5,224	1,048
Sapan wood ....piculs..	2,059	17,224	3,444
Shark-skins ....pieces..	489	17,117	3,423
Sheepskins ....pieces..	800	385	77
Shell, (tortoise) ....piculs..	47	3,411	678
Ship-chandleries, (boxes) ....boxes..	582	22,735	4,480
Shirtings, gray ....pieces..	4,750	46,100	2,305
red ....pieces..	10,051	103,469	5,112
white ....pieces..	11,006	156,014	7,799
Silk goods ....pieces..	180	1,080	54
Soap ....boxes..	72	2,134	426
Spanish stripes ....pieces..	250	1,500	75
Spelter ....piculs..	5,385	94,596	4,729

Statement showing the description, &c., of the imports into Nagasaki—Cont'd.

Description.	Quantity.	Value.	Duty.
Stores .... boxes..	3,123	15,611	2,067
Sugar-candy.................................... piculs..	268	11,815	2,382
Sugar, brown.................................... piculs..	200	3,924	785
white .... piculs..	1,757	39,426	7,883
Sundries .... boxes..	1,009	5,378	1,027
Tin.. piculs..	10,120	661,339	33,066
Tin plates...................................... piculs..	1,190	14,759	2,639
Unicorn.. piculs..	0.50	1,500	300
Velvet .... pieces..	1,017	21,414	1,120
Vermilion .... piculs..	84	15,831	3,164
Woollen blankets .... pieces..	6,910	17,312	863
Total in Japanese taels.................	....	3,552,967	308,334

Piculs of 133⅓ pounds avoirdupois.

Total value of imports 3,552,967 Japanese taels; equal to, at the market value of Mexican dollars, $888,242.

Total amount of duties received on imports 308,334 Japanese taels; equal to, at the treaty value of Mexican dollars, $52,707.

Statement showing the description, quantity, and value of the exports from Nagasaki during the year 1863.

Description.	Quantity.	Value.	Duty.
Antimony .... piculs..	100	200	10
Awati... piculs..	225	9,853	489
Bamboo-ware .... boxes..	1,856	2,191	108
Bronzes .... boxes..	76	1,332	66
Camphor... piculs..	2,877	195,324	10,164
Cassia .... piculs..	213	782	39
Charcoal .... piculs..	15,810	27,481	1,369
Cigars .... pieces..	106,500	479	23
Coal .... piculs..	16,546	25,168	1,256
Cocoons.. packages..	13	8,060	403
Coir .... piculs..	3,404	20,122	1,002
Cotton, manufactured .... pieces..	30,737	39,328	1,695
raw .... piculs..	5,925	322,502	15,621
Crockery and porcelain.................... pieces..	571,099	48,675	2,427
Cuttlefish .... piculs..	4,241	115,405	5,763
Deer-horns .... piculs..	111	2,185	106
Firewood .... piculs..	4,666	2,665	130
Fish, dried .... piculs..	235	8,696	434
Furniture .... pieces..	134	3,095	154
Gall-nuts.. piculs..	951	22,133	1,805
Ginseng .... piculs..	323.31	150,936	7,548
Chinany .... piculs..	403	2,682	181
Honey... piculs..	48	1,184	58
Inks .... piculs..	429	17,104	853
Iron .... piculs..	840	6,840	342
Isinglass .... piculs..	1,917	110,475	5,518
Lacquered ware............................... boxes..	14,503	22,194	1,098
Lobsters .... piculs..	145	5,400	768
Mattings .... pieces..	2,871	802	63
Medicines .... piculs..	2,853	38,571	1,923

Statement showing the description, &c., of the exports from Nagasaki—Cont'd.

Description.	Quantity.	Value.	Duty.
Mushrooms................................piculs..	2,109	169,537	8,445
Oil ....piculs..	435	10,955	547
Orange-peel ....piculs..	266	1,299	64
Paper ....piculs..	1,869	33,961	1,695
Paper umbrellas ....pieces..	11,290	2,202	110
Peas......................................piculs..	2,329	9,916	395
Planks....................................pieces..	1,463,795	274,610	13,716
Pales ....pieces..	63,482	23,261	1,160
Rags ....piculs..	959	1,310	65
Sea-weed..................................piculs..	27,711	288,062	14,398
Sharks' fins ....piculs..	148	6,514	303
Shells ....packages..	542	3,928	194
Silk, (raw) ....piculs..	313,40	291,191	14,559
Soye ....boxes..	250	1,030	51
Stones, (paving)..........................pieces..	19,015	4,233	209
Sulphur...................................piculs..	1,169	6,936	346
Sundries ....packages..	1,640	8,149	403
Tea ....piculs..	29,442	643,197	32,155
Tiles ....pieces..	10,000	295	14
Timber ....pieces..	2,217	2,088	104
Tobacco ....piculs..	5,555	40,646	2,029
Toys ....pieces..	15,324	4,298	214
Vermicelli................................piculs..	1,560	18,536	925
Wax, bees'...............................piculs..	88	9,780	488
vegetable..............................piculs..	10,227	401,384	20,062
Total in Japanese taels.................	....	3,470,182	174,337

Piculs of 133⅓ pounds avoirdupois.

Total value of exports 3,470,182 Japanese taels, equal to, at the market value of Mexican dollars, $867,545 50.

Total amount of duties received on exports 174,337 Japanese taels, equal to, at the treaty value of Mexican dollars, $29,801.

Statement showing the nationality, number, and tonnage of vessels arrived at and departed from Nagasaki during the year 1863.

Nationality.	Arrivals.		Departures.	
	Number of vessels.	Tonnage.	Number of vessels.	Tonnage.
American	48	14,397	39	11,430
British..............................	140	44,417	131	42,308
Dutch..............................	42	12,819	42	12,819
French	20	4,656	19	4,415
Prussian............................	13	3,760	11	3,282
Russian............................	2	542	2	542
Portuguese.........................	1	363	1	363
Total.................	266	80,954	245	75,159

H. Ex. Doc. 60——44

MUSCAT.

ZANZIBAR—WILLIAM E. HINES, *Consul.*

DECEMBER 24, 1863.

I have the honor to enclose herewith a list of export and import trade of this island, to and from what countries. * * * It is made up from official returns of Colonel Playfair, her British Majesty's consul, and is very nearly correct.

Our American trade, you will observe, shows a great falling off from previous years; but there is at present a manifest improvement, and the coming year will, no doubt, show a large increase of exports to the United States.

Statement showing the value of the exports from Zanzibar, together with the names of the countries where shipped, during the year ended July 31, 1863.

	Value.
British India	$477,785
Protected States of India	212,366
Arabia and Persian Gulf	113,696
Coast of Africa and adjacent islands	773,115
France	187,310
Hamburg	227,388
Italy	14,896
United States	186,086
Total	2,192,642

Description and value of the exports to the United States.

	Value.
Cloves	$5,813
Gum copal	15,917
Other gums	217
Hides	67,000
Ivory	87,855
Peppers	5,506
Timber	787
Turtle shell	876
Beeswax	2,115
Total	186,086

Statement showing the value of the imports into Zanzibar, and the names of the countries whence made, during the year ended July 31, 1863.

	Value.
From United Kingdom	$118,312
British India	748,584
Protected States of India	87,100
Arabia and Persian Gulf	50,220
Coast of Africa and adjacent islands	980,372
France	194,350
Italy	34,500

	Value.
From Hamburg	$250, 200
United States	124, 350
Total	2, 588, 288

Statement showing the description and value of the imports from the United States.

	Value.
Arms	$2, 500
China and glassware	200
Flour	2, 500
Miscellaneous	11, 000
Cotton goods	42, 000
Soap	2, 000
Sugar	7, 000
Timber	150
Tobacco	23, 000
Treasure	33, 000
Wines and spirits	1, 000
Total	124, 350

NAVIGATOR'S ISLANDS.

APIA—JOHN E. WILLIAMS, *Acting Consul.*

FEBRUARY 1, 1864.

TRADE REPORT.

There has been a fair amount of business done during the past year; but there being no custom-house, it is impossible to obtain the value of the imports or exports. * * *

In consequence of the failure of the crops there has been a great scarcity of food; the natives have been obliged to live upon cocoa-nuts, hence there has been little cocoa-nut oil made. * * *

Many of the foreign residents within these islands are turning their attention to the cultivation of coffee and cotton, and some of the chiefs are planting; but I fear, owing to the lazy habits of the natives, and their putting too high a value on their labor, that they will not do much.

Statement showing the number and tonnage of vessels of all nationalities arrived and departed from Apia during the year 1863.

Nationality.	Number.	Tonnage.
American	18	5, 339
British and colonial	39	4, 215
French ship-of-war	1	450
Tahiti, under French protectorate	5	590
Hamburg	36	3, 939
Sandwich islands	3	460
Peruvian	1	300
Tongu	1	17
	104	12, 310

Interest on money, 8 to 10 per cent. per annum.
Laborers' wages, $1 per day.
House and ship carpenters, $2 to $3 per day.
House servants, $1 to $1 50 per week.
Sailors, $12 to $18 per month.

SOCIETY ISLANDS.

TAHITI—JOSEPH VANDOR, *Consul.*

MAY 20, 1864.

I have the honor to state that the present season for oranges, limes, and cocoa-nuts, exported from here to San Francisco, has given, in eight American and four Tahitian vessels, the following results : 5,000,000 oranges; 62,000 limes ; 10,800 cocoa-nuts.

The value of said fruits amounted, according to the declarations of the different invoices, to about $6 per one mille, all packed in crates, and the whole quantity exported to $24,104. Among these are not comprised such vessels as have gone to the neighboring independent Society Islands, of which there are three; but I may confidently say that there have been exported, upon the whole, between five and six millions of oranges, limes, and cocoa-nuts, to San Francisco, in a period from the 1st of February to the 1st of May, 1864. All these vessels brought lumber, groceries, and general cargoes from the United States, in exchange for said fruits.

SIAM.

BANGKOK—A. J. WESTERVELT, *Consul,*

DECEMBER 31, 1863.

Statement showing the number, nationality, description and tonnage of vessels, other than American, arrived at and departed from the port of Bangkok during the year 1863.

Nation.	Ships.	Barks.	Brigs.	Schooners.	Steamers	Tons.
British.............	13	47	9	11	1	29,776
American............	19	9	....	2	1	21,774
French.............	4	2	....	....	1	3,126
Hamburg...........	1	14	1	....	....	5,055
Bremen.............	....	7	3	1	....	3,192
Dutch.............	3	21	2	....	1	10,626
Danish.............	3	3	6	4	....	4,522
Swedish.......	....	5	....	....	....	1,764
Portuguese..........	....	2	....	....	....	691
Prussian	....	1	....	....	....	344
Oldenberg..........	....	....	1	1	....	434
Norwegian	....	2	....	....	....	724
Lubeck.............	....	2	....	....	....	662
Total	43	115	22	19	4	82,690

JANUARY 31, 1864.

* * * * * * * * *

I have the honor to transmit for your information a list of foreign vessels and tonnage entered and cleared at the port of Bangkok during the year 1863. I endeavored to get the true value of the imports and exports, but failed in getting the value of the exports in consequence of no statistics being kept by the Siamese officials, most of the import and export cargoes belonging to natives and Chinese merchants.

I send a printed return of the imports, kindly furnished by the inspector of customs, which shows the total value of imports to be $3,775,664 and exports $4,500,000.

* * * * * * * * *

JULY 27, 1864.

* * * * * * * * *

Trade has opened pretty fairly with the United States, two vessels having sailed for it.

The Siamese government having opened their forests to foreigners, there likely will be a great increase in the trade, in teak and mata keen, both used for ship-building.

The natives have been induced to turn their attention to the culture of cotton, as the price is very high and likely to continue, and there will be more shipped this year to foreign markets than all former crops put together. Although the quantity is not large, yet it presages the future in this article, and the country being well adapted to its growth, we may expect it to be cultivated in the upland districts, and more profitable results may be expected than from the cultivation of rice. The quantity that is already known that will be shipped to foreign markets reaches 14,000 piculs.

* * * * * * * * *

OCTOBER 5, 1864.

* * * * * * * * *

During the last four months there have been cleared from this port for the United States four ships with cargoes valued at $130,000, consisting of rice, sugar, timber, and other produce of this country. This is more than ever occurred before; and as the country is developed the trade with the United States will greatly increase. The crop of sugar will be much augmented this season, as machinery has been imported from England and is now being erected; 10,000 acres are represented to be under cultivation, and the rice crop, about which in the early part of the season some apprehensions were entertained, on account of the injurious effects of the dry weather, now gives hopes of a large crop from the late abundant rains.

* * * * * * * * *

BARBARY STATES.

TANGIER—JESSE H. MCMATH, *Consul.*

FEBRUARY 12, 1864.

I have the honor to transmit herewith a return of the exports and imports of the shipping and trade at the several ports of this empire during the year 1862.

The American vessels reported in the returns carried cargoes of wool to the United States. * * * * * * * *

APRIL 2, 1864.

Herewith I transmit the returns of shipping and trade at the different ports of this empire for the year 1863.

The exceptional character of this country makes it impossible to conform with the requisition of the general instructions to consuls within the time allowed for that purpose, there being no statistics nor commercial information published by the Moorish authorities.

Much time and labor are required to collect from the different consulates the necessary commercial information, and such as we get can only be obtained at the close of the year.

The foreign commerce of Morocco is at all times very insignificant, when compared with other countries, and from the peculiar habits of the Moors it is not probable it will be materially increased for some time. There is no direct commerce with the United States; coarse wool, the product of the interior, is reshipped in large quantities to America from Gibraltar, London, and Marseilles.

The staple articles of export from this country are maize, beans, peas, olive oil, cattle, beef, hides, wool, dates, almonds, walnuts, oranges, lemons, limes, bird-seed, wild marjoram, cumin seed, gums, wax, horns, tallow, fowls, eggs, and slippers; besides these, ivory and ostrich feathers, the products of Central Africa, are exported in small quantities.

The principal imports are coarse cotton fabrics, cloths—mostly from England—cochineal, coffee, tea, loaf, crushed, and brown sugars, iron, steel, raw silk, raw cotton, cotton thread, brimstone, saltpetre, lumber, nails, and hardware.

The duty on all articles imported, as heretofore fixed by the Sultan, is ten per cent. *ad valorem*. The duty on all articles of export is fixed by the tariff annexed to the new treaty between Morocco and Spain. Foreign merchants trading in this country claim under that treaty, because it is considered more favorable to commerce than any other treaty with this country.

Horses, mules, asses, and camels cannot be exported without special license from the Sultan. The importation and sale of tobacco are monopolized by the Sultan. In 1863 the Sultan encouraged the cultivation of cotton. American and Egyptian cotton seed was imported from England, and large tracts of crownlands were planted, and quite a number of the more enlightened Moors engaged in the cultivation of this staple on their own account. It is impossible to ascertain the quantity raised, but enough is known to justify the statement that cotton can be successfully cultivated in this country. I have been informed that 200 quintals were shipped from the port of Mazagan and 100 quintals from the port of Saffee to England within the last quarter. It is claimed here to be equal in quality to American cotton; this I doubt. With proper encouragement, its cultivation would greatly benefit this people, but from some cause, altogether unaccountable upon any reasonable hypothesis, the Sultan has within the past two months prohibited the cultivation by private enterprise. This edict will materially affect a number of Europeans residing in this country. Preparation was being made by them to engage in the cultivation of this much-needed staple at the time the Sultan's edict was proclaimed; but in view of it, they will have to abandon the enterprise, for they cannot claim from the Sultan any privilege, not secured by treaty, which he denies his own subjects.   *   *

The privilege of purchasing supplies duty free at all the ports of this empire is accorded to our ships-of-war, and those of other nations.   *   *   *

Statement showing the number, nationality, tonnage, and number of crews of the vessels entered at the several ports of Morocco during the year 1863.

Ports	British vessels				French vessels				Spanish vessels				Portuguese vessels			
	No. of vessels	Tons	No. of crews	Value of cargoes	No. of vessels	Tons	No. of crews	Value of cargoes	No. of vessels	Tons	No. of crews	Value of cargoes	No. of vessels	Tons	No. of crews	Value of cargoes
Tangier	323	49,757	2,655	£256,717	25	5,796	461	£275,494	84	1,804	505	£21,957	17	212	87	£21,226
Tetuan	45	675	181	37,094	3	232	36	1,780	183	881	567	320				
Laroche	51	1,219	110	3,846	5	460	37		37	949	228	334	14	776	93	
Rabat	12	680	82	40,985	17	2,095	131	23,227	2	85	15	4,798	12	478	84	6,704
Daralbeida	55	11,374	790	40,449	39	10,814	916	19,141	4	360	33		96	797	223	42,626
Mazagan	63	10,998	678	87,391	19	5,518	410	11,850	35	3,099	304	21,000	93	1,777	197	661
Saffee	28	4,623	274	13,466	5	1,588	134	3,520	17	1,406	129	4,356	93	2,413	282	7,852
Mogadore	55	14,559	796	231,645	29	7,349	566	67,531	8	990	62	1,388	4	2,395	31	7,438
Total	602	87,265	5,490	685,965	142	33,942	2,691	202,473	370	9,574	1,842	54,123	118	8,848	917	59,707

Statement showing the number, &c., of vessels entered at the several ports of Morocco during the year 1863—Continued.

Ports	Italian vessels				Belgian vessels				Hanoverian vessels				Netherlands vessels				Total value of cargoes imported.
	No. of vessels	Tons	No. of crews	Value of cargoes	No. of vessels	Tons	No. of crews	Value of cargoes	No. of vessels	Tons	No. of crews	Value of cargoes	No. of vessels	Tons	No. of crews	Value of cargoes	
Tangier	16	155	73	£8,361	1	470	94										£585,685
Tetuan																	39,184
Laroche																	10,886
Rabat					1	130	7						1	124			115,806
Daralbeida													1	124		5	32,251
Mazagan	2	220	15													£4,000	190,941
Saffee	1	148	9						1	80	7	£1,900					30,794
Mogadore	1	90	8		1	117	6	£1,560	2	150	9	2,197	1	116	10	4,585	309,394
Total	20	623	105	8,361	3	717	37	1,560	3	230	16	3,397	3	364	21	8,585	1,024,171

Statement showing the number, nationality, tonnage, and number of crews of the vessels cleared from the several ports of Morocco during the year 1863.

Ports	British vessels				French vessels				Spanish vessels				Portuguese vessels			
	No. of vessels	Tons	No. of crews	Value of cargoes	No. of vessels	Tons	No. of crews	Value of cargoes	No. of vessels	Tons	No. of crews	Value of cargoes	No. of vessels	Tons	No. of crews	Value of cargoes
Tangier	319	33,374	2,639	£144,443	24	5,396	440	£37,537	80	1,708	484	£27,247	16	204	83	£8,277
Tetuan	47	900	209	19,150	3	322	36		179	890	551	1,648				
Larache	22	1,247	115	11,376	5	460	37	4,830	36	856	230	5,760	16		104	6,775
Rabatt	12	880	82	13,440	17	2,095	131	47,098					11	870	62	14,000
Daralbeida	55	11,374	720	36,512	39	10,814	916	37,600	4	360	33	1,080	26	409	223	10,016
Mazagan	60	10,116	639	48,100	19	5,209	377	43,720	31	2,946	288	22,000	19	2,797	167	8,900
Saffee	26	4,458	263	30,550	5	1,588	134	1,546	17	1,406	129	4,920	63	1,469	202	12,190
Mogadore	53	12,454	715	282,351	32	7,089	542	58,473	7	602	55	1,235	3	2,413	53	3,577
Total	594	74,803	5,375	565,992	144	32,973	2,613	230,854	356	8,768	1,759	63,910	114	8,425	864	63,635

Statement showing the number, &c., of vessels cleared from the several ports of Morocco during the year 1863—Continued.

Ports	Italian vessels				Belgian vessels				Hanoverian vessels				Netherlands vessels				Total value of cargoes imported.
	No. of vessels	Tons	No. of crews	Value of cargoes	No. of vessels	Tons	No. of crews	Value of cargoes	No. of vessels	Tons	No. of crews	Value of cargoes	No. of vessels	Tons	No. of crews	Value of cargoes	
Tangier	14	130	62	£4,056	1	470	94										£221,560
Tetuan																	201,798
Larache																	28,741
Rabatt					1	130	7	£1,000					1	124	5	£300	74,638
Daralbeida	9	220	15	2,114									1	124	6		88,322
Mazagan	2	304	19	5,520					1	80	7						128,140
Saffee	1	90	8	940	1	117	6										50,196
Mogadore													1	116	10	4,610	355,108
Total	19	754	104	12,630	3	717	37	5,842	1	80	7		3	364	21	4,910	967,703

Statement showing the value of the exports, also the nationality, tonnage, number of crews and of vessels, cleared from the ports of Morocco during the year ended December 31, 1862.

Ports	British vessels				French vessels				Spanish vessels				Portuguese vessels			
	No. of vessels	Tons	Crews	Value of cargo	No. of vessels	Tons	Crews	Value of cargo	No. of vessels	Tons	Crews	Value of cargo	No. of vessels	Tons	Crews	Value of cargo
Tangiers	382	21,176	2,170	£150,335	18	2,600	976	£22,155	36	473	237	£15,716	12	60	36	£3,285
Tetuan	46	1,350	227	4,536	1	38	5	1,180	41	363	182	633	9	230	17	1,706
Larache	98	1,639	92	19,116	3	333	21	3,902	70	1,608	464	7,393	16	638	113	5,435
Rabatt	8	469	52	7,545	14	1,433	123	3,536	4	215	28	32,982	9	446	64	3,400
Darelbeida	51	8,835	504	30,044	38	10,215	975	57,789	9	164	17	1,258	97	2,384	229	33,840
Mazagan	115	13,794	853	91,213	15	4,767	375	14,876	12	985	94	12,600	66	5,161	575	5,880
Saffee	62	8,798	518	85,116	12	3,002	325	11,085	21	1,768	181	9,518	10	1,091	89	5,600
Mogadore	35	10,675	618	145,000	95	8,886	754	57,567	9	692	68	3,566	1	102	7	3,600
Total	797	66,866	5,034	532,905	196	30,974	2,754	172,090	195	6,967	1,271	83,596	143	10,312	1,130	47,146

Ports	Italian vessels				American vessels				Norwegian vessels				Belgian vessels				Netherland vessels				Total Value of cargoes
	No. of vessels	Tons	Crews	Value of cargo	No. of vessels	Tons	Crews	Value of cargo	No. of vessels	Tons	Crews	Value of cargo	No. of vessels	Tons	Crews	Value of cargo	No. of vessels	Tons	Crews	Value of cargo	
Tangiers	7	140	35	£5,094																	£196,515
Tetuan	1	90	7																		6,349
Larache	1	222	9	1,933																	33,980
Rabatt																					49,498
Darelbeida	5	539	43	2,700	2	1,320	36	£3,880													99,721
Mazagan	4	544	37	3,880	1	157	8	7,500	1	259	9	£650	1	117	6	£600	2	200	13	£1,340	146,409
Saffee																					122,639
Mogadore									1	278	9	1,600	1	117	6	3,498					213,231
Total	18	1,535	131	13,537	3	1,477	44	11,380	2	537	18	2,250	2	234	12	4,098	2	200	13	1,340	868,342

Statement showing the value of the imports, also the nationality, tonnage, number of crews and of vessels, entered the ports of Morocco during the year ended December 31, 1862.

Ports	British vessels				French vessels				Spanish vessels				Portuguese vessels			
	No. of vessels	Tons	Crews	Value of cargo	No. of vessels	Tons	Crews	Value of cargo	No. of vessels	Tons	Crews	Value of cargo	No. of vessels	Tons	Crews	Value of cargo
Tangiers	271	30,906	2,119	£224,58	23	4,290	426	£84,845	36	475	233	£29,982	12	60	36	£6,400
Tetuan	49	1,402	239	38,85	1	38	5	1,362	41	362	188		9	230	17	1,890
Larache	59	1,353	149	90,34	3	333	21		70	1,608	464	559	17	665	132	18,493
Rabatt	7	401	47	14,87	14	1,453	123	18,867	5	164	17	440	9	380	64	22,117
Darulbeida	51	8,635	504	13,81	38	10,915	975	96,291	9	280	36	44,885	97	2,344	980	1,123
Mazagan	118	14,393	863	152,81	18	5,749	447	60,000	12	985	94		66	5,303	580	30,000
Saffee	68	9,224	598	56,60	11	2,699	219	1,030	21	1,798	181	2,400	12	1,304	106	3,470
Mogadore	38	11,343	657	196,40	25	9,312	766	29,522	9	657	68	6,340	2	904	14	637
Total	631	68,343	5,146	719,620	133	34,269	2,982	291,807	196	6,299	1,275	84,599	147	10,713	1,168	85,059

Ports	Italian vessels				American vessels				Norwegian vessels				Belgian vessels				Netherland vessels				Total value of cargoes
	No. of vessels	Tons	Crews	Value of cargo	No. of vessels	Tons	Crews	Value of cargo	No. of vessels	Tons	Crews	Value of cargo	No. of vessels	Tons	Crews	Value of cargo	No. of vessels	Tons	Crews	Value of cargo	
Tangiers	6	190	30	£8,689					1	259	9		1	117	6	250	2	200	13	4,860	£354,174
Tetuan	1	90	7	900																	43,369
Larache	1	232	9																		39,778
Rabatt																					100,656
Darulbeida					9	1,320	36						2	234	12	1,938					112,069
Mazagan	5	520	43		1	157	8														246,181
Saffee	4	544	37	410					1	278	9										73,150
Mogadore	1	90	8																		228,737
Total	18	1,605	134	9,999	3	1,477	44		2	537	18		3	351	18	2,188	2	200	13	4,860	1,198,129

April 21, 1864.

I have the honor to forward the following abstract of my report of the shipping and of the imports and exports of this regency for the year 1863. It is due to say that my statistical information is furnished by our consular agents from the seven most important Tunisian ports, and is taken by them from the local custom-house officers; but I am assured by trustworthy merchants, who possess ample means for obtaining practical knowledge, that the imports and exports of the regency are probably five or six times greater than here represented. Statute laws establish import and export duties—the former at 3 per cent. ad valorem, and the latter at from 3 to 75 per cent.; but these laws are virtually nullified by those appointed to enforce them, and the custom-house revenues of the government are small.

The invoice of imports amounts to $4,500,000, which exceeds the invoice of the previous year by more than $1,000,000.

The invoice of exports amounts to $5,050,000, which exceeds the invoice of the previous year by more than $2,000,000.

The imports coming from France amount to $2,150,000; those from England and Malta to $1,200,000, and those from Italy to $670,000.

The exports to France amount to $2,260,000; those to England and Malta to $950,000, and those to Italy to $800,000.

Olive oil and wool were the most important articles of export, and next to these grain, red caps, (shesheas,) and cattle. Cotton culture received a new impulse last year; 300 bales were exported, and preparations are made to raise ten times that amount this season.

There is a law prohibiting the exportation of horses, and the export duty on many articles is so heavy as to amount to a prohibition.

No direct trade is carried on at present with America, but many American articles find their way here through Malta, Leghorn, and Marseilles, and a cargo of wool was sent last year to New York, *via* Liverpool.

The crops of 1863 were generally abundant, and the country exhibited signs of material improvement.

LIBERIA.

Monrovia—A. Hanson, *Consul General*.

Statement showing the description, quantity, and value of the imports at the port of Monrovia, from the United States and other countries, during the fiscal year ended September 30, 1864.

Description.	From the United States.		From other countries.	
	Quantity.	Value.	Quantity.	Value.
Cotton....................yards..	10,312	$2,304 76	102,554	$10,027 59
Pork....................barrels..	101	1,806 45	31	507 15
Beef..........................do....	114	635 00	28	422 40
Flour.........................do....	614	5,486 03	54	394 32
Bacon..................pounds..	29,200	2,996 39	....	....
Hams.........................do....	23,791	2,437 22	4,636	620 58
Fish......................barrels..	692	5,506 99	4	15 00
Corn meal ....do....	16¼	93 07	....	....
Lard ....pounds..	2,220	432 32	472	58 89

Table showing the description, quantity, and value of imports—Continued.

Description.	From the United States.		From other countries.	
	Quantity.	Value.	Quantity.	Value.
Butter......................tins..	772	$818 42	91	$442 74
Sugar ....pounds..	1,581	278 21	2,000	470 09
Tea ....do....	156	177 70	426	277 30
Tobacco......................hhds..	47	22,469 42	36¼	11,749 73
Hake, (fish)..............barrels..	22,438	1,040 92	....	....
Herrings....................boxes..	1,760	838 75	....	....
Hats....:..................dozens..	182	765 12	11	128 90
Clothing.....................do....	1	126 76	95	1,038 90
Spirits....................gallons..	3,603	2,118 85	17,401	5,992 95
Candles.....................boxes..	62	135 32	211	433 10
Brass......................pounds..	2,605¼	1,042 20	11,174	3,526 96
Iron.........................do....	1,400	91 00	43,807	1,702 24
Powder.......................kegs..	....	....	10,807	8,791 88
Nails........................do...	205	1,207 87	22	146 31
Satin stripes..............pieces..	....	....	7,180	3,465 00
Tom coffees, (cotton goods)....do..	....	....	5,575	3,834 64
Rumalls ....do.........do..	....	....	9,672	5,783 08
White baffs, (cotton)........pieces..	....	....	2,582	3,569 60
Madras handkerchiefs ....do..	6	10 00	3,759	4,227 32
Umbrellas...................dozen..	13¼	127 62	49¼	696 13
Paint........................kegs.	62	127 25	39	103 70
Guns ....dozen..	42	49 70	480	8,312 60
Brooms.....................dozen..	41	75 63	....	....
Shoes..................doz. pairs..	247¼	2,588 30	26	394 30
Lumber.......................feet..	52,317	901 19	....	....
Ale........................barrels..	27	294 33	334	2,027 76
Fancy goods	....	563 14	....	2,541 48
Tubs.......................nests..	70	239 75	....	....
Trunks......................do...	4	111 50	14	116 48
Soap.......................boxes..	571	521 63	896	666 30
Pipes.......................do..	....	....	326	366 44
Cheese....................pounds..	1,640	87 63	600	88 02
Socks and hose..........doz. pairs..	23¼	81 82	25	63 20
Biscuit ....tins..	155	223 84	8	16 00
Kerosene....................do...	59	259 90	8¼	78 88
Axes ....dozen..	10	85 75	224	215 20
Linen......................yards..	55	23 80	....	....
Flannel......................de...	1,151	257 78	1,272	412 60
Medicines...................	....	1,057 64	....	45 00
Wines.....................boxes..	81	337 00	256	1,448 40
Cider........................do...	20	55 00	....	....
Chairs.....................dozen..	4	106 50	....	....
Handkerchiefs, (red).........pieces..	....	....	1,645	1,334 40
Crockery...................dozen..	....	....	6,829	3,251 00
Salt.........................tons..	....	....	345	746 73
Bread.....................barrels..	....	....	51	280 40
Beads.....................pounds..	....	....	2,871	948 05
Spool cotton...............dozen..	54	41 62	197	116 32
Knives.......................do....	....	....	143	86 50
Paint oil..................gallons..	....	....	417	282 29
Cutlasses ....dozen..	....	....	3,459	1,183 00
Miscellaneous................	....	2,321 13	....	6,125 72
Total......	....	63,358 22	....	99,572 17
Grand total................	....	....	....	$162,930 39

Statement showing the description, quantity, and value of merchandise exported from the port of Monrovia to the United States and other countries for the year ended September 30, 1864.

Description.	United States.		Great Britain.		Hamburg.	
	Quant'y.	Value.	Quant'y.	Value.	Quant'y.	Value.
Palm oil ....galls..	91,887	$36,330 22	58,976	$23,590 40	176,187	$70,475 80
Camwood..........tons..	27	1,266 58	1¼	63 75	5	3,949 64
Sugar ....lbs..	215,506	9,875 20	41,754	2,067 75	7,424	371 20
Sirup and molasses.galls..	9,232	1,593 90	8,433	414 06		
Palm kernels .....bush..			438	257 90	15,824	9,209 40
Hides .....No..	196	81 00	46	24 00		
Country cloths .....No..			610	488 00		
Coffee ....lbs..	11,606	2,370 14	2,166	433 25	300	60 00
Lumber ....feet..			3,500	140 00		
Ivory.............lbs..	755	593 50			984	636 97
Cotton.............lbs..	800	320 00				
Rice ....bush..						
Total.............		52,430 54		27,499 11		84,703 01

Statement—Continued.

Description.	Holland.		Sierra Leone.		Total.	
	Quant'y.	Value.	Quant'y.	Value.	Quant'y.	Value.
Palm oil ....galls..	2,850	$721 21	3,066	$1,442 40	333,506	$132,560 03
Camwood..........tons..					113¼	5,279 97
Sugar .....lbs..			41,535	2,492 10	306,219	14,826 25
Sirup and molasses.galls..			350	140 00	18,015	2,147 96
Palm kernels .....bush..			395	244 00	16,657	9,711 30
Hides .....No..					242	105 00
Country cloths .....No..			3,324	2,650 45	3,934	3,138 45
Coffee ....lbs..			100	23 00	14,172	2,886 39
Lumber ....feet..			2,853	99 85	6,353	239 85
Ivory.............lbs..	169	87 80			1,908	1,318 27
Cotton.............lbs..					800	320 00
Rice ....bush..			75	75 00	75	75 00
Total.............		809 01		7,166 80		172,606 47

CHINA.

SWATOW—J. C. A. WINGATE, *Consul.*

Summary of duties paid at Swatow during the year ended December 31, 1863

Nationality.	No. of vessels.	Tonnage.	Coast trade duty.	Import duty.	Export duty.	Tonnage dues.	Total.
			Tls. m. c.c.	*Tls. m. c.c.*	*Tls. m. c.c.*	*Tls. m. c.c.*	*Tls. m. c.c.*
British.....	248	96,985	14,681 3 5 0	135,581 9 8 5	55,312 7 1 1	5,485 4 0 0	211,061 4 4 6
American..	29	14,055	5,516 1 4 5	1,146 3 2 6	17,922 7 4 5	1,025 2 0 0	25,610 4 1 6
Sundry	127	41,290	17,565 9 5 5	5,839 2 0 9	60,971 6 3 0	5,007 8 0 0	89,384 5 9 4
Total....	404	152,330	37,763 4 5 0	142,567 5 2 0	134,207 0 8 6	11,518 4 0 0	326,056 4 5 6

Comparative statement showing the nationality, number, and tonnage of vessels entered and cleared from Swatow for the year ended December 31, 1863.

Nationality.	ENTERED INWARDS.						CLEARED OUTWARDS.					
	With cargo.		In ballast.		Total.		With cargo.		In ballast.		Total.	
	No.	Tons.	No.	Tons.	No.	Tons.	No.	Tons.	No.	Tons.	No.	Tons.
British......	195	78,775	53	18,210	248	96,985	145	56,514	103	40,471	248	96,985
American....	27	13,091	2	964	29	14,055	19	9,350	10	4,705	29	14,055
Sundry......	117	38,770	10	2,520	127	41,290	76	25,372	51	15,918	127	41,290
Total......	339	130,636	65	21,694	404	152,330	240	91,236	164	61,094	404	152,330

Statement showing the number and destination of vessels cleared from Swatow with cargoes of sugar for the year ended December 31, 1863.

Destination.	No. of vessels.	Brown.	White.	Total.
		Piculs.	Piculs.	Piculs.
Newchwang......................	8	3,110	1,424	4,534
Tien-tsin......................	10	5,395	15,223	20,618
Chefoo......................	29	14,045	13,763	27,808
Shanghai......................	65	198,741	168,101	366,842
Ningpo......................	4	12,223	2,324	14,547
Foochow......................	16	302	4,045	4,347
Amoy......................	3	47	515	562
Singapore......................	6	1,612	386	1,998
Total......................	139	235,475	205,781	441,256

Comparative statement showing the import and export trade at the port of Swatow during the years 1862 and 1863.

Imports.	1862.	1863.	Decrease.	Increase.
Shirtings, gray ....pieces..	41,895	29,859	12,036	....
Shirtings, white..................do...	15,105	10,547	4,558	....
Shirtings, spotted..................do...		18	....	18
T-cloths, 24 yards ....do...	31,595	10,717	20,878	....
Cambrics ....do...	....	559	....	559
Chintz..................do...	....	469	....	469
Cottons, dyed ....do...	1,688	6,673	....	4,985
Damasks ....do...	1,015	230	785	....
Drills, American..................do...	2,488	2,300	188	....
Handkerchiefs ....dozen.	1,752	2,728	....	976
Linen ....pieces...	159	314	....	155
Muslin ....do...	....	259	....	259
Velvet ....do...	....	1,897	....	1,897
Camlets, English ....do...	1,391	1,348	43	....
Camlets, Dutch..................do...	16	27	....	11
Camlets, imitation ....do...	....	835	....	835
Lastings ....do...	1,271	922	349	....
Long ells ....do...	2,969	3,155	....	186
Spanish stripes ....do...	1,281	1,997	....	716
Metals—Iron, nail-rod, and bar..piculs..	6,104	3,050	3,054	....
Iron wire..................do...	....	27	....	27
Lead ....do...	795	1,132	....	337
Tin ....do...	1,997	3,694	....	1,697
Composition ....do...	....	599	....	599
Cotton yarn..................do...	5,310	3,804	1,506	....
Opium, Malwa..................chests..	1,978½	2,216½	....	238

Imports.	1862.	1863.	Decrease.	Increase.
Opium, Patna.................chests..	1,251½	1,527½	....	275½
Bean cake ....piculs..	470,513	1,048,659	....	578,146
Beans and peas................do...	93,432	212,156	....	118,725
Cotton, native................do...	34,970	42,921	....	7,951
Hemp ....do...	686	496	190	....
Mangrove bark ....do...	60	1,848	....	1,788
Manure cakes ....do...	2,867	3,424	....	557
Nankeens.....................do...	951	1,339	....	388
Pepper, black ....do...	1,494	1,845	....	351
Pepper, white ....do...	62	147	....	85
Ratans.......................do...	1,301	1,657	....	356
Rice.........................do...	23,139	12,210	10,949	....
Silk piece goods ....do...	137	121	16	....
Tea ....do...	....	222	....	222
Vermicelli....................do...	4,262	6,074	....	1,812
Estimated value of articles above enumerated.	$5,055,371	$7,043,277	....	$1,987,906
Estimated value of articles not enumerated in the above list.	143,704	283,462	....	139,758
Total value of import trade	5,199,075	7,326,739	....	2,127,664

Exports.

Exports.	1862.	1863.	Decrease.	Increase.
Betel leaf ....piculs..	754	999	....	245
Capoor cutchery ....do...	1,169	378	791	....
Chinaware, coarse ....do...	22,725	23,517	....	792
Earthenware...................do...	1,064	2,142	....	1,078
Grass cloth...................do...	455	1,131	....	676
Hemp thread ....do...	494	314	180	....
Leather ....do...	456	364	92	....
Paper ....do...	43,980	84,735	....	40,755
Potato flour...................do...	20,427	14,873	5,554	....
Shoes.........................pairs..	50,139	53,639	....	3,500
Sugar, brown ....piculs..	247,465	236,082	11,383	....
Sugar, white ....do...	206,513	204,901	1,612	....
Tobacco ....do...	7,482	7,372	110	....
Tobacco leaf ....do...	373	381	....	8
Vegetables ....do...	11,610	8,134	3,476	....
Estimated value of articles above enumerated.	$3,026,691	$3,080,808	....	$54,117
Estimated value of articles not enumerated in the above list.	183,577	254,269	....	70,692
Total value of export trade.........	3,210,268	3,335,077	....	124,809

Shipping.	1862.		1863.		Decrease.	Increase.
	Vessels.	Tons.	Vessels.	Tons.	Tons.	Tons.
Inward with cargo	214	83,138	339	130,636	....	47,498
Inward in ballast..............	37	11,776	65	21,694	....	9,918
Outward with cargo	175	66,477	240	91,236	....	24,759
Outward in ballast	70	26,261	164	61,094	....	34,833

Comparative statement—Continued.

Summary.	1862.	1863.	1863.	
			Decrease.	Increase.
	Mex. dolls.	*Mex. dolls.*	*Mex. dolls.*	*Mex. dolls.*
Value of import trade	5, 199, 075	7, 326, 739	....	2, 127, 664
Value of export trade.................	3, 210, 268	3, 335, 077	....	124, 809
Total	8, 409, 343	10, 661, 816	....	2, 252, 473

SHANGHAI—G. F. SEWARD, *Consul.*

Summary statement showing the value of the import and export trade at the port of Shanghai for the year ended December 31, 1863.

VALUE OF IMPORT TRADE.

              £ *s.* *d.*
General imports .... Tls. 61,704,099.1 *a* 6*s.* 4¼*d.=* 19,603,906 9 8½
Opium imports:
 Malwa—29,987 chests, (equal to 29,987.00 piculs,) average rate, tls. 538.. Tls. 16,133,006.0
 Patna—6,864 chests, (equal to 8,236.80 piculs,) average rate, tls. 500...................................... Tls. 4,118,400.0 } *a* 6*s.* 4¼*d.=* 6,434,040 8 11½
Treasure imported for the year .... Tls. 11,556,600.0 *a* 6*s.* 4¼*d.=* 3,671,628 2 6

                  29,709 575 1 2¼

VALUE OF EXPORT TRADE.

              £ *s.* *d.*
General exports... Tls. 38,485,465.3 *a* 6*s.* 4¼*d.=* 12,227,153 0 9

VALUE OF RE-EXPORT TRADE.

              £ *s.* *d.*
General re-exports.. Tls. 35,583,654.9 *a* 6*s.* 4¼*d.=* 11,305,223 14 6
Opium re-exports:
 Malwa—10,415 chests, (equal to 10,415.00 piculs,) average rate, tls. 538 .... Tls. 5,603,270.0
 Patna—191 chests, (equal to 229.90 piculs,) average rate, tls. 500 ....,........ Tls. 114,600.0 } *a* 6*s.* 4¼*d.=* 1,816.614 18 11½
*Treasure re-exported for the year........................ Tls. 17,176,631.0 *a* 6*s.* 4¼*d.=* 5,457,158 16 1½

                  18,578.997 9 7½

* The treasure returned as re-exported is treasure which arrived during 1863 and the preceding year and which was exported during 1863 to other ports in China and to Japan.

Summary statement showing the tonnage and value of trade at the port of Shanghai from July 12, 1854, to December 31, 1863.

Date.	VALUE OF TRADE.				
	Imports.			Re-exports.	Exports.
	General.	Opium.	Total.		
	Taels.	*Taels.*	*Taels.*	*Taels.*	*Taels.*
Year ending June 30, 1855..................	3,507,524	*9,113,454	12,620,978	....	24,549,062
Year ending June 30, 1856..................	6,492,299	*11,529,308	18,021,607	....	23,427,215
Half year ending December 31, 1856.......	5,189,821	*5,571,000	10,760,821	....	20,530,337
Year ending December 31, 1857	15,863,393	*11,252,514	30,115,907	....	33,344,435
Year ending December 31, 1858.............	19,017,049	*15,822,320	34,839,369	....	30,623,759
Year ending December 31, 1859.............	20,635,130	*15,397,350	36,032,480	†2,899,558	36,670,608
Year ending December 31, 1860.............	26,225,588	*14,857,440	41,083,028	†11,759,164	31,363,880
Year ending December 31, 1861.............	33,702,814	12,138,232	45,840,846	†21,630,724	28,236,733
Year ending December 31, 1862.............	46,701,584	18,604,140	65,305,721	†30,365,519	47,569,966
Year ending December 31, 1863.............	61,704,099	20,251,406	81,955,505	†35,563,654	38,485,465

Date.	TONNAGE OF SHIPPING—ENTERED INWARDS.							
	British vessels.		American vessels.		Sundry vessels.		Total vessels.	
	No.	*Tons.*	*No.*	*Tons.*	*No.*	*Tons.*	*No.*	*Tons.*
Year ending June 30, 1855	213	71,971	77	49,943	66	19,336	356	141,250
Year ending June 30, 1856	287	86,224	81	40,425	121	28,938	489	155,587
Half year ending December 31,1856.	163	49,064	38	30,908	87	17,107	288	97,099
Year ending December 31, 1857	302	115,409	61	44,850	270	45,354	633	205,613
Year ending December 31, 1858	290	120,205	97	56,280	367	66,139	754	214,624
Year ending December 31, 1859	376	142,008	177	75,228	373	69,864	926	287,100
Year ending December 31, 1860	494	143,609	248	93,365	365	64,180	1,007	304,154
Year ending December 31, 1861	810	229,894	359	95,858	637	93,907	1,806	419,659
Year ending December 31, 1862	1,532	390,189	806	226,056	560	107,943	2,898	724,138
Year ending December 31, 1863	1,790	530,921	820	272,428	790	160,960	3,400	964,309

Date.	TONNAGE OF SHIPPING—CLEARED OUTWARDS.							
	British vessels.		American vessels.		Sundry vessels.		Total vessels.	
	No.	*Tons.*	*No.*	*Tons.*	*No.*	*Tons.*	*No.*	*Tons.*
Year ending June 30, 1855..........	133	54,463	46	43,041	44	14,089	223	111,593
Year ending June 30, 1856..........	277	81,814	81	43,446	114	28,730	472	153,990
Half year ending December 31,1856.	145	45,748	25	17,703	80	15,721	250	79,172
Year ending December 31, 1857.....	169	66,149	35	28,101	94	19,993	298	114,243
Year ending December 31, 1858.....	174	77,496	56	38,270	148	39,029	378	154,795
Year ending December 31 1859.....	383	150,016	179	78,184	377	61,509	939	289,709
Year ending December 31, 1860.....	485	138,068	235	95,071	252	60,429	972	293,568
Year ending December 31, 1861.....	782	229,775	344	92,305	621	86,115	1,747	408,195
Year ending December 31, 1862.....	1,521	389,280	805	226,056	560	107,943	2,896	723,279
Year ending December 31, 1863.....	1,810	554,716	884	287,021	853	155,153	3,547	996,890

* The values of the opium trade for the years preceding 1861 have not been derived from this office. Opium customs business was not done through this office until the end of 1860, when the importation of the drug was legalized by the tariff rules attached to the new treaties.
† Exclusive of opium re-exported to Chinese ports.

Summary statement showing the nationality, number, and tonnage of vessels entered at and cleared from Shanghai for the half year ended June 30, 1863.

Nationality.	ENTERED INWARDS.						CLEARED OUTWARDS.					
	With cargo.		In ballast.		Total.		With cargo.		In ballast.		Total.	
	No.	Tons.	No.	Tons.	No.	Tons.	No.	Tons.	No.	Tons.	No.	Tons.
British	518	223,609	113	17,471	631	241,080	468	181,125	161	60,838	627	241,963
Ningpo boats, &c., under British flag	244	18,799	87	4,839	331	28,638	221	19,104	113	5,935	334	25,039
American	231	106,597	26	6,915	257	115,512	187	91,639	125	44,101	312	135,740
Ningpo boats, &c., under American flag	129	8,029	49	3,614	178	11,643	154	10,591	56	3,218	210	13,809
Sundry	259	73,847	10	2,717	269	76,564	168	48,290	85	22,773	253	71,065
Ningpo boats, &c., under various flags	79	4,183	15	578	94	4,761	46	2,654	35	1,762	81	4,416
Chinese—Ningpo boats	74	3,612	10	479	84	4,091	79	3,781	4	900	83	3,981
Total	1,534	440,676	310	36,613	1,844	477,289	1,321	357,184	579	138,929	1,900	494,013

Summary statement showing the nationality, number, and tonnage of vessels entered at and cleared from Shanghai for the half year ended December 31, 1863.

Nationality.	ENTERED INWARDS.						CLEARED OUTWARDS.					
	With cargo.		In ballast.		Total.		With cargo.		In ballast.		Total.	
	No.	Tons.	No.	Tons.	No.	Tons.	No.	Tons.	No.	Tons.	No.	Tons.
British	546	232,991	120	21,403	666	253,694	513	220,779	197	55,896	710	276,685
Ningpo boats, &c., under British flag	131	10,315	31	2,194	162	12,509	115	9,534	94	1,575	139	11,109
American	220	132,252	19	2,771	242	135,023	176	102,174	60	26,447	236	128,621
Ningpo boats, &c., under American flag	124	9,039	19	1,211	143	10,250	93	6,846	33	2,005	196	8,851
Sundry	223	65,395	18	3,887	241	69,282	171	51,613	61	17,464	232	69,077
Ningpo boats, &c., under various flags	18	1,018	7	667	25	1,645	16	1,021	13	861	29	1,882
Chinese—Ningpo boats	64	3,769	13	808	77	4,577	75	4,232			75	4,238
Total	1,336	454,079	220	32,941	1,556	487,020	1,159	396,199	388	104,178	1,547	500,377

Summary statement of duties paid at Shanghai during the year ended December 31, 1863.

	Imports	Exports	Tonnage dues	Total
	T. m.c.c	*T. m.c.c*	*T. m.c.c*	*T. m.c.c*
During half year ended June 30, 1863	342,812 0 4 7	373,973 4 8 7	81,543 2 0 0	798,328 7 3 4
During half year ended December 31, 1863	254,848 4 4 3	382,380 6 0 3	98,244 8 5 0	735,473 8 9 6
During the year ended December 31, 1863, on opium landed	597,660 4 9 0	756,354 0 9 0	179,788 0 5 0	1,533,802 6 3 0
During the year ended December 31, 1863, half or coast trade duties				717,104 3 8 9
During the year ended December 31, 1863,				275,714 4 5 0
				*2,526,621 4 6 9

* Equivalent to taels 2,814,656 3 1 6 Shanghai syees, at 6s. 4½d. per tael = £894,539 15s. 4d.

Statement showing the quantity, value, and destination of the silk exported from Shanghai for the half year ended June 30, 1863.

Destination.	Raw.			Thrown.			Japan.*			Total.			Coarse.			Refuse.			Cocoons.		
	Bales.	Piculs.	Ct.	Bales.	Piculs.	Ct.	Bales.	Piculs.	Ct.	Bales.	Piculs.	Ct.	Bales.	Piculs.	Ct.	Bales.	Piculs.	Ct.	Bales.	Picula.	Ct.
Great Britain, direct	645	517	60				228	391	36	873	908	96				418	925	13	160	226	60
United States	178	149	18	60	57	90				178	142	18	78	64	21	493	153	84			
Hong Kong for foreign ports	8,641	6,958	53	14	10	96	4,757	3,711	86	13,458	12,728	69	98	22	40	1	1	73			
Coast ports	64	51	21							78	78	17									
Total	9,528	7,669	38	74	68	86	4,985	4,033	22	14,567	13,771	40	106	86	61	612	1,080	70	160	226	60

* In addition to the silk in this column, which is all re-exports, there were 19 bales transshipped to G. Britain, 30 bales to the United States, and 3,356 bales to Hong-Kong for foreign ports.

For the half year ended December 31, 1863.

Destination.	Raw.			Thrown.			Japan.*			Total.			Coarse.			Refuse.			Cocoons.		
	Bales.	Piculs.	Ct.	Bales.	Piculs.	Ct.	Bales.	Piculs.	Ct.	Bales.	Piculs.	Ct.	Bales.	Picula.	Ct.	Bales.	Piculs.	Ct.	Bales.	Picula.	Ct.
Great Britain, direct	3,006	2,363	89				190	120	84	3,196	2,514	73	23	53	15	551	673	94	2	3	40
United States	265	212	51				185	147	58	450	360	09				11	9	11			
Manila	39	31	20							39	31	90							48	76	11
Hong Kong for foreign ports	17,501	13,994	68	77	75	89	1,497	2,038	26	19,075	16,038	83	1	1	80						
Coast ports	364	293	69	20	16	68				384	310	37									
Total	21,175	16,855	97	97	92	57	1,872	2,306	68	23,144	19,255	22	24	53	95	562	882	35	50	79	51

* In addition to the silk in this column, which is all re-exports, there were 66 bales transshipped to G. Britain, 17 bales to the United States, and 3,256 bales to Hong-Kong for foreign ports.

Statement showing the description, quantity, and value of the silk exported from Shanghai for the year ended December 31, 1863.

Description	Great Britain, direct.			Hong Kong for foreign ports.			United States.			Manilla.			Coast ports.			Total.		
	Bales.	Piculs.	Cts.	Bales.	Piculs.	Cts.	Bales.	Piculs.	Cts.	Bales.	Piculs.	Cts.	Bales.	Piculs.	Cts.	Bales.	Piculs.	Cts.
Raw	3,651	2,911	49	26,142	20,883	01	443	354	69		31	90	428	344	90	30,703	94,355	93
Thrown	418	442	90	137	133	79							34	37	64	171	181	43
Japan, (exclusive of transshipment)	23	53	15	6,254	5,750	12	185	147	58	39						6,339	98	90
Coarse	969	1,799	37	79	65	01							98	92	40	130	140	98
Refuse	168	320	00	1		73	204	162	95							1,174	1,963	05
Cocoons				48	76	11										210	306	11

Statement showing the export of tea from Shanghai for the half year ended June 30, 1863.

Destination	Congou.		Souchong.		Oolong.		Flowery Pekoe.		Brick.		Total black.		Sorts, unclassed Japan.		Young Hyson.		Hyson.		Hyson skin.		Twankay.		Imperial.		Gunpowder.		Total green.	
	Pic'ls.	Cts.	Pic'ls.	Cts.	Pic'ls.	Cts.	Pic'ls.	Cts.	Pic'ls.	Cts.	Pic'ls.	Cts.	Pic'ls.	Cts.	Pic'ls.	Cts.	Pic'ls.	Cts.	Pic'ls.	Cts.	Pic'ls.	Cts.	Pic'ls.	Cts.	Pic'ls.	Cts.	Pic'ls.	Cts.
Great Britain, direct	64,187	67	530	18	597	12	428	48	7,940	06	73,313	51	1,175	74	18,989	92	7,370	92	199	66	2,152	37	3,445	07	11,158	55	44,092	93
United States	99	29	28	71	109	90					85	90	1,323	00	20,746	96	2,183	78	243	57	936	04	3,461	43	4,602	61	34,658	93
Hong Kong and coast ports	2,814	18					87	12	1,066	54	3,967	84	322	11	477	83	746	61	270	91	356	91	89	137	4,185	61	4,329	98
Australia	1,804	31									1,804	31					134	19	64	63	1,865	34	18	57	18	57	3,004	08
Montreal	1,552	46	340	03	419	88			2	94	1,314	61			8,842	72	1,201	19	62	30	1,374	99	1,067	61	2,681	34	15,949	45
Japan															360	80	46	19			97	22	94	52	59	75	518	48
Total	69,473	91	598	99	1,056	90	517	84	9,006	60	80,654	17	2,820	85	49,417	39	13,205	00	944	97	7,432	97	8,294	54	18,707	63	100,823	35

Total.

Green.
Great Britain, direct	5,878,984	lbs.
United States	4,618,172½	lbs.
Hong Kong and coast ports	576,381½	lbs.
Australia	267,304	lbs.
Montreal	2,033,260	lbs.
Japan	69,130¾	lbs.

13,443,113¾ lbs.

Black.
Great Britain, direct	9,775,134¾	lbs.
United States	33,853	lbs.
Hong Kong and coast ports	259,043	lbs.
Australia	240,574¾	lbs.
Montreal	175,281¼	lbs.

10,753,889¼ lbs.

Total.
Green	15,654,086¾	lbs.
	4,652,026¾	lbs.
	1,105,426¾	lbs.
	507,778¾	lbs.
	2,208,541½	lbs.
	69,130¾	lbs.

94,197,009½ lbs.

Statement showing the export of tea from Shanghai for the half year ended December 31, 1863.

Destination.	Congou.	Souchong.	Oolong.	Flowery Pekoe.	Brick.	Total black.	Sorts, unclassed Japan.	Young Hyson.	Hyson.	Hyson skin.	Twankay.	Imperial.	Gunpowder.	Total green.
	Pic'ls. Cts.	*Pic'ls. Cts.*	*Pic'ls. Cts.*	*Pic'ls. Cts.*	*Pic'ls. Cts.*	*Pic'ls. Cts.*	*Pic'ls. Cts.*	*Pic'ls. Cts.*	*Pic'ls. Cts.*	*Pic'ls. Cts.*	*Pic'ls. Cts.*	*Pic'ls. Cts.*	*Pic'ls. Cts.*	*Pic'ls. Cts.*
Great Britain, direct	246,421 69	743 32	1,376 48	271 46	7,344 78	236,157 73	6,092 40	8,576 00	1,748 95	38 81	1,198 56	3,254 32	7,504 42	28,413 46
United States	86 90	....	326 52	....	....	413 42	3,285 17	14,072 66	3,912 96	146 82	1,173 64	3,702 54	3,766 02	30,059 81
Hong Kong and coast ports	3,174 56	....	....	84 89	13,017 37	16,276 82	791 41	2,190 58	1,557 64	....	234 60	13 52	32 83	4,820 58
Bombay	....	....	....	62 75	....	62 75	....	....	20 06	....	....	....	....	20 06
Total	249,683 15	743 32	1,703 00	419 10	20,362 15	272,910 72	10,168 98	24,839 24	7,239 61	185 63	2,006 80	6,970 38	11,303 27	63,313 91

	Black.	*Green.*	*Total.*
Great Britain, direct	34,154,364 lbs.	3,788,461½ lbs.	37,942,825½ lbs.
United States	55,122¾ lbs.	4,007,974¾ lbs.	4,063,097½ lbs.
Hong Kong and coast ports	2,170,242¾ lbs.	642,744 lbs.	2,812,986¾ lbs.
Bombay	8,366¾ lbs.	2,674¾ lbs.	11,041½ lbs.
Total	36,388,076 lbs.	8,441,854¾ lbs.	44,829,950¾ lbs.

Summary statement of the opium trade at the port of Shanghai for the year ended December 31, 1863.

Imports.	Malwa.		Patna and Benares.		Duty.
	Chests.	*Weight.*	*Chests.*	*Weight.*	*Haiquan taels.*
Imported and stored on board receiving vessels	29,893	29,893.00	6,670	8,004.00	*
Imported direct to the shore	94	94.00	194	232.80	*
Total	29,987	29,987.90	6,864	8,236.80	*
Landed from receiving vessels and intended chiefly for local consumption	14,474½	14,474,50	5,825	6,989.50	643,923'0 0 0
Re-exports—					
Transhipped from receiving vessels for Yang-tsze ports	3,455½	3,455.50	38	45.60	73,181 3 8 9
Transhipped from receiving vessels for coast ports	6,941½	6,941.50	103	123.60	*
Re-exported direct from the shore	18	18.00	50	60.00	*
Total	10,415	10,415.00	191	229.20	73,181 3 8 9
Total amount of duties collected on opium for 1863	....	....	....	....	717,104 3 8 9

AMOY.

Statement showing the nationality of vessels, the quantity and value of the exports of teas from Amoy to the United States during the year ended September 30, 1864.

EXPORTS.

Nationality of vessels.	Where bound.	Quantity.	Value.	Teas.
		Pounds.		
British	New York	361,007	$81,911 22	Teas.
Hamburg	Do	408,007	82,207 92	do
Bremen	Do	333,291	64,450 61	do
Danish	Do	395,861	73,211 48	do
Hamburg	Do	258,816	56,987 84	do
British	Do	418,225	97,575 97	do
Do	Do	489,709	119,691 53	do
American	Do ..... partial cargo	454,639	92,688 05	do
Sundry transhipments	Do	471,242	93,717 35	do
Total to the United States		3,590,797	762,441 97	....

Total export of teas from Amoy during the above year, 6,921,208 pounds.

HANKOW—WILLIAM BRECK, *Consul.*

SEPTEMBER 2, 1864.

*   *   *   *   *   *   *   *   *

About three and a half years have elapsed since this port was opened to foreign trade, and the vast resources of the interior of China known to the world. The navigation of the Yangtze is now familiar to river pilots. Nankin has been abandoned by the Taiping rebels, and the whole river, from this city to Shanghai, is now unobstructed. Trade on the Yangtze up to this point has not answered the anticipations formed in the earlier stages of business. Freights for steamers have become very scarce, and rates have fallen from $26 66 per ton to Shanghai to $2 66, and the latter is the established rate.

There are thirty-two established houses or *houghs* here, of which three are American.

The foreign population numbers about three hundred. Six months since there were twelve American steamers running regularly on the river between Shanghai and this port. There are now but six, together with five British steamers.

In my judgment, there will be no improvement so long as trade is restricted as it is at present. Free trade on the Yangtze and at all the ports opened to foreigners would greatly stimulate business. Large cities between this and Shanghai are closed to foreign trade, thus cutting off intercourse and business so easy and natural by steam navigation. Until these barriers are removed the full advantages of the opening of the Yangtze to foreign trade can never be realized.

Statement showing the nationality, tonnage, and number of vessels entered at, and cleared from, Hankow for the year ended December 31, 1863.

Nationality and class of vessels.	ENTERED INWARDS.						CLEARED OUTWARDS.					
	With cargo.		In ballast.		Total.		With cargo.		In ballast.		Total.	
	No.	Tons.	No.	Tons.	No.	Tons.	No.	Tons.	No.	Tons.	No.	Tons.
British—												
Steamers under Shanghae river steamer pass	76	40,372	6	2,556	82	42,928	79	41,023	2	792	81	41,815
Steamers, ships, and lorchas under Chinkiang pass	95	4,503	21	3,392	46	7,895	37	6,891	4	350	41	7,941
Junks under special junk pass	5	250	3	150	8	400	44	4,305	7	332	86	4,637
Rafts under special junk pass											44	
American—												
Steamers under Shanghae river steamer pass	163	130,071	9	4,888	172	134,959	162	129,528	9	4,425	171	133,953
Lorchas under Chinkiang pass	93	2,848	24	1,340	47	4,188	39	2,420	1	63	40	2,489
Junks under special junk pass			2	100	2	100	192	11,174¾	1	25	183	11,199¼
Rafts under special junk pass							13				13	
French—												
Lorchas under Chinkiang pass	6	418	4	939	10	657	8	493			8	493
Junks under special junk pass							42	2,207	4	160	46	2,367
Rafts under special junk pass							3				3	
Total	298	178,462	69	12,665	367	191,127	698	198,039¾	28	6,146	726	204,185¾

Summary of duties paid at Hankow during the year ended December 31, 1863.

	Tls.	m.	c.	c.
Steamers under the Shanghae river pass	1,175,986	4	3	6
Vessels under the Chinkiang pass	65,273	0	0	1
Junks and rafts under the special junk pass	52,743	2	5	6
Total	1,314,002	6	9	3

NOTE.—This discrepancy between vessels entered inwards and cleared outwards is owing, on the one hand, to the rafts which cleared from Hankow, and of course never returned, and also to the large number of Hankow-built junks which cleared from Hankow, and either never returned, or returned under the Chinese flag; and, on the other hand, to certain vessels which arrived, but did not clear before 1st January, 1864, and which are therefore included in the inward and not in the outward return.

Summary statement showing the destination of vessels under the Chinkiang pass, cleared at the port of Hankow during the year 1863.

	Chinkiang.	Ningpo.	Shanghai.	Shanghai and Ningpo.	London.	Total.
British	3	27	6	....	5	41
American	5	29	5	1	....	40
French	....	5	3	....	....	8
Total.........	8	61	14	1	5	89

Destination of native craft and rafts under the special junk pass, cleared at the port of Hankow during the year 1863.

	KIUKIANG.		CHINKIANG.		SHANGHAI.		Total.
	Junks.	Rafts.	Junks.	Rafts.	Junks.	Rafts.	
British	3	4	20	38	63	2	130
American	1	....	149	12	43	1	206
French	....	....	12	2	34	1	49
Total	4	4	181	52	140	4	385

CANTON—O. H. PERRY, *Consul.*

Summary statement showing the tonnage of the British and American vessels entered and cleared at the port of Canton during the year 1863 ; also the tonnage duties, and value of the imports, exports, and coast trade.

Period.	Tonnage.	Coast trade.	Imports.	Exports.	Tonnage dues.	Total.‡
*British.**		*Taels. m. c. c.*	*Taels. m. c. c.*	*Taels. m. c. c.*	*Taels. m. c. c.*	*Taels. m. c. c.*
First half year........	40,836	3,584 8 5 9	36,117 4 4 8	216,349 1 2 6	5,202 3 0 0	257,668 8 7 4
Second half year	39,460	2,041 0 0 6	19,122 6 0 9	181,757 0 0 1	5,929 5 0 0	206,800 1 1 0
American.†						
First half year	81,561	7,401 2 0 7	112,060 2 5 6	72,926 2 0 5	2,529 8 0 0	187,516 2 6 1
Second half year	110,687	8,022 3 5 1	64,940 2 0 2	114,025 5 9 6	1,192 4 0 0	180,158 1 9 8
Sundry,						
First half year........	13,336	1,815 8 0 2	2,344 0 8 8	57,097 9 9 7	2,002 4 0 0	61,444 4 8 5
Second half year	15,399	1,377 9 9 0	2,451 4 5 4	28,169 4 4 8	2,106 2 0 0	32,727 1 0 2
Total..............	301,279	24,243 2 1 5	237,036 0 5 7	670,325 3 7 3	18,953 6 0 0	926,315 0 3 0

* Including 22,651 tons river steamers and lorchas.   † Including 172,170 tons river steamers.
‡ These totals do not include coast trade duty.

Period.					Black.	Green.	Total.
	Piculs. cts.	*Piculs. cts.*	*Piculs. cts.*		*Lbs.*	*Lbs.*	*Lbs.*
1st half year...	83 21	937 07	922 00		11,112,512	3,480,956	14,593,468
2d half year...	212 91	4,767 07	2,990 12		6,931,404	2,938,863	9,870,267
Total.......	296 12	5,704 14	3,912 12	695 71	18,043,916	6,419,819	24,463,735

* One picul is 133⅓ pounds avoirdupois.

Résumé of the import and export trade of Canton for the year 1863.

VALUE OF IMPORT TRADE.

			£	s.	d.
First half year ....Mexican dollars..	5,620,795, at 4s. 9¼d., =	1,346,648	16	0¼
Second half year...do........	3,884,490, at 4s. 9¼d., =	934,705	8	1½
Total..	9,505,285	=	2,281,354	4	2

VALUE OF EXPORT TRADE.

			£	s.	d.
First half year ....Mexican dollars..	7,629,512, at 4s. 9¼d., =	1,827,903	16	4
Second half year...do........	8,453,550, at 4s. 9¼d., =	2,034,135	9	4½
Total..	16,083,062	=	3,862,039	7	8½

MACAO—WILLIAM P. JONES, *Consul.*

JUNE 30, 1864.

* * * The trade of this port has been rather brisk for several months, and I have heard many regrets expressed that the state of our commerce prevented or discouraged freighters from taking American charters. There is no questioning the fact, *ceteris paribus*, American carriers are the favorites on the China coast, and we may well hope to regain our former ascendency after the present domestic troubles are concluded, as fast as our ship-builders and owners can come forward to occupy the field.

DECLINE OF THE CHINESE REBELLION.

It is the prevailing impression in this community that the Taiping rebellion is doomed to recede into the southwest, the ancient home and never-failing retreat of nearly all Chinese insurgency, and that before another summer the export trade of China will experience a great revival. But whether Macao will share very largely in this expected revival is highly problematical; yet with the present encouraging policy of its authorities, and the marked energy and ambition of our new governor, the general trade of China will scarcely advance without an accompanying tide of prosperity for this ancient port.

HAWAIIAN ISLANDS.

HILO—JOHN WORTH, *Acting Consul.*

SEPTEMBER 30, 1864.

I have the honor in this my annual report from this consulate to state that under the new constitution of this kingdom, promulgated on the 20th day of August last, the legislative body is not called to assemble until the 19th day of October next, consequently there are no changes in the commercial system of this kingdom to report.

The exports from this island to the United States direct are confined to a few small shipments of late, consisting of sugar, molasses, pulu, amounting to some $3,500. Articles of export generally consist of sugar, molasses, hides, goat-skins, wool, arrowroot, coffee, pulu. These articles are shipped to Honolulu, thence to market, principally in American vessels, which bring as return cargoes American and English goods as imports. The value of exports or imports I am not able to state. The coffee crop is yearly decreasing, owing to blight. There were exported from Honolulu to San Francisco, principally from this island, from January 1 to September 30, 1864, about 36,000 pounds of pulse, invoiced at 6½ cents per pound. There has been in active operation on this island the last year four sugar plantations, which have manufactured about 900 tons of sugar. Two more will commence manufacturing in from one to two months. It is estimated that the six plantations will manufacture the succeeding season at least 20,000 tons of sugar, with a proportion of molasses. The planters find great difficulty in procuring a sufficient number of laborers, and are taking preliminary steps to procure labor from abroad. These plantations are owned as follows, viz: Three by American capitalists; two by Chinese, and one by German. Steps are being taken to export direct from this port to San Francisco, and should the attempt prove successful will be the means of decreasing the expense of shipping the products of this island considerably. Some feeble attempts have been made within the past few months in raising cotton, but as yet without much success. No doubt there are portions of this island where cotton might be successfully raised by persons experienced in its culture. Tobacco, also, might be raised to a considerable extent, but the scarcity of labor will prevent any great amount of these articles being produced at present. The Hawaiians, as a people, are fast fading away, and these islands must ere long be inhabited by foreigners. Whale ships, the arrival of which may be expected in one month, will give some impetus to trade, which now is, to say the least, not active. A number of these ships, however, may be expected to visit San Francisco this fall, that they may communicate earlier with their owners in regard to shipment of the season's catch, as they are unacquainted with the movements of the rebel privateers.

Exchange on the United States is from par to 2½ discount, payable in gold; payable in currency, unsalable, as the rate must necessarily rule so high.

HAYTI.

CAPE HAYTIEN—ARTHUR FULSOM, *Consul.*

SEPTEMBER 30, 1864.

I have the honor of enclosing herewith my consular returns for the year and quarter ended September 30, 1864.

＊   ＊   ＊   ＊   ＊   ＊   ＊   ＊   ＊   ＊

It will be perceived there is a great diminution in the quantity of coffee exported from Hayti this year from the last, which is owing to a very short crop the last year; it will also be seen that the figures of imports from the United States have augmented at this place, caused, first, by high prices in the United States, secondly and principally, by the Dominicans getting their supplies from this place, in consequence of their ports being blockaded. There is also an augmentation of our exports of tobacco, wax, and hides, received from the Dominicans in exchange for their supplies drawn from this place.

The present crop of coffee looks favorable for a full average. The disproportion of exports to the United States in comparison to the imports continues to be the same: the coffee and logwood are still shipped to Europe, and the difference is made up, as before, by drafts on Europe and gold.

Statement showing the number of vessels entered at and cleared from Gonaives with cargoes to and from the United States during the several quarters of the year ended September 3, 1864.

Quarter ended—	ENTERED.			CLEARED.		
	No.	Cargoes.	Value.*	No.	Cargoes.	Value.*
December 31, 1863...	9	Provisions and lumber..	$108, 632 92	11	Haytian produce.	$638,659 88
March 31, 1864............	9	..........do	126, 169 85	7	.......do	493,753 25
June 30, 1864.............	6	..........do	82, 096 00	8	.......do	1,378,659 59
September 30, 1864	9	..........do	152, 500 98	11	.......do	842,911 17
Total.................	33	....	469, 399 75	37	....	3,353,983 89

* In Haytian currency, at 13¼ cents each.

Produce shipped to United States: Logwood, 4,757,600 lbs.; cotton, 257,645 lbs.; coffee, 4,640 bags—600,146 lbs.; mahogany, 12,234 feet; hides, 990; honey, 844 gallons.

Entered: 9 American vessels, 1,503 tons; 24 foreign vessels, 3,434 tons. Class of American vessels: 1 bark, 5 brigs, 3 schooners.

Summary statement showing the imports and exports of Gonaives during the year ended September 30, 1864.

IMPORTS.		
Description.	Quantity.	Value.
33 American vessels ....Haytian currency..	....	$469, 399 75
28 foreign vessels ....do........	....	111, 277 00
American cotton ....tons..	4, 987	....
American gold	....	6, 953 00

EXPORTS.							
To—	Coffee.	Logwood.	Cotton.	Mahogany.	Hides.	Honey.	Wax.
	Lbs.	Lbs.	Lbs.	Feet.	No.	Gallons.	Lbs.
United States.....................	600, 146	4, 757, 600	257, 214	12, 234	996	844	......
Europe..............................	2, 978, 536	2, 075, 350	183, 818	157, 214	137	....	2, 305
Total.........................	3, 578, 682	6, 832, 950	441, 032	169, 448	1, 133	844	2, 305

Statement showing the comparative value of cotton shipped from the port of St. Marc during the several months of the year 1863.

Month.	Direct export	Coastwise.
January	$5,866	$3,919
February		13,916
March	73,122	110,674
April	125,782	59,536
May	156,038	52,966
June		82,892
July	234,671	91,615
August		96,136
September		71,473
October	13,091	55,063
November		95,210
December	1,436	200
Total	610,006	663,601

Statement showing the description and quantity of exports from Jacmel for the year ended September 30, 1864, compared with those of the previous fiscal year.

Description.	1864.		1863.	
	Quantity.		Quantity.	
	Bags.	Pounds.	Bags.	Pounds.
Coffee	62,446	7,359,548	88,111	10,283,792
Logwood		6,229,100		5,683,700
Braziletto		2,900		5,300
Cotton ....bales..	34	} 48,715	823	17,233
Do..................bales..	222			
Orange peal	10	} 60,235	175	12,978
Do.....................cases..	845			
Shell ....cases..	2	118	2	104
Mahogany ....logs..	475	88,497	437	40,409
Coffee		600		
Yellow wax	10	1,082		

MEXICO.

VERA CRUZ—D. L. LANE, *Consul.*

Statement showing the description, quantity, and value of exports of Vera Cruz to the United States for quarter ended March 31, 1864; also the names of the countries where produced and port whither sent, (compiled from official documents.)

Countries where produced.	Description and quantity.	Value, including charges and costs.	Port whither sent.
Mexico	15 packages grana......................	$2,108 09	New York.
Do	13 bags cochineal and 1 bag coffee	1,861 71	Do.
Do	15 packages grana and 146 hides.	2,485 35	Do.
Do	10 packages grana......................	1,448 21	Do.
Do	25 packages grana......................	3,805 87	Do.
Do	10 packages grana......................	1,516 20	Do.
Do	10 packages grana......................	1,516 20	Do.
Do	410 ox and cow hides...................	783 22	Do.
Do	10 seroons cochineal and 2 bales jalap	1,505 36	Do.
Do	214 wet and 345 dry ox and cow hides....	1,032 70	Do.
Do	3,331 pounds rags....................	16 65	Do.
Do	4,800 Vanilla beans and 4 bales jalap.	686 12	Do.
Do	135 packages goatskins	7,362 60	Do.
Do	37 dry ox hides.......................	80 00	Do. '
Do	541 bales goat skins	27,958 85	Do.
Do	20 seroons of cochineal	2,857 09	Do.
Do	10 bales cochineal	1,463 53	Do.
Do	249 bales goatskins.....................	11,946 46	Do.
Do	10 bales of jalap	1,214 28	Do.
Do	600 bales cotton, 800 hides, and 3 bales deerskins	38,415 89	Do.
Do	20 bales cotton	1,216 55	Do.
Do	644 bales cotton and 3,426 hides	52,468 40	Do.
Do	531 bales cotton and 845 hides	34,272 00	Do.
Do	119 bales of cotton	7,386 89	Do.
Do	21 bales blanca grana..................	1,485 12	Do.
Do	480 hides.............................	1,107 00	Do.
Do	85 bales of goatskins	4,608 48	Do.
Do	142 bales cotton, $10,887 24; and 12 bales jalap, $1,345 88..................	12,233 12	Do.
Do	22 seroons cochineal	3,215 30	Do.
Do	4 bales jalap	643 70	Do.
United States....	600 sacks of oats........................	179 09	Do.
Mexico	30 bales of cotton	2,374 82	Do.
Do	296 bags of cochineal...................	23,852 87	Do.
Do	518 bales raw cotton....................	46,810 86	Do.
Do	303 bales cotton	28,018 40	Do.
Do	1 bale deerskins	54 48	Do.
Do	10 bales grana	1,454 07	Do.
Do	1 bag of coffee, in transitu	56 36	Do.
Do	135 bales goatskins	7,552 41	Do.
Do	64 bales raw cotton....................	5,787 15	Do.
United States....	2,475 barrels sour American flour	5,073 75	Do.
Mexico	92 packages merchandise................	3,488 00	Do.
Do	23 bales cotton, 46 bales of rags, and 1 bale of hides......................	1,589 50	Do.
Do	939 dry ox and cow hides	1,726 04	Do.
Do	2 seroons of añil	363 75	Do.
Do	15 seroons of grana	2,118 44	Do.
Do	11,242 lbs. old metal and 43 bales rags ...	1,440 70	Do.
Do	753 dry ox and cow hides	1,478 29	Do.
Do	10 seroons cochineal...................	1,451 69	Do.
Do	59 sacks of walnuts	183 73	Do.
Total	....	363,755 34	

TAMPICO—FRANKLIN CHASE, *Consul.*

APRIL 25, 1864.

I have the honor to enclose herewith the return of the arrivals and departures of American vessels at this port during the quarter ended March 31, 1864. *   *

All foreign vessels arriving at this port are compelled to deliver the manifest from the custom-house of the port of their departure; hence I have found it impossible to obtain the necessary information to make an estimate of their inward cargoes without incurring an unreasonable expense.

ACAPULCO—LEWIS S. ELY, *Consul.*

SEPTEMBER 30, 1863.

I have no material changes to note, since the last annual report, of the commercial matters at this port.   *   *   *   *   *   *

Much uncertainty prevails among the commercial men of this port. But a very limited amount of imports has been made from the United States, the principal articles being flour from San Francisco and machinery from New York, the machinery being employed in the manufacture of sugar and preparing cotton for the market.

No changes have taken place in exports, save a falling off in the amount of hides shipped to the United States, and a large increase in the amount of cotton exported.

Much attention is being paid to the culture of this article in western Mexico. The texture of the staple is *fair*, and bears an even average value in the eastern market. The soil here is well adapted to the growth of cotton, and the climate is not unfavorable. A drain upon the amount required for home consumption has been the result of the high price abroad.

The amount shipped from this port the present season is as follows: bales, 7,095, equal to 1,036,444 pounds; cost, ready for shipment, $269,475 44, being 26 cents per pound.

Tabular statement showing the description, country of production, destination, and value of exports from the port of Acapulco for the quarter ended December 31, 1863.

Description.	Destination.	Country of production.	Value.
Ox hides	New York...........	Mexico	$4,069 50
502 bales of cotton	New York...........	Mexico	30,288 15
Total...................	....	....	34,357 65

Statement showing the number of vessels, with description and value of cargoes shipped from the port of Acapulco to New York, from March 31 to November 20, 1864.

No.	Description.	Value.
3	Ox hides...	$2,394 10
20	Cotton...	271,374 00
		273,768 10

GUAYMAS—FARRELLY ALDEN, *Vice-Consul.*

SEPTEMBER 30, 1864.

* * * * The imports are nearly all from San Francisco, and consist of steam-engines, stamp mills, mining tools and materials, lumber, and gold coin. 874 passengers arrived by steamers during the last twenty months, and 512 departed. The exports are gold and Mexican silver dollars, hides, silver ore and copper ore. The latter will probably increase greatly.

One or other of the ocean steamers Oregon, Sierra Nevada, and John L. Stephens, from ——— ——— line between San Francisco and Guaymas, has been making a round trip every forty days since November, 1862. This regular steam communication is rapidly increasing trade with San Francisco, the registered tonnage for the past fiscal year amounting to $17,864, in ten steamers, one bark, two brigs, and twelve schooners. The steamer rates are $12 per ton, except on ores, which are $8, and passage $100. They touch at Cape St. Lucas and Mazatlan, returning via La Paz, Mazatlan, and Cape St. Lucas. Eastern letters, when indorsed "via San Francisco," come by this line many months sooner than when this precaution is omitted, as I have already informed you, on the 6th instant, in despatch No. 1.

Imports for Arizona, as far west as Tucson, come through this port, paying regular Mexican duties, and are taken from here through in wagons, over an excellent natural road, at $66 to $125 per ton. The important privilege granted by Governor Pesquira, to transport goods duty free to and from Arizona through this State, owing to the abuse of the privilege, is now restricted to all, except special permits for United States quartermasters' shipments.

From recent explorations it has been found that Tucson can be reached by a good natural wagon road of 225 miles from the harbor of Libertad, while the distance from the port of Guaymas is double.

The capital employed by citizens of the United States in Sonora is mostly in mining pursuits, and amounts to more than one million dollars already expended in that branch of business alone. The following are the most prominent incorporated companies of citizens of the United States to develop mines in his State, giving the name of each company, its expenditures and improvements, viz:

Names of companies incorporated in United States.	Expended.	Steam mills, No. of stamps.	Progress and present condition.
San Marcial, silver	$80,000	10	Yielding profits.
Tecoripu, silver	75,000	10	Mill stopped.
Fernandez, silver	30,000	10	Erecting machinery.
Taste, silver	50,000	10	Erecting machinery.
Mina Prieta, silver	200,000	15	Mill stopped.
Libertad, silver	35,000	10	Ready to run.
Germanica, silver	161,000	14	Refining ores.
Mina Blanca, silver	75,000	15	Erecting machinery.
Coral Viejo, silver	35,000	5	Refining ores.
Rio Chico, silver	28,000	8	Erecting and mining.
Dios Parell, silver	70,000	10	No funds.
Crucecitas, silver	250,000	25	Needs funds.
Chipionena, silver	32,000	....	Testing value.
Mercedes, silver	18,000	....	Exploring mines.
Nacosari, copper	10,000	....	Shipping 47 per cent. ores.
Favorita, copper	5,000	....	Mining and smelting.
Soyope, silver	24,000	....	Abandoned.
Tirisa, silver	7,000	....	Running adit 825 feet.
	1,185,000	142	

For the last two years I have been exploring the different mining districts of Sonora, and believe it must rank high as a mineral State. At present she is almost paralyzed, laboring under a mining panic, caused by the general stock panic, extending from Durango to British Columbia. Sonora has plenty of well-known mines that will pay good profits on a sufficient capital judiciously expended in thoroughly opening them, erecting reduction works suitable to their extent and peculiar class of ores, with a skilful reduction, especially the rebellious ores. Experience is gradually overcoming the difficulties of profitable reduction.

Sonora has many valuable copper mines, but that of Nacosari attracts the most attention. I found truly a monster mine, such as would make copper " kind," if it were not for want of cheap transportation. It is situated 250 miles northeast of Guaymas, and about 50 miles north of Oposura. The vein is nearly vertical, well defined between walls of primitive rock, and is nineteen feet wide. The quartz cropping entered northwest and southeast, several thousand yards transversely of a mountain, about 3,000 feet altitude above the adjacent valleys, with its summit 6,000 feet above the level of the sea. It has many open cuts, from two to eight yards deep, all exposing its huge and constant vein of copper sulphurets, evenly disseminated. The assays range from 19 to 65 per cent. copper; but the average of thirteen tons, tested in San Francisco, according to the established mode at Swansea, was $47\frac{80}{100}$ per cent. copper and $62\frac{50}{100}$ silver per ton. The current price for copper ore in San Francisco is $4\frac{50}{100}$ for each one per cent. copper, and as it costs but $1 per ton to mine this ore at Nacosari, $70 for transportation 450 miles, on mules, to the port of Guaymas, and $8 by steamer, or $5 by sail, to San Francisco, it pays a fair profit to ship the ore. The amount of such ore is only limited by nineteen feet wide, miles in length, and depth unlimited. The Nacosari Company owns fourteen hundred varas in length of the vein, which is mined eighteen hundred and sixty feet deep—the same as the great silver mine of Valenciana, at Guanajuato—and doubtless would produce ores containing over 14,000,000 tons of copper. It may be asked, Why has not this mine been long since developed? The causes are the indolence of the Mexicans, difficulties of transportation, and its being the hot-bed of the Apaches.

The cotton culture of Sonora is stimulated by the high price and home demand to supply a factory of sixty-four looms at San Miguel. Four farmers in its vicinity sold their crop, amounting to 578 tons unginned or seed cotton, at eleven cents per pound. The factory will be in full operation by January next, when the company intend selling coarse unbleached shirtings of four yards to the pound of raw cotton at twenty-two cents per yard, in eight months' time, or discounting at one per cent. per month. The factory has lain idle for an age, owing to the wars and litigation, &c.   *   *   *   *

I earnestly recommend that some of our enterprising mariners should run a line of steam propellers from here to Acapulco to carry the mails, passengers, specie, and light freights down, and returning with the mails, passengers, light freights, and tropical products, touching regularly at the most important intermediate ports, such as Santa Barbara, Altata, Mazatlan, San Blas, and Manzanilla. This would be found immediately to yield very great profits. The freights on specie alone would amount to between forty and fifty thousand dollars annually.   *   *   *   *   *   *   *

MINATITLAN—R. C. M. HOYT, *Consul,*

SEPTEMBER 30, 1863.

I have the honor to submit the following for the annual report of this consular district.   *   *   *   *   *   *   *   *

The commerce that was formerly carried on between this port and the interior is at present entirely cut off, and the usual prices formerly established for goods imported, the productions of the country exported, and their transportation to and from the interior before the blockade of all inland communication, now have become so deranged and disconnected that I find it impossible to arrive at anything like an approximation of actual valuations. The demand for every article bought and sold, either foreign or domestic, is governed entirely by the immediate requirement for present consumption and not by the price, so that, in reality, legitimate commerce is now obsolete. I cannot account for this otherwise than that the inhabitants have become so accustomed to revolutions and usurpations of bad and designing men, that they do not desire to have any surplus of clothing or household goods on hand, as many of them fly from the towns and villages on the approach of either military party, either from fear or a participation in some of the various political intrigues so common in this country.

The arrivals of vessels during the past year have been four ships, twenty barks, forty-five brigs, eight schooners, and one steamer, of the aggregate tonnage of 20,074 tons—one steamer, five barks, ten brigs, and four schooners being under the flag of the United States; aggregate tonnage 5,580 tons.

The departures during the last year have been one steamer, one ship, sixteen barks, thirty-seven brigs, and seven schooners, aggregate tonnage 15,600 tons; of which one steamer, four barks, eleven brigs, and four schooners were under American colors. Arrivals and departures of armed vessels, which have been entirely French vessels, are not included in the above enumerations.

I do not find in this consulate any record of an annual report later than 1859 which gives the imports $264,449, and the exports $101,731 50, while the past year exhibits for imports $449,400, and for exports $357,173. I account for the increase of the trade of this port by the gradual decrease of exports of mahogany from Honduras, the wood there being, at present, a long distance from the usual places of shipment, while here large quantities yet remain easy of access, and the shipment of which is really the basis of all mercantile transactions here.

The principal articles of import from the United States are flour, sugar, lard, butter, cheese, hams, and lumber, and a variety of hardware; and I think I may say, in justice, that the United States furnish eleven-twelfths of all the groceries and all the flour consumed in this district, a considerable quantity of which is distributed along the isthmus, a portion reaching even the city of Tehuantepec, on the Pacific shore. The dry goods trade is almost entirely monopolized by Great Britain, the manufacturers of that country studying the desires and tastes of the inhabitants of this, and furnishing them with an article inferior in fabric to that made in the United States, but in length and width manufactured to suit their purposes, the prints being generally of better colors than the American.

The only articles exported from this point in any quantities are mahogany, cedar, fustic, hides, and indigo.

There have been exported from this port and its dependencies during the last year 14,772 tons of mahogany, cedar, and fustic wood, of which 12,257 tons went to England, 2,365 to the United States, and 150 to Hamburg.

Nearly all the indigo goes to England, and seven-eighths of the hides, I think I can safely say, to the United States. The average rates of freights during the last year to the United States have been $8 per ton measurement, and $17 to England.

The average market prices during the past year have been for mahogany and cedar $12 per ton, for fustic $13 per ton, indigo $1 12½ per pound, and $2 each for hides.

I am not aware of any articles being prohibited from admission into this port

H. Ex. Doc. 60——46

since last year, and under the tariff of 1856, (which is now in operation,) except arms of every description, munitions of war, and an article known both in this and other countries as the machette, large quantities of which are manufactured in the United States. The machette somewhat resembles a sword, but is really the only agricultural implement used in this part of the country.

The prohibition of these articles extends to all nations and all vessels, both national and foreign, unless especially ordered for use of government.

All articles imported pay the same duty, there being no difference made between foreign and national vessels.

Tonnage dues are paid at the rate of $1 75 for every foot the vessel draws coming in and the same amount out. Twelve dollars for pilot-boats, from three dollars to four dollars for office dues of the captain of the port, and four dollars for stamped paper, three dollars for municipal dues.

There are no warehouse or sanitary regulations.

Employment of capital of American citizens in this consular district is entirely engrossed in the cutting and shipping of mahogany, cedar, and fustic woods, and general commercial pursuits. The article of indigo is manufactured in the district of Tehuantepec and brought here for shipment. This portion of Mexico is known as the terra caliento (hot land,) and is undoubtedly one of the best agricultural districts in the country. The resources, if properly developed, would produce extravagant results for permanent investments, the soil and climate being admirably adapted to the culture of tobacco, rice, cotton, coffee, cocoa, corn, and sugar-cane. The only impediment to make this one of the richest portions of Mexico is the scarcity of labor.

Statement showing the number, tonnage, and nationality of the vessels entered and cleared at the port of Minatitlan during the year ended September 30, 1864, together with the description and value of their cargoes.

INWARD.

Nationality of vessels.	No.	Tons.	Cargo.	Value.
American	1	198	Assorted	$20,000 00
British vessels from United States...	....	....	....do....................	16,621 00
British	23	2,971	....do....................	55,000 00
Hanoverian	3	481	....do....................	....
	27	3,650		91,621 00

OUTWARD.

Nationality of vessels.	No.	Tons.	Cargo.	Value.
American	1	198	Mahogany and hides.	$2,999 75
In British vessels to United States ..	....	....		23,663 90
British	23	2,971	Mahogany and fustic....	39,217 23
Hanoverian	3	481	Mahogany and fustic....	6,734 00
	27	3,650		72,614 98

TABASCO—J. H. MANSFIELD, *Consul.*

SEPTEMBER 30, 1863.

In compliance with the 153d article of consular instructions, I have the honor to bring before the notice of the department the following observations respecting the agriculture and commerce of this state. The principal element in the agricultural industry of Tabasco is, as I presume, well known to the department from the official reports of consular officers preceding me, the cultivation of the cacao bean. The home demand for this product is, however, so great, and the price so high, that it has never hitherto been exported to foreign countries, and its production therefore has no influence on our trade with Tabasco except in an indirect way, from the greater or lesser local prosperity which a productive or unproductive year may occasion, and thus raise or lower the demand for foreign goods and luxuries.

During the last few years, the crop has been almost a complete failure, and prices have ranged very high in consequence—say, at the present, $35 per cargo of 75 pounds weight. Admirably suited as are the soil and climate of Tabasco for the cultivation of this bean, it would appear to me that some gross error must exist in the method of its culture. The inhabitants are, however, wedded to their old system and would admit of no innovation in this respect, even if such were proposed to them. Besides cacao, a great amount of capital is expended on cattle-raising, which indeed may be considered as second only to cacao-growing, in its importance to the agricultural interests of Tabasco. The cattle are consumed in the state, but their hides form an article of export to our country, the price ranging from $1 25 to $1 50 each, according to size and quality.

Coffee, corn, rice, &c., are freely produced, but merely for home consumption. I may quote prices, coffee $18 a quintal, corn $1 per sonti of 400 ears, and rice from $1 50 to $2 50 per arroba of 25 pounds weight. Tobacco, which is extensively grown in the state, may be divided into two distinct qualities, viz., "tobaco de corral" and "tobaco de monte." The first named is grown on land specially and highly manured for the purpose. The second on forest land, which has been merely cleared of its growth by fire, or by the "machette" or axe. The first bears a much higher price than the second, which is inferior to it in size and quality. Both descriptions are subdivided into different classes. The price of the first named varies, according to class, from 16 to 41 cents per pound; the second from 6¼ to 25 cents. Exports of both leaf and manufactured tobacco have at times been made to our country, but by far the greater portion is either consumed in the state or sent to Vera Cruz, and thence transmitted to the interior. Manufactured cigars vary in price, according to the quality and description of tobacco from which they are made, from $6 to $24 per thousand.

Although but few sugar plantations exist in Tabasco, its soil and climate are peculiarly fitted for the production of this article, and I believe that no finer cane than is here grown can exist elsewhere. Whilst in Louisiana the cane requires to be sown every year, and in the island of Cuba every three years, in Tabasco it remains in the ground, without its productive quality being in the least diminished, for eight, ten, or more years. Sugar production is very limited in the state, and barely sufficient for home consumption. A coarse kind of brown sugar, called "panela," has, however, been at times exported to our country for refining purposes. I believe that a very lucrative field is open to enterprising foreigners in the establishment of a few well conducted sugar plantations in this state. Prices of this article range as follows:

White sugar, 1st quality, $2 50 to $3 12½ per arroba; 2d quality, $2 25 per arroba; brown sugar, 1st quality, $1 75 per arroba; cucuruchos, 1st quality, $1 to $1 25 per arroba; panela, 1st quality, $2 80 to $3 50 per cwt.

No alteration has taken place since my appointment to this consulate, in the general regulations affecting our commercial intercourse with this country, unless, indeed, General Forey's decree prohibiting the exportation of gold or silver metals, both coined and uncoined, may be considered as such.   *   *   *

I regret that it is not in my power to furnish the department with any data respecting the commerce of Tabasco with other foreign countries during the

past year. On the evacuation of this city by the liberal troops, on the 18th of
June last, they carried with them, or previously sent away, all the custom-house
records and other state papers, and these have subsequently been either lost or
destroyed, so that no means exist of my obtaining correct information on the
subject. From my own observation, I should say, however, that a direct trade
with England and other European countries is on the increase. Our own trade
would appear to be stationary, although, if we take into consideration the various causes which must have necessarily affected American commerce during
the past year, the fact of there having been no marked decline would seem to
be far from unsatisfactory, more especially if it is taken into consideration that
both the internal and foreign commerce of Tabasco has been suffering from
marked depression during the last few months, owing to the disturbed and unsettled state of the country.
    The port of Las Bocas, in this state, which two years back had been opened
to commerce by a decree of President Juarez, has been closed by an order of
the present governor of the state, Edward G. Arevalo. This, however, will
hardly affect American interest, and is merely a temporary measure, as such orders must, in the regular course of things, emanate from the supreme government.
By another decree of President Juarez foreign vessels were permitted to engage in the coasting trade of this country. Although up to the present time no
counter order has been issued by the authorities at present exercising the supreme government, I have had some little trouble in obtaining an order for the
discharge of two American vessels from Sisal to this port, laden with salt, it
having been at first refused by the new authorities at the custom-house. I am
given to understand that a supreme order forbidding such coasting trade in
foreign bottoms may be soon expected.   *   *   *   *

PASO DEL NORTE—HENRY E. CUNIFFE, *Consul.*

OCTOBER 1, 1863.

    The trade with my consular district has greatly declined in the past year
from various causes—the principal of which are the internal revolutions of the
country, the war with France, and the present rebellion in the United States—
Trade has been, in a great degree, paralyzed, and the amount of imports the pre
ceding year do not exceed the sum of $50,000. The articles imported consist
of a general assortment of dry goods from the United States, to supply the immediate consumption of the country. These come in wagons by way of Santa
Fé, as the San Antonio trade has closed since the existence of the rebellion.
The imports are generally consumed here, but occasionally portions are sent to
Chihuahua and the interior towns in this state. The exports consist chiefly of
corn and wheat for the United States government, Mexican sugar, soap, and the
wine of the country in small quantities. The export trade is with El Paso
county, Texas, and New Mexico, and is chiefly conducted on a specie basis;
there is but little barter in the exchange of commodities. The exports are much
less than in former years, and the causes of decline the same as those which had
caused the reduction in the imports. There is a great scarcity in gold and
siver coin, and, as it is the only currency, and United States paper, if taken at
all, is at a very great discount, traffic is greatly impeded. The export trade of
grain is most important at this point, as the supplies for the United States
troops in Texas and the southern portion of New Mexico must, in a great degree, come from the state of Chihuahua, and the want of gold and silver coin is
severely felt in its purchase, and great loss must necessarily result in trading
with a people who cannot or will not appreciate the proper value of the paper
issues. It is almost impossible to fix the average price of the staple commodi-

ties of corn and wheat here. These necessarily fluctuate according to the demand and the amount produced each season. In favorable seasons the price is low, and at harvest time will not go over $1 per bushel; but this has been a season of most extraordinary drought, and the frosts have set in more than a month earlier than usual. The crops here are raised by irrigation, and the amount produced is governed by the capacity of the Rio Grande to furnish water for that purpose. There is usually a short rainy season during the months of July, August, and September, which greatly aids in the production of the crops; but this season the rains totally failed; outside of the influence of irrigation the country presents the appearance of a parched desert. The Rio Grande is almost dry. There is no running water in the channel. A large expanse of the river-bed presents only the appearance of dry sand, and what little water can be found in the channel is collected in diminishing pools. The mills have for a long time been stopped, and the prospect of their grinding again looks very remote. I have been informed these droughts are, apparently, becoming more frequent. I know of no articles of trade prohibited under the Mexican tariff; and powder and all munitions of war are exempt from duty. The average duty on imports is ten per cent. at this port. The only custom-house regulations here for the importation of goods is, the procuring of a pass for their entrance, when they are inspected at the custom-house, and the duties assessed are paid, as above stated, at an average of ten per cent.

OCTOBER 10, 1864.

Since my last annual report there has been no change in the revenue laws at this port. Trade is gradually decreasing. The exports almost wholly consist of grain for the use of the United States troops. There is no inducement for merchants, or others, to come to this place; notwithstanding that it has been less affected by the war of intervention than any other portion of the republic, yet every branch of industry is prostrated.

*　*　*　*　*　*　*

LA PAZ—FRANCIS B. ELMER, *Consul.*

OCTOBER 2, 1864.

*　*　*　*　*　*

The commercial affairs of this Territory have not, during the year just closed, kept pace with the anticipations expressed in my last annual review. The main causes of this failure have already been given in my quarterly reports.

The trade with San Francisco, heretofore the only American port in direct communication with this, has not increased in the ratio predicted, although a large steamer has been making regular trips between the two places, occupying forty days in performing the circuit. The reason of this is, obviously, the unsettled condition of public affairs, and the consequent feeling of insecurity, and does not arise from any lack of material with which to enlarge its scope.

The trade, direct and indirect, through Mazatlan with Europe, presents no new features, excepting a small diminution in the amount of imports, arising from the increased intercourse with San Francisco, whence many articles, heretofore supplied from England and Germany, have been obtained.

It will be difficult, however, for the merchants of San Francisco to compete successfully with the markets of Europe so long as the present rate of duties continues, and the expenses attending shipments "in bonds" remain undiminished. European merchants in Mexico are satisfied with less profits than were formerly expected, and seem disposed to adopt any policy necessary to prevent successful competition.

The main reason, it seems to me, why American merchants here have failed to obtain a more considerable share of the commercial advantages offered by Mexico, arises from their undertaking to establish themselves in the country without having European connexions, or the advantages—superior, in many respects, so far as this country is concerned—of the European markets. The speculative, hazardous, and impetuous tendencies of our people do not operate so well here as elsewhere. Europeans entering this country for the purposes of trade are content, through the training received at home, to establish themselves in a small way, and acquire wealth and influence after many years of patient industry and gradual advancement. Our people in Mexico, as a class, have different ideas, and experience, as a general thing, different results.

There are times when goods can be bought in San Francisco—the only American port at present holding commercial relations with this portion of Mexico—at prices sufficiently reduced to leave a good margin for profit, though that market is so variable a great risk must be run by their establishing themselves with the expectation of drawing all their supplies from that source.

While trade, which is so closely connected with, and dependent upon, the other material interests of a country, has shown but little advancement, the mining concerns of the Territory have failed to realize my predictions, for the reasons heretofore given. About eight hundred tons of silver and copper ore have been shipped to San Francisco during the past year, and upwards of one thousand tons to Europe.

Two Hamburg, one English, and one Bremen bark have entered the port during that period, and filled up, partially, with ores, and partially with pearl shells and hides. A few more hides have been shipped than during the year previous, and about the same quantity of pearl shells. The pearl product has not varied perceptibly. These things are unaffected by the causes referred to, except, perhaps, remotely, as their export is entirely in the hands of French and German houses, and require the previous outlay of no capital.

The export of salt, heretofore a very important interest, has almost entirely ceased, owing to the low rate at which the people of Alta California and Oregon are manufacturing for themselves, and the troubles on the other side have prevented shipments in that quarter. Owing to the causes referred to, there are at this time a great many Americans in the Territory in destitute circumstances, and have to be supported, in many instances, by their countrymen. They have come here, in most instances, to obtain work in the mines, and having failed, are unable to return; some kind of sickness is apt to follow, and, as the unfortunate victims have no claim upon the government, and cannot expect assistance from the native people, the burden upon their fellow-countrymen is likely to become a considerable one.

The condition of things here, which you will understand to be, on the whole, unpropitious, must greatly improve, I feel assured, as soon as the present uncertainty regarding affairs on the other side along the coast is removed, and what is to be done with this peninsula becomes definitely known. Many of the mines are certainly rich, and are known to be so by there being sufficient capital to work them.   *   *   *   *   *   *   *   *

NICARAGUA.

SAN JUAN DEL NORTE—B. S. COTRELL, *Consul.*

JULY 25, 1864.

The government of Nicaragua has issued a decree levying a tax of one per cent. on all India-rubber exported which shall be gathered within the limits of the republic from and after the 14th of May, 1864. But little of this article remains to be collected within this territory, and this law will be of small consequence.

JANUARY 18, 1865.

In compliance with your regulations, I submit the following report of the foreign commerce of this port for the year ended November 30, 1864:

There is no custom-house at this place, although the captain of the port requires all invoices of merchandise imported for sale and consumption here to be presented to him, and he keeps a list of the arrivals of all vessels that visit this port. He likewise collects a duty on all articles imported for sale here of 10 per cent., with the exception of gunpowder and manufactured tobacco, on the former of which 15 per cent. is collected, and on the latter 20 per cent. The custom-house for the Atlantic side of the republic is located at Fort San Carlos, at the head of the San Juan river, some ninety miles direct from this port, where all kinds of merchandise destined for the interior are entered and duties collected. The duties on most imports for sale in the interior are 40 per cent. Brandy, gin, &c., are charged one dollar a gallon, or 20 cents per bottle. Flour, machinery, agricultural implements, and printed books are admitted duty free.

Merchandise of almost every description is imported into the republic, the greater part of which consists of English and French dry goods, Italian and French wines, liquors, oils, &c. Beef, flour, and provisions are brought from the United States.

During the past year there have been imported for consumption
at this port merchandise to the value of................... $100,070 08
For sale and consumption in the interior.................... 502,363 27
Money imported for this port.............................. 2,000 00
Money imported for the interior 50,000 00
                                                          _____
                                                          654,433 35
There have also been exported during the same period products
of this country, &c., to the value of...................... 474,970 50
                                                          _____
Leaving a balance in favor of imports of.................... 179,462 85

The prices of products are: hides, $2 each; deer-skins, 75 cents, or 30 cents per pound; indigo, $1 25 for first quality; Brazilwood, per ton, $30 to $35; India-rubber, 23 to 30 cents per pound; coffee, 18 cents; cotton, 10 to 20 cents; cocoa, 20 cents; sarsaparilla, 20 cents; tortoise shell, $2 to $3 per pound.

Six American steamers and one sailing vessel have arrived here during the year, besides English, French, and Italian vessels.

                                                          Tons.
The total amount of American tonnage arrived during the year
amounted to 14,127
Tonnage of all other nations............................... 16,579
                                                          _____
Total of American and foreign 30,706

Freights to New York are as follows: hides, 25 cents each; deer-skins, 2 cents; Brazilwood, $12 per ton; India-rubber, ¾ cent per pound; coffee, 1 cent; indigo, 1 cent; cotton, ¾ cent. Heavy freight is from $8 to $10 per ton.

There are 15 cents per ton levied on all vessels which enter this harbor, excepting ships-of-war and the Central American Transit Company's vessels, which enter free by contract.

The currency is the same as for years past, the dollar being the standard of value.

There is no fixed rate of exchange, no bonded warehouses, nor any sanitary regulations.

Cotton-planting in the interior is now quite an extensive business, in which many Americans, French, Italians, &c., are engaged. But it is not possible to state what their success has yet been.

Indigo and coffee are likewise cultivated to the same extent as for years past.

Cocoa is not produced to any considerable extent beyond the necessities of home consumption.

Business at this port, as well as in the interior, has increased an hundred per cent. and more during the past year, and it is not unreasonable to assign as the cause the successful operation of the Central American Transit Company.

Great improvements have been made at this port within the last two years. Many new and substantial buildings have been erected, among which are several fine dwellings, a government house, and a Roman Catholic church.

Tabular statement showing the estimated value of the exports at San Juan del Norte for the year ended November 30, 1864.

EXPORTS PURCHASED AT SAN JUAN.		EXPORTS DIRECT FROM THE INTERIOR.	
Description.	Value.	Description.	Value.
Beef hides......................	$1,455 00	Beef hides....................	$45,104 50
Deer-skins.....................	460 80	Deer-skins....................	54,403 76
India-rubber..................	92,723 96	Indigo	94,252 00
Tortoise shell	6,388 00	Brazilwood	898 80
Sarsaparilla	350 00	India-rubber	3,885 76
Old copper....................	281 75	Cotton	21,047 70
Old iron machinery	21,437 62	Cocoa	15,299 70
Tobacco, manufactured........	5,100 00	Coffee	8,492 60
Cocoa-nuts	92 60	Old copper...................	1,332 50
		Tobacco, manufactured.......	240 00
		Gold	99,063 25
		Peruvian bark	28 20
		Rouron, (hard wood)	2,592 00
		Hide clippings	40 00
Total	128,289 73	Total	346,680 77

Statement showing the estimated value of the imports at San Juan del Norte for the year ended November 30, 1864.

Imports at San Juan $102,070 08
Imports for the interior at San Juan 552,363 27

654,433 35

CORINTO—R. L. HILL, *Consul.*

JANUARY 20, 1864.

Statement showing the exports from and imports into the port of Corinto, in the republic of Nicaragua, for the year ending December 31, 1863.

Total value of exports..............................		$243,882
Value of imports on which duties were charged........	$151,780	
Value of imports entered duty free..................	65,000	
		216,780
Excess of exports		27,102

The imports on which duties are collected consist of dry goods, boots and shoes, clothing, hardware, iron, and nails—almost exclusively from England, some few being purchased in Panama, being English goods—liquors, wine, and ale, mostly from France, with some from California.

Those articles that come duty free are machinery, agricultural implements, and mining tools, all from the United States. Regarding the imports that are free of duty from the United States, the value is estimated by the officials, and no particular pains taken to get at the real value.

From what I have seen, and also learned from other Americans, I am satisfied that the value of these articles is more than double that which is put down in the record. For example, they estimated a corn-shelling machine, a few days since, at $4, worth at least $10 at the place of manufacture; and a large roller and coulter plough at $5, worth in New York $11 at least. The same errors run through the whole list. Cast-steel drills were estimated at 10 cents per pound, worth 25 cents in New York; and cast-steel hammers at 12 cents that cost 46 cents in New York.

The exports consist of coffee, cotton, sugar, indigo, and tobacco, mostly to England ; cocoa and spice to France ; hides and deer-skins mostly to the Atlantic United States ; lumber to California ; woods to the United States and Europe, and corn and rice to other Central American states. But it is impracticable to get an exact statement of each article without too much expense.

UNITED STATES OF COLOMBIA.

The decree of which the following is a translation, communicated by the United States minister at Bogota, is published for the information of all interested :

[Translation.]

Manuel Murillo, President of the United States of Colombia: In use of the powers given to the executive power by section 1, article 1, of the laws of the 14th of May last, authorizing certain fiscal operations, I decree:

ARTICLE 1. The duties on imports are increased one-fifteenth per cent. on the articles comprehended in the fourth class of the tariff annexed to the code of custom-houses, approved May 29, 1864.

ART. 2. The provisions of this decree shall take effect from the first day of November next.

Given in Bogota, July 15, 1864.

M. MURILLO.

ANTONIO DEL REAL,
Secretary of Finance and Ways and Means.

PANAMA—A. R. McKEE, *Consul.*

DECEMBER 31, 1863.

I enclose herewith my annual report for the year ended September 30, 1863. I regret that I have to inform you that no change has been made in the internal regulations of this government, by which I might have been able to furnish the department with perfect statistics of imports and exports. In consequence of this neglect of the government of the United States of Colombia, I have been compelled to ascertain, in the best possible manner, the value of commerce destined for this port and in transitu. I can add nothing of a new feature to my report of the year ended September 30, 1862, as to character of inward and outward cargoes. No new banks have been inaugurated. Bills of exchange on England and elsewhere in Europe and United States maintain about the same premiums. It will be observed that there is great increase in trade from New York to San Francisco. I hope our merchants will cultivate and encourage a trade with the south Pacific and Central America. A little prudence and foresight would, without doubt, increase the trade with those countries one hundred fold. I would suggest to the American merchant the propriety of sending experienced men to those countries, well versed in the English and Spanish languages, with samples of manufactures, and instructed to cultivate the kindest feeling with citizens, merchants, &c., &c.

AGRICULTURE.

A spirit of improvement is manifest in this department. Many persons have planted cotton, and, by its cultivation in a limited way, proved that this country is well adapted to its growth.

The president of this state earnestly lent himself to the development of this important agricultural experiment, and now desires to press the matter forward if he can procure seed.   *   *   *   *   *

The culture of sugar-cane is a success. Dr. Kratscherill, a naturalized American, grows and manufactures it with unprecedented profit. Nothing has transpired to impede commerce since my last report. This government, with a commendable spirit, is doing all in its power to aid and facilitate the advance of agricultural and commercial interests.

Statement showing the description, quantity, value, and country of production of the exports from Panama to the United States during the quarter ended December 31, 1863.

Description and quantity.	Value.	Country where produced.
5,003 hides, weight 77,279 pounds	$8,044 61	New Granada.
Deer-skins, packages, bales, and bundles	1,690 76	New Granada.
Deer-skins, 2 bales, and 111 pieces India-rubber...........	1,275 80	New Granada.
India-rubber, 137 pieces, and charges....................	810 40	New Granada.
India-rubber in bales, packages, and bundles, &c	13,902 20	New Granada.
Guayaquil cocoa, 75 sacks................................	1,397 00	Ecuador.
Cocoa, 36 sacks, and charges............................	641 36	Ecuador.
Coffee, 9 bags, 1,253 pounds	213 01	Costa Rica.
Tortoise shell, 14 lbs. at $3	42 00	....
Gum opium, 5 pounds, at $7	35 00	....
Old copper, 80 bundles, 3 casks, and 14,425 pounds......	2,163 75	....
Indigo, 18 seroons, 2,700 pounds	2,578 50	Central America.
Bark, 24 packages.......	576 00	New Granada.
Bark in seroons, packages, and bales, 25,150 pounds......	5,030 00	New Granada.
Total amount..................................	38,400 39	

NOTE.—17 burners, American manufacture, received per North Star and returned, value $56. 32 sacks cocoa, 5,950 pounds, at 14 cents, in lieu of No. 163. 1 case goods, United States manufacture, returned to New York; certificate of goods sent back to New York.

Statement showing the description, quantity, and value of the exports of Panama to the United States for the quarter ended June 30, 1864; also the names of the countries where produced and whither sent. (Compiled from official documents.)

Country of production.	Description and quantity.	Value, including costs and charges.	Countries whither sent.
New Granada....	5 barrels of slush, $40 50; and 5 sacks un-ginned cotton, $37 75................	$78 25	New York.
New Granada....	566 hides, 2,592 lbs., $1,102 25; 1 bundle deer-skins, 329 lbs., $128 04; 156 pieces India-rubber, 7,292 lbs., $1,292 56.....	2,522 85	New York.
United States....	9 cases calicoes, 17,035 yards, $2,725.....	2,725 00	San Francisco.
New Granada....	3 boxes and 1 barrel old copper, 700 lbs. net, and charges................	86 50	New York.
New Granada and Costa Rica	7 bags coffee, 895 lbs., $143; 10 pieces and 1 bag India-rubber, 320 lbs., at 18 cents per lb., $57 60................	200 60	Do.
Costa Rica......	2 bags of coffee, 258 lbs., at 14 cents per lb.	36 12	Do.
Europe	33 gold and silver watches............	543 00	Do.
Costa Rica......	33 bags coffee, 4,158 lbs., at 11 cents per lb.	457 38	Do.
Costa Rica......	162 bags coffee, 20,422 lbs., at 12 cents per lb.; and charges, $62 50..........	2,513 14	Do.
New Granada....	3 bales deer-skins	49 00	Do.
New Granada....	20 bales India-rubber, 5,110 lbs., at 17 cents, $868 70; 1 bale of deer-skins, 196 lbs., at 35 cents, $68 60......	937 30	Do.
Costa Rica .,....	110 sacks coffee, 14,182 lbs., at 14 cents per lb	1,985 48	Do.
Costa Rica......	30 sacks coffee, 3,780 lbs., at 15 cts. per lb.	567 00	Do.
New Granada....	11 bales deer-skins, 1,159 lbs., at 32 cents per lb., and charges	373 38	Do.
New Granada....	1,170 hides, 18,289 lbs	2,103 25	Do.
New Granada....	286 hides, 5,165 lbs.	609 63	Do.
Chili	9 kegs wine, 144 gallons............	108 00	Do.
Costa Rica......	11 sacks coffee, 1,450 lbs............	270 00	Do.
New Granada....	30 lbs. turtle shell, $90; 41 pieces and 1 sack India-rubber, $526............	616 00	Do.
Costa Rica......	40 sacks coffee, 6,125 lbs............	644 25	Do.
New Granada....	303 hides, 5,579 lbs., and 1 bale deer-skins, 123 lbs	598 40	Do.
Costa Rica......	100 sacks coffee, 12,900 lbs., at $12\frac{1}{2}$ cents, and charges	1,627 90	Do.
Costa Rica	5 sacks coffee, 640 lbs., and charges......	108 90	Do.
Costa Rica......	61 sacks coffee, 7,745 lbs., and charges ...	1,248 50	Do.
New Granada....	351 bags pearl shells, 34,000 lbs., at 4 cts., and charges	1,362 50	Do.
New Granada....	519 hides, 9,129 lbs., $1,000 92; 1 bale deer-skins, 249 lbs., $120 89..........	1,121 81	Do.
New Granada....	4 bales tobacco, 500 lbs., at 27 cents per lb.	135 00	Do.
Costa Rica......	9,850 lbs. coffee, at 13 cents, $1,280 50; and 4 sacks of coffee, 510 lbs., $71 40..	1,351 90	Do.
New Granada....	62 bales and 1 bag of India-rubber, 6,522 lbs., at 15 cents................	978 30	Do.
New Granada....	2,000 lbs. pearl shells, $82 50; and 40,200 lbs. pearl shells, at 1¾ cent per lb	786 00	Do.
New Granada....	375 hides, 6,968 lbs., $788 25; 2 bales deer-skins, 304 lbs., $108 44; and 6 bales India-rubber, $139......................	1,035 69	Do.

Statement showing the exports of Panama, &c.—Continued.

Country of production.	Description and quantity.	Value, including costs and charges.	Countries whither sent.
New Granada....	6 bales India-rubber, 1,553 lbs., at 16 cts., $248 48; 2 bales deer-skins, $90; and 5,940 lbs. pearl shells, $103 95.........	$442 43	New York.
Ecuador	100 bales bark, 10,000 lbs., at 20 cts. per lb.	2,000 00	Do.
Ecuador	40 seroons bark, 4,200 lbs	1,008 00	Do.
New Granada....	300 hides, 5,388 lbs., $587 18; and 5 bales deer-skins, 514 lbs., $185 04	772 22	Do.
New Granada....	2,200 lbs. India-rubber..................	399 25	Do.
New Granada....	1 bale deer skins, 136 lbs., $40 50; and 1 box, 3 bales, 372 pieces India-rubber, 18,845 lbs., at 14 cents, $2,638 30	2,678 80	Do.
New Granada....	3 seroons of bark, 316 lbs., at 25 cents per lb., and charges.....................	87 50	Do.
Total amount..	....	35,169 23	

NOTE.—1 bale cotton and 1 package locks returned to New York.

SABANILLA—W. A. CHAPMAN, *Consul.*

Statement showing the description, quantity, and value of the exports from Sabanilla, also the countries sent to, from September 1, 1862, to December 31, 1863.

Description.	Weights, kilogrammes.	Packages and bales.	Value.
Cotton	81,526	....	$22,323
Starch	2,174	....	255
Balsam tolu	2,640	....	1,445
Coffee......................................	234,380	....	80,901
Hides	222,384	....	34,037
India-rubber	9,050	....	2,620
Cedar logs..................................	....	750........	7,150
Divi-divi	150,000	....	420
Corn	75,360	....	3,910
Fustic......................................	689,360	....	10,081
Peruvian bark	....	3,842 bales.	150,188
Cotton seed.................................	36,810	....	1,298
Tobacco.....................................	....	73,089 bales	2,753,590
Ivory nuts..................................	720,200	....	7,124
Total	....	....	3,075,342

DESTINATION.

Germany	$2,782,488
West Indies...	4,819
United States...	103,182
France	46,316
England...	138,532
Total...	3,075,337

VENEZUELA.

MARACAIBO—RICHARDS A. EDES, *Consul.*

Statement showing the description, quantity, and value of the imports from the United States into Maracaibo during the year ended December 31, 1863.

Description.	Quantity.	Value.
Flour	4,245 barrels and 4,295 sacks	$136,440
Lard	483 cases	12,075
Butter	373 cases	7,190
Beef	421 barrels	10,525
Soap	2,380 boxes	5,950
Florida water	1,420 boxes	8,520
Paints and oils	21 barrels, 50 kegs, and 119 packages	4,000
Drugs	84 barrels, 408 boxes, and 121 packages	18,000
Hardware	117 cases	4,000
Naval stores	58 cases, 60 barrels, and 33 hogsheads	6,700
Provisions	1,389 packages	12,000
Dry goods	40 packages and 2 bales	4,300
Fire-crackers	500 boxes	2,500
Machinery		5,000
Copper sheathing	5 packages	1,250
Pine lumber		1,200
Sundries		17,000
Total in Venezuela currency		256,650

Summary statement showing the description, quantity, and value of the exports at the port of Maracaibo to the United States during the quarter ended September 30, 1864. (Compiled from authenticated invoices.)

Description.	Quantity.	Value.
Coffee	9,976 bags, 1,190,552 lbs	$231,523 80
Cocoa	221 bags, 22,100 lbs	13,027 70
Hides	1,994 pieces, 55,211 lbs	6,332 94
Fustic	103 tons	3,118 38
Skins	15 packages, 1,500 lbs	856 44
Balsam	5 cases, 800 lbs	311 93
Quina	8 cases, 776 pounds	180 30
Old copper	1 case, 288 lbs	65 45
Total amount		255,416 94

Statement showing the description, quantity, and value of the exports from Maracaibo during the year ended June 30, 1864.

TO—	COFFEE Lbs.	COFFEE Value	COCOA Lbs.	COCOA Value	HIDES No.	HIDES Value	DIVI-DIVI Lbs.	DIVI-DIVI Value	FUSTIC Tons	FUSTIC Value	STRAW HATS Doz.	STRAW HATS Value	TOBACCO Lbs.	TOBACCO Value	BALSAM COPAIBA Lbs.	BALSAM COPAIBA Value
Hamburg	2,976,766	$460,418 60	1,141	$420 00			627,500	$6,275 00	32	$389 00			96,837	$11,261 10	19,500	$5,143 00
Liverpool	180	29 70					72,330	592 00	698	9,215 00						
Fal. cuth	556,172	86,981 04					134,700	2,386 00	36	563 00	26		4,535	1,143 00		
Bordeaux	468,800	54,500 00							294	4,952 00		$300 00				
Belle Isle	277,600	45,300 00							12	150 00						
Marseilles	3,569,599	567,648 04	16,193	12,529 00	1,804	$3,500 00	662,300	9,292 00	776	9,515 00	167	1,100 00				
Havre	1,704,750	281,434 50			1,807	3,850 00	213,400	3,230 00	387	5,992 00	632	9,000 00				
Leghorn	958,842	132,865 50			1,000	2,150 00	91,400	1,113 00	140	1,550 00	794	4,017 50	2,300	622 00		
Cadiz	337,600	54,500 00														
Lisbon	1,956,300	304,800 00														
New York	6,540,413	997,964 00	66,100	24,800 00	700	1,800 00	43,900	449 00	57	680 00	1,643	15,756 78	19,564	6,847 40	17,464	3,652 50
Turpan, Mexico			85,600	35,000 00	21,285	46,075 50			130	1,841 00						
Vera Cruz			284,730	122,319 00					54	360 00						
Tampico			98,500	40,000 00					37	700 00	500	10,000 00				
St. Thomas	9,800	1,280 00					175,900	2,600 00	1,811	21,985 00		18,073 00				
Curacoa	49,109	15,287 12	400	200 00							1,570		2,500	50 00	36,904	
Total	19,475,891	3,063,008 00	555,664	235,268 00	96,596	57,375 50	2,021,430	25,837 00	4,464	58,092 00	5,352	58,247 28	77,936	19,923 50	36,904	8,995 50

Statement—Continued.

TO—	SKINS No.	SKINS Value	TIMBER Qrs.	TIMBER Value	WOOL Lbs.	WOOL Value	STARCH Lbs.	STARCH Value	COTTON Lbs.	COTTON Value	QUINA Lbs.	QUINA Value	SUGAR Cargoes	SUGAR Value	SUNDRIES Value	TOTAL Value
Hamburg									7,500	$900 00	2,200	$250 00			$233 50	$477,865 90
Liverpool															235 00	16,854 70
Fal. cuth															301 00	89,640 04
Bordeaux															43 00	62,183 00
Belle Isle																45,450 00
Marseilles															85 00	603,579 04
Havre			4	$40 00											305 00	304,493 00
Leghorn	2	$6 00									3,666	400 00			434 00	142,536 00
Cadiz															10 00	54,580 00
Lisbon																308,380 00
New York	2,323	900 00	3	18 00					1,100	600 00	1,200	120 00			300 00	1,098,848 68
Turpan, Mexico															224 50	35,000 00
Vera Cruz																122,679 00
Tampico																40,000 00
St. Thomas	20,038	4,645 00	98	450 00	1,467	$3,360 00	21,577	$1,203 00							60 00	12,490 00
Curacoa			1,788	1,189 50									520	$2,223 00	1,544 00	72,292 62
Total	22,363	5,551 00	1,888	1,630 50	1,467	3,360 00	21,577	1,203 00	8,600	1,500 00	7,066	810 00	520	2,223 00	3,847 00	3,466,671 98

Statement showing the description, quantity, and value of the exports from Maracaibo for the year ended June 30, 1864.

Description.	Quantity.	Value.
Coffee..lbs..	19,475,891	$3,003,008 00
Cocoa..lbs..	555,664	235,268 00
Hides ....number..	26,596	57,375 50
Divi-divi ....lbs..	2,021,430	25,837 00
Fustic ....tons..	4,464	58,092 00
Straw hats ....doz..	5,352	58,247 28
Tobacco leaf.......................................lbs..	77,936	19,923 50
Balsam copaiba ....lbs..	36,904	8,995 50
Skins ....number..	22,363	5,551 00
Timber ....pieces..	1,888	1,630 50
Wool ....lbs..	1,487	3,360 00
Starch ....lbs..	21,577	1,203 00
Cotton ....lbs..	8,600	1,500 00
Corn ....lbs..	23,940	525 00
Lignumvitæ..tons..	107	740 00
Brazilwood ....tons..	14	200 00
Dyewood..tons..	49	630 00
Quina bark ....lbs..	7,066	810 00
Bitters ....bottles..	1,344	510 00
Cocoa-nuts ....number..	21,900	242 00
Cocoa-nut oil ....bottles..	1,410	205 00
Sugar ....hhds..	230	2,223 00
Horns ....number..	2,500	75 00
Fish bladders ....lbs..	2,806	350 50
Old copper ....lbs..	1,459	184 50
Cigars ....number..	11,000	70 00
Preserves ....lbs..	75	40 00
Palm leaves ....number..	2,900	75 00
Total value for the year................................		3,486,871 28

Statement showing the number, nationality, and aggregate tonnage of vessels entered at Maracaibo during the year ended December 31, 1863.

Where from.	Venezuelan.	Holland.	French.	Danish.	English.	Hamburg.	Italian.	Spanish.	United States.	Oldenburg.	Hanoverian.	Bremen.	Total.
Ambada........		1			1								2
Curaçoa........	1	56	1	1	4		1	2	2				68
Guaranao	2												2
Hamburg				2									2
Laguayra	2	12	2	1				1					18
Leghorn........							1						1
Liverpool					1	1				1			3
Marseilles			14				2						16
New York				4	3								7
Porto Cabello...	5												5
St. Thomas.....	2	3	5	5	1	3			1	1	1	1	23
Porto Prince....					1								1
Vera Cruz		1											1
Coro		4											4
Number	12	77	22	13	11	4	4	3	3	2	1	1	153
Tons...........	612	4,625	5,065	2,993	1,634	712	911	212	594	355	182	169	18,064

Statement showing the number, nationality, and aggregate tonnage of vessels cleared from Maracaibo during the year ended December 31, 1863.

Where for.	Venezuelan.	Dutch.	French.	Danish.	English.	Italian.	Hamburg.	Spanish.	United States.	Oldenburg.	Hanoverian.	Bremen.	Total.
Bellisle			1										1
Curaçoa	3	51			4			1	2				61
Falmouth				1									1
Guarano	2	1											3
Hamburg		2		6			3			2	1		14
Jacmel					1								1
Laguayra	4	10											14
Leghorn						4							4
Liverpool					1							1	2
Marseilles			16										16
New York				5	4								9
Porto Cabello	1												1
Rio Hacha		1											1
St. Thomas	1	1			1			1					4
Tampico		1											1
Coro		4											4
Vera Cruz		3											3
Number	11	74	17	12	11	4	3	2	2	2	1	1	140
Tons	561	4,444	4,006	2,813	1,634	911	587	142	350	355	182	169	16,154

Statement showing the average price of the principal articles of export at the port of Maracaibo for the year ended June 30, 1864.

Coffee	per quintal	$16 12½
Cocoa	per pound	43
Hides, dry	do	10
salted	do	9
Divi-divi	per quintal	1 50
Fustic	per ton	13 50
Palm hats	per dozen	5 to 12 00
Balsam copaiba	per pound	25½
Goat skins	each	43
Tobacco	per pound	36½
Quina	do	14
Sarsaparilla	per quintal	25 00
Cocoanut oil	per gallon	77

Terms of sale.—Exports generally cash; imports 9 to 12 months' credit.

Freights.—On coffee to the United States 50 cents per 100 lbs.; on hides, 20 cents each; other articles 25 cents per cubic foot.

Statement showing the amount of duties levied upon articles of export at the port of Maracaibo.

Cotton	per quintal	$2 00
Starch	do	1 20
Indigo	per pound	10
Balsam copaiba	do	6

Oil (cocoa-nut)	80 bottles	$2 50
Oil (sarsaparilla)	per pound	06
Horns	per 100	25
Asses	each	4 00
Horses	do	16 00
Cocoa	per quintal	4 00
Coffee	do	1 56
Barley	do	1 00
Cocoa-nuts	per 100	25
Hides	each	75
Deer-skins	do	25
Tiger-skins	do	1 50
Goat-skins	do	10
Divi-divi	per quintal	15
Ship timber	value	15 pr. ct.
Corn	per quintal	12½
Mules	each	12 00
Lignumvitæ	per ton	1 50
Fustic	do	1 00
Dyewood	do	1 50
Quina	per quintal	2 00
Straw hats	per dozen	75
Bulls and oxen	each	4 00
Tobacco leaf	per quintal	3 00
Gums and other medical substances	do	4 00
Vanilla	per pound	50
Sarsaparilla	per quintal	6 00
Sole leather	per side	75
Articles not specified	ad valorem	10 per cent.
Cows	prohibited	

Currency.—The value of the dollar currency of Venezuela is 75 cents, estimated in American coin.

Coin.—American dollar is worth $1 34; American half-eagle, $6 68; British sovereign, $6 50; doubloon of South America, $21; five-franc pieces, $1 25.

Exchange—On New York, par for American coin. On London and Paris, is generally procured at the markets of St. Thomas and Laguayra.

SEPTEMBER 30, 1864.

* * * During the year ended July 30, 1864, there have been no revolutions or popular outbreaks to interfere with the general prosperity of the country; and for that period the amount of business of the port of Maracaibo has increased fully 30 per cent. over any previous year.

The principal article of export is coffee; and in that article alone it is estimated 210,000 quintals have been shipped from this port during the last year; showing an increase of about 50,000 quintals over any previous year.

Of hides, cocoa-skins, dyestuffs, &c., which comprise the articles of export, the increase has been nearly as great; and it is asserted that Maracaibo will, before a long period, become the greatest exporting port in Venezuela, should the commerce of this part of the republic not be disturbed by civil war or rebellion. It must be observed, however, that a large portion of the increased trade of the past year was owing to the blockade of this port from November, 1862, to May, 1863, thereby throwing a large portion of the business of that period into that of the year ended March 30, 1862.

The importance of Maracaibo consists alone in its location, as this province produces almost nothing. But this port being situated at the head of the lake of Maracaibo, is the point for shipment and trade for the adjoining provinces of Truxillo, Merida, and Barquesimento, as well as from the large exportation of the republic of United States of Colombia, bordering upon Venezuela; from San José de Cucuta, in Colombia, nearly one-third of the coffee shipped from this port is received, and the entire foreign business of that important point carried on through this city, the lake of Maracaibo, and the numerous small rivers emptying into it, affording an easier mode of transit than is afforded by any other route for goods to and from that portion of Colombia.

Merchandise from foreign countries intended for that city is required by the transit law of Maracaibo to be delivered at the custom-house of this city; whence, after examination, it is again shipped for Colombia, under a transit certificate given by the collector of customs here, certified by the consul of Colombia, showing the quantity, description, and value of the said merchandise. The goods so certified and indorsed, when received at Cucuta, Cereto, &c., are examined and compared with the accompanying certificate; and if found to agree therewith, the collector of customs there certifies to that effect, describing particularly the goods referred to, which certificate, when received at the custom-house of Maracaibo indorsed by the Venezuelan consul at Cucuta, releases the importer or shipper from the payment of any duties upon the goods. A charge, however, is made at the custom-house here for storage, which amounts to 2½ per cent. upon the import duties upon the merchandise.

The direct trade between Venezuela and the United States, at this port, during the past year has somewhat increased, although the carrying has been done entirely by foreign bottoms instead of American, as formerly; yet it will be seen, by reference to the table herewith enclosed, that in spite of the evil effects of the civil war in the United States the amount of both the exports to and imports from the United States have been fully equal to, if not in excess of, any previous year.

I regret that I can obtain no reliable information of the entire amount of trade with European countries, beyond the fact of a general increase. With France particularly is an increase noticeable, there being at this time sixty-two vessels trading regularly between this port and the ports of France, carrying to that country fully one-third of the entire crop annually exported from this consular district; whereas, in 1859 there was but a single vessel engaged in that trade.

In relation to agriculture, manufactures, and mineral wealth of this part of Venezuela very little of interest can be said. The people of this state, like those of nearly all the South American republics, are jealous of improvements and innovations upon old customs and usages. And in the matter of progress by the application of science to the development of the wealth and resources of the country, little or nothing has as yet been done. The soil is fertile in the extreme; and, in the varieties of climate which exist in the neighboring provinces of Truxillo and Merida, are capable of yielding, with but little care, almost everything which can be produced in more temperate latitudes. Many articles of consumption which at present are supplied from abroad can be produced here without difficulty. For instance, flour, which pays an enormous import duty; the wheat for its manufacture could be advantageously grown here; but there are no flouring mills in the country.

MINERALS.

It is asserted that there exist, in this part of Venezuela, mines of iron, coal, and gold, of considerable extent and value; none of which have yet been developed, nor are they likely to be unless through the instrumentality of foreign capital and enterprise.

MANUFACTURES.

With the exception of straw hats and an inferior quality of grass cloth used for bagging and other similar purposes, nothing is manufactured here; and for machinery of all kinds and manufactured articles of every description, this country is entirely dependent on foreign nations.

INTERNAL IMPROVEMENTS.

In regard to internal improvements, the country is, probably, not so far advanced as her neighbors. In this portion of the republic there are no railroads, telegraphs, improved public highways, or public works of any kind; in fact, nothing to denote the enlightened enterprise and advancement of the present time.

THE CULTIVATION OF COTTON.

Within the past year, owing to the continuation of the civil war in the United States, and the consequently high price of cotton, many persons in this state have turned their attention to the cultivation of that article. The soil is peculiarly adapted to that species of cultivation, and some years ago specimens of the cotton grown in this province were pronounced, in European markets, nearly equal to sea-island cotton of the United States. A small quantity has annually been produced here, but, owing to the uncertain state of the country, the civil war, want of reliable labor and machinery, the production of the staple has not been prosecuted with much energy, and latterly has been quite neglected; so that cotton has almost ceased to be an article of export from this part of Venezuela. Now, however, in all probability, it may again become a most important product of this state. A large number of acres are planted with it, both in this province and upon the neighboring Indian coast. A considerable amount of money also has been invested in the enterprise; and persons of such energy and ability are engaged in the undertaking as to give assurance of success. But the difficulty to be apprehended is the want of sufficient reliable labor; and it is to be feared that when the crops may be ready for picking, laborers may not be obtainable to secure it. To guard against this contingency many of the emancipated blacks of the island of Curaçoa have been induced, by the offer of higher wages, to immigrate to this state; but by no means in sufficient num bers to satisfy the demand for labor which the cultivation of cotton has created. It is impossible, therefore, to form a correct opinion in regard to planting, but it is presumable that the business will be profitable.

POPULATION, CLIMATE, ETC.

The population of the city of Maracaibo may be estimated at 32,000, and that of the remainder of the province 43,000; making a total population for the state of Zulia of about 75,000. But no reliable census has ever been taken, and it is impossible to do more than return an estimate. The climate of this city and vicinity cannot be considered worse than that of ports in the West Indies and upon the Spanish main. Besides, this city is not so subject to the visitations of that terrible scourge, the yellow fever, which so fearfully ravages other places in this part of the world; but the continued, intense heat at all seasons of the year renders this a dangerous place of residence for foreigners, and, in all probability, the mortality is as great here among foreign-born citizens as in any part of the world. In the adjoining provinces of Truxillo and Merida it is different; the climate there is represented as being healthy, cool, and invigorating.

Of the merchants engaged in trade at this port, one firm only can be considered an American house, and of that the senior partner is a subject of Holland. All the merchants, however, residing here—principally Germans—are, to a certain extent, engaged in business with the United States. They are old-established firms, possessing large capital and credit.

The "patents," or licenses for transacting business in Maracaibo, which formerly ranged from $100 to $500 annually, will, under the late decree of the President of the republic, which I have had the honor to forward to the department, exceed, in some cases, $5,000.   *   *   *

Of the business of Maracaibo the peculiar feature is the lake trade; everything, including the fruits and provisions for daily consumption, as well as the entire export, being brought to the city from different localities on the lake, in numerous small sailing vessels of from one to eighty tons burden. Some years ago an American obtained a contract for navigating the lake with steamers, which contract he carried out for a considerable time with success, having two small iron steamers. The contractor, however, at length died; one boat was lost, and the other disabled; the business fell into other hands, and was finally abandoned. At present, owing to the enormous increase of this trade, a line of steamers has become a necessity, and several of the merchants here have proposed to establish a line, provided they may have the privilege of sailing their vessels under some foreign flag. This request, however, does not suit the views of the government, and has been denied; and, consequently, a transit line of such great importance to commercial interests will, doubtless, not be carried into effect.

The communication between Maracaibo and other ports of the republic was sustained by means of small schooners until recently, running to Porto Cabello and Laguayra. A much-needed improvement has, however, taken place. Within the last six months a steamer has been placed on the line, sailing under the English flag, and making two trips each month. It is said that another steamer will shortly be added to the line, affording additional facilities for trade and transit between the different parts of the country. This line affords the only communication by steam which this port possesses, either coastwise or with foreign countries.

A line of propellers is contemplated between Maracaibo and the city of New York, but for various reasons the establishment of this line will have to be postponed for the present. The character and amount of port charges levied upon vessels from foreign ports entering that of Maracaibo are as follows:

On each ton, custom-house measurement, entering and clearing, 50 cents each, (which is an increase of about 15 per cent. on American vessels) $1 00
Pilotage fees, per foot each way, $4 .... 8 00
Stamped paper, seals, &c. 4 00
Interpreter's fee, (greater in proportion to manifest) 3 00
Health visit 3 00
Captain of the port 3 00
Light-house duty, (per ton)   06

The duty last mentioned has been exacted for many years from all foreign vessels trading to this port for the purpose of erecting a light-house near the bar, where it is very much needed; but although the authorities have long since collected sufficient in amount to erect the building, they nevertheless continue to exact the duty, and it does not appear likely that this much-desired work will be accomplished for many years to come. At the place contemplated a foundation was made many years ago; but there the work ceased, and although disasters to vessels crossing the bar are of frequent occurrence, causing great loss of property, yet the government appears indisposed or unable to do anything towards completing such an important work.

National vessels coming from foreign ports pay the same duties as foreign vessels, excepting such vessels as may have been built at this port, which by law are exempted for ten years from the payment of tonnage duties. Two or three vessels sailing to Caracas and other near ports enjoy the benefit of this exception, but for several years past no vessels have been built here, except the small craft intended for traffic upon the lake.

The depth of water on the bar at the mouth of the straits which connect the lake of Maracaibo with the gulf of Venezuela is from 13 to 16 feet.

The distance from the bar to this city is 21 miles. Vessels, however, drawing more than 11 feet of water cannot approach this port, owing to the obstructions presented by the shoals of the Soblasos, the channel through which carries a depth of less than 12 feet at high water. Foreign vessels-of-war of heavy draught of water have anchored at the bar, while the officers and a portion of the crew came up to this city in the boats. All vessels arriving at this port are required to produce an authenticated bill of health, otherwise they are subjected to a fine, and also to be quarantined for a considerable length of time.

THE WILD INDIANS.

Adjoining the province of Maracaibo, and lying between it and the Rio Hacha, in Colombia, and bordering upon the gulf of Venezuela, there is an extent of country, consisting of about 12,000 square miles, called Goajora, of which there is little known. It is inhabited solely by tribes of wild Indians, who are represented as fierce and warlike, and who have succeeded in preserving their independence against every effort heretofore made to subjugate them. Their number is supposed to exceed 40,000, and their warriors are said to be excellent horsemen, well acquainted with the use of the bow and spear, as well as the handling of fire-arms. They are frequently at war among themselves, and formerly have made incursions into the territory of the whites. Along the coasts there are some excellent ports, rarely visited, however, and it is said that fine coral and figs are to be there found in abundance. In the interior of the Goajora territory there are well-wooded highlands and extensive plains, peculiarly adapted to the growth and propagation of cattle, horses, and mules, of which there exists large numbers. A small trade is carried on between the people of this city and the nearest of these Indians, consisting in the exchange of blankets and trinkets for their cattle and horses. But as dealing with them is attended with some danger, the trade has never been of any considerable extent. The navigation of the gulf of Venezuela, upon the west side of which this Indian territory is situated, is at times perilous. Vessels have been driven ashore upon that coast frequently, and in every case the cargoes have been plundered and destroyed, the crews managing to escape in the boats.

I herewith enclose a statement of exports from and imports into this port from the United States for the year ended June 30, 1864, marked No. 1; also, average price of principal articles, marked No. 2; also, statement of arrival at and departure of vessels of all nations from this port for the same period, marked No. 3; table of duties on articles of export, marked No. 4; statement of exports from Maracaibo to all countries for the year ended as above, marked No. 5

PUERTO CABELLO—CHARLES H. LOEHR, *Consul*.

MAY 7, 1864.

Enclosed I beg to remit you two statements specifying the articles generally imported at and exported from this port.

Comparative statement touching the consumption of the staple products of the United States as well as of other countries at the United States consular district of Puerto Cabello.

UNITED STATES.

· Furniture, bricks, flour, biscuits, brooms, cotton shirtings, madapollams, checks, cordage, oakum, baskets, sperm candles, tar, turpentine, resin, rice, hams, lard, codfish, ale, cider, varnish, pitch, twilled and plain unbleached domestics,* potatoes, black pepper, butter, cheese, ice, oysters, onions, pickles, medicines, screens, shoes, hay, lumber, bar-iron, scales, stationery, beaver and felt hats, kerosene oil, lamps, chandeliers, globes, shades, tubes, wick, wheel-barrows, tiles, vegetables, preserved fruit, apples, gold and silver coins.

GREAT BRITAIN.

Cotton goods, canvas, ironmongery and cutlery, earthenware and miscellaneous other articles, such as wheels, zinc, sheet-lead, tin sheets, copper sheeting and nails, ink-powders, powder in kegs and canisters, buck and small shot, blunderbusses, fish-hooks, pistols, fowling-pieces, salampores, paints and oil, venoms, ship-blocks of all sorts, silk parasols and handkerchiefs and other silk goods, tapes, ribbons, thread and braces, ladies' boots and shoes, silk and beaver hats, steel pens, brushes, ale, sugar, soda-water, tin ware.

HANSEATIC TOWNS.

Bricks, lime, cordage, tar, resin, oakum, gin, beer, brandy, empty demijohns, butter, hams, potatoes, sausages, linen, platillas, britannias, creas, drills, checks, stockings, socks, corks, stationery and British manufactures, which it appears are sent from Hull to Hamburg, and there shipped for Puerto Cabello at much less expense than if embarked at Liverpool.

DENMARK.

French wines, brandy, gin, British manufactures, some German linen goods, spices and teas from the East Indies, and a mixture of the productions of various other countries.

FRANCE.

Liquors, oil, composition-candles, preserved fruit, ladies' bonnets, shoes, silk hats, some coarse earthenware, wines, brandy, gin, silks, jewelry, perfumery, masks, toys, and other trifling articles.

UNITED STATES OF COLOMBIA.

A considerable number of mules and horses are brought from Colombia by land through the provinces of "Casanare" and "Barinas," but no vessels from that republic or direct importations of any description.

SPAIN.

Brandy, wines, preserved fruit, vinegar, garlic, nuts, oil, leeches, paper, Spanish cards, and some silks.

---

*The unbleached domestics from the United States are in great demand and preferred to British fabrics of the same class.

Statement showing all the articles of production usually exported to the United States and Europe from the port of Puerto Cabello.

Asses, cotton,* cocoa-nuts and oil, cocoa,* coffee,* copper (old) and ore, ceba-dilla, deer-skins,* divi-divi, dyewood, fustic, horned cattle,* horses and mares, hides, (cattle,) dried,* gold of New Providencia,* indigo,* Ipizapa hats, lignum-vitæ, leaf tobacco,* mules, oil of copaiba,* oil of sassafras, Peruvian bark, starch, skins of tigers,* skins of other animals, sarsaparilla, tonquin beans,* vanilla.

SEPTEMBER 1, 1864.

* * .* The tariff published in 1858, and revised per decree of November 16, 1861, is still in force. * * * * * *

The difference is an augmentation of 18 per cent. currency. Articles which formerly paid 32 per cent. pay now 50 per cent. Both import and export duties are payable in cash.

Articles free of duty are rice, corn, beans, peas, and all sorts of nutritious grains.

This country is supplied almost exclusively from the United States with flour and all sorts of provisions. The usual term of credit on dry goods is six months, and on provisions four months; and if the sale is effected for cash, one per cent. per month of discount is generally allowed when the amount of the purchase is over $50.

The customary charge of commission for the purchase of produce is 5 per cent. for Europe and $2\frac{1}{2}$ per cent. for the United States; storage, 1 per cent. on both.

The true value of the dollar currency of this republic of Venezuela is seventy-four $\frac{42}{100}$ cents estimated in American or Spanish silver dollars. Our gold coins circulate with as much facility as the Spanish gold doubloons of different stamps circulate for 16 dollars. Spanish ones are considered of superior standard, and command sometimes a premium of $2\frac{1}{2}$ to 5 per cent. Some silver coins of the United States of fifty cents and twenty-five cents, stamped as late as 1853, are considered of less value, and circulate for only $62\frac{1}{2}$ cents and $31\frac{1}{4}$ cents cy., when older ones circulate for $67\frac{3}{6}$ cents and $33\frac{1}{6}\frac{3}{6}$ cents cy.

For the great facility in circulation there exists in favor of the small 21 s. gold coin of one dollar a premium of $\frac{6}{8}$ cent, circulating freely for $134\frac{6}{8}$ cy. as a silver dollar.

Agriculture, which, during the late war, has been in every branch entirely neglected or abandoned to the care of the women, is now receiving a fresh impulse from the organization of a national agricultural society now in progress.

Reports about the coffee and cotton crop of the present year in this and the neighboring provinces are favorable, yet the deliveries of these chief staple articles are at present very limited.

The cocoa and indigo crops, according to reports from the custom-house and all the best estates generally, situated not far from the sea-coast, in alluvial soil, are constantly decreasing, for reasons best known to the natives themselves.

SEPTEMBER 2, 1864.

I have the honor to transmit you enclosed the following documents, viz:

Table showing the total exports of Venezuelan produce from Puerto Cabello, from 1857 to 1863, to the port of New York, to the port of Philadelphia, to the port of Baltimore, and a recapitulatory statement of exports from this port to the United States ports from 1857 to 1863.

*To the United States.

Summary tabular statement showing the description and quantity of the exports of Venezuelan produce from Puerto Cabello to the United States, from 1857 to 1863, inclusive, and to September 2, 1864.

Years.	Coffee.	Hides.	Hide cuttings.	Deer, tiger, goat, and sheep skins.	Indigo.	Cocoa.	Cotton	Sugar.	Fustic.	Lignumvitæ.
	Bags.	No.	Lbs.	No.	Lbs.	Bags.	Bales.	Bags.	Tons.	Tons.
1857 ..	52,572	106,705	2,200	24,384	37,614	87	190	336	372½⁸⁹⁹	71
1858 ..	61,159	95,323	377	12,588	63,623	412	......	4,019	118₁⁴⁴₀₀₀	82½⁹⁹⁹
1859 ..	74,491	83,644	2,245	2,700	35,084	584	......	4,290	157½⁸⁸⁸	37
1860 ..	53,879	88,451	3,032	1,007	8,500	1,126	......	......	60	3½⁹⁹⁹
1861 ..	56,256	68,976	848	1,025	4,600	422	4,017	......	81	6
1862 ..	46,802	57,226	1,840	5,058	1,900	202	245	......	19½⁹⁹⁹	......
1863 ..	57,103	38,486	1,391	7,614	1,884	382	1,624	......	....	30
1864 ..	60,996	36,602	......	11,106	1,410	173	467	......	....	39½⁴⁴⁴

SUNDRIES.—Copper, old and ore, cotton seeds, sweetmeats, jewelry, rice, beans, chocolate, bitters, peanuts, fruits, artificial flowers, birds' feathers, cocoa-nuts, oysters, tortoiseshells, hats, boards, woods, palm oil, spices, &c.

Comparative statement showing the number and tonnage of the vessels entered at and cleared from Puerto Cabello, together with the value of the inward and outward cargoes for the several quarters of the years 1863 and 1864.

1863.

Quarters ended.	Vessels.	Tonnage.	Imports.	Exports.
January 1.........................	12	2,384⁸⁸	$139,568 65	$297,843 27
March 31.........................	10	2,326²⁴	132,262 43	261,312 35
June 30..........................	10	2,369⁸⁴	23,983 25	95,933 03
September 30......................	2	732⁴⁴	4,265 51	21,327 55
Total.........................	34	7,812⁵⁸	300,079 84	676,416 20

The foregoing gives us a difference of $400,002 11 of imports and $889,914 75 of exports in favor of the year ending September 30, 1864.

1864.

Quarters ended.	Vessels.	Tonnage.	Imports.	Exports.
January 1.........................	9	2,753½⁴	$34,398 61	$173,307 54
March 31.........................	15	3,733⁸⁹	182,366 10	628,918 00
June 30..........................	15	3,077⁹⁴	253,702 67	680,269 26
September 30......................	12	2,696⁸⁴	229,614 57	83,836 15
Total.........................	51	12,261⁸⁸	700,081 95	1,566,330 95

The above difference appears to have arisen from the blockade of this port, that occurred for four months of the year, depressing not only our own trade, but the general commerce of the place, and from the total change of government, which created a want of confidence in all mercantile classes.

Statement showing the number of arrivals and departures of vessels of all nationalities at and from Puerto Cabello during the year ended June 30, 1864.

ARRIVALS.

Nationality.	No.	Nationality.	No.
United States	26	Holland	15
British	42	Hamburg	20
Spanish	18	Bremen	1
Italian	1	Hanover	2
French	19		
Danish	18	Total number of vessels	162

ENTERED.

	No.		No.
From the United States	43	From Marseilles	1
From Hamburg	28	From Barcelona	7
From Liverpool	19	From Malaga	7
From Newcastle	2	From Genoa	3
From Cardiff	4	From Amsterdam	2
From Bordeaux	9	From the West Indies	35
From Havre	2	Total	162

CLEARED.

	No.		No.
For the United States	43	For Barcelona	9
For Hamburg, Altona, and the channel	34	For Trieste	3
For Bremen	2	For Malaga and San Sebastian	1
For Liverpool	9	For Genoa and Vigo	3
For Bordeaux	7	For Amsterdam	1
For Havre	6	For the West Indies	25
For Nantes	1	Vessels in port	17
For Marseilles	1	Total number of vessels	162

REMARK.—The coasting trade is confined solely to Venezuelan vessels, but foreign vessels may engage in it by changing flag.

Statement showing the description and quantity of the exports of Puerto Cabello, together with the names of the countries whither sent, during the year ending June 30, 1864.

COFFEE.

	Pounds.
United States	6,769,910
France	5,099,110
Spain	1,031,590
Italy	675,190
England	137,450
Germany, Hamburg, and Altona	7,217,440
Bremen	605,792
Trieste	964,100
Total	22,500,582

COCOA.

	Pounds.
United States	34,430
France	175,071
Spain	257,077
West Indies	9,020
Total	475,598

COTTON.

	Pounds.
United States	58,534
England	957,083
Hamburg	596,019
Bremen	12,000
France	230,888
Spain	144,804
Italy	664
Total	1,999,992

INDIGO.

	Pounds.
Bremen	3,236
Spain	4,900
Total	8,136

HIDES.

	Number.
United States	31,112
Spain	12,171
Italy	2,333
France	127
Hamburg	72
Total	45,815

	Pounds.
Cotton exported during the year ending June 30, 1864	1,999,992
during July, 1864	561,431
up to August 17, 1864	120,000
Total	2,681,423

SUMMARY.

Coffee	pounds..	22,500,582
Cocoa	do....	475,598
Hides	number..	45,815
Cotton	pounds..	1,999,992
Indigo	do....	8,136

SEPTEMBER 8, 1864.

I have the honor to lay before the department the following remarks upon this port, its commerce, &c., obtained during the six months since I entered upon my consular duties at this port, as an addition to my commercial reports transmitted previously with despatch No. 28, dated the 1st instant.

    *   *   *   *   *   *

The total value of the trade of the port of Puerto Cabello amounts to $3,967,499 04, of which $577,806 04 were imports and $3,389,693 were exports, divided among the nations as follows:

IMPORTS.

United States $271,350 00
Great Britain 113,770 08
France 32,616 35
Spain 16,068 00
Germany 119,174 87
Holland 5,151 00
Curaçoa 18,528 74
St. Thomas 1,147 00

    Total 577,806 04

EXPORTS.

Countries.	Coffee.	Cotton.	Cocoa.	Hides.	Total.
United States	$359,552	$121,475	$22,763	$111,780	$815,571
Great Britain	21,334	130,824	....	....	152,158
France	388,084	35,152	105,966	450	529,652
Spain	173,696	44,843	212,644	18,330	449,513
Germany	1,293,865	60,793	26,080	1,374	1,382,112
Italy	34,191	....	26,496	....	60,687
Total	2,270,722	393,087	393,949	131,934	3,389,693

The duties collected on said amount of exports were $912,468.

Had this port not been blockaded during the months of August, September, October, and November, the general trade of the past year would have exhibited a considerable increase over previous years.

I have already stated that the dollar currency of Venezuela is estimated at 74-42/100 cents in United States or Spanish dollars, remarking that this country has no circulating medium or metallic currency of its own stamp, with the exception of a small quantity of copper cents, and consequently depends entirely upon the imports of foreign coins, mostly United States, English, and French for such medium, the respective values of which are fixed by law.

On American money there is a profit on its importation of 7½ per cent., on English 4 per cent., and on French 2½ per cent., which, if again exported, will bear a proportionate loss, with the addition of 2 per cent. duty.

All kinds of merchandise or products of Venezuela exported to foreign countries are invariably purchased for cash, without any discount whatever, and such purchases are made by the merchants as circumstances may present, either for their own account or for the account of others. No bounties are allowed on articles exported to foreign countries, either in national or foreign vessels. The customary charge of commission for purchasing and shipping goods of different descriptions, viz., 2½ per centum without brokerage, is debited in the invoice of shipment as a charge upon the purchaser. A statement of the usual and customary expenses in detail attending the purchase and shipment of merchandise I hereby subjoin, which becomes a separate charge, and, aside from the original cost, to be paid by the shipper or purchaser.

COFFEE.

Bag (empty) for 110 pounds net, each .... $0 40 this currency.
Weighing, regulating porterage and shipping, per bag .. 25 " "

Export duty per 100 pounds........................ $1 25 this currency.
Storage, one per cent. on first cost.
Consul's certificate to invoice and currency........... 3 50 U.S. money.
Commission 2½ per cent. on cost and charges.

HIDES (RAW.)

Washing, porterage, beating, marking, and shipping, each, $0 18¾ this currency.
Export duty, each................................ 75 "   "
Storage 1 per cent. on first cost.
Certificates of consul to invoice and currency......... 3 50 U. S. money.
Commission 2½ per cent. on cost and charges.

COCOA.

Bags, (empty,) each per 110 pounds .... $0 50 this currency.
Preparing, weighing, porterage, and shipping per bag
    of 110 pounds................................... 25 ..   ..
Storage 1 per cent. on first cost.
Consul's certificate to invoice and currency........... 3 50 U. S. money.
Commission 2½ per cent. on cost and charges.

COTTON.

Weighing and porterage, &c., per bale.............. $0 12½ this currency.
Export duty per bale (100 pounds)................. 50 "   "
Storage 1 per cent. on first cost.
Consul's certificate to invoice and currency.......... 3 50 U. S. money.
Commission 2½ per cent. on cost and charges.

INDIGO.

Making seroon, each............................. $1 00 this currency.
Raw hide for serooning, about 10 pounds, at the current
    price of hides.
Inspection, per seroon........................... 50 ..   ..
Storage 1 per cent. on first cost.
Consul's certificate to invoice and currency.......... 3 50 U. S. money.
Commission 2½ per cent. on cost and charges.

FUSTIC, LIGNUMVITÆ, AND OTHER WOODS.

Weighing, porterage, and shipping, per ton.......... $1 25 this currency.
Storage 1 per cent. on first cost.
Export duty per ton.............................. 1 80 "   "
Consul's certificate to invoice and currency.......... 3 50 U. S. money.
Commission 2½ per cent. on cost and charges.

BROWN SUGAR.

Bag (empty,) each .... $0 18¾ this currency.
Weighing and shipping, per bag................... 18¾ "   "
Export duty, 25 per cent. on the market price as fixed
    monthly.
Consul's certificate to invoice and currency.......... 3 50 U. S. money.
Commission 2½ per cent. on cost and charges.

DEER AND GOAT SKINS.

Opening, beating, poisoning, baling, and shipping each
skin . . . . $0 04 this currency.
Export, per skin . . . . 25 " "
Storage, 1 per cent. on first cost.
Consul's certificate to invoice and currency . . . . 3 50 U. S. money.
Commission 2½ per cent. on cost and charges.

The quantity of goods on hand now may value about $2,000,000. The rate of profits on sales varies from 25 to 75 per cent. according to circumstances.

The productions of the interior places and towns in this country, of which this port is an outlet, are almost without exception forwarded from thence by the producers or their agents, at their own cost and expense, and sold to the shipping merchant of this place, including consequently in the selling price all expense of transportation, &c., until placed in store here.

The trade of Puerto Cabello depends on the interior provinces for consumption of imports and supply of exportable articles. The whole internal trade in produce is possessed by the natives, but the export trade to the United States, Europe and the West Indies is in the hands of foreigners, with a few very trifling exceptions. The American citizens at this consulate are principally employed in commercial pursuits.

The exports consist chiefly of coffee, cattle hides, deer, goat, and tiger skins, cocoa, indigo, fustic, lignumvitæ and other woods, with partial quantities of cotton, chocolate, cocoa-nuts, &c., which are embarked for the States and Europe.

Formerly large shipments of indigo and tobacco were made, of which vestiges are to be met with in every part of the country, but the frequent revolutions that occur in this country have ruined those plantings, and seriously affected every other branch of cultivation.

The agriculture of the province consists of coffee, cocoa, sugar-cane, rice, Indian corn, plantains, yams, and yarca, sweet potatoes, beans, peas, &c., but the climate is too hot for producing wheat, oats, barley and potatoes. The soil everywhere is well adapted for coffee, cotton, cocoa, and breeding cattle.

The political difficulties in the United States have given a fresh impulse to the cultivation of cotton.

There is abundance of woods in the country fit for furniture of all kinds, and for house and ship-building, but the whole is almost useless for the want of capital and laborers; there are also inexhaustible forests of caoutchouc trees, and innumerable medicinal plants of every description, unheeded.

Manufactures, like every other branch in this quarter, are in their infancy, and not likely to improve while the country remains in the hands of the natives, who are now inoculated with the spirit of revolution. The articles manufactured are tallow candles, very common soap, coarse brown sugar, cheese, casada bread, and rum, all of them for local consumption and for exportation; grass hammocks, cables, bitters, and straw hats.

The value of the mineral wealth distributed over the whole country is yet to be discovered. Gold, silver, lead, quicksilver, and, in the canton of Yaracuy, copper, have been found, but only the latter has been attended to by an English company that exports about 200,000 pounds annually to Great Britain, via Liverpool and Falmouth.

The climate in this district is variable; the heat before sunrise is seldom under 78° of Fahrenheit, and at 2 or 3 in the afternoon rises to 90° or 92° during six months in the year. The coolest months are November, December, January, and February. During the past year this port has been unusually healthy. There has been no yellow fever or any other contagious or pestilential disease whatever.

The following statement shows the present rate of duties or tariff on exports, as per decree dated November 16, 1861:

Asses	each..	$4 00
Cocoa	per 100 pounds..	3 00
Cocoa-nuts	per 100..	25
Cabadilla	per 100 pounds..	1 00
Coffee	do........	1 25
Cotton	do........	50
Divi-divi	do........	15
Dyewood	per ton..	1 50
Fustic	do....	1 00
Horns	per 100..	25
Horses and mares	each..	16 00
Indigo	per pound..	1 11
Hides { each....................		75
{ or about, per 100 pounds..		3 00
Ipijapa hats	per dozen..	2 00
Lignumvitæ	per ton..	1 80
Mules	each..	12 00
Oil of copaiba	per pound..	6 00
Oil of cocoa-nuts	per 80 bottles—large..	2 50
Oil of sassafras	per pound..	6
Peruvian bark	per 100 pounds..	2 00
Starch	do........	1 20
Skins: deer	each..	25
tiger	do....	1 50
of other animals	per pound..	10
Sarsaparilla	per 100 pounds..	6 00
Tobacco leaf	do........	3 00
Vanilla	per pound..	50

Articles not specified in the above pay 10 per cent. ad valorem.

The subsidiary contribution of 10 per centum, which formerly was imposed by an act of Congress dated July 1, 1857, has been abolished.

Articles prohibited to be exported are cows.

Articles prohibited to be imported into this country, from anywhere, are powder, lead, arms of any description, salt, coffee, cocoa, indigo, rum, except in bottles; also sugar, for a limited term.

Articles free from import duty are maize, rice, beans, peas, and animals for the improvement of the breed.

The excessively high duties on imports now levied have produced an active contraband trade between Curaçoa, San Thomas, and Venezuela; but it is impossible to ascertain its extent or value.

The municipal interference with imports and exports also induced smuggling and the concealment, by every possible means, of their value. Therefore the custom-house accounts probably do not show more than three-fourths of the real extent of the trade.

The weights are English, and so is the liquid measure by the imperial gallon; but the cloth and land measure is by the Spanish vara of 33 inches. The league is 6,666 varas.

The exchange at this port is invariably at the rate of 134 cents to the American or Spanish dollar.

The actual prices-current of the staple articles of export from this country are at present as follows:

		Marq's currency.
Coffee, washed, average	per quintal, or 100 pounds..	$17 00
unwashed, average	do........do........	16 00
Cotton, average	do........do........	66 00
Cocoa, superior	per fanega of 100 pounds..	39 00
inferior	do........do........	34 00
Indigo	per pound..	1 50
Hides, raw	per quintal..	11 00
Deer-skins	per pound..	30
Goat-skins	do.....	20
Fustic	per ton of 2,000 pounds..	25 00
Lignumvitæ	do......do........	18 00
Brown sugar, average	per pound..	7½

*   *   *   *   *   *

Prices paid for American lots of coffee from September, 1863, to September, 1864.

		Per 100 lbs. this currency.
1863—September		$15 50 to $16 00
October		15 25 to 15 75
November		15 25 to 16 00
December		15 25 to 15 75
1864—January		15 25 to 15 75
February		15 00 to 15 75
March		15 00 to 15 75
April		14 75 to 15 50
May		15 25 to 17 25
June		17 00 to 17 50
July		17 00 to 18 00
August		16 00 to 17 00
September		15 75 to 17 00

BRAZIL.

RIO DE JANEIRO—JAMES MONROE, *Consul.*

MARCH 31,, 1864.

*   *   .   *   *   *   *

I have the honor to transmit to the department my annual report, containing such information as the imperfect means at my command have enabled me to obtain and the thorough and often-repeated researches of my predecessors have left to me.

The report is accompanied by six statistical tables, marked A, B, C, D, E, F, respectively.

Table A exhibits the importation and consumption of flour in Rio de Janeiro in 1863. Table B shows the export of produce for the same year. Table C the monthly exportation of coffee, sugar, and hides, for the years 1861, 1862, and 1863. Table D the value of the exports from Rio Janeiro for the financial years 1860–'61, 1861–'62, 1862–'63. Table E the arrivals and departures of vessels of all nations from 1857 to 1863, inclusive of both years. Table F contains sundry items useful for reference.

At the end of every quarter during the past year I have forwarded to the department returns of the arrival and departure of American vessels and their cargoes. The subjoined brief summary is made up from these returns.

During the year 1863 the number of American vessels which arrived at this port from Baltimore was 28; from Boston, 10; from New York, 12; from Philadelphia, 5; from foreign ports, 32. Total, 87.

During the same year the number of vessels which cleared from this port for Baltimore was 27; for Boston, 1; for New York, 6; for Philadelphia, 3; for California, 8; for Portland, (Oregon,) 1; for Hampton roads, 1; for foreign ports, 43. Total, 90.

During the year there were two American vessels condemned and sold in this port.

The aggregate tonnage of all the American vessels which arrived was 60,268 tons.

Thus the whole number of American vessels which entered this port during the year 1863 was only 87; while it will be seen by reference to table F that the number in 1862 was 145, and in 1861 was 287, more than three times as many as in the first-named year. It is not necessary to dwell upon the causes of this decrease, for they are sufficiently evident. Full and frequent reports have been made during the year from this and other consulates on the coast, and from the legation of the United States in this empire, of the ravages of the Alabama and other rebel privateers in the neighborhood of Brazil. On the very highway between our great commercial ports and this city our vessels, in large numbers, have been burnt or captured and converted into privateers. As a consequence, the rates of insurance upon American vessels have immensely increased, and it is now almost impossible for such vessels to command freight upon any terms. Many American vessels which formerly visited this port have been kept at home idle; a still larger number has been sold, and their flag has been changed.

But while the labors and responsibilities of my office have been considerably diminished in one direction by the falling off of our commerce, they have been greatly increased in another by the extraordinary cares and duties which the peculiar condition of our country has imposed upon me. At one time large numbers of American seamen, from vessels destroyed by the rebel privateers, were brought into this port upon neutral ships, and thrown upon this consulate for support. To provide suitably for these destitute fellow-countrymen at as small an expense to the government as was practicable, and to secure a return home at a time when there were few American vessels in port, required constant and earnest attention. The large increase in the correspondence of the office with our consuls at other ports and other official personages, in consequence of the presence of privateers upon the coast, the wants of American war steamers that have visited Rio Janeiro, and the ever-shifting places of the lawsuit in the case of the "Richmond vessels," which has been continued through my term of office thus far, have kept my time fully and often anxiously occupied. Full reports upon all these topics have been forwarded to the department as occasion has required.

The total importation of flour in Rio Janeiro during the year 1863 amounted to 319,852 barrels, of which 241,362 barrels were from the United States. The number of barrels imported from the United States in 1862 was 261,865, and in 1861 302,061.

There were exported from this city in 1863 1,353,273 bags of coffee, against 1,487,583 bags for 1862, and 2,064,335 bags for 1861. This decrease of exportation has been due to a falling off in the crops. During both the years last named all the coffee raised in this province which was not required for home consumption was exported at high prices. The decrease in the amount of the crops has been due, in part, to unfavorable seasons and the ravages of an insect which attacks the tree, and sometimes the flower and newly-formed fruit, but still more to defective modes of agriculture and the want of labor. The lack of laborers might be in part supplied by the introduction of suitable machinery. This has been done to a small extent; but improvements of this kind seem to spread slowly among the great plantations in the interior. The partial failure of the crops upon many old estates is no doubt owing to the continued cropping of many successive years without making the necessary returns to the soil.

While the exportation of coffee from this port to the United States in 1861 was 756,355 bags, in 1862 it was but 394,656 bags, and in 1863 only 388,875 bags. The causes of this decrease in the consumption of coffee in our country are too well understood to require explanation here. It is a striking example of the manner in which important events in countries widely separated become related to each other—events having no common origin in material or political causes, or in the plans of any human intelligence—that the falling off in the coffee crop of Brazil for the past three years has been nearly balanced by the decrease in the demand for the article in the United States. When the coffee first began to fail in this country it was supposed that the supply would not be nearly adequate to the demand for exportation. But this opinion was not verified by the result. The principal decrease in the crop occurred from 1861 to 1862, when it amounted to 576,752 bags; and the decrease in the consumption of Rio coffee in the United States for the same period was 361,699 bags—nearly three-fifths of the whole amount. I may add, in this connexion, that good judges here are of the opinion that the coffee crop which is now ripening, and the earlier portion of which will soon appear in the market, is much larger than that of either of the two preceding years. Dealers are already asking the question where this crop is to be sold. May we not indulge the hope that a satisfactory answer will be found before many months have passed in the increased demand for the article in our country which will result from the establishment of a permanent and prosperous peace, upon the basis of submission in all the States to the authority of the government?

The business of the carrying trade between the United States and Brazil was formerly done almost, if not quite wholly by American vessels, and under the American flag. The two years last past have witnessed a great change in this respect. By reference to the books of the consulate, we find that in the year 1862, out of 261,865 barrels of flour imported into this city from the United States, 203,591 barrels were conveyed under the American flag; and in 1863 the flag carried only 122,515 barrels imported, out of a total of 241,362 barrels.

There were 394,656 bags of coffee exported to the United States in 1862, but only 145,446 bags upon American bottoms; while in 1863 our vessels exported only 66,717 bags, out of 388,875 bags.

These facts in regard to exports and imports may be arranged conveniently for reference in the following tables:

Importation of flour into Rio de Janeiro during the years 1862 and 1863.

1862:

	Barrels.
From the United States—	
On American vessels	203,591
On foreign vessels	58,274
Total	261,865
From other countries	69,685
Total of imports	331,550

H. Ex. Doc. 60——48

1863:

	Barrels.
From the United States—	
On American vessels	122, 515
On foreign vessels	118, 847
Total	241, 362
From other countries	78, 490
Total of imports	319, 852

Exportation of coffee from Rio de Janeiro during the years 1861, 1862, and 1863.

1861:

	Bags.
To the United States	756, 355
Total exports of coffee for 1861	2, 064, 335

1862:

To the United States—	
On American vessels	145, 446
On foreign vessels	249, 210
Total	394, 656
Decrease from 1861	361, 699
To other countries	1, 092, 927
Total exports of coffee for 1862	1, 487, 583
Decrease from 1861	576, 752

1863:

	Bags.
To the United States—	
On American vessels	66, 717
On foreign vessels	322, 158
Total	388, 875
To other countries	964, 398
Total exports of coffee for 1863	1, 353, 273

There has been a great deal of discussion in Brazil since 1862 in regard to the cultivation of cotton; and it is generally understood that during the past year a large amount of capital in the several provinces of the empire has been devoted to this object. A considerable breadth of land has been set apart for this purpose, seed imported, and suitable machinery purchased. There has not been time enough, however, as yet, for the result of this activity to show itself in commercial or agricultural reports, which in this country are not often brought down to very late dates; but I confidently expect that the next annual report from this consulate will exhibit a large amount of cotton among the exports of Brazil.

There has been no change since my arrival in Rio Janeiro in the regulations of this port, or in the laws imposing duties upon imports.

In 1862 the legislative assembly of the empire passed a law authorizing the executive department of the government to remove, should it be thought expedient, the restrictions which have prevented foreign vessels from engaging in the coastwise trade between the different ports of Brazil. * * *

No American can reside long in Rio Janeiro without having forced upon his attention the great benefits which England and France have derived from regular steam communication with this city, nor without desiring that the same advantages might be secured for his own country.

Imports and consumption of flour at Rio Janeiro in 1863.

Months.	Receipts from the United States.	From elsewhere.	Total receipts.	Shipped coastwise and re-exported.
	Barrels.	*Barrels.*	*Barrels.*	*Barrels.*
January	23,316	4,440	27,756	7,312
February	19,447	4,226	23,673	9,534
March	33,247	10,771	44,018	11,775
April	27,034	9,957	36,991	11,022
May	8,741	8,301	17,042	11,185
June	15,371	2,140	17,511	9,249
July	20,384	3,806	24,190	11,410
August	11,868	9,988	21,856	10,835
September	11,139	12,607	23,746	9,261
October	22,855	6,381	29,236	17,646
November	25,818	5,673	31,491	3,437
December	22,142	200	22,342	9,544
Total barrels	241,362	78,490	319,852	122,210
Stock in all hands on January 1, 1863			65,000	
				384,852
Shipped coastwise and re-exported in 1863			122,210	
Stock in all hands on January 1, 1864			40,000	
				162,210
Consumption during 1863				222,642

Exports of produce from Rio Janeiro for the year 1863.

Countries.	Coffee.	Rosewood.	Hides.
UNITED STATES.	*Bags.*	*Logs.*	*Pieces.*
New York	272,422	3,313	....
Baltimore	63,805	....	....
San Francisco, California	17,094	....	....
Philadelphia.....................................	5,167	126	....
Delaware Breakwater, for orders...............	3,016	....	....
Hampton Roads, for orders.....................	4,000	....	....
Sandy Hook, for orders.........................	1,650	....	....
Nassau, for orders	6,915	....	....
Havana, for orders..............................	6,806	....	....
St. Thomas, for orders	8,000	....	....
Total..	388,875	3,439	....
EUROPE.			
Antwerp	19,409	....	....
Hamburg and Altoona...........................	29,727	2,198	21
North of Europe	122,340	6	200
Channel, for orders.............................	321,754	1,033	21,000
North of France.................................	129,560	9,930	25,336
Bordeaux..	24,522	....	....
Liverpool..	12,331	791	....
London	3,492	382	200
Lisbon, for orders...............................	17,065	....	....
Portugal	6,223	1,974	1,785
Cadiz, for orders	3,600	....	....
Mediterranean	216,390	484	18,213
Total	906,413	16,798	66,755
ELSEWHERE.			
Cape of Good Hope	42,098	....	....
River Plata......................................	10,440	....	80
Matamoras, Mexico..............................	4,000	....	....
Valparaiso.......................................	1,358	132	....
Havana	....	....	104
Gaspè, Canada	89	....	....
Total..	57,985	132	184
RECAPITULATION.			
United States	388,875	3,439	....
Europe	906,413	16,798	66,755
Elsewhere	57,985	132	184
Grand total	1,353,273	20,369	66,939

Table of monthly exports of coffee, sugar, and hides for the years 1861, 1862, 1863.

MONTHS.	COFFEE									SUGAR			HIDES		
	1861.			1862.			1863.			1861.	1862.	1863.	1861.	1862.	1863.
	United States.	Europe.	Elsewhere.	United States.	Europe.	Elsewhere.	United States.	Europe.	Elsewhere.						
	Bags.	Bags.	Bags.	Bags.	Bags.	Bags.	Bags.	Bags.	Bags.	P'kges.	P'kges.	P'kges.	Pieces.	Pieces.	Pieces.
January	50,039	109,563	557	33,255	93,663	5,236	34,045	60,765	9,585	265	9,306	2,604	7,070	13,461	7,528
February	75,333	97,589	2,325	60,853	93,992	7,970	11,638	60,307	389	142	19,398	6,890	1,000	13,449	7,400
March	54,309	87,084	5,573	43,490	44,949	3,283	37,814	61,670	7,301	95	11,597	584	10,100	1,296	9,704
April	112,060	71,857	6,127	37,685	60,148	3,980	95,390	79,038	6,211	388	9,776	6,970	6,645	650	4
May	126,491	161,630	3,191	31,888	57,398	2,726	99,305	65,896	1,648	754	7,404	2,238	15,886	800	2,381
June	85,493	118,846	6,198	23,164	56,990	6,835	35,333	68,409	9,753	7,690	3,782	3,247	6,491	11,575	7,994
July	62,546	145,706	6,098	34,957	68,547	916	12,574	64,469	2,038	9,182	1,571	937	8,353	12,563	12,050
August	14,516	73,421	2,127	9,024	145,680	1,180	13,359	66,988	3,439	11,040	10,058	1,946	4,996	6,909	8,947
September	76,431	158,744	7,280	85,398	85,398	3,595	45,638	97,964	3,931	33,998	9,153	4,794	7,347	991	8,907
October	29,900	140,495	7,953	97,738	118,935	2,533	41,004	102,511	5,142	16,077	7,188	7,098	3,497	6,380	4,998
November	78,553	101,635	2,453	21,953	140,368	5,130	62,385	105,751	5,432	90,088	5,964	12,469	3,881	8,064	3,123
December	21,113	45,111	250	56,402	76,331	3,529	36,390	74,255	3,816	10,678	4,056	22,810	4,908	454	
Total	756,355	1,311,140	38,790	394,676	1,042,759	50,165	388,875	905,413	57,985	100,281	99,403	78,447	77,914	75,605	68,212

Table showing the exportation from Rio Janeiro for the financial years 1860–'61, 1861–'62, and 1862–'63.

Articles.	From July 1, 1862, to June 30, 1863.	From July 1, 1861, to June 30, 1862.	From July 1, 1860, to June 30, 1861.
Coffee	$21,465,945	$24,062,280	$25,954,157
Diamonds	1,200,000	1,439,100	1,253,160
Gold bars	1,000,000	1,058,013	808,539
Sugar	608,459	888,606	943,533
Rosewood		940,050	326,799
Tobacco		926,750	418,794
Hides	298,630	969,511	221,731
Brandy		85,453	39,468
Horsehair		23,475	21,410
Woods		12,878	18,433
Gold dust		7,662	5,687
Rice		2,936	1,959
Sundries	1,902,466	597,080	435,499
Total	$26,405,500	$28,933,002	39,741,386

Destination.	From July 1, 1862, to June 30, 1863.	From July 1, 1861, to June 30, 1862.	From July 1, 1860, to June 30, 1861.
Great Britain		$7,165,980	$6,565,627
United States		5,519,004	17,976,466
France		5,197,866	5,318,971
English Channel		3,535,133	4,912,453
Denmark and colonies		1,690,819	1,383,149
Sweden and Norway		1,039,817	1,388,043
Spain		857,788	73,855
Hanseatic cities		835,008	994,931
Portugal		715,619	501,555
River Plate		645,003	735,065
Belgium		631,655	674,097
Russia		273,584	380,110
West Indies		190,400	
Austria		177,081	970,518
Mediterranean		130,591	320,139
Turkey		104,043	400,139
Sardinia		97,555	141,004
Chili		32,615	37,381
Prussia		30,360	
Baltic ports			56,643
Consumption of the port			31,430
Total	$28,405,500	$28,923,002	39,741,386

NOTE.—It has been found impossible to obtain the necessary statistics to complete this table, and it is therefore forwarded in an imperfect condition. The values in the first column of the sheet are estimated, but must be nearly correct.

Table showing the arrivals and departures of vessels of all nations in the port of Rio Janeiro from 1857 to 1863.

Years.	FROM FOREIGN PORTS.		BOUND TO FOREIGN PORTS.	
	Vessels.	Tonnage.	Vessels.	Tonnage.
1857	1,172	405,068	1,116	533,687
1858	1,141	375,168	922	507,347
1859	1,198	334,799	977	481,722
1860	1,173	406,620	993	485,859
1861	1,129	406,816	947	463,367
1862	1,003	338,384	824	383,390
1863	1,029	320,944	767	367,268

Years.	ENTERED COASTWISE.				CLEARED COASTWISE.			
	Vessels.	Steamers.	Total.	Tonnage.	Vessels.	Steamers.	Total.	Tonnage.
1857	2,172	437	2,609	352,770	2,260	423	2,683	309,376
1858	1,902	442	2,344	292,846	1,889	411	2,300	269,862
1859	1,847	419	2,266	287,740	1,084	139	1,223	206,281
1860	1,890	388	2,278	290,561	2,040	376	2,416	343,926
1861	2,047	413	2,460	316,625	2,128	456	2,584	366,439
1862	1,901	425	2,326	311,604	2,124	402	2,526	308,174
1863	1,660	358	2,018	295,922	1,759	399	2,158	331,868

Table of sundry items useful for reference.

Year.	No. of American vessels arrived.	Imports of flour from the Unit'd States.	From elsewhere.	Total imports of flour.	Consumption of flour.	Stock of flour in all hands, January 1.	Prices of first-quality flour on January 1.	Flour re-export'd	Exchange on England, January 1.
		Bbls.	Bbls.	Bbls.	Bbls.	Bbls.		Bbls.	Pr. 1$000
1854	219	176,723	34,703	211,426	166,821	25,000	23$000.........	56,605	28d to 28¼d.
1855	332	227,306	73,562	300,868	163,599	13,000	25$ a 25$500	70,269	28d to 28¼d.
1856	295	301,729	15,675	317,404	185,627	80,000	22$ a 25$000....	151,716	27½d to 28d.
1857	273	355,858	15,846	371,704	223,621	60,000	25$000....	128,083	27½d.
1858	257	372,976	29,179	402,155	237,841	80,000	18$ a 20$000....	144,524	25d.
1859	306	336,133	32,459	368,592	258,258	100,000	15$ a 16$000....	135,334	26½d to 27d.
1860	249	268,748	34,610	303,358	249,358	75,000	16$ a 17$000....	89,000	25½d to 25½d.
1861	287	302,061	82,934	384,995	247,121	40,000	23$....	97,874	27½d to 27½d.
1862	145	261,865	69,685	331,550	236,670	80,000	....	109,840	27½d to 27½d.
1863	87	241,362	78,490	319,852	222,642	65,000	....	122,210	27½d to 27½d.
1864						40,000	....		27½d.

PERNAMBUCO—THOMAS ADAMSON, jr., *Consul.*

NOVEMBER 14, 1864.

   *   *   The collection and arrangement of the commercial statistics which I have the honor to submit herewith have involved an amount of labor which no one could imagine who has had no personal experience in attempting to gather information of that kind in Brazil.   *   *

I beg leave to offer a few remarks in description of the port of this city before reviewing the statistical tables which accompany this my annual report.

The port of Pernambuco, generally spoken of by residents as the city of Recife, is at the confluence of the rivers Capabaribe and Beberibe. The channel formed by the union of these rivers constitutes the harbor of this port. It is confined on the west by the coast, and on the east by a natural wall, or reef, (*recife*, whence the name of the city,) of rocks.

This channel, which, near the Recife bridge, has a depth of from fifteen to twenty feet, varies in depth as it approaches the bar, having from ten to fifteen feet of water in the widest places, and from thirty to thirty-five feet in the narrower parts. The greatest depth is found close to the reef, which is nearly vertical on the side towards the land, and lessens gradually in approaching the shore. The reefs appear to be of a quartz rock and fragments of shells, united together during the lapse of centuries by a silicious, calcareous cement, and extend from the neighborhood of Bahia to Cape St. Roque, appearing, in some places, above the level of the sea, and in others entirely submerged, and running almost parallel to the coast. Near this port the reef is generally above the level of high tide.

From the "Ilha Dapina," or cocoanut island south of this port, the reef follows nearly a right line in the direction N. 25° E. up to th ebar, being the distance of a trifle over two and a half miles. Between the "Ilha Dapina" and the bar, at a distance of about twelve hundred yards from the former, there is a depression in the reef of sixty yards in extent, called the "bavuta das jangadas," which was formerly used as a place of entrance and exit for the jangadas, and other small craft common here. This outlet has been closed artificially. From the bavuta das jangadas the reef appears above the level of high water and follows the same general direction for a distance of 3,130 yards to Fort Picao, which is built on the reef. This fort is a small work and has long since ceased to be occupied. About one hundred yards north of the fort, and on the end of the prominent part of the reef, is situated the light-house of the Picao bar, and eighty yards north of the light-house is the rock called the "tartaruga," (turtle.) North of this rock is a depression in the reef, forming the channel, by which vessels of moderate size generally enter the harbor. The width of this channel is about 120 yards. The flow of the tide through this channel arrests, to some extent, the sands brought down by the river, and forms the Picao bar spoken of. Vessels drawing eighteen feet of water can cross this bar at high tide. North of this channel the reef again elevates itself for a distance of 500 yards; but this portion of its extent is always covered with from six to eight feet of water. The reef then disappears entirely for a distance of over half a mile, and here the river forms the "barra do poco." On two-thirds of this bar the depth of water is from eighteen to twenty-five feet, and on the remainder only fifteen feet.

Between this bar and the shore is the "poco," or well, which is a very deep body of water. North of "barra do poco," to some distance above Olinda point, the reef rises again, but is entirely covered with water to the depth of from six to eight feet. This harbor is entirely the work of nature; and, if some judicious efforts were made to improve it, might be deepened so as to admit vessels of almost any tonnage.

To illustrate clearly the extent and value of the trade of this port I have prepared with the greatest care the following tabular statements:

Tabular statement, showing the exportations from the port of Pernambuco during the year ended June 30, 1864, and comparison of the same with the three preceding years.

Statement of the value of the exports of the province of Pernambuco to foreign countries and to ports of the empire for the year ended June 30, 1864, compared with seven preceding years.

Statement of the total exports from the port of Pernambuco to the United States during the year ended June 30, 1864; the quantity and value of each article free on board, (including expenses, commissions, export duties, &c.,) and the ports to which shipped.

Comparative statement of exports of sugar from Pernambuco during the last ten crop years.

Statement of the value of importations of foreign merchandise at the port of Pernambuco during the year ended June 30, 1864, compared with the preceding year.

Statement of goods imported from the United States in American vessels and entered for consumption at the port of Pernambuco during the year ended June 30, 1864, compared with the previous year.

Statement of goods imported from the United States in other than American vessels and entered for consumption at the port of Pernambuco during the year ended June 30, 1864, compared with the preceding year.

Total entries of flour at the port of Pernambuco during the year ended June 30, 1864.

Importations of jerked beef at Pernambuco during the last ten years.

Importation of codfish at Pernambuco during the last ten years.

Statement of foreign shipping at the port of Pernambuco during the year ended June 30, 1864, and comparison of the same with three preceding years.

Statement showing the national flags under which the above foreign shipping entered and cleared at the port of Pernambuco, with number of vessels, tonnage, and crews under each flag.

Statement of coastwise navigation at the port of Pernambuco during the year ended June 30, 1864, and comparison of the same with the three preceding years.

Estimate of the population of Brazil in the year 1860, and the relative proportion of slave to free.

From table No. 1 it will be seen that the exports of cotton during the year ended June 30 amounted to 396,886 arrobas, which, in bales of five arrobas each, is nearly 80,000 bales, against 52,000 bales in 1862–'63, and 25,000 bales in 1861–'62.

From the most reliable information that I can gain, I estimate the total crop of this province for the current year at 110,000 bales; and the three provinces of Alagoas, Parahiba, and Ceara, which are within this consular jurisdiction, will, together, probably produce an equal quantity. For the year ending June 30, 1865, it is believed safe to estimate the cotton crop of the four provinces at from 300,000 to 320,000 bales. Stimulated by the high price of this staple, it is being extensively planted by small farmers and by a class of poor people who are a kind of dependents of the large landholders, and are known as "moradores," which is about the same as squatter in our western country. These people produce only a few arrobas of cotton to each family; just enough to supply them with a little clothing and the very few actual necessaries of life which nature does not produce spontaneously for them. I believe it is safe to say that nine-tenths of the cotton produced in this and the adjacent provinces is the result of free labor. The production might be enormously increased if any care was given to the cultivation; but I doubt if a single plough can be found in the hands of any cotton-grower in this province. The ground is cleared by cutting down and burning the dense vegetation which covers it, holes are made in the ground with a hoe at four or five feet distance from each other, the seed is dropped in, the earth put over it with a push and a stamp of the foot, and nature does the rest. The cotton-tree is here a perennial; it gives its best crop in the third year, after which the yield becomes smaller, and in the fifth year it is generally cut down and the ground replanted. The only instance of thoroughly intelligent farming that I have seen in Brazil was on the estate of the Baron de Mana, at Sapapemba, twelve miles from the city of Rio de Janeiro. This estate, containing nearly five thousand acres, is managed in partnership by

Mr. Hayes, an American gentleman, from Connecticut, who has brought to bear the results of his very thorough studies in agricultural chemistry, botany, and mechanics. At Sapapemba I saw fourteen ploughs take the field each day, and Mr. Hayes informed me that he had ordered fifty more ploughs from the United States. There I saw about fifty acres of land well ploughed, harrowed, and planted with cotton, and was told that only two weeks previous the same land was covered with a dense growth of vines, bushes, and small trees of the country. There can be no doubt of successful results where cotton is thus cultivated intelligently; for, notwithstanding the rude methods employed here, nothing that the planters have grown during the last three years has paid so well as cotton.

If our domestic difficulties should, happily, be brought to a close before Brazilians become fully awakened to the importance of a more intelligent mode of cultivating the soil, our superiority as growers of cotton will not be rivalled here.

This empire possesses the natural advantages of soil and climate, excellently well adapted to the cultivation of cotton, and if the people were generally energetic and intelligent, they might make Brazil the great source of cotton supply for the world; but it is hardly probable that they will improve their resources to any great extent during this century. In one sense Brazil may be said to be improving rapidly—that is, very rapidly in comparison with fifty years gone by; but the word progress as understood in the United States is not known here.

The climate, the races from which the people spring, the religion of the state, and the lack of a system of popular education, each has its effect in retarding the march of improvement.

The people, excepting those of the higher ranks, and the dwellers in large towns, are not educated; they have not acquired the wants of a high state of civilization, and not having any expensive tastes to be gratified, they see no necessity for great exertion. I believe, therefore, they will cease to compete with us to any great extent if we resume our former production before they become rich enough to have acquired many new wants.

SUGAR.

By reference to table No. 4, it will be seen that the exports of sugar during the past year have been less than the average of the ten preceding years. Persons who have opportunities for examining into the cultivation of sugar, which I have not, inform me that the same system of cultivation is in vogue now as was a hundred years since. There are, however, probably a few exceptions to this. On two or three estates within the circle of my own observation the plough has superseded the hoe to a great extent. Some little improvement has been made in setting sugar pans, and in economizing fuel, and, perhaps, slight improvements in the distillation of rum from the molasses. Many sugar planters have planted cotton instead of increasing the extent of their cane fields, and there is nothing to indicate that the coming crop of sugar will be any greater than the last one. If superior modes of cultivation were adopted, and improvements made in the process of manufacturing the sugar, this would probably be one of the most profitable things that could be grown in this province.

There is, perhaps, no part of the world better adapted to the cultivation of sugar than this, but the sugar planters do not appear to be a very prosperous people. There are various obstacles in the way of collecting debts from the proprietors of sugar estates, unless the amount be large enough to swallow up the estate. The consequence is that they can only borrow money at usurious rates of interest, and they are frequently extravagant in their habits, and, therefore, borrowers. A "senhor do engenho," as the proprietor of a sugar estate is called, is generally looked upon as a little lord in his district, and men who are ambitious to wield the power and have the importance of a senhor do engenho enter the business on borrowed capital. There are a variety of reasons why the culture of sugar is not more extensive, and no good reason why it might not be a very prosperous business. At present the want of cheap transportation to market is a very serious drawback, excepting near the coast or on some navigable streams. The usual load, or carga, as it is here called, for a horse or mule is two bags, of 160 pounds each, of either sugar or cotton. The average value of a carga of cotton during the past six months may be roughly estimated at two hundred and fifty milreis, (reis 250||100,) while the carga of sugar was worth but thirty milreis, (reis 30||000.)

Valuing at 1,200 reis, or 65 cents per day, the time and labor of a man and horse—and by city ordinance each horse is required to have an attendant—it will be seen that the cost of transportation of a carga of cotton from a distance requiring twelve days for the round trip would be a fraction under six per cent. on the value, while the carriage of a carga of sugar would cost almost fifty per cent.

Unfortunately for this province, the only railroad it possesses was located, through the interest of influential parties, on a route which, while it serves the purposes of a few individuals, has made it of but little avail to the greater part of the planting population. I do not deny that it has been of great benefit to those who owned lands near its route, but it most certainly has not produced a tithe of the good results that might have been realized by locating it on other than a line parallel with and near to the coast.

There are no wagon roads worth speaking of in this province. I only know of one that is practicable in a carriage to the distance of twenty-five miles inland from the city, and everything is transported on the backs of horses and mules. Even a huge sugar pan is carried on two strong poles between two horses, and this antiquated mode of conveyance is the only one, notwithstanding the fact that there are no mountains or other serious natural difficulties to prevent wagon roads being both well and cheaply made. However, the people appear satisfied; their fathers and grandfathers managed to get on, and they believe they can do so as well as those who have gone before them. I do not mean to disparage the Brazilians, in fact I have lived here long enough to make me feel an interest in the country, but it is saddening to see a country possessing such wonderful natural advantages so far behind the spirit of the age.

I have before referred to the Sapapemba estate, near the city of Rio de Janeiro. There I discovered that the new modes of cultivation adopted by the enterprising manager of that estate were exerting a very beneficial influence throughout a large extent of territory around. Planters came from a long distance to see the ploughs, scythes, mowing machine, and corn-sheller of the Yankee farmer. Some were convinced of the utility of what they saw, and an American dealer in agricultural implements told me that he had sold out a large invoice of ploughs in a very short time.

With increased facility of communication, by means of a good line of steam vessels, Brazil and the United States would be mutually benefited. Brazilians would gladly visit the United States if it were made easy for them to do so, and a portion of the money which they now expend in the capitals and watering places of Europe would be expended among the people of the United States; many would be induced to visit our country to observe the manner in which we cultivate cotton and sugar, and a demand for American cotton gins, sugar mills, ploughs, &c., could hardly fail to follow. Our merchants would visit this country, see its immense capabilities, and enrich themselves while assisting to develop its resources. But it is not necessary to enlarge upon this subject now; it has been brought before our legislators by abler pens than mine, and a very trifling subsidy has been promised by our government. If the Brazilian government should grant the subsidy asked of it the line will soon be in operation, and this consulate will be able to make a better exhibit of the "American trade" of this port than that contained in tables Nos. 6 and 7, to which I have the honor to invite your attention. From these tables you will perceive that the quantity of goods brought to this port from the United States during the past year is somewhat smaller than in the preceding year, and of our trade with Brazil seven-eighths have been under foreign flags.

I have endeavored to make the accompanying tabular statements speak for themselves, by comparing the trade of several years, thus showing in what kind of articles we are being supplanted by other nations, as well as those of which the consumption of American product is increasing.

A few remarks, however, in regard to the articles usually exported from the United States to Brazil may not be out of place. In flour the United States are the principal source of supply. Trieste flour is, however, considered better than that from the United States, and readily commands from one to two dollars more per barrel. This market requires the very finest qualities of flour, and shippers will always do better by selecting the very best brands that can be found.

Kerosene oil has become an important item in our trade with Brazil, and generally affords the shipper a good profit. In comparing Brazilian prices with the cost in the United States it must not be forgotten that our "currency" has for some time past been steadily depreciating in value, while that of Brazil has been equivalent to gold.

Our exports of lard and butter to Brazil are not so large as they should be, owing, perhaps, to the fact that shippers have too frequently sent poor articles to this market, instead of the best possible, and have, therefore, had to sell at a loss. If the farmers of our great west would learn the method of preparing butter for exportation as practiced in the best Irish dairies, from whence the best butter sold here comes, they might make a very remunerative business of it. For this market it should be sent in small packages, of not over twenty-five pounds each.

Persons who wish to build up a trade between the United States and Brazil should remember that the reputation of our goods and products has been injured, unfortunately, by the shipment of imitations and imperfect articles.

Tables 8, 9, and 10 will, I trust, be found both useful and interesting; they show very correctly the quantities of each of the three principal articles of food imported into this province. It will be noticed that the consumption of jerked beef has increased during the last few years, while that of codfish has diminished. It is said that the jerked beef has improved in quality latterly, while the price is so low as to induce its consumption in preference to fish in some degree.

Tables Nos. 11, 12, and 13 are taken from the books of the custom-house. They cost me both trouble and expense, and I hope will be found interesting. It therefore only remains for me to forward you with this the annual reports of the consular agencies at Ceara and Maceio, dependencies of this consulate.

*   *   *   *   *   *   *   *   *

Statement showing the value of importations of foreign merchandise at the port of Pernambuco during the year ended June 30, 1864, compared with the preceding year, (compiled from custom-house book.)

Articles.	1863–'64.	1862–'63.
	Value, in Brazilian currency.	Value, in Brazilian currency.
	Reis.	*Reis.*
Oils	115,823‖248	84,858‖947
Codfish	498,282 880	588,756 346
Spirituous liquors...........................	164,651 964	147,536 080
Boots and shoes.	214,775 734	170,944 650
Meats	612,998 142	691,149 339
Coals.	154,150 000	240,414 000
Hats	421,146 305	297,098 596
Hides and skins	159,249 975	91,908 015
Drugs and medicines........................	81,130 883	87,628 835
Flour	969,597 470	1,636,729 750
Hardware	600,380 946	345,961 056
Iron and steel	48,333 630	27,918 520
Glass and queensware......................	243,439 055	209,263 882
Machinery	10,696 220	12,762 000
Butter and lard	579,162 692	531,658 332
Manufactures of—		
Cotton	5,486,362 027	5,427,457 211
Wool	565,004 870	484,427 680
Silk	246,679 359	203,827 786
Linen	339,336 513	220,299 575
Mixed material	595,919 883	336,341 969
Gold and silver ware	92,962 840	201,629 449
Paper and pasteboard	119,026 729	106,921 971
Powder	118,950 000	111,200 000
Clothing	167,715 477	134,679 756
Salt	17,373 400	25,341 800
Wines	626,735 836	473,008 820
Specie	2,908,819 085	819,939 100
Sundries	2,238,770 432	2,018,285 982
	18,397,475‖595	15,727,949‖387

Statement showing the value of the above articles received from each foreign country.

Countries.	1863–'64.	1862–'63.
	Value.	Value.
	Reis.	*Reis.*
United States	864,725‖896	1,793,466‖000
Great Britain	10,583,068 146	8,310,377 321
France	4,083,467 904	2,888,777 567
Portugal	1,097,645 153	876,005 931
Hanseatic cities	581,672 699	586,362 710
Uruguay and river Plate	581,790 560	608,678 516
Austria	167,870 380	152,657 066
Spain	165,243 784	229,743 278
Italy	68,581 063	37,315 084
Belgium	67,455 640	105,254 350
Holland	28,227 508	40,033 984
Sweden and Norway	4,770 150	....
Via other parts of the empire	102,956 112	99,277 580
	18,397,475‖595	15,767,949‖387

NOTE.—The values as given above are far less than the real values. Invoices are not shown at the custom-house, and this is therefore only the *estimate* of value made by officials. I would increase it by one-third.

Statement showing the goods imported from the United States in American vessels, and entered for consumption at the port of Pernambuco, during the year ended June 30, 1864, compared with previous year.

Articles.	1863–'64.		1862–'63.	
	Quantity.	Value.	Quantity.	Value.
Flour........................barrels..	9,500	$80,375	71,314	$572,852
Lard..........................kegs..	400	1,900	1,550	5,960
Crackers.......................do...	500	562	5,236	6,673
Kerosene......................cases..	350	2,255	1,068	10,250
Wrapping paper................reams..	600	192	6,998	2,095
Blacking.....................barrels..	27	831	32	1,034
Rosin...........................do....	....	....	77	2,000
Soap.........................boxes..	525	3,500	225	1,500
Pitch.......................barrels..	120	2,700	25	600
Tar.............................do....	100	1,200	....	....
Nails..........................kegs..	....	....	125	741
Tea..........................chests..	....	....	433	12,920
Sundries	....	23,515	....	38,676
Total	....	117,030	....	655,301

Statement showing the description, number of packages, weight or measure with the value of the imports, from the United States, in other than American vessels. and entered for consumption at the port of Pernambuco, during the year ended June 30, 1864, compared with previous year.

Articles.	1863–'64.			1862–'63.		
	Number of packages.	Weight or measure.	Value.	Number of packages.	Weight or measure.	Value.
Flour	72,885 barrels		$628,840	23 430 barrels		$193,000
Kerosene	1,480 cases	20.800 gallons	13,253	249 cases		2,475
Lard	2,550 kegs	75,903 pounds	10,464	1,185 kegs		4,562
Machinery			10,374			
Drugs and medicines			9,251			
Lumber		274,218 feet	6,836	40,387 feet		1,010
Tea	565 packages	21,442 pounds	5,960	75 packages		1,500
Crackers	3,650 kegs		5,025	600 kegs		750
Paper, wrapping	14,966 reams		4,603	5,231 reams		1,569
Blacking	80 barrels	9,957 dozen	2,806	20 barrels		640
Nails	320 kegs		1,694			
Bran	1,282 bags		1,486			
Carriages	6 carriages		1,236			
Lamps	20 packages		498			
Cornmeal	20 barrels		338			
Chairs		3 dozen	134			
Shoes	1 case	60 pairs	128			
Butter				40 firkins		500
Candles				20 boxes		200
Rosin				50 barrels		1,300
Soap				63 boxes		425
Specie			22,700			20,000
Sundries			13,500			13,500
Total			725,556			241,431

Tabular statement showing the exportations from the port of Pernambuco during the year ended June 30, 1864, and comparison of the same with the three preceding years, (compiled from official documents and custom-house books.)

Articles.	Unit of quantity.	1863-'64				1862-'63			
		Quantity.	Value.	Medium price.	Duties.	Quantity.	Value.	Medium price.	Duties.
			Reis.	*Reis.*	*Reis.*		*Reis.*	*Reis.*	*Reis.*
To foreign countries:									
Rum	Canadas	301,062	116,073‖700	385	8,125‖156	548,522	154,957‖020	282	10,846‖903
Cotton	Arrobas	394,942	8,928,236 062	82‖657	625,676 415	256,649	4,327,974 383	16‖803	302,962 426
Sugar, white	do	762,149	2,699,617 409	3 542	188,973 082	996,036	2,956,029 477	2 977	395,922 964
Sugar, Muscovado	do	2,491,494	6,172,599 498	2 473	431,381 900	2,381,858	4,297,565 936	1 796	300,830 003
Hides, salted	Pounds	2,810,700	390,634 070	139	97,344 331	3,293,416	471,114 899	143	32,977 979
Hides, dry	do	572,725	57,455 780	100	9,681 897	208,178	29,437 150	141	2,060 358
Diamonds	Grains								
Molasses	Canadas	85,596	16,962 800	198	1,187 396	153,450	30,630 000	199	2,144 128
Gold, in bars	Oitavas					402	447 900	3 600	14 472
Silver, in bars	Ounces	455	729 600	1 603	14 599	4,720	7,500 400	1 588	150 008
Leather	Sides	5,707	16,159 200	2 830	1,132 654	7,030	19,733 600	2 807	1,381 352
Other articles			75,004 003		4,672 529		175,394 711		3,660 064
Total			18,453,435‖142		1,291,129‖952		12,471,784‖766		863,950 857
To ports of the empire:									
Rum	Canadas	150,127	66,781‖580	444		91,989	30,453‖576	334	
Cotton	Arrobas	2,444	56,575 967	23 149		498	10,456 612	90 997	
Sugar, white	do	533,383	1,936,534 263	3 499		326,874	1,144,525 459	1 958	
Sugar, Muscovado	do	14,769	35,489 906	2 403		21,947	38,307 680	1 745	
M, green and dry salted	Pounds								
Hides, dried and not salted	Pounds	8,782	2,098 440	239		31	7 360	237	
Molasses	Canadas	3,506	708 800	202		5,147	1,027 000	199	
Leather	Sides	56,315	163,763 400	2 808		24,850	72,719 450	2 926	
Sundries			1,213,866 489				519,686 404		
Total			3,475,780‖845				1,817,063‖541		

Tabular statement showing the exportations from the port of Pernambuco—Continued.

Articles.	Unit of quantity.	1861-62.				1860-61.			
		Quantity.	Value.	Medium price.	Duties.	Quantity.	Value.	Medium price.	Duties.
To foreign countries:			*Reis.*	*Reis.*	*Reis.*		*Reis.*	*Reis.*	*Reis.*
Rum	Canadas	494,633	174,618,130	353	12,223,430	459,513	204,295,000	445	12,420,999
Cotton	Arrobas	116,517	1,207,864,057	10,366	84,545,075	79,596	684,825,626	7,850	35,745,771
Sugar, white	do.	1,979,518	3,917,276,492	3 061	274,210,340	583,469	3,113,627,438	3 656	138,989,253
Sugar, Muscovado	do.	3,103,942	6,331,185,981	2 041	443,183,843	1,611,715	3,730,874,331	2 308	321,717,554
Hides, salted	Pounds	3,523,901	579,911,130	168	36,964,488	2,794,287	562,840,932	208	35,251,345
Hides, dry	do.	40,138	7,784,040	153	544,881	106,410	32,213,540	303	1,867,805
Diamonds	Grains					58	580,000	5 000	1 400
Molasses	Canadas	150,966	30,983,040	205	2,167,485	180,571	43,998,910	243	8,792,743
Gold, in bars	Oitavas					85	597,500	3 500	975
Silver, in bars	Ounces	694	1,198,080	1 920	32,961	8,331	11,561,000	1 310	921,919
Leather	Hides	4,446	11,457,600	2 589	709,932	6,570	19,133,904	9 763	1,030,974
Other articles			96,630,183		6,622,687		71,560,904		5,027,786
Total			12,339,599,003		864,286,102		7,424,534,061		464,376,904
To parts of the empire:									
Rum	Canadas	263,077	134,609,800	391		314,354	140,887,228	448	
Cotton	Arrobas	19,353	199,834,088	10 560		12,145	98,030,260	8 017	
Sugar, white	do.	548,939	1,711,305,936	3 116		769,586	2,886,131,160	3 750	
Sugar, Muscovado	do.	47,496,944	47,496,944	3 044		335,669	935,968,980	3 132	
Hides, green and dry, salted	Pounds	7,525	1,462,400	197		1,200	270,000	225	
Hides, dry, and not salted	do.	3,979	671,300	919		9,367	686,600	320	
Molasses	Canadas	3,090	622,300	201		2,367	618,540	320	
Leather	Hides	49,454	125,118,400	2 589		43,366	152,277,000	320	
Sundries			730,940,751				590,584,334	9 904	
Total			3,682,617,917				4,775,053,092		

NOTE.—The values given above are those fixed every week by the custom-house, and upon which an export duty is assessed, viz.: on sugar, 7 per cent. and 90 reis per arroba; cotton, 12 per cent. and 90 reis per arroba; hides, 15 per cent. per arroba; rum, 7 per cent. and 20 reis per canada; other articles, 12 per cent. By adding 25 per cent. to the above value you find about the actual value of the goods. On board the vessels all charges and expenses paid.

Statement showing the total exports from the port of Pernambuco to the United States during the year ended June 30, 1864, the quantity and value of each article free on board, (including expenses, commissions, export duties, &c., &c.,) and the port to which shipped, made up from invoices presented for verification at the United States consulate, Pernambuco.

PORTS TO WHICH SHIPPED.

Articles of export.	New York.			Philadelphia.			Baltimore.			Total.		
	No. pack'ges or pieces.	Weight.	Value.	No. pack'ges or pieces.	Weight.	Value.	No. pack'ges or pieces.	Weight.	Value.	No. pack'ges or pieces.	Weight.	Value.
			Reis.			*Reis.*			*Reis.*			*Reis.*
Sugar	27,751 bags	142,493 arrobas	371,007||190	19,505 bags	97,525 arrobas	274,427||840	22,090 bags	113,100 arrobas	327,800||866	69,346 bags	353,123 arrobas	973,325||848
Cotton	1,122 bales	5,087,32 arch	166,660||638	949 bales	4,857,13,82 ar	192,857,390				2,071 bales	10,39491,32s	359,498,098
Waste cotton	18 bales	104 arrobas	389,000							18 bales	104 arrobas	389,000
Hides	11,720 hides	364,448 lbs.	73,708,980	10,749 hides	319,393 lbs.	64,567,703				22,469 hides	683,841 lbs.	138,271,683
Goat-skins	8,354 skins	3,871,080	3,871,030							8,354 skins		3,871,080
Coffee, (Rio Janeiro).	322 bags	1,610 arrobas	15,450,000							322 bags	1,610 arrobas	15,450,000
Old iron		365 tons.	10,493,415		35 tons.	1,077,980					400 tons.	11,562,695
Old yellow metal		5,078 lbs.	1,407,000								5,078 lbs.	1,407,000
Old copper		1,712 lbs.	543,580								1,712 lbs.	543,580
Old lead		896 lbs.	78,000								896 lbs.	78,000
Old sails			1,467,640									1,467,640
Old rope		3,672 lbs.	313,000								3,672 lbs.	313,000
Rum	72 bales	21,686 lbs.	985,750							72 bales	21,686 lbs.	985,750
Liquid India-rubber	2 pipes		904,750							2 pipes		904,750
Cotton seed	15 bbls.		1,290,000							15 bbls.		1,290,000
Castor oil	8 bbls.		119,550							8 bbls.		119,550
Cashka nuts	10 tins	890 lbs.	123,000							10 tins	390 lbs.	123,000
	3 bags		2,500							3 bags		2,500
Total			658,069||063			462,910||117			327,890||866			1,418,870||106

Number of vessels of each nationality employed in carrying the above freight, and value under each flag.

No.	Nationality.	Value of freight.
4	American	Reis 165,905||226
1	Austrian	32,515,000
23	British	961,081,538
5	Brazilian	187,792,781
1	Danish	32,975,619
34		1,418,870||106

NOTE.—One arroba =32,98 lbs.   One milreis (rate 1||000)=54. 15 cents United States gold currency.

Statement showing the value of the exports of the province of Pernambuco to foreign countries, and to ports of the empire, for the year ended June 30, 1864, compared with seven preceding years. (Compiled from official documents.)

To foreign countries:	1863-'64	1862-'63	1861-'62	1860-'61	1859-'60	1858-'59
	Reis.	*Reis.*	*Reis.*	*Reis.*	*Reis.*	*Reis.*
United States	1,155,971||753	1,277,399||591	853,491||003	347,357||692	1,740,068||920	2,233,142||464
Argentine Republic	818,270 678	1,493,955 026	968,986 892	1,006,315 390	1,769,473 820	1,625,781 333
Austria						114,474 972
Belgium						
Chili	583,962 124	454,067 000	465,738 500	454,433 250	453,757 400	786,309 876
Denmark						4,020 400
France	2,434,116 998	995,614 785	1,963,017 221	944,341 689	1,629,331 740	1,946,672 998
Great Britain	8,668,531 986	5,988,640 303	5,840,933 759	2,961,915 638	3,058,710 810	5,945,018 681
Hanseatic Cities			14,933 480	196 500		36 000
Holland		907 000	4,337 675	130 000	3,497 880	600 000
Italy	32,969 125		953,730 448	87,628 180	74,747 060	313,961 972
Portugal	3,180,954 770	1,863,745 866	1,960,592 923	1,286,106 059	63,430 380	1,491,851 943
Peru					1,809,749 660	
Spain	2,517,921 733	1,037,118 172	154,746 183	30,999 119	69,433 160	76,006 100
Sweden and Norway		72,928 568	85,575 431	129,668 977	268,912 100	186,193 329
Turkey						
Uruguay	44,490 675	15,117 205	61,797 192	161,397 949	144,744 040	6,326 700
For consumption on foreign vessels	6,765 310	5,691 270	11,766 283	10,951 468	26,941 880	35,272 481
Total	18,453,456||149	12,471,784||766	12,339,859||003	7,444,534||081	11,105,818||140	14,005,565||549

	1857-'58	1856-'57	Difference in value compared with preceding year.		Difference in value compared with average of 7 preceding years.	
			Greater.	Less.	Greater.	Less.
	Reis.	*Reis.*	*Reis.*	*Reis.*	*Reis.*	*Reis.*
United States	635,739||030	1,562,081||926		191,427||858		85,349||490
Argentine Republic	9,098,634 025	1,985,729 754		695,684 348		447,427 356
Austria	80,150 000					57,803 567
Belgium	25 500					3 643
Chili	592,896 500	701,340 561	149,895||194		34,641||683	
Denmark	11,589 600					2,931 438
France	1,629,505 483	1,312,286 747	1,447,508 223		943,863 040	
Great Britain	5,443,623 054	5,085,500 652	3,400,191 663		4,033,925 803	
Hanseatic Cities	2,061 900	78 920				3,964 854
Holland	667,533 772	68,313 859				91,734 859
Italy			32,969 125		185,319 349	207,591 711
Portugal	71,050 000	2,998,555 674	317,208 904			
Peru	191,408 787			207 000		10,150 000
Spain	73,883 778	495,735 350	1,460,103 561		2,944,690 729	
Sweden and Norway	65,097 000	664,611 218				211,581 914
Turkey						9,399 571

Statement showing the value of the exports of the province of Pernambuco, &c.—Continued.

	1857–'58.	1856–'57.	Difference in value compared with preceding year.		Difference in value compared with average of 7 preceding years.	
			Greater.	Less.	Greater.	Less.
To foreign countries:	*Reis.*	*Reis.*	1857–'58.		1858–'59.	
			Reis.	*Reis.*	*Reis.*	*Reis.*
Uruguay	192,314‖233	37,929‖600	29,373‖470			44,313‖170
For consumption on foreign vessels	47,740 791	59,944 537	1,074 040			18,643,361
Total	14,259,309‖383	15,963,865‖798				
			1860–'61.		1859–'60.	1858–'59.
To ports of the empire:	*Reis.*	*Reis.*	*Reis.*		*Reis.*	*Reis.*
Para	363,247‖059	138,528‖353	217,696‖977	148,932‖848	166,943‖223	126,208‖675
Maranham	26,023,064	6,137 160	94,126 617	68,723 500	90,579 689	62,303 527
Ceara	73,972 909	31,788 927	77,230 669	101,662 022	89,028 846	90,257 195
Rio Grande del Norte	126,644 871	41,309 120	61,145 601	63,918 147	80,542 114	86,356 256
Parahiba	205,389 477	89,950 184	206,690 681	166,963 976	389,995 169	944,963 011
Alagoas and Macelo	493,407 571	301,878 308	283,690 080	179,020 070	345,009 177	164,068 242
Sergipe			656 398			
Bahia	90,472 530	52,634 296	61,156 328	67,981 671	940,155 384	152,258,299
Rio de Janeiro	1,137,581 712	657,676 122	1,910,210 539	9,996,381 709	3,106,990 688	3,032,619 538
Santa Catharina	29,849 495	60 000		30,511 590		
San Pedro do Sul	986,715 659	497,191 161	729,654 399	928,957 560	1,072,111 665	754,464 077
Total	3,475,820‖845	1,817,083‖541	2,882,617‖917	4,775,053‖063	5,463,648‖957	3,712,792‖110

	1857–'58.	1856–'57.	Difference in value compared with preceding year.		Difference in value compared with average of 7 preceding years.	
			Greater.	Less.	Greater.	Less.
Para	171,669‖055	905,763‖196	224,718‖719		195,383‖965	50,704‖397
Maranham	145,969 757	139,956 975	19,885 904			7,986 919
Ceara	106,552 464	72,303 839	42,183 982			
Rio Grande del Norte	72,798 677	58,922 088	83,133 751		59,460 558	
Parahiba	203,641 640	191,399 599	905,319 983		95,998 441	
Alagoas and Macelo	185,431 983	104,982 588	191,599 983		268,604 173	
Sergipe	1,004 500	7,376 140				1,290 948
Bahia	201,764 094	929,708 458	37,838 304			56,050 110
Rio de Janeiro	3,021,736 814	1,833,716 367	479,905 590			985,464 727
Santa Catharina	29,849 495		426 000			8,145 573
San Pedro do Sul	1,196,576 985	765,399 307	371,594 498		29,389 210	
Total	6,272,896‖194	3,608,003‖587				

Statement showing the nationality of the foreign shipping entered and cleared at the port of Pernambuco, with the number of vessels, tonnage, and crews under each flag, during the year ended June 30, 1864, and comparison of the same with the three preceding years.

ENTERED.

Nationality.	1863-'64.			1862-'63.			1861-'62.			1860-'61.		
	Vessels.	Tonnage.	Crews.	Vessels.	Tonnage.	Crews.	Vessels.	Tonnage.	Crews.	Vessels.	Tonnage.	Crews.
United States	12	3,420	151	37	10,085	354	51	13,476	564	51	17,191	604
Arg. Republic	3	662	27	2	560	21	1	276	11			
Austria	2	653	23	3	939	31						
Belgium				1	349	15				1	309	15
Brazil	10	2,583	104	3	640	42	1	270	10			
Bremen	2	615	21				2	496	18	2	666	25
Chili							2	547	19			
Denmark	20	3,236	152	7	1,254	58	12	2,158	118	9	1,745	85
France	50	35,034	3,063	49	35,367	3,030	59	38,506	3,087	53	38,681	3,216
Great Britain	182	89,992	4,709	167	69,953	4,664	175	72,300	4,077	166	70,124	4,131
Greece										1	205	11
Hamburg	6	974	48	10	1,761	88	12	2,226	120	7	1,167	66
Hanover	5	973	42	3	519	26	3	367	23	2	246	13
Holland	8	1,456	65	8	1,309	71	8	1,480	55	8	1,433	66
Italy,(Papal States)	3	540	30	6	1,001	63	8	1,563	89	1	176	12
Lubeck				1	301	10						
Norway				3	1,007	32	2	758	19	1	217	9
Oldenburg	4	807	33							3	594	25
Portugal	58	14,374	750	55	13,524	723	45	10,613	612	41	15,557	836
Prussia							1	182	7	1	171	9
Russia							1	419	13			
Sardinia										3	414	26
Spain	35	5,912	405	40	7,029	470	22	3,912	246	26	4,413	293
Sweden	3	707	30	6	1,400	56	7	1,695	73	5	1,118	57
Uruguay	1	215	9	1	133	9	1	217	11			
Total	404	169,153	9,682	402	147,221	9,763	413	151,463	9,172	381	154,420	9,499

CLEARED.

Nationality.	1863-'64.			1862-'63.			1861-'62.			1860-'61.		
	Vessels.	Tonnage.	Crews.	Vessels.	Tonnage.	Crews.	Vessels.	Tonnage.	Crews.	Vessels.	Tonnage.	Crews.
United States	14	4,608	159	36	11,835	391	46	14,169	456	52	22,060	613
Arg. Republic	2	454	17	2	658	19	1	180	8			
Austria	2	695	22	3	1,180	31						
Belgium				1	605	13				1	304	10
Brazil	24	7,469	291	12	2,618	136				10	2,444	198
Bremen	2	686	23				2	606	17	2	723	94
Chili							2	815	29			
Denmark	21	4,243	159	6	1,345	42	12	3,376	101	10	3,123	100
France	50	37,571	3,081	49	36,311	3,118	62	43,182	3,141	51	39,376	3,151
Great Britain	174	103,007	4,630	172	86,640	4,561	169	87,946	4,025	166	86,356	4,095
Greece										1	295	11
Hamburg	5	1,176	42	8	1,865	79	10	2,990	101	8	1,790	73
Hanover		694	94	2	618	19	3	548	18	3	611	20
Holland	1	2,891	99	7	1,637	50	8	1,847	63	8	1,851	67
Italy,(Papal States)	3	776	29	7	1,801	72	6	1,772	68	1	326	12
Lubeck				1	407	10						
Norway				3	1,085	30	2	763	21	1	342	9
Oldenburg	5	1,375	49							3	764	25
Portugal	59	19,048	774	55	17,337	676	47	14,891	654	39	17,540	839
Prussia							1	203	7			
Russia							1	671	13			
Sardinia										3	603	26
Spain	36	8,862	426	37	9,645	431	29	6,872	332	20	4,844	247
Sweden	2	557	19	4	1,534	44	8	2,634	82	5	1,754	51
Uruguay	1	271	12									
Total	414	194,383	9,856	406	179,191	9,652	409	183,465	9,129	384	185,106	9,503

NOTE.—Anchorage dues on vessels with cargoes inwards and outwards, 300 reis per ton; with cargo inwards, leaving in ballast, or *vice versa*, 150 reis per ton, Brazil measurement.

Statement showing the number of foreign vessels, with their tonnage and crews, entered and cleared at the port of Pernambuco during the year ended June 30, 1864, and comparison of the same with the three preceding years.

ENTERED.

Countries whence arriving and whither clearing.	1863-'64.			1862-'63.			1861-'62.			1860-'61.		
	No. of vessels.	Tonnage.	No. of crews.	No. of vessels.	Tonnage.	No. of crews.	No. of vessels.	Tonnage.	No. of crews.	No. of vessels.	Tonnage.	No. of crews.
United States	52	11,352	491	47	11,989	456	47	11,741	476	39	12,629	462
Great Britain and possess'ns	129	65,579	3,458	142	48,571	3,050	152	50,501	2,682	179	61,568	3,310
France and possessions	37	25,870	2,324	31	19,837	1,634	40	22,527	1,713	28	20,132	1,670
Portugal and possessions	38	8,888	500	36	8,233	492	36	7,714	496	28	8,452	493
Argentine Republic	23	4,087	236	14	2,538	156	17	3,306	179	23	5,063	240
Spain and possessions	14	2,524	126	19	2,969	204	8	1,122	81	5	659	58
Austria	11	2,002	102	9	1,904	86	5	1,393	58	5	676	44
Hanse Towns	12	1,385	78	13	2,356	113	12	1,946	116	8	1,327	73
Italy	3	540	30	4	688	44	5	867	57	3	390	28
Peru	2	543	25									
Sweden and Norway	1	230	10				4	1,082	51	1	197	11
Netherlands and possessions	1	185	9	3	611	29	3	467	26	2	362	19
Belgium	3	502	29	3	399	29	4	748	29	6	944	53
Denmark and possessions										2	841	31
Chili							1	280	14			
China												
Mexico												
Venezuela												
Ports of the empire*	78	38,466	2,231	81	47,106	3,460	79	47,769	3,214	52	41,114	3,017
Total	404	162,153	9,682	402	147,221	9,753	413	151,463	9,172	381	154,420	9,499

CLEARED.

Countries whence arriving and whither clearing.	1863-'64.			1862-'63.			1861-'62.			1860-'61.		
	No. of vessels.	Tonnage.	No. of crews.	No. of vessels.	Tonnage.	No. of crews.	No. of vessels.	Tonnage.	No. of crews.	No. of vessels.	Tonnage.	No. of crews.
United States	35	9,856	335	42	13,176	369	33	10,211	319	25	8,241	256
Great Britain and possess'ns	123	75,257	3,427	97	47,008	2,369	154	67,661	2,660	96	47,449	2,160
France and possessions	41	28,799	2,352	27	19,667	1,569	56	30,363	1,898	31	21,715	1,696
Portugal and possessions	51	17,668	685	48	15,491	602	39	12,127	558	34	14,078	682
Argentine Republic	29	6,572	324	36	9,009	385	21	5,227	213	35	8,331	387
Spain and possessions	28	7,141	333	18	4,736	202	10	2,260	108	8	2,678	93
Austria										1	288	9
Hanse Towns												
Italy				1	241	12	7	1,724	76	2	290	17
Peru												
Sweden and Norway				1	426	10	1	435	12	2	571	15
Netherlands and possessions												
Belgium	1	348	15				1	248	9			
Denmark and possessions	1	213	8				10	2,915	95	15	4,721	146
Chili	10	3,017	102	7	3,129	90	6	2,912	76	5	1,870	58
China	1	132	17	1	289	9						
Mexico							1	261	8	1	298	10
Venezuela							1	204	13	2	521	19
Ports of the empire*	94	45,390	2,258	128	65,949	4,035	69	46,917	3,084	127	74,055	3,955
Total	414	194,383	9,856	406	179,121	9,652	409	183,465	9,129	384	185,106	9,503

* Vessels coming from other ports of the Empire to finish discharging here. Vessels discharged at other ports coming here for freight. Vessels partially discharged here going to other ports with balance of cargo, and those going to other ports to load.

Statement showing the coastwise navigation of the port of Pernambuco during the year ended June 30, 1864, and comparison of the same with the three preceding years.

Provinces where from and whither bound.	ENTERED											
	1863-'64.			1862-'63.			1861-'62.			1860-'61.		
	No. of vessels.	Tonnage.	No. of crews.	No. of vessels.	Tonnage.	No. of crews.	No. of vessels.	Tonnage.	No. of crews.	No. of vessels.	Tonnage.	No. of crews.
Para	26	21,737	1,254	24	21,661	1,187	24	19,785	1,172	24	21,367	1,354
Maranham	6	1,160	63	7	1,250	74	9	1,679	95	10	1,835	116
Ceara	59	10,865	918	61	12,038	864	59	14,999	1,021	59	11,535	787
Rio Grande del Norte	113	6,241	589	19	1,891	138	22	2,010	176	38	2,293	232
Parahiba	290	10,421	1,237	1	155	7	10	699	57	2	56	8
Alagoas	396	19,665	2,076	39	10,447	638	43	11,620	694	30	9,352	549
Sergipe	10	2,979	191				1	108	8			
Bahia	23	3,800	227	30	2,679	196	15	2,667	153	20	2,807	182
Rio de Janeiro	66	39,941	1,871	60	19,768	1,638	69	39,140	1,575	77	36,545	1,996
San Paulo												
Parana												
Santa Catharina	6	919	59	1	743	10				1	196	11
Rio Grande do Sul	61	13,307	710	56	12,386	657	43	8,366	480	59	10,011	691
Ports of the Interior	1,150	33,297	5,064	13	2,427	182	9	898	70	3	315	21
Total	2,206	156,639	14,279	301	84,845	5,591	304	94,971	5,501	316	96,242	5,879

Provinces where from and whither bound.	CLEARED.											
	1863-'64.			1862-'63.			1861-'62.			1860-'61.		
	No. of vessels.	Tonnage.	No. of crews.	No. of vessels.	Tonnage.	No. of crews.	No. of vessels.	Tonnage.	No. of crews.	No. of vessels.	Tonnage.	No. of crews.
Para	37	25,649	1,502	39	22,067	1,234	24	19,785	1,172	33	25,366	1,496
Maranham	4	578	37	4	623	39	10	1,883	109	6	830	49
Ceara	66	10,365	843	61	11,222	891	62	15,085	978	85	12,893	642
Rio Grande del Norte	104	5,786	508	19	3,016	155	24	2,318	193	11	687	56
Parahiba	267	9,959	1,158	1	195	9	8	384	40	2	52	6
Alagoas	389	21,943	2,113	35	10,170	611	42	11,149	664	29	9,277	539
Sergipe	5	1,262	96	1	56	5	1	109	8	1	141	8
Bahia	10	1,155	91	14	1,237	117	12	1,958	112	13	1,460	102
Rio de Janeiro	53	25,996	1,415	53	25,734	1,399	69	39,505	1,639	81	34,302	1,923
San Paulo	1	175	10							1	201	9
Parana										1	126	12
Santa Catharina	4	695	44	1	123	10						
Rio Grande do Sul	58	13,159	654	48	10,368	557	48	9,464	545	40	8,178	436
Ports of the Interior	1,150	32,834	5,068	14	2,793	195	8	850	64	4	522	35
Total	2,148	148,858	13,539	283	87,604	5,152	308	95,490	5,524	307	93,965	5,313

Statement showing the total quantity of wheat flour, with its value and the countries whence shipped, entered at the port of Pernambuco, during the year ended June 30, 1864.

Countries.	Quantity.	Value, estimated at average price of United States flour.
United States .... barrels..	82,365	$709,215
Trieste ....do....	18,124	156,108
Newfoundland ....do....	3,020	26,012
Havre and Bordeaux ....do....	2,870	24,720
Brazilian ports.......................................do....	8,548	73,627
Total..	114,947	989,682

NOTE.—The flour from Brazilian ports was chiefly American, sent here because of the high price at this port. The value of United States flour was given to me by the merchants as the actual cost in United States currency, (paper.)

Statement showing the importations of codfish at Pernambuco during the last ten years, (year ended June 30.)

Drums.

1854-'55	119,307
1855-'56	140,633
1856-'57	155,226
1857-'58	209,871
1858-'59	248,385
1859-'60	167,716
1860-'61	154,948
1861-'62	139,580
1862-'63	94,281
1863-'64	82,175
Total	1,512,122

Statement showing the importations of jerked beef at Pernambuco, together with the quantity and the countries whence shipped, during the last ten years, (year ended June 30.)

Years.	WHERE FROM.		Total.
	Rio Grande do Sul.	River Plate.	
	Arrobas.	*Arrobas.*	*Arrobas.*
1854-'55..........................	170,017	34,956	204,973
1855-'56..........................	112,055	64,862	176,917
1856-'57..........................	203,564	117,853	321,417
1857-'58..........................	305,703	85,385	391,088
1858-'59..........................	288,587	159,236	447,823
1859-'60..........................	391,443	200,574	592,917
1860-'61..........................	539,336	167,576	706,912
1861-'62..........................	569,287	162,666	731,953
1862-'63..........................	802,352	153,591	955,943
1863-'64..........................	750,203	164,963	915,166
Total	4,132,547	1,311,662	5,444,209

Comparative statement showing the exports of sugar from Pernambuco, and the names of countries where shipped, during the last ten years, (year ended September.)

Countries.	1863-'64.	1862-'63.	1861-'62.	1860-'61.	1859-'60.	1858-'59.	1857-'58.	1856-'57.	1855-'56.	1854-'55.	Average.
	Tons.	Tons.	Tons.	Tons.	Tons.	Tons.	Tons.	Tons.	Tons.	Tons.	Tons.
Africa	......	......	24	......	......	......	30	9	19	5	11
Bremen and Hamburg	......	......	24	......	......	......	......	......	100	929	38
England and English Channel, for orders	22,400	18,335	21,539	16,529	7,728	23,285	19,528	16,189	18,298	11,590	17,530
France	3,442	9,979	11,691	5,681	3,899	10,709	5,620	5,899	4,723	11,566	6,782
Genoa	349	57	727	1,112	......	1,391	4,099	1,508	3,525	3,107	1,999
Gibraltar, for orders	......	923	3,981	996	......	2,966	3,713	101	3,579	3,105	1,990
Holland and Belgium	......	......	......	......	......	......	......	11	11	181	53
Portugal and Azores	8,106	10,051	6,444	7,097	6,188	6,112	7,657	9,554	7,804	7,678	7,709
Buenos Ayres	3,039	6,750	4,639	4,346	5,966	5,883	5,820	7,468	4,691	4,994	5,369
Spain	71	445	96	......	254	314	206	271	1,560	36	111
Sweden and Norway	......	......	......	......	......	464	202	1,085	943	1,341	479
Trieste	......	......	......	......	......	......	459	435	......	688	528
United States	4,849	4,925	6,139	1,736	9,450	11,417	1,974	7,592	4,064	4,905	5,897
Valparaiso	1,961	2,602	1,509	2,063	900	3,901	1,880	3,159	3,308	4,715	2,956
Ports of the empire	6,839	9,833	7,976	15,331	13,183	9,421	14,002	8,555	6,923	6,768	9,885
Total	53,089	56,899	64,802	54,846	47,572	75,169	63,251	65,291	57,491	59,104	59,740

Statement showing the estimated population of Brazil in the year 1860.

Provinces.	Free population.	Slave population.	Proportion of slaves to free persons.
Amazonas	68,000	1,000	1 to 68
Para	300,000	20,000	1 to 15
Maranham	330,000	70,000	1 to 4.714
Piauhy	200,000	20,000	1 to 10
Ceara	504,000	36,000	1 to 14
Rio Grande del Norte	200,000	25,000	1 to 8
Farahiba	250,000	30,000	1 to 8.137
Pernambuco	1,040,000	260,000	1 to 4
Alagoas	250,000	50,000	1 to 5
Sergipe	220,000	55,000	1 to 4
Bahia	1,100,000	300,000	1 to 3.666
Espirito Santo	50,000	15,000	1 to 3.333
Rio de Janeiro	1,000,000	400,000	1 to 2.500
San Paulo	700,000	80,000	1 to 8.750
Parana	80,000	20,000	1 to 4
St. Catharina	135,000	15,000	1 to 9
Rio Grande do Sul	380,000	40,000	1 to 9.500
Minas	1,200,000	250,000	1 to 4.800
Goyaz	205,000	15,000	1 to 13.666
Matto Grossa	95,000	5,000	1 to 19
Total	8,307,000	1,707,000	

PARA—SAMUEL G. POND, Consul.

DECEMBER 31, 1863.

Statement showing the number and nationality of foreign vessels arrived at and departed from Para during the quarter ended December 31, 1863, together with a description of their cargoes and value, inward and outward.

| | VESSELS | | | | | CARGOES | | | | | |
| | | | | | | Inward | | | Outward | | |
Classes.	Where from.	Where built.	Where belonging.	Where bound.	Owners.	Where produced.	Description.	Values.	Where produced.	Description.	Values.
Schooner	New York.	Foreign	Foreign	New York.	British.	United States.	Flour and sundries.	$12,889 19	Province of Para.	Rubber and deer-skins	$33,173 14
Brig	do.	do.	do.	do.	do.	do.	do.	36,365 94	do.	do.	98,659 70
Schooner	do.	do.	do.	do.	Brazilian	do.	do.	12,212 14	do.	do.	11,101 98
Brig	do.	do.	do.	do.	British	do.	do.	10,039 57	do.	do.	19,695 15
Brig	do.	do.	do.	do.	Brazilian	do.	do.	16,980 70	do.	do.	16,501 74
Schooner	do.	do.	do.	do.	British	do.	do.	11,249 54	do.	do.	30,602 48
Brig	do.	do.	do.	do.	do.	do.	do.	16,141 31	do.	do.	44,506 42
Brig	do.	do.	do.	do.	do.	do.	do.	18,445 22	do.	do.	46,058 86
Brig	do.	do.	do.	do.	do.	do.	do.	69,598 69	do.	do.	65,908 75
Total								203,201 53			294,131 22

MARANHAM—WILLIAM H. EVANS—*Consul.*

DECEMBER 31, 1863.

Statement showing the description, value, country of production, and port of destination, of the exports from Maranham during the quarter ended December 31, 1863.

Description.	Value.	Country of production.	Port of destination.
Old copper..	$528 82	Brazil.......	New York...
Hides	10,197 20	....do.......	....do......

OCTOBER 22, 1864.

I have the honor to submit the following commercial statistics for the year ended September 30, 1864:

No. 1. Showing the receipts of cotton from the interior of the province and the amount exported from the port of Maranham during the years 1861–'62, 1862–'63, and 1863–'64.

No. 2. Statement showing the destination of exports of cotton from this port during the same period.

No. 3. Statement of the value of exports from this port to the United States during the years 1861–'62, 1862–'63, and 1863–'64.

No. 4. Table showing the value of the trade of Maranham with foreign nations for the financial year of 1862–'63.

No. 5. Table showing the arrivals and departures of vessels and the total value of trade for the financial years of 1860–'61, 1861–'62, and 1862–'63.

No. 6. Statement of the arrivals and departures of foreign vessels for the financial year of 1862–'63.

No. 7. Statement of the arrivals and departures of vessels engaged in the coasting trade for the financial year of 1862–'63.

It will be seen, from the enclosed cotton reports that the increase in the number of bales exported from this port during the past year, as compared with the previous year, amounts to 5,736 bales. Bales average 200 pounds each, making in pounds the amount entered:

	Pounds.
For 1863–'64	8,927,800
1862–'63..	7,576,600
Increase...	1,351,200

The value of the cotton exported from this port during four years, each ending 31st August, is exhibited as follows:

1860–'61..	1,440,827‖966 reis.
1861–'62..	2,062,664 269 "
1862–'63..	4,037,796 533 "
1863–'64	5,133,485 000 "

The advance price of cotton has failed to increase the production in this province to the extent anticipated. The soil is well adapted, and the plant being a perennial requires less labor than in many other cotton-growing countries. But these advantages, with the remunerative prices, seem to have stimulated only a slightly extended cultivation. Labor is not easily attained; the population is small, the poorer class not disposed to steady employment; many subsist on the spontaneous productions of the soil, and, so long as they do not suffer, are not likely to acquire industrious habits. There is, therefore, little hope of a speedy increase in the production of cotton in this portion of the country.

Excepting in the article of cotton, the statistics exhibit no change, either in the general commerce of the port or in trade with the United States, worthy of special notice.

There has been no change in any of the regulations of this port affecting commerce.

Statement showing the number of bales of cotton (of 200 pounds each) received from the interior of this province and the number exported from the port of Maranham during the years 1861–'62, 1862–'63, and 1863–'64, each ending 31st of August.

Months.	1861–'62.		1862–'63.		1863–'64.	
	Entered.	Exported.	Entered.	Exported.	Entered.	Exported.
Estimated stock September 1, 1861	8,217	....	....	....	....	....
September............	2,281	2,614	1,711	1,522	859	130
October.............	1,951	3,346	4,867	1,385	3,512	1,584
November...........	2,537	2,479	6,741	3,178	8,276	4,964
December...........	5,938	3,606	7,846	5,260	9,358	6,800
January.............	4,370	2,912	5,576	2,448	7,948	6,567
February............	1,528	2,054	8,054	9,029	3,718	5,226
March............	3,395	2,492	2,543	3,396	3,388	8,611
April...............	2,116	8,467	1,376	3,741	2,436	3,837
May...............	1,893	5,359	1,706	2,444	1,589	3,117
June...............	1,433	2,634	470	2,431	1,911	1,440
July...............	1,971	335	1,363	1,547	957	457
August.............	1,625	2,701	630	1,936	687	1,320
	39,255					
Total for 12 months— Sept. 1 to Aug. 31..	31,038	38,999	37,883	38,317	44,639	44,053

Table showing the destination and amount of exports of cotton from the port of Maranham during the years 1861, 1862, 1863, (ending December 31,) and to August 31, 1864.

To—	1861.	1862.	1863.	1864.
	Bales.	Bales.	Bales.	Bales.
Liverpool	22,582	25,022	38,683	22,618
Oporto...................................	10,471	11,028	2,805	3,598
Barcelona	550	809	936	1,464
Liverpool	574	789	349	486
New York................................	....	431	1,283	418
Havre	25	220	1,394	1,991
Total	34,202	38,299	45,450	30,575

Statement showing the articles exported to the United States, (under authenticated invoices,) and their value in American currency, during the years 1861-'62, 1862-'63, and 1863-'64, each ended September 30.

Articles.	Value, including costs and charges.		
	1861-'62.	1862-'63.	1863-'64.
Hides	$56, 438 00	$50, 006 45	$38, 353 68
Cotton...	14, 523 00	62, 055 00	32, 688 08
Balsam copaiba...................................	2, 404 50	2, 125 80	6, 828 14
Sugar	....	583 00	3, 657 44
Rice	....	2, 679 22	....
Goat-skins......................................	....	250 25	....
Brazilian rum...................................	....	237 18	....
Old metal	980 41	486 54	729 54
Total	74, 345 91	118, 423 44	82, 256 88

Table showing the value of the trade of Maranhan with foreign nations for the financial year of 1862-'63.

Nations.	Value of imports.	Value of exports.
	Milreis.	*Milreis.*
Great Britain.....................................	2, 106, 647‖445	3, 126, 255‖179
France	722, 559 747	206, 634 810
Portugal...	358, 139 761	1, 131, 850 965
United States....................................	277, 051 615	209, 430 960
Spain..	53, 883 276	47, 829 650
Belgium..	39, 132 044	....
Austria..	17, 184 560	....
Hanseatic cities.................................	29, 803 480	....
Total	3, 604, 401‖928	4, 722, 001‖564

Statement showing the number of arrivals and departures of vessels, and the total value of exports from and imports to the port of Maranhan during the financial years 1860-'61, 1861-'62, and 1862-'63.

Years.	No. of arrivals.	No. of departures.	Total value of imports.	Total value of exports.
			Milreis.	*Milreis.*
1860-'61	73	72	2, 891, 800‖812	2, 049, 384‖582
1861-'62	67	62	3, 263, 470 049	2, 757, 912 372
1862-'63	85	87	3, 604, 401 928	4, 722, 001 564

Table showing the number of arrivals and departures of vessels from the port of Maranham during the financial year of 1862–'63, together with their nationality, tonnage, and number of crews.

Nationality.	ENTERED.			CLEARED.		
	No. of vessels.	Tonnage.	No. of crews.	No. of vessels.	Tonnage.	No. of crews.
Brazilian	3	529	33	3	529	29
American	8	2,123	70	7	1,376	39
Danish	3	361	20	3	691	19
French	15	3,093	188	16	4,369	187
Hamburg	2	562	18	1	206	8
Holland	1	187	6	1	265	6
British	32	11,105	411	33	15,106	434
Norwegian	2	415	23	2	882	23
Portuguese	16	5,633	247	18	8,674	264
Russian	1	470	14	1	590	14
Spanish	2	315	23	2	379	21
Total	85	24,793	1,053	87	33,067	1,044

Table showing the coast trade of Maranham during the financial year of 1862–'63.

Where from and where bound.	ENTERED.			CLEARED.		
	No. of vessels.	Tonnage.	No. of crews.	No. of vessels.	Tonnage.	No. of crews.
Ceara	13	3,300	344	14	3,850	375
Para	95	4,204	466	32	3,783	459
Parahiba	9	1,033	89	10	1,140	99
Pernambuco	7	1,220	71	8	1,352	77
Total	124	9,757	970	64	10,125	1,010

CEARA—JOSÉ SMITH DE VASCONCELLES, *Consular Agent.*

Summary statement showing the value of imports at the port of Ceara, and the countries whence shipped, from June 30, 1863, to June 30, 1864.

IMPORTATION DIRECT.

	Value in reis.
Great Britain	1,020,081‖770
Hamburg	116,561 333
United States	40,679 736
Portugal	90,549 540
France	170,676 160
• Total	1,438,548 539
Importation coastwise	610,691 466
Total	2,049,240‖005

Statement showing the description, quantity, and value of the exports from the port of Ceara, also the names of the ports where shipped, from June 30, 1863, to June 30, 1864.

PORTS.	COFFEE.		SUGAR.		HIDES.		COTTON.	
	Quantity.	Value.	Quantity.	Value.	Quantity.	Value.	Quantity.	Value.
	Arrobas.	*Reis.*	*Arrobas.*	*Reis.*	*Hides.*	*Reis.*	*Arrobas.*	*Reis.*
New York	2,039.19	13,449||680	1,353.12	2,988||220	1,000	4,800||000	666.31	13,914||200
London		3,557 000			2,510	12,550 000		
Liverpool	53,003.99	334,399 160	103,675.04	195,615 400	47,699	277,105 800	56,897.03	1,178,653 020
English Channel	5,128.03	34,123 030	9,197.00	9,498 900	3,045	13,376 000	5,797.11	125,598 500
Hamburg	13,757.98	88,547 180	4.00	6 400	3,504	16,419 900	913.15	4,357 600
Marseilles	92,884.12	143,420 920						
Havre	3,468.09	21,983 340	1,926.00	2,890 160	2,090	10,032 000	2,453.27	55,220 480
Oporto	6,128.98	36,776 860	9,734.94	15,504 980	2,551	11,526 800	1,568.06	35,837 140
Lisbon			5,962.21	10,718 020				
Total	106,963.16	670,250||340	127,858.29	226,450||680	62,399	398,519||500	67,395.29	1,413,500||940

Statement showing the description, quantity, and value of the exports, &c.—Continued.

PORTS.	FUSTIC.		INDIA-RUBBER.		CALFSKINS.		VEGETABLE WAX.		CARNEAUBA ROOT.	
	Quantity.	Value.	Quantity.	Value.	Quantity.	Value.	Quantity.	Value.	Quantity.	Value.
	Arrobas.	*Reis.*	*Arrobas.*	*Reis.*	*Skins.*	*Reis.*	*Arrobas.*	*Reis.*	*Arrobas.*	*Reis.*
London	1,080.00	345||600	4.00	40||000						
Liverpool	4,280.00	1,364 400	2,537.16	27,496 840	50	5||000	5,411.00	32,466||000	6.16	271||000
English Channel	850.00	304 000	622.13	6,964 380						
Hamburg	140.00	44 800								
Marseilles	100.00	50 000								
Lisbon	2,000.00	400 000								
Total	8,460.00	2,478||800	3,163.29	34,501||290	50	5||000	5,411.00	32,466||000	6.16	271||000

Statement showing the nationality, tonnage, number of vessels, and their crews, arrived at and departed from the port of Ceara, from January 1, 1864, to June 30, 1864.

Nationality.	Tonnage.	No. of vessels.	No. of crews.
British	3,118	13	131
Hamburg	120	1	6
Norwegian	235	1	9
French	133	1	11
Danish	150	1	7
Portuguese	216	1	14
American, (war steamer, 7 guns)	1,032	1	....
Total	5,004	19	178

Statement showing the nationality, tonnage, number of vessels, and their crews, arrived at and departed from the port of Ceara, from January 1 to December 31, 1863.

Nationality.	Tonnage.	No. of vessels.	No. of crews.
French	784	4	48
British	4,009	14	161
Hanoverian	491	3	19
Hamburg	321	2	15
Danish	430½	4	26
Holland	100	1	5
Portuguese	736	2	28
Norwegian	273	1	8
Total	7,144½	31	310

MACAYO—J. BOESTELMANN, *Consular Agent.*

Statement showing the description and quantity of the exports from the port of Macayo, together with the nationality and number of vessels, and their destination, during the year ended June 30, 1864.

Nationality.	Number of vessels.	Cotton.		Sugar.			Number of hides.	Destination.
		Bags.	Arrobas.	Bags.	Arrobas.	Tons.		
British	24	39,423	206,794	23,145	127,771	1,825	7,383	Liverpool.
Do	8	....	....	34,827	194,681	2,781	....	Channel.
Do	1	....	....	4,984	28,062	401	....	Greenock.
Do	1	....	....	4,338	23,097	330	....	Clyde.
Hamburg	1	920	5,001	....	....	....	824	Liverpool.
Sweden	1	1,037	5,757	....	....	....	....	Do.
Do	1	....	....	2,690	14,413	206	....	Channel.
Dutch	1	....	....	2,804	16,951	242	....	Do.
Brazil	1	1,069	5,570	1,733	8,890	127	233	Liverpool.
Portugal	1	....	....	3,500	19,211	274	....	Channel.
Danish	1	....	....	3,000	16,046	229	....	Do.
Total	41	42,449	223,052	80,951	449,122	6,415	8,440	

H. Ex. Doc. 60——50

Summary statement showing the exports from the port of Macayo during the year ended June 30, 1864.

Destination.	Cotton.			Sugar.			Hides.
	Bags.	Arrobas.	Tons.	Bags.	Arrobas.	Tons.	
United Kingdom & Channel, for orders..	42,449	223,052	3,186	80,951	449,122	6,415	8,440
Portugal, for orders...................	....	....	....	2,994	16,865	241	600
Total	42,449	223,052	3,186	83,945	465,987	6,656	9,040
Coastwise:							
Pernambuco	557	2,998	43	....	....		....
Rio de Janeiro......................	....	....	....	11,229	58,330	} 960	....
Rio Grande do Sul..................	....	....	....	1,247	8,881		....
Total............................	43,006	226,050	3,229	96,421	533,198	7,616	9,040
Compared with year ended June 30,'63-	49,430	265,938	3,799	165,958	897,686	12,815	8,491
Compared with year ended June 30,'62-	43,200	237,675	3,395	175,500	965,315	13,790	9,690
Compared with year ended June 30,'61-	26,456	145,568	2,080	108,227	595,290	8,504	8,887

SANTOS—CHARLES F. DE VIVALDI, *Consul.*

Statement showing the value of the merchandise imported to and exported from the port of Santos during the fiscal year ended June 30, 1863.

IMPORTS OF FOREIGN MERCHANDISE.

From the United States (directly)........................	$15,000 00
From all other nations "........................	1,042,340 58
From all countries, by way of Rio Janeiro..................	4,924,003 97
Brazilian imports from various ports of Brazil..............	545,630 32
Total imports.	6,526,974 87

EXPORTS.

To the United States.....................................	$403,862 00
To all other countries (ports of Brazil included).............	4,823,517 99
Total exports....................................	5,227,379 99
Total imports and exports.........................	11,754,354 86
Excess of imports over exports........	1,299,594 88

Statement showing the arrival and departure of vessels of all nations at the port of Santos during the fiscal year ended June 30, 1863.

Nationality.	ENTERED.			CLEARED.		
	No. of vessels.	Crews.	Tonnage.	No. of vessels.	Crews.	Tonnage.
Brazilian steamers.................	180	3, 628	43, 599	180	3, 628	43, 599
Brazilian sailing vessels	62	318	3, 613	67	338	3, 920
Austrian sailing vessels...........	1	11	432	1	11	432
Belgian sailing vessels	1	9	306	1	9	306
Bremen sailing vessels	3	27	918	3	27	918
Danish sailing vessels	13	113	3, 548	13	112	3, 548
British sailing vessels..............	32	294	10, 529	31	285	10, 173
French sailing vessels	6	67	2, 472	6	65	2, 472
Hamburg sailing vessels	16	157	5, 300	16	157	5, 300
Hanoverian sailing vessels	1	9	315	1	9	315
Holland sailing vessels	3	24	764	3	24	764
Lubeck sailing vessels	1	10	323	1	9	323
Mecklenburg sailing vessels	2	17	615	2	16	615
Norwegian sailing vessels	6	59	2, 089	6	57	2, 089
Portuguese sailing vessels.........	4	42	1, 147	4	39	1, 147
Prussian sailing vessels............	3	33	1, 019	3	33	1, 019
Roman sailing vessels.............	1	9	319	1	19	319
Swedish sailing vessels............	14	137	5, 390	14	131	5, 390
Total.......................	349	4, 964	82, 621	353	4, 969	82, 579

REMARKS.—The Brazilian vessels engaged exclusively in coasting trade. No American merchant vessels entered the port of Santos since May 11, 1862. Of all other nations entered with sundries, 25; with salt, 33; with coal, 1; with railway iron, 21; with ballast, 27. Cleared, with cargoes of coffee, 77; in ballast, 31.

Comparative statement showing the direct importation of merchandise into the port of Santos from foreign countries during the years 1861, 1862, and 1863, the quantity received from each country, its official tariff value, and the Brazilian duty levied on each article.

Articles.	Weight or measure	Countries whence imported.	1860–'61.		1861–'62.		1862–'63.		Brazil'n duty; all ad valorem.
			Quantity.	Value.	Quantity.	Value.	Quantity.	Value.	
Ale	Canadas	Great Britain	2,074	1,440 702	13,229	10,695 960	64,564	51,291 000	50 per cent.
Ale	do	Hanse Cities	4,064	3,113 160	10,539	8,852 800	14,153	11,799 488	Do.
Ale	do	United States			128	53 760			Do.
Bagging	Pounds	Great Britain	123,533	32,949 333	138,463	36,976 543	137,019	35,222 991	30 per cent.
Do	do	Hanse Cities	108,291	98,677 601	34,063	9,083 723			Do.
Butter	do	United States	2,687	1,078 800	1,411	578 000			Do.
Do	do	Great Britain	9,916	3,974 400	14,302½	5,707 267	6,853	2,741 600	40 per cent.
Do, (star)	do	Hanse Cities	4,947	1,688 800			7,136	2,944 400	Do.
	do	United States	7,540	4,090 000	3,112	1,866 800	30,339	18,022 600	Do.
Cheese	do	Hanse Cities	4,202	2,101 400	3,405	2,373 000	6,577	4,005 200	30 per cent.
Do	do	Great Britain			2,641	1,445 000	1,118	670 800	Do.
Do	do	United States	510	204 000	881	351 867	5,452	3,183 170	Do.
Do	do	Great Britain	5,542	3,316 800	1,496	668 000	2,305	922 000	Do.
Cigars	do	Hanse Cities	950	150 000					40 per cent.
Do	do	Great Britain	390	1,170 000	50	200 000	2,957	8,966 000	Do.
Do	do	United States	870	810 000	1,484	5,810 668			Do.
Clothing	do	Hanse Cities		620 000	462	1,780 989			Do.
Do	do	Fast Berlin		310 350					Do.
Do	do	Hanse Cities		150 000					Free.
Coal	Tons	Great Britain	739	10,958 000			660	10,592 000	Free.
Coal	do	Hanse ditto	300	3,608 000				4,139 115	30 per cent.
Cotton goods	Yards	Great Britain	949,384	81,109 666	262,963	37,705 99	257,831	113,896 992	Do.
Do	do	Hanse Cities	29,758	14,404 004	95,725	34,129 473	47,070	52,870 143	Do.
Do	do	United States	91,718	7,105 929	1,350	891 530			Do.
Drugs and medicines	do	Great Britain		582 982		258 680		923 290	Do.
Do	do	Hanse Cities		1,509 607		2,575 988		6,351 200	10 per cent.
Earthen and China ware	Pounds	Oast Berlin	261,064	94,551 827	227,595	21,912 104	186,906	17,520 960	Do.
Do	do	Hanse Cities	515	229 474			7,619	817,470	Do.
Flour, American	Barrels	United States	2,564	90,321 950	9,514	23,699 840	1,000	9,000 000	10 per cent.
Flour, Trieste	Arrobas	Austria	7,884 15-39	23,653 400					Do.
Fish, cod	Quintals	United States	171 8-128	1,430 620					Do.
Do	do	Great Berlin	17 64-128	1,150 883	1,429	1,300 000	4,399½	9,992 400	40 per cent.
Furniture, house	Canadas	United States	161	320 400	81	3,150 400	4,529	1,259 800	50 per cent.
Gin	do	Hanse Cities	34,	81 600	99,104	3,102 000	54,529	8,170 800	30 per cent.
Glassware	Pounds	Great Britain	92,392	4,953 063		5,800 600	40,063	9,607 711	Do.
Do	do	Hanse Cities		2,369 000		2,665 655	90,449	8,928 894	Do.
Do	do	Belgium	1,963	406 000			3,617	843 970	Do.
Hams	do	United States							

Article	Unit	Country						Duty
Hams	do.	Great Britain	906	46 000	3,690	861 035	7,009	Do.
Hams	do.	Hanse Cities	1,924	438 917	1,873	438 166	2,373	Do.
Hardware	do.	Great Britain	76,840	15,707 339	136,554	22,525 768	119,768	Do.
Do.	do.	Hanse Cities	8,613	961 434	16,049	2,525 768	41,228	Do.
Do.	do.	Portugal			1,408	563 330		Do.
Hats	do.	Great Britain	397	3,139 000	820	1,495 834	1,554	10 per cent.
Hose	do.	Hanse Cities	7,843	1,857 700	130	1,374 666	3,394	Free.
Hose	do.	Great Britain			7,245	1,481 000	7,461	10 per cent.
Iron, railroad	Tons	do.		782,753 383	31,542	964,455 739	4,527	Free.
Iron in bars	Arrobas	do.	3,155	6,315 130	765	255 000		10 per cent.
Do.	do.	Hanse Cities			1,890	600 167	431	Do.
Liquors	do.	do.						50 per cent.
Do.	do.	Great Britain	149	454 400	417	835 000	523	Do.
Do.	do.	Hanse Tow.	109	492 600			664	Do.
Do.	Canadas	United States	150	459 450	351	1,687 200	143	Do.
Lard	do.	Canadas						30 per cent.
Lead shot	Arrobas	United States	105 15-32	597 340	322	4,833 333	59 16-32	Do.
Do.	Quintals	Hanse Cl. &	46 6-198	730 700	171 84-198	2,572 705	50	Do.
	do.	Great Britain			2,822 1-2	2,822 200	194 106-198	Do.
Meats, preserved	Pounds	Hanse Cities	354	187 966	8,689 1-2	3,574 667	7,181	30 per cent.
Oil of olives	Canadas	Portugal	1,598	530 667	1,931		6,539	30 per cent.
Oil, linseed	Pounds	Great Britain	3,310	9,333 000	2,454	494 666	6,915	Do.
Paper	do.	Hanse Cities	10,904			1,383 000	4,990	10 per cent.
Do.	do.	United States	1,625	188 500		461 900	4,618	Do.
Do.	do.	Great Britain	9,790	867 800		1,465 134	7,504	Do.
Do.	do.	Hanse Cities				818 304	1,004	30 per cent.
Do.	do.	Belgium			3,767	412 750	1,497	Do.
Piano-fortes	do.	France				117 440	696	Do.
Do.	do.	Hanse Cities	23	9,880 000	16		97	Do.
Do.	R.	Buenos Ayres	4	1,600 000	1	11,000 000	1	Do.
Powder, gun	do.	Great Britain	22,400	11,800 000	12,465	8,077 000	68,508	40 per cent.
Potatoes	Quintals	Portugal	51,400	1,375 800	371	547 960	1,316 812	10 per cent.
Pine lumber	Feet	United States	96,699	1,295 400	190,300	4,783 901	48,658 111-198	30 per cent.
Salt	Alqueires	Portugal	17,880	57,185 400	202,360	107,910 200	904,889	30 per cent.
Salt	do.	Spain	10,000	10,728 900	93,540	98,333 400	101,770	Do.
Salt	do.	France		6,000 000	46,160	93,440 400	57,197	Do.
Salt	do.	Hanse Cities	7,898	4,728 800			17,254	Free.
Saltpetre	Arrobas	Italy	7,190 30-32	612 000	481 8-32	1,940 000	385 98-29	Free.
Do.	do.	United States					497 30-32	Free.
Shoes	Pairs	Great Britain	940	240 000	180	478 000	1,296	10 per cent.
Do.	do.	Hanse Cities	50	200 000	2,015	4 085 250	3,853	Do.
Do.	do.	Hanse Cities			341	1,938 000		40 per cent.
Silk goods	Pounds	Great Britain					677 3-4	Do.
Do.	do.	Portugal					130 1-2	30 per cent.
Silver ware	Octaves	Great Britain	160	128 000	31	90 000	2,898	5 per cent.
Do.	Pounds	United States					910	30 per cent.
Sugar, crushed	Arrobas	Hanse &.					2,448	10 per cent.
Tar	do.	United States	1,614	2,491 000	128	192 000	567	Do.
Tea	Pounds	Great Britain	300	300 000			96	30 per cent.
Tea	do.	Portugal					959	Do.

Comparative statement showing *the direct importation of merchandise, &c.*—Continued.

Articles.	Weight or measure.	Countries whence imported.	1860-'61. Quantity.	1860-'61. Value.	1861-'62. Quantity.	1861-'62. Value.	1862-'63. Quantity.	1862-'63. Value.	Brazil's duty; all ad valorem.
Tin plates	Arrobas	Great Britain			185	835|024	1,509	6,799|985	20 per cent.
Do.	do.	Hanse Cities			400	1,800 000	400	1,800 000	Do.
Tin ware	Pounds	Great Britain	9,390	7,458|000					30 per cent.
Do.	do.	Hanse Cities			283	324 600			Do.
Various merchandise not specified		Different nations		129,676 999		215,557 383		258,739 165	
White lead	Arrobas	Hanse Cities	449 25-39	1,779 000	1,333 4-32	3,999 350	2,380 2-39	7,159 810	10 per cent.
Do.	do.	Great Britain	103 16-32	681 000			145 21-32	438 180	Do.
Wine	Canadas	Hanse Cities	95	85 760	456	2,190 900	2,999	533 440	50 per cent.
Do.	do.	Hanse Cities	96	412 900	1,065	2,126 900	1,339	4,721 440	Do.
Wine	do.	Portugal	19,965	13,392 640	40,758	96,368 780	60,627	46,461 140	Do.
Wine	do.	France	1,189	748 160			32,150	13,945 560	Do.
Wine	do.	Spain	12,837	8,215 890					Do.
Wine	do.	Belgium					231	570 080	Do.
Woollen goods	Yards	Great Britain	3,920	8,643 135	3,782	4,029 667	1,953	9,726 617	30 per cent.
Do.	do.	Hanse Cities					7,907	19,622 892	Do.
Total values				1,374,950 983		1,777,903 628		2,018,803 842	

Statement showing the value of Brazilian and foreign merchandise imported to and exported from the port of Santos during the fiscal year ended June 30, 1864.

Direct importation of foreign goods from foreign ports........	$796, 888 27
Indirect importation of foreign merchandise, *via* Rio de Janeiro,	4, 414, 803 47
Importation of Brazilian merchandise from ports of the empire of Brazil..	619, 447 57
Total importation.............................	5, 831, 139 31

EXPORTATION.

To the United States.................................	560, 223 76
To all other foreign countries...........................	2, 814, 861 60
To Rio de Janeiro and other ports of the empire of Brazil...	225, 867 50
Total exportation.............................	3, 600, 952 86
Excess of imports over exports	2, 230, 186 45

Statement showing the indirect importation of foreign goods at the port of Santos, by way of Rio de Janeiro, during the fiscal year ended June 30, 1864; also the quantity and market value of each article.

Articles.	Weight or measure.	Quantity.	Value.	
			Brazilian milreis.	American dollars.
Ale	Gallons	86,565	173,361,800	93,875 42
Anvils		1,290	4,196,000	2,234 93
Baggings	Pieces	5,265	67,920,000	36,778 68
Barley	Arrobas	572	2,864,000	1,550 85
Biscuits	do	564	3,264,000	1,767 46
Blacking	Dozens	3,890	6,890,000	3,730 93
Bonnets, ladies'		4,126	21,432,700	11,605 81
Books, blank	Volumes	28,296	16,378,500	8,868 95
Books, printed	do	5,949	8,146,800	4,411 49
Buttons			8,779,880	4,754 30
Brassware	Pounds	24,344	9,737,600	5,272 91
Brushes	Dozens	3,212	18,256,500	9,885 89
Butter	Pounds	48,264	61,817,900	33,474 39
Candles			58,483,000	31,668 54
Canes, walking		8,613	10,919,900	5,913 12
Caps, men's and boys'		12,382	11,283,000	6,109 75
Caps, percussion	Thousands	10,864	10,876,400	5,889 57
Carpets and mats			6,735,000	3,647 00
Carriages		36	10,830,000	5,864 44
Cheese		4,628	6,664,800	3,608 98
Chinaware			193,250,300	104,645 03
Cigars and cigarettes	Hundreds	4,547	6,125,800	3,317 12
Codfish	Quintals	6,293	32,511,000	17,604 70
Clothing, ready-made	Pieces	5,934	52,827,900	28,606 30
Clocks		626	7,512,000	4,067 74
Chocolate	Pounds	3,926	4,685,000	2,536 92
Coal	Tons	10	180,000	97 47
Combs, fine	Dozens	1,119	13,474,000	7,296 17
Combs, common	do	1,622	6,488,000	3,513 25
Copper plates	Pounds	32,526	9,875,700	5,347 69
Copper ware	do	24,193	12,429,200	6,730 41
Cotton manufactures			1,899,757,080	1,028,718 45
Drugs and medicines			80,410,900	43,542 50
Engravings			2,838,294,660	1,536,936 55
Fire-arms	Pieces	2,664	26,640,000	14,425 56
Fire-works			10,129,800	5,485 22
Flour, nearly all American	Barrels	7,329	148,856,000	80,605 54
Flowers, artificial			8,342,600	4,517 52
Fruit, dried			34,573,100	18,721 38
Furniture, house			46,114,700	24,971 11
Furs			26,413,000	14,302 64
Galloons, gold, silver, and spurious			16,921,400	9,162 95
Glassware			104,746,800	56,720 39
Gin	Gallons	15,216	16,536,400	8,954 46
Gloves	Dozen pairs	7,788	24,284,000	13,149 78
Hams	Pounds	12,843	6,421,500	3,477 24
Hardware			477,181,100	258,393 56
Harness and saddlery			8,626,000	4,670 97
Hats		28,147	78,340,000	42,421 11
Hoes		30,734	16,953,500	9,180 32
Ice	Pounds	5,952	372,000	201 43
Ink			9,078,200	4,915 84
Instruments of arts and sciences			20,196,200	10,936 24
Iron, in bars	Quintals	8,636	69,168,000	37,454 47
Jewelry			87,810,000	47,549 11
Lard	Arrobas	334	4,008,000	2,170 33
Lead, in bars	Quintals	1,190	5,866,000	3,176 44
in shot	do	662	13,246,000	7,172 70
in other forms	Pounds	16,526	4,986,300	2,699 99
Leather			70,897,500	38,390 98
Linen manufactures			746,953,220	404,476 25
Liqueurs			36,531,300	19,781 70
Living animals		38	5,700,000	3,086 55
Looking-glasses		9,470	37,388,500	20,245 87
Lumber, pine	Dozen planks	829	8,948,000	4,845 34
Machinery			86,329,300	46,747 31
Matches	Gross	6,564	5,041,200	2,729 80
Meats, preserved			14,394,000	7,794 35
Meats, salted	Arrobas	3,626	6,223,000	3,369 73
Meats, sweet	do	1,246	19,936,800	10,795 77
Minium, or red lead	do	1,768	7,126,800	3,859 16
Needles	Thousands	11,836	14,203,200	7,691 03

Statement showing the indirect importation of foreign goods, &c.—Continued.

Articles.	Weight or measure.	Quantity.	Value.	
			Brazilian mil-reis.	American dollars.
Olive oil	Gallons	28,132	56,264,000	30,466 95
Onions			2,847,000	1,541 65
Paintings		826	2,649,000	1,434 43
Paper of various kinds	Reams	7,728	36,633,000	19,836 78
Pewter	Arrobas	1,642	11,642,000	6,304 14
Pewter ware	Pounds	19,368	15,494,400	8,390 22
Pens, steel	Gross	12,339	18,678,000	10,114 14
Perfumery			21,632,400	11,713 94
Piano-fortes		125	48,525,000	26,276 28
Playing cards	Dozens	830	4,876,800	2,640 78
Potatoes	Bushels	3,724	5,446,000	2,949 00
Powder	Pounds	6,564	10,846,000	5,873 12
Quiltings	Yards	27,793	46,884,300	25,387 84
Salt	Bushels	35,586	11,659,200	6,313 45
Saltpetre	Arrobas	893	8,137,200	4,406 29
Sewing silk	Pounds	964	14,352,000	7,771 62
Shoes	Pairs	21,999	57,384,600	31,073 76
Silk manufactures			658,315,400	356,477 78
Silver ware			6,615,400	3,582 23
Spirits of turpentine	Pounds	11,364	13,636,800	7,384 33
Spurs	Dozen	5,133	16,496,000	8,932 58
Sugar, crushed	Arrobas	465	2,503,000	1,355 38
Tar	do	1,962	5,886,000	3,187 27
Tea	Pounds	5,628	5,862,000	3,174 28
Thread	do	15,346	17,684,410	9,576 10
Tin plates	Boxes	2,368	36,473,000	19,750 13
Tobacco			4,892,000	2,649 01
Umbrellas		2,384	12,013,000	6,505 04
Various articles, not specified			794,026,010	429,966 16
Vinegar	Gallons	29,646	59,292,000	32,106 61
Watches, gold and silver		884	18,864,000	10,214 85
Wines of various qualities	Gallons	179,040	269,673,500	146,028 20
White lead	Arrobas	985	5,910,000	3,200 96
Woollen manufactures			673,474,500	364,686 44
Total			8,152,915,000	4,414,803 47

Statement showing the description, quantity, tariff value, Brazilian duty, together with the name of country whence derived, of each article of foreign merchandise imported into Santos during the fiscal year ended June 30, 1864.

Articles.	Weight or measure.	Country whence imported.	Quantity.	Tariff value in Brazilian milreis.	Duty levied at Santos.
Ale	Canadas	Great Britain	73,129	59,005,440	50 per ct.
Do	do	Hanse Cities	94,731	20,774,460	50 per ct.
Baggings	Pounds	Great Britain	139,287	34,420,337	30 per ct.
Do	do	Hanse Cities	46,512	12,266,534	30 per ct.
Blankets	Arrobas	Great Britain	103 13-32	2,363,619	30 per ct.
Do	do	Hanse Cities	20 15-32	528,733	30 per ct.
Books, blank	Pounds	do	278½	371,336	30 per ct.
Do	do	Ports of Brazil	51	51,000	30 per ct.
Books, printed	do	Hanse Cities	3	4,500	10 per ct.
Do	do	Portugal	106	159,000	10 per ct.
Butter	do	Great Britain	5,432	2,172,800	30 per ct.
Do	do	Hanse Cities	8,791	3,516,400	30 per ct.
Cables and ropes	Arrobas	Great Britain	587 29-32	2,723,624	30 per ct.
Do	do	Portugal	97 16-32	390,000	30 per ct.
Candles, wax	Pounds	do	512	512,000	30 per ct.
Candles, stearine	do	Great Britain	2,160	1,260,000	40 per ct.
Do	do	Hanse Cities	5,504	3,302,400	40 per ct.
Cheese	do	Great Britain	1,409	845,400	30 per ct.
Do	do	Hanse Cities	4,353	1,741,200	30 per ct

Statement showing the description, quantity, tariff value, &c.—Continued.

Articles.	Weight or measure.	Country whence imported.	Quantity.	Tariff value in Brazilian milreis.	Duty levied at Santos.
Chinaware.	Pounds.	Great Britain	261, 898	23, 050, 327	30 per ct.
Do	...do	Hanse Cities	1, 279	566, 467	30 per ct.
Do	...do	Ports of Brazil	2, 795½	1, 745, 902	30 per ct.
Cigars.	...do	Hanse Cities	647	2, 588, 000	30 per ct.
Do	...do	Italy	19	76, 000	30 per ct.
Clocks		Hanse Cities	92	1, 115, 200	30 per ct.
Clothing		Great Britain		3, 029, 750	40 per ct.
Do		Hanse Cities		8, 596, 000	40 per ct.
Do		Ports of Brazil		672, 000	40 per ct.
Coal	Tons	Great Britain	177	2, 042, 600	Free.
Do		Hanse Cities	78	937, 000	Free.
Codfish	Quintals	...do	188-128	108, 370	10 per ct.
Cotton manufactures	Varas	Great Britain	135, 912	48, 195, 160	30 per ct.
Do	...do	Hanse Cities	63, 711	28, 090, 333	30 per ct.
Do	...do	Ports of Brazil	4, 382½	1, 165, 567	30 per ct.
Divers goods not specified		Different nations		75, 158, 171	....
Dried fruit	Pounds	Portugal	11, 634	2, 192, 221	30 per ct.
Do	...do	Hanse Cities	706	111, 434	30 per ct.
Drugs and medicines		Great Britain		1, 885, 414	30 per ct.
Do		Hanse Cities		4, 989, 646	30 per ct.
Do	Pounds	Portugal	256	198, 000	30 per ct.
Fire-arms		Hanse Cities	25	250, 000	30 per ct.
Furniture, house		...do		6, 718, 959	40 per ct.
Gin	Canadas	Great Britain	595	1, 688, 800	50 per ct.
Do	...do	Hanse Cities	4, 521½	9, 849, 400	50 per ct.
Glassware.	Pounds.	Great Britain	4, 958	1, 498, 350	30 per ct.
Do	...do	Hanse Cities	76, 177	6, 871, 138	30 per ct.
Do	...do	Ports of Brazil	2, 000	1, 050, 000	30 per ct.
Hams	...do	Great Britain	582	135, 800	30 per ct.
Do	...do	Hanse Cities	4, 901	1, 143, 568	30 per ct.
Hardware	...do	Great Britain	159, 970	24, 521, 921	30 per ct.
Do	...do	Hanse Cities	67, 638	7, 433, 078	30 per ct.
Do	...do	Ports of Brazil	2, 378	431, 134	30 per ct.
Hats.		Hanse Cities	2, 169	4, 777, 108	30 per ct.
Instruments, optical		Great Britain	1	16, 000	30 per ct.
do		...do	1	400, 000	10 per ct.
mathematical		Hanse Cities	159	591, 000	10 per ct.
musical		...do	44	315, 000	30 per ct.
musical, for church		Ports of Brazil	1	7, 000, 000	30 per ct.
Iron, in bars	Arrobas	Hanse Cities	100	120, 000	10 per ct.
in bars	...do	Great Britain	2, 199 31-32	2, 129 960	10 per ct.
rails for railway	Tons	...do	4, 233	564, 502, 100	Free.
materials for railway	Arrobas	...do	998	6, 703, 477	Free.
Jewelry		Hanse Cities		1, 262, 000	5 per ct.
Leadshot	Quintals	Great Britain	21039-128	3, 154, 571	30 per ct.
Do	...do	Hanse Cities	100	1, 500, 000	30 per ct.
Leather	Pounds	Great Britain	1, 520	1, 894, 000	10 per ct.
Do	...do	Hanse Cities	6, 689	7, 870, 400	10 per ct.
Linen manufactures	Varas	Great Britain	4, 399	4, 388, 730	30 per ct.
Do	...do	Hanse Cities	16, 737	9, 383, 994	30 per ct.
Linseed oil.	Pounds	Great Britain	19, 194	3, 838, 800	10 per ct.
Do	...do	Hanse Cities	4, 243	848, 600	10 per ct.
Linseed oil, for railway	...do	Great Britain	14, 361	2, 872, 200	Free.
Liqueurs not specified	Canadas	...do	1, 072	4, 800, 800	50 per ct.
Do	...do	Hanse Cities	973	4, 426, 000	50 per ct.
Lumber, railroad		Great Britain		1, 368, 000	Free.
Machines, various kinds		...do	9	2, 156, 400	10 per ct.
Do		Hanse Cities	2	450, 000	30 per ct.
Matches.	Pounds	Great Britain	664½	39, 900	30 per ct.
Olive oil.	Canadas	Portugal	4, 169	5, 549, 335	30 per ct.
Do	...do	Great Britain	300	300, 000	30 per ct.
Oil of various kinds	Pounds	Ports of Brazil	15, 785	5, 261, 667	30 per ct.
Onions.	Arrobas	Hanse Cities	2, 112	2, 113, 610	30 per ct.
Do	...do	Portugal	3, 116 30-32	3, 117, 244	30 per ct.
Paper, writing	Pounds	Great Britain	9, 102	2, 656, 500	30 per ct.
Do	...do	Hanse Cities	17, 726	3, 444, 544	30 per ct.
Percussion caps	...do	...do	1, 067	1, 600, 500	30 per ct.
Do	...do	Great Britain	314	471, 000	30 per ct.
Perfumery.		Hanse Cities		313, 334	30 per ct.
Piano-fortes		...do	31	10, 400, 000	30 per ct.
Do		Great Britain	5	2, 000, 000	30 per ct.
Pine lumber	Feet	Hanse Cities	362, 064	14, 291, 511	30 per ct.
Do	...do	Great Britain	507	10, 694	30 per ct.
Potatoes.	Quintals	Portugal	1, 148 80-128	2, 304, 390	10 per ct.

Statement showing the description, quantity, tariff value, &c.—Continued.

Articles.	Weight or measure.	Country whence imported.	Quantity.	Tariff value in Brazilian milreis.	Duty levied at Santos.
Potatoes	Quintals	Hanse Cities	292 59-128	584, 810	10 per ct.
Powder	Pounds	Great Britain	65, 888	32, 944, 250	40 per ct.
Shoes	Pairs	...do	2, 114	3, 853, 300	40 per ct.
Do	...do	Hanse Cities	780	1, 441, 200	40 per ct.
Salt	Alqueires	France	91, 598	55, 578, 800	Free.
Do	...do	Portugal	60, 815	36, 409, 725	Free.
Do	...do	Italy	42, 057	25, 234, 200	Free.
Do	...do	Spain	27, 903	16, 758, 000	Free.
Do	...do	Ports of Brazil	13, 200	7, 920, 800	Free.
Saltpetre	Arrobas	Great Britain	594 16-32	1, 478, 400	10 per ct.
Do	...do	Hanse Cities	407-32	122, 700	10 per ct.
Silk manufactures	Pounds	Great Britain	238½	3, 223, 334	30 per ct.
Do	...do	Hanse Cities	504	7, 665, 668	30 per ct.
Steam-engines		Great Britain	1	10, 000, 000	Free.
Steel	Arrobas	...do	369 13-32	1, 431, 500	Free.
Tea	Pounds	Hanse Cities	1, 457	2, 185, 500	30 per ct.
Tin plates	Arrobas	Great Britain	398 21-32	1, 791, 765	20 per ct.
Umbrellas		Hanse Cities	335	1, 858, 400	30 per ct.
Vinegar	Canadas	Portugal	5, 857	1, 755, 755	40 per ct.
White lead	Arrobas	Hanse Cities	682 28-32	2, 048, 610	10 per ct.
Do	...do	Great Britain	250 12-32	749, 610	10 per ct.
Wines	Canadas	Portugal	87, 501½	56, 037, 640	50 per ct.
Do	...do	France	13, 170½	8, 429, 120	50 per ct.
Do	...do	Hanse Cities	2, 341	4, 721, 040	50 per ct.
Do	...do	Great Britain	1, 161	2, 789, 120	50 per ct.
Do	...do	Italy	833	533, 120	50 per ct.
Do	...do	Ports of Brazil	27, 227	17, 805, 120	50 per ct.
Wire cable, for railway	Pounds	Great Britain	54, 971	29, 716, 330	Free.
Woollen manufactures	Varas	Hanse Cities	17, 636	19, 362, 414	30 per ct.
Do	...do	Great Britain	9, 578	7, 736, 901	30 per ct.
Do	...do	Ports of Brazil	4, 382½	4, 318, 934	30 per ct.
Total				1, 471, 631, 158	

Statement showing the arrival and departure of vessels of all nations at the port of Santos during the fiscal year ended June 30, 1864.

Nationality.	ENTERED.			CLEARED.		
	No. of vessels.	Crew.	Tonnage.	No. of vessels.	Crew.	Tonnage.
Brazilian	207	3, 622	37, 086	202	3, 582	36, 036
Argentine	1	10	405	1	10	405
Bremen	6	44	1, 875	6	45	1, 893
Danish	9	65	2, 951	9	67	2, 951
British	17	127	5, 253	20	162	6, 669
French	7	55	1, 961	6	50	1, 684
Hanoverian	2	20	1, 139	1	5	248
Hamburg	11	96	3, 647	11	103	3, 647
Holland	8	48	2, 039	8	46	2, 153
Italian	1	10	391	1	11	391
Norwegian	9	75	4, 227	10	91	4, 522
Oldenburg	2	11	550	2	24	550
Oriental	1	10	229	1	9	229
Prussian	2	15	490	2	15	630
Portuguese	3	30	1, 425	3	28	1, 425
Russian	1	7	246			
Swedish	12	99	5, 130	13	111	5, 737
Total	299	4, 344	69, 044	296	4, 359	69, 170

REMARKS.—Of the Brazilian vessels that *entered*, 139 were steamers and 67 sailing vessels; of those that *cleared*, 139 steamers and 60 sailing vessels. With the exception of one (sailing) that entered from a foreign port with salt and three (sailing) that cleared for foreign ports with cargoes of coffee, all Brazilian vessels were engaged in coastwise trade. No American merchant vessels have been at this port since May 11, 1862. Of all other nations, entered with merchandise, 53; in ballast, 40; cleared with coffee for the United States, 10; all other countries, 55; in ballast, 32.

Comparative statement showing the exportation of coffee from the port of Santos to the United States and all other countries from July 1, 1857, to June 30, 1864.

Destination.	1857-'58.	1858-'59.	1859-'60.	1860-'61.	1861-'62.	1862-'63.	1863-'64.	Total.
United States........bags*.	26,600	36,040	37,773	42,822	23,385	23,992	35,902	226,514
English channel ......do...	88,521	122,693	205,884	127,088	177,522	211,713	154,438	1,087,859
Hamburg and Altona.do...	17,596	16,768	24,773	37,722	31,322	17,586	....	145,767
Antwerp.............do...	....	....	2,650	4,500	....	....	....	7,150
France ....do...	6,125	3,050	10,260	31,770	30,894	15,636	10,966	108,701
Mediterranean, &c....do...}	6,642	1,600	11,703	17,170	24,808	15,000	11,627	88,550
Lisbon................do...}								
Bremen . ...do...	10,510	....	....	....	....	....	....	10,510
Total each year.........	155,994	183,801	294,893	256,572	287,931	283,927	212,933	†1,675,051

* Each containing 160 pounds.   † Or, 268,008,160 pounds.

OCTOBER 22, 1864.

Herewith I transmit my annual report to the department. * * * Owing to the fact that no commercial statistics of any sort are published here or at San Paulo (the capital of this province) relating to the trade of my consular district. I must confess that, until very recently, it has been utterly impossible for me to obtain such facts and materials as to furnish the Department of State with a reliable commercial report.

PROVINCE OF SAN PAULO.

The province of San Paulo is one of the richest and most important divisions of the Brazilian empire. It is situated between the 20th and 26th degrees of south latitude, comprising an area of about 75,000 square miles, and containing a population of about 650,000 inhabitants, fully one-half of whom, unfortunately, are slaves.

The boundaries are, on the north the provinces of Rio de Janeiro and Menas Geraes, on the south the province of Parana, on the northwest the Parana river divides it from the provinces of Matto Grosso and Goyaz, and on the southeast the Atlantic extends for nearly three hundred miles. This province, with the exception of a narrow border of low lands and small islands on the sea-coast, is an elevated plateau, slowly inclining inland towards the river Parana.

The Sierra de Mar, or great Cordilheira, which runs along the whole coast of Brazil, is in this province, a most stupendous sea cliff which rises abruptly to the height of 2,500 feet the above level of the sea. Its direction is very nearly parallel to the sea-coast, and, as no stream of any importance finds its way down the sierra, so no opening or pass of any account occurs to break the uniformity of the level of the summit. To open easy communications between the interior of the province and this port a good carriage road was built many years since by the intelligent and energetic inhabitants of San Paulo ; and now a grand trunk railroad is in course of construction, which, starting from this city of Santos, is to penetrate into the very heart of the province. To overcome the great obstacles offered by the physical construction of the Sierra de Mar, above alluded to, the economical system of inclined planes has been adopted. Three very substantial engine-houses have been erected at three equally distant places from each other up the Sierra, on the railroad line, where, very powerful steam-engines being stationed, the railway trains are to be pulled up the mountain by the stationary steam-machines, by means of a strong wire cable. These stationary machines are already in operation; and, thus far, the results have fully satisfied the most sanguine expectations of the friends of so dangerous a system of building railroads. The whole line of the railroad is already far advanced towards its final completion. It is expected that in less than twelve months the line will be thrown open to the public.   *   *   *   *

I do not entertain the least doubt that, through the operation of this new line of railroad, Santos will become, in a very few years, one of the most important commercial cities of this empire, and the people of the province of San Paulo add immensely to their already great wealth.

AGRICULTURE.

Although the cultivation of the soil, in this portion of the world, is carried on in the most obsolete and absurd system of hoeing instead of ploughing the ground, yet, on account of the extraordinary fertility of the lands and exceeding mildness of climate, I have to admit that agriculture in this province has produced the most successful results. The farmers are by far the richest and most influential portion of the community; the crops are generally very fair, and oftentimes, as in the current year, exceedingly large.   *   *   *

For many years past coffee has been the principal and almost the sole article of general culture among the planters of this section of Brazil. The crop of the current year is the largest ever raised, being generally estimated at four millions of arrobas, or eight hundred thousand bags, containing 160 pounds each. The planters have already commenced to send down this new crop to Santos for shipment. Its great excess over that of previous years will much add to the prosperity of the province. In fact, by a glance at table I, attached to the present despatch, it will be seen that the largest amount of coffee raised and exported during the last seven years was that of 1859–'60, viz: 294,893 bags. By this simple comparison an idea can be formed of the exceedingly good fortune of this people. The cultivation of cotton, also, although just in its beginning, has been this year, and fairly promises for the next to be, very productive. The present crop is declared to exceed one hundred thousand arrobas, or over 3,200,000 pounds, and that of next year, considering the very vast surface of ground which has been cultivated with this plant, is expected to be at the least four times as great. Nevertheless, the fact that the best farming districts of the interior of the province are wholly destitute of carriage roads, and, consequently, the only means of transporting the cotton to the distant seaport for shipment is by mule-back, (a ruinously expensive one,) is conclusive evidence that the cultivation of cotton, as a general pursuit in the province of San Paulo, will continue just so long as the abnormal and enormous present prices of this staple will warrant and no longer. So soon as the exportation of large quantities of cotton is resumed at our southern ports, and, as a legitimate result, the unnaturally high prices cease to rule the cotton trade, it will be clearly seen that, however desirable it may be that Brazil be encouraged in the cultivation of cotton for the benefit of the world, the Brazilian planters of this province will gladly repudiate a cultivation ceased there to be profitable, and return to the raising of coffee, always so remunerative, and with little competition to fear. The few whose cotton fields are near the Santos railway, and to whom transportation will be cheap, may be excepted.

COMMERCE.

The port of Santos, as well as many cities in the interior of this consular district, offers the most flattering prospects for success to American commercial enterprise. All these can easily be made consumers of American goods, and paying customers of American mercantile firms; for, as a general rule, the Brazilians entertain a very high opinion of everything American, and would much prefer to purchase of Americans.

Notwithstanding this, not one American merchant vessel has entered the port
of Santos since the 11th of May, 1862, and not one pound of American merchandise was imported directly from the United States during the entire fiscal
year ended June 30, 1864.   *   *   *

RIO GRANDE DO SUL—AARON YOUNG, jr., *Consul,*

NOVEMBER 1, 1864.

In accordance with sections 152, 153 and 154, of general instructions to consular officers, I have the honor to lay before the department the following report
upon this port, its commerce, trade, &c., not only for the year since I entered
upon my official duties, but also for some previous years, in order to more fully
illustrate the importance of this district in its commercial relations with the
United States.

As little is known in the States respecting this southern province of Brazil,
I have endeavored to procure and have incorporated much useful information,
particularly relating to the topography, geology, agriculture, climate, scientific
discoveries, &c.   *   *   *   *   *   *

Although the rebellion has driven our shipping completely from these shores,
still the commerce has been respectably kept up by neutral flags, and the trade
has been but slightly diminished so far as the bulk of exports and imports are
concerned, although at small profits to the parties engaged.

The tables exhibiting commercial relations with this district are as complete
as circumstances would allow. In the exports, the invoices certified at this consulate give the exact amount, but of the imports from the States arriving in
foreign vessels no correct information could be obtained. Such, however, as is
furnished, before and after the rebellion broke out, show respectable footings.

The amount of exports for the year ending September 30, 1864, as certified
at the consulate, is 1,743,198||350 reis, or $871,599 17. This is a large ex-
portation, greater than any year since 1859, when it was $1,092,189 26. The
imports from the States the same year were $515,903 29. In 1860, $635,461 40.

In regard to the Brazilian tariff, which has been several times revised, but
not materially since the 19th of September, 1860, there is more or less complaint.
Many of its exactions are illiberal, or perhaps more illiberally administered. The
export duties on dry and salted hides and jerked beef, &c., are seven per cent.
ad valorem to the government and three per cent. to the district, making ten
per cent.; and as it is now on all exports from the district, these duties have
to be paid in national money, which obtains a premium of five to eight per cent.
It is obvious that such restrictions on the manufactories of the district are highly
detrimental to its interest. Among the tables will be found an abstract from the
tariff which affects importation from the States.

Remarks.—The province of Rio Grande do Sul, or São. Pedro, is the most
southerly district of the empire of Brazil. It is bounded on the north by the
province of St. Paul, where it is separated by the rivers Pelotas and Uruguay;
on the northeast by the province of St. Catherine; on the east and southeast by
the Atlantic ocean, and west by the republic of Uruguay; it lies between 27°
30' and 32° 30' south latitude and 50° and 57° west longitude, the whole province being about the size of the New England States.

Its coast.—The coast extends upwards of four hundred miles, and throughout its whole length presents an almost unvaried shore, of so much monotony
in character as to require the utmost patience and vigilance on the part of the
navigator in approaching it. The soil is very light, chiefly sand, which moves
with every wind, and scarcely affording vegetation except here and there a

clump of struggling shrubs and low trees, there being on the whole coast, from Cape Santa Martha Grande to Cape Santa Maria, no objects sufficiently remarkable to guide the mariner excepting the highlands about the former, the general appearance and islands at the latter, the castillos rocks and hills near thereto, and, finally, the light-house and watch-tower of Rio Grande.

Harbor of refuge.—On this whole extent of coast there can scarcely be said to be a single harbor of refuge, and even that of Rio Grande can never be approached except in the most favorable weather, and cannot then be safely entered without great care on the part of the master in observing the signals and understanding them, as well as the rules and regulations particularly laid down for guidance. It is the common remark of all mariners approaching this coast that the entrance to Rio Grande harbor is the worst part of the whole voyage.

Bars of Rio Grande.—These are on the direct line of the coast at the mouth of the river or outlet of the lakes, and about nine miles from the city. The width of these bars and banks may be assumed to be, measuring from shore to shore, about the same width as the river, which is from two to three miles. These bars and banks, subject to daily (though not serious) changes, are not, from the nearest approach of a vessel, visible at all. For some years past there has been a gradual changing to the westward of the principal bar. Every change, however, is readily discovered and easily understood by the pilots, who are constantly sounding, and the Brazilian government is zealous and active in every duty commensurate with the importance of guarding against any dangers in passing to or from this port.

All the employés of the pilotage during the time they remain in that service are considered as belonging to the war marine, and as such subject to the regulations and discipline of the navy.

The banks surrounding the bar are composed of fine sand, and changes are constantly recurring. Every severe storm to the observer on the coast would seem almost to obliterate the last opening to this port. But the velocity of the tidal currents, sometimes six to eight knots an hour, sweeps a clear channel from the sea, and vice versa.

Topography.—From the city or Rio Grande, directly westward and southwestward, the lay of the land is flat, composed of sand and loam, mingled with marine shells, the dust and bones of the numerous herds of cattle that roam over its surface, and here and there spotted with sand-hills, some of them covered with an impenetrable shrubbery, wide plains of low grass, swamps of thatch-grass and clumps of trees, which latter afford the "openings" for agricultural operations. Such a scene of waste land with its occasional oases is the immense tract which forms the east and southeast borders of the province, of a length hardly less than the coast, and of a breadth, including the lakes, on an average of thirty miles.

Further westward and to the northward of this apparently barren section the contour of the country becomes more rolling, hilly and mountainous, diversified with large streams and rivers, ponds and lakes, rich in vegetation and timber and mineral wealth, but very sparsely settled, as indeed is the whole province.

Population, cities, and towns.—The population of the province of Rio Grande do Sul is estimated at 420,000, of whom 40,000 are slaves. It is the seventh of the twenty provinces of Brazil in number of inhabitants, and the fourth in empire in commercial importance.   *   *   *   *

Porto Alegre, the capital of the province, is situated at the head of the lake, (Patos,) distance about 160 miles from Rio Grande, and has a population of 25,000. It has communication by mail steamers, once a week, with the port, and is also reached by sailing vessels drawing nine feet of water. The city is well laid out and is represented as being a picturesque and beautiful place, and its trade yearly increasing.

so that this cause may not affect the climate, and in nearly the same latitude
north and south of the equator.

Countries.	Latitude.	Mean annual temperature.	Mean winter temperature.	Mean summer temperature.	Different temperature.
	o '	o	o	o	?
Bagdad, Asia.....................	N. 33 19	73	42	93	44
Calcutta, Asia....................	N. 22 33	82	72	86	14
Cairo, Africa.....................	N. 30 2	72	58	85	27
New Orleans, United States........	N. 29 51	69	55	82	27
Cape Good Hope...................	S. 34 11	66	58	74	16
Rio Janeiro	S. 22 54	73	68	79	11
Rio Grande	S. 32 7	67	61	73	12

Although Rio Grande city is 10° further south, its mean annual temperature
is only 6° less, mean winter 7°, mean summer 6°, and the difference between
the winter and summer 1° less than Rio de Janeiro. In regard to what is
called the *dry* and *rainy* season, none can be said to exist to any marked degree,
nor are storms, including thunder-showers, ever so severe as further south and
north. Indeed, every atmospheric change, every gale and every storm, appear
with moderation and pursue the even tenor of their way as quietly as promised
in the programme; and seldom, not an annual phenomenon, does hail fall, or
frost or ice form. I have observed each of them but once.

In regard to winds, the most prevalent are the north northeast and the south-
southwest, which often vary to the true northeast and southwest; the former
being more common in summer and the latter in winter. The northeast wind,
never so forcible as the latter, is often rainy, and continues from 12 to 48 hours.
The southwest is more violent, always commencing in a sudden gust and gradually relaxing its force. The *pampero*, which is a southwest wind, is the common local wind of this coast, and is seldom severe enough on land to merit particular attention. At sea, however, it is sometimes a dreadful blast, and frightful
in the extreme.

One important misfortune to the husbandman in Rio Grande is the severity
of occasional seasons of drought, not so much in parching the vegetation as
causing a scarcity of water for the immense herds of this region; many die
from this cause alone. The year past and the summer of the present, years
1863 and 1864, serious droughts were experienced.

Dews and fogs, particularly the latter, occur but seldom. The temperature
of the day and night is too even. In regard to the former there is nothing
perceptible; yet clothing and shoe-leather require frequent airing and sun-
ning to prevent mildew, if suspended against brick walls, and are not exempt
from moisture even in draws for many weeks.

GEOLOGY.

Little is correctly known respecting the geology of this district; no survey
has ever been made; yet the mineral indications are excellent.

Geologically considered, the coast of this province, in nearly its whole extent,
may be regarded as an immense sand down, having its origin in the deltas of
the rivers which flow into the lakes Patos and Mirim, and it now forms the
westerly shore of these lakes, and of course the ancient sea-coast of the province. For thousands of years this work has been going on. The more than

twenty rivers flowing from the highlands and mountainous regions, nearly all pursuing a direct easterly course, annually discharge millions upon millions of tons of sedimentary matter into these lakes, obliterating them so gradually that in the lifetime of a man scarcely any change is observed. Yet the work goes on, every cubic foot of water from the mouths of these rivers loaded with sediment, every breath of wind and every dash of the sea is perpetually building up, not only this wide barrier between the sea and the lakes, but making rapid inroads upon them.

The lesson is highly instructive, and has its parallel only in the Ganges, the Nile, and the Mississippi. The waters of the lakes are very turbid, and scarcely more than brackish for the most part. The light sand and mud which compose this immense formation is filled with marine shells and vegetable matter as far inland as the whole plain extends, viz., to the easterly coast of these lakes, and the fossils brought to light by artesian well-boring are interesting relics of the depth and stupendous formation of the great delta of the Rio Grande do Sul.

COAL.

It has been known for several years that coal existed in this district; but until the present year little has been said or done about mining operations.

The coal mines of the *Arroios dos Ratos*, near Porto Alegre, have been worked only experimentally, and the result seems yet unproductive of any enterprise on the part of the proprietors.

Within the past year new indications of very extensive coal fields have been discovered; and from the surveys made, as well as trial and quality of the coal, the discovery will, no doubt, prove very beneficial to Brazil if facilities are opened to bring it to market.

"The coal mines of Candiota," quoting the language of the report just published, "in the opinion of a distinguished English geologist, have no rival in the world." This coal field is situated about one hundred miles west from this city, "in the valleys of *Rios Candiota é Jaguarago Chico*, and covers an area of 1,800 square miles. "Here a single bed at sight presents a face of sixty-five feet perpendicularly, of pure bituminous coal, directly exposed on the margin of a river bank, and may be easily extracted by the pick, and other tools and agents generally used for such purposes, and carted away, requiring no earth-digging, nor any of the machinery applicable as in other mines of the world." Coal sells in this port for 10||12 per ton, imported from England. Perhaps the whole empire of Brazil imports 250,000 to 300,000 tons annually.

Sandstone of excellent quality for flagging, limestone for marble, iron granite, lead, and even copper, is abundant; and every day is revealing new and important discoveries, indicating great mineral wealth in the province.

AGRICULTURE.

The immense agricultural resources of the province, the breadth of land capable of yielding most any product of any climate, has, of late years, scarcely awakened the general interest among the native inhabitants so commonly observed in countries of older growth, but of far less capability to produce the requirements their population demand. Here the agricultural products are almost wholly derived from the foreign population, while the native give almost exclusive attention to the rearing of cattle and horses.

There is, however, a satisfactory change being made, and the wooden plough and ordinary case-knife (for cutting grass) are rapidly giving way for the iron plough and scythe. When slavery shall have been supplanted by free labor, and the people taught to work for themselves, this province will become the most important agricultural district of the empire.

Of most garden vegetables two crops a year are raised, and no season of the year is without them. Oranges of two or three species, lemons, citrons, quinces, apples, pears, figs, bananas, apricots, grapes of two or three species, are more abundant than the demand, and are, hence, sold at a price that would scarcely pay their gathering, and are, consequently, left to perish in the more remote parts of the country, away from the centres of trade.

The growth of cotton, tobacco, and the sugar-cane is receiving considerable attention; and it has been satisfactorily demonstrated that in the growth of these products alone, the soil, the climate, and everything that favors these valuable plants, no country, not even excepting South Carolina, can be more favorable. Of cotton and tobacco two crops may be raised annually; and a fact worthy of great importance and highly encouraging to the cultivation of the former is, that this plant, an annual in the southern United States, here partakes the perennial order, lasting two or three years, and may be continued in its growth almost indefinitely by simple cuttings and slips.

The present year, 1864—at the time I am writing this report—large tracts of land are being made available for the cotton-seed, and the most promising results are expected. Seeds from the "Manchester Cotton Supply Association,", embracing every variety from the southern United States, and other countries, have been most fully disseminated, and individual and government interest is doing everything to stimulate and encourage its growth.

Two articles grown and largely consumed in this province. as well as exported, need to be mentioned. These are the Mandioca flour, farina, and erba matte. The former is extensively used as a wholesome bread, and the latter as a wholesome tea, or beverage. The consumption of these two articles obtains among all classes throughout Brazil and the river Plata, and their production and manufacture seems to be large, yielding no inconsiderable profit to the producers, and a source of considerable revenue to the country. Large exportations are made to the neighboring provinces and the river Plata, and also to England.

Agricultural tools and implements are also now largely imported from the United States, and in this branch of importation there is an increasing demand. The liberal policy of this government in allowing this importation free, or at a mere nominal tax, has allowed importers to dispose of such articles at a small profit above cost, and at prices that now make purchasers.

PORTS OF ENTRY.

By decree of Brazilian government there are but two ports of entry for this district, viz: Porto Alegre and Rio Grande do Sul. Formerly, San José do Norte was also a port of entry, but it has now been merged into that of Rio Grande do Sul, a branch, however, being left for the collection of taxes. The harbor of Rio Grande is amply capacious for any number of light-draught vessels, while directly opposite the city, at the north village, shipping of any draught getting over the bar may anchor. It is not advisable, however, that any vessel should visit this port drawing over 10½, hardly 11, feet of water, as the chances are very uncertain in *getting over the bar*, and may be detained inside or out, several days, or even weeks. *Six inches of draught over eleven feet may keep a vessel in or out, not only for weeks, but months.*

Porto Alegre, at the head of Lake Patos, and about 160 miles from Rio Grande city, cannot be reached by vessels drawing over nine feet of water. Few of the vessels navigating the lakes draw over six or seven feet, the Lake Patos, especially, having many shallow banks, or bars; the channel, however, such as it is, is clearly defined by buoys and beacons. Few foreign vessels visit Porto Alegre, and these are mostly Danish and Hanseatic, with cargoes from Hamburg, to supply the colonies in that section, which have now become quite large. It is safe to estimate the German population at the head of the lake at 20,000 souls, and immigration still continues annually to the number of several hundred. The whole German population of the province may be assumed to be about one-tenth—that is, 42,000.

CURRENCY AND EXCHANGE.

The *milrea*, in which the prices in the tables are affixed, is assumed to be *fifty cents*, estimated in American or Spanish silver dollars. The coin in circulation in this district is almost exclusively South and North American. English, French, and German coins are seldom seen in ordinary business transactions. The following table embraces all the metal currency, and value in *reis*, reported in newspapers of the district:

Portuguese.	English.	Value in reis currency.	Value in U. S. currency.
Oncas.......................	Ounces doubloon	32‖000	$16 00
Pesos.............	Dollar................	2‖000	1 00
Patacoes....	Dollar......	2‖000	1 00
Pecas America 5 dollars........	Half eagle American 5-dollar gold piece................	10‖000	5 00
Meios presos Bolivianos........	40-cent piece.............	800 reis	40
Quarter dollar Americano	Quarter dollar......	500 reis	25
Colunarios bespenhoes.........	....	300 reis	25
Quinta de patacão dito.........	22-cent piece.............	440 reis	22
Umpreso Boliviano	Half dollar......	1‖000	50

Exchange on London, 25¾d. per 1‖000.
　　　　Hamburg, 630 reis per banco.
　　　　Paris, 365 to 370 reis per franc.
　　　　New York, 90 cents on the dollar.

National money ranges from 5 to 8 per cent.; Brazilian paper money is required to pay duties in custom-house and some other departments. For a year past it has been a premium of 8 per cent. Bills on Rio de Janeiro obtain a premium of 3 to 5 per cent., payable in ten to sixty days after sight, usually ninety days.

FREIGHTS.

To Rio de Janeiro, 300 reis per arroba (32 lbs.)
　　Bahia,　　　　400　　"　　"　　"
　　Pernambuco,　　500　　"　　"　　"
　　England, salted hides, 50 to 55 shillings per ton.
　　　　bone ash,　　42　　"　　"　　"
　　United States, dry hides, ¾ cent per pound.
　　　　salted　　½　　"　　"
　　　　hair,　　　¾　　"　　"
　　　　wool,　　　1　　"　　"

Five per cent. primage gold.

Most vessels from the United States come and return under special contract, so much for the round trip.

On all exports a duty of 10 per cent. is exacted—7 per cent. to the government and 3 per cent. to the province.

CUSTOM-HOUSE RECEIPTS.

The following table exhibits the revenue of the custom-house of the city of Rio Grande do Sul for the month of September, 1864, compared with the corresponding month of the two previous years, 1862 and 1863.

September.	1862.	1863.	1864.
	Reis.	*Reis.*	*Reis.*
Imports	79,822‖667	81,583‖598	142,499‖600
Port charges..................	739‖200	480‖650	944‖600
Exportation..................	14,762‖389	15,050‖843	22,648‖964
Interior	381‖940	546‖490	2,934‖648
Total....................	95,706‖196	97,661‖584	169,024‖810

The following table exhibits the average price of the chief articles of export of Rio Grande do Sul.

Price in reis currency.

Bacon..	per arroba..	4‖000
Beef, "jerked"..................................	per arroba..	2‖800
Beans, black....................................	per sack..	8‖000
Bone ash.......................................	per barrel..	2‖000
Hair, horse.....................................	per arroba..	9‖200
Hair, cow......................................	per arroba..	9‖200
Hides, dry ox..................................	per pound..	200
Hides, dry cow.................................	per pound..	200
Hides, salted cow..............................	per pound..	110
Hides, salted ox...............................	per pound..	110
Hides, horse dry...............................	each..	3‖000
Hides, horse salt...............................	per pound..	080
Hide cuttings..................................	per arroba..	1‖000
Horns, ox.....................................	per 100..	7‖000
Horns, cows...................................	per 100..	1‖500
Hoofs...	per arroba..	400
Grease in pipes................................	per arroba..	3‖800
Horses..	each..	40‖000
Mares...	each..	10‖000
Mules...	each..	24‖000
Mandioca flour................................	sack..	4‖000
Indian corn, red...............................	sack..	3‖200
Indian corn, white.............................	sack..	3‖200
Matte (erba matte).............................	arroba..	3‖000
Rum, caxaca...................................	pipe..	120‖000
Shinbones.....................................	per 1,000..	10‖000
Tallow, melted.................................	arroba..	4‖800
Tallow candles.................................	arroba..	6‖500
Wool, clean....................................	arroba..	11‖000
Wool, dirty....................................	arroba..	7‖000

N. B.—1 arroba=32.277 pounds British.
1 sack=2.219 bushels imperial.
The price in reis divided by 20 will give the price in dollars and cents.

From the above table it will be seen that the articles exported from Rio Grande do Sul consist almost entirely of the products of cattle. From Porto Alegre the articles are more varied by the addition of agricultural products, which formerly were of little amount, but are now annually increasing not only from that district, but throughout the whole province. Mules, horses, and cattle have the past two years been exported to the West Indies and other islands.

Exports from Porto Alegre for 1861.

Bacon	arrobas	1,732
Bacon	flitches	145
Beans, sweet	sacks	1,374
Beans, large	do	1,328
Beans, small	do	63,882
Bone ash	arrobas	13,300
Caxaca, (cane spirits)	pipes	140
Fire-wood	sticks	574,430
Grease	arrobas	3,060
Hair	do	3,518
Hair	bales	1,294
Hides	number	129,496
Horns	do	185,175
Laths	dozens	527
Corn	sacks	66,278
Corn	in ear	2,275
Corn flour	sacks	2,746
Mandioca flour	do	125,660
Matte tea	arrobas	2,805
Matte tea	in hides	14,157
Planks, large	dozens	293
Planks, small	do	2,618
Potatoes	sacks	858
Rafters	number	3,193
Saddles	pairs and parcels	357
Starch	sacks	1,113
Sugar cakes	barrels	373
Tallow	arrobas	7,040
Tallow	barrels	67
Tiles	number	660,960
Timber	do	7,567
Jerked beef	arrobas	119,993

Shipping—navigation—foreign trade.

Since the commencement of the rebellion the carrying trade in United States vessels has rapidly declined. Through fear of piratical interference many were sold, and not a few changed their flag.

For the year ending September 30, 1864, there have been only two arrivals at and two departures from this port.

The following table exhibits United States vessels inward and outward for the years 1860, 1861, 1862, and 1863:

Port of Rio Grande do Sul.

Year.	Quarter.	Arrivals.	Departures.	No. sold in port.
1860......	1st quarter.	8	7	0
"	2d "	5	8	0
"	3d " .	11	8	0
"	4th "	8	9	2
Total......	....	32	32	2
1861......	1st quarter.	4	4	1
"	2d "	8	4	2
"	3d "	14	7	3
"	4th "	17	14	2
Total......	....	43	29	8
1862......	1st quarter.	15	8	3
"	2d "	3	9	3
"	3d "	5	3	1
"	4th "	4	3	1
Total......	....	27	23	8
1863......	1st quarter.	5	5	1
"	2d "	2	1	0
"	3d "	2	2	0
"	4th "	0	0	0
Total......	....	9	8	1

The arroba is 32,277 pounds, British. The sack is 2,219 bushels, imperial.

The large increase of United States vessels at this port in the first three foregoing years is due to the derangement of the coasting trade at home, although this increase was not large compared with the two or three years previous. Except for the year 1862, the number is scarcely more than an average. In 1859 there were thirty-three arrivals and twenty-eight departures, and the year preceding 1858, in the last three quarters, nineteen arrivals and ten departures.

The number of vessels from foreign ports to Rio Grande do Sul is quite large at all times, which, added to the great number of coast and lake vessels in the harbor, give a thrifty appearance of traffic.

A large number of vessels come from Spain and Portugal loaded with salt and other products of those countries, also from Hamburg, Havre, Antwerp, and Marseilles. From Great Britain, coal and hardware, woollen, cotton, and linen goods are largely imported, and from Austria (Trieste and Fiume) considerable flour. From the United States, flour, lard, kerosene, wooden ware, clocks, and agricultural tools and machinery.

The number of vessels visiting this port in 1861 was 173, with an aggregate tonnage of 29,591, and number of crews 1,367. Of this number of vessels forty-three were American, seven Brazilian, and the balance foreign.

The same year, *outward* 147, tonnage 24,586, crews 1,140; American twenty-nine, Brazilian seven, and the balance foreign.

The same year the arrivals of British vessels were thirty-two and departures twenty-seven.

Coasting trade, exports of Rio Grande and Porto Alegre.

The trade coastwise of Rio Grande do Sul consists almost exclusively of jerked beef, grease and tallow, shipped to the northern provinces, especially to Rio, Pernambuco, Bahia, &c. The total value of these exports in 1860 amounted to 6,713,477||000 reis or $3,156,738 50.

The following table will exhibit the extent of this trade for *one month* ending September, 1864:

Ports, exported.	Vessels.	Jerked beef.	Grease.	Tallow.
	No.	*Arrobas.*	*Arrobas.*	*Arrobas.*
Rio de Janeiro..................	8	61,025	10,794	7,902
Paraugua	13	143,403	1,531	2,755
Bahia..................	10	113,408	1,286	977
Paremagua.....................	1	600	....	....
	32	318,436	13,611	11,634

The value of the above estimate by the average market export prices is, jerked beef 636,870||000 reis, grease 51,720||800 reis, and tallow 54,679||800 reis.

The coasting trade between the ports of Brazil is conducted almost exclusively by Brazilian vessels, although there are no important restrictions against foreign vessels. A few United States vessels have taken freights coastwise.

The following table exhibits the coasting trade for 1861:

1861.	VESSELS INWARD.			VESSELS OUTWARD.		
Ports.	Number of vessels.	Tonnage.	Number of crew.	Number of vessels.	Tonnage.	Number of crew.
Rio Grande..........						
Brazilian vessels.....	196	38,364	2,048	160	31,269	1,635
Foreign vessels	....	....	....	2	425	20
Porto Alegre..........						
Brazilian	69	12,462	782	66	11,999	743
Total	265	50,826	2,830	228	43,693	2,398

In the following table will be found the average price of a few of the principal articles of import and export for the first six months of the years 1861 and 1864:

Average market price in currency reis.

Months.	OX AND COW HIDES, per pound.				Coal, per ton.		Flour, per barrel.		Salt, per bushel.	
	Dried.		Salted.							
	1861.	1864.	1861.	1864.	1861.	1864.	1861.	1864.	1861.	1864.
January	345	240	165	125	27‖500	20‖000	26‖500	20‖000	1‖260	500
February	345	240	167	125	25‖500	20‖000	30‖000	20‖000	1‖280	400
March	350	240	172	130	28‖400	23‖000	35‖000	20‖000	1‖300	400
April	322	245	166	132	35‖000	23‖000	30‖000	21‖500	1‖400	400
May	320	240	175	132	43‖000	23‖000	30‖000	21‖500	1‖640	700
June	320	240	180	138	50‖000	23‖000	31‖000	21‖500	2‖000	800

Comparative table of the slaughter of cattle for the years 1862 and 1863, and also for the same period in 1863 and 1864 in the countries below:

1862–'63.

Uruguay	691, 370 head.
Buenos Ayres	259, 800 "
Entre Rios	228, 500 "
Corrientes	24, 000
Rio Grande	420, 000 "
Porto Alegre	40, 000
Total	1, 663, 670

1863–'64.

Uruguay	602, 500 head.
Buenos Ayes	318, 600 "
Entre Rios	353, 000 "
Corrientes	26, 000 "
Rio Grande	536, 000 "
Porto Alegre	45, 000 "
Total	1, 895, 100

Comparative table of the exportation, not including Porto Alegre, from the district for the years 1860, 1861, 1862, and 1863.

Years.	Dry hides.	Salted hides.	Jerked beef.	Fat.
			Arrobas.	Arrobas.
1860	329, 463	374, 290	1, 759, 705	254, 559
1861	243, 526	362, 207	1, 768, 522	228, 472
1862	406, 095	448, 848	1, 913, 530	294, 476
1863	486, 771	466, 694	2, 111, 155	360, 383

Exportation from the 1st of January to the 30th September, 1864.

Months.	Dry hides.	Salted hides.	Jerked beef.	Tar.
			Arrobas.	*Arrobas.*
January	66,328	23,045	145,504	16,683
February	43,890	42,363	85,549	99,358
March	28,924	23,815	93,183	12,545
April	54,730	41,550	247,641	14,918
May	47,844	79,176	216,393	58,225
June	18,293	78,184	227,862	20,718
July	17,114	72,535	183,731	68,403
August	16,793	31,369	284,498	42,965
September	23,469	26,815	393,430	32,047
Total	317,385	419,482	1,777,846	285,862

Table of merchandise imported from foreign countries in Rio Grande do Sul in the year 1863.

Ale and beer, 3,365 barrels.
Brooms, 2,762 dozen.
Biscuits, 156 tons and 56 boxes.
Billiard tables, 5.
Buckets and pails, 660 dozen.
Beef preserved in bags, 72 packages.
Butter, 445 barrels.
Corks, 117 packages.
Clothing, ready-made, 45 cases.
Clocks, 47 cases.
Coal, 3,941 tons.
Cordage, 441 packages.
Cement, 184 barrels.
Copper, in sheets, 54 boxes.
Corn-shellers, 50.
Cotton goods, 1,432 boxes.
Crockery-ware, 1,309 crates.
Cheese, 148 packages.
Candles, 1,872 boxes.
Drugs, 226 packages.
Furniture, all kinds, 616 boxes.
Flour, 24,328 barrels and 777 bags.
Fruits—olives, walnuts, almonds, filberts, and sweetmeats, 6,361 boxes and bags.
Fire-crackers, 80 boxes.
Fish, dry and pickled, 426 cases and barrels.
Gin, 2,959 boxes, 1,907 demijohns, 141 barrels, and 4,740 (garrafoes) large bottles.
Gunpowder, 320 cases.
Glass, 968 cases.
Hardware, 2,483 boxes and cases.
Hams, 17 barrels, 11 boxes, and 206 cases.
Kerosene, 484 boxes or 4,840 gallons.
Lard, 2,719 barrels and 600 half-barrels.
Lime, 213 barrels.
Looking-glasses, 33 boxes.

Liquors—cognac, absinthe, &c., 500 boxes and 4 barrels.
Linseed oil, 217 barrels.
Lumber—boards, 190,026 feet.
    "   plank, 175 feet.
Maccaroni, 2,213 boxes.
Miscellaneous and sundries, 1,257 boxes.
Medicines, 22 cases.
Machines, sewing, 36 boxes.
Oars, 1,170.
Olive oil, 503 casks, 680 boxes, and 121 demijohns, Mediterranean.
Orange water, 40 cases.
Oysters, — cases.
Paints in cases, 20 cases and boxes.
Preserves, 56 boxes.
Perfumeries and soap, 584 boxes.
Peas, split, 20 cases and boxes.
Porcelain brick, 1,400.
Paper, 1,366 reams, 379 bales, and 132 boxes.
Pianos, 21.
Rice, 320 packages.
Rosin, 247 barrels.
Salt, 593,830 bushels.
Sail-cloth, 22 bales.
Silks, 62 boxes.
Shoes, 87 cases.
Spices, 33 boxes.
Small wares, 319 packages.
Soda, 1,125 barrels.
Tea, 277 chests.
Tin, 155 boxes.
Turpentine, 135 boxes.
Tar, 214 barrels and 80 half barrels.
Tubs, 41 nests.
Woollens, 598 boxes.
Worsteds, 259 boxes.
Wax, 64 boxes.
Wines—Portuguese, 686 pipes, 2,659 barrels, and 300 cases; French, 492 pipes, 119 quarter do., 647 barrels, and 967 cases; Spanish, 1,908 pipes, 64 quarter do., 1,719 barrels, and 967 cases; Champagne, 590 cases and 170 baskets.
    Vinegar, 6 pipes, 95 barrels, 225 demijohns.

Statistical table of exportation from Rio Grande do Sul to foreign countries in the year 1863.

Articles exported.	Belgium.	United States.	France.	Spain.	Hamburg.	England.	Portugal.	Total.
Ox and cow hides, dry............?...	4,383	163,143	21,993	91,813	2,139	42,483	88,805	414,759
Do. do. salted..............	3,671	19,345	64,998	4,788	8,997	356,375	11,471	471,645
Kips.........................	....	15,138	....	437	....	77	35,336	50,988
Horse-hides, dry..............	33	637	50	....	....	113	165	998
Do. salted.............	....	6,494	....	....	5,154	16,537	1,042	29,227
Horns, ox....................	5,995	163,157	84,195	11,000	20,700	409,447	60,655	755,149
Horns, cow...................	8,000	8,018	37,251	8,120	6,500	157,723	57,384	282,996
Shinbones...................	....	287,500	10,000	....	....	539,000	....	836,500
Hoofs...............arrobas*.	380	200	300	....	....	2,630	....	3,510
Bone ash................tons.	....	....	....	....	....	2,630	....	2,630
Hide cuttings............arrobas	1,725	5,438	2,788	....	1,736	10,356	....	22,043
Wool.....................arrobas.	1,274	26,865	1,388	....	467	6,001	34	36,029
Hair.....................arrobas.	512	19,175	12,597	1,138	1,006	14,965	2,034	44,427
Fat.....................arrobas.	....	....	396	....	....	10,943	2,104	12,673
Bones...................	....	2,500	....	....	....	115,470	....	117,970

* The arroba is 32,377 lbs. British.

Imports and exports of Rio Grande do Sul for the years 1859, 1860, 1861, 1862, and 1863, in United States' vessels.

IMPORTS.

(To exhibit the gradual increase and diminution the years are made up into quarters.)

Years.	Months.	Kind of goods.	Valuation.
1859..	Jan., Feb., Mar	Flour, lard, and salt	$74,646 83
	April, May, June ...	Flour, lard, salt, and domestics	150,541 90
	July, Aug., Sept....	Flour, domestics, and lumber................	83,738 56
	Oct., Nov., Dec	Salt, lumber, and lard	216,038 25
		Total...................	524,965 54
1860..	Jan., Feb., Mar	Wines, salt, flour, and lard.................	$134,468 98
	April, May, June ...	Wines, salt, lumber, and domestics	147,122 39
	July, Aug., Sept ...	Rice, salt, and lumber	625,453 27
	Oct., Nov., Dec	Flour, salt, lime, and coals................	108,957 66
		Total...................	656,002 30
1861..	Jan., Feb., Mar	Flour, salt, lard, and rice	$58,311 00
	April, May, June ...	Lumber, domestics, and salt................	104,418 11
	July, Aug., Sept....	Salt, wine, flour, and sundries..............	108,761 67
	Oct., Nov., Dec.....	Salt, wine, flour, and coal................	77,460 00
		Total	348,950 78
1862..	Jan., Feb., Mar	Salt, coals, and ballast....................	$21,725 00
	April, May, June ...	Salt, lumber, and flour.......................	16,650 00
	July, Aug., Sept....	Lard, lumber, and flour........................	69,543 10
	Oct., Nov., Dec	Ballast and salt	17,700 00
		Total...................	125,618 10

Imports and exports of Rio Grande do Sul, &c.—Continued.

Years.	Months.	Kind of goods.	Valuation.
1863..	Jan., Feb., Mar	Flour, ballast, and salt.........................	$30,783 00•
	April, May, June...	Flour, ballast, and land	13,500 00
	July, Aug., Sept....	Flour, land, and sundries	31,891 00
	Oct.,.Nov., Dec	No vessels this quarter.	
		Total	76,174 00

EXPORTS.

Years.	Months.	Kind of goods.	Valuation.
1859..	Jan., Feb., Mar	Hides, bone ash, and matté.................	$387,260 00
	April, May, June ...	Hides, horses' bones, and hair	133,500 00
	July, Aug., Sept....	Hides, horns, and hair	339,016 26
	Oct., Nov., Dec	Bone ash, hides, and ballast.................	251,583 00
		Total..........................	1,111,359 26
1860..	Jan., Feb., Mar	Hides, bone ash, and matté	$133,384 00
	April, May, June ...	Hides, jerked beef, and bones................	234,711 00
	July, Aug., Sept....	Hides, horns, and timber....................	203,936 39
	Oct., Nov., Dec	Hides, wool, and bone ash	228,143 55
		Total	800,174 94
1861..	Jan., Feb., Mar	Timber, hides, and wool	$74,310 00
	April, May, June ...	Bone ash, hides, and hair	113,592 75
	July, Aug., Sept....	......do.......do	36,870 00
	Oct., Nov., Dec	Matté, lumber, and timbers	175,450 00
		Total	400,222 75
1862..	Jan., Feb., Mar	Ballast, hides, and hair	$205,600 00
	April, May, June...	Wool, bones, and hair	212,800 00
	July, Aug., Sept....	Hides and wool	114,236 38
	Oct., Nov., Dec	Hides, wool, and hair............!...........	68,300 00
		Total	600,936 38
1863..	Jan., Feb., Mar	Hides, wool, and matté	$106,301 50
	April, May, June ...	Hides and jerked beef.....................	9,500 00
	July, Aug., Sept....	Hides, wool, and hair......................	65,175 77
	Oct:, Nov., Dec	No vessels this quarter.	
		Total	108,977 27

DIRECT TRADE WITH THE UNITED STATES.

Imports and exports of Rio Grande do Sul in United States vessels.

IMPORTS FROM UNITED STATES.

Years.	Months.	. Kind of goods.	Value.
1859..	Jan., Feb., Mar	Flour, lard, and domestic goods	$71,456 83
	April, May, June ...	......do..........do	147,191 90
	July, Aug., Sept....	Flour, lard, and lumber	83,'116 56
	Oct., Nov., Dec	Flour, lard, and domestics	214,138 00
		Total...........................	515,903 29
1860..	Jan., Feb., Mar	Flour, lard, and lumber.....................	$130,005 58
	April, May, June ...	Domestics and lumber	146,544 89
	July, Aug., Sept....	Domestics and flour	264,953 27
	Oct., Nov., Dec	Lard, rice, and flour	93,957 66
		Total...........................	635,461 40
1861..	Jan., Feb., Mar	Flour and rice ....,......	$57,711 00
	April, May, June ...	Flour, lumber, and lard....................	103,268 11
	July, Aug., Sept....	Flour, domestics, and lard	100,761 67
	Oct., Nov., Dec	Flour	50,700 00
		Total...........................	312,440 78
1862..	Jan., Feb., Mar	Flour and lard	$13,600 00
	April, May, June ...	.....do....do	14,500 00
	July, Aug , Sept....	Flour and lumber	69,543 10
	Oct., Nov., Dec	Flour and lard	16,900 00
		Total ....,..................	114,543 10
1863..	Jan., Feb., Mar	Flour and lard	$29,730 00
	April, May, June ...	......do ....,.....	13,500 00
	July, Aug., Sept....	......do	31,891 00
	Oct., Nov., Dec	No vessels this quarter.	
		Total...........................	75,121 00

EXPORTS TO UNITED STATES.

Years.	Months.	. Kind of goods.	Value.
1859..	Jan., Feb., Mar ...:	Hides, horns, and hair ....:...	$374,000 00
	April, May, June ...	.....do........do	132,300 00
	July, Aug., Sept....	.....do........do	337,898 26
	Oct., Nov., Dec	.....do........do	247,991 00
		Total	1,092,189 26
1860..	Jan., Feb., Mar ...	Hides, hair, and bone ash	$125,216 00
	April, May, June...	Hides, hair, and bones	205,711 00
	July, Aug., Sept....	Hides, hair, and bone ash	195,436 39
	Oct., Nov., Dec	.....do......do......do	2,000 00
		Total........:...............	228,363 39

Imports and exports of Rio Grande do Sul, &c.—Continued.

Years.	Months.	Kind of goods.	Value.
1861..	Jan., Feb., Mar	Horns, hides, and hair	$68,710 00
	April, May, June ...	Bone ash, hides, and hair...................	66,092 75
	July, Aug., Sept....	Hides and hair..............................	18,500 00
	Oct., Nov., Dec	Bone ash, hides, and hair	81,000 00
		Total	234,302 75
1862..	Jan., Feb., Mar ...:	Hides and hair	$115,500 00
	April, May, June ...	Wool, hides, and hair...........	180,000 00
	July, Aug., Sept....	....do....do	114,236 38
	Oct., Nov., Dec	....do....do	68,300 00
		Total	478,036 38
1863..	Jan., Feb., Mar	Hides, wool, and hair.......................	$92,801 50
	April, May, June ...	No vessels this quarter.	
	July, Aug., Sept....	Hides and wool	65,173 77
	Oct., Nov., Dec	No vessels this quarter.	
		Total	157,975 27

Tariff on imports at the port of Rio Grande do Sul.

Articles.	Duty.	Articles.	Duty.
	Milreis.		*Milreis.*
Ale and porter ....per doz.	1|390	Lard, American............per lb.	45
Brooms, corn ....do...	700	Lime ....ad. val.	¼ p'r c't
Butter, English and French..per lb.	140	Lead, shot.................per qtl.	4|500
Candles, composition and sperm do..	280	Lumber, American prime..per M.	5 840
" wax....................do..	300	Matches.................per gross.	630
Chairs, wood-seat.........per doz.	8 100	Nails, cut, assorted.......per lb.	40
" cane-seat.............do...	13 500	Oil, olive................per pipe.	64 000
Coal.......................per ton.	180	" " refined ....per doz.	1 500
Codfish ....per qtl.	900	" linseed ....per qt.	45
Cordage, Russian...........do...	4 800	Pails, painted............per doz.	4 100
" Manila...... ......do...	4 800	Pitch, N. A...........per arroba.	200
" Coir ....do...	4 800	Pepper, black.............per lb.	70
Cotton thread .... per lb.	720	Rice ....do..	120
Cheese, Dutch ....do..	120	Rosin....................per bbl.	4 200
Duck cotton ....per yd	150	Raisins..................per box.	1 250
Domestics, American:		Salt ....per bush.	10
Stripes in cases ....do..	150	Tar, Swedish and Amer'n..per bbl.	1 900
" in bales ....do..	150	Tubs.....................per nest.	5 000
Denims in cases...........do..	150	Vermicelli................per lb.	1 400
" in bales...........do..	150	Vinegar..................per pipe.	24 000
Drillings, bleached ....do..	150	Wicking ....per lb.	26
" brown ....do..	150	Turpentine, spirits ....per bbl.	15
" blue ....do..	150	Tea......................per lb.	520
Cotton flannel ....do..	300	Wrapping paper.........per ream.	80
Osnaburgs, flannel..........do..	300	White lead ....per lb.	14
Shirtings, India-head ....do..	300	Wines—Lisbon, &c.....per pipe.	88 000
" Tremont ....do..	300	Champagne ....per doz.	2 400
Flour—all brands.........per bbl.	900	Shoe blacking ....do..	500
Gin in jugs and demijohns..per doz.	1 400	Clocks, wood ....each.	2 400
Hams, Portuguese ....per lb.	50	Sewing machines..........ad. val.	5 p'r c't
" American ....do..	70	Agricult'l implem'ts generally.do ..	2 p'r c't
" Hamburg ....do..	70	Machinery, new.............do ..	2 p'r c't
Sheetings, I. H.............per yd.	150	Kerosene ....per gall.	500
" Tremont ....do..	150		

ATLANTIC STEAMERS.

At present Rio Grande enjoys the benefit of steam communication with Rio de Janeiro twice a month and with Montevideo monthly, performing, however, the former voyages very irregularly, so far as meeting the English and French mail steamers for Europe. Dilatoriness on the part of the Brazilian company, who own this part of the line, is the only cause; not so much, however, for the want of speed, as it would seem, but rather in vexatious delays in port. A line of American steamers between the ports of New York and Rio de Janeiro, and thence to this port and Montevideo, is very much needed. That such a line would not only facilitate commerce between the States and Brazil, but be the means of opening up an increased trade, there can be no doubt. England and France now enjoy complete monopoly in trade with Brazil, and nothing will give us like advantages till this facility of communication is obtained. Speedy communication even from this port with the United States would much increase the traffic and stimulate the now dormant industry of the district beyond calculation; for, of all countries to whom this people look to for amelioration and advantages in mechanical skill and improvements in husbandry, that one is the United States.

H. Ex. Doc. 60——52

Already the indomitable energy of our country is sensibly felt, and every day this fact is being developed by the eagerness and curiosity attached to everything of American skill and ingenuity.

The sewing machine, the plough, the corn-sheller, scales, cotton-gins, wheel-barrows, clocks, and a host of other articles, which, until within the last few years only, and some of them within the present year, have found their way to this market, is proof positive of the estimation in which our manufactures are held and looked after.

At present the balance of trade is against the United States, and it always has been, for no cargo of flour and lard, the chief imports, can pay for a cargo of hides. An increase in variety of imports and an increase of facilities for making our manufactures known, will soon cancel cargoes, and, perhaps, reap the balance of trade.

Nothing will effect this but steam. Every arrival from the United States will bring something new, and every return a demand.

INTERNAL IMPROVEMENTS.

No works of public character are at present going on. A strong effort has been and is still being made to construct a railway to Pelotas, Bage, and thence to Candiota coal mines; but many years will elapse before this important measure will find sufficient enterprise and capital. Railways and electric telegraphs are unknown in Rio Grande do Sul.

GENERAL REMARKS.

In conclusion I may add that, notwithstanding the great revulsion of business all the world over, and those more immediate or proximate causes which may result in disturbances on the frontier of this district, the trade and business of the province are still flourishing. There is no present reason to suppose that the products of the district will be lessened, or that the supply will not be equal to the demand. I am informed that there is a larger number of cattle, in good condition, the present killing season, than usual; and the supposition, from the present low prices of hides, would seem reasonable.

The exports to the United States have diminished in consequence of the high price of gold and exchange.

Merchants are looking anxiously to the United States for a return of "good old times." I may say that shipments generally are made with considerate cautiousness; and the rise and fall of gold, which means exchange, is watched with eagerness.

URUGUAY.

MONTEVIDEO—H. TUTTLE, *Consul.*

JANUARY 9, 1864.

    ●   ●   ●   ●   ●

I beg to communicate to the department, that by a law recently enacted by this government, and which went into operation the first instant, for the purpose (as expressed) of increasing the revenue to meet the interest, and to liquidate a portion of the principal of the public debt, which has been largely augmented through the efforts of the government to suppress the revolutionary proceedings of General Flores since May last, important modifications of the tariff are made by the imposition of additional import and export duties, and the establishment of tonnage dues, viz:

1. A duty of three per cent. *ad valorem* is imposed upon all imports hitherto duty free, with the following exemptions only, viz: printing and lithographic

presses and implements ; printing paper; printed books and maps; geographical globes ; steam vessels in pieces, to be put together in the country; machinery and implements for the study of the natural sciences and mathematics; gold and silver, coined or in bars ; precious stones unset ; animals for the improvement of the species; articles styled " produce of the country;" wooden staves and hoops; empty casks; seeds and plants; passenger's baggage; wearing apparel, and articles of use ; tools and personal effects of immigrants; the effects introduced for the use of foreign diplomatic agents accredited to the government during the first six months of their residence, provided that the governments that they represent shall make the same concession to the diplomatic agents of the republic, and articles that the executive may deem useful for divine worship.

Lumber, the leading article imported from the United States, formerly duty free, is chargeable by this law with three per cent. duty, and machinery and agricultural implements the same.

2. An additional import duty of three per cent. is imposed upon all (former) duty-paying articles. Under this head are the general articles imported from the United States, as kerosene, alcohol, starch, refined sugar, chairs, cordage, &c.

3. An export duty of two per cent. is lev ed upon articles formerly duty free, as flour, jerked beef, &c., &c., and an additional export duty of two per cent. upon all other exports without exception, formerly paying but four per cent. upon valuation. Custom-house valuations upon imports, upon which the duties are levied, are fixed at about ten per cent. below the market wholesale prices.

4. Tonnage dues, which were abolished about three years since, are by this law re-established, and twenty cents per ton are levied upon all sea-going merchant vessels, national and foreign, which shall receive or discharge cargo, excepting only the packets.

In regard to the commercial operations of the country, there are no new features to report. Hides and wool continue to be the leading articles of export. These products, especially the latter, continue largely to increase in amount from year to year. Notwithstanding the existence of a civil war in the country for the past eight months, these staples have come forward freely, and the stock now on hand is considerably in excess of that of last year at the same period.

A large proportion of these products are exported to the United States. Owing to the depredation of the privateers upon our commerce, our vessels have been unable for some time past to obtain homeward freights at this port, the bulk of exports to the United States being shipped in foreign bottoms. Partly from the same cause the number of our vessels and amount of tonnage have sensibly diminished at this port during the past two quarters.

I append the following comparative statement of the shipping and tonnage of the leading commercial nations at this port for the year 1863, except the Spanish, which I was unable to obtain.

Nations.	Vessels inward bound.			Vessels outward bound.		
	No. of vessels.	Tonnage.	Crews.	No. of vessels.	Tonnage.	Crews.
American	80	50,258	1,263	76	47,205	1,250
Brazilian	108	28,224	1,884	113	29,711	1,968
British	146	57,519	3,357	142	55,081	3,217
Dutch	42	9,330	359	41	9,578	362
French	111	45,216	3,056	114	45,603	3,042
Italian	122	34,256	1,618	115	31,762	1,445
Total	609	224,803	11,537	601	218,940	11,284

PERU.

TUMBEZ—DENISON CARD, *Consul.*

SEPTEMBER 1, 1864.

I have the honor to submit my annual report upon the trade, commerce, &c., of this port.

As the department is doubtless aware, the only American commerce carried on at this port is the furnishing of "recruits to whaling vessels, and the trade incident thereto, as limited and defined by treaty; as porte minor," no direct importations are allowed beyond those limits.

By the operation of causes growing out of the internal war in the United States, and the want of success of the whale fishery, there have been very few whaling vessels sent to this coast for the past three years, and most of those previously here have returned home; so that there has been a falling off in the number of vessels visiting this port of nearly fifty per cent. in each year. In 1861, there were eighty-three American vessels entered at this consulate; in 1862, forty-four; in 1863, twenty-five; and the number for the present year will not probably exceed one-half that of 1863. The exports to the United States are extremely limited. Since the first of September, 1863, there have been shipped from this port to New York 34 barrels whale oil, 1,082 pounds goat-skins, and 104 bullock-hides; total invoice valuation $1,006 13.

The agriculture of the district depending upon this port cannot be said to be in a prosperous condition. The experiments in the cultivation of tobacco, referred to in my last annual report, were an entire failure. Although the quantity raised was satisfactory, the quality, either from deficiencies in the soil or climate, or want of knowledge of its proper preparation for market, was so inferior that the capital and labor expended were a total loss.

The present year considerable attention has been paid to the culture of cotton, but the scarcity and high price of labor, and the comparatively small returns received, with the inferior quality of the article produced, seem to render any considerable profit extremely doubtful. The principal agricultural productions of this district have been heretofore sweet potatoes and pumpkins or squashes. These were of a very superior quality, and being afforded at a moderate price, large quantities were purchased by the American shipping. But the crops of even these have materially decreased from deterioration of the soil by continued successive plantings of the same crops. And as the only arable grounds are narrow strips on the banks of the river moistened by the annual freshets, new grounds of any great extent cannot be brought into use without expensive artificial irrigation. The crops of the articles named are said to be less than one-half what they were ten years ago, and the price more than double. But another cause has contributed materially to decrease production, and thus to enhance prices, the present year. The unusual malignancy of the diseases which prevailed during the four months following the first of April last resulted in the death of nearly one-tenth of the entire population of the district, and rendered ineffective a much larger proportion of the laborers at the time when their services were required in planting the crops.

Further explorations in the locality where indications of petroleum had been discovered, seem to have satisfied the proprietors that a sufficient quantity cannot be procured to warrant any attempt at manufacturing kerosene, and the enterprise has been abandoned.

I know of no branches of agriculture or commerce in which investments could be advantageously made in this district.

*   *   *   *   *   *   *   *

The agricultural resources of Ecuador are boundless, but neglected and embarrassed by several causes. The mountainous character of much of the country is unadapted to wagon or rail roads, and all travel and transportation are effected by horses, mules, asses, bullocks, and lamas, upon narrow paths, often worn twenty and thirty feet deep, and which, during three or four months of rainy weather, are dangerous, and in many places impassable.

In the days of the Incas the entire country was highly cultivated in all departments of industry, and filled with improvements fitted to their style of civilization. The vestiges of these witnessed during my journey, both in architecture and the arts, demonstrate this fact beyond question; and the idea is unreservedly settled in my conviction that the ancient Pagan government had effected more for the substantial interests of the country and the happiness of the people than the *de facto* government of the Roman church from the Spanish invasion to the present hour. Even the best and wealthiest of the population live, in one sense, from hand to mouth, and, amid abundant elements of independence and enjoyment, are unhappy and uncertain of their political and personal liberty. This is the chief reason why the commercial, agricultural, and mineral resources of one of the finest and most productive regions of the globe lie dormant and undeveloped.

In the interior of Ecuador I met entire communities of Indians, who were unmixed descendants of the ancient Inca race, who could understand no foreign tongue, and could only speak the Inca or Quichua language—soft and pleasing accents, which struck the ear with peculiar satisfaction.

All the Indian tribes, though differing somewhat in personal appearance, are docile, kind, and industrious, and they perform the entire labor of the agricultural districts and the menial services required by cities and towns. Under a well-organized and benign system of government they would become a most valuable element in the industrial development of that rich country.

The second field of research, which more especially invited me to explore Ecuador, is strictly scientific, and as the results of my observations may tend to increase cosmographical knowledge, I will briefly state their results. Having observed the coast of South America from 14° south latitude, and the Andes from 5° 20′ south to the equator, and carefully studied their geological characters and many of the extinct volcanoes, besides Cotopaxi, which was in a state of unusual activity, and Pichincha, which still exhibits igneous life, I have arrived at the following conclusions, viz: That the Andes, as lofty as their general configuration may be, are only the remains of vast table-lands which in former ages stretched over the western hemisphere and occupied areas now covered by the Pacific ocean; that they were never elevated or upheaved, as is generally supposed by geological writers, but, on the contrary, are, in all their irregularities, generally speaking, (exceptions to be named hereafter,) the effect of sudden and violent depressions or subsidences: that, from the fossils in my possession taken from compact silt several hundred feet below the surface of the valley of Riobamba, at the height of 9,000 feet above the sea, in the ravine of Tungshi, the fact becomes established that mastodons and other extinct animals existed upon those ancient plains, and that their extinction in South America was probably simultaneous with their extinction in Asia by the movements of vast bodies of water occasioned by a *sudden change* of axis in the rotation of the globe; that the formation of volcanoes, and the elevation of volcanic mountains (the exceptions referred to above) are comparatively late, and among the last events in the geological history of the Andes; that, as a final and grand result, our planet, considering its successive revolutions of surface, must have possessed, when vegetable and animal life was *originated*, a much greater diameter in all directions, probably from 50 to 100 miles greater, than at present, and that the changes from time to time have been on so vast a scale, by its reduction of size through sudden subsidences of surface into subterranean cavities embracing immense areas or entire hemispheres, as to produce equally sudden changes of its poles of rotation and similar movements of oceans to reach new beds.

Planets, like all other bodies in equilibrium and free to gravitate toward central points, will and must suddenly change their equilibrium and axes of rotation when the matter composing their surfaces changes its position in a similar manner.

Applying these sequences to the important geological problems that have heretofore puzzled science and required solution, all of them melt into obvious results of these great antecedent causes, and previous confusion settles into fixed law.

In the course of my journey I obtained many insects, some of which may be new to our entomologists.

While in Riobamba I ascertained from Dr. James Taylor, an English gentleman, who for many years has been acquainted with the forests of Ecuador, that the Indians employ in the cure of intermittent fevers the bark of a tree called "muravilla," in preference to the "cinchona" or "Peruvian bark," and that from the analysis of a chemist in Quito it was found to contain saline products whose efficacy possessed four times the medicinal force of quinine. While in Quito I learned that it was unknown to Professor William Jameson, the distinguished Scotch botanist residing there.

Believing a full scientific knowledge of such a tree might be of commercial value and of exceeding usefulness to the human race, I ascertained its habitat, and at the risk of limb and life, on account of rain, precipitous roads, and deep mud, visited the ridges of the Cordillera, where it grows, and, guided by an Indian, obtained sufficient bark from the tree to determine its principles and medicinal virtues, through our own chemists, on my return to the United States. I have since learned that the tree has been described by my friend Richard Spruce, esq., an eminent British botanist, who has travelled many years in this country, and recently returned to London, but I cannot ascertain that any special note has been taken of its commercial and medicinal value.   *   *   *

ARGENTINE REPUBLIC.

BUENOS AYRES—H. R. HELPER, *Consul.*

OCTOBER 15, 1864.

In the tabular statements which accompany this despatch may be found a very considerable amount of miscellaneous commercial information.
*   *   *   *   *   *   *

Some of the tables comprise information which, though not strictly commercial, seemed to me to be worthy of synoptical record in this connexion, while, on the other hand, there is an entire absence of many mercantile and other facts which I have diligently but unsuccessfully sought for.
*   *   * The average rates of freights hence to the United States are, in ordinary times, about six hard dollars per ton of forty cubic feet. The articles of merchandise which are usually shipped by this rule, that is to say, by measurement, are wool, hair, skins, and hide-cuttings. The freights on dry

and salted hides, which are, I believe, invariably shipped by weight, are generally three-fourths of one cent per pound for the dry, and three-eighths of one cent for the salted.

Whether imported or exported in Argentine bottoms or in foreign bottoms, the duties on merchandise at the custom-house in Buenos Ayres are equal.

The Argentine law requiring the payment of an export duty of ten per cent. on all the leading articles of produce shipped hence is still in force.

Mercantile transactions in Buenos Ayres are usually attended with many peculiarities, which are difficult to explain, and which, even when explained in the clearest possible manner, cannot be easily understood by persons residing far from the river Plate.

Prices of commodities here, as elsewhere, fluctuate on the bases of supply and demand.

Dry ox and cow hides are now selling in Buenos Ayres at an average of about 38 rials, of eight to the dollar of seventeen to the doubloon, for a pesada of 35 pounds, duty paid; while the average price of salted ox and cow hides at this time is about 36 rials, of eight to the dollar of seventeen to the doubloon, for a pesada of 60 pounds, subject to a duty of 10 per cent. ad valorem.

Each dry horsehide, subject to duty, averages in price about 40 dollars currency, while the present average price of each salted horsehide, also subject to duty, is about 17 rials, of eight to the dollar of sixteen to the doubloon.

The average price of wool in this market, taking the quantity and quality as it comes from an undivided flock of sheep, is at this time about 95 currency dollars per arroba of 25 pounds, subject to the export duty of 10 per cent.

The currency dollars here mentioned are worth little less than four cents each.

Jerked beef is selling here now, for exportation to Brazil and Cuba, at about 23 rials, of eight to the dollar of sixteen to the doubloon, per quintal of 100 pounds, subject to a duty of 10 per cent. ad valorem.

Weights and measures in Buenos Ayres are the same as those used in Spain.

Wool, hides, and jerked beef are the staple exports; these excepted, all the other Argentine exports are of comparative insignificance.

Frequent attempts have been made here from time to time to preserve mess beef for the European markets, but thus far every effort to that end has proved a most miserable failure. Just now, however, two gentlemen from the United States are entering extensively into the business, under an improved process, and there is much reason to hope and believe that they will ultimately meet with success.

Agriculture in this country is in a very backward condition. All the ordinary cereals, vegetables, and fruits grow well when even moderately cultivated, but as a rule the implements used in husbandry are grotesquely rude and antique, and the people, whether as employers or employés, have, it would seem, no genius for manual labor.

The Cotton-Supply Association of England, through their agents in this country, have been moving heaven and earth in their efforts to facilitate the production of cotton in the provinces of the La Plata, but all, as yet, to little or no purpose.   *   *   *   *   *   *

Two or three cotton planters, from the southern section of our own country, have recently arrived here with the intention of thoroughly testing the adaptation of certain promising portions of the territory of this country for the cultivation of cotton, and although I shall not be at all surprised to hear of the failure of their experiments, yet, owing to their better knowledge of the business, the chances of success are, I think, with them rather than with the English.

Except in the grinding of grain, and in the making of crucifixes, candy, and macaroni, there is not, to my knowledge, any manufacturing worthy of mention going on in this country.

Eight or ten wealthy American merchants reside somewhat permanently in this city, and are extensively engaged in trade between here and the United States.

Since the year 1819 only 811 American citizens have been registered in this consulate, and of these, and of others not registered, there are, perhaps, not more than 700 now residing in all the provinces of the Argentine Republic.

A census of this republic was projected several months since, but, for some unexplained reason, the government has not yet adopted the measures requisite for its completion.

The population is swollen little except by natural increase, but this is very rapid. Last year immigration, which flowed hence chiefly from Ireland and Italy, added to the population only a fraction over 10,000.

Eight diplomatic and twenty-six consular representatives of foreign nations are now stationed in the city of Buenos Ayres, which, despite much intrigue and opposition, still maintains its distinction as the capital of the Argentine Republic. Of the newspapers and periodicals of all classes published in this city, there are twenty-four; churches, twenty-six, all Catholic except one Episcopal, one Presbyterian, one Lutheran, and one Methodist. Insurance companies, native and foreign, nine or ten.   *   *   *   Wholesale merchants, 204; retail merchants, in the several departments of business, 1,034.   *   *   *

At the present time the city of Buenos Ayres, which is intersected by ninety-six streets running at right angles, and which is supposed to contain a population of about 150,000, is in a most flourishing condition. Many new and commodious houses are in process of construction, the streets are well paved, gas has been extensively introduced, wealth and fashion, for this part of the world, are in surprising prominence, and, withal, there is here a luxury and extravagance of living unequalled, perhaps, in any other part of the southern hemisphere.

Statement showing the nationality and the number of merchant vessels, with their tonnage, respectively, which entered the port of Buenos Ayres with cargoes* during the year 1862.

Nationality.	No. vessels.	Ton'ge.	Nationality.	No. vessels.	Ton'ge.
Argentine Republic.....	23	5,514	Norway.............	4	1,613
Belgium	7	1,700	Oldenburg ......·....	7	1,969
Brazil.................	38	7,829	Paraguay	1	329
Bremen	9	3,412	Portugal............	4	646
Chili.................	1	259	Prussia	4	1,021
Denmark.............	16	2,883	Russia..............	2	700
France...............	75	26,862	Spain...............	116	24,149
Great Britain	84	27,042	Sweden.............	6	1,703
Hamburg	17	3,524	United States........	105	46,644
Hanover	5	953	Uruguay............	5	1,070
Holland..............	49	10,556			
Italy.................	64	16,314	Total..........	642	186,692

* In addition to which, twenty (20) vessels under various national flags entered the port in ballast.

Statement showing the nationality and number of merchant vessels, with their tonnage, respectively, which cleared from the port of Buenos Ayres with cargoes* during the year 1862.

Nationality.	No. of vessels.	Tonnage.	Nationality.	No. of vessels.	Tonnage.
Argentine Republic	31	7,935	Norway	1	261
Austria.	1	126	Oldenburg	3	677
Belgium	7	1,901	Paraguay	1	329
Brazil	30	6,272	Portugal	4	709
Chili	1	709	Prussia	4	1,620
Denmark	24	2,663	Russia	3	1,048
France	64	22,867	Spain	96	20,436
Great Britain	83	25,953	Sweden	6	2,009
Hamburg	10	1,857	United States..........	78	35,327
Hanover	4	715	Uruguay	7	1,513
Holland	35	7,034			
Italy	63	15,008	Total..............	559	157,959
Mecklenburg	3	990			

* In addition to which, 139 vessels, under various national flags, cleared from the port in ballast.

Statement showing the official value of the imports into Buenos Ayres during the year 1862, together with the several countries whence the same were brought, and the particular amount brought from each; and also the amount of custom-house duties paid thereon.

Countries whence the imports were brought.	Official value of the imports.	Duties paid at the custom-house in Buenos Ayres.
Belgium	$7,198,711	$1,041,107
Brazil	42,075,335	7,401,763
Chili	3,781,027	705,548
Cuba	12,586,954	2,508,034
France	90,684,014	13,900,897
Germany	23,242,935	3,181,091
Great Britain	93,868,681	12,628,271
Holland	10,015,527	1,962,842
India	2,207,898	255,825
Italy	16,204,259	2,845,749
Paraguay	14,893,208	2,889,602
Portugal	202,940	10,147
Prussia	575,132	28,258
Spain	34,490,564	5,941,795
United States...............................	30,812,411	3,706,869
Uruguay....................................	40,644,633	6,983,511
Total.................................	423,474,229	65,991,299
In American gold, about.......................	16,287,470	2,538,126

IMPORTS FROM THE UNITED STATES.

Statement showing the description, quantity, and official value of the principal articles of merchandise imported into Buenos Ayres from the United States during the year 1862.

Articles.	Quantity.	Official value.
Lumber, (including masts and spars, not measured)...feet..	17,064,368	$14,454,149
Flour........quintals..	27,257	3,270,840
Provisions, assorted................	....	1,752,737
Sugar, refined...........lbs..	785,335	1,590,305
Furniture	....	1,345,913
Alcohol ....galls..	64,765	909,998
Hardware	....	898,676
Lamps	....	659,454
Drugs	....	635,335
Starch ....lbs..	360,632	632,170
Kerosene oil............galls..	20,614	463,865
Shipchandlery	....	429,416
Implements and machinery	....	381,723
Tea ....lbs..	38,324	338,101
Cotton fabrics	....	295,859
Paints	....	237,092
Boots and shoes	....	219,228
Haberdashery	....	210,021
Twine and thread ....lbs..	58,411	179,822
Candle-wick ....lbs..	39,722	177,748
Fire-crackers............boxes..	3,428	128,780
Rice............lbs..	141,260	126,100
Sundries	....	1,545,079
Total	....	30,812,411
In American gold, about................	....	1,185,092

Statement showing the principal articles of merchandise and the number or quantity of the same exported from Buenos Ayres during the fifteen years, from 1849 to 1863, respectively, and also the countries to which the exportations were made.

Countries	Year	Dry hides		Salted hides		Wool		Sheepskins		Horse-hair		Tallow and mare's grease	
		Cow.	Horse.	Cow.	Horse.	Bales.	Bags.	Bales.	Dozens.	Bales.	Serons and bags.	Pipes.	Boxes.
United States	1849	784,701	8,009	192,734	7,676	13,008	1,955	1,493	....	800¼	539	....	....
	1850	603,989	13,474	137,184	20,363	12,249	2,666	2,020	106	909	1,217	199½	....
	1851	572,109	14,037	194,471	20,363	15,749	699	1,371	....	726	356	9	....
	1852	397,433	955	106,640	25,107	7,847	194	1,185	....	1,050	1,303	1,061½	371
	1853	959,164	1,965	96,590	7,196	8,016	364	198	198	763	550	1,435	69
	1854	312,985	6,072	55,645	44,419	9,096	363	774	....	1,101	1,174	46	....
	1855	312,185	781	41,927	13,061	6,438	307	125	....	735	1,190	....	....
	1856	300,519	1,377	59,819	91,035	6,065	35	191	....	1,040	294	20	500
	1857	292,758	1,011	16,518	31,125	8,494½	535	36	....	537	541	960	....
	1858	418,596	5,199	2,349	20,581	6,494½	585	49	....	559	463	....	....
	1859	501,237	2,085	22,318	9,576	11,776	257	60	....	708	561	1	2
	1860	301,560	1,369	735	623	13,157	352	80	....	870	40	....	....
	1861	131,569	910	1,007	....	5,759	974	39	....	983	902	....	....
	1862	408,413	1,995	....	1,910	16,446	53	380	....	683	175	....	....
	1863	594,888	1,945	5,348	....	23,239	169	50	....	599	....	....	....
Great Britain	1849	33,494	9,989	517,386	195,045	4,898	1,070	989	....	1,339	495	17,130	37,050
	1850	25,843	3,660	387,998	102,865	1,391	386	339	....	960	673	11,055	17,337
	1851	48,698	1,564	547,840	57,303	999	970	444	....	1,171	354	19,265	4,095
	1852	11,503	1,290	363,114	53,005	3,946	379	313	....	897	909	23,950	7,609
	1853	33,999	6,937	285,577	106,656	5,584	1,197	754	....	914	738	16,978	3,644
	1854	9,990	407	263,321	67,738	5,120	1,925	850	18	1,192	999	30,951	8,929
	1855	8,982	8,532	196,481	63,490	1,046½	151	647	8	1,140	533	9,004½	698
	1856	53,983	8,532	222,950	91,543	4,919	31	1,948	....	676	128	9,426	742
	1857	8,343	14,701	213,354	64,949	5,999	59	1,594	....	885	254	9,763½	8,887
	1858	17,069	16,095	322,715	91,543	6,685	....	1,831	3	1,451	1,190	9,954	3,778
	1859	5,973	10,901	980,686	86,168	3,039½	989½	1,007	....	1,631	....	13,954½	5,077
	1860	17,516	2,953	226,535	172,716	2,040	1,907	2,257	11½	1,133	366	12,106	5,947
	1861	17,965	96,655	130,406	92,692	5,892	763	703	....	1,704	699	8,911	6,788
	1862	54,253	11,909	255,970	138,009	7,806	1,163	9,911	....	736	873	6,355	4,232
	1863				100,722	10,384	600	2,101	40		116		
France	1849	944,808	7,997	79,708	144	3,357	7	1,682	....	686	96	812	6,449
	1850	397,729	3,191	85,308	7,254	3,035	63	1,168	....	897	857	394	2,745
	1851	188,390	1,285	90,344	10,416	671	....	1,439	....	873	979	369	755
	1852	189,198	1,989	87,692	4,713	3,639	....	2,280	....	451	130	288	319
	1853	62,978	1,461	44,583	4,497	4,658	56	2,376	....	927	503	563	646
	1854	90,455	1,066	48,979	21,763	3,899	2	3,054	....	339	68	144	1,608

Statement showing the principal articles of merchandise and the number or quantity of the same exported from Buenos Ayres, during the fifteen years from 1849 to 1863, respectively, &c.—Continued.

Countries	Years	Dry hides Cow.	Dry hides Horse.	Salted hides Cow.	Salted hides Horse.	Wool Bales.	Wool Bags.	Sheepskins Bales.	Sheepskins Dozens.	Horse-hair Bales.	Horse-hair Serons and bags.	Tallow and mare's grease Pipes.	Boxes.
France—Continued	1855	104,073	1,971	30,639	96,643	8,250	4	4,737	52½	623½	104	167	928
	1856	71,867	5,683	36,745	36,502	8,018	133	4,250	43	634	119	617½	1,065
	1857	84,953	21,086	47,689	74,080	4,642½	12	4,444	80	1,156	575	1,389½	1,905
	1858	83,230	15,366	40,684	94,982	13,139	117	5,744		999	67	188	569
	1859	83,744	28,996	55,186	11,704	13,339½	180	8,900		587	12	708½	474
	1860	167,072	18,498	43,937	33,653	14,040	274	7,165		654	158	1,909½	1,482
	1861	139,869	12,549	47,005	40,539	16,310	194	7,719		759	144	871	3,108
	1862	135,291	10,950	96,658	94,784	13,391	49	8,656		676	190	1,890	5,960
	1863	96,192	12,982	59,437	14,303	19,957	197	10,458		1,258	14	2,824	7,748
Germany, Holland, and Belgium	1849	613,416	750	81,678	224	1,119	164	37		341	77	182½	989
	1850	535,353	941	67,195	107	1,954	143	10		479	55	385	975
	1851	589,639	9,051	85,545	560	770	3	13		386	19	105½	40
	1852	374,394	2,041	94,553	1,554	2,873	487			103		280	524
	1853	948,440	690	34,078	4,298	3,176	9	16		138	10	162	4
	1854	285,686	4,944	52,541	11,066	3,011	3	38		394	34	983	3
	1855	189,772	1,139	50,529	16,176	7,962	69	510		366	19	277	665
	1856	900,668	9,206	91,983	22,766	14,796	76	1,787		305	308	553½	1,360
	1857	907,298	12,983	93,597	6,795	13,404	4	452		947	50	1,494½	
	1858	942,921	3,134	41,539	1,090	13,140	946	91	6	90	9	4	50
	1859	250,052	8,100	89,104	6,341	15,729½	507	927		594	9	365	928
	1860	373,798	8,684	98,955	6,820	15,373	344	248		353	13	1,024	813
	1861	288,363	9,883	77,305	2,957	31,998	490	284		465	7	1,843½	564
	1862	384,480	3,959	171,595	15,391	33,543	33	598		443	97	3,070½	728
	1863	166,283		63,458				787				4,934	
Italy	1849	11,523	18,380	4,949	16,636	243	53	5		145	138	37	34
	1850	131,123	2,630	66,648	80	695	158	44	8	41	963	9	1,994
	1851	135,980	13,787	55,417		683	304	54	43	11	931	44	949
	1852	175,674		74,417		585	74	14		48	405	159½	378
	1853	89,357	1,600	52,113	791	469	11	52		98	98	137	573
	1854	76,605	4,270	13,763	1,945	9,234		70		47	158	994½	1,350
	1855	98,915	4,399	32,370	2,096	706	101	401		50	155	144	3,325
	1856	74,798	5,997	93,382	3,967	983	3	118		71	339	171½	3,877
	1857	71,867	5,477	85,219	13,383	963	35	38		43	236	4	3,310
	1858	194,865	5,628	33,680	3,889	713	34	139	12	47	218	404½	1,929
	1859	83,627	6,667	10,600	4,298	617	59	7			397	39	2,253
	1860	170,879		8,994	18,035								4,174

	1861	1862	1863
Spain	1,846	2,759	328

	1849	1850	1851	1852	1853	1854	1855	1856	1857	1858	1859	1860	1861	1862	1863
Totals of each year	40,683	50,523	47,005	91,403	14,589	29,973	28,787	26,547	28,815	65,300	65,364	47,647	65,447	38,333	

Exportations from Buenos Ayres to Brazil, to Cuba, and to ports on the coast of the Pacific.

Years	BRAZIL. Dry and salted hides.	CUBA. Dry and salted hides.	BRAZIL. Jerked beef.	CUBA. Jerked beef.	BRAZIL. Tallow and mare's grease.		BRAZIL. Tallow and mare's grease.		PACIFIC PORTS.* Tallow and mare's grease.	
			Quintals.	Quintals.	Pipes.	Bozas.	Pipes.	Bozas.	Pipes.	Bozas.
1849	32,798	6,694	948,098	305,450	457	402		1,831	33¼	7,097
1850	7,746	3,522	138,720	254,011	7½	150		1,757		5,800
1851	1,506	4,069	160,958	270,915	28¾	238	90	2,168	14	7,094
1852	2,759	2,019	234,985	295,095	478½	290		2,101	56	3,635
1853	2,176	1,623	129,431	206,184	993			643		2,309
1854	1,818	1,908	81,645	241,414	1,797	449	98	911		2,384
1855	2,579	1,069	126,617	150,889½	2,037 5-6	3,921	63	1,958	9¾	5,852
1856	1,278	1,623	97,565	189,736	2,210	693	18	580	118	491
1857	1,195	1,054	100,447½	237,302	1,213		18	940		1,300
1858	3,725	1,556	117,409	166,191½	1,004	546	971	884		3,399
1859	2,069	2,735	98,284	384,028½	427	291	129	1,348	363	3,374
1860	3,054	2,829	98,854½	312,648½	701	849	453½	1,166		1,195
1862	3,009	1,690	169,559½	129,533	129¾	68	69	567		551
1863	2,967	2,419	145,397	225,194	18	95		2,202		2,027
	1,565	2,980	98,455	923,878½	349½	303		1,640	150¾	

* Also during the year 1863, to ports on the Pacific, 30 dry hides and 2,300 quintals of jerked beef.

VALUE OF EXPORTS.

Statement showing the official value of Argentine and Buenos Ayrean exports during the year 1862, together with the several countries which received the same, and the particular amount received by each.

Countries which received the exports.	Official value of the exports from the Argentine republic, including those from Buenos Ayres.	Official value of the exports exclusively from Buenos Ayres.
Belgium	$100,019,735	$88,215,380
Brazil	5,578,840	5,297,560
Chili	34,810	34,810
Cuba	8,636,605	8,537,880
France	61,631,563	52,670,145
Germany	1,410,450	1,406,360
Great Britain	59,406,053	43,884,445
Holland	6,254,680	5,908,800
Italy	15,342,955	8,358,752
Paraguay	38,820	38,820
Spain	17,152,987	5,647,740
United States	64,135,978	37,128,780
Uruguay	2,138,790	2,101,760
Total	341,782,266	259,431,232
In American gold, about	13,130,087	9,978,128

DUTIES PAID AT THE CUSTOM-HOUSE.

Statement showing the amount of duties levied and collected at the custom-house in Buenos Ayres during the year 1862 on imports and exports, respectively.

Countries.	Duties on imports.	Duties on exports.	Total duties.
Belgium	$1,041,107	$4,410,664	$5,451,771
Brazil	7,401,763	264,868	7,666,631
Chili	705,548	1,740	707,288
Cuba	2,508,031	426,894	2,934,925
France	13,900,897	2,624,372	16,525,269
Germany	3,181,091	70,318	3,251,409
Great Britain	12,628,270	2,188,188	14,816,458
Holland	1,962,842	295,430	2,258,272
India	255,825	....	255,825
Italy	2,845,749	416,967	3,262,716
Paraguay	2,889,601	1,941	2,891,542
Portugal	10,147	....	10,147
Prussia	28,258	....	28,258
Spain	5,941,785	282,362	6,224,147
United States	3,706,865	1,841,599	5,548,464
Uruguay	6,983,511	104,600	7,088,111
	65,991,290	12,929,943	79,921,233
Additional duties on imports and exports	7,108,955	10,383,160	17,492,115
Sundry duties from various sources	1,930,303	147,138	2,077,441
Totals, city of Buenos Ayres	75,030,548	23,460,241	98,490,789
Miscellaneous duties, including those collected at the custom-house in San Nicholas	....	....	19,528,512
Grand total, province of Buenos Ayres	....	....	118,019,301
In American gold, about	....	....	11,539,204

EXPENSES OF ENTRANCE AND CLEARANCE. (A.)

Statement showing the ordinary charges which attend the entrance and clearance of a merchant vessel of 1,000 tons, drawing eighteen feet, in the port of Buenos Ayres, September 30, 1864.

Entrance.

Pilotage* from Point Indio $150 00
Light dues, Point Indio and Ortiz bank 62 50
Entry at custom-house 10 75
                            $223 25

Clearance.

Stamps for opening register for loading 10 00
Clearing from the custom-house and from the office of the captain of the port 14 50
Light dues, English bank and Lobos island 62 50
Pilotage down the river 75
                            162 00

*Although the rates of pilotage here given are those fixed by the regular tariff, yet shipmasters meeting rival pilots are often piloted on terms more favorable to the owners of the vessels.

Consular fees.

1,000 tons, at 1 cent	$10 00	
Two certificates for entry, $2 each	4 00	
Deposit of register	2 00	
Spanish roll	2 00	
Recording crew	50	
		$18 50
Total in gold or silver		403 75

EXPENSE OF ENTRANCE AND CLEARANCE. (B.)

Statement showing the ordinary charges which attend the entrance and clearance of a merchant vessel of 500 tons, drawing fifteen feet, in the port of Buenos Ayres, September 30, 1864.

Entrance.

Pilotage* from Point Indio	$90 00	
Light dues, Point Indio and Ortiz bank	31 25	
Entry at the custom-house	10 75	
		$132 00

Clearance.

Stamps for opening register for loading	10 00	
Clearing from the custom-house and from the office of the captain of the port	14 50	
Light dues, English bank and Lobos island	31 25	
Pilotage down the river	45 00	
		100 75

Consular fees.

500 tons, at one cent	5 00	
Two certificates for entry, $2 each	4 00	
Deposit of register	2 00	
Spanish roll	2 00	
Recording crew	50	
		13 50
Total in gold or silver		246 25

*Although the rates of pilotage here given are those fixed by the regular tariff, yet shipmasters meeting rival pilots are often piloted on terms more favorable to the owners of the vessels.

H. Ex. Doc. 60——53

RAILROADS.

Statement showing the number of miles of railroad in actual operation, and the number of miles of railroads projected or in course of construction, in the Argentine Republic September 30, 1864.*

Name of railway.	Most distant points or places connected or proposed to be connected.	Miles projected.	Miles in operation.	Capital subscribed, in £'s stg.	Government guarantee.		
					Maximum cost not to exceed—	Term of years.	Rate of Int.
							p.c
Western Buenos Ayres..	Buenos Ayers and Mercedes..	62½	43	£500,000	....	..	..
Northern Buenos Ayres..	Buenos Ayres & San Fernando	17	17	250,000	£150,000	20	7
Southern Buenos Ayres..	Buenos Ayres and Chascomas	75	..	750,000	700,000	40	7
Buenos Ayres & Eusevada	Buenos Ayres and Eusevada..	30	..	Comp. not formed	......(†)......	..	..
Central Argentine........	Rosario and Cordova........	247	..	1,600,000	6,400 per mile.	40	7
Eastern Argentine	Concordia and Mercedes......	200	..	Comp. not formed	13,353 per mile	40	7

* There are, I regret to have to say, no canals nor telegraphs in this country. † No guarantee granted.

REMARKS.

The four first lines of railways in this list are in the province of Buenos Ayres. The fifth is in the province of Santa Fe and Cordova. The sixth is in the provinces of Entre Rios and Corrientes.

First line. This line belongs to the province of Buenos Ayres. Two branches are now spoken of—one to Chivilcoy, thirty-six miles from Mercedes, westward; the other to Navarro and Lobos. The western line is soon to be offered for sale for £500,000, cash down.

Second line. A bill for the prolongation of this line to Zarate has already passed the legislature. Zarate is on the river Parana.

Third line. This line may be lengthened on the same terms to Dolores, sixty miles southward, whenever the government desires it.

Fourth line. Although no company has yet been formed, the concessionaire is now building the first section to the Boca and Banacas, a distance of about four miles.

Fifth line. This company has a free grant of three miles of land on each side of the line, and also the preference to go to the Andes and to the Pacific.

Sixth line. Concordia is on the Uruguay, about 270 miles from Buenos Ayres; and Mercedo is in the province of Corrientes. This line is to be divided into two sections, at Monte Caseros; and the second section will not be undertaken until the first shall have earned an income of three and a half per cent. net.

Statement showing the nationality and number of foreign vessels arrived at and departed from Buenos Ayres from or to the United States for the quarter ended March 31, 1864, together with a description and value of the inward and outward cargoes.

INWARD CARGOES.

Nationality.	No. of vessels.	Description.	Value.
Bremen...........	1	179,821 ft. spruce and pine..................	$5,300
England...........	1	22 boxes chains, 1 bale medicines, and sundries.	750
Do...............	1	230,558 feet pine..........................	7,000
Do...............	1	84,025 feet lumber, 272 boxes starch, and sundries.	4,200
Do...............	1	171,441 ft. pine, 88,787 ft. spruce, and sundries.	7,020
Do...............	1	184,294 ft. pine, 61,723 ft. spruce...........	4,299
Do...............	1	540,040 ft. lumber, 10 boxes merchandise....	10,320
Denmark.........	1	127,156 ft. lumber, 100 kegs nails, and sundries.	4,500
Belgium..........	1	2,241 pieces lumber, 500 boxes kerosene oil, and sundries.	6,500
Total.........	9	Total imports in foreign vessels.........	49,889
		Total imports in American vessels.......	173,612
		Total inward.......................	223,501

OUTWARD CARGOES.

Nationality.	No of vessels.	Description.	Value.
England..........	1	759 bales wool, 11,896 dry hides.............	$156,665
Hamburg........	1	692 bales wool, 2,000 dry hides.............	101,850
Holland...........	1	273 bales wool, 1,001 dry hides, 17 bales sheep-skins.	44,741
Denmark.........	1	290 bales wool, 1,500 dry hides.............	43,585
Italy..............	1	20,234 dry hides, 288 bales wool, 26 bales nutria-skins, and sundries.	105,242
England..........	1	13,656 dry hides, 479 bales wool, 28 bales goat-skins, and sundries.	127,415
Holland..........	1	215 bales wool, 600 dry hides..............	30,904
Do.............	1	344 bales wool, 71 dry hides..............	36,092
England..........	1	448 bales wool, 2,000 dry hides.............	69,929
Do.............	1	10,900 dry hides, 298 bales and 1 bag of wool, 2,227 carpincho skins, and sundries.	73,833
Holland...........	1	350 bales wool, 500 dry ox and cow hides....	40,920
England..........	1	11,000 dry hides, 459 bales wool, 23 bales goat-skins, 1,500 river hog-skins.	96,957
Argentine Republic.	1	620 bales wool, 3,670 dry hides.............	89,946
England..........	1	104 bales wool, 3,793 dry hides.............	24,426
Do.............	1	1,500 dry hides, 140 bales wool.............	65,838
Do.............	1	616 bales wool, 18,532 dry hides.............	138,041
Do.............	1	22,392 dry hides, 191 bales, 11 ceroons and 16 packages wool, and sundries.	104,953
Do.............	1	575 bales wool, 10,363 dry hides.............	111,677
Denmark..........	1	211 bales wool, 600 dry hides..............	32,958
England..........	1	258 bales wool, 2,523 dry hides, 49 bales hair, 3 bales nutria-skins.	52,676
Denmark..........	1	275 bales wool, 1,000 dry hides.............	43,054
Hanover..........	1	347 bales wool, 560 dry hides..............	45,780
Prussia...........	1	326 bales wool, 9,730 dry hides.............	76,750
Argentine Republic.	1	610 bales wool, 6,450 dry hides.............	94,117

OUTWARD CARGOES—Continued.

Nationality.	No. of vessels.	Description.	Value.
Denmark..........	1	238 bales wool, 12 bales nutria skins, 500 dry hides.	$33,822
Hamburg	1	436 bales wool, 2,000 dry hides..............	63,237
England	1	4,515 dry hides, 352 bales wool, 28 bales hair, and sundries.	61,821
Italy..............	1	7,600 dry hides, 564 bales wool, 1 bale goat-skins, 1 bale sheepskins.	108,944
Hanover	1	290 bales wool......................	34,346
Argentine Republic.	1	358 bales wool, 3,000 dry hides, 65 bales and 1 package of hair, and 2 bales feathers.	52,960
England	1	594 bales wool, 2,920 dry hides	90,091
Do	1	572 bales wool, 5,955 dry hides.............	99,934
Do	1	708 bales wool, 1,215 dry hides.............	94,391
Italy	1	402 bales wool, 9,318 dry hides, 169 dry kips, 19 cases feathers.	80,213
England	1	223 bales wool, 11,178 dry hides.............	61,130
Do	1	620 bales wool, 8,635 dry hides, 18 bales goat-skins	114,961
Argentine Republic.	1	467 bales wool, 4,915 dry hides..............	76,060
Total	37	Total exports in foreign vessels............	2,780,259
		Total exports in American vessels.,........	253,154
			3,033,413
		Total inward in foreign and American vessels.	223,501
		Excess of exports.......................	2,809,912

Statement showing the nationality and number of foreign vessels arrived at and departed from Buenos Ayres from or to the United States for the quarter ended June 30, 1864, together with a description and value of the inward and outward cargoes.

INWARD CARGOES.

Nationality.	No. of vessels.	Description.	Value.
Denmark..........	1	78 boxes sawing machines, and sundries......	$4,000
England	1	173,548 feet lumber, 37,500 shingles	3,528
Do	1	211,500 feet spruce......	6,100
Do	1	222,591 feet lumber, 5,440 pickets, and sundries.	5,440
Argentine Republic.	1	652 barrels flour, 30,863 ft. oak, 188,138 ft. pine, and sundries.	44,140
England	1	2,198 pieces lumber, 80 boxes shoes, and sundries.	8,012
Argentine Republic.	1	2,739 barrels and 300 half barrels flour........	19,000
Hamburg	1	164,278 feet pine boards, 31,148 feet planks, and sundries.	12,079
	8	Total in foreign vessels..................	102,299
		Imports in American vessels	10,015
		Total inward......................	112,314

OUTWARD CARGOES.

Nationality.	No. of vessels.	Description.	Value.
Holland	1	517 bales wool, 4,999 dry hides, 1 bale feathers.	$84,565
Bremen	1	8,071 dry hides, 283 bales and 8 ceroons wool, 3,728 wild pig-skins, and 2 bales nutria-skins.	40,637
England..........	1	401 bales, 37 ceroons and 2 bags wool, 4,855 dry hides.	53,386
Do	1	504 bales wool, 23 bales goat-skins, 1,149 dry kip-skins, 120 chiquas wool, and sundries.	83,697
Holland..........	1	10,402 dry hides, 66 bales wool, 4 bales nutria-skins, 5 bales hair, and sundries.	44,629
Argentine Republic.	1	457 bales and 3 bags wool, 41 bales hair, 5,819 dry hides, and sundries.	88,861
England.	1	9,584 dry hides, 164 bales and 5 packages wool, and sundries.	67,410
Do	1	4,984 dry hides, 280 bales and 22 chiquas wool.	59,224
Do	1	379 bales wool, 557 kip-skins, 3,502 dry hides, 2 bales feathers.	64,452
Argentine Republic.	1	551 bales and 7 ceroons wool, 2,432 dry hides..	89,942
England	1	9,025 dry hides, 364 bales wool, 33 bales goat-skins, and sundries.	128,145
Do	1	11,366 dry hides, 102 bales wool, 1,000 dry horse-hides, 5 bales nutria-skins.	54,746
	12	Total exports in foreign vessels	859,694
		Total exports in American vessels.........	149,760
			1,009,454
		Total inward...........................	112,314
		Excess of exports......................	897,140

The total number of the principal flouring mills in the city and province of Buenos Ayres, September 30, 1864, was 21, at a cost of $39,500,000, in currency, or, in American gold, about $1,519,231.

The total number of immigrants that arrived in Buenos Ayres during the six years from 1858 to 1863, inclusive, were as follows:

1858	4,654	1861	6,301
1859	4,735	1862	6,716
1860	5,656	1863	10,258

The total number of American vessels sold at Buenos Ayres since January, 1862, is 17; total tonnage, 6,309.

PART II.

NAVIGATION AND COMMERCE

OF THE

UNITED STATES WITH FOREIGN COUNTRIES

DURING THE

YEAR ENDED SEPTEMBER 30, 1864.

NAVIGATION AND COMMERCE OF THE UNITED STATES WITH FOREIGN COUNTRIES DURING THE YEAR ENDED SEPTEMBER 30, 1864.

[MADE UP FROM CONSULAR RETURNS.]

COUNTRY, CONSULATE, NAME OF CONSUL, AND DATE OF RETURNS.	VESSELS.				CARGOES.						
	ENTERED.		CLEARED.		INWARD.				OUTWARD.		
	No.	Where from.	No.	Where for.	No.	Description.	Value.	No.	Description.	Value.
BRITISH DOMINIONS. LIVERPOOL—*T. H. Dudley.* Quarter ended December 31, 1863.*	31	In port	12	New York	12	Before reported		7	Gen eral merchandise	
			2	Boston	2	do		3	Salt	
			1	Bath	1	do		2	Coal and salt	
			1	Gibraltar	1	do		1	Salt	
			1	Point de Galle	1	do		1	Coal	
			1	Rangoon	1	do		1	Salt, rin, coal	
			8	Sold	8	do		3	Coal	
			5	In port	5	do		8	Sold	
								5	In port	
	30	New York	21	New York	30	9813 tons flour, 1,599,474 bushels and 33,851 bags grain, 43 packages tallow, 700 barrels ore, 35 090 staves, 90 casks steel, 230 drs cedar, 1,190½ tons logwood, 83 logs mahogany, 47 ales rags, 105 ales cotton, 756 cases sewing machines, 181 barrels paper clay, 2,300 boxes prepared corn, 4,226 sacks and 320 barrels oil cake, 1,131 bags pem, 1,513 boxes cake, 30 half-chests tea.		21	In port	
			2	Cardiff				1	General	
			6	In port				2	Ballast	
								6	In port	
	9	Portland	1	New ork }	9	83,351 pieces deals, battens, beds, &c., 10,934 pieces d-als, 4,970 battens, 3,368 planks, 24,825 palings.		1	Coals	
			1	In port }				1	In port	
	8	St. John, N. B.	5	New York	8	185,673 pieces d-als, 13,263 pieces boards, 22 202 pieces scantling, 99,406 pieces deal ends, 46,000 palings.		5	General merchandise	
			2	Sold				2	Sold	
			1	In port				1	In port	
	1	Glasgow Dock	1	Havana	1	Ballast		1	Coals and iron	
	2	St. George, N. B.	1	Boston	2	66,769 pieces deals, battens, and ends, 8,000 palings.		2	General merchandise	
			1	In port.				1	In port	
	1	Dublin	1	Sold	1	Ballast		1	Sold	
	1	Bangor	1	New York	1	573,828 feet drain, 11,926 feet deal ends, 174,399 feet lair.		1	General merchandise	
	3	Fleetwood	1	Sold	1	Ballast		1	Sold	
			2	In port	2	do		2	In port	

1	Londonderry	New York	...do...
2	Callao	In port	2,816 tons and 1,600 casks guano
3	San Francisco	New York	56,542 sacks 125,905 bushels wheat, 170 packages, 99 casks, and 27 tierces tallow, 24 bales wool, 85 packages ore, 192 barrels and 132 sacks copper ore, 47 sacks silver ore
		Sold	19,300 bags rice
1	Manimain	In port	50,675 bags rice
3	(jhb)	Sold	
2	Rangoon	Port	47,598 bags ho, 229 pieces teak timber
1	Bucktanche	New York	6,486 deals, 1,759 ends, 1,610 deal scantlings, 2,339 deal boards
2	Shediac	In port	23,377 pieces deals and battens, 13,717 pieces deals and scantling, 2,736 pieces deal ends
1	Rockland	Sold	13,776 pieces deals, 1,054 pieces deal ends, 25,540 pieces palings, 10,800 laths
1	Port Louis	In port	104 tea planks, 21,235 nige rice, 1,000 nige tah
1	Bassein	...do...	2630 bags rice
1	Alicante	...do...	348,703 kilos Ex opio gm, 1 package raisins, 1 package figs, 1 package almonds
1	Point de Preaux	Wrecked	Put ask
1	Put back disabled	In port	
100		100	

30	In port	Calcutta	Before reported
		Aden	...do...
10		Valparaiso	...do...
1		Calders	...do...
1		Cardiff	...do...
1		Bath	...do...
1		Baltimore	...do...
1		In port	...do...
1		Sold	...do...
3		New York	1,246,359 bushels wheat, 39,065 bags wheat, 93,697 barrels flour, 2,553 bushels peas, 2,526 bags peas, 300 barrels paper clay, 9,107 boxes and 301 barrels bacon, 2,559 tierces and 18 barrels beef, 160 firkins butter, 19,542 boxes cheese, 100 barrels and 1 cask bams, contents unknown, 2 casks bams
7		Cardiff	
21	New York	In port	
1		Sold	
16			
39	New York	39	

Disposition column:
General merchandise — 1
In port — 2
General merchandise — 3
In port — 1
Sold — 1
In port — 2
General merchandise — 1
In port — 2
Sold — 1
In port — 1
...do. — 1
...do. — 1
Wrecked — 1
In port — 1
100

Salt — 4
General — 9
Coal — 4
Coal, salt, and etc. — 1
Ballast — 2
In port — 3
Sold — 7

General merchandise — 21
Ballast — 1
Sold — 1
In port — 16

Quarter ended Mar. 31, 1864†.

* Entered: 62 ships, 7 barks—69, and 31 in port. Cleared: 50 ships, 2 barks—52, 17 sold, 1 wrecked, and 30 in port. Aggregate tonnage entered, 76,017.
† Entered: 56 ships, 1 bark—57, and 30 in port. Cleared: 46 ships, 1 bark—47, 9 sold and 39 in port. Aggregate tonnage entered, 70,769.

Navigation and commerce of the United States with foreign countries—British Dominions.

COUNTRY, CONSULATE, NAME OF CONSUL, AND DATE OF RETURN.	VESSELS.				CARGOES.					
	ENTERED.		CLEARED.		INWARD.			OUTWARD.		
	No.	Where from.	No.	Where for.	No.	Description.	Value.	No.	Description.	Value.
Quarter ended March 31, 1864—Continued.										
	1	Amsterdam	1	Sold	1	200 oars, 100 tierces lard, 123 hogsheads tallow, 258 packages and 447 barrels tallow, 866 sacks and 90 bags oil cake, 196 hogsheads and 14 tierces sugar, 35 bales and 44 bags rags, 110 tons copper ore, 650 barrels copper ore, 125 barrels chrome ore, 175 bags cotton seed, 648 tons logwood, 45,840 hogshead staves, 5,551 bundles laths, 1,130 pieces oak plank.		1	Sold	
	1	Chanaral	1	In port	1	Ballast.		1	In port	
	1	Akyb	1	Havana	1	56,566 quintals copper ore		1	Coal	
	1	Howland's Island	1	In port	1	9,000 bags rice		1	In port	
	2	St. John, N. B.	2	...do...	2	850 tons guano		2	...do...	
						53,185 pieces deals and battens, 12,283 pieces deal ends, 21,352 pieces boards.				
	1	New river	1	...do...	1	23,195 pieces deal ends and battens		1	...do...	
	1	Newburyport	1	New York	1	Ballast		1	General merchandise	
	7	San Francisco	6	Rio de Janeiro	7	122,640 sacks and 52,849 bags wheat, 763 casks tallow, 943 sacks copper ore, 1,115 barrels and 22 sacks ore, 51 bales wool.		6	Coal	
				In port					In port	
	2	Philadelphia	1	Philadelphia	2	77,542 bushels wheat, 74 hogsheads bark, 1,171 barrels flour, 296 barrels pork, 6 hogsheads leaf tobacco, 260 bags cotton seed.		1	General cargo	
				In port				1	In port	
	1	St. John via New York.	1	...do...	1	33,259 pieces deals and deal ends, 11,000 palings.		1	...do...	
	87		87		87			87		
Quarter ended June 30, 1864*.	20	In port	20	New York	20	Before reported		18	General merchandise	
	14		1	Philadelphia	1	...do...		1	General cargo	
			3	Boston	3	...do...		1	Coal	
			1	Calcutta	1	...do...		1	Salt	
			6	Sold	6	...do...		3	General cargo	
			3	In port	3	...do...		1	Salt and soda ash	
								6	Salt	
								3	Sold	
								3	In port	

37	New York	26	New York	37,010 bags wheat, 644,740 bushels wheat, 30,546 barrels flour, 31,318 boxes bacon, 100 tierces beef, 2,434 barrels pork, 59,087 pieces deals, 2,340 hogshead staves, 72 bales cotton, 1,400 ship knees, 292 barrels copper ore, 277 bags clover seed, 221 hogsheads tallow, 18 casks, 227 barrels, 24 tierces tallow, 100 tierces lard, 121 hogsheads tobacco, 29 bales rags, 25 bales wool, 675 barrels prepared corn, 1,600 coils rope, 9,371 pieces boards, 5,795 pieces scantling, 222 bushels peas, 8 cases mouldings, 216 bales gunny cloth, 1,691 bags bark, 7 hogsheads bark, 73 tons logwood.	26	General cargo
		9	In port	198,441 bushels wheat, 4,512 bags wheat, 977 boxes bacon, 1,750 barrels flour, 372 barrels pork, 27,662 bushels peas, 584 horse hides, 3,600 pipe staves.	9	In port
1	Calcutta	2	Sold	Sold. 3,387 barrels jute, 3,411 bags rice, 9,512 bags linseed, 364 bags poppy seed.	2	Sold
		1	New York		1	Coal
7	San Francisco	2	Boston	102,543 bags and 53,792 bush. wheat, 2,855 bags flour, 1,136 half sacks flour, 296 casks and 98 boxes tallow, 40 bales wool.	5	General cargo
		2	New York			
		1	Rio Janeiro			
2	New Orleans	2	New York	72 bags and 67 bales cotton.	2	In port
1	Baltimore	1	Balt ... re	17 hogsheads tobacco, 1,686 barrels flour.	2	General cargo
		1	do.		1	do.
2	Baker's Island	1	Boston	1,600 tons guano	1	In port
		1	In port		1	General cargo
1	Howland's Island	1	New York	1,900 do.	2	do.
3	Philadelphia	2	Philadel pia	30,678 bushels wheat, 377 bags clover seed, 18 tierces hams, 18 casks tallow, 3 barrels flour, 50 tierces beef, 94 tierces lard, 1 box books.		
1	Maulmain	1	In port	Teak timber, 700 bags cutch.	1	In port
1	Rangoon	1	Sold	20,005 bags rice	1	Sold
2	St. John	2	In port	14,418 deals and battens, 1,726 pieces deal ends, 418 pieces scantling.	1	In port
			do.		2	General cargo
92		92			92	

* Entered: 57 ships, 1 bark—58, and 34 in port. Cleared: 64 ships, 10 sold, in port 18. Aggregate tonnage entered, 73,022.

Navigation and commerce of the United States with foreign countries—British Dominions.

COUNTRY, CONSULATE, NAME OF CONSUL, AND DATE OF RETURNS.	VESSELS				CARGOES					
	ENTERED.		CLEARED.		INWARD.			OUTWARD.		
	No.	Where from.	No.	Where for.	No.	Description.	Value.	No.	Description.	Value.
Quarter ended September 30, 1864.*	21	In port	3	Sold	3	Before reported		3	Sold	
			3	In port	3	do		3	In port	
			11	New York	7	do		7	General cargo	
					2	do		2	do	
					2	do		2	Salt	
					1	do		1	General coal	
	47	New York	2	Philadelphia	1	do		1	Coal	
			1	Rangoon	47	1,462,223 bush. wheat, 114,496 bags ditto, 41,699 bbls. flour, 4,745 bbls. copper ore, 244½ tons ditto, 597 tcs. beef, 1,151 pcs. timber, 29,229 pcs. tas, 137 hhds. and 15 bbl. tallow, 22,483 sacks oil-cake, 225 bales cotton, 496 sacks linseed cake, 842 bales gunny cloth, 1,860 bales hemp, 1,019 bbls. crude, and 1,600 bbls. refined petroleum, 406 hhds. tobacco, 18,369 bush. and 2,187 bags peas, 700 sewing machines, 2,574 boxes clocks, 5 bales wool, 2,276 tcs lard, 229,674 bush. and 3,223 bags corn, 74,222 bush. and 5,337 bags Indian corn, 500 tons logwood.		30	General cargo	
			1	Boston				4	do	
			26	New York				1	Coal, iron, and salt	
			21	In port				1	Salt	
								21	In port	
	3	San Francisco	1	Boston	3	95,362 bags wheat, 92 sacks lead ore, 258 bags copper ore, 42 boxes and 11 casks tallow, 1 bbl. jeweller's sweepings.		1	General cargo	
			2	Singapore				2	Coals	
	3	Philadelphia	3	Philadelphia	3	61,684 bush. wheat, 1,145½ bush. Indian corn, 63 hhds. quercitron bark, 7,755 bbls. flour, 363 bags oil cake, 286 casks tallow, 100,000 locust tree nails, 105 tcs. lard.		2	General cargo	
								1	In port	
	1	Quebec	1	do	1	3,934 pcs. staves, 15 cords hemlock lathwood, 3,168 pcs. deals.		1	General cargo	
	5	Rangoon	1	In port	5	87,276 bags rice, 937 dry hides, 3,502 bags and 315 boxes cutch.		5	In port	
	13	St. John's, N. B.	1	Cardiff	13	83 tons copper, 9,934 pieces staves, 415,034 pcs. deals, 286,600 palings, 329 boxes preserved lobsters.		1	To Cardiff for cargo	
			1	Genoa				1	Coal	
			1	Bath				1	do	
			1	New York				1	Salt	
			1	Sold				1	Sold	
			8	In port				8	In port	

3	Akyab	3	...do	3
1	Camden, Me	1	51,654 bags rice, 550 bags linseed, 2,996 bundles rattans.	1
1	Cuba	1	12,754 spruce deals, 1,833 deal ends, 9,980 palings, 521 pcs. deals.	...do
1	St. George, N. B.	1	557 hhds., 56 tcs., 21 bbls. molasses, 14,792 deals and battens, 9,262 deal ends, 6,905 pine and spruce boards, 19,000 palings.	General cargo	1
	Baltimore			In port	1
	In port				
1	Matanzas	1	...do	1,111 hhds., 81 tcs., 34 bbls. molasses	...do	1
1	Calais	1	...do	20,161 d-als, 1,594 deal ends, 466 battens, 2,778 boards, 46,475 pickets.	...do	1
1	Bangor	1	...do	21,029 pcs. deals, 1,338 deal ends, 995 pcs. boards, 94,180 pcs. palings, 31,000 pcs. lathwood.	...do	1
102		102		102		102
	BRISTOL—Z. Eastman.					
3	**Quarter ended December 31, 1863.†** In port	3	New York	3	Before reported	3	$69,000 00
1	New York	1	Cardiff	1	Wheat, flour, and corn	1	$75,000 00	2	2,300 tons railroad iron	$9,000 00
1	Opwick	1	...do	1	Copper and barley	1	6,000 00	1	Put in for repairs
1	Charontini	1	...do	1	Deals	1	90,000 00	1	...do
1	Nyham	1	...do	1	...do	1	15,000 00	1	...do
1	Hemansend	1	...do	1	...do	1	15,000 00	1	...do
1	St. John's	1	Newport	1	...do	1	19,000 00	1	...do
1	Havre	1	In port	1	Ballast	1		1	In port
1	Gloucester	1	...do	1	...do	1		1	...do
1	Huum	1	...do	1	Deals	1		1	...do
12		12		12		12	13,480 00	12	13,480 00
						162,480 00		162,480 00
3	**Quarter ended March 31, 1864.‡** In port	3	Sold	3	Before reported	3		1	Sold
1	Galata	1	Cardiff	1	...do	1		1	Ballast
1	St. George	1	Barletta	1	...do	1	22,000 00	1	850 tons railroad iron	25,000 00
			Newport	1	18,400 bushels barley	1	28,000 00	1	Ballast
			...do	1	480 standard deals	1		1	...do
5		5		5		5	50,000 00	5		25,000 00
1	**Quarter ended June 30, 1864.§** St. John's	1	In port	} 3	500 standard deals, sugar, 2,000 tons guano,	} 3	190,000 00	3	In port	95,000 00
1	Clenfuegos	1	...do						
1	Callao	1	...do						
3		3		3		3	190,000 00	3	

* Entered: 72 ships, 7 barks, 1 steamer—81, and 21 in port. Cleared: 49 ships, 3 barks—52, 4 sold, and 46 in port. Aggregate tonnage entered, 22,152.
† Entered: 5 ships, 1 brig, 3 barks—9, and 3 in port. Cleared: 3 ships, 1 brig, 2 barks, 3 class not given—9, and 3 in port. Aggregate tonnage entered, 5,462.
‡ Entered: 1 bark, 1 ship, 3 and 3 in port. Cleared: 2 barks, 2 ships—4, and 1 sold. Aggregate tonnage entered, 1,482.
§ Entered: 2 ships, 1 bark—3. Cleared: None. Aggregate tonnage entered, 3,514.

Navigation and commerce of the United States with foreign countries—British Dominions.

COUNTRY, CONSULATE, NAME OF CONSUL, AND DATE OF RETURNS.	VESSELS				CARGOES					
	ENTERED		CLEARED		INWARD			OUTWARD		
	No.	Where from.	No.	Where for.	No.	Description.	Value.	No.	Description.	Value.
Quarter ended September 30, 1864.*	3	In port	2	Newport	2	Before reported		2	Ballast	
	2	New York	1	Cardiff	2	do		1	do	
			1	do	1	General cargo	$100,000 00	1	do	
			1	In port	1	do	90,000 00	1	In port	
		Bangor	1	Cardiff	1	400 standard deals	99,000 00	1	Ballast	
		Portland	1	do	1	300 standard deals	15,000 00	1	do	
	2	Callao	1	In port	1	1,300 tons guano	78,000 00	1	Ballast	
			1	Portsmouth	1	1,800 tons guano	108,000 00	1	In port	
	1	St. John's	1	In port	1	500 standard deals	25,000 00	1	In port	
	10		10		10		438,000 00	10		
GLOUCESTER—J. Jones.										
Quarter ended December 31, 1863.†	1	Burisouke	1	Cardiff	1	Deals	8,400 00	1	Ballast	
	1	St. Andrews	1	Bristol	1	do	16,500 00	1	do	
	2		2		2		24,900 00	2		
2d, 3d, and 4th quarters		No arrivals		No departures						
CARDIFF—C. D. Cleveland.										
Quarter ended December 31, 1863.‡	5	In port	1	Cape de Verde	1	Before reported		1	Coal	$4,000 00
			1	Hong Kong	1	do		1	do	1,125 00
			1	Sold	1	do		1	Sold; took English flag	
			1	Rangoon	1	do		1	Coal	2,500 00
			1	Malta	1	do		1	do	3,000 00
	6	Antwerp	3	Glasgow	3	Ballast		3	490 tons coal	12,725 00
			1	Mire	1	do		1	960 tons coal	2,650 00
			1	Rio de Janeiro	1	do		1	1,250 tons coal	3,125 00
	4	London	1	In port	1	do		1	In port	
			1	New York	1	do		1	1,780 tons coal	4,450 00
			1	do	1	do		1	1,018 tons iron	30,540 00
			1	Hong Kong	1	do		1	1,766 tons coal	4,430 00
	5	Bristol	1	Bermuda	1	do		1	400 tons coal	1,000 00
			1	Algerine	1	do		1	250 tons coal	650 00
			2	New York	2	do		2	I	23,750 00
			1	Alexandria	1	do		1	740 tons coal	1,875 00
			1	In port	1	do		1	In port	
	2	Bordeaux	1	Montevideo	1	do		1	1,150 tons coal	2,775 00

3	Marseilles	1	Ancona	do	630 tons iron	18,900 00
3	Valencia	2	Malta	do	1,750 tons coal	4,380 00
		1	In port	do	In port	
		1	Ceylon	do	1,700 tons coal	4,520 00
		1	Sold	do	Sold; took English flag	
1	Londonderry	1	In port	do	In port; took English flag	
1	Gloucester	1	New York	do	1,330 tons coal	3,300 00
1	Hamburg	1	Asphawall	do	692 tons coal	1,744 00
1	White Haven	1	Callao	do	1,390 tons coal	2,340 00
1	Havre	1	Montevideo	do	600 tons coal	1,500 00
1	St. John's, N. B.	1	New York	do	900 tons coal	2,250 00
		1	Naples	do	1,000 tons coal	2,250 00
34		**34**				**139,519 00**

5	In port	1	Rio de Janeiro	Before reported	Coal and iron	101,050 00
		1	Marseilles	do	do	
		1	San Francisco	do	do	
		1	Naples	do	do	
		4	Baltimore	Ballast	5,500 tons iron	165,000 00
8	London	4	New York	do		
		2	Cape Good Hope	do	4,970 tons coal	12,425 00
		2	Baltimore	do	do	
		1	In port	do	In port	6,955 00
		2	New York	do	2,700 tons coal	36,000 00
5	Antwerp	1	Rio de Janeiro	do	2,300 tons iron	
		1	Sold	do	Sold; took English flag	
		1	In port	do	In port	
		1	New York	do	1,300 tons iron	49,000 00
2	Liverpool	1	Alexandria	do	Coal	3,000 00
1	Algeirus	1	Algeirus	do	Coal	1,000 00
1	Dunkirk	1	In port	do	In port	
1	Hamburg	1	Sold	do	Sold; took English flag	
1	Cork	1	Genoa	do	Coal	
1	Riot	1	New York	do	do	2,000 00
1	Dublin	1	do	210 tons grass and ore	1,300 tons iron	39,000 00
1	Santander	1	Civita Vecchia	Ballast	Coal	900 00
1	Gile Munds	1	In port	do	In port	
1	Limerick	1	do	do	do	
1	New Dieppe	1	New York	do	Sold; took English flag	30,000 00
2	do	1	In port	do	1,000 tons iron	
2	Havre	1	New York	do	In port	45,000 00
		1	Sold	do	1,300 tons iron	
		1		do	Sold; took English flag	
34		**34**			685 00	**453,330 00**

* Entered: 6 ships, 1 bark—7, and 3 in port. Clear—3: 3 ships, 2 barks—7, and 3 in port. Aggregate tonnage entered, 5,906.

† Entered and cleared 1 bark, 1 ship—2. Aggregate tonnage entered, 1,059.

‡ Entered: 21 ships, 5 barks, 3 brigs—29, and 5 in port. Cleared: 18 ships, 6 barks, 3 brigs—27, 2 sold, and 5 in port. Aggregate tonnage entered, 24,368.

§ Entered: 22 ships, 6 barks, 1 brig—29, and 5 in port. Cleared: 21 ships, 2 barks, 1 brig—24, 4 sold, and 6 in port. Aggregate tonnage entered, 25,822.

Navigation and commerce of the United States with foreign countries—British Dominions.

COUNTRY, CONSULATE, NAME OF CONSUL, AND DATE OF RETURN.	VESSELS.				CARGOES.						
	ENTERED.		CLEARED.		INWARD.			OUTWARD.			
	No.	Where from.	No.	Where for.	No.	Description.	Value.	No.	Description.	Value.
Quarter ended June 30, 1864.*	5	In port	5	New York	5	Before reported		5	Coal and iron	$71,715 00
	7	London	5	do	5	Ballast		3	5,262 tons coal	13,730 00
								2	2,600 tons iron	80,000 00
								1	187 tons coal	2,890 00
	4	Havre	1	San Francisco	1	d.		1	a plat	
			1	In port	1	do		2	3,300 tons coal	9,300 00
			2	Rio Janeiro	2	do		2	3,300 tons iron	107,300 00
	3	Antwerp	2	New York	2	d.		1	3,410 tons coal	9,350 00
				Cape Verde				1	1,720 tons coal	3,160 00
	1	Dunkirk	1	Montevideo	1	do		1	1,100 tons coal	3,000 00
	1	Nantes	1	Rio Janeiro	1	do		1	1,200 tons coal	3,000 00
	3	Rotterdam	1	New York	1	do		1	1,000 tons coal	2,742 00
			2	In port	2	do		2	In port	
	1	Glasgow	1	Rio Janeiro	1	do		1	1,650 tons coal	4,950 00
	25		**25**		**25**			**25**		319,337 00
Quarter ended September 30, 1864.†	2	In port	2	Hamburg	2	Before reported		1	Not at sail	
			1	Antwerp	1	do		1	do	4,300 00
	1	Newport	1	Naples	1	Ballast		1	1,200 tons coal	46,440 00
	1	St. Nazaire	1	New York	1	do		1	500 tons iron, 220 tons coal	5,120 00
	6	Bristol	4	do	4	do		4	1,000 tons iron, 3,280 tons coal	73,600 00
			1	Lisbon	1	do		1	1,200 tons coal	3,600 00
			1	Bahia	1	do		1	1,740 tons coal	5,980 00
	3	Antwerp	1	Cape de Verd.	1	do		1	1,760 tons coal	5,980 00
			1	Cape Good Hpe	1	Grass		1	1,050 tons coal	3,130 00
			1	In port	1	Ballast		1	In port	
	1	Bordeaux	1	Rio Janeiro	1	do		1	1,220 tons coal	3,680 00
	2	Gloster	1	Alexandria	1	do		1	250 das coal	750 00
			1	Boston	1	do		1	1,000 tons coal	3,000 00
	1	Genoa	1	Rio de Janeiro	1	Grain	$19,465 00	1	1,820 tons coal	5,460 00
	1	New York	1	Boston	1	Ballast		1	606 tons coal	1,818 00
	1	Dunkirk	1	Cape Gd oodHope	1	do		1	920 tons coal	2,760 00
	2	Havre	1	Cape de V'rde.	1	do		1	1,450 ton coal	4,350 00
			1	Sagua la Grande	1	do		1	470 das coal	1,410 00
	1	Cork	1	Cape de Verde.	1	do		1	1,600 tons coal	4,800 00
	1	Liverpool	1	Rio de Janeiro	1	do		1	1,208 tons coal	3,624 00
	1	Gestif Mude.	1	Rio Grande	1	do		1	150 tons coal	450 00
	2	London	2	New York	2	do		2	2,530 tons coal	7,590 00
	1	Portland	1	Montevideo	1	Deals		1	900 tons coal	2,700 00

NEWPORT.—J. N. Kucp.

Quarter ended December 31, 1863.‡

1	Portsmouth	1	New York	Ballast		1	700 tons coal	9,100 00
1	Hamburg	1	In port	do		1	In port	
29		**29**			19,465 00	**29**		**188,659 00**

3	Bristol	1	Point de Galle	Ballast		1	Sold; took English flag	3,365 00
		1	Malta	do		1	1,347 tons coal	
		1	Buenos Ayres	do		1	Sold; took English flag	
		3	New York	do		3	4,049 tons railroad iron	101,470 00
5	London	1	Malta	do		2	1,946 tons coal	4,980 00
		1	Aden	do			Sold; took English flag	
		1	Genoa	124 standard deals	4,620 00	1	590 tons coal	1,300 00
1	St. John, N. B	1	Bombay	Ballast		1	Sold; took English flag	
1	Marseilles							
10		**10**			4,090 00	**10**		**110,895 00**

Quarter ended March 31, 1864.§

5	London	5	Malta	Ballast		1	1,098 tons coal	2,720 00
		3	New York	do		3	2,500 tons railroad iron	19,384 00
		1	San Francisco	do		1	960 tons railroad iron	94,000 00
1	St. John, N. B	1	Genoa	134 standard deals	4,690 00	1	590 tons coal	1,302 00
4	Bristol	1	Malta	Ballast		1	1,347 tons coal	3,365 00
		1	Buenos Ayres	do		1	9k took English flag	
		1	Genoa	do		1	820 tons coal	4,500 00
		1	Port Said	do		1	465 tons coal	1,160 00
1	Marseilles	1	Bombay	do		1	Sold; took English flag	
2	Liverpool	1	G-noa	do		1	992 tons coal	2,490 00
1	Antwerp	1	Rio de Janeiro	do		1	1,600 tons railroad iron	48,000 00
1	Cork	1	New York	do		1	1,700 tons coal	4,750 00
15		**15**			4,690 00	**15**	In port	**104,559 00**

Quarter ended June 30, 1864.‖

1	Cork	1	New York	Ballast		1	1,505 tons railroad iron, 943 tons coal	45,150 00
1	Bremen	1	do	do		1	1,098 tons railroad iron	39,840 00
1	St. Nazaire	1	do	do		1	1,330 tons railroad iron	39,900 00
3	London	2	Buenos Ayres	do		3	4,134 tons railroad iron	132,040 00
1	Dunkirk	1	New York	do		1	775 tons railroad iron	92,250 00

* Entered: 19 ships, 1 bark—20, and 5 in port. Cleared: 20 ships, 2 barks—22, and 3 in port. Aggregate tonnage entered, 18,695.
† Entered: 18 ships, 3 brigs, 6 barks—27, and 2 in port. Cleared: 18 ships, 3 brigs, 6 barks—27, and 2 in port. Aggregate tonnage entered, 19,512.
‡ Entered: 9 ships, 1 bark—10. Cleared: 7 ships, 3 sold—10. Aggregate tonnage entered, 8,119.
§ Entered: 12 ships, 3 barks—15. Cleared: 11 ships, 3 barks—14, and 1 in port. Aggregate tonnage entered, 11,567.
‖ Entered: 8 ships, 2 barks—10. Cleared: 7 ships, 2 barks—9, and 1 in port. Aggregate tonnage entered, 8,945.

Navigation and commerce of the United States with foreign countries.—British Dominions.

COUNTRY, CONSULATE, NAME OF CONSUL, AND DATE OF RETURNS.	VESSELS				CARGOES					
	ENTERED		CLEARED		INWARD			OUTWARD		
	No.	Where from.	No.	Where for.	No.	Description.	Value.	No.	Description.	Value.
Quarter ended June 30, 1864—Continued.	2	Elba	1	Jamaica	1	495 tons iron ore	$1,235 00	1	594 tons coal	$1,310 00
	1	Havro	1	Cardiff	1	Ballast		1	Ballast	
			1	New York	1	do		1	In port	
	10		10		10		1,235 00	10		272,490 00
Quarter ended September 30, 1864.*	4	Havre	3	New York	3	Ballast		3	2,814 tons coal, (1 in port)	$3,420 00
			1	In port	1	do		1	Coal, (in port)	
	1	Bristol	1	Matanzas	1	do		1	649 tons coal	1,625 00
	1	London	1	Sold	1	do		1	Sold; took English flag	
	1	Antwerp	1	Rio Janeiro	1	do		1	1,060 tons coal	2,730 00
	2	Rotterdam	1	Montevideo	1	do		1	1,211 tons coal	3,025 00
			1	In port	1	do				
	2	Gloucester	1	In port	1	do		5	Coal and railroad iron, (in port)	
			1	In port	1	do				
	1	Liverpool	1	In port	1	148 standard deals	4,440 00			
	1	St. George								
	13		13		13		4,440 00	13		90,820 00
SWANSEA.—H. Morice. (Bristol consulate.)										
1st and 2d quarters		No arrivals		No departures						
3d quarter		No report								
MILFORD HAVEN.—A. B. Harries. (Bristol consulate.)										
...ded September 30, 861,†	2	Havre	1	Cape de Verde	1	Ballast		1	Patent fuel	5,900 00
1st and 2d quarters		No arrivals		No departures						
3d and 4th quarters		No reports								

Port and quarter	No.	Entered from	Inward cargo	No.	Tonnage	No.	Cleared for	Outward cargo	No.	Value
FALMOUTH.—A. Fox.										
Quarter ended December 31, 1863;†	1 7	In port Akyab	Before reported 10,450 tons rice, 350 tons teak wood	1 9	Unknown	1 9	Vlaardingen Bremen Bordeaux Liverpool London Havre	Be Same as inward cargo	1 9	
	9	Rangoon								
	10			10		10			10	
Quarter ended March 31, 1864.§	1	Galatz	18,400 bushels barley	1	Unknown	1	Bristol	Same as inward cargo	1	
Quarter ended June 30, 1864.		No arrivals					No departures			
Quarter ended September 30, 1864.‖	1	Rangoon	1,550 tons rice	1	Unknown	1	Liverpool	Same as inward cargo	1	
PLYMOUTH.—T. W. Fox.										
1st, 2d, and 3d quarters		No arrivals					No departures			
Quarter ended September 30, 1864.¶	1	Bangor	906 standard deals	1	7,416 00	1	Cardiff	Ballast	1	
NEWCASTLE-ON-TYNE.—J. H. McClaney.										
Quarter ended December 31, 1863.**	1 1 1 3	In port Havre Antwerp London	Before reported Ballast do do do	1 1 1 2 1	Coal	6	Newport New York Boston New Haven New York		6	$10,696 72
	6			6		6				10,696 72
Quarter ended March 31, 1863.††	1 1 3	London Antwerp Hamburg	Ballast do do do do	1 1 1 1 1		1 1 3	Sold New York Singapore Wellington Rio Janeiro	Sold General cargo 1,000 tons 4,049 tons coal		27,478 68 6,863 12
	5			5		5			5	34,342 00

* Entered: 10 ships, 3 barks—13. Cleared: 4 ships, 2 barks—6, 1 sold. Aggregate tonnage entered, 11,476.
† Entered: 1 ship, 1 bark—2. Cleared: 1 ship, 1 not stated. Aggregate tonnage entered, 1,209.
‡ Entered: 7 ships, 2 barks—9, and 1 in port. Cleared: 8 ships, 2 barks—10. Aggregate tonnage entered, 7,150 78-95.
§ Entered and cleared: 1 bark. Tonnage, 389 65-95. ‖ Entered and cleared: 1 ship. Tonnage, 999 47-95.
¶ Entered: 3 ships, 2 barks—5, and 1 in port. Cleared: 3 ships, 3 barks—6. Aggregate tonnage entered, 4,060.
** Entered: 4 ships, 9 barks, and 1 sold. Cleared: 4 ships, and 1 sold. Aggregate tonnage entered, ——
†† Entered: 4 ships, 1 bark—5. Cleared: 4 ships, 1 bark—5.
¶ Entered and cleared: 1 bark. Tonnage, 521.

Navigation and commerce of the United States with foreign countries—British dominions.

COUNTRY, CONSULATE, NAME OF CONSUL, AND DATE OF RETURNS.	VESSELS				CARGOES					
	ENTERED		CLEARED		INWARD			OUTWARD		
	No.	Where from.	No.	Where for.	No.	Description.	Value.	No.	Description.	Value.
Quarter ended June 30, 1864.	1	Leith	1	New York	1	Ballast		1	} 3,176 tons coals and chemicals.	$17,189 00
	1	Dundee	1	Boston	1	do		1		
	1	Dunkirk	1	Rio Janeiro	1	do		1		
	3		3		3			3		17,189 00
Quarter ended September 30, 1864.†	4	London	1	Beverly	1	Ballast		5 }	5,337 tons coal.	13,115 70
	1	Bremen	3	New York	3	do				
			1	Montevideo	1	do				
	5		5		5			5		13,115 70
LEITH.—N. McLaughlin.										
Quarter ended December 31, 1863.		No arrivals.		No departures.						
Quarter from November 14, 1863, to March 21, 1864.	3	Callao	1	Sold	} 3	3,550 tons guano	$203,990 00	1	Sold	} 9,490 00
			1	Genoa				1	1,400 tons coal	
			1	United States				1	Ballast	
	3		3		3		203,990 00	3		9,490 00
Quarter ended June 30, 1864.	1	Callao	1	Sold	1	1,300 tons guano		1	Sold; took British flag	
4th quarter		No report								
CORK.—E. G. Eastman.										
1st and 2d quarters		No report								
Quarter ended June 30, 1864.	1	In port	1	New York	1	Before reported		1	In distress	56,000 00
	1	Callao	1	Leith	1	1,400 tons guano		1	Same as inward cargo	76,000 00
			1	In port	1	1,900 tons guano		1	In port	500,000 00
	1	Cardenas	1	Bristol	1	500 hhds. sugar		1	Same as inward cargo	100,000 00
	1	Manilmain	1	Glasgow	1	500 logs teak timber		1	do	
	5		5		5			5		732,000 00

Quarter ended September 30, 1864.¶	8	Callao	Guano	3	
	1	Philadelphia	...do	2	
	1	Cardenas	...do	1	
	2	Bangor	...do	1	740,500 00
	1	Matanzas	...do	1	
	1	Akyab	...do	1	
	1	Cardiff	...do	1	
	1	St. John	...do	1	
	1	New York	...do	1	
		Galway		3	
		Bristol		2	
		Limerick		1	
		New London		1	
		In port		1	{15 {2 Same as inward cargo
		London		1	In port
		Hamburg		1	
		Gloucester		1	
		Cardiff		1	
		Liverpool		1	
		London		1	
		In port		1	
		Dublin		1	
		Liverpool		1	
	17			17	740,500 00	17
BELFAST.—J. Young.					
Quarter ended December 31, 1865.**	1	In port	New York	1	Before reported	1 Ballast
2d quarter.		No report			
3d and 4th quarters.		No arrivals	No departures		
LONDONDERRY.—A. Henderson.					
Quarter ended December 31, 1865.††	1	New York	Liverpool	1	Flour and Indian corn	29,240 00	1 Ballast
2d and 3d quarters.		No reports	No reports		
4th quarter.		No arrivals	No departures		
HULL.—H. J. Atkinson.					
Quarter ended December 31, 1865.‡‡	2	In port	New York	2	Before reported, 1,477 sacks flour, 2,356 bags wheat, 397 logs rosewood, 53 logs mahogany, 35 bags copper ore.	2 2,500 tons coal
	1	San Francisco	Boston	1		1 220 tons coal
	3			3		3

* Entered and cleared: 3 ships. Aggregate tonnage entered, 2,409. † Entered and cleared: 4 ships, 1 schooner.—5. Aggregate tonnage entered, 3,792.
‡ Entered: 2 ships, 1 bark.—3. Cleared: 2 ships, 1 sold. Aggregate tonnage entered, 2,455. § Entered: 1 ship. Cleared: 1 ship. Cleared: 1 sold. Tonnage, 896 62-95.
‖ Entered: 3 ships, 1 bark—4, and 1 in port. Cleared: 3 ships, 1 bark—4, and 1 in port. Aggregate tonnage entered, 2,853. ** 1 bark in port. Cleared: 1 bark.
¶ Entered: 9 ships, 7 barks, 1 brig—17. Cleared: 7 ships, 7 barks, 1 brig—15, and 2 in port. Aggregate tonnage entered, 11,494.
†† Entered and cleared: 1, class not given. Tonnage, 673. ‡‡ Entered: 1, class not given; 2 in port. Cleared: 3, class not given. Aggregate tonnage entered, 1,196 75-95.

Navigation and commerce of the United States with foreign countries—British Dominions,

COUNTRY, CONSULATE, RANK OF CONSUL, AND DATE OF RETURNS.	VESSELS.				CARGOES.					
	ENTERED.		CLEARED.		INWARD.			OUTWARD.		
	No.	Where from.	No.	Where for.	No.	Description.	Value.	No.	Description.	Value.
HULL.—*H. J. Atkinson*—Continued.										
Quarter ended March 31, 1864.*	1	Bangor	1	In port	1	Deals		1	In port	
3d and 4th quarters		No reports								
SUNDERLAND.—*H. Brown.*										
Quarter ended December 31, 1863.†	1	In port	1	Boston	1	Before reported		} 3	3,929 tons coal	$5,474 04
	1	London	1	Genoa	1	Ballast				
	1	Antwerp	1	Portland	1	...do				
	3		3		3			3		5,474 04
Quarter ended March 31, 1864.‡	1	Manlmain	1	King George's S'd	1	1,276 tons timber	$81,790 40	1	1,690 tons coal	2,963 90
Quarter ended June 30, 1864.§	3	London	2	Shanghai	} 4	Ballast		4	6,109 tons coal	10,376 96
	1	Antwerp	1	Rio Janeiro						
			1	King George's S'd						
	4		4		4			4		10,376 96
Quarter ended September 30, 1864.‖	1	Antwerp	1	Rio Janeiro	1	Ballast		1	1,466 tons coal	2,316 80
	1	Manlmain	1	Sold	1	...do		1	Sold	
	2		2		2			2		2,316 80
COWES.—*T. Harling.*										
Quarter ended December 31, 1863.¶	5	Callao	5	Hamburg	5	Guano		5	Waiting orders	
	1	Basnein	1	Amsterdam	1	Rice		1	...do	
	6		6		6			6		

Station and quarter		Whence arrived		Whither bound		Cargo			Remarks
Quarter ended March 31, 1864.**	2	Callao	1	Hamburg	1	Guano		1	Waiting orders
	2		1	Dunkirk	1	do.		1	Put in for supplies
Quarter ended June 30, 1864.††	2	Callao	2	Hamburg	2	Guano		2	Put in for orders
	1		1		1			1	
Quarter ended September 30, 1864.		No arrivals		No departures					Put in for orders
WEYMOUTH.—W. Roberts. 1st, 2d, 3d, and 4th quarters.		No arrivals		No departures					
PORTSMOUTH.—J. Garrett. 1st, 2d, 3d, and 4th quarters.		No arrivals		No departures					
SOUTHAMPTON.—J. Britten. 1st, 2d, 3d, and 4th quarters.		No arrivals		No departures					
LLANELLY.—R. Duncan. 1st, 2d, 3d, and 4th quarters.		No arrivals		No departures					
DUNDEE.—J. Smith. Quarter ended December 31, 1863.‡‡	1	Buenos Ayres	1	Sold	1	450 tons bones and ashes	21,780 00	1	Sold
2d quarter.		No report							
Quarter ended June 30, 1864.§§	1	Callao	1	Androssan	1	900 tons guano	45,272 00	1	Ballast
4th quarter.		No report							
GLASGOW.—W. L. Underwood. 1st quarter.		No report							

* Entered: 1, class not given. Cleared: 1 in port. Tonnage, 940. † Entered: 2 ships, and 1 in port. Cleared: 3 ships. Aggregate tonnage entered, 2,776.
‡ Entered and cleared: 1 ship. Tonnage, 973. § Entered and cleared: 4 ships. Aggregate tonnage entered, 3,775.
‖ Entered: 2 ships. Cleared: 1 ship; 1 sold. Aggregate tonnage entered, 1,504. ¶ Entered: 6, class not given. Cleared: not reported. Aggregate tonnage entered, 4,697.
** Entered: 2, class not given. Cleared: not reported. Aggregate tonnage entered, 1,202. †† Entered: 1 ship. Cleared: 1 in port. Tonnage, 833.
‡‡ Entered: 1, class not given. Cleared: 1 sold. Tonnage, 266 80-95. §§ Entered and cleared: 1, class not given. Tonnage, 552 4-95.

Navigation and commerce of the United States with foreign countries—British Dominions.

COUNTRY, CONSULATE, NAME OF CONSUL, AND DATE OF RETURNS.	VESSELS				CARGOES					
	ENTERED.		CLEARED.		INWARD.			OUTWARD.		
	No.	Where from.	No.	Where for.	No.	Description.	Value.	No.	Description.	Value.
Quarter ended March 31, 1861.*	2	In port	2	Sold	2	Before reported.		2	1,693 tons pig iron and sundries.	$29,200 00
	1	Maulmain				Teak.		1	Sold and took British flag.	25,725 00
	6	New York	3	New York	3	56,332 bushels wheat, 373 bbls. flour, 6,000 staves, and sundries.	$69,549 00	2	1,515 tons pig iron, vinegar, alum, and sundries.	
					1	Not reported.		1	In port.	
			3	In port	3	89,471 bushels wheat, 15,900 staves, 5,595 bbls. flour, 500 bbls. lard, and sundries.	157,105 00	3	In port.	
	9		9		9		226,657 00	9		53,995 00
Quarter ended June 30, 1864.†	4	In port	4	New York	4	Before reported.		4	1,900 tons pig iron, 1,968 tons iron, spirits, tar, &c.	53,020 00
	1	Callao	1	Cardiff	1	2,850 tons guano	199,500 00	1	Ballast.	
	2	Maulmain	1	Boston	2	1,222 logs, 165 plank, and 700 pieces teak timber, 1,750 boxes catch.	10,000 00	1	...do.	
	3	New York	1	In port	2	66,143 bushels wheat, 4,071 barrels flour, 750 tins lard, staves, bacon, and tallow.	136,361 00	1	In port.	37,175 00
			2	New York				2	1,760 tons pig iron, 47,539 yards linen, iron, and corkwood.	
			1	In port	1	940 bbls. flour, 15,600 bushels wheat, tallow, lard, &c.	68,900 00	1	In port.	10,000 00
	1	Aberdeen	1	Boston	1	53,000 staves, tallow, lard, &c.		1	700 tons pig iron	100,195 00
					1	Ballast				
	11		11		11		414,761 00	11		
GIBRALTAR—H. J. Sprague. Quarter ended December 31, 1863.†	3	Boston	2	Marseilles	10	Rum, logwood, coal, fruit, marble, bark, flour, tobacco, grain, salt.	Unknown.	8	Inward cargoes	
	1	Cardiff	1	Malaga						
	1	Mn	1	Cadiz						
	1	Valencia	1	New York						
	1	Leghorn	1	...do.						
	1	Liverpool	1	Cadiz	1	Ballast		3	Ballast	
	1	Trapani	1	Boston						
	1	Galati	1	Cork						
	1	Hyeres	1	Boston						
	11		11		11			11		

Quarter ended March 31, 1864.§

No.	Port	No.	Inward cargo		No.	Outward cargo
2	Boston					
1	Philadelphia					
1	Cardiff					
4	Messina					
1	Genoa					
9		9	Tobacco, rum, petroleum, railway iron, flour, fruit, marble, &c.	Unknown.	9	Same as inward cargo

Quarter ended June 30, 1864.||

No.	Port	No.	Inward cargo	No.	Outward cargo
1	Licata	1	Sulphur	1	Sulphur
3	Messina	2	Fruit and salt	2	Fruit and salt
2	Boston	1	do.	1	do.
1	Malta	1	Tobacco and staves	1	Tobacco.
1	Almeria	1	Flour and tobacco	1	Ballast
1	Cardiff	1	Coal	1	Coal.
1	Sumatra and Pernambuco	1	Pepper	1	Pepper
1	Cape Good Hope				
1	Marseilles				
2	New York	1	Tobacco, &c.	1	Tobacco, &c.
	do.	1	Flour and tobacco.	1	Tobacco.
1	Trapani	1	Salt	1	Salt.
11		11		11	

Quarter ended September 30, 1864.¶

No.	Port	No.	Inward cargo	No.	Outward cargo
2	Palermo	1	Fruit, &c.	1	Fruit, &c.
	Messina	1	do.	1	do.
	New York	1	do.	1	do.
1	Fayal	1	Lumber	1	Lumber.
1	Maulmain	1	fiber	1	Timber.
	London	1		1	Staves
	Malaga	1	hides and tobacco.	1	Sulphur
1	New York			1	Staves
1	Licata	1	Sulphur	1	Cotton-seed.
1	Boston	1	Fibre and staves.		
	Falmouth	1	Salt		
1	Alexandria				
9		9		9	

St. Helena.—G. Gerard.

Quarter ended December 31, 1863.**

No.	Port	No.	Inward cargo	Value	No.	Outward cargo
4	Whaling	4	1,870 barrels sperm and whale oil	88,000 00		
2	Maulmain	1	Rice	30,000 00		
	Liverpool	1	fiber	30,000 00		
	Falmouth	1	Rice	30,000 00		
	Liverpool	1	Petroleum	30,000 00		
1	Mauritius	1	General cargo.	150,000 00		
1	Manila	1	Sugar and hemp	45,000 00		
1	Benetin	1	Rice.	150,000 00		
1	Akyab	1	do.	150,000 00	12	Same as inward cargoes.
12		12		583,000 00	12	583,000 00

583,000 00

Navigation and commerce of the United States with foreign countries—British Dominions.

COUNTRY, CONSULATE, NAME OF CONSUL, AND DATE OF RETURN.	VESSELS				CARGOES					
	ENTERED		CLEARED		INWARD			OUTWARD		
	No.	Where from.	No.	Where for.	No.	Description.	Value.	No.	Description.	Value.
Quarter ended March 31, 1864.*	3	Calcutta	3	London	3	Coffee and general cargo	$700,000 00	3	Same as inward cargo	$700,000 00
	9	Whaling	6	Whaling	9	6,950 barrels sperm and whale oil	310,000 00	8	Same as inward cargo	965,000 00
				In port				1	In port	
			2	New Bedford						
	1	Padang	1	Boston	1	Coffee	150,000 00	1	Same as inward cargo	150,000 00
	1	Shanghai	1	New York	1	Tea and silk	40,000 00	1	do.	40,000 00
	1	Capetown	1	Desolation isle	1	Cattle	9,000 00	1	do.	9,000 00
	1	Singapore	1	New Bedford	1	210 barrels sperm oil	10,000 00	1	do.	10,000 00
	1	Louanda	1	In port	1	General cargo	16,000 00	1	In port	16,000 00
	1	Manila	1	New York	1	Hemp, hides, cigars.	150,000 00	1	Same as inward cargo.	150,000 00
	18		18		18		1,385,000 00	18		1,294,000 00
Quarter ended June 30, 1864.†	2	In port	1	Boston	2	Before reported		2	Wool, copper, old iron, stores, whaling equipment.	9,000 00
	4	Whaling	1	Whaling	2					
	1	Seg Harbor	5	Whaling	5	2,375 barrels whale and sperm oil	133,000 00	5	Same as inward cargo	107,000 00
	1	Meulmain	1	Falmouth	1	Teak timber.	25,000 00	1	do.	25,000 00
	1	Calcutta	1	Boston.	1	General cargo.	40,000 00	1	do.	40,000 00
	9		9		9		188,000 00	9		181,000 00
Quarter ended September 30, 1864.‡	2	Whaling	2	Whaling	2	Sperm and whale oil	10,000 00	2	Same as inward cargo	10,000 00
	4	Bassein	4	Falmouth	4	Rice.	175,000 00	4	do.	175,000 00
	2	Akyab	2	do.	2	do.	105,000 00	2	do.	105,000 00
	1	Meulmain	1	do.	1	Teak timber.	30,000 00	1	do.	30,000 00
	3	Rangoon	3	Boston.	3	Rice	135,000 00	3	do.	135,000 00
	1	Manila	1	Cork.	1	Sugar and indigo	230,000 00	1	do.	230,000 00
	1	Padang			1	General cargo	200,000 00	1	do.	200,000 00
	14		14		14		885,000 00	14		865,000 00
CAPETOWN.—*W. Graham.* Quarter ended December 31, 1863.§	1	In port	1	Sydney	1	Before reported		1	Part inward cargo	
	1	Whaling	1	Whaling	1	Cargo not discharged.		1	Inward cargo	
	1	Cardiff	1	Calcutta	1	970 tons coal.		1	Ballast	
	1	Montevideo.	1	Ascension	1	Mules.	11,640 00	1	In port	
	1	Masulipatam	1	New York.	1	Cargo not discharged.	3,110 00	1	inward cargo	
	5		5		5		13,750 00	5		13,750 00

Quarter ended March 31, 1864.‖	2	Boston	1	Algoa Bay	1	Cargo not landed	29,416 38	1	Inward cargo
	1	New York	1	Singapore	1	General cargo	37,439 07	1	Not stated
			1	New York	1	...do...		1	Wool and skins
	3		3		3		66,853 45	3	19,202 50
									19,202 50
From March 31 to September 30, 1864.	1	New York	1	China	1	Ballast		1	Ballast
	1	Mauritius	1	Sold	1	...do...		1	Sold
	2		2		2			2	
PORT ELIZABETH.—J. C. Hess. Quarter ended December 31, 1863.		American vessels under foreign flags reported.							
Quarter ended March 31, 1864.¶	1	Rio de Janeiro	1	New York	1			1	Wool and skins
									84,129 64
2d and 3d quarters.		No arrivals.		No departures.					
MAURITIUS.—W. R. G. Mellon. Quarter ended December 31, 1863.**	7	In port	3	Condemned	3	Before reported		3	Condemned
			1	Sold	1	...do...		1	Sold
			2	London	2	...do...		2	Inward cargo
			1	Manilmain	1			1	Ballast
	5	Cruising	{ 1	Condemned	5	972 barrels oil..	35,000 00	{ 1	Condemned
			{ 4	Cruising				{ 4	Inward cargo
	1	Honolulu	1	Cork	1	1,250 tons guano	37,500 00	1	Cargo of condemned ship
	2	Calcutta	{ 1	Calcutta	{ 2	3,200 tons rice.	148,000 00	{ 1	Ballast
			{ 1	In port				{ 1	In port
	15		15		15		220,500 00	15	
Quarter ended March 31, 1864.††	1	Calcutta	1	Calcutta	1	1,500 tons rice.	68,000 00	1	Ballast
Quarter ended June 30,1864.‡‡	3	Capetown	1	Shanghai	1	Ballast		1	Ballast
			2	Singapore	2	...do...		2	...do...

* Entered: 5 ships, 12 barks, 1 brig—18. Cleared: 1 brig—18, and 2 in port. Aggregate tonnage entered, 8,753 75-95.
† Entered: 4 barks, 1 brig, 2 ships—7, and 2 in port. Cleared: 4 barks, 2 brigs, 3 ships—9. Aggregate tonnage entered, 2,995.
‡ Entered and cleared: 10 ships, 4 barks—14. Aggregate tonnage entered, 10,182.
§ Entered: 2 ships, 3 barks—5, and 1 in port. Cleared: 2 ships, 3 barks—5, and 1 in port. Aggregate tonnage not given.
‖ Entered and cleared: 3—class and tonnage not given. ¶ Entered: 1—class and tonnage not given. Cleared: not stated.
** Entered: 4 ships, 4 barks—8, and 7 in port. Cleared: 4 ships, 5 brig—9; sold, 1; condemned, 4, and 1 in port. Aggregate tonnage entered, 2,317.
†† Entered and cleared: 1 ship. Tonnage, 796.
‡‡ Entered: 5 ships, 2 barks, 1 schooner, 3 steamers—11. Cleared: 4 ships, 1 bark, 1 schooner, 3 steamers—9 and 2 in port. Aggregate tonnage entered, 6,541 56-93.

Navigation and commerce of the United States with foreign countries—British Dominions.

COUNTRY, CONSULATE, NAME OF CONSUL, AND DATE OF RETURNS.	VESSELS				CARGOES					
	ENTERED		CLEARED		INWARD			OUTWARD		
	No.	Where from.	No.	Where for.	No.	Description.	Value.	No.	Description.	Value.
Quarter ended June 30, 1864.	2	Boston	1	Batavia	1	Ice and sundries	$35,000 00	1	Part inward cargo and ballast	
	1	Manila	1	In port	1	Assorted cargo	35,000 00	1	In port	
	1	Port Alfred	1	New York	1	Hemp, sugar, and indigo	113,000 00	1	Inward cargo	
	2	Cruising	1	Fishing	1	6 tons fish	450 00	1	Ballast	
	1	Calcutta	2	Cruising	2	975 bbls. sperm, 50 bbls. whale oil	45,875 00	2	Inward cargo	
	1	Port Louis	1	Calcutta	1	1,450 tons rice	65,000 00	1	Ballast	
			1	In port	1	Hemp, sugar, and indigo	113,000 00	1	In port	
	11		11		11		407,325 00	11		
Quarter ended September 30, 1864.*	2	In port	1	Penang	1	Before reported		1	Ballast	
	3	Cruising	1	New York	1	do.		1	Inward cargo	
			3	Cruising	3	5,250 barrels oil	125,000 00	3	do.	
	5		5		5		125,000 00	5		
BOMBAY—G. W. Kittridge. Quarter ended December 31, 1865.†	3	Calcutta	2	Calcutta	2	General cargo and salt		2	Ballast and salt	
	1	Madras	1	Maulmain	1	Timber		1	Ballast	
	7	Maulmain	1	Bassein	1	Sugar		1	Sugar	
			2	Maulmain	2	General cargo and timber		2	Ballast	
			5	In port	5	Timber		5	In port	
	1	Rangoon	1	Maulmain	1	do.		1	Ballast	
	12		12		12			12		
2d, 3d, and 4th quarter. CALCUTTA—N. P. Jacob.		No report.								
Quarter ended December 31, 1865.‡	17	In port	1	New York	1	Before reported	Not given.	1	Saltpetre, linseed, cowhides, &c.	Not given.
			1	Boston	6	do.		1	do.	
			6	London	1	do.		6	Linseed, jute, rapeseed, &c.	
			1	Liverpool	1	do.		1	Linseed, jute, rice, &c.	
			1	Port Elizabeth	1	do.		1	Rice, &c.	
			1	Mauritius	2	do.		1	Rice, gram, dholl, &c.	
			2	Bombay	2	do.		2	Rice, wheat, sugar, &c.	
			2	Sold	2	do.		2	Rice, gram, sugar, &c.	
			2	Columbo				2	Sold; took British flag.	
	3	Singapore	1	Boston	1	Ballast		1	Saltpetre, linseed, hides, &c.	

2	Boston	Sold	2	Ice and sundries	2	Sold; took British flag.
2	Port Louis	In port	2	Ballast	1	In port.
1	Muscat	Hong Kong	1		1	Saltpetre, rice, cloves.
1	Montevideo	London	1	do.	1	Linseed, rice, jute, &c.
1	Liverpool	Singapore	1	Salt	1	Rice, gunny bags, soap, &c.
1	Mauritius	Boston	1	Ballast	1	Saltpetre, linseed, hides.
3	Moulmein	Sold	3	Timber	1	Sold; took British flag.
		In port	2	In port	2	Saltpetre, linseed, hides, &c.
1	Colombo	do.	1	do.	1	In port.
1	Shields	do.	1	do.	1	do.
1	Buenos Ayres	Boston	1	Coal	1	Saltpetre, linseed, hides.
1	Bombay	In port	1	Tobacco and ballast	1	In port.
1	Hong Kong	do.	1	Salt and ballast	1	do.
1	Port Adelaide	do.	1	Ballast	1	do.
1	Rio de Janeiro	do.	1	Horns and ballast	1	do.
				Ballast	1	do.
38			38		38	

11	In port	Bombay, Cochin and Tellochery.	1	Before reported	1	Rice, jute, and goat-skins.
		London.	1		1	Tobacco, jute, sugar, and rice.
1			1	do.	1	Tobacco leaf, linseed, rice, jute cuttings.
1	Bombay	Bom.	3	do.	3	General cargo and merchandise.
2	Kurrachee	Sold	4	do.	4	Sold; took British flag.
		New York	1	Ballast	1	General cargo and merchandise.
3	Colombo	Boston	2	215 tons salt	2	General cargo and merchandise.
		Sold	1	Bal st.	1	do.
		In port	1	do.	1	Sold; took British flag.
3	Singapore		3	do.	3	In port.
2	Mauritius	do.	4	do.	1	Sold; took British flag.
1	Cochin	In port	1	Coir yarn and copper	1	In port.
1	Boston		1	Ice and apples	1	do.
1	Newport	Sold	1	Ballast	1	do.
1	Liverpool	do.	1	Salt	2,420 00	Sold; took British flag.
1	Moulmein		1	China timber	75,000 00	do.
1	Madras	Burnt	1	Ice and tobacco	1	Burnt; wreck sold.
1	Hong Kong	Sold	1	do.	1	Sold; took British flag.
1	Shanghai	In port	1	Ballast	1	In port.
30			30		77,420 00	30

Quarter ended Mar. 31, 1864.§

* Entered: 2 ships, 1 bark—3, and 2 in port. Cleared: 3 ships, 2 barks—5. Aggregate tonnage entered, 963 15-95.
† Entered: 10 ships, 2 barks—12. Cleared: 5 ships, 2 barks—7, and 5 in port. Aggregate tonnage entered, 8,569.
‡ Entered: 16 ships, 4 barks, 1 brig—21, and 17 in port. Cleared: 19 ships, 1 bark, 1 brig, 1 schooner—22, 5 sold, and 11 in port. Aggregate tonnage entered, 16,160.
§ Entered: 16 ships, 3 barks—19, and 11 in port. Cleared: 8 ships, 3 barks—11. 1 ship burnt 7 ships and 2 barks in port. Ag're tonnage entered, 17,436 45-95.

Navigation and commerce of the United States with foreign countries—British Dominions.

COUNTRY, CONSULATE, NAME OF CONSUL, AND DATE OF RETURNS.	VESSELS.				CARGOES.					
	ENTERED.		CLEARED.		INWARD.			OUTWARD.		
	No.	Where from.	No.	Where for.	No.	Description.	Value.	No.	Description.	Value.
Quarter ended June 30, 1864.	9	In port	1	New York	1	Before reported		1	9,223 mds. saltpetre, 8,059 cwt. linseed, 10,000 cowhides, 2,999 buffalo-hides, 27,350 goat-skins, 37,500 gunny bags, 8 cwt. ginger, 9 cwt. deers' horns, 394 cwt. shell-lac, 529 rolls coir matting, 70 cwt. cocoa-nut oil, 3,322 cwt. jute.	
			4	Boston	4	do.		4	21,864 mds. saltpetre, 57,858 cwt. linseed, 14,800 do., 3,310 bn do., 990 goat-skins, 277,150 gunny bags, 298 cwt. ginger, 1,811 ct. do., 152 cwt. shellac, 385 cwt. kokerdye, 299 mds. indigo, 982 cwt. oak, 844 cwt. jute, 884 cwt. castor oil, 37 cwt. india-rubber, 369 cwt. cotton, 137 cwt. senna leaves, 5 cwt. gum tragacanth, 10 pieces rug, 1 case cigars.	
			1	Mauritius	1	do.		1	740 mds. gram, 38,900 mds. rice.	
			1	Maulmain	1	do.		1	Ballast.	
			2	Sold	2	do.		2	Sold; took British flag.	
	2	Shanghai	2	do.	2	Ballast.		2	do. ... do.	
	1	Galle, Ceylon	1	Boston	1	do.		1	4,113 mds. saltpetre, 30,403 cwt. linseed, 13,300 cowhides, 960 buffalo-hides, 137,500 gunny bags, 500 cwt. ginger, 41 mds. indigo, 76 cwt. india-rubber.	
	1	Hong Kong	1	do.	1	do.		1	6,117 mds. saltpetre, 12,699 cwt. linseed, 5,800 cowhides, 440 buffalo-hides, 16,000 goat-skins, 75,000 gunny bags, 298 cwt. ginger, 448 cwt. shellac, 127 cwt. lac-dye, 385 cwt. india-rubber, 1,875 cwt. jute, 294 cwt. castor oil.	
	3	Singapore	1	do.	1	do.		1	4,634 mds. saltpetre, 14,897 cwt. linseed, 4,900 buffalo-skins, 590,000 goat-skins, 906,250 gunny bags, 370 cwt. cotton, 100	

	Port			Destination / Status		Value		Cargo
3	New York	3	In port / New York	...do...	2 / 1		2 / 1	cwt. lac dye, 34 maunds indigo, 803 cwt. jute. / In port.
				...do...			1	10,000 cwt. linseed, 31 maunds indigo, 6,426 cwt. jute.
3	Liverpool	1	Boston	Lumber, mahogany, tobacco	2	$68,000 00	1	6,530 mds. saltpetre, 6,811 cwt. linseed, 1,500 cowhides, 2,600 buffalo hides, 15,000 goat skins, &c.
1	Maulmain	1 1 2 1	In port / Sold / In port / Maulmain	Salt, &c... / Teak timber, &c...	3 / 1	73,000 00 / 21,500 00	1 / 1 / 2 / 1	In port. / Sold; took British flag. / In port. / 180 mds. dholl, 109 cwt. seeds, 30 casks wine, 49 cwt. lines and twine, 5 casks cutlery, 98 cwt. nails, 100 mds. peas, 150 bags fuller's earth, 349 cwt. sugar, 138 bundles tobacco leaf, 18,900 gunny-bags.
5 1 1	Boston / Put back / Bombay	1 4 1 1	Sold / In port / Put back / In port	Ice, general merchandise... / In distress... / Ballast...	5 1 1	180,000 00	1 4 1 1	Sold. / In port. / In distress. / In port.
30		30			30	341,500 00	30	
10	In port...	4	Boston...	Before reported...	4		4	16,762 mds. saltpetre, 145,995 cwt. linseed, 51,000 cowhides, 10,810 buffalo hides, 154,560 goat skins, 410,850 gunny bags, 10,024 pieces gunny cloth, 836 cwt. ginger, 4,609 sheep skins, 370 cwt. shellac, 153 cwt. lac dye, 291 mds. indigo, 407 cwt. turmeric, 750 bundles twine, 8,103 cwt. jute, 793 cwt. India-rubber, 1 box tea, 1 bale seersucker, 51 dozen chatties, 2,000 casks claret, 1,629 mds. saltpetre, 3,563 cwt. linseed, 5,000 cowhides, 2,930 buffalo hides, 72 cwt. button lac, 110 mds. shellac, 92 cwt. twine, 569 pieces door-mats, 1 case cashmere shawls, 3,536 cwt. jute, 2,436 maunds rice.
	New York...	1	New York...	...do...	1		1	
1	Hull...	1	Hull...	...do...	1		1	16,611 cwt. linseed.

Quarter ended September 30, 1864.†

* Entered: 18 ships, 2 barks, 1 brig—21, and 9 in port. Cleared: 10 ships, 2 barks, 1 brig—13, 7 sold, and 10 in port. Aggregate tonnage entered, 16,359 9-95.
† Entered: 6 ships, and 10 in port. Cleared: 10 ships, 1 bark—11, and 5 in port. Aggregate tonnage entered, 5,506 18-95.

Navigation and commerce of the United States with foreign countries—British Dominions.

COUNTRY, CONSULATE, NAME OF CONSUL, AND DATE OF RETURNS.	VESSELS				CARGOES					
	ENTERED		CLEARED		INWARD			OUTWARD		
	No.	Where from.	No.	Where for.	No.	Description.	Value.	No.	Description.	Value.
Quarter ended September 30, 1864—Continued.		In port	2	London	2	Before reported		2	39,594 cwt. linseed, 963 cwt. rapeseed, 539 cwt. molasses, 2,703 cwt. turmeric, 663 cwt. jute, 1,319 wt. sugar, 2,410 cwt. jute.	
	1	Bremerhaven	1	Sold	1	...do		1	Sold.	
			1	In port	1	...do		1	17,925 cwt. rice, 964 cwt. rapeseed, 4,004 cwt. poppy-seed	
			1	London	1	Ballast		1	In port	
	1	Mauritius	1	In port	1	...do		1	In port	
	1	Sydney	1	...do	1	...do		1	13,666 cwt. linseed, 15,000 cwt. 3,002 cwt. rape	
	1	Point de Galle	1	London	1	...do		1	cwt. linseed, 2,002	
	1	Melbourne	1	In port	1	...do		1	In port	
	1	Liverpool	1	...do	1	1,113 tons salt.	$10,000 00	1	In port	
	16		16		16		10,000 00	16		
AKYAB—J. Bullock. Quarter ended December 31, 1863.*	1	In port	1	London	1	Before reported		1	Inward cargo.	R.60,000
	1	Singapore	1	Singapore	1	Ballast		1	122,356 baskets rice	
	1	Sydney	1	Bassein	1	...do		1	Ballast	*
	1	Rio de Janeiro	1	Falmouth	1	...do		1	In port	
	4		4		4			4		R.60,000
Quarter ended March 31, 1864.†	1	In port	1	Falmouth	1	Before reported		1	Rice	
	2	Singapore	2	In port	2	...do				
	1	Dunedin	1	Falmouth	1	Ballast				
	1	Antwerp	1	...do	1	...do				
	1	Rotterdam	1	...do	1	...do				
	1	Madras	1	...do	1	...do		2	In port.	R.508,180
	1	Cape Good Hope	1	...do	1	...do		9	924,164 baskets rice.	
	1	Melbourne	1	...do	1	...do				
	1	China	1	...do	1	...do				
	2	Not stated	2	...do	2	...do				
	12		12		12			12		R.508,180

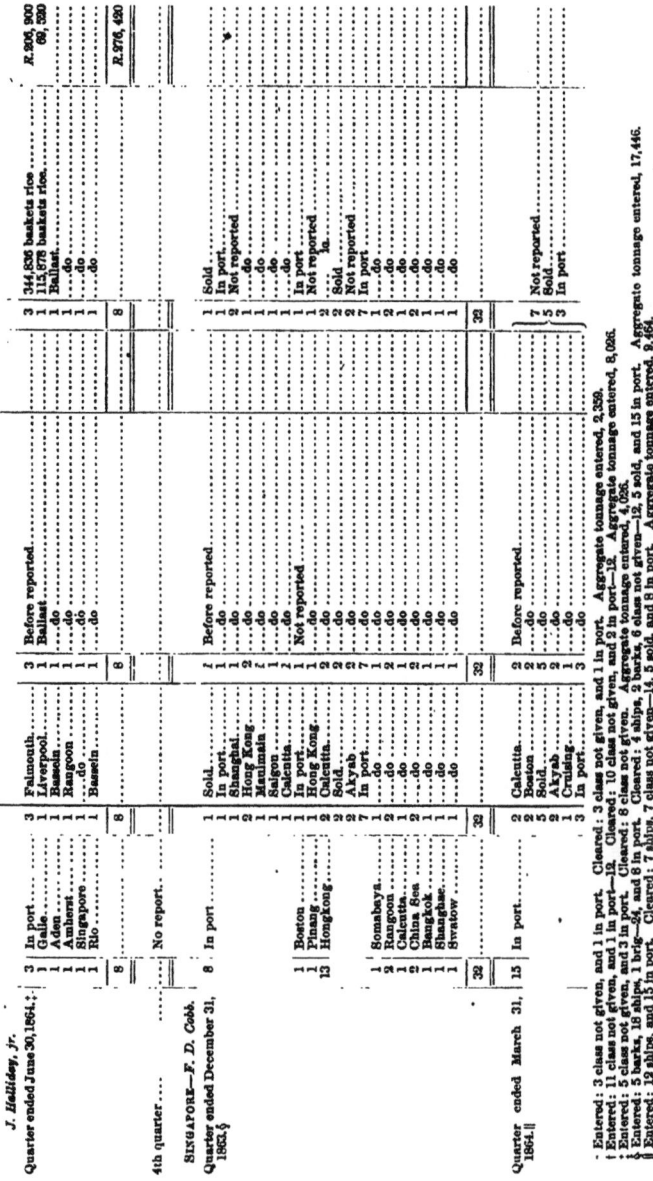

J. Halliday, jr.

Quarter ended June 30, 1864.‡

3	In port	3	Falmouth	3	Before reported	3	344,830 baskets rice R.205,900
1	Gale	1	Liverpool	1	Ballast	1	115,578 baskets rice 69,590
1	Aden	1	Bassein	1	...do	1	Ballast
1	Amherst	1	Rangoon	1	...do	1	...do
1	Singapore	1	...do	1	...do	1	...do
1	Rio	1	Bassein	1	...do	1	...do
8		8		8		8	R.276,490

4th quarter .... | No report.

SINGAPORE—F. D. Cobb.

Quarter ended December 31, 1863.§ | 8 | In port

1	Boston	1	Sold	1	Before reported	1	Sold
1	Pinang	1	In port	1	...do	1	In port
13	Hongkong	2	Shanghai	2	...do	2	Not reported
		1	Hong Kong	1	...do	1	...do
		1	Maulmain	1	...do	1	...do
1	Bombay	2	Saigon	2	...do	1	...do
2	Rangoon	1	Calcutta	1	Not reported	1	In port
2	Calcutta	1	In port	1	...do	1	Not reported
2	China Sea	2	Hong Kong	2	...do	2	Sold
1	Bangkok	2	Calcutta	2	...do	2	Not reported
1	Shanghae	7	Sold	7	...do	7	In port
1	Swatow	2	Akyab	2	...do	2	...do
		2	In port	2	...do	1	...do
		1	...do	1	...do	1	...do
		1	...do	1	...do	1	...do
		1	...do	1	...do	1	...do
		1	...do	1	...do		
32		32		32		32	

Quarter ended March 31, 1864.|| | 15 | In port

2	Calcutta	2	Before reported	7	Not reported
2	Boston	2	...do	5	Sold
5	Sold	5	...do	3	In port
2	Akyab	2	...do		
1	Cruising	1	...do		
3	In port	3	...do		

Aggregate tonnage entered, 17,446.

* Entered: 3 class not given, and 1 in port. Cleared: 3 class not given, and 1 in port. Aggregate tonnage entered, 2,259.
† Entered: 11 class not given, and 1 in port—12. Cleared: 10 class not given, and 1 2 in port—12. Aggregate tonnage entered, 8,026.
‡ Entered: 5 class not given, and 3 in port. Cleared: 8 class not given, and 3 in port. Aggregate tonnage entered, 4,026.
§ Entered: 5 barks, 18 ships, 1 brig—24, and 8 in port. Cleared: 4 ships, 2 barks, 6 class not given—12, 5 sold, and 15 in port. Aggregate tonnage entered, 17,446.
|| Entered: 12 ships, and 15 in port. Cleared: 7 ships, 7 class not given—14, 5 sold, and 8 in port. Aggregate tonnage entered, 9,464.

Navigation and commerce of the United States with foreign countries—British Dominions.

Quarter ended March 31, 1864—Continued.

VESSELS				CARGOES					
ENTERED		CLEARED		INWARD			OUTWARD		
No.	Where from.	No.	Where for.	No.	Description.	Value.	No.	Description.	Value.
3	Hong Kong	2	Calcutta	2	Not reported		7	Not reported	
4	Cardiff	1	In port	1	do		5	In port	
		3	Akyab	3	do				
1	Bassein	1	In port	1	do				
1	Penang	1	Diamond Island	1	do				
1	Bangkok	1	Akyab	1	do				
1	Swatow	1	In port	1	do				
1	Batavia	1	do	1	do				
27		27		27			27		

Quarter ended June 30, 1864*.

VESSELS				CARGOES					
ENTERED		CLEARED		INWARD			OUTWARD		
No.	Where from.	No.	Where for.	No.	Description.	Value.	No.	Description.	Value.
8	In port	2	Manila	2	Before reported		16	Not reported	
		1	New York	1	do		2	In port	
2	Hong Kong	1	Hong Kong	1	do				
2	Shanghai	1	Boston	1	do				
		1	Akyab	1	do				
		2	Sold	2	Not reported				
1	New York	1	Hong Kong	1	do				
1	Batavia	1	Bangkok	1	do				
1	Bangkok	1	Boston	1	do				
1	Rangoon	1	New York	1	do				
1	Amoy	1	Hong Kong	1	do				
1	Boston	1	In port	1	do				
		1	Hong Kong	1	do				
		1	Shanghai						
18		18		18			18		

Quarter ended September 30, 1864.†

VESSELS				CARGOES					
ENTERED		CLEARED		INWARD			OUTWARD		
No.	Where from.	No.	Where for.	No.	Description.	Value.	No.	Description.	Value.
2	In port	1	Batavia	1	Before reported		1	Ballast	
		1	Rangoon	1	do		1	do	
3	New York	2	Hong Kong	1	Ballast		1	do	
		1	In port	1	General cargo	22,000	1	In port	
1	Bassein	1	Falmooth	1	22,000 piculs rice		1	do	
2	Batavia	1	In port	2	General cargo		1	do	
1	Penang	2	Whampoa	1	Ballast		1	500 piculs raisin, 346 tons timber	
9		9		9		22,000	9		22,000

HONG KONG.—H. N. Congar.

Quarter ended December 31, 1863.‡

Vessels entered:

No.	Whence	No.	Cargo
33	In port	33	Before reported
8	Shanghai	8	General cargo, cotton, and passengers
6	San Francisco	6	General cargo, flour, and wheat
3	New ..... do	3	Ballast
2	Macao	2	General cargo
2	New York	2	Coal
2	Sydney	2	General cargo
2	Singapore	2	Ballast
2	Yoko.	2	General cargo and ballast
1	Macao	1	do
1	Nagasaki	1	Cotton
1	Jpan	1	Rice
1	Bangkok	1	General cargo
1	Kanagawa	1	Chinese passengers
1	Melbourne	1	General cargo
1	Foochau	1	Coal
1	Sunderland	1	General do
1	Ningpo	1	Lumber, &c.
1	Chfoo	1	Rice
1	Amoy	1	Coal
1	Reenter.		
1	Sual		
1	Cardiff		
72		**73**	

Vessels cleared:

No.	Whither	No.	Cargo
20	In port	20	In port
17	Singapore	17	Ballast, sundries, and passengers
7	Shanghai	7	do
5	Sold	5	Coal cargo, coal, &c.
4	Macao	4	Sold
3	Whampoa	3	Ballast
2	San Francisco	2	Ballast and sundries
2	Manila	2	General cargo and passengers
2	Nagasaki	2	Ballast
1	Sual	1	General cargo
1	Kanagawa	1	Ballast
1	Java	1	General cargo
1	Calcutta	1	Ballast
1	Bangkok	1	do
1	Chinese passengers	1	Rice
1	Ningpo	1	General cargo
1	General cargo	1	Ballast
1	Coal		
1	Lumber, &c.		
1	Rice		
1	Coal		
73		**73**	

Quarter ended March 31, 1864.§

Vessels entered:

No.	Whence	No.	Cargo
20	In port	6	Before reported
1	Calcutta	1	do
3	Sual	3	do
4	San Francisco	2	do
1	Yokohama	8	Re.
1	Sydney	1	do
1	Liverpool	1	do
1	Shanghai	1	do
2	New York	1	do
1	Amoy	1	General cargo and passengers
3	Whampoa	3	do
	Singapore	1	Coal
	Manila	1	do
	In port	2	General cargo
	Saigon	1	do
	Sual	1	Ballast
	Manila	1	do
6		**73**	

Vessels cleared:

No.	Cargo
20	In port
17	Sold; took Portuguese flag
5	Sold; took English flag
5	Condemned
3	Not stated
2	do
8	In port
1	Ballast
1	do
1	In port
1	Ballast
3	In port
1	Coal and spars
1	Ballast
1	In port
2	Ballast
2	In port
1	Sold; took British flag
1	Ballast
73	

* Entered: 7 ships, 2 steamers, 1 bark—10, and 8 in port. Cleared: 6 ships, 2 steamers, 8 class not reported—16, and 2 in port. Aggregate tonnage entered, 8,240.

† Entered: 2 steamers, 2 ships, 3 barks—7, and 2 in port. Cleared: 2 steamers, 1 bark, 1 class not given—4 in port. Aggregate tonnage entered, 5,461.

‡ Entered: 3 steamers, 26 ships, 8 barks, 2 brigs, 1 schooner—40, and 33 in port. Cleared: 4 steamer, 30 ships, 12 barks, 1 brig, 1 schooner—48, 5 sold, and 20 in port. Aggregate tonnage entered, 33,219.

§ Entered: 1 steamer, 10 ships, 11 barks—22, and 20 in port. Cleared: 1 steamer, 10 ships, 5 barks—16, 19 in port, 6 sold, 1 condemned—total, 42. Aggregate tonnage entered, 29,792.

Navigation and commerce of the United States with foreign countries—British Dominions.

COUNTRY, CONSULATE, NAME OF CONSUL, AND DATE OF RETURNS.	VESSELS				CARGOES					
	ENTERED		CLEARED		INWARD			OUTWARD		
	No.	Where from.	No.	Where for.	No.	Description.	Value.	No.	Description.	Value.
Quarter ended March 31, 1864—Continued.	2	Whampoa	1	Shanghai	1	Ballast		1	Ballast	
	1	Cardiff	1	In port	1	do.		1	In port	
	2	Manila	1	do.	1	Coal.		1	do.	
			1	Piolo.	3	Lumber and timber		1	Ballast	
			1	In port	1	do.		1	In port	
	42		42		42			42		
Quarter ended June 30, 1864.	19	In port	4	Sold.	4	Before reported		4	Sold; took English flag	
			6	Not stated.	2	do.		3	In port	
			1	San Francisco	6	do.		8	do.	
			1	Singapore	1	do.		12	General cargo and passengers	
			1	Foo-chow-foo	1	do.		8	Ballast.	
			2	Bangkok	1	do.		2	Sundries.	
			1	Manila	1	do.		1	Rice	
	1	Manila	1	Sual.	2	do.				
	4	Shanghai	1	Kanagawa.	1	do.				
			1	Whampoa	1	General cargo.				
			1	Manila	1	do.				
			1	Shanghai	1	do.				
	9	Whampoa	2	Whampoa	3	Rice and timber				
			3	San Francisco	3	Coal.				
	3	New York.	3	In port	1	Ballast				
	1	Sual.	1	Shanghai	2	Ice.				
	2	Boston	1	Foo-chow-foo	2	Sugar				
			1	Manila	1	Rice.				
	1	Newchwang.	1	In port	1	Peas				
	3	Singapore	1	do.	1	Coal				
	1	Cardiff	1	do.	1	Rice.				
	1	Bangkok.	1	do.						
	38		38		38			38		
Quarter ended September 30, 1864.	11	In port	1	Manila	1	Before reported		9	Not stated.	
			1	New York.	2	do.		2	In port.	
			1	Bangkok.	1	do.				
			2	Whampoa.	1	do.				
			1	Siam.	1	do.				

2	Singapore	1	Calcutta	...do	1	Not stated	
		2	Sold	...do	1	...do	
1	New York	1	Manila	Not stated	2	...do	
1	Chefoo	1	Shanghai	General cargo	1	In port	
1	Whampoa	1	In port	Cotton	1	...do	
2		1	...do	Ballast	1	In port	
1	Puget Sound	1	Manila	...do	1	Ballast	
1	Bangkok	1	In port	Lumber	1	In port	28,975 00
1	Newchwang	1	Whampoa	Rice	1	General cargo	51,900 00
1	Shanghai	1	In port	Pease	1	Not stated	
1	Swatow	1	Shanghai	General cargo	1	In port	11,000 00
		1	In port	Ballast			
22		22			22		

MELBOURNE.—*W. Blanchard.*
Quarter ended December 31, 1863.‡

7	In port	3	Otago	Before reported			2	Horses, sheep
		1	Callao	...do			2	Tea, wine, &c.
		1	Sydney	...do			1	Ballast
		1	China	...do			1	Part of inward cargo
		1	Sold	Sold			1	Sheep
							1	Sold

2	Boston	1	Otago	Notions, &c.	140,505 00	2	Horses and drays	37,150 00
		4	Akyab	Timber, carriages	100,430 00	1	Ballast	
4	Otago	1	Otago	Ballast		4	Salt, sheep, horses, fodder	46,850 00
1	Newcastle	1	...do			1	Sheep, fodder	11,850 00
2	San Francisco	1	In port	Grain and provisions	33,755 00	1	Forage	1,800 00
		1	Otago	Flour, grain, &c.	95,300 00	1	In port	
3	Sydney	3	In port	Ballast		1	Sheep, fodder	15,700 00
3	New York			Oats and timber	75,575 00	3	In port	
30		20			445,765 00	20		201,725 00

Quarter ended March 31, 1864.§

4	In port	1	San Francisco	Before reported		1	Ballast	
9	San Francisco	2	Newcastle	...do		2	Blankets, oats, beer	31,630 00
		1	Sold	...do		1	Oats, beer, &c.	51,250 00
2	San Francisco	1	Newcastle	Oats and wheat	42,950 00	1	Oats	42,700 00
		3	Sold	Oats, wheat, &c.	29,625 00	3	Sold	42,980 00
4	Otago	2	Otago	Hay	1,005 00	1	Sheep and fodder	
		1	Bluff Harbor	Ballast		1	Sold	
1	Antwerp	1	Callao	Timber	25,750 00	1	Ballast	

* Entered: 3 steamers, 10 ships, 6 barks—19, and 19 in port. Cleared: 3 steamers, 19 ships, 8 barks—23, 4 sold, and 11 in port. Aggregate tonnage entered, 13,007.
† Entered: 5 ships, 4 barks, 2 steamers—11, and 11 in port. Cleared: 4 ships, 3 steamers, 9 class not given—15, and 7 in port. Aggregate tonnage entered, 9,262.
‡ Entered: 7 ships, 5 barks, 1 brig—13, and 7 in port. Cleared: 8 ships, 5 barks, 2 class not given—if, 1 sold, and 4 in port. Aggregate tonnage entered, 10,176.
‡ Entered: 6 ships, 3 barks—9, and 4 in port. Cleared: 6 ships, 4 barks—0, 3 sold, and in port. Aggregate tonnage entered, 6,317.

Navigation and commerce of the United States with foreign countries—British Dominions.

COUNTRY, CONSULATE, NAME OF CONSUL, AND DATE OF RETURNS.	VESSELS				CARGOES					
	ENTERED		CLEARED		INWARD			OUTWARD		
	No.	Where from.	No.	Where for.	No.	Description.	Value.	No.	Description.	Value.
Quarter ended March 31, 1864—Continued.	1	Philadelphia.	1	Newcastle.	1	Timber.	$23,400 00	1	In port.	
	1	New Zealand.	1	Sold.	1	Wheat and bran.	25,350 00	1	Sold.	
	13		13		13		159,060 00	13		$167,860 00
Quarter ended June 30, 1864.*	1	In port.	1	Newcastle.	1	Before reported.		1	Ballast.	
	1	Bluff Harbor.	1	New Zealand.	1	Ballast.		1	Sheep and fodder.	15,200 00
	2	Boston.	1	do.	1	Timber.	8,545 00	1	Provisions and general cargo.	33,675 00
	1	Gothenburgh.	1	Calcutta.	1	Tobacco, timber, &c.	66,900 00	1	Ballast.	
	1	Newcastle.	1	Caliao.	1	Timber.	35,121 00	1	do.	
	2	New Zealand.	1	Newcastle.	1	Coals.	5,050 00	1	do.	
			2	In port.	2	Ballast.		2	In port.	
	8		8		8		115,616 00	8		48,675 00
Quarter ended September 30, 1864.†	2	In port.	1	New Zealand.	1	Ballast.		1	Ballast.	
	4	Newcastle.	1	Newcastle.	1	do.		1	do.	
			3	China.	1	1,054 tons coal.	7,905 00	1	In port.	
			1	Newcastle.	3	1,825 tons coal.	13,687 00	3	do.	
			1	do.	1	600,000 feet lumber.	30,124 42	1	Ballast.	
					1	Flour and walnuts.	80,000 00	1	300 tons miscellaneous.	6,000 00
	8		8		8		131,716 00	8		6,000 00
PORT ADELAIDE—J. W. Smith. Quarter ended December 31, 1863.‡	1	Vancouver's isl'd.	1	Brisbane.	1	400 tons lumber.		1	400 tons flour and wheat.	3,000 00
	1	Puget's Sound.	1	Sydney.	1	500 tons lumber.		1	500 tons flour and wheat.	4,000 00
	1	Bangor.	1	India.	1	1,300 tons lumber.	7,000 00	1	380 tons flour and wheat.	2,500 00
	1	Newcastle, N.S.W	1	Gerona.	1	400 tons coal.	600 00			
	4		4		4		7,600 00	4		9,500 00
Quarter ended March 31, 1864.§	1	Wallerro.	1	Auckland.	1	45 tons copper.	19,360 00	1	500 tons cornis.	33,880 00
	1	Puget's Sound.	1	Sydney.	1	600 tons lumber.	14,520 00	1		
	2		2		2		33,880 00	2		33,880 00
2d and 4th quarters.		No report.								

QUEBEC.—C. S. Ogden.

6 months ended December 31, 1863.||

ENTERED — No.	Whence	Cargo	Value	CLEARED — No.	Whither	Cargo	Value
1	New Orleans	Ballast		1	Liverpool	Deals, pipe staves, and ends	20,000 00
1	Bordeaux	...do...		1	London	...do...	10,000 00
1	Providencetown	800 bushels oysters	400 00	1	Prince Edward's	Flour, ballast	150 00
3			400 00	3			30,150 00

2d quarter...... No report.

Quarter ended June 30, 1864.¶

ENTERED — No.	Whence	Cargo	Value	CLEARED — No.	Whither	Cargo	Value
1	Philadelphia	Ballast		1	Liverpool	468 standard dry deals	12,000 00

4th quarter...... No report.

ST. JOHN'S, N. F.—C. O. Leach.

Quarter ended December 31, 1863.**

ENTERED — No.	Whence	Cargo	Value	CLEARED — No.	Whither	Cargo	Value
1	Whaling cruise	290 barrels oil, 3,500 lbs. bone	8,000 00	1	New London	Inward cargo	

Quarter ended March 31, 1864.††

ENTERED — No.	Whence	Cargo	Value	CLEARED — No.	Whither	Cargo	Value
1	Hamburg	3,722 bags bread, 20,000 bricks	8,000 00	1	New York	12 tons cod oil, 40 tons fish and bone manure, 1,092 quintals codfish, 505 barrels herring, 474 hides, 133 calfskins, 4 tierces salmon, 13,812 lbs. tea, 60 tons old iron, &c.	90,330 00

Quarter ended June 30, 1864.‡‡

ENTERED — No.	Whence	Cargo	Value	CLEARED — No.	Whither	Cargo	Value
1	New York	657 barrels flour, 66 barrels pork	6,000 00	1	Cow Bay	Ballast	
1	Rockland	925 casks lime, 14 tons hay, 1,500 feet lumber	1,220 00	1	Lingan	...do...	
2	New London	Whaling outfit		2	Hudson's Bay	Whaling outfit	
4			7,220 00	4			

Quarter ended September 30, 1864.§§

ENTERED — No.	Whence	Cargo	Value	CLEARED — No.	Whither	Cargo	Value
1	Bangor	314 tons hay, bricks	1,150 00	1	Glace Bay	Ballast	
1	Baltimore	80 bbls. beef and pork, 1,133 bbls. flour	6,000 00	1	Boston	Old iron, junk, fish, &c.	3,000 00
1	New London	Whaling outfit	575 00	1	Hudson's Bay	Whaling outfit	
1	Rockland	1,100 barrels lime, 30,000 laths, 3,000 bricks, 5 tons hay	11,000 00	1	Lingan	Ballast	
1	Philadelphia	1,900 barrels flour		1	Cow Bay	...do...	
1	Whaling voyage	400 bbls. oil, 6,000 lbs. bone		1	New London	Inward cargo	3,000 00
6			18,725 00	6			

H. Ex. Doc. 60——3*

* Entered: 5 ships, 1 brig, 1 bark—7, and 1 in port. Cleared: 5 ships, 1 brig—6, and 2 in port. Aggregate tonnage entered, 5,019.
† Entered: 4 ships, 1 bark, 1 brig—6, and 2 in port. Cleared: 3 ships, 1 bark—4, and 4 in port. Aggregate tonnage entered, 4,866.
‡ Entered and cleared: 4, class not given. Aggregate tonnage entered, 1,937 79-95. § Entered and cleared: 2, class not given. Aggregate tonnage entered, 939.
|| Entered and cleared: 2 ships, 1 schooner—3. Aggregate tonnage entered, 3. Tonnage, 999 31-95.
¶ Entered and cleared: 1 brig. Tonnage, 190. ** Entered and cleared: 1 brig. Tonnage, 497. †† Entered and cleared: 1 schooner. Tonnage, 1,868.
‡‡ Entered and cleared: 4 schooners. Aggregate tonnage entered, 431. §§ Entered and cleared: 1 brig, 5 schooners—6. Aggregate tonnage entered, 934.

Navigation and commerce of the United States with foreign countries—British Dominions.

COUNTRY, CONSULATE, NAME OF CONSUL, AND DATE OF RETURNS.	VESSELS.				CARGOES.					
	ENTERED.		CLEARED.		INWARD.			OUTWARD.		
	No.	Where from.	No.	Where for.	No.	Description.	Value.	No.	Description.	Value.
HALIFAX—*M. M. Jackson.*										
Quarter ended December 31, 1863.*	1	New York...	1	Cape Breton...	1	925 barrels flour and merchandise.	$2,500 00	1	Ballast........	
	3	Gloucester.	3	Newfoundland	3	Flour, provisions, &c., for fisheries	12,000 00	3	....do........	
	4		4		4		14,500 00	4		
Quarter ended March 31, 1864.†	1	Boston......	1	Sold........	1	Ballast........		1	Sold........	
	1	Eastport....	1	Eastport....	1	4,450 boxes smoked herring.	500 00	1	Ballast........	$2,500 00
	1	Newfoundland			1	492 barrels herring	2,500 00	1	Inward cargo	2,500 00
	3		3		3		3,000 00	3		2,500 00
Quarter ended June 30, 1864.‡	1	New York...	1	Halifax......	1	Flour, pork, apples, sugar.	10,000 00	1	Ballast........	
	3	Camden......	1	Calais......	1	Lime........	1,160 00	1	....do........	
			1	Pictou......	1	....do........	800 00	1	....do........	
	1	Baltimore...	1	Glace Bay...	1	....do........	720 00	1	....do........	
	1	Beverly.....	1	Baltimore...	1	Flour.......	8,416 00	1	....do........	
	1	Boston......	1	Fishing Banks	1	Fishing supplies.		1	....do........	
	1	Prince Ed. Island	1	Prince Ed. Island	1	Merchandise.	400 00	1	....do........	
	1	Boston......	1	Boston......	1	....do........	1,000 00	1	....do........	
	1	Eastport....	1	Eastport....	1	Herring......	900 00	1	....do........	
	1	Rockland....	1	Tignish, C. B.	1	Lime........	600 00	1	....do........	
	1	Provincetown	1	Newfoundland	1	Codfish......	1,575 00	1	....do........	
	11		11		11		25,571 00	11		
Quarter ended September 30, 1864.§	1	Rockland....	1	Lingan......	1	600 barrels lime.	500 00	1	Ballast........	
	1	Thomaston..	1	Eastport....	1	585.....do....	530 00	1	2,175....salt.	3,800 00
	1	Kingston....	1	Pictou......	1	642 punchoons molasses	8,000 00	1	Ballast........	
	9	Boston......	9	Charlottetown	9	300 barrels flour, 50 bbls. meal and merchandise.	4,000 00	9	Flour, fish, and merchandise.	12,500 00
	1	New York...	1	Kingston....	1	175 tons moulding sand.	800 00	1	Ballast........	
	1	Baltimore...	4	Cape Breton.	4	655 bbls. flour, 900 bbls. bread	7,000 00	4	....do........	
	6	Charlottetown	9	Pictou......	1	Flour, merchandise, &c.	8,000 00	9	2,000 bbls. fish and merchandise	65,500 00
			9	Charlottetown	1	Alcohol and merchandise	300 00	4	Merchandise.	
	1	Bangor......	1	Bridgeport..	1	23,000 bricks.		1	Ballast........	
	14		14		14		28,130 00	14		$81,800 00

PICTOU.—B. H. Norton.

Quarter ended December 31, 1863.‖

No.	Where from (cleared)	No.		No.	Cargo		No.	Cargo	Value
3	Boston	1	Boston						
1	Nantucket	1	Warren						
1	Pembroke	1	Somerset						
1	Wareham	1	Nantucket						
1	Spain	1	Wareham						
2	Ireland	1	..do	10	Ballast		10	3,864 tons coal	9,660 00
1	France	1	Boston						
		1	Somerset						
		1	Somerset						
		1	Boston						
10		10		10			10		9,660 00

2d quarter. No report.

Quarter ended June 30, 1864.¶

No.	Where from	No.	Cleared	No.	Cargo	Value	No.	Cargo	Value
1	Rockland	1	Prince Ed. Island	1	800 barrels lime	800 00	1	Ballast	
5	New York	3	New York				5	3,177 tons coal	6,857 50
		5	Somerset		Ballast				
13	Boston	9	Boston		do		2	1,365 ..do	3,385 50
		2	Fall River		do		4	In port	
		1	Providence		do		4	do	
		1	New Bedford		do		3	do	
1	Portland	1	Portland		do		1	do	
1	New London	1	Portsmouth		do		1	Ballast	
2	Halifax	1	Prince Ed. Island		do		1	In port	
1	Quebec	1	Wareham		do		1	Ballast	
1	Prince Ed. Island	1	New York		do		1	In port	
		1	Bangor						
25		25		25		800 00	25		10,943 00

Quarter ended September 30, 1864.**

No.		No.		No.			No.	Cargo	Value
15	In port	1	Providence	1	Before reported		1	409 tons coal	1,072 50
		1	Portsmouth	1	do		1	144 ..do	380 00
		1	New York	1	do		1	444 ..do	1,110 00
		1	Bangor	1	do		1	158 ..do	398 00
		6	Boston	6	do		6	3,206 ..do	8,015 00
		2	Fall River	2	do		9	755 ..do	1,890 00
		1	New Bedford	1	do		1	366 ..do	915 00
		1	Wareham	1	do		1	198 ..do	480 50
		1	Portland	1	do		1	357 ..do	692 50

* Entered and cleared: 4 schooners. Aggregate tonnage entered, 494 79-95.   † Entered: 1 sloop, 2 schooners—3. Cleared: 2 schooners, 1 sold. Aggregate tonnage entered, 214.
‡ Entered and cleared: 9 schooners, 2 steamers—11. Aggregate tonnage entered, 1,499 67-95.   § Entered and cleared: 6 schooners, 8 steamers—14. Aggregate tonnage entered, 7,301.
¶ Entered and cleared: 1 ship, 2 barks, 4 brigs, 3 schooners—10. Aggregate tonnage entered, 2,794.
‖ Entered: 11 barks, 8 brig, 4 schooners, 2 steamers—25. Cleared: 4 barks, 3 brigs, 1 schooner, 2 steamers—10, and 15 in port. Aggregate tonnage entered, 7,780.
** Entered: 20 barks, 35 brigs, 38 schooners, 2 steamers—105, and 15 in port. Cleared: 21 barks, 40 brigs, 23 schooners, 2 steamers—86, and 34 in port. Aggregate tonnage entered, 27,491.

Navigation and commerce of the United States with foreign countries—British Dominions.

PICTOU.—B. H. Norton. Quarter ended September 30, 1864—Continued.

COUNTRY, CONSULATE, NAME OF CONSUL, AND DATE OF RETURNS.	VESSELS				CARGOES					
	ENTERED		CLEARED		INWARD			OUTWARD		
	No.	Where from	No.	Where for	No.	Description	Value	No.	Description	Value
	31	Boston	9	Boston	9	Ballast		9	5,194 tons coal	$12,995 00
			4	Providence	4	do		4	1,511..do	3,777 50
			1	Dighton	1	do		5	925..do	2,562 50
			5	Pembroke	5	do		1	1,199..do	2,997 50
			1	Somerset	1	do		1	340..do	850 00
			1	New York	1	do		1	1,040..do	9,600 00
			1	New Haven	1	do		1	300..do	750 00
			1	Wareham	1	do		1	222..do	630 00
			1	Portland	1	do		1	351..do	877 50
			1	Glace Bay	6	do		6	Ballast	
	1	Bucksport	6	In port	1	do		4	In port	
	10	Eastport	1	New York	4	do		4	225 tons coal	970 00
			4	Pembroke	5	do		1	948..do	2,372 00
			1	New York	1	do		5	500..do	2,000 00
	15	Portland	5	In port	6	do			In port	727 50
			1	Pembroke	8	do		1	591 tons coal	
			6	Portland	1	do		6	1,786..do	4,465 00
	14	New York	8	In port	1	do		8	In port	
			1	New Haven	1	do		1	402 tons coal	1,005 00
			4	Boston	1	do		1	1,360..do	3,400 00
			1	Providence	1	do		1	834..do	2,085 00
			1	Wareham	1	do		1	402..do	1,005 00
			1	New York	4	do		1	813..do	2,032 00
			1	Somerset	3	240 barrels lime	$192 00	1	420..do	1,050 00
			1	Glace Bay		Ballast		4	Ballast	
	1	Rockland	4	In port	1	do		1	In port	
	10	Providence	1	New Haven	1	do		3	102 tons coal	255 00
			3	Providence	1	do		1	960..do	2,400 00
			1	Fall River	1	do		1	480..do	1,200 00
			1	Bangor	1	do		1	350..do	875 00
			1	Wareham	2	do		1	270..do	677 00
			1	Boston	2	do		1	330..do	825 00
			1	Dighton	1	do		2	301..do	502 50
	2	Thomaston	2	In port	1	do		2	In port	
	1	Buffalo	2	do	1	do		2	do	
	2	New Haven	1	New York	1	do		1	Ballast	
	2	New Bedford	1	In port	1	do		2	In port	
			2	New Bedford	1	do		1	354 tons coal	494 80
			1	Glace Bay	1	do		1	Ballast	
	1	Lubec	1	Pembroke	1	do		1	301 tons coal	502 50

No.	Port entered	No.	Port cleared	Cargo / remarks	Value	No.	Cargo	Value
1	Searport	1	Gardiner			1	200....do	750 00
2	Fall River	1	Providence			1	450....do	1,125 00
		1	Boston			1	336....do	837 00
2	Norwich	1	Norwich			1	334....do	1,057 00
1	Edgartown	1	In port			1	166 tons coal	460 00
1	Wiscasset	1	Wareham			1	In pt	
2	Somerset	2	In port			2	do	
1	Cruising	1	do			1	Bat	
1	Halifax	1	Cruising			1	150 tons coal	397 50
1	Teneriffe	1	Wareham			1	334....do	885 00
1	Prince Ed. Island	1	Boston			1	In port	
2	Fishing	1	In port			2	Fishing supplies	
		1	Eng					
130		130			192 00	130		74,757 00

ST. JOHN, N.B.—J. Q. Howard.
Quarter ended December 31, 1861.*

No.	Port entered	No.	Port cleared	Cargo / remarks	Value	No.	Cargo	Value
8	In port	3	Liverpool	Before reported		1	642 deals	10,972 00
		3	Penarth roads	do		3	943 deals	13,488 00
		1	Wilmington	do		1	200,000 laths and palings	561 00
21	Eastport	21	Eastport	do		21	Passengers	
6	Boston	2	Boston	Passengers, 30 barrels apples	160 00	1	50,000 pine boards and spruce	2,561 00
				30 barrels flour, 10 barrels apples		1	104,700 feet pine boards	1,820 00
1	Portland	1	Portland	167 tons coal	1,670 00	1	20,000 boards, 494,000 laths	1,828 00
1	London	1	London	Ballast		1	415 standard deals	6,640 00
1	Philadelphia	1	Philadelphia	do		1	Deals and scantling	885 00
1	Washington	1	Washington	do		1	192,000 feet pine lumber	1,000 00
2	Philadelphia	2	Philadelphia	do		2	120,000 feet pine boards	1,185 00
		1	Boston	do		1	120 M O'ds., &c., 100 M pickets, &c.	600 00
3	Philadelphia	1	Queenstown	292½ tons coal	2,625 00	1	594 standard deals	500 00
		1	Baltimore	908 tons coal	2,080 00	1	313,000 feet boards and laths	1,334 00
		1	Eastport	175 tons coal	1,750 00	1	Ballast	
9	New York	1	Philadelphia	Ballast		9	Took British flag	
		1	Took British flag	do		1	248,000 feet boards, 457 deals	9,812 00
9	London	2	Liverpool	do		9	1,022 standard deals	16,038 00
1	Frenchman's Bay	1	London	do		1	130,000 boards and scantling	1,300 00
1	Cherryfield	1	Boston	30 tons iron	150 00	1	4,224 feet boards and plank	1,130 00
1	New Orleans	1	Took British flag	Ballast		1	Took British flag	
1	Portland	1	Philadelphia	236 tons coal	2,360 00	1	116 M b'ds, 62 M laths, 25 tons iron	1,200 00
1	Baltimore	1	Washington	125,000 feet oak timber	6,000 00	1	40,000 scantling, 129,000 boards	2,100 00
1	Bath	1	In port	Ballast		1	In port	
1	Calais	1	do	do		1	do	
1	Waldoboro'	1	London	do		1	469 standard deals	7,504 00
54		54			16,395 00	54		85,732 68

* Entered: 22 steamers, 12 schooners, 8 ships, 3 brigs, 1 bark—46, and 8 in port. Cleared: 10 ships, 2 barks, 4 brigs, 22 steamers, 12 schooners—50, 2 sold, and 2 in port. Aggregate tonnage entered, 98,541.

Navigation and commerce of the United States with foreign countries—British Dominions.

COUNTRY, CONSULATE, NAME OF CONSUL, AND DATE OF RETURNS.	VESSELS.					CARGOES.					
	ENTERED.		CLEARED.			INWARD.			OUTWARD.		
	No.	Where from.	No.	Where for.	No.	Description.	Value.	No.	Description.	Value.	
St. Johns, N. B.—J. Q. Howard.											
Quarter ended March 31, 1864.*	3	In port.	1	London.	1	Before reported			933 standard deals	$15,414 00	
			1	Liverpool	1	do.			In port.		
	5	Eastport.	1	In port.	1			5	Passengers	2,740 00	
	4	Thomaston.	5	Eastport.	5	Passengers—35 barrels flour	$175 00	1	137,000 pine lumber	1,147 00	
			1	Boston.	1	White oak timber	5,900 00	1	200,000 boards and scantling		
			1	Philadelphia.	1	160 tons timber	3,840 00	1	In port.		
	3	Machias.	2	In port.	2	Ballast.		1	7,000 feet spruce boards	1,047 00	
			2	Boston.	2	Flour and meal	1,731 00	2	In port.		
	1	Portland.	2	In port.	2	Ballast.		2	114,000 shipping boards	1,435 00	
	1	London.	1	Boston.	1	do.		1	In port.		
	1	New Orleans.	1	do.	1	do.		1	do.		
	18		18		18		10,946 00	18		21,773 00	
Quarter ended June 30, 1864.†	7	In port.	1	Eastport.	1	Before reported		1	Ballast.		
			3	Liverpool	3	do.		3	1,458 standard deals	25,190 88	
			1	Melbourne.	1	do.		1	do.	4,900 00	
			2	Boston.	2	do.		2	210. do.	685 00	
	26	Eastport.	25	Eastport.	25	Passengers.		25	625 poles.		
			1	Philadelphia.	1	Ballast.		1	Passengers	591 00	
	10	Boston.	3	Boston.	3	12 barrels flour and general cargo	2,184 00	3	Pine boards.	9,077 00	
			2	New York.	2	550 poles, 106,000 feet boards		2	550 poles, 106,000 feet boards		
			1	Penarth river.	1	do.		1	154,000 feet lumber, 330 poles.	1,670 00	
			1	Philadelphia.	1	do.		1	410 standard deals	8,200 00	
	4	New York.	1	Liverpool	1	do.		1	300,000 boards and pickets	10,600 00	
			1	Providence	1	do.		1	530 standard deals.	10,111 87	
			1	In port.	1	do.		1	104,671 feet pine boards & plank.		
	3	Philadelphia.	3	Liverpool	3	do.		3	In port.		
			1	In port.	1	do.		1	447 standard deals	8,940 00	
	3	Machias.	2	Liverpool	2	do.		2	619 standard deals	11,934 00	
			1	New York.	1	60 barrels flour.	480 00	1	In port.		
	1	Providence.	1	Boston.	1	Ballast.		1	860 poles.	860 00	
	3	Bath.	2	Liverpool.	2	do.		2	Lumber.	5,395 00	
			1	In port.	1	do.		1	851 standard deals.	14,840 00	
									In port.		

	Port	Cargo	Value	No.	Cargo	Value
1	New Orleans	do.		1	421 standard deals.	8,210 00
1	Fort Monroe	do.		1	In port.	140 00
1	Jonesport	do.		1	140 poles.	140 00
1	Baltimore	961 tons oak timber.	5,271 00	1	112,800 laths.	639 00
1	Centreville	125 ...... do.	2,500 00	1	120,000 feet lumber.	9,892 00
1	Belfast	Ballast.		1	81,000 ... do.	
1	Havana	3,500 sugar.	3,500 00	1	120,000 feet pine boards.	2,655 00
1		216 tons oak timber.	5,184 00	1	Laths and paling.	2,400 00
1	Salem			1		738 00
1		Ballast.		1	340,000 boards and pickets.	836 00
66			19,059 00	66		114,580 16

Quarter ended September 30, 1864.‡

	Port	Cargo	Value	No.	Cargo	Value
8	In port	Before reported.		6	2,445 standard deals.	48,988 00
		do.			500 ... do.	10,040 00
		do.			383 ... do.	7,360 00
30	Eastport	Passengers.		26	Passengers.	
3		Ballast.		1	In port.	740 00
				1	115,555 feet boards and scantling.	
8	Boston	do.		1	Ballast.	
1		do.		1	134,000 palings.	492 00
1		do.		1	144 standard deals.	2,880 00
1		do.		1	78,558 feet lumber.	749 00
1		20 barrels flour.	110 00	1	955 ship knees, 52 barrels ore.	927 00
3		144 tons coal.	1,008 00	3	1,250 spruce poles.	680 00
		Ballast.				
6	Machias	do.		6	2,350 spruce poles, 800 railroad sleepers.	1,490 00
4		do.		3	1,525 standard deals.	0,300 00
3	New York	do.				
2		do.		2	812 ... do.	
1	Bath	d.		1		16,940 00
2	Belfast	do.		2	490,000 laths.	970 00
2		do.		1	118,037 feet pine	1,564 00
2		do.		2	214,000 ... do.	2,346 00
	Maryland	240 tons oak timber.	8,890 00		450,375 pickets.	531 54
1		145 sticks oak timber.		1	485 standard deals.	9,700 00
2	Newburyport	Ballast.		2	In port.	
1		920 tons oak timber.	4,200 00	1	880,000 laths.	430 00
1	Bangor	Ballast.		1	190 standard deals.	800 00
1	Camden	do.		1	45,000 boards and scantling.	358 00
1	Citoler	do.		1	1,502,000 laths.	541 00
1	Frankfort	3ds. sugar; 87 hhds., 25 tierces, and 52 barrels molasses.	8,920 00	1	53,000 feet boards.	859 00
1	Fort Monroe	295 tons coal.	9,950 00	1	486 standard deals.	9,730 00
1	Jonesboro'	Ballast.		1	204,000 palings.	500 00
1	Philadelphia	200 tons coal.	1,400 00	1	Ballast.	
1	Portsmouth	Ballast.		1	90,000 superficial feet deals.	550 00

* Entered: 3 ships, 4 steamers, 1 srk, 7 schooners—15, and 3 in port. Cleared: 2 ships, 4 steamers, 5 schooners—11, and 7 in port. Aggregate (tonnage) entered, 8,294.
† Entered: 25 steamers, 14 ships, 18 schooners, 1 brk, 1 brig—59, and 7 in port. Cleared: 36 steamers, 9 ships, 2 barks, 1 brig, 30 schooners—58, and 8 in port. Aggregate tonnage entered, 36,729.
‡ Entered: 8 ships, 96 steamers, 2 barks, 3 brigs, 96 schooners—67, and 8 in port. Cleared: 15 ships, 96 steamers, 2 barks, 3 brigs, 23 schooners—69, and 6 in port. Aggregate tonnage entered, 33,731.

Navigation and commerce of the United States with foreign countries—British Dominions.

COUNTRY, CONSULATE, NAME OF CONSUL, AND DATE OF RETURNS.	VESSELS				CARGOES					
	ENTERED.		CLEARED.		INWARD.			OUTWARD.		
	No.	Where from.	No.	Where for.	No.	Description.	Value.	No.	Description.	Value.
ST. JOHNS, N. B.—J. Q. Howard. Quarter ended September 30, 1864—Continued.	1	Providence	1	Boston	1	73 barrels flour	$401 00	1	107,000 feet lumber	$966 00
	1	St. Andrews	1	In port	1	Ballast		1	In port	
	1	Thomaston	1	...do.	1	135 tons oak timber	2,000 00	1	...do.	
	75		75		75		29,169 00	75		153,112 54
BERMUDA—C. M. Allen. Quarter ended December 31, 1863.*	1	Philadelphia	1	Cond'd and sold	1	Coal	1,376 00	1	Condemned and sold	40,000 00
	1	New Bedford	1	Rio de Janeiro	1	Lumber and general cargo	40,000 00	1	Inward cargo	
	2		2		2		41,376 00	2		40,000 00
2d quarter		No report								
Quarter ended June 30, 1864.†	1	In port	1	New York	1	Before reported		1	Part of inward cargo	4,000 00
	2	Whaling	1	Condemned	1	60 barrels oil	2,400 00	1	Condemned	
	1	New York	1	In port	1	250 ...do.	10,000 00	1	In port	
	1	New York	1	Sold	1	Dry goods, &c.	11,700 00	1	Ballast	
	2	Boston	1	Boston	1	40 tons general cargo	1,300 00	1	Sold—took English flag	9,000 00
	1	Bangor	2	Boston	2	20,000 feet lumber and general cargo	3,300 00	2	Sold 250 bbls. vegetables, dry goods, &c.	
			1	Turk's island	1	250,000 feet lumber	6,300 00	1	In port	
	8		8		8		34,800 00	8		13,000 00
4th quarter		No report								
NASSAU, N. P.—T. Kirkpatrick. 1st, 2d, and 3d quarters		No reports								
Quarter ended September 30, 1864.‡	2	Boston	1	New York	1	General cargo	8,575 85	1	Leather, cotton, &c.	3,451 90
		New York	1	Boston	1	Provisions	3,794 80	1	Cigars, fish, &c.	1,756 80
	4		2	New York	2	Ice, brick, lumber, &c.	3,388 00	2	Iron, cotton, salt.	6,180 00

IRAGUA (Bahama).—D. Sargent.

1st, 2d, and 3d quarters.

No.	Port	No.	Cleared for	Cargo	Value	No.	Cargo	Value
3	Bath, Me.	1	Havana	Put in for coal, &c.		1	Inward cargo	
1	St. Thomas	1	in port	Provisions, lumber, &c.	16,000 00	1	in port	
4	Key West	3	Holmes' Hole	Ice, provisions, lumber	7,996 84	3	29,000 bushels salt	
		2	St. Thomas	Coffee, rum, sugar	3,115 90	2	Ballast	2,898 40
1	Havana	1	Key West	Shoes, turtle, &c.	710 40	1	do	
1	Harbor Island	1	Sold	Ballast		1	Sold	
		1	in port	do		1	in port	
		1	Key West	do	1,700 70	1	Ballast	
			Sold	Flour, &c.			Sold	
16		16			45,980 89	16		14,985 80

No reports.

Quarter ended September 30, 1864.§

No.	Port	No.	Cleared for	Cargo	Value	No.	Cargo	Value
1	Martinique	1	Bangor	Ballast		1	4,149 bushels salt	539 37
1	Baltimore	1	U.S. of Colombia	Stranded	48 00	1	Stranded	3,650 31
1	Jamaica	1	Boston	Ballast		1	90,387 bushels salt	
3		3				3		3,189 08

TURK'S ISLAND.—J. C. Crisson.

Quarter ended December 31, 1863.‖

No.	Port	No.	Cleared for	Cargo	Value	No.	Cargo	Value
1	Madeira	1	United States	Ballast		1	10,520 bushels salt	789 75
1	Trinidad	1	do	Shingles		1	10,872 bushels salt	763 54
9	St. Thomas	9	Salt Cay	Ballast		1	Ballast	389 15
		1	do	do		1	4,180 bushels salt	1,361 53
4	Guadaloupe	2	Salt Cay	Assorted cargo	500 00	4	14,940 bushels salt	2,018 48
		9	United States	Ballast		9	95,530 bushels salt	
11	St. Croix	11	do	Assorted cargo		8	9,128 bushels salt	733 54
9	Porto Rico		do			3	58,554 bushels salt	58,554 90
	Boston	1	Trujillo	in port		1	in port	
				Inward cargo	5,000 00		Inward cargo	4,000 00
1	New York	1	Condemned	General cargo	7,000 00	1	Condemned	902 85
1	Cape Haytien	1	United States	Ballast		1	8,690 bushels salt	729 53
1	Cayenne	1	do	do		1	8,558 bushels salt	690 91
		1	do	do		1	8,602 bushels salt	
26		26			19,848 00	26		17,331 98

* Entered: 1 ship, 1 bark—2. Cleared: 1 ship, and 1 condemned. Aggregate tonnage entered, 756 98-95.

† Entered: 1 steamer, 1 bark, 1 brig, 4 schooners—7, in port 1. Cleared: 1 brig, 3 schooners—4, 1 sold, 1 condemned, 2 in port. Aggregate tonnage entered, 939 49-95.

‡ Entered: 1 ship, 1 bark, 2 brigs, 8 schooners, 4 sloops—16. Cleared: 6 schooners, 2 brigs, 1 bark, 1 sloop—11, 2 sold, 3 in port. Aggregate tonnage entered, 3,147.

§ Entered: 2 schooner, 2 barks—3. Cleared: 1 schooner, 2 barks—3, and 3 in port. Aggregate tonnage entered, 704.

‖ Entered: 8 barks, 11 brig, 7 schooners—26. Cleared: 8 barks, 11 brig, 4 schooners—23, and 3 in port. Aggregate tonnage entered, 5,986.

SALT CAY.—A. W. Harriott.

Quarter ended December 31, 1863.§

No.	Cleared to	No.	Cargo	Value	No.	Entered from	Cargo	Tonnage
2	Porto Rico	2	do assorted cargo		2	Newburyport	8,490 bushels salt	1,231 68
1	Ponce, P. R.	1	75 barrels assorted cargo	600 00	1	Hartford	5,584 bushels salt	784 26
3	New York	3	700 barrels assorted cargo	5,000 00	2	New York	{16,514 bushels salt / 10 barrels old copper}	2,597 38
			Ballast		1		Old iron, &c.	1,510 75
					1		450 barrels assorted cargo	3,300 00
1	Boston	1	900 barrels assorted cargo	2,000 00	1	Truxillo		
14		14		11,600 00	14			16,650 33

Quarter ended March 31, 1864.|| (Block — 12)

No.	Port	No.	Cargo	Value	No.	Port	Cargo	Tonnage
2	St. Croix	2	Not stated		1	Newport, R. I.	10,162 1 sal ... salt	815 46
2	Cape Haytien	2	do	99 90	1	New Haven	3,764 bushels salt	341 96
			946 barrels lime		1	Philadelphia	13,352 bushels salt	1,037 98
3	Mayaguez	3	Not stated		1	New Haven	14,678 bushels do.	1,176 74
2	Grand Turk	2	do		1	Boston	14,740 bushels salt	1,937 58
1	Ponce	1	do		2	Newburyport	957 bushels salt	735 86
1	Curacao	1	do		1	New Haven	6,388 bushels salt	576 48
1	St. Thomas	1	do		1	Philadelphia	11,684 bushels salt	937 98
12	In port	12	do	99 90	12	In port	In port.	6,557 76

Quarter ended March 31, 1864.|| (Block — 5)

No.	Port	No.	Cargo	Value	No.	Port	Cargo	Tonnage
1	In port	1	Not stated		1	Not stated	13,120 bble salt	1,249 85
2	St. Thomas	1	Before reported		1	Holmes' Hole	5,424 bushels salt	517 76
1	Arroyo, P. R.	1	Ballast		1	Boston	6,138 bushels salt	895 61
1	Ponce, P. R.	1	do		1	New York	984 bushels salt	851 15
			do		1	New London	9,160 bushels salt	1,010 10
5		5			5			4,214 49

Quarter ended June 30, 1864.¶

No.	Port	No.	Cargo	Value	No.	Port	Cargo	Tonnage
2	Mayaguez	2	Ballast		2	Baltimore		
2	Grand Turk	2			1	Bangor		
1	Havana	1			1	Boston		
1	Key West	1			1	Bath		
1	Belfast	1	do		1	Philadelphia	77,036 bushels salt	
1	Martinique	1	Hay, lumber, and flour	300 00	1	Belfast		10,481 10
1	Georgetown	1	Ballast		1	New York		
1	Ponce	1	do		1	do		
10		10			10	Baltimore		10,481 10

4th quarter.... No report. .... | 10,481 10

* Entered: 5 brigs, 2 barks, 9 schooners—16, and 3 in port. Cleared: 4 brigs, 2 barks, 12 schooners—18, and 1 in port. Aggregate tonnage entered, 2,823 60-95.
† Entered: 5 schooners, 1 bark, 1 brig—7, and 1 in port. Cleared: 5 schooners, 1 bark, 2 brigs—8. Aggregate tonnage entered, 1,341 47-95.
‡ Entered and cleared: 2 barks, 6 brigs, 6 schooners—14. Aggregate tonnage entered, 2,909 39-95.
§ Entered: 2 barks, 8 brigs, 2 schooners, and 1 in port—12. Cleared: 2 barks, 7 brigs, 2 schooners—11, and 1 in port. Aggregate tonnage entered, 3,346 65-95.
|| Entered: 4 brigs, and 1 in port. Cleared: 5 brigs. Aggregate tonnage entered, 1,061 14-95.
¶ Entered and cleared: 1 ship, 5 brigs 4 schooners—10. Aggregate tonnage entered, 2,339 75-95.

Navigation and commerce of the United States with foreign countries—British Dominions.

COUNTRY, CONSULATE, NAME OF CONSUL, AND DATE OF RETURNS.	VESSELS.				CARGOES.					
	ENTERED.		CLEARED.		INWARD.			OUTWARD.		
	No.	Where from.	No.	Where for.	No.	Description.	Value.	No.	Description.	Value.
EAST HARBOR, (Turk's Isl'd.) E. Jones.										
Quarter ended December 31, 1863.*	1	Porto Rico	1	Boston	1	Not stated		1	8,500 bushels salt	$982 50
	1	Guadaloupe	1	do	1	do		1	5,000 bushels salt	402 50
	1	St. Martin's	1	Philadelphia	1	do		1	7,000 bushels salt	562 50
	1	Trinidad	1	do	1	do		1	Wrecked	
	1	Miragoane	1	Wrecked	1	do		1	Wrecked	
	1	St. Lucia	1	Baltimore				1		
	6		6		6			6		1,647 50
A. Morrison.										
Quarter ended March 31, 1864.†	1	In port	1	United States	1	Before reported		1	5,530 bushels salt	535 50
	1	Trinidad	1	Philadelphia	1	Ballast		1	8,400 bushels salt	662 50
	2		2		2			2		1,198 00
Quarter ended June 30, 1864.‡	1	Barbadoes	1	Grand Turk	1	Ballast		1	434 bushels salt	45 57
Quarter ended September 30, 1864.§	1	Porto Rico	1	Baltimore	1	Ballast		{2}	10,639 bushels salt	1,380 84
	1	Curacoa	1	Philadelphia	1	do				
	2		2		2			2		1,380 84
ST. CHRISTOPHER—E. De Isle.										
Quarter ended December 31, 1863.‖	1	Guadaloupe	1	St. Martin's	{2}	2,300 barrels breadstuffs	$17,000 00	1	Ballast	
	1	New York	1	New York	1	Ballast		1	1,064 barrels salt	966 00
	1	Barbadoes	1	..do				1	2,937 barrels salt	734 25
	3		3		3		17,000 00	3		1,000 25
Quarter ended March 31, 1864.¶	1	Beaufort	1	Beaufort	1	140,000 shingles and staves	1,300 00	1	Ballast	
	1	New York	1	Banaco	1	1,100 barrels breadstuffs	8,000 00	1	In port	
	2		2		2		9,300 00	2		

Quarter ended June 30, '64,**

No.	Whence	No.	Imports	Value	No.	Exports	Value
1	Granada	1	1,000 barrels breadstuffs	10,000 00	1	Ballast	
1	Sombrero	1	300 tons guano	3,000 00	1	300 tons guano	3,000 00
2		2		13,000 00	2		3,000 00

Quarter ended September 30, 1864.††

No.	Whence	No.	Imports	Value	No.	Exports	Value
1	Nevis	1	100 barrels breadstuffs	800 00	1	Ballast	
2	New York	1	1,000 barrels breadstuffs	10,000 00	1	1,000 barrels salt	300 00
		1	800 barrels breadstuffs	1,200 00	1	Ballast	
3		3		12,000 00	3		300 00

ANTIGUA.—M. Galody.
1st and 2d quarters.

No arrivals. — No departures.

Quarter ended June 30, 1864,‡‡

No.	Whence	No.	Imports	Value	No.	Exports	Value
2	Baltimore	§2	Flour, corn, meal, lard, butter, and other provisions	}17,965 00	2	Ballast	
					1	Porto Rico	
					1	Spanish Main	
2		§2		17,965 00	2		

Quarter ended September 30, 1864.§§

No.	Whence	No.	Imports	Value	No.	Exports	Value
2	Baltimore	2	Provisions	22,000 00	2	Ballast	
1	Philadelphia	1	....do	15,000 00	1	Condemned and sold	
3		3		37,000 00	3		

BARBADOES.—W. J. Trowbridge.
Quarter ended December 31, 1863.‖‖

No.	Whence	No.	Imports	Value	No.	Exports	Value
14	New York	17	100 bbls. apples, 168 bbls. bread, 100 bbls. beef, 300 half bbls. beef, 40 dos. brooms, 2,468 bags bread, 325 kegs butter, 3,343 bags corn, 244 bbls. crackers, 8,355 bbls. corn meal, 7 carriages, 633 boxes candles, 360 boxes cheese, 12,783 bbls. flour, 29 boxes fish, 10 tierces hams, 209 firkins lard, 30 bbls. oil, 140 bags oil-cakes, 356 puncheons oil meal, 639 bbls. pork, 2,020 bbls. potatoes, 2,850 bags peas, 658 bbls. peas, 30 doz. pails, 59 bbls. mackerel, 4,069 staves, 10,435 shooks, 81 kegs tobacco.	196,800 00	14	1,760 puncheons molasses, 1 bbl. molasses, 77 bbls., 16 tierces, 1,594 bbls. sugar, 195 bags cocoa, 104 tons iron, 152,021 lbs. metals, 1,449 lbs. rags, 436 hides, 926 skins, 14 bbls. grease. Ballast.	88,055 73
2	Philadelphia						
1	Boston				3		
17		17		196,800 00	17		88,055 73

Navigation and commerce of the United States with foreign countries—British Dominions.

COUNTRY, CONSULATE, NAME OF CONSUL, AND DATE OF RETURNS.	VESSELS.				CARGOES.			
	ENTERED.		CLEARED.		INWARD.		OUTWARD.	
	No.	Where from.	No.	Where for.	No.	Description.	Value.	No.	Description.	Value.

COUNTRY, CONSULATE, NAME OF CONSUL, AND DATE OF RETURNS.	No.	Where from.	No.	Where for.	No.	Description.	Value.	No.	Description.	Value.
Quarter ended March 31, 1864.*	2	New Haven	2	New York	2	250 boxes cheese, 150 pails lard, 350 bbls. corn meal, 100 cases matches, 100 kegs corn, 30 kegs tobacco, 1,513 bbls. flour, 150 bbls. crackers, 100 bbls. pork, 50 ½ bbls. beef, 398 bbls., and 150 bags bread, 1,963 bbls. and 350 bags peas, 62 puncheons oil meal, 360 shooks.	$31,800 00	2	900 shooks, 28 bushels peas, 800 bbls. flour, 80 cases matches, 62 bags cocoa, 46 bags arrow root, 24 bhds. and 30 tcs. sugar, 975 hides, 1,360 skins, 256 puncheons molasses.	$23,000 00
	10	New York	1	Trinidad	1	3,726 shooks, 100 puncheons oil meal, 60 boxes Florida water.	6,000 00	1	3,726 shooks, 100 puncheons oil meal.	5,500 00
			5	Porto Rico	5	550 boxes cheese, 100 kegs butter, 300 tins lard, 90 cases matches, 50 bags corn, 50 kegs tobacco, 2,800 bbls. flour, 150 bbls. potatoes, 650 bbls. crackers, 175 bbls. beef, 698 bags and 290 bbls. bread, 690 bags and 175 bbls. peas, 3,177 bbls., 83 pun'k, & 50 casks peas, 6,724 shooks.	72,500 00	3	3,825 shooks, 700 bbls. flour, 25 bbls. beef.	9,600 00
								2	Ballast	
			4	New York	4	400 boxes cheese, 150 pails butter, 499 tins lard, 70 cases matches, 690 bags corn, 35 kegs tobacco, 3,131 bbls. flour, 25 doz. buckets, 750 bbls. crackers, 290 bbls. pork, 175 half bbls. beef, 925 bbls. and 450 bags bread, 550 bags and 80 bbls. peas, 890 bbls. meal, 100 punch'ns oil meal, 2,578 shooks, 25 bbls. oil, 40 bags oil cake, 50 doz. brooms.	69,000 00	3	394 bags cocoa, 50 bags arrow root, 32 tierces, 56 hhds., and 360 bbls. sugar, 466 punch'n molasses, 300 bbls. oil, 50 tons metals, 100 tons iron, 1,130 lbs. coffee, 16,384 lbs. lead.	42,490 00
	3	Philadelphia	1	St. Martin's	1	250 bbls. flour, 350 bbls. meal, 220 lbs. crackers, 12 cases hams, 357 tins lard, 50 bags bread, 100 bags corn, 50 kegs beef, 20 kegs butter, 600 boxes candles, 25 bbls. oil, 600 do.	8,000 00	1	Ballast	8,000 00
			2	Turk's Island.	2	66 bags bread, 60 bags peas, 75 hams, 54 half bbls. and 36 kegs beef, 100 bags and 95 casks corn, 400 boxes candles, 103 kegs and 165 tins lard, 20 tierces hams.	30,000 00	2	do	
	2	Provincetown	2	Whaling	2	195 bbls. oil	10,000 00	2	do	

No.	Whence	No.	Imports	Value	No.	Whither	Exports	Value
2	Boston	1	300 tons ice...... 100 kegs butter, 80 bbls. mackerel, 200 boxes candles, 150 boxes herring, 1,500 shooks.	6,000 00 / 90,000 00	1 / 1	Cuba. / Turk's island.	do...... / do......	12,000 00
1	Baltimore	1	1,050 bbls. flour, 1,300 bbls. meal, 50 bags peas, 250 bags corn, 96 bags bread, 410 tins lard, 300 boxes shingles.	15,000 00	1	Trinidad	300 bbls. meal, 1,050 bbls. flour, 50 bags peas, 250 bags corn, 410 tins lard, 300 boxes cheese.	18,500 00
4	Whaling	4	690 bbls. oil.	34,500 00	2	Whaling	370 barrels oil.	18,500 00
94		94		292,800 00	24			111,090 00
	No report.							
12	New York	10	1,173 bbls. pork, 680 boxes cheese, 350 kegs butter, 400 tins and 250 pails lard, 219 cases matches, 1,800 bags corn, 350 boxes candles, 8 hhds. and 60 kegs tobacco, 6,632 bbls. flour, 39 doz. buckets, 150 bbls. potatoes, 1,475 bbls. crackers, 75 bbls. and 300 half bbls. beef, 50 bbls. and 1,025 bags bread, 100 bbls. and 50 bags split peas, 315 bbls. and 1,675 bags peas, 175 puncheons and 7,543 bbls. meal, 50 bbls. kerosene oil, 3,973 bbls. shooks, 448 cases, 260 tins, and 35 bbls. oil, 107 hhds. oatmeal, 50 bbls. mackerel, 5,860 hoops, 100 sides sole leather, 10 quarter casks wine, 3 bbls. beans.	223,609 00	10	New York	48 bbls. and 50 tins arrowroot, 63 tons iron, 5 tons and 1,370 lbs. iron, 1,622 puncheons and 20 tierces molasses, 439 crates hides and goatskin, 340 goat and 38 calf skins, 1 box turtle-shell.	53,330 00
		1	137 bbls. pork, 929 bbls. flour, 600 bbls. meal, 100 bbls. crackers, 30 bbls. peas, 25 bbls. beef, 10 bbls. oil, 1,250 bags corn, 250 bags peas, 100 tins lard, 9 hhds. and 30 kegs tobacco, 35 cases matches, 125 bags bread, 93 puncheons oatmeal, 325 shooks, 300 tins oil, 2 carriages.	99,176 00	1	Trinidad	Ballast	
		1	150 bbls. pork, 1,089 bbls. flour, 800 bbls. meal, 150 bbls. crackers, 50 bbls. split peas, 250 bags peas, 200 bags corn, 50 bags bread, 10 hhds. and 125 kegs tobacco, 100 kegs butter, 100 tins lard, 130 cases kerosene oil, 390 shooks, 18 —— oil meal.	98,000 00	1	St. Martin's.	......do......	

3d quarter......

Quarter ended September 30, 1864.†

* Entered: 7 brigs, 10 barks, 7 schooners—34. Cleared: same as above. Aggregate tonnage entered, 4,666 35-95.
† Entered and cleared: 6 brigantines, 9 barks, 2 schooners—17. Aggregate tonnage entered, 4,163 5-95.

Navigation and commerce of the United States with foreign countries—British Dominions.

COUNTRY, CONSULATE, NAME OF CONSUL, AND DATE OF RETURNS.	VESSELS.						CARGOES.						
	ENTERED.		CLEARED.				INWARD.			OUTWARD.			
	No.	Where from.	No.	Where for.	No.		Value.	Description.	No.	Description.	No.	Value.	
Quarter ended September 30, 1864—Continued.	3	New York......	1	Anguilla......	1		$36,183 00	128 bbls. pork, 25 bbls. beef, 748 bbls. flour, 251 bbls. meal, 25 bbls. peas, 100 bbls. crackers, 34 kegs tobacco, 250 bags corn, 200 bags peas, 120 bags bread, 15 cases matches, 40 puncheons oil meal, 737 shooks, 200 boxes cheese.	1	Ballast	1	$53,330 00	
			2	Turk's Island......	2		42,500 00	294 bbls. spork, 1,614 bbls. flour, 1,228 bbls. meal, 300 bbls. crackers, 600 bags corn, 200 kgs bread, 3 hhds, 25 tkgs, and 20 boxes lime, 90 half-bbls. bef, 45 cases ahes, 1,000 shooks, 105 bales hay, 75 puncheons oil meal, 25 bbls. peas, 90 bbls. apes, 65 boxes shoes, 30 dos. buckets, 60 tins lard, 55 tins butter, 4 tins ham, 50 cheese candles, 30 cases kerosene oil.		......do......	2		
	1	Philadelphia......	1	Nevis	1		18,000 00	350 lbs. flour, 400 lbs. meal, 50 bbls. crackers, 20 bbls. pork, 104 bags bread, 200 bags beans, 500 bags corn, 90 hhds. ale, 25 puncb's oil meal, 265 tins lard, 232 kegs butter, 20 tierces ham, 25 boxes cheese, 150 boxes and 120 half-boxes candles, 20 bbls. oil, 25 half-bbls beef, 20 quarter-casks wine.	1	......do......	1		
	1	Rio Grande......	1	Baltimore	1		1,900 00	38 mules.	1		1		
	17		17		17		369,398 00		17		17		
TRINIDAD.—E. H. Fitz. Quarter ended December 31, 1863.*	1	In port......	1	Baltimore	1			Before reported	1	Ballast	1		
	2	Boston......	1	Boston	1			Description not given					
			1	Turk's Island	1			......do......					
	4	Philadelphia......	1	......do......	1			......do......					
			1	Sombrero	1			......do......					
			1	Cuba......	1		99,250 00	......do......	2	Cocoa......		2,962 49	
	1	New York......	1	Philadelphia......	1			......do......	6	Ballast			
			1	Cuba......	1			......do......					

No.	Entered from	No.	Cleared to	No.	Cargo	Value	No.	Cargo / remarks	Value
Quarter ended March 31, 1864.									
1	Baltimore	1	Baltimore	1	...do...		9	Ballast	9,922 43
Barbadoes — Quarter ended March 31, 1864.†									
9	Barbadoes	9	Jamaica	9		99,250 00	9		
2	New York	1	Porto Rico	1	Shooks and oil meal	7,500 00	1	Cocoa and shooks	9,718 05
1	Boston	2	New York	1	Shooks	7,500 00	1	Sugar, &c.	7,228 52
1	Portland	1	Cuba	1	Ice and provisions	7,000 00	1	Ballast	
1	Philadelphia	1	New York	1	Shooks	10,000 00	1	...do...	
4	Baltimore	3	Cuba	1	Shooks and provisions	6,000 00	1	...do...	
1	Baltimore	1	In port	1	Flour and provisions	7,000 00	3	In port	
		1	...do	3	Flour and meal	31,500 00	1	...do	16,976 57
				1		13,500 00			
10		10		10		90,000 00	10		
3d and 4th quarters — No reports									

KINGSTON, (Canada.)—J. N. Camp.

No.	Entered from	No.	Cleared to	No.	Cargo	Value	No.	Cargo / remarks
Quarter ended December 31, 1863.‡								
2	Philadelphia	2	Philadelphia	2	Provisions		1	Logwood
3	Machias	1	New York	1	Lumber	90,000 00	6	Not stated
1	Boston	1	Philadelphia	1	221,521 feet lumber			
1	Baltimore	1	Cuba	1	Ice, apples, and tobacco			
		1	Baltimore	1	Ballast			
7		7		7			7	
Quarter ended March 31, 1864.§								
3	Machias	3	New York	3	4,3629 feet late pine lumber	3,180 39	1	Logwood, pimento, and coffee
1	Gloucester	1	Rustan	1	Provisions, candles, and lumber	3,341 25	4	Not stated
1	Philadelphia	1	Philadelphia				1	Coffee, pimento, and wood
1	Black River, Ind.	1	Aspinwall	1	Ballast		2	U. R. mail and passengers
2	New York	2	Manzanilla, Cuba	2	Passengers		2	Ballast
2	Boston			2	Ice and candles			
10		10		10			10	
Quarter ended June 30, 1864.||								
1	Navass	1	Navass	1	Ballast	5,521 64	1	Laborers and supplies
1	New York	1	New York	1	Provisions and sundries		1	Ballast
1	Baltimore	1	Cienfuegos	1	Provisions			
3		3		3			3	

* Entered: 3 barks, 3 schooners, 2 brigs—8, and 1 in port. Cleared: 3 barks, 3 schooners, 3 brigs—8. Aggregate tonnage entered, 2,007.
† Entered: 9 barks, 6 brigs, 2 schooners—10. Cleared: 1 bark, 5 brigs—6, and 4 in port. Aggregate tonnage entered, 2,313.
‡ Entered and cleared: 1 bark, 6 brigs—7. Aggregate tonnage entered, 1,671. § Entered and cleared: 2 steamers, 5 brigs, 3 schooners—10. Aggregate tonnage entered, 5,960.
|| Entered and cleared: 2 brigs, 1 schooner—3. Aggregate tonnage entered, 585.

Navigation and commerce of the United States with foreign countries—British Dominions.

COUNTRY, CONSULATE, NAME OF CONSUL, AND DATE OF RETURNS	VESSELS				CARGOES					
	ENTERED		CLEARED		INWARD			OUTWARD		
	No.	Where from.	No.	Where for.	No.	Description.	Value.	No.	Description.	Value.
Quarter ended September 30, 1864.*	2	Navassa.	2	Navassa.	2	Ballast.		2	Water for laborers at Navassa.	
	2	Boston.	1	Inagua.	1	600 tons ice, candles, tobacco.		1	In port.	
	1	Newport, Wales.	1	In port.	1	Provisions and sundries.		1	Not stated.	
			1	Belize.	1	500 tons coal.		1	Ballast.	
	5		5		5		Not stated.	5		
KINGSTON, (Jamaica.)—F. H. Ruggles.										Not stated.
Quarter ended December 31, 1864.†	2	Philadelphia.	2	Kingston.	7	Assorted cargoes, provisions, lumber, breadstuff.		1	Logwood.	
	3	Machias.	3	...do...				5	Not given.	
	1	Boston.	1	...do...			Not stated.	1	Ballast.	
	1	Baltimore.	1	West Indies.	1	Ballast.		1	In distress.	
	1	Kingston.	1	New York.						
	8		8		8			6		
Quarter ended March 31, 1864.‡	3	Machias.	1	New York.	1	125,000 feet of lumber.	Not stated.	1	100 tons logwood, 546 bags pimento, 88 bags coffee, 89 bbls. coffee, 22 bales rags.	
			1	N.Y. via Black River.	1	136,698 feet lumber.	2,180 39			
			1	N.Y. via Port Morat.	1	168,000 feet lumber.		1	Part inward cargo.	
	1	Gloucester.	1	Ruatan.	1	General cargoes.	3,341 25			
	1	Philadelphia.	1	Philadelphia.	1	Ballast.		1	Passengers.	
	1	Elk River.	1	New York.	2	Passengers.		1	Ballast.	
	2	New York.	2	Aspinwall.	2	Ice and sundries.	5,521 64	2		
	2	Boston.	2	Manzanilla.						
	10		10		10			10		
Quarter ended June 30, 1864.§	1	Navassa.	1	Navassa.	1	Ballast.		1	Laborers for guano digging.	
	1	New York.	1	New York.	1	140 half bbls. tongues, 10 bbls. lard, 800 bbls. and 100 half bbls. wheat flour, 23 quarter casks wine, 117 bbls. corn meal, 125 bbls. bread, 250 kegs lard, 100 boxes cheese, 9 bbls.		1	Ballast.	

1	Baltimore	1	In port	malt, 100 boxes starch, 1 bale hops, 15 cases lamp matches, 400 boxes tallow candles, 2 boxes carriage materials, 6 bundles rims, 27 boards, 2 boxes merchandise.		1	In port		1
				817 bbls. flour, 300 bbls. corn meal, 100 bbls. pork, 50 bbls. and 20 kegs crackers, 300 bags corn.					

Quarter ended September 30, 1864.||

3		3				3			3
2	Navassa	2	Navassa	Ballast.		2	Water for laborers at Navassa. Ballast		2
2	Boston	1	Inagua	600 tons ice, 300 boxes candles, 25 boxes tobacco, 100 packages butter.		1	Ballast		1
		1	In port	155 bbls. flour, 32 bbls. beans, 67 bbls. potatoes, 72 bbls. haddock, 20 boxes cheese, 3 casks glassware, 3 bbls. do., 130 pailslard, 25 half bbls. pork tongues, 10 half bbls. beef, 3 bbls. onions, 14 bbls. pilot bread, 39 kegs butter, 70 cases and 10 bbls. kerosene oil, 2 cases hoop skirts, 27 boxes preserved fish, 130 bbls. pork, 950 boxes candles, 17 bbl. beef, 200 boxes red herrings.		1	In port		

1	Newport, Wales	1	Belize	Coals.		1	In port		1
5		5				5			5

DEMARARA.—C. G. Hannah.
Quarter ended December 31, 1863.
No report.

Quarter ended Mar. 31, 1864.¶

1	In port	1	New York	Before reported...	5,769 92	1	181 hogsheads sugar.	13,949 48	1
1	Boston	1	Turk's Island	36,688 feet spruce scantling, 100,563 feet white pine lumber, 1,156 shooks, hay, and general provisions.		1	Ballast		1
1	New York	1	New York	66 barrels flour, 100 barrels corn meal, 50 barrels pork, 200 pailslard, 100 boxes candles, 900 sugar hogsheads shooks, 10,000 wooden hoops, 98 barrels pilot bread, 100 boxes cheese, 10 barrels crackers, 39 bales hay, 6 puncheons oil meal, 6 tierces hams, and general provisions.	14,882 07	1	99 hogsheads, 10 tierces, and 40 barrels sugar, 39 puncheons molasses.	10,837 14	1
3		3			20,651 99	3		24,786 62	3

* Entered: 1 bark, 6 brigs—7. Cleared: 6 brigs, 1 in port. Agg. ton. ent., 1,740. † Entered: 1 bark, 6 brigs, 1 in distress—8. Cleared: 1 bark, 6 brigs—7. Agg. ton. ent., 1,873 7-95.
‡ Entered and cleared: 3 schooners, 5 brigs, 2 steamers—10. Agg. ton. entered, 5,957. § Entered: 2 brigs, 1 schooner—3. Cleared: 2 brigs, and 1 in port—3. Agg. ton. entered, 565.
|| Entered: 3 barks, 1 brig, 1 schooner—5. Cleared: 2 barks, 1 brig—3, and 2 in port. Aggregate tonnage entered, 1,131 91-95.
¶ Entered: 1 bark, 1 brigantine—2, and 1 in port. Cleared: 2 barks, 1 brigantine—3. Aggregate tonnage entered, 490 72-95.

Navigation and commerce of the United States with foreign countries—British Dominions.

COUNTRY, CONSULATE, NAME OF CONSUL, AND DATE OF RETURNS.	VESSELS				CARGOES					
	ENTERED.		CLEARED.		INWARD.			OUTWARD.		
	No.	Where from.	No.	Where for.	No.	Description.	Value.	No.	Description.	Value.
Quarter ended June 30, 1864*.	5	Boston	2	Turk's Island	2	318 tons rice, 10 barrels mess pork, 100 dozen pails, 139,290 feet lumber, 350 shooks, 100 tins lard, 235 mils flour, 200 bags corn.	$12,517 27	2	Ballast	
			1	Bangor	1	93,000 feet white pine lumber, 50 barrels beef, 25 barrels pork.		1	50 barrels sugar, 1,000 cocoa-nuts	$674 84
			1	Manzanilla	1	100 tins lard, 100 dozen pails, 12,588 feet white pine lumber, 200 ... shingles, too, and ... onions.	5,080 82	1	Ballast	
			1	In port	1	108,172 feet late pine lumber, 300 cks, 100 dozen ... qk, 50 bales hay, 235 ... mils flour, 200 bags corn.	6,893 54	1	In port	
	6	New York	2	New York	2	100 barrels pork, 200 pails lard, 502 ... mils flour, 100 barrels corn ... 200 half ... mils beef, 250 ... pilot bread, 50 barrels any bread, 25 barrels peas, 280 ... mils potatoes, 6 tierces h... ms, 100 boxes cheese, ..., 100 bxs. candles, 100 cases ..., 600 reams paper, 200 ... hoops, &c.	16,680 87	2	223 hogsheads, 31 tierces, 446 barrels sugar, 38 puncheons molasses, 141,066 pounds old metal.	31,910 44
			1	Trinidad de Cuba	1	700 barrels flour, 7,500 ... lets oak staves, provisions, and general supplies.	18,852 51	1	Ballast	
			1	Barbadoes	1	132 barrels pork, 50 barrels beef, 75 half barrels beef, 200 tins lard, 150 boxes cheese, 1,175 barrels flour, 829 bundles shooks.	19,751 05	1	416 casks molasses	10,893 70
			1	Cienfuegos	1	525 tins lard, 233 half barrels beef, 560 boxes candles, 560 barrels flour, 225 barrels bread, 17,700 white oak staves, general provisions.	21,991 91	1	Ballast	
			1	In port	1	100 barrels pork, 200 half barrels beef, 1,017 barrels flour, 250 barrels bread, 170 barrels potatoes, 300 shooks, 12,300 hoops, 200 tins lard, 100 boxes cheese, 100 reams paper, and general cargo.	20,145 17	1	In port	
	1	Rio Grande	1	Pedro Keyes	1	30 miles.	2,500 00	1	Ballast	
	1	Montevideo	1	St. Thomas	1	83 mules and horses.	3,500 00	1	do	
	1	Bangor	1	In port	1	155,000 feet white pine lumber, 4,000 cedar shingles.	3,141 00	1	In port	
	14		14		14		131,054 14	14		43,479 98

Quarter ended September 30, 1864.†	3	In port	1	Before reported		1	220 hogsheads, 46 tierces, and 56 barrels sugar, 22 puncheons molasses	26,713 33
	1	Queenstown	1	do		1	6,559 feet green-heart timber	3,360 00
	1	New York	1	do		1	136 puncheons molasses, 100 bags rice	3,937 99
	6	New York	4	506 barrels pork, 900 boxes cheese, 300 pails lard, 90 cases matches, 50 bags and 900 barrels corn, 900 boxes candles, 1,696 barrels flour, 150 barrels potatoes, 59 barrels and 353 half barrels beef, 210 barrels bread, 5 tierces ham, 311 bags meal, 900 bundles and 472 shooks, 10 half barrels mackerel, 1,800 reams paper, 3 hogsheads tobacco, 17,500 shingles.	43,081 74	4	2,506 pounds old copper, 4,530 pounds old brass, 221 pounds lead, 563,335 pounds old iron, 2,415 pounds old pewter, 354 casks and 12 barrels molasses.	14,527 72
	1	St. Thomas	1	220 barrels flour, 672 shooks, 26,400 red oak staves, 26,400 white oak staves, 5,880 headings.	8,563 49	1	Ballast	
	2	Baltimore	1	In port	29,600 30	1	In port	
			1	Baltimore	25,947 00	1	168,395 pounds old iron	956 19
	1	In port	1	General cargo, lumber, and provisions 2,372 barrels flour, 230 barrels meal, 400 firs lard, 407 boxes candles, 50 bags bran, 351 bundles shooks, 12,000 feet lumber.	10,471 87	1	In port	
	1	Turk's Island	1	400 barrels cornmeal, 237 barrels pork, 117,500 feet boards and plank. 275 tons ice and general provisions	3,094 57	1	Ballast	
	12		12		119,968 97	12		49,495 23

St. George, N.B.—A. Sprague.

Quarter ended December 31, 1863.‡	16	Boston	12	Ballast		12	585,000 feet boards, 20,000 palings, 159,000 laths, 147,000 feet lumber, 1,400 barrels lime.	5,412 30
			1	do		1	90,000 feet boards	900 00
		Portland	1	do		1	90,000 feet boards, 25,000 laths	460 00
		Providence	1	do		1	Ballast	
		Ellsworth	1	do		1	800,000 feet deals	6,400 00
	2	Liverpool	1	do		1	40,000 feet boards	430 00
		Portland	1	do		1	72,000 feet boards, 30,000 laths	948 00
	1	Boston	1	do		1	130,000 feet boards, 10,000 palings.	1,940 00
	2	Providence	2	do		2	194,000 feet boards	
	10	do	8	do		8	606,177 feet boards, 580,000 laths	7,211 47
		Boston	1	do		1	Hackmatack timber and knees.	
		Portland	1	do		1	40,000 feet boards.	
	3	Lubec	1	do		1	250,000 feet boards, 70,000 laths.	1,000 00
		S. W. Harbor	3	do		3	Hackmatack timber and knees.	1,278 00
	1	Rockland	1	do		1	Timber, knees, plank, laths.	1,085 25

* Entered: 5 barks, 1 brig, 1 schooner. Cleared: 4 barks, 1 brig, 1 schooner, 5 brigantines—11, and 3 in port. Aggregate tonnage entered, 3,590 49-95.
† Entered: 4 brigs, 2 barks, 3 brigantines—9, and 3 in port. Cleared: 4 brigantines, 2 barks, 4 brigs—10, and 2 in port. Aggregate tonnage entered, 1,903 35-95.
‡ Entered and cleared: 4 ships, 36 schooners—40. Aggregate tonnage entered, 8,016 70-95.

Navigation and commerce of the United States with foreign countries—British Dominions.

COUNTRY, CONSULATE, NAME OF CONSUL, AND DATE OF RETURNS.	VESSELS				CARGOES					
	ENTERED		CLEARED		INWARD			OUTWARD		
	No.	Where from	No.	Where for	No.	Description	Value	No.	Description	Value
Quarter ended December 31, 1863—Continued.	3	New York	2	Liverpool	2	Ballast		2	1,797,000 deals, 36,000 palings	$12,700 00
	1	Portland	1	Bristol	1	do		1	960,000 deals, 4,000 palings	7,000 00
	1	Ellsworth	1	Boston	1	do		1	90,000 feet boards	900 00
			1	do	1	do		1	90,000 feet boards, 150,000 laths	600 00
	40		40		40			40		51,085 82
Quarter ended Mar. 31, 1864.	1	Portsmouth	1	London	1	Ballast		1	900,000 feet spruce deals	7,900 00
	1	Goldsboro'	1	Boston	1	do		1	755 barrels lime	377 50
	4	Eastport	1	New York	1	do.		1	100,056 feet spruce deals	1,990 66
			1	New Haven	1	do		1	100,000 feet boards, 90,000 laths	618 00
			1	Eastport	1	do		1	105,000 feet boards, 10,000 laths	954 00
	1	Boston	1	Providence	1	do		1	900,000 feet boards and plank	9,000 00
	2	Cherryfield	1	Boston	1	do		1	755 barrels lime	377 50
			2	do	2	do		2	187,284 feet boards and plank	1,691 95
	9		9		9			9		14,419 61
Quarter ended June 30, 1864.†	16	Eastport	4	Providence	4	Ballast		4	388,000 feet boards and plank, 36,000 laths	3,987 80
			1	Bridgeport	1	do		1	111,373 feet boards	1,670 60
			2	Eastport	2	do		2	Timber knees, sleepers, laths. 40,000 feet boards, 22,000 feet spool stuff	1,289 75 / 1,040 00
			5	Boston	5	do		5	975,000 feet boards and plank	3,995 50
			2	Mystic	2	do		2	250 railroad ties, 7,000 ft. laths. 150 ship knees, 137 spars, DO tons 1 oak matack timber	4,656 50
	2	St. Andrews	2	Stonington	2	do		2	6,600 laths, 209,371 ft. boards	1,892 81
			1	New York	1	do		1	100 tons hacktm't oak timber	500 00
	2	Ellsworth	2	Boston	2	do		2	7000 feet beds and plank	900 00
	2	Boston	7	do	7	do		7	133,000 ft. do., 72,000 laths	1,139 80
								7	900 cdr railroad ties, 361,000 ft. boards, 465,000 laths	2,994 00
	2	Providence	1	Philadelphia	1	do		1	900 ship knees, 190 tons timber	1,145 00
			1	Providence	1	do		1	90,000 feet spruce plank	1,040 00
			1	Newport	1	do		1	100,000 feet boards, 8,000 clapboards, 11,000 laths	9,171 00
		Goldsboro'	1	Providence		do				
			2	Boston		do				

No.	District	No.	Whither	Cargo	No.	Value	No.	Cargo	Value
1	St. Stephen		1	Stonington	do			1	921 ship knees, 5,000 boards	550 00
2	S. W. Harbor		1	Newport	do			1	90,000 ft. boards, 50,000 shingles	2,670 00
			1	Providence	do			1	140,000 feet boards and plank	2,100 00
36			36			36		36		35,513 76
	Quarter ended September 30, 1864.‡									
7	Eastport		1	New London	Ballast			1	80,000 feet	560 00
			2	Philadelphia	do			2	77 tons timber, 162,000 ft. b yrds	1,915 00
			1	Eastport	do			1	65,000 feet boards	565 64
			2	Mystic	do			1	120 tons timber	1,040 00
1f	Boston		10	Boston	do			2	150,000 ft. boards, 100,000 laths	980 00
				...do	do			10	475,000 feet boards, 1,500 laths	4,880 00
			1	Bristol	do			1	740 feet deals	4,800 00
			1	Boston	do			1	740 barrels lime	370 00
4	S. W. Harbor		1	Newport	do			1	83,000 feet boards, 33,000 pickets	834 13
			1	Providence	do			1	90,000 feet plank	1,080 00
1	Providence		1	do do	do			1	140,000 feet deals, 40,000 laths	1,440 00
1	Newburyport		1	Philadelphia	do			1	200,000 feet boards	3,000 00
1	Western Isles		1	Ed.	do			1	9 ... feet deals	3,430 00
1	Portsmouth		1	Boston	do			1	240,000 laths	240 00
1	Cherryfield		1	Providence	do			1	75,000 ft. boards, 100,000 shingles	2,600 00
1	Goldsboro'		1	New York	do			1	140 tons	1,120 00
			1	Boston	do			1	740 barrels lime	370 00
28			28			28		28		29,334 77

HAMILTON, (BERMUDA)—J. L. Darrell.

1	Bangor	Quarter ended December 31, 1863.§	1	Philadelphia	Lumber	1	2,600 00		Ballast	
	No report	2d and 3d quarters								

St. George's, (Bermuda) C. M. Allen.

1	Whaling	Quarter ended September 30, 1864.‖	1	Whaling	40 barrels oil	1	1,600 00	1	Whaling gear	
	No report	1st, 2d, and 3d quarters								
2	In port	Quarter ended September 30, 1864.¶	1	Whaling	Before reported			1	Ballast	
			1	Turk's Island	...do			1	...do	

* Entered and cleared: 1 ship, 8 schooners—9. Aggregate tonnage entered, 2,107 19-95.
† Entered and cleared: 1 brig, 25 schooners—26. Aggregate tonnage entered, 3,839 30-95.
‡ Entered and cleared: 2 barks, 96 schooners—98. Aggregate tonnage entered, 4,296 4-95.
§ Entered and cleared: 1 brig. Tonnage, 198 37-95. ‖ Entered and cleared: 1 brig. Tonnage, 143 45-95.
¶ Entered: 1 bark, 1 brig, 1 schooner—3. Cleared: 2 barks, 2 brig, 1 schooner—5. Aggregate tonnage entered, 649 43-95.

Navigation and commerce of the United States with foreign countries—British Dominions.

COUNTRY, CONSULATE, NAME OF CONSUL, AND DATE OF RETURNS.	VESSELS — ENTERED		VESSELS — CLEARED		CARGOES — INWARD			CARGOES — OUTWARD		
	No.	Where from.	No.	Where for.	No.	Description.	Value.	No.	Description.	Value.
Quarter ended September 30, 1864—Continued.	1	Machais	1	Turk's Island	4	150 M feet lumber	$7,500 00	1	Ballast	$830 00
	1	Sydney	1	Philadelphia	1	332 tons coal	830 00	1	332 tons coal	
	1	Boston	1	Turk's Island	1	240 tons ice and general cargo	2,400 00	1	Ballast	
	5		5		5		10,730 00	5		830 00
BELIZE—C. A. Lea. 1st quarter.		No report.								
Quarter ended Mar. 31 1864.*	1	Boston	1	Boston	1	Lumber and provisions	5,945 88	1	Logwood, mahogany, sponges	2,682 00
	1	New Orleans	1	Rustan	1	Provisions	4,000 00	1	Ballast	1,050 00
	1	Not stated	1	Matamoras	1	Cotton	22,500 00	1	Logwood	
	3		3		3		32,445 88	3		3,732 00
Quarter ended June 30, 1864.†	1	New Orleans	1	Belize	1	Provisions	5,700 00	1	12 tons logwood	122 00
	1	Boston	1	In port	1	Ice, lumber, and provisions	4,376 00	1	In port	
	2		2		2		10,076 00	2		122 00
Quarter ended September 30, 1864.‡	1	In port	1	Boston	1	Before reported		1	196 tons logwood, old iron, &c.	3,651 98
	1	Langor	1	Belize	1	General merchandise and lumber	6,441 05	1	164 tons logwood, 5 tons old iron, 1 box coffee	2,353 98
	1	Boston	1	do	1	Ice, lumber, and provisions	4,200 22	1	151 tons logwood, 11½ tons rosewood, 26 bales ——, and sundries	3,841 00
	1	Kingston	1	In port	1	In ballast	30,000 00	1	In port	
	1	New Orleans	1	do	1	Provisions, hay, and merchandise		1	do	
	5		5		5		40,641 27	5		9,846 96
BASSEIN—J. Henderson. Quarter ended December 31, 1863.§	1	Akyab	1	Singapore	1	Ballast		1	33,000 bags rice	30,000 00
Quarter ended March 31, 1864.‖	1	Rangoon	1	Europe	1	Ballast		1	Sold, took British flag	
	1	Gibraltar	1	do	1	do		2	46,630 bags rice	
	1	Antwerp	1	do	1	do				
	3		3		3			3		

Period / Port	No.	Whence	Cargo inward	No.	Ballast / cargo	Value	No.	Cargo
Quarter ended June 30, 1864.¶	2	Singapore	Not stated	2	Ballast		2	Rice
	1	Aden	do	1	do		1	do
	3	Hong-Kong	do	3	do		3	do
	1	Not stated	do	1	do		1	do
	1	Bombay	do	1	do		1	do
	1	Akyab	do					do
	9			9			9	
4th quarter		No report						
POINT DE GALLE.—J. Black.								
1st quarter		No report						
Quarter ended March 31, 1864.**	1	Sunderland	Akyab	1	1,300 tons coal	10,400 00	1	Ballast
	2	Liverpool	do	1	1,307 tons coal	10,456 00	1	do
			Rangoon	1	1,511 tons coal	12,088 00	1	do
	3			3		32,944 00	3	
3d and 4th quarters		No report						
MAULMAIN.—W. Brooke.								
From September 1 to December 31, 1865.††	1	Isle of Bourbon	Bombay	1	Ballast		1	563 tons teak timber.
	1	Bombay	do	1	do		1	399 tons teak timber.
	1	Shanghai	Calcutta	1	do		1	921 tons teak timber.
	1	Anjer	Bombay	1	do		1	852 tons teak timber, 1½ maunds tobacco.
	3	Singapore	...do	1	do		1	1,109 tons teak timber, 150 bags rice.
	1	Galle	Kurrachee	1	do		1	635 tons teak timber.
	1	Aden	Singapore	1	do		1	31,395 baskets rice.
	2	Madras	Calcutta	1	do		1	319 tons teak timber.
			Bombay	1	do		1	722 tons teak timber.
			Cork or Falmouth	1	do		1	1,524 tons teak timber, 27 tons cutch.
	1	Buenos Ayres & Monte Video.	Sold	1	do		1	Sold.
			Calcutta	1	do		1	1,045 tons teak timber.
	1	Mauritius	Cork, Falmouth, &c.	1	do		1	1,023 tons teak timber.

* Entered and cleared : 1 brig. 2 schooners—3. Aggregate tonnage entered, 425.
† Entered : 1 brig, 1 schooner.—2. Cleared : 1 schooner, and 1 in port. Aggregate tonnage entered, 337.
‡ Entered : 1 ship, 3 barks—4, and 1 in port. Cleared : 2 barks, 1 brig—3, and 2 in port. Aggregate tonnage entered, 1,409.
§ Entered and cleared : 1, class not given. Tonnage, 527. || Entered and cleared : 2 class not given, 1 sold. Aggregate tonnage entered, 2,019 90-95.
¶ Entered and cleared : 9, class not given. Aggregate tonnage entered, 7,979 61-95. ** Entered and cleared : 3, class not given. Aggregate tonnage entered, 2,999.
Entered : 16, class not given. Cleared : 13 class not given, 1 sold—14, and 2 in port. Aggregate tonnage entered, 12,254.

Navigation and commerce of the United States with foreign countries—British Dominions.

COUNTRY, CONSULATE, NAME OF CONSUL, AND DATE OF RETURNS.	VESSELS				CARGOES					
	ENTERED.		CLEARED.		INWARD.			OUTWARD.		
	No.	Where from.	No.	Where for.	No.	Description.	Value.	No.	Description.	Value.
From September 1 to December 31, 1863—Continued.	1	Cape Good Hope.	1	United Kingdom.	1	Ballast		1	1,449 tons teak timber, 700 bags cutch.	
	1	Hong Kong and Singapore.	1	In port.	1	do		1	In port.	
	1	Rio Janeiro.	1	do.	1	do		2	do.	
	16		16		16					
From January 1 to June 30, 1864.*	8	Bombay	4	United Kingdom.	4	Ballast		2	3,342 tons teak timber, 1,098 boxes cutch.	
			3	Bombay.	3	do				
			1	Calcutta.	1	do				
	1	Calcutta.	1	United Kingdom.	1	do		1	750 tons teak timber.	
	1	Buenos Ayres.	1	In port.	1	do		1	In port.	
	10		10		10			10		
4th quarter.	No report.									
SEYCHELLES.—C. Dupuy.										
From July 1, 1863, to March 31, 1864.†	1	Whaling	1	Whaling	1	920 barrels sperm oil		1	920 barrels sperm oil	
3d and 4th quarters	No report.									
HOBART TOWN.—D. McPherson, jr.										
Quarter ended December 31, 1863;	3	Whaling	3	Whaling	1	Whaling stores	80,000 00	1	Called for supplies	
					2	2,050 barrels sperm oil, 60 barrels black oil.		2	1,450 barrels sperm oil	
					3		80,000 00	3		
2d, 3d, and 4th quarters	No report.									

Port / Period	Entered No.	Whence	Cargo	Value	No.	Cargo	Cleared No.	Whither	Cargo	Value	No.	Cargo	Value
SIMON'S BAY.—J. M. Hoets.													
1st, 2d, and 3d quarters	No report						No report						
Quarter ended September 30, 1864.§	1	Cardiff	1,600 tons coal	24,000 00	1	Ballast	1	Maulmain		107,000 00			
	1	Zanzibar	Ivory, dates, &c	83,000 00	1	Inward cargo	1	Providence					
	2				2		2						
NATAL.													
1st, 2d, and 3d quarters	No report						No report						
Quarter ended September 30, 1864.‖	1	Whaling	1,056 gallons of oil, 1,300 lbs. bone		1	Ballast	1	Whaling					
MOSSEL BAY.—E. Eger.													
1st, 2d, 3d, and 4th quarters	No arrivals						No departures						
VICTORIA, V.I.—A. Francis.													
Quarter ended December 21, 1863.¶	18	San Francisco	Merchandise and provisions	47,800 00	5	San Francisco	6	San Francisco	Ballast and merchandise		3	Ballast and merchandise	18,648 66
			Ballast		1				Ballast		2	Ballast	
									Coal		1	Coal	
	41	Port Angelos	Ballast	1	11	Port Angelos	11	Nanaimo	Ballast	1 9462 00	11	Ballast	
			Produce and lumber	15,360 00	26		40	Port Angelos	do	15,360 00	1	do	13,668 82
			Passengers		7				Ballast and merchandise		19	Ballast and merchandise	
			Ballast		1				Ballast		21	Ballast	
	2	N. Dungeness	Produce	750 00	2	San Francisco	1		Merchandise	750 00	1	Merchandise	3,500 00
	2	Sandwich Islands	do	1,730 00	2	Port Angelos	2		do	1,730 00	2	do	181 32
			do	3,900 00	1	do			do	3,900 00	1	do	336 44
	1	China	Sugar and molasses	5,800 00	1	do	1		Ballast	5,800 00	1	Ballast	
	1	Queen Charlotte'n Island	Ballast		1		1		do		1	do	
	65			268,802 00	65		65				65		35,337 26

* Entered: 10, class not given. Cleared: 9, class not given. Aggregate tonnage entered, 3,781 58-95.
† Entered and cleared: 1, class not given. Tonnage, 397 40-95.
‡ Entered and cleared: 3 barks. Aggregate tonnage entered, 985.
§ Entered and cleared: 1 ship, 1 bark.—2. Aggregate tonnage entered, 1,376.
‖ Entered and cleared: 1 schooner. Tonnage, 382.
¶ Entered and cleared: 18 barks, 20 sloops, 23 schooners, 7 steamers, 3 brigs—65. Aggregate tonnage entered, 13,368.

Navigation and commerce of the United States with foreign countries—British Dominions.

COUNTRY, CONSULATE, NAME OF CONSUL, AND DATE OF RETURNS.	VESSELS				CARGOES					
	ENTERED.		CLEARED.		INWARD.			OUTWARD.		
	No.	Where from.	No.	Where for.	No.	Description.	Value.	No.	Description.	Value.
Quarter ended March 31, 1864.*	13	San Francisco	8	Port Angelos	8	Merchandise	$145,950 00	8	Ballast	$17,327 50
			5	San Francisco	4	Castle, $2,500; merchandise, $31,250	33,750 00	3	2,690 tons coal	8,734 11
					1	Ballast		1	Merchandise	
	37	Port Angelos	36	do	1	Lumber	450 00	1	Ballast	
				Port Angelos	27	Lumber and produce	14,060 00	1	Ale, porter, &c	2,728 69
					9	Ballast and passengers		11	Castings, molasses, merchandise	2,416 12
								25	Ballast and passengers	
	50		50		50		194,210 00	50		31,106 42
Quarter ended June 30, 1864†	10	San Francisco & Astoria	8	San Francisco & Astoria	10	Merchandise and produce	416,841 00	8	Furs, wood, coal, and merchandise.	102,999 42
	51	Port Angelos	53	Port Angelos	51	Produce	70,570 00	53	Merchandise	14,411 41
	61		61		61		487,411 00	61		117,410 83
Quarter ended September 30, 1864‡	53	Port Angelos	51	Port Angelos	36	Rince, coal, lumber, &c	33,472 90	18	Merchandise	5,464 24
					15	Ballast and passengers		33	Ballast and passengers	
	22	San Francisco	2	Astoria	2	Ballast	108,226 27	2	Mdndise	9,865 98
			9	San Francisco	9	Produce, merchandise, &c		8	Furs, merchandise, &c	26,652 72
								1	Ballast	
	6	Astoria	12	Port Angelos	12	do	196,996 84	12	do	791 12
			1	Astoria	1	do	23,000 00	1	Merchandise	
			2	Port Angelos	2	do	14,128 00	1	Ballast	
			4	San Francisco	4	do	25,680 00	4	do	
	2	Port Madison	2	Port Angelos	2	Ballast		2	do	
	83		83		83		401,628 01	83		42,914 06
ZANTE, (GREECE)—A. S. York.										
1st and 2d quarters	No report.									
Quarter ended June 30, 1864	No arrivals		No departures.							
4th quarter	No report.									

HAVRE—J. O. Putnam.

Quarter ended December 31, 1863.§

No.	Whence	No.	Cargo	Value	No.	Disposition
5	In port....		Before reported....			Sold....
			....do		2	Ballast
			....do		2	Wines, dry goods, &c.
2	Sold....	2	Known.		1	
2	New York....	2	7,004 sacks wheat, 38,371 sacks rice, 98,885 deals, 3,400 tons guano, &c.			
1	Akyab....	1	21,042 bushels wheat			
		9	584 bbls. flour, 250 cases prepared flour.			
1	Honfleur....	1	380 casks tallow	31,563 00		
2	Rangoon....	1	285 casks lard	9,212 00		
		1	162 bbls. pearlash	10,640 00		Ballast
2	New York....	2	18 bbls. gum...	50,736 00	2	Wines, dry goods, &c.
1	Rimouski....	1	200 sacs pork	8,965 00	2	Sold....
2	Chincha Islands..	1	66 hhds. and 500 sacks quercitron oak.	8,400 00	4	In port
1	Sold; in port..	1	38 bales hops	5,712 00		
1	Hamburg....	1	2969 cdls. 1,216 tpes pine	3,040 00		
1	Akyab....	3	421 bbls. goldsmiths sweepings	40,498 00		
			47 cases sewing machines	6,300 00		
			231 packages staves	6,298 00		
			5,042 packages laths	6,795 60		
			2,963 unwrought oars	751 25		
			482 superior bars	523 50		
			64,640 staves....	3,696 00		
			5 bbls. Indian corn	18 75		
			100 bales vegetable hair	1,800 00		
15		15		195,444 50	15	

Quarter ended March 31, 1864.‖

No.	Whence	No.	Cargo	Value	No.	Disposition
4	In port....		Before reported....			Sold....
			....do		1	Ballast
1	Sold....	1	....do		2	....do
2	Calino....	2	221 hhds. and 1 case tobacco.		1	
1	Cardiff....	1	73,695 pounds lard	110,750 00		
2	New York....	7	12,832 pounds tallow	5,895 80	1	Wine, dry goods, &c....
5	Calino....		54 bbls. jewellers' dust.	1,995 90	2	Ballast
			414 bbls. pearlash.	8,100 00	4	In port
			100 bbls. potash.	18,620 00		
			30 bales hops	4,500 04		
			12 logs palissander wood.	2,000 00		
			32 casks whale oil.	300 00		
				1,120 00		

Aggregate tonnage entered, 8,998 94-95.

* Entered and cleared: 21 schooners, 7 steamers, 11 sloops, 5 barks, 2 ships, 4 brigs—50. Aggregate tonnage entered: 10,781.
† Entered and cleared: 28 schooners, 21 sloops, 3 barks, 9 brigs, 7 steamers—61. Aggregate tonnage entered, 7,820.
‡ Entered and cleared: 21 sloops, 30 steamers, 4 brigs, 7 barks, 21 schooners—83. Aggregate tonnage entered, 17,861.
§ Entered: 8 ships, 1 schooner, 1 bark—10, and 5 in port. Cleared: 7 ships, 1 schooner—8, 2 sold, 1 condemned, and 4 in port. Aggregate tonnage entered, 8,998 94-95.
‖ Entered: 7 ships, and 4 in port. Cleared: 7 ships, and 4 in port. Aggregate tonnage entered, 7,986 43-85.

Navigation and commerce of the United States with foreign countries—French Dominions.

COUNTRY, CONSULATE, NAME OF CONSUL, AND DATE OF RETURNS.	VESSELS.					CARGOES.						
	ENTERED.		CLEARED.			INWARD.			OUTWARD.			
	No.	Where from.	No.	Where for.	No.	Description.	Value.	No.	Description.	Value.		
Quarter ended March 31, 1864—Continued.						2,541 sacks and 26 hhds. quercitron bark.	$19,095 90					
						1,090 packages laths	1,306 00					
						79,692 staves	3,983 10					
						1,050 oars	525 00					
	11		11		11		177,492 10	11				
Quarter ended June 30, 1864*.	4	In port	3	Cardiff	3	Before reported		3	Ballast			
			1	New York	1	do		1	Wines, dry goods, &c.			
					8	114 bbls. potash	5,130 00					
						215 hhds. tobacco	199,436 00					
						60 bales cotton	28,800 00					
						125 hhds. and 3,353 sacks quercitron bark.	11,547 90					
	5	Callao	1	Cardiff		1,175 casks tallow	58,750 40					
			4	In port		4,586 casks lard	102,796 40					
			4	New York		628 white pine plank	2,552 00	1	Wines, dry goods, &c.			
	3	New York	2	In port		190 bbls. pigs' bristles	2,582 00	1	Ballast			
						53 bales hops	2,875 00	6	In port			
						50 bbls. gold-smiths' dust.	13,500 00					
						6 cases buckskin	225 00					
						25 bbls. salt beef	150 00					
						250 logs cedar wood	3,750 00					
						2,000 bbls. petroleum oil	25,000 00					
						30 logs maple wood	70 00					
						14 bbls. sausage skins	1,442 00					
						12,000 staves, 485 oars						
						6,700 tons guano	380,000 00					
	12		12		12		769,495 60	12				
Quarter ended September 30, 1864.†	6	In port	3	Cardiff	3	Before reported		2	Wines, dry goods, &c.			
			1	Akyab	1	do		4	Ballast			
			2	New York	2	2,540 bbls. petroleum oil	31,750 00					
					10	1,395 hides	4,185 00					
						2,363 hhds. tobacco	1,417,800 00					
						355 bbls. potash	15,975 00					
						41 bbls. pearlash	1,845 00					

4	New York	1	do		548 casks of tallow	15,344 00	
		1	Cardiff		2,542 casks of lard	56,940 00	
		2	In port		4,670 bbls. flour	98,080 00	
		1	Akyab		41 bbls. pork	8,200 00	
		1	In port		100 bbls. pigs' bristles	3,000 00	
2	Callao	1	Cardiff		33 lbs. wax	7,920 00	
		1	do		36 hhds. and 555 sacks quercitron bark	2,340 00	
1	Baltimore	1	In port		196 packages palm leaves	196 00	
1	Philadelphia				62 logs maple end	2,976 00	
1	St. John's				855 logs other chinet wood	25,650 00	
1	Quebec				284 packages staves	284 00	
					1,535 cars	1,353 00	
					43 cases preserved meats	3,010 00	
					56 bales hair	2,800 00	
					50 discs hops	2,500 00	
					3 cases cigars	600 00	
					2 sewing machines	50 00	
					247,844 staves	24,784 00	Wines, dry goods, &c.
					97 bbls. gol'lsmiths' dust	14,550 00	Ballast
							In port
16		16		16		1,672,072 00	16 $30,300 00
							30,300 00

BORDEAUX—C. Davisson.
Quarter ended December 31, 1863†

2	In port	1	New Orleans	1	Before reported	163,940 10	1 429 tons wine, fruit in brandy
1	Baltimore	1	Cardiff	1	do		1 Ballast
1	Akyab	1	do		1,625 hhds. tobacco, 18,000 staves		5 do
		1	In port	1	807 — rice	19,368 00	4 do
4		4		4		183,308 00	4 30,300 00

Quarter ended March 31, 1864.§

1	In port	1	Sold	1	Before reported	12,375 00	1 Sold
1	Trieste	1	New York	1	947,500 staves		1 457 tons wine, brandy, &c
1	Sagua	1	In port	1	13,600 staves	8,160 00	1 In port
3		3		3		20,535 00	3 27,000 00
							27,000 00

Quarter ended June 30, 1864‖

1	In port	1	New York	1	Before reported		1 666 tons wine, brandy, porcelain, and corks
1	Callao	1	In port	1	1,300 tons guano	78,000 00	1 In port
2		2		2		78,000 00	2 40,170 00
							40,170 00

* Entered: 8 ships, and 4 in port. Cleared: 6 ships, and 6 in port. Aggregate tonnage entered, 8,317 75-95.
† Entered: 6 ships, 3 barks, 1 brig—10, and 6 in port. Cleared: 10 ships, 1 bark, 1 brig—12, and 4 in port. Aggregate tonnage entered, 8,205 30-95.
‡ Entered: 2 ships, and 2 in port. Cleared: 2 ships, 1 bark—3, and 1 in port. Aggregate tonnage entered, 1,813 73-95.
§ Entered: 1 brig, 1 schooner—2, and 1 in port. Cleared: 1 schooner; 1 sold, and 1 in port. Aggregate tonnage entered, 807 11-95.
‖ Entered: 1 ship, and 1 in port. Cleared: 1 brig, and 1 in port. Tonnage, 856 89-95.

Navigation and commerce of the United States with foreign countries—French Dominions.

COUNTRY, CONSULATE, NAME OF CONSUL, AND DATE OF RETURNS.	VESSELS.				CARGOES.					
	ENTERED.		CLEARED.		INWARD.			OUTWARD.		
	No.	Where from.	No.	Where for.	No.	Description.	Value.	No.	Description.	Value.
Quarter ended September 30, 1864.*	1	In port	1	Cardiff	1	Before reported		1	Ballast	
NANTES—*J. De La Montagne.* 1st, 2d, and 3d quarters		Not reported								
Quarter ended September 30, 1864.b	1	Chincha Islands	1	In port	1	Guano	$108,000 00	1	In port	
LA ROCHELLE—*T. Hyatt.* 1st quarter		No report								
2d and 3d quarters		No arrivals		No departures						
4th quarter		No report								
CETTE—*L. S. Nahmens.* 1st quarter		No report								
Quarter ended March 31, 1864.;	2	New York	1	Palermo	1	71,000 staves, 90 tierces lard	85,637 00	1	Ballast	$300 00
			1	Messina	1	79,900 staves	14,754 00	1	150 tons salt	300 00
	2		2		2		100,391 00	2		
d quarter		No report								
Quarter ended September 30, 1864.§	2	New York	1	Licata	1	12,000 staves, 61 boxes hams, 958 hhds. and 3 bbls. tallow.	164,600 00	1	Ballast	
			1	Messina	1	13,900 staves, 519 hhds. lard, 50 bbls. lard.	87,723 00	1	do.	
	2		2		2		252,323 00	2		

Origin	No.	Destination / Port	No.	Cargo	Value	No.	Remarks
1st quarter....... DUNKIRK.—F. B. Morrill.‖		No report.					
Six months, from January 1 to June 30, 1864. Chincha	8	Newport / Cardiff / Gothenburg / Shields / London	1,3,1,1,... (8)	Guano....		8	Ballast.
4th quarter.......	8	No report.	8			8	Ballast.
MARSEILLES.—G. W. Van Horn. Quarter ended December 30, 1863.¶							
In port	2	Akyab	1	Before reported	110,097 00	1	Ballast.
		Cardiff	1	do..... staves	129,850 00	1	do.
New York	5	Hyeres	2	Rum, alcohol, lard, staves	78,650 00	2	do.
		Messina	3	Tobacco, staves, beef	131,910 00	1	In port.
Boston	5	In port	1	Rum, alcohol, logwood	27,350 00	1	Ballast.
		Girgenti	1	Lard and staves	15,840 00	1	do.
		Palermo	1	Quercitron bark, logwood	110,000 00	1	do.
Mannheim	1	Cardiff	1	Teak timber	13,200 00	1	do.
Gudava	3	do	1	11,000 railroad sleepers		1	do.
		Messina	2	9,500 ...do	11,400 00	2	do.
Baltimore		Baltimore		1,375 hhds. tobacco & quercitron bark	405,600 00	1	do.
	17		17		1,033,867 00	17	
Quarter ended March 31, 1864.							
In port	2	Messina	2	Before reported			
Trieste	1	...do	1	40,000 staves, 960 pieces timber	6,400 00		
New York	1	Palermo	1	2,351 bbls. lard, 1,000 staves	78,530 00		
Callao	2	Licata	1	800 tons guano	32,000 00		
		Leghorn	1	1,000...do	40,000 00		
Cardiff	1	Carthagena	1	1,000 tons coal	8,000 00	9	Ballast.
Philadelphia	2	Messina	1	2,472 bbls. petroleum, 43 hhds. quercitron.	98,020 00		
Fiume	1	Palermo	1	2,800 bbls. petroleum.	98,000 00		
		In port	1	55,000 staves.	5,000 00	1	In port.
	10		10		223,950 00	10	
Quarter ended June 30, 1864.††							
In port	2	Carthagena	1	Before reported		1	Ballast.
		St. Petersburg	1	...do		1	250 casks chloride of lime. 107 casks thistles.
					10,980 00		10,980 00

* Entered: 1 ship. Cleared: 1 ship. † Entered: 1 ship. Cleared: None. Tonnage, 1,170. ‡ Entered and cleared: 2 barks. Aggregate tonnage entered, 865 33-95.

‡ Entered and cleared: 2 barks. Aggregate tonnage entered, 884 66-94. Entered and cleared: 6 ships, 2 barks—8. Aggregate tonnage entered, 5,387 28-95.

¶ Entered: 2 ships, 8 barks—15, in port 2. Cleared: 5 ships, 8 barks, 2 brigs—15, in port 2. Aggregate tonnage entered, 6,998.

↓ Entered: 3 ships, 6 barks—8, and 2 in port. Cleared: 3 ships, 5 barks, 2 brigs—9, and 1 in port. Aggregate tonnage entered, 3,563.

†† Entered: 2 ships, 1 brig—3, in port 2. Cleared: 2 ships, 1 bark, 1 brig—4, 1 in port. Aggregate tonnage entered, 1 494.

H. Ex. Doc. 60——5*

Navigation and commerce of the United States with foreign countries—French Dominions.

COUNTRY, CONSULATE, NAME OF CONSUL, AND DATE OF RETURNS.	VESSELS				CARGOES					
	ENTERED		CLEARED		INWARD			OUTWARD		
	No.	Where from.	No.	Where for.	No.	Description.	Value.	No.	Description.	Value.
MARSEILLES.—G. W. Van Horn. Quarter ended June 30, 1864—Continued.	1	Sumatra	1	In port	1	610 tons pepper	$54,900 00	1	In port.	
	1	New York	1	Sold	1	190,000 slaves	9,600 00	1	Sold and took French flag	
	1	Oporto	1	Palermo	1	Ballast		1	Ballast.	
	5		5		5		64,500 00	5		$10,290 00
Quarter ended September 30, 1864.	1	In port	1	Sumatra	1	Before reported		1	Ballast.	
	5	Philadelphia	1	Malaga	1	1,940 bbls. petroleum	48,500 00	1	do	
			1	Licata	1	1,860 .... do	46,500 00	1	Sold and took Italian flag	
			1	Sold	1	3,464 .... do	98,600 00	1	Ballast	
			1	Cadiz	1	2,817 .... do	70,425 00	1	In port	
			1	In port	1	1,457 .... do	35,425 00	1	100 tons logwood, &c.	23,650 00
	2	New York	1	Mala	1	40,000 staves, 302 tons logwood, &c.	34,630 00	1	In port.	
	1	Gudava	1	In port	1	19,000 railroad sleepers	22,800 00	1	do.	
	1	Leghorn	1	do	1	35,000 staves	2,800 00	1	do.	
	1	Taganrok	1	do	1	6,400 charges wheat	44,800 00	1	do.	
	11		11		11		382,480 00	11		22,650 00
TOULON.—A. Schuing. 1st, 2d, and 3d quarters.		No reports.		No departures.						
Quarter ended September 30, 1864.		No arrivals.		No departures.						
ST. PIERRE, (Miquelon,)—G. Hughis. Quarter ended December 31, 1863.	1	Gloucester	1	Fortune Bay	1	Not stated		1	Not stated.	
	1	Bangor	1	Cape Breton	1	General merchandise	1,318 00	1	Ballast.	
	2	New York	1	New York	1	Assorted provisions and lumber	16,000 00	1	do.	
			1	Placentia Bay	1	General cargo		1	Same as inward cargo	
	4		4		4		17,318 00	4		

	No.		No.	Cargo	Value	No.	Cargo	Value	No.
2d quarter......		No report							
St. Pierre, (Miquelon).— J. P. Frecker.									
Quarter ended June 30, 1864.‡									
Gloucester...	1	Fishing voyage...	1	Not stated...			Not stated...		1
Bangor...	2	Picton...	1	Lumber...			Ballast...		1
		Lingan...	1	...do...			Not stated...		1
Fishing voyage..	1	Fishing voyage..	1	Not stated...					1
	4		4		3,740 00	4			4
Quarter ended September 30, 1864.§									
New Foundland...	1	Trading voyage...	1	General cargo...			Inward cargo...		1
Miquelon...	1	Fishing voyage...	1	Not stated...	1,900 00		Not stated...		1
Bangor...	2	Lingan...	1	Lumber...	3,300 00		Ballast...		1
		Sydney...	1	...do...			...do...		2
Fishing voyage..	2	Fishing voyage..	2	Not stated...			Not stated...		
	6		6		5,200 00	6			6
St. Pierre, (Martinique).— W. P. Green.									
1st quarter		No report							
Quarter ended March 31, 1864.‖									
New York...	3	Mayaguez...	1	Assorted provisions...	4,000 00		} Ballast...		} 3
		Porto Rico...	1	Provisions and shooks...	10,000 00				
		Anguilla...	1	1,213 shooks...	2,000 00				
	3		3		16,000 00	3			3
Quarter ended June 30, 1864.¶									
New York...	4	Barracoa...	1	Breadstuffs...	12,000 00		Ballast...		1
		Grand Cayman...	1	Assorted provisions...	7,500 00		...do...		1
		Guadaloupe...	1	Flour, meal, &c...	12,000 00		Part of inward cargo...	5,500 00	1
		New York...	1	Provisions and shooks...	20,000 00		403 puncheons molasses...	11,359 50	1
Philadelphia...	1	St. Martin...	1	Breadstuffs...	18,000 00		Part of inward cargo...	2,500 00	1
	5		5		69,500 00	5		19,359 50	5

* Entered: 2 ships, 4 barks, 3 brigs, 1 schooner—10, and 1 in port. Cleared: 2 ships, 1 bark, 3 brigs—6, and 5 in port. Aggregate tonnage entered, 5,125.

† Entered and cleared: 3 schooners, 1 bark—4. Tonnage entered, 548 39-95.

‡ Entered and cleared: 4 schooners. Aggregate tonnage entered, 461.

§ Entered and cleared: 6 schooners. Aggregate tonnage entered, 512.

‖ Entered and cleared: 3 bark. Aggregate tonnage entered, 608 39-95.

¶ Entered and cleared: 2 ships, 3 schooners—5. Aggregate tonnage entered, 984 69-95.

Navigation and commerce of the United States with foreign countries—French Dominions.

COUNTRY, CONSULATE, NAME OF CONSUL, AND DATE OF RETURNS.	VESSELS				CARGOES					
	ENTERED		CLEARED		INWARD			OUTWARD		
	No.	Where from.	No.	Where for.	No.	Description.	Value.	No.	Description.	Value.
ST. PIERRE, (Martinique.) *W. F. Gibson.*										
Quarter ended September 30, 1864.*	1	Barbadoes	1	New York	1	Assorted provisions	9,500 00	1	94 puncheons molasses	2,609 16
	2	New York	1	Grand Cayman	1	do	9,000 00	1	Provisions	2,500 00
	1	Philadelphia	1	New York	1	do	19,000 00	1	Ballast	
			1	St. Barts				1	Provisions	4,000 00
	4		4		4		37,500 00	4		9,109 16
ST. MARTIN.—*G. Roy.*										
1st and 2d quarters		No reports								
Quarter ended June 30, 1864.†	1	Martinique	1	Sombrero	1	Not stated		1	Not stated	
	2	New York	1	Baracoa	1	Flour and provisions	5,765 40	1	do	
	2		2		2		5,765 40	2		
4th quarter		No report								
GUADALOUPE.—*H. Thionville.*										
Quarter ended December 31, 1863.‡	3	Philadelphia	1	St. Kitts	1	Provisions and shooks	9,266 00	1	Ballast	
			2	Portland	1	Coal and flour	5,427 00	1	do	
	1	Portland	1	Buenos Ayres	1	Coal	2,687 00	1	do	
					1	Shooks and kerosene	6,000 00	1	In port	
	4		4		4		23,380 00	4		
Quarter ended March 31, 1864.§	1	Seamport	1	Stockton	1	147,040 feet white pine lumber		1	Ballast	
Quarter ended June 30, 1864‖.	3	New York	3	Baracoa	3	Flour and provisions	27,998 38	3	Ballast	
4th quarter		No arrivals		No departures						

NICE—*W. Slade.*
1st, 2d, 3d, and 4th quarters.

SPANISH DOMINIONS.

CADIZ—*E. S. Eggleston.*

Quarter ended December 31, 1863.¶

No arrivals.		No departures.				
3	In port	Pomeron	Before reported		1	Ballast
		Canaries	do		1	Inward. do
		Malaga	do		1	Ballast
1	Boston	Tarragona	Staves	10,000 00	1	Inward cargo
6	New York	Malaga	Provisions, staves, and rum		1	Ballast
		Boston	Staves and rum	10,000 00	1	Wine and salt	10,686 30
		Palermo	Staves	30,720 00	2	Salt	3,250 00
		Alicata	Staves and lumps	49,000 00	1	Ballast
1	Bremen	In port	Staves, rum, and oil	24,000 00	1	In port	3,250 00
2	Gibraltar	Boston	Ballast	20,400 00	1	Salt	4,750 00
		Montevideo	do	23,620 00	{2}	do
		Boston	do			
13		13		157,740 00	13		99,876 30

Quarter ended March 31, 1864.**

1	In port	Alicata	Before reported	26,160 00	1	Ballast	1,965 00
3	Boston	Boston	Staves		{3}{1}	
3	New York	Messina	Ballast		4	Salt
2		do				
		In port	Staves and oil	21,240 00	2	In port	1,965 00
7		7		47,400 00	7		

Quarter ended June 30, 1864.††

2	In port	Messina	Before reported		1	Ballast	1,279 00
		Boston	do			Salt	9,690 16
1	Nantes	do	Staves and oil	51,800 00	{13}	Wine and salt	3,877 50
6	New York	Gloucester	Staves	19,380 00	1	Salt and cork	4,041 50
		New York	Ballast		2	In port
		In port				
9		9		71,180 00	9		18,878 16

Quarter ended September 30, 1864.‡‡

| 2 | In port | Boston | Before reported | 62,777 00 | 2 | 493 lasts of salt | 2,541 00 |
| 5 | New York | do | 445,800 staves, 300 bbls. provisions, 8 hhds. hams | | 5 | 1,200½ lasts of salt | 6,037 50 |

* Entered and cleared: 1 bark, 2 schooners, 1 brig—4. Aggregate tonnage entered, 705 67-95. † Entered and cleared: 2 schooners. Aggregate tonnage entered, 207.
‡ Entered: 1 brig and 3 barks—4. Cleared: 1 brig, 2 barks—3, and 1 in port. Aggregate tonnage entered, 5,196 40-95.
§ Entered and cleared: 1 schooner. Tonnage, 197. ‖ Entered and cleared: 3 schooners. Aggregate tonnage entered, 511 92-95.
¶ Entered: 6 barks, 3 ships, 1 schooner—10, and 3 in port. Cleared: 8 barks, 3 ships, 1 schooner—12, and 1 in port. Aggregate tonnage entered, 5,289 6-95.
** Entered: 6 barks, and 1 in port. Cleared: 5 barks, and 2 in port. Aggregate tonnage entered, 2,940 92-95.
†† Entered: 1 ship, 6 barks—7, and 2 in port. Cleared: 1 ship, 6 barks—7, and 2 in port. Aggregate tonnage entered, 3,397.
‡‡ Entered: 1 ship, 9 barks, 1 brig—11, and 2 in port. Cleared: 1 ship, 9 barks, 1 brig—11, and 2 in port. Aggregate tonnage entered, 4,838 10-95.

Navigation and commerce of the United States with foreign countries—Spanish Dominions.

COUNTRY, CONSULATE, NAME OF CONSUL, AND DATE OF RETURN.	VESSELS				CARGOES					
	ENTERED		CLEARED		INWARD			OUTWARD		
	No.	Where from.	No.	Where for.	No.	Description.	Value.	No.	Description.	Value.
Quarter ended September 30, 1864—Continued.	5	New York	2	Cardiff	2	105,900 staves, 755 hhds. tobacco	$125,900 00	2	Ballast	
			1	New York	1	98,000 staves, 300 bbls. provisions	11,400 00	1	200 tons of salt	$1,000 00
			1	In port	1	140,000 staves, 300 bbls. provisions	25,900 00	1	In port	
	1	Malaga	1	Barcelona	1	75,500 staves	9,600 00	1	Inward cargo	9,600 00
			1	In port	1	Ballast		1	In port	
	13		13		13		234,677 00	13		19,178 50
MALAGA—J. R. Geary. Quarter ended December 31, 1861.*	2	In port	2	New York	2	Before reported		2	Fruit, &c.	80,676 00
	2	Cadiz	2	San Francisco	2	Ballast		2	do.	49,398 00
	2	New York	1	Messina	1	80,400 staves	10,452 00	1	do.	34,329 00
	1	Tarragona	1	Sold	1	53,400 staves	6,942 00	1	Ballast	
	1	Gibraltar	1	Boston	1	2,340 staves	421 00	1	Sold	
	1	Boston	1	Messina	1	45,530 staves	5,530 00	1	Fruit	20,136 00
								1	Ballast	
	9		9		9		93,345 00	9		184,539 00
2d and 3d quarters	No report.									
Quarter ended September 30, 1864.†	6	New York	1	Goree	1	64,000 staves	10,000 00	1	Ballast	
			2	Cagliari	2	333,320 staves	34,000 00	2	do.	
			1	Alicata	1	72,600 staves	11,000 00	1	do.	
			1	New York	1	56,880 staves	9,000 00	1	Fruit	17,751 00
	2	Boston	1	In port	1	58,560 staves	9,000 00	1	In port	
			1	New York	1	In transitu		1	Fruit	33,976 00
	1	Marseilles	1	New York	1	89,159 staves	13,000 00	1	Ballast	
	1	Gibraltar	1	In port	1	Ballast		1	Fruit	22,869 00
	1	Cagliari	1	Boston	1	71,360 staves	10,000 00	1	In port	
	1	Baltimore	1	In port	1	4,500 staves; in transitu	600 00	1	Fruit	8,397 00
					1	91,230 staves	9,000 00	1	In port	
	12		12		12		105,600 00	12		81,993 00

ALICANTE—W. L. Gire.

Quarter	Entered No.	Whence	Entered value	Cleared No.	Whither	Cargo	Cleared value	Ballast No.	Remarks	Value
Quarter ended December 31, 93;‡	2	Bordeaux		{1 / 1}	Cadiz / Liverpool	23,628 railroad sleepers, 2,150 telegraph posts, 36 bbls. spirits of turpentine.		{1 / 1}	Ballast. 350 tons Esparto grass.	6,000 00
	2			2				2		6,000 00
Quarter ended March 31, 1864.§	1	Tarragona		1	New York	665 barrels wine, 90 bags nuts, 452 bundles licorice root.		1	Inward cargo, 1,041 gallons licorice root.	2,784 60
3d quarter		No report.								

DENIA—I. Morand.

Quarter	Entered No.	Whence	Entered value	Cleared No.	Whither	Cargo	Cleared value	Ballast No.	Remarks	Value
Quarter ended September 30, 1864.‖	1 / 1	Antwerp / New York		1 / 1	Cardiff / New York	1,312 tons railroad iron ... / 48,480 pieces staves, 1,826 pieces oak plank, 15 dozen chairs.	9,842 65	1 / 1	350 tons Esparto grass ... / 580 casks wine, 1,127 cwt. licorice root, 160 bundles mats.	5,600 00 / 11,569 17
	2			2			9,842 65	2		17,169 17
1st, 2d, 3d, and 4th quarters		No arrivals.				No departures.				

BARCELONA—J. A. Licia.

Quarter	Entered No.	Whence	Entered value	Cleared No.	Whither	Cargo	Cleared value	Ballast No.	Remarks	Value
Quarter ended December 31, 1863.¶	1 / 1	In port / Cardiff		1 / 1	Trapani / Licata.	Before reported 800 tons coal.	8,000 00	1 / 1	Ballast. / ...do.	
	2			2			8,000 00	2		8,000 00
3d quarter		No arrivals.				No departures.				
Quarter ended June 30, 1864.**	1	New York		1	Palermo	85,000 staves.	11,175 00	1	Ballast.	11,175 00
4th quarter		No arrivals.				No departures.				

* Entered : 5 barks, 1 brig, 1 schooner—7, and 2 in port. Cleared : 7 barks, 1 brig—8, and 1 sail. Aggregate tonnage entered, 2,302.
† Entered : 1 ship, 10 barks, 1 brig—12. Cleared : 1 ship, 7 barks, 1 brig—9, and 3 in port. Aggregate tonnage entered, 4,653.
‡ Entered and cleared : 2 ships. Aggregate tonnage entered, 1,469.   § Entered and cleared : 1 brig. Tonnage entered, 198.
‖ Entered and cleared : 1 ship, 1 bark—2. Aggregate tonnage entered, 1,259.   ** Entered and cleared : 1 bark. Tonnage, 570 47.95.
¶ Entered : 1 bark, and 1 in port. Cleared : 1 bark, 1 ship—2. Aggregate tonnage entered, 1,833 61.95.

Navigation and commerce of the United States with foreign countries—Spanish Dominions.

COUNTRY, CONSULATE, NAME OF CONSUL, AND DATE OF RETURN	VESSELS				CARGOES					
	ENTERED		CLEARED		INWARD			OUTWARD		
	No.	Where from.	No.	Where for.	No.	Description.	Value.	No.	Description.	Value.
TARRAGONA—*J. A. Little.* Quarter ended September 31, 1862.*	2	In port	1	Malaga and San Francisco.	2	Before reported		1	320 ½-pipes and 250 ½-pipes wine.	$9,882 00
			1	Licata				1		
	1	Boston and Cadiz.	1	In port	1	32,000 pipe and 94,000 hhd. staves.	$4,685 00	1	In port.	
	3		3		3		6,685 00	3		9,882 00
Quarter ended March 31, 1864.†	1	In port	1	Messina	1	Before reported		1	Ballast	
	2	New York	1	do	1	59 M staves	6,750 00	1	Wine, licorice, and nuts.	9,000 00
			1	New York	1	37½ M. staves	6,000 00	1		
	3		3		3		12,750 00	3		9,000 00
Quarter ended June 30, 1864.		No arrivals		No departures						
4th quarter.		No report.								
HAVANA—*W. T. Minor.* 1st, 2d, 3d, and 4th quarters.		No reports.								
MATANZAS—*H. C. Hall.* Quarter ended December 31, 1862.‡	8	In port	4	New York	4	Before reported		4	1,028 hhds, 44 tierces, 17 bbls, 2,385 boxes sugar, 501 hhds. molasses, 84 bales tobacco.	113,954 06
			1	Philadelphia	1	do		1	16 hhds. and 4,447 boxes sugar, 7 bales tobacco.	10,397 19
			1	Boston	1	do		1	414 hhds. and 98 tierces molasses.	8,569 94
			1	Cardenas	1	do		1	Ballast.	
			1	Bristol, R. I.				1	143 hhds. molasses, 15 tierces and 14 bbls. honey.	4,077 44
	20	Portland	1	Remedios	1	General cargo	6,500 00	1	Ballast.	
			2	Cardenas	2	Cooperage	15,350 00	2	do.	
			8	Portland	8	Cooperage, lumber, box shooks.	53,450 00	4	do. 975 bbls, 133 tierces, and 20 bbls molasses, 384 boxes sugar, 98 M cigars.	90,703 96

No.	Port	No.	Port	Cargo	Value	No.	Cargo	Value
1		1	Havana	Cooperage	7,900 00	1	Ballast	
6		1	Sagua la Grande	do	8,150 00	1	do	
		1	Philadelphia	do	8,200 00	1	do	
		1	Inagua Island	do	6,900 00	1	do	
		5	In port	Cooperage and shooks		5	In port	
	Sierra Morena	1	Portland	Cooperage and machinery, &c.	27,720 00	1	Molasses in transit	
	Philadelphia	3	Philadelphia	General cargo, machinery, &c.	47,300 00	1	325 hhds. and 25 tierces molasses, 5 M cigars.	7,700 56
2		1	Sagua la Grande	do	14,600 00	2	Ballast.	2,014 59
3	Baltimore	2	Baltimore	Provisions and cooperage	24,600 00	1	100 boxes sugar in transit.	
	Boston	1	In port	General cargo	9,275 00	1	In port.	21,450 63
		1	Portland	Ice and general cargo.	6,225 00	1	274 hhds. sugar, 55 hhds. molasses.	
		1	Boston		6,000 00	1	In port.	10,946 66
1	New York	1	New York	do	6,000 00	1	44 hhds. 39 tierces molasses and sundries.	17,949 15
						2	211 hhds. 53 boxes sugar, 17 bbls. honey.	
2	Bristol, R.I.	1	In port	do	5,975 00	1	In port.	5,498 31
2	Bangor, Me.	1	Bristol, R.I.	Potatoes, &c.	4,000 00	1	229 hhds. and 25 bbls. molasses.	3,387 31
1	New York	1	Fall River	do.	3,500 00	1	76 hhds. molasses, 63 boxes sugar.	
1	Trinidad	1	Philadelphia	Lumber	4,850 00	1	In port	
		1	In port	Lumber, box shooks		1	Sold.	
		1	Sold.	Ballast		1	In port	
		1	In port	do.				
46		**46**			**269,995 00**	**46**		**223,039 00**

MATANZAS—A. G. Biddle.
Quarter ended March 31, 1864.§

No.	Port	No.	Port	Cargo	Value	No.	Cargo	Value
11	In port	4	Philadelphia	Before reported		10	2,033 hhds. and 125 tierces molasses, 2 M cigars, &c.	114,289 73
		1	Baltimore	do		1	Ballast.	
		1	Boston	do.				
		2	New York	do.				
		1	Portland	do.				
29	Portland	5	Portland	do.		19	278 hhds. 38 tierces, and 31 bbls. molasses, sugar, 25 M cigars, and sundries.	233,704 49
		4	New York	Box shooks, lumber, &c	150,581 00	10	In port.	
		4	Boston					
		3	Bangor					
		3	Philadelphia					
		10	Cardenas					
			In port					
11	Port Royal, Key West, Tortugas, and Pensacola.	4	New York	Ballast		4	Sugar and molasses	89,990 99
		1	Boston	do		3	Ballast	
		1	Remedios.	do		4	In port.	
		1	Cardenas	do				
		4	In port.	do				

* Entered: 1 brig, and 9 in port. Cleared: 1 schooner, 1 brig—2, and 1 in port. Tonnage, 368 69-95.
† Entered: 1 bark, 1 schooner—2, and 1 in port. Cleared: 2 barks and 1 schooner—3. Aggregate tonnage entered, 564 89-95.
‡ Entered: 25 brigs, 9 barks, 3 schooners, 1 steamboat—38, and 8 in port. Cleared: 19 brigs, 19 bark, 3 schooners—34, 1 sold and 11 in port. Aggregate tonnage entered, 10,685 56-95.
§ Entered: 3 ships, 30 barks, 54 brigs, 16 schooners, 1 steamboat—104, and 11 in port. Cleared: 2 ships, 21 barks, 40 brigs, 10 schooners—74, 1 sold, and 30 in port. Aggregate tonnage entered, 31,418 72-95.

Navigation and commerce of the United States with foreign countries—Spanish Dominions.

COUNTRY, CONSULATE, NAME OF CONSUL, AND DATE OF RETURN.	VESSELS				CARGOES					
	ENTERED		CLEARED		INWARD			OUTWARD		
	No.	Where from.	No.	Where for.	No.	Description.	Value.	No.	Description.	Value.
Quarter ended March 31, 1864—Continued.	1	Sagua la Grande	1	Fall River	1	Ballast		1	153 hhds., 4 tierces, and 89 bbls. molasses.	$4,275 10
	8	Philadelphia	1	New York	8	Cooperage, provisions, &c	$97,949 00	6	297 hhds. and 70 boxes sugar, 60 hhds. molasses and sundries.	100,606 75
			5	Philadelphia				2	In port	
			2	In port						
	14	Havana	1	Providence	11	Empty casks, cooperage, lumber, and shooks.	10,499 00	9	789 hhds., 86 tierces, and 29 bbls. molasses, 50 hhds. and 50 bbls. sugar, &c.	171,139 89
			1	Newport						
			1	Portland						
			1	Philadelphia				2	In port	
			7	New York						
			2	In port						
	1	Wiscasset	1	New York	1	Box shooks	3,950 00	1	570 hhds. sugar, 491 hhds. molasses.	57,004 88
	1	Boston	1	Boston	1	Cooperage	8,199 09	1	418 hhds., 78 tierces, and 96 bbls. molasses.	19,156 53
	3	Bristol	2	Bristol	2	Cooperage, &c	9,640 00	2	Molasses	18,091 23
			1	In port	1	General cargo	3,900 00	1	In port	
	1	Brownsville	1	New York	1	Ballast		1	372 hhds. and 42 tierces molasses.	10,694 41
	9	New Orleans	1	Baltimore	1	do		1	343 hhds. and 66 bbls. sugar, 3 hhds. molasses.	94,639 83
			1	Philadelphia	1	do		1	Ballast	
			1	New Orleans	1	do		1	1,170 bbls. molasses.	11,254 93
			1	Sagua la Grande	3	Empty casks and lumber		3	Ballast	
			5	In port	2	Ballast	4,085 00	2	do	
					1	do		1	In port	
	1	Bermudas	1	New York	1	Cooperage	3,894 00	1	205 hhds. melado, 265 hhds. and 89 bbls. sugar.	29,836 01
	1	Cardenas	1	Belfast	1	do	7,930 00	1	44 hhds. molasses	1,460 67
	7	New York	1	Remedios	1	Ballast		1	Ballast	
			1	Sold				1	Sold	
			2	New York	2	Cooperage and empty casks	10,870 00	2	Sugar, melado, molasses, honey.	73,252 07
	3	Baltimore	3	In port	3	Box shooks, cooperage, &c	17,000 00	3	In port	
			1	Portland	2	Cooperage	7,225 00	1	30 hogsheads and 50 barrels molasses.	1,983 05
	2	Frankfort	2	In port	2	Cooperage and general cargo	19,113 00	2	In port	
	2	Cardenas			2	Casks and lumber	6,600 00	2	Ballast	
	1	Laguna	1	In port	1	Ballast		1	In port	
	104		104		104		370,968 00	104		953,610 50

Quarter ended June 30, 1864.*

30	In port	1	Sagua la Grande	1	Before reported	1	Ballast.	467,082 78
		12	New York	12	do	12	Sugar, molasses, honey, &c.	37,387 38
		2	Boston	2	do	2	335 hhds. and 100 boxes sugar, 375 hhds. and 30 tcs. molasses.	
		6	Philadelphia	6	do	6	Sugar, molasses, old iron, &c.	91,617 94
		2	Baltimore	2	do	2	370 hhds. and 58 boxes sugar, 84 hhds. and 30 bbls. molasses.	37,694 04
		1	Bristol	1	do	1	185 hhds., 3 tierces, and 8 bbls. molasses.	6,004 94
11	New Orleans	1	New Orleans	1	do	1	1,713 bbls. molasses.	14,842 91
		5	Portland	5	do	5	Sugar, molasses, cigars.	74,548 59
		3	New York	3	Ballast	3	675 hhds. and 56 tierces molasses, 725 hhds. melado, 1,237 dozen pineapples.	68,885 70
		7	Philadelphia	7	do	1	Ballast.	6,848 64
						1	259 hhds. molasses and 58 tierces molasses.	
1	Tortugas	1	In port	1	do	6	Ballast.	
1	Pensacola	1	New York	1	do	1	In port.	53,130 66
11	Key West	1	do	1	do	1	564 hhds. and 446 boxes sugar.	16,366 44
		1	Sagua la Grande	1	do	1	571 hhds. and 61 tierces molasses.	
		1	Boston	1	do	1	Ballast.	11,500 25
		6	New York	6	do	6	405 hhds. and 36 tierces molasses.	81,037 34
							2,310 hhds. and 258 tcs. molasses.	90,146 07
							820 boxes sugar	
16	Portland	1	Remedios	1	do	1	Ballast.	38,598 55
		2	Philadelphia	2	do	2	987 hhds. and 115 tcs. molasses.	34,865 45
		3	Boston	3	Box shooks, cooperage, &c.	3	927 hhds. and 107 tcs. molasses.	59,303 21
		3	Portland	3	do	3	1,077 hhds. and 57 tcs. molasses.	
		3	Coastwise	3	do	3	95 hhds. and 404 boxes sugar, 60 bales tobacco.	5,130 77
		2	New York	2	do	2	125 boxes sugar and 60 hhds. molasses.	41,900 54
8	Boston	5	In port	5	do	5	845 hhds. and 92 tierces molasses.	
		3	Boston	3	do	3	320 hhds. and 197 boxes sugar.	56,612 98
						3	In port.	
							806 hhds. and 73 tcs. 61 bbls. molasses, 973 hhds. and 122 boxes sugar.	
5	Vera Cruz	2	New York	2	do	2	504 hhds. and 125 boxes sugar.	60,960 68
	Tabasco	2	Coastwise	2	do	2	226 hhds. and 64 tierces molasses.	13,205 45
	Laguna	1	Philadelphia	1	do	1	Ballast.	98,166 93
	Matamoras	4	New York	4	Ballast	4	344 hhds. and 40 tierces molasses.	5,853 31
1	Sierra Morena	1	Philadelphia	1		1	565 hhds. and 330 boxes sugar, 1,232 hhds. and 148 tcs. molasses.	
		1	Portland	1	Cargo in transitu.	1	512,120 lbs. old iron	11,457 19
2	Newport	2	Coastwise	2	General cargo, cooperage, &c.	2	335 hhds., 30 tierces, and 10 bbls. molasses.	27,171 31
1	Baltimore	1	Baltimore	1	General cargo.	1	Ballast.	
							253 hhds. and 160 boxes sugar.	

* Entered: 4 ships, 33 barks, 34 brig, 13 schooners—74, and 39 in port. Cleared: 5 ships, 27 barks, 44 brig, 12 schooners—84, and 10 in port. Aggregate tonnage entered, 28,697 51-95.

Navigation and commerce of the United States with foreign countries—Spanish Dominions.

COUNTRY, CONSULATE, NAME OF CONSUL, AND DATE OF RETURNS.	VESSELS.				CARGOES.					
	ENTERED.		CLEARED.		INWARD.			OUTWARD.		
	No.	Where from.	No.	Where for.	No.	Description.	Value.	No.	Description.	Value.
Quarter ended June 30, 1864—Continued.										
	1	Providence	1	New York	1	Cooperage	$4,900 00	1	569 hhds., 58 tierces, and 26 bbls. molasses.	$17,911 75
	8	New York	7	do	7	Cooperage, empty casks, &c	16,819 00	7	25,366 doz. pineapples, 594 hhds. and 1,457 bxs. sugar, 384 hhds., 101 tcs., and 75 bbls. molasses.	166,779 00
	3	Philadelphia	1	In port	1	Box shooks and cooperage	9,300 00	1	In port	34,255 99
			1	New York	1	Cooperage and provisions	9,145 00	1	378 hhds. and 33 boxes sugar, 80 hhds. molasses.	16,977 58
	2	Bristol	1	Philadelphia	1	do	5,340 00	1	466 hhds. and 35 tierces molasses.	7,541 63
			1	In port	1	Cooperage and lard	8,800 00	1	In port	
			1	Bristol	1	Cooperage	9,900 00	1	184 hhds., 9 tierces, and 111 bbls. molasses.	
	1	Ellsworth	1	Baltimore	1	Hoops	3,430 00	1	265 hhds. and 27 tierces molasses.	11,336 63
	1	Bath	1	In port	1	Lumber	3,675 00	1	In port	
	1	Machias	1	do	1	Ice	9,500 00	1	do	
			1	Philadelphia	1	Lumber	3,250 00	1	290 hhds. and 45 tierces molasses.	10,563 65
	104		104		104		221,674 00	104		1,706,994 63
Quarter ended September 30, 1864.*										
	10	In port	3	Portland	3	Before reported		3	1,379 hhds., 142 tcs., and 61 bbls. molasses.	39,404 96
			2	Philadelphia	2	do		2	669,728 lbs. old iron, 579 hhds. and 58 tierces molasses.	25,927 39
			2	Boston	2	do		2	811 hhds. and 81 tcs. molasses.	93,340 97
			2	Cork	2	do		1	2,100 boxes sugar and 1,966 hhds. molasses.	98,284 00
			1	Falmouth	1	do				
	4	Machias	3	Philadelphia	3	Lumber	$3,425 00	4	Ballast	
	1	Newport	1	Portland	1	General cargo	5,498 00		do	
	11	Portland	2	Sagua la Grande	2	Lumber and cooperage		5	42 bhds. sugar, 1,333 hhds. and 114 tierces molasses.	39,537 77
			3	Boston	3	do	69,375 00	3	Ballast	
			3	Portland	3	do		3	In port	
			3	Philadelphia	3	do		1	196 hhds. and 40 tcs. molasses.	
	3	Philadelphia	1	In port	1	General cargo and cooperage		1	In port	12,091 45
			2	Philadelphia	2	do	19,982 00	1	In cart	
	2	Boston	1	Boston	1	General cargo	17,960 00	1	89 hhds. molasses	
			1	Philadelphia	1	do		1	Ballast	2,320 02
	2	Bath	1	Baire	1	Ice, lumber, &c	11,000 00	1	do	
			1	In port	1	Lumber	16,550 00	1	In port	
	3	Bangor	2	Philadelphia	2	do		2	do	
			1	In port	1	do		1	Ballast	

No.	Where from	Where to	Cargo	No.	Value	No.	Cargo	Value
4	Baltimore	Baltimore	{ Gen'l cargo, lumber, and cooperage.	2	23,158 00	2	do	10,071 44
1	Searsport	In port	Lumber	2	5,375 00	3	412 hhds. and 31 tcs. molasses.	
1	New York	Philadelphia	General cargo	1	11,000 00	1	In port	
1	Newport, Eng	In port	650 tons coal	1	4,875 00	1	do	
2	Havana	Cork	Ballast	1		1	do	
		Palmouth	do			1	1,731 boxes sugar and 1,250 hhds. molasses.	
45				45	208,158 00	45		321,129 98

CARDENAS.—N. Cross.

1st quarter .... No report

Quarter ended March 31, 1864.

No.	Where from	Where to	Cargo	No.	Value	No.	Cargo	Value
9	In port	Philadelphia	Before reported	3		9	Molasses and sugar	100,159 41
		Portland	do	5		1	Molasses	3,394 63
1	Ellsworth	New York	Box shooks	1	3,550 00	1	do	8,040 17
17	Havana	Portland	Ballast	1		3	do	93,496 39
		Newport	do	3		1	do	9,605 89
		Boston	do	1		1	do	18,937 13
		New York	do	1			do	
		Philadelphia	Box shooks	1	3,100 00	3	do	31,445 43
		Portland	Ballast	2		1	do	6,920 00
						1	do	9,643 31
			Lumber			1	do	9,644 63
			Ballast		3,000 00	4	In port	
26	Portland	Philadelphia	Box shooks	2	9,950 00	2	Sugar and molasses	33,525 17
		Portland	Cooperage and box shooks	6	94,750 00	6	do	75,775 33
		New York	Cooperage	3	13,170 00	3	Molasses	33,557 01
		Havana	do	1	6,500 00	1	Ballast	
		Remedios	do	1	4,500 00	1	do	
		Boston	Box shooks	5	19,000 00	5	Molasses and sugar	82,509 00
		Boston	Cooperage and box shooks	7	4,900 00	7	Molasses and sugar	27,269 11
		In port	do	3	27,900 00	3	In port	49,146 66
3	Baltimore	Baltimore	do	3	12,500 00	3	Sugar and molasses	9,844 22
4	Matanzas	Portland	Cooperage	1		1	Molasses	11,563 01
		Belfast	Ballast	1		1	Sugar	
2	Belfast	In port	do	2		2	In port	95,367 29
		Philadelphia	Box shooks	1	4,500 00	1	Sugar	
3	Boston	Matanzas	Cooperage, box shooks, provisions.	1	11,000 00	1	Inward cargo	95,085 94
		Boston	do	3	7,500 00	3	Molasses	44,367 75
		Baltimore	do	1	4,800 00	2	Sugar	36,524 70
8	Boston	New York	do	1	7,500 00	1	do	
		In port	Lumber and assorted cargo.	2		2	In port	

* Entered: 9 barks, 21 brigs, 5 schooners—35, and 10 in port. Cleared: 11 barks, 18 brigs, 5 schooners—34, and 11 in port. Aggregate tonnage entered, 9,912 4-95.

‡ Entered: 22 barks, 53 brigs, 18 schooners—93, and 9 in port. Cleared: 13 barks, 40 brigs, 19 schooners—72, and 30 in port. Aggregate tonnage entered, 23,559 21-95.

Navigation and commerce of the United States with foreign countries—Spanish Dominions.

COUNTRY, CONSULATE, NAME OF CONSUL, AND DATE OF RETURNS.	VESSELS				CARGOES					
	ENTERED		CLEARED		INWARD			OUTWARD		
	No.	Where from	No.	Where for	No.	Description	Value	No.	Description	Value
Quarter ended March 31, 1864—Continued.	14	New Orleans	1	Portland	1	Ballast		1	Molasses	$12,394 46
			2	New Orleans	2	Empty casks	$530 00	2	...do	10,910 16
			1	Philadelphia	1	Ballast		1	...do	16,821 79
			2	New York	2	Empty barrels	900 00	2	Sugar and molasses	53,998 79
			8	In port	6	Empty barrels	3,600 00	6	In port	
					2	Ballast		2	...do	
	5	Philadelphia	3	Philadelphia	3	Box shooks and cooperage	11,700 00	3	Sugar and molasses	46,535 94
			2	In port	2	Provisions and cooperage	6,500 00	2	In port	
	3	New York	1	Sagua	1	Empty hogsheads	900 00	1	Ballast	
			2	In port	2	Assorted cargo and empty hogsheads	8,100 00	2	In port	
	5	Key West	4	New York	4	Ballast		4	Sugar and molasses	71,756 53
			1	Sagua	1	do		1	Ballast	
	1	Frankfort	1	Frankfort	1	Box shooks	3,600 00	1	Molasses	8,364 39
	1	Pensacola	1	New York	1	Ballast		1	Molasses and sugar	17,064 33
	1	Sierra Morena	1	Portland	1	Molasses	2,500 00	1	Inward cargo	
	1	Culaba	1	In port	1	Shooks	2,500 00			
	1	Bristol	1	do	1	Provisions		1	In port	
	102		102		102		909,350 00	102		911,979 16
Quarter ended June 30, 1864*.	30	In port	10	New York	10	Before reported		30	Sugar, molasses, honey, cigars, old copper, old iron, &c.	538,944 19
			3	Philadelphia	3	do				
			8	Portland	8	do				
			4	Boston	4	do				
			1	Bristol	1	do				
			1	Baltimore	1	do				
			1	Bangor	1	do				
			1	New Orleans	1	do				
	3	Matanzas	2	Newport	2	Lumber	$2,500 00	3	Molasses	95,495 33
			1	Boston	1	Ballast				
	10	Key West	2	Portland	2	do		2	Molasses	13,740 40
			2	Philadelphia	2	do		2	Ballast	
	15	New Orleans	3	New York	3	do		3	Sugar and molasses	78,055 90
			1	Frankfort	1	do		1	Molasses	8,630 16
			1	Sierra Morena	1	do		1	Ballast	
			1	Sagua	1	do		1	...do	13,963 90
			1	Portland	1	do		1	Molasses	
			1	In port	1	do		1	In port	11,949 57
			1	Frankfort	1	do		1	Molasses	13,337 63
			1	Portland	1	do		1	...do	

No.	Port	No.	Cargo	No.	Value	No.	Cargo	Value
19	Portland	6	do	6			Sugar and molasses	157,777
		1	do	1			Fruit	1,126 35
		1	do	1			do	21,283 65
	New Orleans	1	Lard	1	500 00		Ballast	8,170 52
	Sierra Morena	2	Ballast	2			Molasses	34,066 61
	Baltimore	3	do	1			do	
	Boston	3	Box shooks and lumber	3	9,500 00		Sugar and molasses	46,253 91
	Philadelphia	6	Box shooks and cooperage	5	22,500 00		do	77,948 59
9	Havana	2	Box shooks and lumber	2	5,500 00		Sugar and molasses	35,949 38
	Sagua	2	Lumber	2	5,500 00		Ballast	
	Portland	1	Box shooks	1	4,000 00		Molasses	16,129 96
	In port	5	Ballast	4	19,500 00		In port	
4	Philadelphia	3	Ballast	3			Molasses	42,699 30
	New York	2	do	2			Sugar and molasses	52,679 68
	Boston	1	do	1			Molasses	52,279 46
	Bangor	1	do	1			Molasses	9,244 00
	Portland	1	do	1			Molasses	7,064 56
4	Philadelphia	2	Assorted cargo	2	10,000 00		Sugar	54,987 69
	New York	1	Cooperage	1	2,500 00		Molasses	13,392 98
	In port	1	Assorted cargo	1	10,000 00		In port	
	New York	1	Empty hogsheads	1	1,000 00		Sugar and molasses	19,622 70
	Philadelphia	1	Hoops	1	2,500 00		Molasses	11,823 84
	Sagua	1	Lumber	1	15,000 00		Ballast	
	Sierra Morena	1	Assorted cargo	1			Molasses in transit	
6	Portland	6	Molasses in transit	6			Sugar	93,173 38
6	Philadelphia	2	Ballast	2	1,500 00		do	55,396 39
	New York	1	Empty hogsheads	1	3,000 00		Ballast	
	Sagua	2	Assorted cargo	2	95,000 00		In port	
1	In port	1	do	1	9,000 00		Sugar and molasses	90,596 14
1	Baltimore	1	Lumber	1			Inward cargo	
1	Newport	2	Provisions	2	2,500 00		In port	
1	Bristol	1	Cooperage	1	3,000 00		do	
	Bangor	1	Lumber	1				
110		110		110	149,500 00	110		1,415,267 14
11	In port	5	Before reported	5		11	Molasses, sugar, &c.	141,070 96
	Boston	3	do	3				
	Philadelphia	1	do	1				
	Portland	1	do	1				
	Falmouth	1	do	1				
7	Portland	2	Lumber	2	5,500 00	2	Molasses	11,571 04
	New York	1	do	1	3,500 00	1	do	16,540 27
	Portland	1	do	1	2,500 00	1	do	10,096 91
	Boston	2	do	2	6,000 00	2	do	50,273 99
	In port	1	Box shooks	1	4,500 00	1	In port	

Quarter ended September 30, 1864.†

* Entered: 14 barks, 51 brigs, 15 schooners—80, and 30 in port. Cleared: 6 barks, 50 brigs, 13 schooners—99, and 11 in port. Aggregate tonnage entered, 17,846 66-95.
† Entered: 16 brigs, 1 bark, 11 not cleared, 3 schooners—30, and 9 in port. Aggregate tonnage entered, 5,930 87-95.

Navigation and commerce of the United States with foreign countries—Spanish Dominions.

COUNTRY, CONSULATE, NAME OF CONSUL, AND DATE OF RETURNS.	VESSELS				CARGOES							Value.
	ENTERED.		CLEARED.		INWARD.			OUTWARD.				
	No.	Where from.	No.	Where for.	No.	Description.	Value.	No.	Description.	Value.		
Quarter ended September 30, 1864—Continued.												
	2	Sierra Morena	2	Portland	2	Molasses in transitu		2	Molasses			$15,637 98
	2	Havana	1	New York	1	Ballast		1	do			11,092 37
			1	Portland	1	do		1	do			7,783 08
	1	New Orleans	1	Newport	1	do		1	do			8,183 90
	2	Bangor	2	New York	2	Lumber	$5,000 00	2	Sugar and molasses			23,968 90
	1	Frankfort	1	Boston	1	do	3,000 00	1	Molasses			7,840 74
	1	Vera Cruz	1	New York	1	Ballast		1	Ballast			
	1	Philadelphia	1	do	1	Cooperage	4,500 00	1	Sugar			24,991 04
	1	New York	1	Boston	1	Assorted cargo	95,000 00	1	Molasses			12,855 08
	1	Boston	1	do	1	do	15,000 00	1	Molasses			12,679 99
	1	Matanzas	1	Portland	1	Ballast		1	do			11,531 07
	1	Baltimore	1	In port	1	Lumber		1	In port			
	32		**32**		**32**		8,500 00	**32**				337,119 00
Sagua la Grande—J. H. Homer.												
Quarter ended December 31, 1863.												
	1	In port	1	Philadelphia	1	Before reported		1	412 hhds., 61 tierces, 1 bbl. sugar			31,452 49
	1	Cardenas	1	New York	1	Ballast		2	653 hhds., 4 tierces, 1 bbl. sugar			43,630 01
	2	Matanzas	1	do	1	do		3	1,022 hhds., 1 tierce sugar			70,746 94
	1	Searsport	1	Philadelphia	2	Lumber and shooks		3	271 hhds., 28 tcs., 6 bbls. molasse.			7,085 45
	3	Philadelphia	1	New York	3	Cooperage and mahogany	32,258 53	1	In port			
	1	Fall River	3	In port	4	General cargo		1	do			34,745 66
	1	Havana	1	New York	1	Ballast		1	500 hogsheads, 1 tes., 37 boxes sugar, 20 tierces molasses.			187,630 57
	10		**10**		**10**		32,258 53	**10**				
Quarter ended March 31, 1864.												
	4	In port	3	Philadelphia	3	Before reported		3	694 hhds. and 51 tcs. sugar, 198 hhds. and 63 bbls. molasse.			55,942 85
			1	Matanzas	1	do		1	Ballast			
	4	Philadelphia	2	Philadelphia	2	Cooperage	10,362 44	2	711 hhds., 45 tcs., 6 bbls. sugar			59,215 11
			1	Cardenas	1	Cargo in transit		1	Cargo in transit			
	2	Boston	1	In port	1	General cargo	3,927 00	1	In port			17,356 15
			1	New York	1	Cooperage	4,209 00	1	213 hhds., 13 tcs., 2 bbls. sugar, and 60 bbls. molasses.			
			1	Boston	1	General cargo	14,900 00	1	1 625hhd. and 4 tierces sugar, and 208 hhds. and 19 tcs. molasses.			19,155 87
	2	Baltimore	2	Baltimore	2	Cooperage	8,113 00	2	431 hhds. and 31 tcs. sugar, and 160 hhds. molasses.			26,044 94

	Port		Status		Cargo		Description	Amount	Value
2	Newport	1	Newport	1	...do	1	235 hds., 10 tierces, and 22 bbls. mol ses.	1,160 97	7,871 04
1	Frankfort	1	In port.	1	Lumber		In port. 1177 hds., 30 tierces, and 50 bbls. molasses.	2,500 00	4,990 25
		1	Frankfort	1	...do		908 hhds. sugar, 50 hhds. and 18 tcs. molasses,	1,600 00	
1	Bucksport	1	New York	1	Cooperage		484 hhds. 1 tce., 1 bbl. sugar.	7,300 00	15,942 26
2	Cardenas	1	...do	1	Ballast	1	In port. 929 hhds. and 40 tcs. sugar, and 60 hhds. mses.		34,312 50
1	Machiasport	1	Boston	1	Lumber	1	408 hhds. sugar.	3,900 00	19,926 60
2	Havana	1	New York	1	Ballast	1	In port. 465 hhds., 35 tcs., and 30 bbls. molasses.		29,313 05
5	Key West	1	In port.	1	...do	1			16,019 90
		1	Philadelphia	1	...do				
1	Fall River	4	In port.	4	...do	4	In port.	3,997 00	8,335 00
3	Matanzas	3	Remedios.	1	Ballast	1	Ballast	1,678 00	10,668 08
1	Bristol	3	In port.†	3	In port	3	In port.	3,788 97	
1	New Orleans	1	...do	1	Cooperage	1	...do	7,882 97	11,743 63
4	Portland	1	Remedios.	1	Empty barrels	1	108 hogsheads sugar		
		1	Boston	1	Lumber	1	333 hhds., 18 tcs., and 2 barrels molasses.	3,500 00	
		1	New York.	1	Cooperage	1	336 hhds., 39 tcs., and 3 barrels molasses.	3,283 00	
		1	In port.	1	Lumber	1	In port	3,562 00	
36		36		36		36		83,502 38	346,189 94

Quarter ended June 30, 1864:								
14	In port.	7	New York.	7	Before reported	7	2,935 bhds., 925 tcs., 7 bbls, and 120 boxes sugar; 794 bhds., 39 tcs., and 66 lbs. molasses.	853,964 54
		1	Bristol	1		1	307 bhds., 20 tcs., and 23 > bls. m...	11,780 12
		2	Philadelphia.	2	...do	2	453 bhds, 100 boxes sugar; 427 bhds., 48 tcs., 100 bbls. molar's,	59,050 79
		1	Frankfort.	1	...do	1	234 bhds. and 41 tcs. mses.	8,246 37
		1	Portland.	1	...do	1	565 bhds. and 60 does sugar.	43,216 94
		1	Boston.	1	...do	1	291 bhds. 2 tces, and 90 bbls.	11,394 63
		1	An ordered port.	1	...do	1	533 bhds., 97 tcs., 11 bbl. mo-ses, and 75 gllons shy.	8,359 57
13	Havana	7	New York.	7	Ballast	7	3,599 bhds., 131 tcs., 13 rm. tcs. gar, and 491 hhds., 5 tces.	259,685 63
6		6	Philadelphia.	6	do	6	2,115 hhds. 1 red, 1 bbl. 207 boxes sugar, and 562 hhds. 50 tcs.	187,042 74

*Entered: 5 barks, 3 brigs, 1 schooner—9, and 1 in port. Cleared: 5 barks, 1 brig—6, and 4 in port. Aggregate entered, 2,878 59-95.
†Entered: 4 barks, 19 brigs, 9 schooners—32, and 4 in port. Cleared: 2 barks, 13 brigs, 7 schooners—22, and 14 in port. Aggregate tonnage entered, 8,365 11-95.
‡Entered: 19 barks, 27 brigs, 14 schooners—60, and 14 in port. Sisred: 18 barks, 33 brigs, 14 schooners—64, and 10 in port. Aggregate tonnage entered, 18,367 83-95.

Navigation and commerce of the United States with foreign countries—Spanish Dominions.

COUNTRY, CONSULATE, NAME OF CONSUL, AND DATE OF RETURN.	VESSELS.				CARGOES.					
	ENTERED.		CLEARED.		INWARD.			OUTWARD.		
	No.	Where from.	No.	Where for.	No.	Description.	Value.	No.	Description.	Value.
Quarter ended June 30, '64—Continued.	7	Havana	2	Boston	2	Ballast		2	1,134 hhds., 99 tcs., 4 bbls. sugar, and 100 bbls molasses.	$956 30
			1	Frankfort	1	do		1	300 bxs. sugar, 34 hhds. molasses.	8,834 87
			2	In port	2	do		2	In port.	
			2	Baltimore	2	do		3	596 hhds. and 63 tierces sugar	45,375 54
	6	Philadelphia	3	Philadelphia					892 kds., 74 tcs. sugar, and 110 hhds. molasses.	75,847 61
			1	New York	6	Cooperage	$36,187 00	1	100 hhds. and 42 tierces molasses.	17,279 56
			4	In port, Philadelphia	4	Ballast		2	In port	
	14	Key West	7	New York	7	do		4	2,025 hhds., 91 tcs., and 251 bbls. molasses.	79,481 95
								7	420 hhds., 220 tcs., 92 bbls. 530 boxes sugar, 515 hhds., 41 tcs. sugar, and 63 tgls., dry, 2 tks. molasses.	356,336 48
			9	Boston	9	do		9	812 hhds., 80 tcs., 2 tks. molasses.	99,744 89
	3	New York	1	In port	1	do		1	In port	
			2	New York	2	Cooperage		1	556 hhds., 59 tcs., 1 bbl. sugar.	45,103 57
			1	In port	1	Ballast		1	In port	
	2	New Orleans	2	New York	2	do	10,364 00	9	627 hhds., 10 tcs., 61 bbls. sugar, 300 boxes sugar, 50 bbls. molasses.	59,064 90
	2	Boston	2	Boston	2	Sugar	5,456 00	3	18 hhds. sugar, and 649 hhds., 45 tcs. molasses.	28,541 91
	3	Matanzas	1	New York	1	Ballast		3	1,495 hhds., 75 tcs., 1 bbl. sugar, and 156 hhds. molasses.	119,738 13
	3	Newport	2	Boston	2	General, ago	12,072 93	2	471 hhds., 10 tcs. sugar, and 91 hhds. molasses.	18,417 56
			1	Newport	1	Ballast		1	In port	
			1	Boston						
	1	Fall River	1	Fall River	1	General, ago	3,437 00	1	219 hhds. and 46 bbls. molasses.	8,722 90
	3	Cardenas	1	Providence	1	allast		1	274 hhds., 27 tcs., and 90 bbls. molasses.	9,127 63
	1	Portland	1	Boston	1	do		1	272 hhds. and 56 bbls. molasses.	10,244 35
	1	Baltimore	1	In port	1	do		1	In port	
			1	do					do	
			1	Baltimore	1	Cooperage	5,977 49	1	206 bbls., 26 tcs. sugar, and 60 hhds. molasses.	93,947 29
	1	Mariel	1	Philadelphia	1	do	5,375 00	1	226 hhds., 30 tcs. sugar, and 196 hhds. 6 tcs. molasses.	91,679 93
	71		71		71		79,060 37	71		

Quarter ended September 30, 1864.*

	No.		No.	Cargo	Value	No.	Description	Value
In port	10	Portland	1	In port		1	231 hhds., 14 tcs., and 22 bbls. molasses.	10,386 06
		Fall River	1	....do		1	496 hhds. and 26 bbls. molasses.	19,930 00
		New York	3	....do		3	879 hhds. 42 tcs. sugar, 157 hhds. 11 tcs., 180 bbls. molasses.	70,007 33
		Philadelphia	5	....do		5	2,252 bbds. 156 tcs. sugar, and 312 hhds., 10 tcs., 24 bbls. molasses.	178,195 07
Portland	3	New York	3	Lumber and cooperage	15,500 00	1	415 bhds. and 38 tcs. molasses.	14,947 56
		Philadelphia	1			1	Ballast.	
		In port	1			1	In port.	
Havana	4	Philadelphia	3	Ballast		3	729 hhds., 25 tcs., 3 bbls sugar, and 302 hhds., 20 tcs., 20 bbls molasses.	68,338 43
Baltimore	1	New York	1	....do		1	495 hhds., 3 tcs., 3 bbls., 124 boxes sugar, and 2 bbls. molasses.	40,513 15
Baltimore	1	Baltimore	1	Lumber	4,361 10	1	293 hhds. and 35 tcs. molasses.	10,491 94
Matanzas	1	Newport	1	Ballast		1	297 hhds., 13 tcs., and 28 bbls. molasses.	9,922 63
Philadelphia	3	Philadelphia	2	Cooperage and general cargo	18,041 31	2	393 hhds., 42 tcs. sugar, and 427 hhds., 23 tcs., 46 bbls. molasses.	46,185 49
Boston	1	In port	1	General cargo	11,722 00	1	In port, 118 hhds., 8 tcs., and 190 bbls. molasses.	5,812 65
	23		23		49,624 41	23		474,649 58

SANTIAGO DE CUBA—E. F. Wallace.

Quarter ended December 31, 1863.†

	No.		No.	Cargo	Value	No.	Description	Value
In port	1	Baltimore	1	Before reported		1	Sugar.	26,964 80
Charlottetown	1	Boston	1	Fish		1	Ballast.	10,403 75
Baltimore	1	Baltimore	1	General cargo	10,000 00	1	Sugar.	14,389 44
St. Thomas	1	New York	1	Coal	2,500 00	1	....do.	
Cherryfield	1	Manzanillo	1	Lumber	6,800 00	1	Ballast.	
New York	1	New York	1	Cooperage	6,500 00	1	Sugar.	7,991 45
Kingston	1	Philadelphia	1	In distress		1	Sugar.	
Guantanamo	2	Philadelphia	1			1	In distress.	11,615 53
Boston	1	Boston	1	Ice	5,000 00	1	Cedar logs, &c.	
	9		9		30,800 00	9		71,257 97

Quarter ended March 31, 1864.‡

	No.		No.	Cargo	Value	No.	Description	Value
Philadelphia	2	Cienfuegos	1	Cooperage	4,000 00	1	Ballast.	42,808 45
Boston	2	In port	1	Assorted cargo	8,500 00	1	In port, hides, and rags.	8,980 63
New York	1	Boston	2	Ice and provisions	5,850 00	2	Sugar, hides, and rags.	
		Portland	1	Cooperage and provisions	18,000 00	1	Sugar, partial cargo.	
	5		5		36,350 00	5		51,789 08

* Entered: 4 barks, 8 brigs, 1 schooner—13, and 10 in port.   Cleared: 8 barks, 10 brigs, 3 schooners—21, and 2 in port.   Aggregate tonnage entered, 3,001 46-95.
† Entered: 1 schooner, 4 brigs, 3 barks—8, and 1 in port.   Cleared: 5 brig, 1 schooner, 3 barks—9.   Aggregate tonnage entered, 2,194.
‡ Entered: 2 barks, 1 brig, 2 schooners—5.   Cleared: 2 barks, 1 brig, 1 schooner—4, and 1 in port.   Aggregate tonnage entered, 1,231.

Navigation and commerce of the United States with foreign countries—Spanish Dominions.

COUNTRY, CONSULATE, NAME OF CONSUL, AND DATE OF RETURNS.	VESSELS.					CARGOES.						
	ENTERED.		CLEARED.		INWARD.			OUTWARD.				
	No.	Where from.	No.	Where for.	No.	Description.	Value.	No.	Description.	Value.	No.	Description.	Value.

	No.	Where from.	No.	Where for.	No.	Description.	Value.	No.	Description.	Value.
Quarter ended June 30, 1864.*	1	In port	1	Philadelphia	1	Before reported			$19,000 00	1	Sugar	$3,113 16
	3	Baltimore	2	Baltimore	3	Cooperage and lumber		2	do	41,386 74
			1	In port				1	In port	
	9	New York	1	New York	1	Cooperage	10,000 00	1	Sugar and honey	29,832 33
			1	Portland	1	Lumber	4,000 00	2	Sugar	30,234 58
	3	Boston	2	Boston	2	Lumber and provisions	16,000 00	2	Sugar, rum, rags, and fustic	28,818 95
			1	Cienfuegos	1	Lumber	6,000 00	1	Ballast	
	9		9		9		55,000 00	9		132,391 76
Quarter ended September 30, 1864.†	1	In port	1	Baltimore	1	Before reported		1	Sugar	29,059 51
	1	Machias	1	Boston	1	Lumber	3,000 00	1	Ballast	
	1	Boston	1	Cienfuegos	1	Ice	4,000 00	1	do	
	1	Portland	1	Baltimore	1	Lumber	4,000 00	1	Sugar	29,815 32
	1	New York	1	New York	1	Provisions	6,000 00	1	do	14,087 52
	5		5		5		17,000 00	5		72,962 35
TRINIDAD, (CUBA.)—E. R. Fitz. Quarter ended December 31, 1863.‡	2	Boston	1	Turk's Island	1	Ice and provisions	16,000 00	1	Ballast	1,577 10
			1	Boston	1	do	8,500 00	1	Cocoa	
	1	New York	1	Cuba	1	Provisions, &c	6,500 00	1	Ballast	
	1	Baltimore	1	Jamaica	1	Flour, meal, &c	14,000 00	1	do	
	4	Philadelphia	2	Philadelphia	2	Flour and provisions	25,000 00	1	Cocoa	685 32
			1	Sombrero	1	Flour and meal	12,500 00	1	Ballast	
			1	Cuba	1	Flour and provisions	16,750 00	1	do	
	8		8		8		99,250 00	8		2,262 42
2d quarter		No report								
Quarter ended June 30, 1864.§	4	In port	1	Philadelphia	{ 4	Before reported		{ 1	Molasses and cocoa	17,094 57
			2	Orchilla				3	Ballast	
			1	Sombrero				1	do	
	1	Baltimore	1	Porto Rico	1	Flour, pork, &c	18,000 00			

No.	Port	No.	Port	Cargo	Value	No.	Cargo	Total
2	Barbadoes	2	New York	Port, meal, shooks	7,000 00	2	Molasses	26,540 51
3	Philadelphia	1	Sombrero	Flour, &c.	9,500 00	1	Ballast	....
..	....	2	In port	Provisions, &c.	24,000 00	2	In port	....
1	Boston	1	Boston	Ice and provisions	10,000 00	1	Cocoa	3,272 53
11		11			65,500 00	11		46,907 61

Quarter ended September 30, 1864.‖

No.	Port	No.	Port	Cargo	Value	No.	Cargo	Total
2	In port	2	Orchilla	Before reported	....	2	Ballast	26,310 00
2	Barbadoes	2	New York	Guano	3,300 00	2	Cocoa, old metals, and rags	26,310 00
3	Philadelphia	1	Orchilla	Breadstuffs	72,000 00	1 }	Ballast	....
1	Baltimore	1	Baltimore	....do	22,500 00	1	In port	....
1	Boston	1	Bonair	Ice and provisions	10,000 00	1	do.	....
1	Bangor	1	Bonair	Lumber	6,000 00	1	do.	....
10		10			113,800 00	10		26,310 00

ST. JOHN'S, (PORTO RICO.)—
J. I. Hyde.

Quarter ended December 31, 1863.¶

No.	Port	No.	Port	Cargo	Value	No.	Cargo	Total
1	In port	1	Arecibo	Before reported	....	1	Ballast	10,071 00
5	Baltimore	2	Baltimore	Provisions and general cargo	26,270 00	2	Sugar and oranges	....
3	....	3	Arecibo	Provisions and general cargo	29,069 00	1	In port	13,315 00
1	New York	1	Turk's Island	Provisions and general cargo	18,955 00	2	Molasses and sugar	....
1	Philadelphia	1	Mayaguez	....do	6,189 00	1	Ballast	....
						1	....do.	....
						1	In port	23,386 00
8		8			80,483 00	8		23,386 00

Quarter ended March 31, 1864.**

No.	Port	No.	Port	Cargo	Value	No.	Cargo	Total
2	In port	1	Mayaguez	Before reported	....	1	Sugar and molasses	10,146 00
..	....	1	Turk's Island	....do.	12,131 00	1	Ballast	14,480 00
2	Baltimore	1	Baltimore	General cargo	14,040 00	1	Sugar and molasses	3,443 00
2	New York	1	Arecibo	....do.	3,792 00	1	do.	11,841 00
..	....	1	New York	....do.	15,265 00	1	do.	1,874 00
..	....	1	Mayaguez	....do.	....	1	Molasses	....
6		6			45,228 00	6		41,784 00

* Entered: 3 schooners, 4 brigs, 1 bark—8, and 1 in port. Cleared: 4 schooners, 3 brigs, 1 bark—8, and 1 in port. Aggregate tonnage entered, 1,894.
† Entered: 3 brigs, 1 bark—4, and 1 in port. Cleared: 4 brigs, 1 bark—5. Aggregate tonnage entered, 954.
‡ Entered and cleared: 3 barks, 2 brigantines, 3 schooners—8. Aggregate tonnage entered, 2,007.
§ Entered: 6 barks, 1 brig—7, and 2 in port. Cleared: 5 barks, 1 brig, 2 schooners—9, and 2 in port. Aggregate tonnage entered, 1,838.
‖ Entered: 4 barks, 4 brigs—8, and 2 in port. Cleared: 5 bark, 4 brigs—9, and 1 in port. Aggregate tonnage entered, 1,871.
¶ Entered: 3 brigs, 2 schooners, 2 barks—7, and 1 in port. Cleared: 1 brig, 2 schooners, 2 bark—5, and 2 in port. Aggregate tonnage entered, 1,324.
** Entered: 1 brig, 2 schooners, 1 bark—4, and 2 in port. Cleared: 2 brigs, 3 schooners, 1 bark—6. Aggregate tonnage entered, 730.

Navigation and commerce of the United States with foreign countries—Spanish Dominions.

COUNTRY, CONSULATE, NAME OF CONSUL, AND DATE OF RETURNS.	VESSELS.				CARGOES.					
	ENTERED.		CLEARED.		INWARD.			OUTWARD.		
	No.	Where from.	No.	Where for.	No.	Description.	Value.	No.	Description.	Value.
Quarter ended June 30, 1864.*	1	Canary Islands	1	New York	1	Dripstones, fish, &c.	$6,326 49	1	Sugar and molasses	$41,543 39
	1	Portland	1	New York, via Mayaguez.	1	Shooks and lumber	7,636 19	1	Ballast	
	1	Trinidad	5	Baltimore, one via Mayaguez.		Ballast			Sugar and molasses	95,199 33
	4	Baltimore			4	General cargo	56,346 32	4	Sugar, molasses, and coffee.	93,235 53
	7		7		7		70,108 99	7		159,978 45
Quarter ended September 30, 1864.†	1	New York	1	New York	1	Ice and provisions	7,131 75	1	Ballast	
	2	Baltimore	1	Baltimore	1	Lumber and general cargo.	8,378 86	1	Sugar	14,569 14
			1	New York	1	General cargo	15,804 00	1	Sugar and molasses	2,534 37
	3		3		3		31,314 61	3		17,103 51
GUAYAMA, (PORTO RICO.)—C. H. Vargas.										
Quarter ended December 31, 1863.‡	1	In port	1	Mayaguez	1	Before reported	15,800 00	1	110 hhds. and 2 bbls. sugar	6,338 00
	2	Norwich	2	Norwich	2	Cooperage and provisions.	10,000 00	2	Lignumvitæ, old iron, &c.	5,130 00
	2	New Haven	1	Turk's Island	1	do	10,000 00	1	Ballast	
	1	Baltimore	1	Ponce	1	do	10,000 00	1	Part inward cargo.	6,000 00
	1	Cherryfield	1	Turk's Island	1	do	7,000 00	1	Ballast	
			1	In port	1	Lumber	3,500 00	1	In port	
	7		7		7		46,300 00	7		14,488 00
Quarter ended March 31, 1864.§	1	In port	1	New York	1	Before reported	8,500 00	1	65 tons lignumvitæ	612 00
	2	New York	2	In port	2	Provisions and cooperage.	8,500 00	2	In port	
	1	Calais	1	Ponce	1	Lumber and cooperage	30,000 00	1	Inward cargo	4,000 00
	1	New Haven	1	New Haven	1	Provisions and specie	9,000 00	1	Sugar and molasses	94,945 00
	1	Norwich	1	Norwich	1	do	9,000 00	1	196 casks molasses, 18 boxes	7,698 00
	1	New London	1	Mayaguez	1	Ballast and specie	18,000 00	1	Inward cargo	12,000 00
	7		7		7		69,500 00	7		48,555 00
Quarter ended June 30, 1864.‖	2	In port	1	New Haven	} 2	Before reported		2	Sugar and molasses	98,640 00
	1	Portland	1	New York	1	Lumber	5,000 00	1	do ...do	24,124 00
			1	Ponce, N. York.						

				Inward cargo	Value		Outward cargo	Value
2	Machias	2	New York	...do...		2	...do...	34,223 00
2	New Haven	2	New Haven	...do...		2	...do...	28,176 00
1	Norwich	1	In port / Norwich	Cooperage, provisions, and specie / do	8,500 00 / 65,000 00 / 11,000 00	{2 / 1} / 1	In port / do / Molasses	8,758 00
8		**8**			**89,500 00**	**8**		**123,921 00**

Quarter ended September 30, 1864.¶

1	In port.	1	New Haven	Before reported	16,000 00	1	Sugar and molasses	98,552 00
1	New Haven	1	Ponce.	Provisions	18,000 00	1	Part of inward cargo	8,000 00
1	Norwich	1	Humacao.	Cooperage and provisions		1	Molasses	4,406 00
3		**3**			**34,000 00**	**3**		**40,958 00**

MATAGUEZ.—J. C. Coze.
Quarter ended December 31, 1865.**

				Inward cargo	Value		Outward cargo	Value
3	New York	1	New Haven, via T.I. / Nw Mn, via Nw dn.	Provisions and specie	10,810 00	1	37 puncheons molasses	985 00
4	Newburyport	1	Turk's Island	Provisions, lumber, and specie	13,534 00	1	Ballast	
		3	Newburyport	Provisions and cooperage / Provisions, cooperage, and specie	9,710 00 / 35,800 00	1 / 3	...do... / ...do...	2,047 00
2	Baltimore	1	In port / Baltimore, via Arecibo	Provisions and cooperage	7,600 00	1	63 quintals coffee, 20 hhds. sugar	
		1	Baltimore	Provisions, cooperage, and specie	26,058 00	1	In port / Ballast	
1	Salinas de Caom. P. R.	1	New York	Provisions and cooperage	12,553 00	1	250,000 oranges	86 00
			To complete cargo			1	73 hhds. sugar	4,190 00
4	New Haven	1	Nw Mn, via Arecibo	Provisions and cooperage	7,300 00	1	14 ...	959 00
		1 / 2	Turk's Island / Nw dn / Turk's Island	...do...do...	10,800 00 / 20,460 00	1 / 2	6,000 oranges, &c. / Ballast	244 00
3	Cherryfield	1	Bn	Lumber.	3,500 00	1	...do...	
		1	Nw York	...do...	2,800 00	1	...do...	
2	Philadelphia	2	Philadelphia	...do... / Provisions, lumber, and sundries	1,850 00 / 30,200 00	1 / 2	...do... / Provisions, lumber, and sundries	3,369 00
1	Ponce, P. R.	1	Ballast	Ballast		1	261,000 oranges, 4,700 cocoanuts, 31 hhds. sugar	1,184 00
1	St. Domingo	1	New Haven	Cooperage and stuff	1,209 00	1	203,000 oranges, 5 hhds. sugar	889 00
						1	211,000 oranges	
21		**21**			**194,184 00**	**21**		**14,733 00**

* Entered and cleared: 2 barks, 4 brigs, 1 schooner—7. Aggregate tonnage entered, 1,508.
† Entered and cleared: 2 schooners, 1 brig—3. Aggregate tonnage entered, 513.
‡ Entered: 1 bark, 1 brig, 4 schooners—6, and 1 in port. Cleared: 1 bark, 1 brig, 4 schooners—6, and 1 in port. Aggregate tonnage entered, 1,397 45-95.
§ Entered: 3 brigs, 2 barks, 2 schooners—6, and 1 in port. Cleared: 3 brigs, 1 bark, 1 schooner—5, and 2 in port. Aggregate tonnage entered, 1,336 19-95.
‖ Entered: 1 brig, 2 barks, 3 schooners—6, and 2 in port. Cleared: 2 brigs, 2 barks, 3 schooners—7, and 1 in port. Aggregate tonnage entered, 1,397 61-95.
¶ Entered: 2 schooners, and 1 in port. Cleared: 2 schooners, 1 bark—3. Aggregate tonnage entered, 388 23-95.
** Entered: 10 brigs, 11 schooners—21. Cleared: 10 brigs, 10 schooners—20, and 1 in port. Aggregate tonnage entered, 3,853 64-95.

Navigation and commerce of the United States with foreign countries—Spanish Dominions.

COUNTRY, CONSULATE, NAME OF CONSUL, AND DATE OF RETURNS.	VESSELS				CARGOES					
	ENTERED		CLEARED		INWARD			OUTWARD		
	No.	Where from.	No.	Where for.	No.	Description.	Value.	No.	Description.	Value.
MAYAGUEZ.—J. C. Cox— Continued.										
Quarter ended March 31, 1864.										
	1	In port	1	Newburyport	1	Before reported	$55,310 00	1	Ballast	$61,359 00
	6	New Haven	5	New Haven	5	Provisions, cooperage, and specie	10,850 00	5	389 hhds. sugar, 999 pun's mol's	
			1	In port	1	Provisions and specie	9,600 00	1	In port	11,000 00
	2	Newburyport	2	Newburyport	1	Provisions, lumber, and furniture	6,800 00	1	80 hhds. sugar, 185 punc's mol's	8,432 00
	1	Barbadoes	1	New York	1	Provisions	1,670 00	1	78 ... do ... 95 ... do	17,492 00
	2	St. John's, P. R.	1	Philadelphia	1	Cooperage		1	100 ... do ... 338 ... do	9,964 00
			1	New York	1	To complete cargo		1	150 hhds. sugar	10,623 00
	2	Machias	1	Cienfuegos	1	Lumber	3,649 00	1	306 puncheons molasses	
			1	In port	1	... do	3,240 00	1	Ballast	
	2	New York	1	New York	2	Provisions, cooperage, and specie	11,730 00	1	In port	7,554 00
			1	In port	1	Provisions and lumber	10,300 00	1	210 puncheons molasses	
	1	Martinique	1	New York	1	Ballast		1	In port	15,904 00
	1	Ponce	1	Baltimore	1	Provisions	14,881 00	1	467 pun. molasses, 41 qtls. coffee	15,559 00
	1	Santa Cruz	1	In port	1	Ballast		1	30 ... do ... 208 hhds. sugar	
	1	St. Thomas	1	New Haven	1	Rum, &c		1	In port	8,469 00
			1	New York	1	Provisions and cooperage	9,125 00	1	78 hhds. sugar, 107 pun. molasses	7,368 00
								1	75 ... do ... 51 ... do	
	21		21		21		130,135 00	21		173,614 00
Quarter ended June 30, 1864.										
	4	In port	1	New York	1	Before reported		1	382 puncheons molasses	13,160 00
			1	Philadelphia	1	... do		1	105 hhds. sugar	7,791 00
			1	Newburyport	1	... do		1	121 hhds. sugar, 113 pun. mol's	12,503 00
	6	New Haven	5	New Haven	5	Provisions, lumber, cooperage, and specie	106,014 00	1	150 ... do ... 906 ... do	19,632 00
								5	743 ... do ... 755 ... do	93,912 00
	4	Newburyport	4	In port	1	Provisions and lumber	7,850 00	1	In port	50,300 00
				Newburyport	1	... do	42,806 00	4	323 hhds. sugar, 244 pun. mol's, 144 b'ls cotton, at 46.50, & 75 cts.	
	2	New York	2	New Haven	2	Provisions, lumber, and specie	31,473 00	2	946 hhds. sugar, 122 pun. mol's, 37 quintals coffee	92,845 00
	1	Machias	3	Baltimore, direct	1	Lumber	2,975 00	3	130 hhds. sugar, 272 pun. mol's	20,168 00
	5	Baltimore	1	Baltimore, via Turk's Island	3	Provisions, cooperage, &c	47,745 00	1	772 ... do ... 60 ... do	66,879 00
					1	... do	16,629 00	1	Ballast	
	1	Philadelphia	1	In port	1	Provisions and lumber	16,439 00	1	In port	91,183 00
			1	Phila, via Guauica.	1	Provisions, lumber, and specie	13,078 00	1	220 hhds. sugar, 60 pun. mol's, 10 quintals coffee, &c	

No.	Port	No.	From	Cargo (cleared)	Value	No.	Cargo (in port)	Value
1	St. Domingo	1	New Haven	Cooperage and specie	9,500 00	1	14 hhds. sugar, 70 pun. molasses	4,274 00
1	St. John's, P. R.	1	Portland	Ballast	3,022 00	1	322 puncheous molasses	12,656 00
1	Cherryfield	2	New York	178,000 feet lumber			Ballast	
26		26			299,531 00	26		345,303 00
Quarter ended September 30, 1864;								
2	In port	1	New Haven	Before reported		1	Sugar and molasses	4,036 00
3	New Haven	1	Baltimore, via Turk's island.	do.		1	Ballast	
		2	New Haven, via Gaunles and Ponce.					
4	Newburyport	2	Newport, via Turk's Island.	Provisions, lumber, and cooperage	67,771 00	3	Sugar, molasses, cocoanuts	25,755 00
1	Baltimore	1	Baltimore, via Turk's Island.	Provisions, lumber, furniture, &c.	62,074 00	4	Sugar, molasses, and ballast	21,620 00
				Provisions and lumber	12,038 00	1	Ballast	
1	Philadelphia	1	Philadelphia, via Gaunles.	do. ...... do.	16,363 00	1	Sugar and molasses	21,182 00
11		11			164,246 00	11		72,393 00
MANILA.—J. Russell. Quarter ended December 31, 1863.§								
2	In port	2	Not stated.	Before reported		2	Sugar and hemp	148,055 00
2	Hong Kong	1	San Francisco.	Ballast		1	do.	77,512 00
1	Batavia	1	In port.	do.		1	In port	95,642 00
1	Vancouver's Isl'd.	1	New York.	do.		1	Sugar and hemp	
		1	In port.	Lumber	13,500 00	1	In port	
6		6			13,500 00	6		319,209 00
Quarter ended March 31, 1864.‖								
1	In port	1	Boston.	Before reported		1	Sugar and hemp	91,603 00
1	San Francisco	1	San Francisco.	Flour and grain	30,000 00	1	do.	6,339 00
1	Vancouver's Isl'd.	1	do.	Timber	41,000 00	1	do.	74,634 00
3	Hong Kong	2	New York.	Ballast		2	do.	157,902 00
2	Shanghae.	1	New York.	do.		1	In port	
		1	In port.	do.		1	Sugar and hemp	73,418 00
1	Tagnbas?	1	Hong Kong.	do.		1	Timber	25,623 00
9		9			71,000 00	9		429,538 00

* Entered: 3 barks, 8 brig, 9 schooners—30, and 1 in port. Cleared: 3 barks, 6 brigs, 8 schooners—17, and 4 in port. Aggregate tonnage entered, 3,993 37-95.
† Entered: 7 brigs, 15 schooners—22, and 4 in port. Cleared: 9 brigs, 15 schooners—24, and 2 in port. Aggregate tonnage entered, 3,887 29-95.
‡ Entered: 3 brigs, 6 schooners—9, and 2 in port. Cleared: 3 brigs, 8 schooners—11. Aggregate tonnage entered, 1,552 2-95.
§ Entered: 3 ships, 1 bark—4, and 2 in port. Cleared: 4 ships, and 2 in port. Aggregate tonnage entered, 3,916.
‖ Entered: 1 brig, 6 ships, 1 bark—8, and 1 in port. Cleared: 5 ships, 1 brig, 1 bark—7, and 2 in port. Aggregate tonnage entered, 6,250.

Navigation and commerce of the United States with foreign countries—Spanish Dominions.

COUNTRY, CONSUL, NAME OF CONSUL, AND DATE OF RETURNS.	VESSELS ENTERED No.	Where from	CLEARED No.	Where for	CARGOES INWARD No.	Description	Value	OUTWARD No.	Description	Value
MANILA.—J. Russell—Continued.										
Quarter ended June 30, 1864.*	2	In port	2	Not stated	2	Before reported		2	Sugar and hemp	$187,347 00
	4	Hong Kong	1	San Francisco	2	Ballast		1	...do	87,432 00
			1	In port	1	..do		2	In port	
	2	Singapore	2	New York	1	do		1	Sugar and hemp	253,622 00
	1	San Francisco	1	...do	1	do		1	...do	98,322 00
	1	Shanghai	1	...do	1	do		1	In port	
								1	...do	
	10		10		10			10		567,743 00
Quarter ended September 30, 1864.‡	4	In port	2	Not stated	2	Before reported		1	Not stated	
			1	New York	1	..do		2	Sugar and hemp	180,748 80
	2	San Francisco	1	San Francisco	2	do		2	...do	130,106 48
	2	Hong Kong	2	New York	2	Ballast		1	In port	
	1	Foochow	1	New Bedford	2	do		1	Sugar and hemp	133,861 97
			1	In port	1	do		1	In port	
	9		9		9			9		444,719 25
SANTANDER.—R. C. Hassock.										
Quarter ended December 31, 63.‡	1	Villa Real	1	In port	1	380 tons copper ore	$14,000 00	1	In port	
Quarter ended March 31, 1864.§	1	In port	1	Cardiff	1	Before reported		1	220 tons iron ore & esparta grass	1,150 00
3d and 4th quarters		No arrivals		No departures						
PORT MAHON.—H. B. Robinson.										
1st, 2d, and 3d quarters		No reports								
4th quarter		No arrivals		No departures						

	No.	Entered, whence	No.		No.	Cleared, whither		No.		Value
GUANTANAMO.—F. Badell. Quarter ended December 31, 1863.‖	1 / 1 / 1	In port / Cuba / Philadelphia	3		1 / 1 / 1	Philadelphia / Boston / Philadelphia, via Cuba	Before reported / Ballast / Machinery	3	} 12,000 00 — 3 — Sugar	53,749 84
Quarter ended Mar. 31, 1864.¶	1 / 1	Cuba / New York	2	Sugar / Cooperage	1 / 1	Portland / In port		3	12,000 00 — 1 — Sugar; 5,400 00 — 1 — In port	53,749 84; 17,366 06; 17,366 06
Quarters ended June 30, 1864, and September 30, 1864.**	2	Cuba	2	Ballast / Sugar / do. / Ballast / Sugar / do.	1 / 1 / 1 / 1 / 1	Philadelphia / Boston / Trinidad / Boston / London	Ballast / Sugar / Cooperage / do. / Ballast	5	5,400 00; 6,000 00; 4,500 00 — total 10,500 00 — 5	15,893 68; 23,548 43; 20,171 18; 21,684 00; 81,297 31
ARECIBO.—C. F. Storer. 1st and 2d quarters.		No report.								
Quarter ended June 30, 1864.††	2 / 1	Baltimore / St. John's, P.R.	3	Provisions / Ballast	2 / 1	Baltimore / do.	Sugar and molasses / do.	3	21,304 00 — 2; 21,304 00 — 1	35,768 79; 9,814 48; 45,583 27
Quarter ended September 30, 1864.‡‡	1	St. John's, P.R.	1	Ballast	1	Baltimore	Loading	1		
NAGUABO, HUMACAO, FAJARDO.—W. Haddock. 1st, 2d, and 3d quarters.		No report.								
Quarter ended September 30, 1864.§§	1 / 1	New York / Norwich	2	Ballast / Molasses	1 / 1	St. John's / Arroyo	199 casks molasses / 86 casks and 2 bbls. molasses	2	5,000 00 — 1; 5,000 00 — 2	10,807 40; 3,683 08; 14,490 48

Navigation and commerce of the United States with foreign countries—Spanish Dominions.

COUNTRY, CONSULATE, NAME OF CONSUL, AND DATE OF RETURNS.	VESSELS.					INWARD.		CARGOES.		OUTWARD.		
	ENTERED.		CLEARED.									
	No.	Where from.	No.	Where for.	No.	Description.	No.	Value.	No.	Description.	Value.	
CIENFUEGOS.—*G. Barrió.*												
1st and 2d quarters.		No report.										
Quarter ended June 30, 1864.*	6	In port.	1	Liverpool.	1	Before reported.						
			2	New York.	2				2	1,367 hhds., 57 tierces, and 12 bbls. sugar.	$68,665 78	
			3	Boston.	3	do.			3	108 hhds., 9 tierces, and 3 bbls. molasses; 1,148 hhds., 91 tierces, and 2 bbls. sugar.	79,848 60	
	8	New Orleans.	3	Trinidad de Cuba.	3	Ballast.			3	Ballast.		
			3	New York.	3	do.			1	1,462 hhds. and 138 tierces sugar.	112,187 91	
			1	Philadelphia.	1	do.			1	601 hhds. and 1 tierce sugar.	43,761 23	
			1	Boston.	1	do.			1	300 hhds., 17 tierces, and 10 bbls. molasses; 651 hhds. and 63 tierces sugar.	56,781 10	
	2	St. Thomas.	1	New York.	1	do.			1	391 hhds. and 39 tierces sugar.	31,134 57	
	4	Portland.	1	In port.	1	do.			1	In port.		
			1	Portland.	1	140,000 feet boards.			1	258 hhds. and 21 tierces molasses.	13,996 07	
			1	Philadelphia.	1	Cooperage.	$2,000 00		1	300 hhds., 17 tierces molasses, and 40 hhds. sugar.	14,806 79	
							3,500 00		1	494 hhds. and 51 tierces sugar.	39,585 48	
	1	New York.	1	New York.	1	do.	4,500 00		1	In port.		
	1	Machias.	1	In port.	1	do.	9,700 00		1	422 hhds. and 21 tierces sugar.	34,819 36	
	5	Aspinwall.	1	New York.	1	182,000 feet lumber.	4,000 00		1	336 hhds. and 35 tierces sugar.	26,175 50	
			1	Trinidad de Cuba.	1	Ballast.	2,300 00		1	Ballast.		
			1	Boston.	1	do.			1	539 hhds. and 53 tierces sugar.	37,787 64	
			2	New York.	2	do.			2	274 hhds., 10 tierces, and 40 bbls. molasses.	9,946 60	
	4	Philadelphia.	4	In port.	4	do.			4	485 hhds. and 43 tierces sugar.	43,233 18	
			4	Philadelphia.	4	Cooperage.	17,100 00		4	72 hhds. all sugar, 1,653 hhds. sugar.	135,220 44	
	1	Demarara.	1	Boston.	1	Ballast.			1	175 tierces, and 96 bbls. sugar.		
									1	268 hhds., 96 tierces, and 21 bbls. molasses.	9,390 64	
	1	St. Jago.	1	do.	1	40,000 feet lumber.	900 00		1	443 hhds. and 38 tierces sugar.	30,058 36	
	2	Boston.	2	do.	2	General cargo and ballast.	9,000 00		2	580 hhds. and 50 tierces sugar, 139 hhds., 14 tierces, and 6 bbls. molasses.	45,049 07	
	1	Rio de Janeiro.	1	Philadelphia.	1				1	24 hhds. molasses, 380 hhds., 34 tierces, and 1 bbl. sugar.	31,707 55	

Period	Arrivals	From	Arrivals cargo	Value	Departures	To / remarks	Departures cargo	Value
4th quarter...	No report.							
ZAZA.—J. F. Zayas.								
1st and 2d quarters...	No report.							
Quarter ended June 30, 1864.‡	1	Aspinwall	Ballast.		1	New York	Sugar.	41,525 74
	1	Vera Cruz	do.		1	...do.	...do.	25,470 15½
	3	New York	Assorted cargo.		3	...do.	Not stated.	
	5				5			66,995 89½
4th quarter:	No report.							
TENERIFFE.—W. H. Dabney.								
1st quarter.	No arrivals.				No departures.			
2d and 3d quarters.	No report.							
Quarter ended September 30, 1864.‡	1	Chirm Bay	Whaling.	200 bbls. sperm and whale oil.	6,000 00	1	200 bbls. sperm and whale oil.	6,000 00
	1	Boston	Picton.	200,000 feet lumber.	6,000 00	1	Ballast.	6,000 00
	2				12,000 00	2		6,000 00
VALENCIA.—G. Kent.								
Quarter ended December 31, 1863.§	2	In port	Delaware Break-water.	Before reported.	.....	1	Ballast.	104,780 00
	2	Callao	New York.	do.		1	...do.	8,000 00
			Cardiff.	1,612 tons guano.		1	...do.	13,026 00
	2	New York	In port.	72,900 pipe staves.		1	In port.	56,355 00
			Palermo.	108,546 pipe staves.		1	Ballast.	
			In port.	867 tons guano.		1	In port.	
	6					6		182,161 00
Quarter ended March 31, 1864.‖	2	In port	Sicily.	Before reported.		1	Ballast.	
			Cardiff.	do.		1	Sold; took British flag.	
	2					2		

* Entered: 16 barks, 11 brigs, 3 schooners—30, and 6 in port. Cleared: 18 barks, 12 brigs, 3 schooners—33, and 3 in port. Aggregate tonnage entered, 9,345.
† Entered and cleared: Not stated. Tonnage not stated. ‡ Entered and cleared: 1 brig, 1 schooner—2. Aggregate tonnage entered, 383.
§ Entered: 2 ships, 2 barks—4, and 2 in port. Cleared: 3 ships, 1 bark—4, and 2 in port. Aggregate tonnage entered, 2,996 94-95.
‖ Entered: 2 in port. Cleared: 1 bark, and 1 sold. Tonnage before reported.

Navigation and commerce of the United States with foreign countries—Spanish Dominions.

COUNTRY, CONSULATE, NAME OF CONSUL, AND DATE OF RETURNS.	VESSELS				CARGOES					
	ENTERED		CLEARED		INWARD			OUTWARD		
	No.	Where from.	No.	Where for.	No.	Description.	Value.	No.	Description.	Value.
3d quarter........		No report.								
Quarter ended September 30, 1864.*	2	Callao........	1	Boston........	1, 1	} 2,318 tons guano........	$163,670 00			
			1	Cardiff........				2	Ballast........	
	2		2		2		163,670 00	2		
PONCE, P. R.—J. C. Gallaher. Quarter ended December 31, 1863.†	2	New Haven........	1	New Haven........	1	Provisions, &c........	5,900 00	1	Sugar, molasses, and tobacco....	$2,529 12
	2	Cherryfield........	1	Mayaguez........	1	Provisions and cooperage........	9,450 00	1	Ballast........	
	1	Arroyo........	2	Turk's Island........	2	Lumber........	5,300 00	2	....do........	
	3	New York........	1	New Haven........	1	Provisions and cooperage........	8,000 00	1	Old iron and copper........	1,591 53
	3	Baltimore........	1	Turk's Island........	1	....do........	6,500 00	1	Cotton........	533 69*
			2	In port........	2	....do........	17,500 00	2	In port........	
			1	Turk's Island........	2	....do........	17,440 00	2	Old iron, copper, &c........	162 39
			1	In port........	1	....do........	10,600 00	1	In port........	
	11		11		11		79,990 00			6,146 93
Quarter ended March 31, 1864.‡	3	In port........	2	New York........	2	Before reported........		2	Oranges, castor oil, &c........	653 75
	1	Arroyo........	1	Turk's Island........		....do........		1	Ballast........	
	1	Trinidad........	1	....do........		Lumber........	5,400 00	1	....do........	
	5	New Haven........	4	New Haven........		Ballast........		4	Sugar and mol mss........	
			1	New York........	4	Provisions and cooperage........	24,100 00	1	Molasses........	47,631 88
	1	Philadelphia........	1	Philadelphia........	1	Provisions........	7,000 00	1	Sugar........	7,896 98
	3	Barbadoes........	1	New York........	1	Provisions and shooks........	9,000 00	1	Molasses........	14,858 93
			1	In port........		Ballast........		1	In port........	
			1	Mayaguez........		....do........		1	Ballast........	
	1	Portland........	1	Portland........	1	Prov. bbls and shooks........	5,500 00	1	....do........	12,458 90
	1	New York........	1	New York........	1	....do........	9,800 00	1	Sugar and molasses........	6,028 48
	1	Bucksport........	1	....do........	1	....do........	9,500 00	1	Sugar and molasses........	13,745 47
	1	Seaport........	1	....do........	1	Lumber........	2,600 00	1	Sugar........	23,632 05
						....do........		1	....do........	4,270 34
	18		18		18		66,300 00	18		129,998 01
Quarter ended June 30, 1864.§	1	In port........	1	New York........	1	Before reported........		1	Molasses........	12,467 02
	5	New York........	5	San Francisco........	1	Provisions........		1	Sugar and molasses........	61,430 57

No.	Port	No.	Where to	No.	Cargo (cleared)	Value	No.	Cargo (entered)	Value
3	Barbadoes	1	New Haven	1	...do	8,482 00	1	...do	17,996 81
		1	Hartford	1	Provisions and lumber	7,150 00	1	...do	17,362 51
1	Arroyo	2	New York	2	Provisions	21,894 00	2	...do	14,978 54
		1	New Haven	1	Ballast		2	Sugar	30,789 42
4	New Haven	1	Hartford	1	Molasses and sugar	41,824 00	1	do	7,881 83
		3	New York	3	...do		3	...do	43,734 24
		1	New Haven	1	Provisions, cooperage, and lumber		1	In port	
			In port		In port				
13		13		13		87,850 00	13		197,031 54

Quarter ended September 30, 1864.‖

No.	Port	No.	Where to	No.	Cargo (cleared)	Value	No.	Cargo (entered)	Value
1	In port	1	New Haven	1	Before reported		1	Sugar, molasses, and cotton	18,808 26
2	Guanica	1	New York	1	} Sugar and molasses		2	...do	46,054 00
1	New York	1	New Haven	1	Provisions	10,150 00	1	Ballast	
1	Middletown	1	New Haven	1	Provisions and lumber	7,300 00	1	...do	17,068 84
1	Arroyo	1	New Haven	1	Provisions	6,900 00	1	Sugar and molasses	21,166 91
1	New Haven	1	New Haven	1	...do	6,900 00	1	Sugar	
1	Baltimore	1	Turk's Island	1	Provisions and cooperage	3,900 00	1	Coffee	11,276 34
1	Mechias	1	Turk's Island	1	Lumber		1	In port	
	In port		In port						
9		9		9		41,350 00	9		114,374 35

MANZANILLO DE CUBA.—M. R. Esqy.
July 1 to December 31, 1863.¶

No.	Port	No.	Where to	No.	Cargo (cleared)	Value	No.	Cargo (entered)	Value
2	Kingston	1	Boston	1	Ballast		1	Palmleaf and cocoawood	9,916 75
		1	New York	1	...do		1	Cedar, palmleaf, mats, &c.	10,906 38
2	New York	2	...do	2	Provisions and cooperage		2	Honey, palmleaf, mats, &c.	15,514 75
1	Boston	1	Boston	1	Provisions		1	Sugar, palmleaf, mats, &c.	5,650 82
1	Portland	1	...do	1	...do		1	Honey, lancewood, mahogany	11,357 83
2	St. Jago de Cuba	1	Ballast	1	Ballast		1	Cedar, cocoawood, palmleaf, &c.	9,164 95
		1	New York	1	Sugar		1	Cedar, leaf tobacco, palmleaf	8,392 78
1	St. Croix	1	...do	1	Ballast		1	Honey, tobacco, cedar, palmleaf	9,616 39
9		9		9			9		80,520 65

From January 1 to June 30, 1864.*

No.	Port	No.	Where to	No.	Cargo (cleared)	Value	No.	Cargo (entered)	Value
1	Nuevitas	1	New York	1	Ballast		1	Sugar, molasses, honey, timber	6,608 68
2	Boston	2	Boston	2	Provisions and cooperage		2	Cocoawood, molasses, "sugar"	14,469 02
2	Kingston	2	...do	2	Ballast		2	Molasses, sugar, cocoawood	32,693 24
3	New York	3	New York	3	Provisions		1	Honey, molasses, sugar, timber	22,445 18
			In port					In port	

* Entered and cleared: 2 ships. Aggregate tonnage entered, 1,684 87-95.
† Entered: 6 brigs and 5 schooners—11. Cleared: 4 brigs, 4 schooners—8, and 3 in port. Aggregate tonnage entered, 2,111 46-95.
‡ Entered: 3 barks, 8 brigs, 4 schooners—15, and 3 in port. Cleared: 3 barks, 10 brigs, 5 schooners—17, and 1 in port. Aggregate tonnage entered, 2,871 39-95.
§ Entered: 2 barks, 6 brigs, 4 schooners—12, and 1 in port. Cleared: 3 barks, 5 brigs, 4 schooners—12, and 1 in port. Aggregate tonnage entered, 2,519 77-95.
‖ Entered: 6 brigs, 2 schooners—8, and 1 in port. Cleared: 6 brigs, 2 schooners—8, and 1 in port. Aggregate tonnage entered, 1,548 91-95.
¶ Entered and cleared: 5 brigs, 2 barks—9. Aggregate tonnage entered, 2,136.
** Entered and cleared: 6 brigs, 2 schooners, 1 bark—9. Aggregate tonnage entered, 2,216.

Navigation and commerce of the United States with foreign countries—Spanish Dominions.

COUNTRY, CONSULATE, NAME OF CONSUL, AND DATE OF RETURN	VESSELS				CARGOES					
	ENTERED		CLEARED		INWARD			OUTWARD		
	No.	Where from.	No.	Where for.	No.	Description.	Value.	No.	Description.	Value.
From January 1 to June 30, 1861—Continued.	1	St. Domingo	1	In port	1	Ballast		1	In port	
	9		9		9			9		76,916 10
4th quarter		No report.								
GRAND CANARY.—*F. G. Manley.*										
Quarter ended December 31, 1863.*	1	Boston	1	Cape de Verde	1	Lumber, tobacco, rum, &c.	$9,000 00	1	Inward cargo	$8,050 00
	2	Bermudas	2	To sea	2	Ballast		2	Ballast	
	3	Fayal	3	...do	3	...do		3	...do	
	1	Bangor	1	St. Thomas	1	Lumber		1	...do	
	7		7		7		9,000 00	7		8,050 00
Quarter ended March 31, 1864.‡	1	Provincetown	1	To sea	1	Not stated	5,000 00	1	Not stated	
	1	Madeira	1	Porto Rico	1	180,000 ft. lumber, 30 bbls. flour	11,000 00	1	Flagstones and filters	3,000 00
	1	Boston	1	Cadiz	1	300,000 ft. lumber, tobacco, manila, and chairs.		1	Ballast	
	3		3		3		16,000 00	3		3,000 00
3d and 4th quarters		No reports.		No departures						
BILBAO.—*D. Evans.*										
1st, 2d, 3d, and 4th quarters		No arrivals								
LAS PALMAS.—*F. W. Manley.*										
Quarter ended December 31, 1863.‡	1	Boston	1	Cape de Verde	1	Lumber, tobacco, rum, &c.	9,000 00	1	Lumber, tobacco, rum, &c.	8,050 00
	2	Bermudas	2	To sea	2			2		
	3	Fayal	3	...do	3			3		
	1	Bangor	1	St. Thomas	1	Lumber		1		
	7		7		7		9,000 00	7		8,050 00

	Arrivals		Value		Departures	Remarks
2d, 3d, and 4th quarters	No reports					
PORTUGUESE DOMIN'S.						
LISBON.—C. A. Mearns.						
Quarter ended December 31, 1863.§	In port 1; Chanaral, Chile 1; New York 1 — 3	Before reported; 1,186 tons copper ore; General cargo	60,000 00; 9,000 00 — 69,000 00	3	Boston, via Cadiz 1; Liverpool 1; In port 1 — 3	Ballast; Put back in distress; In port
Quarter ended Mar. 31, 1864.	In port 1	Before reported		1	Condemned and sold 1	Condemned and sold
3d quarter.	No arrivals				No departures	
Quarter ended September 30, 1864.‖	Antwerp 1; Cardiff 1 — 2	1,800 tons railroad iron; 1,197 tons coal	72,000 00; 3,000 00 — 75,000 00	2	Akyab 1; In port 1 — 2	Ballast; In port
OPORTO.—H. W. Diman.						
1st and 2d quarters.	No arrivals				No departures	
Quarter ended June 30, 1864.¶	New York 1	250 staves; wheat	21,540 00	1	Marseilles 1	Ballast
4th quarter.	No arrivals				No departures	
FUNCHAL.—R. Bayman.						
1st and 2d quarters.	No reports					
Quarter ended June 30, 1864.**	New York 1	300 barrels flour, $2,600; 7,622 bushels corn, $10,300.	12,900 00	1	Messina 1	Ballast
4th quarter.	No report.					

* Entered and cleared: 2 brigs, 3 schooners, 2 barks—7. Aggregate tonnage entered, 1,136 19-95.
† Entered and cleared: 1 schooner, 1 brig, 1 bark—3. Aggregate tonnage entered, 905 40-95.
‡ Entered and cleared: 2 barks, 2 brigs, 3 schooners—7. Aggregate tonnage entered, 1,136 13-95.
§ Entered: 1 ship, 1 schooner—2, and 1 in port. Cleared: 1 ship, 1 schooner—2, and 1 in port. Aggregate tonnage entered, 953 38-95.
‖ Entered: 2 ships. Cleared: 1 ship, and 1 in port. Aggregate tonnage entered, 1,905.
¶ Entered and cleared: 1 brig. Tonnage, 285.
** Entered and cleared: 1 schooner. Tonnage, 293.

Navigation and commerce of the United States with foreign countries—Portuguese Dominions.

COUNTRY, CONSULATE, NAME OF CONSUL, AND DATE OF RETURNS.	VESSELS				CARGOES					
	ENTERED		CLEARED		INWARD			OUTWARD		
	No.	Where from.	No.	Where for.	No.	Description.	Value.	No.	Description.	Value.
FAYAL.—*C. W. Dabney.*										
Quarter ended December 31, 1863.*	4	In port........	1	Boston........	1	Before reported........		1	Inward cargo; put in for repairs.	$37,446 06
	8	Whaling......	8	Whaling......	3	....do........		3	Whaling implements........	
	1	Boston........	1	....do........	8	45,828 gallons sperm oil	$30,410 80	8	....do........	
	1	Liverpool.....	1	St. Michael's.	1	Lumber, &c........	4,000 00	1	Inward cargo........	4,000 00
				In port........	1	General cargo........	80,000 00	1	In port........	
	14		14		14		114,410 00	14		41,446 06
Quarter ended Mar. 31, 1864.†	1	In port........	1	New York.....	1	Before reported........		1	Inward cargo........	60,000 00
	1	Whaling......	1	Whaling......	1	3,194 gallons sperm oil	3,438 40	1	Whaling implements........	
	1	Calcutta......	1	In port........	1	Jute, linseed, &c......	54,000 00	1	In port........	
	1	Callao........	1	....do........	1	1,900 tons guano......	75,000 00	1	....do........	
	1	London........	1	....do........	1	Iron and general cargo.	22,000 00	1	....do........	
	1	Boston........	1	....do........	1	Lumber, tobacco, &c...	12,400 00	1	....do........	
	6		6		6		167,836 40	6		60,000 00
Quarter ended June 30, 1864.‡	4	In port........	2	London........	2	Before reported........		1	Inward cargo........	54,000 00
			1	Boston........	1	....do........		1	Part inward cargo......	74,800 00
			.1	Palermo......	1	....do........		1	Ballast........	
	15	Whaling......	15	Whaling......	13	80,904 gallons sperm and whale oil, 2,557 pounds whalebone.	80,229 80	1	Inward cargo........	13,400 00
					2	Whaling implements......		10	Whaling implements........	
	1	Callao........	1	Havre........	1	900 tons guano........	48,000 00	5	Inward cargo; in for orders.	34,083 00
								1	Inward cargo; in for supplies.	48,000 00
	20		20		20		128,229 60	20		223,083 00
Quarter ended September 30, 1864.§	43	Whaling......	43	Whaling......	36	Sperm and whale oil and bone....	176,003 50	15	Inward cargo; called for orders and provisions.	61,085 00
					7	Whaling implements......		27	Whaling implements........	
	1	Boston........	1	Gibraltar.....	1	Corn, lumber, &c......	28,680 00	1	Part of inward cargo......	16,795 50
	1	Akyab........	1	Falmouth.....	1	1,600 tons rice......	64,000 00	1	....do........ In distress.	8,672 00
	1	New York.....	1	Gibraltar.....	1	Flour and staves......		1	Part of inward cargo; in distress.	40,000 00
								1	Inward cargo; put in for supplies.	
	46		46		46			46		1,206, 0413 20

ST. PAUL DE LOANDA.—J. T. Bradbery.

Quarter ended December 31, 1863.

Entered		Cleared		Cargo	Value	In port	Description	Value
1	In port	1	Amherst	Before reported		1	Ballast	
2	Cardiff	1	Akyab	1,652 tons coal	17,000 00	1	...do	
1	Benguela	1	Callao	1,319 tons coal	13,401 00	1	In port	
1	Salem	1	Salem	Assorted cargo		1	400 tons palm oil	12,819 26
1	Whaling	1	St. Thomas	...do	12,000 00	1	Assorted cargo	3,150 00
		1	Whaling	60 barrels sperm oil	3,150 00	1	Same as inward cargo	
6		6			45,551 00	6		15,969 26

Quarter ended Mar. 31, 1864.

Entered		Cleared		Cargo	Value	In port	Description	Value
1	In port	1	Callao	Before reported		1	Ballast	9,000 00
1	Salem	1	Benguela	Rum, flour, chairs, lumber	14,000 00	1	In part inward cargo	18,000 00
1	St. Thomas	1	Salem	Palm and fish oil, gum copal	6,000 00	1	Inward cargo and African produce	16,000 00
1	Boston	1	St. Helena	Rum, provisions, &c.	20,000 00	1	Part inward cargo	
4		4			40,000 00	4		43,000 00

Quarter ended June 30, 1864.

Entered		Cleared		Cargo	Value	In port	Description	Value
1	Benguela	1	In port	Fish oil, gum, &c.	9,000 00	1	In port	9,000 00

Quarter ended September 30, 1864.

Entered		Cleared		Cargo	Value	In port	Description	Value
1	In port	1	In port	Before reported		1	Part inward cargo, oil, hides	13,000 00
1	St. Helena	1	Ambrizette	Assorted cargo	10,000 00	1	Gum, oil, hides, &c.	10,000 00
1	Ambrizette	1	Boston	Peanuts, oil, gum, hides	16,000 00			
3		3			26,000 00	3		23,000 00

MACAO.—W. P. Jones.

Quarter ended December 31, 1863.

Entered		Cleared		Cargo	Value	In port	Description	Value
6	Hong Kong	4	Sold	Ballast		4	Sold; took Portuguese flag	45,000 00
		2	Japan	...do			Guns and ammunition	
1	New York	1	Hong Kong	General cargo	3,000 00	1	General cargo	90,000 00
1	Shanghai	1	...do	Coal, ammunition, hides	90,000 00	1	Coal and hides	
1	Canton & Whampoa	1	Canton & Whampoa	Chinese passengers		1	Ballast	
				General cargo and passengers	200,000 00	1	General cargo and passengers	50,000 00
9		9			233,000 00	9		115,000 00

2d quarter. .... No report.

* Entered: 1 ship, 7 barks, 2 schooners—10, and 4 in port. Cleared: 1 ship, 10 barks, 2 schooners—13, and 1 in port. Aggregate tonnage entered, 3,161.
† Entered: 2 ships, 3 barks—5, and 1 in port. Cleared: 1 ship, 1 bark—2, and 4 in port. Aggregate tonnage entered, 2,456.
‡ Entered: 2 ships, 13 barks, 1 schooner—16, and 4 in port. Cleared: 4 ships, 15 barks, 1 schooner—20. Aggregate tonnage entered, 4,708.
§ Entered and cleared: 5 ships, 29 barks, 1 brig, 8 schooners—43. Aggregate tonnage entered, 12,432.
|| Entered: 3 ships, 2 barks—5. Cleared: 2 ships, 2 barks, 1 brig—4. Aggregate tonnage entered, 837.   ** Entered: 1 bark, and 1 in port. Tonnage, 325.
¶ Entered: 2 barks, 1 brig—3, and 1 in port. Cleared: 1 ship, 2 barks, 1 brig, 2 steamers—9. Aggregate tonnage, 5,191 40-95.
†† Entered and cleared: 2 brigs, and 1 in port. Aggregate tonnage entered, 508.   ‡‡ Entered and cleared, 4 ships, 2 barks, 1 brig, 2 steamers—9.

Navigation and commerce of the United States with foreign countries—Portuguese Dominions, Belgium, Netherlands.

COUNTRY, CONSULATE, NAME OF CONSUL, AND DATE OF RETURNS	VESSELS				CARGOES					
	ENTERED		CLEARED		INWARD			OUTWARD		
	No.	Where from.	No.	Where for.	No.	Description.	Value.	No.	Description.	Value.
Quarter ended June 30, 1864.*	1	Manila	1	Japan	1	Passengers and freight	$250,000 00	1	Passengers and freight	$250,000 00
	1	Canton	1	Canton	1		250,000 00	1		250,000 00
	2		2		2			2		180,000 00
Quarter ended September 30, 1864.†	2	Canton	2	Canton	2	Passengers and freight	300,000 00	2	Passengers and freight	
BELGIUM.										
ANTWERP.—*A. F. Crawford.*										
Quarter ended December 31, 1863.‡	10	In port	6	Cardiff	6	Before reported		8	Ballast	
			1	Sunderland	1	do		1	Sold; took English flag	
			1	East Indies	1	do		1	Sold; took Hamburg flag	
			9	Sold	2	do				
	1	Akyab	1	Cardiff	1	1,965 tons rice	50,690 00	1	Sold; took English flag	50,690 00
	9	Callao	2	Shields	9	13,877 tons guano	902,005 00	3	Ballast	902,005 00
			6	In port				6	In port	
	20		20		20		952,695 00	20		952,695 00
Quarter ended Mar. 31, 1864.§	6	In port	3	Cardiff	3	Before reported		5	Ballast	
			1	Rotterdam	1	do		1	Sold; took Belgian flag	
			1	Newport, Eng	1	do				
	1	Almeria	1	Sold	1	400 tons marble, &c.	2,400 00	1	Ballast	2,400 00
	3	Callao	1	Port Said	3	4,250 tons guano	276,250 00	2	do	276,250 00
			1	Cardiff				1	In port	
			1	Rotterdam						
			1	In port						
	10		10		10		278,650 00	10		278,650 00
Quarter ended June 30, 1864.‖	1	In port	1	Cardiff	1	Before reported		1	Ballast	
	11	Callao	5	do	11	19,803 tons guano	1,287,195 00	5	do	43,144 00
			5	New York				5	Passengers and general cargo	
			1	In port				1	In port	
	1	Carthagena	1	do	1	1,905 tons zinc ore	94,100 00	1	do	
	13		13		13		1,311,295 00	13		43,144 00

1864.¶

	No.	Where from	Cargo	No.	Value	Remarks
		New York	Lisbon	1		Ballast
			Callao	1		Railroad iron
			Cardiff	1		Passengers
			Akyab	2		
			Chinchas	1		
		Callao	Cardiff	1	51,000 00	
			Sold	3		Ballast
			In port	24		Sold
	29		before reported	29		In port
	1	New York	36,417 tons guano	1	3,022,405 00	
	3	Akyab	2,922 barrels petroleum	1	49,222 00	541 tons window-glass
			3,350 tons rice	3	130,000 00	In port
	39			39	3,201,657 00	69,000 00

GHENT.—M. J. Leissen.
For the past two years.

No arrivals. — No departures.

NETHERLANDS.

AMSTERDAM.—T. Breicker.
Quarter ended December 31, 1863.**

| | 2 | Bassein | 40,350 bags rice | 2 | Not stated | Ballast |

2d and 3d quarters.

No arrivals. — No departures.

Quarter ended September 30, 1864.††

| | 1 | Bassein | In port | 22,130 bags rice | 1 | |

ROTTERDAM.—G. E. Wiss.
Quarter ended December 31, 1863.‡‡

	3	In port	Sold	Before reported	3	Sold; took Netherlands flag
	2	Akyab	Akyab	2,150 tons rice	2	Ballast
			England		1	do.
			Sold		1	Sold; took Hamburg flag
	5				5	

Quarter ended March 31, 1864.§§

| | 2 | Antwerp | Sold | Ballast | 2 | Sold |

* Entered and cleared: 1 ship, and cleared: 1 steamer.—2. Tonnage not given.
† Entered: 10 ships, and 10 in port. Cleared: 11 ships, 3 sold, and 6 in port. Aggregate tonnage entered, 9,936 46-95.
‡ Entered: 2 ships, 1 brig, 1 bark—4, and 6 in port. Cleared: 7 ships, 1 brig, 1 bark—9, and 1 in port. Aggregate tonnage entered, 2,912 80-95.
§ Entered: 12 ships, and 1 in port. Cleared, 7 ships, and 6 in port. Aggregate tonnage entered, 12,043 18-95.
¶ Entered: 31 ships, 2 barks—33, and 6 in port. Cleared: 9 ships, 3 sold, 27 in port. Aggregate tonnage entered, 33,633 85-95.
** Entered and cleared: 2 ships. Aggregate tonnage, 2,226.
†† Entered: 2 ships, and 3 in port. Cleared: 2 ships, and 3 sold. Aggregate tonnage entered, 1,474 60-95.
‡‡ Entered: 2 ships, and 3 in port. Cleared: 2 sold. Tonnage, 1,607.
§§ Entered: 1 ship, 1 bark—2. Cleared: 2 sold. Tonnage, 1,607.

‖ Entered and cleared: 2 steamers. Tonnage not given.
†† Entered: 1 ship, and 1 in port. Tonnage, 898.

Navigation and commerce of the United States with foreign countries—Netherlands.

COUNTRY, CONSULATE, NAME OF CONSUL, AND DATE OF RETURNS.	VESSELS.				CARGOES.							
	ENTERED.		CLEARED.		INWARD.			OUTWARD.				
	No.	Where from.	No.	Where for.	No.	Description.	Value.	No.	Description.	Value.		Value.
Quarter ended June 30, 1864.*	4	Callao	3	Cardiff	3	2,350 tons guano		3	Ballast			
	2	Baltimore	1	Sold	1	900 tons guano		1	Sold; took Norwegian flag			
			2	In port	2	1,999 hhds. tobacco, 1,350 bbls. flour, 338 bags bark, 27,950 staves, 38 hhds. tobacco stems, 1,107 oars.		2	In port			
	6		6		6			6				
Quarter ended September 30, 1864.†	2	In port	1	Cardiff	1	Before reported		1	Ballast			
	2	Callao	1	New York	1	do		1	General cargo			
			1	In port	1	1,800 tons guano		1	In port			
	3	Akyab	1	Sold	1	750 tons guano		1	Sold			
			1	do	1	1,000 tons rice		1	do			
			1	Akyab	1	950 tons rice		1	Ballast			
	1	Baltimore	1	In port	1	900 tons rice		1	In port			
			1	England	1	1,425 hhds. tobacco, 50 bbls. beef, 100 bbls. flour, 400 bags bark, 9,990 staves.		1	Ballast			
	8		8		8			8				
BATAVIA.—J. P. Pels.												
Quarter ended December 31, 1863.‡	1	Boston	1	Manila	1	216 cases chairs, 1 machine	$3,659 03	1	Not stated			$14,968 82
	1	Rio de Janeiro	1	Boston	1	791 tons ice, (not received)		1	{ 1,000.17 piculs ratans			7,309 48
									{ 72.82 piculs rubber			51,911 98
									{ 3,946.95 piculs sugar			
	2		2		2		3,659 03	2				74,190 28
Quarter ended March 31, 1864.§	1	Otago	1	Singapore	1	Ballast		1	2,472.48 piculs ratans			37,778 34
Quarter ended June 30, 1864.‖	1	Anjer	1	do	1	do		1	Ballast			
	1	Rio de Janeiro	1	Boston	1	do		1	{ 5,988.02 piculs sugar			456 14
									{ 853.46 piculs ratans			
									{ 348.05 piculs pepper			
									{ 46.93 piculs India-rubber			
	2		2		2			2				456 14

	No.	From	No.	To	No.	Cargo	Value	No.	Cargo	Value
Quarter ended September 30, 1864.¶	1	Mauritius	1	Singapore	1	General merchandise	7,000 00	{1,1	2,700 picls rajans / Part of inward cargo	13,777 00 / 3,500 00
	1	Manila	1	New York	1	Hemp and sugar, &c.	25,000 00	1	In distress	
	1	Pernambuco	1	Singapore	1	1,300 bbls. flour, &c.		1	Part of inward cargo	5,000 00
	1	Boston	1	In port	1	Ice, flour, tobacco, &c.		1	In port	
	4		4		4		32,000 00	4		24,277 00
CURACAO.—R. E. Morse.										
Quarter ended December 31, 1863.*	1	Bangor	1	Portland	1	Lumber	1,300 00	1	Ballast	
	1	Puerto Cabello	1	New York	1	Ballast	3,640 00	1	do	
	1	Philadelphia	1	Turk's Island	1	520 tons coal	5,460 00	1	do	
	1	New York	1	Bonaire	1	General cargo	2,000 00	1	do	
	1	Barbadoes	1	Whaling cruise	1	Whale oil		1	Whaling cruise	
	5		5		5		12,400 00	5		
2d quarter		No report								
Quarter ended June 30, 1864.††	1	Baltimore	1	New York	1	Provisions	17,344 70	1	907 bbls. salt, 30 hhds. sugar, 30	121 71
	1	New York	1	do	1	do		1	478 bbls. salt, 30 hhds. sugar, 246 dozen hats, 119 bales coffee, 246 goat-skins, 346 hides, 100,000 cigars.	19,611 16
	2		2		2		17,344 70	2		19,732 87
Quarter ended September 30, 1864.‡‡	1	Barbadoes	1	Bath	1	Ballast	14,670 72	1	Salt	3,329 00
	1	New York	1	New York	1	Provisions	7,408 96	1	Salt, skins, rags, &c.	5,740 98
	2	Bangor	2	Turk's Island / Bonaire	2	Timber		2	Ballast	
	4		4		4		12,078 98	4		8,962 98
PARAMARIBO.—H. Sawyer.										
1st quarter		No report.								

* Entered: 4 ships, 2 barks—6. Cleared: 2 ships, 1 bark—3. 1 sold and 2 in port. Aggregate tonnage entered, 3,597 51-95.

† Entered: 5 ships, 1 bark—6, and 2 in port. Cleared: 3 ships, 1 bark—4, 2 sold, and 2 in port. Aggregate tonnage entered, 4,725 43-95.

‡ Entered and cleared: 1 ship, 1 bark—2. Aggregate tonnage entered, 1,463 12-95. § Entered and cleared : 1 ship. Tonnage, 716 81-95.

|| Entered : 3 ships, 1 bark—4. Aggregate tonnage entered, 1,281 52-95.

** Entered and cleared : 2 ships, 1 bark—3, and 1 in port. Aggregate tonnage entered, 3,180 30-95.

†† Entered and cleared: 3 schooners, 1 bark, 1 propeller—5. Aggregate tonnage entered, 1,363 40-95. ‡‡ Entered and cleared : 2 schooners. Aggregate tonnage entered, 283 10-95.

Entered and cleared: 1 bark, 1 schooner, 2 brigs—4. Aggregate tonnage entered, 1,123 96-95.

Commerce and navigation of the United States with foreign countries—Netherlands—Hanse Towns.

COUNTRY, CONSULATE, NAME OF CONSUL, AND DATE OF RETURNS.	VESSELS.				CARGOES.					
	ENTERED.		CLEARED.		INWARD.			OUTWARD.		
	No.	Where from.	No.	Where for.	No.	Description.	Value.	No.	Description.	Value.
Quarter ended March 31, 1864.*	1	In port	1	Boston	1	Before reported		1	Sugar and molasses	$10,386 14
	7	Boston	6	do.	6	Provisions	$90,358 88	5	do.	57,379 51
			1	In port	1	do.		1	In port	
								1	Ballast	
	8		8		8		90,358 88	8		67,765 65
3d quarter		No report								
Quarter ended September 30, 1864.†	1	In port	1	Boston	1	Before reported		1	Sugar and molasses	14,343 85
	8	Boston	5	do.	5	Provisions	64,889 14	5	Sugar, molasses, and cocoa	60,254 27
			3	In port	3	do.	38,400 00	3	In port	
	1	Brazil	1	Brazil	1	Cattle	3,000 00	1	Ballast	
	1	Cherryfield	1	Boston	1	Timber	7,500 00	1	do.	18,284 50
	1	Taken up here	1	do.				1	Sugar, molasses, and cocoa	92,882 39
	12		12		12		113,789 14	12		
HANSE TOWNS. BREMEN.—F. W. Speck.										
Quarter ended December 31, 1863.‡	3	In port	1	Sold	3	Before reported		1	Sold	
			1	Rangoon				1	do.	
			1	Cadiz				1	Ballast	
	1	Akyab	1	In port	2	33,726 bags rice		2	In port	
	1	Mauritius	1	do.						
	5		5		5			5		
Quarter ended March 31, 1864.§	2	In port	1	Akyab	1	Before reported		1	Ballast	
			1	Newport	1	do.		1	do.	
	2		2		2			2		
Quarter ended June 30, 1864.‖	1	In port	1		1	Before reported		1	In port	

HAMBURG.—J. H. Anderson.

3			In port		1	Ballast
		1	29,157 bags rice		1	In port
		3			3	
8	Callao	1	7,329 tons guano	373,160 00	{3 1 4}	Ballast. Sold. In port
	Havre	1				
	Shields	1				
	Cardiff	4				
	In port	8		373,160 00	8	
Quarter ended March 31, 1864.††						
4	In port	1 2 1	Before reported		{1 2 1}	Sold. Ballast. In port
	Sold					
	Newcastle					
	In port	4			4	
Quarter ended June 30, 1864.‡‡						
1	In port	1	Before reported		1	Sold
4	Callao	1 1 1 1	7,400 tons guano		{1 3}	Ballast. General cargo
	Gothenburg					
	Rio de Janeiro					
	Buenos Ayres					
	New York	5			5	
Quarter ended September 30, 1864.§§						
1	In port	1	Before reported		1	General cargo
3	Callao	1 1 1	2,000 tons guano	116,000 00	1	do
	do		1,100 tons guano	63,800 00	1	Ballast
	Cardiff		800 tons guano	46,400 00	1	do
	Siderhamn		1,327 blocks cedar wood, 869 pieces red wood, 8,400 lbs. pearl shells, 10,547 lbs. silver ore	30,418 50	1	do
1	Point Arenas	1				
5		5		256,618 50	5	

* Entered: 3 barks, 2 brigs, 2 schooners—7, and 1 in port. Cleared: 3 barks, 3 brigs, 2 schooners—7, and 1 in port. Aggregate tonnage entered, 1,194 25-95.
† Entered: 1 bark, 5 brigs, 4 schooners—11, and 1 in port. Cleared: 1 bark, 3 schooners, 5 brigs—9, and 3 in port. Aggregate tonnage entered, 2,169 14-95.
‡ Entered: 2, class not given, and 3 in port. Cleared: 1, class not given, 2 sold, and 1 in port. Aggregate tonnage entered, 1,509 77-95. § In port. ‖ Entered: 9 ships in port 1. Cleared: 2 ships, in port 1. Aggregate tonnage entered, 1,552
¶ Entered: 2, in port. Cleared: 2 ships. Tonnage before reported.
†† Entered: 6 ships, 3 barks—8. Cleared: 3 ships, 1 sold, and 4 in port. Aggregate tonnage entered, 6,484 67-95.
‡‡ Entered: 4 in port. Cleared: 1 ship, 1 bark—2, 1 sold, and 1 in port. Tonnage before reported. —— §§ Entered: 4 ships, 1 in port. Cleared: 5 ships. Aggregate tonnage entered, 3,49079-95.

Navigation and commerce of the United States with foreign countries—Danish Dominions.

COUNTRY, CONSULATE, NAME OF CONSUL, AND DATE OF RETURNS.	VESSELS.						CARGOES.						
	ENTERED.		CLEARED.		INWARD.				OUTWARD.				
	No.	Where from.	No.	Where for.	No.	Description.	Value.	No.	Description.	Value.			
DANISH DOMINIONS. COPENHAGEN.—*L. A. Heckscher.*													
Quarter ended December 31, 1863.*	1	Cronstadt	1	New York	1	General cargo	Unknown.	1	In port				
Quarter ended March 31, 1864.‡	1	Not given	1	Not given	1	General cargo		1	Put in for repairs				
3d and 4th quarters		No report											
CHRISTIANSTED.—*E. H. Perkins.*													
Quarter ended December 31, 1863.‡	1	Bangor	1	Turk's Island	1	White pine lumber	3,200 00	1	Ballast				
	1	New Haven	1	...do...	1	White pine boards, shooks, hoops, &c.	7,189 00	1	25 puncheons rum	871 68			
	2		2		2		10,389 00	2		871 68			
Quarter ended March 31, 1864.§	1	New Haven	1	Porto Rico	1	Meal, flour, provisions, &c.	6,000 00	1	Rum	1,415 01			
	1	New York	1	Baracoa, Cuba.	1	Meal, flour, cooperage	3,258 10	1	Ballast				
	1	Wilmington, Del.	1	In port.	1	...do... ...do...	13,000 00	1	In port				
	3		3		3		23,258 10	3		1,415 01			
Quarter ended June 30, 1864.‖	1	In port.	1	New York.	1	Before reported		1	Sugar, rum, molasses.	14,788 64			
	1	New York.	1	New Haven	1	Meal, flour, provisions	7,590 00	1	Molasses	8,307 41			
	1	Wilmington, Del.	1	New York.	1	Meal, flour, lumber	13,250 00	1	Sugar, molasses, rum.	13,307 86			
	3		3		3		20,840 00	3		36,403 91			
Quarter ended September 30, 1864.¶	2	New York	1	New York.	1	Assorted provisions	11,226 25	1	Molasses, hides and skins.	6,373 75			
	2	Bangor	1	In port.	1	Flour and provisions	23,212 86	1	In port				
			1	Turk's Island	1	Lumber	3,249 43	1	Ballast				
			1	New Haven	1	Fish and lumber	3,929 20	1	Molasses	3,361 43			
	4		4		4		43,617 74	4		9,735 18			

FREDERICKSTAD.—*Wm. P. Moore.*

	From		To		Inward cargo	Value		Outward cargo	Value
Quarter ended December 31, 1863.*									
1	New York	1	Mansanilla, Cuba	1	105 puncheons meal, 115 bbl. pork, 100 bbl. flour.	10,323 00	1	Ballast	
1	Bangor	1	Turk's Island	1	127 M feet boards, 349,000 shingles.	3,386 00	1	do	
2		2		2		13,709 00	2		
Quarter ended March 31, 1864.††									
1	New York	1	Santa Cruz	1	Meal, flour, hoops, &c.	8,471 75	1	Ballast	
Quarter ended June 30, 1864.‡‡									
2	Wilmington	1	Turk's Island	1	407 puncheons and 149 bbls. meal, 225 puncheons corn, 20,000 wood hoops.	14,861 35	1	Ballast	12,701 44
		1	New York	1	317 puncheons meal, 200 bbls. flour, 50 bbls. pork, 6,000 wood hoops.	11,257 00	1	393 casks and 33,543 gallons molasses, 3 bbls. sugar.	12,701 44
2		2		2		26,118 35	2		12,701 44
Quarter ended September 30, 1864.§§									
1	Barbadoes	1	New York	1	Ballast		1	40 puncheons rum, 169 casks molasses, 1 anchor and 2 chains	8,935 13
1	Wilmington, Del.	1	Santa Cruz	2	293 puncheons and 66 bbls. molasses, 250 bbls. flour, 20 half bbls. beef.	16,198 82	1	Ballast	
2		2		2		16,198 82	2		8,935 13

ELSINORE.—*G. P. Hassen.*

	From		To		Inward cargo	Value		Outward cargo	Value
Quarter ended December 31, 1863.‖‖									
1	Nyhaven	1	Bristol						
1	Hermosand	1	do	3	Cargoes untouched.		3	Same as inward cargoes.	
1	Cronstadt	1	Boston						
3		3		3			3		
2d quarter.									
	No arrivals.		No departures.						
Quarter ended June 30, 1864.¶¶									
1	New York	1	New York						
2	Boston	2	Cronstadt	5	Unknown.		5	Unknown.	
2	Cronstadt	1	New York						
		1	Boston						
5		5		5			5		
4th quarter.									
	No report.		No report.						

* Entered: 1 bark, and 1 in port. Tonnage, 503 56-95.   † Entered and cleared: 1 bark. Tonnage, 503 56-95.   ‡ Entered and cleared: 2 brigs. Aggregate tonnage entered, 368 61-95.
§ Entered: 2 brigs, 1 schooner. Cleared: 1 brig, 1 schooner—3, and 1 in port. Aggregate tonnage entered, 502 66-95.
‡ Entered: 2 brigs, and 1 in port. Cleared: 3 brigs. Aggregate tonnage entered, 584 85-95.   ¶ Entered: 4 brigs. Cleared: 3 brigs, and 1 in port. Aggregate tonnage entered, 713 80-95.
** Entered and cleared: 1 brig, 1 brigantine. Aggregate tonnage entered, 431 26-95.   †† Entered and cleared: 1 brig. Tonnage, 199 16-95.
‡‡ Entered and cleared: 2 schooners. Aggregate tonnage entered, 408 34-95.   §§ Entered and cleared: 1 bark, 1 brigantine. Aggregate tonnage entered, 463 44-95.
‖‖ Entered and cleared: 3 barks. Aggregate tonnage entered, 1,412.   ¶¶ Entered and cleared, 5 barks. Aggregate tonnage entered, 2,361.

Navigation and commerce of the United States with foreign countries—Danish Dominions.

COUNTRY, CONSULATE, NAME OF CONSUL, AND DATE OF RETURNS.	VESSELS.				CARGOES.					
	ENTERED.		CLEARED.		INWARD.			OUTWARD.		
	No.	Where from.	No.	Where for.	No.	Description.	Value.	No.	Description.	Value.
SANTA CRUZ.—C. Huger. 1st, 2d, and 3d quarters. From November 5, 1863, to September 30, 1864.*		No reports								
	3	New York	2	New York	2	General cargo		2	Timber, sugar, molasses, &c.	
	2	Havana	1	In port	1	Merchandise		1	In port	
	7	St. Thomas	1	Liverpool	1	Ballast		1	Timber, honey, and rum	
			1	Trinidad	1	do		1	Ballast	
			1	Queenstown	1	do		1	Mahogany	
			1	London	1	do		1	do	
	9	Santiago	4	New York	4	do		4	Molasses, honey, sugar, &c.	
			1	Trinidad	1	do		1	Ballast	
			5	Queenstown	5	do		5	Mahogany, honey, timber	
	1	Martinique	1	Falmouth	1	do		3	Timber, sugar, and honey	
	1	Aspinwall	3	New York	3	do		1	do....do.	
	1	Trinidad	1	do	1	do		1	do....do.	
			1	In port	1	do		1	Sugar and molasses	
								1	In port	
	24		24		24			24		250,000 00
ST. THOMAS.—J. T. Edgar. Quarter ended December 30, 1863.†	3	In port	3	Philadelphia	3	Before reported		3	Not stated	
	3	Philadelphia	3	New York / Turk's Island	3	Coal	15,300 00	3	Ballast	
	1	Bombay	1	New York	1	General cargo	200,000 00	1	General cargo	900,000 00
	1	Demarara	1	Baltimore	1	Sugar	50,000 00	1	Sugar	50,000 00
	1	Bahia	1	Turk's Island	1	Ballast		1	Ballast	
	1	Canary Islands	1	do		do			do	
	1	St. Kitts	1	In port	1	Salt and cocoa	5,000 00	2	In port	
	2	Boston	1	do	9	General cargo	12,500 00	9	do	
	1	St. Croix	2	do	1	Ballast		1	do	
	14		14		14		282,800 00	14		250,000 00
Quarter ended March 31, 1864.‡	4	In port	1	New York	4	Before reported		1	Salt and cocoa	5,000 00
	2	Philadelphia	2	Turk's Island				3	Ballast	
	1	New York	1	Boston	1	General cargo	9,000 00	1	do	
			1	Turk's Island	1	Ballast	4,000 00	1	do	4,000 00
			1	Avon Island	1	General cargo				
			1	Mayaguez						

No.	Where from	No.	Where to	Cargo	Value	Value
1	China	1	In port	Tea	50,000 00	
1	Shields	1	New York	Coal	5,000 00	
1	Trinidad	1	Philadelphia	Guano	4,000 00	
1	Turk's Island	1	do	Salt	2,000 00	4,000 00
1	Cadiz	1	In port	do	2,500 00	
1	St. Eustatia	1	Whaling	Whale oil	1,200 00	1,200 00
1	Montevideo	1	New York	Ballast		
15		15			73,700 00	21,200 00

Quarter ended June 30, 1864, §

No.	Where from	No.	Where to	Cargo	Value	Value
2	In port	2	Boston	Here reported		Not stated
1	St. Michael's	1	New York	do		
3	New York	1	Cuba	Oranges	20,500 00	General cargo 3,500 00
			do	General cargo		Ballast
1	Cruise	1	Hartford	Whale oil	4,000 00	Whale oil 4,000 00
1	Orchilla	1	Prov'l estova	Ballast		Ballast
2	Demerara	1	do	Provisions	3,000 00	do
		1	Bangor	do		In port
2	St. Eustatia	2	In port	Ballast	2,000 00	Ballast
2	Dog Island	1	Cruise	1 Mle oil		do
1	Boston	1	Orchilla	Ballast		
		2	C do / Bonaceo	General cargo	14,000 00	Lumber, &c.
1	St. Martin	1	In port	Lumber	2,000 00	In port
				Ballast		
16		16			45,500 00	7,500 00

Quarter ended September 30, 1864, ‖

No.	Where from	No.	Where to	Cargo	Value
2	In port	1	Nassau	Before reported	Not stated
2	Orchilla	2	Orchilla	Ballast	Ballast
1	Martinique	1	do	do	do
2	New York	2	Turk's Island	General cargo	
1	Granada	1	St. Croix	Ballast	do
1	Boston	1	Turk's Island	do	do
1	Frankfort	1	do	General cargo	do
1	Trinidad	1	Frankfort	Ballast	do
1	Bermuda	1	Baltimore	do	do
1	St. Eustatia	1	St. Martin's	do	do
1	St. Michael's	1	do	do	do
1	Dominica	1	Turk's Island	do	
		1	Baltimore		
16		16			

* Entered: 24—class not given. Cleared: 22—class not given. Tonnage not given.
† Entered: 6 brigs, 4 ships, 2 barks, 2 schooners—11, and 3 in port. Cleared: 5 brigs, 2 schooners, 1 ship, 1 bark—8, 1 not stated, and 4 in port. Aggregate tonnage entered, 3,419.
‡ Entered: 2 ships, 4 barks, 2 brigs, 5 schooners—11, and 4 in port. Cleared: 1 ship, 2 barks, 4 brigs, 6 schooners—13, and 2 in port. Aggregate tonnage entered, 3,500.
§ Entered: 12 schooners, 1 brig, 1 bark—14, and 2 in port. Cleared: 1 ship, 1 bark, 1 brig, 11 schooners—14, and 2 in port. Aggregate tonnage entered, 1,672.
¶ Entered: 2 schooners, 1 brig, 1 bark, 1 steamer—14, and 2 in port. Cleared: 8 schooners, 4 brigs, 3 barks—15, and 1 in port. Aggregate tonnage entered, 2,471.
‖ Entered: 7 schooners, 4 brigs, 2 barks, 1 steamer—14, and 2 in port. Cleared: 8 schooners, 4 brigs, 3 barks—15, and 1 in port. Aggregate tonnage entered, 2,471.

Navigation and commerce of the United States with foreign countries—Sweden and Norway, Russia.

COUNTRY, CONSULATE, NAME OF CONSUL, AND DATE OF RETURNS.	VESSELS.				CARGOES.					
	ENTERED.		CLEARED.		INWARD.			OUTWARD.		
	No.	Where from.	No.	Where for.	No.	Description.	Value.	No.	Description.	Value.
SWEDEN AND NORWAY. GOTTENBURG.—N. W. Thomas, jr. Quarter ended December 31, 1863.*	1	London	1	Australia	1	Ballast		1	509 119-185 standard deals	$20,347 00
2d and 3d quarters.		No reports.								
4th quarter. St. Bartholomew.—R. B. Dinzey.		No arrivals		No departures						
1st and 2d quarters.		No reports.								
Quarter ended June 30, 1864.†	1	Martinique	1	Philadelphia	1	Breadstuffs and provisions	$1,444 75	1	Ballast	812 10
	1	St. Kitts	1	New York	1	White pine lumber	144 00	1	Fruit	812 10
	2		2		2		1,588 75	2		
Quarter ended September 30, 1864.‡	1	Barbados	1	Boston	1	Fish and shoes	161 00	1	Fruit	413 16
	1	St. Kitts	1	Baltimore	1	Provisions	767 90	1	Fruit and old iron	308 12
	1	Martinique	1	Philadelphia	1	Breadstuffs	3,171 51	1	Cotton and skins	650 98
	3		3		3		4,099 71	3		1,371 57
RUSSIA. AMOOR RIVER.—H. G. O. Chase. Quarter ended December 31, 1863.		No arrivals		No departures						
2d quarter.		No report.								
Quarter ended June 30, 1864.§	1	Boston	1	Hakodadi	1	300 tons assorted cargo	46,449 98	1	Same as inward cargo	
	1	Hakodadi	1	San Francisco	1	do	10,000 00	1	10 tons assorted cargo	
	1	San Francisco		do	970	do	82,511 00	1	road, oil, &c	

Period	No.	Whence	No.	Whither	Cargo (cleared)	Value	No.	Cargo (entered)	Value
Quarter ended September 30, 1864.‖	1 1 1 3	Boston Hakodadi San Francisco	1 1 1 3	Hakodadi do San Francisco	300 tons assorted cargo 100......do 270......do		1 1 1 3	45 tons coal 10 tons assorted cargo 160 tons coal, oil	500 00 .... 5,000 00 5,500 00
CRONSTADT.—A. Wilkins. Quarter ended December 31, 1863.¶	1	Newcastle	1	London	380 casks cement, 120 casks soda, 35,000 fire-bricks.	46,449 96	1	4,011 poods clean hemp, 250 pieces mats.	
	1	Boston	1	Boston	107 bales sarsaparilla, 368 tons logwood.	10,000 00	1	18,944 lbs. sheet iron, 3,159 poods clean hemp, 5,687 lbs. flax tow, 344 poods horse hair, 2,660 pieces mats.	
	1	London	1	New York	Ballast.	22,511 00	1	10,099 lbs. sheet iron, 3,168 poods clean hemp, 6,292 lbs. rags, 135 lbs. bristles, 235 poods red leather, 847 pieces still cloth, 80 pieces ravens duck, 350 pieces mats, 407,050 arsheents crush.	
	3		3			78,960 26	3		
2d quarter.....	3	No report.....	3						
Quarter ended June 30, 1864.**	2	Boston.....	1	Boston	400 bales sarsaparilla, 250 boxes logwood extract, 431 tons logwood.		1	19,970 poods sheet iron, 5,329 poods flax tow, 1,646 poods cordage, 900 poods oakum, 672 poods horse hair, 272 poods bristles, 94 poods red leather, 885 pieces sailcloth, 750 pieces ravens duck, 1,710 pieces mats, 2,839 poods Lima wood, 27 poods tortoise shell.	
	1	Boston.....	1	Boston	164 tons logwood, 150 barrels petroleum, 3 cases wine.		1	670 poods sheet iron, 653 poods flax, 193 poods flax tow, 242 poods cordage, 12,640 poods junk, 1,576 poods rags, 4,300 poods tar, 382 poods bristles, 60 cbm's linseed, 1,776 pieces sailcloth, 500 pieces ravens duck, 50 pieces fam's, 1,200 pieces mats, 90,000 arsheens crush, 17,959 ditto diapers.	

* Entered and cleared: 1 ship. Tonnage, 1,695 57.95.   † Entered and cleared: 1 brig, 1 schooner—2. Aggregate tonnage, 442.

‡ Entered and cleared: 2 schooners, 1 brig—3. Aggregate tonnage entered, 401.

§ Entered: 3 in port end of last quarter. Cleared: Not stated. Aggregate tonnage, 605 87.95.

‖ Entered: 3 in port June 30. Cleared: 1 bark, 1 schooner, 1 brig—3. Aggregate tonnage before reported.

¶ Entered and cleared: 2 barks, 1 schooner—3. Aggregate tonnage entered, 1,157 83.95.

** Entered: 5 barks. Cleared: 4 barks, and 1 in port. Aggregate tonnage entered, 2,662 47.95.

Navigation and commerce of the United States with foreign countries—Russian Dominions.

COUNTRY, CONSULATE, NAME OF CONSUL, AND DATE OF RETURNS.	VESSELS.					CARGOES.					
	ENTERED.		CLEARED.			INWARD.			OUTWARD.		
	No.	Where from.	No.	Where for.	No.	Description.	Value.	No.	Description.	Value.	
CRONSTADT.—*A. Wilkins.* Quarter ended June 30, 1864—Continued	2	New York	2	New York	2	296 tons logwood, 5,100 boxes logwood extract, 171 bales sarsaparilla.		2	24,404 pods sheet iron, 13,799 pods clean hemp, 3,041 pods cordage, 1,301 pods flax, 18,351 pods junk, 636 pods bristles, 225 pods feathers, 636 pods oakum, 1,377 pods horse hair, 130 pods felt, 2,400 pieces sailcloth, 2,689 pieces ravens' duck, 100 pieces flem., 2,760 pieces mats, $77,000 sheena crash.	
	1	Marseilles	1	In port	1	250 barrels chloride of lime, 107 casks bristles.		1	In port		
	5		5		5			5			
Quarter ended September 30, 1864.*	1	In port	1	Marseilles	1	Before reported		1	14,130 pods rags, 800 pieces mats		
	1	Boston	1	In port	1	83 tons logwood, 580 bales sarsaparilla, 1 reaper and appurtenances.		1	In port		
	2		2		2			2			
ODESSA.—*T. C. Smith.* 1st, 2d, and 3d quarters		No arrivals		No departures							
Quarter ended September 30, 1864.†	1	Redout Kale	1	Palmouth	1	Ballast		1	6,700 chetwerts Indian corn	$25,000 00	
REVEL.—*H. B. Stacy.* 1st and 2d quarters		No report									
3d and 4th quarters		No arrivals		No departures							
STETTIN.—*C. J. Sundell.* 1st, 2d, 3d, and 4th quarters		No arrivals		No departures							

AUSTRIA.

TRIESTE.—R. Hildreth.

Quarter ended December 31, 1863.‡	2	New York	1	962 tons logwood	2,576 00	1	Staves and timber	27,974 40
			1	Ballast		1	Staves	11,160 00
	2		2		2,576 00	2		39,134 40

Quarter ended Mar. 31, 1864.§

	Boston	1	654 bags pepper	7,838 18	}
1			150 cases petroleum oil	1,004 00	} Ballast
			596 tons St. Domingo logwood	6,169 38	}
	New York	1	150 cases petroleum oil	1,756 00	
1			303 tons St. Domingo logwood	10,004 00	
			200 bags pimento	1,686 94	
			3,050 bags pepper	23,901 94	
2		2		51,484 44	2		2,082 00

3d quarter. — No report.

Quarter ended September 30, 1864.‖

1	Cleveland	1	250 tons wheat	10,800 00	1	22,000 feet boards	6,600 00
2	Boston	1	Ballast		1	94,000 staves	6,016 00
	In port	1	In port		1	In port	
3		3		10,800 00	3		12,616 00

ITALY.

BRINDISI.—J. S. Redfield.

1st, 2d, and 3d quarters. — No reports.

4th quarter. — No arrivals. No departures.

ANCONA.—L. Ujhazi.

Quarter ended December 31, 1863.¶

2	Cardiff	1	Railroad iron	Unknown	1	Ballast
	Segua	1	do.	do.	1	do.
2		2			2	

* Entered: 1 bark—in port 1. Cleared: 1 bark—in port 1. † Entered and cleared: 1 ship. Tonnage, 306 79-95.
‡ Entered and cleared: 2 barks. Aggregate tonnage entered, 658 65-95. § Entered and cleared: 1 bark, 1 ship.—2. Aggregate tonnage entered, 1,009 26-95.
‖ Entered: 3 barks. Cleared: 2 barks, and 1 in port. Aggregate tonnage entered, 990. ¶ Entered and cleared: 1 brig, 1 bark. Aggregate tonnage entered, 756 30-95.

Navigation and commerce of the United States with foreign countries—Italy.

COUNTRY, CONSULATE, NAME OF CONSUL, AND DATE OF RETURNS.	VESSELS				CARGOES					
	ENTERED.		CLEARED.		INWARD.			OUTWARD.		
	No.	Where from.	No.	Where for.	No.	Description.	Value.	No.	Description.	Value.
2d, 3d, and 4th quarters		No report.								
CAGLIARI.—E. Persia. Quarter ended December 31, 1863.*	1	Genoa	1	Boston	1	Ballast		1	385 67-100 tons salt, $597 61; 10,000 lemons, $51 16.	$648 77
2d and 3d quarters		No arrival.		No departures.						
Quarter ended September 30, 1864.†	1 / 2	Messina / Malaga	1 / 2	Boston / do	1 / 2	Staves / Ballast	$800 00	1 / 2	300 tons salt / 1,183 186-1,000 tons salt	449 19 / 1,763 53
	3		3		3		800 00	3		2,212 74
GENOA.—D. H. Wheeler. Quarter ended December 31, 1863.‡	2 / 2	In port / Androsain	1 / 1 / 1 / 1 / 1 / 1 / 1	Trapani / Boston / Leghorn / New York / Trapani / In port / do	1 / 1 / {2} / 1 / 1 / 1	Before reported / do / 1,150 tons pig iron, 799 tons coal / 1,300 tons guano / 630 tons nitrate of soda / 1,600 tons coal	29,236 00 / 91,000 00 / 37,800 00 / 12,800 00	1 / 1 / {1} / 1 / 1 / 1 / 1	Ballast / Pasta, marble, and rags / Ballast / Pasta, marble, and rags / Ballast / In port / do	3,431 76 / 4,666 46
	7		7		7		163,836 00	7		8,098 22
Quarter ended Mar. 31, 1864.§	1 / 2	In port / Newport	1 / 1 / 1 / 1 / 1	Philadelphia / Newport / In port / do / do	1 / 1 / 1 / 1 / 1	Before reported / 510 tons coal / 1,347 tons coal / 2,940 barrels petroleum / 800 tons coal, 5 crates crockery	4,160 00 / 10,776 00 / 41,704 00 / 6,325 00	1 / 1 / 1 / 1 / 1	Marble and pasta / Ballast / In port / do / do	3,337 69
	5	Philadelphia / Cardiff	5		5		69,965 00	5		3,337 69
Quarter ended June 30, 1864.‖	9 / 2	In port / Newport	1 / 1 / 1	Philadelphia / Trapani / England	1 / 2	Before reported / do / 2,700 tons coal, 80 tons railroad iron	71,744 00	1 / 1 / 1	Olive oil, lemons, and marble / Ballast / do	10,986 00

Port	No.	Port	No.	Cargo	Value	No.	Cargo	Value
Leith	1	...do	1	1,485 tons coal	10,395 00	1	...do	8,100 66
Philadelphia	1	Philadelphia	1	1,514 barrels petroleum	27,250 00	1	199 cases lemons, rags, marble	
	6		6		59,389 00	6		18,386 66
Quarter ended September 30, 1864.¶								
SPEZZIA.—W. T. Rice.								
Callao	1	Callao	1	2,900 tons guano	143,000 00	1	Ballast	
New York	1	In port	1	1,800 barrels petroleum	31,000 00	1	In port	
	2		2		174,000 00	2		
Quarter ended December 31, 1863.								
2d, 3d, and 4th quarters.........		No reports						
LEGHORN.—A. J. Stevens.								
Liverpool	1	Leghorn	1	Coal	6,531 00	1	Ballast	
Quarter ended December 31, 1863.††								
In port	1	New York	1	Before reported		1	Before reported	5,940 73
Spezzia	1	In port	1	Ballast		1	...do	
Genoa	1	...do	1	...do		1	...do	
	3		3			3		5,940 73
Quarter ended March 31, 1864.‡‡								
In port	2	Philadelphia	1	Before reported		1	Marble, rags, soap, &c	34,595 54
		Boston	1	...do		1	...do	
Cardiff	1	...do	1	600 tons coal		1	...do	7,900 23
Marseilles	1	In port	1	Ballast		1	In port	
	4		4			4		42,495 77
Quarter ended June 30, 1864.§§								
In port	1	Boston	1	Before reported		1	Marble and rags	41,541 91
Naples	1	In port	1	Ballast		1	In port	
	2		2			2		41,541 91

* Entered and cleared: 1, class not given. Tonnage, 498.   † Entered and cleared: 2 barks.

‡ Entered: 4 ships, 1 bark—5, and 2 in port. Cleared: 3 ships, 2 class not given—5, and 2 in port. Aggregate tonnage entered, 1,449.

§ Entered: 3 ships, 3 barks—4, and 1 in port. Cleared: 1 bark, 4 in port. Aggregate tonnage entered, 2,083 6-95.

‖ Entered: 3 ships, 1 bark—4, and 2 in port. Cleared: 1 ship, 1 bark, 2 class not given—4, sold 2. Aggregate tonnage entered, 2,891 5-95.

¶ Entered: 1 ship, 1 bark—2, and 1 in port. Cleared: 1 ship, and 1 in port. Aggregate tonnage entered, 1,401.   ** Entered and cleared: 1 bark. Tonnage, 640 70-95.

†† Entered: 1 ship, 1 bark—2, and 2 in port. Cleared: 1 bark, and 2 in port. Aggregate tonnage entered, 1,163.

‡‡ Entered: 1 ship, 1 bark—2, and 2 in port. Cleared: 1 ship, 2 barks—3, and 1 in port. Aggregate tonnage entered, 1,102.

§§ Entered: 1 ship, and 1 in port. Cleared: 1 ship, and 1 in port. Tonnage, 659.

Navigation and commerce of the United States with foreign countries—Italy.

COUNTRY, CONSULATE, NAME OF CONSUL, AND DATE OF RETURNS.	VESSELS.						CARGOES.					
	ENTERED.		CLEARED.		INWARD.			OUTWARD.		
	No.	Where from.	No.	Where for.	No.	Description.	Value.	No.	Description.	Value.
Quarter ended September 30, 1864.*	1	In port	1	New York	1	Before reported		1	Marble, rags, and straw	$21,771 70
	1	Malaga	1	do	1	Ballast		1	do	15,305 20
	1	New York	1	Marseilles	1	Tobacco and staves		1	Slaves	
	3		3		3			3		37,076 90
Messina.—F. W. Behn.										
Quarter ended December 31, 1863.†	2	Licata	1	New York	1	Not stated		1	200 cantars brimstone, 225 bales rags, 3,550 boxes fruit.	16,950 00
			1	Boston	1	do		1	1,000 cantars brimstone, 550 boxes lemons, 3,985 boxes oranges.	9,270 00
	1	Barcelona	1	New York	1	do		1	384 cantars brimstone, 75 bales rags, 50 bbls. canary seed, 350 bags filberts, 100 bags hemp-seed, 300 boxes and 300 bags almonds, 50 half-pipes olive oil, 115 bags walnuts, 3,409 boxes lemons.	17,845 00
	6	Marseilles	2	Boston	2	do		2	1,290 cantars brimstone, 200 bags seed, 225 bags filberts, 200 bags sumac, 40 bales rags, 8,980 boxes fruit.	21,330 00
	1	Philadelphia	1			do		1	640 do cantars brimstone, 300 boxes almonds, 50 bags hemp- seed, 111 bags walnuts, 10 bags canary seed, 41 saki! Sesame, 700 boxes citron 3,960 boxes oranges.	9,585 00
	2	Malaga	3	In port	3	do		3	In port	
			1	New York	1	do		1	512 cantars brims one, 100 boxes almonds, 100 bags filberts, 100 bags walnuts, 980 boxes lemons, 2,960 boxes oranges.	8,635 00
	3	Tangier	1	In port	1	do		1	In do	
			3	do	3	do 129,300 box shooks, 8,050 pine boards, 4180 large nails.	$16,700 00	3		

1864.‡

Port	No.	Destination	No.	Cargo (outward)		No.	Cargo	Value
							boxes and 75 bags almonds, 92 bags walnuts, 200 bags filberts, 13,405 boxes oranges, 2,100 boxes lemons, 10 cases licorice, 2 casks argols, 1 cask tartar, 18 jars essences, 12 casks pumice-stone.	
	2	New York	2	do		2	1,000 cantars brimstone, 90 cantars corkwood, 400 boxes and 49 bags almonds, 900 bags filberts, 7,560 boxes oranges, 1,700 boxes lemons, 130 bales rags, 50 bags canary seed, 25 casks olive oil.	31,800 00
	2	Boston	2	do		2	312 cantars brimstone, 250 bags sumac, 7,340 boxes oranges, 2,400 boxes lemons, 122,444 kilograms salt.	16,125 00
Cette		do	1	Ballast		1	250 bags walnuts, 1,300 cantars brimstone, 30 bags filberts, 50 boxes macaroni, 120 bales rags, 38 cantars corkwood, 1,100 boxes lemons, 4,259 boxes oranges.	16,875 00
		New York	1	do		1	7 cantars corkwood, 200 boxes almonds, 300 bags filberts, 250 bales rags, 1,250 boxes lemons, 3,750 boxes oranges.	17,500 00
Gibraltar	2	Boston	2	7,200 staves, 5,000 box shooks, 763 bbls. flour, 300 kegs nails, 120 pieces mahogany, 1 hhd. tobacco.	9,948 00	2	1,152 cantars brimstone, 550 bags sumac, 25 cantars corkwood, 50 bags walnuts, 7,630 boxes oranges, 1,900 boxes lemons, 5 casks argols, 12 jars essences.	22,425 90
Marseilles	4	New York	1	Ballast		1	460 cantars brimstone, 10 jars essence, 3 bags dried lemon-peel, 500 boxes lemons, 4,500 boxes oranges.	9,000 00
	2	Philadelphia	2	do		2	1,712 cantars brimstone, 200 bags sumac, 6 cantars corkwood, 2,725 boxes oranges, 1,843 boxes lemons, 50 bales rags, 50 bags hempseed, 30 cases licorice paste, 50 cases pumice-stone, 25 casks olive oil.	25,485 00
Tarragona	1	In port / Boston	1 / 1	do / do		1 / 1	In port: 448 cantars brimstone, 200 bags sumac, 310 boxes lemons, 3,305 boxes oranges.	10,250 00

* Entered and cleared: 1 ship, 2 barks—3. Aggregate tonnage entered, 937.
† Entered: 8 barks, 5 brigs, 1 schooner—14. Cleared: 4 barks, 2 brigs, 1 schooner—7, and 7 in port. Aggregate tonnage entered, 4,518.
‡ Entered: 1 ship, 14 barks, 3 brigs—18, and 7 in port. Cleared: 1 ship, 16 barks, 6 brigs—23, and 2 in port. Aggregate tonnage entered, 6,383.

Navigation and commerce of the United States with foreign countries—Italy.

COUNTRY, CONSULATE, NAME OF CONSUL, AND DATE OF RETURNS.	VESSELS				CARGOES					
	ENTERED		CLEARED		INWARD			OUTWARD		
	No.	Where from.	No.	Where for.	No.	Description.	Value.	No.	Description.	Value.
	1	Tarragona	1	New York	1	Ballast		1	1,500 boxes lemons, 3,027 boxes oranges.	$7,775 00
	1	Malta	1	Boston	1	..do..		1	700 cantars brimstone, 1,200 boxes lemons, 3,564 boxes oranges.	9,500 00
	1	Portland	1	..do..	1	38,000 box shooks.	$5,000 00	1	3 casks argols, 1,133 boxes lemons, 3,053 boxes oranges.	7,700 00
	3	Cadiz	2	New York	2	Ballast		2	969 cantars brimstone, 14 cantars corkwood, 300 boxes almonds, 75 bags walnuts, 100 bags filberts, 5,613 boxes oranges, 360 boxes lemons, 25 bbls. canary seed, 100 kgs lam. seed, 22 cases essences, 5 kgs dried.	21,740 00
	1	Naples	1	In port	1	..do..		1	512 cantars brimstone, 1,200 boxes lemons, 3,340 boxes oranges.	8,500 00
			1	New York	1	7,440 staves.	352 00	1		
	1	Smyrna	1	Boston	1	Ballast		1	2 cases brimstone, 60 bags walnuts, 70 bags walnuts, 300 boxes hams, 306 boxes oranges.	15,125 00
	1	Licata	1	..do..	1	..do..		1	1,600 cantars brimstone, 1 bag hemp-seed, 49 boxes almonds, 1,000 boxes lemons, 1,996 boxes oranges.	13,470 00
	25		25		25		15,300 00	25		264,100 00
Quarter ended June 30, 1864.	2	In port	2	Boston, New York	2	Before reported		2	1,247 boxes lemons, 3,753 boxes oranges, 800 cantars brimstone, 300 bags filberts, 15 cases essences, 3,868 boxes fruit.	22,290 00
	1	Smyrna	1	Palermo	1			1	Ballast	
	1	Malta	1	Boston	1			1	170 bags hempseed, 20 pipes lemon juice, 3,535 boxes fruit.	8,900 00
	1	Licata	1	Messina	1			1	1,600 cantars brimstone, 250 bales rags.	8,835 00
	5		5		5			5		40,025 00

	Port	No.	Cargo (entered)	Value	No.	Cargo (cleared)	Value
Quarter ended September 30, 1864.†							
1	Gibraltar	1	25 hhds. tobacco, 1,005 bbls. flour, 90 logs mahogany.	12,876 00	1	Ballast	
1	Licata						
1	Cette		In port.		2	Ballast	
3		3	Ballast	12,876 00	3		12,876 00
NAPLES—J. T. Howard.							
1st quarter	No report.						
Quarter ended Mar. 31, 1864.‡							
1	New York	1	300 barrels flour and stores.	2,100 00	1	Ballast	
1	Boston	1	1,200 tons coal.	12,000 00	1	do.	
1	Bath	1	1,800 tons railroad iron.		1	do.	
3		3		14,100 00	3		14,100 00
Quarter ended June 30, 1864.§							
1	New York	1	650 hhds. tobacco.		1	do.	
Quarter ended September 30, 1864.∥							
1	Cardiff	1	1,389 tons coal.	4,189 98	1	do.	
PALERMO—L. Monti.							
Quarter ended December 31, 1863.¶							
3	New York	3	Ballast		3	Brimstone, sumac, rags, oranges, &c.	73,745 00
1	Cette	1	do.		1	Lemons and sundries.	12,950 00
1	Bangor	{1	Philadelphia		{1	Sicilian produce.	8,725 00
3		3	41,915 bundles shooks.	11,905 00	2	In port.	
2	Marseilles	2	do.		2	Sicilian produce.	25,213 00
1	Valencia	1	do.		1	In port.	
1	Cadiz	1	do.		1	do.	
11		11		11,905 00	11		120,633 00
Quarter ended Mar. 31, 1864. **							
4	In port	2	Philadelphia		2	Before reported.	19,922 10

1,140 sacks brimstone, 200 bags sumac, 4 stars and 100 bags cork, 200 boxes shelled a. lmds, 94 bags walnuts, 110 segiliberia, 4,241 boxes oranges, 1,500 boxes lemons, 200 bales rags, 98 bags canary seed, 33 bags hemp-seed.

* Entered: 3 barks, and 2 in port. Cleared: 5 barks. Aggregate tonnage entered, 563. † Entered: 3 barks. Cleared: 1 bark, and 2 in port. Agg. tonnage entered, 1,118.
‡ Entered and cleared: 2 ships, 1 bark—3. Aggregate tonnage entered, 2,152. § Entered and cleared: 1, class not given. Tonnage, 699.
∥ Entered and cleared: 1 ship, Tonnage, 745. ¶ Entered: 1 ship, 8 barks, 2 brigs—11. Cleared: 1 ship, 4 barks, 2 brigs—7, and 4 in port. Aggregate tonnage entered, 4,884.
** Entered: 1 ship, 8 barks, 1 brig—10, and 4 in port. Cleared: 1 ship, 11 barks, 1 brig—13, and 1 in port. Aggregate tonnage entered, 4,302.

Navigation and commerce of the United States with foreign countries—Italy.

COUNTRY, CONSULATE, NAME OF CONSUL, AND DATE OF RETURNS.	VESSELS				CARGOES					
	ENTERED		CLEARED		INWARD			OUTWARD		
	No.	Where from.	No.	Where for.	No.	Description.	Value.	No.	Description.	Value.
Quarter ended Mar. 31, 1864—Continued.	4		2	New York...	2	Before reported.		2	2,940 cantars brimstone, 2,091 bags sumac, 404 boxes shelled almonds, 50 bags nuts, 136 bags walnuts, 189 bags filberts, 8,060 ubs oranges, 2,358 bxs. lemons, 200 bales rags, 71 bags canary seed.	$33,996 60
		Licata...	1	Philadelphia...	1	Ballast...		1	600 stars brimstone, 400 bags 1 antr. 17 ars corked, 100 bales rags, 200 boxes shelled almonds, 150 bags filberts, 200 boxes oranges, 800 boxes lemons.	22,132 51
	1		1	Boston....	1	...do...		1	200 cantars brimstone, 1,500 bags sumac, 50 pipes wine, 3,200 bxs. oranges, 30 bxs. lemons.	19,263 13
	1		2	New York....	2	...do...		2	250 cantars brimstone, 2,300 bags sumac, 14 cantars corkwood, 250 bags almonds, 250 bags filberts, 20 pipes wine, 100 bx. shelled almonds, 5,840 bxs oranges, 2,710 bxs. lemons.	32,375 96
	1	Bangor...	1	New York....	1	Shooks....	$5,500 00	1	500 tars brimstone, 2,594 bxs. oranges, 1,660 boxes lemons.	6,371 54
	1	Cette....	1	...do....	1	Ballast...		1	1,580 cantars brimstone, 1,000 bags sumac, 175 bales rags, 100 bags hempseed, 250 bags almonds, 200 bags filberts, 50 bags canary seed, 120 boxes shelled almonds, 345 boxes oranges, 1,985 boxes lemons.	18,245 51
	1	Marseilles....	1	...do....	1	...do....		1	540 cantars brimstone, 500 bags sumac, 175 bales rags, 50 bags hempseed, 100 boxes maccaroni, 2,042 boxes oranges, 2,061 bxs. lemons.	15,465 16
	1	Trieste....	1	...do....	1	...do....		1	500 bags sumac, 100 bxs. shelled almonds, 53 bags almonds, 100 bags filberts, 50 bags canary seed, 100 bags hempseed, 2,150 bxs. oranges, 1,850 bxs. lemons.	10,621 78

Smyrna	2	Boston	1	...do...	1	1,050 bags sumac, 30 cantars corkwood, 100 bxs. maccaroni, 3,000 bxs. oranges, 2,000 bxs. lemons	13,325 17
	14	In port	1	In port	1		191,718 76
	14		14		14		5,500 00

Quarter ended June 30, 1864.*

Licata	1	New York	1	Ballast	1	75 bales rags, 2,500 bxs. oranges, 1,500 boxes lemons	10,750 57
Malta	2	Boston	1	...do...	1	290 bags sumac, 28 bags cork, 255 bags filberts, 10 casks argols, 63 pipes wine, 27 jars lemon oil, 100 bags hempseed, 50 boxes maccaroni, 400 boxes oranges, 2,960 boxes lemons	18,721 20
	1	New York	1	...do...	1	1,920 cantars brimstone, 550 bags sumac, 50 bags corks, 94 bags almonds, 39 bags filberts, 21 pipes wine, 14 casks lemon juice, 28 bags canary seed, 101 bags hempseed, 2,560 boxes lemons	16,821 71
Cadiz	1	...do...	1	...do...	1	500 cantars brimstone, 800 bags sumac, 100 bags almonds, 163 bags filberts, 24 pipes wine, 100 bags hempseed, 1,049 boxes oranges, 2,241 boxes lemons	15,725 87
Messina	1	...do...	1	...do...	1	12 pipes wine, 1,735 bxs. oranges, 2,560 boxes lemons	7,719 30
Fayal	1	Boston	1	Tobacco, petroleum, and lumber	1	600 cantars brimstone, 550 bags sumac, 149 bags hempseed, 50 boxes maccaroni, 295 boxes oranges, 3,159 boxes lemons	14,723 19	12,101 83
Barcelona	1	New York	1	Ballast	1	1,290 cantars brimstone, 1,750 bags sumac, 11 cantars corkwood, 240 bales rags, 29 casks argols, 18 casks lemon juice, 250 bags canary seed, 489 boxes oranges, 1,089 boxes lemons	32,374 40
Marseilles	1	...do...	1	...do...	1	1,290 cantars brimstone, 550 bags sumac, 50 bales rags, 50 pipes wine, 50 bags canary seed, 93 boxes maccaroni, 30 casks olive oil, 214 bxs. oranges, 1,586 bxs. lemons	16,089 05
	8	New York	8		8		14,723 19	130,303 93
Licata	1	New York	1	Ballast	1	Brimstone, sumac, and rags	32,882 00

Quarter ended September 30, 1864.†

*Entered: 7 barks, 1 brig—8. Cleared: 7 barks, 1 brig—8. Aggregate tonnage entered, 2,946.

†Entered and cleared: 1 bark. Tonnage, 536.

Navigation and commerce of the United States with foreign countries—Italy—Turkey.

COUNTRY, CONSULATE, NAME OF CONSUL, AND DATE OF RETURNS.	VESSELS				CARGOES					
	ENTERED		CLEARED		INWARD			OUTWARD		
	No.	Where from.	No.	Where for.	No.	Description.	Value.	No.	Description.	Value.
TARANTO.—A. J. De Zepi. 1st, 2d, 3d, and 4th quarters		No arrivals		No departures						
GIRGENTI.—L. Granet. (Palermo consulate.) 1st, 2d, and 3d quarters		No reports								
Quarter ended September 30, 1864.*	1	Smyrna	1	Messina	1	Ballast			} Brimstone	$10,880 00
	1	Genoa	1	New York	1	do		2		
	2		2		2					10,880 00
TRAPANI.—O. Tubino. (Palermo consulate.) 1st, 2d, and 3d quarters		No reports								
Quarter ended September 30, 1864.†	2	Genoa	2	Boston	2	Ballast				
	1	Barcelona	1	New York	1	do				
	1	Valencia	1	New York	1	do			16,579 salms salt	10,695 06
	1	Malta	1	Portland	1	do				
	2	Naples	1	Bath	1	do				
			1	Boston	1	do				
	7		7		7			7		10,695 06
LICATA.—J. Mastroeni. (Palermo consulate.) 1st, 2d, and 3d quarters		No reports								
Quarter ended September 30, 1864.‡	1	Malta	1	New York, via Palermo.						
	1	Aragona	1	do.						
	1	Barcelona	1	New York, via Barcelona.						
	2	Cadiz	2	do.						
	1	Smyrna	1	New York, via Palermo.						

TURKEY.

BEIRÛT.—J. A. Johnson.

	Entered		Cleared					Remarks	Value
1st, 2d, and 3d quarters.	4	Marseilles	1	Boston, via Palermo, via...					
	1	Trieste	3	New York, via Palermo, via					
	1	Cette	1	Boston, via Palermo, via					
	1	Malaga	1	New York, via Palermo, via					
			1	...do...					
	13		13				13	30,380 cantars brimstone	60,780 00
							13		60,780 00

Quarter ended September 30, 1864.§ — No arrivals since Sept. 30, 1862.

CONSTANTINOPLE.—C. W. Goddard.

	Entered			Cleared		Value		Remarks
	1	Boston	1	Boston	6,937 pounds cordage, 8,600 pieces boards, 250 pieces furniture.	$10,380 99	1	Went to Cyprus for cargo.

Quarter ended December 31, 1863.‖

Entered			Cleared				Remarks
2	Gudawa, Russia	8,278 railroad sleepers, 10,000 staves	2	Marseilles	Same as inward cargo	2	do
1	Galatz	2,235 quarters barley	1	Cork	...do...	1	
3			3			3	

Quarter ended March 31, 1864.¶

Entered			Cleared		Remarks
1	Malta	Ballast	1	Gudawa	1 Ballast
1			1		3

Quarter ended June 30, 1864.*

Entered			Cleared			Remarks
1	Barletta	Ballast	1	Kertch	Ballast	1 Ballast
1	Port Said	...do...	1	Trieste	...do...	1 ...do...
2			2			2

Quarter ended September 30, 1864.††

Entered			Cleared			Remarks
1	Alexandria	Ballast	1	Redout Kale	Ballast	1 Ballast
1	Redoot Kale	18,500 railroad sleepers	1	Marseilles	18,500 railroad sleepers	1 18,500 railroad sleepers
1	Taganrog	3,408 quarters wheat	1	Marseilles	3,408 quarters wheat	1 3,408 quarters wheat
3			3			3

CYPRUS.—T. J. Barclay.

1st, 2d, and 3d quarters. — No reports.

...ended September 30, 1864.‡‡

Entered			Cleared		Remarks
1	Not stated	Not stated	1	Not stated	1 Not stated

* Entered and cleared: 2 barks. Aggregate tonnage entered, 592.
† Entered and cleared: 10 barks, 2 schooners, 1 ship—13. Aggregate tonnage entered, 5,876.
‡ Entered and cleared: 2 barks, 1 brig—3. Aggregate tonnage entered, 1,066.
§ Entered and cleared: 2 barks. Aggregate tonnage entered, 1,015.
Cleared: 1, class not stated. Tonnage, not stated.
‖ Entered and cleared: 6 ships, 1 bark—7. Aggregate tonnage entered, 6,253 15-95.
¶ Entered and cleared: 1 bark. Tonnage, 479 79-95.
** Entered and cleared: 1 ship. Tonnage, 1,100.
†† Entered and cleared: 1 bark, 2 ships—3. Aggregate tonnage entered, 2,395 34-95.

Navigation and commerce of the United States with foreign countries—Turkey—Liberia—Muscat.

COUNTRY, CONSULATE, NAME OF CONSUL, AND DATE OF RETURNS.	VESSELS				CARGOES					
	ENTERED		CLEARED		INWARD			OUTWARD		
	No.	Where from.	No.	Where for.	No.	Description.	Value.	No.	Description.	Value.
GALATZ.—F. Wippermann.										
Quarter ended December 31, 1861.	1	Port Said	1	England	1	Ballast		1	Barley	$7,000 00
2d quarter.		No report								
3d and 4th quarters.		No arrivals		No departures						
SMYRNA.—J. Bing.										
Quarter ended ?ber 31, 1863.†	3	In port	3	Boston	3	Before reported		3	Figs, wool, gums, &c	148,000 00
	1	Boston	1	Boston	1	Rum, brandy, canvas, &c	28,000 00	1	Ballast	
	4		4		4		28,000 00	4		148,000 00
Quarter ended March 31, 1864.‡	3	Boston	1	Sicily	1	Gunny cloth, rum, lamps, domestics, furniture.	35,000 00	1	Ballast	
			1	Palermo	1	Alcohol, gunny cloth, glassware, petroleum, cotton seeds and glue.	20,000 00	1	Wool, gum, and spges	52,000 00
			1	..do	1	Gunny cloth, flour, cotton gin, petroleum, and furniture.	30,000 00	1	Ballast	
	1	Boston and Malta			1	Gunny cloth, staves, missionary goods.	20,000 00	1	..do	
	4		4		4		105,000 00	4		52,000 00
Quarter ended June 30, 1864.§	1	Boston	1	Sicily	1	Gunny cloth, coal oil, chairs, furniture, glassware, pails, brooms, and tubs.	15,240 00	1	Ballast	
J. Griffin.										
Quarter ended September 30, 1864.‖	2	Boston	1	In port	1	Rum, lumber, bricks	9,500 00	1	In port	
			1	In port	1	Gunny cloth, furniture, petroleum, ironware.	12,000 00	1	..do	
	2		2		2		21,500 00	2		
LIBERIA. MONROVIA.—J. Seys.										
From January 1, 1864, to February 22, 1864.¶	1	In port	1	Boston	1	Before reported		1	17,758 gallons palm oil, 1.00† lbs. ivory, 947 lbs. sugar.	6,046 79

A. Hansen.

From February 22, 1864, to March 31, 1864.

					Outward cargo			Inward cargo	
New York	1	Grand Bass	1		Tobacco, provisions, &c	26,000 00	1	Part of inward cargo	20,000 00
		Grand Bass	1		Palm oil	26,000 00	1	Inward cargo	20,000 00
	2		2				2		

Quarter ended June 30, 1864.††

Basas	1	Boston	1	Outward cargo, having come in to finish loading		1	Palm oil, ivory, sugar, gum copal, camwood, coffee.	9,323 27
New York	2	Basas	1	Tobacco, provisions, and lumber	10,000 00	1	Inward cargo, coffee.	12,000 00
		New York	1	Outward cargo, having come in to finish loading.		1	Palm oil, wood, sugar, ivory, coffee.	
	3		3			3		21,323 27

Quarter ended September 30, 1864.‡‡

New York	1	Grand Bass	1	Provisions, tobacco, rum, dry goods.	10,000 00 / 17,000 00	1	Part of inward cargo.	12,000 00

MUSCAT.

ZANZIBAR.—W. E. Hines.

Quarter ended December 31, 1863.§§

New York, via Cape Town.	1	Bombay.	1	400 barrels flour, 24 cases shoes, 500 tins crackers, 300 oars, 95 scale-beams, 1 bbl. lanterns, 90 boxes candles, 92 cases clocks, 4 sewing machines, &c.	8,850 00	1	396 barrels flour, 24 cases shoes, 975 oars, 90 boxes candles, 51 cases clocks, 4 sewing machines, 11 pieces ivory, &c.	6,452 00

2d quarter.

No report.

Quarter ended June 30, 1864.‖‖

Muscat.	1	Providence.	1	702 pairs shoes	874 38	1	3,000 frails dates	10,316 60
				1 trunk, 359 clocks	919 00		125 pieces ivory	13,672 40
				3,000 frails dates	10,316 60		503 pieces ebony	6,912 47
							5,794 hides	6,049 43
							197 bales pepper	1,989 19
							1,167 packages sugar	639 25
							140 bundles coir jums	281 03
							237 pieces ivory, 403 pieces Scrivellos ivory, 11 pieces Glendi ivory.	38,926 15
	1	Aden.	1	100 boxes tobacco	7,000 00	1	In port.	
Boston.				125 dozen chairs	780 00			
				100 boxes sugar	2,800 00			
				500 kegs paint	1,000 00			
				1,200 tins biscuit	2,400 00			
				100 boxes clocks	2,000 00			

* Entered and cleared: 1 bark. Tonnage entered, 382 59-95.
† Entered and cleared: 4 barks. Aggregate tonnage entered, 1,574.
‡ Entered: 2 barks. Cleared: 2 barks in port.
§ Entered and cleared: 2 barks. Aggregate tonnage entered: 321 75-95.
‖ Entered and cleared: 2 bark. Tonnage: 265 0-95.
¶ Entered: 2 barks. Cleared: 1 bark, 1 in port—2. Aggregate tonnage entered, 911 93-95.

¶ Entered: 1 bark, and 3 in port—4. Cleared: 4 barks. Tonnage: 487.
† Entered and cleared: 1 bark. Tonnage, 279.
‡ Entered: 1 in port. Cleared: 1 bark. Tonnage before reported.
§ Entered and cleared: 2 barks, 1 brig—3. Aggregate tonnage entered, 669 13-95.
‖ Entered and cleared: 1 bark. Tonnage, 416 49-95.

Navigation and commerce of the United States with foreign countries—Muscat—Siam—China.

COUNTRY, CONSULATE, NAME OF CONSUL, AND DATE OF RETURNS.	VESSELS.				CARGOES.					
	ENTERED.		CLEARED.		INWARD.			OUTWARD.		
	No.	Where from.	No.	Where for.	No.	Description.	Value.	No.	Description.	Value.
Quarter ended June 30, 1864—Continued.						150 barrels flour	$1,500 00			
						4 dozen scale beams.	900 00			
						boards, boxes, &c.	5,800 00			
						200 boxes domestics	25,000 00			
	2		2		2		60,989 92	2		$77,766 00
Quarter ended September 30, 1864.*	1	In port	1	Aden	1	Before reported		1	57 tons ebony, 751 bags gum copal, 500 bags cloves, 600 frs. clove stems, 24,250 hides, 3,180 goat skins, 5 carriages, 60 bales cottons, 75 boxes tobacco, 500 frs. ivory, and sundries.	54,357 00
	1	Aden	1	Salem	1	57 tons ebony, 751 bags gum copal, 200 bags cloves, 600 frs. clove stems, 24,250 hides, 3,180 goat skins, ivory, goat skins, coffee, gum myrrh.	39,223 50	1	57½ tons ebony, 1,502 frs. gum copal, 203 bags cloves, 5,094 pounds ivory, 600 frs. clove stems, 24,250 hides, 3,180 goat skins, 398 coir jums, 450 frs. stems, 498 frs. peppers, 832 goat skins, 74 frs. gum myrrh, 700-pounds turtle shell, 3,328 Scrivelloes ivory, 8 frs. ivory.	55,946 33
	2		2		2		39,223 50	2		110,303 33
SIAM.										
BANGKOK.—*S. W. Virgin.*										
Quarter ended December 31, 1863.†	10	Hong Kong	3	Sold	3	Ballast		3	Sold	
			2	Singapore	2	do		2	Ballast	
	1	Shanghai	5	In port	5	do		5	In port	
	1	Montevideo	1	Sold	1	do		1	Sold	
	1	Put back	1	In port	1	do		1	In port	
			1	do	1	do		1	do	
	13		13		13			13		
Quarter ended March 31, 1864.‡	1	Montevideo	1	In port	1	Ballast		1	In port	
	1	Saigon	1	Saigon	1	do		1	Ballast	
	6	Hong Kong	1	Sold	1	do		1	Sold · took Siamese flag.	

	No.	Ports			Cargo	No.	Value	Value
		In port	3		9 cases sundries	1		
		Singapore	1		do	2		
		Hong Kong	1		do	1		
		In port	2		do	2		12,000 00
Shanghai	2				Ballast			
					8,000 piculs rice			
Quarter ended June 30, 1864,§	6	In port	10			10		12,000 00
		Singapore	1			1		7,800 00
		Shanghai	1		1,493 piculs white sugar	1		13,639 60
					2,800 piculs sapan wood, 5,798 bags rice, 723 bags rosewood, 98 bags dried fruit.			
In port	6	Sold	2		Sold	2		25,566 00
		Hong Kong	2		In port	1		
					8,080 piculs rice, 121 piculs tin, 3,172 piculs sapan wood, 81 piculs cotton, sundries.	1		
		St. Thomas	1		125 tons coal, 6 kegs tobacco, 15 barrels bread, 18 cases claret.	1	2,340 00	46,048 98
Hong Kong	1				27,366 bags rice, 2,952 bags sugar, 246 bags stick-lac, 15 boxes gamboge, 5 boxes gum Benjamin, 1,815 buffalo hides, 4,506 buffalo horns, 7,036 sticks sapan wood.			
		In port	1		Ballast	1		
		do	1		do	2		
Shanghai	1							
Singapore	1							
	8	In port	9			9	2,340 00	93,074 56
		Hong Kong	2		Before reported	3		89,188 00
Quarter ended September 30, 1864,‖	3	San Francisco	1		4,200 piculs rice, 1,200 piculs sepan wood, 100 piculs paddy, 3,480 feet teak plank, 210 piculs teak timber, 281 piculs rosewood.			
		New York	1		100 tons coal, 6 boxes merchandise	1	1,406 00	26,317 00
Hong Kong	3				17,460 83-100 piculs rice, 7104 piculs sapan wood, 10 rolls matting, camphor wood, and sundries.	1		
		In port	2		Ballast	2		108,505 00
	6		6		In port	6	1,406 00	

CHINA.

AMOY.—O. R. Bradford.

	No.	Port			Cargo	No.		Value
Chefoo	1	Hong Kong	1		Chinese cargo	1		50,789 00
Newchwang	1	do	1		3,500 piculs bean-cake	1		9,900 00
					Ballast			
					do			

* Entered: 1 bark, and 1 in port. Cleared: 2 barks. Tonnage, 495 51-95.
† Entered: 5 barks, 7 ships, 1 schooner—13. Cleared: 3 barks, 3 ships—6, and 7 in port. Aggregate tonnage entered, 9,715.
‡ Entered: 1 steamer, 2 barks, 4 ships, 1 brig, 1 boat—9. Cleared: 1 steamer, 1 bark, 1 ship—3, 1 sold, and 6 in port. Aggregate tonnage entered, 5,689 21-95.
§ Entered: 2 ships, 1 brig—3, and 6 in port. Cleared: 4 ships, 2 sold, and 3 in port. Aggregate tonnage entered, 2,341 38-95.
‖ Entered: 1 ship, 9 barks—?, and 3 in port. Cleared: 3 ships, 1 brig—4, and 2 in port. Aggregate tonnage entered, 1,555 88-95.
¶ Entered: 2 barks, 1 ship—3. Cleared: 2 barks, and 1 in port. Aggregate tonnage entered, 1,579 24-95.

Navigation and commerce of the United States with foreign countries—China.

COUNTRY, CONSULATE, NAME OF CONSUL, AND DATE OF RETURNS	VESSELS				CARGOES					
	ENTERED		CLEARED		INWARD			OUTWARD		
	No.	Where from.	No.	Where for.	No.	Description.	Value.	No.	Description.	Value.
Quarter ended December 31, 1863—Continued.	1	Hong Kong	1	In port	1	Chinese assorted cargo	$13,949 00	1	In port	
	3		3		3		74,631 00	3		
Quarter end of March 31, 1864.*	1	In port	1	Hong Kong	1	Before reported		1	Ballast	
	1	Foochow	1	Sold	1	Ballast		1	Sold; took British flag	
	1	Hong Kong	1	In port				1	In port	
	3		3		3			3		
Quarter ended June 30, 1864.†	1	In port	1	Shanghai	1	Before reported	37,540 00	1	Ballast	
	1	Shanghai	1	Singapore	1	Chinese cottons and linens	63,698 00	1	...do	
	1	Swatow	1	In port	1	...do		1	In port	
	3	Newchwang	1	Swatow		Ballast		1	Ballast	
			1	Talienwhan	3	Bean-cake and general cargo	33,910 00	1	General cargo	$13,050 00
			1	Newchwang				1	Assorted Chinese cargo	7,390 00
			1	Chefoo				1	Ballast	
	7		7		7		135,148 00	7		20,250 00
Quarter ended September 30, 1864.‡	1	In port	1	Foochow	1	Before reported		1	454,639 lbs. tea	92,088 00
	2	Newchwang	2	In port	2	General Chinese cargo	33,456 00	2	In port	
	4	Shanghai	1	Honland's Isl'd	1	Ballast		1	Ballast	
			1	Foochow	1	...do		1	General Chinese cargo	24,161 00
	1	Swatow	1	Shanghai	1	General Chinese cargo	26,550 00	1	In port	
			1	In port	1	For repairs		1	...do	
			1	...do	1	Ballast				
	8		8		8		60,006 00	8		116,849 00
TIENTSIN—J. N. Limeburgher. 1st, 2d, and 3d quarters.		No reports								
Quarter ended September 30, 1864.§	1	Foochow	1	Foochow	1	General cargo		1	General cargo	
	2	Swatow	2	Newchwang	2	...do		2	Cotton	
	3		3		3			3		

CANTON.—O. H. Perry.							
Quarter ended December 31, 1863.‖	3	Hong Kong		2	Ballast		
	4	Running on the river.		1	Ratans and sundries		
				4	Passengers, &c.		
Quarter ended March 31, 1864.¶	7			7			
3d quarter	1	Hong Kong		1	Ballast		
Quarter ended September 30, 1864.**		No report.					
	3	Hong Kong		3	Ballast		
	4	Running on the river.		4	Not stated		
FOOCHOWFOO.—W. H. Carpenter.	7			7			
Quarter ended December 31, 1863.††	7	In port		4	Before reported	60,397 00	4	Spars and lumber	47,350 00
				3	do		2	General cargo	7,570 00
	21	Shanghai		3	Nankeens, cotton, and general cargo		3	Ballast	
				14	Ballast	63,600 00	14	Spars, paper, lumber, poles, nankeens, and general cargo.	854,140 00
	2	Hong Kong		2	General cargo and medicine		2	General cargo	128,307 00
	2	In port		2	In port	115,850 00	2	In port	79,650 00
	2	Ningpo		2	General cargo and sundries	119,480 00	2	General cargo	192,800 00
	3	Hong Kong		3	do		3	General cargo and sundries	192,800 00
	1	N. Port		1	Ballast		1	Lumber	5,000 00
	1	Kanagawa		1	do		1	Sundries	13,000 00
	1	Chefoo		1	do		1	Sugar, &c.	20,555 00
	36			36		252,397 00	36		748,372 00
Quarter ended March 31, 1864.‡‡	9	Ningpo		2	Ballast	71,628 00	2	General cargo and poles	3,473 00
	8	Shanghai		5	do		8	10,595 poles, paper, and lumber	94,400 00
				3	Nankeens, general cargo, &c.	8,900 00	1	Ballast	
	1	Amoy		1	General cargo			Sold	
§§	1	Sold		1	Put back				

* Entered: 1 ship, 1 steamer—2, and 1 in port. Cleared: 1 ship, 1 bark—2, and 1 in port. Aggregate tonnage entered, 1,296 96-95.
† Entered: 1 ship, 4 barks, 1 brig—6, and 1 in port. Cleared: 1 ship, 4 barks, 1 brig—6, and 1 in port. Aggregate tonnage entered, 2,887 54-95.
‡ Entered: 1 ship, 4 barks, 1 brig, 1 steamer—7, and 1 in port. Cleared: 2 ships, 1 bark, 1 brig—4, and 4 in port. Aggregate tonnage entered, 3,027 39-95.
§ Entered and cleared: 3, class not known. Aggregate tonnage entered, 1,165.
¶ Entered and sued: 2 barks, 1 ship, 4 steamers—7. Aggregate tonnage entered, 3,955 13-95.
‖ Entered and cleared: 1 ship. Tonnage, 1,357 19-95. Entered and cleared: 2 ships, 1 bark, 4 steamers—7. Aggregate tonnage entered, 4,090 22-95. Aggregate
†† Entered: 9 ships, 19 barks, 6 steamer, 1 boat—29, and 7 in port. Cleared: 11 ships, 19 barks, 6 steamer, 1 schooner, 3 boats, 1 brig—34, and 2 in port. Aggregate
tonnage entered, 22,910.
‡‡ Entered: 6 ships, 10 barks, 2 lorchas, 10 barks, 1 steamer, 1 schooner—30, and 12 in port. Cleared: 18 barks, 8 ships, 2 steamers, 2 lorchas, 1 schooner—31, and 1 sold. Aggregate
tonnage ind. 15,644.
§§ And cargo and tonnage not reported in the previous quarter.

Navigation and commerce of the United States with foreign countries—China.

COUNTRY, CONSULATE, NAME OF CONSUL, AND DATE OF RETURNS.	VESSELS.					CARGOES.						
	ENTERED.		CLEARED.		INWARD.			OUTWARD.				
	No.	Where from.	No.	Where for.	No.	Description.	Value.	No.	Description.	Value.		
Quarter ended March 31, 1864—Continued.	14	Shanghai	14	Shanghai	5	Silks and nankeens	$83,960 00	12	Poles and lumber	$49,422 00		
	3	Ningpo	3	Ningpo	9	Ballast		2	Ballast	13,270 00		
	1	Kanagawa	1	Shanghai	3	...do		3	Paper and lumber	50,000 00		
	2	Ports and tonnage not given.	2	New York	1	...do		1	2,450 picols tea	8,548 00		
					2			2	Poles and lumber			
	39		39		39		164,488 00	32		219,275 00		
A. L. Clarke.												
Quarter ended June 30, 1864.*	4	In port	4	Shanghai	{ 11	Nankeens	} $35,000 00	4	Bean-cake, 12,235 poles, sugar	28,800 00		
	1	Ningpo	1	...do	{ 3	Before reported		1	Sugar	10,000 00		
	13	Shanghai	13	...do	1	Ballast		13	Poles, paper, and sugar	31,040 00		
	1	Hong Kong	1	Fewchwang	3	Nankeens	36,300 00	1	paper	700 00		
					1	Ballast						
	19		19		19		91,300 00	19		70,540 00		
Quarter ended September 30, 1864.†	1	Tientsin	1	Chefoo	1	Ice	4,000 00	1	Paper	10,519 00		
	10	Shanghai	8	Shanghai	4	Lumber, 1,215 bs. nankeens and cotton	} 42,000 00	8	Poles	57,300 00		
					1	Ballast		{	850,700 lbs. tea	202,920 00		
					1	...do		1	Ballast			
	1	Ningpo	1	New York	1	300 picols bones	600 00	1	Assorted cargo	1,200 00		
	1	Amoy	1	Not stated	1	Ballast		1	251,900 lbs. tea	50,000 00		
	1	Chefoo	1	New York	1	Sundries	18,000 00	1	Paper	32,000 00		
			1	Chefoo								
	14		14		14		64,600 00	14		342,939 00		
KIUKIANG.—H. G. Bridges.												
Quarter ended December 31, 1863.‡	2	Shanghai	1	Shanghai	1	General cargo		1	Tea and general cargo			
			1	Chinkiang	1	...do		1	...do			
	2		2		2			2				
Quarter ended March 31, 1864.‡	1	Shanghai	1	Shanghai	1	General cargo		1	General cargo			
Quarter ended June 30, 1864.‡	1	Shanghai	1	Shanghai	1	General cargo		1	General cargo			

Quarter ended September 30, 1864.‡

NINGPO.—W. P. Mangum.

Quarter ended December 31, 1864.§

	42 Shanghai		42 Hankow and Shanghai		42 General cargo		42 Tea and general cargo	
	In port	92	In port	5	Before reported		In port	5
			Sold	3	do		Sold	3	13,504 00
			Shanghai	12	do		General cargo	11	
	Foochow	5	Hong Kong	1	do		Ballast	1	35,000 00
			Hankow	1			Cotton	1	1,000 00
			Sibul	1	do		General cargo	1	10,113 00
	Shanghai	46	Sold	4	Sugar and general cargo	19,425 00	do	3	
			In port	1	Ballast		In port	1	
			Shanghai	27	General cargo	99,092 00	Ballast	1	
			Foochow	15	do	31,095 00	General cargo	27	40,700 00
			Hankow	1	Ballast		do	14	31,004 00
			Kinkiang	1	General cargo	640 00	Ballast	1	
			Sold	1	do	650 00	General cargo	1	2,000 00
	Hankow	1	In port	1	do	2,666 00	do	1	1,200 00
	Simi	2	Hankow	1	do	3,648 00	In port	1	
			Hong Kong	1	11,038 piculs rice	34,000 00	Sold	1	2,176 00
	Ningpo	1	Shanghai	1	General cargo		600 bags cotton	1	19,800 00
			In port	1	Ballast	1,900 00	Ballast	1	
							In port	1	
		77		**77**		**195,046 00**		**77**	**156,497 00**

Quarter ended March 31, 1864.‖

	42 Shanghai		42 Hankow and Shanghai		42 General cargo		42 Tea and general cargo	
	In port	8	Sold	4	Before reported		Sold; oak Chinese flag	4	
			Shanghai	3	do		General cargo	1	1,250 00
			Tsingtsing	1	do		Ballast	1	
	Shanghai	29	Shanghai	21	Rice and general cargo	109,825 00	Pig, ash, and general cargo	21	63,915 10
			Foochow	1		1,200 00	...took Chinese flag	1	1,000 00
			Sold	1	Coal cargo	6,500 00			
	Hong Kong	1	In port	6	Opium and general cargo	20,625 00	In port	6	
	Foochow	6	Shanghai	1	6,485 bags rice	20,455 00	Ballast	1	
			Foochow	1	Lumber and 1 iper	8,281 00	Bean cake	2	520 00
			Shanghai	2	Paper and general cargo	9,730 00	Oranges and olives	2	3,300 00
			Kanagawa	1	do	10,000 00	Ballast	1	
	Hankow	4	Sold	1	General cargo	8,000 00	Sold; took English flag	1	
			Shanghai	1	Drugs and general cargo	7,009 00	Copper, cash	3	2,425 00
	Sea	1	In port	2	General ego	12,000 00	In port	1	
			do		Flag-store	65 00	do	1	
		49		**49**		**213,710 00**		**49**	**72,610 00**

* Entered: 8 ships, 1 brig, 4 barks, 2 schooners—15, and 4 in port. Cleared: 11 ships, 3 barks, 1 brig, and 2 schooners—19. Aggregate tonnage entered, 10,016.
† Entered and cleared: 2 barks, 2 schooners, 9 ships, and 1 lorchin—14. Aggregate tonnage entered, 9,1[..].
‡ Class of vessels and tonnage not given.
§ Entered: 7 steamers, 44 boats, 1 ship, 1 brig, 2 barks—55, and 22 in port. Cleared: 7 steamers, 41 boats, 1 brig, 1 ship, 14 class not given—65, 4 sold, and 8 in port. Aggregate tonnage entered, 5,756.
‖ Entered: 6 steamers, 3 barks, 32 boats—41, and 8 in port. Cleared: 5 steamer, 3 barks, 26 boats—34, 6 sold, and 9 in port. Aggregate tonnage entered, 5,091.

Navigation and commerce of the United States with foreign countries—China.

COUNTRY, CONSULAT, NAME OF CONSUL, AND DATE OF RETURNS.	VESSELS				CARGOES					
	ENTERED		CLEARED		INWARD			OUTWARD		
	No.	Where from.	No.	Where for.	No.	Description.	Value.	No.	Description.	Value.
NINGPO.—*E. C. Lord.* Quarter ended June 30, 1864*.	9	In port...	6	Shanghai...	6	Before reported...		6	General cargo...	$47,129 00
			1	Hankow...	1	do		1	do	3,690 00
			2	In port...	2	do		2	In port...	
	35	Shanghai...	31	Shanghai...	24	Rice, opium, and general cargo.	$139,290 00	21	Tea, sugar, copper, cash, &c.	150,519 00
			1	Hankow...	1	General cargo...	5,000 00	1	General cargo...	3,000 00
			3	In port...	10	Ballast...		4	In port...	
	5	Hankow...	1	Shanghai...	1	1,400 piculs gypsum.	650 00	9	Ballast...	
								1	Salt fish...	467 00
			4	In port...	4	General cargo...	14,458 00	4	In port...	
	49		49		49		159,398 00	49		204,798 00
Quarter ended September 30, 1864.†	10	In port...	4	Shanghai...	4	Before reported...		4	General cargo...	11,400 00
			3	Hankow...	3	do		3	do	11,000 00
			3	In port...	3	do		3	In port...	
	3	Hankow...	1	Shanghai...	1	General cargo...	6,253 00	1	General cargo...	9,500 00
			2	In port...	1	do	6,614 00	2	In port...	
	1	Tientsin...	1	Foochow...	1	Bones...	2,500 00	1	do	500 00
	77	Shanghai...	73	Shanghai...	73	Opium, treasure, and general cargo.	908,371 00	73	Silk, tea, treas'rs, and gen'l cargo.	1,371,528 00
			2	Sold...	2	Lumber and general cargo.	6,300 00	2	Sold...	
			2	In port...	2	General cargo...	3,000 00	2	In port...	
	91		91		91		1,397,388 00	91		1,397,388 00
SWATOW.—*J. C. A. Wingate.* Quarter ended December 31, 1863;	6	In port...	1	Shanghai...	1	Before reported...		1	8,925 piculs sugar...	65,980 00
			2	Hong Kong...	2	do		2	Ballast...	
			2	Chefoo...	2	do		2	Paper, sugar, and sundries.	99,976 00
	1	Shanghai...	1	Singapore...	1	do		1	Sundries...	18,000 00
	3	Chefoo...	1	Hong Kong...	2	Cotton...	25,000 00	1	Ballast...	
			2	In port...	2	Bean cakes, &c...	33,600 00	2	In port...	
			1	Sold...	1	do	14,050 00	1	Sold...	
	10		10		10		72,650 00	10		113,556 00
Quarter ended March 31, 1864.§	2	In port...	1	Sold...	1	Before reported...		1	Sold; took English flag...	
			1	In port...	1	do		1	In port...	
	1	Chefoo...	1	Chefoo...	1	Bean cake and sundries	18,500 00	1	Sugar and paper...	16,000 00

No.	Port	No.	Destination	No.	Cargo	Value	No.	Cargo	Value
1	Shanghai	1	Hong Kong	1	...do		1	Ballast	
1	Purchased	1	Singapore	1	Purchased in port	16,000 00	1	Sundries	7,000 00
1	Hong Kong	1	In port	1	Spars and coal	4,800 00	1	In port	
6		6		6		39,300 00	6		23,000 00
Quarter ended June 30, 1864.									
2	In port	2	Chefoo	1	Before reported		1	7,627 pkgs. paper, 3,419 pkgs. china-ware, 1,500 bags sugar.	
2	Chefoo	2	Newchwang	1	...do		2	10,314 pkgs. paper, 1,415 bags sugar, 61 — sundries.	10,000 00
			Chefoo	1	1,120 piculs bean cake, 485 bales cotton, 162 bales sundries.		1	In port	
				1	14,000 piculs bean cake, 457 bales cotton, 543 bales sundries.				
1	Shanghai	1	In port	1	995 bales cotton, 57 bales sundries.		1	Ballast	
1	Amoy	1	Amoy	1	Ballast		1	In port	10,000 00
6		6		6			6		
Quarter ended September 30, 1864.									
2	In port	1	...do	1	Before reported		1	2,179 bags sugar, 3,568 pkgs. paper, 151 pkgs. sundries.	
		1	Amoy	1	...do		1	2,506 bags sugar, 528 pkgs. paper, 244 pkgs. sundries.	
4	Newchwang	1	...do	1	9,500 bean cake, 3,330 bags peas.		1	Ballast	
		1	Amoy	1	13,000 bean cakes		1	...do	
		1	Hong Kong	1	Peas		1	Inward cargo	
		1	In port	1	13,800 bean cake, 54 piculs peas, 5 bales cotton.		1	In port	
4	Chefoo	1	...do	1	950 bean cake, 221 bales cotton, 136 bales sundries.		1	3,410 bags sugar, 3,341 pkgs. paper, 291 pkgs. sundries.	
		1	Newchwang	1	9,300 bean cake, 486 bales cotton, 692 packages sundries.		1	806 bags sugar, 35 pkgs. medicines, 15 pkgs. tumeric.	
		1	Hong Kong	1	4,704 bean cake, 4,920 piculs peas.		1	Ballast	
		1	In port	1	6,926 piculs peas, 328 bales cotton, 757 bales sundries.		1	In port	
10		10		10			10		
HANKOW.—W. Breck. Entire year of 1865.									
172	Shanghai	171	Shanghai and Chinkiang		Not given			Not given	
49	Chinkiang and Shanghai	233	Shanghai	417			417		
196	Not stated	13	Chinkiang						
417		417		417					

* Entered: 28 boats, 12 steamers—40, and 9 in port. Cleared: 26 boats, 13 steamers—39, and 10 in port. Aggregate tonnage entered, 6,944.

† Entered: 67 steamers, 14 luggers—81, and 10 in port. Cleared: 67 steamers, 10 luggers—77, 2 sold, and 7 in port. Aggregate tonnage entered, 34,604.

‡ Entered: 1 ship, 3 barks—4, and 6 in port. Cleared: 6 barks, 1 schooner—7, 1 sold, and 2 in port. Aggregate tonnage entered, 2,061.

§ Entered: 3 barks, 1 schooner—4, and 2 in port. Cleared: 2 barks, 1 schooner—3, 1 sold, and 2 in port. Aggregate tonnage entered, 2,061.

‖ Entered: 4 barks, and 2 in port. Cleared: 4 barks, and 2 in port. Aggregate tonnage entered, 7,434.

¶ Entered: 8 barks, and 2 in port. Cleared: 8 barks, and 2 in port. Aggregate tonnage entered, 3,066.

** Entered and cleared: 171 steamers, 40 lorchas, 193 junks, 13 rafts—417. Aggregate tonnage entered, 139,247.

Navigation and commerce of the United States with foreign countries—Japan—Burmah.

COUNTRY, CONSULATE, NAME OF CONSUL, AND DATE OF RETURNS.	VESSELS. ENTERED.		VESSELS. CLEARED.		CARGOES. INWARD.			CARGOES. OUTWARD.		
	No.	Where from.	No.	Where for.	No.	Description.	Value.	No.	Description.	Value.
JAPAN.										
HAKODADI.—*E. E. Rice.*										
Quarter ended December 31, 1863.*	1	Amoor river	1	San Francisco	1	Unknown		1	Unknown	
	5	Shanghai	5	Shanghai	5	...do		5	...do	
	2	Nagasaki	2	Nagasaki	2	...do		2	...do	
	8		8		8			8		
Quarter ended March 31 and June 30, 1864.†	2	Nagasaki	1	Shanghai	1	Ballast		1	Sold to Japanese government	
			1	Nagasaki	1	...do		1	Ballast	
	1	Honolulu	1	Arctic ocean	1	Whaling stores		1	Whaling stores	
	6	Cruise	6	...do	6	...do		6	...do	
	2	Shanghai	1	Amoor river	1	...do		1	...do	
	1	San Francisco	1	Kin-siu coast	1	...do		1	...do	
			1	Amoor river	1	Assorted merchandise		1	Assorted merchandise	
	12		12		12			12		
4th quarter	No report									
KANAGAWA.—*G. S. Fisher.*										
Quarter ended December 31, 1863.‡	4	Hong Kong	1	New York	1	Ballast		1	1,200 tons rags and tea	$24,497 90
			1	In port		Furniture and coal		1	In port	
			1	Hong Kong	1	Passengers		1	229 packages sundries	
	7	Shanghai	3	San Francisco	2	Lead, 1 propeller, 3,500 plates spelter, 80 rifles		3	1,700 tons lumber, &c., 2,959 pkgs. tea, raw cotton, and silk	47,491 80
			1	Ningpo	1	Stores		1	150 tons tea, &c., 1,451 pkgs. tea and rags	14,405 04
	1	Nagasaki	2	San Francisco				2		
	2	San Francisco	1	In port	1			1	In port	
			1	Shanghai	1			1	700 tons lumber	
			1	In port	1			1	In port	
			1	Shanghai	1			1		
	14		14		14			14		86,394 04
2d quarter	No report									

Quarter ended June 30, 1864.§	3	In port	2	Shanghai	2	Not stated		2	Not stated	
	1	San Francisco		San Francisco		...do		1	...do	
	1	Bonin Islands		Cruise		...do		1	...do	
	1	Nagasaki	1	Nagasaki	1	...do		1	...do	
	1	Hong Kong	1	In port	1	...do		1	In port	
	1	Shanghai		...do		...do		1	...do	
	8		8		8			8		
4th quarter		No report.								
NAGASAKI.—J. G. Welsh.										
1st quarter		No report.								
Quarter ended March 31, 1864.‖	5	In port	4	Shanghai	4	Before reported		4	Lumber, seaweed, charcoal, crockery, sundries	4,520 00
			1	Sold	1	...do		2	Sold; took English flag	
	5	Shanghai	2	Shanghai	2	Medicine, sugar, lead, English goods, sundries	$4,348 00	2	Lumber, crockery, ginseng, tea, tobacco, seaweed, &c.	7,967 00
			1	Hakodadi	1	Ballast	2,287 43	1	Ballast	
			2	In port	2	Coal and merchandise		1	In port	
	1	Hong Kong	1	Sold	1	Ballast, 196 picals cloves	1,757 00	1	...do	
								1	Sold; took Japanese flag	
	11		11		11		8,392 43	11		12,487 00
Quarter ended June 30, 1864.¶	2	In port	2	Hakodadi	2	Before reported		1	Tobacco, bricks, sundries	428 15
								1	Ballast	
	11	Shanghai	9	Shanghai	7	General cargoes	43,647 00	9	Lumber, tea, tobacco, crockery, medicine, seaweed, sundries	78,599 73
	1	Kanagawa	2	Kanagawa	4	Ballast		2	In port	
			1	In port	1	...do		1	Ballast	
	14		14		14		43,647 00	14		79,027 88
4th quarter		No report.								
BURMAH.										
RANGOON.—G. Bullock.										
Quarter ended December 31, 1863.**	3	Singapore	3	Singapore	2	Ballast		2	19,942 bags rice	
					1	General cargo		1	Sold; took British flag	
	1	Galle	1	Cork for orders	1	Ballast		1	930 tons timber, 96,201 viss cutch	

* Entered and cleared : 3 brigs, 4 barks, 1 schooner—8. Aggregate tonnage entered, 2,604.
† Entered and cleared : 2 steamers, 5 barks, 2 ships, 2 schooners, 1 brig—12. Aggregate tonnage entered, 3,307.
‡ Entered : 3 ships, 7 barks, 3 brigs, 1 schooner—14. Cleared : 3 ships, 5 barks, 5 brigs, 1 schooner—11, and 3 in port. Aggregate tonnage entered, 7,493 66-95.
§ Entered : 1 brig, 3 barks, 1 steamer—5, and 3 in port. Cleared : 2 brigs, 1 schooner, 2 barks, 1 steamer—6, and 2 in port. Aggregate tonnage entered, 2,069 41-95.
‖ Entered : 3 steamers, 1 bark, 1 brig, 1 schooner—6, and 5 in port. Cleared : 1 steamer, 4 barks, 1 brig, 1 schooner—7, 2 sold, 2 in port. Aggregate tonnage entered, 1,738 17-95.
¶ Entered : 2 steamers, 1 ship, 8 barks, 1 brig—12, and 2 in port. Cleared : 3 steamers, 7 barks, 1 brig, 1 schooner—12, and 2 in port. Aggregate tonnage entered, 5,528 45-95.
** Entered : 7, class not given. Cleared : 5, class not given, and 2 in port. Aggregate tonnage entered, 4,902.

Navigation and commerce of the United States with foreign countries—Burmah—Hawaiian Islands.

COUNTRY, CONSULATE, NAME OF CONSUL, AND DATE OF RETURNS.	VESSELS.						CARGOES.						
	ENTERED.		CLEARED.		INWARD.				OUTWARD.			
	No.	Where from.	No.	Where for.	No.	Description.	Value.	No.	Description.	Value.		
Quarter ended December 31, 1863—Continued.	1	Mauritius	1	Bassein	1	do		1	3,199 bags rice			
	1	Aden	1	Bombay	1	do		1	In port			
	1	Madras	1	do	1	do		1	do			
	7		7		7			7				
Quarter ended March 31, 1864.*	2	In port	2	Bombay	2	Before reported		2	In port			
	2	Liverpool	1	Liverpool	1	Coals		1	50,000 baskets rice			
			1	In port	1	Coals		1	In port			
	1	London	1	Falmouth	1	Ballast		1	957 hides, 50,300 baskets rice			
	1	Cardiff	1	Chefoo	1	Coals		1	50,920 baskets rice			
	2	Bombay	1	Bombay	1	Ballast		1	556 tons timber			
			1	In port	1	do		1	In port			
	1	Madras			1	do		1	31,200 baskets rice			
	1	Havre			1	do		1	9,300 bags rice, 2,000 hides			
	1	Aden	1	In port	1	do		1	In port			
	1	Galle	1	do	1	do		1	do			
	12		12		12			12				
Quarter ended June 30, 1864.†	6	In port	3	Bombay	3	Before reported		3	Not stated			
			1	Liverpool	1	do		1	do			
			1	Aden	1	do		1	do			
			1	Galle	1	do		1	6,610 bas cdta rice, 103,300 cutch.			
	1	Buenos Ayres	1	Falmouth	1	Ballast						
	4	Singapore	1	Liverpool	4	Ballast		4	63,492 baskets r cd, 34,970 cutch, 7,289 pieces sapan wood, 5,492 bales rataan.			
			3	Falmouth								
	1	Akyab	2	do	2	Ballast		1	24,770 baskets rice			
	3	Not stated	1	do	1	do		3	44,792 da rice			
	1	New York	1	New York	1	Coals		1	Ballast			
	1	Galle	1	Unknown	1	Ballast		1	31,100 baskets rice, 19 — timber			
	1	Aden	1	In port	1	do		1	In port			
	1	Cochin	1	Liverpool	1	do		1	13,810 baskets rice			
	2	London	1	Boston	1	Coals		1	21,449 baskets rice			
			1	Falmouth	1	Coals		1	In port			
	1	Bombay	1	do	1	Ballast		1	do			
	22		22		22			22				

Quarter ended September 30, 1864;

No.	Where	No.	Inward cargo	Value	No.	Outward cargo	Value
3	In port		Before reported		1	Not stated	$18,830 97
1	London	Aden		do		1	do	48,864 95
2	Aden	London		do		1	do	17,257 90
2	Bombay	Falmouth		do		2	985 tons rice, cutch	72,056 59
		...do				1	2,286 tons rice, cutch	6,600 00
		Bombay				1	Ballast	
		Europe				1	846½ tons square timber and planking	
1	Bassein	Bassein		For repairs		1	For repairs	
1	San Francisco	Boston		Ballast		1	Ballast	
10			**10**			**10**		

HAWAIIAN ISLANDS.
HONOLULU.—A. Caldwell.
Quarter ended December 31, 1864.§

No.	Where	No.	Inward cargo	Value	No.	Outward cargo	Value
4	In port	Boston	1	Before reported		1	Sperm and whale oil, and Hawaiian produce	
		Micronesia	1	do		1	Ballast	
		Cruise and bone	1	do		1	Whale oil and bone	
		San Francisco	1	do		1	Hawaiian produce	
11	San Francisco	...do	4	General merchandise	$22,455 63	4	Whale oil and bone, and Hawaiian produce	
		Hong Kong	1	Cargo for China, and general merchandise	17,190 31	1	Cargo for China, and Hawaiian produce	
		Howland's Island	2	Ballast		2	Ballast	
		Kanagawa	1	Cargo for Japan, and general merchandise	3,500 00	1	Cargo for Japan	
		Melbourne	1	Cargo for Australia	9,119 70	1	Cargo for Australia	
		In port	1	In port		1	In port	
		Baker's Island	1	Whale and sperm oil		1	Ballast	
15	Arctic sea	Coast of California	4	Sperm and whale oil, and bone	138,506 58	4	Whaling gear	159,719 02
		Cruise and bone	4	do	169,997 13	4	Sperm and whale oil, and bone	
		Cruise south	6	do	226,167 97	6	Whaling gear	
		Sold	1	Whale oil and bone	23,186 60	1	Sold	
10	Ochotsk sea	Cruise and bone	2	Sperm and whale oil, and bone	31,200 57	2	Sperm and whale oil	46,054 94
		Coast of California	2	do	72,702 64	2	Whaling gear	
		Cruise south	3	do	54,081 86	3	Sperm and whale oil, bone, &c.	28,996 50
2	Sea	In port	1	do	10,656 96	1	In port	
		Howland's Island	1	Ballast		1	Ballast	
2	Shanghai	In port	1	Whaling gear		1	In port	
3	Hilo	Howland's Island	2	In port		2	Ballast	22,500 90
		Coast of California		Whale oil and bone	22,500 90		Inward cargo	
2	Lahaina	Cruise south	1	Ballast	11,363 28	1	Whaling gear	
		...do	1	Sperm and whale oil, and bone	47,499 99	1	do	
		In port	1	do	34,069 59	1	In port	
1	Boston	Sold	1	General merchandise	54,922 50	1	Sold	

* Entered: 10, class not given, and 2 in port. Cleared: 8, class not given, and 4 in port. Aggregate tonnage entered, 6,865.
† Entered: 16, class not given, and 6 in port. Cleared: 19, class not given, and 3 in port. Aggregate tonnage entered, 12,351.
‡ Entered: 9, class not given, and 3 in port. Cleared: 12, class not given. Aggregate tonnage entered, 5,682.
§ Entered: 22 ships, 21 barks, 2 brigs—68, and 4 in port. Cleared: 21 ships, 29 barks, 3 brigs—48, 2 sold, and 4 in port. Aggregate tonnage entered, 21,550.

Navigation and commerce of the United States with foreign countries—Hawaiian Islands.

COUNTRY, CONSULATE, NAME OF CONSUL, AND DATE OF RETURNS.	VESSELS ENTERED — No.	ENTERED — Where from.	CLEARED — No.	CLEARED — Where for.	CARGOES INWARD — No.	INWARD — Description.	INWARD — Value.	OUTWARD — No.	OUTWARD — Description.	OUTWARD — Value.
Quarter ended December 31, 1863—Continued	1	Port Angelos	1	Victoria and Teekalet	1	Lumber	$1,884 04	1	Ballast	$447 77
	1	Teekalet	1	Teekalet	1	...do	4,290 00	1	Hawaiian produce	
	52		52		52		1,015,337 55	52		421,386 74
Quarter ended Mar. 31, 1864*:	4	In port	4	Arctic and South seas	4	Before reported		4	Whaling craft and gear	
	14	San Francisco	8	San Francisco	8	General merchandise	131,785 23	8	567 gallons sperm oil, 6,888 lbs. whale-bone, and Hawaiian produce.	163,925 20
	2	New London	2	Hong Kong	2	Cargoes for China	9,467 92	2	Inward cargo; Hawaiian produce	
	1	Philadelphia	2	In port	1	General merchandise		1	In port	3,730 00
	3	Port Angolos	1	Shanghai	1	Ballast		1	...do	
	6	New Bedford	1	Baker's Island	1	Cargo for China		1	Inward cargo	
	1	Edgartown	1	Sold	1	Ballast		1	Ballast	
	1	Hilo	1	In port	1	General merchandise	13,452 40	1	Sold; took Hawaiian flag	
	1	Whaling cruise	1	East Indies	1	Whaling craft and gear		1	In port	
	7	Coast of California	1	Victoria	1	Ballast		1	Ballast	
			1	Shanghai	1	Lumber		1	...do	
			1	Teekalet	1	Cargo for China	1,700 39	2	Inward cargo	
			2	Ochotsk sea		Lumber		2	Hawaiian produce	539 73
			2	Arctic sea		4,147 gallons sperm oil, &c.	1,894 81	2	Inward cargo	
			2	In port		49,298 gallons sperm oil, 16,848 gallons whale oil, 5,000 pounds bone.	3,912 31	2	Whaling craft and gear	3,402 00
			1	Arctic sea		3,150 gallons sperm and 50,400 gallons whale oil, 2,500 pounds bone.	56,266 28	2	In port	
			1	Teekalet	2	1,575 gallons sperm and 50,400 gallons whale oil.	28,094 00	1	Sailing craft and gear	
			1	In port	2	Ballast	24,601 50	1	Hawaiian produce	1,099 48
			7	...do	1	Ballast		1	In port	
					1	3,151 gallons sperm oil.	2,835 00	7	...do	
					7	96,075 gallons whale oil.	44,194 50			
	40		40		40		318,126 34	40		172,696 41
Quarter ended June 30, 1864†:	13	In port	9	Arctic sea	9	Before reported		10	Whaling gear	
			1	Ochotsk sea	1	...do		1	Sperm and whale oil, and produce	26,389 88
			1	San Francisco	1	...do		2	Sold; took Hawaiian flag	
			2	Sold	2	...do				

No.		No.		No.		No.	Sperm and whale oil.		Whaling gear.
8	New Bedford	7	Arctic sea	8	Sperm and whale oil	8	22,097 02	Whaling gear	21,010 50
6	Lahaina	1	O. mk sea	6	Sperm and whale oil, and bone	6	68,886 50	do	
		1	O. mk sea						
5	Hilo	5	Arctic sea	5	do	5	27,694 80	do	17,262 00
5	Coast of California			5	do	5	15,787 78	Whale oil and gear	2,875 00
1	Paita	1	do	1	Sperm oil	1	15,412 50	Whaling craft and gear	
1	Sea	1	do	1	do	1	3,402 00		
1	St. Catharine's	1	do	1	do	1	850 50	do	
1	King's Mills Isl'd	1	Sold	1	Ballast	1		Sold; t ok Hawaiian flag.	
1	Howland's Island	1	In port	1	do	1		In port	266 95
1	La Paz	1	San Francisco	1	do	1		Hawaiian salt.	
2	Teekalet	2	Teekalet	2	do				
			Port Angelos	2	Lumber from United States	2	4,013 34	Hawaiian produce	1,008 90
1	Sydney	1	San Francisco	7	Cargo for San Francisco	7		Inward cargo	191,784 91
19	San Francisco	7	do	6	General merchandise	6	108,643 69	Sperm and whale oil, &c.	
		6	Baker's Island	2	Ballast	2		Ballast	4,..
		2	Howland's Island	1	do	1		do	19,184 52
		1	Portland	1	Lumber	1	2,750 00	Hawaiian produce	161,467 17
			New Bedford	1	Ballast	1		Sperm and whale oil; Hawaiian produce,	
2		2	In port	1	General merchandise	2	43,620 27	In port	
65	**Quarter ended September 30, 1864.;**	**65**		**65**		**65**	**313,158 40**		**434,299 83**
3			In port	1	Before reported	1		Ballast	
		1	Honolulu	2	do	2		Hawaiian produce	46,822 14
16	San Francisco	8	San Francisco	8	Gen eral cargo	8	120,381 09	do	151,557 08
		2	Hong Kong	2	Cargoes for China	2		Inward cargoes	
		1	Howland's Island	1	Ballast	1		Ballast	
		3	Baker's Island	3	do	3		do	
2	Port Angelos	2	In port	2	General cargoes	2	65,302 27	do	
1	Howland's Island	1	Port Angelos	2	Lumber	2	9,513 35	Ballast	
1	Baker's Island	1	Howland's Island	1	Ballast	1			
1	Astoria	1	Baker's Island	1	do	1		Hawaiian produce	24,634 35
1	New London	1	Astoria	1	General	1	3,300 00	Ballast	
1	Mazatlan	1	do	1	do	1	1,991 96	Ballast	
1	Boston	1	Phoenix Island	1	Cargo for Great Britain	1		Bad cargo	
		1	Cork	1	General cargo	1	54,116 70	In port	222,693 57
27		**27**	In port	**27**		**27**	**247,608 37**		
3	Arctic ocean	1	New Bedford	1	800 bbls. sperm and 2,000 bbls. whale oil, 17,000 lbs. bone.	1	91,650 00	200 bbls. sperm and 2,000 bbls. whale oil, 39,925 lbs. bone.	126,037 00
	HILO.—J. Worth. Quarter ended December 31, 1863.§	1	Honolulu & cruise	1	900 bbls. whale oil, 10,000 lbs. bone.	1	40,515 00	900 bbls. whale oil.	25,515 00
		1	Kawacha & cruise	1	200 bbls. sperm and 600 bbls. whale oil, 7,000 lbs. bone.	1	38,350 00	200 bbls. sperm and 600 bbls. whale oil.	29,400 00

* Entered: 11 ships, 20 barks, 1 brig, 4 schooners—38, and 4 in port. Cleared: 6 ships, 15 barks, 1 brig, 2 schooners—26, 1 sold, and 13 in port. Aggregate tonnage entered, 15,041.

; Entered: 23 ships, 27 barks, 1 brig, 1 schooner—52, and 13 in port. Cleared: 26 ships, 32 barks, 1 schooner—59, 3 sold, and 3 in port. Aggregate tonnage entered, 26,247.

‡ Entered: 9 ships, 14 barks, 1 schooner—24, and 3 in port. Cleared: 10 ships, 13 barks, 1 schooner—24, and 3 in port. Aggregate tonnage entered, 13,092.

§ Entered: 5 ships, 1 bark—6. Cleared: 5 ships, and 1 in port. Aggregate tonnage entered, 2,282.

Navigation and commerce of the United States with foreign countries—Hawaiian Islands.

COUNTRY, CONSULATE, NAME OF CONSUL, AND DATE OF RETURNS.	VESSELS				CARGOES					
	ENTERED		CLEARED		INWARD			OUTWARD		
	No.	Where from.	No.	Where for.	No.	Description.	Value.	No.	Description.	Value.
Quarter ended December 31, 1863.	2	Ochotsk sea	2	Kawacha & cruise	2	29 bbls. sperm and 350 bbls. whale oil, 4,000 lbs. bone.	$16,981 00	2	21 bbls. sperm and 250 bbls. whale oil, 4,000 lbs. bone.	$16,913 00
	1	Honolulu	1	Coast of California	1	Ship stores.	....	1	In port.	....
	6		6		6		187,676 00	6		197,865 00
Quarter ended March 31, 1864.*	1	Teekelet	1	Honolulu	1	25,300 feet lumber.	2,300 00	1	Lumber	900 00
	2	New Bedford	2	In port	2	290 bbls. sperm oil	14,011 80	1	In port	....
	5	Coast of California	2	Hawaii	2	1,250 bbls. whale and sperm oil	43,030 00	1	1,250 bbls. whale and sperm oil	29,030 00
	1	Gulf of California	1	In port	3	1,440 bbls. whale oil	43,900 00	3	In port	....
				do.	1	180 bbls. whale oil	5,400 00	1	do.	....
	9		9		9		103,941 60	9		39,930 00
Quarter ended June 30, 1864.†	6	In port	6	Cruise	6	Before reported	....	6	390 bbls. sperm, 1,620 bbls. w. oil	45,911 00
	1	Paita	1	Arctic ocean	1	15 bbls sperm, and 170 bbl. whale oil	5,865 00	1	15 bbls. sperm, 15 bbls. whale oil	1,062 60
	7	New Bedford	7	Cruise	1	Stores	....	6	Stores	....
	1	Talcahuano	1	do.	1	75 bbls. sperm oil	4,595 00	1	25 bbls. sperm oil	9,300 00
	1	Port Angeles	1	Honolulu	1	Stores	....	1	Stores	....
	1	La Paz, Cal.	1	do.	1	34,300 feet lumber	3,200 00	1	16,000 feet lumber	1,400 00
					1	Passengers.	....	1	Passengers	....
	17		17		17		13,660 00	17		50,003 60
Quarter ended September 30, 1864.‡	1	Teekelet	1	Honolulu	1	25,000 feet lumber, 2 bales blankets, 2 bales burlaps, &c.	3,658 00	1	12,000 feet lumber	1,100 00
	2	San Francisco	2	San Francisco	2	105,000 feet lumber, $10,000 specie, lime, cement, &c.	15,400 00	2	25,344 lbs. sugar, 10,296 gallons molasses, $10,000 in specie, 16,725 lbs. pulee, 42 hhds. tallow, hides, &c.	14,025 25
	3		3		3		19,058 00	3		15,125 29
LAHAINA.—E. Perkins.										
Quarter ended December 31, 1863.§	3	Ochotsk	2	Coast of California	2	500 bbls. sperm and 950 bbls. whale oil, 5,000 lbs. bone, &c.	22,995 25	2	Inward cargoes	22,035 25
			1	Honolulu	1	4,964 bbls. sperm and 700 bbls. whale oil, 9,500 lbs. bone.	19,162 00	1	Same as inward cargo	19,162 00

				Value		Part inward cargo.	Value
Quarter ended March 31, 1864.‖							
2	Arctic ocean	1	Coast of California	606 lbs. sperm and 1,300 bbls. whale oil, 20,000 lbs. bone.	35,667 00	1	Part inward cargo	19,067 00
		1	Honolulu	156 lbs. sperm and 2,275 bbls. whale oil, 15,000 lbs. bone.	45,786 00	1	...do	45,786 00
5		5			193,630 25	5		104,070 25
Quarter ended March 31, 1864.‖							
3	Lower California	3	Arctic ocean	75 bbls. sperm, 1,520 bbls. whale oil.	12,942 40	2	In port	
1	South Pacific, &c.	1	...do	40 bbls. sperm and 400 bbls. whale oil, 4,000 lbs. be.	9,758 00	1	...do	
1	Coast South America and South Pacific.	1	...do	220 bbls. sperm and 10 bbls. whale oil.	6,481 00	1	...do	
1	San Francisco	1	Honolulu	Ballast		1	Ballast	
6		6			28,481 40	6		
Quarter ended June 30, 1864.¶							
5	In port	5	Arctic ocean	Before reported		5	190 bbls. sperm and 1,880 bbls. whale oil.	29,969 00
2	Coast of California	2	Ochotsk sea	1,300 bbls. whale oil	19,470 00	2	1,400 bbls. whale oil.	19,490 00
1	Honolulu	1	Arctic ocean	20 bbls. sperm and 400 bbls. whale oil.	6,356 00	1	Same as inward cargo	6,356 00
2	South Pacific	2	...do	440 bbls. sperm, 1,800 bbls. whale oil.	38,177 00	2	...do	38,177 00
10		10			64,003 00	10		93,935 00
4th quarter	...No report.							
DOMINICAN REPUBLIC.—W.G. W. Jaeger.							
St. Domingo City.							
Quarter ended December 31, 1863.**							
1	New Haven	1	Porto Rico	Provisions	5,900 00	1	Ballast	
Quarter ended March 31, 1864.††							
1	New York	1	Mayaguez	Provisions	5,100 00	1	Lignumvitæ.	1,040 00
Quarter ended June 30, 1864.‡‡							
1	New Haven	1	New York, via Turk's Island.	Provisions	6,143 00			
2	New York			Ice	478 00	} 3	Ballast	
1		1	Cuba	Ice	589 00			
3		3			7,203 00	3		

* Entered: 4 barks, 5 ships—9. Cleared: 2 ships, 1 bark—3, and 6 in port. Aggregate tonnage entered, 3,477 24-95.

† Entered: 9 barks, 5 ships, 1 schooner—11, and 6 in port. Cleared: 11 barks, 5 ships, 1 schooner—17. Aggregate tonnage entered, 3,434.

‡ Entered and cleared: 1 bark, 1 brig, 1 schooner—3. Aggregate tonnage entered, 330.   § Entered and cleared: 4 ships, 1 bark—5. Aggregate tonnage entered, 1,845 14-95.

‖ Entered: 2 ships, 3 barks, 1 schooner—6. Cleared: 1 schooner, and 5 in port. Aggregate tonnage entered, 1,027 98-95.

¶ Entered: 2 barks, 3 ships—5, and 5 in port. Cleared: 1 bark, 3 ships—4, 6 not stated. Aggregate tonnage, 1,356 59-95.

** Entered and cleared: 1 schooner. Tonnage, 144.   †† Entered and cleared: 1 schooner. Tonnage, 144.

‡‡ Entered and cleared: 2 schooners, 1 brig—3. Aggregate tonnage entered, 510.

Navigation and commerce of the United States with foreign countries—Dominican Republic, Hayti.

COUNTRY, CONSULATE, NAME OF CONSUL, AND DATE OF RETURNS.	VESSELS ENTERED — No.	ENTERED — Where from.	CLEARED — No.	CLEARED — Where for.	CARGOES INWARD — No.	INWARD — Description.	INWARD — Value.	OUTWARD — No.	OUTWARD — Description.	OUTWARD — Value.
4th quarter		No American vessels arrived or departed.								
HAYTI.										
CAPE HAYTIEN.—A. Folsom.										
Quarter ended December 31, 1863.*	8	Philadelphia	6	Turk's Island	7	3,598 tons coal		7	Ballast	
	5	Boston	5	Boston	1	353 tons deals	$13,961 00	1	27 tons, (of what not stated)	$293,776 00
					5	Provisions		3	326 tons logwood	64,846 00
								2	170 tons logwood and coffee	385,210 00
	13		13		13	...Spanish currency	91,961 00	13	...Haytien currency	753,852 00
Quarter ended March 31, 1864.†	2	Boston	2	Boston	2	Provisions	40,124 00	2	241 tons logwood and coffee	202,975 00
Quarter ended June 30, 1864.§	4	do.	3	do.	3	do.	54,643 00	3	Logwood	233,069 00
		Boston	1	In port	1	Coal		1	In port	
	4		4		4	...Haytien currency	54,643 00	4	...Haytien currency	253,069 00
Quarter ended September 30, 1864.‖	2	In port	2	Boston	2	Before reported		2	30 tons logwood; 105 tons coffee and logwood	4,259 00
	1	Philadelphia	1	Philadelphia	1	537 tons coal		1	Ballast	
	1	Boston	1	Boston	1	Provisions	38,173 00	1	179 tons logwood	27,678 00
	4		4		4	...Haytien currency	38,173 00	4	...Haytien currency	31,937 00
GONAIVES.—A. Hildenbeck.										
Quarter ended December 31, 1863.¶	2	Boston	2	Boston	2	Provisions and lumber	$5,467 77	2	Logwood and cotton	$97,330 81
Quarter ended March 31, 1864.**	1	New York	1	New York	1	Provisions	19,646 00	1	Mahogany, logwood	252,181 40
	3	Boston	2	Boston	3	do.	29,960 78	2	Cotton, logwood	
			1	In port				1	In port	
	4		4		4	...Haytien currency	49,106 78	4	...Haytien currency	252,181 40
Quarter ended June 30, 1864.††	1	In port	1	Boston	1	Before reported		1	Logwood	13,150 39

Quarter ended September 30, 1864.‡‡	2	Machias........	1	Miragoane.........; Port de Paix.......; ...do........	1 1	Lumber.......; Provisions		3,553 00; 2,576 27; 20,539 27	1 1 1	110 tons cotton and logwood...; 80 tons logwood...; 39 tons cotton and logwood...	75,763 41; 17,220 00; 99,430 00
	1	Boston........	3		3			26,675 98	3		192,413 41
JACMEL—C. Morenia. Quarter ended December 31, 1863.§§	2	New York......	2	New York......	2	Provisions......		24,064 14	2	290,000 lbs. logwood, 21 bales cotton, 2,000 brazilletto wood.	28,013 32
	1	Boston........	1	Boston........	1	...do		10,766 14	1	67,851 lbs. coffee, 59,750 lbs. logwood.	122,805 74
	3		3		3			34,830 28	3		151,819 06
2d quarter........		No report.									
Quarter ended June 30, 1864‖‖‖	3	Boston........	2	Boston........	3	Provisions......; Gold.........		31,882 43; 10,000 00	2 1	1,337 bags coffee, 120,000 lbs. logwood.; In port.	213,568 66
	1	New York......	1 1	In port...; New York...	1	Provisions		10,028 00	1	120,000 pounds logwood	11,743 16
	4		4		4			51,910 43	4		225,311 82
Quarter ended September 30, 1864.¶¶	3	Boston........	2	Boston........	3	Provisions, &c......		21,869 03	2	256,000 lbs. logwood, 460 bags coffee.; In port.	135,213 53
	1	Port au Prince	1 1	In port...; New York...	1	...do			1 1	Inward cargo.	
	4		4		4			21,869 03	4		135,213 53
PORT AU PRINCE—H. Conrad. Quarter ended December 31, 1863.***	1	In port...	1	Port au Prince...	1	Before reported.		6,131 58	1	30,000 pounds logwood.	2,436 93
	4	Bangor...	2	Miragoane	2	34,636 feet lumber.		4,392 10	2	110,000 pounds logwood.	8,194 28
			1	Inagua...	1	256,956 feet lumber.		2,885 00	1	50,600 pounds logwood.	3,771 81
	3	Boston...	1	New York...	1	175,000 feet lumber.		12,940 00	1	460,000 pounds logwood.	36,890 00
			1	St. Marc.	1	Provisions.		8,133 60	1	50,000 pounds logwood.	4,709 50
			1	Miragoane	1	...do		18,151 85	1	15,000 pounds logwood.	1,449 35
			1	Inagua	1	...do		13,338 18	1	50,000 pounds logwood.	3,728 43
	1	New York...	1	New York	1	...do		26,183 00	1	50,000 pounds logwood.	15,318 00
	1	Philadelphia	1	St. Marc.	1	...do			1	180,000 pounds logwood.	2,969 40
										40,000 pounds logwood.	50,304 78
										98,549 pounds coffee.	
	10		10		10			92,115 31	10		129,602 48

* Entered and cleared: 5 barks, 5 brigs, 3 schooners—13. Aggregate tonnage entered, 4,151. † Entered and cleared: 1 brig, 1 schooner—2. Aggregate tonnage entered, 416.
‡ Haytien currency.
§ Entered: 3 schooners, 1 bark. Cleared: 2 schooners, 1 bark—4. Cleared—4. Aggregate tonnage entered, 881.
‖ Entered: 1 brig, 1 bark—2, in port 2. Cleared: 2 brigs, 2 barks—4. Aggregate tonnage entered, 549. ¶ Entered and cleared: 2 brigs. Aggregate tonnage entered, 343 68-95.
** Entered: 3 schooners, 1 brig—4. Cleared: 1 brig—1, in port 1. Aggregate tonnage entered, 528 18-95.
†† Entered: 1 schooner, in port. Cleared: 1 schooner. ‡‡ Entered and cleared: 2 brigs, 1 bark—3. Aggregate tonnage entered, 579.
§§ Entered and cleared: 3 schooners. Aggregate tonnage entered, 464 66-95. ‖‖ Entered: 4 schooners. Cleared: 3 schooners, and 1 in port. Aggregate tonnage entered, 512 4-95.
¶¶ Entered: 4 schooners. Cleared: 3 schooners, and 1 in port. Aggregate tonnage entered, 606 2-95.
*** Entered: 6 brigs, 3 schooners—9, and 1 in port. Cleared: 6 brigs, 4 schooners—10. Aggregate tonnage entered, 1,891 73-95.

Navigation and commerce of the United States with foreign countries—Hayti, Mexico.

COUNTRY, CONSULATE, NAME OF CONSUL, AND DATE OF RETURNS.	VESSELS				CARGOES					
	ENTERED		CLEARED		INWARD			OUTWARD		
	No.	Where from.	No.	Where for.	No.	Description.	Value.	No.	Description.	Value.
3d quarter		No report.								
Quarter ended June 30, 1864*	1	Calais	1	Boston	1	116,320 feet lumber	22,169 58	1	274,600 pounds logwood	221,717 86
	2	Boston	1	Inagua	1	Provisions	8,471 00	1	1,932 bags coffee	337,353 82
			1	Condemned	1	do	12,518 00	1	Condemned	
	2	New York	1	Miragoane	1	do	44,893 44	1	80,000 pounds logwood	6,356 79
			1	St. Marc	1	do	17,914 00	1	60,000 pounds logwood	4,832 84
	2	Portland	2	Miragoane	2	326,937 feet lumber	6,896 00	2	211,000 pounds logwood	17,169 83
	7		7		7	United States currency	92,862 02	7	Haytien currency	387,494 14
4th quarter		No report.								
ST. MARC.—F. A. Baker. Quarter ended December 31, 1863.†	1	Port au Prince	1	Boston	1	Ballast		1	150,000 pounds logwood	
	1	Boston	1	do	1	General cargo		1	82,000 pounds logwood, 5,000 lbs. lignumvitæ	
	2		2		2			2		
Quarter ended March 31, 1864.‡	1	Boston	1	Boston	1	General cargo	8,945 67	1	89,000 pounds logwood, 22,000 pounds lignumvitæ, 5,660 lbs. coffee, 35 dry hides, 390 pounds copper	1,574 00
	1	Port au Prince	1	New York	1	Ballast		1	200,000 pounds logwood	1,201 00
	2		2		2		8,945 67	2		2,775 00
Quarter ended June 30, 1864.§	1	Boston	1	Boston	1	General cargo	8,000 00	1	100,000 pounds logwood, 17,649 pounds coffee, 98 lbs. copper	3,174 00
4th quarter		No report.								

MEXICO.

ACAPULCO—L. S. Ely.

Quarter ended December 31, 1863.‖

No.	Whence	No.	Whither	Cargo	Tonnage	No.	Remarks
12	Panama	12	San Francisco	6,318 passengers	8,700 00	12	Not stated
9	San Francisco	9	Panama	3,880 passengers	9,600 00	9	do
1	Baltimore	1	Callao	1,450 tons coal	9,600 00	1	Ballast
1	Boston	1	do	1,600 tons coal	8,300 00	1	do
1	New York	1	China	1,550 tons coal	8,760 00	1	do
2	Philadelphia	1	In port	1,460 tons coal	14,000 00	1	do
1	Hull	1	do	2,000 tons coal	14,000 00	1	In port
				2,000 tons coal		1	do
27		27			63,360 00	27	

Quarter ended March 31, 1864.¶

No.	Whence	No.	Whither	Cargo	Tonnage	No.	Remarks
2	In port	2	Callao	Before reported		9	@5 passengers
10	Panama	10	San Francisco	4,085 passengers		9	For ?
				In for supplies.		1	1,291 passengers.
10	San Francisco	10	Panama	1,291 passengers	3,000 00	9	Ballast.
				Assorted merchandise.	9,150 00	1	do
1	Baltimore	1	Boston	1,450 tons coal	22,540 00	2	In port.
2	New York	2	Callao	3,220 tons coal			
25		25			34,690 00	27	

Quarter ended June 30, 1864.*

No.	Whence	No.	Whither	Cargo	Tonnage	No.	Remarks
2	In port	2	Callao	Before reported.		2	Not stated.
10	Panama	10	San Francisco	5,840 passengers		10	5,840 passengers.
9	San Francisco	9	Panama	2,990 passengers.	19,995 00	9	2,990 passengers.
2	Panama	2	Callao	2,906 tons cal.	10,095 00	2	Ball.
1	Hull	1	do	1,900 tons cal.	8,946 00	1	do
1	Baltimore	1	do	1,491 tons coal.		1	do
25		25			38,871 00	25	

Quarter ended September 30, 1864.††

No.	Whence	No.	Whither	Cargo	Tonnage	No.	Remarks
1	Put back	1	Callao	Before reported.		1	Not stated.
8	Panama	8	San Francisco	2,950 passengers		8	do
9	San Francisco	8	Panama	980 ...	14,000 00	8	do
1	Mazatlan	1	San Francisco	Assorted merchandise.	6,000 00	1	do
1	Baltimore	1	do	bales cotton.	7,940 00	1	do
2	Unknown	1	Callao	1,243 tons cal.		1	do
		1	Panama	920 passengers.		1,1	do
		2	Unknown				
22		22			27,940 00	22	

* Entered: 3 schooners, 1 bark, 3 brigs—7. Cleared: 3 schooners, 1 bark, 2 brigs—6, and 1 condemned. Aggregate tonnage entered, 1,463.58-95.
† Entered and cleared: 2 schooners. Aggregate tonnage entered, 291.45-95. ‡ Entered and cleared: 2 schooners, 3 ships. Aggregate tonnage entered, 263.
§ Entered and cleared: 1 schooner. Tonnage, 110 6-95. ‖ Entered: 21 steamers, 6 ships—27. Cleared: 20 steamers, 5 ships—25, and 2 in port. Aggregate tonnage entered, 49,999.
¶ Entered: 19 steamers, 5 ships—24, and 2 in port. Cleared: 20 steamers, 5 ships—25, and 2 in port. Aggregate tonnage entered, 49,254.
** Entered: 19 steamers, 4 ships—23, and 2 in port. Cleared: 21 steamer, 4 ship—25. Aggregate tonnage entered, 52,971.
†† Entered: 18 steamers, 2 schooners, 1 ship—21, and 1 in port. Cleared: 18 steamer, 2 schooners, 2 ships—22. Aggregate tonnage entered, 45,301.

H. Ex. Doc. 60——10*

Navigation and commerce of the United States with foreign countries—Mexico.

COUNTRY, CONSULATE, NAME OF CONSUL, AND DATE OF RETURN.	VESSELS				CARGOES					
	ENTERED.		CLEARED.		INWARD.			OUTWARD.		
	No.	Where from.	No.	Where for.	No.	Description.	Value.	No.	Description.	Value.
GUAYMAS.—F. Alden. Quarter ended December 31, 1863.*	4	San Francisco	{5}	San Francisco	4	Merchandise, machinery, mining tools, lumber, and 173 passengers.		2	Ballast	
	1	Rio Colorado			1	Ballast		3	Specie, hides, silver ore, copper ore, and 63 passengers.	
	5		5		5			5		
Quarter ended March 31, 1864.†	4	San Francisco	3	San Francisco	4	Specie, merchandise, machinery, and 150 passengers.		2	Specie, ore, and 150 passengers.	
	1	Rio Colorado	3	La Paz	1	Lumber		4	Ballast	
	1	Mazatlan			1	Ballast				
	6		6		6			6		
Quarter ended June 30, 1864.‡	7	San Francisco	5	San Francisco	5	Merchandise, machinery, tools, and 139 passengers.		3	Specie, ore, hides, and 126 passengers.	
	1	Rio Colorado	1	La Paz	1	Powder		1	Powder	
	1	Altata	2	Rio Colorado	2	Ballast		5	Ballast	
			1	Altata	1	Army stores for Arizona				
	9		9		9			9		
Quarter ended September 30, 1864.§	4	San Francisco	3	San Francisco	4	Merchandise, machinery, lumber, and 78 passengers.		2	Specie and 73 passengers.	
	1	Rio Colorado	2	La Paz	1	Ballast		3	Ballast	
	5		5		5			5		
LA PAZ.—F. R. Elmer. Quarter ended December 31, 1863.‖	10	San Francisco	2	San Francisco	2	180 tons wines, liquors, mining machinery, &c.	$11,000 00	2	800 tons salt	$3,500 00
			5	Gulf ports	5	408 tons wines, liquors, provisions, machinery, &c.	64,000 00	4	Passengers and salt	250 00
			1	Cruise	1	40 tons wines, liquors, &c.	4,500 00	1	In port	
			1	Whaling & sealg	1	80 tons lumber and mining supplies.	6,500 00	1		
			1	Colorado river				1	300 tons salt, 25 tons ore.	
	10		10		10		86,000 00	10		3,750 00

Quarter ended March 31, 1864.¶	1	In port	1	Before reported	55,250 00	1	Not stated
	10	San Francisco	7	384 tons mining supplies, machinery, and general merchandise.		5	Passengers
						2	45 tons silver ore
				Cruise		1	50 tons copper ore
	1	Manzanillo	1	Le Paz	17,000 00	1	In port
			1	In port		2	
			2	San Francisco		1	
	19		12		72,250 00	12	
Quarter ended June 30, 1864.**	1	San Francisco and Guaymas	1	Ballast		1	
	2	San Francisco, Mazatlan, and Guaymas.	2	Miscellaneous cargo	18,000 00	1	A few tons silver ore
						1	40 tons gold and silver ore
	1	San Francisco	1	Mining supplies, mach'ry, & lumber	21,000 00	1	
	4		4		39,000 00	4	
Quarter ended September 30, 1864.††	6	San Francisco	3	Mining machinery, &c	26,900 00	2	Silver ore and passengers
		Not stated	2	do	22,000 00	1	Passengers
						1	Not stated
	1	For supplies	1	Not s ted		1	do
	6		6		48,900 00	6	For supplies
MANZANILLO.—W. H. Blake.							
Quarter ended December 31, 1865.‡‡	3	San Francisco	2	1,005 passengers		3	Not stated
			1				
	3		3			3	
Quarter ended March 31, 1864.§§	3	Panama	3	Passengers and general cargo		3	Not stated
	2	Piedra Blanca	2	do		2	
	4	San Francisco	3	Passen gers and general cargo, flour, tools, machinery.	39,000 00	1	
			1			9	
	9		9		29,000 00	9	
3d and 4th quarters		No report					

* Entered and cleared: 3 steamers, 2 schooners—5. Aggregate tonnage entered, 3,951.   † Entered and cleared: 2 steamers, 1 bark, 3 schooners—6. Aggregate tonnage entered, 3,038.
‡ Entered and cleared: 3 steamers, 1 brig, 5 schooners—9. Aggregate tonnage entered, 6,075.   § Entered and cleared: 2 steamers, 2 schooners, 2 schooners, 1 bark—5. Aggregate tonnage entered, 4,797.
¶ Entered: 3 steamer, 1 ship, 1 bark, 5 schooners—10. Cleared: 3 steamers, 1 ship, 1 bark, 4 schooners—9, and 1 in port. Aggregate tonnage entered, 4,477 71-95.
** Entered: 2 steamships, 1 bark, 8 schooners—11, and 1 in port. Cleared: 2 steamers, 1 bark, 8 schooners—11, and 1 in port. Aggregate tonnage entered, 3,307 71-95.
†† Entered: 2 steamers, 2 schooners—4. Cleared: 2 steamers, 1 schooner, 1 not stated. Aggregate tonnage entered, 4,780.
‡‡ Entered: 4 steamers, 2 schooners—6. Cleared: 3 steamers, 1 schooner—4, and 2 in port. Aggregate tonnage entered, 5,647 99-95.
§§ Entered and cleared: 3 steamers. Aggregate tonnage entered, 7,400.   §§ Entered: 4 steamers, 2 sloops, 3 barks—9. Cleared: not reported. Aggregate tonnage entered, 9,280.

Navigation and commerce of the United States with foreign countries—Mexico.

COUNTRY, CONSULATE, NAME OF CONSUL, AND DATE OF RETURNS.	VESSELS				CARGOES					
	ENTERED		CLEARED		INWARD			OUTWARD		
	No.	Where from.	No.	Where for.	No.	Description.	Value.	No.	Description.	Value.
MAZATLAN.—R. R. Carman.										
Quarter ended December 31, 1863.*	2	La Paz	1	La Paz	1	General merchandise		1	In port	
			1	In port	1	90 tons salt		1	Ballast	
	9	San Francisco	1	Manzanillo	1	68,000 feet lumber		1	Lumber and merchandise, 100	$16,000 00
			2	La Paz	2	200 tons general merchandise and machinery, &c.	$26,000 00	2	tons machinery, &c.	
			4	Guaymas	4	850 tons ditto	260,000 00	4	550 tons general merchandise	
			2	Mazatlan	1	200 tons ditto	200,000 00	1	In port	
	3	Guaymas			1	Ballast		1	do.	
			3	San Francisco	1	do.		1	Rock from mines	
					1	do.		1	30 tons gen. mer'dise and specie	
					1	30 tons gen. merchandise and specie	100,000 00			
	14		14		14		586,000 00	14		16,000 00
2d quarter	No report									
Quarter ended June 30, 1864.†	8	San Francisco	4	Guaymas	4	1,110 tons general merchandise	196,000 00	4	780 tons general merchandise	144,000 00
			2	Altata	2	Ballast		2	Ballast	
			1	Carmen island	1	250 tons general merchandise	30,000 00	1	8 tons machinery	1,200 00
			1	Navachista	1	Ballast		1	Ballast	
	2	La Paz	2	San Francisco	2	Specie	200,000 00	2	Specie, &c.	97,000 00
	10		10		10		426,000 00	10		242,200 00
Quarter ended September 30, 1864.‡	4	San Francisco	1	La Paz	1	110 tons general merchandise	13,000 00	1	90 bales cotton	16,000 00
			2	Guaymas	1	160 tons ditto	98,000 00	1	General merchandise	56,000 00
	3	La Paz	1	Manzanillo	1	General merchandise		1	In distress	
	1	Pt Colorado	3	San Francisco	1	Ballast		1	Ballast	
			1	Europe	3	$100,000; 330 tons gen. merchandise.	226,500 00	3	Specie and cotton	480,000 00
						800 tons dyewoods	30,000 00		Dyewoods	30,000 00
	8		8		8		255,500 00	8		582,000 00
MINATITLAN.—R. C. M. Hoyt.										
Quarter ended December 31, 1863.§	1	New York	1	New York	1	Assorted cargo	20,000 00	1	In port	
Quarter ended March 31, 1864.‖	1	In port	1	New York	1	Before reported		1	210 tons mahogany	6,999 75

3d and 4th quarters......... | No report.........

TABASCO.—J. H. Mansfield.

1st quarter......... | No report.........

	Whither	Cargo	No.	Value	Cargo	Value
Quarter ended March 31, 1864.¶						
2	New York	Ballast	2	......	4531 tons logwood	4,535 00
Quarter ended June 30, 1864.						
1	New Orleans	Ballast	1	......	183 tons mahogany, 300 tons logwood, 291 hides	3,081 00

4th quarter......... | No report.........

MEXICO.—F. Chase.

	Whence	Cargo	No.	Value	Cargo	Value
Quarter ended December 31, 1863.†						
3	New Orleans	Assorted cargoes	3	11,085 00	Plantains	397 50
1	New York	...do......	1	6,850 00	Hemp	6,396 97
4			4	17,935 00		6,773 77
Quarter ended March 31, 1864.‡						
4	New Orleans	Flour, &c.	4	3,454 15	Fruit and sarsaparilla	654 58
2	New York	...do......	3			
		...do......	2		Hides and hemp	17,087 44
6			6	3,454 15		17,742 02
Quarter ended June 30, 1864.§§						
2	New York......	Assorted cargo...	1		Ballast	27 00
1	Brazos Sgo.	Not stated......	1		...do......	
4	New Orleans......	...do......	1		Fruit......	
		Assorted cargo......	3	12,092 61	Not stated	458 45
					Fruit and sarsaparilla	485 45
7			7	12,092 61		
Quarter ended September 30, 1864.‖						
6	New Orleans......	Assorted cargo......	7	23,941 67	Fruit.........	332 47
1	Sold		2		Sold......	
1	New York......	Ballast......	1		Ballast......	
1	Matamoras......	...do......	5		...do......	250 00
2	Santiago......	...do......	1		Fruit.	
	Sold......	...do......	1		Sold.	582 47
11			11	23,941 67		

* Entered: 7 schooners, 6 steamers, 1 brig—14. Cleared: 4 schooners, 6 steamers, 1 brig—11, and 3 in port. Aggregate tonnage entered, 7,886 46-95.
† Entered and cleared: 5 steamers, 3 ships, 1 schooner, 1 brig—10. Aggregate tonnage entered, 12,622 72-95.
‡ Entered and cleared: 2 schooners, 5 steamers, 1 ship—8. Aggregate tonnage entered, 10,491 76-95. § Entered: 1 brig. Cleared: 1 brig in port. Tonnage, 193 3-95.
‖ Entered: 1 in port. Cleared: 1 brig. Tonnage before reported. ¶ Entered and cleared: 1 brigantine, 1 bark—2. Aggregate tonnage entered, 514.
** Entered and cleared: 1 schooner. Tonnage, 199. †† Entered and cleared: 3 schooners, 1 steamer—4. Aggregate tonnage entered, 415 8-95.
‡‡ Entered and cleared: 6 schooners. Aggregate tonnage entered, 498. §§ Entered and cleared: 6 schooners, 1 steamer—7. Aggregate tonnage entered, 550.
‖‖ Entered: 8 schooners, 2 steamers, 1 sloop—11. Cleared: 7 schooners, 1 steamer, 1 sloop—9; 2 sold. Aggregate tonnage entered, 480.

Navigation and commerce of the United States with foreign countries.—Mexico, Honduras.

COUNTRY, CONSULATE, NAME OF CONSUL, AND DATE OF RETURNS.	VESSELS				CARGOES					
	ENTERED		CLEARED		INWARD			OUTWARD		
	No.	Where from.	No.	Where for.	No.	Description.	Value.	No.	Description.	Value.
VERA CRUZ—M. D. L. Lane.										
Quarter ended December 31, 1863.*	2	New York	1	Frontera	1	Lumber		1	Ballast	
	1	Havana	1	Cuba	1	Ice		1	do	
	1	Wilmington	1	Honduras	1	Assorted cargo		1	do	
	1	Beauport	1	Cuba	1	Railroad ties		1	do	
	1	Philadelphia	1	do	1	Lumber		1	do	
			1	Brownsville	1	Railroad ties				
	6		6		6			6		
Quarter ended Mar. 31, 1864.†	2	New York	1	Havana	1	Lumber		1	Ballast	
	3	New Orleans	1	Cienfuegos	1	do		1	do	
	1	Portland	1	Cuba	1	Railroad ties		1	do	
			1	Frontera	1	do		1	do	
			1	Cienfuegos	1	Lumber		1	do	
			1	Matanzas						
	6		6		6			6		
Quarter ended June 30 and September 30, 1864.‡	{2	Havana	7	Vera Cruz	7	Assorted cargo and sleepers	$1,470 37	{6	Ballast	$11,169 17
	2	New York						1	In port	
	4}	New Orleans								
	7		7		7			7		
HONDURAS. OMOA—C. R. Follin.										
Quarter ended December 31, 1863.§	1	Boston	1	Boston	1	Lumber and provisions	$1,448 90	1	Sarsaparilla, hides, deer-skins, turtle-shell, fustic, India-rubber.	
Quarter ended Mar. 31, 1864.‖	1	Belize	1	Belize	1	Ballast		1	90 tons fustic	320 00
	1	Boston	1	Boston	1	Lumber and provisions	1,448 90	1	Produce	17,690 45
	2		2		2		1,448 90	2		18,010 45

	No.			No.			No.		Value
Quarter ended June 30, 1864.¶‡‡	1	Boston	......	1	Boston	Lumber and provisions......	1	Hides, sarsaparilla, India-rubber..	13,697 45
Quarter ended September 30, 1864.**	2	Boston	......	2	Boston	Ballast...... Assorted cargo.....	1 1	Produce...... Fustic......	10,794 16 15,463 45
	9			2			2		26,257 71
NICARAGUA. **SAN JUAN DEL SUR. CORIN-TO.—B. L. Hill.**									
Quarter ended December 31, 1863.††	6 1 4 11	Panama...... San Francisco... San José......	......	1 10 11	San José...... La Union...... San Francisco... Panama......	Unknown...... General cargo.....	1 10 11	Unknown...... General cargo.....	2,076 93
Quarter ended Mar. 31, 1864.‡‡	7 6 13	San José...... Panama......	......	7 6 13	Panama...... San José......	General cargo...... ...do......	7 6 13	Not stated...... ...do......	......
Quarter ended June 30, 1864.§§	5 3 3 11	Guatemala...... Salvador......	......	3 3 3 11	Panama...... San José...... Panama...... San José......	Not stated...... ...do...... ...do...... ...do......	3 3 3 11	Not stated...... ...do...... ...do...... ...do......	......
Quarter ended September 30, 1864.‖‖	4 3 7	San José...... Panama......	......	4 3 7	Panama...... San José......	General cargo...... ...do......	3 4 7	Cotton, coffee, hides, indigo... Unknown......	......

* Entered and cleared: 2 brigs, 1 schooner, 1 ship, 2 barks—6. Aggregate tonnage entered, 1,502 45-95.
† Entered and cleared: 3 barks, 3 brigs, 1 schooner—6. Aggregate tonnage entered, 3,092 5-95.
‡ Entered: 1 brig, 4 schooners, 1 bark, 1 ship—7. Cleared: 1 brig, 3 schooners, 1 bark, 1 ship—6, and 1 in port. Aggregate tonnage entered, 2,418 76-95.
¶ Entered and cleared: 1 brig. Tonnage, 145 49-95. ‡‡ Entered and cleared: 1 steamer, 1 brig—2. Aggregate tonnage entered, 205 45-95.
†† Entered and cleared: 10 steamers, 1 brig—11. Aggregate tonnage entered, 9,973.
‡‡ Entered and cleared: 13 steamers. Aggregate tonnage entered, 27,560.
§§ Entered and cleared: 11 steamers. Aggregate tonnage entered, 11,660.
‖‖ Entered and cleared: 7 steamers. Aggregate tonnage entered, 7,440.

COUNTRY, CONSULATE, NAME OF CONSUL, AND DATE OF RETURNS.	VESSELS.				CARGOES.					
	ENTERED.		CLEARED.		INWARD.			OUTWARD.		
	No.	Where from.	No.	Where for.	No.	Description.	Value.	No.	Description.	Value.
SAN JUAN DEL NORTE.—B. S. Cottrell.										
Quarter ended December 31, 1863.*	1	In port	1	New York	1	Before reported		1	Ballast	
	2	New York	2	...do	2	Assorted cargo		2	Hides, skins, &c.	$30,032 96
	3		3		3			3		30,032 96
2d quarter.		No arrivals.		No departures.						
Quarter ended June 30, 1864.†	1	Georgetown	1	In port	1	Ballast		1	In port	
Quarter ended September 30, 1864;‡	3	New York	2	New York	2	Passengers		2	Passengers	
			1	In port	1	...do		1	In port	
	3		3		3			3		
U. S. OF COLOMBIA. **PANAMA.—A. R. McKee.**										
Quarter ended December 31, 1863.§	2	In port	1	San Francisco	1	Before reported		1	Assorted merchandise	318,700 00
	11	San Francisco	1	Central America	1	...do		1	...do	32,400 00
			9	San Francisco	11	842 sacks potatoes; 52 sacks onions	$1,859 40	9	...do	3,711,300 00
						30 packages merchandise	3,363 90			
						181 packages express freight	100,473 95			
						18 cases natural curiosities	8,000 00			
						25 flasks quicksilver	1,147 50			
						2,226 packages tea	24,800 00			
						43 packages deer-skins	5,144 00			
						95 bales drills	12,000 00			
						17 bales silks	5,958 21			
						1,046 bundles whalebone	164,705 90			
						1404 barrels flour	388 50			
						720 hides	2,160 00			
						23 cases walrus teeth	1,200 00			
						44 bags silver ore	3,100 00			
						1,941 bales wool	3,989 39			
						Treasure	900,962 38			
							10,525,041 73			

					Imports			Exports	
1	New York	2	In port	1	Ballast and stores		2	In port	
1	Buenaventura	1	San Francisco	1	do		1	Assorted merchandise	708,800 00
2	Baltimore	1	Buenaventura	2	,344 tons ore	50,304 00	1	Ballast, &c	
		1	Chincha Islands		do		1	do	
1	Boston	1	In port	1	1,104 tons ed	17,664 00	1	In port	
5	Central America	1	Chincha Islands	1	36 sacks pea...	144 00	1	Ballast	
		4	Central America	5	653 ceroons cochineal	94,950 00	4	Assorted merchandise	727,500 00
					303 sacks coffee	6,060 00			
					231 dox deer-skins	7,985 00			
					90 bales cotton	1,180 00			
					9,638 hides	28,974 00			
					10 cans silver ore	300 00			
					181 packages sugar	120 00			
					309 do	2,550 00			
					do	120 00			
						565,350 00			
					99 ceroons cocoa	1,455 00			
					26 cases cigars	635 00			
					52 cans balsam				
					31 bales Bt. tiber	4,160 00			
					14 bales hats and mats	1,640 00			
					Lumber and general produce	1,365 00			
					57 kgs mhandise	9,680 00			
					Specie	3,475 00			
						142,358 90			
23	In port	1	In port	23		11,999,959 88	1	In port	5,498,700 00

Quarter ended Mar. 31, 1864.||

5	In port	2	San Francisco	2	Before reported		2	Assorted merchandise	1,350,250 00
		1	In port	1	do		1	In port	
		1	Chincha Islands	1	do		1	Ballast	
13	San Francisco	11	San Francisco	13	866 sacks potatoes; 36 sacks onions	1,883 84	11	Assorted merchandise	906,280 00
					16 packages merchandise	13,131 60		do	4,691,950 00
					154 packages personal effects	80,498 72			
					262 packages tea	6,444 00			
					84 bales deer and other skins	6,475 90			
					194 bundles whalebone	20,000 00			
					330d barrels flour	961 58			
					12,845 hides	38,649 00			
					144 sacks silver ore	16,013 51			
					681 sacks wool	62,659 32			
					42 bales cotton	6,692 50			
					8 bales and boxes furs	3,876 90			
					7 cases cigars	2,080 00			
					6 packages silk-worms	1,025 00			
					335 packages copper ore	6,256 06			

* Entered: 2 schooners, and 1 in port. Cleared: 3 schooners. Aggregate tonnage entered, 566 8-95. Tonnage, 199 27-95.
† Entered: 2 steamers, 1 brig—3. Cleared: 2 steamers, and 1 in port. Aggregate tonnage entered, 2, 960 76-95.
‡ Entered: 1 brig, 3 ships—31, and 2 in port. Cleared, 1; 16 steamers, 1 brig—19, and 4 in port. Aggregate tonnage entered, 33, 272 3-95.
§ Entered: 17 steamers, 1 brig, 3 ships—21, and 2 in port. Cleared: 16 steamers, 1 brig—32, and 5 in port. Aggregate tonnage entered, 37, 364 77-95.
|| Entered: 19 steamers, 2 ships, 1 schooner—22, and 5 in port. Cleared: 19 steamers, 2 ships, 1 schooner—22, and 5 in port. Aggregate tonnage entered, 37, 364 77-95.

Navigation and commerce of the United States with foreign countries—U. S. of Colombia.

COUNTRY, CONSULATE, NAME OF CONSUL, AND DATE OF RETURNS.	VESSELS.					CARGOES.					
	ENTERED.		CLEARED.		INWARD.		OUTWARD.				
	No.	Where from.	No.	Where for.	No.	Description.	Value.	No.	Description.	Value.	
Quarter ended Mar. 31, 1864—Continued.											
	2	New York	2	In port		Treasure for Panama	$119,709 25				
			1	Chincha Islands		Treasure for New York	3,301,943 47	2	In port		
						Treasure for England	8,175,608 34	1	do		
						Treasure for Havana	8,000 00	1	Ballast		
	1	Buenaventura	1	Buenaventura				1	do		
	6	Central America	5	Central America	3, 604 16-90 tons coal		57,676 80	5	General cargo	$443,010 00	
						Passengers					
					130 serons cochineal		23,850 00				
					9,594 sacks coffee		190,480 00				
					130 packages deer-skins		4,550 00				
					1,657 bales cotton		95,390 00				
					10,648 hides		32,064 00				
					61 ceroons silver ore		3,500 00				
					48 packages sugar		7,860 00				
					362 bags rice		3,655 00				
					31 ceroons cocoa		380 00				
					9,361 ceroons indigo		504,890 00				
					94 cans balsam		7,760 00				
					61 bales India-rubber		1,338 00				
					926 pieces lumber, produce, &c.		34,191 98				
					Treasure for England		107,565 00				
					2 bales tobacco		70 00				
	1	In port	1	In port				1	In port		
	37		37		37		12,947,530 77	37		6,680,500 00	
Quarter ended June 30, 1864.	5	In port	1	Stationary	1	Before reported		1	General merchandise	608,000 00	
			2	San Francisco	2	do	2,925 29	2	Ballast		
			1	Chincha Islands	1	do	4,218 66	1	In port		
	12	San Francisco	10	San Francisco	12	do	104,210 00	10	General merchandise	3,689,540 00	
					869 sacks potatoes; 18 sacks onions						
					46 packages merchandise						
					163 packages personal effects		87,366 82				
					3,495 packages tea						
					97 bales deer and other skins		10,434 24				
					66 bales whalebone		5,769 00				
					500 hides		2,000 00				
					593 bags silver ore		19,211 30				

No.	Destination / Cargo	Value	In port
	1,561 sacks wool	181,736 94	
	23 bales cotton	1,950 00	
	45 bales, &c., of furs	37,131 43	
	175 bales old pper.	1,060 00	
	1,189 flasks quicksilver	49,071 25	
	94 cases diving materials	99 27	
	10 sheep		
	Treasure for Panama	80,000 00	
	Treasure for New York	2,356,790 00	
	Treasure for England	7,182,676 16	
	Treasure for Punta Arenas	7,000 00	
	10,000 feet lumber.	350 00	
2 / 4	Central America — In port. General merchandise		842,460 00
5			
	489 packages sustainment	223,350 00	
	11,269 sacks coffee	927,380 00	
	158 packages deer skins	5,635 00	
	1,725 bales cotton	81,270 00	
	12,566 hides	36,568 00	
	18 cerrous silver ore	380 00	
	30 bags rice and 20 bags cocoa	790 00	
	58 cerrons indigo	8,700 00	
	4,045 packages sugar	40,450 00	
	128 cans balsam	10,940 00	
	140 packages India-rubber	6,108 00	
	1,064 packages produce and mdse.	19,397 21	
	44 boxes plants	300 00	
	17 boxes cigars	350 00	
	Specie	96,937 27	
1 / 2 / 1	New York. South Pacific. Cape St. Lucas.		
	In port. Chincha Islands. In port.—do.	46,616 00 / 90,498 00	
	Ballast		
26		10,959,381 16	5,140,000 00
5	Quarter ended September 30, 1864.†		
1	Before reported	10,765,704 78	
1	do.	4,597 57	
2	do.	994,599 80	
	Treasure		
	796 bags potatoes, 43 bags onions	1,400 00	
	2,297 bales wool	96,889 00	
	30 fur skins	9,486 30	
	147 packages personal effects	2,557 00	
	290 flasks quicksilver	3,000 00	
	296 bags silver ore	16,964 27	
	161 half chests tea	9,450 00	
	91 bales merchandise		
12	San Francisco — 130 pieces machinery		
10 / 2	In port. Stationary General cargo—do.		1,953,800 00 / 233,385 00
	In port. General merchandise		5,165,400 00

* Entered: 16 steamers, 2 ships, 3 schooners—21, and 5 in port. Cleared: 17 steamers, 3 ships, 1 schooner—21, and 5 in port. Aggregate tonnage entered, 34,456 6-95.

† Entered: 18 steamships, 1 schooner—19, and 5 in port. Cleared: 18 steamships, and 6 in port. Aggregate tonnage entered, 35,438 45-95.

Navigation and commerce of the United States with foreign countries—U. S. of Colombia.

COUNTRY, CONSULATE, NAME OF CONSUL, AND DATE OF RETURNS.	VESSELS				CARGOES					
	ENTERED		CLEARED		INWARD			OUTWARD		
	No.	Where from.	No.	Where for.	No.	Description.	Value.	No.	Description.	Value.
Quarter ended September 30, 1864—Continued.	1	New York	1	San Francisco		25 bales cotton	$11,951 90			
	1	Guayaquil	1	Guayaquil		25ea fura	23,355 41			
	5	Central America.	5	Central America.		25 seco skins	10,541 37			
						94 bags pper ore	875 00			
						71 cas ica	785 58			
						82 cases iac	519 00			
						4 bales hay	28			
						17 cases samples	3,063 50	1	General merchandise	$677,700 00
						11 bars lead and fur	3,750 00	1	In port	
						7 cases i lpao goods	1,000 00	5	General merchandise	985,636 06
						1 file	26,000 00			
					1	Ballast 1 sail				
					1	492 cervons i sail	402,820 00			
					5	1,225 packages merchandise	126,900 00			
						1,514 bags coffee	30,125 00			
						1,696 bales cotton	63,620 00			
						3,296 hides	9,888 00			
						275 cervons silver	10,130 00			
						137 bales deer-skins	4,805 00			
						153,000 feet lumber	775			
						111 cases cigars	3,990 00			
						100 cases balsam	8,000 00			
						43 cases sugar	430 00			
						45 cervons indigo	6,750 00			
						50 bags rice	760 00			
						35 bags cocoa	700 00			
						24 barrels turpentine	600 00			
						14 bales India-rubber	1,120 00			
						12 packages spice	174,742 88			
						16 packages sundries	670 00			
						7 cases natural history	350 00			
						7 packages meal	210 00			
	24		24		24		12,126,886 64	24		8,315,991 08
SABANILLA.—*W. A. Chapman.* 1st, 2d, and 3d quarters.		No report.								

No.	Whither	No.	Whence	Articles imported	Value	No.	Articles exported	Value
Quarter ended September 30, 1864. *								
1	New York	1	River Magdalena	Ballast		1	River Magdalena	
1	...do...	1	New Orleans	...do...		1	Ballast	
2		2				2		
VENEZUELA. **LA GUAYRA.—G. Ulrich.** 1st and 2d quarters.....	Foreign vessels only reported.							
Quarter ended June 30, 1864. †								
1	Philadelphia	1	Philadelphia	Butter and lard	34,332 14	1	1,000 sacks coffee	16,053 43
1	Baltimore	1	Baltimore	Provisions	18,069 00	1	1,000 sacks coffee	21,125 50
5	England	3	Philadelphia	General cargo	269,145 00	3	6,264 sacks coffee	149,550 59
				Gold	173,515 00		2,938 hides, 4,223 bales skins	50,993 98
2	New York	2	New York	General cargo	65,611 00	2	2,539 sacks coffee	
7		7			560,672 14	7		237,723 50
Quarter ended September 30, 1864. ‡								
4	Philadelphia	4	Philadelphia	4,113 barrels flour, 5,350 kegs lard, 1,054 bags wheat, 300 bxs. candles, 75 barrels and 25 bxs. tallow, 897 bags corn.	169,979 89	3	4 bags coffee and gold, 8 casks palm oil, 156 bags wheat, and 220,570 44 American gold.	28,347 44
						1	Ballast.	10,665 89
8	New York	8	New York	1,700 barrels flour, 9,194 kegs lard and butter, 1,300 barrels flour and butter, 1,020 bags wheat, 160 boxes tallow, 2,000 boxes soap, 2,540 bags corn.	217,803 16	3	79 sacks coffee, 36 boxes of old type, 39 bales cotton merchandise, deer-skins, &c.	
						5	Ballast.	
12		12			387,783 05	12		39,013 33
PUERTO CABELLO.—C. H. Loehr.								
Quarter ended December 31, 1863. §								
4	New York	4	New York	Not given.	55,027 71	2	Not given.	43,603 89
1	In port.	1	In port.			1	Ballast.	
						1	In port.	118,842 69
5	Philadelphia	4	Philadelphia	...do...	79,370 90	4	Not given.	
1	In port.	1	In port.	...do...		1	In port.	
9		9			134,398 61	9		162,446 58
Quarter ended Mar. 31, 1864. ‖								
1	Philadelphia	1	Philadelphia	Before reported.		2	Not given.	130,761 20
1	New York	1	New York					
2	In port.	2				2	Not given.	

* Entered: 2 steamers. Cleared: 1 steamer, and 1 on River Magdalena. Aggregate tonnage entered, 464 64.95.
† Entered and cleared: 4 barks, 2 brigs, 1 schooner—7. Aggregate tonnage entered, 1,479.
‡ Entered and cleared: 4 barks, 8 brigs—12. Aggregate tonnage entered, 3,146.
§ Entered: 9, class not given. Cleared: 7, class not given, and 2 in port. Aggregate tonnage entered, 2,601 49-95.
‖ Entered: 13, class not given, and 3 in port. Cleared: 13, class not given, and 3 in port. Aggregate tonnage entered, 3,513 12-95.

Navigation and commerce of the United States with foreign countries—Venezuela.

COUNTRY, CONSULATE, NAME OF CONSUL, AND DATE OF RETURNS	VESSELS — ENTERED No.	Where from	CLEARED No.	Where for	CARGOES — INWARD No.	Description	Value	OUTWARD No.	Description	Value
Quarter ended Mar 31, 1864—Continued	6	Philadelphia	5	Philadelphia	5	Not given	81,940 05	5	Not given	$255,715 37
	1	New York	1	New York	1	do.	12,800 50	1	do.	47,298 12
	2	Baltimore	1	do.	1	do.	14,622 50	1	do.	18,811 75
	1	Liverpool	1	In port	1	do.	7,810 00	1	In port	28,829 23
	2	Windsor	1	New York	1	do.	9,087 75	1	Not given	143,210 93
	1	Copenhagen	1	do.	1	do.	21,280 40	1	do.	14,231 40
			1	in port	1	do.	10,913 45	1	in port	
			1	do.	1		5,987 00			
							8,500 00			
	15		**15**		**15**		172,901 35	**15**		628,918 00
Quarter ended June 30, 1864.*	3	In port	1	Baltimore.	{3		146,121 21	3	5,817 bags coffee, 391 hides.	117,528 58
	6	Philadelphia	2	New York	6	General cargo		6	19,134 bags coffee, 3,444 hides, 1,188 deer-skins, 11,879 lbs. cotton, $10,265 American gold, 12 lbs. chocolate, 2,000 bags.	491,845 93
			6	Philadelphia						
			1	New York	1	Assorted merchandise.	17,800 00	1	1,150 bags coffee.	25,682 66
			2	Hamburg	1	do.	19,080 85	1	1,897 bags coffee.	28,230 12
			1	New York	{3	General cargo.	56,973 33	{2,635 bags coffee 880 deer-skins, 560 bags.		46,481 40
								1	Ballast.	
			1	Baltimore.	1	do.	13,928 28	1	In port	40,510 57
								1	1,778 bags coffee, 12,420 lbs. liga-mumvitæ.	
	15		**15**		**15**		253,702 67	**15**		680,989 26
Quarter ended September 30, 1864.†	1	In port	1	New York	1	Before reported		1	1,123 bags coffee, 2,928 deer-skins, 2,979 hides.	36,903 10
	5	Philadelphia	5	Philadelphia	5	50 boxes cheese, 30 barrels beef, 490 dozen brooms, 4 boxes perfumery, 74 packages drugs, 329 boxes dry goods, 6 boxes stationery, 3,480 barrels flour, 300 boxes codfish, 345 kegs lard, 320 kegs butter, 39 boxes chairs, 70 kegs vinegar, 5,360 feet lumber, 274 bales rope, 220 boxes candles, 1,015 boxes soap, 12 wheel-barrows, 1,000 gallons petroleum.	106,845 61	4	478 hides, 30 casks palm oil, $20,000 American gold, 2,160 empty wheat bags. Ballast.	40,004 05

	Whence	No.	Cargo	Value	No.	Remarks / Cargo	Value
3	New York	3	86 bxs. hardware, 119 bxs. matches, 35 barrels kerosene oil, 750 boxes fire-crackers, 200 boxes Florida water, 350 packages provisions.	65,206 25	2	$2,000 American gold, 220 doubloons, 2 cotton gins, 840 wheat bags, (return goods.)	6,929 00
			1,800 barrels flour, 15 packages drugs, 320 boxes codfish, 210 boxes chairs, 600 kegs vinegar, 3,117 feet lumber, 300 boxes candles, 1,200 boxes soap, 500 gallons petroleum, 200 boxes fire-crackers, 200 boxes Florida water, 200 boxes tobacco, 140 packages tobacco, 3 coaches, 16 boxes machinery, 4 cotton gins, 250 barrels tallow, 150 bags beans.		1	Ballast.	
1	St. Thomas	1	35 boxes hardware, 10 barrels beef, 12 boxes castor oil, 30 boxes perfumery, 720 barrels flour, 300 kegs lard, 100 boxes cheese, 4 bundles harness, 2 packages drugs, 100 bxs. codfish, 40 packages provisions.	14,587 09	1	...do...	
1	Bremen	1	1,000 barrels flour, 4 boxes hardware, 50 packages dry goods, 150 kegs lard, 300 kegs butter, 8 tierces hams, 20 pkgs. drugs, 40 pkgs. provisions.	16,254 62	1	...do...	
1	Amsterdam	1	20 boxes felt hats, 410 demijohns liquors, 120 boxes dry goods, 200 boxes candles, 35 boxes coarse earthenware, 100 boxes perfumery, 120 boxes ladies' shoes, 300 boxes boots and shoes.	96,721 00	1	...do...	
12		12		259,614 57	12		83,836 15

BRAZIL.

BAHIA.—T. F. Wilson.

Quarter ended December 31, 1863.‡	In port			Before reported		Ballast.	
2	Pernambuco	1	Callao	do	1	Sugar.	19,298 00
			Boston		1		
3		3	Rio Plata	Ballast.	3	Ballast.	19,298 00
Quarter ended Mar. 31, 1864.§	Boston	1	Boston	Flour, &c.	1	Hides, &c.	28,905 00
1		1			1		19,000 00
Quarter ended June 30, 1864.∥	Boston	1	In port	Flour, &c.	1	In port	29,573 52
1	Cardiff	1		1,800 tons coal.	1	...do...	
2		2			2		29,573 52
4th quarter	No report.						

*Entered: 5 barks, 3 brigs, 4 schooners—12, and 3 in port. Cleared: 5 barks, 3 brigs, 6 schooners—14, and 1 in port. Aggregate tonnage entered, 2,649 46-95.
†Entered: 3 barks, 7 brigs, 2 schooner—11, and 1 in port. Cleared: 3 barks, 7 brigs, 2 schooners—12, Aggregate tonnage entered, 2,541 89-95.
‡Entered: 1 schooner, and 2 in port. Cleared: 1 ship, 1 bark, 1 schooner—3. Tonnage, 151. Aggregate tonnage, 1,521.
§Entered and cleared: 1 bark. Tonnage, 358. ∥Entered: 1 ship, 1 bark—2, and 2 in port.

Navigation and commerce of the United States with foreign countries—Brazil.

COUNTRY, CONSULATE, NAME OF CONSUL, AND DATE OF RETURNS.	VESSELS — ENTERED No.	ENTERED Where from.	CLEARED No.	CLEARED Where for.	CARGOES — INWARD No.	INWARD Description.	INWARD Value.	OUTWARD No.	OUTWARD Description.	OUTWARD Value.
MARANHAM.—W. H. Evans.										
1st and 2d quarters		No report								
Quarter ended June 30, 1861.*	1	New York	1	New York	1	211 barrels flour, 500 reams paper, 30 bbls. salt pork, 55 bbls. kerosene oil, 149 cases hardware, 150 tins soda biscuit, domestics, &c.	$10,000 00	1	Part inward cargo	$2,500 00
4th quarter		No report								
PARA.—J. R. Bond.										
1st and 2d quarters		No report								
Quarter ended June 30, 1864.†	1	New York	1	New York	1	Ballast		1	Rubber and annatto	17,723 32
4th quarter		No report								
PERNAMBUCO.—T. Adamson.										
Quarter ended December 31, 1863;	1	In port	1	Philadelphia		Before reported			Ballast	
	2	Baltimore	1	Bahia	1	917 bbls. flour, 300 kegs crackers, &c.	7,645 00	1	...do...	
			1	Valparaiso	1	1,500 bbls. flour and sundries.	46,000 00	1	Inward cargo, 2,500 bags sugar.	56,000 00
			1	Baltimore	1	1,710 bbls. flour, 100 kegs lard.	16,413 00	1	2,820 bags sugar	50,377 00
	2	Rio de Janeiro	1	do.	1	Ballast		1	4,080 bags sugar	29,816 00
			1	In port.	1	...do...		1	In port.	
	6		6		6		70,058 00	6		106,393 00
Quarter ended March 31, 1864.§	1	In port	1	Baltimore		Before reported		1	2,350 bags sugar	18,111 00
	1	Philadelphia	1	Rio Janeiro	1	1,734 barrels flour and machinery.	16,000 00	1	Machinery	
	1	Sumatra	1	Gibraltar.	1	Pepper		1	Inward cargo.	
	3		3		3		16,000 00	3		18,111 00
Quarter ended June 30, 1864.‖	1	Whaling cruise.	1	Whaling cruise.	1	175 barrels sperm oil		1	ward cargo.	
	1	New York	1	Telcahuano	1	Assorted cargo		1	...do...	
	2	Boston	1	Rio Janeiro	1	40 bbls. rock oil, 3,405 bbls. flour.	33,870 00	2	40 bbls. rock oil, 1,494 bbls. flour.	14,730 00
			1	Batavia	1	Assorted cargo.		1	ward cargo.	
	4		4		4		33,870 00	4		14,730 00

Quarter ended September 30, 1864.¶							
Bangor	1	Valparaiso	160,000 feet lumber		1	Ballast	3,500 00
Bravo	1	In port	Whaling stores		1	In port	4,000 00
Boston	1	...do	70,000 feet lumber		}	...do	37,000 00
			2,900 barrels flour				
	3				3		44,500 00
RIO GRANDE DO SUL—A. Young, jr.							
1st quarter	No report.						946 00
Six months ended June 30, 1864.*							
Baltimore	2	West Indies	Flour, coal oil, lard, and lumber		1	82 mules	21,686 21
					1	In port	
	2				2		21,686 21
4th quarter	No report.						946 00
RIO JANEIRO—J. Monroe.							
Quarter ended December 31, 1863.††							
New York	2	In port	General cargo		...	In port	
ndlif	2	California	Ballast		1	Ballast	
		Callao	Coal		1	..do	
		Maine	1,908 tons coal		1	..do	
Guinby	1	Whaling	Coal		1	..do	
St. Catherine's	4	Baltimore	Ballast		4	13,305 bags coffee	275,780 00
Baltimore	8	Pernambuco	14,412 bbls flour		2	Ballast	
		In port	3,470 barrels		2	Inward cargo	
Callao	1	Antwerp	2,910 sks flour and sundries		1	Ballast	36,000 00
Boston	3	Calcutta	Cargo not landed		1	In port	
		In port	593 barrels apples, ice, &c		1	Inward cargo	
		do	900 barrels apples				
			Cargo not landed				
	18				18		311,780 00
Quarter ended March 31, 1864.‡‡							
In port	...	In port			18		226,185 00
Boston	3	India	Ice, apples, lumber		1	Ballast	15,000 00
		Batavia	Lumber and sundries		2	Ballast and sundries	15,000 00
		California	Cargo not landed		1	Inward cargo	
		Augora Bay	1,720 barrels flour		2	Coffee, &c	18,500 00
Baltimore	7	Montevideo	150 barrels flour and sundries		1	Ballast	17,000 00
§§4		18			18		224,235 00

H. Ex. Doc. 60——11*

* Entered and cleared: 1 brig. Tonnage, 186.
† Entered and cleared: 1 schooner. Tonnage, 186.
‡ Entered: 3 barks, 1 brigantine, 1 schooner—5, and 1 in port. Cleared: 3 barks, 1 brigantine, 1 schooner—5, and 1 in port. Aggregate tonnage entered, 1,644 25-95.
§ Entered: 1 bark, 1 ship—2, and 1 in port. Cleared: 2 barks, 1 ship—3. Aggregate tonnage entered, 761 77-95.
|| Entered and cleared: 4 barks. Aggregate tonnage entered, 1,231 31-95. ¶ Entered: 2 barks, 1 brig—3. Cleared: 1 bark, and 2 in port. Aggregate tonnage entered, 991 35-95.
** Entered: 1 brig, 1 schooner—2. Cleared: 1 brig, and 1 in port. Aggregate tonnage entered, 352.
†† Entered: 9 ships, 8 barks, 1 steamer—18. Cleared: 6 ships, 7 barks, 1 steamer—14, and 4 in port. Aggregate tonnage entered, 14,223.
‡‡ Entered: 4 ships, 8 barks, 1 brig—13. Cleared: 3 ships, 6 barks, 1 brig—10, and 3 in port. Aggregate tonnage entered, 7,282.
§§ Not reported in this quarter.

Navigation and commerce of the United States with foreign countries—Brazil.

COUNTRY, CONSULATE, NAME OF CONSUL, AND DATE OF RETURNS.	VESSELS				CARGOES					
	ENTERED		CLEARED		INWARD			OUTWARD		
	No.	Where from.	No.	Where for.	No.	Description.	Value.	No.	Description.	Value.
Quarter ended March 31, 1864—Continued.	1	Cardiff	1	Hampton Roads	1	2,900 barrels flour	$30,200 00	1	3,400 bags coffee	$48,996 00
	1	Pernambuco	2	Baltimore	2	5,738 barrels flour	72,500 00	2	5,686 bags coffee	
	1	Philadelphia	2	In port	2	7,300 barrels flour	95,000 00	2	In port	
			1	do	1	1,743 tons coal	17,000 00	1	do	
			1	Philadelphia	1	Machinery	20,000 00	1	Ballast	
			1	California	1	Cargo not landed		1	Inward cargo	
	13		13		13		300,200 00	13		973,161 00
Quarter ended June 30, 1864.*	3	Cardiff	1	Callao	1	1,249 tons coal		1	Ballast	
	7	Baltimore	2	In port	2	3,294 tons coal		2	In port	
	2	Boston	7	Baltimore	7	22,060 barrels flour	224,730 00	7	24,877 bags coffee	550,090 00
	1	Newport	1	Callao	1	Ballast		1	Ballast	
	1	Liverpool	1	do	1	1,426 barrels flour, &c.	26,260 00	1	do	
	1	Shields	1	Callao	1	1,700 tons coal		1	Ballast	
	1	New York	1	In port	1	1,390 tons coal		1	In port	
			1	do	1	1,555 tons coal		1	do	
					1	General cargo				
	16		16		16		260,990 00	16		550,090 00
Quarter ended September 30, 1864.†	6	Baltimore	4	Baltimore	4	12,351 barrels flour.	120,690 00	3	3,000 bags coffee	63,000 00
	3	Cardiff	2	In port	2	Flour, lumber, &c		3	Ballast	
	3	New York	3	Callao	3	4,599 tons coal	109,500 00	3	In port	
	1	Philadelphia	3	California	1	Cargo not landed	45,920 00	3	Ballast	
	1	Boston	2	In port	2	do		2	Same as inward cargo	
	1	Pat abt.	1	California	1	do		1	In port	
	1	Sunderland	1	River Platte	1	Outward cargo		1	Same as inward cargo	
	1	New do	1	California	1	1,717 tons coal	17,170 00	1	Same cargo	
	1	Hamburg	1	India	1	1,030 tons coal	10,300 00	1	In port	
	1	...pool	1	In port	1	Dry goods	25,000 00	1	do	
			1	do	1	1,815 tons coal	18,150 00	1	do	
			1	do						
	19		19		19		346,730 00	19		63,000 00
SONSONATE.—J. Mahl. 1st, 2d, 3d, and 4th quarters.		No arrivals.		No departures.						

	Arrivals			Departures		
ST. CATHARINE's.—B. Lindsey.						
1st quarter..........	No report....			No report....		
Quarter ended March 31, 1864.‡	1 Sag Harbor....	971 barrels oil....	1 Cruise....	Same as inward cargo....		
	4 New Bedford....	3,000 lbs. whalebone, 1,550 bbls. oil.	4 New Bedford....	do....do....		
	1 Montevideo....	United States war steamer.	1 Rio de Janeiro....	War steamer.		
	6		6			
Quarter ended June 30, 1864.§	4 New Bedford....	4,590 barrels oil.	6 Cruise....	Same as inward cargo.		
	1 Mattapoisett....	650....do.....	1 Home....	In port....		
			1 ....do....	Same as inward cargo.		
	7		7			
Quarter ended September 30, 1864.‖	2 In port....	Before reported....	2 New Bedford....	1,980 barrels oil		
	1 Sag Harbor....	400 barrels oil....	1 Cruise....	400....do....		
	1 New Bedford....	30....do....	1 New Bedford....	30....do....		
	4		4			
ACAJUTLA.—J. Mask.						
1st quarter....	No report....			No report....		
2d quarter....	No arrivals....			No departures....		
3d and 4th quarters....	No reports....					
PERU.						
CALLAO.—J. E. Lovejoy.						
Quarter ended December 31, 1863.¶	7 Montevideo....	Ballast....	2 France....	2,900 tons guano....	66,000 00
	11 San Francisco....	....do....	5 Antwerp....	6,300....do....	189,000 00
		....do....	4 ....do....	5,600....do....	166,000 00
		....do....	3 Hamburg....	3,300....do....	99,000 00
		....do....	2 France....	2,600....do....	78,000 00
		....do....	2 Antwerp....	2,300....do....	69,000 00
		....do....	2 England....	2,300....do....	66,000 00

* Entered: 9 ships, 6 barks, 1 brig—16. Cleared: 4 ships, 5 barks, 1 brig—10, and 6 in port. Aggregate tonnage entered, 10,547.
† Entered: 12 ships, 6 barks, 1 brig—19. Cleared: 5 barks, 5 ships, 1 brig—11, and 8 in port. Aggregate tonnage entered, 13,451.
‡ Entered and cleared: 5 barks, 1 steamer—6. Aggregate tonnage entered, 1,596.
§ Entered: 5 barks, 2 ships—7. Cleared: 5 barks, 1 in port. Aggregate tonnage entered, 2,072.
‖ Entered: 2 barks—2 in port. Cleared: 3 barks, 1 ship—4. Aggregate tonnage entered, 530.
¶ Entered and cleared: 54 ship, 6 barks—60. Aggregate tonnage entered, 57,906.

Navigation and commerce of the United States with foreign countries—Peru.

COUNTRY, CONSULATE, NAME OF CONSUL, AND DATE OF RETURNS.	VESSELS				CARGOES					
	ENTERED		CLEARED		INWARD			OUTWARD		
	No.	Where from.	No.	Where for.	No.	Description.	Value.	No.	Description.	Value.
CALLAO.—J. E. Loosley. Quarter ended December 31, 1863—Continued.										
	1	Melbourne	1	France	1	Ballast		1	1,400 tons guano	842,000 00
	10	Rio Janeiro	7	Antwerp	7	do		7	9,900...do	297,000 00
			1	France	1	do		1	1,800...do	54,000 00
			1	Hamburg	1	do		1	700...do	21,000 00
			2	England	1	do		1	1,600...do	48,000 00
	5	Valparaiso			1	General cargo, (burned by the Alabama.)	$50,000 00	1	Burned	
			1	Boston	1	Ballast		1	900 tons guano	27,000 00
			1	Antwerp	1	do		1	1,000 tons rice	30,000 00
			1	Acapulco	1	do		1	1,500 tons guano	45,000 00
	5	Buenos Ayres	3	Antwerp	1	829 tons coal	29,000 00	2	2,000 tons sal.	60,000 00
			2	Antwerp	2	Ballast		2	3,400 tons guano	102,000 00
	4	Cardiff	4	England	3	do		2	1,800...do	54,000 00
	1	Bangor	1	France	3	499 tons coal	64,400 00	4	5,500...do	165,000 00
	2	Gibraltar	1	Hamburg		Lumber	50,000 00	1	800...do	24,000 00
			1	Genoa	2	Ballast		3	2,900...do	90,000 00
	2	Acapulco	1	Antwerp	1	do		2	3,400...do	102,000 00
	2	Bahia	1	England	1	do		2	380...do	117,000 00
	2	Panama	2	Antwerp	2	do				
	1	Payta	1	England	1	Oil and stores		1	1,000...do	30,000 00
	1	King George's Sd	1	France	1	Ballast		1	800...do	24,000 00
	1	Hamburg	1	England	1	do		1	1,200...do	36,000 00
	1	New Zealand	1	Antwerp	1	do				
	60		60		60		183,400 00	60	75,600 tons	2,268 000 00
Quarter ended March 31, 1864.*										
	3	Acapulco	2	England	2	Ballast		2	2,600 tons guano	78,000 00
			1	Antwerp	1	do		1	1,600...do	48,000 00
	3	Cardiff	2	England	3	4,901 tons coal	59,970 00	3	4,400...do	132,000 00
			1	Hamburg						
	1	King George's Sd	1	England	1	Ballast		1	1,300...do	39,000 00
	1	Montevideo	1	do	1	do		1	1,300...do	39,000 00
	1	New York	1	San Francisco	1	1,700 tons coal	25,500 00	1	1,700 tons coal	25,500 00
	1	New Zealand	2	Antwerp	2	Ballast		1	1,400 tons guano	42,000 00
	4	Panama	1	Spain	1	do		4	5,400...do	153,000 00
			1	England	1	do				

Quarter ended June 30, 1864.†

No.	Port	No.	From	No.	Cargo	Value	Cargo (guano, etc.)	Value
9	Puerno Arenas	1	Antwerp	1	...do		200 tons sugar	16,000 00
3	Rio Janeiro	1	San Francisco	1	Lumber	10,000 00	1,400 ton guano	42,000 00
7	San Francisco	3	England	3	Cedar and shells, 1,400 tons	18,045 00	4,400...do	132,000 00
		4	Antwerp	4	Ballast		5,900...do	177,000 00
		1	France	1	General cargo		1,600...do	48,000 00
		1	England	1	Hat	11,565 00	1,800...do	54,000 00
		1	Hamburg	1	do		1,700...do	51,000 00
1	St. Paulo Loando	1	Antwerp	1	do		1,400...do	42,000 00
27		**27**		**27**		**125,080 00**	**27**	**1,118,500 00**

No.	Port	No.	From	No.	Cargo	Value	Cargo (guano, etc.)	Value
3	Acapulco	2	England	2	Ballast		3,300 tons guano	99,000 00
2	Buenos Ayres	1	Hamburg	1	do		1,300...do	39,000 00
11	San Francisco	1	England	1	do		1,600...do	48,000 00
		1	Hamburg	1	do		1,600...do	48,000 00
		10	Antwerp	10	70,000 feet lumber	98,000 00	16,200...do	450,0000
9	Havre	1	England	9	Ballast		3,100...do	93,000 00
3	Montevideo	1	Spain	1	do		1,200...do	00000
		1	Genoa	1	do		400...do	30,000 00
		1	England	1	do		980...do	30,001 00
1	Cardiff	1	do	1	1,400 tons coal		42...do	94,000 00
1	Coquimbo	1	Hamburg	1	Ballast	91,000 00	1,400...do	9000
1	Nantes	1	Antwerp	1	do		1,000...do	36,000 00
1	Melbourne	1	England	1	do		1,200...do	36,000 00
2	Panama	1	Antwerp	1	do		1,000...d	30,000 00
1	Caldera	1	England	1	do		2,300...d	00,000 00
1	Valparaiso	1	do	1	200,000 feet	80,000 00	1,400...do	4800
1	Cruise	1	Cruise	1	Oil ... their		900...do	30,000 00
1	Rio Janeiro	1	England	1	Ballast		900...do	30,000 00
1	London	1	do	1	do		Oil	
2	Genoa	1	Genoa	1	do		2,000 tons guano	60,000 00
							1,500...do	45,000 00
							1,300...do	39,000 00
33		**33**		**33**		**129,000 00**	**33**	**1,380,000 00**

Quarter ended September 30, 1864.‡

No.	Port	No.	From	No.	Cargo	Value	Cargo (guano)	Value
4	Acapulco	1	England	1	Ballast		33,500 tons guano	1,045,000 00
3	Valparaiso	3	Germany	3	do			
8	San Francisco	9	England	3	3,300 tons general cargo	125,000 00		
		1	Germany	1	Ballast			
		5	Barbadoes	5	do			
		1	England	1	do			
4	Rio Janeiro	2	Genoa	1	do			
		1	Germany	2	do			
		1	England	1	do			
		1	France	1	do			
			Germany	1	do			
26		**26**		**26**		**125,000 00**	**26**	**1,045,000 00**

Aggregate tonnage entered, 34 160.

* Entered and cleared: 26 ships, 1 brig—27. Aggregate tonnage entered, 28,142. † Entered and cleared: 30 ships, 3 barks—33.
‡ Entered and cleared: 26 ships. Aggregate tonnage entered, 25,878.

COUNTRY, CONSULATE, NAME OF CONSUL, AND DATE OF RETURNS.	VESSELS				CARGOES					
	ENTERED		CLEARED		INWARD			OUTWARD		
	No.	Where from.	No.	Where for.	No.	Description.	Value.	No.	Description.	Value.
CALLAO.—*J. F. Lovejoy.* Quarter ended September 30, 1864—Continued.	1	London	1	England	1	Ballast				$1,045,000 00
	2	Panama	1	do	1	do				
	1	Melbourne	1	Germany	1	do				
	1	Caldera	1	England	1	do				
	1	Coquimbo	1	do	1	do				
	1	Malta	1	Genoa	1	do				
	96		96		96		$121,000 00	26		
PAITA.—*C. F. Winslow.* Quarter ended December 31, 1863.*	1	In port	1	Cruise	1	Before reported		1	Condemned and sold	
	7	Cruise	7	do	7	6,960 barrels whale oil	380,876 87	7	Inward cargoes	
	8		8		8		380,876 87	8		
Quarter ended March 31, 1864.†	2	Tumbez	2	Cruise	2	950 barrels sperm oil	44,887 50	2	Not stated	
	1	Callao	1	Sold	1	Ballast		1	Sold	
	1	Cruise	1	Cruise	1	50 barrels sperm oil	2,362 50	1	Not stated	
	4		4		4		47,250 00	4		
Quarter ended June 30, 1864.‡	1	Cruise	1	Cruise	1	600 barrels sperm oil	21,000 00	1	Not stated	
Quarter ended September 30, 1864.§	4	Tumbez	4	Cruise	2	170 barrels whale oil		2	Not stated	
	1	Cruise	1	do	2	3,020 barrels sperm oil		3	1,880 barrels sperm oil	
	5		5		5			5		

TUMBEZ.—D. Card.

Quarter ended December 31, 1863.||	14	Cruise	12 / 1 / 1	Cruise / New Bedford / In port	14	5,230 barrels sperm oil, 335 barrels whale oil	169,985 00	13 / 1	Same as inward cargo	169,985 00
	14				14			14	In port	169,985 00
Quarter ended March 31, 1864.¶	1 / 1	In port / Cruise	1 / 1	Cruise	2	Before reported. 100 bbls. sperm and 40 bbls. whale oil	3,600 00	1 / 1	300 bbls. sperm & 10 bbls. w. oil / 100 bbls. sperm oil	9,590 00 / 3,000 00
	2				2		3,600 00	2		12,590 00
Quarter ended June 30, 1864.		No report.								
Quarter ended September 30, 1864.**	7 / 1	New Bedford / Fairhaven	8	Cruise	8	3,715 bbls. sperm & 220 bbls. whale oil	118,404 25	8	Same as inward cargo	
	8				8		118,404 25	8		

CHILI.

TALCAHUANO.—J. H. Trumbull.

1st quarter.		No report.								
Quarter ended March 31, 1864.††	28	Cruise	10 / 1 / 3 / 23 / 1 / 1	New Bedford / Falmouth / Cruise / In port / San Francisco / do	27	90,385 barrels sperm oil / 4,930 barrels whale oil / 120,500 pounds whalebone / Ballast / General cargo / 1,125 tons coal		16 / 1 / 13	Same as inward cargo / Sold—took Chili flag / In port	
	1 / 1	Boston / New York			30			30		
	30									
Quarter ended June 30, 1864.‡‡	13	In port	5 / 1 / 7 / 3	New Bedford / Dartmouth / On a cruise / New Bedford	30	Before reported / do / do		29	Same as inward cargo	
	3	0 cts.								

* Bared: 7 ships—1 condemned. Cleared: 7 ships. Aggregate tonnage entered, 2,292.
† Entered: 3 ; do, 1 steamer—4. Cleared: 3 bark, 1 sold—4. Aggregate tonnage entered, 951.
‡ Entered: 1 ship. Cld: 1 ship. Tonnage, 436.
§ Ent and cleared: 4 ships—1 lay off the harbor. Aggregate tonnage entered, 1,251 78-95.
|| Entered: 5 ships, 9 barks—14. Cleared: 5 ships, 8 barks—13, 1 in port. Aggregate tonnage entered, 4,386.
¶ Entered: 1 bark, and 1 in port. Cleared: 2 barks. Tonnage, 180.
** Entered and cld: 3 ships, 5 barks—8. Aggregate tonnage entered, 2,408.
†† Entered: 22 barks, 7 ships—30. Cleared: 11 barks, 5 ship—16, 1 sold, and 13 in port. Aggregate tonnage entered, 10,971.
‡‡ Entered: 3 ships, 7 barks, 1 schooner—11, and 13 in port. Cleared: 3 ships, 6 barks, 1 schooner, 13 clms not given—23, and 1 sold. Aggregate tonnage entered, 3,081.

Navigation and commerce of the United States with foreign countries—Chili, Bolivia, Argentine Republic.

COUNTRY, CONSULATE, NAME OF CONSUL, AND DATE OF RETURN.	VESSELS				CARGOES					
	ENTERED		CLEARED		INWARD			OUTWARD		
	No.	Where from.	No.	Where for.	No.	Description.	Value.	No.	Description.	Value.
TALCAHUANO.—*J. H. Trumbull.* Quarter ended June 30, 1864—Continued.	6	Cruise	4	Cruise	9	5,010 barrels sperm oil, 480 barrels whale oil.				
			1	Matapoilesti						
	1	Valparaiso	1	Valparaiso	1	Ballast		1	Sold—took Chilian flag	
	1	New London	1	Sold	1	General merchandise		1	Ballast	
			1	Cruise						
	24		24		24			24		
Quarter ended September 30, 1864.*	1	Baltimore	1	Baltimore	1	Hides, wool, copper	$30,000 00	1	Same as inward cargo	
	1	New York	1	Valparaiso	1	199 tons merchandise	30,000 00	1	do...do	
	2		2		2			2		
BOLIVIA. COBIJA.—*L. Joel.* 1st quarter		No report								
2d, 3d, and 4th quarters	1	Valparaiso	1	Paquica & Cork, for orders.	1	Ballast		1	1,400 tons guano	$14,000 00
ARGENTINE REPUBLIC. BUENOS AYRES.—*H. Q. Helper.* Quarter ended December 31, 1863.†	9	In port	1	Sold	1	Before reported		1	Sold	
			1	New York	1	do		1	13,950 dry hides and sundries	$8,845 00
	1	Ellsworth	1	Callao	1	484,339 ft. lumber, 99,000 shingles	8,905 00	1	Ballast	
	3	Baltimore	1	New York	1	431,118 ft. white lumber	9,758 00	1	do	
			2	In port	2	100,000 ft. lumber, 15,000 ft. hard wood 783 bbls. flour.	56,648 00	9	In port	
	1	Parnas	1	New York	1	Ballast		1	Ballast	8,600 00
	1	Searsport	1	India	1	340,000 ft. pine and spruce, &c	8,600 00	1	do	5,970 00
	1	Portland	1	Sold	1	1,000 boxes kerosene oil	5,970 00	1	Sold	7,794 00
	1	New Bedford	1	In port	1	268,000 ft. spruce and pine lumber	7,794 00	1	In port	
	10		10		10		96,899 00	10		58,845 00

Quarter ended March 31, 1864.‡

Port	No.	Whence/Whither	No.	Cargo	Value	No.	Cargo	Value
In port	3	Baltimore	1	Before reported		} 2	27,110 dry hides and sundries	105,937 00
		Sold	1	do		1	Sold	
New York	2	New York	1	do		1	1 929 dry hides and sundries	79,659 00
Montevideo	1	In port	1	1,881 bbls. flour and sundries		1	In port	
Mas	1	Sold	1	1,250 bbls. sugar and sundries		1	Sold	
Troon	1	Boston	1	Ballast	41,501 00	1	555 bales wool, 1,000 dry hides	67,558 00
Portland	2	India	1	264,417 ft. pine lumber	65,541 00	1	Ballast	
		Callao	1	400 tons coal	5,384 00	1	do	
		In port	1	469,733 ft. lumber	7,293 00	1	In port	
Rosario	1	Sold	1	265,661 ft. lumber	8,550 00	1	Sold	
Ellsworth	1	Callao	1	Ballast	9,600 00	1	Ballast	
Bahre	1	Sold	1	264,000 ft. lumber, 69,000 shingles	6,250 00	1	Sold	
		Callao	1	2,862 boxes kerosene oil, &c.	99,386 00			
	13		13		173,612 00	13		253,154 00

Quarter ended June 30, 1864.§

Port	No.	Whence/Whither	No.	Cargo	Value	No.	Cargo	Value
In port	2	Lima	1	Before reported		1	Ballast, wool, skins, hair, &c.	83,904 00
		New York	1	do		1	Hides, skins, hair, &c.	65,836 00
Montevideo	1	do	1	Ballast		1	Hides, wool, and skins.	
Portland	1	In port	1	447,195 ft. lumber, 157,000 shingles	10,015 00	1	In port	
	4		4		10,015 00	4		149,760 00

Quarter ended September 30, 1864.‖

Port	No.	Whence/Whither	No.	Cargo	Value	No.	Cargo	Value
In port	1	Callao	1	Before reported		1	Ballast	
Higuentes	1	England	1	630 tons bones and bone salt	7,000 00	1	Inward cargo	7,000 00
New York	5	Callao	1	442,090 ft. lumber	8,448 00	1	Ballast	
		In port	4	General cargo, lumber, shooks, machines	99,700 00	1	In port	
		do	1	Rails, &c.	9,000 00	1	do	
Newport	1	do	2	548,710 ft. lumber, &c.	10,900 00	2	do	
Seanport	2	do	2	320,000 ft. lumber and general cargo	18,528 00	2	do	
Boston	2							
	12		12		83,306 00	12		7,000 00

ROSARIO—B. Upton.

1st quarter

Port	No.	Whence/Whither	No.	Cargo	Value	No.	Cargo	Value
No report		No report						

Quarter ended March 31, 1864.¶

Port	No.	Whence/Whither	No.	Cargo	Value	No.	Cargo	Value
Portland	1	Buenos Ayres	1	Lumber	8,500 00	1	Ballast	

3d and 4th quarters

Port	No.	Whence/Whither	No.	Cargo	Value	No.	Cargo	Value
No report								

* Entered and cleared: 1 ship, 1 bark—2 Aggregate tonnage entered, 709.
† Entered: 5 barks, 1 schooner, 1 brig, 1 ship—8, and 2 in port. Cleared: 4 barks, 1 schooner—5, 2 sold, and 3 in port. Aggregate tonnage entered, 3,521.
‡ Entered: 9 barks, 1 ship—10, and 3 in port. Cleared: 1 brig, 2 ships, 4 barks—7, 4 sold, and 2 in port. Aggregate tonnage entered, 5,829.
§ Entered: 9 barks, and 2 in port. Cleared: 3 barks, and 1 in port. Aggregate tonnage entered, 1,050.
‖ Entered: 1 schooner, 6 barks, 4 ships—11, and 1 in port. Cleared: 2 barks, 1 schooner—3, and 9 in port. Aggregate tonnage entered, 6,409.
¶ Entered and cleared: 1 bark. Tonnage, 369.

Navigation and commerce of the United States with foreign countries—Uruguay, Africa, Society Islands.

COUNTRY, CONSULATE, NAME OF CONSUL, AND DATE OF RETURNS.	VESSELS.				CARGOES.					
	ENTERED.		CLEARED.		INWARD.		OUTWARD.			
	No.	Where from.	No.	Where for.	No.	Description.	Value.	No.	Description.	Value.
URUGUAY. MONTEVIDEO—*H. Twill.* Quarter ended December 31, 1863.*	4	In port	1	Valparaiso	1	Before reported		1	Ballast	
			2	Callao	2	do		2	do	
	1	Bangor	1	Searsport				1	do	$3,468 00
	1	Hull, (England)	1	Cape Town	1	300,000 ft. lumber	$6,000 00	1	100 mules	
			1	Callao	1	1,270 tons coal	13,700 00	1	Ballast	
	1	Portland	1	Buenos Ayres	1	225,000 ft. lumber, 1,000 boxes kero-	13,900 00	1	1,000 boxes kerosene oil	8,000 00
						sene oil.				
	1	Ellsworth	1	In port	1	590,000 ft. lumber	16,294 00	1	In port	
	1	Buenos Ayres	1	do	1	Ballast		1	do	
	1	Put back	1	do				1	do	
	1	St. John's, N. B.	1	do	1	300,000 ft. lumber	9,000 00	1	do	
	1	New York	1	San Francisco	1	Assorted merchandise	300,000 00	1	Inward cargo	300,000 00
	1	Philadelphia	1	In port	1	454,000 ft. lumber	14,528 00	1	In port	
	1	Searsport	1	do	1	459,000 ft. lumber	14,259 00	1	do	
	14		14		14		388,881 00	14		311,468 00
Quarter ended March 31, 1864.†	6	In port	1	Amherst	1	Before reported		1	Ballast	
			3	New York	3	do		3	do	
			1	Buenos Ayres	1	do		1	do	
			1	Condemned	1	do		1	Condemned	
	1	Ellsworth	1	St. Thomas	1	400,000 ft. lumber	11,900 00	1	Ballast	
	1	Buenos Ayres	1	Amherst	1	Ballast		1	do	
	1	Bangor	1	Valparaiso	1	200,000 ft. lumber	19,200 00	1	200,000 ft. lumber	4,000 00
	1	Boston	1	Callao	1	600,000 ft. lumber, &c.	98,100 00	1	Ballast	
	1	Portland	1	Buenos Ayres	1	464,000 ft. lumber, &c.	14,100 00	1	Inward cargo	14,100 00
	1	Bordeaux	1	Callao	1	470,000 ft. lumber		1	Ballast	
	1	Baltimore	1	In port	1	9,500 bbls. flour, &c.	30,000 00	1	In port	
	1	Isl'd of Ascension	1	do	1	Ballast		1	Inward cargo	49,550 00
	1	Whaling	1	Whaling	1	1,150 bbls. whale oil	42,550 00	1	Inward cargo	60,650 00
	15		15		15		131,050 00	15		60,650 00
Quarter ended June 30, 1864;	2	In port	1	Buenos Ayres	1	Before reported		1	Ballast	
			1	Unknown		do		1	90 mules and 5 horses	3,010 00

No.	Whence	No.	Cargo (entered)	Value	No.	Remarks (cleared / in port)	Value
2	Buenos Ayres	2	Ballast	106,250 00	2	Ballast	3,210 00
1	Callao	1	1,700 tons guano		1	In port in distress	
5	In port	5		106,250 00	5		3,210 00

Quarter ended September 30, 1864.§

No.	Whence	No.	Cargo (entered)	Value	No.	Remarks (cleared / in port)	Value
1	Cardiff	1	Before reported		1	Condemned	
1	Rio de Janeiro	1	1,000 tons coal	10,000 00	1	Ballast	
1	Hamburg	1	1,585 tons coal	15,950 00	1	In port	40,000 00
1	New York	1	Assorted merchandise	50,000 00	1	Part inward cargo	17,326 00
1	do.	1	476,000 ft. lumber	17,326 00	1	Inward cargo; called for orders	
5		5		93,276 00	5		57,326 00

AFRICA.
GABOON RIVER.—H. May.||

1st quarter .... No report.

Quarter ended March 31, 1864.||

No.	Whence	No.	Cargo (entered)	Value	No.	Remarks (cleared)	Value
1	Windward coast	1	200 lbs. ivory, 200 tons camwood, 3,618 gals. palm oil, 104 lbs. metal, 2,000 lbs. tobacco, 1,000 lbs. soap.	3,823 38	1	New York. — 238 lbs. ivory, 200 tons barwood, 10,329 lbs. rubber, 4 tons camwood, 60 lbs. yellow wax, 3,618 gals. palm oil, 104 lbs. copper, 357 lbs. metal.	3,923 00

Quarter ended June 30, 1864¶.

No.	Whence	No.	Cargo (entered)	Value	No.	Remarks (cleared)	Value
1	Acera	1	84 bbls. flour, 1,000 lbs. tobacco and provisions.	1,318 00	1	St. Thomas. — 130 tons barwood, 1,039 lbs. ginger, 700 lbs. coffee, 2,410 gals. palm oil.	1,555 61

4th quarter .... No report.

SOCIETY ISLANDS.
PAPIETI.—J. Vander.

1st, 2d, and 3d quarters .... No report.

Quarter ended September 30, 1864.**

No.	Whence	No.	Cargo (entered)	Value	No.	Remarks (cleared / in port)	Value
1	In port	1	Wrecked; cargo sent to Valparaiso.		1	Wrecked. — 990 bbls. oil	40,000 00
1	San Francisco	1	General cargo	6,000 00	1	In port	40,000 00
2		2		6,000 00	2		40,000 00

* Entered: 6 ships, 1 schooner, 3 barks—10, and 4 in port. Cleared: 6 ships, 2 barks—8, and 6 in port. Aggregate tonnage entered, 6,755 16-95.
† Entered: 5 ships, 4 barks—9, and 6 in port. Cleared: 8 ships, 3 barks, 1 schooner—12, 1 condemned, and 2 in port. Aggregate tonnage entered, 4,972 35-95.
‡ Entered: 1 ship, 2 barks—3, and 2 in port. Cleared: 4 barks, and 1 in port. Aggregate tonnage entered, 2,064 64-95.
§ Entered: 3 ships, 1 bark—4, and 1 in port. Cleared: 2 ships, 1 bark—3, 1 condemned, and 1 in port. Aggregate tonnage entered, 3,325 55-95.
|| Entered and cleared : 1 bark. Tonnage entered, 25.
¶ Entered and cleared : 1 brig. Tonnage, 147.
** Entered: 1 brigantine, and 1 in port, wrecked. Cleared, none. Tonnage, 180.

Navigation and commerce of the United States with foreign countrie—Society Islands.

COUNTRY, CONSULATE, NAME OF CONSUL, AND DATE OF RETURNS.	VESSELS.				CARGOES.					
	ENTERED.		CLEARED.		INWARD.			OUTWARD.		
	No.	Where from.	No.	Where for.	No.	Description.	Value.	No.	Description.	Value.
TAHITI—J. Vander.										
Quarter ended December 31, 1863.*	4	Whaling cruise	4	Cruise	4	Sperm oil	$63,000 00	4	Inward cargoes	
	1	San Francisco	1	In port	1	Lumber and general cargo	5,000 00	1	In port	
	5		5		5		98,000 00	5		57,554 12
Quarter ended March 31, 1864.†	1	In port	1	San Francisco	1	Before reported		1	400,000 oranges, 10,000 limes.	$2,503 00
	3	San Francisco	3	...do	3	Provisions, lumber, &c.	38,066 00	2	1,000,000 oranges, 30,000 limes. Ballast.	5,037 00
	1	Puget's sound	1	In port	1	Lumber	2,500 00	1	In port	
	1	Whaling cruise	1	Whaling cruise	1	Sperm oil	16,000 00	1	Sperm oil	16,000 00
	1	New Zealand	1	...do	1	Provisions and stores	32,000 00	1	Provisions and stores.	32,000 00
	1	Mazatlan	1	San Francisco	1	Ballast		1	350,000 oranges, 10,000 limes.	2,014 12
	8		8		8		88,566 00	8		57,554 12
Quarter ended June 30, 1864.‡	1	In port	1	San Francisco	1	Before reported		1	Oranges, limes, &c.	3,530 00
	2	New Zealand	1	Whaling cruise	1	Stores; in for repairs		1	Inward cargo, cocoa-nuts	5,000 00
	1	Valparaiso	1	San Francisco	1	General cargo	5,000 00	1	...do	1,967 00
	2	Puget's sound	1	Sydney, N. S. W.	1	Lumber	7,000 00	1	Called for supplies.	4,500 00
	1	La Paz (Mexico)	1	San Francisco	1	Potatoes and ballast	4,600 00	1	Oranges, limes, &c.	873 00
	3	Whaling cruise	2	Cruise	3	Sperm oil and provisions; came in for repairs.	18,000 00	2	Same as inward cargo.	13,000 00
			1	Wrecked				1	Wrecked; most of cargo saved.	
	8		8		8		35,100 00	8		29,170 00
4th quarter		No report								

* Entered: 2 ships, 2 barks, 1 brig—5. Cleared: 2 ships, 2 barks—4, and 1 in port. Aggregate tonnage entered, 1,613.

† Entered: 1 ship, 2 barks, 1 brig, 3 schooners—7, and 1 in port. Cleared: 1 ship, 1 bark, 2 brigantines, 3 schooners—7, and 1 in port. Aggregate tonnage entered, 1,489 13-95.

‡ Entered: 2 ships, 4 barks, 2 schooners—8. Cleared: 1 ship, 4 barks, 2 schooners—7, and 1 wrecked. Aggregate tonnage entered, 2,297

RECAPITULATION.

Showing the navigation of the United States with each consulate in each foreign country during each quarter of the year ended September 30, 1864, as far as data have been furnished by consular returns received at the statistical bureau of the Department of State.

(For aggregate values of cargoes, inward and outward, descriptions and quantities of merchandise, aggregate tonnage entered, and other minor details, the tabular statements must be consulted.)

COUNTRY AND CONSULATE.	NAME OF CONSUL.	NUMBER OF VESSELS.									
		FIRST QUARTER.		SECOND QUARTER.		THIRD QUARTER.		FOURTH QUARTER.		AGGREGATE.	
		Entered.	Cleared.	Entered.	Cleared.	Entered.	Cleared.	Entered.	Cleared.	Entered.	Cleared.
BRITISH DOMINIONS.											
Liverpool	T. H. Dudley	69	52	57	47	58	64	81	52	265	215
Bristol	Z. Eastman	9	9	2	4	3		7	7	21	20
Gloucester	J. Jones	1	1							1	1
Cardiff	C. D. K........ Mad	29	27	29	24	20	23	27	27	105	100
Newport	J. N. K........ sup.	10	7	15	14	10	9	13	6	48	36
Swansea	H. Morice							2	2	2	2
Milford Haven	A. B. Harries			1	1						
Falmouth	A. Fox	9	10					1	1	11	12
Plymouth	T. W. Fox							1	1	1	1
Newcastle-on-Tyne	J. H. McChesney	5	8	5	4	3	3	5	5	18	18
Leith	N. McLaughlin								1	4	2
Cork	E. G. Eastman			3	2	4	4	17	15	21	19
Belfast	J. Young	1	1							1	1
Thierry	A. Henderson	1	3	1						2	3
Hull	H. J. Atkinson	2	3	1		4	4	2	1	9	9
Sunderland	H. Brown			2		1					
Cowes	T. ...... Esq.										
Weymouth	W. Robberts										
.... nth	J. Garratt										
Southampton	J. Britton										
......	R. Duncan										
Dundee	J. Smith	1				1	1	1		2	1
Glasgow	W. L. Underwood	11	11	7	5	7	9	9	9	15	15
Gibraltar	H. J. Sprague	12	12	18	16	7	11	9*	14	40	40
St........ ža	G. Gerard	5	5	3	3	2	2	14		51	51
...... ath	W. Graham			1				1		10	10
Port ...... Bith	Y. C. Hree......									1	
Mauritius	W. R. G. Millen	8	9	1	1	11	9	3	5	23	24
Bombay	G. W. Kittridge	12	7	1						12	7

* Six months.

Recapitulation—Continued.

COUNTRY AND CONSULATE.	NAME OF CONSUL.	FIRST QUARTER.		SECOND QUARTER.		THIRD QUARTER.		FOURTH QUARTER.		AGGREGATE.	
		Entered.	Cleared.	Entered.	Cleared.	Entered.	Cleared.	Entered.	Cleared.	Entered.	Cleared.
BRITISH DOMINIONS—Continued.											
Calcutta	N. P. Jobe	21	22	19	11	21	13	6	11	67	57
Akyab	J. Bullock	3	3	11	10	5	8			19	21
Singapore	F. D. Cobb	24	12	12	14	10	18	7	4	53	46
Hong Kong	H. N. Gager	40	48	22	16	19	23	11	15	92	102
Port Adelaide	W. Blanchard	13	15	9	9	7	6	6	4	35	34
	J. W. Smith	4	4	2	2					6	6
St. John, N. F	C. S. Ogden	3	3							4	4
Halifax	C. O. Leach	1	4	1	1	1	1	6	6	12	12
Pictou	M. M. Jackson	4	4	3	2	11	4	14	14	32	31
St. John, N. B.	B. H. Norton	10	10			25	10	105	86	140	106
Bermuda	J. Q. Howard	46	50	15	11	59	58	67	69	187	188
Inagua, N. P.	C. M. Allen	2	1			7	4			9	11
	T. Kirkpatrick							16	11	13	5
Turk's Island	J. C. Crismon	26	23	16	18	7	8	14	14	63	63
Salt Cay	A. W. Hartlett	12	11	4	5	10	10	3	2	96	96
East Harbor	E. Jones	6	2	1	2	1	1	3	3	10	7
St. Christopher	E. Delisle	3	3	2	1	2	2	17	17	10	4
Antigua											5	5
Barbadoes	W. J. Trowbridge	17	17	24	24					58	58
Trinidad	E. H. Pitt	8	9	10	6			7	6	18	15
Kingston, Jamaica	J. N. Camp	7	7	10	10	3	3	5	10	27	26
Demerara	F. H. Pitt			2	2	14	11	9	10	55	28
	C. G. Hanson			8	9	36	36	98	98	55	94
St. George, N. B.	A. Sprague	40	40	2	3			1	1	113	113
Hamilton, (Bermuda)	J. L. Gill	1	1	9	9					2	2
St. George, (Bermuda)	C. N. Allen							3	3	3	3
Belize	C. S. Leas	1	1	3	3	2	1	4	3	9	7
Bassein	J. Henderson			3	3	9	9			12	12
Point de Galle	J. Bk.	16	13	*10	*9					12	3
	W. Brook	11	11							96	96
Seychelles	C. Dupuy	3	3							3	1
	D. McPherson, Jr							2	2	3	3
Natal	J. M. Hotze							1	1	1	1

Place	Officer	65	65	50	50	61	61	63	83	259	259
Mossel Bay	E. Eager										
Victoria, V. I.	A. Frances										
Zante	A. S. York										
FRENCH DOMINIONS.											
Havre	J. O. Putnam	10	8	7	7	8	6	10		35	35
Bordeaux	C. Davison	2	3	2	1	1	1	1	12	5	5
Nantes	J. De la Montagnie									1	
La Rochelle	J. Hirt										
Cette	L. S. Nahmens	8	8	2	2			2	2	4	4
Marseilles	F. B. Morell	8	9	4	3	15	15	10	6	8	8
Dunkirk	G. W. Van Horn									36	34
Toulon	A. Schenking	4	4								
St. Pierre, Miquelon	G. Hughs					4	4	6	6	14	14
St. Pierre, Martinique	W. P. Given			3	3	5	5	4	4	12	12
St. Martin's	C. Ray			1	1	3	3			9	9
Guadaloupe	H. Thlorville	4				3	3			7	7
Nice	W. Sladd										
SPAIN.											
Cadiz	E. B. Eggleston	10	12	6	5	7	7	11	11	34	35
Malaga	J. R. Geary	7	8	1	1			12	9	19	17
Alicante	W. L. Giro	2	2					2	2	5	5
Denia	J. Morand										
Barcelona	J. A. Little	1	2	3	3	1	1			3	3
Tarragona	J. A. Little	1	2							5	5
Havana	W. T. Minor	38	34	104	73			35	34	251	225
Matanzas	H. C. Hall	9	9	93	72	74	84	21	30	194	201
Cardenas	N. Cross	8	8	38	22	80	90	13	21	114	113
Sagua la Grande	J. H. Harman	8	8	5	4	60	64	4	5	25	26
Santiago de Cuba	E. F. Wallace					8	8	8	9	21	22
Trinidad, Cuba	E. B. Pitt	6	6	6	6	7	7	3	3	21	21
St. John, Porto Rico	J. J. Hyde	6	6	5	5	6	6	2	3	90	73
Guayama, Porto Rico	H. H. Verges	21	30	17	20	24	24	9	11	72	72
Mayaguez	J. C. Cox	4	4	1	8	6	6	5	7	25	24
Manila	J. Russel	1	1	7	7	8	8			1	1
Santander	R. C. Hannah			1	1						
Port Mahon	H. D. Robinson	2	3	2	2						
Guantanamo	F. Badell					3	3	1		4	3
Arecibo	C. F. Storer					3	5	1	5	4	
Nagnabo											
Hermanao	W. Haddocks			2	2			2			
Fajardo											
Cienfuegos	G. Barrio	4	4			30	33	2	2	30	33
Teneriffe	J. F. Zayas					5	5			5	5
Zaza	W. H. Dabney							2	2	2	2
Valencia	G. Kent	11	8	15	17	18	18	8	8	46	45
Ponce, P. R.	J. C. Gallaher	9	9			9	9	8	8	18	18
Manzanillo, Cuba	M. R. Essy										

* Six months.   † Nine months.

Recapitulation—Continued.

NUMBER OF VESSELS.

COUNTRY AND CONSULATE.	NAME OF CONSUL.	FIRST QUARTER.		SECOND QUARTER.		THIRD QUARTER.		FOURTH QUARTER.		AGGREGATE.	
		Entered.	Cleared.	Entered.	Cleared.	Entered.	Cleared.	Entered.	Cleared.	Entered.	Cleared.
SPAIN—Continued.											
Grand Canary	F. G. Manley	7	7	3	3					10	10
Bilbao	D. Evans	7	7							7	7
Las Palmas	F. W. Manley										
PORTUGAL.											
Lisbon	C. A. Monroe	2	2					2	1	4	3
Oporto	H. W. Diman									1	1
Funchal	R. Bajnan	10	13	5		16				77	81
Fayal	C. W. Dabney	6	5	3	2	1	20	46	46	12	11
St. Paul de Loanda	J. T. Bradberry	9	9		4	2	2	2	2	13	13
Macao	W. P. Jones										
BELGIUM.											
Antwerp	A. W. Crawford	10	11	4	9	12	7	33	9	59	36
Ghent	N. J. Levison										
NETHERLANDS.											
Amsterdam	T. Breicker	2	2	2		6	3	1	4	3	2
Rotterdam	G. E. Wiss	2	2	1	1	2	2	6	3	16	9
Batavia	J. P. Pels	2	2			2	2	4	4	9	8
Curacoa	R. E. Morse	5	5	7	7			11	9	11	11
Paramaribo	H. Sawyer									18	16
HANSE TOWNS.											
Bremen	F. W. Specht	3	1	1	2	4	4	2	5	5	5
Hamburg	J. H. Anderson	8	3	3	2			4	5	16	14
DENMARK.											
Copenhagen	L. A. Hecksher	1	2	1	1	2	3	4	4	2	1
Christianstad	E. H. Perkins	2		3	2	2		9	3	11	10
Frederickstad	W. P. Moore	2		1	1					7	7

Elsinore	G. P. Hansen														8
Santa Cruz	C. Huger														*22
St. Thomas	J. T. Edgar	11	9	11	13	14	14	14	15	50	51				
SWEDEN AND NORWAY.															
Gothenburg	W. W. Thomas, Jr.	1	1							1	1				
St. Bartholomew	R. B. Diney					2	2	3	3	5	5				
RUSSIA.															
Amoor river	H. G. O. Chase	3	3				5				6				
Cronstadt	A. Wilkins					3		1	3	9	8				
Odessa	T. C. Smith					4		1	1	1	1				
Revel	H. B. Stacy														
PRUSSIA.															
Stettin	C. J. Sundell								1						
AUSTRIA.															
Trieste	J. Hildreth	2	2	2	2		3	3	1	7	5				
ITALY.															
Brindisi	J. S. Redfield	1	1							1	1				
Ancona	L. Ulhani	1	1					2	2	3	3				
Cagliari	E. Pernis	5	5	4	1	4	4	1	1	1	1				
Genoa	D. H. Wheeler	1	1	8	3	1	1	3	3	8	8				
Spezzia	W. T. Rice	2	1	18	23	3	1	1	1	5	36				
Leghorn	A. J. Stevens	14	7	3	3	1	3	1	1	30	5				
Messina	F. W. Behn			10	13	8	8	8	2	29	29				
Naples	J. T. Howard	11	7						7	7	7				
Palermo	L. Monti							13	13	13	13				
TURKEY.															
Beirut	J. A. Johnson	3	3	1	1		2	1	1	9	1				
Constantinople	C. W. Goddard							3	3	1	9				
Cyprus	J. J. Barclay	1	1	4	4	1		1	1	1	1				
Galatz	F. Wippermann	1								8	1				
Smyrna	J. Bing					3	3	2		6	9				
LIBERIA.															
Monrovia	J. Seys			2	2	3		1	1	6	7				

* From November 5, 1863, to September 30, 1864.

Recapitulation—Continued.

COUNTRY AND CONSULATE.	NAME OF CONSUL.	FIRST QUARTER.		SECOND QUARTER.		THIRD QUARTER.		FOURTH QUARTER.		AGGREGATE.	
		Entered.	Cleared.	Entered.	Cleared.	Entered.	Cleared.	Entered.	Cleared.	Entered.	Cleared.
MUSCAT.											
Zanzibar	W. E. Hines	1	1			2	1	1	2	3	4
SIAM.											
Bangkok	G. W. Virgin	13	6	9	3	3	4	3	4	28	17
CHINA.											
Amoy	O. W. Bradford	3	2	2	2	6	6	7	4	18	14
Tientsin	J. N. Stembdrgher	7	7	1	1			3	3	3	3
Canton	O. H. Perry	29	34	20	31	15	19	7	7	15	15
Foo-chow-foo	W. H. Carpenter							14	14	83	98
Kiukiang	H. G. Bridges										
Ningpo	W. P. Mangum	55	65	41	34	40	39	81	77	217	215
Swatow	J. C. A. Wingate	4	7	4	3	4	4	8	8	90	92
Hankow	W. Breck									*417	*417
JAPAN.											
Hakodadi	E. F. Rice	8	8	†12	†12	5	6			90	90
Kanagawa	G. S. Fisher	14	11	6	7	12	12			19	17
Nagasaki	J. G. Walsh									18	19
BURMAH.											
Rangoon	G. Bullock	7	5	10	8	16	19	9	12	48	44
HAWAIIAN ISLANDS.											
Honolulu	A. Caldwell	48	46	36	26	52	59	24	24	169	155
Hilo	J. Worth	6	5	9	3	11	17	3	3	98	98
Lahaina	E. Perkins	5	5	6	1	5	10			16	16
DOMINICAN REPUBLIC.											
St. Domingo city	W. G. W. Jaeger	1	1	1	1	3	3			4	4

NUMBER OF VESSELS.

HAYTI.												
Cape Hayden	A. Folsom	29	21	4	9	3	2	2	4	13	13	
Gonaives	A. Hildembeck	9	9	3	3	1	3	3		9	9	
Jacmel	G. Moravia	9	11	3	4	3				3	3	
Port au Prince	H. Conrad	16	16			6	4	2	2	10	9	
St. Marc	F. A. Bethan	5	5			1	1			2	2	
MEXICO.												
Acapulco	L. S. Ely	95	94	29	21	25	23	23	23	25	27	
Guaymas	F. Alden	25	25	5	5	9	9	6	6	5	5	
La Paz	F. B. Elsner	28	31	4	6	4	4	11	11	9	10	
Manzanillo	W. H. Blake	3	13				10		9	3	3	
	B. R. Carman	29	32							11	14	
Mas.	B. C. M. Hoyt										11	
Sio	J. H. Mansfield	1	1	8	8	10	10	1	2			
Tampico	F. Chase	3	3		11	1	1	6	6		4	
Ven Cruz	M. D. L. Lane	98	98	9	9	7	7	6	5	6	6	
		18	19			16	17					
HONDURAS.												
Omoa	C. R. Follin	6	6	2	2	1	1	2	2	1	1	
NICARAGUA.												
San Juan del Sur, Coriate	B. L. Hill	42	42	7	7	11	11	13	13	11	11	
San Juan del Norte	B. S. Cottrell	6	5	3	2		11			3	2	
NEW GRANADA.												
Panama	A. R. McKee	80	83	18	19	21	21	22	22	19	21	
Sabanilla	W. A. Chapman	2	2	2	2							
VENEZUELA.												
La Guayra	G. Ulrich	19	19	12	12	7	7	12	12	7	9	
Puerto Cabello	C. H. Bar	45	44	12	11	14	12		12			
BRAZIL.												
Bahia	T. F. Wilson	4	4			1	2	1	1	3	1	
Maranham	W. H. Evans	1	1			1	1					
Para	J. B. Bond	1	1	3	3	4	4	3	2	5	5	
Pernambuco	T. Adamson	15	14					11	12			
Rio Grande del Sur	A. Gieg, Jr.	2	2					10	13	14		
Rio Janeiro	J. Monroe, Jr.	45	76	11	19	10	16	19				
Sonsonate	J. Mathé											
St. Catharine's	B. Ley	16	15	4	2	6	7	6	6	18	18	
Aoqtila	J. Mathé											

Lightning Source UK Ltd.
Milton Keynes UK
UKHW011002210219
337574UK00005B/510/P